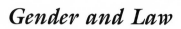

Gender and Law

Gender and Law
Theory, Doctrine, Commentary
Fourth Edition

Katharine T. Bartlett

Dean and A. Kenneth Pye
Professor of Law
Duke University School of Law

Deborah L. Rhode

Ernest W. McFarland Professor of Law
Director, Center on Ethics
Stanford University

ASPEN
PUBLISHERS

76 Ninth Avenue, New York, NY 10011
http://lawschool.aspenpublishers.com

Printed in the United States of America.

1 2 3 4 5 6 7 8 9 0

ISBN 0-7355-5741-1

Library of Congress Cataloging-in-Publication Data

Bartlett, Katharine T.
    Gender and law : theory, doctrine, commentary / Katharine T. Bartlett,
Deborah L. Rhode. — 4th ed.
        p. cm.
    ISBN 0-7355-5741-1
    1. Women — Legal status, laws, etc. — United States — Cases. 2. Sex and law — United
States — Cases. 3. Sex discrimination against women — Law and legislation — United
States — Cases. 4. Feminist jurisprudence — United States.   I. Rhode, Deborah L.
II. Title.

KF478.A4B37 2006
346.7301'34 — dc22

                                                                            2006015568

About Aspen Publishers

Aspen Publishers, headquartered in New York City, is a leading information provider for attorneys, business professionals, and law students. Written by preeminent authorities, our products consist of analytical and practical information covering both U.S. and international topics. We publish in the full range of formats, including updated manuals, books, periodicals, CDs, and online products.

Our proprietary content is complemented by 2,500 legal databases, containing over 11 million documents, available through our Loislaw division. Aspen Publishers also offers a wide range of topical legal and business databases linked to Loislaw's primary material. Our mission is to provide accurate, timely, and authoritative content in easily accessible formats, supported by unmatched customer care.

To order any Aspen Publishers title, go to *http://lawschool.aspenpublishers.com* or call 1-800-638-8437.

To reinstate your manual update service, call 1-800-638-8437.

For more information on Loislaw products, go to *www.loislaw.com* or call 1-800-364-2512.

For Customer Care issues, e-mail *CustomerCare@aspenpublishers.com*; call 1-800-234-1660; or fax 1-800-901-9075.

Aspen Publishers
a Wolters Kluwer business

Summary of Contents

Contents

2   *Substantive Equality*   *151*

3 *Nonsubordination* 399

4 *Difference Theory*   *637*

6 *Non-Essentialism*   *963*

Preface

Many topics from traditional law school courses such as employment law, family law, criminal law, and constitutional law have special relevance to women. Studying these topics within their conventional legal categories can provide systematic coverage of those substantive areas of law that are central to women's lives. Some excellent courses on gender and law proceed in this fashion. The risk of this approach, in the view of the authors of this book, is that it suggests (1) that sex discrimination law can be sliced off from the larger fields of law of which it is but one of many parts, (2) that once removed and consolidated, the parts form a coherent body of law worthy of separate academic study, and (3) that the salient categories in that body of law are the different spheres of women's life to which law is (separately) applied, such as the workplace, the family, and the jury box.

The insights of feminist legal theory over the past two decades pose an implicit challenge to a cut-and-paste approach, by demonstrating the importance of the overall structure and assumptions of law (including the categories it uses to divide one area of law from another) in maintaining a gendered society. The organization of this book into different perspectives reflects the authors' view that what makes gender and law an academic subject worthy of a separate course of study is less that some laws have particular relevance to women, than that *across legal categories* there are different possibilities for defining the relationship between law and gender that have important theoretical and practical consequences.

The perspectives represented in this book are not mutually exclusive, nor are they fully formed or "total" theories of law and gender. They draw from and play off one another. The field is still in a healthy stage of evolution and has been changing through the life of each edition of this book. We have maintained the same six categories used in the first edition, with only slight modifications in terminology: formal equality, substantive equality, nonsubordination (or dominance theory), difference theory, autonomy, and non-essentialism. Each perspective draws on cases and readings from a cross-section of legal materials. Thus, for example, while much of Title VII is covered in Chapter 1 on formal equality, the issue of affirmative action is covered as an example of substantive equality in Chapter 2, issues of work and family are covered both in Chapter 2 and in relation to difference theory in Chapter 4, the topic of sexual harassment appears in Chapter 3 as an example of nonsubordination theory, and the issue of bifurcating race and sex claims in Title VII cases exemplifies one type of "essentialism" in Chapter 6. Likewise, while the conventional "women's" subjects such as family law, employment, reproductive rights, and rape are well covered, the book also includes topics in civil procedure, legal ethics, federal sentencing guidelines, tort remedies, and other subject areas and interdisciplinary materials that help demonstrate the implications of the various frameworks highlighted in the book.

A few principles have guided the preparation of these materials. Their order is, for the most part, cumulative. For example, a student must understand the principles of formal equality before fully appreciating the impulse toward, and potential limitations of, substantive equality. Similarly, knowledge of both formal and substantive equality is a prerequisite to a firm grasp of the concepts incorporated in the nonsubordination approach. The book is also interactive. In early chapters, the student is asked to consider questions for which later materials may give fuller answers; as the book progresses, the student is asked to return to questions previously examined under an earlier perspective. In this sense, the book is an ongoing unraveling and reweaving of interconnected designs, rather than a straight-seamed assembly of a single, finished fabric.

The approach of this book works best if the student attempts to be both open to, and critical of, each approach studied. As will become clear in this book, we find significant value *and* serious limitations in each of the perspectives presented. We urge students to join in the creative effort begun in these course materials to formulate approaches that offer the greatest potential for understanding and improving existing law and practice. Toward this end, we welcome disagreement with whichever of our own preferences may surface in the textual notes or in the choice of cases and readings. On the other hand, it is our hope that the search for the *best* approach — an enterprise that usually emphasizes distinctions and contrasts — does not blind the student to the overlap and similarities between the various perspectives offered. It seems unlikely that social progress will be made on gender issues as a consequence of one perspective trumping another. The premise of this book is that a fuller understanding, and at least partial acceptance, of numerous perspectives on law and gender is the most promising precondition for meaningful reform.

Finally, a word on the editing of this book. Additions to, deletions from, and other alterations to quoted material are indicated by brackets and ellipses, except that footnotes and citations are deleted without notice. Where retained, the original footnote numbers are used. Paragraph breaks and the order of paragraphs are occasionally modified without notice to make edited excerpts coherent.

Katharine T. Bartlett
Deborah L. Rhode

June 2006

Acknowledgments

This book has been a truly collaborative effort, involving an expanding circle of colleagues, friends, and students. A substantial debt is owed to Angela Harris, co-author of the second and third editions, whose other commitments made her unable to continue as an active partner in this fourth edition; this edition carries forward her considerable investment in the materials on work and family, domestic violence, rape, and essentialism.

The book also bears the stamp of another round of research assistants, including Jessica Bodger, Elizabeth Gilbert, and Ryan Higgins from Duke Law School, and Tamar Kricheli Katz, Aarti Kotak, Elizabeth Pederson, and Christopher Walker from Stanford Law School — all of whom, like their predecessors, contributed greatly to the research and thought that went into this edition. We are also grateful for the extraordinarily able administrative assistance of Janse Haywood, Sharon Nash, and Cheril Pulliam from Duke, and Mary Tye from Stanford.

We also thank the following authors and copyright holders for permission to use their works:

Kathryn Abrams, Gender Discrimination and the Transformation of Workplace Norms, 42 Vand. L. Rev. 1183 (1989). Reprinted by permission of the author and Vanderbilt Law Review.

Kathryn Abrams, Sex Wars Redux: Agency and Coercion in Feminist Legal Theory, 95 Colum. L. Rev. 304 (1995). Reprinted by permission.

Kathryn Abrams, Social Construction, Roving Biologism, and Reasonable Women: A Response to Professor Epstein, 41 DePaul L. Rev. 1021 (1992). Reprinted by permission.

American Bar Association Commission on Women in the Profession, The Unfinished Agenda: A Report on the Status of Women in the Legal Profession (2001). Reprinted by permission.

Elvia R. Arriola, Law and the Gendered Politics of Identity: Who Owns the Label "Lesbian," 8 Hastings Women's L.J. 1 (1997). Reprinted from Hastings Women's Law Journal. Copyright © 1996 by University of California, Hastings College of the Law.

Katharine K. Baker, Gender, Genes and Choice: A Comparative Look at Feminism, Evolution, and Economics, 80 N. C. L. Rev. 465 (2002). Reprinted by permission.

Katharine T. Bartlett, Feminist Legal Methods, 103 Harv. L. Rev. 829 (1990). Copyright © 1990 by the Harvard Law Review Association. Reprinted by permission.

Mary E. Becker, Patriarchy and Inequality: Toward a Substantive Feminism, 1999 U. Chi. L. F. 21. Reprinted by permission.

Leslie Bender, A Lawyer's Primer on Feminist Theory and Tort, 38 J. Legal Educ. 3 (1988). Copyright © 1988 by the Association of American Law Schools. Reprinted by permission.

Leslie Bender, From Gender Difference to Feminist Solidarity: Using Carol Gilligan and an Ethic of Care in Law, 15 Vt. L. Rev. (1990). Reprinted by permission.

Kingsley R. Browne, Sex and Temperament in Modern Society: A Darwinian View of the Glass Ceiling and the Gender Gap, 37 Ariz. L. Rev. 974 (1995). Copyright © 1996 by the Arizona Board of Regents. Reprinted by permission.

Kingsley R. Browne, Women at War: An Evolutionary Perspective, 49 Buff. L. Rev. 51 (2001). Reprinted by permission.

Devon W. Carbado & Mitu Gulati, The Fifth Black Woman, 11 J. Contemp. Legal Issues, 701 (2001). Reprinted by permission.

Martha Chamallas, Listening to Dr. Fiske: The Easy Case of *Price Waterhouse v. Hopkins,* 15 Vt. L. Rev. 89 (1990). Reprinted by permission.

Donna K. Coker, Heat of Passion and Wife Killing: Men Who Batter/Men Who Kill, 2 S. Cal. L. & Women's Stud. 71 (1992). Reprinted by the permission of the author and the Southern California Review of Law and Women's Studies.

Shannon DeRouselle, Welfare Reform and the Administration for Children's Services: Subjecting Children and Families to Poverty and Then Punishing Them For It, 25 N.Y.U. Rev. L. & Soc. Change 403 (1999). Reprinted by permission.

Mary C. Dunlap, Sexual Speech and the State: Putting Pornography in Its Place, 17 Golden Gate U. L. Rev. 359 (1987). Reprinted by permission of the author and Golden Gate University Law Review.

Maxine Eichner, On Postmodern Feminist Legal Theory, 36 Harv. C.R.-C.L. L. Rev. 1 (2001). Reprinted by permission.

Richard A. Epstein, Gender Is for Nouns, 41 DePaul L. Rev. 981 (1992). Reprinted by permission.

Susan Estrich, Rape, 95 Yale L.J. 1087 (1986). Reprinted by permission of the author, The Yale Law Journal Company, and Fred B. Rothman & Company.

Holly B. Fechner, Three Stories of Prostitution in the West: Prostitutes' Groups, Law, and Feminist "Truth," 4 Colum. J. Gender & L. 26 (1994). Permission granted by the Columbia Journal of Gender & Law.

Lucinda Finley, Female Trouble: The Implications of Tort Reform for Women, 64 Tenn. L. Rev. 847 (1997). Reprinted by permission of the author and the Tennessee Law Review Association, Inc.

Martha Albertson Fineman, Cracking the Foundational Myths: Independence, Autonomy, and Self-Sufficiency, 8 Am U. J. Gender Pol'y & L. 13 (1999). Reprinted by permission.

Martha Albertson Fineman, The Autonomy Myth: A Theory of Dependency (2004). Reprinted by permission.

Karla Fischer, Neil Vidmar, & René Ellis, The Culture of Battering and the Role of Mediation in Domestic Violence Cases, 46, SMU L. Rev. 2117 (1993). Reprinted by permission from the SMU Law Review and the Southern Methodist University School of Law.

Janet Halley et al, Gender, Sexuality, and Power: Is Feminist Theory Enough?, 12 Colum. J. Gender & L. 601 (2003). Reprinted by permission.

Angela P. Harris, Race and Essentialism in Feminist Legal Theory, 42 Stan. L. Rev. 581 (1990). Reprinted by permission.

Heidi I. Hartmann, Patricia A. Roos, & Donald Treiman, An Agenda for Basic Research on Comparable Worth. Reprinted from Comparable Worth: New Directions for Research (Heidi I. Hartmann ed.) Reprinted by permission of the authors and National Academy Press, Washington, D.C.

L. Camille Hébert, The Economic Implications of Sexual Harassment for Women, 3 Kan. J. L. & Pol'y 41 (Spring 1994). Reprinted by permission.

Ronald K. Henry, "Primary Caretaker": Is It a Ruse?, 17 Fam. Advoc. 53 (Summer 1994). Copyright © 1995 American Bar Association. Reprinted by permission.

Tracey E. Higgins, "By Reason of Their Sex": Feminist Theory, Postmodernism, and Justice, 80 Cornell L. Rev. 1536 (1995). Reprinted by permission.

Nan D. Hunter & Sylvia A. Law, Brief Amici Curiae of Feminist Anti-Censorship Taskforce et al. In *American Booksellers Association v. Hudnut*, 21 U. Mich. J. L. Ref. 69 (Fall 1987-Winter 1988). Reprinted by permission.

Rosemary Hunter, Afterword: A Feminist Response to the Gender Gap in Compensation Symposium, 83 Geo. L.J. 147 (1993). Reprinted with the permission of the publisher, Georgetown University and Georgetown Law Journal, Copyright © 1994.

Herma Hill Kay, Equality and Difference: The Case of Pregnancy, 1 Berkeley Women's L.J. 1 (1985). Copyright © 1985 by California Law Review. Reprinted by permission.

Michael Kimmel, Integrating Men Into the Curriculum, 4 Duke J. Gender Law & Pol'y 181 (1997). Reprinted by permission.

Judith Koons, Motherhood, Marriage and Morality: The Pro-Marriage Moral Discourse of American Welfare Policy, 19 Wis. Women's L.J. 1 (2004). Reprinted by permission.

Karen M. Kramer, Note, Rule by Myth: The Social and Legal Dynamics Governing Alcohol-Related Acquaintance Rape, 47 Stan. L. Rev. 115 (1994). Copyright © 1994 by the Board of Trustees of the Leland Stanford Junior University.

Linda Hamilton Krieger, The Content of Our Categories, 47 Stan. L. Rev. 1161 (1995). Reprinted by permission.

Gerda Lerner, The Meanings of Seneca Falls, 1848-1998, 45 Dissent 34 (Fall 1998). Reprinted by permission of the author.

Dorchen Liedholdt, Prostitution: A Violation of Women's Human Rights, 1 Cardozo Women's L.J. 133 (1993). Reprinted by permission.

Catharine A. MacKinnon, Afterword, in Directions in Sexual Harassment Law (Catharine A. MacKinnon & Reva B. Siegel eds., 2004). Reprinted by permission.

Catharine A. MacKinnon, Feminism Unmodified: Discourses on Life and Law. Reprinted by permission of the author and Harvard University Press. Copyright © 1987 by the President and Fellows of Harvard College.

Catharine A. MacKinnon, Pornography as Defamation and Discrimination, 71 B.U. L. Rev. 793 (1991). Reprinted by permission of the author and Boston University Law Review.

Catharine A. MacKinnon, Sexual Harassment of Working Women (1979). Reprinted by permission of the author and Yale University Press.

Catharine A. MacKinnon, Toward a Feminist Theory of the State. Reprinted by permission of Catharine A. MacKinnon and Harvard University Press. Copyright © 1989 by Catharine A. MacKinnon.

Catharine A. MacKinnon, Women's Lives, Men's Laws (2005). Reprinted by permission.

Martha R. Mahoney, Legal Images of Battered Women: Redefining the Issue of Separation, 90 Mich. L. Rev. 4 (1991). Copyright © 1991 by The Michigan Law Review Association. Reprinted with permission of the author and Michigan Law Review.

Mari J. Matsuda, Beside My Sister, Facing the Enemy: Legal Theory Out of Coalition, 43 Stan. L. Rev. 1183 (1991). Reprinted by permission.

Carrie Menkel-Meadow, Portia in a Different Voice: Speculation on a Woman's Lawyering Process, 1 Berkeley Women's LJ. 39 (1985). Copyright © 1985 by California Law Review, Inc. Reprinted by permission.

Carlin Meyer, Sex, Sin, and Women's Liberation: Against Porn-Suppression, 72 Tex. L. Rev. 1097 (1994). Copyright © 1994 by the Texas Law Review Association. Reprinted by permission.

L. Amede Obiora, Bridges and Barricades: Rethinking Polemics and Intransigence in the Campaign Against Female Circumcision, 47 Case W. Res. L. Rev. 275 (1997). Copyright: Case Western Reserve Law Review. Reprinted by permission.

Richard A. Posner, Conservative Feminism 1989 U. Chi. Legal F. 191. Reprinted by permission.

Margaret Jane Radin, The Pragmatist and the Feminist, 63 S. Cal. L. Rev. 1699 (1990). Reprinted with the permission of the author and Southern California Law Review.

Judith Resnik, On the Bias: Feminist Reconsiderations of the Aspirations for Our
    Judges, 61 S. Cal. L. Rev. 1877 (1988). Reprinted with the permission of the
    Southern California Law Review and the author.

Deborah L. Rhode, Sex in Schools, Who's Minding the Adults, in Directions in
    Sexual Harassment Law (Catharine A. MacKinnon & Reva B. Siegel eds.,
    2004). Reprinted by permission.

Deborah L. Rhode, Speaking of Sex: The Denial of Gender Inequality (1997).
    Reprinted by permission of the Harvard University Press. Copyright © 1997
    by Deborah L. Rhode.

Deborah L. Rhode, Occupational Inequality, Duke L.J. 1207 (1988). Reprinted
    by permission.

Cookie Ridolfi, Statement on Representing Rape Defendants, unpublished
    manuscript, July 26, 1989, Santa Clara University School of Law. Reprinted
    by permission.

Dorothy Roberts, Spiritual and Menial Housework, 9 Yale J. L. & Feminism 51
    (1997). Reprinted by permission of the Yale Journal of Law & Feminism, Inc.

Cristina M. Rodriguez, Clearing the Smoke-Filled Room: Women Jurors and the
    Disruption of an Old-Boys' Network in Nineteenth-Century America, 108
    Yale L.J. 1805 (1999). Reprinted by permission of The Yale Law Journal
    Company and William S. Hein Company.

Carol M. Rose, Women and Property: Gaining and Losing Ground, 78 Va. L. Rev.
    421 (1992). Reprinted with permission of the author, Virginia Law Review
    Association, and Fred B. Rothman & Company.

Judy Scales-Trent, Equal Rights Advocates: Addressing the Legal Issues of
    Women of Color, 3 Berkeley Women's L.J. 34 (1998). Reprinted by
    permission.

Kim Lane Scheppele, The Re-Vision of Rape Law, 54 U. Chi. L. Rev. 1095 (1987).
    Reprinted by permission.

Elizabeth M. Schneider, The Violence of Privacy, 23 Conn. L. Rev. 973 (1991).
    Reprinted by permission of the author and Connecticut Law Review.

Vicki Schultz, Life's Work, 100 Colum. L. Rev. 1881 (2000). Copyright © Vicki
    Schultz. Reprinted by permission.

Marjorie Maguire Shultz, Reproductive Technology and Intent-Based Parent-
    hood: An Opportunity for Gender Neutrality, 1990 Wis. L. Rev. 297.
    Copyright © 1990 by Wisconsin Law Review. Reprinted by permission.

Reva Siegel, Reasoning from the Body: A Historical Perspective on Abortion
    Regulation and Questions of Equal Protection, 44 Stan. L. Rev. 261 (1992).
    Copyright © 1992 by the Board of Trustees of the Leland Stanford Junior
    University.

Katharine Silbaugh, Turning Labor into Love: Housework and the Law, 91 NW U.
    L. Rev. 1 (1996). Reprinted by permission.

Elizabeth Cady Stanton, Susan B. Anthony, & Matilda Joslyn Gage, eds., History
    of Woman Suffrage (1985 reprint edition), Declaration of Sentiments, Seneca
    Falls Convention (July 1848); Address of Elizabeth Cady Stanton to the New
    York Legislature (Feb. 14, 1854); Reminiscences by Frances D. Gage of
    Sojourner Truth at the Akron Convention (May 1851); Susan B. Anthony's

post-trial comments in United States v. Anthony (1873). Reprinted by permission of Ayer Company Publishers, Inc., P.O. Box 958, Salem, N.H., 03079.

Susan Sturm, Second Generation Employment Discrimination: A Structural Approach, 101 Colum. L. Rev. 458 (2001). Reprinted by permission.

Madhavi Sunder, Piercing the Veil, 112 Yale L.J. 1399 (2003). Reprinted by permission.

Rena K. Uviller, Father's Rights and Feminism: The Maternal Presumption Revisited, 1 Harv. Women's L.J. 107 (1978). Copyright © 1978 by the President and Fellows of Harvard College.

Leti Volpp, Feminism Versus Multiculturalism, 101 Colum. L. Rev. 1881 (2001). Reprinted by permission.

Amy L. Wax, Against Nature — On Robert Wright's "The Moral Animal," 63 U. Chi. L. Rev. 307 (1996). Reprinted by permission.

Carol Weisbrod, Images of the Woman Juror, 9 Harv. Women's L.J. 59 (1986). Copyright © 1986 by the President and Fellows of Harvard College. Permission granted by the author and the Harvard Women's Law Journal.

Robin L. West, The Difference in Women's Hedonic Lives: A Phenomenological Critique of Feminist Legal Theory, 3 Wis. Women's L.J. 81 (1987). Reprinted by permission.

Robin L. West, The Supreme Court 1989 Term, Foreword: Taking Freedom Seriously, 104 Harv. L. Rev. 43 (1990). Reprinted by permission.

Joan Williams, Toward a Reconstructive Feminism: Reconstructing the Relationship of Market Work and Family Work, 19 N. Ill. U. L. Rev. 89 (1998). Reprinted by permission.

Joan Williams, Do Wives Own Half? Winning for Wives After *Wendt*, 32 Conn. L. Rev. 249 (1999). Reprinted by permission.

Verna L. Williams, Reform or Retrenchment? Single-Sex Education and the Construction of Race and Gender, 2004 Wis. L. Rev. 15. Reprinted by permission.

Wendy W. Williams, The Equality Crisis: Some Reflections on Culture, Courts, and Feminism, 7 Women's Rts. L. Rep. 175 (1982). Reprinted with permission of the author and the Women's Rights Law Reporter.

Gender and Law

1 Formal Equality

Formal equality is a principle of equal treatment: individuals who are alike should be treated alike, according to their actual characteristics rather than assumptions based on their sex, race, ethnicity, sexual orientation or other impermissible characteristics. It is a principle that can be applied either to a single individual, whose right to be treated on his or her own merits reflects values of individual autonomy, or to a group, whose members claim the entitlements of other similarly situated groups. What makes an issue one of *formal* equality is that the claim is limited to treatment *in relation to* another, similarly situated individual or group and does not extend to a demand for some particular, *substantive* treatment.

This chapter begins with historical materials from first-wave legal feminism, setting forth the basic outline of women's claim for equal rights. In the nineteenth century, the focal point for the emerging theory of formal equality for women was woman's suffrage, resolved successfully in the passage of the Nineteenth Amendment in 1920. The Nineteenth Amendment left untouched, however, a broad range of legal restrictions and practices that discriminated on the basis of sex.

Most of the chapter then explores the constitutional and statutory doctrines developed to dismantle these restrictions using formal equality principles. Beginning with a series of decisions by the U.S. Supreme Court in the early 1970s, this dismantling drew heavily from earlier civil rights cases, and much of the development of the law in this area was directed toward determining to what extent the standard of review for sex-based classifications would mirror standards developed in the civil rights domain. Eventually, the Court settled on the standard that a classification based on sex "must serve important governmental objectives and must be substantially related to achievement of those objectives," Craig v. Boren, 429 U.S. 190, 197 (1976), or, as later stated, that it be supported by "an exceedingly persuasive justification." See J.E.B. v. Alabama ex rel. T.B., 511 U.S. 127, 136 (1994). Within this "intermediate" standard of review, courts have assessed state-created sex-based classifications by examining their purposes and determining how well the classification "fits" its underlying objectives.

In reviewing the legitimacy of sex-based classifications, a chief concern has been the accuracy of the underlying assumptions. When a classification is based on overbroad or otherwise inaccurate stereotypes about women, it generally fails. Even when the assumptions are to some extent accurate, the classification may be invalid. Some classifications are invalid because even if true *of women in general*, they may not be true *of each individual woman* who, in appropriate cases, should be able to prove she is qualified for the opportunity or benefit on the same terms as a man. Some classifications based on stereotypes may be impermissible even if true (or partially true) because they help to perpetuate the stereotypes, thereby reinforcing the discriminatory reality that make them plausible. Finally, even if the classifications are based on real differences between men and women, they may fail if their use is not substantially related to the purpose they purport to serve.

Some problems of sex equality are masked because the rule or practice is based on criteria that appear to be sex-neutral, such as height and weight requirements, but have a disproportionate impact on women. In these cases, the principle that likes be treated alike requires that such criteria be justified by the actual requirements of the job, not stereotyped expectations. Formal equality insists not only that those who are similarly situated be treated alike, but that overgeneralizations not dictate who appears to be similarly situated to whom.

Formal equality applies to sex-based classifications that discriminate against men, as well as those that discriminate against women. In formal equality terms, the goal is equal treatment for all, not just women. Extending formal equality principles to rules that discriminate against men might be justified, even on a woman-centered basis, on the ground that such rules promote attitudes and expectations about women, including their dependency or status as victims, that disadvantage them in many contexts. Those who offer this rationale may favor formal equality as a strategy, but insofar as their choice of principle is based on its woman-centered result, they have stepped beyond formal equality and have their foot in the door of substantive equality, examined in Chapter 2.

Throughout this chapter it is important to keep in mind both the benefits and the limitations of formal equality. As will be apparent, much has been accomplished and many societal inequities can be addressed on formal equality grounds. But what is left after formal equality has done its work? Look critically not only at formal equality as an analytical tool of gender reform but at the criticisms made against it. To what extent do these criticisms identify defects in formal equality analysis, and to what extent might they reflect, instead, the failure to apply formal equality analysis properly? Which objections are ones of principle? Which ones are differences of strategy? Is there a distinction?

A. HISTORICAL FOUNDATIONS FOR WOMEN'S CLAIM TO FORMAL EQUALITY

United States v. Anthony (1873)

History of Woman Suffrage, vol. II, 1861-1876, at 688-689
(Elizabeth Cady Stanton, Susan B. Anthony & Matilda Joslyn Gage eds.,
reprint ed. 1985)

[The following is an excerpt of comments made by Susan B. Anthony, in open court, the day after a verdict was directed against her for voting in violation of section 19 of the Civil Rights Act of 1870, 16 Stat. 144, a statute intended to prohibit multiple voting by white voters in order to dilute black votes.]

Miss ANTHONY: All my prosecutors, from the 8th Ward corner grocery politician, who entered the complaint, to the United States Marshal, Commissioner, District Attorney, District Judge, your honor on the bench, not one is my peer, but each and all are my political sovereigns; and had your honor submitted my case to the jury, as was clearly your duty, even then I should have had just cause of protest, for not one of those men was my peer; but, native or foreign, white or black, rich or poor, educated or ignorant, awake or asleep, sober or drunk, each and every man of them was my political superior; hence, in no sense, my peer. Even, under such circumstances, a commoner of England, tried before a jury of lords, would have far less cause to complain than should I, a woman, tried before a jury of men. Even my counsel, the Hon. Henry R. Selden, who has argued my cause so ably, so earnestly, so unanswerably before your honor, is my political sovereign. Precisely as no disfranchised person is entitled to sit upon a jury, and no woman is entitled to the franchise, so, none but a regularly admitted lawyer is allowed to practice in the courts, and no woman can gain admission to the bar—hence, jury, judge, counsel, must all be of the superior class.

Judge HUNT: The Court must insist—the prisoner has been tried according to the established forms of law.

Miss ANTHONY: Yes, your honor, but by forms of law all made by men, interpreted by men, administered by men, in favor of men, and against women; and hence, your honor's ordered verdict of guilty, against a United States citizen for the exercise of "that citizen's right to vote," simply because that citizen was a woman and not a man. But, yesterday, the same man-made forms of law declared it a crime punishable with $1,000 fine and six months' imprisonment, for you, or me, or any of us, to give a cup of cold water, a crust of bread, or a night's shelter to a panting fugitive as he was tracking his way to Canada. And every man or woman in whose veins coursed a drop of human sympathy violated that wicked law, reckless of consequences, and was justified in so doing. As then the slaves who got their freedom must take it over, or under, or through the unjust forms of law, precisely so now must women, to get their right to a voice in this Government, take it; and I have taken mine, and mean to take it at every possible opportunity.

Judge HUNT: The Court orders the prisoner to sit down. It will not allow another word.

Miss ANTHONY: When I was brought before your honor for trial, I hoped for a broad and liberal interpretation of the Constitution and its recent amendments, that should declare all United States citizens under its protecting aegis — that should declare equality of rights the national guarantee to all persons born or naturalized in the United States. But failing to get this justice — failing, even, to get a trial by a jury not of my peers — I ask not leniency at your hands — but rather the full rigors of the law.

Judge HUNT: The Court must insist — (Here the prisoner sat down.)

Judge HUNT: The prisoner will stand up. (Here Miss Anthony arose again.) The sentence of the Court is that you pay a fine of one hundred dollars and the costs of the prosecution.

Miss ANTHONY: May it please your honor, I shall never pay a dollar of your unjust penalty. All the stock in trade I possess is a $10,000 debt, incurred by publishing my paper — *The Revolution* — four years ago, the sole object of which was to educate all women to do precisely as I have done, rebel against your man-made, unjust unconstitutional forms of law, that tax, fine, imprison, and hang women, while they deny them the right of representation in the Government; and I shall work on with might and main to pay every dollar of that honest debt, but not a penny shall go to this unjust claim. And I shall earnestly and persistently continue to urge all women to practical recognition of the old revolutionary maxim, that "Resistance to tyranny is obedience to God."

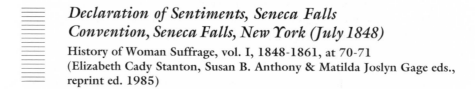

Declaration of Sentiments, Seneca Falls Convention, Seneca Falls, New York (July 1848)

History of Woman Suffrage, vol. I, 1848-1861, at 70-71
(Elizabeth Cady Stanton, Susan B. Anthony & Matilda Joslyn Gage eds., reprint ed. 1985)

When, in the course of human events, it becomes necessary for one portion of the family of man to assume among the people of the earth a position different from that which they have hitherto occupied, but one to which the laws of nature and of nature's God entitle them, a decent respect to the opinions of mankind requires that they should declare the causes that impel them to such a course.

We hold these truths to be self-evident: that all men and women are created equal; that they are endowed by their Creator with certain inalienable rights; that among these are life, liberty, and the pursuit of happiness; that to secure these rights governments are instituted, deriving their just powers from the consent of the governed. Whenever any form of government becomes destructive of these ends, it is the right of those who suffer from it to refuse allegiance to it, and to insist upon the institution of a new government, laying its foundation on such principles, and organizing its powers in such form, as to them shall seem most likely to effect their safety and happiness. Prudence, indeed, will dictate that governments long established should not be changed for light and transient causes; and accordingly all experience hath shown that mankind are more disposed to suffer, while evils are sufferable, than to right themselves by abolishing the forms to which they were accustomed. But when a long train of abuses and usurpations, pursuing invariably the same object evinces a design to reduce them under absolute despotism, it is their duty to throw off such government, and to provide new guards for their future security. Such has been the patient sufferance of the women under this government, and such is now the necessity which constrains them to demand the equal station to which they are entitled.

The history of mankind is a history of repeated injuries and usurpations on the part of man toward woman, having in direct object the establishment of an absolute tyranny over her. To prove this, let facts be submitted to a candid world.

He has never permitted her to exercise her inalienable right to the elective franchise.

He has compelled her to submit to laws, in the formation of which she had no voice.

He has withheld from her rights which are given to the most ignorant and degraded men — both natives and foreigners.

Having deprived her of this first right of a citizen, the elective franchise, thereby leaving her without representation in the halls of legislation, he has oppressed her on all sides.

He has made her, if married, in the eye of the law, civilly dead.

He has taken from her all right in property, even to the wages she earns.

He has made her, morally, an irresponsible being, as she can commit many crimes with impunity, provided they be done in the presence of her husband. In the covenant of marriage, she is compelled to promise obedience to her husband, he becoming, to all intents and purposes, her master — the law giving him power to deprive her of her liberty, and to administer chastisement.

He has so framed the laws of divorce, as to what shall be the proper causes, and in case of separation, to whom the guardianship of the children shall be given, as to be wholly regardless of the happiness of women — the law, in all cases, going upon a false supposition of the supremacy of man, and giving all power into his hands.

After depriving her of all rights as a married woman, if single, and the owner of property, he has taxed her to support a government which recognizes her only when her property can be made profitable to it.

He has monopolized nearly all the profitable employments, and from those she is permitted to follow, she receives but a scanty remuneration. He closes against her all the avenues to wealth and distinction which he considers most honorable to himself. As a teacher of theology, medicine, or law, she is not known.

He has denied her the facilities for obtaining a thorough education, all colleges being closed against her.

He allows her in Church, as well as State, but a subordinate position, claiming Apostolic authority for her exclusion from the ministry, and with some exceptions, from any public participation in the affairs of the Church.

He has created a false public sentiment by giving to the world a different code of morals for men and women, by which moral delinquencies which exclude women from society, are not only tolerated, but deemed of little account in man.

He has usurped the prerogative of Jehovah himself, claiming it as his right to assign for her a sphere of action, when that belongs to her conscience and to her God.

He has endeavored, in every way that he could, to destroy her confidence in her own powers, to lessen her self-respect, and to make her willing to lead a dependent and abject life.

Now, in view of this entire disfranchisement of one-half the people of this country, their social and religious degradation — in view of the unjust laws above mentioned, and because women do feel themselves aggrieved, oppressed, and fraudulently deprived of their most sacred rights, we insist that they have immediate admission to all the rights and privileges which belong to them as citizens of the United States.

In entering upon the great work before us, we anticipate no small amount of misconception, misrepresentation, and ridicule; but we shall use every instrumentality within our power to effect our object. We shall employ agents, circulate tracts, petition the State and National legislatures, and endeavor to enlist the pulpit and the press in our behalf. We hope this Convention will be followed by a series of Conventions embracing every part of the country.

Gerda Lerner, *The Meaning of Seneca Falls, 1848-1998*
Dissent, Fall 1998, at 35, 37-39

By selecting the Declaration of Independence for their formal model and following its preamble almost verbatim, except for the insertion of gender-neutral language, the organizers of the convention sought to base their main appeal on the democratic rights embodied in the nation's founding document. They also put the weight and symbolism of this revered text behind what was in their time a radical assertion: "We hold these truths to be self-evident: that all men and women are created equal."

The feminist appeal to natural rights and the social contract had long antecedents on the European continent, the most important advocate of it being Mary Wollstonecraft. Her work was well known in the United States, where the same argument had been well made by Judith Sargent Murray, Frances Wright, Emma Willard, Sarah Grimke and Margaret Fuller.

The second fundamental argument for the equality of women was religious. As stated in the Declaration:

> Resolved, That woman is man's equal — was intended to be so by the Creator, and the highest good of the race demands that she should be recognized as such.

And one of the "grievances" is:

He [man] has usurped the prerogative of Jehovah himself, claiming it as his right to assign to her a sphere of action, when that belongs to her conscience and her God.

The feminist argument based on biblical grounds can be traced back for seven hundred years prior to 1848, but the women assembled at Seneca Falls were unaware of that fact.... They did know the Quaker argument, especially as made in her public lectures by Lucretia Mott. They had read Sarah Grimke's Letters on the Equality of the Sexes, and several of the resolutions in fact followed her text. They knew the biblical argument by Ann Lee of the Shakers and they echoed the anti-slavery biblical argument, applying it to women.

The Declaration departed from precedent in its most radical statement:

The history of mankind is a history of repeated injuries and usurpations on the part of man toward woman, having in direct object the establishment of an absolute tyranny over her.

The naming of "man" as the culprit, thereby identifying patriarchy as a system of "tyranny," was highly original, but it may have been dictated more by the rhetorical flourishes of the Declaration of Independence than by an actual analysis of woman's situation....

The Declaration claimed universality, even though it never mentioned differences among women. Future woman's rights conferences before the Civil War would rectify this omission and pay particular attention to the needs of lower class and slave women.

While grievances pertaining to woman's sexual oppression were not explicitly included in the Declaration of Sentiments, they were very much alive in the consciousness of the leading participants. Elizabeth Cady Stanton had already in 1848 begun to include allusions to what we now call "marital rape" in her letters and soon after the Seneca Falls convention made such references explicit, calling on legislatures to forbid marriage to "drunkards." She soon became an open advocate of divorce and of the right of women to leave abusive marriages. Later woman's rights conventions would include some of these issues among their demands, although they used carefully guarded language and focused on abuses by "drunkar/ds." This was a hidden feminist theme of the mainstream woman's temperance movement in the 1880s and caused many temperance women to embrace woman suffrage. What we now call "a woman's right to her body" was already on the agenda of the nineteenth-century woman's rights movement.

It was the confluence of a broad-ranging programmatic declaration with a format familiar and accessible to reformers that gave the event its historical significance. The Seneca Falls convention was the first forum in which women gathered together to publicly air their own grievances, not those of the needy, the enslaved, orphans or widows. The achievement of a public voice for women and the recognition that women could not win their rights unless they organized, made Seneca Falls a major event in history.

Elizabeth Cady Stanton, Address to the Legislature of the State of New York (February 14, 1854)

History of Woman Suffrage, vol. I, 1848-1861, 595, 595-599, 602-605 (Elizabeth Cady Stanton, Susan B. Anthony & Matilda Joslyn Gage eds., reprint ed. 1985)

The tyrant, Custom, has been summoned before the bar of Common-Sense. His majesty no longer awes his multitude — his sceptre is broken — his crown is trampled in the dust — the sentence of death is pronounced upon him. All nations, ranks and classes have, in turn, questioned and repudiated his authority; and now, that the monster is chained and caged, timid woman, on tiptoe, comes to look him in the face, and to demand of her brave sires and sons, who have struck stout blows for liberty, if, in this change of dynasty, she, too, shall find relief. Yes, gentlemen, in republican America, in the nineteenth century, we, the daughters of the revolutionary heroes of '76, demand at your hands the redress of our grievances — a revision of your State Constitution — a new code of laws. Permit us then, as briefly as possible, to call your attention to the legal disabilities under which we labor.

1st. Look at the position of woman as woman. It is not enough for us that by your laws we are permitted to live and breathe, to claim the necessaries of life from our legal protectors — to pay the penalty of our crimes; we demand the full recognition of all our rights as citizens of the Empire State. We are persons; native, free-born citizens; property-holders, tax-payers; yet we are denied the exercise of our right to the elective franchise. We support ourselves, and, in part, your schools, colleges, churches, your poor-houses, jails, prisons, the army, the navy, the whole machinery of government, and yet we have no voice in your councils. We have every qualification required by the Constitution, necessary to the legal voter, but the one of sex. We are moral, virtuous, and intelligent, and in all respects quite equal to the proud white man himself and yet by your laws we are classed with idiots, lunatics, and negroes; and though we do not feel honored by the place assigned us in fact, our legal position is lower than that of either; for the negro can be raised to the dignity of a voter if he possess himself of $250; the lunatic can vote in his moments of sanity, and the idiot, too, if he be a made one, and not more than nine-tenths a fool; but we, who have guided great movements of charity, established missions, edited journals, published works on history, economy, and statistics; who have governed nations, led armies, filled the professor's chair, taught philosophy and mathematics to the savants of our age, discovered planets, piloted ships across the sea, are denied the most sacred rights of citizens, because, forsooth, we came not into this republic crowned with the dignity of manhood! . . .

Now, gentlemen, who would fain know by what authority you have disfranchised one-half the people of this State? You who have so boldly taken possession of the bulwarks of this republic, show us your credentials, and thus prove your exclusive right to govern, not only yourselves, but us. . . . Can it be that here, where we acknowledge no royal blood, no apostolic descent, that you, who have declared that all men were created equal — that governments derive their

just powers from the consent of the governed, would willingly build up an aristocracy that places the ignorant and vulgar above the educated and refined — the
alien and the ditch-digger above the authors and poets of the day — an aristocracy
that would raise the sons above the mothers that bore them? Would that the men
who can sanction a Constitution so opposed to the genius of this government,
who can enact and execute laws so degrading to womankind, had sprung,
Minerva-like, from the brains of their fathers, that the matrons of this republic
need not blush to own their sons!

 . . . [Y]ou place the negro, so unjustly degraded by you, in a superior position
to your own wives and mothers; for colored males, if possessed of a certain
amount of property and certain other qualifications, can vote, but if they do
not have these qualifications they are not subject to direct taxation; wherein
they have the advantage of woman, she being subject to taxation for whatever
amount she may possess. (Constitution of New York, Article 2, Sec. 2.) But, say
you, are not all women sufficiently represented by their fathers, husbands, and
brothers? Let your statute books answer the question.

 [W]e demand in criminal cases that most sacred of all rights, trial by a jury of
our own peers. . . .

 Shall an erring woman be dragged before a bar of grim-visaged judges,
lawyers, and jurors, there to be grossly questioned in public on subjects which
women scarce breathe in secret to one another? Shall the most sacred relations of
life be called up and rudely scanned by men who, by their own admission, are so
coarse that woman could not meet them even at the polls without contamination?
[A]nd yet shall she find there no woman's face or voice to pity and defend? Shall
the frenzied mother, who, to save herself and child from exposure and disgrace,
ended the life that had but just begun, be dragged before such a tribunal to
answer for her crime? How can man enter into the feelings of that mother?
How can he judge of the agonies of soul that impelled her to such an outrage
of maternal instincts? How can he weigh the mountain of sorrow that crushed
that mother's heart when she wildly tossed her helpless babe into the cold waters
of the midnight sea? Where is he who by false vows thus blasted this trusting
woman? Had that helpless child no claims on his protection? Ah, he is freely
abroad in the dignity of manhood, in the pulpit, on the bench, in the professor's
chair. The imprisonment of his victim and the death of his child, detract not a
tithe from his standing and complacency. His peers made the law, and shall lawmakers lay nets for those of their own rank? Shall laws which come from the
logical brain of man take cognizance of violence done to the moral and affectional
nature which predominates, as is said, in woman?

 Statesmen of New York, whose daughters guarded by your affection, and
lapped amidst luxuries which your indulgence spreads, care more for their nod-
ding plumes and velvet trains than for the statute laws by which their persons and
properties are held — who, blinded by custom and prejudice to the degraded
position which they and their sisters occupy in the civil scale, haughtily claim
that they already have all the rights they want, how, think ye, you would feel
to see a daughter summoned for such a crime — and remember these daughters
are but human — before such a tribunal? Would it not, in that hour, be some
consolation to see that she was surrounded by the wise and virtuous of her own

sex; by those who had known the depth of a mother's love and the misery of a lover's falsehood; to know that to these she could make her confession, and from them receive her sentence? If so, then listen to our just demands and make such a change in your laws as will secure to every woman tried in your courts, an impartial jury. At this moment among the hundreds of women who are shut up in prisons in this State, not one has enjoyed that most sacred of all rights — that right which you would die to defend for yourselves — trial by a jury of one's peers.

2d. Look at the position of woman as wife. Your laws relating to marriage — founded as they are on the old common law of England, a compound of barbarous usages, but partially modified by progressive civilization — are in open violation of our enlightened ideas of justice, and of the holiest feelings of our nature. If you take the highest view of marriage, as a Divine relation, which love alone can constitute and sanctify, then of course human legislation can only recognize it. Men can neither bind nor loose its ties, for that prerogative belongs to God alone, who makes man and woman, and the laws of attraction by which they are united. But if you regard marriage as a civil contract, then let it be subject to the same laws which control all other contracts. Do not make it a kind of half-human, half-divine institution, which you may build up, but can not regulate. Do not, by your special legislation for this one kind of contract, involve yourselves in the grossest absurdities and contradictions.

... The wife who inherits no property holds about the same legal position that does the slave on the Southern plantation. She can own nothing, sell nothing. She has no right even to the wages she earns; her person, her time, her services are the property of another. She can not testify, in many cases, against her husband. She can get no redress for wrongs in her own name in any court of justice. She can neither sue nor be sued. She is not held morally responsible for any crime committed in the presence of her husband so completely is her very existence supposed by the law to be merged in that of another. Think of it; your wives may be thieves, libelers, burglars, incendiaries, and for crimes like these they are not held amenable to the laws of the land, if they but commit them in your dread presence. For them, alas! there is no higher law than the will of man....

[The discussion of the position of the widow is deleted.]

... 4th. Look at the position of woman as mother. There is no human love so strong and steadfast as that of the mother for her child; yet behold how ruthless are your laws touching this most sacred relation. Nature has clearly made the mother the guardian of the child; but man, in his inordinate love of power, does continually set nature and nature's laws at open defiance. The father may apprentice his child, bind him out to a trade, without the mother's consent — yea, in direct opposition to her most earnest entreaties, prayers and tears.

He may apprentice his son to a gamester or rum-seller, and thus cancel his debts of honor. By the abuse of this absolute power, he may bind his daughter to the owner of a brothel, and, by the degradation of his child, supply his daily wants; and such things, gentlemen, have been done in our very midst. Moreover, the father, about to die, may bond out all his children wherever and to whomsoever he may see fit, and thus, in fact, will away the guardianship of all his children from the mother. The Revised Statutes of New York provide that "every father, whether of full age or a minor, of a child to be born, or of any living child under the age of twenty-one years, and unmarried, may by his deed or last will, duly executed, dispose of the custody and tuition of such child during its minority, or for any less time, to any person or persons, in possession of remainder."...Thus, by your laws, the child is the absolute property of the father, wholly at his disposal in life or at death.

In case of separation, the law gives the children to the father; no matter what his character or condition. At this very time we can point you to noble, virtuous, well-educated mothers in this State, who have abandoned their husbands for their profligacy and confirmed drunkenness. All these have been robbed of their children, who are in the custody of the husband, under the care of his relatives, whilst the mothers are permitted to see them but at stated intervals....

By your laws, all these abominable resorts are permitted. It is folly to talk of a mother moulding the character of her son, when all mankind, backed up by law and public sentiment, conspire to destroy her influence. But when woman's moral power shall speak through the ballot-box, then shall her influence be seen and felt....

Many times and oft it has been asked us, with unaffected seriousness, "What do you women want? What are you aiming at?" Many have manifested a laudable curiosity to know what the wives and daughters could complain of in republican America, where their sires and sons have so bravely fought for freedom and gloriously secured their independence, trampling all tyranny, bigotry, and caste in the dust, and declaring to a waiting world the divine truth that all men are created equal. What can woman want under such a government? Admit a radical difference in sex, and you demand different spheres — water for fish, and air for birds.

It is impossible to make the Southern planter believe that his slave feels and reasons just as he does — that injustice and subjection are as galling as to him — that the degradation of living by the will of another, the mere dependent on his caprice, at the mercy of his passions, is as keenly felt by him as his master. If you can force on his unwilling vision a vivid picture of the negro's wrongs, and for a moment touch his soul, his logic brings him instant consolation. He says, the slave does not feel this as I would. Here, gentlemen, is our difficulty: When we plead our cause before the law-makers and savants of the republic, they can not take in the idea that men and women are alike; and so long as the mass rest in this delusion, the public mind will not be so much startled by the revelations made of the injustice and degradation of woman's position as by the fact that she should at length wake up to a sense of it.

If you, too, are thus deluded, what avails it that we show by your statute books that your laws are unjust — that woman is the victim of avarice and power? What avails it that we point out the wrongs of woman in social life; the victim of passion and lust? You scorn the thought that she has any natural love of freedom burning in her breast, any clear perception of justice urging her on to demand her rights.

Would to God you could know the burning indignation that fills woman's soul when she turns over the pages of your statute books, and sees there how like feudal barons you freemen hold your women. Would that you could know the humiliation she feels for sex, when she thinks of all the beardless boys in your law offices, learning these ideas of one-sided justice—taking their first lessons in contempt for all womankind—being indoctrinated into the incapacities of their mothers, and the lordly, absolute rights of man over all women, children, and property, and to know that these are to be our future presidents, judges, husbands, and fathers; in sorrow we exclaim, alas! for that nation whose sons bow not in loyalty to woman. The mother is the first object of the child's veneration and love, and they who root out this holy sentiment, dream not of the blighting effect it has on the boy and the man. The impression left on law students, fresh from your statute books, is most unfavorable to woman's influence; hence you see but few lawyers chivalrous and high-toned in their sentiments toward woman. They can not escape the legal view which, by constant reading, has become familiarized to their minds: "*Femme covert*," "dower," "widow's claims," "protection," "incapacities," "incumbrance," is written on the brow of every woman they meet.

But if, gentlemen, you take the ground that the sexes are alike, and, therefore, you are our faithful representatives—then why all these special laws for woman? Would not one code answer for all of like needs and wants? Christ's golden rule is better than all the special legislation that the ingenuity of man can devise: "Do unto others as you would have others do unto you." This, men and brethren, is all we ask at your hands. We ask no better laws than those you have made for yourselves. We need no other protection than that which your present laws secure to you.

In conclusion, then, let us say, in behalf of the women of this State, we ask for all that you have asked for yourselves in the progress of your development, since the Mayflower cast anchor beside Plymouth rock; and simply on the ground that the rights of every human being are the same and identical. You may say that the mass of the women of this State do not make the demand; it comes from a few sour, disappointed old maids and childless women.

You are mistaken; the mass speak through us. A very large majority of the women of this State support themselves and their children, and many their husbands too. . . .

Now, do you candidly think these wives do not wish to control the wages they earn—to own the land they buy—the houses they build? To have at their disposal their own children, without being subject to the constant interference and tyranny of an idle, worthless profligate? Do you suppose that any woman is such a pattern of devotion and submission that she willingly stitches all day for the small sum of fifty cents, that she may enjoy the unspeakable privilege, in obedience to your laws, of paying for her husband's tobacco and rum? Think you the wife of the confirmed, beastly drunkard would consent to share with him her home and bed, if law and public sentiment would release her from such gross companionship? Verily, no! Think you the wife with whom endurance has ceased to be a virtue, who, through much suffering, has lost all faith in the justice of both heaven and earth, takes the law in her own hand, severs the unholy bond, and turns her back forever upon him whom she once called husband, consents to the law that in such an hour tears her child from her—all that she has left on earth to love and cherish? The drunkards' wives speak through us, and they number 50,000. Think you that the woman who has worked hard all her days in helping her husband to accumulate a large property, consents to the law that places this wholly at his disposal? Would not the mother whose only child is bound out for a term of years against her expressed wish, deprive the father of this absolute power if she could?

For all these, then, we speak. If to this long list you add the laboring women who are loudly demanding remuneration for their unending toil; those women who teach in our seminaries, academies, and public schools for a miserable pittance; the widows who are taxed without mercy; the unfortunate ones in our work-houses, poor-houses, and prisons; who are they that we do not now represent? But a small class of the fashionable butterflies, who, through the short summer days, seek the sunshine and the flowers; but the cool breezes of autumn and the hoary frosts of winter will soon chase all these away; then they, too, will need and seek protection, and through other lips demand in their turn justice and equity at your hands.

Notes

1. Sameness or Difference? To what extent do the arguments by Elizabeth Cady Stanton, Susan B. Anthony, and the drafts of the Declaration of Sentiments assume that women are the same as men, and to what extent do they assume women's differences? What other important assumptions are made? To what extent have these been carried over to contemporary gender debates?

2. Women and Slavery. How have feminists used slavery, or the position of African Americans, in their own favor? Note the compound references to slaves and slavery by Stanton. Women are like slaves to the extent they are subject to the unjust laws of men, and thus women are justified in resisting their oppression. But they are also higher than slaves; thus Stanton is outraged that (white) men place the "negro . . . in a superior position to [their] own wives and mothers." Later suffragettes used even more explicit arguments about the desirability of diluting the Negro vote as a rationale for supporting women's suffrage. As an example, historian Sara M. Evans quotes one Southern suffragist at a 1903 NAWSA convention as saying that "[t]he enfranchisement of women would insure immediate and durable white supremacy, honestly attained." Evans, Born for Liberty: A History of Women in America 155 (1989).

The limitations of the analogy between slavery and women's subordination are examined in other chapters of this book, especially Chapter 6, pp. 964-978. See generally Serena Mayeri, A Common Fate of Discrimination: Race-Gender Analogies in Legal and Historical Perspective, 110 Yale L.J. 1045 (2001); bell hooks, Ain't I a Woman: Black Women and Feminism 139 (1981) ("white women have used comparisons between 'women' and 'blacks' to exclude black women and to deflect attention away from their own racial caste system"); Joyce E. McDonnell, Beyond Metaphor: Battered Women, Involuntary Servitude, and the Thirteenth Amendment, 4 Yale J.L. & Feminism 207, 207-208 (1992) ("No matter how rhetorically useful [the metaphor of women as slaves] may have seemed then or may seem now, it was and remains grossly inaccurate and inherently racist"). In the nineteenth-century context, is the analogy between women's status and that of slaves ever useful?

3. Second Wave Feminism. If modern feminism was born in the United States over the fight for suffrage, it was reborn in the 1960s after a housewife and former labor union journalist named Betty Friedan published The Feminine Mystique (1963). The book, which became an instant best-seller, reported the results of Friedan's interviews with affluent graduates of Smith College, then suburban housewives. Despite their material privilege, these women were deeply unhappy: "desperately in search of stimulation and challenge, some had sexual affairs, others spent their time shopping and accumulating consumer goods, and still others gulped tranquilizers, cooked gourmet meals, or scrutinized their children as though they were rare insects." Ruth Rosen, The World Split Open 4 (2000). Friedan called their common, pervasive unhappiness "the problem that has no name." Id.

The 1950s had been a time in which domesticity rhetoric — celebrating the heterosexual nuclear family with a male breadwinner and female housewife as the source of American prosperity and happiness and as a bulwark against world Communism — was all-pervasive. Experts agreed that homemaking was one of the highest professions a woman could aspire to, and harshly criticized women who worked outside the home. Ruth Rosen reports, for example:

> In their influential anti-Communist best-seller, The Modern Woman: The Lost Sex (1947), Ferdinand Lundberg and Marya Farnham typically laid society's problems on women's defiant determination to pursue outside interests and careers. The authors argued that an "independent" woman was an oxymoron, single women were sick, and childless women were "emotionally disturbed." "All spinsters," they concluded, "[should] be barred by law from having anything to do with the teaching of children on the ground of emotional incompetence."

Id. at 26.

Yet even throughout the quiescent 1950s, women active in labor unions and other left-wing movements had preserved a familiarity with "the woman question." In the 1960s and 1970s, younger women working in the civil rights movement and the new student Left movements began increasingly to turn their organizing skills and intellectual and political radicalism to espousing "women's liberation," based on a fundamental equality between the sexes. For an engrossing account of what happened next, see generally Rosen, supra; see also William H. Chafe, The Road to Equality: 1962-Today, in No Small Courage: A History of Women in the United States 529-586 (Nancy F. Cott ed., 2000). Materials in this chapter represent many of the key legal outcomes of these efforts, while subsequent chapters reflect theories that developed once the basic civil rights structure for gender quality was in place.

4. Bibliographic Note. Women's history, including the history of efforts to achieve gender equality in the United States, is a rich literature, to which this casebook cannot begin to do justice. Among the most basic sources are: Gail

Collins, America's Women (2003); A Companion to American Women's History (Nancy A. Hewitt ed., 2002); No Small Courage: A History of Women in the United States (Nancy F. Cott ed., 2000); Eleanor Flexner & Ellen Fitzpatrick, Century of Struggle: The Woman's Rights Movement in the United States (enlarged ed. 1996); Joan Hoff, Law, Gender, and Injustice: A Legal History of U.S. Women (1991); Sara M. Evans, Born for Liberty: A History of Women in America (1989); Nancy Woloch, Women and the American Experience (1984); Linda K. Kerber, Women of the Republic: Intellect and Ideology in Revolutionary America (1980); Gerda Lerner, The Majority Finds Its Past (1979); Ellen Carol DuBois, Feminism and Suffrage: The Emergence of an Independent Women's Movement in America 1848-1869 (1978); Barbara J. Harris, Beyond Her Sphere: Women and the Professions in American History (1978).

B. FORMAL EQUALITY AND THE CONSTITUTIONAL RIGHT TO EQUAL PROTECTION OF THE LAW

1. The Right to Equal, Individualized Treatment

Reed v. Reed
404 U.S. 71 (1971)

Mr. Chief Justice BURGER delivered the opinion of the Court.

Richard Lynn Reed, a minor, died intestate in Ada County, Idaho, on March 29, 1967. His adoptive parents, who had separated sometime prior to his death, are the parties to this appeal. Approximately seven months after Richard's death, his mother, appellant Sally Reed, filed a petition in the Probate Court of Ada County, seeking appointment as administratrix of her son's estate.

Prior to the date set for a hearing on the mother's petition, appellee Cecil Reed, the father of the decedent, filed a competing petition seeking to have himself appointed administrator of the son's estate. The probate court held a joint hearing on the two petitions and thereafter ordered that letters of administration be issued to appellee Cecil Reed.... The court treated §15-312 and §15-314 of the Idaho Code as the controlling statutes and read those sections as compelling a preference for Cecil Reed because he was a male.

Section 15-312 designates [in order of priority] the persons who are entitled to administer the estate of one who dies intestate. In making these designations, that section lists 11 classes of persons who are so entitled and provides, in substance, that the order in which those classes are listed in the section shall be determinative of the relative rights of competing applicants for letters of administration. One of the 11 classes so enumerated is "[t]he father or mother" of the person dying intestate. Under this section, then, appellant and appellee, being members of the same entitlement class, would seem to have been equally entitled to administer their son's estate. Section 15-314 provides, however, that:

[o]f several persons claiming and equally entitled [under § 15-312] to administer, males must be preferred to females, and relatives of the whole to those of the half blood.

In issuing its order, the probate court implicitly recognized the equality of entitlement of the two applicants under § 15-312 and noted that neither of the applicants was under any legal disability; the court ruled, however, that appellee, being a male, was to be preferred to the female appellant "by reason of Section 15-314 of the Idaho Code." In stating this conclusion, the probate judge gave no indication that he had attempted to determine the relative capabilities of the competing applicants to perform the functions incident to the administration of an estate. It seems clear the probate judge considered himself bound by statute to give preference to the male candidate over the female, each being otherwise "equally entitled."

Sally Reed appealed [and the Idaho Supreme Court upheld the statute]....

[W]e have concluded that the arbitrary preference established in favor of males by § 15-314 of the Idaho Code cannot stand in the face of the Fourteenth Amendment's command that no State deny the equal protection of the laws to any person within its jurisdiction.

In applying that clause, this Court has consistently recognized that the Fourteenth Amendment does not deny to States the power to treat different classes of persons in different ways.... The Equal Protection Clause of that amendment does, however, deny to States the power to legislate that different treatment be accorded to persons placed by a statute into different classes on the basis of criteria wholly unrelated to the objective of that statute. A classification "must be reasonable, not arbitrary, and must rest upon some ground of difference having a fair and substantial relation to the object of the legislation, so that all persons similarly circumstanced shall be treated alike." Royster Guano Co. v. Virginia, [253 U.S. 412, 415 (1920)]. The question presented by this case, then, is whether a difference in the sex of competing applicants for letters of administration bears a rational relationship to a state objective that is sought to be advanced by the operation of § 15-312 and § 15-314.

In upholding the latter section, the Idaho Supreme Court concluded that its objective was to eliminate one area of controversy when two or more persons, equally entitled under § 15-312, seek letters of administration and thereby present the probate court "with the issue of which one should be named." The court also concluded that where such persons are not of the same sex, the elimination of females from consideration "is neither an illogical nor arbitrary method devised by the legislature to resolve an issue that would otherwise require a hearing as to the relative merits . . . of the two or more petitioning relatives. . . ." [465 P.2d at 638].

Clearly the objective of reducing the workload on probate courts by eliminating one class of contests is not without some legitimacy. The crucial question, however, is whether § 15-314 advances that objective in a manner consistent with the command of the Equal Protection Clause. We hold that it does not. To give a mandatory preference to members of either sex over members of the other, merely to accomplish the elimination of hearings on the merits, is to make the very kind of arbitrary legislative choice forbidden by the Equal Protection Clause of the Fourteenth Amendment; and whatever may be said as to the positive values of avoiding intrafamily controversy, the choice in this context may not lawfully be mandated solely on the basis of sex. . . .

Reversed and remanded.

≡ *Frontiero v. Richardson*
≡ 411 U.S. 677 (1973)

Mr. Justice BRENNAN announced the judgment of the Court in an opinion in which Mr. Justice DOUGLAS, Mr. Justice WHITE, and Mr. Justice MARSHALL join.

The question before us concerns the right of a female member of the uniformed services to claim her spouse as a "dependent" for the purposes of obtaining increased quarters allowances and medical and dental benefits under 37 U.S.C. §§ 401, 403, and 10 U.S.C. §§ 1072, 1076, on an equal footing with male members. Under these statutes, a serviceman may claim his wife as a "dependent" without regard to whether she is in fact dependent upon him for any part of her support. . . . A servicewoman, on the other hand, may not claim her husband as a "dependent" under these programs unless he is in fact dependent upon her for over one-half of his support. . . . [T]he question for decision is whether this difference in treatment constitutes an unconstitutional discrimination against servicewomen in violation of the Due Process Clause of the Fifth Amendment. A three-judge District Court for the Middle District of Alabama, one judge dissenting, rejected this contention and sustained the constitutionality of the provisions of the statutes making this distinction. 341 F. Supp. 201 (1972). . . . We reverse. . . .

In an effort to attract career personnel through reenlistment, Congress established . . . a scheme for the provision of fringe benefits to members of the uniformed services on a competitive basis with business and industry. [Under this scheme] a member of the uniformed services with dependents is entitled to an increased "basic allowance for quarters" and . . . a member's dependents are provided comprehensive medical and dental care.

Appellant Sharron Frontiero, a lieutenant in the United States Air Force, sought increased quarters allowances, and housing and medical benefits for her husband, appellant Joseph Frontiero, on the ground that he was her "dependent." Although such benefits would automatically have been granted with respect to the wife of a male member of the uniformed services, appellant's application was denied because she failed to demonstrate that her husband was dependent on her for more than one-half of his support. Appellants then commenced this suit, contending that, by making this distinction, the statutes unreasonably discriminate on the basis of sex in violation of the Due Process Clause of the Fifth Amendment. In essence, appellants asserted that the discriminatory impact of the statutes is twofold: first, as a procedural matter, a female member is required to demonstrate her spouse's dependency, while no such burden is imposed upon male members; and, second, as a substantive matter, a male member who does not provide more than one-half of his wife's support receives benefits, while a similarly situated female member is denied such benefits. Appellants therefore sought a permanent injunction against the continued enforcement of these statutes and an order directing the appellees to provide Lieutenant Frontiero with the same housing and medical benefits that a similarly situated male member would receive.

Although the legislative history of these statutes sheds virtually no light on the purposes underlying the differential treatment accorded male and female members, a majority of the three-judge District Court surmised that Congress might reasonably have concluded that, since the husband in our society is generally the "breadwinner" in the family—and the wife typically the "dependent" partner—"it would be more economical to require married female members claiming husbands to prove actual dependency than to extend the presumption of dependency to such members." [341 F. Supp. 201, 207 (1972).] Indeed, given the fact that approximately 99% of all members of the uniformed services are male, the District Court speculated that such differential treatment might conceivably lead to a "considerable saving of administrative expense and manpower." Id.

At the outset, appellants contend that classifications based upon sex, like classifications based upon race, alienage, and national origin, are inherently suspect and must therefore be subjected to close judicial scrutiny. We agree and, indeed, find at least implicit support for such an approach in our unanimous decision only last Term in Reed v. Reed [404 U.S. 71 (1971)]....

[The Court reviews the attitude of "romantic paternalism" discussed in *Reed*.] As a result of notions such as these, our statute books gradually became laden with gross, stereotyped distinctions between the sexes and, indeed, throughout much of the 19th century the position of women in our society was, in many respects, comparable to that of blacks under the pre-Civil War slaves codes. Neither slaves nor women could hold office, serve on juries, or bring suit in their own names, and married women traditionally were denied the legal capacity to hold or convey property or to serve as legal guardians of their own children.- ... And although blacks were guaranteed the right to vote in 1870, women were denied even that right... until adoption of the Nineteenth Amendment half a century later.

It is true, of course, that the position of women in America has improved markedly in recent decades. Nevertheless, it can hardly be doubted that, in part because of the high visibility of the sex characteristic, women still face pervasive, although at times more subtle, discrimination in our educational institutions, in the job market and, perhaps most conspicuously, in the political arena....

Moreover, since sex, like race and national origin, is an immutable characteristic determined solely by the accident of birth, the imposition of special disabilities upon the members of a particular sex because of their sex would seem to violate "the basic concept of our system that legal burdens should bear some relationship to individual responsibility...." Weber v. Aetna Casualty & Surety Co. [406 U.S. 164 (1972)]. And what differentiates sex from such non-suspect statuses as intelligence or physical disability, and aligns it with the recognized suspect criteria, is that the sex characteristic frequently bears no relation to ability to perform or contribute to society. As a result, statutory distinctions between the sexes often have the effect of invidiously relegating the entire class of females to inferior legal status without regard to the actual capabilities of its individual members.

We might also note that, over the past decade, Congress has itself manifested an increasing sensitivity to sex-based classifications. In [Title VII] of the Civil Rights Act of 1964, for example, Congress expressly declared that no employer, labor union, or other organization subject to the provisions of the Act shall discriminate against any individual on the basis of "race, color, religion, sex, or national origin." Similarly, the Equal Pay Act of 1963 provides that no employer covered by the Act "shall discriminate . . . between employees on the basis of sex." And §1 of the Equal Rights Amendment, passed by Congress on March 22, 1972, and submitted to the legislatures of the States for ratification, declares that "(e)quality of rights under the law shall not be denied or abridged by the United States or by any State on account of sex." Thus, Congress itself has concluded that classifications based upon sex are inherently invidious, and this conclusion of a coequal branch of Government is not without significance to the question presently under consideration. . . .

With these considerations in mind, we can only conclude that classifications based upon sex, like classifications based upon race, alienage, or national origin, are inherently suspect, and must therefore be subjected to strict judicial scrutiny. Applying the analysis mandated by that stricter standard of review, it is clear that the statutory scheme now before us is constitutionally invalid.

The sole basis of the classification established in the challenged statutes is the sex of the individuals involved. . . .

[T]he Government concedes that the differential treatment accorded men and women under these statutes serves no purpose other than mere "administrative convenience." In essence, the Government maintains that, as an empirical matter, wives in our society frequently are dependent upon their husbands, while husbands rarely are dependent upon their wives. Thus, the Government argues that Congress might reasonably have concluded that it would be both cheaper and easier simply conclusively to presume that wives of male members are financially dependent upon their husbands, while burdening female members with the task of establishing dependency in fact.[22]

The Government offers no concrete evidence, however, tending to support its view that such differential treatment in fact saves the Government any money. In order to satisfy the demands of strict judicial scrutiny, the Government must demonstrate, for example, that it is actually cheaper to grant increased benefits with respect to all male members, than it is to determine which male members are in fact entitled to such benefits and to grant increased benefits only to those members whose wives actually meet the dependency requirement. Here, however, there is substantial evidence that, if put to the test, many of the wives of male members would fail to qualify for benefits. And in light of the fact that the dependency determination with respect to the husbands of female members is presently made solely on the basis of affidavits rather than through the more costly

---

22. It should be noted that these statutes are not in any sense designed to rectify the effects of past discrimination against women. . . . On the contrary, these statutes seize upon a group — women — who have historically suffered discrimination in employment, and rely on the effects of this past discrimination as a justification for heaping on additional economic disadvantages.

hearing process, the Government's explanation of the statutory scheme is, to say the least, questionable.

In any case, our prior decisions make clear that, although efficacious administration of governmental programs is not without some importance, "the Constitution recognizes higher values than speed and efficiency." Stanley v. Illinois, 405 U.S. 645, 656 (1972). And when we enter the realm of "strict judicial scrutiny," there can be no doubt that "administrative convenience" is not a shibboleth, the mere recitation of which dictates constitutionality.... We therefore conclude that, by according differential treatment to male and female members of the uniformed services for the sole purpose of achieving administrative convenience, the challenged statutes violate the Due Process Clause of the Fifth Amendment insofar as they require a female member to prove the dependency of her husband.

Reversed.

Mr. Justice STEWART concurs in the judgment, agreeing that the statutes before us work an invidious discrimination in violation of the Constitution. Reed v. Reed [404 U.S. 71].

Mr. Justice REHNQUIST dissents for the reasons stated by Judge Rives in his opinion for the District Court, Frontiero v. Laird, 341 F. Supp. 201 (1972).

Mr. Justice POWELL, with whom THE CHIEF JUSTICE and Mr. Justice BLACKMUN join, concurring in the judgment....

It is unnecessary for the Court in this case to characterize sex as a suspect classification, with all of the far-reaching implications of such a holding. Reed v. Reed, [404 U.S. 71 (1971)], which abundantly supports our decision today, did not add sex to the narrowly limited group of classifications which are inherently suspect.... In my view, we can and should decide this case on the authority of *Reed* and reserve for the future any expansion of its rationale.

There is another, and I find compelling, reason for deferring a general categorizing of sex classifications as invoking the strictest test of judicial scrutiny. The Equal Rights Amendment, which if adopted will resolve the substance of this precise question, has been approved by the Congress and submitted for ratification by the States. If this Amendment is duly adopted, it will represent the will of the people accomplished in the manner prescribed by the Constitution.... It seems to me that this reaching out to pre-empt by judicial action a major political decision which is currently in process of resolution does not reflect appropriate respect for duly prescribed legislative processes....

Orr v. Orr
440 U.S. 268 (1979)

Mr. Justice BRENNAN delivered the opinion of the Court.

The question presented is the constitutionality of Alabama alimony statutes which provide that husbands, but not wives, may be required to pay alimony upon divorce.

On February 26, 1974, a final decree of divorce was entered, dissolving the marriage of William and Lillian Orr. That decree directed appellant, Mr. Orr, to pay appellee, Mrs. Orr, $1,240 per month in alimony. On July 28, 1976, Mrs. Orr initiated a contempt proceeding in the Circuit Court of Lee County, Ala., alleging that Mr. Orr was in arrears in his alimony payments. On August 19, 1976, at the hearing on Mrs. Orr's petition, Mr. Orr submitted in his defense a motion requesting that Alabama's alimony statutes be declared unconstitutional because they authorize courts to place an obligation of alimony upon husbands but never upon wives. The Circuit Court denied Mr. Orr's motion and entered judgment against him. . . . Relying solely upon his federal constitutional claim, Mr. Orr appealed the judgment. . . . We now hold the challenged Alabama statutes unconstitutional and reverse. . . .

The fact that the classification expressly discriminates against men rather than women does not protect it from scrutiny. Craig v. Boren, [429 U.S. 190 (1976)]. "To withstand scrutiny" under the Equal Protection Clause, "'classifications by gender must serve important governmental objectives and must be substantially related to achievement of those objectives.'" Califano v. Webster, [430 U.S. 313, 316-317 (1977)]. . . .

Appellant views the Alabama alimony statutes as effectively announcing the State's preference for an allocation of family responsibilities under which the wife plays a dependent role, and as seeking for their objective the reinforcement of that model among the State's citizens. . . .

The opinion of the Alabama Court of Civil Appeals suggests other purposes that the statute may serve. Its opinion states that the Alabama statutes were "designed" for "the wife of a broken marriage who needs financial assistance," 351 So. 2d at 905. This may be read as asserting either of two legislative objectives. One is a legislative purpose to provide help for needy spouses, using sex as a proxy for need. The other is a goal of compensating women for past discrimination during marriage, which assertedly has left them unprepared to fend for themselves in the working world following divorce. We concede, of course, that assisting needy spouses is a legitimate and important governmental objective. We have also recognized "[r]eduction of the disparity in economic condition between men and women caused by the long history of discrimination against women . . . as . . . an important governmental objective," Califano v. Webster [supra]. It only remains, therefore, to determine whether the classification at issue here is "substantially related to achievement of those objectives." Id.

Ordinarily, we would begin the analysis of the "needy spouse" objective by considering whether sex is a sufficiently "accurate proxy," Craig v. Boren [supra], for dependency to establish that the gender classification rests "'upon some ground of difference having a fair and substantial relation to the object of the legislation,'" Reed v. Reed, [404 U.S. 71, 77 (1971)]. Similarly, we would initially approach the "compensation" rationale by asking whether women had in fact been significantly discriminated against in the sphere to which the statute applied a sex-based classification, leaving the sexes "not similarly situated with respect to opportunities" in that sphere, Schlesinger v. Ballard, [419 U.S. 498, 508 (1975)]. Compare Califano v. Webster, [supra] and Kahn v. Shevin, [416 U.S. 351, 353 (1974)], with Weinberger v. Wiesenfeld, [420 U.S. 636, 648 (1975)].

But in this case, even if sex were a reliable proxy for need, and even if the institution of marriage did discriminate against women, these factors still would "not adequately justify the salient features of" Alabama's statutory scheme.... Under the statute, individualized hearings at which the parties' relative financial circumstances are considered already occur.... There is no reason, therefore, to use sex as a proxy for need. Needy males could be helped along with needy females with little if any additional burden on the State. In such circumstances, not even an administrative-convenience rationale exists to justify operating by generalization or proxy. Similarly, since individualized hearings can determine which women were in fact discriminated against vis-à-vis their husbands, as well as which family units defied the stereotype and left the husband dependent on the wife, Alabama's alleged compensatory purpose may be effectuated without placing burdens solely on husbands. Progress toward fulfilling such a purpose would not be hampered, and it would cost the State nothing more, if it were to treat men and women equally by making alimony burdens independent of sex. "Thus, the gender-based distinction is gratuitous; without it, the statutory scheme would only provide benefits to those men who are in fact similarly situated to the women the statute aids," Weinberger v. Wiesenfeld [420 U.S. at 653], and the effort to help those women would not in any way be compromised.

Moreover, use of a gender classification actually produces perverse results in this case. As compared to a gender-neutral law placing alimony obligations on the spouse able to pay, the present Alabama statutes give an advantage only to the financially secure wife whose husband is in need. Although such a wife might have to pay alimony under a gender-neutral statute, the present statutes exempt her from that obligation. Thus, "[t]he [wives] who benefit from the disparate treatment are those who were . . . nondependent on their husbands," Califano v. Goldfarb, [430 U.S. 199, 221 (1977)] (Stevens, J., concurring in judgment). They are precisely those who are not "needy spouses" and who are "least likely to have been victims of . . . discrimination," id., by the institution of marriage. A gender-based classification which, as compared to a gender-neutral one, generates additional benefits only for those it has no reason to prefer cannot survive equal protection scrutiny.

Legislative classifications which distribute benefits and burdens on the basis of gender carry the inherent risk of reinforcing the stereotypes about the "proper place" of women and their need for special protection.... Thus, even statutes purportedly designed to compensate for and ameliorate the effects of past discrimination must be carefully tailored. Where, as here, the State's compensatory and ameliorative purposes are as well served by a gender-neutral classification as one that gender classifies and therefore carries with it the baggage of sexual stereotypes, the State cannot be permitted to classify on the basis of sex. And this is doubly so where the choice made by the State appears to redound — if only indirectly — to the benefit of those without need for special solicitude. Reversed and remanded.

[The concurring opinions by Justices Blackmun and Stevens are omitted. The dissenting opinion by Justice Powell urging abstention, and the dissenting opinion by Justice Rehnquist, with whom the Chief Justice joined, urging that the plaintiff has no standing because he is a nondependent spouse who is not in a position to benefit from a sex-neutral statute, are also omitted.]

2. The Right to Equal Group Treatment

≡ *Stanton v. Stanton*
≡ 421 U.S. 7 (1975)

Mr. Justice BLACKMUN delivered the opinion of the Court.

This case presents the issue whether a state statute specifying for males a greater age of majority than it specifies for females denies, in the context of a parent's obligation for support payments for his children, the equal protection of the laws guaranteed by § 1 of the Fourteenth Amendment.

[The case is an appeal arises from divorce proceedings, following a stipulated judgment requiring, among other things, that the father pay child support to the mother for a daughter and a son. The father discontinued support payments for the daughter when she turned 18, even though under Utah Code Ann. § 15-2-1 (1953) he was required to support the son until he reached the age of 21. Pursuant to the challenged statute establishing different support obligations toward female and male children, the Supreme Court of Utah affirmed the denial of the mother's motion for further support.] ...

We find it unnecessary in this case to decide whether a classification based on sex is inherently suspect. ... *Reed* we feel, is controlling here. ... "A classification 'must be reasonable, not arbitrary, and must rest upon some ground of difference having a fair and substantial relation to the object of the legislation, so that all persons similarly circumstanced shall be treated alike.'" ... The test here, then, is whether the difference in sex between children warrants the distinction in the appellee's obligation to support that is drawn by the Utah statute. We conclude that it does not. It may be true, as the Utah court observed and as is argued here, that it is the man's primary responsibility to provide a home and that it is salutary for him to have education and training before he assumes that responsibility; that girls tend to mature earlier than boys; and that females tend to marry earlier than males. The last mentioned factor, however, under the Utah statute loses whatever weight it otherwise might have, for the statute states that "all minors obtain their majority by marriage"; thus minority, and all that goes with it, is abruptly lost by marriage of a person of either sex at whatever tender age the marriage occurs.

Notwithstanding the "old notions" to which the Utah court referred, we perceive nothing rational in the distinction drawn by § 15-2-1 which, when related to the divorce decree, results in the appellee's liability for support for Sherri only to age 18 but for Rick to age 21. This imposes "criteria wholly unrelated to the objective of that statute." A child, male or female, is still a child. No longer is the female destined solely for the home and the rearing of the family, and only the male for the marketplace and the world of ideas. ... Women's activities and responsibilities are increasing and expanding. Coeducation is a fact, not a rarity. The presence of women in business, in the professions, in government and, indeed, in all walks of life where education is a desirable, if not always a necessary, antecedent is apparent and a proper subject of judicial notice. If a specified age of minority is required for the boy in order to assure him parental support while he attains his education and training, so, too, is it for the girl. To distinguish between the two on educational grounds is to be self-serving: if the female is not to be supported so long as the male, she hardly can be expected to attend school as long as he does, and bringing her education to an end earlier coincides with the role-typing society has long imposed. And if any weight remains in this day to the claim of earlier maturity of the female, with a concomitant inference of absence of need for support beyond 18, we fail to perceive its unquestioned truth or its significance, particularly when marriage, as the statute provides, terminates minority for a person of either sex. . . .

[Whether the common law age of 21 applies to both children or the remedy for the unconstitutional inequality is to treat males as adults at age 18] is an issue of state law to be resolved by the Utah courts on remand. . . .

[The dissenting opinion by Mr. Justice Rehnquist is omitted.]

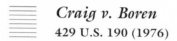

Craig v. Boren
429 U.S. 190 (1976)

Mr. Justice BRENNAN delivered the opinion of the Court, with whom Mr. Justice POWELL, Mr. Justice STEVENS, Mr. Justice BLACKMUN (in part), and Mr. Justice STEWART concurred.

The interaction of two sections of an Oklahoma statute . . . prohibits the sale of "nonintoxicating" 3.2% beer to males under the age of 21 and to females under the age of 18. The question to be decided is whether such a gender-based differential constitutes a denial to males 18-20 years of age of the equal protection of the laws in violation of the Fourteenth Amendment.

This action was brought in the District Court for the Western District of Oklahoma on December 20, 1972, by appellant Craig, a male then between 18 and 21 years of age, and by appellant Whitener, a licensed vendor of 3.2% beer. The complaint sought declaratory and injunctive relief against enforcement of the gender-based differential on the ground that it constituted invidious discrimination against males 18-20 years of age. A three-judge court . . . sustained the constitutionality of the statutory differential and dismissed the action. . . . We reverse. . . .

To withstand constitutional challenge . . . classifications by gender must serve important governmental objectives and must be substantially related to achievement of those objectives. . . . We accept for purposes of discussion the District Court's identification of the objective underlying [the statutes in question] as the enhancement of traffic safety. Clearly, the protection of public health and safety represents an important function of state and local governments. However, appellees' statistics in our view cannot support the conclusion that the gender-based distinction closely serves to achieve that objective and therefore the distinction cannot under [Reed v. Reed, 404 U.S. 71 (1971)] withstand equal protection challenge.

The appellees introduced a variety of statistical surveys. First, an analysis of arrest statistics for 1973 demonstrated that 18-20-year-old male arrests for "driving under the influence" and "drunkenness" substantially exceeded female arrests for that same age period. Similarly, youths aged 17-21 were found to be overrepresented among those killed or injured in traffic accidents, with males again numerically exceeding females in this regard. Third, a random roadside survey in Oklahoma City revealed that young males were more inclined to drive and drink beer than were their female counterparts. Fourth, Federal Bureau of Investigation nationwide statistics exhibited a notable increase in arrests for "driving under the influence." Finally, statistical evidence gathered in other jurisdictions, particularly Minnesota and Michigan, was offered to corroborate Oklahoma's experience by indicating the pervasiveness of youthful participation in motor vehicle accidents following the imbibing of alcohol. Conceding that "the case is not free from doubt," 399 F. Supp. at 1314, the District Court nonetheless concluded that this statistical showing substantiated "a rational basis for the legislative judgment underlying the challenged classification." Id., at 1307.

Even were this statistical evidence accepted as accurate, it nevertheless offers only a weak answer to the equal protection question presented here. The most focused and relevant of the statistical surveys, arrests of 18-20-year-olds for alcohol-related driving offenses, exemplifies the ultimate unpersuasiveness of this evidentiary record. Viewed in terms of the correlation between sex and the actual activity that Oklahoma seeks to regulate — driving while under the influence of alcohol — the statistics broadly establish that .18% of females and 2% of males in that age group were arrested for that offense. While such a disparity is not trivial in a statistical sense, it hardly can form the basis for employment of a gender line as a classifying device. Certainly if maleness is to serve as a proxy for drinking and driving, a correlation of 2% must be considered an unduly tenuous "fit." [12] Indeed, prior cases have consistently rejected the use of sex as a decisionmaking factor even though the statutes in question certainly rested on far more predictive empirical relationships than this.

Moreover, the statistics exhibit a variety of other shortcomings that seriously impugn their value to equal protection analysis. Setting aside the obvious methodological problems, [14] the surveys do not adequately justify the salient features of Oklahoma's gender-based traffic-safety law. None purports to measure the use and dangerousness of 3.2% beer as opposed to alcohol generally, a detail that is of particular importance since, in light of its low alcohol level, Oklahoma apparently considers the 3.2% beverage to be "nonintoxicating." . . . Moreover, many of the studies, while graphically documenting the unfortunate increase in driving while

---

12. Obviously, arrest statistics do not embrace all individuals who drink and drive. But for purposes of analysis, this "underinclusiveness" must be discounted somewhat by the shortcomings inherent in this statistical sample, see n. 14, infra. In any event, we decide this case in light of the evidence offered by Oklahoma and know of no way of extrapolating these arrest statistics to take into account the driving and drinking population at large, including those who avoided arrest.

14. The very social stereotypes that find reflection in age-differential laws, see Stanton v. Stanton, 421 U.S. 7, 14-15 (1975), are likely substantially to distort the accuracy of these comparative statistics. Hence, "reckless" young men who drink and drive are transformed into arrest statistics, whereas their female counterparts are chivalrously escorted home.... Moreover, the Oklahoma surveys, gathered under a regime where the age-differential law in question has been in effect, are lacking in controls necessary for appraisal of the actual effectiveness of the male 3.2% beer prohibition. In this regard, the disproportionately high arrest statistics for young males — and, indeed, the growing alcohol-related arrest figures for all ages and sexes — simply may be taken to document the relative futility of controlling driving behavior by the 3.2% beer statute and like legislation, although we obviously have no means of estimating how many individuals, if any, actually were prevented from drinking by these laws.

under the influence of alcohol, make no effort to relate their findings to age-sex differentials as involved here. Indeed, the only survey that explicitly centered its attention upon young drivers and their use of beer — albeit apparently not of the diluted 3.2% variety — reached results that hardly can be viewed as impressive in justifying either a gender or age classification.[16]

There is no reason to belabor this line of analysis. It is unrealistic to expect either members of the judiciary or state officials to be well versed in the rigors of experimental or statistical technique. But this merely illustrates that proving broad sociological propositions by statistics is a dubious business, and one that inevitably is in tension with the normative philosophy that underlies the Equal Protection Clause. Suffice to say that the showing offered by the appellees does not satisfy us that sex represents a legitimate, accurate proxy for the regulation of drinking and driving. In fact, when it is further recognized that Oklahoma's statute prohibits only the selling of 3.2% beer to young males and not their drinking the beverage once acquired (even after purchase by their 18-20-year-old female companions), the relationship between gender and traffic safety becomes far too tenuous to satisfy *Reed*'s requirement that the gender-based difference be substantially related to achievement of the statutory objective.

We hold, therefore, that under *Reed*, Oklahoma's 3.2% beer statute invidiously discriminates against males 18-20 years of age. . . .

[The opinion of Mr. Justice Powell, concurring, is deleted.]

Mr. Justice STEVENS, concurring.

There is only one Equal Protection Clause. It requires every State to govern impartially. It does not direct the courts to apply one standard of review in some cases and a different standard in other cases. Whatever criticism may be leveled at a judicial opinion implying that there are at least three such standards applies with the same force to a double standard. . . .

In this case, the classification is not as obnoxious as some the Court has condemned,[1] nor as inoffensive as some the Court has accepted. It is objectionable because it is based on an accident of birth, because it is a mere remnant of the now almost universally rejected tradition of discriminating against males in this age bracket, and because, to the extent it reflects any physical difference between

---

16. The random roadside survey of drivers conducted in Oklahoma City during August 1972 found that 78% of drivers under 20 were male. Turning to an evaluation of their drinking habits and factoring out nondrinkers, 84% of the males versus 77% of the females expressed a preference for beer. Further 16.5% of the men and 11.4% of the women had consumed some alcoholic beverage within two hours of the interview. Finally, a blood alcohol concentration greater than .01% was discovered in 14.6% of the males compared to 11.5% of the females. "the 1973 figures, although they contain some variations, reflect essentially the same pattern." 399 F. Supp., at 1309. Plainly these statistical disparities between the sexes are not substantial. Moreover, when the 18-20 age boundaries are lifted and all drivers analyzed, the 1972 roadside survey indicates that male drinking rose slightly whereas female exposure to alcohol remained relatively constant. Again, in 1973, the survey established that "compared to all drivers interviewed, . . . the under-20 age group generally showed a lower involvement with alcohol in terms of having drunk within the past two hours or having a significant BAC (blood alcohol content)." [Id.] In sum, this survey provides little support for a gender line among teenagers and actually runs counter to the imposition of drinking restrictions based upon age.

1. Men as a general class have not been the victims of the kind of historic, pervasive discrimination that has disadvantaged other groups.

males and females, it is actually perverse.[4] The question then is whether the traffic safety justification put forward by the State is sufficient to make an otherwise offensive classification acceptable.

The classification is not totally irrational. For the evidence does indicate that there are more males than females in this age bracket who drive and also more who drink. Nevertheless, there are several reasons why I regard the justification as unacceptable. It is difficult to believe that the statute was actually intended to cope with the problem of traffic safety,[5] since it has only a minimal effect on access to a not very intoxicating beverage and does not prohibit its consumption. Moreover, the empirical data submitted by the State accentuate the unfairness of treating all 18–20-year-old males as inferior to their female counterparts. The legislation imposes a restraint on 100% of the males in the class allegedly because about 2% of them have probably violated one or more laws relating to the consumption of alcoholic beverages. It is unlikely that this law will have a significant deterrent effect either on that 2% or on the law-abiding 98%. But even assuming some such slight benefit, it does not seem to me that an insult to all of the young men of the State can be justified by visiting the sins of the 2% on the 98%. . . .

[The opinions of Mr. Justice Blackmun and Mr. Justice Stewart, concurring, and the opinion of Mr. Justice Burger, dissenting, are deleted.]

Mr. Justice REHNQUIST, dissenting. . . .

I think the Oklahoma statute challenged here need pass only the "rational basis" equal protection analysis . . . and I believe that it is constitutional under that analysis.

Most obviously unavailable to support any kind of special scrutiny in this case, is a history or pattern of past discrimination, such as was relied on by the plurality in [Frontiero v. Richardson, 411 U.S. 677 (1973)] to support its invocation of strict scrutiny. There is no suggestion in the Court's opinion that males in this age group are in any way peculiarly disadvantaged, subject to systematic discriminatory treatment, or otherwise in need of special solicitude from the courts.

The Court does not discuss the nature of the right involved, and there is no reason to believe that it sees the purchase of 3.2% beer as implicating any important interest, let alone one that is "fundamental" in the constitutional sense of invoking strict scrutiny. . . .

It is true that a number of our opinions contain broadly phrased dicta implying that the same test should be applied to all classifications based on sex, whether affecting females or males. . . . However, before today, no decision of this Court has applied an elevated level of scrutiny to invalidate a statutory discrimination harmful to males, except where the statute impaired an important

---

4. Because males are generally heavier than females, they have a greater capacity to consume alcohol without impairing their driving ability than do females.
5. There is no legislative history to indicate that this was the purpose. . . . [This discrimination] represented nothing more than the perpetuation of a stereotyped attitude about the relative maturity of the members of the two sexes in this age bracket. . . .

personal interest protected by the Constitution.[1] There being no such interest here, and there being no plausible argument that this is a discrimination against females,[2] the Court's reliance on our previous sex-discrimination cases is ill-founded. It treats gender classification as a talisman which — without regard to the rights involved or the persons affected — calls into effect a heavier burden of judicial review.

The Court's conclusion that a law which treats males less favorably than females "must serve important governmental objectives and must be substantially related to achievement of those objectives" apparently comes out of thin air. The Equal Protection Clause contains no such language, and none of our previous cases adopt that standard. I would think we have had enough difficulty with the two standards of review which our cases have recognized — the norm of "rational basis," and the "compelling state interest" required where a "suspect classification" is involved — so as to counsel weightily against the insertion of still another "standard" between those two. How is this Court to divine what objectives are important? How is it to determine whether a particular law is "substantially" related to the achievement of such objective, rather than related in some other way to its achievement? Both of the phrases used are so diaphanous and elastic as to invite subjective judicial preferences or prejudices relating to particular types of legislation, masquerading as judgments whether such legislation is directed at "important" objectives or, whether the relationship to those objectives is "substantial" enough. I would have thought that if this Court were to leave anything to decision by the popularly elected branches of the Government, where no constitutional claim other than that of equal protection is invoked, it would be the decision as to what governmental objectives to be achieved by law are "important," and which are not. As for the second part of the Court's new test, the Judicial Branch is probably in no worse position than the Legislative or Executive Branches to determine if there is any rational relationship between a classification and the purpose which it might be thought to serve. But the introduction of the adverb "substantially" requires courts to make subjective judgments as to operational effects, for which neither their expertise nor their access to data fits them. And even if we manage to avoid both confusion and the mirroring of our own preferences in the development of this new doctrine, the thousands of judges in

1. In Stanley v. Illinois, 405 U.S. 645 (1972)...the Court struck down a statute allowing separation of illegitimate children from a surviving father but not a surviving mother, without any showing of parental unfitness. The Court stated that "the interest of a parent in the companionship, care, custody, and management of his or her children 'come[s] to this Court with a momentum for respect lacking when appeal is made to liberties which derive merely from shifting economic arrangements.'" In Kahn v. Shevin, 416 U.S. 351 (1974)...the Court upheld Florida's $500 property tax exemption for widows only. The opinion of the Court appears to apply a rational-basis test....

2. I am not unaware of the argument from time to time advanced, that all discriminations between the sexes ultimately redound to the detriment of females, because they tend to reinforce "old notions" restricting the roles and opportunities of women. As a general proposition applying equally to all sex categorizations, I believe that this argument was implicitly found to carry little weight in our decisions upholding gender-based differences. See Schlesinger v. Ballard, 419 U.S. 498 (1975); Kahn v. Shevin, 416 U.S. 351 (1974). Seeing no assertion that it has special applicability to the situation at hand, I believe it can be dismissed as an insubstantial consideration.

other courts who must interpret the Equal Protection Clause may not be so fortunate. . . .

Notes

1. Individualized-Based and Group-Based Equality. Cases such as *Reed* and *Orr*, involving matters as to which individualized hearings already take place, presented relatively favorable sites for the origins of modern sex discrimination law. In a context of individualized decisionmaking where the state already held hearings, it had little to gain in using sex as a proxy, and arguably little to lose in being prevented from doing so. Moreover, disregarding the sex of the individual should produce sounder results, given the underlying legitimate goals in cases such as *Reed*, *Orr*, and *Frontiero*.

By contrast, *Craig* and *Stanton* arose in the context of questions that do not lend themselves easily to individualized fact-finding. There are many such matters, including the right to vote, marry, drive, serve in the military, and attend public schools, as well as to drink alcoholic beverages (*Craig*) and to receive financial support from one's parents (*Stanton*). In such cases, individualized decisionmaking is not an alternative, and sex in some matters may be a good proxy for characteristics the state would otherwise find hard to measure. With these cases, then, the Court began to confront the problems with stereotypes that have some basis in fact. Being true may make the classifications a good fit with the state's underlying substantive objectives, but decisions based on them only reinforce and perpetuate the inequality they reflect.

At a distance of three decades, these cases do not seem so difficult, but at the time they were decided, most members of the all-male Court did not perceive them as straightforward. The recently released papers of Justice Blackmun offer a window into how one of those who voted ultimately to overturn the gender preference in *Reed* viewed the case and the arguments underlying it. The brief in *Reed*, on which Ruth Bader Ginsburg had collaborated as an advocate, argued that the probate code compounded the "subordination of women." It claimed that "American women have been stigmatized historically as an inferior class and are today subject to pervasive discrimination. . . . A person born female continues to be branded inferior for this congenital and unalterable condition of birth." Blackmun found the brief "mildly offensive and arrogant" and out of proportion in what he considered "a very simple little case." It was "much ado about nothing" since the estate in dispute amounted to less than $1000. However, Blackmun also recognized that it was meant as a "test case" and he was prepared to join the majority because "there can be no question that women have been held down in the past in almost every area." He advised the Court to write "brief and simple opinion" and hoped that "we do not get into a long and emotional discussion about women's rights." For the full story, see Linda Greenhouse, Becoming Justice Blackmun: Harry Blackmun's Supreme Court Journey 209-211 (2005).

Was the Court's decision to write a "brief and simple" opinion in *Reed* the right choice? How much guidance does it provide about what is wrong with sex-based classifications and which ones might pass constitutional scrutiny? Does

Blackmun's reference to "emotional" arguments about women's rights reflect the same kinds of stereotypes that underpinned the classifications in *Reed*, *Orr*, and the cases that followed?

2. The Role of Stereotyping. The articulated standard in these cases, at least from *Craig* forward, is that the challenged classification must serve important governmental objectives and bear a substantial relationship to the achievement of those objectives. At the same time, note the frequency with which the Supreme Court's analysis focuses on the harm of stereotyping, rather than on the imperfect fit between valid objectives and the classification. Consider the following:

> [T]he components of the intermediate scrutiny standard — a practice "substantially related to an important governmental objective" — have rarely been the moving parts in a Supreme Court sex discrimination decision. Rather, the bulk of work in these decisions has been done by what readers of the opinions may be tempted to treat as mere decorative rhetorical flourish — the proposition that there are constitutional objections to "gross, stereotyped distinctions between the sexes," that is to say, to "classifications based on sex . . . premised on overbroad generalizations." To determine whether there is unconstitutional sex discrimination, one need generally ask only two questions: (1) Is the rule of practice at issue sex-respecting, that is to say, does it distinguish on its face between males and females? and (2) Does the sex-respecting rule rely on a stereotype? In the constitutional . . . law of sex discrimination, "stereotype" has become a term of art by which is simply meant any imperfect proxy, any overbroad generalization. For a sex-respecting rule to withstand constitutional scrutiny by the Court, it seems to be at least necessary and usually sufficient that it embody some perfect proxy. That is to say, the assumption at the root of the sex-respecting rule must be true of either all women or no women or all men or no men; there must be a zero or a hundred on one side of the sex equation or the other.

Mary Anne Case, "The Very Stereotype the Law Condemns": Constitutional Sex Discrimination Law as a Quest for Perfect Proxies, 85 Cornell L. Rev. 1447, 1449-1450 (2000).

Does Case's analysis fit the cases set forth so far? Reconsider the analysis after reading Personnel Administrator of Massachusetts v. Feeney, infra, and United States v. Virginia, infra. What about cases where the Court sustains the classification? Aren't stereotypes involved in Kahn v. Shevin, infra, and Rostker v. Goldberg, infra?

3. Remedying Formal Equality Defects. Formal equality defects often can be eliminated in more than one way. Formal gender neutrality could be achieved in *Orr* either by eliminating alimony for both husbands and wives, or by leaving the state's system of individualized alimony determinations in place and extending eligibility to dependent husbands. 440 U.S. at 282. The latter alternative, which is the option Alabama chooses, presents the classic "won the battle but lost the war" scenario for Mr. Orr: he prevails on the constitutional point, but remains liable for alimony (albeit under a different, gender-neutral regime). Should his lawyer have advised him of this likelihood? If adequately counseled, what would a rational client do in his circumstances? Note also that the formal equality principles applied in *Craig* and *Stanton* did not compel any particular resolution: the state could use the higher age or the lower age or some other age altogether, just so long as they used the same age for both males and females.

Frontiero also presents the rule-maker with options — either require all employees to demonstrate dependency, or extend dependency benefits to all spouses. The first option would have the same effect as the ultimate result in *Orr*: all spouses would have to show dependency in order to receive the attendant benefits. Instead, the court decides to extend the presumption of dependency to all spouses, putting the burden on Congress to eliminate the presumption if it so chose. Thus while, as in *Orr*, a benefit previously available only to members of one sex was extended to both, in *Frontiero* the effect of extending the benefit is to give a windfall to some employees — female as well as male. It seems clear enough why Mr. Orr should not have the relief to which he was not entitled — escape from alimony obligations — simply because other husbands (dependent ones) were victims of unconstitutional discrimination: Mr. Orr was not like those other, dependent husbands. It may seem less clear that Sharron Frontiero and her husband should receive dependency benefits when her husband was not a dependent, simply because some other potential claimants, who also were not dependent, were receiving them. Another way of looking at this issue is that while in *Reed*, *Orr*, *Craig*, and *Stanton* the Court forces the state to abandon gender-based stereotypes and adopt an approach that is *more accurate*, in *Frontiero* extension of the presumption actually renders the fringe-benefit scheme *less accurate*. Is this a problem, constitutionally speaking? Is it consistent with the analysis set forth in note 2, above, by Mary Anne Case?

As the cases in the next note reveal as well, courts have been reluctant to resolve violations of formal equality in the sex discrimination context by "leveling down" the benefits or treatment to the lowest common denominator. The appropriate approach in such cases may well turn on the type of discrimination one is trying to address. Deborah Brake argues that there are three circumstances in which leveling down might be appropriate:

> (1) where the injury from the discrimination is a formal equality injury that may be remedied by the end of differential treatment; (2) where some leveling down is necessary to set a sustainable baseline consistent with equal concern; and (3) where the benefit at issue is so distorted by privilege that equal concern requires the relinquishment, rather than the extension, of unjust privilege.

Deborah L. Brake, When Equality Leave Everyone Worse Off: The Problem of Leveling Down in Equality Law, 46 Wm. & Mary L. Rev. 513, 524 (2004). In other situations, she argues, making everyone worse off is not a cure for inequality, but an exacerbation of it. Id. at 524-525. Can you think of some examples of each of these categories?

4. Distinguishing Employment-Based Dependency Benefits from Social Welfare. Subsequent to *Frontiero*, two cases challenged sex-based classifications in the Social Security Act that illustrate the complexity of eliminating sex discrimination in the context of government benefits programs. Weinberger v. Wiesenfeld, 420 U.S. 636 (1975), concerned a provision that provided spousal benefits only to widows, not widowers, without respect to need and without the opportunity for a widower to show that he was dependent on his wife. The Court, in an opinion also written by Justice Brennan, held that "given the purpose of enabling the surviving parent to remain at home to care for a child, the gender-based distinction . . . is entirely irrational." 420 U.S. at 651. Amendments following *Wiesenfeld* extended survivors' benefits to widowers, but only if they showed that they received at least one-half of their support from their deceased wives. In the case challenging the extra burden imposed on widowers, Califano v. Goldfarb, 430 U.S. 199 (1977), the plaintiff-widower could not establish dependency according to this standard, which he claimed violated equal protection since a similarly situated nondependent widow was eligible for benefits without such a showing. As in *Frontiero*, the person challenging the statute sought dependency benefits even though he wasn't a dependent, on the grounds that a similarly situated person of the other sex, by virtue of the sex-based presumption, would have received (equally undeserved) benefits.

In defense of the statutory presumption in *Goldfarb*, the government attempted to distinguish the case from *Frontiero* by arguing that the benefit in question was not a contractual benefit that impermissibly used sex as a proxy for dependency but rather a social welfare scheme defining different standards of eligibility based on the differing social welfare needs of widowers and widows. Support for this argument was sought from a prior United States Supreme Court case, Kahn v. Shevin, 416 U.S. 351 (1974), which had upheld a $500 property tax exemption for widows, but not widowers, on the grounds that women faced financial needs at the death of their spouses not equal to those faced by men. (This case is excerpted in Chapter 2, p. 152.) Rather than face the reasoning of *Kahn* directly, Justice Brennan, writing for the Court in *Goldfarb*, distinguished the case by determining that the purpose of the statutory scheme at issue was to determine dependency, not need, and thus that *Frontiero* controlled, rather than *Kahn*.

Justice Stevens, in a separate concurring opinion in *Goldfarb*, applied the single-standard form of equal protection review he urged in *Craig*. Under this standard, a sex-based classification may sometimes be sufficiently rational to pass constitutional muster, but not if its actual purposes, as may be revealed by its actual effects, are improper ones. In *Goldfarb*, Justice Stevens found the presumption irrational after determining that for the administrative convenience of processing the applications of the estimated 90 percent of widows who are dependent, "perhaps $750 million" in payments are made to the remaining, nondependent widows. 430 U.S. at 220. Given this costly trade-off, Justice Stevens concluded that the "actual reason" for the presumption was neither administrative convenience nor redressing the "legacy of economic discrimination" against women; it was, rather, the accidental byproduct of a traditional way of thinking about females.... In my judgment, something more than accident is necessary to justify the disparate treatment of persons who have as strong a claim to equal treatment as do similarly situated surviving spouses.

430 U.S. at 223. Following this line of analysis, Justice Stevens found nothing worth salvaging in *Kahn* and noted that it was effectively ignored, if not explicitly overruled, by *Wiesenfeld*. See also Wengler v. Druggists Mut. Ins. Co., 446 U.S. 142 (1980) (Missouri statute granting worker's compensation death benefits to widows, but not widowers, without proof of actual dependency violates equal protection).

Further amendments by Congress to the Social Security Act eliminated the need to prove dependency for widowers, but to avoid the possible windfall for plaintiffs such as Goldfarb who may have pensions based both on their own previous employment and that of their wives, Congress imposed a requirement that an individual's own pension be set off against any entitlement acquired through one's spouse's employment. In order to protect the reliance interests of female employees who may have planned their retirements based on the "double" benefits potentially available to them under pre-1977 law, this offset provision was delayed for *women* for five years. This sex-based, five-year exemption from the pension offset requirement was itself challenged in Heckler v. Mathews, 465 U.S. 728 (1984). In an opinion written also by Justice Brennan, the exemption was upheld as a "temporary" effort to protect "reasonable reliance interests" through "reasoned analysis" rather than "archaic generalizations about the roles and abilities of men and women." 465 U.S. at 750. Is this reasoning persuasive? Does it meet the requirements of formal equality? Is the exemption an example of a "perfect proxy"?

5. Who Is the Protected Victim? One question in some of these cases is who the victim of discrimination is. In *Goldfarb* and *Frontiero*, for example, is it the female wage-earner whose benefits are lower because her husband is not presumed to be a dependent, or the male dependent himself? Justice Brennan in *Goldfarb* determined that since the benefits were based upon contributions made by a female employee on the basis of her earnings, the discrimination was, as in *Frontiero*, a discrimination against female employees. Justice Rehnquist, in a part of his dissenting opinion in *Goldfarb* that was joined by four other Justices, reasoned that the discrimination at issue was a discrimination against those for whom dependency benefits were sought, i.e., men.

What are the consequences? None, if you think that discrimination against men should be analyzed the same as discrimination against women. But Justice Rehnquist's view in his dissenting opinion in *Craig* (and other early cases) was that when the "victim" of the discrimination is male, the constitutional standard of review appropriate to other forms of "social welfare legislation" — i.e., the rational basis test — is all that is required (and that administrative convenience satisfies this standard). Consider this position, in light of the Court's view, shared by Chief Justice Rehnquist, that affirmative action plans designed to eliminate the effects of past discrimination against racial minorities be subject to the same strict standard as rules and practices that exclude or disadvantage those minorities. See pp. 167-170 in Chapter 2.

One approach to the "victim" problem is reflected in such cases as *Orr* and *Craig*, but found frivolous by Justice Rehnquist in footnote 2 to his dissent in *Craig*: to assume that women are harmed not only by discrimination against them, but also by discrimination that favors them, when this discrimination is based on, and thus perpetuates, traditional stereotypes. How would you evaluate this proposition?

6. The Equal Rights Amendment. The Equal Rights Amendment (the "ERA") referred to in both Justice Brennan's and Justice Powell's opinions in *Frontiero* failed by three states to gain the support of two-thirds (38) of the states by the Congressional deadline of June 30, 1982 (a date already extended three years beyond the original 1979 deadline). The simple language of the proposed amendment read: "Equality of rights under the law shall not be denied or abridged by the United States or by any state on account of sex." It was assumed that the passage of the ERA would have mandated a stricter review of classifications based on sex, amounting in effect to the kind of "strict scrutiny" favored by four Justices in *Frontiero*. For a comprehensive analysis of how the ERA would have been applied, see Barbara A. Brown et al., The Equal Rights Amendment: A Constitutional Basis for Equal Rights for Women, 80 Yale L.J. 871 (1971). The ERA did not itself resolve fundamental issues about when sexual differences warrant different treatment. See Ruth Bader Ginsburg, Sexual Equality Under the Fourteenth and Equal Rights Amendments, 1979 Wash. U. L.Q. 161, 176 ("No one can predict with complete assurance how the Amendment will be interpreted and applied . . ."). As a result, the significance of its passage — or its loss — was perhaps more symbolic than anything else. Id. at 177.

The viability of the ERA over 20 years after it failed the ratification process is still a debated topic. The ratification of the 27th Amendment (Congressional Pay Amendment) in 1992, more than 200 years after it was originally proposed, may offer encouragement for a revival of the ERA. See Brannon P. Denning & John R. Vile, Necromancing the Equal Rights Amendment, 17 Const. Comment 593 (2000); Allison L. Held et al., The Equal Rights Amendment: Why the ERA Remains Legally Viable and Properly Before the States, 3 Wm. & Mary J. Women & L. 113 (1997). Some scholars contest whether there is still a need for the ERA in light of the significant advancement of women since its failure. See Mary Anne Case, Reflections on Constitutionalizing Women's Equality, 90 Cal. L. Rev. 765 (2002); David A. Strauss, Comment, The Irrelevance of Constitutional Amendments, 114 Harv. L. Rev. 1457 (2001); Martha Craig Daughtrey, Seventy-five Years Madison Lecture: Women and the Constitution: Where We Are at the End of the Century, 75 N.Y.U. L. Rev. 1 (2000). The Amendment has been reintroduced in Congress periodically since the turn of the twenty-first century. See Carolyn B. Maloney, Here Comes the ERA Again, Ms., Summer 2005, at 23. A national poll taken on Women's Equality Day (which commemorates the anniversary of passage of the women's suffrage amendment) found that 96 percent of Americans supported legal protection of women's rights; 82 percent believed that those rights were already protected under the United States Constitution;

and 69 percent (including 58 percent of Republicans) supported amending the Constitution to include language that specifically protects women. Chris Lombardi, Women's Equality Day Poll Finds Support for ERA, www.womensenews.org, August 27, 2002. Given such support, why has passage proved so difficult? What is at stake? Should the Amendment be a priority for the women's rights movement?

A number of individual states enacted their own versions of the ERA into their constitutions: Utah in 1896, Wyoming in 1890, and fourteen others between 1970 and 1977. See Beth Gammie, State ERAs: Problems and Possibilities, 1989 U. Ill. L. Rev. 1123, 1125-1126 (1989). Early reviews of decisions under state equal rights amendments found no systematic relation between results, rationales, and formal standards. Some gender classifications have survived strict scrutiny under these amendments. See Deborah L. Rhode, Justice and Gender 92 (1989). Does that suggest that the importance of a federal Equal Rights Amendment would be largely symbolic? If so, how should that affect debate on its priority for women's rights organizations. Ellen Goodman argues that while an ERA wouldn't change the average woman's life overnight, "words matter.... At the very least, a discussion would jumpstart the dormant debate about a stalled movement." Ellen Goodman, Ironies of the Equal Rights Battle, Boston Globe, Dec. 14, 2003, at D11. Do you agree?

3. The Right to Be Free of Indirect Discrimination

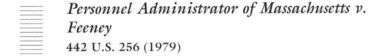

Personnel Administrator of Massachusetts v. Feeney
442 U.S. 256 (1979)

Mr. Justice STEWART delivered the opinion of the Court.

This case presents a challenge to the constitutionality of the Massachusetts veterans' preference statute . . . on the ground that it discriminates against women in violation of the Equal Protection Clause of the Fourteenth Amendment. Under [this statute], all veterans who qualify for state civil service positions must be considered for appointment ahead of any qualifying nonveterans. The preference operates overwhelmingly to the advantage of males.

The appellee Helen B. Feeney is not a veteran. She brought this action pursuant to 42 U.S.C. §1983, alleging that the absolute preference formula established in [the Massachusetts statute] inevitably operates to exclude women from consideration for the best Massachusetts civil service jobs and thus unconstitutionally denies them the equal protection of the laws. The three-judge District Court agreed, one judge dissenting. . . .

The Federal Government and virtually all of the States grant some sort of hiring preference to veterans. The Massachusetts preference, which is loosely termed an "absolute lifetime" preference, is among the most generous. It applies to all positions in the State's classified civil service, which constitute approximately 60% of the public jobs in the State. It is available to "any person, male or female, including a nurse," who was honorably discharged from the United States Armed Forces after at least 90 days of active service, at least one day of which was during "wartime." Persons who are deemed veterans and who are otherwise qualified for a particular civil service job may exercise the preference at any time and as many times as they wish....

The appellee has lived in Dracut, Mass., most of her life. She entered the workforce in 1948, and for the next 14 years worked at a variety of jobs in the private sector. She first entered the state civil service system in 1963, having competed successfully for a position as Senior Clerk Stenographer in the Massachusetts Civil Defense Agency. There she worked for four years. In 1967, she was promoted to the position of Federal Funds and Personnel Coordinator in the same agency. The agency, and with it her job, was eliminated in 1975.

During her 12-year tenure as a public employee, Ms. Feeney took and passed a number of open competitive civil service examinations. On several she did quite well, receiving in 1971 the second highest score on an examination for a job with the Board of Dental Examiners, and in 1973 the third highest on a test for an Administrative Assistant position with a mental health center. Her high scores, however, did not win her a place on the certified eligible list. Because of the veterans' preference, she was ranked sixth behind five male veterans on the Dental Examiner list. She was not certified, and a lower scoring veteran was eventually appointed. On the 1973 examination, she was placed in a position on the list behind 12 male veterans, 11 of whom had lower scores. Following the other examinations that she took, her name was similarly ranked below those of veterans who had achieved passing grades.

Ms. Feeney's interest in securing a better job in state government did not wane. Having been consistently eclipsed by veterans, however, she eventually concluded that further competition for civil service positions of interest to veterans would be futile. In 1975, shortly after her civil defense job was abolished, she commenced this litigation....

The sole question for decision on this appeal is whether Massachusetts, in granting an absolute lifetime preference to veterans, has discriminated against women in violation of the Equal Protection Clause of the Fourteenth Amendment....

The cases of Washington v. Davis, [426 U.S. 229 (1976)], and Arlington Heights v. Metropolitan Housing Dev. Corp., [429 U.S. 252 (1977)], recognize that when a neutral law has a disparate impact upon a group that has historically been the victim of discrimination, an unconstitutional purpose may still be at work. But those cases signaled no departure from the settled rule that the Fourteenth Amendment guarantees equal laws, not equal results. Davis upheld a job-related employment test that white people passed in proportionately greater numbers than Negroes, for there had been no showing that racial discrimination entered into the establishment or formulation of the test. *Arlington Heights* upheld a zoning board decision that tended to perpetuate racially segregated housing patterns, since, apart from its effect, the board's decision was shown to be nothing more than an application of a constitutionally neutral zoning policy. Those principles apply with equal force to a case involving alleged gender discrimination.

When a statute, gender-neutral on its face, is challenged on the ground that its effects upon women are disproportionably adverse, a twofold inquiry is thus appropriate. The first question is whether the statutory classification is indeed neutral in the sense that it is not gender-based. If the classification itself, covert or overt, is not based upon gender, the second question is whether the adverse effect reflects invidious gender-based discrimination.... In this second inquiry, impact provides an "important starting point," [429 U.S. at 266], but purposeful discrimination is "the condition that offends the Constitution." Swann v. Charlotte-Mecklenburg Board of Education, [402 U.S. 1, 16 (1971)]....

The District Court made two central findings that are relevant here: first, that [the statute] serves legitimate and worthy purposes; second, that the absolute preference was not established for the purpose of discriminating against women. The appellee has thus acknowledged and the District Court has thus found that the distinction between veterans and nonveterans drawn by [the statute] is not a pretext for gender discrimination....

Veteran status is not uniquely male. Although few women benefit from the preference the nonveteran class is not substantially all female. To the contrary, significant numbers of nonveterans are men, and all nonveterans — male as well as female — are placed at a disadvantage. Too many men are affected by [the statute] to permit the inference that the statute is but a pretext for preferring men over women.... The dispositive question, then, is whether the appellee has shown that a gender-based discriminatory purpose has, at least in some measure, shaped the Massachusetts veterans' preference legislation....

Discriminatory intent is...either...a factor that has influenced the legislative choice or it is not. The District Court's conclusion that the absolute veterans' preference was not originally enacted or subsequently reaffirmed for the purpose of giving an advantage to males as such necessarily compels the conclusion that the State...intended nothing more than to prefer "veterans." Given this finding, simple logic suggests that an intent to exclude women from significant public jobs was not at work in this law. To reason that it was, by describing the preference as "inherently nonneutral" or "gender-biased," is merely to restate the fact of impact, not to answer the question of intent....

The basic distinction between veterans and nonveterans, having been found not gender-based, and the goals of the preference having been found worthy, [the statute] must be analyzed as is any other neutral law that casts a greater burden upon women as a group than upon men as a group. The enlistment policies of the Armed Services may well have discriminated on the basis of sex.... But the history of discrimination against women in the military is not on trial in this case.

The decision to grant a preference to veterans was of course "intentional." So, necessarily, did an adverse impact upon nonveterans follow from that decision. And it cannot seriously be argued that the Legislature of Massachusetts could have been unaware that most veterans are men. It would thus be disingenuous to say that the adverse consequences of this legislation for women were unintended, in the sense that they were not volitional or in the sense that they were not foreseeable.

"Discriminatory purpose," however, implies more than intent as volition or intent as awareness of consequences.... It implies that the decisionmaker, in this case a state legislature, selected or reaffirmed a particular course of action at least in part "because of," not merely "in spite of," its adverse effects upon an identifiable group.[25] Yet, nothing in the record demonstrates that this preference for veterans was originally devised or subsequently re-enacted because it would accomplish the collateral goal of keeping women in a stereotypic and predefined place in the Massachusetts Civil Service.

To the contrary, the statutory history shows that the benefit of the preference was consistently offered to "any person" who was a veteran. That benefit has been extended to women under a very broad statutory definition of the term veteran. The preference formula itself, which is the focal point of this challenge, was first adopted — so it appears from this record — out of a perceived need to help a small group of older Civil War veterans. It has since been reaffirmed and extended only to cover new veterans. When the totality of legislative actions establishing and extending the Massachusetts veterans' preference are considered...the law remains what it purports to be: a preference for veterans of either sex over non-veterans of either sex, not for men over women.

Veterans' hiring preferences represent an awkward — and, many argue, unfair — exception to the widely shared view that merit and merit alone should prevail in the employment policies of government. After a war, such laws have been enacted virtually without opposition. During peacetime, they inevitably have come to be viewed in many quarters as undemocratic and unwise. Absolute and permanent preferences, as the troubled history of this law demonstrates, have always been subject to the objection that they give the veteran more than a square deal. But the Fourteenth Amendment "cannot be made a refuge from ill-advised...laws."...The substantial edge granted to veterans by [the Massachusetts statute] may reflect unwise policy. The appellee, however, has simply failed to demonstrate that the law in any way reflects a purpose to discriminate on the basis of sex.

The judgment is reversed, and the case is remanded for further proceedings consistent with this opinion....

Mr. Justice STEVENS, with whom Mr. Justice WHITE joins, concurring.... If a classification is not overtly based on gender, I am inclined to believe the question whether it is covertly gender-based is the same as the question whether its adverse effects reflect invidious gender-based discrimination. However the question is phrased, for me the answer is largely provided by the fact that the number of males disadvantaged by Massachusetts' veterans' preference (1,867,000) is sufficiently large — and sufficiently close to the number of disadvantaged females (2,954,000) — to refute the claim that the rule was intended to benefit males as a class over females as a class.

---

25. This is not to say that the inevitability or foreseeability of consequences of a neutral rule has no bearing upon the existence of discriminatory intent. Certainly, when the adverse consequences of a law upon an identifiable group are as inevitable as the gender-based consequences of [the statute at issue in this case], a strong inference that the adverse effects were desired can reasonably be drawn. But in this inquiry — made as it is under the Constitution — an inference is a working tool, not a synonym for proof. When, as here, the impact is essentially an unavoidable consequence of a legislative policy that has in itself always been deemed to be legitimate, and when, as here, the statutory history and all of the available evidence affirmatively demonstrate the opposite, the inference simply fails to ripen into proof.

Mr. Justice MARSHALL, with whom Mr. Justice BRENNAN joins, dissenting....

That a legislature seeks to advantage one group does not, as a matter of logic or of common sense, exclude the possibility that it also intends to disadvantage another. Individuals in general and lawmakers in particular frequently act for a variety of reasons.... Absent an omniscience not commonly attributed to the judiciary, it will often be impossible to ascertain the sole or even dominant purpose of a given statute.... Thus, the critical constitutional inquiry is not whether an illicit consideration was the primary or but-for cause of a decision, but rather whether it had an appreciable role in shaping a given legislative enactment....

Moreover, since reliable evidence of subjective intentions is seldom obtainable, resort to inference based on objective factors is generally unavoidable.... To discern the purposes underlying facially neutral policies, this Court has therefore considered the degree, inevitability, and foreseeability of any disproportionate impact as well as the alternatives reasonably available....

In the instant case, the impact of the Massachusetts statute on women is undisputed. Any veteran with a passing grade on the civil service exam must be placed ahead of a nonveteran, regardless of their respective scores. The District Court found that, as a practical matter, this preference supplants test results as the determinant of upper level civil service appointments.... Because less than 2% of the women in Massachusetts are veterans, the absolute-preference formula has rendered desirable state civil service employment an almost exclusively male prerogative....

As the District Court recognized, this consequence follows foreseeably, indeed inexorably, from the long history of policies severely limiting women's participation in the military....

The legislative history of the statute reflects the Commonwealth's patent appreciation of the impact the preference system would have on women, and an equally evident desire to mitigate that impact only with respect to certain traditionally female occupations. Until 1971, the statute and implementing civil service regulations exempted from operation of the preference any job requisitions "especially calling for women."... In practice, this exemption, coupled with the absolute preference for veterans, has created a gender-based civil service hierarchy, with women occupying low-grade clerical and secretarial jobs and men holding more responsible and remunerative positions....

Thus, for over 70 years, the Commonwealth has maintained, as an integral part of its veterans' preference system, an exemption relegating female civil service applicants to occupations traditionally filled by women. Such a statutory scheme both reflects and perpetuates precisely the kind of archaic assumptions about women's roles which we have previously held invalid.... The Court's conclusion to the contrary — that "nothing in the record" evinces a "collateral goal of keeping women in a stereotypic and predefined place in the Massachusetts Civil Service" — displays a singularly myopic view of the facts established below.[3]

---

3. Although it is relevant that the preference statute also disadvantages a substantial group of men, see [opinion of Stevens, J., concurring], it is equally pertinent that 47% of Massachusetts men over 18 are veterans, as compared to 0.8% of Massachusetts women. Given this disparity, and the indicia of intent noted,... the absolute number of men denied preference cannot be dispositive, especially since they have not faced the barriers to achieving veteran status confronted by women....

To survive challenge under the Equal Protection Clause, statutes reflecting gender-based discrimination must be substantially related to the achievement of important governmental objectives.... Appellants here advance three interests in support of the absolute-preference system: (1) assisting veterans in their readjustment to civilian life; (2) encouraging military enlistment; and (3) rewarding those who have served their country.... Although each of those goals is unquestionably legitimate, the "mere recitation of a benign, compensatory purpose" cannot of itself insulate legislative classifications from constitutional scrutiny. Weinberger v. Wiesenfeld, [420 U.S. 636, 648 (1974)]. And in this case, the Commonwealth has failed to establish a sufficient relationship between its objectives and the means chosen to effectuate them.

With respect to the first interest, facilitating veterans' transition to civilian status, the statute is plainly overinclusive.... By conferring a permanent preference, the legislation allows veterans to invoke their advantage repeatedly, without regard to their date of discharge. As the record demonstrates, a substantial majority of those currently enjoying the benefits of the system are not recently discharged veterans in need of readjustment assistance.

Nor is the Commonwealth's second asserted interest, encouraging military service, a plausible justification for this legislative scheme. In its original and subsequent re-enactments, the statute extended benefits retroactively to veterans who had served during a prior specified period.... If the Commonwealth's "actual purpose" is to induce enlistment, this legislative design is hardly well suited to that end.... For I am unwilling to assume what appellants made no effort to prove, that the possibility of obtaining an ex post facto civil service preference significantly influenced the enlistment decisions of Massachusetts residents. Moreover, even if such influence could be presumed, the statute is still grossly overinclusive in that it bestows benefits on men drafted as well as those who volunteered.

Finally, the Commonwealth's third interest, rewarding veterans, does not "adequately justify the salient features" of this preference system.... Where a particular statutory scheme visits substantial hardship on a class long subject to discrimination, the legislation cannot be sustained unless "'carefully tuned to alternative considerations.'"... Here, there are a wide variety of less discriminatory means by which Massachusetts could effect its compensatory purposes. For example, a point preference system, such as that maintained by many States and the Federal Government, or an absolute preference for a limited duration, would reward veterans without excluding all qualified women from upper level civil service positions. Apart from public employment, the Commonwealth, can, and does, afford assistance to veterans in various ways, including tax abatements, educational subsidies, and special programs for needy veterans.... Unlike these and similar benefits, the costs of which are distributed across the taxpaying public generally, the Massachusetts statute exacts a substantial price from a discrete group of individuals who have long been subject to employment discrimination, and who, "because of circumstances totally beyond their control, have [had] little if any chance of becoming members of the preferred class." 415 F. Supp. at 499....

I would affirm the judgment of the court below.

NOTE ON NONDISCRIMINATORY AND
DISCRIMINATORY INTENT

Did the Idaho and Alabama legislatures in *Reed* and *Orr* "intend" to disadvantage people because of their sex? Probably not, but the point of these cases is that laws based on stereotyped thinking about women are unacceptable, even if—perhaps *especially* if—they are unintentional.

Why, then, in *Feeney*, does the Court allow to stand a system that has a substantially disproportionate impact against women—a much greater practical impact, indeed, than the statutes in *Reed* and *Orr*? One explanation is that, when a rule or practice is facially neutral, it is less clear than when an explicit sex-based distinction is made that discrimination *on the basis of sex* has actually occurred. A showing of discriminatory intent establishes discrimination when it is not otherwise evident.

Should intent be required in order to establish the presence of sex discrimination in cases such as *Feeney*? On the one hand, as noted above, without such a requirement we may be unsure whether discrimination based on sex has actually occurred or whether there is a more benign explanation. On the other hand, rules and practices that are not explicitly sex-based but that have a disproportionate, negative impact against women may be even more dangerous than cases of explicit sex-based discrimination; the stereotypes that guide decisionmaking in such cases may be more hidden and thus easier to perpetuate. In fact, Title VII of the Civil Rights Act of 1964, explored later in this chapter, requires that rules and practices in the employment context that have a disparate impact on women be justified by their job-relatedness, regardless of the "intent" of the employer. See Dothard v. Rawlinson, 433 U.S. 321 (1977), excerpted on p. 100.

Ironically, some direct or explicit sex-based classifications are actually "saved" by the intention to discriminate. For example, in Rostker v. Goldberg, 453 U.S. 57 (1981), the Supreme Court upheld a male-only draft registration system on the theory that, since females could not serve in combat, they were not likely to be subjected to future drafts. The fact that the reasons for the exclusion of women were well reviewed in the legislative history meant that the statute was not an "accidental by-product" of narrow, outmoded stereotypes about women, but a deliberate, reasoned choice. 453 U.S. at 74. *Rostker* is discussed on pp. 628-630 in Chapter 3. Similarly in Mississippi University for Women v. Hogan, 458 U.S. 718 (1982), the Court's conclusion that an all-female state-supported nursing school was a violation of equal protection turned in part on the origins of the school and stereotyped notions about what it was appropriate to train women to do. Justice O'Connor suggests in her opinion for the Court that if the intent had been to compensate women for the disadvantage they experienced in their educational or employment opportunities, another result might have followed. See 458 U.S. at 728-729. *MUW* is further discussed in Chapter 2 at pp. 275-276. An example in the affirmative action context is Contractors Ass'n of Eastern Pennsylvania v. City of Philadelphia, 6 F.3d 990, 1010 (3d Cir. 1993), cert. denied, 519 U.S. 1113 (1997) (affirmative action plan favoring women will pass intermediate scrutiny if it is shown to be "a product of analysis rather than a stereotyped reaction based on habit").

To the extent that a showing of discriminatory intent seems analytically desirable, what should be required to establish it? In *Feeney*, the fact that few women performed military service was a "neutral fact" used to disprove discriminatory intent. Was this analysis sound?

Some suggest that disparate impact analysis—because it does not require proof of motive—is aimed at smoking out discriminatory states of mind that may not be otherwise apparent. Others view this analysis as addressing the structural barriers that are a product of past discrimination that are unintentional but lingering. See Richard A. Primus, Equal Protection and Disparate Impact: Round Three, 117 Harv. L. Rev. 493, 515 (2003). The issues of intent and unconscious discrimination are explored further on pp. 74-83 in this chapter in the context of employment discrimination cases. See Section B.

Putting Theory into Practice

1-1. The following exchange is reported as part of a voir dire examination conducted by a judge in a criminal case in a municipal court in California:

> *The Court*: Miss Bobb, what is your occupation?
> *Miss Bobb*: I'm an attorney.
> *The Court*: And in your practice do you practice criminal law as well as civil law?
> *Miss Bobb*: No, I practice entirely bankruptcy law.
> *The Court*: All right. Is there a Mr. Bobb?
> *Miss Bobb*: I have some difficulty with that question because I've noticed only the women have been asked to answer that.
> *The Court*: Yes, I know. Do you have a Mr. Bobb—is there a Mr. Bobb?
> *Miss Bobb*: Are you going to [poll] the men to see if they care to disclose—
> *The Court*: No, I'm just going to ask you if you have a husband or not. Do you have a husband?
> *Miss Bobb*: I don't care to answer it then. What's relative to women is relative to men.
> *The Court*: Yes, I know. What is your husband's occupation?
> *Miss Bobb*: I don't care to answer that.
> *The Court*: I instruct you to answer.
> *Miss Bobb*: I don't think I should.
> *The Court*: I've got—you understand that you'll be in contempt of Court—jury—you're an attorney, you understand these rules, don't you?
> *Miss Bobb*: No, I do not understand why only the women are asked certain questions and the men aren't asked the same questions.
> *The Court*: The question to you, Mrs. Bobb—you're an attorney at law, you understand the rules and regulations of—of—of being an attorney. And the question to you now simply is: What is your husband's occupation?
> *Miss Bobb*: I refuse to answer.
> *The Court*: You're held in contempt of Court, Mrs. Bobb.

Bobb v. Municipal Court, 192 Cal. Rptr. 270, 270-271 (Cal. App. 1983). To what extent will formal equality principles provide relief to Mrs. Bobb? Is Mrs. Bobb's resistance reasonable?

1-2. In response to acts of violence in and around school occurring between warring factions of rival gangs, a school board instituted a ban on students wearing or displaying any gang symbol. This ban is interpreted in one school to bar males, but not females, from wearing earrings, because some males who wear earrings do so as a sign of gang allegiance while earrings on females do not have any gang significance. Does the rule offend formal equality principles?

1-3. A Veterans Administration rule requires that all chaplains at VA hospitals be "ordained" clergy members. The requirement is shown to have a disparate impact on women since in the Roman Catholic church, among others, women cannot be ordained as priests. Does the rule offend formal equality principles?

C. FORMAL EQUALITY IN EMPLOYMENT

1. The Equal Pay Act: Formal Equality Paradigm?

EEOC v. Madison Community Unit School District No. 12
818 F.2d 577 (7th Cir. 1987)

POSNER, Circuit Judge.

The Equal Employment Opportunity Commission brought this suit against the school district of Madison, Illinois, charging that the district was paying female athletic coaches in its high school and junior high school less than male coaches, in violation of the Equal Pay Act of 1963. That Act . . . forbids an employer to

> discriminate . . . between employees on the basis of sex by paying wages to employees . . . at a rate less than the rate at which he pays wages to employees of the opposite sex . . . for equal work on jobs the performance of which requires equal skill, effort, and responsibility, and which are performed under similar working conditions, except where such payment is made pursuant to [(i) a seniority system; (ii) a merit system; (iii) a system which measures earnings by quantity or quality of production; or] (iv) a differential based on any other factor other than sex: Provided, That an employer who is paying a wage rate differential in violation of this subsection shall not, in order to comply with the provisions of this subsection, reduce the wage rate of any employee.

29 U.S.C. §206(d)(1). . . .

The trial brought out the following facts:

[Luvenia] Long was paid substantially less for coaching girls' track than Steptoe, a man, was paid for coaching boys' track. Although the boys' track program included more students and had more meets than the girls', Steptoe had two assistant coaches compared to Long's one, and as a result Long and

Steptoe devoted approximately equal time to their coaching jobs. Long also coached the girls' tennis team, and Jakich, a man, the boys' tennis team; and Jakich was paid more than Long even though there were no significant differences between the teams in number of students, length of season, or number of practice sessions; however, the boys' team played almost twice as many matches as the girls' team. Long was also assistant coach of the girls' basketball team one year and received lower pay than Tyus, the male assistant coach of the boys' track team. The district judge found that the work of the two assistant coaches was substantially equal and required the same skill, effort, and responsibility — except that Long worked longer hours than Tyus. [Carol] Cole, who coached the girls' volleyball, girls' basketball, and girls' softball teams, was paid less for coaching volleyball than the male coach of the boys' soccer team, less for coaching basketball than the male coach of the boys' soccer team, and less for coaching softball than the male coach of the boys' baseball team. Also, as assistant coach of the girls' track team she was paid less than the assistant coach of the boys' track team. In all of these cases the judge found that the work of the female coach and her male counterpart was the same in skill, effort (including time), and responsibility. Any potential differences in effort and responsibility stemming from the fact that the boys' teams were sometimes larger and played longer seasons were, he found, offset by the fact that the head coaches of the boys' teams had more assistants than their female counterparts. . . .

The first question we must decide is whether the pairs of jobs that the district judge compared in finding unequal pay are sufficiently similar to be "equal work" within the meaning of the Equal Pay Act. The Act is not a general mandate of sex-neutral compensation. It does not enact "comparable worth" — the principle that wages should be based on "objective" factors, rather than on market conditions of demand and supply which may depress wages in jobs held mainly by women relative to wages in jobs held mainly by men. See American Nurses' Assn. v. Illinois, 783 F.2d 716, 718-20 (7th Cir. 1986). A female secretary paid less than a male janitor cannot complain under the Equal Pay Act that the disparity in their wages is not justified by "objective" factors such as differences in skill, responsibility, and effort. . . . The Act requires equal pay only when men and women are performing "equal work on jobs the performance of which requires equal skill, effort, and responsibility, and which are performed under similar working conditions." 29 U.S.C. § 206(d)(1). The working conditions of a janitor are different from those of a secretary, and so are the skills and responsibilities of the two jobs. The Act does not prohibit paying different wages even if the result is to pay a woman less than a man and by doing so "underpay" her because the difference in the wage rate is greater than necessary to compensate the male for any greater skill, effort, or responsibility required by, or any inferior working conditions encountered in, his job.

Thus the jobs that are compared must be in some sense the same to count as "equal work" under the Equal Pay Act; and here we come to the main difficulty in applying the Act: whether two jobs are the same depends on how fine a system of job classifications the courts will accept. If coaching an athletic team in the Madison, Illinois school system is considered a single job rather than a congeries of jobs, the school district violated the Equal Pay Act prima facie by paying female holders of this job less than male holders, and the only question is whether the district carried its burden of proving that the lower wages which the four female coaches received were lower than the wages of their male counterparts because of a factor other than sex. If on the other hand coaching the girls' tennis team is considered a different job from coaching the boys' tennis team, and a fortiori if coaching the girls' volleyball or basketball team is considered a different job (or jobs) from coaching the boys' soccer team, there is no prima facie violation. So the question is how narrow a definition of job the courts should be using in deciding whether the Equal Pay Act is applicable.

We can get some guidance from the language of the Act. The Act requires that the jobs compared have "similar working conditions," not the same working conditions. This implies that some comparison of different jobs is possible. It is true that similarity of working conditions between the jobs being compared is not enough to bring the Act into play — the work must be "equal" and the jobs must require "equal" skill, effort, and responsibility, as well as similar working conditions. But since the working conditions need not be "equal," the jobs need not be completely identical.

Estimating and comparing the skill, effort, responsibility, and working conditions in two jobs are factual determinations. . . . We can overturn them, therefore, only if they are clearly erroneous. . . . The district judge found (among other things) that coaching a girls' tennis team is sufficiently like coaching a boys' tennis team, coaching a girls' softball team is sufficiently like coaching a boys' hardball team, and, indeed, coaching a girls' volleyball or basketball team is sufficiently like coaching a boys' soccer team, to allow each pair of jobs to be described as involving equal work, as requiring equal skill, effort, and responsibility, and as being performed under similar working conditions. . . .

There are pitfalls in allowing any comparisons between different jobs, and they are illustrated by this case. One is a tendency to focus entirely on the measurable differences and ignore the equally or more important but less readily measurable ones. The witnesses in this case concentrated on the amount of skill and time required for coaching girls' and boys' teams and paid little attention to responsibility. It may be true that because the boys' teams tend to have more assistant coaches than the girls' teams, the head coaches of the boys' teams put in no more time than the head coaches of the girls' teams even when the boys' teams are larger and play more matches. But normally there is greater responsibility (one of the dimensions in which the statute requires equality between the jobs compared) if you have a staff than if you don't. That is one reason why the president of a company is paid more than a junior executive who, lacking staff assistance, may work longer hours. "Direction of others as well as value of commodity worked upon and overall importance of assignment may be considered as part of an [employee's] job responsibility." 109 Cong. Rec. 9209 (1963) (remarks of Congressman Goodell).

Another difference tends to be ignored when effort, which is hard to measure, is equated to time, which is easy to measure. Boys and girls differ on average in strength, speed, and perhaps other dimensions of athletic ability; there may also be important differences in their attitudes toward athletic competition. The differences between boys and girls in athletic aptitude and interest may make coaching a boys' team harder — or easier — than coaching a girls' team; there can be no confidence that the two jobs require equal effort. The district judge set aside this consideration by ruling that a difference in the sex of students, customers, etc., can't be used to justify a pay difference under the Equal Pay Act. But this is wrong. The reference to "factor other than sex" refers to the sex of the employee, not the sex of the employer's customers, clients, or suppliers. . . . Suppose that the school district happened to have just male, or just female, coaches and paid coaches more for coaching boys' teams than girls' teams. Men paid less than other men for coaching, or women paid less than other women, could not complain of a violation of the Equal Pay Act. . . . The Act did not seek to eliminate whatever differences between the sexes might make it harder to coach a boys' team than a girls' team. If it is harder (we are not saying it is harder — we are just discussing possibilities), the statutory requirement of equal effort is not met and the differential in pay is outside the scope of the Act.

Nevertheless, we are unwilling to hold that coaches of girls' and boys' teams can never be found to be doing equal work requiring equal skill, effort, and responsibility and performed under similar working conditions. Above the lowest rank of employee, every employee has a somewhat different job from every other one, even if the two employees being compared are in the same department. So if "equal work" and "equal skill, effort, and responsibility" were taken literally, the Act would have a minute domain. . . .

But the words "very much alike," "closely related," or, as the cases sometimes say, "substantially equal" — even the words "virtually identical" — are not synonymous with "identical." . . . There is a gray area, which we must be vigilant to police, between "very much alike," which is within the scope of the Act, and "comparable," which is outside; for it is plain that Congress did not want to enact comparable worth as part of the Equal Pay Act of 1964. . . .

The courts have thus had to steer a narrow course. The cases do not require an absolute identity between jobs, but do require substantial identity. The line is a fine, perhaps imperceptible, one. . . .

Whatever answer we might give, if we were the finders of fact, to the question whether coaching a girls' tennis team and coaching a boys' tennis team are sufficiently alike to be equal work within the meaning of the Act, we cannot, on the record compiled in this case (a potentially important qualification), deem the district court's determination clearly erroneous. . . .

Boys' teams might of course be greater revenue producers than girls' teams. Jacobs v. College of William & Mary, 517 F. Supp. 791, 797 (E.D. Va. 1980), aff'd without opinion, 661 F.2d 922 (4th Cir. 1981), relied on this factor. . . . But *Jacobs* involved college teams. Madison has only one revenue-producing team, the boys' high-school basketball team, and the plaintiffs do not complain about the higher wage that the head coach of that team received — they acknowledge that his job is not the same as that of any female coach. . . .

For those of us whose knowledge of athletic coaching is confined to newspaper and television accounts of the travails of professional and college coaches, the idea of homogenizing the coaching profession in the manner attempted by the plaintiffs and accepted by the district judge is discordant. But we must, by an effort of imagination, place ourselves in a different world, that of small-town high-school and junior-high-school athletics, where the coach's task is not to compete for money in a high-pressure environment but to impart elementary athletic skills and norms of sportsmanship to adolescents. Given these modest goals, a finding that the coaching of boys' and of girls' tennis involves inconsequential differences in skill, effort, responsibility, and working conditions is not so improbable that we can set it aside. . . . Although we conclude that there is no objection in principle to comparing different coaching jobs, the record of the present case does require us to distinguish between coaching boys' and girls' teams of the same sport and coaching boys' and girls' teams of different sports. The judge equated coaching girls' basketball and girls' volleyball to coaching boys' soccer (and, in the assistant-coach comparisons, girls' basketball with boys' track), without regard for the fact that Madison treats coaching a different sport as a different coaching job irrespective of the sex of either the coach or the team. . . . We are willing to assume that hardball and fast-pitch softball — similar sports played under similar rules — are the same sport for purposes of the Equal Pay Act. See Brennan v. Woodbridge School District, 74 Labor Cases ¶33,121, at p. 46,627 (D. Del. 1974). But given the wage differentials among the male coaches, we cannot make this assumption for volleyball and soccer, or for basketball and soccer. Another consideration is the arbitrariness of the particular comparisons suggested by the plaintiffs. In 1980 Long, as girls' track coach, received the same wage as the male coach of the boys' soccer team. How was the school district to know that a court would think basketball and soccer or volleyball and soccer a closer pair than track and soccer? We vacate the findings of the district judge with respect to a violation of the Equal Pay Act in the comparison between boys' soccer and girls' volleyball, boys' soccer and girl's basketball, and boys' track and girls' basketball.

With this exception we conclude that the plaintiffs did establish a prima facie case of violation of the Equal Pay Act, and we move on to consider defenses, of which only one ("factor other than sex") is relevant. Madison argues that the sex of the teams is a factor other than sex, and though the district court thought this wrong, we disagree as we have said; the factor other than sex to which the Act refers is a factor other than the employee's sex. . . . If Madison, having decided for reasons unrelated to the sex of the coaches that coaches of male teams should be paid more than coaches of female teams, neither prohibited nor even discouraged women from coaching male teams, the difference in pay between male coaches of boys' teams and female coaches of girls' teams would be due to a decision unrelated to the sex of the coaches. But Madison discouraged women, including Cole and Long, from applying to coach boys' teams, which not only adds a reason related to the sex of the coaches for a difference in pay between men and women to a reason related solely to the sex of the team members, but also casts doubt on the bona fides of the school district's claim to have based the difference in the pay of coaches of male and of female teams solely on the sex of the team members. . . . There was contrary evidence: a woman once was hired to coach the boys' tennis team and was paid the same as her male predecessor; several times men were hired to coach girls' teams and paid the same as female coaches of those teams. But such job offers were very rare prior to the EEOC's investigation, and the district judge was entitled to find their evidentiary significance outweighed by the evidence that women were discouraged from applying to coach boys' teams.

The reason for discouraging women from coaching boys' teams was that the school authorities were concerned about the "locker room problem." This may or may not be a good reason... but it does suggest that women receive less pay than men for doing what the district court found was equal work within the meaning of the Equal Pay Act because they are women; their sex makes them ineligible to receive the higher wage that men receive for equal work. Even if the school district is entitled to insist that coaches and coached be of the same sex, if the work of each coach is the same and the reason for the difference in pay is the difference in the sex of the coach, the Equal Pay Act is violated. An employer cannot divide equal work into two job classifications that carry unequal pay, forbid women to compete for one of the classifications, and defend the resulting inequality in pay between men and women by reference to a "factor other than [the] sex" of the employees.... It would not be the sexual segregation that had caused the inequality in pay, but a decision to pay men more for doing the same work as women (albeit with a "clientele" of a different sex from the women's "clientele")....

Notes

1. **The Wage Gap.** Although the wage gap between women's and men's earnings has been slowly eroding, it remains significant. Adjusting for hours worked (but not for differences in education, experience, or time in the workforce), women's median weekly earnings in 1979 were 63 percent those of men. By 2004, the figure was 80 percent. U.S. Department of Labor, Bureau of Labor Statistics, Women in the Labor Force: A Databook 47 (May 2005), at 47, www.bls.gov/cps/wlf-databook2005.htm. The gap is narrower among African Americans (89 percent) and Hispanics (87 percent). Id. At current rates of change, it would take an estimated half century to achieve gender parity. Institute on Women's Policy Research, Women's Economic Status in the States: Wide Disparities by Race, Ethnicity, and Region (2004).

Women, of course, have not all benefited equally from the shrinking of the wage gap. For instance, although earnings for women with college degrees have increased more than earnings for males with college degrees, the wage disparity between men and women with higher education continues to be larger than it is for the overall population (75 percent for college degrees, 77 percent for doctoral degrees, and 65 percent for professional degrees, respectively). Id. at 48-49. Similarly, while women now constitute about half of the workforce in occupations typified by high earnings (executive, administrative, and managerial positions), these female employees earn only 71 percent of what their male colleagues earn and are underrepresented in the best-paid positions. Id. at 50. With the exception of Asians, women of color are at the bottom of the economic scale. In 2004, the median weekly earnings for men and women broken down by race were: Asian men, $708; Asian Women, $613; white men, $657; white women, $584; African-American men, $525; African-

American women, $505; Hispanic or Latino men, $456; Hispanic or Latino Women, $419. U.S. Dept. of Labor, Women in the Labor Force, supra, at 46, Table 16.

The disparity for older women is greater than for younger women. For example, full-time working women in the 16-24 age bracket earned on average 93 percent of what men earn; women in the 55-64 age range earn only 73 percent. U.S. Dept. of Labor, Bureau of Labor Statistics, Highlights of Women's Earnings in 2003, Report 978 (2004). Particularly in higher paid occupations, including law, the gender gap increases over women's life cycle. See the discussion of women lawyers in note 4 below, at p. 54.

Part of the explanation for the gender gap in wages is the concentration of women in lower-paying occupations. More than three-quarters of women work in two of six job occupational categories: technical, sales, and administrative support; and managerial and professional specialties. Within these categories, almost two-thirds work in the lowest paying area of administrative support. U.S. Dep't of Labor, Bureau of Labor Statistics, Highlights of Women's Earnings in 2000, Report 952, at 2 (August 2001). Women make up the vast majority of the labor force in low-paying fields such as secretaries and administrative assistants (98 percent) and childcare workers (96 percent). U.S. Census Bureau, Evidence from Census 2000 About Earnings by Detailed Occupation for Men and Women 11 (2004). Additionally, women in managerial and professional specialties are more likely to work in relatively lower paying fields. Women constitute about 14 percent of architects and engineers, and 86 percent of paralegals. Even in the same fields, women earn less; the gap for lawyers is 73 percent; for CEOs, 70 percent; for bartenders, 81 percent; and for nurses, 87 percent. U.S. Department of Labor, Bureau of Labor Statistics, Household Data Annual Averages, Table 39 (2004). See Not All Paychecks Are Equal, L.A. Times, March 20, 2005, at M2. Even female dishwashers earn on average $2000 less per year than male dishwashers. U.S. Census Bureau, supra, at 11. According to IRS data, the ratio of men to women earning over $1 million is 13 to 1; among those earning $500,000 to $1 million, the ratio is 10 to 1, and among those earning $200,000 to $500,000, 9 to 1. See Peter Sailer et al., Income by Gender and Age from Information Returns 96-97 (I.R.S. 2002), discussed in David Cay Johnston, As Salary Grows, So Does a Gender Gap, N.Y. Times, May 12, 2002, at § 3, p. 8.

The wage disparity between male and female employees is greater if part-time employees are included; over one-quarter of women are part-time employees, compared with only 11 percent of men. These jobs tend to be paid less on a pro rata basis than full time jobs, and carry fewer benefits. As noted below, women are also more likely to take time out of the labor force, typically for family reasons, which disrupts their earning potential. A majority of women (52 percent) but only 16 percent of men had at least one complete calendar year outside of the labor force. When all of these factors are taken into account, women on average earned only 38 percent of what men earned during the period 1983-1998. Even women who were in the paid labor force for the entire period earned only 57 percent. Men without high school diplomas earned more than women with college degrees; women with graduate degrees earned about the same as male high school graduates. Stephen J. Rose & Heidi I. Hartman,

Still a Man's Labor Market: The Long Term Earnings Gap iii-iv, 18 (Institute for Women's Policy Research, 2004), discussed in Jeff Madrick, Economic Scene, N.Y. Times, June 10, 2004, at C2. For frequently updated data on U.S. employment patterns by race, sex, and age, see the websites of the U.S. Bureau of Labor Statistics at http://www.bls.gov/data/home.htm and the National Commission on Pay Equity, http://www.pay-equity.org. Further analysis of issues relating to part-time and contingent labor appears on pp. 246-247.

   2. The Formal Equality Paradigm. The Equal Pay Act of 1963 is a paradigmatic application of formal equality principles. As its title suggests, the Act requires equal pay for equal work. The main interpretative task is defining what work is equal. It obviously would be unfair to allow employers to circumvent the Act by minor variations in job titles or job descriptions. Thus, the Act has been applied to require the same wages for different job classifications entailing substantially equal duties and involving comparable skill, responsibility, and effort. See 29 C.F.R. § 1620 (2003). See, e.g., Mehus v. Emporia State Univ., 326 F. Supp. 2d 1213 (D. Kan. 2004) (female volleyball coach performed work substantially equal to male basketball coaches, even though basketball revenue and ticket sales were larger than volleyball revenue and ticket sales); Aldrich v. Randolph Central School Dist., 963 F.2d 520 (2d Cir.), cert. denied, 506 U.S. 965 (1992) (female "cleaners" and male "janitors" do essentially equal work, and the use of a civil service examination and classifications system for custodian's position is not a "factor other than sex").

   Successful Equal Pay Act cases, however, are relatively rare, particularly in cases involving upper-level employees. The main problem with administrative and executive positions is the difficulty of finding a close enough comparison employee. See, e.g., Juliene James, The Equal Pay Act in the Courts: A De Facto White-Collar Exemption, 79 N.Y.U. L. Rev. (2004); Mary E. Graham & Julie L. Hitchkiss, A Systematic Assessment of Employer Equal Employment Opportunity Efforts as a Means of Reducing the Gender Earnings Gap, 12 Cornell J.L. & Pub. Pol'y 169 (2002). Courts generally require the plaintiff in an Equal Pay Act suit to identify a particular employee who is earning more for the same work, and it is more difficult to compare the substance of white-collar jobs. A representative example is Georgen-Saad v. Texas Mutual Insurance Co., 195 F. Supp. 2d 853 (W.D. Tex. 2002). There, the plaintiff, a Senior Vice President of Finance, alleged underpayment in comparison with other senior vice presidents in the company. The court dismissed that claim on the ground that "the assertion that any one of these jobs requires 'equal skill, effort, and responsibility' . . . cannot be taken seriously. . . . These are Senior Vice Presidents in charge of different aspects of Defendant's operation; these are not assembly-line workers or customer-service representatives." Id. at 857. In the court's view, the Equal Pay Act could deal with "commodity-like" work, not the functions of high-level executives. Id. at 857. See also Stopka v. Alliance of American Insurers, 141 F.3d 681 (7th Cir. 1998) (jobs of five male vice presidents required insurance skills that were substantially different from responsibilities of only female vice president whose job required administrative skills, even though all division vice presidents were ranked equally under Alliance's Salary Administration Program); Houck v. Virginia Polytechnic Institute, 10 F.3d 204 (4th Cir. 1993) (affirming dismissal of suit by university professor who had used statistical evidence to establish a composite match of male professors, but failed to single out an actual individual with the same qualifications). But see Lawin-McEleney v. Marist College, 239 F.3d 476 (2d Cir. 2001) (female professor's use of statistical averages from pool of entire college faculty could establish liability when there were only three other professors in her department); McMillan v. Massachusetts Society for the Prevention of Cruelty to Animals, 140 F.3d 288 (1st Cir. 1998) (statistical averages from sample of 46 veterinarians employed at the MSPCA over a period of ten years permissible to determine whether employer's conduct conformed to a general pattern of discrimination).

Plaintiffs can also bring wage discrimination claims under Title VII, but the Bennett Amendment to Title VII, 42 U.S.C. § 2000e-2(h), limits liability to claims that would be recognized under the Equal Pay Act. The relationship between the two Acts is explored in City of Los Angeles, Dept. of Water & Power v. Manhart, 435 U.S. 702, 711-714 (1978), set forth on p. 253 in Chapter 2. Some commentators believe that the overlap between the statutes leads to confusion about their requirements, and encourages courts to demand proof of discriminatory intent in both Equal Pay Act and Title VII cases, even though only the latter statute requires such evidence. See Peter Avery, The Diluted Equal Pay Act: How Was It Broken? How Can It Be Fixed?, 56 Rutgers L. Rev. 849 (2004).

The Equal Pay Act addresses unjustified wage differentials based on sex but does not deal with gender biases that underlie the disparities. For example, the Act would not encompass discriminatory behavior that may have prevented women from becoming coaches of male sports teams at Madison Community Unit School. Such claims would proceed under Title VII of the Civil Rights Act of 1964, discussed in the next section.

3. Factors Justifying Differences in Pay. How should courts treat pay disparities that are attributable to market conditions and practices? Consider an employer's willingness to match a worker's salary at a previous position. This common practice is, on the one hand, a practical response to competitive market conditions; on the other hand, it serves to immunize pay disparities that begin elsewhere and to perpetuate the social conditions that the Equal Pay Act was designed to eliminate. The problem is aggravated by the fact that women do not negotiate as effectively as men for their own salaries. See Linda Babcock & Sara Laschever, Women Don't Ask: Negotiation and the Gender Divide (2003). One illustrative study found that male Carnegie Mellon graduates were eight times more likely to negotiate a starting salary than their female classmates. See Betsy Morris, How Corporate America Is Betraying Women, Fortune, Jan. 10, 2005, at 70.

Courts have not been uniform in their approaches to wage disparities based on matching offers and similar market forces. Compare, e.g., Wernsing v. Illinois Dep't of Human Servs., 427 F.3d 466 (7th Cir. 2005) (court "not even slightly tempted" to change its longstanding position that prior salary may be taken into account when setting an employee's starting pay); Brinkley v. Harbour Recreation Club, 180 F.3d 598 (4th Cir. 1999) (pay differential between plaintiff and male replacement hire reflected salary history and market demand and thus was not a factor related to sex), with Glenn v. General Motors Corp., 841 F.2d 1567 (11th Cir. 1988), cert. denied, 488 U.S. 948 (1988) (rejecting employer justification for wage disparity based on male clerks' transfer from higher paying positions than female clerks).

In Corning Glass Works v. Brennan, 417 U.S. 188 (1974), the Supreme Court rejected an employer's claim that market forces justified higher pay for night workers where women had previously been excluded from such positions. 417 U.S. at 205-207. This approach parallels Judge Posner's analysis in Madison, which rejects market explanations if women have not had equal access to the higher-paying jobs. Is this logical? Consider that question in light of the discussion of market forces and pay equity on pp. 198-203 in Chapter 2.

How would you evaluate compensation systems that confer advantages on workers who are "heads of households"? Some employment benefits such as family medical insurance and tuition waivers have such criteria. What underlies these preferences? Could an employer justify the system by showing that heads of household have more stable work histories? Or that these employees have greater economic needs, and that allocating benefits in this fashion maximizes employee satisfaction? Such rationales are quite familiar but they have long justified paying women less than men. See, e.g., Colby v. J.C. Penney Co., Inc., 811 F.2d 1119, 1127-1128 (7th Cir. 1987) (Judge Posner expressing skepticism about business justification for rule). Nonetheless, head-of-household fringe benefits have been upheld. See, e.g., Colby v. J.C. Penney Co., Inc. 926 F.2d 645 (7th Cir. 1991); EEOC v. J.C. Penney Co., Inc., 843 F.2d 249 (6th Cir. 1988).

In 2002-2003, head coaches of women's teams at Division I NCAA schools earned only 62 percent of what coaches of men's teams earned. Corey Bray, 2002-2003 NCAA Gender-Equity Report, at 12, available at http://www.ncaa.org/library/research/gender_equity_study/2002-03/2002-03_gender_equity_report.pdf (2004). Should differences in athletic team revenues justify differences in salaries? Judge Posner in *Madison* sees no problem with a revenue-based criterion as long as women have equal access to the higher paid coaching jobs. Under his analysis, however, failure to treat male and female applicants equally not only would violate Title VII, but it would also help establish an equal pay claim because: (1) it means the woman's sex is a reason for the difference in pay; and (2) it "casts doubt on the bona fides" of the employer's justifications for gender disparities in compensation.

Under this approach, what follows from the fact that in college athletics, women hold less than two percent of the coaching jobs in men's sports in all divisions? See R. Vivian Acosta & Linda Jean Carpenter, Women in Intercollegiate Sport: A Longitudinal, National Study-Twenty Seven Year Update 1977-2004 (2004), at 2, available at http://webpages.charter.net/womeninsport/Acosta-Carp_2004.pdf. Moreover, women's share of coaching jobs for women's teams has declined in recent years. Prior to Title IX, women held over 90 percent of the jobs coaching female athletes. Possibly as a result of Title IX working to improve salaries in coaching positions for women's teams, in 2004, women held only 44 percent of the head coaching jobs for women's intercollegiate teams. Id. at 12. Women hold 41 percent of all intercollegiate athletic administrative positions, and only 18.5 percent of head administrator jobs. Id. at 25. See also Robert Drago et al., Final Report for CAGE: The Coaching and Gender Equity Report 11 (August 15, 2005), available at http://lsir.la.psu.edu/workfam/CAGE.htm.

Does this suggest that rules designed to promote equal opportunity have been ineffective in college athletic employment? Will a reliance on market defenses for differential pay insulate these gender inequalities from review? The 1997 Equal Employment Opportunity Commission Enforcement Guidelines for interpreting Equal Pay Act claims to speak on this problem. The Guidelines insist on "equality in opportunity" and place special burdens on defendant educational institutions in justifying gender disparities in compensation for coaches. See Enforcement Guidance on Sex Discrimination in the Compensation for Sports Coaches in Educational Institutions, EEOC Notice No. 915.002, Empl. Prac. Guide (CCH) Section 3, ¶5527 (Oct. 10, 1997), analyzed in Mel Narol & Joseph A. Martin, A New Defense to the Old Defenses? The EEOC Equal Pay Act Guidelines, 9 Marq. Sports L.J. 175 (1998). Under these Guidelines, in order to justify differential salaries based on differential revenues from male and female sports, the institution must establish that the "revenue discrepancy in no way relates to: (1) institutional discrimination in opportunity, or (2) societal discrimination." In effect, a school must show that (1) the female coach was provided the same opportunities as the male coach to become a revenue producer, and (2) the incongruity in revenue production is not related to lesser interest in female sports, lesser resources devoted to women's athletic programs, or historically discriminatory notions concerning women. The Guidelines also focus on traditional "factor other than sex" defenses, such as the "prior salary defense," the "marketplace defense," and the "additional duties," defense. In each case, the Guidelines make it more difficult for defendant institutions to escape liability by requiring that the "factor other than sex defense is not an element underlying the wage differential either expressly or by implication." Id. Other issues implicated by revenue-producing sports are raised in the discussion of Title IX on pp. 308–310 in Chapter 2.

Should all equal pay defendants have to prove that market-related forces are not themselves a result of discriminatory underpinnings? See, e.g., Charles B. Craver, If Women Don't Ask: Implications for Bargaining Encounters, the Equal Pay Act, and Title VII, 102 Mich. L. Rev. 1104 (2004) (suggesting that societal forces may discourage women from demanding equal pay, and that employers should be held liable for knowingly exploiting women's market vulnerability). For an economic analysis, see Lawrence M. Spizman, The Economist's Role in Equal Pay Act Litigation, 11 J. Legal Econ. 69, 72-73 (2002) (suggesting that courts may improperly fail to consider differential resources invested in male and female workers when evaluating market forces defenses).

Congress has considered but failed to adopt a variety of proposals that would strengthen equal pay enforcement. See, e.g., Fair Pay Act of 1999 (FPA) S. 702, 106th Cong. (1999); H.R. 1271, 106th Cong. (1999) (eliminating the catchall "factor other than sex" defense for all wage discrimination claims and replacing the "substantially equal work" standard of comparability with what the drafters intend to be a broader standard of "equivalent work"); Fair Pay Act of 2005, S. 840, 109th Cong. (2005). See also Paycheck Fairness Act, S. 841, 109th Cong. (2005) (proposed legislation requiring increased Equal Pay Act enforcement, pay negotiation training for women, and the collection of pay information from employers). Commentators have also proposed a variety of methods to reduce job segregation and increase employer accountability. See, e.g., Graham & Hitchkiss, supra (proposing requirements that employers report annual wage and hiring statistics for all employees). For discussion of pay equity strategies, see pp. 193-208 in Chapter 2.

4. Equal Pay for Women Lawyers? As noted earlier, Department of Labor statistics find a gender gap in weekly earnings for lawyers of 73 percent. U.S. Dept. of Labor, Household Data, supra. Although some qualitative evidence suggests that law firm interviewers are more concerned about the marital status and reproductive intentions of women than of men, male and female law graduates seem to fare about the same in initial hiring and compensation processes. However, a gap grows over time. A representative study of Colorado lawyers found that salaries for full-time female lawyers during their first three years of practice were 92 percent of salaries of full-time male lawyers when controlled for years of experience. For lawyers with ten to twenty years of practice, the figure was 74 percent. Nancy Reichman & Joyce S. Sterling, Gender Penalties Revisited 3, 8-11 (Colorado Women's Bar Ass'n 2004), http://cwba.org. See also Nancy J. Reichman & Joyce S. Sterling, Sticky Floors, Broken Steps, and Concrete Ceilings in Legal Careers, 14 Texas Journal of Women and the Law 27 (2004). Similarly, a study of University of Michigan Law school graduates found that salaries of female lawyers were, on average, 71 percent of salaries of male lawyers with equivalent years in practice. For lawyers with fifteen years of experience, the gap was 61 percent. In both the Colorado and Michigan studies, the gap for more experienced lawyers had not narrowed over the previous six to ten years. Id. at 9, 11, citing Eric Freedman, Pay Gap Narrows for Black Lawyers, Remains Wide for Women, Capital News Service, December 5, 2003. See also Virginia Valian, The Cognitive Basis of Gender Bias, 65 Brook. L. Rev. 1037, 1039 (1999) (despite rough equality in entry-level salaries, study of 500 corporate law departments found that income for male general counsel averaged $205,097, while females averaged $152,412).

Do such statistical disparities demonstrate sex-based discrimination? This is an issue of longstanding dispute. Some researchers attribute the gender disparity in earnings to women's different choices and the lower number of hours worked. See, e.g., Bernard F. Lentz & David N. Laband, Sex Discrimination in the Legal Profession 32 (1995). Other experts conclude that studies controlling for various personal characteristics such as education and experience, or employment context, such as sector, specialty, or firm size, consistently leave some portion of the disparity unexplained. See Reichman & Sterling, supra, at 10-11. Researchers also generally find significant differences in the returns to men and women for factors influencing income, like education and family status. For example, one study found that in both small and large firms, men received large income premiums from attaining partnership while the impact of partnership on women's incomes was statistically insignificant. Wynn R. Huang, Gender Differences in the Earnings of Lawyers, 30 Colum. J.L. & Soc. Probs. 267, 302 (1997). Men also obtained higher income premiums from attending a prestigious law school. Id. at 304-305. So too, when controlling for hours worked and other work-related factors, marriage and children are associated with a rise in income for men but not for women. Joni Hersch, The New Labor Market for Lawyers: Will Female Lawyers Still Earn Less? 10 Cardozo Women's L.J. 1, 3 (2003). Some of these patterns may be changing as more women enter the profession and focus increased attention to gender equity. Id.

Although part of the gender disparity in earning reflects women's over-representation in lower-earning specialties such as family law, public interest law, and government service, most research finds that occupational segregation is not the primary cause of the gender wage gap. Huang, supra, at 301, 308, 309; Reichman & Sterling, supra, at 10-11. Cf. Jo Dixon and Caroll Seron, Stratification in the Legal Profession: Sex, Sector, and Salary, 29 L. & Soc'y Rev. 381 (1995) (finding gender differences in returns to human and social capital but noting that disparities are less pronounced in government, which employs a greater percentage of women than the private sector and does not tie compensation to billable hours or business development).

Further discussion of gender inequalities in the legal profession appears on pp. 682-685, 694-697 in Chapter 4. Additional analysis of factors affecting opportunities for women in upper-level employment appears in Section 2 below. Further analysis of explanations for the wage gap appears in the materials on pay equity on pp. 198-203 in Chapter 2.

Putting Theory into Practice

1-4. As head coach of the University of Southern California women's basketball team, Marianne Stanley led her team to four national championships. In 1993, she sought a salary increase from $60,000 to $150,000, to match that paid to George Raveling, the head coach of the men's basketball team. At that time, she had brought her team to the previous three NCAA Tournaments where it advanced to the round of 16 in 1993 and the final eight in 1992. She was named PAC-10 Coach-of-the-Year in 1993. Raveling's team had never won a national championship and did not have as good an NCAA Tournament record.

Both head coaches recruited student athletes, coached basketball, provided academic guidance to team members and supervised their coaching staffs. Coach Raveling was under more pressure to increase the number of spectators in order to help alleviate the million-and-a-half dollar deficit in the athletic department. The pressure was created by the media, public, and the school's administration and donors, which made the men's basketball team a potential source of funds and school loyalty, while the women's basketball team was not viewed as such. The average number of spectators for a men's basketball game was 4,103; for a women's game the average was 762. Stanley made herself available for public appearances but was not required to make any specific number of them, while Raveling's contract required participation in at least twelve outside speaking engagements per year and availability to the media for interviews.

While Stanley was head coach, the USC women's basketball program produced just under $60,000 in revenue. During the same period, the men's basketball program produced revenue of over $4.5 million from ticket sales, broadcast right fees, cable television right fees, PAC-10 conference revenue sharing, guarantees from away games, post season revenue sharing, and endowment income. Supporters of the men's team donated close to $100,000, as compared to under $13,000 by supporters of the women's team.

Stanley had 17 years of coaching experience, as compared to Raveling's 31 years' coaching experience and nine years of marketing and promotional experience outside of coaching.

Does the Equal Pay Act require that USC pay Stanley as much as it pays Raveling? See Stanley v. Univ. of Southern California, 13 F.3d 1313 (9th Cir. 1994), aff'd, 178 F.3d 1069 (9th Cir. 1999), cert. denied, 528 U.S. 1022 (1999) ("Stanley II") (no). Despite the EEOC's 1997 Enforcement Guidelines directing all equal-skill analyses to focus only on those abilities necessary to perform coaching-related duties, the *Stanley II* decision did not reveal how Raveling's worth as an author or media figure related to his coaching ability, nor did the court look at USC's history of resource allocation in areas like public relations. See Andrea M. Giampetro-Meyer, Recognizing and Remedying Individual and Institutional Gender-based Wage Discrimination in Sport, 37 Am. Bus. L.J. 343 (2000). See also Ira Berkow, NCAA Tournament: Sports of The Times — Auriemma Helps Pave The Way at UConn, N.Y. Times, April 2, 1995, §8, p. 2 (male coach of national championship women's basketball team paid $80,000, compared with $150,000 for male coach of national championship men's basketball team).

Stanley went on to become head women's basketball coach at the University of California at Berkeley, where she was paid the same as the men's basketball coach. See Diane Heckman, On the Eve of Title IX's 25th Anniversary: Sex Discrimination in the Gym and Classroom, 21 Nova L. Rev. 545, 600 n.321 (1997). Is this proof of discrimination, or of a well functioning market? She left after four seasons with a losing record, and amidst much controversy. After a college coaching career that included Southern Cal, Berkeley, Stanford, and Penn, Stanley moved to the pros, where she coached the Washington Mystics for two seasons, and then became an assistant coach for the New York Liberty. Vicki L. Friedman, Where Are They Now?, The Virginian Pilot, Feb. 26, 2005, at C7.

1-5. A national clothing store chain has separate departments for women and men's clothing. The merchandise in the men's department is, on average, of higher price and better quality than the merchandise in the women's department, and the store's gross revenues and profit margin is greater for men's clothing. Only male sales personnel work in the men's department; only female personnel work in the women's department. Their salaries reflect base payments plus incentives pegged to the value of the garments sold. Female saleswomen, who receive lower salaries than male salesmen, have challenged the compensation system under the Equal Pay Act. They do not challenge the job segregation, which the store justifies in terms of customer's discomfort at having sales personnel of a different sex in fitting rooms. The company acknowledges that the basic functions of male and female sales personnel is the same, but defends its incentive system as a practice "other than sex," and one that is widespread in the sales industry. What are the best arguments in defense of store policy? Against? How should the court decide? See Hodgson v. Robert Hall Clothes, Inc., 473 F. 2d 589 (3d Cir.), cert. denied sub nom. Brennan v. Robert Hall Clothes, Inc., 414 U.S. 866 (1973) (rejecting Equal Pay claim).

1-6. The all-female nursing faculty at a major university sues the university for violation of the Equal Pay Act, arguing that the skill, effort, and responsibility of their jobs are functionally equivalent to the salaries of the majority-male, higher-paid faculties at the university's law and medical schools. Should they prevail?

2. Title VII: Finding the Limits of Formal Equality

The linchpin of employment discrimination law is Title VII of the Civil Rights Act of 1964, §701 et seq., as amended, 42 U.S.C. §2000e et seq. (1994). The primary purpose of this legislation was to end employment discrimination based on race, and the customary story told is that sex was added by opponents of the bill hoping to defeat it. Note, Developments in the Law — Employment Discrimination and Title VII of the Civil Rights Act of 1964, 84 Harv. L. Rev. 1109, 1167 (1971). This story is disputed by Katherine M. Franke, who argues that the addition of sex to Title VII was the culmination of a "rich congressional legislative history concerning the equal rights of women." See Franke, The Central Mistake of Sex Discrimination Law: The Dissaggregation of Sex from Gender, 144 U. Pa. L. Rev. 1, 16 (1995).

Two theories of employment discrimination have emerged under Title VII. The *disparate treatment* theory addresses employment rules or decisions that treat an employee less favorably than others explicitly because of the employee's race, sex, religion, or national origin. Traditionally, when determining whether there has been disparate treatment based on sex, courts have applied the *McDonnell Douglas/Burdine* framework. See McDonnell Douglas Corp. v. Green, 411 U.S. 792 (1973) (race discrimination); Texas Dep't of Community Affairs v. Burdine, 450 U.S. 248 (1981) (sex discrimination). Under this framework, to establish a prima facie case, a woman must prove that (1) she was qualified for the position under dispute, or was performing her job at a level that rules out the possibility of firing for inadequate job performance; (2) she was not hired, or suffered some other adverse job action by the employer; and (3) someone with roughly equivalent qualifications was hired instead of her, or replaced her. *McDonnell Douglas*, 411 U.S. at 802; *Burdine*, 450 U.S. at 252-254. If the case is based on a charge of retaliatory action, she must prove (1) she engaged in a protected activity known to the employer; (2) thereafter she was subjected to an adverse employment decision by the employer; and (3) there was a causal link between the two. See Mattern v. Eastman Kodak Co., 104 F.3d 702, 705 (5th Cir. 1997), cert. denied, 522 U.S. 932 (1997). A prima facie case creates a rebuttable presumption that the employer's actions were discriminatory, shifting the burden of producing evidence to the employer to articulate some legitimate, non-discriminatory (or non-retaliatory) reason for the adverse action. If such a reason is offered, plaintiff may still establish that it was a pretext. See further discussion on pp. 74-75.

Disparate treatment cases may be brought not only as individual claims, but also as "pattern and practice" claims of systematic disparate treatment against women. In a pattern and practice case, the plaintiff has the initial burden of demonstrating that unlawful discrimination has been the regular policy of the employer. A prima facie pattern and practice case shifts the burden to the employer to show that the employee's proof is inaccurate or insignificant, or to provide a nondiscriminatory explanation for the apparently discriminatory result. An often raised and fairly successful defense to pattern and practice claims backed up by statistical data is that women have a "lack of interest" in the employment in question. See, e.g., EEOC v. Sears, Roebuck & Co., 628 F. Supp. 1264 (N.D. Ill. 1986), aff'd, 839 F.2d 302 (7th Cir. 1988). The Sears case is further discussed on pp. 171-172 in Chapter 2.

If the plaintiff meets her burden of proving that the employer has discriminated against her based on her sex, the employer's only defense in a disparate treatment case is to prove that a sex-based requirement or restriction is a bona fide occupational qualification (BFOQ), which is reasonably necessary to the normal operation of its business. While a number of different tests for the BFOQ defense exist, basically the defense requires the employer to show that "the essence of the business operation would be undermined" by hiring employees without the qualification in question. See Diaz v. Pan American World Airways, Inc., 442 F.2d 385 (5th Cir.) (1971), cert. denied, 404 U.S. 950 (1971). See also UAW v. Johnson Controls, Inc., 499 U.S. 187 (1991), set forth on p. 124.

The second theory under Title VII is *disparate impact* discrimination. Under this theory the plaintiff must show that a facially neutral job requirement or policy impacts disproportionately on women and that this requirement or policy is not related to job performance. See, e.g., Dothard v. Rawlinson, 433 U.S. 321 (1977), infra. Unlike discriminatory impact cases brought under the United States Constitution, see *Feeney*, supra, the plaintiff need not show discriminatory intent under Title VII. Once disparate impact is shown, the burden shifts to the employer to either refute the elements of the plaintiff's case, or demonstrate that the facially neutral job requirement is justified by a business necessity. See Griggs v. Duke Power Co., 401 U.S. 424 (1971). The *Griggs* standard, though undermined by subsequent cases, was essentially reinstated by the Civil Rights Act of 1991. In moving beyond explicitly sex-based discriminations to the effects of particular, facially neutral policies or practices, the disparate impact theory is a significant step beyond the disparate treatment theory. It potentially reaches a large number of cases in which it is the consequences of rules and not their formal structure or discriminatory intent that are objectionable. To the extent the approach focuses on the results of a rule rather than its form, it more closely fits the model of substantive, rather than formal, equality. See Chapter 2.

Title VII has been a significant tool in helping women gain access to areas of employment previously closed to them. Title VII has eliminated explicit exclusions of women from employment (see, e.g., Laffey v. Northwest Airlines, Inc., 567 F.2d 429 (D.C. Cir. 1976), cert. denied, 434 U.S. 1086 (1978) (prohibiting exclusion of women applicants from positions as "pursers")); restrictions that impose additional requirements on women that are not imposed on men (see, e.g., Phillips v. Martin Marietta Corp., 400 U.S. 542 (1971) (employer cannot hire men with pre-school-age children and exclude women in the same category)); and job requirements assuming male qualifications that are not necessary for successful job performance (see, e.g., Dothard v. Rawlinson, 433 U.S. 321 (1977) (invalidating height and weight requirements not sufficiently correlated to job requirements of prison guards)). Title VII has had greater difficulty, even under disparate impact analysis, with rules that are based on women's actual differences from men. Such questions tend to divide into two separate phases of Title VII analysis: (1) the definitional question of whether the claimed discrimination constitutes "discrimination on the basis of sex"; and (2) the question of whether, even if a classification is sex discrimination, it is nonetheless justified because of its relationship to legitimate business concerns of the employer. Although these questions take different forms depending on their position in the proof process, in an important sense they amount to the same thing: are women being treated differently from similarly situated men? Do the analyses provided in the cases that follow satisfactorily answer this question?

a. What Is Discrimination "Based on Sex"?

Price Waterhouse v. Hopkins
490 U.S. 228 (1989)

Justice BRENNAN announced the judgment of the Court and delivered an opinion, in which Justice MARSHALL, Justice BLACKMUN, and Justice STEVENS join.

Ann Hopkins was a senior manager in an office of Price Waterhouse when she was proposed for partnership in 1982. She was neither offered nor denied admission to the partnership; instead, her candidacy was held for reconsideration the following year. When the partners in her office later refused to repropose her for partnership, she sued Price Waterhouse under Title VII . . . charging that the firm had discriminated against her on the basis of sex in its decisions regarding partnership. Judge Gesell in the Federal District Court for the District of Columbia ruled in her favor on the question of liability . . . and the Court of Appeals for the District of Columbia Circuit affirmed. . . . We granted certiorari to resolve a conflict among the Courts of Appeals concerning the respective burdens of proof of a defendant and plaintiff in a suit under Title VII when it has been shown that an employment decision resulted from a mixture of legitimate and illegitimate motives. . . .

Ann Hopkins had worked at Price Waterhouse's Office of Government Services in Washington, D.C., for five years when the partners in that office proposed her as a candidate for partnership. Of the 662 partners at the firm at that time, 7

were women. Of the 88 persons proposed for partnership that year, only 1 —
Hopkins — was a woman. Forty-seven of these candidates were admitted to the
partnership, 21 were rejected, and 20 — including Hopkins — were "held" for
reconsideration the following year. Thirteen of the 32 partners who had submitted comments on Hopkins supported her bid for partnership. Three partners
recommended that her candidacy be placed on hold, eight stated that they did not
have an informed opinion about her, and eight recommended that she be denied
partnership.

In a jointly prepared statement supporting her candidacy, the partners in
Hopkins' office showcased her successful 2-year effort to secure a $25 million
contract with the Department of State, labeling it "an outstanding performance"
and one that Hopkins carried out "virtually at the partner level." Despite Price
Waterhouse's attempt at trial to minimize her contribution to this project, Judge
Gesell specifically found that Hopkins had "played a key role in Price Waterhou-
se's successful effort to win a multi-million dollar contract with the Department of
State." Indeed, he went on, "[n]one of the other partnership candidates at Price
Waterhouse that year had a comparable record in terms of successfully securing
major contracts for the partnership."

The partners in Hopkins' office praised her character as well as her accom-
plishments, describing her in their joint statement as "an outstanding professional" who had a "deft touch," a "strong character, independence and
integrity." Clients appear to have agreed with these assessments. At trial, one
official from the State Department described her as "extremely competent, intelligent," "strong and forthright, very productive, energetic and creative." Another
high-ranking official praised Hopkins' decisiveness, broadmindedness, and "intellectual clarity"; she was, in his words, "a stimulating conversationalist." Evaluations such as these led Judge Gesell to conclude that Hopkins "had no difficulty
dealing with clients and her clients appear to have been very pleased with her
work" and that she "was generally viewed as a highly competent project leader
who worked long hours, pushed vigorously to meet deadlines and demanded
much from the multidisciplinary staffs with which she worked."

On too many occasions, however, Hopkins' aggressiveness apparently spilled
over into abrasiveness. Staff members seem to have borne the brunt of Hopkins'
brusqueness. Long before her bid for partnership, partners evaluating her work
had counseled her to improve her relations with staff members. Although later
evaluations indicate an improvement, Hopkins' perceived shortcomings in this
important area eventually doomed her bid for partnership. Virtually all of the
partners' negative remarks about Hopkins — even those of partners supporting
her — had to do with her "interpersonal skills." Both "[s]upporters and opponents of her candidacy," stressed Judge Gesell, "indicated that she was sometimes
overly aggressive, unduly harsh, difficult to work with and impatient with staff."

There were clear signs, though, that some of the partners reacted negatively
to Hopkins' personality because she was a woman. One partner described her as
"macho"; another suggested that she "overcompensated for being a woman"; a
third advised her to take "a course at charm school." Several partners criticized
her use of profanity; in response, one partner suggested that those partners
objected to her swearing only "because it's a lady using foul language." Another

supporter explained that Hopkins "ha[d] matured from a tough-talking somewhat masculine hard-nosed mgr to an authoritative, formidable, but much more appealing lady ptr candidate." But it was the man who, as Judge Gesell found, bore responsibility for explaining to Hopkins the reasons for the Policy Board's decision to place her candidacy on hold who delivered the coup de grace: in order to improve her chances for partnership, Thomas Beyer advised, Hopkins should "walk more femininely, talk more femininely, dress more femininely, wear makeup, have her hair styled, and wear jewelry."

Dr. Susan Fiske, a social psychologist and Associate Professor of Psychology at Carnegie-Mellon University, testified at trial that the partnership selection process at Price Waterhouse was likely influenced by sex stereotyping. Her testimony focused not only on the overtly sex-based comments of partners but also on gender-neutral remarks, made by partners who knew Hopkins only slightly, that were intensely critical of her. One partner, for example, baldly stated that Hopkins was "universally disliked" by staff, and another described her as "consistently annoying and irritating"; yet these were people who had had very little contact with Hopkins. According to Fiske, Hopkins' uniqueness (as the only woman in the pool of candidates) and the subjectivity of the evaluations made it likely that sharply critical remarks such as these were the product of sex stereotyping — although Fiske admitted that she could not say with certainty whether any particular comment was the result of stereotyping. Fiske based her opinion on a review of the submitted comments, explaining that it was commonly accepted practice for social psychologists to reach this kind of conclusion without having met any of the people involved in the decisionmaking process.

In previous years, other female candidates for partnership also had been evaluated in sex-based terms. As a general matter, Judge Gesell concluded, "[c]andidates were viewed favorably if partners believed they maintained their femin[in]ity while becoming effective professional managers"; in this environment, "[t]o be identified as a "women's lib[b]er" was regarded as [a] negative comment." In fact, the judge found that in previous years "[o]ne partner repeatedly commented that he could not consider any woman seriously as a partnership candidate and believed that women were not even capable of functioning as senior managers — yet the firm took no action to discourage his comments and recorded his vote in the overall summary of the evaluations."

Judge Gesell found that Price Waterhouse legitimately emphasized interpersonal skills in its partnership decisions, and also found that the firm had not fabricated its complaints about Hopkins' interpersonal skills as a pretext for discrimination. Moreover, he concluded, the firm did not give decisive emphasis to such traits only because Hopkins was a woman; although there were male candidates who lacked these skills but who were admitted to partnership, the judge found that these candidates possessed other, positive traits that Hopkins lacked.

The judge went on to decide, however, that some of the partners' remarks about Hopkins stemmed from an impermissibly cabined view of the proper behavior of women, and that Price Waterhouse had done nothing to disavow reliance on such comments. He held that Price Waterhouse had unlawfully discriminated against Hopkins on the basis of sex by consciously giving credence and effect to partners' comments that resulted from sex stereotyping. Noting that Price Waterhouse could avoid equitable relief by proving by clear and convincing evidence that it would have placed Hopkins' candidacy on hold even absent this discrimination, the judge decided that the firm had not carried this heavy burden.

The Court of Appeals affirmed the District Court's ultimate conclusion, but departed from its analysis in one particular: it held that even if a plaintiff proves that discrimination played a role in an employment decision, the defendant will not be found liable if it proves, by clear and convincing evidence, that it would have made the same decision in the absence of discrimination. Under this approach, an employer is not deemed to have violated Title VII if it proves that it would have made the same decision in the absence of an impermissible motive, whereas under the District Court's approach, the employer's proof in that respect only avoids equitable relief. We decide today that the Court of Appeals had the better approach, but that both courts erred in requiring the employer to make its proof by clear and convincing evidence. . . .

[The separate concurring opinions of Justice O'Connor and Justice White are omitted.]

Justice KENNEDY, with whom THE CHIEF JUSTICE AND Justice SCALIA join, dissenting. . . .

The ultimate question in every individual disparate-treatment case is whether discrimination caused the particular decision at issue. Some of the plurality's comments with respect to the District Court's findings in this case, however, are potentially misleading. As the plurality notes, the District Court based its liability determination on expert evidence that some evaluations of respondent Hopkins were based on unconscious sex stereotypes,[5] and on the fact that Price Waterhouse failed to disclaim reliance on these comments when it conducted the partnership review. The District Court also based liability on Price Waterhouse's failure to "make partners sensitive to the dangers [of stereotyping], to discourage comments tainted by sexism, or to investigate comments to determine whether they were influenced by stereotypes."

Although the District Court's version of Title VII liability is improper under any of today's opinions, I think it important to stress that Title VII creates no independent cause of action for sex stereotyping. Evidence of use by decisionmakers of sex stereotypes is, of course, quite relevant to the question of discriminatory intent. The ultimate question, however, is whether discrimination

---

5. The plaintiff who engages the services of Dr. Susan Fiske should have no trouble showing that sex discrimination played a part in any decision. Price Waterhouse chose not to object to Fiske's testimony, and at this late stage we are constrained to accept it, but I think the plurality's enthusiasm for Fiske's conclusions unwarranted. Fiske purported to discern stereotyping in comments that were gender neutral — e.g., "overbearing and abrasive" — without any knowledge of the comments' basis in reality and without having met the speaker or subject. "To an expert of Dr. Fiske's qualifications, it seems plain that no woman could be overbearing, arrogant, or abrasive: any observations to that effect would necessarily be discounted as the product of stereotyping. If analysis like this is to prevail in federal courts, no employer can base any adverse action as to a woman on such attributes." [825 F.2d 458, 477 (D.C. Cir. 1987)] (Williams, J., dissenting). Today's opinions cannot be read as requiring factfinders to credit testimony based on this type of analysis. . . .

caused the plaintiff's harm. Our cases do not support the suggestion that failure to "disclaim reliance" on stereotypical comments itself violates Title VII. Neither do they support creation of a "duty to sensitize." As the dissenting judge in the Court of Appeals observed, acceptance of such theories would turn Title VII "from a prohibition of discriminatory conduct into an engine for rooting out sexist thoughts." [825 F.2d 458, 477 (1987) (Williams, J., dissenting).]

Employment discrimination claims require factfinders to make difficult and sensitive decisions. Sometimes this may mean that no finding of discrimination is justified even though a qualified employee is passed over by a less than admirable employer. In other cases, Title VII's protections properly extend to plaintiffs who are by no means model employees. As Justice Brennan notes, courts do not sit to determine whether litigants are nice....

The language of Title VII and our well-considered precedents require this plaintiff to establish that the decision to place her candidacy on hold was made "because of" sex. Here the District Court found that the "comments of the individual partners and the expert evidence of Dr. Fiske do not prove an intentional discriminatory motive or purpose," and that "[b]ecause plaintiff has considerable problems dealing with staff and peers, the Court cannot say that she would have been elected to partnership if the Policy Board's decision had not been tainted by sexually based evaluations." Hopkins thus failed to meet the requisite standard of proof after a full trial. I would remand the case for entry of judgment in favor of Price Waterhouse.

Ezold v. Wolf, Block, Schorr & Solis-Cohen
983 F.2d 509 (3d Cir. 1992), cert. denied, 510 U.S. 826 (1993)

HUTCHINSON, Circuit Judge.

Wolf, Block, Schorr and Solis-Cohen (Wolf) appeals from a judgment of the United States District Court for the Eastern District of Pennsylvania granting relief in favor of Nancy O'Mara Ezold (Ezold) on her claim that Wolf intentionally discriminated against her on the basis of her sex in violation of Title VII... when it decided not to admit her to the firm's partnership effective February 1, 1989....

I

Ezold sued Wolf under Title VII alleging that Wolf intentionally discriminated against her because of her sex when it decided not to admit her to the firm's partnership.... The district court held that the nondiscriminatory reason articulated by Wolf for its rejection of Ezold's candidacy—that her legal analytical ability failed to meet the firm's partnership standard—was a pretext.... The court...awarded Ezold back pay in the amount of $131,784.00 for the period from her resignation on June 7, 1989 to January 31, 1991. The parties agreed that if the court's November 27, 1990 and March 15, 1991 orders were affirmed on appeal, Ezold would be instated as a partner....

II

Ezold was hired by Wolf as an associate on a partnership track in July 1983. She had graduated in the top third of her class from the Villanova University School of Law in 1980 and then worked at two small law firms in Philadelphia.... Ezold was hired at Wolf by Seymour Kurland, then chairman of the litigation department. The district court found that Kurland told Ezold during an interview that it would not be easy for her at Wolf because "she was a woman, had not attended an Ivy League law school, and had not been on law review."... [She] was assigned to the firm's litigation department. From 1983-87, Kurland was responsible for the assignment of work to associates in the department. He often delegated this responsibility to partner Steven Arbittier.... The district court found that Arbittier assigned Ezold to actions that were "small" by Wolf standards....

Senior associates within two years of partnership consideration are evaluated annually; non-senior associates are evaluated semi-annually. The firm's partners are asked to submit written evaluations on standardized forms.... Ten criteria of legal performance are listed on the forms in the following order: legal analysis, legal writing and drafting, research skills, formal speech, informal speech, judgment, creativity, negotiating and advocacy, promptness and efficiency. Ten personal characteristics are also listed: reliability, taking and managing responsibility, flexibility, growth potential, attitude, client relationship, client servicing and development, ability under pressure, ability to work independently, and dedication. As stated by Ian Strogatz, Chairman of the Associates Committee: "The normal standards for partnership include as factors for consideration all of the ones...that are contained [on] our evaluation forms."...

[A lengthy discussion of the firm's evaluation procedures is omitted.]

The firm's partners evaluated Ezold twice a year as an associate and once a year as a senior associate from October 1983 until the Associates Committee determined that it would not recommend her for partnership in September 1988. The district court found that "in the period up to and including 1988, Ms. Ezold received strongly positive evaluations from almost all of the partners for whom she had done any substantial work."... Ezold's overall score in legal skills in the 1988 bottom line memorandum before the Associates Committee was a "G" for good [the second highest rating on a 5-part scale ranging from exceptional to unacceptable]....

Evaluations in Ezold's file not mentioned by the district court show that concerns over Ezold's legal analytical ability arose early during her tenure at the firm. In an evaluation covering the period from November 1984 through April 1985, Arbittier wrote:

> I have discussed legal issues with Nancy in connection with [two cases]. I found her analysis to be rather superficial and unfocused. I am beginning to doubt that she has sufficient legal analytical ability to make it with the firm.... She makes a good impression with people, has common sense, and can handle routine matters well. However these traits will take you just so far in our firm. I think that due to the nature of our practice Nancy's future here is limited....

That same year Schwartz wrote:

> I have worked a great deal with Nancy since my last evaluation....Both cases are complex, multifaceted matters that have presented novel issues to us. While her enthusiasm never wanes and she keeps plugging away — I'm often left with a product that demonstrates uncertainty in the analysis of a problem. After extensive discussions with me, the analysis becomes a little more focused, although sometimes I get the sense that Nancy feels adrift and is just marching as best she can to my analytical tune....In my view her energy, enthusiasm and fearlessness make her a valuable asset to us. While she may not be as bright as some of our best associates, her talents will continue to serve us well.

...Also in 1985, partner Donald Joseph rated Ezold's legal analytical ability as marginal and wrote "its [sic] too early to tell but I have been disappointed on her grasp of the problem, let alone performance."...

During her next evaluation period from April through November 1985, Ezold received similar negative evaluations. Arbittier, Robert Fiebach and Joseph rated her legal analytical abilities as marginal. Arbittier wrote:

> She took a long time getting [a summary judgment brief] done and I found it to be stilted and unimaginative. One of the main issues—dealing with the issue of notice—she missed completely and did not grasp our position....Also, in considering whether to file a defensive motion...she failed to cite me to a clause in the agreement that was highly relevant leaving me with the impression that the motion could not succeed. I think Nancy tries hard and can handle relatively straight-forward matters with a degree of maturity and judgment, but when she gets into more complicated areas she lacks real analytical skill and just does what she is told in a mechanical way. She is not up to our minimal Wolf, Block standards....

Boote made the following report on his performance review with Ezold after this evaluation period:

> Nancy appeared to accept the judgment, albeit a little grudgingly, that her analytical, research and writing ability was not up to our standards and that she should focus on the types of matters that she can handle effectively....We made it very clear to Nancy that if she pursues general civil litigation work she is not on track toward partnership and that her only realistic chance for partnership in our opinion is to develop a good reputation for herself in one of the specialized areas of practice....

In the evaluation period covering November 1985 to April 1986, Boote wrote the following to the Associates Committee:

> Nancy continues to get mixed reviews. Her pluses are that she is mature, courageous, pretty good on her feet and has the capacity to inspire confidence in clients. Her minuses are that there is doubt about her analytic and writing ability....In considering Nancy's prospects for the long range, I think we should bear in mind that we have made mistakes in the past in letting people go to other firms who really could have filled a valuable niche here. Whether Nancy is such a person, of course, remains to be seen....

A summary of Ezold's performance review from October 1986 prepared by Schwartz stated:

> Nancy was advised that several of the lawyers feel she has made very positive progress as a lawyer, Sy [Kurland] being one of them. However, he told her that other lawyers had strong negative sentiments about her capabilities and they feel she has a number of shortcomings in the way of complicated analysis of legal problems and in being able to handle the big complicated corporate litigation, and therefore, does not meet the standard for partnership at Wolf, Block. . . . Both Sy and I urged Nancy to seriously consider looking for employment elsewhere as she may not be able to turn the tide. . . .

Although several partners saw improvement in Ezold's work, negative comments about her analytical ability continued up until, and through, her 1988 senior associate evaluation, the year she was considered for partnership. . . .

[In the 1988 review] the Associates Committee voted 9-1 not to recommend Ezold for Category VI partnership.

. . . It did vote, however, to recommend her for the status of "Group VII" special partner that the firm had heretofore made available to associates who are valuable but fall below the firm's high standards for full partnership. The continuing existence of that category was, however, then under review by the firm's Executive Committee. It was in fact later eliminated.

Out of a total of eight candidates in Ezold's class, five male associates and one female associate were recommended for regular partnership. One male associate, Associate X, was not recommended for either regular or special partnership. . . . Ezold resigned from the firm on June 7, 1989. . . .

IV

Ezold claims Wolf intentionally discriminated against her because of her sex. . . . [She] litigated this case as a pretext case, which is governed by McDonnell Douglas Corp. v. Green, 411 U.S. 792, 802 (1973) and Texas Dep't of Community Affairs v. Burdine, 450 U.S. 248, 252-56 (1981). . . . The plaintiff must first establish by a preponderance of the evidence a prima facie case of discrimination. *Burdine*, 450 U.S. at 252. . . . The plaintiff can establish a prima facie case by showing that she is a member of a protected class; that she was qualified for and rejected for the position; and that non-members of the protected class were treated more favorably. . . . After the plaintiff has established a prima facie case, the burden shifts to the defendant to produce evidence of a legitimate, nondiscriminatory reason for the employee's rejection. *Burdine*, 450 U.S. at 252. . . . If the defendant's evidence creates a genuine issue of fact, the presumption of discrimination drops from the case. *Burdine*, 450 U.S. at 254-55. . . . Then, the plaintiff, since she retains the ultimate burden of persuasion, must prove, by a preponderance of the evidence, that the defendant's proffered reasons were a pretext for discrimination. *Burdine*, 450 U.S. at 257. . . .

The parties do not dispute the district court's conclusion of law that Ezold demonstrated a prima facie case, in particular that she was "qualified" for admission to the partnership. . . . In Title VII cases involving a dispute over "subjective" qualifications, we have recognized that the qualification issue should often be resolved in the second and third stages of the *McDonnell Douglas/Burdine* analysis, to avoid putting too onerous a burden on the plaintiff in establishing a prima facie case. . . . We agree with the district court's conclusion that favorable evaluations from partners with whom Ezold worked, and a score of "G" on her 1988 bottom line memo, demonstrate that she was qualified for partnership consideration. . . .

The defendant may rebut the presumption of discrimination arising out of the plaintiff's prima facie case by producing evidence that there was a "legitimate, nondiscriminatory reason" why the plaintiff was rejected. *Burdine*, 450 U.S. at 254; *McDonnell Douglas*, 411 U.S. at 802. . . . The burden then shifts to the plaintiff to show that the defendant's articulated reasons are pretextual. Id. at 256. This burden merges into the plaintiff's ultimate burden of persuading the court that she has been the victim of intentional discrimination. Id. The plaintiff must demonstrate "by competent evidence that the presumptively valid reason[ ] for [the alleged unlawful employment action was] in fact a coverup for a . . . discriminatory decision." *McDonnell Douglas*, 411 U.S. at 805. Explicit evidence of discrimination — i.e., the "smoking gun" — is not required. . . . A plaintiff can establish pretext in one of two ways: "either directly by persuading the court that a discriminatory reason more likely motivated the employer or indirectly by showing that the employer's proffered reason is unworthy of credence." *Burdine*, 480 U.S. at 256.

In proving that the employer's motive was more likely than not the product of a discriminatory reason instead of the articulated legitimate reason, sufficiently strong evidence of an employer's past treatment of the plaintiff may suffice. . . . The employer's "general policy and practice with respect to minority employment" may also be relevant. . . . Alternately, if a plaintiff produces credible evidence that it is more likely than not that "the employer did not act for its proffered reason, then the employer's decision remains unexplained and the inferences from the evidence produced by the plaintiff may be sufficient to prove the ultimate fact of discriminatory intent." . . .

Wolf's articulated nondiscriminatory reason for denying Ezold's admission to the partnership was that she did not possess sufficient legal analytical skills to handle the responsibilities of partner in the firm's complex litigation practice. Ezold attempted to prove that Wolf's proffered explanation was "unworthy of credence" by showing she was at least equal to, if not more qualified than, similarly situated males promoted to partnership. She also contended that her past treatment at the firm showed Wolf's decision was based on a discriminatory motive rather than the legitimate reason of deficiency in legal analytical ability that the firm had articulated.

V . . .

The district court compared Ezold to eight successful male partnership candidates. . . . It found:

> The test that was put to the plaintiff by the Associates Committee that she have outstanding academic credentials and that before she could be admitted to the most

junior of partnerships, she must demonstrate that she had the analytical ability to handle the most complex litigation was not the test required of male associates....

The district court then concluded:

Ms. Ezold has established that the defendant's purported reasons for its conduct are pretextual. The defendant promoted to partnership men having evaluations substantially the same or inferior to the plaintiff's, and indeed promoted male associates who the defendant claimed had precisely the lack of analytical or writing ability upon which Wolf, Block purportedly based its decision concerning the plaintiff. The defendant is not entitled to apply its standards in a more "severe" fashion to female associates.... Such differential treatment establishes that the defendant's reasons were a pretext for discrimination....

Wolf says this finding of pretext is wrong. Analyzing its contentions, we perceive two reasons why this is so. First, the ... only evidence in the record that Wolf considered Ezold's academic record is limited to the original decision to hire Ezold and to assignments given to Ezold early in her employment with Wolf, issues we consider in Part IX, infra. Second, in its analysis, the district court did not focus on Wolf's articulated reason for denying Ezold partnership — lack of analytic ability to handle complex litigation. Instead, the district court first substituted its own general standard for the qualities Wolf believed were essential to law firm partnership. Then, applying its own incorrect standard of comparison, the district court did not realize that a comparison of Ezold's legal analytic ability with that of the successful males could not support a finding of pretext. Overall, Ezold's evaluations in that category were not as good as that of even the least capable male associate who was offered a partnership position....

VII...

The record does not show that anyone was taken into the partnership without serious consideration of their strength in the category of legal analytic ability.... Wolf reserves for itself the power to decide, by consensus, whether an associate possesses sufficient analytical ability to handle complex matters independently after becoming a partner. It is Wolf's prerogative to utilize such a standard.... The partnership evaluation process at Wolf, though formalized, is based on judgment, like most decisions in human institutions. A consensus as to that judgment is the end result of Wolf's formal process. In that process, the Associates Committee has the role of collecting and weighing hundreds of evaluations by partners with diverse views before reaching its consensus as to a particular associate's abilities.... The differing evaluations the partners first submit to the Associates Committee are often based on hearsay or reputation. No precise theorem or specific objective criterion is employed....

Were the factors Wolf considered in deciding which associates should be admitted to the partnership objective, as opposed to subjective, the conflicts in various partners' views about Ezold's legal analytical ability that this record shows might amount to no more than a conflict in the evidence that the district court as factfinder had full power to resolve. . . . [The difficulty in this case] is the lack of an objective qualification or factor that a plaintiff can use as a yardstick to compare herself with similarly situated employees. . . .

When an employer relies on its subjective evaluation of the plaintiff's qualifications as the reason for denying promotion, the plaintiff can prove the articulated reason is unworthy of credence by presenting persuasive comparative evidence that non-members of the protected class were evaluated more favorably, i.e., their deficiencies in the same qualification category as the plaintiff's were overlooked for no apparent reason when they were promoted to partner.

A plaintiff does not establish pretext, however, by pointing to criticisms of members of the non-protected class, or commendation of the plaintiff, in categories the defendant says it did not rely upon in denying promotion to a member of the protected class. Such comments may raise doubts about the fairness of the employer's decision. "The fact that a court may think that the employer misjudged the qualifications of the applicant does not in itself expose him to Title VII liability, although this may be probative of whether the employer's reasons are pretexts for discrimination." *Burdine*, 450 U.S. at 259. . . . Evidence establishing such incredibility must show that the standard or criterion the employer relied on was "obviously weak or implausible." . . . Ezold's evidence does not make this showing. . . .

The district court's failure to consider the negative evaluations of Ezold's legal analytic ability because the partners making them had little contact with Ezold cannot be excused in the face of the credence the district court gave to positive comments about Ezold's ability from those who likewise had little or no contact with her. While a factfinder can accept some evidence and reject other evidence on the basis of credibility, it should not base its credibility determination on a conflicting double standard.

Moreover, . . . [t]here is no evidence that Wolf's practice of giving weight to negative votes and comments of partners who had little contact and perhaps knew nothing about an associate beyond the associate's general reputation was not applied equally to female and male associates. . . .

VIII

[The court next reviews the evaluations of other associates selected for partnership, including negative comments about their analytical abilities. It concludes that the district court erred in not crediting the many favorable evaluations of these associates, and in not giving adequate weight to the negative comments about Ezold.] . . .

Because the evaluation files contain insufficient evidence to show that Ezold was evaluated more severely than the male associates, Ezold has not shown that Wolf's proffered reason for failing to promote her was "unworthy of credence." We therefore hold that the district court's ultimate finding of pretext cannot be sustained on this basis.

IX

We must, however, still consider certain additional evidence which Ezold says directly establishes that Wolf's articulated reason was a pretext by showing that a discriminatory reason more likely motivated its decision not to admit her to the partnership. . . .

This Court has recognized that when an employer discriminatorily denies training and support, the employer may not then disfavor the plaintiff because her performance is affected by the lack of opportunity. . . . Even if we assume that Ezold received "small" cases at the beginning of her tenure at Wolf, however, there is no evidence this was the result of sex discrimination. Her evaluations indicate, rather, that it may have been her academic credentials that contributed to her receipt of less complex assignments. For example, Davis stated that "the Home Unity case was the first really fair test for Nancy. I believe that her background relegated her to . . . matters (where she got virtually no testing by Wolf, Block standards) and small matters." . . . It is undisputed that Arbittier opposed hiring Ezold because of her academic history and lack of law review experience. In one of Ezold's early evaluations, Kurland wrote: "She has not, in my view, been getting sufficiently difficult matters to handle because she is not the Harvard Law Review type. . . . We must make an effort to give her more difficult matters to handle." . . . He also stated: "I envisioned . . . her when I hired her as a 'good, stand-up, effective courtroom lawyer.'" . . . In urging the Executive Committee to reconsider Ezold's candidacy Magarity wrote:

> [The] perception [that she is not able to handle complex cases] appears to be a product of how Sy Kurland viewed Nancy's role when she was initially hired. For the first few years Sy would only assign Nancy to non-complex matters, yet, at evaluation time, Sy, and some other partners, would qualify their evaluations by saying that Nancy does not work on complex matters. . . .

Nancy was literally trapped in a Catch 22. The Chairman of the Litigation Department would not assign her to complex cases, yet she received negative evaluations for not working on complex matters. . . . While it would be unfortunate if these academic and intellectual biases were perpetuated after the decision was made to hire Ezold, academic or intellectual bias is not evidence of sex discrimination. The district court made no finding that Ezold was given small assignments because of her sex. . . .

The district court found that when Ezold suggested to Schwartz in her early years at Wolf that an unfairness in case assignments may have occurred because she was a woman, Schwartz replied: "Nancy, don't say that around here. They don't want to hear it. Just do your job and do well." . . . This statement, made years before the 1988 decision to deny Ezold partnership, does not show that Wolf's evaluation of her legal ability was pretextual. . . .

Ezold also points to a preliminary injunction matter early in her career that was reassigned to a man after she had been the sole volunteer. The district court found that Arbittier reassigned the injunction to a man "without explanation." . . . Arbittier, however, testified that he realized the case needed a more senior associate and so reassigned it. This too occurred early in Ezold's employment at Wolf and there is nothing in the record to show that it had any connection with Ezold's failure to attain partnership. . . .

The district court also found that when Ezold first got to the firm in 1983, she and a male associate not on partnership track were assigned to sort out a large group of minor cases previously handled by an associate who had left the firm. This finding fails to support the district court's ultimate finding of pretext. The assignment was made on an as-needed basis to fill the void created when the associate working on the matters had left. Additionally, the district court failed to recognize that Arbittier gave Ezold full authority to reassign the matters to other male associates and administer the whole affair. The small bankruptcy matters to which the district court refers were later reassigned by Kurland at Ezold's request. Kurland testified that he did this "both to free Nancy up a little and to give some demonstration that we [were] making an effort to change the nature of her assignments." . . .

Finally, the district court found that by allowing partners to bypass the formal assignment system, Kurland and Arbittier "prevented the plaintiff from securing improved assignments . . . [and] impaired her opportunity to be fairly evaluated for partnership." . . . The fact that Wolf's formal assignment process was often bypassed does not support the district court's finding of pretext. Title VII requires employers to avoid certain prohibited types of invidious discrimination, including sex discrimination. It does not require employers to treat all employees fairly, closely monitor their progress and insure them every opportunity for advancement. "Our task is not to assess the overall fairness of [Wolf's] actions." . . . It is a sad fact of life in the working world that employees of ability are sometimes overlooked for promotion. Large law firms are not immune from unfairness in this imperfect world. The law limits its protection against that unfairness to cases of invidious illegal discrimination. This record contains no evidence that Wolf's assignment process was tainted by a discriminatory motive. . . .

[T]he district court held that the four specific instances of conduct . . . evidenced a discriminatory animus and supported its finding of pretext. . . . It did not hold that these instances of conduct provided an independent or alternative basis for its finding, but viewed them only as support therefor.

The first instance of conduct on which the district court relied was that Ezold "was evaluated negatively for being too involved with women's issues . . . specifically her concern about the [firm's] treatment of paralegals," while Fiebach [a male partner] was not reproached for raising the "women's issue" of part-time employment. . . . Ezold's perception was that the firm mistreated its paralegals by overworking and underpaying them and that treatment would not have occurred but for the fact that they were predominantly women. The court's finding on this matter refers to a 1986 evaluation submitted by Schwartz, one of Ezold's partnership supporters, in which he wrote: "Judgment is better, although it still can be clouded by over-sensitivity to what she misperceives as 'womens' [sic] issues." . . . Schwartz testified, however, that he was not criticizing Ezold for raising the issue of the firm's treatment of paralegals, but for her misperception that this was a "women's issue." Moreover, the fact that Fiebach . . . was not criticized for encouraging discussion of part-time employment is not probative of whether the partnership decision concerning Ezold was gender-based. This evidence is of marginal value. . . .

The second instance of conduct on which the district court relied was "the fact that a male associate['s] sexual harassment of female employees at the Firm was seen as insignificant and not worthy of mention to the Associates Committee in its consideration of that male associate for partnership." . . . While it is undisputed that the male associate, Associate X, engaged in some form of harassment of female employees, the district court's finding about Wolf's attitude towards it is unsupported by the evidence and thus clearly erroneous. The record shows that Strogatz, then Chairman of the Associates Committee, met with Associate X concerning these incidents, and that a memorandum was placed in his personnel file. There was testimony that the incident was reported to the associate's department chairman and to the Associates Committee. The record also indicates that the incident occurred after the Associates Committee decided it was unlikely to recommend Associate X for partnership in any event. There is no evidence Wolf viewed the incident as "insignificant." This incident is not evidence that the firm harbored a discriminatory animus against either women generally or Ezold specifically. It lends no support to the district court's finding of pretext.

The district court found that Ezold was "evaluated negatively for being 'very demanding,' while several male associates who were made partners were evaluated negatively for lacking sufficient assertiveness in their demeanors." . . . The criticisms of Ezold's assertiveness related to the way in which she handled administrative matters such as office and secretarial space, and not legal matters. . . . In particular, David Hofstein's evaluation of Ezold in 1984 stated:

> My one negative experience did not involve legal work. When my group moved to the south end of the 21st floor, Nancy had a fit because she had to move. As I. Strogatz and our [Office Manager] know, Nancy's behavior was inappropriate and I think affected everyone's perception of her. Dealing with administrative matters professionally is almost as important as dealing with legal matters competently, and at least in that instance, Nancy blew it. . . .

The district court refers to criticisms of male associates for lacking assertiveness, but in connection with their handling of legal matters. The district court was comparing apples and oranges. The record shows that male associates were also criticized for their improper handling of administrative problems. . . . The district court also quotes an evaluation of Ezold as a "prima donna" on administrative matters, but leaves out the full context of the statement which compares her to a male associate: "Reminds me of [a male associate] — very demanding, prima donna-ish, not a team player." . . .

The district court's finding that this evidence supports its conclusion that Ezold was treated differently because of her gender is clearly erroneous. An "unfortunate and destructive conflict of personalities does not establish sexual discrimination." Bellissimo [v. Westinghouse Elec. Corp.], 764 F.2d 175, 182 (3d Cir. 1985). Further, by the time of Ezold's final evaluation in 1988, there was no mention of her attitude on administrative matters. Rosoff testified that in independently reviewing the Associate Committee's decision not to recommend

Ezold for partnership, he disregarded the criticisms of her handling of administrative matters from earlier years as "ancient history." . . . There is again no evidence that this incident played any role in Wolf's decision to deny Ezold's admission to the partnership.

Finally, the district court found that Ezold was the target of several comments demonstrating the firm's differential treatment of women. The district court found the following:

During the selection process . . . Mr. Kurland told Ms. Ezold that it would not be easy for her at Wolf, Block because she did not fit the Wolf, Block mold since she was a woman, had not attended an Ivy League law school, and had not been on law review. Mr. Kurland and Ms. Ezold stated that at one of the meetings with Ms. Ezold, only Ms. Ezold and he were present. . . .

Ezold did not raise this reference at a subsequent lunch with associate Liebenberg, a woman, and Schwartz, nor did she express concern over Wolf's treatment of women. Although Kurland denied making the statement, the district court resolved this credibility issue in Ezold's favor and we will not disturb it.

Wolf argues that this comment made in 1983 before Ezold accepted the job is not probative on whether its partnership decision five years later was gender-based. In Roebuck v. Drexel University, 852 F.2d at 733, the plaintiff alleged racial discrimination in the denial of tenure and we considered the probative value of evidence of a discriminatory attitude on the part of a key decisionmaker. There, the president of the university exercised a significant influence on the decisionmakers and had made the final tenure decision. He had also made two statements reflecting racial bias. Id. We held, although the "statements standing alone, occurring as they did over five years before the final denial of tenure, could not suffice to uphold a finding [of discrimination], they do add support, in combination with the other evidence, to the ultimate conclusion." Id. . . . Here, however, as we have painstakingly pointed out, other evidence of sex discrimination is lacking. In any event, Kurland made this comment before Ezold began her employment at Wolf, five years before the partnership decision. The comment's temporal distance from the decision Ezold says was discriminatory convinces us it is too remote and isolated to show independently that unlawful discrimination, rather than Wolf's asserted reason, more likely caused the firm to deny Ezold the partnership she sought in 1988.

Kurland himself had left the firm in January 1988, before Ezold's 1988 evaluation and before the Associates Committee and the Executive Committee denied her admission to the partnership. Thus, he did not take part in the final decision to deny Ezold's admission to the partnership, although he had consistently supported her candidacy despite his recognition of other partners' perceptions about her legal analytical ability. Stray remarks by non-decisionmakers or by decisionmakers unrelated to the decision process are rarely given great weight, particularly if they were made temporally remote from the date of decision. . . .

X

We have reviewed the evidence carefully and hold that it is insufficient to show pretext. Despite Ezold's disagreement with the firm's evaluations of her abilities, and her perception that she was treated unfairly, there is no evidence of sex discrimination here. The district court's finding that Wolf's legitimate non-discriminatory reason was incredible because Ezold was evaluated more severely than male associates because of her gender, as well as its finding that Wolf's requirement that she possess analytical skills sufficient to handle complex litiga-tion was a pretext for discrimination, are clearly erroneous and find no support in the evidence. Finally, this record also lacks sufficient direct evidence of discrimi-natory animus to sustain a finding that Wolf more likely had a discriminatory motive in denying Ezold's admission to the partnership.

XI

Accordingly, we will reverse the judgment of the district court in favor of Ezold and remand for entry of judgment in favor of Wolf.

Notes

1. *Price Waterhouse* **Modified.** The *Price Waterhouse* rule, which gave employers a defense to a discrimination claim if they show a nondiscriminatory motive for reaching the same employment decision, was modified by the Civil Rights Act of 1991. Under the Act, even if an employer demonstrates that it "would have taken the same action in the absence of the impermissible motivating factor" it may be held liable, although remedies are limited to declaratory relief, injunctive relief, and attorney's fees. Financial damages, reinstatement, hiring, or promotion are not available. See 42 U.S.C. §§ 2000e-2(m), 2000e-5(g)(2)(B) (1994). Relief issues in *Price Waterhouse* and *Ezold* are discussed in note 5, infra.

2. **"Mixed-Motives" and "Pretext" Discrimination.** Proof of discrimina-tory intent in disparate treatment cases has traditionally taken two main forms: "pretext" and "mixed-motives" discrimination. *Ezold* is an example of a pretext claim; in response to circumstantial evidence of discrimination, the employer offered proof that the employment action was justified, which the plaintiff then tried to prove was a pretext for the underlying discrimination. If pretext had been shown, the original "mandatory presumption" proof mechanism of *McDonnell Douglas/Burdine* would have meant that a ruling was required in favor of Ezold. More recent case law merely permits a finding of discriminatory motive based on pretext, but does not require it. See Reeves v. Sanderson Plumbing Products, Inc., 530 U.S. 133 (2000).

Price Waterhouse is an example of a mixed-motives claim. Direct evidence was presented of the partners' discriminatory motivation in denying plaintiff partnership, along with the nondiscriminatory reasons offered by the firm. This evidence of discrimination served to shift the burden to the firm to show that the employment action would have been the same absent the discriminatory motives.

The difference between mixed-motive and pretext claims was substantially reduced when the United States Supreme Court interpreted the 1991 Amend-ments to Title VII to allow proof of a mixed-motive case by circumstantial evidence alone. See Desert Palace, Inc. v. Costa, 539 U.S. 90, 99 (2003) (involving warehouse worker who claimed that she was singled out for "intense stalking" by one of her supervisors, received harsher discipline than men for the same conduct, and was not treated as well as men were in the assignment of overtime). Would this precedent have made it easier for Nancy Ezold to prove her case? For an analysis of the relationship between *Costa* and the viability of the *McDonnell Douglas* framework for proving discrimination, see Michael J. Zimmer, The New Discrimination Law: *Price Waterhouse* is Dead, Whither *McDonnell Douglas?*, 53 Emory L.J. 1887, 1932-1940 (2004). Among the subsequent cases involving sex discrimination claims that have struggled with the application of *Costa*, see Rowland v. American General Finance, 340 F.3d 187, 192 (4th Cir. 2003) (reversing and remanding a case originally tried under pretext analysis because *Costa* "makes clear" that a request to try the case as a mixed-motive case should have been granted); Stegall v. Citadel Broadcasting Co., 350 F.3d 1061, 1071 (9th Cir. 2003) (applying both mixed-motive analysis and *McDonnell Douglas* analysis to plaintiff's case); Allen v. City of Pocahontas, 340 F.3d 551, 557-558 n.5 (8th Cir. 2003), cert. denied, 540 U.S. 1182 (2004) (applying *McDonnell Douglas* and stating that it is unnecessary to determine whether *Costa* changes *McDonnell Douglas'* framework, because the outcome of the case would be the same under either standard).

Is the Civil Rights Act's liability-but-no-damages rule an appropriate response when an employer has both discriminatory and nondiscriminatory motives? On the one hand, it would seem desirable to discourage employers from acting on discriminatory impulses. See Susan Bisom-Rapp, Of Motives and Maleness: A Critical View of Mixed Motive Doctrine in the Title VII Sex Discrimination Cases, 1995 Utah L. Rev. 1029, 1040. On the other hand, liability seems unreasonable in a case in which an employer's action was otherwise justified, the employee has not been injured, and no damages can be established. Is the current approach a good compromise?

3. Determining and Proving Intent in Disparate Treatment Cases. Note that establishing discrimination in disparate treatment cases under Title VII requires proof of discriminatory intent or motive. When an employment rule or practice is facially discriminatory, this showing of discriminatory intent is not an issue (just as there is no issue with facially discriminatory rules challenged under the Equal Protection Clause). In *Price Waterhouse*, the trial court found that the firm had discriminated against Hopkins on the basis of sex "by consciously giving credence and effect to partners' comments that resulted from sex stereotyping." 490 U.S. at 237. Is this a kind of constructive intent? See Martha Chamallas, Deepening the Legal Understanding of Bias: On Devaluation and Biased Prototypes, 74 S. Cal. L. Rev. 747, 753-774 (2001) (in some disparate treatment cases, it is enough to show that gender "caused" the employer to treat the plaintiff differently). In the case, the only way out for the employer was to show that the same employment decision would have been made on other permissible grounds; under the Civil Rights Act of 1991, this would not have been enough to avoid liability, although it may have avoided damages. The trial court in *Ezold* also found bias, but the appellate court was not persuaded that discrimination played a role at all; it found that Ezold was denied partnership because of legitimate (albeit subjective) factor of lack of legal analytical ability.

How does one prove discriminatory intent, when evidence of discrimination is only circumstantial? Consider the following:

> [T]he characteristics traditionally associated with women are at odds with many characteristics traditionally associated with professional success such as assertiveness, competitiveness, and business judgment. Some lawyers and clients still assume that women lack sufficient aptitude for complex financial transactions or sufficient combativeness for major litigation. Particularly in high stakes matters, risk averse managers are often reluctant to gamble on female practitioners.
>
> Yet professional women also tend to be rated lower when they depart from traditional stereotypes and adopt "masculine," authoritative styles. Negative evaluations are particularly likely when the evaluators are men, or the role is one typically occupied by men.
>
> As a consequence, female lawyers often face a double standard and a double bind. They risk appearing too "soft" or too "strident," too "aggressive" or "not aggressive enough." And what appears assertive in a man often appears abrasive in a woman. . . .
>
> The force of traditional stereotypes is compounded by the subjectivity of performance evaluations and by other biases in decisionmaking processes. People are more likely to notice and recall information that confirms prior assumptions than information that contradicts them. Attorneys who assume that working mothers are less committed tend to remember the times they left early, not the nights they stayed late.
>
> A related problem is that people share what psychologists label a "just world" bias. They want to believe that, in the absence of special treatment, individuals generally get what they deserve and deserve what they get. Perceptions of performance are frequently adjusted to match observed outcomes. Individuals are also motivated to interpret information in ways that maintain their own status and self-esteem.

ABA Commission on Women in the Profession, The Unfinished Agenda: A Report on the Status of Women in the Legal Profession 15-16 (2001). See also Virginia Valian, Why So Slow: The Advancement of Women 133 (1998). Considering that only one of fifty-five litigation partners was a woman, is it reasonable for the partners to believe that there was no discrimination in Ezold's case?

Interviews of the parties in *Ezold* following the decision in the case are reasonably persuasive that the partners did not think that they discriminated against Nancy Ezold on account of her sex. Wolf Block itself was founded partly in response to anti-Semitism, and the firm considered itself sensitive to all forms of discrimination. See Deborah L. Rhode, "What's Sex Got to Do With It": The Challenge of Diversity in the Legal Profession, in Legal Ethics: Law Stories 233, 234 (Deborah L. Rhode & David Luban eds., 2005). Whereas Ezold and her supporters concluded that she was equally or better qualified than many of the men promoted to partnership, Wolf Block and its supporters believed she "just didn't meet the firm standard for legal analytical ability." Id. at 243 (quoting Wolf Block partner Roberta Liebenberg, the department's only female partner). Another partner, Mark Dichter, explained that if anything was unfair, it was not that the firm discriminated but simply that the standards of evaluating associates were unclear. Id. at 244.

Is it possible to know if the courts are free of bias? The district court judge was an Irish Catholic graduate of Temple Law School, as was Nancy Ezold. Rhode, supra, at 250. He examined evaluations of associates who were granted partnership, pointing out many received very critical comments. For instance, he noted that one partner wrote that "if [Associate A] is made a partner, I will never again submit an evaluation. . . . I believe his intellectual laziness will someday embarrass us." Other associates were described as, for example, "very lazy," having "abandoned ship" on an assignment, "sloppy at times," and "wishy washy and immature." Id. at 239.

In contrast, the Third Circuit Court of Appeals consisted of justices arguably more similar to the partners at Wolf Block. In fact, multiple justices knew Wolf Block's appellate counsel, Arlin Adams, because he himself was a retired member of the appellate court. Rhode, supra, at 251. Instead of focusing on evidence that supported Ezold's claim, the appellate court summarized favorable evidence about male associates and unfavorable evidence about Ezold. Id. at 240. It also found evidence about a sexual harassment incident and remarks about Ezold having a low chance at making partner because she was a woman to be unpersuasive and not indicative of a pattern of discrimination. Id at 241. What would Ezold have to have shown to win at the appellate level?

It is often noted that the likelihood of bias in performance evaluations is greater in settings where women constitute a minority of the workforce, the applicant pool, and the senior management. When women constitute a substantial percentage of the work force, their performance ratings are consistently higher. See Valian, supra, at 139-140 (reviewing studies); Robin J. Ely, The Power in Demography; Women's Social Construction of Gender Identity at Work, 38 Acad. Management J. 589 (1995). The expert testimony of Dr. Susan Fiske in the *Price Waterhouse* case, introduced to explain the influence of gender stereotypes in Price Waterhouse's decision, was built in part on the influential work of Rosabeth Moss Kanter, Men and Women of the Corporation (1977), which established that groups constituting 15 percent or less of an organization are particularly vulnerable to stereotyping.

> Fiske stated that when there is dramatic underrepresentation of a group, the token individuals are much more likely to be thought about in terms of their social category. People expect token individuals to fit preconceived views about the traits of the group. . . . When a token person behaves in a way that is counterstereotypical — for example, when a woman acts in an aggressive, competitive, ambitious, independent, or active way — she is more likely to be regarded as uncaring or lacking in understanding. This does not mean that women can play safe by conforming to conventional stereotypes. The Catch 22 or double bind of the powerless group is that stereotypes associated with nondominant groups are also traits that are not highly valued in the organization. A woman who acts womanly acts in a way that may cast doubt on her competence and effectiveness; a woman who is thought to be too masculine may be regarded as deviant.
>
> In describing how persons respond to an individual whose behavior is incongruent with prevailing stereotypes, Fiske referred to Kanter's four "role traps." Under this scheme, the dominant male group perceives token women as mothers, seductresses, iron maidens, or pets. . . . The role trap most applicable to Hopkins was

that of the "iron maiden." ... Under Fiske's theory, the explicitly sex-based comments describing Hopkins were a predictable response to her status as a token woman who did not fit the conventional feminine mold. ...

An additional cue Fiske found which indicated that stereotyping was influencing decisionmaking was the intensity of the negative reaction toward Hopkins. ... Claims were made, for example, that Hopkins was universally disliked, potentially dangerous, and likely to abuse authority. Fiske contrasted these extremely negative comments with positive comments by others in the organization who seemed to describe the same behavior. Supporters found Hopkins as "outspoken, sells her own ability, independent, [has] the courage of her convictions." Detractors found her "overbearing, arrogant, abrasive, runs over people, implies she knows more than anyone in the world about anything and is not afraid to let anybody know it." Fiske's testimony on this phenomenon of "selective perception" suggested that the differing reactions to Hopkins were not simply a function of the slice of Hopkins' behavior that each individual evaluator had witnessed. Instead, when all the evidence was in, the "real" Ann Hopkins might still not clearly emerge from putting all the pieces together. Fiske's use of Kanter's role traps also demonstrated how other people can contribute to the social construction of the personality of an individual. This made it more difficult to separate Hopkins' "real" personality from the environment in which she worked.

Martha Chamallas, Listening to Dr. Fiske: The Easy Case of Price Waterhouse v. Hopkins, 15 Vt. L. Rev. 89, 96-99 (1990).

Is this testimony persuasive? Of what? If Dr. Fiske's theory is accepted, would employers safely be able to make suggestions to female employees for improving their deficiencies that could be linked to traditional gender roles? What if a woman *is* ineffective because she is too assertive? Or not assertive enough? See Deborah Dyson, Note, Expert Testimony and Subtle Discrimination in the Workplace: Do We Now Need a Weatherman to Know Which Way the Wind Blows?, 34 Golden Gate U. L. Rev. 37, 68-69 (2004) (arguing that expert testimony may be necessary to explain the problem of subtle discrimination, but that experts must be careful not to draw links between sexism in general and discrimination in the particular case at hand).

Yet without testimony of this sort, it is difficult to imagine how most employees could refute an employer's non-discriminatory justifications for an adverse decision. Smoking guns like the charm school comment are increasingly rare. As one court put it, employers of even "minimal sophistication" will "neither admit discriminatory . . . [conduct] nor leave a paper trail demonstrating it." Riordan v. Kempiners, 831 F.2d 690, 697 (7th Cir. 1987). Managers who appear lacking in such sophistication are often counseled by human resources personnel to ensure that written performance reviews include concrete examples of employee weaknesses and avoid stereotypical characterizations.

Susan Sturm argues that unconscious bias and patterns of interaction have largely replaced deliberate intentional discrimination as the foundations of contemporary discriminatory employment practices. See Susan Sturm, Second Generation Employment Discrimination: A Structural Approach, 101 Colum. L. Rev. 458, 460 (2001). For more on cognitive bias, including sources on the subject, see Jerry Kang, Trojan Horses of Race, 118 Harv. L. Rev. 1489 (2005).

Can the low percentage of women in the plaintiff's work category itself be probative of discrimination?

> Glass ceiling cases are rarely stronger than this. At the time when Price Waterhouse withheld her promotion, all but 7 of the firm's 662 partners were male. Hopkins billed more hours and brough in more business than any other person nominated for partnership in the year of her reject, and clients generally had given her high ratings.... Several men who obtained partnerships [in the year that Hopkins did not] were characterized as "abrasive," "overbearing," or "cocky." No one mentioned charm school for them.

Deborah Rhode, Speaking of Sex 161 (1997). Is this analysis convincing, even without expert evidence about unconscious discrimination?

In evaluating claims of sex discrimination, what significance should be given to "stray remarks" like those alleged in *Ezold*? Courts have reached inconsistent results. Compare Plotke v. White, 405 F.3d 1092 (10th Cir. 2005) (holding that evidence that male supervisors referred to a woman physician as "Jane" instead of "Dr." and called her a "femi-Nazi" were relevant and precluded summary judgment, even though they were not directly related to the termination decision); Santiago-Ramos v. Centennial P.R. Wireless Corp., 217 F.3d 46 (1st Cir. 2000) (evidence of several remarks that questioned the ability of women to have children and still remain committed to work as well as blatant statements that the employer preferred hiring unmarried, childless women because they were more committed to their work is sufficient to prove pretext in a sex discrimination case contesting termination of a woman who expressed the desire to have another child in the near future) with Sreeram v. La. State Univ. Med. Ctr., 188 F.3d 314 (5th Cir. 1999) (in upholding decision against a terminated surgical resident claiming discrimination on the basis of sex and national origin, the court found irrelevant remarks by her evaluators such as that "her difficulties in the program were 'cultural'"; a concern by one superior about why women would put themselves through surgical residency particularly if they plan on having children because, "they're constantly tired, and they don't have time to put on their makeup and put on clothes and do a lot of things girls need to do. . . ."; and the observation of one superior that "she is not accepted well by the "'good old boys'"); Heim v. State of Utah, 8 F. 3d 1541, 1546 (10th Cir. 1993) (holding comment by supervisor, "Fucking women, I hate having fucking women in the office," insufficient to show discrimination because it appeared directed at "women in general," rather than at plaintiff).

It has been argued that members of outsider groups, such as women and minorities, perceive themselves as subject to negative stereotypes and thus are "likely to feel the need to do significant amounts of 'extra' identity work to counter those stereotypes." Devon W. Carbado & Mitu Gulati, Working Identity, 85 Cornell L. Rev. 1259, 1262 (2000). Carbado and Gulati note that engaging in "signaling strategies" is common, such as when one acts harried and tired to overcome the impression that one is not busy, or sends an e-mail late at night to indicate that one has worked late. Id. at 1260. Additional strategies that members of outsider groups may employ — strategies that may actually compromise their own identities and have other psychic costs—include heterosexual "performances" to avoid suspicion of homosexuality, passing up social events that might suggest to avoid racial "cliquishness," and laughing at racist or sexist jokes to show that one can take a joke, is not obsessed with his or her outsider status, and can make others feel comfortable. Id. at 1277, 1286, 1290, 1302.

Evidence suggests that when members of subordinate groups do succeed at climbing the employment ladder, incentives exist for them to differentiate and isolate themselves from less successful members and to conform with existing workplace landscapes instead of trying to change them. Devon W. Carbado & Mitu Gulati, Race to the Top of the Corporate Ladder: What Minorities Do When They Get There, 61 Wash. & Lee L. Rev. 1645 (2004). In Ezold's case, many women at the firm expressed support for her privately but none would testify on her behalf, given the potential damage to their own careers. Rhode, "What's Sex Got to Do with It?," supra, at 246. The only female partner in the department, Roberta Liebenberg, voted against Ezold's promotion. Liebenberg was involved in women's issues in the community and was deeply offended by suggestions that she was enjoying her position as the only woman partner. However, she did acknowledge being limited in her ability to assist other women in the firm. Id. at 247-248. Should Liebenberg have had special responsibilities or aiding women in addition to juggling her own demand work and family life? Is that the obligation of women who gain positions of power any more than it is the job of similar men? Should engagement in behaviors that compromise one's identity or one's ability to be honest and forthright be evidence of discrimination? When discrimination is proven, should these behaviors count as evidence of damages?

4. What Works to Eliminate Discrimination? What mechanisms are most effective in eliminating job bias against women? Opinions on this subject are diverse. Legal scholar Richard Epstein has argued that employer self-interest is a sufficient check against gender bias. A free market rewards efficiency, he argues, and since it is inefficient for employers to discriminate against qualified workers, women do not need law to guarantee equal opportunity. If they are not advancing at the same rate as men, the reason must be sex-based differences in female employees' choices and capabilities. Epstein, Forbidden Grounds: The Case Against Employment Discrimination Laws (1992). Similarly, some argue that employers should be allowed to intentionally discriminate (such as when hiring only those who appeal to the employers customers) if doing is more efficient or saves the employer a reasonable amount of money. Ernest F. Lidge III, Financial Costs as a Defense to an Employment Discrimination Claim, 58 Ark. L. Rev. 1 (2005). Others suggest that the economic market is not always efficient and that illogical personal preferences for non-minorities cause employers to discriminate against minorities and minorities to limit themselves to fields of work with less discrimination. See, e.g., Scott A. Moss, Women Choosing Diverse Workplaces; A Rational Preference with Disturbing Implications for Both Occupational Segregation and Economic Analysis of Law, 27 Harv. Women's L.J. 1 (2004). For comparable arguments in the wage context, see Chapter 2, pp. 200-203.

Feminists have argued that law needs to be more proactive in addressing subtle but pervasive barriers. One possibility would be to create two-tiered remedies similar to those applicable for personal injuries. Under such a framework, proof of intentional discrimination in disparate treatment cases would entitle a plaintiff to full compensation, including punitive damages where appropriate. Proof of unintentional discrimination would result in more restricted remedies such as legal costs, back pay and reinstatement. Linda Hamilton Krieger, The Content of Our Categories: A Cognitive Bias Approach to Discrimination and Equal Employment Opportunity, 47 Stan. L. Rev. 1161, 1243 (1995); David Benjamin Oppenheimer, Negligent Discrimination, 141 U. Pa. L. Rev. 899 (1993). In this latter category of unintended bias, a variation of the current mixed-motives standard would apply. The test would be whether an employee's group status in fact made a difference, not whether the employer intended that it make a difference in the adverse decision. Krieger, supra, at 1243. Employers would have a defense to such claims of discrimination if that could establish that they were not negligent — i.e., that they had taken affirmative steps to identify, remedy, and prevent bias. Under such a limited liability option, plaintiffs would no longer face the evidentiary difficulties and expense of proving invidious intent, and defendants would no longer suffer the stigma and remedial costs that attach to such a judgment. Employers would also have incentives to take proactive steps to prevent bias in order to refute claims of negligence.

Other commentators believe that the most promising approach to reducing gender inequality in the workforce is to shift emphasis away from after-the-fact enforcement of antidiscrimination prohibitions and to rely more on improving an employers' capacities to identify, prevent, and redress unconscious bias and exclusionary practices. Consider the following:

> Second generation claims frequently involve patterns of interaction among groups within the workplace that, over time, exclude nondominant groups. This exclusion is difficult to trace directly to intentional, discrete actions of particular actors. . . .
>
> [Take the example of a large law firm that] aggressively recruits women at the entry level and [yet] fails to track patterns in work assignment and promotion so [that] the firm's management [was] largely unaware of any problem until [the following] complaints arose: . . . differences in patterns of work assignment and training opportunities among men and women; tolerance of a sexualized work environment by partners who are otherwise significant "rainmakers"; routine comments by male lawyers, particularly in the predominantly male departments, on the appearance, sexuality, and competence of women; harsh assessments of women's capacities and work styles based on gender stereotypes; avoidance of work-related contact with women by members of particular departments; and hyper-scrutiny of women's performance by some, and the invisibility of women's contributions to others. These complaints coincide with a concern about low morale and productivity among diverse work teams. Upon examination, the firm discovers dramatic differences in the retention and promotion rates of men and women in the firm.
>
> The problems of bias described in this scenario result from ongoing patterns of interaction shaped by organizational culture. These interactions influence workplace conditions, access, and opportunities for advancement over time, and thus constitute the structure for inclusion or exclusion. They cannot be traced solely to the sexism of a single "bad actor." Nor can they be addressed by disaggregating the problem into

discrete legal claims. The overall gender impact of this conduct may be discernible only if examined in context and in relation to broader patterns of conduct and access. The absence of systematic institutional reflection about these patterns and their impact on workplace conditions, access, and opportunity for advancement contributes to their cumulative effect. The overall organizational culture affects the extent to which particular acts produce bias in a given workplace. Comments or behavior occurring in conjunction with sex segregation and marginalization may be discriminatory, while the same statements may produce little gender exclusion in a more integrated context....

[These] second generation problems cannot be reduced to a fixed code of specific rules or commands that establishes clear boundaries governing conduct. Instead, their resolution requires a different process, namely problem solving. That process identifies the legal and organizational dimensions of the problem, encourages organizations to gather and share relevant information, builds individual and institutional capacity to respond, and helps design and evaluate solutions that involve employees who participate in the day-to-day patterns that produce bias and exclusion. An effective system of external accountability, including judicial involvement as a catalyst, would encourage organizations to identify and correct these problems without creating increased exposure to liability, and to learn from other organizations that have engaged in similar efforts.

A rule-enforcement approach to regulating second generation problems discourages this type of proactive problem solving. That approach treats regulation as punishing violations of predefined legal rules and compliance as the absence of identifiable conduct violating those rules. Rules developed externally and imposed unilaterally, whether by courts or other regulatory bodies, cannot adequately govern the range of circumstances implicated by the general principle of nondiscrimination, or account for how those circumstances will shape the law's meaning in context. Any rule specific enough to guide behavior will inadequately account for the variability, change, and complexity characteristic of second generation problems. General rules, unless linked to local structures for their elaboration in context, provide inadequate direction to shape behavior. This is particularly true for more subtle and less familiar problems, such as second generation discrimination. Externally-imposed solutions also founder because they cannot be sufficiently sensitive to context or integrated into the day-to-day practice that shapes their implementation. Yet, internally generated solutions are often insufficiently attentive to their normative implications, or to the connection between those local practices and the general antidiscrimination norm.

In a rule-enforcement process, problems tend to be redefined as discrete legal violations with sanctions attached. Fear of liability for violation of ambiguous legal norms induces firms to adopt strategies that reduce the short-term risk of legal exposure rather than strategies that address the underlying problem. They accomplish this in significant part by discouraging the production of information that will reveal problems, except in the context of preparation for litigation. Under the current system, employers producing information that reveals problems or patterns of exclusion increase the likelihood that they will be sued. Thus, lawyers counsel clients not to collect data that could reveal racial or gender problems or to engage in self-evaluation, because that information could be used to establish a plaintiff's case. Similarly, the rule-enforcement approach to compliance induces plaintiffs' lawyers and advocates to view information about institutional problems and failures as a potential basis for establishing liability. It thus encourages these important legal actors to overlook ways of using that information proactively to develop accountability systems and promote constructive structural change.

Fundamentally, the rule-enforcement model encourages lawyers to see issues as potential legal claims, rather than as problems in need of systemic resolution. This narrow focus on avoiding liability diverts attention from the structural dimensions underlying the legal violations, as well as the organizational patterns revealed through aggregating claims. . . .

Susan Sturm, Second Generation Employment Discrimination: A Structural Approach, 101 Colum. L. Rev. 458, 468, 470-471, 475-476 (2001).

Professor Sturm, among others, proposes that employers should be obligated to establish systems to collect information on recruitment, hiring, promotion, retention, and quality of life issues; monitor evaluation, assignment, and mentoring practices; provide adequate diversity training, family leave, and alternative schedule policies; and hold managers accountable for their performance in achieving diversity-related goals. See Sturm, supra, at 462-465, 493-568. Could such measures have made a difference to Nancy Ezold?

For further analysis of the relational and organizational dimensions of work culture and the "meaningful programs for reform" that employers should be pressured to devise, see Tristin K. Green, Work Culture and Discrimination, 93 Cal. L. Rev. 623, 684 (2005).

5. Remedies for Title VII Sex Discrimination Claims. Prior to the Civil Rights Act of 1991, compensatory and punitive damages were available for victims of racial discrimination but not discrimination based on sex. The 1991 Act provides for compensatory and punitive damages for victims of intentional, disparate treatment sex discrimination, but with caps, ranging from $50,000 if the employer has between 15 and 100 employees, to $300,000 for employers who have more than 500 employees. 42 U.S.C. § 1981(b) (1994). These damages are still not available in disparate impact cases of sex discrimination. The caps do not apply to race discrimination awards. Back pay is not subject to the damage caps because, like reinstatement and injunctive relief, it is considered equitable relief. After much confusion, the Supreme Court has decided that front pay — money awarded for lost compensation during the period between judgment and reinstatment or in lieu of reinstatement — is not subject to the damages cap of the 1991 Act. See Pollard v. E.I. du Pont de Nemours, 532 U.S. 843 (2001).

Higher damages may be available under state non-discrimination statutes. See Rush v. Scott Specialty Gases Inc., 930 F. Supp. 194 (E.D. Pa. 1996) (after finding $3 million punitive damages in sexual harassment suit to be excessive, remitting case for $2.7 million, after noting that Title VII limit would be $300,000).

On remand in *Price Waterhouse*, among other things, Judge Gesell ordered that Ann Hopkins be instated as a partner, 737 F. Supp. 1202 (D.D.C. 1990), aff'd, 920 F.3d 967 (D.C. Cir. 1990). Her story and its aftermath, in her own words, can be found in Ann Branigar Hopkins, So Ordered: Making Partner the Hard Way (1996). Lawyer Elizabeth Hishon, who was discriminated against in a law firm partnership decision (see note 6, infra), did not seek injunctive relief and settled her case against King and Spalding out of court. See Julie Tamminen, Law Firms Face New Challenges in Their Role as Employers: Hishon Opened the Door to Civil Rights Litigation Against Partnerships, 17 Legal Economics 41 (March 1991).

Attorney's fees and costs are also available to the prevailing party at the court's discretion. See 42 U.S.C. § 2000e-5(k) (1994). This rule has been interpreted to mean that a prevailing plaintiff will be awarded attorney's fees in all but "special circumstances." Attorney's fees are awarded to successful defendants only if the court finds the claim was frivolous, unreasonable, or groundless, or that "the plaintiff continued to litigate after it clearly became so." Christiansburg Garment Co. v. EEOC, 434 U.S. 412, 422 (1978). Costs are available as a matter of course to the prevailing party, although they need not be awarded if it would be inequitable. In Ezold's case, she agreed to pay for the appeal's costs of $12,810.25 but contested the trial expenses of $24,822.22, in part because her suit raised significant public policy issues. Rhode, "What's Sex Got To Do With It," supra, at 228. In deciding to split the cost between the parties, the Court explained that it was a "close case, concerning difficult legal issues regarding proof of discrimination" and expressed concern that "astronomical costs not become a deterrent against the assertion of legitimate disputes." Id. (citing Ezold v. Wolf, Block, Schorr and Solis-Cohen, 157 F.R.D. 13, 17-18 (E.D. Pa. 1994).

Is it fair for courts to order the prevailing party to pay in order to encourage legitimate actions by parties not involved in the case? Consider that defendants may have had more at stake than just money. Unlike most discrimination claims which are quietly settled, Ezold's case left a lengthy, publicly available paper trail and attracted widespread media coverage. Id. at 217. The co-chair of Wolf Block's executive committee, Charles Kopp, explained that the firm's reputation was on the line and settling the case would suggest that the firm was guilty of discrimination. Id. at 231. In his opinion, anything short of a prevailing court opinion would have hurt recruitment efforts and damaged the firm's reputation. Id. Is splitting court costs a good compromise to protect both plaintiffs' and defendants' rights?

6. The "Glass Ceiling," Title VII, and Professional Partnerships. *Price Waterhouse* and *Ezold* illustrate the difficulties in applying an equal opportunity principle to subjective job criteria that are especially prevalent in upper-level employment. Should the under-representation of women in management and executive positions be of concern under a formal equality approach? Or should the law be indifferent to gender disparities in results, so long as the same criteria are applied to each individual? Reconsider these questions in light of the materials on upper-level employees under the Equal Pay Act on pp. 50-51 in this chapter; on pay equity theories on pp. 198-208 in Chapter 2; on the sociobiological debate about gender differences described on pp. 644-658 in Chapter 4; and on the barriers confronting women in the legal profession described on pp. 682-685, 694-701, 719-721 in Chapter 4.

A threshold question in *Price Waterhouse* and *Ezold* is the extent to which Title VII regulates employment practices by partnerships. The United States Supreme Court, in Hishon v. King & Spalding, 467 U.S. 69 (1984), held that the decision by a private law firm whether to offer partnership to a law associate falls under Title VII because opportunities for partnership constituted a term or privilege "linked directly with an [associate's] status as an employee." Id. at 76. It is not clear, however, whether Title VII covers an employment package which, from the outset, decouples partnership consideration from performance as an associate. Justice Powell, in a concurring opinion in *Hishon*, stated his view that absent a claim based on the law firm's promise of partnership consideration, Title VII would not apply to such decisions.

> The relationship among law partners differs markedly from that between employer and employee — including that between the partnership and its associates. The judgmental and sensitive decisions that must be made among the partners embrace a wide range of subjects [including participation in profits, work assignments, approval of commitments in bar association, civil and political activities, questions of billing, and acceptance of new clients]. The essence of the law partnership is the common conduct of a shared enterprise.

476 U.S. at 79-80 & n.3 (Powell, J., concurring).

Subsequent cases have confirmed that, even if Title VII covers the partnership decision, it may not cover treatment of partners by the partnership, at least when the partner has equity in the partnership, has a significant degree of management over the partnership, and is subject to liability. See, e.g., Wheeler v. Main Hurdman, 825 F.2d 257 (10th Cir. 1987), cert. denied, 484 U.S. 986 (1987); see also EEOC v. Sidley Austin Brown & Wood, 315 F.3d 696, 703-707 (7th Cir. 2002) (partners are still employees when they lack equity in the partnership, receive regular salary, and lack meaningful management over the partnership). Similarly, the EEOC issued guidelines in 2000 that would bring Title VII into play when "the individual is subject to the organization's control," although they would not apply when "the individual acts independently and participates in managing the organization." See EEOC Compliance Manual, ¶7110, §2-III-A.1.d (2000). To what extent should a partnership's First Amendment associational rights take precedence over equal opportunity guarantees? See problem 1-17 on p. 148.

7. Alternative Dispute Resolution. An increasing number of employment contracts and professional partnerships now include mandatory arbitration clauses. Generally, so long as basic due process requirements are met and the employee is not in the transportation industry, such clauses and policies are upheld. See Circuit City Stores, Inc. v. Adams, 532 U.S. 105 (2001). Typically, proponents of arbitration point to data suggesting that it is faster and less expensive than litigation and that it may allow plaintiffs to adjudicate claims that would be too costly to bring to court. For an analysis of data suggesting that arbitration is reasonable and fair, see David Sherwyn et al., Assessing the Case for Employment Arbitration: A New Path for Empirical Research, 57 Stan. L. Rev. 1557 (2005).

Concerns exist about mandatory arbitration. Organizations such as the Equal Employment Opportunity Commission, the American Arbitration Association, and the National Academy of Arbitration all oppose compelling parties to arbitrate based on employment agreements predating the dispute. In their view, the reason is that the process permits little judicial oversight and reflects structural biases favoring employers. Arbitration awards can be set aside ordinarily only upon a showing of fraud, corruption, or misconduct. Yet the procedures that give rise to such awards are systematically skewed. According to the EEOC:

> As a "repeat player," the employer has an advantage over the employee, who is less able to make an informed selection of an arbitrator or be savvy regarding other aspects of the system.
>
> The arbitrator also is likely to be influenced by the fact that it is the employer who is the potential source of future business. . . . [A survey] of non-union, employment law cases . . . found the more frequently an employer used arbitration, the better it fared in the outcome. . . .
>
> "Unlike voluntary post-dispute arbitration — which must be fair enough to be attractive to the employee — the employer imposing mandatory arbitration is free to manipulate the arbitral mechanism to its benefit," the [EEOC concluded in a July 10, 1997 statement]. "The terms of the private agreement defining the arbitrator's authority and the arbitral process are characteristically set by the more powerful party, the very party that the public law seeks to regulate."
>
> "When employees are forced into private, employer-designed arbitration systems to resolve their discrimination claims, there is no public accountability or decisions that are made up for employers who violate the law," [EEOC Chairman Gilbert Casellas said in the July 1997 statement].

Nancy Montwieler, EEOC Policy Guidance Reaffirms Opposition to Mandatory Arbitration, 66 U.S. Law Week (BNA) 2055-2056, July 22, 1997.

The problems are said to be compounded by the frequent lack of procedural safeguards in the appointment and oversight of arbitrators. While the American Arbitration Association and American Bar Association developed a "due process protocol" to ensure that parties have right to counsel of their choice and access to discovery, the protocol does not recommend that opinions be published or that appeals be allowed, and the protocol is not mandatory. A further complaint is that the vast majority of the arbitrators selected by the industry are white men over the age of sixty who have little in common with plaintiffs. See Stephan Landsman, ADR and the Cost of Compulsion, 57 Stan. L. Rev. 1593, 1597 (2005) (examining this and other limitations and sources of bias in compulsory arbitration and court-ordered ADR); Jean Sternlight, Creeping Mandatory Arbitration: Is It Just?, 57 Stan. L. Rev. 1631 (2005) (arguing that mandatory arbitration is unjust in a number of different ways).

The growing use of mandatory arbitration has generated a growing body of legal challenges. See Martha Neil, Litigation Over Arbitration, ABA J., Jan. 2005, at 50. For a listing of many of the cases and law review articles, see David Sherwyn et al., supra, at 1558-1563.

Should Congress ban compulsory arbitration clauses entirely? Or should courts insist on compliance with standards developed by independent organizations like the American Arbitration Association, which provide for protections such as written decisions, adequate discovery, enforcement of applicable laws and selection of neutral arbitrators? According to some commentators, "ADR procedures that are fair in form as well as fact will not need to be compulsory. And procedures that fail to meet that standard do not belong in a system that implicates fundamental human rights." Deborah L. Rhode, Arbitration Pitfalls for Women, National L.J., Jan. 31, 2000, at A21.

The rising cost of arbitration has led some companies to substitute waivers of jury trials in employment contracts. See Jane Spencer, Waiving Your Right to a Jury Trial, Wall St. J., Aug. 17, 2005, at D1. Does this raise concern for victims of discrimination? Most studies suggest that although judges and juries tend to reach similar conclusions on liability, jury damage awards are greater. Id.

Even if a plaintiff is bound by a mandatory arbitration agreement, the Equal Employment Opportunities Commission, as a public agency and nonparty to the agreement acting under independent statutory authority, can seek victim-specific as well as class-action relief against an employer. E.E.O.C. v. Waffle House, Inc., 534 U.S. 279 (2002).

Jespersen v. Harrah's Operating Company, Inc.
392 F.3d 1076 (9th Cir. 2004), aff'd, 2006 U.S. App. LEXIS 9307 (9th Cir. April 14, 2006)

TASHIMA, Circuit Judge:

Plaintiff Darlene Jespersen, a bartender at Harrah's Casino in Reno, Nevada, brought this Title VII action alleging that her employer's policy requiring that certain female employees wear makeup discriminates against her on the basis of sex. The district court granted summary judgment for Harrah's, holding that its policy did not constitute sex discrimination because it imposed equal burdens on both sexes. . . . [W]e affirm.

Darlene Jespersen was a bartender at the sports bar in Harrah's Casino in Reno, Nevada, for nearly 20 years. She was an outstanding employee. Over the years, Jespersen's supervisors commented that she was "highly effective," that her attitude was "very positive," and that she made a "positive impression" on Harrah's guests. Harrah's customers repeatedly praised Jespersen on employee feedback forms, writing that Jespersen's excellent service and good attitude enhanced their experience at the sports bar and encouraged them to come back.

Throughout the 1980s and '90s Harrah's encouraged its female beverage servers to wear makeup, but wearing makeup was not a formal requirement. Although Jespersen never cared for makeup, she tried wearing it for a short period of time in the 1980s. But she found that wearing makeup made her feel sick, degraded, exposed, and violated. Jespersen felt that wearing makeup "forced her to be feminine" and to become "dolled up" like a sexual object, and that wearing makeup actually interfered with her ability to be an effective bartender (which sometimes required her to deal with unruly, intoxicated guests) because it "took away [her] credibility as an individual and as a person." After a few weeks, Jespersen stopped wearing makeup because it was so harmful to her dignity and her effectiveness behind the bar that she could no longer do her job. Harrah's did not object to Jespersen's choice not to wear makeup and Jespersen continued to work at the sports bar and receive positive performance reviews for over a decade.

In February 2000, Harrah's implemented its "Beverage Department Image Transformation" program at 20 Harrah's locations, including its casino in Reno. The goal of the program was to create a "brand standard of excellence" throughout Harrah's operations, with an emphasis on guest service positions. The program imposed specific "appearance standards" on each of its employees in guest services, including heightened requirements for beverage servers. All beverage servers were required to be "well groomed, appealing to the eye, be firm and body toned, and be comfortable with maintaining this look while wearing the specified uniform." In addition to these general appearance standards applicable to both sexes, there were gender-specific standards for male and female beverage servers. Female beverage servers were required to wear stockings and colored nail polish, and they were required to wear their hair "teased, curled, or styled." Male beverage servers were prohibited from wearing makeup or colored nail polish, and they were required to maintain short haircuts and neatly trimmed fingernails....

In order to enforce [its new appearance] standards, Harrah's required each beverage service employee to attend "Personal Best Image Training" prior to his or her final uniform fitting. At the conclusion of the training, two photographs (one portrait and one full body) were taken of the employee looking his or her "Personal Best." Each employee's "Personal Best" photographs were placed in his or her file and distributed in his or her supervisor. The supervisors used the "Personal Best" photographs as an "appearance measurement" tool, holding each employee accountable to look his or her "Personal Best" on a daily basis. Jespersen acknowledged receipt of the policy and committed to adhere to the appearance standards for her position as a beverage bartender in March 2000.

Shortly thereafter, however, the "Personal Best" standards were amended such that in addition to the existing appearance standards, all female beverage servers (including beverage bartenders) were required to wear makeup.[2] As before, male beverage servers were prohibited from wearing makeup. Because of her objection to wearing makeup, Jespersen refused to comply with the new policy. In July 2000, Harrah's told Jespersen that the makeup requirement was mandatory for female beverage service employees and gave her 30 days to apply for a position that did not require makeup to be worn. At the expiration of the 30-day period, Jespersen had not applied for another job, and she was terminated.

After exhausting her administrative remedies with the Equal Employment Opportunity Commission, Jespersen brought this action alleging that Harrah's makeup requirement for female beverage servers constituted disparate treatment sex discrimination in violation of [Title VII]. The district court granted Harrah's motion for summary judgment, holding that the "Personal Best" policy did not run afoul of Title VII because (1) it did not discriminate against Jespersen on the basis of "immutable characteristics" associated with her sex, and (2) it imposed equal burdens on both sexes. Jespersen timely appealed....

In order to prevail on a Title VII disparate treatment sex discrimination claim, an employee need only establish that, but for his or her sex, he or she

---

2. The amended policy required that "[m]ake up (foundation/concealer and/or face powder, as well as blush and mascara) must be worn and applied neatly in complimentary colors," and that "[l]ip color must be worn at all times."

would have been treated differently.... Although the employee must prove that the employer acted intentionally, the intent need not have been malevolent....

We have previously held that grooming and appearance standards that apply differently to women and men do not constitute discrimination on the basis of sex. In Baker v. Cal. Land Title Co., 507 F.2d 895 (9th Cir. 1974), employees challenged their employer's rule banning men, but not women, from having long hair. Id. at 896. We concluded that grooming and dress standards were entirely outside the purview of Title VII because Congress intended that Title VII only prohibit discrimination based on "immutable characteristics" associated with a worker's sex. Id. at 897 ("Since race, national origin and color represent immutable characteristics, logic dictates that sex is used in the same sense rather than to indicate personal modes of dress or cosmetic effects.").... Because grooming and dress standards regulated "mutable" characteristics such as hair length, we reasoned, employers that made compliance with such standards a condition of employment discriminated on the basis of their employees' appearance, not their sex.

Our later cases recognized, however, that an employer's imposition of more stringent appearance standards on one sex than the other constitutes sex discrimination even where the appearance standards regulate only "mutable" characteristics such as weight. Gerdom v. Continental Airlines, Inc., 692 F.2d 602, 605-606 (9th Cir. 1982). In Frank v. United Airlines, Inc., 216 F.3d 845 (9th Cir. 2000) (en banc), a class of female flight attendants challenged their employer's weight restrictions as a violation of Title VII because women were held to more strict weight limitations than were men. The employer insisted that all employees maintain a weight that corresponded to the "desirable" weight for their height as determined by an insurance company table, but women were required to maintain the weight corresponding to women of "medium" build, whereas men were permitted to maintain the weight corresponding to men of "large" build. Id. at 848. The employer argued that because the weight restrictions were mere "appearance" standards, they were not subject to Title VII. Id. at 854. We rejected the employer's argument, holding that "[a] sex-differentiated appearance standard that imposes unequal burdens on men and women is disparate treatment that must be justified as a BFOQ." Id. at 855; see also Carroll v. Talman Fed. Sav. & Loan Ass'n, 604 F.2d 1028, 1032 (7th Cir. 1979) (holding that employer's policy requiring female employees to wear uniforms but permitting male employees to wear "appropriate business attire" of their choosing was sex discrimination in violation of Title VII). Although employers are free to adopt different appearance standards for each sex, they may not adopt standards that impose a greater burden on one sex than the other. Frank, 216 F.3d at 855.

Although in *Frank* we characterized the weight standards at issue as "appearance standards," id., we have, as yet, had no occasion to apply the "unequal burdens" test to gender-differentiated dress and grooming requirements. In *Frank* and *Gerdom*, we were called upon only to compare the relative burdens of different weight limitations imposed on male and female employees. In those cases our task was simple because it was apparent from the face of the policies at issue that female flight attendants were subject to a more onerous standard than were males. See *Frank*, 216 F.3d at 854; *Gerdom*, 692 F.2d at 608.

In order to evaluate the relative burdens the "Personal Best" policy imposes, we must assess the actual impact that it has on both male and female employees. In doing so we must weigh the cost and time necessary for employees of each sex to comply with the policy. Harrah's contends that the burden of the makeup requirement must be evaluated with reference to all of the requirements of the policy, including those that burden men only, such as the requirement that men maintain short haircuts and neatly trimmed nails. Jespersen contends that the only meaningful appearance standard against which the makeup requirement can be measured is the corresponding "no makeup" requirement for men. We agree with Harrah's approach. Because employers are permitted to apply different appearance standards to each sex so long as those standards are equal, our task in applying the "unequal burdens" test to grooming and dress requirements must sometimes involve weighing the relative burdens that particular requirements impose on workers of one sex against the distinct requirements imposed on workers of the other sex.

Jespersen contends that the makeup requirement imposes "innumerable" tangible burdens on women that men do not share because cosmetics can cost hundreds of dollars per year and putting on makeup requires a significant investment in time. There is, however, no evidence in the record in support of this contention.... Even if we were to take judicial notice of the fact that the application of makeup requires some expenditure of time and money, Jespersen would still have the burden of producing some evidence that the burdens associated with the makeup requirement are greater than the burdens the "Personal Best" policy imposes on male bartenders, and exceed whatever "burden" is associated with ordinary good-grooming standards. Because there is no evidence in the record from which we can assess the burdens that the "Personal Best" policy imposes on male bartenders either, Jespersen's claim fails for that reason alone.

Jespersen also contends that even if Harrah's makeup requirement survives the "unequal burdens" test, that test should be invalidated in light of the Supreme Court's decision in Price Waterhouse v. Hopkins, 490 U.S. 228 (1989). In *Price Waterhouse*, the Supreme Court held that an employer may not force its employees to conform to the sex stereotype associated with their gender as a condition of employment. Id. at 250-251.

Following *Price Waterhouse*, we have held that sexual harassment of an employee because of that employee's failure to conform to commonly accepted gender stereotypes is sex discrimination in violation of Title VII. In Nichols v. Azteca Restaurant Enter., Inc., 256 F.3d 864 (9th Cir. 2001), a male waiter at a restaurant sued his employer under Title VII for sexual harassment. The waiter contended that he was harassed because he failed to conform his behavior to a traditionally male stereotype. Id. at 874. Noting that *Price Waterhouse* "sets a rule that bars discrimination on the basis of sex stereotypes," we concluded that the harassment and abuse was actionable under Title VII because the waiter was systematically abused for failing to act "as a man should act" and for walking and carrying his tray "like a woman." Id. at 874-875. Similarly, in Rene v. MGM Grand Hotel, Inc., 305 F.3d 1061 (9th Cir. 2002) (en banc), we held that a man stated a claim for sexual harassment under Title VII where he alleged that he was the victim of assaults "of a sexual nature" by his co-workers because of stereo-typical assumptions. Id. at 1068.

Although *Price Waterhouse* held that Title VII bans discrimination against an employee on the basis of that employee's failure to dress and behave according to the stereotype corresponding with her gender, it did not address the specific question of whether an employer can impose sex-differentiated appearance and grooming standards on its male and female employees. Nor have our subsequent cases invalidated the "unequal burdens" test as a means of assessing whether sex-differentiated appearance standards discriminate on the basis of sex.... In short, although we have applied the reasoning of *Price Waterhouse* to sexual harassment cases, we have not done so in the context of appearance and grooming standards cases, and we decline to do so here....

Finally, we note that we are, in any event, bound to follow our en banc decision in *Frank*, in which we adopted the unequal burdens test. *Price Water-house* predates *Frank* by more than a decade and, presumably, the *Frank* en banc court was aware of it when it adopted the unequal burdens test. Thus, *Price Waterhouse* does not qualify as an "intervening decision" which could serve as a basis for overruling *Frank*....

We hold that under the "unequal burdens" test, which is this Circuit's test for evaluating whether an employer's sex-differentiated appearance standards constitute sex discrimination in violation of Title VII, Jespersen failed to intro-duce evidence raising a triable issue of fact as to whether Harrah's "Personal Best" policy imposes unequal burdens on male and female employees.

The judgment of the district court is affirmed.

THOMAS, Circuit Judge, dissenting:

I respectfully dissent.... Harrah's required Darlene Jespersen to wear makeup to work. She refused because the cost — measured in time, money, and personal dignity — was too high. Harrah's fired her. The majority holds that Jespersen failed to raise a triable issue of fact as to whether Harrah's policy imposes unequal burdens on men and women. In fact, Jespersen easily satisfied her burden. A reasonable fact-finder could determine that Harrah's acted because of Jespersen's sex under not just one theory, but two. First, Harrah's fired Jesper-sen because of her failure to conform to sex stereotypes, which is discrimination based on sex and is therefore impermissible under Title VII. Second, Jespersen created a triable issue of fact as to whether the policy imposed unequal burdens on men and women, because the policy imposes a requirement on women that is not only time-consuming and expensive, but burdensome for its requirement that women conform to outdated and impermissible sex stereotypes.

The Harrah's policy is far more stringent than simply asking female employees to wear some makeup. The policy essentially requires women to wear a uniform of makeup including at least mascara, blush, lipstick, and foundation. In fact, accord-ing to the "image consultant" who helped implement the policy, wearing makeup "completes" the "uniformed look" of women beverage servers.... Thus, while men are held accountable to look as clean, have their hair as neat, and have their clothes as tidy and fitted as in their photo, women are held accountable to do all these things as well as be "properly made up," as they are in the post-makeover photo.

The majority attempts to distinguish this case from *Price Waterhouse* and *Nichols* because this is not a sexual harassment case. But neither was *Price Waterhouse*, in which the adverse employment action taken against the plaintiff was that she was denied partnership. 490 U.S. at 233. Even if it were, that would not matter. The question of whether an action is "because of sex" is separate from the question of whether the action constitutes an adverse employment action actionable under Title VII. . . .

The majority also suggests that *Price Waterhouse* only applies in certain contexts and did not address sex-differentiated appearance and grooming standards. In Price Waterhouse v. Hopkins, the plaintiff was denied partnership at a prestigious accounting firm where she had excelled because she didn't act femininely enough, and was specifically faulted for not wearing makeup. 490 U.S. at 235. Jespersen was fired from a job she also excelled at, for exactly the same reason. The distinction created by the majority opinion leaves men and women in service industries, who are more likely to be subject to policies like the Harrah's "Personal Best" policy, without the protection that white-collar professionals receive.

Title VII does not make exceptions for particular industries, and we should not write them in. Pervasive discrimination often persists within an industry with exceptional tenacity, and the force of law is sometimes required to overcome it. See *Gerdom*, 692 F.2d at 606-607 (describing the history of litigation over gender discrimination in the airline industry). When a company acts to enforce sexual stereotypes through grooming standards, it is not immune from *Price Waterhouse* liability; to the contrary, such actions fall precisely within the heartland of *Price Waterhouse*.

Even if *Price Waterhouse* did not apply in the grooming and appearance context, Harrah's was not entitled to summary judgment, for Jespersen created an issue of material fact as to whether the Harrah's policy is a grooming standard that imposes unequal burdens on men and women, in violation of Title VII. *Frank*, 215 F.3d at 855. . . .

The majority opinion's holding that the burdens imposed by all of Harrah's appearance policy requirements must be compared to each other does not follow from prior case law permitting employers to maintain sex-differentiated appearance standards that do not impose unequal burdens. Under the majority opinion's methodology, a sex-differentiated appearance requirement that unfairly burdens women, such as a requirement that women meet more stringent weight limits than men, *Frank*, 216 F.3d at 855, could be permissible if the employer unfairly burdened men via another sex-differentiated appearance requirement, for instance, by requiring men to wear contacts but permitting women to wear glasses, id.

Rather than permit all sorts of sex discrimination as long as it "balances out" for both genders, I would instead compare individual sex-differentiated appearance requirements that correspond to each other, given that Title VII prohibits employers from taking adverse employment actions "because of . . . sex." . . . Harrah's hair length requirement and ponytail prohibition for men should be compared to the requirement that women wear their hair "teased, curled, or styled" every day and that their hair be "worn down" at all times. Similarly, Harrah's requirement that men keep their hands and fingernails clean and trimmed and not wear colored nail polish should be compared with the rule allowing women to have longer nails, although not of "exotic length," and allowing them to wear clear, white, pink, or red nail polish. Finally, the requirement that women wear makeup and lip color at all times should be compared to the prohibition on makeup for men. If the makeup requirement for women is compared to the clean face requirement for men, there can be no dispute that Jespersen created an issue of material fact as to whether the burdens are unequal. "A rule which applies only to women, with no counterpart applicable to men, may not be the basis for depriving a female employee who is otherwise qualified of her right to continued employment." *Gerdom*, 692 F.2d at 606.

Furthermore, the majority neglects burdens other than time and money that are imposed by the policy. The sex-stereotyping inherent in certain appearance standards is a burden that falls more heavily on one sex than the other. Thus, we have recognized that the unequal burdens test does not permit sex-differentiated appearance standards that denigrate one gender based on sex stereotypes. See *Gerdom*, 692 F.2d at 606 (quoting *Carroll*, 604 F.2d at 1032-1033) ("In *Carroll*, which involved a requirement to wear uniforms, the court noted that while there is nothing offensive about uniforms per se, requiring only female employees to wear them is 'disparate treatment . . . demeaning to women . . . based on offensive stereotypes prohibited by Title VII.'").

Jespersen testified very compellingly to the burdens she personally felt in complying with the makeup policy, explaining that it required her to conform with a feminine stereotype that she felt had nothing to do with making drinks. Given her stellar customer and supervisor evaluations, Jespersen is obviously not alone in this analysis. Sex-differentiated appearance standards stemming from stereotypes that women are unfit for work, fulfill a different role in the workplace, or are incapable of exercising professional judgment systematically impose a burden on women, converting such stereotypes into a stubborn reality. See Nevada Dep't of Hum. Res. v. Hibbs, 538 U.S. 721, 736 (2003) (noting that "mutually reinforcing stereotypes create [ ] a self-fulfilling cycle of discrimination").

This is not to say that all gender-differentiated appearance requirements are prohibited; what violates Title VII are those that rest upon a message of gender subordination. The distinction is apparent in the history of our case law on grooming and appearance standards under Title VII. When early challenges to requirements that men keep their hair short arose in the federal courts, those requirements stemmed not from gender subordination, but from fear of a youth counterculture. See Willingham v. Macon Tel. Publ'g Co., 507 F.2d 1084, 1087, 1092 (5th Cir. 1975). Similarly, we have held that requiring men to wear neckties is permissible under Title VII, Fountain v. Safeway Stores, Inc., 555 F.2d 753, 755 (9th Cir. 1977). However, we have held that requiring women to wear contacts while men may wear glasses, *Frank*, 216 F.3d at 855, maintain a lower relative weight than men, id., or wear uniforms while men wear appropriate business attire, id. (citing *Carroll*, 604 F.2d at 1032) is impermissible under Title VII.

Finally, even if all appearance requirements for men are compared to all appearance requirements for women, and even if the burdens engendered by sex-stereotyping are neglected, a reasonable jury could easily conclude that having to wear approximately as much makeup as one was wearing post-makeover, in addition to teasing, curling, or styling one's hair every day, constitutes more of a burden than having to keep one's hair short and cut one's fingernails. All of these activities are ones with which fact-finders have everyday familiarity. . . .

A reasonable fact-finder could conclude that the Harrah's makeup require-ment imposes an unequal burden on women, that Jespersen was fired for failure to conform to a sex stereotype, or both. Darlene Jespersen should be allowed to present her case to a jury. Therefore, I respectfully dissent.

Notes

1. "Sex-Plus" Analysis. Employment criteria that impose "neutral requirements" on a sex-specific basis are often referred to as "sex-plus" require-ments. The first sex-plus case decided by the United States Supreme Court was Phillips v. Martin Marietta, 400 U.S. 542 (1971), which held that an employment policy precluding women with pre-school-age children from certain jobs, but not men, violated Title VII.

Workplace rules that impose sex-specific hair length, makeup, or dress codes are also examples of "sex plus" requirements but, with the few exceptions noted in *Jespersen*, they have been uniformly upheld. Setting the stage was Willingham v. Macon Telegraph Publ'g Co., 507 F.2d 1084 (5th Cir. 1975), holding that employers may impose different hair length standards on male and female employees as long as "both sexes are being screened with respect to a neutral fact, i.e., grooming in accordance with generally accepted community standards of dress and appearance." 507 F.2d at 1092. Reasoning that the addition of "sex" to the categories of discrimination prohibited by Title VII appeared to have been an afterthought, the court concluded that "Congress in all probability did not intend for its proscription of sexual discrimination to have significant and sweep-ing implications," 507 F.2d at 1090, and, accordingly, narrowed the scope of Title VII to the limitation of opportunities based on "immutable characteristics": "[A] hiring policy that distinguishes on some other ground, such as grooming codes or length of hair, is related more closely to the employer's choice of how to run his business than to equality of employment opportunity." 507 F.2d at 1091.

The *Willingham* court distinguished *Phillips* by concluding that Congress' intent was to guarantee equal job opportunity for males and females, not the ability to dress or wear one's hair alike. 507 F.2d at 1091. It also noted that the decision whether to have children, implicated in *Phillips*, is a fundamental right, while the right to wear one's hair a certain length is not. See 507 F.2d at 1091. Is this a satisfactory distinction?

The number of "sex-plus" suits per year doubled between 1990 and 2004, with seventy-four successful verdicts between 1999 and 2005. Dee McAree, 'Sex-Plus' is Hot, 179 N.J. L.J. 1117 (2005). Although an increasing number of men have also brought sex-plus suits, most successful claims have been brought by women who claim to be treated differently because they have children or of child-bearing age. See, e.g., Back v. Hastings on Hudson Union Free School Dist., 365 F.3d 107 (2d Cir. 2004).

2. Appearance Standards and Sex Stereotypes. In the first instance, one might expect a formal equality approach to disapprove sex-specific dress and appearance standards, insofar as such standards impose requirements on members of one sex (e.g., make-up, skirts, or short hair) that are not imposed on the other. Instead, courts like *Willingham* re-characterized the the issue as whether employers are allowed to expect their employees — both male and female — to conform to reasonable community standards of dress and appearance.

Many commentators have pointed out that this reliance on community standards can reinforce the very stereotypes that Title VII was intended to eliminate. Karl Klare, for example, argues that "in using [phrases like commonly accepted social norms or generally accepted community standards of dress and appearance], the courts are of course referring to mainstream or conventional norms, which in our society are thoroughly sexist and patriarchal." Karl E. Klare, Power/ Dressing: Regulation of Employee Appearance, 26 New Eng. L. Rev. 1395, 1417-1418 (1992). Building on this critique, Katharine T. Bartlett argues that the question should be whether dress and appearance requirements, or any stereotyping messages they may convey, disadvantage women in the workplace. See Bartlett, Only Girls Wear Barrettes: Dress and Appearance Standards, Community Norms, and Workplace Equality, 92 Mich. L. Rev. 2541 (1994). David B. Cruz goes even further, arguing that *all* differential dress and appearance standards should be improper under Title VII, since they all depend in one way or another on sex-based stereotypes. See Cruz, Making Up Women: Casinos, Cosmetics, and Title VII, 5 Nev. L.J. 240 (2004).

Some others take more cautious stances, arguing that holding men and women to the same appearance standards may not be appropriate or necessary to stop sex subordination and stereotyping. Robert Post offers a "sociological account" that attempts to describe how courts address appearance regulations less from some abstract determination of what is discriminatory and what is not, than from some practical sense of what social practices it is desirable for the law to help transform. See Post, Prejudicial Appearances: The Logic of American Antidiscrimination Law, 88 Cal. L. Rev. 1 (2000). Kimberly Yuracko argues for a power-access approach in which courts should focus on ending status-based hierarchy. See Yuracko, Trait Discrimination as Sex Discrimination: An Argument Against Neutrality, 83 Tex. L. Rev. 167 (2004). This approach would have courts prohibit appearance-based discrimination only when it is a product of gender norms or expectations that are incompatible with sex equality. In some situations this might require interfering with apparently neutral standards; in others, Yuracko argues, holding men and women to the same appearance standards may actually hinder women in the workplace by devaluing what is traditionally feminine or by requiring androgyny at the cost of individual liberty. Id. at 199. See also Deborah Brake, When Equality Leaves Everyone Worse Off: The Problem of Leveling Down in Equality Law, 46 Wm. & Mary L. Rev. 513 (2004) (arguing that "leveling down" often leaves everyone worse off and that equality evaluations should include additional considerations).

Should sex-specific appearance standards ever be allowed?

In May of 2005 the Ninth Circuit voted to rehear Jespersen's case en banc. Jespersen v. Harrah's Operating Co., 409 F.3d 1061. The Court explained that the first decision would not be precedent except to the extent adopted by the en banc court. In June of 2005, the Court heard oral arguments and asked plaintiffs to answer questions about, among other things, what courts should do when traditional dress codes require men and women to wear differently-priced clothing or when traditional women's clothing highlights femininity. See Cathy Gellis, Judge Kozinski Asks, And I Answer, De Novo Online News, Jun. 29, 2005, available at http://www.blogdenovo.org/archives/2005_06.html. How might the answers to these questions be relevant? What questions should the en banc Court have asked?

3. The Impact of Discrimination Based on Appearance. Appearance matters. One study found that attractive attorneys, regardless of qualification and experience, earned more than their less attractive counterparts, and that the disparity increases over time. See Jeff E. Biddle & Daniel S. Hamermesh, Beauty, Productivity and Discrimination: Lawyers' Looks and Lucre, 16 J. Lab. Econ. 172, 185-190 (1998). Research evaluating all occupations indicates that attractive people tend to make 14 percent more per hour than their below average counterparts. Kristie M. Engemann & Michael T. Owyang, So Much for That Merit Raise: The Link between Wages and Appearance, Q. Rev. Bus. & Econ. Conditions, April 2005, at 10.

Furthermore, according to a recent poll, while 33 percent of Americans think that laws should protect unattractive people from hiring discrimination, 39 percent believe that employers should be allowed to discriminate based on appearance. Press Release, Employment Law Alliance, National Poll Shows Public Opinion Sharply Divided on Regulating Appearance — From Weight to Tattoos — in the Workplace, Mar. 22, 2005 (on file with the Employment Law Alliance). Many believe that looks may be especially relevant in management positions and service industries because clients and customers prefer attractive persons. An increasing number of employers have adopted hiring practices based on attractiveness, which are generally upheld even when they are stricter or more burdensome for one sex. See, e.g., Jordan D. Bello, Attractiveness as a Hiring Criteria: Savvy Business Practice or Racial Discrimination, 8 J. Gender, Race & Just. 483, 483 (2004). Claims of discrimination by plaintiffs who claim they were discriminated against for being too attractive and dressing too sexy also have been largely unsuccessful. See, e.g., Goodwin v. Harvard College, No. 03-11797JLT (D. Mass. 2005) (finding against plaintiff who claimed she was fired for not conforming to the stereotypical conservative image of a librarian).

Should it be relevant whether an employee's appearance can be directly tied to the success of the business? In Craft v. Metromedia, Inc. 572 F. Supp. 868 (W.D. Mo. 1983), rev'd in part, 766 F.2d 1205 (8th Cir. 1985), a local television station anchorwoman, Christine Craft, filed suit against her employer after she was moved to another, off-camera position because producers found her hair and makeup to be inappropriate. Craft claimed that she was judged by harsher standards, as a woman, than male anchors were judged. The station responded not with station managers' subjective judgments about Craft's appearance, but with audience research including focus groups and a scientific telephone survey, which showed that the plaintiff's appearance had an adverse impact on her acceptance among viewers. The court determined that she was properly reassigned due to the demonstrated negative viewer response. Id. at 879. For Craft's own account of her experience, see Craft, Too Old, Too Ugly, and Not Deferential to Men (1988).

Assuming that viewer surveys demonstrate public prejudice and stereotyping, should the station be entitled to rely on them? Further discussion of the role of customer preferences in establishing employer defenses to sex discrimination claims follows the Wilson v. Southwest Airlines case on p. 107.

Some employers have taken proactive steps to neutralize how clients perceive workers. For instance, one technology company finds that by informing clients that they will be working with a top employee, the clients focus less on the employee's appearance and more on their work. Michael Barrier, Should Looks Count? Are You Discriminating Against Employees Because of their Appearance?, HR Mag. Sept. 1, 2004, at 64. For the argument that unless appearance discrimination is eliminated, the economy will be deprived of well-qualified workers, and qualified workers will be deprived of meaningful work, see Kari Horner, A Growing Problem: Why the Federal Government Needs to Shoulder the Burden in Protecting Workers from Weight Discrimination, 54 Cath. U. L. Rev. 589, 593-595 (2005). Other commentary in favor of statutory protection of physical appearance includes Stacey S. Baron, Note, (Un)lawfully Beautiful: The Legal (De)construction of Female Beauty, 46 B.C. L. Rev. 359 (2005); Elizabeth M. Adamitis, Note, Appearance Matters: A Proposal to Prohibit Appearance Discrimination in Employment, 75 Wash. L. Rev. 195 (2000). Commentary opposed to such protection includes James J. McDonald, Jr., Civil Rights for the Aesthetically-Challenged, 29 Employee Rel. L.J. 118 (2003).

As a general matter, is a person's appearance something, like intelligence, that produces different opportunities that, as a society, we must simply accept? Or is it an unfair basis for discrimination that we should attempt to eliminate, as a matter of law? Does it matter that research shows that beauty standards appear to be innate? See Nancy Etcoff, Survival of the Prettiest: The Science of Beauty 31-32 (1999) (describing study of babies who responded consistently to features based on faces rated for attractiveness by symmetry, balance and other standard measures).

Even if appearance-based discrimination constitutes discrimination based on sex, an employer may argue that the discrimination is justified by business considerations. Section b. on p. 100 addresses standards an employer must meet to show that a sex-related job requirement is justified as a "bona fide occupational qualification" (BFOQ) or a business necessity.

4. Weight. Weight also matters. One recent study indicates that, overall, women earn 0.6% less family income for each one percent increase in body mass. See Stephanie Armour, Your Appearance, Good or Bad, Can Affect Size of Your Paycheck, USA Today, July 20, 2005, at 1B (referring to Dalton Conley & Rebecca Glauber, Gender, Body Mass, and Economic Status (forthcoming

2005) (Working Paper No. 11343 on file with National Bureau of Economic Research)). Significantly, chronic obesity is more common in women than in men. See Vivian M. Dickerson, Focus on Primary Care Evaluation, Management, and Treatment of Obesity in Women, 56 Obstetrical & Gynecological Survey 650 (October 2001). Overweight women average nine percent less per hour than average-sized women. John Cawley, The Impact of Obesity on Wages, 39 J. Hum. Res. 451, 468 (2004).

Weight limits have been a common appearance requirement in some occupations. Notorious until recently were weight restrictions imposed on flight attendants. These weight restrictions were uniformly upheld in the courts, even though the standards for men took into account large frame sizes while the standards for women presupposed women of small or medium build. See, e.g., Jarrell v. Eastern Airlines, Inc., 430 F. Supp. 884, 889 (E.D. Va. 1977), aff'd mem., 577 F.2d 869 (4th Cir. 1978). See also Delta v. New York St. Div. of Human Rights, 652 N.Y.S.2d 253, 259 (App. Div. 1996), aff'd, 689 N.E.2d 898 (N.Y. 1997) (employer, "particularly those whose business involves contact with the public[,] should be free to express and act upon a concern with the image which their employees communicate by their appearance and demeanor (citation omitted)").

The court in *Jarrell* relied on the "fact" that the weight restrictions for women at issue in that case did not concern an "immutable characteristic":

> Weight gain, unlike height, is a characteristic subject to the reasonable control of most individuals.... [T]here is nothing inherent in womanhood which makes Eastern's weight standards more difficult for women to satisfy than men. To be sure weight control is not as simple as cutting one's hair. Nonetheless, ... "discrimination based on factors of personal preference does not necessarily restrict employment opportunities and thus is not forbidden." [citation omitted].

430 F. Supp. at 892.

This reasoning raises a number of issues. As a threshold matter, should the degree of control an individual can exercise over various job criteria be relevant to a Title VII analysis of "sex-plus" job requirements? Was it relevant in *Phillips*? For a comprehensive argument that the use of the immutability criterion to uphold employment requirements based on sex-based stereotypes violates the language and purpose of Title VII, see Peter Brandon Bayer, Mutable Characteristics and the Definition of Discrimination Under Title VII, 20 U.C. Davis L. Rev. 769 (1987). What about the fact, discussed above, that women have more problem with their weight than men? Further discussion of the immutability criterion in the context of constitutional analysis appears on pp. 614-617 in Chapter 3.

Even if immutability should be relevant to Title VII analysis, how immutable should the characteristic have to be? Studies show that people tend to cling to the belief that obesity is the product of personal choice instead of genetics or environmental factors. Sunaina Assanand et al., Personal Theories of Hunger and Eating, 28 J. Applied Soc. Psych. 998 (1998). Scientists agree that personal choices affect weight. However, there is some also medical scientific evidence that people are genetically predisposed to overeat and store fat. See generally

John C. Peters, et al., From Instinct to Intellect: The Challenge of Maintaining Healthy Weight in the Modern World, 3 Obesity Revs. 69, 70 (2002). There is also evidence that environmental factors are partly responsible for obesity. See Adam Benforado et al., Broken Scales: Obesity and Justice in America, 53 Emory L.J. 1645 (2004). Furthermore, as women age, their weight tends to increase at a more significant rate than men. Robert Pollack Seid, Never Too Thin: Why Women Are at War with Their Bodies 175 (1989).

Of what relevance to this issue is the problem of eating disorders for women? The research indicates that one out of every 200 to 250 women between the ages of 13 and 22 suffers from anorexia and that 12 to 33 percent of female college students struggle with induced vomiting, diuretics, and laxatives. See Susan Bordo, Unbearable Weight: Feminism, Western Culture, and the Body 140 (1993); Lynn S. Chancer, Reconcilable Differences: Confronting Beauty, Pornography, and the Future of Feminism 84-85 (1998). Over ninety percent of anorectics and bulimics are women, as are 80 percent of those who have their intestines partially removed to help control their weight. See http://www.anred.com/stats.html (last updated November 2004). Assume that this disparity arises from the social reality that women's physical appearance is more important, and more limiting, than men's. Is formal equality useful in challenging this reality? What are its limitations?

As noted in *Jespersen*, Frank v. United Airlines, Inc., 216 F.3d 845 (9th Cir. 2000), cert. denied, 532 U.S. 914 (2001), reversed the trend represented by *Jarrell*. The Ninth Circuit Court of Appeals seized upon the fact that men's weight was permitted within a broader range of frame sizes than women, as grounds for invalidating the weight standards of United Airlines. Id. at 845-855.

The cases have split on whether obesity is covered by the Americans with Disabilities Act. Under the ADA, alleged discrimination may be based on an actual or perceived disability. In successful cases, some courts have determined that obesity may be a medical disability. See, e.g., Viscik v. Fowler Equipment Co., Inc., 800 A.2d 826 (N.J. 2002) (obesity plus other medical complications); Cook v. Rhode Island Department of Mental Health, Retardation & Hospitals, 10 F.3d 17 (1st Cir. 1993). Others have held that obesity is not a disability. See, e.g., Whaley v. Southwest Student Transportation, L.C., 2002 U.S. Dist. LEXIS 9103 (N.D. Tex. 2002); Coleman v. Georgia Power Co., 81 F. Supp. 2d 1365 (N.D. Ga. 2000).

Among those arguing that discrimination based on obesity should be prohibited, see Elizabeth Kristen, Comment, Addressing the Problem of Weight Discrimination in Employment, 90 Cal. L. Rev. 57 (2002); Jane Byeff Korn, Fat, 77 B.U. L. Rev. 25, 66-67 (1997); Elizabeth A. Adamitis, Note, Appearance Discrimination in Employment, 75 Wash. L. Rev. 195, 200-203 (2000); Kari Horner, A Growing Problem: Why the Federal Government Needs to Shoulder the Burden in Protecting Workers from Weight Discrimination, 54 Cath. U. L. Rev. 589, 589 (2005).

The state of Michigan, and the cities of Madison, Wisconsin, and Santa Cruz, California, specifically prohibit discrimination on the basis of weight. See Maureen J. Arrigo-Ward, No Trifling Matter: How the Legal System Supports Persecution of the Obese, 10 Wis. Women's L.J. 27, 35 (1995).

5. Sex and Age. Sex and age can be a devastating combination. Evidence suggests that older women experience discrimination that younger women and older men do not face, and that weight and appearance standards may become more burdensome as women age. Even in jobs where appearance is considered less important, older women earn less money than men and younger women, and they may lack opportunities to obtain higher-paying and more prestigious jobs. See Nicole Buonocore Porter, Sex Plus Age Discrimination: Protection Older Women Workers, 81 Denv. U. L. Rev. 79, 94-99 (2003).

Should age, too, be treated as an "immutable characteristic"? See, e.g., Bryan B. Woodruff, Note, Unprotected Until Forty: The Limited Scope of the Age Discrimination in Employment Act of 1967, 73 Ind. L.J. 1295 (1998) (arguing that "for the old, age is an immutable characteristic, just like race and sex"); cf. O'Connor v. Consolidated Coin Caterers Corp., 517 U.S. 368 (1996) (treating age differently than traditional immutable characteristics by requiring more evidence to show a prima facie case for age than for sex or race).

The sex-plus framework (see note 1, p. 94) may have promise for older women. Some argue that since they face unique discrimination, older women, like black women, should be treated as a subset of a protected class and receive the protection of sex-plus analysis under Title VII. See, e.g., Sabina Crocette, Comment, Considering Hybrid Sex and Age Discrimination Claims by Women: Examining Approaches to Pleading and Analysis — A Pragmatic Approach, 28 Golden Gate U. L. Rev. 115 (1998). Recent high-profile cases have rendered successful verdicts for women claiming age and appearance discrimination. See, e.g., Eduardo Porter, UBS Ordered to Pay $29 Million in Sex Bias Lawsuit, N.Y. Times, Apr. 15, 2005, at C4 (reporting on Zubulake v. UBS Warburg LLC., No. 02 Civ. 1243 (S.D.N.Y. March 16, 2005), where defendant bank allegedly called plaintiff "old and ugly").

b. When Is Discrimination a "Bona Fide Occupational *Qualification*"?

Dothard v. Rawlinson
433 U.S. 321 (1977)

Mr. Justice STEWART delivered the opinion of the Court.

Appellee Dianne Rawlinson sought employment with the Alabama Board of Corrections as a prison guard, called in Alabama a "correctional counselor." After her application was rejected, she brought this class suit under Title VII of the Civil Rights Act of 1964 . . . , and under 42 U.S.C. § 1983, alleging that she had been denied employment because of her sex in violation of federal law. . . .

I

At the time she applied for a position as correctional counselor trainee, Rawlinson was a 22-year-old college graduate whose major course of study had been correctional psychology. She was refused employment because she failed to meet the minimum 120-pound weight requirement established by an Alabama statute. The statute also establishes a height minimum of 5 feet 2 inches.

After her application was rejected because of her weight, Rawlinson filed a charge with the Equal Employment Opportunity Commission, and ultimately received a right-to-sue letter. She then filed a complaint in the District Court on behalf of herself and other similarly situated women, challenging the statutory height and weight minima as violative of Title VII and the Equal Protection Clause of the Fourteenth Amendment. A three-judge court was convened. While the suit was pending, the Alabama Board of Corrections adopted Administrative Regulation 204, establishing gender criteria for assigning correctional counselors to maximum-security institutions for "contact positions," that is, positions requiring continual close physical proximity to inmates of the institution. Rawlinson amended her class-action complaint by adding a challenge to Regulation 204 as also violative of Title VII and the Fourteenth Amendment.

Like most correctional facilities in the United States, Alabama's prisons are segregated on the basis of sex. . . . A correctional counselor's primary duty within these institutions is to maintain security and control of the inmates by continually supervising and observing their activities. To be eligible for consideration as a correctional counselor, an applicant must possess a valid Alabama driver's license, have a high school education or its equivalent, be free from physical defects, be between the ages of 20-1/2 years and 45 years at the time of appointment, and fall between the minimum height and weight requirements of 5 feet 2 inches, and 120 pounds, and the maximum of 6 feet 10 inches, and 300 pounds. Appointment is by merit, with a grade assigned each applicant based on experience and education. No written examination is given.

At the time this litigation was in the District Court, the Board of Corrections employed a total of 435 people in various correctional counselor positions, 56 of whom were women. Of those 56 women, 21 were employed at the Julia Tutwiler Prison for Women, 13 were employed in noncontact positions at the four male maximum-security institutions, and the remaining 22 were employed at the other institutions operated by the Alabama Board of Corrections. Because most of Alabama's prisoners are held at the four maximum-security male penitentiaries, 336 of the 435 correctional counselor jobs were in those institutions, a majority of them concededly in the "contact" classification. Thus, even though meeting the statutory height and weight requirements, women applicants could under Regulation 204 compete equally with men for only about 25% of the correctional counselor jobs available in the Alabama prison system. . . .

The gist of the claim that the statutory height and weight requirements discriminate against women does not involve an assertion of purposeful discriminatory motive. It is asserted, rather, that these facially neutral qualifications standards work in fact disproportionately to exclude women from eligibility for employment by the Alabama Board of Corrections. We dealt in Griggs v. Duke Power Co., [401 U.S. 424 (1971)], and Albemarle Paper Co. v. Moody, [422 U.S. 405 (1975)], with similar allegations that facially neutral employment standards disproportionately excluded Negroes from employment, and those cases guide our approach here.

Those cases make clear that to establish a prima facie case of discrimination, a plaintiff need only show that the facially neutral standards in question select applicants for hire in a significantly discriminatory pattern. Once it is thus shown that the employment standards are discriminatory in effect, the employer must meet "the burden of showing that any given requirement (has) . . . a manifest relationship to the employment in question." Griggs v. Duke Power Co., supra, [at 432]. If the employer proves that the challenged requirements are job related, the plaintiff may then show that other selection devices without a similar discriminatory effect would also "serve the employer's legitimate interest in 'efficient and trustworthy workmanship.'" Albemarle Paper Co. v. Moody, supra, [at 425], quoting McDonnell Douglas Corp. v. Green, [411 U.S. 792, 801 (1973)].

Although women 14 years of age or older compose 52.75% of the Alabama population and 36.89% of its total labor force, they hold only 12.9% of its correctional counselor positions. In considering the effect of the minimum height and weight standards on this disparity in rate of hiring between the sexes, the District Court found that the 5'2" requirement would operate to exclude 33.29% of the women in the United States between the ages of 18-79, while excluding only 1.28% of men between the same ages. The 120-pound weight restriction would exclude 22.29% of the women and 2.35% of the men in this age group. When the height and weight restrictions are combined, Alabama's statutory standards would exclude 41.13% of the female population while excluding less than 1% of the male population. Accordingly, the District Court found that Rawlinson had made out a prima facie case of unlawful sex discrimination.

The appellants argue that a showing of disproportionate impact on women based on generalized national statistics should not suffice to establish a prima facie case. They point in particular to Rawlinson's failure to adduce comparative statistics concerning actual applicants for correctional counselor positions in Alabama. There is no requirement, however, that a statistical showing of disproportionate impact must always be based on analysis of the characteristics of actual applicants. . . . The application process might itself not adequately reflect the actual potential applicant pool, since otherwise qualified people might be discouraged from applying because of a self-recognized inability to meet the very standards challenged as being discriminatory. See International Brotherhood of Teamsters v. United States, [431 U.S. 324, 365-367 (1977)]. A potential applicant could easily determine her height and weight and conclude that to make an application would be futile. Moreover, reliance on general population demographic data was not misplaced where there was no reason to suppose that physical height and weight characteristics of Alabama men and women differ markedly from those of the national population.

For these reasons, we cannot say that the District Court was wrong in holding that the statutory height and weight standards had a discriminatory impact on women applicants. . . .

We turn, therefore, to the appellants' argument that they have rebutted the prima facie case of discrimination by showing that the height and weight requirements are job related. These requirements, they say, have a relationship to strength, a sufficient but unspecified amount of which is essential to effective job performance as a correctional counselor. In the District Court, however,

the appellants produced no evidence correlating the height and weight requirements with the requisite amount of strength thought essential to good job performance. Indeed, they failed to offer evidence of any kind in specific justification
of the statutory standards.

If the job-related quality that the appellants identify is bona fide, their purpose could be achieved by adopting and validating a test for applicants that measures strength directly. Such a test, fairly administered, would fully satisfy the
standards of Title VII because it would be one that "measure(s) the person for
the job and not the person in the abstract." Griggs v. Duke Power Co., [401 U.S.
at 436]. But nothing in the present record even approaches such a measurement.

For the reasons we have discussed, the District Court was not in error in
holding that Title VII . . . prohibits application of the statutory height and weight
requirements to Rawlinson and the class she represents.

III

Unlike the statutory height and weight requirements, Regulation 204
[excluding women from maximum security "contact positions"] explicitly discriminates against women on the basis of their sex. In defense of this overt discrimination, the appellants rely on §703(e) of Title VII, 42 U.S.C. §2000e-2(e),
which permits sex-based discrimination "in those certain instances where . . .
sex . . . is a bona fide occupational qualification reasonably necessary to the normal
operation of that particular business or enterprise."

The District Court rejected the bona-fide-occupational-qualification (BFOQ)
defense. . . .

We are persuaded by the restrictive language of §703(e), the relevant legislative history, and the consistent interpretation of the Equal Employment Opportunity Commission that the BFOQ exception was in fact meant to be an
extremely narrow exception to the general prohibition of discrimination on the
basis of sex. In the particular factual circumstances of this case, however, we
conclude that the District Court erred in rejecting the State's contention that
Regulation 204 falls within the narrow ambit of the BFOQ exception.

The environment in Alabama's penitentiaries is a peculiarly inhospitable one
for human beings of whatever sex. Indeed, a Federal District Court has held that
the conditions of confinement in the prisons of the State, characterized by "rampant violence" and a "jungle atmosphere," are constitutionally intolerable. Pugh v.
Locke, 406 F. Supp. 318, 325 (M.D. Ala. (1976)). The record in the present case
shows that because of inadequate staff and facilities, no attempt is made in the
four maximum-security male penitentiaries to classify or segregate inmates
according to their offense or level of dangerousness — a procedure that, according to expert testimony, is essential to effective penological administration. Consequently, the estimated 20% of the male prisoners who are sex offenders are
scattered throughout the penitentiaries' dormitory facilities.

In this environment of violence and disorganization, it would be an over-
simplification to characterize Regulation 204 as an exercise in "romantic paternalism." Cf. Frontiero v. Richardson, [411 U.S. 677, 684 (1973)]. In the usual

case, the argument that a particular job is too dangerous for women may appropriately be met by the rejoinder that it is the purpose of Title VII to allow the individual woman to make that choice for herself. More is at stake in this case, however, than an individual woman's decision to weigh and accept the risks of employment in a "contact" position in a maximum-security male prison.

The essence of a correctional counselor's job is to maintain prison security. A woman's relative ability to maintain order in a male, maximum-security, unclassified penitentiary of the type Alabama now runs could be directly reduced by her womanhood. There is a basis in fact for expecting that sex offenders who have criminally assaulted women in the past would be moved to do so again if access to women were established within the prison. There would also be a real risk that other inmates, deprived of a normal heterosexual environment, would assault women guards because they were women.[22] In a prison system where violence is the order of the day, where inmate access to guards is facilitated by dormitory living arrangements, where every institution is understaffed, and where a substantial portion of the inmate population is composed of sex offenders mixed at random with other prisoners, there are few visible deterrents to inmate assaults on women custodians.

Appellee Rawlinson's own expert testified that dormitory housing for aggressive inmates poses a greater security problem than single-cell lockups, and further testified that it would be unwise to use women as guards in a prison where even 10% of the inmates had been convicted of sex crimes and were not segregated from the other prisoners.[23] The likelihood that inmates would assault a woman because she was a woman would pose a real threat not only to the victim of the assault but also to the basic control of the penitentiary and protection of its inmates and the other security personnel. The employee's very womanhood would thus directly undermine her capacity to provide the security that is the essence of a correctional counselor's responsibility. . . .

The judgment is accordingly affirmed in part and reversed in part, and the case is remanded to the District Court for further proceedings consistent with this opinion. . . .

[The opinion of Mr. Justice Rehnquist, with whom The Chief Justice and Mr. Justice Blackmun joined, concurring in the result and concurring in part, is omitted.]

Mr. Justice MARSHALL, with whom Mr. Justice BRENNAN joins, concurring in part and dissenting in part. . . .

The Court properly rejects two proffered justifications for denying women jobs as prison guards. It is simply irrelevant here that a guard's occupation is dangerous and that some women might be unable to protect themselves

---

22. The record contains evidence of an attack on a female clerical worker in an Alabama prison, and of an incident involving a woman student who was taken hostage during a visit to one of the maximum-security institutions.

23. Alabama's penitentiaries are evidently not typical. Appellee Rawlinson's two experts testified that in a normal, relatively stable maximum-security prison characterized by control over the inmates, reasonable living conditions, and segregation of dangerous offenders, women guards could be used effectively and beneficially. Similarly, an amicus brief filed by the State of California attests to that State's success in using women guards in all-male penitentiaries.

adequately. Those themes permeate the testimony of the state officials below, but as the Court holds, "the argument that a particular job is too dangerous for women" is refuted by the "purpose of Title VII to allow the individual woman to make that choice for herself." . . . Some women, like some men, undoubtedly are not qualified and do not wish to serve as prison guards, but that does not justify the exclusion of all women from this employment opportunity. Thus, "[i]n the usual case," . . . the Court's interpretation of the BFOQ exception would mandate hiring qualified women for guard jobs in maximum-security institutions. The highly successful experiences of other States allowing such job opportunities, see briefs for the States of California and Washington, as amici curiae, confirm that absolute disqualification of women is not, in the words of Title VII, "reasonably necessary to the normal operation" of a maximum security prison.

What would otherwise be considered unlawful discrimination against women is justified by the Court, however, on the basis of the "barbaric and inhumane" conditions in Alabama prisons, conditions so bad that state officials have conceded that they violate the Constitution. . . . To me, this analysis sounds distressingly like saying two wrongs make a right. It is refuted by the plain words of § 703(e). The statute requires that a BFOQ be "reasonably necessary to the normal operation of that particular business or enterprise." But no governmental "business" may operate "normally" in violation of the Constitution. Every action of government is constrained by constitutional limitations. While those limits may be violated more frequently than we would wish, no one disputes that the "normal operation" of all government functions takes place within them. A prison system operating in blatant violation of the Eighth Amendment is an exception that should be remedied with all possible speed, as Judge Johnson's comprehensive order in Pugh v. Locke, [406 F. Supp. 318 (M.D. Ala. 1976)], is designed to do. In the meantime, the existence of such violations should not be legitimatized by calling them "normal." Nor should the Court accept them as justifying conduct that would otherwise violate a statute intended to remedy age-old discrimination.

The Court's error in statutory construction is less objectionable, however, than the attitude it displays toward women. Though the Court recognizes that possible harm to women guards is an unacceptable reason for disqualifying women, it relies instead on an equally speculative threat to prison discipline supposedly generated by the sexuality of female guards. There is simply no evidence in the record to show that women guards would create any danger to security in Alabama prisons significantly greater than that which already exists. All of the dangers with one exception discussed below are inherent in a prison setting, whatever the gender of the guards.

The Court first sees women guards as a threat to security because "there are few visible deterrents to inmate assaults on women custodians." . . . In fact, any prison guard is constantly subject to the threat of attack by inmates, and "invisible" deterrents are the guard's only real protection. No prison guard relies primarily on his or her ability to ward off an inmate attack to maintain order. Guards are typically unarmed and sheer numbers of inmates could overcome the normal complement. Rather, like all other law enforcement officers, prison guards must rely primarily on the moral authority of their office and the threat of future punishment for miscreants. As one expert testified below, common sense, fairness, and mental and emotional stability are the qualities a guard needs to cope with the dangers of the job. . . . Well qualified and properly trained women, no less than men, have these psychological weapons at their disposal.

The particular severity of discipline problems in the Alabama maximum-security prisons is also no justification for the discrimination sanctioned by the Court. The District Court found in Pugh v. Locke, supra, that guards "must spend all their time attempting to maintain control or to protect themselves." 406 F. Supp., at 325. If male guards face an impossible situation, it is difficult to see how women could make the problem worse, unless one relies on precisely the type of generalized bias against women that the Court agrees Title VII was intended to outlaw. For example, much of the testimony of appellants' witnesses ignores individual differences among members of each sex and reads like "ancient canards about the proper role of women." Phillips v. Martin Marietta Corp., [400 U.S. 542, 545 (1971) (Marshall, J., concurring)]. The witnesses claimed that women guards are not strict disciplinarians; that they are physically less capable of protecting themselves and subduing unruly inmates; that inmates take advantage of them as they did their mothers, while male guards are strong father figures who easily maintain discipline, and so on. Yet the record shows that the presence of women guards has not led to a single incident amounting to a serious breach of security in any Alabama institution.[3] And, in any event, "[g]uards rarely enter the cell blocks and dormitories," Pugh v. Locke, 406 F. Supp., at 325, where the danger of inmate attacks is the greatest.

It appears that the real disqualifying factor in the Court's view is "[t]he employee's very womanhood." . . . The Court refers to the large number of sex offenders in Alabama prisons, and to "[t]he likelihood that inmates would assault a woman because she was a woman." . . . In short, the fundamental justification for the decision is that women as guards will generate sexual assaults. With all respect, this rationale regrettably perpetuates one of the most insidious of the old myths about women that women, wittingly or not, are seductive sexual objects. The effect of the decision, made I am sure with the best of intentions, is to punish women because their very presence might provoke sexual assaults. It is women who are made to pay the price in lost job opportunities for the threat of depraved conduct by prison inmates. Once again, "[t]he pedestal upon which women have been placed has . . . , upon closer inspection, been revealed as a cage." Sail'er Inn, Inc. v. Kirby, [485 P.2d 529, 541 (1971)]. It is particularly ironic that the cage is erected here in response to feared misbehavior by imprisoned criminals.[4]

The proper response to inevitable attacks on both female and male guards is not to limit the employment opportunities of law-abiding women who wish to

---

3. The Court refers to two incidents involving potentially dangerous attacks on women in prisons. . . . But these did not involve trained corrections officers; one victim was a clerical worker and the other a student visiting on a tour.

4. The irony is multiplied by the fact that enormous staff increases are required by the District Court's order in Pugh v. Locke, 406 F. Supp. 318 (M.D. Ala. 1976). This necessary hiring would be a perfect opportunity for appellants to remedy their past discrimination against women, but instead the Court's decision permits that policy to continue. Moreover, once conditions are improved in accordance with the *Pugh* order, the problems that the Court perceives with women guards will be substantially alleviated.

contribute to their community, but to take swift and sure punitive action against the inmate offenders. Presumably, one of the goals of the Alabama prison system is the eradication of inmates' antisocial behavior patterns so that prisoners will be able to live one day in free society. Sex offenders can begin this process by learning to relate to women guards in a socially acceptable manner. To deprive women of job opportunities because of the threatened behavior of convicted criminals is to turn our social priorities upside down.[5] . . .

[The opinion of Mr. Justice White, concurring and dissenting, is omitted.]

5. The appellants argue that restrictions on employment of women are also justified by consideration of inmates' privacy. It is strange indeed to hear state officials who have for years been violating the most basic principles of human decency in the operation of their prisons suddenly become concerned about inmate privacy. It is stranger still that these same officials allow women guards in contact positions in a number of nonmaximum-security institutions, but strive to protect inmates' privacy in the prisons where personal freedom is most severely restricted. I have no doubt on this record that appellants' professed concern is nothing but a feeble excuse for discrimination. As the District Court suggested, it may well be possible, once a constitutionally adequate staff is available, to rearrange work assignments so that legitimate inmate privacy concerns are respected without denying jobs to women. Finally, if women guards behave in a professional manner at all times, they will engender reciprocal respect from inmates, who will recognize that their privacy is being invaded no more than if a woman doctor examines them. The suggestion implicit in the privacy argument that such behavior is unlikely on either side is an insult to the professionalism of guards and the dignity of inmates.

Wilson v. Southwest Airlines Co.
517 F. Supp. 292 (N.D. Tex. 1981)

HIGGINBOTHAM, District Judge.

This case presents the important question whether femininity, or more accurately female sex appeal, is a bona fide occupational qualification ("BFOQ") for the jobs of flight attendant and ticket agent with Southwest Airlines. Plaintiff Gregory Wilson and the class of over 100 male job applicants he represents have challenged Southwest's open refusal to hire males as a violation of Title VII. . . .

At the phase one trial on liability, Southwest conceded that its refusal to hire males was intentional. . . . Southwest contends, however, that the BFOQ exception to Title VII's ban on sex discrimination, 42 U.S.C. §703(e), justifies its hiring only females for the public contact positions of flight attendant and ticket agent. The BFOQ window through which Southwest attempts to fly permits sex discrimination in situations where the employer can prove that sex is a "bona fide occupational qualification reasonably necessary to the normal operation of that particular business or enterprise." Id. Southwest reasons it may discriminate against males because its attractive female flight attendants and ticket agents personify the airline's sexy image and fulfill its public promise to take passengers skyward with "love." Defendant claims maintenance of its females-only hiring policy is crucial to the airline's continued financial success. . . .

Factual Background . . .

Southwest was incorporated in March of 1967 and filed its initial application with the Texas Aeronautics Commission ("TAC") in November of 1967 to serve the intrastate markets of Dallas, Houston and San Antonio. Southwest's proposed entry as an intrastate commuter carrier sparked a hostile reaction from the incumbent air carriers serving the Texas market. . . . [A]s a result of the defensive tactics of Southwest's competitors . . . [i]n December of 1970, Southwest had $143 in the bank and was over $100,000 in debt, though no aircraft had ever left the ground.

Barely intact, Southwest, in early 1971, called upon a Dallas advertising agency, the Bloom Agency, to develop a winning marketing strategy. Planning to initiate service quickly, Southwest needed instant recognition and a "catchy" image to distinguish it from its competitors.

The Bloom Agency evaluated both the images of the incumbent competitor airlines as well as the characteristics of passengers to be served by a commuter airline. Bloom determined that the other carriers serving the Texas market tended to project an image of conservatism. The agency also determined that the relatively short haul commuter market which Southwest hoped to serve was comprised of predominantly male businessmen. Based on these factors, Bloom suggested that Southwest break away from the conservative image of other airlines and project to the traveling public an airline personification of feminine youth and vitality. A specific female personality description was recommended and adopted by Southwest for its corporate image: This lady is young and vital . . . she is charming and goes through life with great flair and exuberance . . . you notice first her exciting smile, friendly air, her wit . . . yet she is quite efficient and approaches all her tasks with care and attention. . . .

From the personality description suggested by The Bloom Agency, Southwest developed its now famous "Love" personality. Southwest projects an image of feminine spirit, fun, and sex appeal. Its ads promise to provide "tender loving care" to its predominantly male, business passengers. The first advertisements run by the airline featured the slogan, "AT LAST THERE IS SOMEBODY ELSE UP THERE WHO LOVES YOU." Variations on this theme have continued through newspaper, billboard, magazine and television advertisements during the past ten years.[4]

Bloom's "Love" campaign was given a boost in 1974-1975 when the last of Southwest's competitors moved its operations to the new Dallas/Fort Worth Regional Airport, leaving Southwest as the only heavy carrier flying out of Dallas' convenient and fortuitously named, Love Field.

Over the years, Southwest gained national and international attention as the "love airline." Southwest Airlines' stock is traded on the New York Stock Exchange under the ticker symbol "LUV." During 1977 when Southwest opened five additional markets in Texas, the love theme was expanded to "WE'RE SPREADING LOVE ALL OVER TEXAS."

As an integral part of its youthful, feminine image, Southwest has employed only females in the high customer contact positions of ticket agent and flight

---

4. Unabashed allusions to love and sex pervade all aspects of Southwest's public image. Its T.V. commercials feature attractive attendants in fitted outfits, catering to male passengers while an alluring feminine voice promises in-flight love. On board, attendants in hot-pants (skirts are now optional) serve "love bites" (toasted almonds) and "love potions" (cocktails). Even Southwest's ticketing system features a "quickie machine" to provide "instant gratification."

attendant. From the start, Southwest's attractive personnel, dressed in high boots and hot-pants, generated public interest and "free ink." Their sex appeal has been used to attract male customers to the airline. Southwest's flight attendants, and to a lesser degree its ticket agents, have been featured in newspaper, magazine, billboard and television advertisements during the past ten years. Some attendants assist in promotional events for other businesses and civic organizations. Southwest flight attendants and ticket agents are featured in the company's in-flight magazine and have received notice in numerous other national and international publications. The airline also encourages its attendants to entertain the passengers and maintain an atmosphere of informality and "fun" during flights. According to Southwest, its female flight attendants have come to "personify" Southwest's public image.

Southwest has enjoyed enormous success in recent years.[6] This is in no small part due to its marketing image. Though Southwest now enjoys a distinct advantage by operating its commuter flights out of "convenient" Love and Hobby Fields, the airline achieved a commanding position in the regional commuter market while flying "wing tip to wing tip" with national carriers who utilized the same airport, fares, schedules, and aircraft. The evidence was undisputed that Southwest's unique, feminized image played and continues to play an important role in the airline's success.

Less certain, however, is Southwest's assertion that its females-only hiring policy is necessary for the continued success of its image and its business. Based on two on-board surveys, one conducted in October, 1979, before this suit was filed, and another in August, 1980, when the suit was pending, Southwest contends its attractive flight attendants are the "largest single component" of its success. In the 1979 survey, however, of the attributes considered most important by passengers, the category "courteous and attentive hostesses" ranked fifth in importance behind (1) on time departures, (2) frequently scheduled departures, (3) friendly and helpful reservations and ground personnel, and (4) convenient departure times. . . . Apparently, one of the remaining eight alternative categories, "attractive hostesses," was not selected with sufficient frequency to warrant being included in the reported survey results. . . .

[R]ather than Southwest's female personnel being the "sole factor" distinguishing the airline from its competitors, as Defendant contends, the 1980 survey lists Southwest's "personnel" as only one among five characteristics contributing to Southwest's public image. . . . Accordingly, there is no persuasive proof that Southwest's passengers prefer female over male flight attendants and ticket agents, or, of greater importance, that they would be less likely to fly Southwest if males were hired.

In evaluating Southwest's BFOQ defense, therefore, the Court proceeds on the basis that "love," while important, is not everything in the relationship between Defendant and its passengers. Still, it is proper to infer from the airline's competitive successes that Southwest's overall "love image" has enhanced its

6. From 1979 to 1980, the company's earnings rose from $17 million to $28 million when most other airlines suffered heavy losses. As a percentage of revenues, Southwest's return is considered to be one of the highest in the industry.

ability to attract passengers. To the extent the airline has successfully feminized its image and made attractive females an integral part of its public face, it also follows that femininity and sex appeal are qualities related to successful job performance by Southwest's flight attendants and ticket agents. The strength of this relationship has not been proved. It is with this factual orientation that the Court turns to examine Southwest's BFOQ defense.

Interpretations of the Bona Fide Occupational Qualification...

Early on, the Equal Employment Opportunity Commission ("EEOC"), created by Congress to administer Title VII, pronounced that "the bona fide occupational qualification as to sex should be interpreted narrowly." See EEOC Guidelines on Discrimination Because of Sex, 29 C.F.R. § 1604.2(a) (1965). The agency Guidelines further stated that the BFOQ exception did not justify "the refusal to hire an individual because of the preferences of...the employer, clients or customers," except where necessary for authenticity as provided in § 1604.2(a)(2). Id. at § 1604.2(a)(1)(iii)....

To date, the Commission has steadfastly adhered to its position that customer preference gives rise to a bona fide occupational qualification for sex in one instance only, "(w)here it is necessary for the purpose of authenticity or genuineness...e.g. an actor or actress." Id. at § 1604.2(a)(2) as amended by 45 Fed. Reg. 74676 (Nov. 10, 1980)....

Those courts which have analyzed Title VII's BFOQ exception, however, have broadened its sweep. Consistent with the language of §703(e), courts have held, or stated, that customer preference for one sex may be taken into account in those limited instances where satisfying customer preference is "reasonably necessary to the normal operation of the particular business or enterprise."...

This Circuit's decisions in Weeks v. Southern Bell Tel. & Tel. Co., 408 F.2d 228 (5th Cir. 1969) ("Weeks") and Diaz v. Pan American World Airways, Inc., 442 F.2d 385 (5th Cir.), cert. denied [404 U.S. 950 (1971)] ("Diaz") have given rise to a two step BFOQ test: (1) does the particular job under consideration require that the worker be of one sex only; and if so, (2) is that requirement reasonably necessary to the "essence" of the employer's business. . . . The first level of inquiry is designed to test whether sex is so essential to job performance that a member of the opposite sex simply could not do the same job. . . . As stated in *Weeks*, 408 F.2d at 235: (T)o rely on a bona fide occupational qualification exception, an employer has the burden of proving that he had reasonable cause to believe, that is a factual basis for believing, that all or substantially all women would be unable to perform safely and efficiently the duties of the job involved. The second level is designed to assure that the qualification being scrutinized is one so important to the operation of the business that the business would be undermined if employees of the "wrong" sex were hired. . . . *Diaz*'s "essence of the business" rule has now been adopted by every Circuit that has considered the matter. As the court there explained:

(T)he use of the word "necessary" in Section 703(e) requires that we apply a business necessity test, not a business convenience test. That is to say, discrimination based on sex is valid only when the essence of the business operation would be undermined by not hiring members of one sex exclusively.

Diaz, 442 F.2d at 388 (original emphasis).

Southwest concedes with respect to the *Weeks* test that males are able to perform safely and efficiently all the basic, mechanical functions required of flight attendants and ticket agents . . . Southwest's position, however, is that females are required to fulfill certain non-mechanical aspects of these jobs: to attract those male customers who prefer female attendants and ticket agents, and to preserve the authenticity and genuineness of Southwest's unique, female corporate personality.

A similar, though not identical, argument that females could better perform certain non-mechanical functions required of flight attendants was rejected in *Diaz*. There, the airline argued and the trial court found that being female was a BFOQ because women were superior in "providing reassurance to anxious passengers, giving courteous personalized service and, in general, making flights as pleasurable as possible within the limitations imposed by aircraft operations." 442 F.2d at 387; 311 F. Supp. 559, 563 (S.D. Fla. 1970). Although it accepted the trial court findings, the Court of Appeals reversed, holding that femininity was not a BFOQ, because catering to passengers' psychological needs was only "tangential" to what was "reasonably *necessary*" for the business involved (original emphasis). [442 F.2d at 388.] Characterizing the "essence" or "primary function" of Pan American's business as the safe transportation of passengers from one point to another, the court explained:

> While a pleasant environment, enhanced by the obvious cosmetic effect that female stewardesses provide as well as, according to the findings of the trial court, their apparent ability to perform the non-mechanical functions of the job in a more effective manner than most men, may all be important, they are tangential to the essence of the business involved. No one has suggested that having male stewards will so seriously affect the operation of the airline as to jeopardize or even minimize its ability to provide safe transportation from one place to another.

[442 F.2d at 388.]

Similar reasoning underlay the appellate court's rejection of Pan American's claim that its customers' preference for female attendants justified its refusal to hire males. Because the non-mechanical functions that passengers preferred females to perform were tangential to the airline's business, the court held, "the fact that customers prefer (females) cannot justify sex discrimination." [442 F.2d at 389.] The Fifth Circuit in *Diaz* did not hold that customer preference could never give rise to a sex BFOQ. Rather, consistent with the EEOC's exception for authenticity and genuineness, the Court allowed that customer preference could "be taken into account only when it is based on the company's inability to perform the primary function or service it offers," that is, where sex or sex appeal is itself the dominant service provided.

Diaz and its progeny establish that to recognize a BFOQ for jobs requiring multiple abilities, some sex-linked and some sex-neutral, the sex-linked aspects of the job must predominate. Only then will an employer have satisfied *Weeks'* requirement that sex be so essential to successful job performance that a member of the opposite sex could not perform the job. An illustration of such dominance in sex cases is the exception recognized by the EEOC for authenticity and genuineness. In the example given in [29 C.F.R.] § 1604.2(a)(2), that of an actor or actress, the primary function of the position, its essence, is to fulfill the audience's expectation and desire for a particular role, characterized by particular physical or emotional traits. Generally, a male could not supply the authenticity required to perform a female role. Similarly, in jobs where sex or vicarious sexual recreation is the primary service provided, e.g. a social escort or topless dancer, the job automatically calls for one sex exclusively; the employee's sex and the service provided are inseparable. Thus, being female has been deemed a BFOQ for the position of a Playboy Bunny, female sexuality being reasonably necessary to perform the dominant purpose of the job which is forthrightly to titillate and entice male customers. See St. Cross v. Playboy Club, Appeal No. 773, Case No. CFS 22618-70 (New York Human Rights Appeal Board, 1971) (dicta); Weber v. Playboy Club, Appeal No. 774, Case No. CFS 22619-70 (New York Human Rights Appeal Board, 1971) (dicta). One court has also suggested, without holding, that the authenticity exception would give rise to a BFOQ for Chinese nationality where necessary to maintain the authentic atmosphere of an ethnic Chinese restaurant, Utility Workers v. Southern California Edison, 320 F. Supp. 1262, 1265 (C.D. Cal. 1970).

Application of the Bona Fide Occupational Qualification to Southwest Airlines

Applying the first level test for a BFOQ, with its legal gloss, to Southwest's particular operations results in the conclusion that being female is not a qualification required to perform successfully the jobs of flight attendant and ticket agent with Southwest. Like any other airline, Southwest's primary function is to transport passengers safely and quickly from one point to another.[24] To do this, Southwest employs ticket agents whose primary job duties are to ticket passengers and check baggage, and flight attendants, whose primary duties are to assist passengers during boarding and deboarding, to instruct passengers in the location and use of aircraft safety equipment, and to serve passengers cocktails and snacks during the airline's short commuter flights. Mechanical, non-sex-linked duties dominate both these occupations. Indeed, on Southwest's short-haul commuter flights there is time for little else. That Southwest's female personnel may perform

---

24. Southwest's argument that its primary function is "to make a profit," not to transport passengers, must be rejected. Without doubt the goal of every business is to make a profit. For purposes of BFOQ analysis, however, the business "essence" inquiry focuses on the particular service provided and the job tasks and functions involved, not the business goal. If an employer could justify employment discrimination merely on the grounds that it is necessary to make a profit, Title VII would be nullified in short order.

their mechanical duties "with love" does not change the result. "Love" is the manner of job performance, not the job performed.

While possession of female allure and sex appeal have been made qualifications for Southwest's contact personnel by virtue of the "love" campaign, the functions served by employee sexuality in Southwest's operations are not dominant ones. According to Southwest, female sex appeal serves two purposes: (1) attracting and entertaining male passengers and (2) fulfilling customer expectations for female service engendered by Southwest's advertising which features female personnel. As in Diaz, these non-mechanical, sex-linked job functions are only "tangential" to the essence of the occupations and business involved. Southwest is not a business where vicarious sex entertainment is the primary service provided. Accordingly, the ability of the airline to perform its primary business function, the transportation of passengers, would not be jeopardized by hiring males.

Southwest does not face the situation . . . where an established customer preference for one sex is so strong that the business would be undermined if employees of the opposite sex were hired. Southwest's claim that its customers prefer females rests primarily upon inferences drawn from the airline's success after adopting its female personality. But according to Southwest's own surveys, that success is attributable to many factors. There is no competent proof that Southwest's popularity derives directly from its females-only policy to the exclusion of other factors like dissatisfaction with rival airlines and Southwest's use of convenient Love and Hobby Fields. Nor is there competent proof that the customer preference for females is so strong that Defendant's male passengers would cease doing business with Southwest as was the case in [Fernandez v. Wynn Oil Co., 20 Fair Empl. Prac. Cas. (BNA) 1162 (C.D. Cal. 1979)]. In short, Southwest has failed in its proof to satisfy Diaz's business necessity requirement, without which customer preference may not give rise to a BFOQ for sex. . . .

It is also relevant that Southwest's female image was adopted at its discretion, to promote a business unrelated to sex. Contrary to the unyielding South American preference for males encountered by the Defendant company in *Fernandez,* Southwest exploited, indeed nurtured, the very customer preference for females it now cites to justify discriminating against males. . . . Moreover, the fact that a vibrant marketing campaign was necessary to distinguish Southwest in its early years does not lead to the conclusion that sex discrimination was then, or is now, a business necessity. Southwest's claim that its female image will be tarnished by hiring males is, in any case, speculative at best. . . .

[S]ex does not become a BFOQ merely because an employer chooses to exploit female sexuality as a marketing tool, or to better insure profitability. . . .

Conclusion. . .

Rejecting a wider BFOQ for sex does not eliminate the commercial exploitation of sex appeal. It only requires, consistent with the purposes of Title VII, that employers exploit the attractiveness and allure of a sexually integrated workforce. Neither Southwest, nor the traveling public, will suffer from such a rule. More to the point, it is my judgment that this is what Congress intended. . . .

Notes

1. The Business Necessity Defense. The height and weight job criteria challenged in *Dothard* did not exclude women based directly on their sex; rather, by excluding over 40 percent of the female population while excluding only 1 percent of males, it had a disparate impact on women. Under Title VII, it thus required a business necessity, which the state could not show. The Supreme Court's reasoning is that these criteria were proxies for strength, which could have been more directly, and nondiscriminatorily, measured. How likely do you think it is that substantially more women could qualify under a strength test? See Problem 1-12, infra. Of course, if a disproportionate impact remained, that rule, too, would need to be justifiable under the business necessity test.

In light of the Court's recognition of prison security concerns that led it to uphold the male-only rule in maximum-security areas, what if the defendant had shown that the height and weight restrictions were necessary to create the *appearance* of strength, as vital to prison security as strength itself? Justice Rehnquist, concurring, raises this possibility. See 433 U.S. at 339-341.

The business necessity test is viewed by many courts as being somewhat more lenient on the employer than the BFOQ test. See, e.g., Yuhas v. Libby-Owens-Ford Co., 562 F.2d 496 (7th Cir. 1977), cert. denied, 435 U.S. 934 (1978) (anti-nepotism rule having a disproportionate effect on women was justified by employer concerns that were "far from frivolous" and "plausible"). Other courts treat the two tests as essentially the same. See, e.g., Chambers v. Omaha Girls Club, Inc., 834 F.2d 697 (8th Cir. 1987).

2. BFOQ and Sexual Authenticity. As facially discriminatory exclusions based on sex, the prison regulation excluding women as prison guards in maximum-security areas in *Dothard* and the exclusion of men as flight attendants in *Wilson* are examples of disparate treatment discrimination, which are justified under Title VII only if the sex of the employee in each case is shown to be a bona fide occupational qualification or BFOQ. There are a few "easy" cases where it seems clear that sex is a necessary qualification for a particular job. Only a woman can be a wet nurse, for example, and only a man can be a semen donor. Most other cases are more difficult. Under one recognized category of cases, sex is a BFOQ if the job requires sexual authenticity. 29 C.F.R. § 1604.2(a)(2) (2000).

The most common application arises in the entertainment industry, in circumstances in which an actor's or actress's plausibility depends on sexual identity with the character portrayed. According to *Wilson*, sex may be used to establish a climate of female sex appeal only when the "essence" of the business relates to that sex appeal. What constitutes the "essence" of a business is less clear. For instance, Kimberly A. Yuracko argues that no plausible definition of "essence" can account for allowing customer preference to create a BFOQ in some situations but not in others, and suggests that, instead, courts actually are (1) attempting to promote group-based equality of opportunity by ensuring that men and women face approximately the same number and type of job opportunities, and (2) trying to protect the divide between traditionally sexualized jobs such as a Playboy

Bunny from traditionally nonsexual jobs such as a restaurant server. Yuracko, Private Nurses and Playboy Bunnies: Explaining Permissible Sex Discrimination, 92 Cal. L. Rev. 147 (2004).

It generally is assumed that a topless dancing bar or a Playboy Bunny Club may hire only women dancers, and may discharge an employee for failure to meet the employer's criteria relating to sexual image:

> The "Bunny image" apparently depends upon the physique, attractiveness and beauty of the girl-employee who wears on the job a rabbit-like costume of scanty dimensions, quite unlike the fulsome attire (white gloves and formal dress) worn by the White Rabbit in Lewis Carroll's Alice in Wonderland. A particular employee's "Bunny image" has been rated by [Playboy Clubs International] on a numerical scale as follows: (1) "a flawless beauty"; (2) "exceptionally pretty, perhaps some minor flaw"; (3) "marginal or having some correctible deficiency, which might be weight [or] a cosmetic problem; something that is not of a more lasting, enduring, permanent nature"; (4) "loss of or the absence of the image requirements to be employed as a bunny."

Playboy Clubs Int'l, Inc. v. Hotel & Restaurant Employees & B.I.U., 321 F. Supp. 704 (1971) (discharge of 13 women for "lack of bunny image" not arbitrable under union agreement). A few unreported cases directly upholding sex as a BFOQ for Playboy Bunnies are cited in Guardian Capital Corp. v. New York State Div. of Human Rights, 360 N.Y.S.2d 937 (App. Div. 1974), appeal dismissed, 396 N.Y.S.2d 1027 (N.Y. 1975). *Guardian Capital* itself, however, holds that the replacement by a restaurant of male waiters with waitresses dressed in alluring costumes violates Title VII even if evidence demonstrates that restaurant sales increased slightly after doing so. Ironically, perhaps, it would seem that the more explicitly the employer's business exploits sex for money — and thus arguably the more harmful to women — the more easily sex will be viewed as a BFOQ. See Yuracko, supra, at 196-211; Rachel L. Cantor, Comment, Consumer Preferences for Sex and Title VII: Employing Market Definition Analysis for Evaluating BFOQ Defenses, 1999 U. Chi. Legal F. 493 (1999).

Is it clear that the case for "authentic" movie roles or for Playboy "Bunnies" is more compelling than for female flight attendants in the "Luv" airline?

3. BFOQ and Customer Preferences. Do *Diaz* and *Wilson* suggest that customer preference based on sexual stereotypes can never justify discriminatory conduct? In the lower court decision in *Diaz*, 311 F. Supp. 559 (S.D. Fla. 1970), the airline introduced evidence of a survey indicating that 79 percent of all passengers, male and female, preferred being served by female flight attendants. Expert psychological evidence was also introduced to explain the general preference of airline passengers for female attendants. It posited that the unique experience of being levitated off the ground and transported through the air at high speeds creates feelings of apprehension, boredom, and excitement; that females were psychologically better equipped to cope with these conflicting states and especially adept at relieving passenger apprehension; and that passengers of both sexes responded better to the presence of females. Id. at 565. This and other evidence persuaded the district court that sex was a BFOQ for flight attendants. The Fifth Circuit Court of Appeals took a harder line on the question of customer preferences, however, holding that the airline could take the interpersonal skills of flight attendant applicants into account, but that it could not do so by categorically excluding all men. 442 F.2d 385, 388 (5th Cir.), cert. denied, 404 U.S. 950 (1971).

As noted above, in Craft v. Metromedia, Inc., 572 F. Supp. 868 (W.D. Mo. 1983), rev'd in part, 766 F.2d 1205 (8th Cir. 1985), the court came to a different conclusion when evaluating a local television station's public opinion polls about KMBC anchorwoman Christine Craft. The station conducted audience research including focus groups and a scientific telephone survey, which showed that the plaintiff's appearance had an extremely adverse impact on her acceptance among viewers. The court determined that she was properly reassigned due to the demonstrated negative viewer response. Id. at 879. Is the rejection of the survey evidence in *Diaz* and *Wilson* reconcilable with its use in defending the employer's decision to reassign Christine Craft?

Fernandez v. Wynn Oil Co., 20 Fair Empl. Prac. Cas. (BNA) 1162 (C.D. Cal. 1979), distinguished with some difficulty in *Wilson*, was overturned by the Ninth Circuit Court of Appeals, 653 F.2d 1273 (9th Cir. 1981). The Court of Appeals held that an oil company could not refuse to hire female executives because its South American clients would refuse to deal with them. While the factual basis for this claim was not established in *Fernandez*, the court held that even if it had been, customer preference based on gender stereotypes, cannot justify a sexually discriminatory practice. 653 F.2d at 1276-1277.

4. BFOQ and Privacy Considerations. Courts have also found the BFOQ test satisfied in some cases in which sex-specific hiring accommodates the concern of third parties for privacy or other related interests. In Fesel v. Masonic Home of Delaware, Inc., 447 F. Supp. 1346 (D. Del. 1978), aff'd mem., 591 F.2d 1334 (3d Cir. 1979), for example, nine of the nursing home's female residents signed an affidavit objecting "most strenuously" to male nurses or nurses' aides. The court accepted the employer's defense that female sex was a BFOQ for the nursing positions. Quite a number of cases in the context of hospitals and nursing homes have reached the same conclusion. See, e.g., Jennings v. New York State Office of Mental Health, 786 F. Supp. 376 (S.D.N.Y.), aff'd, 977 F.2d 731 (2d Cir. 1992) (sex is a BFOQ at a state psychiatric hospital for "security hospital treatment assistant" whose duties included feeding, clothing, and cleaning patients, assisting in personal hygiene, and observing patients in bathrooms and bedrooms).

On the one hand, it may be reasonable to hire based on sex when the employment at issue implicates privacy or therapeutic interests that are gender related and the preference does not derive from harmful stereotypes. See Emily Gold Waldman, The Case of the Male OB-GYN: A Proposal for the Expansion of the Privacy BFOQ in the Healthcare Context, 6 U. Pa. J. Lab. & Emp. L. 357, 366-392 (2004) (proposing that employers should be able to hire, for example, only female obstetricians and gynecologists). Hints in UAW v. Johnson Controls, 499 U.S. 187, 206 n.4 (1991) (Blackmun, J.) and 499 U.S. at 219 n.8 (White, J., concurring), set forth below at p. 124, suggest that the United States Supreme Court is inclined to endorse a privacy application of the BFOQ defense.

On the other hand, applying the BFOQ exception in this context would seem to perpetuate age-old stereotypes that Title VII was meant to condemn — i.e., women's role washing and cleaning up after people, and men's role as the skilled professional. Along this vein, see Amy Kapczynski, Same-Sex Privacy and the Limits of Antidiscrimination Law, 112 Yale L.J. 1257 (2003). One recent case suggests that the BFOQ privacy defense is narrow, and only comes into play when hiring members of one sex would undermine the institution's safety and effectiveness. In Slivka v. Camden-Clark Memorial Hospital, 594 S.E.2d 616 (W. Va. 2004), the West Virginia state supreme court struck down a hospital policy to hire only female obstetrics nurses, despite evidence that eighty percent of patients demanded female nurses and female nurses were needed as chaperones for male physicians. The *Slivka* court noted the importance of employers not assuming personal preferences based on dated world views.

When the privacy claim is by a prisoner, rather than a patient or customer, it is likely to get short shrift. See, e.g., Michenfelder v. Sumner, 860 F.2d 328 (9th Cir. 1988); Gunther v. Iowa State Men's Reformatory, 612 F.2d 1079 (8th Cir.), cert. denied, 446 U.S. 966 (1980). When courts do recognize a right to privacy for inmates, they appear to give more respect to women's privacy than to men's. Compare Johnson v. Phelan, 69 F.3d 144 (7th Cir. 1995), cert. denied, 519 U.S. 1006 (1996) (upholding a monitoring policy that allowed female guards to observe male prisoners in various states of undress) and Oliver v. Scott, 276 F.3d 736 (5th Cir. 2002) (concluding that privacy rights did not bar cross-sex surveillance of male prisoners or require shower partitions and that such conditions did not violate equal protection rights), with Everson v. Michigan Department of Corrections, 391 F.3d 737 (6th Cir. 2004) (upholding sex as a BFOQ in Michigan's women's prisons, because the duties required officers to patrol sleeping, shower, and bathroom areas, and Michigan sought to address a deplorable record in caring for its female inmates). For a discussion of such cases, see Rebecca Jurado, The Essence of Her Womanhood: Defining the Privacy Rights of Women Prisoners and the Employment Rights of Women Guards, 7 Am. U. J. Gender, Soc. Pol'y & L. 1 (1999). Is the "favoritism" to women appropriate?

5. Sex as a BFOQ in Counseling Positions. Should the BFOQ defense be recognized in cases in which counseling may be affected by the sex of the counselor? Compare Healey v. Southwood Psychiatric Hospital, 78 F.3d 128 (3d Cir. 1996) (sex is a BFOQ for purposes of scheduling assignments in psychiatric hospital for emotionally disturbed and sexually abused children, because matching of staff and patients is important for parental role modeling and because children who have been sexually abused will disclose their problems more easily to a member of a certain sex, depending on their sex and sex of the abuser); City of Philadelphia v. Pennsylvania Human Relations Comm'n, 300 A.2d 97 (Pa. Comm. Ct. 1973) ("the biological differences between men and women which in turn produce psychological differences" justify counseling jobs using sex as a criterion), with EEOC v. Physicians Weight Loss Centers, 953 F. Supp. 301

(W.D. Mo. 1996) (although 95 percent of customers at a weight loss center were women and some objected to having their measurements taken by a man and did not feel comfortable discussing emotional and physiological issues associated with weight loss with a man, sex was not a BFOQ for center's counselors).

6. **Vulnerability to Rape as a BFOQ.** *Dothard* upholds a sex-based discrimination precluding women from taking positions as prison guards in maximum-security prisons on the grounds that the likelihood of assault, which is a direct consequence of the "employee's very womanhood," would pose a threat to "basic control of the penitentiary." Justice Marshall's dissenting opinion exhausts virtually every tool of traditional equality analysis: it disputes the factual premises of the rule — for example, that woman guards would create a danger to the prison's basic security; it identifies the stereotypes about women as "seductive sexual objects" that are reinforced through the exclusion; and it insists that some women will be able to protect themselves and should be given the chance, as individuals, to prove that ability rather than be foreclosed from an opportunity on the basis of the average characteristics of their sex. It also challenges the quality of the justification offered by the state: inadequate staffing. If you think that this issue in *Dothard* is wrongly decided, is it because the Court failed to apply standard formal equality principles correctly? Or because formal equality does not provide the tools necessary to analyze an exclusion based on factors "unique" to women? Or some other reason?

Is *Dothard* consistent with the other principles set forth in this section? In an important sense, of course, excluding women where they might present temptation for the prisoners is comparable to "consumer preference." Is the concern for prison safety and security sufficiently distinguishable from the kinds of business justifications rejected in other cases? Isn't it just a question of economics? Why should Southwest Airlines be required to forego the income attributable to being the "LUV" airline, while the state of Alabama may defend the limits it places on women's employment opportunities on the grounds that prison conditions are insufficient, under present staffing arrangements? Should courts be more sympathetic when taxpayers are footing the bill and underfunding causes chronic safety problems?

Consider *Dothard* in the context of both Muller v. Oregon, 208 U.S. 412 (1908), and UAW v. Johnson Controls, 499 U.S. 187 (1991), excerpted at p. 121 and p. 124 below. See also Goeseart v. Cleary, 335 U.S. 464 (1948) (barring a woman from working as a bartender unless she was the wife or daughter of the male bar owner).

Putting Theory into Practice

1-7. (a) A 50-lawyer law firm handles, among other things, insurance and employment discrimination defense. A number of the firm's oldest and best clients prefer to work with male attorneys, because they have more confidence in their abilities. Most recently, an insurance client threatened to take his business elsewhere if a Jewish female lawyer, who was assigned to handle a personal injury defense case for his company, was not replaced by one of the firm's "bright, new" (male) attorneys from the court. The client claims that the man will be more effective in the "redneck" Southern town where the case is scheduled for trial. The reassignment is made. Does the woman have a Title VII claim?

(b) The firm also has a practice of assigning women attorneys to employment discrimination cases brought by women claiming sex discrimination, and assigning minority attorneys to employment discrimination cases in which race is an issue. A white male attorney with the firm, believes that this policy in assigning cases reduces his opportunities to excel at the firm. Does he have a Title VII claim?

1-8. Upon her return from a medical leave, Joan was transferred by her employer from a day to an evening shift. She quits and sues the employer. Her claim is that she was discriminated against based on her sex in that the employer "preyed upon [her] wifely instincts" by transferring her to the second shift knowing that she would quit to take care of her husband. Does she have a claim under Title VII? For a related set of facts, see Grube v. Lau Industries Inc., 257 F.3d 723 (7th Cir. 2001).

1-9. Your friend, who is a manager of a cosmetic company, is fired for not firing a female cosmetic associate for "not being hot enough." Can you help him? See Yanowitz v. L'Oreal USA, Inc., 131 Cal. Rptr. 2d 575, 588 (Ct. App. 2003) (finding violation of California Fair Employment and Housing Act on similar facts).

1-10. (a) Although male and female guards serve in men's prisons, in women's prisons only female guards work in positions involving strip searches and surveillance of female inmates while undressed, using toilet facilities, showering and sleeping. In support of the policy, the superintendent of the women's prison testified as follows:

> [W]omen ... when they come in have a history of being very influenced, if not dominated by men in their lives and one of our major goals is to teach them ... self-respect and ... dignity [and that they] have the capability of making their own decisions and living their lives based on their own perceptions of what they want and what their options are. And [if] we established atmospheres where men are playing the primary dominant force ... that's just going to perpetuate that, that's just going to further compound what she's lived with in the past and she will probably defer to the male and that's not something we want her to do.

Torres v. Wis. Dep't of Health & Soc. Servs., 838 F.2d 944 (7th Cir. 1986) (dissenting opinion by Ripple, J.), rev'd en banc, 859 F.2d 1523 (7th Cir. 1988), cert. denied, 489 U.S. 1017, cert. denied, 489 U.S. 1082 (1989). Is sex a BFOQ in this case?

(b) A female prison guard in a small county jail was employed on the first shift for a few years. A state regulation required a female guard to be on duty whenever a female prisoner was present. The majority of all female inmates were brought in during the third shift. The lack of a female guard on duty during that time was a huge expense and inconvenience to the County, as they had to call in a female deputy and pay her overtime to transport the female prisoner to a neighboring county where a female guard was on duty. The County decided to solve this problem by reassigning the female prison guard to the third shift. The guard sues claiming sex discrimination because her reassignment to the third shift occurred solely on the basis of her sex and that shift was the least desirable for employees. Does she have a Title VII claim? See Reed v. County of Casey, 184 F.3d 597 (6th Cir. 1999) (holding that sex was a permissible BFOQ in this instance).

1-11. In 2005, Transition House, New England's first battered women's shelter, caused a stir by hiring a man as the interim executive director. About Women, a collective of psychologists and social workers who were influential in creating shelters including Transition House, wrote a public letter protesting what they termed a "flagrant violation" of the organization's founding principle to establish a space where "women could feel safe from male intrusion and could openly unburden themselves of the experiences of male violence they had undergone without fear of censure, criticism, or inhibition by male presence." Courtney E. Martin, Violence Shelter Considers Hiring Male Director, www.womensnews.org, August 22, 2005. The male interim director responded by noting that he spent his time in administrative offices in a separate location from the shelter and had limited contact with residents. Id. Who is right? If the male director is fired based on the rationale of About Women, would he have a sex discrimination claim?

1-12. A transportation agency requires all foot patrol officers to be able to run 1.5 miles in under 12 minutes and maintain a 42.5 ml/kg/min aerobic capacity. The Agency claims that the qualification is necessary to deter crime. In the years 1991, 1993, and 1996, an average of only 12 percent of women applicants passed the 1.5 mile run compared to 60 percent of male applicants. Is this job qualification a BFOQ? See Lanning v. SEPTA, 2000 U.S. Dist. LEXIS 17612 (E.D. Pa. 2000), 84 Fair Empl. Prac. Cas. (BNA) 1012 (holding requirements valid as a business necessity).

1-13. The management of a new, expensive French restaurant intends to hire only male waiters, in line with the tradition of the "classiest" Continental establishments. If it tries to do so, will it be violating Title VII?

1-14. A prestigious uptown law firm in Manhattan requires women in its receptionist and secretarial positions to wear high heels. Does this violate Title VII?

Does it matter, under Title VII, that high-heeled shoes have been offered as the explanation for the fact that 90 percent of all forefoot surgery is performed on women, and that "seventy-five percent of the problems eventuating in the more than 600,000 . . . [foot] corrections performed annually in the United States either result from or are greatly aggravated by the use of high-fashion footwear.'" See Marc Linder, Smart Women, Stupid Shoes, and Cynical Employers: The Unlawfulness and Adverse Health Consequences of Sexually Discriminatory Workplace Footwear Requirements for Female Employees, J. Corp. L. 295, 296 (Winter

1997). Or that, in addition to the adverse health consequences, high heels have long been used as a symbol of idleness or, in Thorstein Veblen's words, of "the wearer's abstinence from productive employment"? Id. at 329, citing Veblen, The Theory of the Leisure Class: An Economic Study of Institutions 121 (1899).

1-15. Professor V. works for a state university and conducts many research projects under grants obtained through the university. One of these projects is a study of women who have rejected settlement offers by a trust fund set up to satisfy the claims of women injured by the Dalkon Shield inter-uterine birth-control device and who must pursue their claims through non-judicial adjudicatory hearings. The purpose of the project is to study the effectiveness of those hearings and the surrounding process. The research requires lengthy interviews of women claimants both before and after the hearings, with questions that probe, among other things, the intimate details of their sex lives, their sex partners, their contraception histories, and other matters relating to their experiences with the Dalkon Shield. Most of these women have suffered substantial distress and harm as a result of these experiences and many find it understandably difficult to discuss these experiences with strangers.

Professor V. wants to hire only white women, ages 35 to 45, to conduct these interviews. His reason is that the validity of his research requires the interviewer to create a neutral, nonjudgmental atmosphere in which the interviewees feel comfortable talking about one of the most private aspects of their lives. Research has shown that people of virtually every race, sex, and background, including blacks, Hispanics, men, and women, feel most comfortable talking about the intimate details of their lives with middle-aged, white women between the ages of 35 and 45.

He asks your advice. May he hire only white women ages 35 to 45 as interviewers, without violating any laws? Should the law allow him to do so?

1-16. Hooters is an Atlanta-based restaurant chain that hires only female food servers, bartenders, and hosts. These women wear tight short-shorts and tank tops or half-tees with a large-eyed owl on the front. Some shirt backs read "More than a Mouthful." Hooters sells food, drink, posters, T-shirts, calendars, and other products. It also offers an atmosphere of what a spokeswoman described as "good-humored, wholesome sex appeal that the Hooters girls embody." Although it "welcomes" children, the sexy cheerleader image of the Hooters' girls is designed to attract its target audience of adult males.

Does Hooters have a BFOQ defense to a sex discrimination suit brought by male applicants who were rejected for jobs because of their sex?

≡≡≡ *Muller v. Oregon*
≡≡≡ **208 U.S. 412 (1908)**

Mr. Justice BREWER delivered the opinion of the court.

On February 19, 1903, the legislature of the State of Oregon passed an act, . . . the first section of which is in these words:

SEC. 1. That no female (shall) be employed in any mechanical establishment, or factory, or laundry in this State more than ten hours during any one day....

Section 3 made a violation of the provisions of the prior sections a misdemeanor, subject to a fine of not less than $10 nor more than $25. On September 18, 1905, [defendant was charged with violation of the statute for ordering Mrs. E. Gotcher to work more than ten hours per day in defendant's laundry]....

A trial resulted in a verdict against the defendant, who was sentenced to pay a fine of $10. The Supreme Court of the State affirmed the conviction...where-*whereuponthecasewasbroughtthereonwritoferror*.

The single question is the constitutionality of the statute under which the defendant was convicted so far as it affects the work of a female in a laundry....

It is the law of Oregon that women, whether married or single, have equal contractual and personal rights with men....

It thus appears that, putting to one side the elective franchise, in the matter of personal and contractual rights they stand on the same plane as the other sex. Their rights in these respects can no more be infringed than the equal rights of their brothers. We held in Lochner v. New York, 198 U.S. 45 [1905], that a law providing that no laborer shall be required or permitted to work in a bakery more than sixty hours in a week or ten hours in a day was not as to men a legitimate exercise of the police power of the State, but an unreasonable, unnecessary and arbitrary interference with the right and liberty of the individual to contract in relation to his labor, and as such was in conflict with, and void under, the Federal Constitution. That decision is invoked by plaintiff in error as decisive of the question before us. But this assumes that the difference between the sexes does not justify a different rule respecting a restriction of the hours of labor....

In the brief filed by Mr. Louis D. Brandeis, for the defendant in error, is a very copious collection of all these matters, an epitome of which is found in the margin....

The legislation and opinions referred to [above] may not be, technically speaking, authorities,...yet they are significant of a widespread belief that woman's physical structure, and the functions she performs in consequence thereof, justify special legislation restricting or qualifying the conditions under which she should be permitted to toil. Constitutional questions, it is true, are not settled by even a consensus of present public opinion, for it is the peculiar value of a written constitution that it places in unchanging form limitations upon legislative action, and thus gives a permanence and stability to popular government which otherwise would be lacking. At the same time, when a question of fact is debated and debatable, and the extent to which a special constitutional limitation goes is affected by the truth in respect to that fact, a widespread and long continued belief concerning it is worthy of consideration. We take judicial cognizance of all matters of general knowledge.

That woman's physical structure and the performance of maternal functions place her at a disadvantage in the struggle for subsistence is obvious. This is especially true when the burdens of motherhood are upon her. Even when they are not, by abundant testimony of the medical fraternity continuance for a long time on her feet at work, repeating this from day to day, tends to injurious effects upon the body, and as healthy mothers are essential to vigorous offspring, the physical well-being of woman becomes an object of public interest and care in order to preserve the strength and vigor of the race.

Still again, history discloses the fact that woman has always been dependent upon man. He established his control at the outset by superior physical strength, and this control in various forms, with diminishing intensity, has continued to the present. As minors, though not to the same extent, she has been looked upon in the courts as needing especial care that her rights may be preserved. Education was long denied her, and while now the doors of the school room are opened and her opportunities for acquiring knowledge are great, yet even with that and the consequent increase of capacity for business affairs it is still true that in the struggle for subsistence she is not an equal competitor with her brother. Though limitations upon personal and contractual rights may be removed by legislation, there is that in her disposition and habits of life which will operate against a full assertion of those rights. She will still be where some legislation to protect her seems necessary to secure a real equality of right. Doubtless there are individual exceptions, and there are many respects in which she has an advantage over him; but looking at it from the viewpoint of the effort to maintain an independent position in life, she is not upon an equality. Differentiated by these matters from the other sex, she is properly placed in a class by herself, and legislation designed for her protection may be sustained, even when like legislation is not necessary for men and could not be sustained. It is impossible to close one's eyes to the fact that she still looks to her brother and depends upon him. Even though all restrictions on political, personal and contractual rights were taken away, and she stood, so far as statutes are concerned, upon an absolutely equal plane with him, it would still be true that she is so constituted that she will rest upon and look to him for protection; that her physical structure and a proper discharge of her maternal functions — having in view not merely her own health, but the well-being of the race — justify legislation to protect her from the greed as well as the passion of man. The limitations which this statute places upon her contractual powers, upon her right to agree with her employer as to the time she shall labor, are not imposed solely for her benefit, but also largely for the benefit of all. Many words cannot make this plainer. The two sexes differ in structure of body, in the functions to be performed by each, in the amount of physical strength, in the capacity for long-continued labor, particularly when done standing, the influence of vigorous health upon the future well-being of the race, the self-reliance which enables one to assert full rights, and in the capacity to maintain the struggle for subsistence. This difference justifies a difference in legislation and upholds that which is designed to compensate for some of the burdens which rest upon her.

We have not referred in this discussion to the denial of the elective franchise in the State of Oregon, for while it may disclose a lack of political equality in all things with her brother, that is not of itself decisive. The reason runs deeper, and rests in the inherent difference between the two sexes, and in the different functions in life which they perform.

For these reasons, and without questioning in any respect the decision in Lochner v. New York, we are of the opinion that it cannot be adjudged that the act in question is in conflict with the Federal Constitution, so far as it respects the work of a female in a laundry, and the judgment of the Supreme Court of Oregon is affirmed.

UAW v. Johnson Controls, Inc.
499 U.S. 187 (1991)

Mr. Justice BLACKMUN delivered the opinion of the Court.

In this case we are concerned with an employer's gender-based fetal-protection policy. May an employer exclude a fertile female employee from certain jobs because of its concern for the health of the fetus the woman might conceive?

I

Respondent Johnson Controls, Inc., manufactures batteries. In the manufacturing process, the element lead is a primary ingredient. Occupational exposure to lead entails health risks, including the risk of harm to any fetus carried by a female employee.

Before [Title VII] became law, Johnson Controls did not employ any woman in a battery-manufacturing job. In June 1977, however, it announced its first official policy concerning its employment of women in lead-exposure work:

> [P]rotection of the health of the unborn child is the immediate and direct responsibility of the prospective parents. While the medical profession and the company can support them in the exercise of this responsibility, it cannot assume it for them without simultaneously infringing their rights as persons. . . .
>
> Since not all women who can become mothers wish to become mothers (or will become mothers), it would appear to be illegal discrimination to treat all who are capable of pregnancy as though they will become pregnant. . . .

Consistent with that view, Johnson Controls "stopped short of excluding women capable of bearing children from lead exposure," . . . but emphasized that a woman who expected to have a child should not choose a job in which she would have such exposure. The company also required a woman who wished to be considered for employment to sign a statement that she had been advised of the risk of having a child while she was exposed to lead. The statement informed the woman that although there was evidence "that women exposed to lead have a higher rate of abortion," this evidence was "not as clear . . . as the relationship between cigarette smoking and cancer," but that it was, "medically speaking, just good sense not to run that risk if you want children and do not want to expose the unborn child to risk, however small. . . ."

Five years later, in 1982, Johnson Controls shifted from a policy of warning to a policy of exclusion. Between 1979 and 1983, eight employees became pregnant while maintaining blood lead levels in excess of 30 micrograms per deciliter. . . . This appeared to be the critical level noted by the Occupational Health and Safety Administration (OSHA) for a worker who was planning to have a family. See 29 C.F.R. §1910.1025 (1989). The company responded by announcing a broad exclusion of women from jobs that exposed them to lead:

> [I]t is [Johnson Controls'] policy that women who are pregnant or who are capable of bearing children will not be placed into jobs involving lead exposure or which could expose them to lead through the exercise of job bidding, bumping, transfer or promotion rights....

The policy defined "women . . . capable of bearing children" as "[a]ll women except those whose inability to bear children is medically documented." . . . It further stated that an unacceptable work station was one where, "over the past year," an employee had recorded a blood lead level of more than 30 micrograms per deciliter or the work site had yielded an air sample containing a lead level in excess of 30 micrograms per cubic meter. . . .

II

In April 1984, petitioners filed in the United States District Court for the Eastern District of Wisconsin a class action challenging Johnson Controls' fetal-protection policy as sex discrimination that violated Title VII. . . . Among the individual plaintiffs were petitioners Mary Craig, who had chosen to be sterilized in order to avoid losing her job, Elsie Nason, a 50-year-old divorcee, who had suffered a loss in compensation when she was transferred out of a job where she was exposed to lead, and Donald Penney, who had been denied a request for a leave of absence for the purpose of lowering his lead level because he intended to become a father. . . .

The District Court granted summary judgment for defendant-respondent Johnson Controls, 680 F. Supp. 309 (1988), having concluded that while "there is a disagreement among the experts regarding the effect of lead on the fetus," the hazard to the fetus through exposure to lead was established by "a considerable body of opinion"; that although "[e]xpert opinion has been provided which holds that lead also affects the reproductive abilities of men and women . . . [and] and] that these effects are as great as the effects of exposure of the fetus . . . a great body of experts are of the opinion that the fetus is more vulnerable to levels of lead that would not affect adults"; and that petitioners had "failed to establish that there is an acceptable alternative policy which would protect the fetus." . . . The court stated that, in view of this disposition of the business necessity defense, it did not "have to undertake a bona fide occupational qualification's (BFOQ) analysis." . . .

The Court of Appeals for the Seventh Circuit, sitting en banc, affirmed the summary judgment by a 7-to-4 vote. 886 F.2d 871 (1989). . . . We granted certiorari. . . .

III

The bias in Johnson Controls' policy is obvious. Fertile men, but not fertile women, are given a choice as to whether they wish to risk their reproductive health for a particular job. Section 703(a) of the Civil Rights Act of 1964 [Title VII] prohibits sex-based classifications in terms and conditions of employment, in hiring and discharging decisions, and in other employment decisions that adversely affect an employee's status. Respondent's fetal-protection policy explicitly discriminates against women on the basis of their sex. The policy excludes women with childbearing capacity from lead-exposed jobs and so creates a facial classification based on gender....

Nevertheless, the Court of Appeals assumed, as did the two appellate courts who already had confronted the issue, that sex-specific fetal-protection policies do not involve facial discrimination [and thus could be justified under the more lenient business necessity test.] ... That assumption, however, was incorrect.

First, Johnson Controls' policy classifies on the basis of gender and child-bearing capacity, rather than fertility alone. Respondent does not seek to protect the unconceived children of all its employees. Despite evidence in the record about the debilitating effect of lead exposure on the male reproductive system, Johnson Controls is concerned only with the harms that may befall the unborn offspring of its female employees.... This Court faced a conceptually similar situation in Phillips v. Martin Marietta Corp., [400 U.S. 542 (1971)], and found sex discrimination because the policy established "one hiring policy for women and another for men—each having pre-school-age children." [Id. at 544.] Johnson Controls' policy is facially discriminatory because it requires only a female employee to produce proof that she is not capable of reproducing.

Our conclusion is bolstered by the Pregnancy Discrimination Act of 1978 (PDA), 92 Stat. 2076, 42 U.S.C. § 2000e(k), in which Congress explicitly provided that, for purposes of Title VII, discrimination "on the basis of sex" includes discrimination "because of or on the basis of pregnancy, childbirth, or related medical conditions." ... In its use of the words "capable of bearing children" in the 1982 policy statement as the criterion for exclusion, Johnson Controls explicitly classifies on the basis of potential for pregnancy. Under the PDA, such a classification must be regarded, for Title VII purposes, in the same light as explicit sex discrimination. Respondent has chosen to treat all its female employees as potentially pregnant; that choice evinces discrimination on the basis of sex.

[T]he absence of a malevolent motive does not convert a facially discriminatory policy into a neutral policy with a discriminatory effect. Whether an employment practice involves disparate treatment through explicit facial discrimination does not depend on why the employer discriminates but rather on the explicit terms of the discrimination....

We hold that Johnson Controls' fetal-protection policy is sex discrimination forbidden under Title VII unless respondent can establish that sex is a "bona fide occupational qualification."

IV...

The wording of the BFOQ defense contains several terms of restriction that indicate that the exception reaches only special situations. The statute thus limits the situations in which discrimination is permissible to "certain instances" where sex discrimination is "reasonably necessary" to the "normal operation" of the "particular" business. Each one of these terms—certain, normal, particular—prevents the use of general subjective standards and favors an objective, verifiable requirement. But the most telling term is "occupational"; this indicates that these objective, verifiable requirements must concern job-related skills and aptitudes.

The concurrence defines "occupational" as meaning related to a job.... According to the concurrence, any discriminatory requirement imposed by an employer is "job-related" simply because the employer has chosen to make the requirement a condition of employment.... This reading of "occupational" renders the word mere surplusage.... By modifying "qualification" with "occupational," Congress narrowed the term to qualifications that affect an employee's ability to do the job.

Johnson Controls argues that its fetal-protection policy falls within the so-called safety exception to the BFOQ. Our cases have stressed that discrimination on the basis of sex because of safety concerns is allowed only in narrow circumstances. In Dothard v. Rawlinson, [433 U.S. 321 (1977)] this Court indicated that danger to a woman herself does not justify discrimination. [433 U.S. at 335.] We there allowed the employer to hire only male guards in contact areas of maximum-security male penitentiaries only because more was at stake than the "individual woman's decision to weigh and accept the risks of employment."... We also required in *Dothard* a high correlation between sex and ability to perform job functions and refused to allow employers to use sex as a proxy for strength although it might be a fairly accurate one.

Similarly, some courts have approved airlines' layoffs of pregnant flight attendants at different points during the first five months of pregnancy on the ground that the employer's policy was necessary to ensure the safety of passengers.... In two of these cases, the courts pointedly indicated that fetal, as opposed to passenger, safety was best left to the mother....

We considered safety to third parties in Western Airlines, Inc. v. Criswell, [472 U.S. 400 (1985)], in the context of the [Age Discrimination in Employment Act]. We focused upon "the nature of the flight engineer's tasks," and the "actual capabilities of persons over age 60" in relation to those tasks. [472 U.S. at 406.] Our safety concerns were not independent of the individual's ability to perform the assigned tasks, but rather involved the possibility that, because of age-connected debility, a flight engineer might not properly assist the pilot, and might thereby cause a safety emergency. Furthermore, although we considered the safety of third parties in *Dothard* and *Criswell*, those third parties were indispensable to the particular business at issue. In *Dothard*, the third parties were the inmates; in *Criswell*, the third parties were the passengers on the plane. We stressed that in order to qualify as a BFOQ, a job qualification must relate to the "essence," *Dothard*, [433 U.S. at 333] or to the "central mission of the employer's business," *Criswell*, [472 U.S. at 413]....

Third-party safety considerations properly entered into the BFOQ analysis in *Dothard* and *Criswell* because they went to the core of the employee's job performance. Moreover, that performance involved the central purpose of the enterprise.... The concurrence attempts to transform this case into one of customer safety. The unconceived fetuses of Johnson Controls' female employees, however, are neither customers nor third parties whose safety is essential to the business of battery manufacturing. No one can disregard the possibility of injury to future children; the BFOQ, however, is not so broad that it transforms this deep social concern into an essential aspect of batterymaking. . . .

The PDA's amendment to Title VII contains a BFOQ standard of its own: unless pregnant employees differ from others "in their ability or inability to work," they must be "treated the same" as other employees "for all employment-related purposes." 42 U.S.C. § 2000e(k). This language clearly sets forth Congress' remedy for discrimination on the basis of pregnancy and potential pregnancy. Women who are either pregnant or potentially pregnant must be treated like others "similar in their ability . . . to work." [Id.] In other words, women as capable of doing their jobs as their male counterparts may not be forced to choose between having a child and having a job. . . .

We conclude that the language of both the BFOQ provision and the PDA which amended it, as well as the legislative history and the case law, prohibit an employer from discriminating against a woman because of her capacity to become pregnant unless her reproductive potential prevents her from performing the duties of her job. We reiterate our holdings in *Criswell* and *Dothard* that an employer must direct its concerns about a woman's ability to perform her job safely and efficiently to those aspects of the woman's job-related activities that fall within the "essence" of the particular business.[4]

V

We have no difficulty concluding that Johnson Controls cannot establish a BFOQ. Fertile women, as far as appears in the record, participate in the manufacture of batteries as efficiently as anyone else. . . .

VI

A word about tort liability and the increased cost of fertile women in the workplace is perhaps necessary. . . . It is correct to say that Title VII does not prevent the employer from having a conscience. The statute, however, does prevent sex-specific fetal-protection policies. These two aspects of Title VII do not conflict.

More than 40 States currently recognize a right to recover for a prenatal injury based either on negligence or on wrongful death. . . . According to Johnson Controls, however, the company complies with the lead standard developed by OSHA and warns its female employees about the damaging effects of lead. It is worth noting that OSHA gave the problem of lead lengthy consideration and

---

4. The concurrence predicts that our reaffirmation of the narrowness of the BFOQ defense will preclude considerations of privacy as a basis for sex-based discrimination. . . . We have never addressed privacy-based sex discrimination and shall not do so here because the sex-based discrimination at issue today does not involve the privacy interests of Johnson Control's customers. Nothing in our discussion of the "essence of the business test," however, suggests that sex could not constitute a BFOQ when privacy interests are implicated. See, e.g., Backus v. Baptist Medical Center, 510 F. Supp. 1191 (E.D. Ark. 1981), vacated as moot, 671 F.2d 1100 (8th Cir. 1982) (essence of obstetrics nurse's business is to provide sensitive care for patient's intimate and private concerns).

concluded that "there is no basis whatsoever for the claim that women of child-bearing age should be excluded from the workplace in order to protect the fetus or the course of pregnancy." 43 Fed. Reg. 52952, 52966 (1978). See also id. at 54354, 54398. Instead, OSHA established a series of mandatory protections which, taken together, "should effectively minimize any risk to the fetus and newborn child." Id. at 52966. See 29 C.F.R. § 1910.125(k)(ii) (1989). Without negligence, it would be difficult for a court to find liability on the part of the employer. If, under general tort principles, Title VII bans sex-specific fetal-protection policies, the employer fully informs the woman of the risk, and the employer has not acted negligently, the basis for holding an employer liable seems remote at best.

Although the issue is not before us . . . [w]hen it is impossible for an employer to comply with both state and federal requirements, this Court has ruled that federal law pre-empts that of the States. . . .

[Moreover, t]he extra cost of employing members of one sex . . . does not provide an affirmative Title VII defense for a discriminatory refusal to hire members of that gender. See [City of Los Angeles, Dept. of Water & Power v. Manhart, 435 U.S. 702, 716-718, and n.32 (1978)]. Indeed, in passing the PDA, Congress considered at length the considerable cost of providing equal treatment of pregnancy and related conditions, but made the "decision to forbid special treatment of pregnancy despite the social costs associated therewith." . . .

We, of course, are not presented with, nor do we decide, a case in which costs would be so prohibitive as to threaten the survival of the employer's business. We merely reiterate our prior holdings that the incremental cost of hiring women cannot justify discriminating against them.

VII

Our holding today that Title VII . . . forbids sex-specific fetal-protection policies is neither remarkable nor unprecedented. Concern for a woman's existing or potential offspring historically has been the excuse for denying women equal employment opportunities. See, e.g., Muller v. Oregon, [208 U.S. 412 (1908)]. Congress in the PDA prohibited discrimination on the basis of a woman's ability to become pregnant. We do no more than hold that the Pregnancy Discrimination Act means what it says. . . .

The judgment of the Court of Appeals is reversed and the case is remanded for further proceedings consistent with this opinion.

Justice WHITE, with whom The CHIEF JUSTICE and Justice KENNEDY join, concurring in part and concurring in the judgment. . . .

I . . .

Common sense tells us that it is part of the normal operation of business concerns to avoid causing injury to third parties, as well as to employees, if for no other reason than to avoid tort liability and its substantial costs. This possibility of tort liability is not hypothetical; every State currently allows children born alive to recover in tort for prenatal injuries caused by third parties . . . and an increasing number of courts have recognized a right to recover even for prenatal injuries caused by torts committed prior to conception. . . .

The Court dismisses the possibility of tort liability by no more than speculating that if "Title VII bans sex-specific fetal-protection policies, the employer fully informs the woman of the risk, and the employer has not acted negligently, the basis for holding an employer liable seems remote at best." . . . Such speculation will be small comfort to employers. First, it is far from clear that compliance with Title VII will pre-empt state tort liability, and the Court offers no support for that proposition. Second, although warnings may preclude claims by injured employees, they will not preclude claims by injured children because the general rule is that parents cannot waive causes of action on behalf of their children, and the parents' negligence will not be imputed to the children. Finally, although state tort liability for prenatal injuries generally requires negligence, it will be difficult for employers to determine in advance what will constitute negligence. Compliance with OSHA standards, for example, has been held not to be a defense to state tort or criminal liability. . . . Moreover, it is possible that employers will be held strictly liable, if, for example, their manufacturing process is considered "abnormally dangerous." See Restatement (Second) of Torts § 869, comment b (1979).

Dothard and *Criswell* make clear that avoidance of substantial safety risks to third parties is inherently part of both an employee's ability to perform a job and an employer's "normal operation" of its business. . . . On the facts of this case . . . protecting fetal safety while carrying out the duties of battery manufacturing is as much a legitimate concern as is safety to third parties in guarding prisons (*Dothard*) or flying airplanes (*Criswell*).[5]

Dothard and *Criswell* also confirm that costs are relevant in determining whether a discriminatory policy is reasonably necessary for the normal operation of a business. In *Dothard*, the safety problem that justified exclusion of women from the prison guard positions was largely a result of inadequate staff and facilities. See [433 U.S. at 335]. If the cost of employing women could not be considered, the employer there should have been required to hire more staff and restructure the prison environment rather than exclude women. Similarly, in *Criswell* the airline could have been required to hire more pilots and install expensive monitoring devices rather than discriminate against older employees. . . .

The Pregnancy Discrimination Act (PDA), 42 U.S.C. § 2000e(k), contrary to the Court's assertion . . . did not restrict the scope of the BFOQ defense. The PDA was only an amendment to the "Definitions" section of Title VII, 42 U.S.C. § 2000e, and did not purport to eliminate or alter the BFOQ defense. Rather, it merely clarified Title VII to make it clear that pregnancy and related conditions are included within Title VII's antidiscrimination provisions. . . .

---

5. I do not, as the Court asserts, . . . reject the "essence of the business" test. Rather, I merely reaffirm the obvious—that safety to third parties is part of the "essence" of most if not all businesses. Of course, the BFOQ inquiry "'adjusts to the safety factor.'" *Criswell*, [472 U.S. at 413]. . . . As a result, more stringent occupational qualifications may be justified for jobs involving higher safety risks, such as flying airplanes. But a recognition that the importance of safety varies among businesses does not mean that safety is completely irrelevant to the essence of a job such as battery manufacturing.

The Court's narrow interpretation of the BFOQ defense in this case ... means that an employer cannot exclude even pregnant women from an environment highly toxic to their fetuses. It is foolish to think that Congress intended such a result, and neither the language of the BFOQ exception nor our cases require it.[8]

II

Despite my disagreement with the Court concerning the scope of the BFOQ defense, I concur in reversing the Court of Appeals because that court erred in affirming the District Court's grant of summary judgment in favor of Johnson Controls. First, the Court of Appeals erred in failing to consider the level of risk-avoidance that was part of Johnson Controls' "normal operation." ... If the fetal protection policy insists on a risk-avoidance level substantially higher than other risk levels tolerated by Johnson Controls such as risks to employees and consumers, the policy should not constitute a BFOQ.

Second, even without more information about the normal level of risk at Johnson Controls, the fetal protection policy at issue here reaches too far. This is evident both in its presumption that, absent medical documentation to the contrary, all women are fertile regardless of their age ... and in its exclusion of presumptively fertile women from positions that might result in a promotion to a position involving high lead exposure. ...

Third, it should be recalled that until 1982 Johnson Controls operated without an exclusionary policy, and it has not identified any grounds for believing that its current policy is reasonably necessary to its normal operations. ...

Finally, the Court of Appeals failed to consider properly petitioners' evidence of harm to offspring caused by lead exposure in males. ... It seems clear that if the Court of Appeals had properly analyzed that evidence, it would have concluded that summary judgment against petitioners was not appropriate because there was a dispute over a material issue of fact.

Mr. Justice SCALIA, concurring in the judgment.

I generally agree with the Court's analysis, but have some reservations, several of which bear mention.

First, I think it irrelevant that there was "evidence in the record about the debilitating effect of lead exposure on the male reproductive system." ... Even without such evidence, treating women differently "on the basis of pregnancy" constitutes discrimination "on the basis of sex," because Congress has unequivocally said so. ...

---

8. The Court's cramped reading of the BFOQ defense is also belied by the legislative history of Title VII, in which three examples of permissible sex discrimination were mentioned — a female nurse hired to care for an elderly woman, an all-male professional baseball team, and a masseur. ... In none of those situations would gender "actually interfer[e] with the employee's ability to perform the job," as required today by the Court. ... the Court's interpretation of the BFOQ standard also would seem to preclude considerations of privacy as a basis for sex-based discrimination, since those considerations do not relate directly to an employee's physical ability to perform the duties of the job. The lower federal courts, however, have consistently recognized that privacy interests may justify sex-based requirements for certain jobs. ...

Second . . . it would not matter if all pregnant women placed their children at risk in taking these jobs, just as it does not matter if no men do so. . . .

Third . . . [i]t is perfectly reasonable to believe that Title VII has accommodated state tort law through the BFOQ exception. However, all that need be said in the present case is that Johnson has not demonstrated a substantial risk of tort liability — which is alone enough to defeat a tort-based assertion of the BFOQ exception.

Last, the Court goes far afield, it seems to me, in suggesting that increased cost alone — short of "costs . . . so prohibitive as to threaten survival of the employer's business" . . . — cannot support a BFOQ defense . . . I think, for example, that a shipping company may refuse to hire pregnant women as crew members on long voyages because the on-board facilities for foreseeable emergencies, though quite feasible, would be inordinately expensive. In the present case, however, Johnson has not asserted a cost-based BFOQ.

Notes

1. *Johnson Controls* as a Reprieve of the Protective Legislation Debate. In *Muller*, the famous Brandeis brief cited the protective legislation of nineteen states and seven foreign countries, and then brought to the Court's attention

> over ninety reports of committees, bureaus of statistics, commissioners of hygiene, inspectors of factories, both in this country and in Europe, to the effect that long hours of labor are dangerous for women, primarily because of their special physical organization. . . . The matter is discussed in these reports in different aspects, but all agree as to the danger. It would of course take too much space to give these reports in detail. . . . Perhaps the general scope and character of all these reports may be summed up in what an inspector for Hanover says: "The reasons for the reduction of the working day to ten hours — (a) the physical organization of women, (b) her maternal functions, (c) the rearing and education of the children, (d) the maintenance of the home — are all so important and so far reaching that the need for such reduction need hardly be discussed."

208 U.S. 412, 419. The Court notes that the material cited in the Brandeis brief

> may not be, technically speaking, authorities, . . . yet they are significant of a widespread belief that women's physical structure, and the functions she performs in consequence thereof, justify special legislation restricting or qualifying the conditions under which she should be permitted to toil. Constitutional questions, it is true, are not settled by even a consensus of present public opinion . . . At the same time, when a question of fact is debated and debatable . . . a widespread and long continued belief concerning it is worthy of consideration. We take judicial cognizance of all matters of general knowledge.

208 U.S. at 420-421.

Since *Muller*, much of the legal landscape, not to mention "general knowledge," has changed. In *Muller*, the issue was whether the danger to women of a long work day was sufficient enough to overcome the Fourteenth Amendment freedom of contract rights of the employer who had been fined for violating the

Oregon statute, while in *Johnson Controls*, the question was whether the danger to women justified their exclusion from certain job categories under Title VII. The freedom of contract no longer has the recognition it once had and women's equality is now a protected value, both constitutionally and statutorily. Nonetheless, several commentators, along with Justice Blackmun himself, have drawn parallels between fetal protection policies and protective legislation of the nineteenth century, which was also backed by "scientific" data (most notably the Brandeis Brief). See, e.g., Wendy W. Williams, Firing the Woman to Protect the Fetus: The Reconciliation of Fetal Protection with Employment Opportunity Goals Under Title VII, 69 Geo. L.J. 641, 653-655 (1981); Mary E. Becker, From *Muller v. Oregon* to Fetal Vulnerability Policies, 53 U. Chi. L. Rev. 1219, 1221-1243 (1986). Professor Becker argues that the risks against which women were protected in both cases were not weighed against the harm to women of exclusion; women were viewed solely in terms of their reproductive functions; the evidence upon which exclusion was based was weak or uncertain; the possibility that women might be in the best position to make their own decisions about their own safety or that of their potential children was ignored; and, perhaps most tellingly, women tend to be protected only in higher-paying job classifications considered desirable by men. As Becker notes, fetal protection politics are generally absent in jobs typically occupied by women:

> The electronics industry, for example, employs mostly women, and many of these women frequently come into contact with six of the seven substances [the presence of which was used to exclude women from traditionally male jobs in companies such as *Johnson Controls*]: lead, benzene, vinyl chloride, carbon tetrachloride, carbon monoxide, and carbon disulfide. Yet fetal vulnerability policies have not been instituted in this industry. Many women laundry workers and dry cleaners are exposed to carbon disulfide and benzene. Women laboratory technicians are often exposed to benzene and other dangerous chemicals. Infectious agents and chemicals create risks of fetal harm to health care workers and hospital laundry workers. Dental offices are often contaminated by mercury. Pottery painting, a traditionally female job, involves exposure to lead. Yet with the exception of hospitals that fire pregnant x-ray technicians or otherwise restrict their exposure, women are generally allowed to work in women's jobs without restrictions based on fetal safety.

Becker, supra, at 1238-1239.

What conclusions is it fair to draw from this history? See David Kirp, Fetal Hazards, Gender Justice and the Justices: The Limits of Equality, 34 Wm. & Mary L. Rev. 101, 115 (1992) ("Expressions of corporate concern for the plight of fetuses . . . have been highly selective. Businesses that depend heavily on women workers have been much less scrupulous about the dangers they impose on the unborn."); Nicole G. Hoeksma, Note, Regulating Risk: Reproductive Toxins in the Workplace in the Post-Johnson Controls Era, 14 S. Cal. Rev. L. & Women's Studies 289, 294-295 (2005) (suggesting fetal protection policies have caused more harm than good because the "male-intensive" jobs from which women are excluded typically have the best pay and health policies). Some research suggests significant risks to women's reproductive health from extensive exposure to the electromagnetic fields produced by video display terminals. See Cheryl L. Meyer, Video Display Terminals and Reproductive

Complications: Regulatory Issues Concerning Health Care in the Workplace, 9 Wis. Women's L.J. 1 (1994). Why do you suppose employers have not attempted to place restrictions on women's working 8-hour days in front of computer screens?

Should fetal risks, to which the company in *Johnson Controls* said it was responding, be totally irrelevant to the legal validity of the kind of policy at issue in the case? Should fetuses whom the mother does not intend to abort be considered third parties? How do you respond to this commentary:

> [T]he Supreme Court's decision looks decidedly less heroic when regarded, not as a set of principles abstracted from the commonplace but rather as a statement about how to make real — and literally toxic — choices. *Johnson Controls* may have invested nondiscrimination with all the meaning it can be made to carry, but the opinions of the Justices speak more to the inadequacy of equal rights reasoning than to its potential to address the matter at hand. As Judge Easterbrook noted in his dissent: "How much risk is too much is a moral or economic or political question, one ill suited to the processes of litigation and not the sort of question Title VII puts to a judge." (886 F.2d 871, 917 (7th Cir. 1989) (Easterbrook, J., dissenting).) A less formally constrained conception of justice requires a language that honors claims about the public good deeper than merely the right to be treated no worse — or no better — than someone else because of reproductive capacity.

Kirp, supra, at 103.

2. Women Workers and "Choice." The issue of women's choice with respect to fetal protection policies can be posed in different ways. Fetal protection policies do give women one kind of choice — between sterilization and losing their jobs. Professor David Kirp reports on the circumstances under which many women have made such choices, including one woman, Betty Riggs, who submitted to sterilization although she wanted more children, because her marriage was breaking up and she needed the money. Not long after Betty Riggs and four other women were sterilized, the company shut down its pigments department and their jobs were eliminated. Id. at 104-106. The Court in *Johnson Controls*, in invalidating fetal protection policies, concludes that women workers should make their own decisions about whether to assume the risks of the workplace for themselves and their potential offspring. Has the Court, finally, maximized women's choices?

Is there a solution to the *Johnson Controls* problem that would give women greater meaningful choice? Kirp suggests that there are steps Johnson Controls could have taken to both minimize the possibility of fetal damage and preserve greater autonomy for women. For example, it could have lowered the levels of airborne lead in its plants (it had already spent $15 million to lower lead levels but with considerable more money, levels might have been decreased still further); it could have narrowed the number of women subjected to the policy, for example, by lowering the age range (Johnson Controls' policy affected all women between the ages of 17 and 70 unless they could prove their sterility) and by offering the option of regular pregnancy tests with transfer to women who tested positive; and it could have delivered clearer information to women about their risks of lead exposure and measures they might take to reduce it. Kirp, supra, at 109-111.

Deborah Stone suggests, in addition, the possibility of job rotation to reduce reproductive risks for both men and women when they wish to begin their families, and the provision of comprehensive health coverage to employees, including routine monitoring. See Deborah Stone, Fetal Risks, Women's Rights: Showdown at *Johnson Controls*, Am. Prospect 43, 52 (Fall 1990).

The law in the United Kingdom, instead of presupposing that all women will become pregnant, requires employers to assess risks to expectant mothers and their fetuses and then to control the risk if possible. If the risk cannot be controlled, then suitable alternative work or paid leave must be given until the woman is no longer pregnant. See Michael Thomson, Reproductivity, the Workplace and the Gendering of the Body (Politic), 14 Cardozo Stud. L. & Lit. 565, 571 (2004). Would this have worked for Johnson Controls? Should the Court have compelled any of these alternatives? Should Congress enact legislation along these lines? For other regulatory objectives, see Hoeksma, supra, at 304-312.

The industry's early responses to the Court's decision in *Johnson Controls* was not to change anything substantive in the workplace, but to revert to their old "voluntary" plans and seek waivers of liability from their workers. See Laura Oren, Protection, Patriarchy, and Capitalism: The Politics and Theory of Gender-Specific Regulation in the Workplace, 6 UCLA Women's L.J. 321, 371 n.290 (1996). In general, it has been noted that making the workplace safe for all employees has been the least popular option since *Johnson Controls*. See Hoeksma, supra, at 300; Thomson, supra, at 570-574. Similar limitations have hobbled efforts of the Occupational Health and Safety Administration. Since its inception, the agency has only regulated two known reproductive toxicants: lead and ethylene oxide. Hoeksma, supra, at 305.

3. Equality Analysis in *Johnson Controls*. Justice Blackmun compared fertile women to fertile men, concluding that the fetal protection policy violates Title VII because it treats these two groups differently. Justice Blackmun referred in his opinion to evidence that lead exposure may damage sperm as well as ova to strengthen his analysis that men and women are similarly situated and thus the relevant groups for comparison. Would Blackmun's analysis remain intact if the evidence was clear that men did not face the same — or did not face any — reproductive risks? See Williams, supra, at 663 (advocating gender-neutral fetal protection policies because of "uncertainties and ambiguities about harm to fetuses through both sexes," but conceding that if the workplace exposure was not harmful to men, sex-based restrictions might be permissible). Commentators have observed that most reproductive health research focuses on women, and relatively little on men, such that there is little evidence clarifying whether men are at equal risk or not. See, e.g., Hoeksma, supra, at 293; Thomson, supra, at 570-574 (suggesting that because they lack information about men, policymakers often apply restrictive policies only to women, even when there is no evidence that women are more at risk than men).

Justice Scalia did not specify the groups to be compared. In his view, whether or not the Court thought the policy in question was a form of sex discrimination, Congress unequivocally had determined with the Pregnancy

Discrimination Act that it was. For the same reason, Justice Scalia's analysis is not affected by whether or not there are any comparable fetal risks to be passed through male employees.

The Seventh Circuit Court of Appeals, in effect, compared employees who could bear children against employees who could not. As such, the policy was facially sex-neutral and thus could be justified by the "benign" purpose of protecting women's unconceived offspring. See 886 F.2d at 886-887. This approach is similar to the one used by the Supreme Court when it concluded in 1974 that discrimination on the basis of pregnancy (even though only women were thereby affected) was not discrimination between women and men but rather discrimination between pregnant and non-pregnant persons. See Geduldig v. Aiello, 417 U.S. 484 (1974), discussed on pp. 219-221 in Chapter 2. The Pregnancy Discrimination Act reversed *Geduldig* as to whether discrimination on the basis of pregnancy is sex discrimination under Title VII, but left intact the reasoning of the case with respect to constitutional law.

As for other doctrinal components of the Court's analysis, Justice Blackmun identifies as crucial whether the discrimination is "reasonably necessary" to the "normal operation" of the "particular" business and — especially — whether the restriction is an "occupational" requirement related to the "essence" of the employer's business. Each one of these terms, he states, "prevents the use of general subjective standards and favors an objective, verifiable requirement." Is this assessment correct? As to any of these legal determinations, is there any discernible basis upon which to prefer one conclusion over another? Justice Blackmun implicitly accuses *Johnson Controls* of "word play." Does he avoid the game?

4. Potential Tort Liability. The U.S. Supreme Court notes in *Johnson Controls* that some right to recover for prenatal injuries is recognized in at least 40 states. However, such tort remedies for toxic exposure have been limited because of the problems of proving causation and the lack of research on long-term effects. Hoeksma, supra, at 301. Does the Court give employers any reassurance that they will be protected from subsequent tort claims in the event of fetal injury? To the extent it does not, are women being given *too much* choice by being allowed to have it both ways: they may keep their jobs but also sue later if they miscarry or if their babies are born with birth defects attributable to the risks of their employment? Or is this simply a cost to the employer of being engaged in a risky business, which is best dealt with by ordinary business means, such as insurance, or passing the risks of business along to the consumer?

At least one recent case suggests that an employer's reasonable fear of liability may be a defense to a disparate treatment claim. See Chevron U.S.A. v. Echazabal, 536 U.S. 73, 84, 86 n.5 (2002) (holding that the Americans with Disabilities Act did not require employers to hire employees whose physical disability would put them at risk in a particular job, irrespective of their consent, and distinguishing *Johnson Controls* as being concerned with "paternalistic judgments based on the broad category of gender...").

Should mothers themselves be subject to tort liability for harm suffered by a child due to the mother's voluntary exposure to harmful substances during pregnancy?

D. STATE PUBLIC ACCOMMODATIONS LAWS AND FIRST AMENDMENT ASSOCIATIONAL FREEDOMS

Board of Directors of Rotary International v. Rotary Club of Duarte
481 U.S. 537 (1987)

Mr. Justice POWELL delivered the opinion of the Court.

We must decide whether a California statute that requires California Rotary Clubs to admit women members violates the First Amendment.

I

Rotary International (International) is a nonprofit corporation founded in 1905, with headquarters in Evanston, Illinois. It is "an organization of business and professional men united worldwide who provide humanitarian service, encourage high ethical standards in all vocations, and help build goodwill and peace in the world." . . . Individual members belong to a local Rotary Club rather than to International. In turn, each local Rotary Club is a member of International. . . . In August 1982, shortly before the trial in this case, International comprised 19,788 Rotary Clubs in 157 countries, with a total membership of about 907,750. . . .

Individuals are admitted to membership in a Rotary Club according to a "classification system." The purpose of this system is to ensure "that each Rotary Club includes a representative of every worthy and recognized business, professional, or institutional activity in the community." . . . Each active member must work in a leadership capacity in his business or profession. The general rule is that "one active member is admitted for each classification, but he, in turn, may propose an additional active member, who must be in the same business or professional classification." Thus, each classification may be represented by two active members. In addition, "senior active" and "past service" members may represent the same classifications as active members. . . . There is no limit to the number of clergymen, journalists, or diplomats who may be admitted to membership. . . . Subject to these requirements, each local Rotary Club is free to adopt its own rules and procedures for admitting new members. . . .

Membership in Rotary Clubs is open only to men. . . . Herbert A. Pigman, the General Secretary of Rotary International, testified that the exclusion of women results in an "aspect of fellowship . . . that is enjoyed by the present male membership," . . . and also allows Rotary to operate effectively in foreign countries with varied cultures and social mores. Although women are not admitted to membership, they are permitted to attend meetings, give speeches, and receive awards. Women relatives of Rotary members may form their own associations, and are authorized to wear the Rotary lapel pin. Young women between 14 and 28 years of age may joint Interact or Rotaract, organizations sponsored by Rotary International. . . .

In 1977 the Rotary Club of Duarte, California, admitted Donna Bogart, Mary Lou Elliott, and Rosemary Freitag to active membership. International notified the Duarte Club that admitting women members is contrary to the Rotary constitution. After an internal hearing, International's board of directors revoked the charter of the Duarte Club and terminated its membership in Rotary International. The Duarte Club's appeal to the International Convention was unsuccessful.

The Duarte Club and two of its women members filed a complaint in the California Superior Court for the County of Los Angeles. The complaint alleged, inter alia, that appellants' actions violated the Unruh Civil Rights Act, Cal. Civ. Code Ann. § 51 (West 1982).[2] . . .

II

In Roberts v. United States Jaycees, [468 U.S. 609 (1984)], we upheld against First Amendment challenge a Minnesota statute that required the Jaycees to admit women as full voting members. *Roberts* provides the framework for analyzing appellants' constitutional claims. As we observed in *Roberts*, our cases have afforded constitutional protection to freedom of association in two distinct senses. First, the Court has held that the Constitution protects against unjustified government interference with an individual's choice to enter into and maintain certain intimate or private relationships. Second, the Court has upheld the freedom of individuals to associate for the purpose of engaging in protected speech or religious activities. In many cases, government interference with one form of protected association will also burden the other form of association. In *Roberts* we determined the nature and degree of constitutional protection by considering separately the effect of the challenged state action on individuals' freedom of private association and their freedom of expressive association. We follow the same course in this case. . . .

A

The Court has recognized that the freedom to enter into and carry on certain intimate or private relationships is a fundamental element of liberty protected by the Bill of Rights. Such relationships may take various forms, including the most intimate. . . . We have not attempted to mark the precise boundaries of this type of constitutional protection. The intimate relationships to which we have accorded constitutional protection include marriage . . . the begetting and bearing of children . . . child rearing and education . . . and cohabitation with relatives. . . . In determining whether a particular association is sufficiently personal or private to warrant constitutional protection, we consider factors such as size, purpose, selectivity, and whether others are excluded from critical aspects of the relationship. [468 U.S. at 620.]

---

2. The Unruh Civil Rights Act provides, in part: "All persons within the jurisdiction of this state are free and equal, and no matter what their sex, race, color, religion, ancestry, or national origin are entitled to the full and equal accommodations, advantages, facilities, privileges, or services in all business establishments of every kind whatsoever." Cal. Civ. Code Ann. § 51 (West 1982).

The evidence in this case indicates that the relationship among Rotary Club members is not the kind of intimate or private relation that warrants constitutional protection. The size of the local Rotary Clubs ranges from fewer than 20 to more than 900.... There is no upper limit on the membership of any local Rotary Club. About 10 percent of the membership of a typical club moves away or drops out during a typical year.... The clubs therefore are instructed to "keep a flow of prospects coming" to make up for the attrition and gradually to enlarge the membership.... The purpose of Rotary "is to produce an inclusive, not exclusive, membership, making possible the recognition of all useful local occupations, and enabling the club to be a true cross section of the business and professional life of the community."... The membership undertakes a variety of service projects designed to aid the community, to raise the standards of the members' businesses and professions, and to improve international relations. Such an inclusive "fellowship for service based on diversity of interest,"... however beneficial to the members and to those they serve, does not suggest the kind of private or personal relationship to which we have accorded protection under the First Amendment. To be sure, membership in Rotary Clubs is not open to the general public. But each club is instructed to include in its membership "all fully qualified prospective members located within its territory," to avoid "arbitrary limits on the number of members in the club," and to "establish and maintain a membership growth pattern."

Many of the Rotary Clubs' central activities are carried on in the presence of strangers. Rotary Clubs are required to admit any member of any other Rotary Club to their meetings. Members are encouraged to invite business associates and competitors to meetings. At some Rotary Clubs, the visitors number "in the tens and twenties each week."... Joint meetings with the members of other organizations, and other joint activities, are permitted. The clubs are encouraged to seek coverage of their meetings and activities in local newspapers. In sum, Rotary Clubs, rather than carrying on their activities in an atmosphere of privacy, seek to keep their "windows and doors open to the whole world."... We therefore conclude that application of the Unruh Act to local Rotary Clubs does not interfere unduly with the members' freedom of private association.

B

The Court also has recognized that the right to engage in activities protected by the First Amendment implies "a corresponding right to associate with others in pursuit of a wide variety of political, social, economic, educational, religious, and cultural ends." Roberts v. United States Jaycees, [468 U.S. at 622].... For this reason, "[i]mpediments to the exercise of one's right to choose one's associates can violate the right of association protected by the First Amendment...." Hishon v. King & Spalding, [467 U.S. 69, 80 n.4 (1984)] (Powell, J., concurring) (citing NAACP v. Button, [371 U.S. 415 (1963)]; NAACP v. Alabama ex rel. Patterson, [357 U.S. 449 (1958)]). In this case, however, the evidence fails to demonstrate that admitting women to Rotary Clubs will affect in any significant way the existing members' ability to carry out their various purposes.

As a matter of policy, Rotary Clubs do not take positions on "public questions," including political or international issues.... To be sure, Rotary Clubs engage in a variety of commendable service activities that are protected by the First Amendment. But the Unruh Act does not require the clubs to abandon or alter any of these activities. It does not require them to abandon their basic goals of humanitarian service, high ethical standards in all vocations, good will, and peace. Nor does it require them to abandon their classification system or admit members who do not reflect a cross section of the community. Indeed, by opening membership to leading business and professional women in the community, Rotary Clubs are likely to obtain a more representative cross section of community leaders with a broadened capacity for service.

Even if the Unruh Act does work some slight infringement on Rotary members' right of expressive association, that infringement is justified because it serves the State's compelling interest in eliminating discrimination against women. See Buckley v. Valeo, [424 U.S. 1, 25 (1976)] (per curiam) (right of association may be limited by state regulations necessary to serve a compelling interest unrelated to the suppression of ideas). On its face the Unruh Act, like the Minnesota public accommodations law we considered in *Roberts*, makes no distinctions on the basis of the organization's viewpoint. Moreover, public accommodations laws "plainly serv[e] compelling state interests of the highest order." [468 U.S. at 624.] In *Roberts* we recognized that the State's compelling interest in assuring equal access to women extends to the acquisition of leadership skills and business contacts as well as tangible goods and services. [Id. at 626.] The Unruh Act plainly serves this interest. We therefore hold that application of the Unruh Act to California Rotary Clubs does not violate the right of expressive association afforded by the First Amendment. . . .

Justice SCALIA concurs in the judgment.

Justice BLACKMUN and Justice O'CONNOR took no part in the consideration or decision of this case.

Isbister v. Boys' Club of Santa Cruz, Inc.
707 P.2d 212 (Cal. 1985)

GRODIN, Justice. . . .

The Boys' Club of Santa Cruz, Inc., a private nonprofit California corporation, owns and operates a building which includes such recreational facilities as a gymnasium, an indoor competition-size swimming pool, a snack bar, and craft and game areas. The local Club is affiliated with the Boys' Clubs of America, Inc., a congressionally chartered organization. . . .

Only members may use the Club's programs and facilities, but membership is open to all Santa Cruz children between eight and eighteen, so long as they are male. Members pay only a $3.25 annual membership fee. The principal source of funding for the Club—providing approximately 50 percent of its annual budget—is a gift in trust from John T. and Ruth M. Mallery (the Mallery Trust). The Mallerys also donated the money for the Club building. The trial court found that the Mallery Trust was "unrestricted" as to gender. In 1978, after this suit began, the Mallerys made a $200,000 donation which was expressly conditioned on restriction of membership to boys. Remaining funds come from the United Way campaign, an annual golf event, and miscellaneous private donations.

The Club is run by an adult board of directors, officers of the corporation, and a paid staff headed by an executive director. Club members have no power over Club affairs or membership policies.

The Club is unique in northern Santa Cruz County in the range and low cost of the recreational facilities and programs it provides under one roof. No single program or facility open to girls offers a similar range of activities at similar cost.

In 1977, plaintiff girls were denied access to the Boys' Club's membership and facilities solely on the basis of their sex. This action for injunctive and declaratory relief [under the Unruh Act] followed. . . .

1. The Boys' Club is a "business establishment" covered by the Unruh Act. . . .
2. The Boys' Club male-only membership policy is prohibited by the Unruh Act. . . .

The Club contends that its primary purpose — to combat delinquency — is an important social interest best served by concentrating on male youth. It introduced juvenile hall statistics suggesting that Santa Cruz boys are four times more likely than their female counterparts to get into trouble with the law. By extending service to girls, the Club urges, it will have to dilute its efforts with boys, who present the greater social problem.

It was conceded, however, that delinquency affects substantial numbers of girls. There was no evidence that boys need the recreation offered by the Club more than girls, that a sex-segregated "drop-in" recreational facility is more effective in combating juvenile delinquency than one open to both sexes, or that extension of membership to girls would cause an impractical net increase (or decrease) in membership. . . .

The Club suggests that its funding is in jeopardy if its membership policies change. But the trial court found on substantial evidence that the original Mallery Trust, the Club's major financial source, is unrestricted on that score. We recognize with concern that the Mallerys' 1978 gift of $200,000 is conditioned on continuation of the male-only policy. But admission of girls may well produce offsetting new revenue sources. There is no evidence of severe, permanent financial danger should the Club be forced to comply with the Act. In sum, this record provides no basis for an exception to the Act's rule against arbitrary discrimination by "business establishments." . . .

The judgment is affirmed.

BROUSSARD, REYNOSO and CHESNEY, JJ., concur.

[The concurring opinion of Chief Justice Bird is omitted.]

MOSK, Justice, dissenting.
I dissent.

The incredible concept that a private, charitably funded recreational club for boys cannot be allowed to exist as such because it is a "business establishment" would be an irresistible subject for ridicule and humor if it were not so serious in its impact. The majority opinion conjures up visions of young boys, who have been skinny-dipping in their club pool, donning three-piece suits to attend the board meeting of their "business establishment" where they may discuss such matters as the antitrust implications of a proposed takeover of girl scout cookies. Precocious indeed these teen and preteen youngsters must be.

Growing up into a world of sex equality is inevitable for all children, but the court-ordered elimination of traditional childhood activity is an exorbitant price to pay for accelerating the process.

The majority purport to be blithely oblivious to the extended reach of their decision, and disingenuously attempt to restrict their opinion to this one case, involving only this one Boys' Club in this one city. At the same time they appear to implore the Legislature to rescue society from this judicial folly and its consequences. . . . That is a plea I can enthusiastically endorse.

That the ultimate result of this case will strain our social fabric and send shock waves throughout the realm of children's organizations is made clear by the appearance of numerous apprehensive *amici curiae* representing both girls and boys. Girls' organizations throughout California are no more eager for an invasion by boys than are boys' groups for dilution of their programs by compulsory inclusion of girls. . . .

The majority's insouciance is disturbing. No girl's parents who are inclined to be litigious will fail to use this case as authority to demand their daughter's admission to other boys' clubs, the Boy Scouts, Cub Scouts, Young Men's Christian Association, and similar organizations that maintain camps or physical facilities. Conversely, boys could rely on this case to insist on their right to join girls' clubs, the Girl Scouts, Campfire Girls, Young Women's Christian Association, and like groups. There is no rational way to distinguish those situations.

In addition, the majority strike a death knell for fraternities and sororities as they exist on every college campus in California. There is no way any court can read the rationale of the majority opinion and yet deny the right of a male student to join a sorority, or a female student to become a fraternity member. If the Boys' Club of Santa Cruz is a business because it operates a gymnasium and swimming pool, a fortiori sororities and fraternities, which provide and charge for housing accommodations and eating facilities, are business establishments. Similar considerations will probably also affect separate college dormitories.

The natural extension of the majority opinion to women's colleges is even more potentially devastating. If a qualified male student seeks admission to Mills, Mount St. Mary's or Scripps — California's renowned educational institutions for women — there is no rational way in which a court could distinguish his demand from that of the plaintiff herein. Colleges that provide not only classes but living accommodations and food service are arguably more akin to a business establishment than is a recreational boys' club. . . .

Services and facilities are provided by the Boys' Club for a nominal nonprofit fee of $3.25 per year; the relationship between the Boys' Club and its members is essentially gratuitous. The purpose of the Boys' Club — to help boys develop citizenship, leadership, values, health and fitness, personal adjustment and individual growth, and inter-group understanding — is primarily to provide services of a personal and social nature, and the relationship between the Boys' Club and its members is clearly noncommercial. Finally, boys may remain members for years; the relationship is thus continuous. . . .

The effects, tangible and intangible, of the majority opinion in this case are devastating.

First, the club will be required to compel joint use of facilities by boys and girls — swimming, basketball, handball, etc. In the alternative, the club will be required to cut the boys' recreational time in half and restrict their hours in order to accommodate girls: e.g., not a full day on Saturday but only a half day; not two hours after school but only one hour.

Second, the club will be compelled to build an additional locker room, showers, toilets, and other physical facilities. This, of course, will require a considerable expenditure of charitable funds.

Third, while being thus obligated to expand, the club will simultaneously lose a $200,000 gift that is conditioned on a male-only policy. The majority gratuitously declare that the admission of girls "may well produce offsetting new revenue sources." I doubt that my colleagues would enjoy serving on a fund-raising committee seeking to raise a $200,000 "offset" for this purpose in the Santa Cruz community.

Fourth, the majority effectively stifle any community incentive to create and construct a girls' club comparable to the Boys' Club.

Fifth, the Boys' Club may very well lose its national charter. By act of Congress, the Boys' Clubs of America are authorized "to promote the health, social, educational, vocational, and character development of boys throughout the United States of America. . . ." Parenthetically, it may be observed that Congress has chartered other sex-exclusive organizations, e.g., Daughters of the American Revolution . . . , Sons of the American Revolution . . . , and Veterans of Foreign Wars of the United States. . . .

Amicus Boy Scouts of America points out other significant policy considerations overlooked by the majority. By protecting the freedom to base sexual associations on personal affinities, society promotes its pluralism, with all the values that connotes — values such as a diversity of views, a variety of ideas, and preservation of traditions. Here, the plaintiff and her supporters believe that their community will benefit by making certain private facilities with limited capacity and with limited adult supervision available either to children of both sexes or to none at all. Other citizens — those who charitably donated the property and those who charitably maintain it — believe their community will benefit by more narrowly focusing the use of that property on boys, many of whom are disadvantaged.

The value of a pluralistic, democratic society is that it permits members of each group to join with others sharing their views, to pool their resources as they wish, to seek the resources of new members, and to experiment to try to prove the validity of their respective concepts. The charitable donors of the Boys' Club property and funds, and the volunteers who charitably organize and operate the club, have done just that. No law or policy bars plaintiff and others from seeking out charitable contributors who share their views. . . .

Another important factor that the majority have ignored is the policy favoring private charitable contributions, a policy manifested in tax laws and laws authorizing charitable contributions.... The more the state arbitrarily dictates the permissible goals and practices of charitable organizations, the tighter the purse-strings of potential donors are likely to be drawn.

For all of the foregoing reasons I would reverse the judgment.

KAUS, Justice, dissenting....

I feel compelled to express puzzlement at the majority's repeated mention of the fact that there is no comparable facility for girls in the Santa Cruz area. If there were a Girls' Club in Santa Cruz, would the majority be satisfied with "separate but equal" facilities? If there were two boys' clubs, would each have to admit girls? Two boys' clubs and one girls' club? Unless the majority is prepared to suggest that the existence of additional facilities might affect its conclusions, I respectfully submit that the references to the Club's monopoly are of no legal significance....

To establish that the Club is a facility that is generally open to the public, the majority states that it "offers basic recreational facilities to a broad segment of the population, excluding only a particular group expressly recognized by the Act as a traditional target of discrimination." [707 P.2d at 220 (quoting the majority opinion).] Sounds good, but what are the facts? The "broad segment" of the population consists of boys between the ages of eight and eighteen. On the other hand, the "particular" group which is excluded is the rest of humanity. I submit that the only way to reach the conclusion that the Club is "generally open to the public" is to look at the included and excluded groups through different ends of a telescope.

Further, I believe that the Club has demonstrated "a compelling need to maintain single-sex facilities." The majority quite properly holds that section 51 only forbids arbitrary sex discrimination. One would think, then, that if one of the main goals of the Club is the control of juvenile delinquency and those who guide its affairs have made a reasoned decision that this goal is best advanced by a prophylactic application of the Club's limited resources to that group of young-sters from which the majority of serious delinquents seems to come—boys—that is surely not arbitrary.... No reason was given why it is arbitrary to spend the delinquency prevention dollar where it is thought to do the most good....[3]

The majority seeks to improve on the trial court's *ipse dixit* by asserting that because some delinquents are girls, the Club should have proved that "a sex-segregated...facility is more effective in combating juvenile delinquency than one open to both sexes...." Why did the Club have a burden in that respect? If it acted in good faith—and no one claims that it did not—why should it have to prove that a perfectly defensible decision on how to spend its resources has actually proved to be the most effective one?...

Evidently those responsible for the Club's policy have decided that it is beneficial for boys to have some time when they do not have to adjust their behavior to the presence of girls. There is, of course, a vast professional literature on the subject. Who are we to say that it is unreasonable for the Club's manage-ment to believe that there is a rational basis for giving boys a few hours a day when

---

3. I do not claim that the same considerations would be valid if, for example, statistics showed that members of a particular racial group or religion were more prone to turn delinquent. Some suspect classifications are simply more suspect than others and demand greater degrees of justification....

they do not have to carry their machismo on their sleeves? Whether or not we share these views is immaterial. What matters is that we have no right to force contrary theories on those who have devoted considerable time, energy, devotion and financial resources to the problem.

If I may suggest, the basic mistake of the majority opinion is that it views the Club's policies as being pointed toward the exclusion of girls. With that chip on the majority's shoulder, pejoratives come easily. If the court looked at the Club's activities more benignly as providing a service for boys — a service tailored to their needs — it would not find it necessary to reach such a wondrous result.

I therefore dissent.

Notes

1. State and Local Public Accommodations Laws. Since no federal legislation reaches private clubs or associations, challenges to sex-based exclusions from these associations, like *Rotary Club* and *Isbister*, have been brought under state civil rights acts. These acts vary. Some prohibit discrimination only as to places of public accommodation, construed to mean entities that exist at a particular place and thereby excluding organizations that may meet in different locations, such as the Jaycees, Rotary Clubs, and some scouting organizations. Others apply to private clubs only in areas or at functions where nonmembers are present. Some apply only to businesses, although business may be quite broadly construed, as it was in *Isbister*. Some statutes specifically exempt "private" or "distinctly private" clubs. Examples of each of these types of statutes are discussed in Sally Frank, The Key to Unlocking the Clubhouse Door: The Application of Antidiscrimination Laws to Quasi-Private Clubs, 2 Mich. J. Gender & L. 27 (1994).

The federal constitutional issue raised by the application of these statutes is the extent to which the First Amendment protects the rights of individuals to associate in private clubs that discriminate on grounds prohibited by the statutes and to express themselves through these associations. The rights of free association and free expression have long been invoked to protect the activities and privacy of politically unpopular groups, including those involved in the civil rights movement. See, e.g., NAACP v. Alabama ex rel. Patterson, 357 U.S. 449 (1958); NAACP v. Button, 371 U.S. 415 (1963). The question is how far this protection extends, and to whom. In determining the answers to this question, the only limit formal equality would seem to impose is that the criteria applied be neutral, that is, that they do not unfairly privilege one group over another because of the content of their beliefs.

In light of this constraint, the courts' criteria for balancing First Amendment and equality interests may seem paradoxical. For example, the emphasis in *Rotary Club* on size, inclusiveness, openness to the public, and the failure to take positions on public questions means that the more exclusive and "discriminating" an association is, the more likely it will be allowed to discriminate. Similarly, the more connection there is between the exclusion and the expressive purpose of the association, the greater protection the association will enjoy. Thus, a white supremacy organization may be allowed to exclude blacks (but perhaps not women?), and a neo-Nazi group to exclude Jews, but a Rotary Club or Little League organization will not be allowed to so discriminate. Religious organizations, as well, will be given wide range to discriminate in carrying out their rituals, selecting their members, and employing people. See Frank, supra, at 60, 79. The topic of how notions of privacy shield discriminatory behavior is further explored in Chapters 3 and 5.

An Oregon case highlights the importance of the existence of a substantial economic or commercial advantage to the organization's members, under the Oregon Public Accommodations Act. See Lahmann v. Grand Aerie of Fraternal Order of Eagles, 43 P.2d 113 (Or. Ct. App. 2002). Another factor is the connection between the private organization and the organizations on which they are dependent to whom anti-discrimination laws may clearly apply. A New Jersey court held that the highly selective eating clubs at Princeton University are subject to the state anti-discrimination laws, because of their interdependent relationship to the University. Frank v. Ivy Club, 576 A.2d 241 (N.J. 1990). This case may suggest another paradox — the more self-sufficient a group is, the more likely it will be to be left alone.

Obtaining the benefits of a successful discrimination suit against a "private" association may pose greater challenges for the plaintiff than in the employment context. Social and recreational benefits are more difficult to secure, in a meaningful sense, than the economic benefits of a job. While shunning and stigmatization can also be a problem on the job, Title VII specifically addresses those practices, and makes them a further violation of the Act; state and local nondiscrimination rules typically do not address the issue. For an account of the costs to the plaintiffs of one lawsuit to end gender-discriminatory practices at a Massachusetts country club, see Marcia Chambers, The High Price of Victory, N.Y. Times, April 2, 2001, at D1 (describing the ostracism and frustration of plaintiffs in lawsuit to challenge sex discrimination at the Haverhill County Club that led, among other things, to the divorce of one plaintiff, the loss of clients and business to another who was a real-estate agent, and the decision by another plaintiff to abandon the club altogether). The lawsuit is Borne v. The Haverhill Golf & Country Club, 1999 Mass. Super. LEXIS 523 (Nov. 19, 1999).

2. The End of Single-Sex Organizations? Each of the opinions written in *Isbister* seems to assume that the desegregation of organizations such as the Boy Scouts would be regrettable. In California, the exclusion of girls from the Boy Scouts was upheld from challenge under the Unruh Act (under which *Isbister* was decided) on grounds the Boy Scouts was not a business protected by the Act. See Yeaw v. Boy Scouts of America, 64 Cal. Rptr. 2d 85 (Ct. App. 1997). The Boy Scouts still exclude girls, although since 1969 the Explorers have permitted boys and girls, ages 14 through 20, to join. Moreover, since 1988, adult women have been allowed to become Boy Scout troop leaders. The Boy Scouts also exclude homosexuals, a policy which the United States Supreme Court has held is protected by the organization's First Amendment right of expressive association. See Boy Scouts of America v. Dale, 530 U.S. 640 (2000), discussed at pp. 618-621 in Chapter 3.

Financial as well as legal pressures have led a number of formerly all-male associations to expand their membership to women. See Rosanne Calbo, The YWCA as a Single Sex Organization — Would It Survive a Legal Challenge? 22 Golden Gate L. Rev. 715, 717 nn.16-18 (1992). The Boy Scouts have experienced considerable financial consequences of their decision to exclude gays after that exclusion was upheld in *Dale*. See Kate Zernike, Scouts' Successful Ban on Gays is Followed by Loss in Support, N.Y. Times, Aug. 29, 2000, A1 (reporting on withdrawal by cities, corporations, a state-run charity and some United Way agencies, of various types of support including use of parks and schools and funding, as a result of its policy against gay members); David France, Scouts Divided, Newsweek, Aug. 6, 2001, at 44, 47 (noting a 4.5 percent drop in Boy Scout membership in year following *Dale* decision). The Girl Scouts have avoided these consequences by adopting a national guideline against discrimination based on sexual orientation, along with a policy against "'sexual displays' or advocacy of personal lifestyles." Peg Tyre, Where the Girls Are: The Girl Scouts Try a Version of 'Don't Ask, Don't Tell,' Newsweek, Aug. 6, 2001, at 51. Local Girl Scout councils apparently are not dechartered if they violate the national policy. Id.

A widely publicized challenge to Augusta National Golf Club, one of the nation's most prestigious all-male associations, erupted in 2002 when the club hosted the annual Masters tournament. The National Council of Women's Organizations sought unsuccessfully to force major corporate sponsors to withdraw their support if the club did not admit women. Similar pressure by civil rights organizations in the 1970s had forced the integration of the club that hosted the prestigious Professional Golf Association tournament. The Augusta case is chronicled in Martha Burk, Cult of Power: Sex Discrimination in Corporate America and What Can Be Done About It (2005). Why do you suppose that it has been harder to get clubs and corporate sponsors to take sex discrimination seriously than race discrimination?

3. Special Needs of Boys. According to Ruth Mallery, the private donor who funded the Santa Cruz Boys' Club, boys need their own club because they get into more trouble than girls.

> The problem . . . dates back to the days when farms were falling apart and families moved to the cities. While girls still had housework to occupy their time, boys no longer had milking and planting chores to keep them off the streets. Girls also mature faster. . . . Young men need to be around other young men without female pressure.

Jill Wolfson, Santa Cruz Boys' Club Does the Unthinkable: The Invasion of the Girls, San Jose Mercury News, Feb. 27, 1986, at 1D. In addition to withdrawing a $200,000 contribution, Mrs. Mallery attempted to cancel the $15 million trust fund that brought in 75 percent of the club's annual budget, but was not able to do so because there had been no requirement of girls' exclusion in her original gift. Id.

By 1987, 30 percent of the members of the Boys' Club in Santa Cruz were girls, involved in all aspects of the club, including football and baseball. According to one report, there were "no signs of tension between boys and girls." Jill Zuckman, Boys' Club Finds Sugar and Spice, San Jose Mercury News, Aug. 14, 1987, at 1B. The issue of separate classes and programs for girls, on theories similar to Mrs. Mallery's, see Chapter 2, pp. 278-285.

Should *Isbister* apply to private girls' organizations, like the Girl Scouts? Does it matter whether the purpose of the Girl Scouts is to remedy past discrimination or to provide for girls' "special needs"? Which case would be the stronger one? The problems set forth below should be considered again in the context of Chapter 2, which addresses both of these rationales for all-female associations.

Putting Theory into Practice

1-17. Should a private law firm specializing in women's rights litigation be allowed to hire only women associates and partners? Can it decide to take only women clients? Hire only women who fit in with its own female tone and atmosphere? Contribute only to pro-women's political organizations and pro bono activities?

If so, should a private law firm specializing in men's rights litigation be able to make comparable choices that are compatible with their political and social goals?

1-18. The Black Women's Health Imperative is a membership organization dedicated to "health education, research, advocacy and leadership development" for Black women and girls. Its website describes itself as follows:

> Founded in 1983 by health activist Byllye Y. Avery, it has been a pioneer in promoting the empowerment of African American women as educated health care consumers and a strong voice for the improved health status of African American women. The organization is gaining the well-earned reputation as the leading force for health for African American women. Black Women's Health Imperative possesses national stature as the only national organization devoted solely to the health of the nation's 19 million Black women and girls.

http://www.blackwomenshealth.org/site. Its services and programs are all geared toward Black women and girls. Are there any pitfalls the organization needs to be careful to avoid, to escape exposure under the kind of anti-discrimination statutes applied in *Rotary Club* and *Isbister*? What advice would you give the organization? How would you respond to the view propounded in relation to the organization's predecessor organization, the National Black Women's Health Project:

> If African-American women do not exclude white women from their association, their sharing will be chilled by the presence of white women. African-American women will spend valuable time listening to white women defend their actions. In essence, African-American women will spend time concentrating on white women, instead of focusing on themselves. Their communications will become stilted until they are effectively silenced in their own associations.

Pamela J. Smith, We Are Not Sisters: African-American Women and the Freedom to Associate and Disassociate, 66 Tul. L. Rev. 1467, 1511 (1992).

1-19.　A man sues Healthworks, a Massachusetts all-women's health club, for excluding men from membership. Should he win? What arguments would you make on his behalf? On behalf of Healthworks? See Miriam A. Cherry, Exercising the Right to Public Accommodations: The Debate Over Single-Sex Health Clubs, 52 Me. L. Rev. 97 (2000) (against single-sex health clubs); Michael R. Evans, The Case for All-Female Health Clubs: Creating a Compensatory Purpose Exception to State Public Accommodation Law, 11 Yale J.L. & Feminism 307 (1999) (in favor). The plaintiff won the case, see Foster v. Back Bay Spas, Inc., No. 96-7060, 1997 WL634354 (Mass. Super. Ct. Oct. 1, 1997), but the Massachusetts legislature then passed legislation allowing Healthworks to continue operating as an all-women's club, at the same time also allowing men-only health spas to operate. Was this a good idea? If Massachusetts wanted to allow all-women's health clubs, was it also required to allow all-men's health clubs?

1-20.　How do the identity-based student organizations on your campus handle membership and leadership?

2
Substantive Equality

Theories of formal sex equality refer to the form of a rule and require that the rule treat women and men on the same terms without special barriers or favors on account of sex. Formal equality works best in situations when men and women are enough alike that the same rule operates equally well for both. It has been questioned as an approach, however, when men and women are different in some significant respect, and when, as a result of the differences, the same rule leads to unequal outcomes. Theories of substantive equality take account of these differences, and attempt to achieve equality of results or effects. Determining what differences should be taken into account and in what ways is not always an easy matter. Theories of substantive equality reflect multiple types and sources of differences and multiple, sometimes conflicting, substantive goals.

One formulation of substantive equality focuses on remedying the effects of past discrimination. Women historically have been excluded either by law or by gender roles and norms from having certain jobs or earning wages comparable to men's. "Affirmative action" plans designed to increase female representation in traditionally male occupations and "pay equity" schemes designed to restructure wage scales are examples of remedial measures that seek to reverse the effects of past discrimination.

Another type of substantive equality focuses on biological differences between women and men. Only women become pregnant, for example, and pregnancy can disadvantage workers with respect to job opportunities, seniority, and job security. Parental leave provisions and flexible work schedules are examples of measures that aim to neutralize this disadvantage. More radical substantive equality approaches look beyond biological difference and try to change the social expectations and practices that steer women into lower-paying occupational categories, encourage their economic dependence on men, and perpetuate their disproportionate share of caretaking responsibilities.

Many differences between men and women are matters of averages, rather than definitional or categorical differences. Formal rule equality principles will be sufficient to achieve fair and equal outcomes for the exceptional or "non-average"

151

woman who can compete successfully for an opportunity on the same basis as the average man. Other more result-oriented approaches may be required, however, to protect the interests of women as a whole, whose average characteristics or circumstances would otherwise disadvantage them in relation to men. Some argue, for example, that all-female classrooms or sports teams are necessary to ensure equal opportunities for girls and women. Others contend that special rules are required at divorce to recognize women's economic vulnerability and their greater investment in their children.

In considering the examples of substantive equality in this chapter, it is important to note (1) which differences in circumstances or characteristics between men and women are, or should be, significant, (2) which outcomes are just, and (3) which strategies are most likely to lead to those outcomes. Compare the reasoning in these examples with that of formal equality. How different is a substantive equality approach from formal equality? To what extent is it necessary to choose between the two?

A. REMEDYING THE EFFECTS OF PAST DISCRIMINATION

1. Sex-Specific Public Benefits to Remedy Past Societal Discrimination

═══ *Kahn v. Shevin*
═══ 416 U.S. 351 (1974)

Mr. Justice DOUGLAS delivered the opinion of the Court.

Since at least 1885, Florida has provided for some form of property tax exemption for widows. The current law granting all widows an annual $500 exemption...has been essentially unchanged since 1941. Appellant Kahn is a widower who lives in Florida and applied for the exemption to the Dade County Tax Assessor's Office. It was denied because the statute offers no analogous benefit for widowers. [T]he Circuit Court for Dade County, Florida, held the statute violative of the Equal Protection Clause of the Fourteenth Amendment.... The Florida Supreme Court reversed....

There can be no dispute that the financial difficulties confronting the lone woman in Florida or in any other State exceed those facing the man. Whether from overt discrimination or from the socialization process of a male-dominated culture, the job market is inhospitable to the woman seeking any but the lowest paid jobs.[4] There are, of course, efforts under way to remedy this situation.... But firmly entrenched practices are resistant to such pressures, and, indeed, data compiled by the Women's Bureau of the United States Department

---

4. In 1970 while 40% of males in the work force earned over $10,000, and 70% over $7,000, 45% of women working full time earned less than $5,000, and 73% earned less than $7,000. U.S. Bureau of the Census: Current Population Reports, Series P-60, No. 80.

of Labor show that in 1972 a woman working full time had a median income which was only 57.9% of the median for males — a figure actually six points lower than had been achieved in 1955.... The disparity is likely to be exacerbated for the widow. While the widower can usually continue in the occupation which preceded his spouse's death, in many cases the widow will find herself suddenly forced into a job market with which she is unfamiliar, and in which, because of her former economic dependency, she will have fewer skills to offer.

There can be no doubt, therefore, that Florida's differing treatment of widows and widowers "rest[s] upon some ground of difference having a fair and substantial relation to the object of the legislation." [Reed v. Reed...]

This is not a case like Frontiero v. Richardson,... where the Government denied its female employees both substantive and procedural benefits granted males "solely... for administrative convenience." We deal here with a state tax law reasonably designed to further the state policy of cushioning the financial impact of spousal loss upon the sex for which that loss imposes a disproportionately heavy burden....

Affirmed.

Mr. Justice BRENNAN, with whom Mr. Justice MARSHALL joins, dissenting....

In my view... a legislative classification that distinguishes potential beneficiaries solely by reference to their gender-based status as widows or widowers, like classifications based upon race, alienage, and national origin, must be subjected to close judicial scrutiny, because it focuses upon generally immutable characteristics over which individuals have little or no control, and also because gender-based classifications too often have been inexcusably utilized to stereotype and stigmatize politically powerless segments of society. See Frontiero v. Richardson, ...

I agree that, in providing special benefits for a needy segment of society long the victim of purposeful discrimination and neglect, the statute serves the compelling state interest of achieving equality for such groups. No one familiar with this country's history of pervasive sex discrimination against women can doubt the need for remedial measures to correct the resulting economic imbalances.... [T]he purpose and effect of the suspect classification are ameliorative; the statute neither stigmatizes nor denigrates widowers not also benefited by the legislation. Moreover, inclusion of needy widowers within the class of beneficiaries would not further the State's overriding interest in remedying the economic effects of past sex discrimination for needy victims of that discrimination. While doubtless some widowers are in financial need, no one suggests that such need results from sex discrimination as in the case of widows.

The statute nevertheless fails to satisfy the requirements of equal protection, since the State has not borne its burden of proving that its compelling interest could not be achieved by a more precisely tailored statute or by use of feasible, less drastic means. [The statute] is plainly overinclusive, for the $500 property tax exemption may be obtained by a financially independent heiress as well as by an unemployed widow with dependent children. The State has offered nothing to explain why inclusion of widows of substantial economic means was necessary to advance the State's interest in ameliorating the effects of past economic discrimination against women. . . .

By merely redrafting that form to exclude widows who earn annual incomes, or possess assets, in excess of specified amounts, the State could readily narrow the class of beneficiaries to those widows for whom the effects of past economic discrimination against women have been a practical reality.

Mr. Justice WHITE, dissenting.

The Florida tax exemption at issue here is available to all widows but not to widowers. The presumption is that all widows are financially more needy and less trained or less ready for the job market than men. It may be that most widows have been occupied as housewife, mother, and homemaker and are not immediately prepared for employment. But there are many rich widows who need no largess from the State; many others are highly trained and have held lucrative positions long before the death of their husbands. At the same time, there are many widowers who are needy and who are in more desperate financial straits and have less access to the job market than many widows. Yet none of them qualifies for the exemption.

I find the discrimination invidious and violative of the Equal Protection Clause. There is merit in giving poor widows a tax break, but gender-based classifications are suspect and require more justification than the State has offered. . . .

It may be suggested that the State is entitled to prefer widows over widowers because their assumed need is rooted in past and present economic discrimination against women. But this is not a credible explanation of Florida's tax exemption; for if the State's purpose was to compensate for past discrimination against females, surely it would not have limited the exemption to women who are widows. Moreover, even if past discrimination is considered to be the criterion for current tax exemption, the State nevertheless ignores all those widowers who have felt the effects of economic discrimination, whether as a member of a racial group or as one of the many who cannot escape the cycle of poverty. It seems to me that the State in this case is merely conferring an economic benefit in the form of a tax exemption and has not adequately explained why women should be treated differently from men.

I dissent.

NOTE ON "BENIGN" SEX-BASED CLASSIFICATIONS TO REMEDY PAST DISCRIMINATION

As a result of the statute upheld in Kahn v. Shevin, a wealthy widow could receive a $500 property tax exemption while an impoverished widower could not. Can this result be justified under equal treatment principles?

Recall the government benefits cases discussed in the notes to Chapter 1, Section B, such as Frontiero v. Richardson, Weinberger v. Wiesenfeld, and Califano v. Goldfarb. Can Kahn v. Shevin be reconciled with these cases?

Kahn v. Shevin is one of a few benefits cases that have upheld group-based treatment more favorable to women than to men. In another example, Schlesinger v. Ballard, 419 U.S. 498 (1975), the Court sustained the Navy's "up or out" termination policy under which male officers were terminated when passed over for promotion a second time after nine years, while female officers were discharged for non-promotion only after thirteen years. The rationale was compensatory: because women could only be assigned to hospital ships and transports and not to vessels involved in combat, they did not have the same opportunities as men to compile records warranting promotion. In the Court's view, giving female officers a longer period for proving themselves was a permissible means of equalizing their career opportunities. 419 U.S. at 508.

The other principal case along this line is Califano v. Webster, 430 U.S. 313 (1977), a case that upheld a Social Security provision applied to retirements before 1972 that computed old-age benefits under a formula more favorable to women than to men. The benefits for both were determined according to an average monthly wage earned during certain years, but women were given the opportunity of excluding three additional lower earning years than men. In a per curiam opinion, the Court concluded:

> The statutory scheme involved here is more analogous to those upheld in *Kahn* [and Schlesinger v. Ballard] than to those struck down in [Weinberger v. Wiesenfeld, 430 U.S. 636 (1975), and Califano v. Goldfarb, 430 U.S. 199 (1977)]. The more favorable treatment of the female wage earner enacted here was not a result of "archaic and overbroad generalizations" about women . . . or of "the role typing society has long imposed" upon women . . . such as casual assumptions that women are "the weaker sex" or are more likely to be child-rearers or dependents. . . . Rather, "the only discernible purpose of [the statute's more favorable treatment is] the permissible one of redressing our society's longstanding disparate treatment of women." [*Goldfarb*, 430 U.S. at 209 n.8.]
>
> The challenged statute operated directly to compensate women for past economic discrimination. Retirement benefits under the Act are based on past earnings. But as we have recognized: "Whether from overt discrimination or from the socialization process of a male-dominated culture, the job market is inhospitable to the woman seeking any but the lowest paid jobs." [*Kahn*, 416 U.S. at 353.] Thus, allowing women, who as such have been unfairly hindered from earning as much as men, to eliminate additional low-earning years from the calculation of their retirement benefits works directly to remedy some part of the effect of past discrimination. . . .

430 U.S. at 317-318.

How "benign" are the classifications upheld in *Kahn* and *Webster*? In an illuminating international study by Peter Glick and Susan Fiske, some 15,000 men and women were rated on attitudes of hostile and benevolent sexism (an example of the latter would be "women should be cherished and protected by men"). They found that the two forms of sexism were related and together were better predictors of gender inequality than either alone. Peter T. Glick et al., Beyond Gender Prejudice as Simple Antipathy: Hostile and Benevolent Sexism

Across Cultures, 79 J. of Pers. & Soc. Psych. (2000). What are the policy implications of this research?

How good are benign classifications for women? Consider Catharine MacKinnnon's criticism of both equal treatment and "special benefits" approaches to equality:

> The special benefits side of the difference approach has not compensated for the differential of being second class. The special benefits rule is the only place in mainstream equality doctrine where you get to identify as a woman and not have that mean giving up all claim to equal treatment — but it comes close. Under its double standard, women who stand to inherit something when their husbands die have gotten the exclusion of a small percentage of the inheritance tax to the tune of Justice Douglas waxing eloquent about the difficulties of all women's economic situation. If we're going to be stigmatized as different, it would be nice if the compensation would fit the disparity.

Catharine A. MacKinnon, Feminism Unmodified: Discourses on Life and Law 38 (1987). What are the implications of this critique? See Chapter 3.

2. "Affirmative Action" in Employment

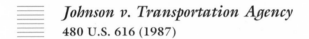

Johnson v. Transportation Agency
480 U.S. 616 (1987)

Justice BRENNAN delivered the opinion of the Court.

Respondent, Transportation Agency of Santa Clara County, California, unilaterally promulgated an Affirmative Action Plan applicable, *inter alia*, to promotions of employees. In selecting applicants for the promotional position of road dispatcher, the Agency, pursuant to the Plan, passed over petitioner Paul Johnson, a male employee, and promoted a female employee applicant, Diane Joyce. The question for decision is whether in making the promotion the Agency impermissibly took into account the sex of the applicants in violation of Title VII of the Civil Rights Act of 1964.... The District Court for the Northern District of California ... held that respondent had violated Title VII. The Court of Appeals for the Ninth Circuit reversed.... We affirm.[2]

I

In December 1978, the Santa Clara County Transit District Board of Supervisors adopted an Affirmative Action Plan (Plan) for the County Transportation Agency. The Plan implemented a County Affirmative Action Plan, which had been adopted, declared the County, because "mere prohibition of discriminatory practices is not enough to remedy the effects of past practices and to permit attainment of an equitable representation of minorities, women

2. No Constitutional issue was either raised or addressed in the litigation below.... We therefore decide in this case only the issue of hte prohibitory scope of Title VII....

and handicapped persons."... Relevant to this case, the Agency Plan provides that, in making promotions to positions within a traditionally segregated job classification in which women have been significantly underrepresented, the Agency is authorized to consider as one factor the sex of a qualified applicant.

In reviewing the composition of its work force, the Agency noted in its Plan that women were represented in numbers far less than their proportion of the County labor force in both the Agency as a whole and in five of seven job categories. Specifically, while women constituted 36.4% of the area labor market, they composed only 22.4% of Agency employees. Furthermore, women working at the Agency were concentrated largely in EEOC job categories traditionally held by women: women made up 76% of Office and Clerical Workers, but only 7.1% of Agency Officials and Administrators, 8.6% of Professionals, 9.7% of Technicians, and 22% of Service and Maintenance Workers. As for the job classification relevant to this case, none of the 238 Skilled Craft Worker positions was held by a woman.... The Plan noted that this underrepresentation of women in part reflected the fact that women had not traditionally been employed in these positions, and that they had not been strongly motivated to seek training or employment in them "because of the limited opportunities that have existed in the past for them to work in such classifications."... The Plan also observed that, while the proportion of ethnic minorities in the Agency as a whole exceeded the proportion of such minorities in the County work force, a smaller percentage of minority employees held management, professional, and technical positions.

The Agency stated that its Plan was intended to achieve "a statistically measurable yearly improvement in hiring, training, and promotion of minorities and women throughout the Agency in all major job classifications where they are underrepresented."... As a benchmark by which to evaluate progress, the Agency stated that its long-term goal was to attain a work force whose composition reflected the proportion of minorities and women in the area labor force.... Thus, for the Skilled Craft category in which the road dispatcher position at issue here was classified, the Agency's aspiration was that eventually about 36% of the jobs would be occupied by women....

The Agency's Plan ... set aside no specific number of positions for minorities or women, but authorized the consideration of ethnicity or sex as a factor when evaluating qualified candidates for jobs in which members of such groups were poorly represented. One such job was the road dispatcher position that is the subject of the dispute in this case....

On December 12, 1979, the Agency announced a vacancy for the promotional position of road dispatcher in the Agency's Roads Division. Dispatchers assign road crews, equipment, and materials, and maintain records pertaining to road maintenance jobs.... The position requires at minimum four years of dispatch or road maintenance work experience for Santa Clara County. The EEOC job classification scheme designates a road dispatcher as a Skilled Craft Worker.

Twelve County employees applied for the promotion, including Joyce and Johnson. Joyce had worked for the County since 1970, serving as an account clerk until 1975. She had applied for a road dispatcher position in 1974, but was deemed ineligible because she had not served as a road maintenance worker. In 1975, Joyce transferred from a senior account clerk position to a road maintenance worker position, becoming the first woman to fill such a job.... During her four years in that position, she occasionally worked out of class as a road dispatcher.

Petitioner Johnson began with the County in 1967 as a road yard clerk, after private employment that included working as a supervisor and dispatcher. He had also unsuccessfully applied for the road dispatcher opening in 1974. In 1977, his clerical position was downgraded, and he sought and received a transfer to the position of road maintenance worker.... He also occasionally worked out of class as a dispatcher while performing that job.

Nine of the applicants, including Joyce and Johnson, were deemed qualified for the job, and were interviewed by a two-person board. Seven of the applicants scored above 70 on this interview, which meant that they were certified as eligible for selection by the appointing authority. The scores awarded ranged from 70 to 80. Johnson was tied for second with a score of 75, while Joyce ranked next with a score of 73. A second interview was conducted by three Agency supervisors, who ultimately recommended that Johnson be promoted. Prior to the second interview, Joyce had contacted the County's Affirmative Action Office because she feared that her application might not receive disinterested review.[5] The Office in turn contacted the Agency's Affirmative Action Coordinator, whom the Agency's Plan makes responsible for, *inter alia*, keeping the Director informed of opportunities for the Agency to accomplish its objectives under the Plan. At the time, the Agency employed no women in any Skilled Craft position, and had never employed a woman as a road dispatcher. The Coordinator recommended to the Director of the Agency, James Graebner, that Joyce be promoted.

Graebner, authorized to choose any of the seven persons deemed eligible, thus had the benefit of suggestions by the second interview panel and by the Agency Coordinator in arriving at his decision. After deliberation, Graebner concluded that the promotion should be given to Joyce. As he testified: "I tried to look at the whole picture, the combination of her qualifications and Mr. Johnson's qualifications, their test scores, their expertise, their background, affirmative action matters, things like that.... I believe it was a combination of all those."...

---

5. Joyce testified that she had had disagreements with two of the three members of the second interview panel. One had been her first supervisor when she began work as a road maintenance worker. In performing arduous work in this job, she had not been issued coveralls, although her male co-workers had received them. After ruining her pants, she complained to her supervisor, to no avail. After three other similar incidents, ruining clothes on each occasion, she filed a grievance, and was issued four pairs of coveralls the next day.... Joyce had dealt with a second member of the panel for a year and a half in her capacity as chair of the Roads Operation Safety Committee, where she and he "had several differences of opinion on how safety should be implemented."... In addition, Joyce testified that she had informed the person responsible for arranging her second interview that she had a disaster preparedness class on a certain day the following week. By this time about 10 days had passed since she had notified this person of her availability, and no date had yet been set for the interview. Within a day or two after this conversation, however, she received a notice setting her interview at a time directly in the middle of her disaster preparedness class.... This same panel member had earlier described Joyce as a "rebel-rousing, skirt-wearing person."...

The certification form naming Joyce as the person promoted to the dispatcher position stated that both she and Johnson were rated as well qualified for the job. The evaluation of Joyce read: "Well qualified by virtue of 18 years of past clerical experience including $3\frac{1}{2}$ years at West Yard plus almost 5 years as a [road maintenance worker]." . . . The evaluation of Johnson was as follows: "Well qualified applicant; two years of [road maintenance worker] experience plus 11 years of Road Yard Clerk. Has had previous outside Dispatch experience but was 13 years ago." . . . Graebner testified that he did not regard as significant the fact that Johnson scored 75 and Joyce 73 when interviewed by the two-person board. . . .

Petitioner Johnson filed a complaint with the EEOC alleging that he had been denied promotion on the basis of sex in violation of Title VII. . . .

II

As a preliminary matter, we note that petitioner bears the burden of establishing the invalidity of the Agency's Plan. . . .

The assessment of the legality of the Agency Plan must be guided by our decision in Steelworkers v. Weber, [443 U.S. 193 (1979)]. In that case, the Court addressed the question whether the employer violated Title VII by adopting a voluntary affirmative action plan designed to "eliminate manifest racial imbalances in traditionally segregated job categories." [Id. at 197.] The respondent employee in that case challenged the employer's denial of his application for a position in a newly established craft training program, contending that the employer's selection process impermissibly took into account the race of the applicants. The selection process was guided by an affirmative action plan, which provided that 50% of the new trainees were to be black until the percentage of black skilled craftworkers in the employer's plant approximated the percentage of blacks in the local labor force. Adoption of the plan had been prompted by the fact that only 5 of 273, or 1.83%, of skilled craftworkers at the plant were black, even though the work force in the area was approximately 39% black. Because of the historical exclusion of blacks from craft positions, the employer regarded its former policy of hiring trained outsiders as inadequate to redress the imbalance in its work force.

We upheld the employer's decision to select less senior black applicants over the white respondent, for we found that taking race into account was consistent with Title VII's objective of "break[ing] down old patterns of racial segregation and hierarchy." Id. at 208. As we stated:

> It would be ironic indeed if a law triggered by a Nation's concern over centuries of racial injustice and intended to improve the lot of those who had "been excluded from the American dream for so long" constituted the first legislative prohibition of all voluntary, private, race-conscious efforts to abolish traditional patterns of racial segregation and hierarchy.

Id. at 204 (quoting remarks of Sen. Humphrey, 110 Cong. Rec. 6552 (1964)).

We noted that the plan did not "unnecessarily trammel the interests of the white employees," since it did not require "the discharge of white workers and their replacement with new black hirees." [443 U.S. at 208.] Nor did the plan create "an absolute bar to the advancement of white employees," since half of those trained in the new program were to be white.... Finally, we observed that the plan was a temporary measure, not designed to maintain racial balance, but to "eliminate a manifest racial imbalance."... As Justice Blackmun's concurrence made clear, *Weber* held that an employer seeking to justify the adoption of a plan need not point to its own prior discriminatory practices, nor even to evidence of an "arguable violation" on its part. Id. at 212. Rather, it need point only to a "conspicuous...imbalance in traditionally segregated job categories." Id. at 209. Our decision was grounded in the recognition that voluntary employer action can play a crucial role in furthering Title VII's purpose of eliminating the effects of discrimination in the workplace, and that Title VII should not be read to thwart such efforts. Id. at 204.

In reviewing the employment decision at issue in this case, we must first examine whether that decision was made pursuant to a plan prompted by concerns similar to those of the employer in *Weber*. Next, we must determine whether the effect of the Plan on males and nonminorities is comparable to the effect of the Plan in that case.

The first issue is therefore whether consideration of the sex of applicants for Skilled Craft jobs was justified by the existence of a "manifest imbalance" that reflected underrepresentation of women in "traditionally segregated job categories." Id. at 197. In determining whether an imbalance exists that would justify taking sex or race into account, a comparison of the percentage of minorities or women in the employer's work force with the percentage in the area labor market or general population is appropriate in analyzing jobs that require no special expertise....Where a job requires special training, however, the comparison should be with those in the labor force who possess the relevant qualifications....

A manifest imbalance need not be such that it would support a prima facie case against the employer...since we do not regard as identical the constraints of Title VII and the Federal Constitution on voluntarily adopted affirmative action plans. Application of the "prima facie" standard in Title VII cases would be inconsistent with *Weber*'s focus on statistical imbalance, and could inappropriately create a significant disincentive for employers to adopt an affirmative action plan....

As the Agency Plan recognized, women were most egregiously underrepresented in the Skilled Craft job category, since none of the 238 positions was occupied by a woman....

[H]ad the Plan simply calculated imbalances in all categories according to the proportion of women in the area labor pool, and then directed that hiring be governed solely by those figures, its validity fairly could be called into question. This is because analysis of a more specialized labor pool normally is necessary in determining underrepresentation in some positions. If a plan failed to take distinctions in qualifications into account in providing guidance for actual employment decisions, it would dictate mere blind hiring by the numbers....

The Agency's plan emphatically did not authorize such blind hiring. It expressly directed that numerous factors be taken into account....

We next consider whether the Agency Plan unnecessarily trammeled the rights of male employees or created an absolute bar to their advancement. In contrast to the plan in *Weber*, which provided that 50% of the positions in the craft training program were exclusively for blacks, . . . the Plan sets aside no positions for women. The Plan expressly states that "[t]he 'goals' established for each Division should not be construed as 'quotas' that must be met." . . . Rather, the Plan merely authorizes that consideration be given to affirmative action concerns when evaluating qualified applicants. As the Agency Director testified, the sex of Joyce was but one of numerous factors he took into account in arriving at his decision. . . . The Plan thus resembles the "Harvard Plan" approvingly noted by Justice Powell in Regents of University of California v. Bakke, [438 U.S. 265, 316-319 (1978)], which considers race along with other criteria in determining admission to the college. As Justice Powell observed: "In such an admissions program, race or ethnic background may be deemed a 'plus' in a particular applicant's file, yet it does not insulate the individual from comparison with all other candidates for the available seats." Id. at 317. Similarly, the Agency Plan requires women to compete with all other qualified applicants. No persons are automatically excluded from consideration; all are able to have their qualifications weighed against those of other applicants.

In addition, petitioner had no absolute entitlement to the road dispatcher position. Seven of the applicants were classified as qualified and eligible, and the Agency Director was authorized to promote any of the seven. Thus, denial of the promotion unsettled no legitimate, firmly rooted expectation on the part of petitioner. . . .

Finally, the Agency's Plan was intended to attain a balanced work force, not to maintain one. The Plan contains 10 references to the Agency's desire to "attain" such a balance, but no reference whatsoever to a goal of maintaining it. . . .

Express assurance that a program is only temporary may be necessary if the program actually sets aside positions according to specific numbers. . . . In this case, however, substantial evidence shows that the Agency has sought to take a moderate, gradual approach to eliminating the imbalance in its work force, one which establishes realistic guidance for employment decisions, and which visits minimal intrusion on the legitimate expectations of other employees. . . .

Justice STEVENS, concurring.

While I join the Court's opinion, I write separately to explain my view of this case's position in our evolving antidiscrimination law and to emphasize that the opinion does not establish the permissible outer limits of voluntary programs undertaken by employers to benefit disadvantaged groups.

I

Antidiscrimination measures may benefit protected groups in two distinct ways. As a sword, such measures may confer benefits by specifying that a person's membership in a disadvantaged group must be a neutral, irrelevant factor in governmental or private decisionmaking or, alternatively, by compelling decisionmakers to give favorable consideration to disadvantaged group status. As a shield, an antidiscrimination statute can also help a member of a protected class by assuring decisionmakers in some instances that, when they elect for good reasons of their own to grant a preference of some sort to a minority citizen, they will not violate the law. The Court properly holds that the statutory shield allowed respondent to take Diane Joyce's sex into account in promoting her to the road dispatcher position. . . .

It remains clear that the [Civil Rights] Act does not require any employer to grant preferential treatment on the basis of race or gender, but since 1978 the Court has unambiguously interpreted the statute to permit the voluntary adoption of special programs to benefit members of the minority groups for whose protection the statute was enacted. . . .

II. . .

Given the interpretation of the statute the Court adopted in *Weber*, I see no reason why the employer has any duty, prior to granting a preference to a qualified minority employee, to determine whether his past conduct might constitute an arguable violation of Title VII. Indeed, in some instances the employer may find it more helpful to focus on the future. Instead of retroactively scrutinizing his own or society's possible exclusions of minorities in the past to determine the outer limits of a valid affirmative-action program — or indeed, any particular affirmative-action decision — in many cases the employer will find it more appropriate to consider other legitimate [diversity-related] reasons to give preferences to members of under-represented groups. Statutes enacted for the benefit of minority groups should not block these forward-looking considerations. . . . The Court today does not foreclose other voluntary decisions based in part on a qualified employee's membership in a disadvantaged group. Accordingly, I concur.

Justice O'CONNOR, concurring in the judgment. . . .

In my view, the proper initial inquiry in evaluating the legality of an affirmative action plan by a public employer under Title VII is no different from that required by the Equal Protection Clause. In either case, consistent with the congressional intent to provide some measure of protection to the interests of the employer's nonminority employees, the employer must have had a firm basis for believing that remedial action was required. An employer would have such a firm basis if it can point to a statistical disparity sufficient to support a prima facie claim under Title VII by the employee beneficiaries of the affirmative action plan of a pattern or practice claim of discrimination. . . .

As I read *Weber* . . . the Court . . . determined that Congress had balanced [its intent to root out invidious discrimination against any person on the basis of race or gender, and its goal of eliminating the lasting effects of discrimination against minorities] by permitting affirmative action only as a remedial device to eliminate actual or apparent discrimination or the lingering effects of this discrimination.

Contrary to the intimations in Justice Stevens' concurrence, this Court did not approve preferences for minorities "for any reason that might seem sensible from a business or a social point of view." . . . I concur in the judgment of the Court.

Justice WHITE, dissenting.

I agree with Parts I and II of Justice Scalia's dissenting opinion. Although I do not join Part III, I also would overrule *Weber.* . . .

Justice SCALIA, with whom THE CHIEF JUSTICE joins, and with whom Justice WHITE joins in Parts I and II, dissenting. . . .

The Court today completes the process of converting [Title VII] from a guarantee that race or sex will *not* be the basis for employment determinations, to a guarantee that it often *will*. Ever so subtly, without even alluding to the last obstacles preserved by earlier opinions that we now push out of our path, we effectively replace the goal of a discrimination-free society with the quite incompatible goal of proportionate representation by race and by sex in the workplace. . . .

I

Several salient features of the plan [at issue in this case] should be noted. Most importantly, the plan's purpose was assuredly not to remedy prior sex discrimination by the Agency. It could not have been, because there was no prior sex discrimination to remedy. The majority, in cataloging the Agency's alleged misdeeds . . . neglects to mention the District Court's finding that the Agency "has not discriminated in the past, and does not discriminate in the present against women in regard to employment opportunities in general and promotions in particular." . . . This finding was not disturbed by the Ninth Circuit.

Not only was the plan not directed at the results of past sex discrimination by the Agency, but its objective was not to achieve the state of affairs that this Court has dubiously assumed would result from an absence of discrimination — an overall work force "more or less representative of the racial and ethnic composition of the population in the community." Teamsters v. United States, [431 U.S. 324, 340, n.20 (1977)]. Rather, the oft-stated goal was to mirror the racial and sexual composition of the entire county labor force, not merely in the Agency work force as a whole, but in each and every individual job category at the Agency. In a discrimination-free world, it would obviously be a statistical oddity for every job category to match the racial and sexual composition of even that portion of the county work force *qualified* for that job; it would be utterly miraculous for each of them to match, as the plan expected, the composition of the entire work force. Quite obviously, the plan did not seek to replicate what a lack of discrimination would produce, but rather imposed racial and sexual tailoring that would, in defiance of normal expectations and laws of probability, give each protected racial and sexual group a governmentally determined "proper" proportion of each job category.

That the plan was not directed at remedying or eliminating the effects of past discrimination is most clearly illustrated by its description of what it regarded as the "Factors Hindering Goal Attainment" — i.e., the existing impediments to the racially and sexually representative work force that it pursued. The plan noted that it would be "difficult"...to attain its objective of across-the-board statistical parity in at least some job categories, because:

> a. Most of the positions require specialized training and experience. Until recently, relatively few minorities, women and handicapped persons sought entry into these positions. Consequently, the number of persons from these groups in the area labor force who possess the qualifications required for entry into such job classifications is limited....
>
> c. Many of the Agency positions where women are underrepresented involve heavy labor; e.g., Road Maintenance Worker. Consequently, few women seek entry into these positions....
>
> f. Many women are not strongly motivated to seek employment in job classifications where they have not been traditionally employed because of the limited opportunities that have existed in the past for them to work in such classifications....

That is, the qualifications and desires of women may fail to match the Agency's Platonic ideal of a work force. The plan concluded from this, of course, not that the ideal should be reconsidered, but that its attainment could not be immediate....

Finally, the one message that the plan unmistakably communicated was that concrete results were expected, and supervisory personnel would be evaluated on the basis of the affirmative-action numbers they produced....[S]upervisors were reminded of the need to give attention to affirmative action in every employment decision, and to explain their reasons for failing to hire women and minorities whenever there was an opportunity to do so....

The fact of discrimination against Johnson is much clearer, and its degree more shocking, than the majority and Justice O'Connor's concurrence opinion would suggest—largely because neither of them recites a single one of the District Court findings that govern this appeal....Worth mentioning, for example, is the trier of fact's determination that, if the Affirmative Action Coordinator had not intervened, "the decision as to whom to promote...would have been made by [the Road Operations Division Director]," ...who had recommended that Johnson be appointed to the position....Likewise, the even more extraordinary findings that James Graebner, the Agency Director who made the appointment, "did not inspect the applications and related examination records of either [Paul Johnson] or Diane Joyce before making his decision," ...and indeed "did little or nothing to inquire into the results of the interview process and conclusions which [were] described as of critical importance to the selection process." ...In light of these determinations, it is impossible to believe (or to think that the District Court believed) Graebner's self-serving statements relied upon by the majority and Justice O'Connor's concurrence, such as the assertion that he "tried to look at the whole picture, the combination of [Joyce's] qualifications and Mr. Johnson's qualifications, their test scores, their expertise, their background, affirmative action matters, things like that." ...It was evidently enough for Graebner to know that both candidates (in the words of Johnson's counsel, to which Graebner assented) "met the M.Q.'s, the minimum. Both were minimally qualified." ...

When asked whether he had "any basis" for determining whether one of the candidates was more qualified than the other, Graebner candidly answered, "No....As I've said, they both appeared, and my conversations with people tended to corroborate, that they were both capable of performing the work."...

After a 2-day trial, the District Court concluded that Diane Joyce's gender was "*the determining factor*"...in her selection for the position. Specifically, it found that "[b]ased upon the examination results and the departmental interview, [Mr. Johnson] was more qualified for the position of Road Dispatcher than Diane Joyce,"...that "[b]ut for [Mr. Johnson's] sex, male, he would have been promoted to the position of Road Dispatcher,"...and that "[b]ut for Diane Joyce's sex, female, she would not have been appointed to the position...." The Ninth Circuit did not reject these factual findings as clearly erroneous....

II

The most significant proposition of law established by today's decision is that racial or sexual discrimination is permitted under Title VII when it is intended to overcome the effect, not of the employer's own discrimination, but of societal attitudes that have limited the entry of certain races, or of a particular sex, into certain jobs....

In fact,...today's decision goes well beyond merely allowing racial or sexual discrimination in order to eliminate the effects of prior societal discrimination. The majority opinion often uses the phrase "traditionally segregated job category" to describe the evil against which the plan is legitimately (according to the majority) directed. As originally used in *Weber*, supra, that phrase described skilled jobs from which employers and unions had systematically and intentionally excluded black workers—traditionally segregated jobs, that is, in the sense of conscious, exclusionary discrimination. [See 443 U.S. at 197-198.] But that is assuredly not the sense in which the phrase is used here. It is absurd to think that the nationwide failure of road maintenance crews, for example, to achieve the Agency's ambition of 36.4% female representation is attributable primarily, if even substantially, to systematic exclusion of women eager to shoulder pick and shovel. It is a "traditionally segregated job category" not in the *Weber* sense, but in the sense that, because of longstanding social attitudes, it has not been regarded by women themselves as desirable work. Or as the majority opinion puts the point, quoting approvingly the Court of Appeals: "'A plethora of proof is hardly necessary to show that women are generally underrepresented in such positions and that strong social pressures weigh against their participation.'"... Given this meaning of the phrase, it is patently false to say that "[t]he requirement that the 'manifest imbalance' relate to a 'traditionally segregated job category' provides assurance...that sex or race will be taken into account in a manner consistent with Title VII's purpose of eliminating the effects of employment discrimination."... There are, of course, those who believe that the social attitudes which cause women themselves to avoid certain jobs and to favor others are as nefarious as conscious, exclusionary discrimination. Whether or not that is so (and there is assuredly no consensus on the point equivalent to our national consensus against intentional discrimination), the two phenomena are certainly distinct. And it is the alteration of social attitudes, rather than the elimination of discrimination, which today's decision approves as justification for state-enforced discrimination. This is an enormous expansion, undertaken without the slightest justification or analysis.

III...

In *Weber* itself... and in later decisions... this Court has repeatedly emphasized that *Weber* involved only a private employer.... [S]tate agencies, unlike private actors, are subject to the Fourteenth Amendment.... [I]t would be strange to construe Title VII to permit discrimination by public actors that the Constitution forbids.

In truth, however, the language of [Title VII] draws no distinction between private and public employers, and the only good reason for creating such a distinction would be to limit the damage of *Weber*. It would be better, in my view, to acknowledge that case as fully applicable precedent, and to use the Fourteenth Amendment ramifications — which *Weber* did not address and which are implicated for the first time here — as the occasion for reconsidering and overruling it....

[H]ollow is the Court's assurance that we would strike this plan down if it "failed to take distinctions in qualifications into account," because that "would dictate mere blind hiring by the numbers."... For what the Court means by "taking distinctions in qualifications into account" consists of no more than eliminating from the applicant pool those who are not even minimally qualified for the job. Once that has been done, once the promoting officer assures himself that all the candidates before him are "M.Q.'s" (minimally qualifieds), he can then ignore, as the Agency Director did here, how much better than minimally qualified some of the candidates may be, and can proceed to appoint from the pool solely on the basis of race or sex, until the affirmative action "goals" have been reached. The requirement that the employer "take distinctions in qualifications into account" thus turns out to be an assurance, not that candidates' comparative merits will always be considered, but only that none of the successful candidates selected over the others solely on the basis of their race or sex will be utterly unqualified. That may be of great comfort to those concerned with American productivity; and it is undoubtedly effective in reducing the effect of affirmative-action discrimination upon those in the upper strata of society, who (unlike road maintenance workers, for example) compete for employment in professional and semiprofessional fields where, for many reasons, including most notably the effects of past discrimination, the numbers of "M.Q." applicants from the favored groups are substantially less. But I fail to see how it has any relevance to whether selecting among final candidates solely on the basis of race or sex is permissible under Title VII....

It is impossible not to be aware that the practical effect of our holding is... effectively [to require] employers, public as well as private, to engage in intentional discrimination on the basis of race or sex. This Court's prior interpretations of Title VII, especially the decision in Griggs v. Duke Power Co., [401 U.S. 424 (1971)], subject employers to a potential Title VII suit whenever there is a noticeable imbalance in the representation of minorities or women in the employer's work force. Even the employer who is confident of ultimately prevailing in such a suit must contemplate the expense and adverse publicity of a trial.... If, however, employers are free to discriminate through affirmative action, without fear of "reverse discrimination" suits by their nonminority or male victims, they are offered a threshold defense against Title VII liability premised on numerical disparities. Thus, after today's decision the failure to engage in reverse discrimination is economic folly, and arguably a breach of duty to shareholders or taxpayers, wherever the cost of anticipated Title VII litigation exceeds the cost of hiring less capable (though still minimally capable) workers. (This situation is more likely to obtain, of course, with respect to the least skilled jobs—perversely creating an incentive to discriminate against precisely those members of the nonfavored groups least likely to have profited from societal discrimination in the past.) It is predictable, moreover, that this incentive will be greatly magnified by economic pressures brought to bear by government contracting agencies upon employers who refuse to discriminate in the fashion we have now approved. A statute designed to establish a color-blind and gender-blind workplace has thus been converted into a powerful engine of racism and sexism, not merely permitting intentional race- and sex-based discrimination, but often making it, through operation of the legal system, practically compelled.

It is unlikely that today's result will be displeasing to politically elected officials, to whom it provides the means of quickly accommodating the demands of organized groups to achieve concrete, numerical improvement in the economic status of particular constituencies. Nor will it displease the world of corporate and governmental employers (many of whom have filed briefs as amici in the present case, all on the side of Santa Clara) for whom the cost of hiring less qualified workers is often substantially less—and infinitely more predictable—than the cost of litigating Title VII cases and of seeking to convince federal agencies by nonnumerical means that no discrimination exists. In fact, the only losers in the process are the Johnsons of the country, for whom Title VII has been not merely repealed but actually inverted. The irony is that these individuals—predominantly unknown, unaffluent, unorganized—suffer this injustice at the hands of a Court fond of thinking itself the champion of the politically impotent. I dissent.

Notes

1. Affirmative Action: Definitions and Background. Affirmative action emerged in U.S. law in 1965, when President Lyndon Johnson approved Executive Order 11246, which was strengthened under President Nixon, and further modified under President Clinton. This order reflects affirmative action in its classic form: a requirement of proactive strategies to increase the representation of targeted groups. See Faye J. Crosby, Affirmative Action is Dead: Long Live Affirmative Action 7 (2004). It requires firms over a certain size doing a certain level of business with the federal government to employ qualified individuals from targeted groups in percentages roughly proportional to their representation in the available applicant pool. If those groups are underrepresented, the employer must develop a corrective plan and make good faith efforts to implement it. Another form of affirmative action involves "set asides" — preferences for targeted groups in the government contracting process. The concept originated in the preferences for small businesses adopted in the 1950s, was extended in the 1970s to encompass minority-owned businesses, and was further extended in the 1980s to include women-owned businesses. See Women's Business and Ownership Act, Pub. L. No. 100-533, 102 Stat. 2689 (1988). The federal government has between 150 and 200 other laws and regulations mandating some form of affirmative action. Most are precatory: they express a desire for proactive strategies but not methods of implementation or sanctions for noncompliance. See Crosby, supra, at 7; C.V. Dale, Congressional Research Service Report to Robert Dole: Compilation and Overview of Federal Laws and Regulations Establishing Affirmative Action Goals or Other Actions Based on Race, Gender, or Ethnicity (1995). About one-fifth of American employees work for the United States government or for contractors and subcontractors who are subject to federal affirmative action requirements. Many more workers are covered by state or local mandates or voluntary private sector plans. Crosby, supra, at 9.

Affirmative action plans vary across multiple dimensions: who they cover; whether they are voluntarily adopted or imposed under law or court order; and what strategies they require. At one end of the spectrum are programs that focus on recruitment and training; they aim to expand the group of qualified applicants. At the other end of the spectrum are quotas for underrepresented groups. In between are various forms of goals, timetables, and tie-breaking preferences that give favorable treatment when applicants are equally qualified. See generally Peter Schuck, Diversity in America 139-140 (2003).

The different opinions in *Johnson* represent the range of judicial perspectives in affirmative action cases. Shifts in the make-up of the Court as well as changes in public attitudes about affirmative action, however, have created considerable uncertainty about the continued legality of preferential treatment. One significant development was the Supreme Court's approach to race-based minority set-aside programs. In a departure from prior precedents, the Supreme Court in City of Richmond v. J.A. Croson Co., 488 U.S. 469 (1989) invalidated under a "strict scrutiny" standard a city ordinance setting aside 30 percent of its contracting work for minority-owned businesses. In so doing, the Court made it clear that the strict standard could be satisfied only by a showing of past discrimination by the city itself. In Adarand Constructors, Inc. v. Pena, 515 U.S. 200 (1995), the Court applied the same standard to a federal government set-aside mandate, reversing its prior deference to Congress in determining how to effectuate equal protection guarantees.

Reversals of government-sponsored affirmative action plans have also occurred at the state level. For example, in 1996, California voters passed the California Civil Rights Initiative (Proposition 209) which prohibits "discrimination against, or . . . preferential treatment to, any individual on the basis of race, sex, color, ethnicity, or national origin in the operation of public employment, public education, or public contracting." Proposition 209 was upheld in both federal and state courts. Coalition for Economic Equity v. Wilson, 110 F.3d 1445-1448 (9th Cir. 1997), cert. denied, 522 U.S. 963 (1997); Hi-Voltage Wire Works,

Inc. v. City of San Jose, 12 P.3d 1068, 1083 (Cal. 2000). Proposition 209 is considered further in the context of education opportunity on p. 186, infra. Other examples of the rollback of affirmative action follow in the notes below.

  2. Affirmative Action and Gender: A Separate Standard? After *Adarand*, a pivotal question is whether affirmative action plans on behalf of women should be reviewed under the same standard as race-based plans. On the one hand, the standard of review is well established: a sex-based classification must serve important governmental objectives and be substantially related to those objectives or, more recently, supported "by an exceedingly persuasive justification." See United States v. Virginia, 518 U.S. 515 (1996), set forth on p. 260 of this chapter. This is intermediate, not strict, scrutiny. On the other hand, given the objective of affirmative action — to reverse the effects of past discrimination and/or to enhance diversity — there is no obvious reason why gender-based affirmative action should be treated more leniently than race-based plans. Indeed, if race is the more suspect category, it seems perverse to impose greater barriers to ending past race discrimination than to eliminating past sex discrimination.

  Courts have not been entirely consistent in dealing with this issue. The Sixth Circuit Court of Appeals has applied the same strict scrutiny to sex-based preferences as the law requires in reviewing race-based preferences. See, e.g., Brunet v. City of Columbus, 1 F.3d 390 (6th Cir. 1993), cert. denied, 510 U.S. 1164 (1994) (striking down preferences to female applicants in the city's fire department, under strict scrutiny test). See also Long v. City of Saginaw, 911 F.2d 1192, 1196 (6th Cir. 1990) (same test applied to both minorities and women). For a recent application of this approach, see Builders Association v. City of Chicago, 298 F. Supp. 2d 725 (N.D. Ill. 2005). See also Mallory v. Harkness, 895 F. Supp. 1556 (S.D. Fla. 1995), aff'd, 109 F.3d 771 (11th Cir. 1997) (invalidating the Florida Bar Board's quota system for filling vacancies on the judicial Nominating Commission to guarantee seats for minorities or women).

  Other Circuit Courts of Appeal, in examining affirmative action plans favoring both minorities and women, have applied intermediate scrutiny to sex-based preferences. See, e.g., Dallas Fire Fighters Association v. City of Dallas, 150 F.3d 438 (5th Cir. 1998), cert. denied, 526 U.S. 1038 (1999); Engineering Contractors Association v. Metropolitan Dade County, 122 F.3d 895 (11th Cir. 1997), cert. denied, 523 U.S. 1004 (1998); Concrete Works, Inc. v. City & County of Denver, 36 F.3d 1513 (10th Cir. 1994), cert. denied, 514 U.S. 1004 (1995). See also Associated Utility Contractors of Maryland v. City of Baltimore, 83 F. Supp. 2d 613 (D. Md. 2000) (set-aside programs for minorities and women both "arbitrary," under strict scrutiny test applied to race-based programs, and under intermediate standard applied to sex-based programs).

  Most of these courts have noted that in establishing an important governmental interest, past discrimination must be shown, but not necessarily discrimination by the governmental entity whose affirmative action plan is in dispute. See, e.g., Ensley Branch, N.A.A.C.P. v. City of Birmingham, 31 F.3d 1548, 1580 (11th Cir. 1994) (gender-conscious affirmative action requires demonstration of "some past discrimination against women, but not necessarily discrimination by the government itself"); Coral Construction Co. v. King County, 941 F.2d 910, 932 (9th Cir. 1991), cert. denied, 502 U.S. 1033 (1992) ("some degree of discrimination must have occurred in a particular field before a gender-specific remedy may be instituted" but intermediate scrutiny "does not require any showing of governmental involvement . . . in the discrimination it seeks to remedy"). Moreover, to an extent not apparent in judicial analysis of race-based affirmative action plans, courts emphasize that the purpose for reviewing gender-based discrimination is to make sure that sex-based rules are not based on archaic stereotypes. See, e.g., Contractors Association of Eastern Pennsylvania v. City of Philadelphia, 6 F.3d 990, 1010 (3d Cir. 1993), cert. denied, 519 U.S. 1113 (1997) (affirmative action plan favoring women will pass intermediate scrutiny if it is shown to be "a product of analysis rather than a stereotyped reaction based on habit").

   3. Public Opinion and Affirmative Action. A wide array of polling data and empirical research is available on affirmative action, both in the employment and the education contexts. (Higher education is explored more fully starting on p. 177, infra.) For a comprehensive survey, see Faye J. Crosby, Affirmative Action is Dead: Long Live Affirmative Action 75-94, 175-220 (2004).

   Whether people say they support affirmative action depends on the way the plan is described, and how the question is asked. In general, support is much lower for quotas or for "preferential treatment" than for other strategies that seek to equalize opportunities or that take qualifications into account. See id. at 75-81. The vast majority of Americans, including about a third of African Americans and over two thirds of Hispanics, say that they are opposed to racial preferences in hiring and promotion. Peter Schuck, Diversity in America 170 (2003). See also Crosby, supra, at 191-193.

   Most surveys reflect between 10 to 20 percent greater popular support for affirmative action programs on behalf of women than for programs on behalf of African Americans. See Dara Z. Strolovitch, Playing Favorites: Public Attitudes Toward Race- and Gender-Targeted Anti-Discrimination Policy, 10 Nat'l Women's Stud. Ass'n J. 27 (Fall 1998). However, the gap is narrower when questions on preferences for women immediately precede questions on preferences for men, which suggests a "reciprocity" effect. Charlotte Steeh & Maria Krysan, The Polls-Trends: Affirmative Action and the Public, 1970-1995, 60 Public Opinion Q. 128, 137 (1996). Those who believe that sex discrimination is no longer a problem or that women's requests for equality are exaggerated tend to oppose preferential treatment. See Francine Tougas et al., Men's Attitudes Toward Affirmative Action Justice and Intergroup Relations at the Crossroads, 8 Soc. Justice Res. 57 (1995).

   Self-interest is also a factor, as was evident in an experiment in which men and women took a test which they thought measured creativity. Test-takers were told that researchers had reason to suspect that the test was biased, in that women who had a certain cut-off score would be preferred for placement in a "high creativity" group over men who scored higher, and men would be included only if not enough qualified women were available. Both men and women who passed the test were more likely to believe that the process was fair than those who failed. Kimberly J. Matheson et al., Reactions to Affirmative Action: Seeking the Basis for Resistance, 30 J. Applied J. Soc. Psych. 1013, 1021 (2000). For other evidence of self-interest, see Strolovitch, supra; Crosby, supra, at 216.

Support for affirmative action is greater when specific practices are described, when policies are characterized in terms of promoting diversity rather than giving preferences, and when socially usefully functions are presented. See Crosby, supra, at 138-141(describing studies).

Should public opinion matter when it comes to evaluating the validity of an affirmative action measure?

4. Women's "Choices": Explanation or Symptom of Gender Inequality? In his dissent in *Johnson*, Justice Scalia attributes women's underrepresentation in traditionally male job categories to women's choices. In his view, it is "absurd" to think that women could be "eager to shoulder pick and shovel." Could he be right? What is the basis for his assumption?

Women's interest in traditionally male occupations was focus of a widely discussed lawsuit by the Equal Employment Opportunity Commission (EEOC) against Sears, Roebuck & Co. in the late 1980s. The suit alleged a nationwide pattern and practice of discriminating against women for commission sales positions. To support its claim, the EEOC offered extensive statistical evidence that women who applied for sales positions were less likely than men with similar qualifications to receive high-paying commission jobs involving "big ticket" items, such as major appliances, furnaces, roofing, and tires. Rather, women disproportionately ended up in non-commission lower-paying jobs selling apparel, linen, toys, paint, and cosmetics. In defending its employment practices, Sears introduced testimony by a female historian, Rosalind Rosenberg, that such patterns were consistent with women's traditional preferences, including their reluctance to work irregular hours, their desire for "social contact and friendship," and their discomfort with the stress of competitive pay structures. The trial court found such evidence more credible than testimony by other historians called by the EEOC, who asserted that women are influenced by the opportunities presented to them, and have been eager to take higher paying nontraditional jobs when such options have been available.

The evidence in the case was also that Sears relied on tests that measured applicants' "vigor" by reference to their views on boxing, wrestling, and swearing, and one witness explained that female employees weren't in higher paid retail sales positions because they "didn't like going outside when it's snowing, raining, or whatever." Sears had taken no steps that might have made the higher paid positions more attractive to women, such as flexible schedules or support programs. EEOC v. Sears, Roebuck & Co., 628 F. Supp. 1264, 1307 (N.D. Ill. 1986), aff'd, 839 F.2d 302 (7th Cir. 1988). Should this evidence have concerned the court? The judgment for Sears was affirmed on appealed, over the dissent of Judge Cudahy who challenged the stereotypes implicit in the court's analysis and its failure to recognize the employer's role in shaping the interests of applicants. 839 F.2d at 361 (Cudahy, J., dissenting).

Is the *Sears* case about stereotypes? Or is there a larger problem?

[T]he liberal approach misses the ways in which employers draw upon societal gender relations to produce sex segregation at work. The liberal prohibition against stereotyping assumes that the problem is that the employer has inaccurately identified the job interests of (at least some exceptional) women who have already formed preferences for nontraditional work. By stopping at this level of analysis, however, liberal courts fail to inquire into or discover the deeper process through which employers actively shape women's work aspirations along gendered lines.... [For example, through] their recruiting strategies, employers do more than simply publicize job vacancies to those who are already interested: They actually stimulate interest among those they hope to attract to the jobs.

Vicki Schultz, Telling Stories About Women and Work: Judicial Interpretations of Sex Segregation in the Workplace in Title VII Cases Raising the Lack of Interest Argument, 103 Harv. L. Rev. 1749, 1808 (1990). To what extent does the affirmative action plan at issue in *Johnson* address Schultz's concern?

Despite affirmative programs, some industries remain highly segregated by sex. Figures from the 2000 census reveal that less than ten percent of precision production, craft, and repair workers are women. U.S. Dep't of Labor, Bureau of Labor Statistics, Highlights of Women's Earnings in 2000, Report 952, at 8 (August 2001). Similarly, less than five percent of transportation and material moving occupations are women, only around ten percent of all engineers are women, and less than twelve percent of those in the farming, forestry, and fishing industries are women. Id. Conversely, over ninety-nine percent of pre-kindergarten and kindergarten teachers are women, and nearly eighty percent of administrative and clerical support are women. Id at 9. Is this a cause of concern, or a neutral fact about preferences?

The "lack of interest" defense that prevailed in *Sears* was more successful in early sex discrimination cases than it was in race discrimination cases, although the statistical gap closed as courts narrowed the ways that statistics could establish a valid claim. Vicki Schultz & Stephen Petterson, Race, Gender, Work, and Choice: An Empirical Study of the Lack of Interest Defense in Title VII Cases Challenging Job Segregation, 59 U. Chi. L. Rev. 1073, 1081, 1097 (1992). Still, analysis of the facts of sampled cases suggests that judges view women's job preferences as more fixed and impervious to employer influence than job preferences of racial minorities. Id. at 1100-1135. Cf. Robert J. Gregory, You Can Call Me a "Bitch" Just Don't Use the "N-Word": Some Thoughts on Galloway v. General Motors Service Parts Operations and Rodgers v. Western-Southern Life Insurance Co., 46 DePaul L. Rev. 741 (1997) (arguing that courts are more likely to find other explanations for sexually harassing behavior and speech than for race-based harassment). Is this surprising? What follows, if anything, from this difference?

For a recent, vigorous defense of the "lack of interest" defense, see Neil Dishman, Defending the Lack of Interest Defense: Why Title VII Should Recognize Differing Job Interests Between the Sexes, 14 Geo. Mason U. Civ. Rts. L.J. 189 (2004).

5. Whose Discrimination May the State Attempt to Remedy? The debate over the validity of voluntary affirmative action plans is partly a debate about whose discrimination an employer may attempt voluntarily to remedy. The *Johnson* case reveals the range of options. To Justice Scalia, past discrimination by the employer itself is all that will justify such voluntary efforts. Justice O'Connor's opinion in *Johnson* does not require proof of past discrimination, but the employer must have had some "firm basis for believing that remedial action is required," e.g., a statistical disparity sufficient to support a prima facie claim of discrimination under Title VII. Justice O'Connor's opinion shifted in *Croson*, where she stated that an "amorphous claim that there has been past discrimination in a particular industry cannot justify use of an unyielding racial quota," 488 U.S. at 499, and in *Adarand* she essentially came over to Justice Scalia's position, having concluded that "all racial classifications...must be analyzed by a reviewing court under strict scrutiny." 515 U.S. at 227. For Justice Brennan, the important factor in *Johnson* is that the Agency had identified a substantial underrepresentation of women in "traditionally segregated job categories"—whatever the cause of that underrepresentation. To Justice Stevens, the past is even less important; it is enough that the employer concludes, on the basis of "forward-looking" considerations, that it would be beneficial to have a more balanced work force.

Note that in Kahn v. Shevin, the Court seemed satisfied that Florida was attempting to address societal discrimination rather than any past acts by the state itself. A difference in *Johnson*, besides the applicability of Title VII, is the existence of a specific "victim" who, according to the district court, would have gotten the job at issue were it not for Santa Clara's "affirmative action" plan. Even Justice Brennan's opinion seems to require that the interests of the non-minority employees not be "unnecessarily trammeled." Under what theory of equality should the cause of significant underrepresentation matter? Under an approach of formal equality, would the employer's own actions be conclusive? If women "choose" not to take advantage of an opportunity to enter a particular male-dominated occupation, does it matter why? Justice Scalia emphasizes the district court's finding that the county had no history of discrimination against women. Some commentators have charged that this finding was "incredible" and evidences the Court's greater difficulty in seeing sex-based discrimination than in seeing discrimination based on race:

> Prior to the affirmative action plan at issue in [Steelworkers v. Weber, 443 U.S. 193 (1979)], 1.83 percent (five out of 275) of the skilled craft workers were blacks in Kaiser's plan....(Compare zero women out of approximately 238 at the Agency prior to the affirmative action plan at issue in *Johnson*.) In *Weber*, the Court reversed the two lower court decisions holding Kaiser's plan illegal and noted that "[j]udicial findings of exclusion from crafts on racial grounds are so numerous as to make such exclusion a proper subject for judicial notice." Women, too, have been traditionally, explicitly, and routinely excluded from crafts, but—unlike the exclusion of blacks which was judicially noticed in *Weber*—women's exclusion was apparently invisible to all the judges deciding *Johnson*.

Mary Becker, Prince Charming: Abstract Equality, 1987 Sup. Ct. Rev. 201, 210. Is this a question of what counts as discrimination or of the capacity to see it?

6. Affirmative Action and the "Merit" Principle. One debate within the court in *Johnson* involves the relative costs and benefits of reducing reliance on ostensibly "objective" definitions of merit. Justice Brennan, citing an amicus curiae brief from the American Society for Personnel Administration, responds to the implicit charge that affirmative action leads to a flood of less qualified women and minority hires:

> It is a standard tenet of personnel administration that there is rarely a single, "best qualified" person for a job. An effective personnel system will bring before the selecting official several fully-qualified candidates who each may possess different attributes which recommend them for selection. Especially where the job is an unexceptional, middle-level craft position, without the need for unique work experience or educational attainment and for which several well-qualified candidates are available, final determinations as to which candidate is "best qualified" are at best subjective.

480 U.S. at 641 n.17.

Justice Scalia rejects this view entirely:

> [Acceptance of the brief's contention] effectively constitutes appellate reversal of a finding of fact by the District Court in the present case ("[P]laintiff was more qualified for the position of Road Dispatcher than Diane Joyce. . . ."). More importantly, it has staggering implications for future Title VII litigation, since the most common reason advanced for failing to hire a member of a protected group is the superior qualification of the hired individual.

480 U.S. at 675 n.5 (Scalia, J., dissenting).

Are you persuaded that Diane Joyce was less "qualified"? Is there an argument that a woman who compiled her record in a workplace with so much gender bias is at least as qualified as a man who scored marginally higher? Although many critics have worried that affirmative action programs will result in less qualified workers and accompanying losses in productivity, the research does not support these concerns. For example, one overview of the studies on point concluded:

> There is virtually no evidence of significantly weaker qualifications of performance among white women in establishments that practice affirmative action. . . . There is some evidence of lower qualifications for minorities hired under affirmative action programs, especially when such qualifications are measured using test scores or educational attainment. Evidence of lower performance among these minorities appears much less consistently or convincingly. . . .

Harry J. Holzer & David Neumark, Assessing Affirmative Action, 38 J. Econ. Lit. 483, 544 (2000). In the most systematic surveys on point, researchers have compared firms with strong affirmative action programs to firms without such commitments, and found no difference in employee performance and favorable differences in market performance. See Harry J. Holzer & David

Neumark, What Does Affirmative Action Do?, 53 Industrial & Labor Relations J. 240 (2000); Crosby, supra, at 111-112.

7. **"Positive Action" in European Law.** In Europe, "positive action" applies only to women, not to blacks or other minorities. Germany, Canada, and the European Union all have explicit constitutional commitments to maintaining gender affirmative action programs, and they have increasingly supported notions of substantive equality. For example, tax breaks are offered to firms who hire women in traditionally men-dominated fields, and advancement plans for women are sometimes mandated. Still, these commitments are mixed with legal rules that reflect the same tensions apparent in U.S. debates on affirmative action. For example, the European Court of Justice has upheld rules of priority for women, but they must have an exception when "reasons specific to an individual [male] candidate . . . [tilted] the balance in his favour." Marschall v. Land Nordrhein-Westfalen, Case C-409/95, 1997 E.C.R. I-6363, at para. 3. In Abrahamsson v. Fogelqvist, the European Court of Justice struck down an affirmative action measure in a case with a strikingly similar fact-pattern to *Johnson*, holding that giving preferential treatment to women was inconsistent with Europe's formal equality principles of equal treatment. Case C-407/98, 2000 E.C.R. I-5539. For recent cases, see Thomas Trelogan et al., Can't We Enlarge the Blanket and the Bed? A Comparative Analysis of Positive/Affirmative Action in the European Court of Justice and the United States Supreme Court, 28 Hastings Int'l & Comp. L. Rev. 39, 40-41 (2004); Christopher D. Totten, Constitutional Precommitments to Gender Affirmative Action in the European Union, Germany, Canada and the United States: A Comparative Approach, 21 Berkeley J. Int'l L. 27 (2003). For further discussion of positive action in the European Union in the context of women's pregnancy and childbearing, see pp. 224-225, 242-246.

8. **Diversity as an Alternative Rationale for Affirmative Action.** Does the goal of diversity offer a better theory for affirmative action than the elimination of past discrimination? Some advocates believe that it does, because it is forward looking; it "ascribes no guilt," requires no admission of prior discrimination, and focuses on the benefits to individuals and institutions. Eugene Volokh, Diversity, Race as Proxy, Religion as Proxy, 43 UCLA L. Rev. 2059, 2060 (1996). By contrast, other commentators claim that the diversity rationale deflects focus from responsibility for prior discrimination. Charles R. Lawrence, Two Views of the River: A Critique of the Liberal Defense of Affirmative Action, 101 Colum. L. Rev. 928, 966-968 (2001). Critics of the diversity rationale also claim that this rationale ignores diversity within groups, and offers no justification for the favored treatment of certain groups under contemporary affirmative action plans. For example, Peter Schuck claims that [a] group can only create diversity value if it possesses certain desired qualities *qua* group. . . . To affirm that a quality inheres in a racial group, however, is to essentialize race in a way that utterly contradicts liberal egalitarian, legal, scientific, and religious values." Peter Schuck, Diversity in America 165 (2003). Moreover, Schuck asks, how much diversity is enough and whose diversity counts?: "doesn't the perspective of Muslim or

fundamentalist Christian applicant have at least as much diversity value as that of a middle-class black or Hispanic?" Id. at 164. Does the Supreme Court give a satisfactory answer in Grutter v. Bollinger, excerpted at p. 177 below?

In an early case relying on diversity justifications for affirmative action, the Federal Communications Commission gave preferences to women in granting construction permits and operation licenses for radio and television stations. The rationale was that women

> are a general population group which has suffered from a discriminatory attitude in various fields of activity, and one which, partly as a consequence, has certain separate needs and interests with respect to which the inclusion of women in broadcast ownership and operation can be of value.

In re Application of Mid-Florida Television Corp., 70 F.C.C.2d 281, 326 (Rev. Bd. 1978), set aside on other grounds, 87 F.C.C.2d 203 (1981). A similar preference for certain racial minorities had been upheld by the United States Supreme Court in Metro Broadcasting, Inc. v. FCC, 497 U.S. 547 (1990), on the grounds that enhancing broadcast diversity was a sufficiently important governmental goal to justify the race-based policy. 497 U.S. at 567-568. *Metro Broadcast* was eventually overruled by *Adarand*, discussed on p. 168, supra. However, the FCC has continued to consider diversity in employment and programming to some extent. See Schuck, supra, at 141-142.

What do you suppose constitutes "women's programming"? What message does programming that is directed toward women tend to send? Assume that women-owned radio and television stations do broadcast more programming directed toward women. Is this likely to help change the attitudes that cause women to be underrepresented in male job categories? Or will "women's programming" perpetuate "archaic stereotypes" about separate women's interests and points of views? In another case striking down broadcasting preferences, dissenting Judge Abner Mikva rejected this last concern.

> [Congress] has not relied on stereotypes of any kind. It has not assumed that women "share some cohesive, collective viewpoint," Metro, [497 U.S. at 582], or that female journalists will approach stories about the federal budget, school prayer, voting rights, or foreign relations any differently than male journalists would.... Nor has Congress endorsed the similarly controversial proposition that men and women think differently about most questions. (If it had, the constitutional issue might be closer: the Fourteenth Amendment does not enact Ms. Betty Friedan's The Second Stage.) It has merely assumed that some female programmers will choose to emphasize different subjects — breast cancer, say, or glass ceilings in the workplace — than male programmers will. The assumption strikes me as innocuous to the point of being obvious.

Lamprecht v. FCC, 958 F.2d 382 (D.C. Cir. 1992) (Mikva, J., dissenting). Is Judge Mikva right that some female programmers will emphasize "different" subjects? Is that assumption "innocuous"? Realistic? Should it justify a sex-based preference? Consider that issue in light of Grutter v. Bollinger, in the next section.

3. Affirmative Action in Higher Education

≡≡≡ *Grutter v. Bollinger*
≡≡≡ 539 U.S. 306 (2003)

Justice O'CONNOR delivered the opinion of the Court, in which Justice STEVENS, Justice SOUTER, Justice GINSBURG, and Justice BREYER joined, and in which Justice SCALIA and Justice THOMAS joined insofar as it is consistent with the views expressed in Part VII of the opnion of Justice THOMAS.

This case requires us to decide whether the use of race as a factor in student admissions by the University of Michigan Law School (Law School) is unlawful.

A

The Law School ranks among the Nation's top law schools. It receives more than 3,500 applications each year for a class of around 350 students. Seeking to "admit a group of students who individually and collectively are among the most capable," the Law School looks for individuals with "substantial promise for success in law school" and "a strong likelihood of succeeding in the practice of law and contributing in diverse ways to the well-being of others." More broadly, the Law School seeks "a mix of students with varying backgrounds and experiences who will respect and learn from each other." . . .

The hallmark of that policy is its focus on academic ability coupled with a flexible assessment of applicants' talents, experiences, and potential "to contribute to the learning of those around them." The policy requires admissions officials to evaluate each applicant based on all the information available in the file, including a personal statement, letters of recommendation and an essay describing the ways in which the applicant will contribute to the life and diversity of the Law School. In reviewing an applicant's file, admissions officials must consider the applicant's undergraduate grade point average (GPA) and Law School Admissions Test (LSAT) score because they are important (if imperfect) predictors of academic success in law school. The policy stresses that "no applicant should be admitted unless we expect that applicant to do well enough to graduate with no serious academic problems."

The policy makes clear, however, that even the highest possible score does not guarantee admission to the Law School. Nor does a low score automatically disqualify an applicant. Ibid. Rather, the policy requires admissions officials to look beyond grades and test scores to other criteria that are important to the Law School's educational objectives. So-called "soft variables" such as "the enthusiasm of recommenders, the quality of the undergraduate institution, the quality of the applicant's essay, and the areas and difficulty of undergraduate course selection" are all brought to bear in assessing an "applicant's likely contributions to the intellectual and social life of the institution."

The policy aspires to "achieve that diversity which has the potential to enrich everyone's education and thus make a law school class stronger than the sum of its parts." The policy does not restrict the types of diversity contributions eligible for "substantial weight" in the admissions process, but instead recognizes "many possible bases for diversity admissions." The policy does, however, reaffirm the Law School's longstanding commitment to "one particular type of diversity," that is, "racial and ethnic diversity with special reference to the inclusion of students from groups which have been historically discriminated against, like African-Americans, Hispanics, and Native Americans, who without this commitment might not be represented in our student body in meaningful numbers. By enrolling a "'critical mass' of [underrepresented] minority students," the Law School seeks to "ensure their ability to make unique contributions to the character of the Law School."

The policy does not define diversity "solely in terms of racial and ethnic status." Nor is the policy "insensitive to the competition among all students for admission to the Law School." Rather, the policy seeks to guide admissions officers in "producing classes both diverse and academically outstanding classes made up of students who promise to continue the tradition of outstanding contribution by Michigan Graduates to the legal profession."

B

Petitioner Barbara Grutter is a white Michigan resident who applied to the Law School in 1996 with a 3.8 grade point average and 151 LSAT score. The Law School initially placed petitioner on a waiting list, but subsequently rejected her application. In December, 1997, petitioner filed suit [alleging] ... her application was rejected because the Law School uses race as a "predominant" factor, giving applicants who belong to certain minority groups "a significantly greater chance of admission than students with similar credentials from disfavored racial groups." Petitioner also alleged that respondents "had no compelling interest to justify their use of race in the admissions process." Petitioner requested compensatory and punitive damages, an order requiring the Law School to offer her admission, and an injunction prohibiting the Law school from continuing to discriminate on the basis of race. . . .

During the 15-day bench trial, the parties introduced extensive evidence concerning the Law School's use of race in the admissions process. Dennis Shields, Director of Admissions when petitioner applied to the Law School, testified that he did not direct his staff to admit a particular percentage or number of minority students, but rather to consider an applicant's race along with all other factors. Shields testified that at the height of the admissions season, he would frequently consult the so-called "daily reports" that kept track of the racial and ethnic composition of the class (along with other information such as residency status and gender). This was done, Shields testified, to ensure that a critical mass of under-represented minority students would be reached so as to realize the educational benefits of a diverse student body. Ibid. Shields stressed, however, that he did not seek to admit any particular number or percentage of under-represented minority students. . . .

Dr. Stephen Raudenbush, the Law School's expert, focused on the predicted effect of eliminating race as a factor in the Law School's admission process. In Dr. Raudenbush's view, a race-blind admissions system would have a "very dramatic," negative effect on underrepresented minority admissions. He testified that in 2000, 35 percent of underrepresented minority applicants were admitted. Dr. Raudenbush predicted that if race were not considered, only 10 percent of those applicants would have been admitted. Under this scenario, underrepresented minority students would have comprised 4 percent of the entering class in 2000 instead of the actual figure of 14.5 percent.

In the end, the District Court concluded that the Law School's use of race as a factor in admissions decisions was unlawful.... Sitting en banc the Court of Appeals reversed....

We granted certiorari... to resolve the disagreement among the Courts of Appeals on a question of national importance. Whether diversity is a compelling interest that can justify the narrowly tailored use of race in selecting applicants for admission to public universities. Compare Hopwood v. Texas, 78 F. 3d 932 (5th Cir. 1996) (Hopwood I) (holding that diversity is not a compelling state interest), with Smith v. University of Wash. Law School, 233 F. 3d 1188 (9th Cir. 2000) (holding that it is).

[Our prior decisions] have never held that the only governmental use of race that can survive strict scrutiny is remedying past discrimination. Nor, since *Bakke*, have we directly addressed the use of race in the context of public higher education. Today, we hold that the Law School has a compelling interest in attaining a diverse student body.

The Law School's educational judgment that such diversity is essential to its educational mission is one to which we defer. The Law School's assessment that diversity will, in fact, yield educational benefits is substantiated by respondents and their amici.... These benefits are substantial. As the District Court emphasized, the Law School' admissions policy promoted "cross-racial understanding," helps to break down racial stereotypes, and "enables [students] to better understand persons of different races." These benefits are "important and laudable," because "classroom discussion is livelier, more spirited, and simply more enlightening and interesting" when the students have "the greatest possible variety of backgrounds."

The Law School's claim of a compelling interest is further bolstered by its amici, who point to the educational benefits that flow from student body diversity. In addition to the expert studies and reports entered into evidence at trial, numerous studies show that student body diversity promotes learning outcomes, and "better prepares students for an increasingly diverse workforce and society, and better prepares them as professionals." Brief for American Educational Research Association et al. as Amici Curiae 3; see, e.g., W. Bowen & D. Bok, The Shape of the River (1998); Diversity Challenged: Evidence on the Impact of Affirmative Action (G. Orfield & M. Kurlaender eds., 2001); Compelling Interest: Examining the Evidence on Racial Dynamics in Colleges and Universities (M. Chang, D. Witt, J. Jones & K. Bakuta eds., 2003).

These benefits are not theoretical but real, as major American businesses have made clear that the skills needed in today's increasingly global marketplace can only be developed through exposure to widely diverse people, cultures, ideas, and viewpoints. Brief for 3M et al. as Amici Curiae 5; Brief for General Motors Corp. as Amicus Curiae 3-4. What is more, high-ranking retired officers and civilian leaders of the United States military assert that, "based on [their] decades of experience," a "highly qualified, racially diverse officer corps . . . is essential to the military's ability to fulfill its principle mission to provide national security." Brief for Julius W. Becton, Jr. et al. as Amici Curiae 27.

Effective participation by members of all racial and ethnic groups in the civic life of our nation is essential if the dream of one Nation, indivisible, is to be realized.

Moreover, universities, and in particular, law schools, represent the training ground for a large number of our Nation's leaders. . . . In order to cultivate a set of leaders with legitimacy in the eyes of the citizenry, it is necessary that the path to leadership be visible open to talented and qualified individuals of every race and ethnicity. All members of our heterogeneous society must have confidence in the openness and integrity of the educational institutions that provide this training. . . .

Access to legal education (and thus the legal profession) must be inclusive of talented and qualified individuals of every race and ethnicity, so that all members of our heterogeneous society may participate in the educational institutions that provide the training and education necessary to succeed in America.

The Law School does not premise its need for critical mass on "any belief that minority students always (or even consistently) express some characteristic minority viewpoint on any issue." Brief for Respondent Bollinger et al. 30. To the contrary, diminishing the force of such stereotypes is both a crucial part of the Law School's mission, and one that it cannot accomplish with only token numbers of minority students. Just as growing up in a particular region or having particular professional experiences is likely to affect an individual's views, so too is one's own, unique experience of being a racial minority in a society, like our own, in which race unfortunately still matters. The Law School has determined, based on its experience and expertise, that a "critical mass" of underrepresented minorities is necessary to further its compelling interest in securing the educational benefits of a diverse student body.

We find that the Law School's admissions program bears the hallmarks of a narrowly tailored plan. . . .

The Law School's goal of attaining a critical mass of underrepresented minority students does not transform its program into a quota. As the Harvard plan described by Justice Powell recognized, there is of course "some relationship between numbers and providing a reasonable environment for those students admitted." Regents of the University of California v. Bakke, 438 U.S. 265, 323 (1978). "Some attention to numbers," without more, does not transform a flexible admissions system into a rigid quota. Nor, as Justice Kennedy posits [in his dissenting opinion], does the Law School's consultation of the "daily reports which keep track of the racial and ethnic composition of the class (as well as of residency and gender), "suggest[] there was no further attempt at individual review save for race itself" during the final stages of the admissions process. To the contrary, the Law School's admissions officers testified without contradiction that they never gave race any more or less weight based on the information contained in these reports. . . . Moreover, as Justice Kennedy concedes, between 1993 and 2000, the number of African-American, Latino, and Native-American students in each class at the Law School varied from 13.5 to 20.1 percent, a range inconsistent with a quota.

That a race-conscious admissions program does not operate as a quota does not, by itself, satisfy the requirement of individualized consideration. When using race as a "plus" factor in university admissions, a university's admissions program must remain flexible enough to ensure that each applicant is evaluated as an individual and not in a way that makes an applicants race or ethnicity the defining feature of his or her application. . . .

Here, the Law School engages in a highly individualized, holistic review of each applicant's file, giving serious consideration to all the ways an applicant might contribute to a diverse educational environment. The Law School affords this individualized consideration to applicants of all races.

The Law School does not, however, limit in any way the broad range of qualities and experiences that may be considered valuable contributions to student body diversity. To the contrary, the 1992 policy makes clear "there are many possible bases for diversity admissions," and provides examples of admittees who have lived or traveled widely abroad, are fluent in several languages, have overcome personal adversity and family hardship, have exceptional records of extensive community service, and have had successful careers in other fields. . . . All applicants have the opportunity to highlight their own potential diversity contributions through the submission of a personal statement, letters of recommendation, and an essay describing the ways in which the applicant will contribute to the life and diversity of the Law School.

What is more, the Law School actually gives substantial weight to diversity factors besides race. The Law School frequently accepts non-minority applicants with grades and test scores lower than underrepresented minority applicants (and other non-minority applicants) who are rejected. See Brief for Respondents, Bollinger et al. 10. This shows that the Law School seriously weighs many other diversity factors besides race that can make a real and dispositive difference for non-minority applicants as well.

We are mindful, however, that "[a] core purpose of the Fourteenth Amendment was to do away with all governmentally imposed discrimination based on race." Palmore v. Sidoti, 466 U.S. 429, 432 (1984). Accordingly, race-conscious admissions policies must be limited in time. This requirement reflects that racial classifications, however compelling their goals, are potentially so dangerous that they may be employed no more broadly than the interest demands. Enshrining a permanent justification for racial preferences would offend this fundamental equal protection principle. We see no reason to exempt race-conscious admissions programs from the requirement that all governmental use of race must have a logical end point. . . . It has been 25 years since Justice Powell first approved the use of race to further an interest in student body diversity in the context of public higher education. Since that time, the number of minority applicants with high grades and test scores has indeed increased. See Tr. of Oral Arg. 43. We expect that 25 years from now, the use of racial preferences will no longer be necessary to further the interest approved today.

[The concurring opinion of Justice Ginsburg in which Justice Breyer joined, is omitted.]

[The opinion of Justice Scalia concurring in part and dissenting in part, in which Justice THOMAS joined, is omitted.]

[The opinion of Justice Thomas concurring in part and dissenting in part, in which Justice Scalia joined Parts I-VII, is omitted.]

[The dissenting opinion of Justice Rehnquist, in which Justice Scalia, Justice Kennedy, and Justice Thomas joined, is omitted.]

[The dissenting opinion of Justice Kennedy is omitted.]

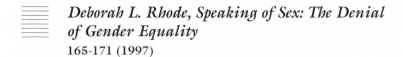

Deborah L. Rhode, Speaking of Sex: The Denial of Gender Equality
165-171 (1997)

[Opponents of affirmative action] believe that it is indefensible on both moral and practical grounds. The moral argument is that allocating educational or employment opportunities on the basis of sex or race compromises fundamental values of individual merit and responsibility. Preferential treatment based on involuntary group characteristics rather than on individual qualifications reinforces precisely the kind of gender and color consciousness that created problems in the first place.

Whatever obligation society has to remedy the effects of discrimination, critics argue, the costs of that remedy should not fall on individual white males who are not personally responsible for injustice. Nor are affirmative action programs appropriate strategies for compensation, since they seldom reach individuals who have suffered most from discrimination. As one opponent of preferential treatment put it, "My parents were impoverished immigrants. Neither they nor we . . . oppressed anyone. Yet my sons are punished." And what's worse, they may be losing out to some upper-middle-class female or nonwhite applicant who looks anything but oppressed. To many commentators, the moral justification for favoritism toward white women is particularly weak because they have not endured the same socioeconomic disadvantages as people of color. From this perspective, the way to achieve gender blindness in society is not to enshrine it in law. As the title of an article by Supreme Court Justice Antonin Scalia suggests, the problem with affirmative action is that "the cure" is worse than "the disease."

The problem with this argument, however, is that it understates both the consequences of the disease and the limitations of other remedies. Opponents' claim that people should be treated on the basis of individual rather than group characteristics sounds right. But it comes several generations too early and several centuries too late. Group treatment has been a pervasive feature of America's social, economic, and political landscape and has exposed white women as well as minorities to systematic injustice. When defenders of affirmative action mention the historical roots and institutional practices that perpetuate inequality "America yawns." Yet such discrimination has left a legacy of underrepresentation that neutral mandates have failed to correct. At this juncture, ignoring racial and gender differences will simply perpetuate them.

We pay homage to equal opportunity and merit selection in principle, but in practice these principles are often not "even accepted, let alone realized." A delightfully ironic example involves a recent admissions controversy at a prominent Ivy League institution. One of its alumni wrote a letter to the campus newspaper claiming that his son had been passed over in the rush to admit less deserving women and minority applicants. It then emerged that while the overall odds of admission were one in seven, for children of alumni they were almost one in two.

Contrary to opponents' claims, most ostensibly "meritocratic" decisions reflect some considerations unrelated to merit or to an individual's own efforts and talents. As is clear from the employment cases [like *Johnson*], bias often creeps into the assessment of even "objective" qualifications. Moreover, family background, economic resources, childhood environment, and societal stereotypes all affect access to the educational and employment opportunities on which those qualifications depend. Susan Faludi, the recipient of multiple journalistic awards, got her first press job through affirmative action. In an earlier era, she notes, the position would probably have gone to the son or nephew of a white male editor. No one would have called it "affirmative nepotism."

So too, "merit" standards are highly imperfect predictors of academic or job performance. Law school admissions is a representative example. Unsuccessful white applicants frequently have protested and sometimes successfully sued institutions that admit nonwhite candidates with slightly lower grade point averages and LSAT test scores. But those criteria are extremely inadequate measures of the qualities that produce successful lawyering. Taken together, grades and test scores predict only about a quarter of the variation in grades among first year law students. And we have no idea how well performance at the beginning of law school measures performance on the job.

What we do know is that most surveyed practitioners think that law schools fail to teach or test many of the interpersonal skills most critical for professional success, such as interviewing and negotiating. As legal educators increasingly have recognized, part of their mission *should* be to teach potential lawyers how to collaborate and communicate with those who are "different." Such a mission requires students with varied backgrounds, experiences, and strengths. Diversity does not compete with educational quality: it enhances it.

The moral case against affirmative action either denies the importance of these values or sidesteps the difficulties of realizing them under race- or gender-blind standards. Neutrality in formal policy cannot correct for bias in social practices. Without affirmative action programs, estimates suggest that less than a fifth of African Americans who graduated from law school in the 1970s would have been admitted. Comparable underrepresentation would persist today. The same is true in a wide array of occupations. The most systematic studies find that affirmative action has significantly expanded employment and educational opportunities for white women and people of color from all socioeconomic backgrounds.

We are, in short, unlikely to achieve a society without race or gender prejudices if we pretend we are already there or that all preferences are equally objectionable. Disfavoring women stigmatizes, stereotypes, and subordinates; disfavoring white males does not. That is not to discount the economic injury or sense of unfairness that individual men may experience. But white males as a group suffer no implications of inferiority or systematic subordination as a result of affirmative action.

Of course, as opponents emphasize, preferential treatment does stigmatize some individuals — its beneficiaries. For that reason, critics often argue that affirmative action, even if morally acceptable, is socially counterproductive. Singling out women for special assistance risks reinforcing the very assumptions of inferiority that society should be trying to eliminate. Selecting those who may not succeed by conventional criteria also risks compromising organizational goals and entrenching negative stereotypes. Even when white women or people of color perform effectively after affirmative action, their success is likely to be devalued. As long as they appear unable to advance without special favors, societal prejudices will persist.

In critics' view, the problem is not simply the inferiority that others attribute to affirmative action recipients. It is also the effect that favoritism has on the recipients themselves. Opponents claim that special treatment erodes recipients' incentives for excellence and their self-esteem when they achieve it. According to Shelby Steele, "affirmative action tells us that . . . preferences can do for us what we cannot do for ourselves." If individuals believe that they owe their positions to favoritism rather than their own achievements, why should they bother to achieve?

The problem with these arguments is not that stigma is insignificant, but rather that critics mistake its causes and solutions. Social science research does indeed show that individuals rate a woman's performance lower when they believe that her selection is based at least partly on sex or race. Under these circumstances, women also devalue their own successes, and are less likely to be interested in continuing in their positions. But such assumptions of inferiority predate preferential treatment and would persist without it. Affirmative action is not responsible for adverse stereotypes. Racism and sexism are. White males who have long benefited from preferences by schools, jobs, and clubs have suffered no discernible loss of self-esteem. Nor have the children of alumni who get special treatment in school admissions; they certainly aren't clamoring for policy changes that would spare their own children such injuries.

What, moreover, is the likely alternative to affirmative action programs? A return to the "neutral" policies that have perpetuated gender and racial hierarchies is hardly preferable. Women who benefit from preferential treatment may experience some stigma, but the absence of women is stigmatizing as well. Many members of underrepresented groups find it demeaning to lose affirmative action opportunities on the ground that they will experience it as demeaning. . . .

A final set of objections to affirmative action involves its cost, not to recipients, but to everyone else. Critics complain that race and gender preferences increase the risk of incompetent performance among beneficiaries and resentment from their competitors. While there is no systematic evidence for the first claim, there is all too much for the second. Affirmative action programs target only those who are basically qualified, and social science research does not find declines in performance as a result of those programs. Nor do studies of employment grievances find evidence of overbroad preferences. One review of some 3,000 recent federal discrimination cases revealed fewer than 100 claims of reverse discrimination, and only six white male litigants prevailed. . . .

[That is not to suggest that affirmative action is] the primary solution for white women and people of color. Critics are right in claiming that limited preferential treatment can too readily pass for gender or racial justice on the cheap. Rather than address the underlying causes of underrepresentation, many decisionmakers have been willing to settle for token efforts at diversity. If we simply hand out a few, usually entry-level positions to the "best black" or "best woman" and call it a day, we haven't solved the problem. We have only masked it.

Yet while critics are right to underscore the limits of affirmative action, it by no means follows that its abolition would improve the situation. It is particularly galling to hear conservative political and business leaders condemn preferential treatment because it "diverts attention from the fundamental problems," such as inadequacies in early education, job training, mentoring, work/family, and antidiscrimination initiatives. Whose attention? Theirs? Many of these opponents of affirmative action are also working to dismantle government programs aimed at the "fundamental" problems.

History suggests that decisionmakers are most likely to develop antidiscrimination strategies when white women and people of color are well represented in the decisionmaking process. Affirmative action is not the only means of promoting diversity among policy leaders. But it is a crucial one. Preferential programs have made an important difference in supplying underrepresented groups with role models, mentors, and spokespersons.

We should, of course, look for ways to reduce the need for affirmative action and the backlash that accompanies it. Tailoring programs carefully may be part of the answer. Dismantling them entirely is not. . . . [T]he goal should be support for flexible goals that seek to attract and retain a critical mass of underrepresented groups. Managers and administrators should be accountable for achieving such objectives and for minimizing backlash that results when diversity serves as a "diplomatic" excuse for rejecting white males. Where there are unnecessary costs connected with affirmative action, then as [President William] Clinton concluded, we should "mend it, not end it."

To reduce gender consciousness in the long run, we cannot live without it in the short run. Some corrective action is essential to counteract the lingering biases that remain. Without affirmative action, policies may be gender-blind but people are not.

Notes

1. The Constitutional Framework for Affirmative Action in Higher Education. In Regents of the University of California v. Bakke, 438 U.S. 265 (1978), the Supreme Court invalidated a state university affirmative action program, but suggested in a pivotal opinion by Justice Powell that race could be one of a number of considerations used to ensure educational diversity. In the aftermath of *Bakke*, lower courts divided on what sorts of racial preferences would pass muster. The issue also proved divisive within the public generally, and eventually, in 1997, California's Proposition 209 banned consideration of race (and sex) entirely. See pp. 168-169, supra. The impact of Proposition 209 on racial diversity at the University of California School of Law School of Law (Boalt Hall) was immediate; the percentage of non-white students fell from 35 percent non-white in 1996, to five percent of the entering class the following year, with the only African-American student a holdover from the prior year. See Ian F. Haney Lopez, Traditional Affirmative Action, 91 Cal. L. Rev. 1139, 1140 (2003). For a narrative-based account of the Boalt experience, see Andrea Guerrero, Silence at Boalt Hall: The Dismantling of Affirmative Action (2002), which is featured in a series of reviews in 91 Cal. L. Rev. 1125-1207 (2003). As a result of adjustments in the admissions policies that reduced the weight attached to the test and grade point averages and gave more weight to various discretionary criteria, by 2002 the number of targeted minorities had grown to 19 percent in the state system. Barbara Whitaker, Admission Up for Minorities in California, N.Y. Times, April 7, 2002, at A25. However, representation of students of color in the state's flagship universities remained lower than it had been before Proposition 209. See Peter Schuck, Diversity in America 183 (2003).

At the same time that the Supreme Court upheld the University of Michigan's law school admissions policy in *Grutter*, six Justices joined the majority in striking down the undergraduate admissions program because it awarded a substantial and fixed number of points toward admission to members of targeted racial and ethnic minority groups. Gratz v. Bollinger, 539 U.S. 244 (2003).

In *Grutter*, four Justices dissented, each writing separately and concurring in some aspects of each others' opinions. Justice Rehnquist viewed the law school's practice as a form of racial balancing, "a carefully managed program designed to ensure proportionate representation of applicants from selected minority groups. 539 U.S. at 386 (Rehnquist, C.J., dissenting). Justice Kennedy agreed, and emphasized the narrow fluctuation in minority admissions. Justices Scalia and Thomas rejected the claim that the state had a compelling interest in diversity. They also emphasized the costs of preferential treatment, including the resentment by disadvantaged white applicants and stigma among minority admits who would be stamped with a "badge of inferiority." 539 U.S. at 373 (Scalia, J., dissenting, quoting *Adarand*, 515 U.S. at 241, Thomas, J., dissenting). Moreover, according to these Justices, even if diversity was a compelling interest, the school had other ways of achieving it, such as reducing reliance LSAT scores, or using a lottery for those who were minimally competent. The law school's reluctance to resort to these strategies reflected a desire to maintain its selectivity, which was not, in the view of Justices Thomas and Scalia, a compelling interest.

2. Critiques of Law School Affirmative Action Programs. Critics of preferential treatment in law school admissions argue that it masks rather than addresses the core problem, which is inadequate educational preparation. This, for example, is the claim of Clint Bolick, director of litigation at the Institute of Justice, which has challenged university affirmative action programs:

> So long as we have a regime of racial preferences that problem is not going to be addressed head-on. . . . When affirmative action is practiced that way it does not have any impact in expanding the pool of qualified applicants, which is what the goal should be. The way affirmative action is practiced today is cosmetic and superficial. It does not offer a systemic cure for serious social problems. It simply reshuffles the deck [among applicants].

Tim Wells, "Affirmative Action in Law Schools: Is It Necessary?," Washington Lawyer, Jan./Feb. 2000, at 46, 48 (quoting Clint Bolick). In Bolick's view, current policies simply enable the most privileged nonwhite candidates to obtain better positions and to attend better law schools than their credentials justify. Id.

How would defenders of preferential treatment respond to these critiques? Should criteria apart from grades and test scores assume more weight in law school admissions? Do U.S. News & World Report rankings foster over-reliance on these latter criteria? How much reliance should schools place on factors such as socioeconomic background and leadership ability, community service, employment experiences, and perseverance in the face of disadvantages? Would greater reliance on such factors leave too much room for idiosyncratic or biased judgments? Is there any truly "neutral" basis on which to weigh relevant characteristics? (See note 6, p. 174.)

3. Public Opinion and Affirmative Action in Education. Opinion polls consistently find that most Americans oppose preferential treatment in higher education, and most disagreed with the Court's holding in *Grutter*. Harris Poll, Public Sharply Divided on Recent Supreme Court Decisions, July 30, 2003 (76 percent of Americans opposed the Court's decision that universities may use race as a factor in admissions; 12 percent of whites, 20 percent of Hispanics, and 60 percent of African Americans supported the ruling). As in the case of affirmative action in the employment context (see pp. 170-171, supra), people are more likely to support specific practices to enhance minority representation than the broader principle of whether African Americans, or women, should be favored over less qualified candidates. See Faye J. Crosby, Affirmative Action is Dead: Long Live Affirmative Action 138-141 (2004); see also Carol M. Swain et al., Life After *Bakke* Where Whites and Blacks Agree: Public Support for Fairness in Educational Opportunities, 6 Harv. Blackletter L.J. 147, 168 (2000) (half of respondents expressed a willingness to prefer a less "qualified" candidate in student admissions when it would serve socially useful functions).

How do you account for the opposition to preferential treatment among many minorities? Consider the views of one self-described "tepid" supporter of affirmative action, a black *Time* editor, Perry Bacon, who objects to placing a burden on students or workers to contribute a "uniquely black viewpoint."

> But the fact is, a Michigan Law School student would learn a lot more about the "unique experience" of blacks in America if he spent a day at an inner-city school in Detroit than he would in a torts class with me. In fact, a white person who grew up poor has an equally or perhaps more diverse perspective, and yet my blackness counts so much more in affirmative action.... Let's stop using this notion of diversity to sidestep the real issue. Colleges don't want more minority student so we can all hold hands and sing *It's a Small World*. Why can't we just say what the real goal is: the creation of a multiethnic élite? I think young minorities can help form that élite. But I want to join that élite and be expected to deliver the "unique experience" of my whole life rather than an assumed experience based solely on the color of my skin.

Perry Bacon, How Much Diversity Do You Want from Me?, Time, July 7, 2003, at 108.

To what extent could the same argument be made about affirmative action for women? What about men in contexts in which they are underrepresented? If a historically all-female college determines to go co-ed, would it be justified in giving preferences to male applicants in order to achieve a "critical mass"?

As in the case of affirmative action in employment, to what extent is public opinion relevant to how courts treat affirmative action in education? See Gail L. Heriot, Strict Scrutiny, Public Opinion, and Affirmative Action on Campus: Should the Courts Find a Narrowly Tailored Solution to a Compelling Need in a Policy Most Americans Oppose?, 40 Harv. J. on Legis. 217 (2003) (although it was right for Supreme Court to ignore public sentiment in ending segregation in education, it should not ignore the public when it favors equal treatment and opposes affirmative action). Even some who favor affirmative action believe that in the effort to establish the legal case for affirmative action, the importance of building a public consensus in favor of affirmative action has been given too little attention. Tomiko Brown-Nagin, Elites, Social Movements, and the Law: The Case of Affirmative Action, 105 Colum. L. Rev. 1436 (2005).

Given the public's opposition to preferential treatment, what accounts for the continued, albeit qualified, support of affirmative action among policy makers and corporate leaders? What should be the relevance of popular opinion surveys for the legal status of affirmative action?

4. Does Affirmative Action Work? A final, highly publicized criticism of law school affirmative action programs is that it bumps minority applicants up into law schools where they are more likely to earn poor grades, drop out, and fail their state bar exams. This concern is based on law professor Richard Sander's statistical survey of black students admitted at twenty law schools in the mid-1990s. Sander concludes that scaling back racial preferences would increase the number of new black lawyers because they would enter schools where they would be better able to succeed. Richard Sander, A Systematic Analysis of Affirmative Action in American Law Schools, 57 Stan. L. Rev. 657 (2004).

Sander's methodology and conclusions have been widely criticized. See, e.g., David Wilkins, A Systematic Response to Systematic Disadvantage: A Response to Sander, 57 Stan. L. Rev. 1915 (2005); David L. Chambers et al., The Real Impact of Eliminating Affirmative Action in American Law Schools: An Empirical Critique of Richard Sander Study, 57 Stan. L. Rev. 1855 (2005). For similar disputes regarding undergraduate admissions, see Harry J. Holzer & David Neumark, Assessing Affirmative Action, 38 J. Econ. Lit. 483, 547-548, 553 (2000).

Women have made substantial progress, partly through the assistance of affirmative action. Law schools are a case in point. Before the mid-1970s, only three law schools had ever had a woman dean and few had more than one or two women faculty. Three decades later, as a result of deliberate attempts to diversity the faculty, 25 percent of full professors and 17 percent of law school deans are women. See Mary Elizabeth Basile, False Starts: Harvard Law School's Efforts Toward Integrating Women Into the Faculty, 1928-1981, 28 Harv. J.L. & Gender 143, 143 (2005). Only about five percent of law faculty and deans are women of color. ABA Commission on Women in the Profession, The Unfinished Agenda: A Report on the Status of Women in the Legal Profession 27 (2001). Still, one study shows that even with affirmative action, white women and men of color have only a slightly better chance of getting a teaching job at prestigious schools than white men with comparable credentials, and that minority women have no advantage at all. See Deborah Jones Merritt & Barbara F. Reskin, Sex, Race, and Credentials: The Truth About Affirmative Action in Law Faculty Hiring, 97 Colum. L. Rev. 199 (1997). Moreover, women are paid less than similarly qualified men with the same status and experience, and women receive tenure at lower rates than men. Basile, supra, at 143. The strongest positive factor relating to initial rank of appointment is a nonemployed spouse. Merritt & Reskin, supra, at 256. White men also are hired to teach more prestigious courses, like constitutional law; women are more likely to be hired to teach trusts and estates, family law, and clinical courses. Id. at 258-267.

5. Defining an Endpoint. Justice O'Connor's *Grutter* opinion indicated that race-conscious programs "must have a logical endpoint," and suggests that in 25 years, it will be "safe to sunset affirmative action." Justice Ginsburg's concurrence notes that this view of temporary preferences is consistent with other nations' approaches. By what criteria should law schools decide when to end preferential treatment in the admission of students? How much diversity is enough?

6. Gender and Affirmative Action in Higher Education. Nationally, the male/female ratio for college enrollments is 43/57, according to a U.S. Census Bureau estimate in 2004. Mary Beth Marklein, Gollege Gender Gap Widens: 57% are Women, USA Today, October 20, 2005, at 1A, 2A. The widening gender gap is especially acute in lower-income categories. Only 40 percent of undergraduates from families with income less than $30,000 are male, and only 36 percent of African Americans in this income category who attend college are male. In contrast, 49 percent of undergraduates from families making $70,000 or more are male. Id.

Some colleges have sought to address this issue with affirmative action for male applicants. At Dickinson College in Pennsylvania, a slight preference for men helped boost the percentage of male undergraduates from 36 percent to 45 percent. The disparity at public universities is greater. The University of North Carolina at Chapel Hill has a male/female ratio of 42/58 and the ratios at the universities of Delaware, Georgia and New Mexico are in a similar range.

It is clear that, under Proposition 209, affirmative action in order to improve gender parity in the University of California system would be illegal. See pp. 168-169, 186, supra. What about at other state colleges and universities? Could the University of Georgia give male applicants extra points in the admissions process, to address its declining percentage of male undergraduates? In Johnson v. Board of Regents of the University of Georgia, 106 F. Supp. 2d 1362, 1375 (S.D. Ga. 2000), an admissions plan favoring males and non-whites was struck down, after a federal district court determined that the University had not shown a sufficiently compelling reason for either aspect of the plan. The University did not appeal the decision invalidating its preference for males; on appeal, the Eleventh Circuit of Appeals upheld the trial court's summary judgment in favor of the plaintiffs on the challenge to the preference for non-whites. *Johnson*, 263 F.3d 1234 (11th Cir. 2001).

7. Gender and Standardized Testing. Notwithstanding the general issue of male under-representation in higher education, there remain issues with gender bias against women in standardized testing. Like the critique of "merit" more generally (see pp. 174-175, supra), the practice of standardized testing is strongly criticized for relying on criteria that appear to be unbiased but are not, and for appearing to be more predictive of future performance than they in fact are. Susan Sturm and Lani Guinier charge, for example, that the SAT, LSAT, and other standardized instruments that purport to test "merit," operate, in fact, to exclude people who could succeed, and do "violence to fundamental principles of equity and 'functional merit' in [the] distribution of opportunities for [educational opportunity]." Sturm & Guinier, The Future of Affirmative Action: Reclaiming the Innovative Ideal, 84 Cal. L. Rev. 953, 957 (1996). Among the criteria they argue are left out of standardized "paper-and-pencil tests" which are indicative of potential of future success are discipline, emotional intelligence, commitment, drive to succeed, reliability, creativity, judgment, honesty, courage, the ability to manage anger, and leadership. Id. at 976. The criteria that are overvalued in relation to their correlation with preparation for higher education or employment, they argue, are the willingness to guess, conformity, and docility. Does this analysis help to explain why women tend to outperform men on grades, and underperform on standardized tests? See id. at 977.

What does it mean that standardized tests are biased? One claim, explored by Sturm and Guinier, is that the tests benefit those from families with high incomes. Sturm & Guinier, supra, at 988 (average family income rises with each 100-point increase in SAT score, except for the highest . . . [category]). Another claim is that the subject matter of the questions favors males. Evidence offered to support this claim includes the following question, which produced a 27 percent gap in favor of boys:

A high school basketball team has won 40 percent of its first 15 games. Beginning with the sixteenth game, how many games in a row does the team now have to win in order to have a 50 percent winning record? (A) 3; (B) 5; (C) 6; (D) 11; (E) 15.

Diane Ravitch, Showdown at Gender Gap, Forbes, April 7, 1997, at 68. Is such a question biased on the basis of sex?

On the LSAT, women trail men by an average of about 1.5 points. See Richard K. Newmann, Jr., Women in Legal Education: A Statistical Update, 73 UMKC L. Rev. 419, 422, Table 2 (2004). The following LSAT question has been identified as an example of gender bias.

Fred is tall, dark, and handsome, but not smart.
People who are tall and handsome are popular.
Popular people either have money or are smart.

Joan would like to meet anyone with money. If the statements above are true, which of the following statements must also be true?

I.   Fred is popular.
II. Fred has money.
III. Fred is someone Joan would like to meet.

(A) I only.
(B) II only.
(C) III only.
(D) I and II only.
(E) I, II, and III.

Leslie G. Espinoza, The LSAT: Narratives and Bias, 1 Am. U. J. Gender & L. 121, 121 (1993). Do you agree that this question is biased?

Other possible sources of testing bias are that women and minorities expect to do worse, and therefore do; these groups respond less well to time pressure and are less likely to guess on answers; the subject matter of the questions is more likely to be familiar to men; and some questions are insensitive and thus distract members of offended groups. William C. Kidder, Portia Denied: Unmasking Gender Bias on the LSAT and Its Relationship to Racial Diversity in Legal Education, 12 Yale J.L. & Feminism 1, 25-34 (2000); Kidder, The Rise of Testocracy: An Essay on the LSAT, Conventional Wisdom, and the Dismantling of Diversity, 9 Tex. J. Women & L. 167 (2000). Which of these explanations, if proved, would constitute gender bias?

In 1996, the Educational Testing Service (ETS) added a writing component to the PSAT to help boost women's scores, after women's success in receiving National Merit Scholarships based on these tests stalled at about 40 percent. See Rigging the Test Scores Justifiably, N.Y. Times, Oct. 14, 1996, at A16. In 2005 ETS added the writing component to the SAT as well. While the College Board, which designs the test, said that it did not add the new writing component to tailor the test towards girls, it admitted that the old SAT often unfairly reflected the potential of young women. Kara Alaimo, New SAT Could Shrink Test's Gender Gap, Women's eNews,

March 15, 2005, at http://www.womensenews.org/article.cfm/dyn/aid/2220/context/archive. Is such a measure "affirmative action"?

One federal court held that the exclusive use of the SAT to select recipients of the New York State Regents Scholarships violates Title IX of the Education Amendments of 1972 and possibly also the federal equal protection clause, because of its disparate impact against females. See Sharif v. New York State Educ. Dep't, 709 F. Supp. 345 (S.D.N.Y. 1989); cf. United States v. Fordice, 505 U.S. 717 (1992) (automatic entrance standard based on American College Testing Program standardized test scores and minimum test scores requirement that failed to take into account high school grades — both of which perpetuated past de jure segregated university system — are "constitutionally problematic"). On this general subject, compare William C. Kidder, How the SAT Creates "Built-In Headwinds": An Educational and Legal Analysis of Disparate Impact, 43 Santa Clara L. Rev. 131 (2002); Andrea L. Silverstein, Standardized Tests: The Continuation of Gender Bias in Higher Education, 29 Hofstra L. Rev. 669 (2000), with Jennifer C. Braceras, Killing the Messenger: The Misuse of Disparate Impact Theory to Challenge High-Stakes Educational Tests, 55 Vand. L. Rev. 1111 (2002); Linda F. Wightman, An Examination of Sex Differences in LSAT Scores From the Perspective of Social Consequences, 11 Applied Measurement in Educ. 255, 274 (1998) (no gender bias exists in the LSAT).

Although the ACT scores for male and female high school seniors narrowed to "within a whisker" by the mid-1990s (see Richard Whitmire, ACT Test Scores Up Third Straight Time: Gender Gap Narrow, Gannett News Service, Aug. 14, 1996), the gender gap in the SAT in 2005 (42 overall points) is no smaller than it was in 1972 (40 points). The math advantage for males (34 points, as compared with 38 points in 1972) continues to be far more significant than the verbal gap (eight points, as compared with two points in 1972). See College Board, 2005 College-Bound Seniors: Total Group Profile Report (2005). See www.collegeboard.com.

In 2001, the median LSAT-GPA correlation was .41, meaning that the test accounted for about 16 percent of variation in first year grades. David A. Thomas, Predicting Law School Academic Performance from LSAT Scores and Undergraduate Grade Point Averages: A Comprehensive Study, 35 Ariz. St. L.J. 1007, 1019 (2003). The same data suggests while the LSAT may be the strongest predictor of first-year grades which — like the LSAT — rely heavily on artificial and time-sensitive tests, undergraduate GPA is a stronger indicator of overall grades in law school. Id. at 1019-1021. Furthermore, many educators believe that the LSAT is not an adequate predictor of success as a lawyer. See Law School Admission Council Aims to Quash Overreliance on LSAT, Wall St. J., March 29, 2001, at 1. Some research also suggests that high scores do not correlate with achievement after law school, as measured by earned income, career satisfaction, or service to the profession and community. David L. Chambers et al., Doing Well and Doing Good: The Careers of Minority and White Graduates of the University of Michigan Law School, 1970-1996, Law Quadrangle Notes, Summer 1999, at 60, 61. Are these sufficient reasons to downplay the LSAT in the law school admissions process?

Putting Theory into Practice

2-1. Your law school's student population is 30 percent men and 70 percent women. Is this a problem? If so, should it be fixed? How? Is your plan legal?

2-2. Your law school has no female African-American faculty. Is this a problem? If so, how should it be fixed? Is your plan legal?

4. "Pay Equity": Challenging the Economic Structure

≡≡≡ *American Nurses' Association v. Illinois*
≡≡≡ 783 F.2d 716 (7th Cir. 1986)

POSNER, Circuit Judge.

This class action charges the State of Illinois with sex discrimination in employment, in violation of Title VII of the Civil Rights Act of 1964 . . . and the equal protection clause of the Fourteenth Amendment. The named plaintiffs are two associations of nurses plus 21 individuals, mostly but not entirely female, who work for the state in jobs such as nursing and typing that are filled primarily by women. The suit is on behalf of all state employees in these job classifications . . . [and claims] that the state pays workers in predominantly male job classifications a higher wage not justified by any difference in the relative worth of the predominantly male and the predominantly female jobs in the state's roster.

In April 1985 the district judge dismissed the complaint [on grounds] that the complaint pleaded a comparable worth case and that a failure to pay employees in accordance with comparable worth does not violate federal antidiscrimination law. The plaintiffs appeal. They argue that their case is not (or perhaps not just) a comparable worth case and that in characterizing the complaint as he did the district judge terminated the lawsuit by a semantic manipulation. . . .

Comparable worth is not a legal concept, but a shorthand expression for the movement to raise the ratio of wages in traditionally women's jobs to wages in traditionally men's jobs. Its premises are both historical and cognitive. The historical premise is that a society politically and culturally dominated by men steered women into certain jobs and kept the wages in those jobs below what the jobs were worth, precisely because most of the holders were women. The cognitive premise is that analytical techniques exist for determining the relative worth of jobs that involve different levels of skill, effort, risk, responsibility, etc. These premises are vigorously disputed on both theoretical and empirical grounds. Economists point out that unless employers forbid women to compete for the higher-paying, traditionally men's jobs — which would violate federal law — women will switch into those jobs until the only difference in wages between traditionally women's jobs and traditionally men's jobs will be that necessary to equate the supply of workers in each type of job to the demand. Economists have conducted studies which show that virtually the entire difference in the average hourly wage of men and women, including that due to the fact that men and women tend to be concentrated in different types of job, can be explained by the fact that most women take considerable time out of the labor force in order to take care of their children. As a result they tend to invest less in their "human capital" (earning capacity); and since part of any wage is a return on human capital, they tend therefore to be found in jobs that pay less. Consistently with this hypothesis, the studies find that women who have never married earn as much as men who have never married. To all this the advocates of comparable worth reply that although there are no longer explicit barriers to women's entering traditionally men's jobs, cultural and psychological barriers remain as a result of which many though not all women internalize men's expectations regarding jobs appropriate for women and therefore invest less in their human capital.

On the cognitive question economists point out that the ratio of wages in different jobs is determined by the market rather than by any a priori conception of relative merit, in just the same way that the ratio of the price of caviar to the price of cabbage is determined by relative scarcity rather than relative importance to human welfare. Upsetting the market equilibrium by imposing such a conception would have costly consequences, some of which might undercut the ultimate goals of the comparable worth movement. If the movement should cause wages in traditionally men's jobs to be depressed below their market level and wages in traditionally women's jobs to be jacked above their market level, women will have less incentive to enter traditionally men's fields and more to enter traditionally women's fields. Analysis cannot stop there, because the change in relative wages will send men in the same direction: fewer men will enter the traditionally men's jobs, more the traditionally women's jobs. As a result there will be more room for women in traditionally men's jobs and at the same time fewer opportunities for women in traditionally women's jobs — especially since the number of those jobs will shrink as employers are induced by the higher wage to substitute capital for labor inputs (e.g., more word processors, fewer secretaries). Labor will be allocated less efficiently; men and women alike may be made worse off.

Against this the advocates of comparable worth urge that collective bargaining, public regulation of wages and hours, and the lack of information and mobility of some workers make the market model an inaccurate description of how relative wages are determined and how they influence the choice of jobs. The point has particular force when applied to a public employer such as the State of Illinois, which does not have the same incentives that a private firm would have to use labor efficiently.

It should be clear from this brief summary that the issue of comparable worth . . . is not of the sort that judges are well equipped to resolve intelligently or that we should lightly assume has been given to us to resolve by Title VII or the Constitution. An employer (private or public) that simply pays the going wage in each of the different types of job in its establishment, and makes no effort to discourage women from applying for particular jobs or to steer them toward particular jobs, would be justifiably surprised to discover that it may be violating federal law because each wage rate and therefore the ratio between them have been found to be determined by cultural or psychological factors attributable to the history of male domination of society; that it has to hire a consultant to find out how it must, regardless of market conditions, change the wages it pays in order to achieve equity between traditionally male and traditionally female jobs; and that it must pay backpay, to boot. We need not tarry over the question of law presented by this example because as we understand the plaintiffs' position it is not that a mere failure to rectify traditional wage disparities between predominantly male and predominantly female jobs violates federal law. The circuits that have considered this contention have rejected it. . . .

The next question is whether a failure to achieve comparable worth — granted that it would not itself be a violation of law — might permit an inference of deliberate and therefore unlawful discrimination, as distinct from passive acceptance of a market-determined disparity in wages. The starting point for analyzing this question must be County of Washington v. Gunther, [452 U.S. 161 (1981)]. Women employed to guard female prisoners were paid less than men employed to guard male prisoners. Since male prison inmates are more dangerous than female ones and since each male guard on average guarded ten times as many prisoners as each female guard, the jobs were not the same. Therefore, paying the male guards more could not violate the Equal Pay Act of 1963, 29 U.S.C. §206(d), which requires equal pay only for equal work. The issue was whether it could violate Title VII, and the Court held that it could. A comparable worth study figured in this conclusion. The plaintiffs had alleged . . . that the county had conducted a comparable worth study and had determined that female guards should be paid 95 percent of what male guards were paid; that it had then decided to pay them only 70 percent; "and that the failure of the county to pay [the plaintiffs] the full evaluated worth of their jobs can be proved to be attributable to intentional sex discrimination. Thus, [the plaintiffs'] suit does not require a court to make its own subjective assessment of the value of the male and female guard jobs, or to attempt by statistical technique or other method to quantify the effects of sex discrimination on the wage rates." [452 U.S. at 181.]

All that this seems to mean, as the dissenting Justices pointed out, is "that even absent a showing of equal work, there is a cause of action under Title VII when there is direct evidence that an employer has intentionally depressed a woman's salary because she is a woman. The decision today does not approve a cause of action based on a comparison of the wage rates of dissimilar jobs." Id. at 204. The relevance of a comparable worth study in proving sex discrimination is that it may provide the occasion on which the employer is forced to declare his intentions toward his female employees. In *Gunther* the county accepted (it was alleged) the recommendation of its comparable worth consultant regarding the male guards — decided to pay them "the full evaluated worth of their jobs" — but then rejected the recommendation regarding the female guards and did so because of "intentional sex discrimination," that is, because they were female, not because they had easier jobs or jobs that, for any reason, the market valued below the guarding of male prisoners (however a comparable worth consultant might value them).

The State of Illinois asks us to limit the teaching of *Gunther* to cases where the employer has accepted the recommendation of the comparable worth consultant with respect to the male job classifications. . . . So limited, [as the majority of the Supreme Court in *Gunther* suggests,] its only effect would be to discourage employers from commissioning comparable worth studies.

Gunther suggests the type of evidence that is sufficient but perhaps not necessary to establish sex discrimination in wages for different work. A more recent case out of the State of Washington, American Federation of State, County & Municipal Employees (AFSCME) v. Washington, 770 F.2d 1401 (9th Cir. 1985), suggests the type of evidence that is insufficient. The state's traditional policy had been to pay state employees the prevailing market rates of pay. Beginning in 1974, however, the state commissioned a series of comparable worth studies, each of which found that employees in predominantly female job classifications were paid about 20 percent less than employees in predominantly male job classifications judged to be of comparable worth. Eventually the state passed legislation providing for the phasing in over a decade of a wage system based on comparable worth. The suit charged that the state's failure to act sooner was a form of discrimination. The case was tried and the plaintiffs won in the district court, but the Ninth Circuit reversed. It held that a decision to pay market wages is not discriminatory, that "comparable worth statistics alone are insufficient to establish the requisite inference of discriminatory motive," ... and that "isolated incidents" of intentional discrimination in the form of help-wanted ads specifying the sex of the applicant were not enough to convert the case into one of wage discrimination across different jobs.

The *AFSCME* case resembles our hypothetical case of the firm accused of sex discrimination merely because it pays market wages. *AFSCME* shows that such a case is not actionable under Title VII even if the employer is made aware that its pattern of wages departs from the principle of comparable worth to the disadvantage of women (plus the occasional male occupant of a traditionally woman's job) and even if the employer is not so much a prisoner of the market that it cannot alter its wages in the direction of comparable worth, as eventually the State of Washington did. The critical thing lacking in *AFSCME* was evidence that the state decided not to raise the wages of particular workers because most of those workers were female. Without such evidence, to infer a violation of Title VII from the fact that the state had conducted a comparable worth study would, again, just discourage such studies.

The plaintiffs can get no mileage out of casting a comparable worth case as an equal protection case. The Supreme Court held in Washington v. Davis, [426 U.S. 229 (1976)], that the equal protection clause is violated only by intentional discrimination; the fact that a law or official practice adopted for a lawful purpose has a racially differential impact is not enough. [Personnel Administrator v. Feeney, 442 U.S. 256 (1979)]....

Knowledge of a disparity is not the same thing as an intent to cause or maintain it; if for example the state's intention was to pay market wages, its knowledge that the consequence would be that men got higher wages on average than women and that the difference might exceed any premium attributable to a difference in relative worth would not make it guilty of intentionally discriminating against women. Similarly, even if the failure to act on the comparable worth study could be regarded as "reaffirming" the state's commitment to pay market wages, this would not be enough to demonstrate discriminatory purpose. To demonstrate such a purpose the failure to act would have to be motivated at least in part by a desire to benefit men at the expense of women.

Neither *Davis* nor *Feeney* were Title VII cases, a point emphasized in Davis. [See 426 U.S. at 238-239.] But when intentional discrimination is charged under Title VII the inquiry is the same as in an equal protection case. The difference between the statutory and constitutional prohibitions becomes important only when a practice is challenged not because it is intended to hurt women (say), but because it hurts them inadvertently and is not justified by the employer's needs — when, in short, the challenge is based on a theory of "disparate impact," as distinct from "disparate treatment" (= intentional discrimination). The plaintiffs in this case, however, have said that they are proceeding on the basis of disparate treatment rather than disparate impact....

So if all that the plaintiffs in this case are complaining about is the State of Illinois' failure to implement a comparable worth study, they have no case and it was properly dismissed....

But the [plaintiffs' mention of] "sex-segregated" [job classifications] blurs the picture. If the state has deliberately segregated jobs by sex, it has violated Title VII....

Paragraph 10 [of the complaint], after summarizing the comparable worth study, says, "Defendants knew or should have known of the historical and continuing existence of patterns and practices of discrimination in compensation and classification, as documented at least in part by the State of Illinois Study." All that the study "documents," however, is that 28 percent of the employees subject to the state's personnel code are employed in 24 job classifications, in each of which at least 80 percent of the employees are of the same sex, and that based on the principles of comparable worth the 12 predominantly female job classifications are underpaid by between 29 and 56 percent. For example, an electrician whose job is rated in the study at only 274 points in skill, responsibility, etc. has an average monthly salary of $2,826, compared to $2,104 for a nurse whose job is rated at 480 points. These disparities are consistent, however, with the state's paying market wages, and of course the fact that the state knew that market wages do not always comport with the principles of comparable worth would not make a refusal to abandon the market actionable under Title VII. But at the very end of paragraph 10 we read, "Moreover, defendants have knowingly and *willfully* failed to take any action to correct such discrimination" (emphasis added), and in the word "willfully" can perhaps be seen the glimmerings of another theory of violation that could survive a motion to dismiss. Suppose the state has declined to act on the results of the comparable worth study not because it prefers to pay (perhaps is forced by labor-market or fiscal constraints to pay) market wages but because it thinks men deserve to be paid more than women. Cf. Crawford v. Board of Education, [458 U.S. 527, 539 n.21 (1982)]. This would be the kind of deliberate sex discrimination that Title VII forbids....

"Willfully" is, however, a classic legal weasel word. Sometimes it means with wrongful intent but often it just means with knowledge of something or other.... After reading the comparable worth study the responsible state officials knew that the state's compensation system might not be consistent with the principles of comparable worth ("might" because there has been no determination that the comparable worth study is valid even on its own terms — maybe it's a lousy comparable worth study). But it would not follow that their failure to implement the study was willful in a sense relevant to liability under Title VII. They may have decided not to implement it because implementation would cost too much or lead to excess demand for some jobs and insufficient demand for others. The only thing that would make the failure a form of intentional and therefore actionable sex discrimination would be if the motivation for not implementing the study was the sex of the employees — if for example the officials thought that men ought to be paid more than women even if there is no difference in skill or effort or in the conditions of work. . . .

Reversed and remanded.

Notes

1. Market Explanations for Job Segregation by Sex. While the Equal Pay Act is aimed primarily at wage differentials between male and female workers doing the same job (see Chapter 1, starting at p. 43 where are found, also, statistics on job segregation between men and women in certain industries), comparable worth — increasingly referred to as pay equity — focuses on wage differentials for different jobs of seemingly equal value. Pay equity strategies may be the best, or only, way to equalize compensation in a labor force that is highly segregated and stratified by sex.

Whether pay equity strategies are justified turns in part on assumptions about the causes of such occupational segregation, which are a matter of long-standing dispute. One cluster of explanations for occupational segregation focuses on workers' different occupational and life-style choices. "Human capital" theorists argue that women anticipate working fewer years than men with more interruptions, and therefore "self-select" into occupations that require lower levels of skill and less educational investment. For a classic formulation, see Solomon W. Polachek, Occupational Self-Selection: A Human Capital Approach to Sex Differences in Occupational Structure, 63 Rev. Econ. & Stat. 60 (1981).

Women are also said to choose occupations that offer lower pay in exchange for more pleasant and less hazardous working conditions, and for more flexible schedules that will accommodate family responsibilities. See Warren Farrell, Why Men Earn More: The Startling Truth About the Pay Gap — and What Women Can Do About It (2005). For women's disproportionate representation in part-time and contingent employment, see pp. 246-247, infra.

The empirical data concerning these theories are mixed. Economist Jane Friesen notes that evidence of compensating differentials for jobs with less favorable working conditions is "weak," except where risk of fatality is involved. See Jane Friesen, Alternative Economic Perspectives on the Use of Labor Market Remedies to Explain the Gender Gap in Compensation, 82 Geo. L.J. 31, 38 (1993). Other gender differences in work patterns are, however, well-established. A comprehensive study by the General Accounting Office concluded that about half the gap between men and women's earnings is due to differences in work patterns — primarily men's longer hours and more continuous work histories — as well differences in employee experience, education, occupation and industry. See General Accounting Office, Women's Earnings: Work Patterns Partially

Explain Difference Between Men's and Women's Earnings (October 2003). Another study of workers between the ages of 24 and 36 across seven industries found that if earnings were adjusted to include not just salaries but also the value of fringe benefits (such as insurance coverage, training/education subsidies, profit sharing, maternity/paternity leave, flexible hours, employer-subsidized child care, and retirement benefits), the gender gap narrowed from 87 percent to 96 percent. See Eric Solberg & Teresa Laughlin, 48 Indus. & Lab. Rel. Rev. 692, 706-707 (1995). This study suggests that women may choose non-wage compensation, at a higher rate than men, particularly family-related benefits.

Under a human capital or market model, pay equity is a cure without a disease, and a dangerous one at that. The argument is that setting wages above market rates in female-dominated occupations will increase the attractiveness of these occupations, thereby making them more competitive. Such salary adjustments may also reduce the number of overall jobs available, because the higher cost of labor will give employers a greater incentive to cut jobs. The end result will be to limit women's access to the jobs they prefer.

An alternative perspective, also grounded in economic theory, is that profit-maximizing employers often "sort" women into lower-paying occupations through barriers in hiring and promotion, when it is too costly or difficult to obtain individualized information about employees' willingness to work and commitment to the labor force. See Friesen, supra, at 47-50, for a review of the literature and alternative models. This model views the segregation of women into lower-paying jobs as a point of equilibrium in a market where wage rate corresponds to anticipated productivity. Employers screen women out of high-paying employment when the cost of turnover or employee "monitoring" is expensive because they assume that women are more likely to leave the workforce and less willing to work extended hours. See id. at 45-47.

The evidence, here, is also mixed. One study found that women leave the paid labor force at a rate approximately three times that of men. See June O'Neill & Solomon Polachek, Why the Gender Gap in Wages Narrowed in the 1980s, 11 J. Lab. Econ. 205, 219 (1993). Economists Stephen Rose and Heidi Hartman, using national data from the Michigan Panel Study of Income Dynamics, found that over a fifteen-year period, 52 percent of women, but only 16 percent of men, had at least one full calendar year with no earnings. Stephen J. Rose & Heidi I. Hartman, Still a Man's Labor Market: The Long-term Earnings Gap iii, 41 (Institute for Women's Policy Research, 2004). The implications of these data, however, are not conclusive because of the interrelationship between turnover and wage rates: "Women's wage rates may be lower because they have higher exogenously determined quit rates, or their quit rates may be higher due to the fact that women earn lower wages because of discrimination or other factors." Friesen, supra, at 47. According to Friesen, the difference in men's and women's quit rates is "eliminated or reversed" when researchers control for characteristics including wages. Id. So, too, in one study involving a large New York insurance firm over a ten-year period, about half the gender gap in departure rates appeared attributable to the women's younger age, inferior education and training, and concentration in lower-level jobs. Nachum Sicherman, Gender Differences in Departures from a Large Firm, 49 Indus. & Lab. Rel. Rev. 484, 493 (1996). Women left for very different reasons than men; for example, 12 percent of women cited family considerations, a reason that men rarely mentioned; six percent of women cited personal health problems or family illness compared with 2.6 percent of men, who almost never mentioned family illness. Id. at 488. For further discussion of sex disparities in work patterns, see Chapter 4, pp. 644-658, 665-678.

As *American Nurses* illustrates, the law generally assumes that job segregation by sex is attributable to nondiscriminatory factors. Is that assumption justified? Catharine MacKinnon puts the relevant question: "Is the economic reality of sex the result of the market working, the market failing to work, or the market not being allowed to work?" Catharine A. MacKinnon, Women's Lives, Men's Laws 151 (2005).

2. Critiques of Market Explanations. One main criticism of these economic models is that they incorporate the very bias they attempt to refute. According to feminist critiques, societal gender bias, unequal distribution of household labor, and wage discrimination lie at the root of the choices women make, including how they develop their human capital. For example, Rose and Hartman ask:

> When women "choose" to spend more time out of the labor market taking care of children than their husbands do, how much of that choice is constrained by lack of affordable, good quality alternative care, women's lower pay or inferior working conditions on the job, their expectations that they won't be promoted anyway, or social norms in their kinship network, religious group, or community?

Rose & Hartmann, supra, at 2. Gillian Hadfield similarly argues that strategies to reduce the wage gap must address the organization of the household, which plays a large part in determining women's "choices" in the labor market and firms' perceptions of women workers. Hadfield, Households at Work: Beyond Labor Market Policies to Remedy the Gender Gap, 83 Geo. L.J. 89, 95-107 (1993).

Rosemary Hunter also emphasizes the broader social forces that economic theories overlook:

> Economic theories are notably ahistorical, and thus they fail to perceive that the phenomenon of gender segregation in the labor market is produced by particular social and historical forces. The majority of women in the labor market today were channeled into certain industries and occupations by social expectations (imposed and conditioned) about what was appropriate work for women (of their color). This channeling process is something far more pervasive and systemic than individual employers' "tastes for discrimination," or even statistical discrimination by employers. Indeed, to the extent that these forms of employer discrimination actually exist, they too arise out of the same social conditions.
>
> In Western societies, labor market work deemed appropriate for women has been, by and large, work that closely resembles women's domestic labor: cleaning, washing, cooking, garment making, socializing young children, nurturing, caring, and serving. There is nothing innate in women that makes them especially suited to these occupations. Gender definitions of work are not biologically based but are

culturally constructed, as demonstrated by the fact that notions of appropriate work for women and men vary across different societies. . . . Gender definitions of work also vary historically. The occupation of secretary was originally a male occupation, and only became "feminized" after the Civil War. Even in new industries, such as computing, gender definitions soon assert themselves — men become programmers and women become operators.

Moreover, a great many women in the labor market today were, as girls, educated to perform "women's work. . . ." Families did not invest in girls' education to the same extent as boys'. Schools taught boys a range of useful market skills, while girls were taught sewing and domestic science. Girls' aspirations to careers were actively dampened and deflected. To label all of this as women's rational "choices" about investment in human capital is repugnant. Indeed, the attractive-sounding concept of "choice" and "preference" in economic models obscure the operations of a patriarchal and racist social system. . . . Human capital and individual choice theories allow white males to ignore the fact that they are the beneficiaries of the most thorough and effective affirmative-action program ever known.

Hunter, Afterword: A Feminist Response to the Gender Gap in Compensation Symposium, 82 Geo. L.J. 147, 149-151 (1993). Theorists who trace the historical processes that Hunter describes note that when jobs become typed as female they lose prestige and wages. Barbara F. Reskin & Patricia A. Roos, Job Queues, Gender Queues (1990). A wide array of historical and cross-cultural data suggest that the same jobs are paid less when they are performed by women rather than men. Deborah L. Rhode, Occupational Inequality, 1988 Duke L.J. 1207, 1220; Margaret Mead, Male and Female: A Study of the Sexes in a Changing World 159-160 (1949).

Mary Becker similarly argues that nondiscrimination remedies will not adequately address sex-based inequality in the workplace because that inequality reflects gender socialization, unconscious bias, and existing distributions of wealth and entitlement. One cannot expect, Becker contends, that job segregation can be addressed through principles of economic efficiency, which accept occupational patterns as freely chosen rather than as problems in need of responses. See Mary Becker, Barriers Facing Women in the Wage-Labor Market and the Need for Additional Remedies: A Reply to Fischel and Lazear, 53 U. Chi. L. Rev. 934 (1986).

Carol M. Rose uses the "prisoner's dilemma" model in game theory to explain why the market does not prevent the systematic undervaluing of women's work. She argues that *perceptions* about what choices women make in comparison to men are as important as any *actual* differences between women and men.

[T]he employment agreement is [a] positive-sum game: the employer values labor more than the wages he or she pays for it, whereas the employee puts a higher value on wage dollars than on the leisure he or she would enjoy otherwise. . . .

How do they split the gains they jointly make from the positive-sum game? In general, the employer might offer Sam a greater portion of those gains. Sam has less taste for cooperation than Louise does, and more tolerance for confrontation, so he can make a more credible threat that he will walk away from a potential job or quit an actual one.

202 ≡≡≡ 2. Substantive Equality

On the other hand, the employer might offer Louise a relatively small share of the collective gains from a labor-wage trade. The employer can rely on her taste for cooperation — her willingness to give up something to be sure that the cooperative relationship will take place or (perhaps a more likely scenario) to be sure that she can take care of others for whom she feels responsible. If Louise is skittish, the employer might offer her the same wage he offers Sam at the outset, in order to bring her into a relationship, but then give her relatively few promotions and pay raises over time. He can rely on the attachments she makes during the course of her employment to weaken her bargaining power over these issues. . . .

It may not matter very much that any difference actually exists between Sam's and Louise's respective tastes. . . . What may matter is that people think such a difference exists. . . . Suppose, [in the employment example] that [Louise] has no such taste and refuses to take such a low cut. Given a sufficiently widespread cultural presumption that women have a greater taste for cooperation than men, the employer will continue to make low bids for women for some time before he changes his mind. Moreover, he may never change his mind at all because at least some Louises will take his low offer, and this will make him think he was right about Louises all along.

Indeed, in a sense the employer may be right, because Louise may be unable to challenge this set of beliefs. If he thinks that she will only face another low bid from Employer B, she may well just accept Employer A's offer. The Louise who insists on something better may well not get a job at all, given a widespread set of beliefs about what her wage demands should be. In other words, it costs her something to try to break the stereotype that affects all the Louises in the labor market. Why, then, should she be the first to stick her neck out to break the pattern, particularly when the effort looks hopeless? This set of beliefs, in short, presents Louise with a collective action problem; her failure to solve that problem only reinforces the belief system.

See Carol M. Rose, Women and Property: Gaining and Losing Ground, 78 Va. L. Rev. 421 (1992).

Rose's description is characteristic of the gender differences in salary negotiations. See Linda Babcock & Sara Laschever, Women Don't Ask: Negotiation and the Gender Divide (2003). Such patterns are commonly reported among lawyers. Surveys find that women lawyers are less likely than their male colleagues to stand up to unfair treatment. Rather than risk being seen as "whiners" or "bitches," they will put up with unequal compensation and advancement opportunities or quit if the situation becomes intolerable. Nancy Reichman & Joyce S. Sterling, Gender Penalties 49 (2004); Paula A. Patton, Women Lawyers: Their Status, Influence and Retention in the Legal Profession, 11 Wm. & Mary J. Women & L. 173, 187 (2005). Do these patterns reflect "market failure"? If so, how might they be corrected?

Market explanations for wage disparities between men and woman may also fail to consider organizational practices that depress wages in female-dominated occupations. These practices, according to sociologists Robert Nelson and William Bridges, include better political mobilization of male workers, better advocacy by male managers for male workers, historical pay practices, systems that benchmark female jobs to other female jobs, and biased job evaluation schemes. See Nelson & Bridges, Legalizing Gender Inequality

(1999), reviewed in Paula England, The Pay Gap between Male and Female Jobs: Organization and Legal Realities, 25 L. & Soc. Inquiry 913, 925-927 (2000).

Is the debate over pay equity primarily empirical or normative? Can it be resolved through economic principles and factual analysis? Or does it turn on values and political commitments?

3. Equalizing Job Classifications. Efforts to reform the wage structure generally rely on some system of evaluation by which to compare different jobs. Such systems have been common in both the public and private sectors since World War II. See Michele Andrisin Wittig & Gillian Turner, Implementing Comparable Worth: Some Measurement and Conceptual Issues in Job Evaluation, in Comparable Worth, Pay Equity, and Public Policy 143-144 (Rita Mae Kelly & Jane Bayes eds., 1988). They are not without criticisms, however. A principal difficulty is how to revalue job characteristics and qualifications in the market, without replicating the gender bias the evaluation system is trying to eliminate.

> Job evaluation systems depend on the ability of raters to describe adequately and fairly the tasks required for incumbents in jobs.... Given the inherently subjective nature of the process,... job descriptions are vulnerable to systematic errors and biases resulting from stereotyping. Thus, to the extent that women's jobs are undervalued or seen as less responsible as a result of cultural stereotyping, job descriptions of women's jobs may... not adequately reflect the abilities required to perform necessary job tasks....
>
> Although existing quantitative job evaluations systems vary in their details, they tend to share certain basic features. A set of attributes of jobs, called compensable factors, is designated and points are assigned to defined levels of each factor....
>
> [T]he relative ranking of jobs is heavily dependent on which attributes of jobs are designated as compensable factors and how much weight each factor is assigned.... Historically, factors and factor weights have been chosen to maximize the prediction of existing pay rates, by capturing the implicit policy underlying a firm's existing pay structure. The difficulty with this approach, however, is that it has the effect of incorporating any existing gender bias in wages and salaries.... Even when factors and factor weights are chosen de novo, there is the possibility that traditional cultural stereotypes as to what is valued enter into the choice of compensable factors or relative weight accorded various factors or both. For example, are coordinating activities, which tend to be characteristic of jobs performed mainly by women, identified as a comparable factor, and, if so, what is its weight relative to that of direct supervision, which tends to be characteristic of jobs performed mainly by men? Is being subjected to consistent interruptions identified as an "unfavorable working condition" comparable to working under noisy conditions? ...
>
> Evaluating the worth of jobs with respect to compensable factors is the final stage of the job evaluation process, and it too is subject to social judgment biases. There is preliminary evidence that, other things being equal, prestigious jobs or those with high salaries are rated more highly on compensable factors than lower-prestige and lower-paying jobs.... This labeling bias is thus likely to result in overestimation of the worth of traditionally male jobs relative to those jobs held mainly by women.

Heidi I. Hartmann, Patricia A. Roos & Donald J. Treiman, An Agenda for Basic Research on Comparable Worth, in Comparable Worth: New Directions for Research 9-12 (Heidi I. Hartmann ed., 1985).

Are there ways to improve such evaluation strategies? Consider the following possibilities:

> The most common job evaluation system involves a "policy-capturing" approach. This system focuses on the *relative worth* of particular positions under existing wage scales, either the employer's own rates or those of similarly situated employers. Through this approach, decisionmakers identify factors relevant to compensation and score jobs in terms of those factors, such as skill, responsibility, and working conditions. Then, statistical regression techniques are used to assess the relative importance of such factors in predicting current wages and to establish a weight for each factor. Each job receives a rating based on its weighted characteristics. This rating can serve as the basis for adjusting pay scales or for setting salaries for new jobs, although decisionmakers may make further modifications in response to market forces.
>
> To pay equity advocates, such a policy-capturing approach is primarily useful for identifying racial or gender biases in an employer's own evaluation system. For example, statistical analysis can indicate the importance an employer attaches to particular factors in male-dominated or gender integrated jobs and determine whether the same factors command the same financial reward in female-dominated positions. . . .
>
> [T]he strengths of this system are also the source of its limitation. . . . Such a framework takes no position on what weight specific employment characteristics *should* assume. It only demands that employers consistently apply their own weighting system across job categories. . . . Although this approach is consistent with antidiscrimination principles reflected in existing legislation . . . it does not accomplish one central objective of pay equity advocates — to challenge societal devaluations of women's work. . . .
>
> A more fundamental challenge to current norms is possible with techniques that focus on *intrinsic worth*. Under such an approach, decisionmakers generally define a priori a set of factors *and* the factor weights that should serve as the basis for salary differentials. Typically, this system will rank job characteristics such as skill effort, responsibility, and working conditions, and then assign points to particular jobs based on their weighted characteristics. Compensation levels can then be adjusted to ensure parity between jobs with similar ratings. By valuing job characteristics without explicit reference to employers' existing salaries or market rates, such techniques often expose underpayment of predominantly female occupations. . . .

Rhode, Occupational Equality, supra, at 1228-1230. Is the "relative worth" concept compatible with market principles? What about "intrinsic worth"? What conceptual or practical problems might arise under the latter approach? Nelson and Bridges' case histories of pay equity legal disputes suggests why feminists have seen job evaluation as both "friend and foe." England, supra, at 917. On the one hand, where women are well organized and well represented in the design of new evaluation structures, they can start to close the compensation gap between men's and women's jobs. On the other hand, in the common circumstances where male managers and male dominated workers' organizations have the most leverage, the "reformed" evaluation systems may simply reinforce and legitimate this gap. Nelson & Bridges, supra.

4. Comparable Worth, Liberal Theory, and Equal Opportunity Principles. Is comparable worth compatible with the liberal theory underpinning equal opportunity principles explored in Chapter 1? Consider the following:

> A liberal discourse on equality centers on the ideal of meritocracy.... Liberal political thought accepts the notion of inequality and hierarchy.... Equality is defined as equal opportunity, and thus, from a liberal perspective, fairness exists when the distribution of individuals within unequal positions reflects their individual qualities — their differential motivation, talent, intelligence, and effort — and not their gender, race, religion, or family background....
>
> [Advanced capitalist society assumes] that there are large and significant differences among individuals in talent and potential; that a complex industrial society requires hierarchies; that competition and differential rewards for various positions within the hierarchies will motivate the most talented people to fill the most central and important positions.

Johanna Brenner, Feminist Political Discourses: Radical Versus Liberal Approaches to the Feminization of Poverty and Comparable Worth, 1 Gender and Soc'y 447, 448-449 (1987).

Are pay equity strategies a challenge to the liberalism and the ostensibly meritocratic hierarchies on which markets are based? In one early decision rejecting a comparable worth claim, the district court concluded:

> This...is case which is pregnant with the possibility of disrupting the entire economic system of the United States of America.... [W]hat we are confronted with here is history...which I have no hesitancy at all in finding has discriminated unfairly and improperly against women. But Congress did not, in my judgment, decide that we were going to roll aside all history and that the Federal Courts should take over the job of leveling out centuries of discrimination.... There isn't a judge in the United States, especially this Judge, qualified to set anybody else's pay. It would be an absolutely hopeless morass....

Lemons v. City of Denver, 17 Fair Empl. Prac. Cas. (BNA) 906, 907-909, aff'd, 620 F.2d 228 (10th Cir. 1978). Brenner sees it differently:

> [C]omparable worth's fundamental claim to legitimacy reinforces an existing ideology: the necessity and validity of meritocratic hierarchy. Rather than questioning the market as an arbiter of wages, comparable worth...aims primarily to rationalize the existing sorting and selecting of individuals into unequal places and does not eliminate market criteria from job evaluation.

Id. at 457.

Other commentators find a more radical potential in the concept of pay equity:

Comparable worth does depart less from a liberal vision of the labor market than I and many others would prefer. However, [b]y demonstrating that the value of work can be an object of struggle, comparable worth reveals that the recognition of skill is itself an inherently political process. In other words, acknowledging the connection between skill and gender may open the wage relationship to greater scrutiny, revealing that what society deems valuable is in fact part of a field of social conflict, determined not by intrinsic value, "natural" merit, or abstract market forces but by power relations. This discovery places comparable worth substantially beyond the meritocratic view of the labor market. . . .

If affirmative action exemplifies the mainstream vision of the labor market, comparable worth . . . may move toward a more radical vision of class transformation. . . . Affirmative action attempts to push women into male fields, and in so doing it implicitly accepts the devaluation of women's work and reinforces the greater social esteem accorded male activity. In contrast, comparable worth contests women's devaluation, extending the focus of radical (or cultural) feminism on rescuing female spheres from the denigration of misogynist culture.

Linda M. Blum, Between Feminism and Labor: The Significance of the Comparable Worth Movement 15, 16-19 (1991). How significant a challenge does the rescue of "female spheres" pose to the liberal, free-market premises of this society? What is the risk that simply tinkering with job evaluation systems will reinforce overly unequal wage hierarchies?

5. Contemporary Pay Equity Initiatives. Did Judge Posner in *American Nurses* successfully distinguish *Gunther*? *Gunther* held that women prison guards who alleged sex-based underpayment stated a cause of action under Title VII. The jobs at issue were not equal: male guards supervised more than ten times as many prisoners per guard as did their female counterparts, who devoted much of their time to "less valuable" clerical duties. Justice Brennan, writing for the majority, emphasized that the Court was not endorsing "the controversial concept of 'comparable worth'" Rather, the majority was relying on the fact that the county had itself undertaken to eliminate pay inequities, had commissioned a study finding that female guards should be paid approximately 95 percent as much as the male guards, and then had paid them only about 70 percent as much. Under these circumstances, "the failure of the county to pay [the female guards] the full evaluated worth of their jobs can be proven to be attributable to intentional sex discrimination." 452 U.S. at 181.

Might *Gunther* have the perverse result of discouraging employers from commissioning a comparable worth study? How likely is it that litigants will prevail without such a study? How would you evaluate the chances that plaintiffs in *American Nurses* could demonstrate an intent to discriminate against female employees? See California State Employees' Ass'n v. State of California, 724 F. Supp. 717 (N.D. Cal. 1989) (requiring plaintiffs to show not only discriminatory intent in initial wage-setting, but also carry-over of this discriminatory intent into current wage structure).

By the beginning of the twenty-first century, approximately 20 states had adjusted their payrolls to correct for sex or race bias, and others had commissioned job evaluation studies to identify such bias. Two states, Minnesota and

Iowa, require comparable pay for equal work in state employment, and Maine requires it for private sectors jobs as well. Other countries, including Sweden, England, Australia, and Ontario, Canada, also have pay equity requirements. Catharine A. MacKinnon, Sex Equality 186 (2001); CindyRichards, Maine Becomes First State Requiring Pay Equity, Women's eNews, http://www.womensenews.com/article.cfm/dyn/aid/500/context/archive (Sept. 17, 2001). European Council Directive 75/117, Article I, provides that the principle of equal pay under Article 119 of the EEC Treaty requires equal pay for "work to which equal value is attributed." Employers subject to these requirements typically have adopted some form of job evaluation along the lines noted earlier.

Most research indicates that such market interventions produce results. A four-year study by the Institute for Women's Policy Research found that pay equity strategies in all twenty surveyed states "were successful in closing the female/male wage gap without substantial negative side effects such as increased unemployment." Heidi I. Hartmann & Stephanie Aaronsen, Pay Equity and Women's Wage Increases: Success in the States, a Model for the Nation, 1 Duke J. Gender L. & Pol'y 69 (1994). Wage ratios rose to between 74 and 88 percent, compared to the national average at the time of the study of 71 percent. See id. at 80. Targeting methods that raised wages in predominantly female job classifications were more cost-effective in producing pay equity than job evaluation systems. See id. at 83. Employment losses were generally minimal (Minnesota experienced a .3 percent decrease in rate of employment growth), and tended to correlate with the rate at which the pay increases were implemented. Gradual phasing was the more successful strategy. See id. at 85. The "substantial negative effects" predicted by critics of comparable worth did not come to pass. See id.

Another study by Deborah Figart and Jane Lapidus projected that nationwide pay equity adjustments could increase women's median wages by about 13 percent and narrow the pay gap by about ten percent. The number of working women living below the poverty level for a family of three would decline by almost 25 percent. See Figart & Lapidus, A Gender Analysis of U.S. Labor Market Policies for the Working Poor, 1 Feminist Economics 60, 65 (1995).

Over the past decade, supporters of such pay equity initiatives have introduced proposals in Congress and in at least 30 states. Richards, supra. The two most recent federal bills are the Fair Pay Act, S. 840, 109th Cong. (2005) and the Paycheck Fairness Act, S. 841, 109th Cong. (2005). As noted in Chapter 1, pp. 53-54, the Fair Pay Act would extend the Equal Pay Act by requiring equal pay for "equivalent jobs" in terms of "skills, effort, responsibility, and working conditions." The Act would also cover disparities by race and national origin, and would expand class action enforcement procedures and permit punitive damages. It would also require disclosure of important employment data to the EEOC. The Paycheck Fairness Act would enhance enforcement of equal pay requirements by limiting the affirmative defense of "factors other than sex" to a "bona fide factor other than sex," which would include only job-related factors such as education or training.

Experts have proposed other strategies. One is to require that federal contractors implement a form of pay equity through an Executive Order paralleling the one that now mandates affirmative action. See the discussion of Executive

Order 11246 at pp. 167-168, supra, and England, supra, at 929 (evaluating proposals by Nelson and Bridges). Another possibility is to provide recognition and incentives for employers to conduct their own pay equity audits. See Business and Professional Women, Employer Pay Self Audit (2005). In the absence of such targeted pay-equity initiatives, Rose and Hartmann identify other strategies that would improve women's earnings, such as paid parental leave for all workers, reduction in working hours, subsidized child care, elimination of the tax system's marriage penalty, and strengthened equal opportunity enforcement, including random audits. Rose & Hartmann, supra, at 35-36. Are these proposals (discussed further on pp. 228-253, realistic in the current political climate?

B. ELIMINATING THE DISADVANTAGES OF WOMEN'S DIFFERENCES

1. Pregnancy

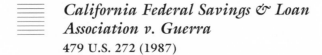

California Federal Savings & Loan Association v. Guerra
479 U.S. 272 (1987)

Justice MARSHALL delivered the opinion of the Court.

The question presented is whether Title VII of the Civil Rights Act of 1964, as amended by the Pregnancy Discrimination Act of 1978, pre-empts a state statute that requires employers to provide leave and reinstatement to employees disabled by pregnancy.

I

California's Fair Employment and Housing Act (FEHA), Cal. Govt. Code Ann. § 12900 et seq. (West 1980 and Supp. 1986), is a comprehensive statute that prohibits discrimination in employment and housing. In September 1978, California amended the FEHA to proscribe certain forms of employment discrimination on the basis of pregnancy . . . now codified at Cal. Govt. Code Ann. § 12945(b)(2) (West 1980). Subdivision (b)(2) . . . requires these employers to provide female employees an unpaid pregnancy disability leave of up to four months. [It has been construed] to require California employers to reinstate an employee returning from such pregnancy leave to the job she previously held, unless it is no longer available due to business necessity. In the latter case, the employer must make a reasonable, good-faith effort to place the employee in a substantially similar job. The statute does not compel employers to provide paid leave to pregnant employees. Accordingly, the only benefit pregnant workers actually derive . . . is a qualified right to reinstatement.

Title VII of the Civil Rights Act of 1964 . . . also prohibits various forms of employment discrimination, including discrimination on the basis of sex.

However, in General Electric Co. v. Gilbert, [429 U.S. 125 (1976)], this Court ruled that discrimination on the basis of pregnancy was not sex discrimination under Title VII. In response to the *Gilbert* decision, Congress passed the Pregnancy Discrimination Act of 1978 (PDA), 42 U.S.C. § 2000e(k). The PDA specifies that sex discrimination includes discrimination on the basis of pregnancy.[6]

II

Petitioner California Federal Savings & Loan Association (Cal Fed) is a federally chartered savings and loan association based in Los Angeles; it is an employer covered by both Title VII and § 12945(b)(2). Cal Fed has a facially neutral leave policy that permits employees who have completed three months of service to take unpaid leaves of absence for a variety of reasons, including disability and pregnancy. Although it is Cal Fed's policy to try to provide an employee taking unpaid leave with a similar position upon returning, Cal Fed expressly reserves the right to terminate an employee who has taken a leave of absence if a similar position is not available.

Lillian Garland was employed by Cal Fed as a receptionist for several years. In January 1982, she took a pregnancy disability leave. When she was able to return to work in April of that year, Garland notified Cal Fed, but was informed that her job had been filled and that there were no receptionist or similar positions available. Garland filed a complaint with respondent Department of Fair Employment and Housing, which issued an administrative accusation against Cal Fed on her behalf.[7] Respondent charged Cal Fed with violating § 12945(b)(2) of the FEHA. Prior to the scheduled hearing before respondent Fair Employment and Housing Commission, Cal Fed, joined by petitioners Merchants and Manufacturers Association and the California Chamber of Commerce, brought this action in the United States District Court for the Central District of California. They sought a declaration that § 12945(b)(2) is inconsistent with and pre-empted by Title VII and an injunction against enforcement of the section. The District Court granted petitioners' motion for summary judgment....

The United States Court of Appeals for the Ninth Circuit reversed....

We granted certiorari ... and we now affirm....

III...

Petitioners argue that the language of the federal statute itself unambiguously rejects California's "special treatment" approach to pregnancy discrimination.... They contend that the PDA forbids an employer to treat pregnant employees any differently from other disabled employees....

---

6. ... Subsection (k) provides, in relevant part: The terms "because of sex" or "on the basis of sex" include, but are not limited to, because of or on the basis of pregnancy, childbirth, or related medical conditions; and women affected by pregnancy, childbirth, or related medical conditions shall be treated the same for all employment-related purposes, including receipt of benefits under fringe benefit programs, as other persons not so affected but similar in their ability or inability to work, and nothing in section 703(h) of this title shall be interpreted to permit otherwise.

[S]ubject to certain limitations, we agree with the Court of Appeals' conclusion that Congress intended the PDA to be "a floor beneath which pregnancy disability benefits may not drop, not a ceiling above which they may not rise." 758 F.2d at 396.

The context in which Congress considered the issue of pregnancy discrimination supports this view of the PDA. Congress had before it extensive evidence of discrimination against pregnancy, particularly in disability and health insurance programs like those challenged in *Gilbert*. . . . Opposition to the PDA came from those concerned with the cost of including pregnancy in health and disability-benefit plans and the application of the bill to abortion, not from those who favored special accommodation of pregnancy. . . .

We . . . find it significant that Congress was aware of state laws similar to California's but apparently did not consider them inconsistent with the PDA. In the debates and Reports on the bill, Congress repeatedly acknowledged the existence of state antidiscrimination laws that prohibit sex discrimination on the basis of pregnancy. Two of the States mentioned [Connecticut and Montana] then required employers to provide reasonable leave to pregnant workers. . . . [B]oth the House and Senate Reports suggest that these laws would continue to have effect under the PDA.

Title VII, as amended by the PDA, and California's pregnancy disability leave statute share a common goal. The purpose of Title VII is "to achieve equality of employment opportunities and remove barriers that have operated in the past to favor an identifiable group of . . . employees over other employees." . . . Rather than limiting existing Title VII principles and objectives, the PDA extends them to cover pregnancy. As Senator Williams, a sponsor of the Act, stated: "The entire thrust . . . behind this legislation is to guarantee women the basic right to participate fully and equally in the workforce, without denying them the fundamental right to full participation in family life." 123 Cong. Rec. 29658 (1977).

Section 12945(b)(2) also promotes equal employment opportunity. By requiring employers to reinstate women after a reasonable pregnancy disability leave, § 12945(b)(2) ensures that they will not lose their jobs on account of pregnancy disability. California's approach is consistent with the dissenting opinion of Justice Brennan in General Electric Co. v. Gilbert, which Congress adopted in enacting the PDA. Referring to Lau v. Nichols, [414 U.S. 563 (1974)], a Title VI decision, Justice Brennan stated:

> [D]iscrimination is a social phenomenon encased in a social context and, therefore, unavoidably takes its meaning from the desired end products of the relevant legislative enactment, end products that may demand due consideration of the uniqueness of the "disadvantaged" individuals. A realistic understanding of conditions found in today's labor environment warrants taking pregnancy into account in fashioning disability policies. [429 U.S. at 159] (footnote omitted).

By "taking pregnancy into account," California's pregnancy disability-leave statute allows women, as well as men, to have families without losing their jobs.

We emphasize the limited nature of the benefits § 12945(b)(2) provides. The statute is narrowly drawn to cover only the period of *actual physical disability* on account of pregnancy, childbirth, or related medical conditions. Accordingly, unlike the protective labor legislation prevalent earlier in this century, § 12945(b)(2) does not reflect archaic or stereotypical notions about pregnancy and the abilities of pregnant workers. A statute based on such stereotypical assumptions would, of course, be inconsistent with Title VII's goal of equal employment opportunity....

Moreover, even if we agreed with petitioners' construction of the PDA, we would nonetheless reject their argument that the California statute requires employers to violate Title VII. Section 12945(b)(2) does not prevent employers from complying with both the federal law (as petitioners construe it) and the state law. This is not a case where "compliance with both federal and state regulations is a physical impossibility,"... or where there is an "inevitable collision between the two schemes of regulation."... Section 12945(b)(2) does not compel California employers to treat pregnant workers better than other disabled employees; it merely establishes benefits that employers must, at a minimum, provide to pregnant workers. Employers are free to give comparable benefits to other disabled employees, thereby treating "women affected by pregnancy" no better than "other persons not so affected but similar in their ability or inability to work." Indeed, at oral argument, petitioners conceded that compliance with both statutes "is theoretically possible."...

IV

Thus, petitioners' facial challenge to § 12945(b)(2) fails....

[The opinions of Justices Stevens and Scalia, concurring in the judgment, are omitted.]

Justice WHITE, with whom THE CHIEF JUSTICE and Justice POWELL join, dissenting.

I disagree with the Court....

[The PDA] mandates that pregnant employees "shall be treated the same for all employment-related purposes" as nonpregnant employees similarly situated with respect to their ability or inability to work. This language leaves no room for preferential treatment of pregnant workers....

Contrary to the mandate of the PDA, California law requires every employer to have a disability leave policy for pregnancy even if it has none for any other disability. An employer complies with California law if it has a leave policy for pregnancy but denies it for every other disability. On its face, § 12945(b)(2) is in square conflict with the PDA and is therefore preempted....

The majority nevertheless would save the California law on two grounds. First, it holds that the PDA does not require disability from pregnancy to be treated the same as other disabilities; instead, it forbids less favorable, but permits more favorable, benefits for pregnancy disability. The express command of the PDA is unambiguously to the contrary, and the legislative history casts no doubt on that mandate.

The legislative materials reveal Congress' plain intent not to put pregnancy in a class by itself within Title VII, as the majority does with its "floor... not a ceiling" approach.... The Senate Report clearly stated:

> By defining sex discrimination to include discrimination against pregnant women, the bill rejects the view that employers may treat pregnancy and its incidents as *sui generis*, without regard to its functional comparability to other conditions. Under this bill, the treatment of pregnant women in covered employment must focus not on their condition alone but on the actual effects of that condition on their ability to work. Pregnant women who are able to work must be permitted to work on the same conditions as other employees; and when they are not able to work for medical reasons, they must be accorded the same rights, leave privileges and other benefits, as other workers who are disabled from working [citation omitted].

The House Report similarly stressed that the legislation did not mark a departure from Title VII principles:

> It must be emphasized that this legislation, *operating as part of Title VII*, prohibits only discriminatory treatment. Therefore, it does not require employers to treat pregnant employees in any particular manner with respect to hiring, permitting them to continue working, providing sick leave, furnishing medical and hospital benefits, providing disability benefits, or any other matter. H.R. 6075 in no way requires the institution of any new programs where none currently exist. The bill would simply require that pregnant women be treated the same as other employees on the basis of their ability or inability to work [citation omitted]....

There is only one direct reference in the legislative history to preferential treatment. Senator Brooke stated during the Senate debate: "I would emphasize most strongly that S. 995 in no way provides special disability benefits for working women. They have not demanded, nor asked, for such benefits. They have asked only to be treated with fairness, to be accorded the same employment rights as men" [citation omitted]. Given the evidence before Congress of the widespread discrimination against pregnant workers, it is probable that most Members of Congress did not seriously consider the possibility that someone would want to afford preferential treatment to pregnant workers. The parties and their *amici* argued vigorously to this Court the policy implications of preferential treatment of pregnant workers. In favor of preferential treatment it was urged with conviction that preferential treatment merely enables women, like men, to have children without losing their jobs. In opposition to preferential treatment it was urged with equal conviction that preferential treatment represents a resurgence of the 19th-century protective legislation which perpetuated sex-role stereotypes and which impeded women in their efforts to take their rightful place in the workplace.... It is not the place of this Court, however, to resolve this policy dispute. Our task is to interpret Congress' intent in enacting the PDA. Congress' silence in its consideration of the PDA with respect to preferential treatment of pregnant workers cannot fairly be interpreted to abrogate the plain statements in the legislative history, not to mention the language of the statute, that equality of treatment was to be the guiding principle of the PDA....

Nor does anything in the legislative history from the Senate side indicate that it carefully considered the state statutes, including those of Connecticut and Montana, and expressly endorsed their provisions. . . . Passing reference to state statutes without express recognition of their content and without express endorsement is insufficient in my view to override the PDA's clear equal-treatment mandate, expressed both in the statute and its legislative history.

The Court's second, and equally strange, ground is that even if the PDA does prohibit special benefits for pregnant women, an employer may still comply with both the California law and the PDA: it can adopt the specified leave policies for pregnancy and at the same time afford similar benefits for all other disabilities. This is untenable. California surely had no intent to require employers to provide general disability leave benefits. It intended to prefer pregnancy and went no further. Extension of these benefits to the entire work force would be a dramatic increase in the scope of the state law and would impose a significantly greater burden on California employers. That is the province of the California Legislature. . . .

Troupe v. May Department Stores Co.
20 F.3d 734 (7th Cir. 1994)

POSNER, Chief Judge.

The plaintiff, Kimberly Hern Troupe, was employed by the Lord & Taylor department store in Chicago as a saleswoman in the women's accessories department. . . . Until the end of 1990 her work was entirely satisfactory. In December of that year, in the first trimester of a pregnancy, she began experiencing morning sickness of unusual severity. The following month she requested and was granted a return to part-time status, working from noon to 5:00 p.m. Partly it seems because she slept later under the new schedule, so that noon was "morning" for her, she continued to experience severe morning sickness at work, causing what her lawyer describes with understatement as "slight" or "occasional" tardiness. In the month that ended with a warning from her immediate supervisor, Jennifer Rauch, on February 18, she reported late to work, or left early, on nine out of the 21 working days. The day after the warning she was late again and this time received a written warning. After she was tardy three days in a row late in March, the company on March 29 placed her on probation for 60 days. During the probationary period Troupe was late eleven more days; and she was fired on June 7, shortly after the end of the probationary period. She testified at her deposition that on the way to the meeting with the defendant's human resources manager at which she was fired, Rauch told her that "I [Troupe] was going to be terminated because she [Rauch] didn't think I was coming back to work after I had my baby." Troupe was due to begin her maternity leave the next day. . . . [A]t argument Lord & Taylor's counsel said that employees of Lord & Taylor are entitled to maternity leave with half pay. . . .

The great, the undeniable fact is the plaintiff's tardiness. Her lawyer argues with great vigor that she should not be blamed — that she was genuinely ill, had a doctor's excuse, etc. That would be pertinent if Troupe were arguing that the Pregnancy Discrimination Act requires an employer to treat an employee afflicted by morning sickness better than the employer would treat an employee who was equally tardy for some other health reason. This is rightly not argued. If an employee who (like Troupe) does not have an employment contract cannot work because of illness, nothing in Title VII requires the employer to keep the employee on the payroll. . . .

Against the inference that Troupe was fired because she was chronically late to arrive at work and chronically early to leave, she has only two facts to offer. The first is the timing of her discharge: she was fired the day before her maternity leave was to begin. . . . Thus, her employer fired her one day before the problem that the employer says caused her to be fired was certain to end. If the discharge of an unsatisfactory worker were a purely remedial measure rather than also, or instead, a deterrent one, the inference that Troupe wasn't really fired because of her tardiness would therefore be a powerful one. But that is a big "if." We must remember that after two warnings Troupe had been placed on probation for sixty days and that she had violated the implicit terms of probation by being as tardy during the probationary period as she had been before. If the company did not fire her, its warnings and threats would seem empty. Employees would be encouraged to flout work rules knowing that the only sanction would be a toothless warning or a meaningless period of probation.

[I]t might appear to be an issue for trial whether it is superior to Troupe's interpretation. But what is Troupe's interpretation? Not (as we understand it) that Lord & Taylor wanted to get back at her for becoming pregnant or having morning sickness. The only significance she asks us to attach to the timing of her discharge is as reinforcement for the inference that she asks us to draw from Rauch's statement about the reason for her termination: that she was terminated because her employer did not expect her to return to work after her maternity leave was up. We must decide whether a termination so motivated is discrimination within the meaning of the pregnancy amendment to Title VII.

Standing alone, it is not. (It could be a breach of contract, but that is not alleged.) . . . We must imagine a hypothetical Mr. Troupe, who is as tardy as Ms. Troupe was, also because of health problems, and who is about to take a protracted sick leave growing out of those problems at an expense to Lord & Taylor equal to that of Ms. Troupe's maternity leave. If Lord & Taylor would have fired our hypothetical Mr. Troupe, this implies that it fired Ms. Troupe not because she was pregnant but because she cost the company more than she was worth to it.

The Pregnancy Discrimination Act does not, despite the urgings of feminist scholars . . . require employers to offer maternity leave or take other steps to make it easier for pregnant women to work . . . to make it as easy, say as it is for their spouses to continue working during pregnancy. Employers can treat pregnant women as badly as they treat similarly affected but nonpregnant employees. . . .

The plaintiff has made no effort to show that if all the pertinent facts were as they are except for the fact of her pregnancy, she would not have been fired. So in the end she has no evidence from which a rational trier of fact could infer that she was a victim of pregnancy discrimination. . . . The Pregnancy Discrimination Act requires the employer to ignore an employee's pregnancy, but . . . not her absence from work, unless the employer overlooks the comparable absences of nonpregnant employees. . . . Of course there may be no comparable absences . . . ; but we do not understand Troupe to be arguing that the reason she did not present evidence that nonpregnant employees were treated more favorably than she is that . . . there is no comparison group of Lord & Taylor employees. . . . We doubt that finding a comparison group would be that difficult. Troupe would be halfway home if she could find one nonpregnant employee of Lord & Taylor who had not been fired when about to begin a leave similar in length to hers. She either did not look, or did not find. Given the absence of other evidence, her failure to present any comparison evidence doomed her case.

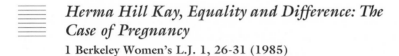

Herma Hill Kay, Equality and Difference: The Case of Pregnancy
1 Berkeley Women's L.J. 1, 26-31 (1985)

Philosophers recognize that, just as the concept of equality requires that equals be treated equally, so it requires that unequals be treated differently. To treat persons who are different alike is to treat them unequally. The concept of formal equality, however, contains no independent justification for making unequals equal. A different concept, that of equality of opportunity, offers a theoretical basis for making unequals equal in the limited sense of removing barriers which prevent individuals from performing according to their abilities. The notion is that the perceived inequality does not stem from an innate difference in ability, but rather from a condition or circumstance that prevents certain uses or developments of that ability. As applied to reproductive behavior, the suggestion would be that women in general are not different from men in innate ability. During the temporary episode of a woman's pregnancy, however, she may become unable to utilize her abilities in the same way she had done prior to her reproductive conduct. Since a man's abilities are not similarly impaired as a result of his reproductive behavior, equality of opportunity implies that the woman should not be disadvantaged as a result of that sex-specific variation.

As applied to the employment context, the concept of equality of opportunity takes on the following form. Let us postulate two workers, one female, the other male, who respectively engage in reproductive conduct. Assume as well that prior to this activity, both were roughly equal in their ability to perform their similar jobs. The consequence of their having engaged in reproductive behavior will be vastly different. The man's ability to perform on the job will be largely unaffected. The woman's ability to work, measured against her prior performance, may vary with the physical and emotional changes she experiences during pregnancy. At times, her ability to work may be unaffected by the pregnancy; at other times, she may be temporarily incapacitated by it. Ultimately, she may require medical care to recover from miscarriage, or to complete her pregnancy by delivery, or to terminate it earlier by induced abortion. In order to maintain the woman's equality of opportunity during her pregnancy, we should modify as far as reasonably possible those aspects of her work where her job performance is adversely affected by the pregnancy. Unless we do so, she will experience employment disadvantages arising from her reproductive activity that are not encountered by her male co-worker. . . .

[P]regnancy differs from sex . . . in that pregnancy is an episodic occurrence, rather than an immutable trait. The category of pregnant persons is a sub-class within the larger category of women. . . . Employers must take those measures that may be reasonably necessary to permit pregnant workers to continue working until delivery, in order to avoid discrimination against them. Women returning from pregnancy leave must be allowed to resume their former status as workers. An episodic view of pregnancy requires that any benefits extended to pregnant workers or restrictions imposed on them be tailored to actual medical need resulting from the pregnancy, and not be triggered by stereotypical notions of what pregnant women should or should not do.

This interpretation of Title VII based on an episodic analysis of biological reproductive differences will permit pregnancy to be recognized as the normal consequence of reproductive behavior that can and should be accommodated in the workplace. Pregnancy is not itself a disability, although an individual pregnant woman may experience disabling symptoms and may require medical care. If she is temporarily impaired from performing at work up to her normal level of ability, the concept of equal employment opportunity embodied in Title VII requires not only that she remain free of resulting job reprisals, but also that she secure compensatory benefits to offset any potential work-related disadvantage. Under this analysis, women will be equal to men in their ability to work and to make reproductive choices. . . .

It follows from this analysis that, for constitutional purposes as well as statutory coverage under Title VII, a discrimination against a woman based on pregnancy is a facial discrimination against her because of her sex. The same intermediate standard of judicial review developed for equal protection sex discrimination cases can be adapted for use in pregnancy discrimination cases. The analysis will, however, be different . . . because there is no matching group of pregnant males to use for purposes of comparison. Instead, the constitutional test must be applied so as to assure pregnant women equality of opportunity to the same extent as that available to males who have engaged in reproductive conduct. Thus, pregnant women may be treated differently from such males if the result is to prevent a disadvantage that might otherwise follow from their condition. . . . [A] reasonable leave provided by a state employer to pregnant workers is not only constitutional, it is constitutionally compelled to avoid discrimination by the state against pregnant workers.

Richard A. Posner, Conservative Feminism
1989 U. Chi. Legal F. 191, 195-198

Where the libertarian is apt to part company with the liberal or radical feminist in the field of employment is over the question whether employers should be forced to subsidize female employees, as by being compelled to offer maternity leave or pregnancy benefits, or to disregard women's greater longevity than men when fixing pension benefits. To the extent that women workers incur higher medical expenses than men (mainly but not entirely due to pregnancy), or live longer in retirement on a company pension, they cost the employer more than male workers do. So the employer should not be required to pay the same wage *and* provide the same package of fringe benefits. (Of course, to the extent that women impose lower costs — for example, women appear to be more careful about safety than men, and therefore less likely to be injured on the job — they are entitled to a correspondingly higher wage or more extensive fringe benefits.) This is not to suggest — which would be absurd — that women are blameworthy for getting pregnant or for living longer than men. It is to suggest merely that they may be more costly workers and that, if so, the disparity in cost should be reflected in their net compensation. If this disparity is not reflected, then male workers are being discriminated against in the same sense in which women would be discriminated against if they received a lower wage than equally productive (and no less costly) male workers. What is sauce for the goose should be sauce for the gander. More than symmetry is involved; we shall see in a moment that laws designed to improve the welfare of women may boomerang, partly though not wholly because of the economic interdependence of men and women.

I anticipate three objections to my analysis. The first is that in speaking of employers' subsidizing women I am taking as an arbitrary benchmark the costs and performance of male workers. I am not. Consider an employer who is female in a hypothetical female-dominated society and whose entire labor force is also female, so that for her the benchmark in setting terms of employment is female. A man applies for a job. He asks for a higher wage on the ground that experience shows that the average male employee's medical costs are lower than the average female employee's medical costs. If the employer refuses to pay him the higher wage, then, assuming that this worker is just as good as the employer's average female worker, the employer is discriminating against him. This should answer the second objection — that nature should not be allowed to determine social outcomes. I agree that natural law does not compel the conclusion that women should be penalized in the marketplace or anywhere else for living longer or for incurring greater medical costs on average than men. But neither is there any reason why men should be penalized for not living as long as women by being forced to pay for women's longer years of retirement. The matter should be left to the market.

The third objection to my analysis is that, in suggesting that the employer be allowed to make cost-justified differentiations based on sex, I am necessarily implying that he should be permitted to treat employees as members of groups whose average characteristics the particular employee may not share, rather than as individuals. That is true. Some women die before some men, just as some women are taller than some men. The difference is that while it is obvious on inspection whether a given woman is taller than a given man — and therefore it would be absurd for an employer to implement a (let us assume valid) minimum-height requirement of 5 feet 8 inches by refusing to accept job applications from women, it is not obvious which women employees will not live as long as which men employees or will not take as much leave or incur as high medical expenses.

Any cost-based differentiation in these areas must be based on probabilistic considerations, of which sex may be the most powerful in the sense of having the greatest predictive power. The average differences between men and women are not invidious, and many cut in favor of women — they are safer drivers, and they live longer, and in a free insurance market would therefore be able to buy liability insurance and life insurance at lower rates than men. Women would not be stigmatized if the market were allowed to register these differences.

It is not even clear, moreover, that women benefit, on balance, from laws that forbid employers to take into account the extra costs that female employees can impose. Such laws discourage employers from hiring, promoting, and retaining women, and there are many ways in which they can discriminate in these respects without committing detectable violations of the employment-discrimination laws.[9] Sometimes there is no question of violation, as when an employer accelerates the substitution of computers for secretaries in response to an increase in the costs of his female employees.

There is an additional point. Most women are married — and many who are not currently married are divorced or widowed and continue to derive a benefit from their husband's earnings. The consumption of a married woman is, as I have noted, a function of her husband's income as well as of her own (in the divorce and widowhood cases as well, for the reason just noted). Therefore a reduction in men's incomes as a result of laws that interfere with profit-maximizing and cost-minimizing decisions by employers will reduce women's welfare as well as men's. Moreover, women who are not married are less likely to have children than women who are married; and where employer benefits are child-related — such as pregnancy benefits and maternity leave — their effect is not merely to transfer wealth from men to women but from women to women. The effect could be dramatic. Compare the situation of a married woman with many children and an unmarried woman with no children. Generous pregnancy benefits and a generous policy on maternity leave will raise the economic welfare of the married woman. Her and her husband's wages will be lower, because all wages will fall in order to finance the benefit, but the reduction will probably be smaller than the benefits to her — in part because the unmarried female worker will experience the same reduction in wages but with no offsetting benefit. Feminists who support rules requiring employers to grant pregnancy benefits and maternity leave may therefore, and I assume unknowingly, be discouraging women from remaining single or childless. Feminists of all persuasions would think it outrageous if the

---

9. Suits for employment discrimination are not a terribly effective remedy. They are rarely worth bringing even when the prospects for winning are good, because, in general, the successful plaintiff can obtain only back pay and reinstatement, not common law damages, and because the filing of an employment discrimination suit identifies the plaintiff as a "troublemaker," thereby making him or her unattractive to future employers. (Many women, I have been told, regard filing a sex-discrimination suit as tantamount to committing professional suicide.) In addition, most discrimination cases are difficult to win, because the plaintiff, unless irrationally willing to invest resources in investigation and proof that are disproportionate to the modest stakes in most such cases, will be hard-pressed to establish the counterfactual proposition essential to victory: for example, that she would not have been fired if she had been male. I am speaking here primarily of disparate-treatment (intentional discrimination) rather than disparate-impact litigation, but the latter will not eliminate most forms of sex discrimination.

government required fertile women to have children, yet many feminists support an oblique form of such a policy — a subsidy to motherhood. They do this, I suspect, because they have not considered the economic consequences of proposals that *appear* to help women.

Notes

1. When Is Pregnancy Discrimination "Based on Sex"? As noted by the Court in *Cal Fed*, Congress enacted the Pregnancy Discrimination Act (PDA) in response to the Supreme Court decision in General Electric Co. v. Gilbert, which held that discrimination on the basis of pregnancy did not amount to discrimination on the basis of sex under Title VII. *Gilbert* followed Geduldig v. Aiello, 417 U.S. 484 (1974), which had challenged the exclusion of pregnancy from an otherwise comprehensive list of disabilities covered by a state disability insurance plan under the equal protection clause. In *Geduldig*, the Court began by taking, as givens, the fundamental principles of the then-existing insurance system and the means by which the costs of the system were spread among workers:

> California intended to establish this benefit system as an insurance program that was to function essentially in accordance with insurance concepts.... Since the program was instituted in 1946, it has been totally self-supporting, never drawing on general state revenues.... The Disability Fund is wholly supported by the one percent of wages annually contributed by participating employees. At oral argument, counsel for the appellant informed us that in recent years between 90% and 103% of the revenue ... has been paid out in disability and hospital benefits....
>
> Over the years California has demonstrated a strong commitment not to increase the contribution rate above the one-percent level [and] to provide the broadest possible disability protection that would be affordable by all employees, including those with very low incomes. Because any larger percentage or any flat dollar-amount rate of contribution would impose an increasingly regressive levy bearing most heavily upon those with the lowest incomes, the State has resisted any attempt to change the required contribution from the one-percent level.

417 U.S. at 492-493. Compare this deference to the status quo, and to insurance concepts to the Court's decision in City of Los Angeles, Dep't of Water & Power v. Manhart, 435 U.S. 702 (1978), set forth on p. 253, infra.

The heart of the Court's analysis in *Geduldig* appears in the now-famous footnote 20 in Justice Stewart's majority opinion:

> [T]his case is ... a far cry from cases like [*Reed*] and [*Frontiero*], involving discrimination based upon gender as such. The California insurance program does not exclude anyone from benefit eligibility because of gender but merely removed one physical condition — pregnancy — from the list of compensable disabilities. While it is true that only women can become pregnant, it does not follow that every legislative classification concerning pregnancy is a sex-based classification.... Normal pregnancy is an objectively identifiable physical condition with unique characteristics. Absent a showing that distinctions involving pregnancy are

mere pretexts designed to effect an invidious discrimination against the members of one sex or the other, lawmakers are constitutionally free to include or exclude pregnancy from the coverage of legislation such as this on any reasonable basis, just as with respect to any other physical condition.

The lack of identity between the excluded disability and gender as such under this insurance program becomes clear upon the most cursory analysis. The program divides potential recipients into two groups—pregnant women and nonpregnant persons. While the first group is exclusively female, the second includes members of both sexes. The fiscal and actuarial benefits of the program thus accrue to members of both sexes.

417 U.S. at 496-497 n.20.

The fact that pregnancy is "unique" means, for the *Geduldig* court at least, that pregnant women are not similarly situated to other, "nonpregnant persons" and thereby excuses explicitly different treatment. This view of uniqueness is consistent with the most formalistic (and content-less) version of the equal treatment model of equality that likes be treated alike. But in ignoring both the link between pregnancy and sex and the similarities between pregnancy and other disabilities with respect to the purposes of disability insurance, the Court seems blind to the reasons for giving classifications based on sex special scrutiny.

Pregnancy, to be sure, is a *real* difference, and unique. But is this a reason to give classifications based on pregnancy less scrutiny?

> Paradoxically, the uniqueness of pregnancy is probably the most important reason why it warrants special protection, for pregnancy's unique identifiability facilitates [the drafting of] laws and regulations based on exactly those generalizations, stereotypes, and assumptions that constitutional doctrine in the area of sex discrimination was intended to curb.... [In particular, the notion in *Geduldig* that pregnancy is unique reinforces assumptions] that women belong in the home raising children; that once women leave work to have babies, they do not return to the labor force; that pregnancy, though it keeps women from working, is not a "disability" but a blessing which fulfills every woman's deepest wish; that women are and should be supported by their husband, not themselves or the state.

Katharine T. Bartlett, Comment, Pregnancy and the Constitution: The Uniqueness Trap, 62 Cal. L. Rev. 1532, 1536, 1563 (1974). Does this reasoning support the result in *Cal Fed*? Compel it? For a more recent application of *Geduldig*, see Bray v. Alexandria Women's Health Clinic, 506 U.S. 263, 271-272 (1993) (applying *Geduldig* in § 1985 challenge to anti-abortion demonstrations and concluding that discrimination against women who seek abortions is not discrimination based on sex). (This case is discussed on pp. 891-894.)

Shortly after winning the *Geduldig* case, California amended its disability benefits plan, first to include "abnormal and involuntary" complications of pregnancy, 1973 Cal. Stats. ch. 1163, and later to eliminate the pregnancy exclusion outright. 1979 Cal. Stats., ch. 663, 3.

Notwithstanding *Geduldig*, the Supreme Court has invalidated on constitutional grounds some rules that discriminate against pregnant women. In the same year *Geduldig* was decided, the Supreme Court held in Cleveland Bd. of Educ.

v. LaFleur, 414 U.S. 632 (1974), that a school system could not conclusively presume that school teachers become physically incapable of being classroom teachers after the fourth month of pregnancy and require them to take (unpaid) maternity leave; the same rule prohibited women from returning to work until their child was at least three months old. The Court's analysis turned on the importance of women's right to bear children and the freedom of personal choice in matters of marriage and family life established in the Court's earlier privacy decisions, such as Roe v. Wade, 410 U.S. 113 (1973), and Griswold v. Connecticut, 381 U.S. 479 (1965). See *LaFleur*, 414 U.S. at 639-640, 650. The next year the court invalidated a Utah law that made pregnant women ineligible for unemployment benefits during any time from 12 weeks before the expected date of delivery to 6 weeks after the child's birth on the assumption that a woman during that period was not able, and thus not available, to work. Turner v. Dep't of Employment Sec., 423 U.S. 44 (1975). The Court in *Turner*, as in *LaFleur*, reasoned that a state rule constitutionally could not burden a woman's childbearing choices by irrebuttably presuming unfitness to work when she was pregnant. Are these decisions consistent with *Geduldig*?

A third case, Nashville Gas Co. v. Satty, 434 U.S. 136 (1977), held that it was a violation of Title VII for an employer to refuse to permit a woman who left work to bear a child to retain the seniority benefits accrued before leaving work. Justice Rehnquist, writing for the Court, explained that while the policy, like the policies at issue in *Geduldig* and *Gilbert*, was facially neutral, it was unlike the policies in those previous cases because it actually favored men over women.

Why was the Court able to see sex discrimination in *Satty* and not in *Geduldig* and *Gilbert*? Could it be that in the one case, women sought benefits for a condition not experienced by men, while in the other, they sought to preserve benefits earned "like a man"?

> Roughly translated, *Gilbert* and *Satty* read together seemed to stand for the proposition that insofar as a rule deprives a woman of benefits for actual pregnancy, that rule is lawful under Title VII. If, on the other hand, it denies her benefits she had earned while not pregnant (and hence like a man) and now seeks to use upon return to her non-pregnant (male-like) status, it has a disproportionate effect on women and is not lawful.

Wendy Williams, The Equality Crisis: Some Reflections on Culture, Courts, and Feminism, 7 Women's Rts. L. Rep. 175, 192-193 (1982). Can *LaFleur* and *Turner* be explained along similar lines?

Is *Cal Fed* consistent with *Johnson Controls* (set forth on p. 124, supra)? It would seem that *Cal Fed* permits special legislation that gives pregnant women employees protection that other disabled employees may not get, while *Johnson Controls* prohibits any special protection. Is the rule that employers may give (may be even required by the state to give) special accommodations that favor pregnant women — accommodations they are free to accept or decline — but they may not protect them in a way that limits the choices available to them? In other words, protections that favor them are fine; protections that may hinder their work opportunities are not? Is this distinction satisfactory?

2. The Feminist Debate over "Equal" vs. "Special" Treatment. While a broad coalition of feminist groups advocated the passage of the PDA, once it was passed the feminist community split over the issue of what the new law meant. Feminists agreed that discrimination *against* pregnant women is sex discrimination, and bad, but disagreed profoundly over the legality and desirability of rules that attempt to eliminate some of the special disadvantages experienced by women as a consequence of pregnancy and childbirth.

What is the case for "special treatment"? As Professor Kay explains, neutral rules do not take adequate account of the extent to which the material realities of women's lives are different from those of men's lives; same treatment, simply put, cannot effectuate equality between men and women when their circumstances are so different.

The case against "special treatment" in favor of "equal treatment" can also be simply stated.

> Pregnancy [is] the centerpiece, the linchpin, the essential feature of women's separate sphere. The stereotypes, the generalizations, the role expectations [are] at their zenith when a woman [becomes] pregnant....
>
> [F]eminists who seek special recognition for pregnancy are starting from the same basic assumption, namely, that women have a special place in the scheme of human existence when it comes to maternity....
>
> The special treatment model has great costs.... [T]he reality [is] that conceptualizing pregnancy as a special case permits unfavorable as well as favorable treatment of pregnancy. Our history provides too many illustrations of the former....

Wendy W. Williams, The Equality Crisis: Some Reflections on Culture, Courts, and Feminism, 7 Women's Rts. L. Rep. 175, 191, 195-196 (1982).

Judge Posner's analysis offers a market-based rationale against "special treatment." Does his analysis have the same consequences as Williams' rationale? To what extent is Judge Posner correct that maternity leave policies "subsidize" women? Are there ordinary employment policies that subsidize men?

3. From "Special Treatment" to Full Accommodation. Professor Kay uses the sex-based uniqueness rationale of her theory to limit, as well as justify, workplace accommodations on behalf of pregnant women. Only during the episode of pregnancy when the women's body functions in a unique way, she states, should the law be allowed to treat women differently from men. Kay, supra, 1 Berkeley Women's L.J. at 34.

Professor Kay's approach is consistent with *Cal Fed*, which permits states to require employers to provide leaves for pregnant and childbearing women, even when leaves are not available for other disabilities, but only as to the sex-unique disability of pregnancy. In cases since *Cal Fed*, courts have overturned women-only childrearing leaves that go beyond the medical aspects of pregnancy- and childbirth-related conditions. See, e.g., Schafer v. Board of Public Educ., 903 F.2d 243 (3d Cir. 1990). *Troupe* represents the prevailing interpretation of the PDA that it requires that pregnant women be treated like other similarly-situated non-pregnant employees, not that pregnancy be accommodated. For a more recent case, see Gorman v. Wells Manufacturing Corp., 209 F. Supp. 2d 970

(S.D. Iowa 2002). Is it realistic to expect Ms. Troupe could meet this standard, even if she was the victim of pregnancy discrimination? See Ruth Colker, Pregnancy, Parenting, and Capitalism, 58 Ohio St. L.J. 61, 80 (1997) ("[w]hat was she supposed to find—a nonpregnant employee with a sudden record of tardiness after a nearly spotless work record who also had scheduled a lengthy leave?").

Commentators have noted that the European Union has recognized that, due to the uniqueness of pregnancy, no comparison group is necessary to establish a discrimination claim. See Jessic Carvey Manners, The Search for Mr. Troupe: The Need to Eliminate Comparison Groups in Pregnancy Discrimination Act Cases, 66 Ohio St. L.J. 209, 225-228 (2005) (discussing European Union cases). See also Judith G. Greenberg, The Pregnancy Discrimination Act: Legitimating Discrimination Against Pregnant Women in the Workforce, 50 Me. L. Rev. 225, 241 (1998) (arguing against need to find comparison group).

A problem more easily handled under the PDA than the *Troupe* situation is the pregnant woman who is a victim of sex stereotyping related to her pregnancy of the birth of her child. In Maldonado v. U.S. Bank, 186 F.3d 759 (7th Cir. 1999), for example, a bank employee was terminated after notifying her supervisor that she was pregnant, because the bank needed a teller who could work the whole summer. In holding that the bank could not take advance adverse action against Maldonado, the court noted that Maldonado had not asked for leave and had even hinted to her supervisor that she might not carry the pregnancy to term. Id at 767-778. The court did allow that:

> under narrow circumstances that we are not convinced are present here, [an employer may] project the normal inconveniences of pregnancy and their secondary effects into the future and take actions in accordance with and in proportion to those predictions.... But an employer cannot take anticipatory action unless it has a good faith basis, supported by sufficiently strong evidence, that the normal inconveniences of an employee's pregnancy will require special treatment.

186 F.3d at 767. For a fuller discussion of *Maldonado*, and the argument that pregnancy discrimination plaintiffs face increasingly high evidentiary standards, see Julie Manning Magid, Pregnant with Possibility: Reexamining the Pregnancy Discrimination Act, 38 Am. Bus. L.J. 819 (2001).

A number of other plaintiffs also have had success with claims in which assumptions were improperly made about their seriousness in the work because they had become pregnant, or had a child. In Back v. Hastings on Hudson, 365 F.3d 107 (2d Cir. 2004), for example, a school psychologist was denied tenure because, she claimed, school personnel had decided that, as a young mother, she would not be able to devote enough of herself to the job. The trial court granted summary judgment to the school district, but the Second Circuit Court of Appeals reversed, even though plaintiff had not produced a comparison male who had been better treated. Id.

In another case, plaintiff was a sales representative who was denied a promotion that went instead to a man. Among the evidence of discrimination was the fact that her supervisor admitted he didn't consider recommending her for promotion because she had children and he didn't think she'd want to relocate her family, though she hadn't told him that and, in fact, had told him frequently how much she wanted to be promoted. The supervisor also, when the plaintiff asked about a promotion, asked her why her husband wasn't going to take care of her. Lust v. Sealy, 383 F.3d 580, 583 (7th Cir. 2004). The plaintiff won at trial and the verdict was upheld on appeal in a decision written by Richard Posner, the same judge who authored the opinion in *Troupe*, although the award was reduced to $150,000—half the maximum statutorily allowed—because the employer had taken steps to remedy the discrimination.

Even where stereotyping is not as obvious as it is in these cases, another theory potentially available under existing law is that the failure to accommodate pregnancy has a disparate impact against women. A strong advocate of this theory is Christine Jolls. See Jolls, Antidiscrimination and Accommodation, 115 Harv. L. Rev. 643 (2001). See also Joan C. Williams & Nancy Segal, Beyond the Maternal Wall: Relief for Family Caregivers Who Are Discriminated Against on the Job, 26 Harv. Women's L.J. 77, 134-136 (2003) (reviewing cases). Few plaintiffs have succeeded under a disparate impact theory. Compare, e.g., EEOC v. Warshawski & Co., 768 F. Supp. 647 (N.D. Ill. 1991) (employer's policy of discharging all first-year employees who requested long-term sick leave disproportionately impacted pregnant women, in violation of PDA), with Pittsnogle v. West Virginia Dep't of Transportation, 605 S.E.2d 796 (W. Va. 2004) (two female consumer service representatives with infant children who were terminated for not attending a three-week out-of-town training session failed to state a disparate impact claim where they presented journal articles that women usually are the primary caretakers of children, but no statistical evidence that their employer's policy had a disparate impact on female consumer service representatives). In *Cal Fed*, the Court specifically had declined to address the disparate impact issue. 479 U.S. 272, 292 n.32. For discussion of women's disproportionate share of caretaking, as well as further workplace reforms and "accommodations," including paid leaves, see the next section beginning on p. 228.

Among those noting the limitations of the PDA, especially insofar as it only attacks invidious discrimination against pregnant women and not the absence of accommodations to their needs, see, e.g., Samuel Issacharoff & Elyse Rosenblum, Women and the Workplace: Accommodating the Demands of Pregnancy, 94 Colum. L. Rev. 2154, 2157 (1994); Maxine Eichner, Square Peg in a Round Hole: Parenting Policies and Liberal Theory, 59 Ohio St. L.J. 133, 141 (1998).

4. European Community Law. European Community law prohibiting discrimination based on pregnancy has developed in a direction far more favorable to the claims of pregnant women. In one case, the nondiscrimination provisions of a Council Directive of the European Community Union were found to be violated when a pregnant woman, hired without disclosing her pregnancy, was discharged, even though the only reason she had been hired was to replace another employee on maternity leave. See Case 32/93, Webb v. Emo Cargo (UK) Ltd., 1994 E.C.R. I-3567. See also Case 394/96, Brown v.

Rentokil, Ltd., 1998 E.C.R. I-4185 (holding that under European Union law, it is direct discrimination for an employer to dismiss an employee at any time during pregnancy or maternity leave for any reason connected to pregnancy, including the inability to do the job because of pregnancy-related illness); Case 177/88, Dekker v. VJV-Centrum, 1990 E.C.R. I-3941 (nondiscrimination provisions violated when employer did not hire pregnant women because the foreseeability of her incapacity meant employer could not have obtained reimbursement from government under Dutch law). These cases go well beyond *Troupe* and the Pregnancy Discrimination Act by eliminating the necessity for comparison to other disabilities; pregnancy is protected regardless of whether other disabilities are protected. As one commentator explains, the European "no comparison necessary" approach places a "badge of protection" on pregnant women, protecting them from employment-based consequences as a result of the pregnancy, whether or not those consequences would flow from other disabilities. See Claire Kilpatrick, How Long Is a Piece of String? European Regulation of the Post-Birth Period, in Sex Equality Law in the European Union, 81, 82-83 (Tamara K. Hervey & David O'Keeffe eds., 1996). Would this be a better approach to pregnancy than the one reflected in *Troupe*? Would it violate the PDA? European Union law is also more accommodating of family caretaking. See pp. 242-246, infra.

5. Pregnancy as a Disability. Coming full circle from a time when feminists fought to establish that pregnancy should not be assumed to be a disabling condition (see, e.g., Cleveland Bd. of Educ. v. LaFleur, 414 U.S. 632 (1974) discussed on pp. 220-221, supra, some have argued that the best way to recognize the disabling disadvantages of pregnancy for women is to include pregnancy as a disability under the Americans with Disabilities Act of 1990, 42 U.S.C. 12101-12213 (1995) ("ADA"), thereby requiring employers to make "reasonable accommodations" for pregnant women.

> The equal treatment model is male-centered because it accepts maleness as the norm and forces women, especially pregnant workers, to compare themselves to men to get any rights. Similarly, the special treatment model is male-centered and reminiscent of protective legislation that has always worked against women's interests.
>
> The reasonable accommodation approach applied to pregnancy avoids these problems. First, [it] is not male-centered, because it requires an individualized, case-by-case assessment — determining what each pregnant woman needs in the circumstances and the reasonableness of accommodating that need. How an employer treats men, or other disabled employees, does not determine a pregnant worker's entitlements. This case-by-case approach eludes strained analogies because each covered person is deserving in her own right, without comparisons to other groups or individuals.
>
> Finally, the reasonable accommodation standard is unlike past protective labor legislation that has worked against women's interests. Under this standard, an employer cannot implement, for example, a blanket policy excluding women from certain jobs, because the need for accommodation must be determined case-by-case. An employer could not force a woman into some "protective" accommodation

because the accommodation must be reasonable and the woman must be willing to accept the accommodation.

D'Andra Millsap, Comment, Reasonable Accommodation of Pregnancy in the Workplace: A Proposal to Amend the Pregnancy Discrimination Act, 32 Hous. L. Rev. 1411, 1434-1435 (1996).

Under current law, pregnancy is ordinarily not a disability under the ADA. See, e.g., Gorman v. Wells Manufacturing Corp., 209 F. Supp. 2d 970 (S.D. Iowa 2002); Gudenkauf v. Stauffer Communications, Inc., 922 F. Supp. 465 (D. Kan. 1996); 29 C.F.R. Pt. 1630, Appendix, Interpretive Guidelines, § 1630.2(h), Physical or Mental Impairment (1996). Some courts, however, have recognized pregnancy-related complications as disabilities under the Act. See Gabriel v. City of Chicago, 9 F. Supp. 2d 274 (N.D. Ill. 1998) (back and stomach pain are disabilities of an abnormal pregnancy); Darian v. University of Mass., 980 F. Supp. 77 (D. Mass. 1997) (severe pelvic bone pain, back pain, and premature uterine contractions are conditions constituting disabilities under the ADA).

Is the line so clear between normal and abnormal pregnancy? Some argue that advancements in medical technology may make it difficult for courts to determine what is a "normal" condition of pregnancy. Amanda G. Wachuta, Note, The ADA Gets Even More Complicated: Analyzing Pregnancy with Complications as a Disability, 52 Drake L. Rev. 471 (2004). Is the disability route even worth taking? See Judith B. Greenberg, The Pregnancy Discrimination Act: Legitimating Discrimination Against Pregnant Women in the Workforce, 50 Me. L. Rev. 225, 250 (1998) ("bringing pregnancy under the ADA would reinvigorate the stereotype of pregnant women as disabled and not fit for work").

6. Breastfeeding and the PDA. Should discrimination based on a woman's breastfeeding be protected by the PDA? Would it be protected within Professor Kay's "episodic approach" to equality? See Kay, supra, at 22, 24 (lactation covered).

Recall that the language of the PDA provides:

> The terms "because of sex" or "on the basis of sex" include, but are not limited to, because of or on the basis of pregnancy, childbirth, or related medical conditions; and women affected by pregnancy, childbirth, or related medical conditions shall be treated the same for all employment-related purposes...as other persons not so affected in their ability or inability to work.

42 U.S.C. § 2000e(k) (1994).

To date, the small number of discrimination claims relating to breastfeeding in the workplace have been unsuccessful. In considering whether one claim alleging the failure of a cable television network to accommodate a woman's breastfeeding schedule was actionable under the PDA, the court reasoned:

> [T]here is and could be no allegation that [plaintiff] was treated differently than similarly situated men. . . . As there were and could be no men with the same characteristic, all that is left . . . is a work environment hostile to breast pumping, not a

work environment that subjected women to treatment less favorable than was meted out to men.

Martinez v. NBC Inc., 49 F. Supp. 2d 305, 310 (S.D.N.Y. 1999). Is the *Martinez* reasoning familiar? Is it a sound application of the PDA? See Henry Wyatt Christrup, Litigating a Breastfeeding and Employment Case in the New Millennium, 12 Yale L.J. & Feminism 263, 279-282 (2000) (use of *Geduldig/Gilbert* reasoning in breastfeeding discrimination cases ignores congressional intent behind the PDA to change the definition of sex discrimination and protect working women from all forms of employment discrimination based on sex).

Why isn't breastfeeding a "related medical condition" within the definition of the PDA? The conventional answer is that breastfeeding is a "choice" related to parenting and the PDA should be limited to "incapacitating medical conditions for which medical care or treatment is usual and normal." Wallace v. Pyro Mining Co., 789 F. Supp. 867, 869 (W.D. Ky. 1990), aff'd, 951 F.2d 351 (6th Cir. 1991); see also Fejes v. Gilpin Ventures, Inc., 960 F. Supp. 1487, 1491 (D. Colo. 1997) (employer's unwillingness to provide a part-time work schedule while employee weaned her newborn was permissible because breastfeeding and childbearing are not conditions related to pregnancy or childbirth within the meaning of the PDA, although they may be "natural 'concomitants' of pregnancy and childbirth").

Should the following argument convince judges to the contrary?

[B]reast milk is by far the healthiest form of nourishment for newborns, conferring immunities against many diseases. Breast feeding also lowers the woman's risk of breast and ovarian cancers, diabetes, and post-menopausal bone loss, and helps reduce unhealthy pregnancy-related weight gain. Thus the law could, but currently does not, view breastfeeding as the final stage of the pregnancy cycle, readjusting the hormonal balance of the woman's body and continuing the developmentally crucial process of nourishment and bonding that began in the womb.

Jendi B. Reiter, Accommodating Pregnancy and Breastfeeding in the Workplace: Beyond the Civil Right Paradigm, 9 Tex. J. Women & L. 1, 2 (1999). Along similar lines, see Greenberg, supra, at 230-231 ("the line between 'biological' and 'non-biological' effects of pregnancy is not self-evident in the way the court would have us believe").

The failure of courts to include breastfeeding discrimination within the PDA might best be viewed as another example of courts' reasoning that child-related decisions are private choices as to which the individual woman or family should bear the full consequences. See Reiter, supra; see also Diana Kasdan, Reclaiming Title VII and the PDA: Prohibiting Workplace Discrimination Against Breastfeeding Women, 76 N.Y.U. L. Rev. 309, 333-336 (2001) (arguing that discrimination against women who are breastfeeding, whether or not is discrimination based a medical condition related to pregnancy, is inconsistent with the broader goal of the PDA to "prevent all forms of sex discrimination against women"). The issue of the significance of whether childbearing and childrearing decisions are matters of private choice is further discussed in Chapter 4, pp. 665-678.

Even if discrimination against a breastfeeding woman could be actionable under the PDA, there is still the problem of what would constitute discrimination—how much "accommodation" is required. Would a nursing mother be entitled to more, or longer, breaks? A special room? Accommodations at the workplace so that she can keep her child with her? All day?

Connecticut, Hawaii and Minnesota now require employers to accommodate the needs of nursing mothers. For a summary of these laws, and others relating to breastfeeding women (including jury duty exemptions and consideration of breastfeeding as a factor in custody and visitation decisions), see Elizabeth N. Baldwin & Kenneth A. Friedman, A Current Summary of Breastfeeding Legislation in the U.S. (July 2005), at http://www.lalccheleague.org/LawBills.html. For proposed legislation, see Melissa R. Vance, La Leche League, Summary of Proposed Breastfeeding Legislation in the United States (July 5, 2005), http://www.lalecheleague.org/Law/proposedsummary.html. Other resources include Shana M. Christrup, Breastfeeding in the American Workplace, 9 Am. U. J. Gender Soc. Pol'y & L. 471 (2001); Lara M. Gardner, A Step Toward True Equality in the Workplace: Requiring Employer Accommodation for Breastfeeding Women, 17 Wis. Women's L.J. 259, 285-288 (2002).

The ability of nursing mothers to breastfeed in public has also been an issue. Some courts have concluded that bans or restrictions on breastfeeding in public do not violate their state's public accommodation nondiscrimination statutes. See, e.g., Derungs v. Wal-Mart Stores, 374 F.3d 428 (6th Cir. 2004) (storeowners or managers of places of public accommodation may restrict breastfeeding in their stores or establishments). Increasingly, state legislatures have acted to protect women who wish to breastfeed in public places. See, e.g., Cal. Civil Code § 43.3 (2006); N.J. Stat. Ann. § 26:4B-4 (2006); Ohio Rev. Code Ann. § 3781.55 (2006) (responding to *Derungs* case). See Brianne Whelan, For Crying Out Loud: Ohio's Legal Battle with Public Breastfeeding and Hope for the Future, 13 J. Gender, Social Pol'y & L. 669 (2005).

2. Work and Family

State v. Bachmann
521 N.W.2d 886 (Minn. Ct. App. 1994)

SCHUMACHER, Judge.

Appellant Suzanne Margie Bachmann claims that the district court erred by denying her motion for postconviction relief on the basis that she was not eligible for work-release privileges. We affirm.

In November 1993, Bachmann pleaded guilty to one count of burglary in the second degree and one count of check forgery. As part of her sentence, she was ordered to spend 90 days in the county jail.

Following her sentencing, Bachmann requested that she be granted work-release privileges while serving her 90-day jail term. Bachmann is not presently employed outside the home. Instead, she wished to be released from jail on weekdays in order to care for her four children and perform other homemaking services for her husband and children, for which her husband agreed to pay her $1.50 per hour. The district court concluded that Bachmann was not eligible for work-release and denied her motion.

Is a homemaker eligible for work-release? . . . Minn. Stat. § 631.425, subd. 3 (1992) provides:

> If the person committed under [the work-release statute] has been regularly employed, the sheriff shall arrange for a continuation of the employment insofar as possible without interruption. If the person is not employed, the court may designate a suitable person or agency to make reasonable efforts to secure some suitable employment for that person. An inmate employed under this section must be paid a fair and reasonable wage for work performed and must work at fair and reasonable hours per day and per week.

Bachmann argues that homemaking is employment within the meaning of this statutory language. We disagree.

Bachmann's homemaking services clearly have economic value. Nevertheless, homemaking is generally not considered employment. For example, in the context of workers' compensation:

> The upkeep and care of a home for one's self and family are not in the category of a trade, business, profession or occupation, as generally understood. A home is not established and maintained in the expectation of pecuniary gain. Such a venture is solely an expense. . . .

Eichholz v. Shaft [208 N.W. 18, 19-20 (Minn. 1926)].

Similarly, in holding that a domestic servant could not picket the home in which he had been employed, the supreme court reasoned:

> The validity of defendant's argument depends upon whether a home, exclusively used as such, may be said to be a place for the carrying on of an industrial or a business enterprise. Obviously the home cannot be so classified.
>
> "The home is an institution, not an industry." . . .

[Barres v. Watterson Hotel Co., 244 S.W. 308, 309, 310 (Ky. Ct. App. 1922).] . . .

And the same result was reached in Anderson v. Ueland, [267 N.W. 517, 518, 927] where we said:

> . . . the home is a sacred place for people to go and be quiet and at rest and not be bothered with the turmoil of industry," and that as such it is "a sanctuary of the individual and should not be interfered with by industrial disputes." We think [this] conception of "home" as "a sanctuary of the individual" is sound. The word is defined as, "the abiding place of the affections, esp. domestic affections"; as "the social unit formed by a family residing together in one dwelling," and as "an organized center of family life."

[State v. Cooper, 285 N.W. 903, 904-905 (Minn. 1939).]

The fact that Bachmann's husband has offered to pay an hourly wage to her does not change our conclusion. First, Bachmann has an obligation to care for her children regardless of whether she is paid to do so. . . . Second, income received by Bachmann is marital property. Thus, Bachmann's husband has a common ownership interest in her income. . . . The Bachmanns have not shown that their proposed wage agreement results in either gain or loss to either person; unlike the typical employment relationship, the economic exchange between the Bachmanns would be purely illusory. . . .

The district court properly concluded that Bachmann was not eligible for work-release to perform homemaking responsibilities for her family.

═══ *Jill Elaine Hasday, Intimacy and Economic*
═══ *Exchange*
119 Harv. L. Rev. 492, 517-519 (2005)

[L]egal efforts to mark the specialness of intimate relationships by limiting or prohibiting economic exchange within them appear to have systematically adverse distributional consequences for women and poorer people, maintaining and increasing distributive inequality. . . .

. . . More specifically, the law's strategies for affirming the distinctiveness of intimacy appear to steadily assume that women — including relatively poor women — need not be compensated for their activities. On this view, women can be deprived of a direct claim to economic assets based on their own activities because they will be supported by other people. In the process, the law helps produce the situation it purports only to describe, making self-support more difficult and enhancing the need to rely on others.

For instance, the law's refusal to enforce interspousal contracts for domestic services is meant to promote the dignity and distinctiveness of the marital relation by declaring its separation from the market. . . . [S]ome women may receive more in the marital support their husbands choose to provide than they would receive if they had a legal right to be paid for their domestic work. . . . The refusal to enforce interspousal contracts for domestic services, [however], ensures that more wives receive their economic assets in the form of provided support (social exchange) rather than legally negotiated compensation (legal exchange) and in this way helps perpetuate married women's dependence on their husbands.

═══ *Katharine Silbaugh, Turning Labor into Love:*
═══ *Housework and the Law*
91 Nw. U. L. Rev. 1, 80-84 (1996)

By failing to enforce contracts between spouses providing wages for housework, the law explicitly prohibits attempts to obtain security for labor on the grounds that bargains in families are inappropriate to the affections of family life. When love motivates work at home, nothing but love should be its reward.

By providing no opportunity for houseworkers to make contributions to the social security system on their own behalf and to combine those contributions with contributions from wage labor, the law denies the houseworker the opportunity to gain a stake in the nation's old-age financial safety net. In social security law, financial security for houseworkers is ensured only through the maintenance of intimate relationships, not through a history of work in the home. By tying full-time houseworkers' social security payments to the length of a marriage, the emotions themselves become the measure of desert within the system.

At the time of divorce, wages are discussed as a part of the contribution to family wealth in dollar amounts, while housework is discussed in any number of ways, but almost never in terms of concrete dollar contributions. Housework can warrant property awards because a houseworker is financially needy, but it is less common for courts to make financial awards because a houseworker is considered to have contributed as much to the material wealth of a family as a wage-earner. If a person contributes both wages and housework, only one of those contributions can be weighed at divorce. Because need and not desert sets the stage for alimony awards at divorce, any surplus wage, beyond the needs of a houseworker spouse, is retained by the wage-earner at the time of divorce, while the houseworker spouse is left without skills that translate into liquidity. When the affections of a marriage have died, the houseworker's stake in the wealth generated by her labor is also lost, including marketable human capital. . . .

The productive nature of housework is implicitly rejected in the failure to tax it as income. By treating the family, rather than the individuals within it, as the taxable unit, we assume a sharing of wealth that is not compelled by law. In tax, divorce, and contract law, we allow one spouse to earn cash and keep it away from the other spouse, but houseworkers have only a limited similar ability to withhold the benefits of their labor from a spouse. The sharing presumed by tax law and upon which benefits can be delivered to a wage-earning tax-payer must result from the emotional bond within a marriage because legal compulsion to share does not exist. . . .

Paid domestic workers, a field populated by immigrant women and women of color, do not receive the protection of basic labor laws in part because they work where expression takes the form of affections rather than of market dealings. Moreover, the wage of a paid domestic worker is driven down by competition with a tax-subsidized unpaid houseworker — the competition, the unpaid houseworker, can do the work for less because there are no taxes.

All other attempts to monetize housework depend on the paid domestic worker's substitution cost. For example, in loss of consortium and wrongful death cases, courts will often accept direct testimony on the costs of hiring a housekeeper, nurse, or child care worker. If those workers' wages are already deflated by tax subsidies to their competition, the low monetary value of housework will be perpetuated throughout the law. At divorce, housework is often understood to have lower economic value than the wage contribution of paid workers, particularly when the paid worker is middle class or richer. The courts' understanding of the value of housework, however, is influenced by a market for paid domestic labor that is itself a product of law.

In all of these ways, the affectionate characterizations of housework are used to justify treatment of the houseworker that leaves her without financial security. Given these consequences of a conception of housework as exclusively an expression of affection, houseworkers would benefit from a fuller conception of housework, one that shows its significant similarities to wage labor.

[In *Bachmann,*]...[t]he work-release statute did not speak to the status of houseworkers one way or the other, but the court found ample support in the law for its understanding that housework is so different from paid work that it cannot be covered by the same statute. This interpretation undoubtedly flies in the face of Suzanne Bachmann's understanding of her position: one suspects that from her first day in jail, the family took on new expenses either from her husband's lost wages or in the form of child care expenses. Bachmann certainly would understand that the money lost was a result of work that she could no longer do.

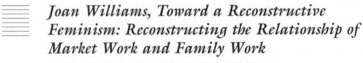

Joan Williams, Toward a Reconstructive Feminism: Reconstructing the Relationship of Market Work and Family Work
19 N. Ill. U. L. Rev. 89, 89-93 (1998)

Domesticity remains the entrenched, almost unquestioned, American norm and practice. As a gender system it has two defining characteristics. The first is its organization of market work around the ideal of a worker who works full-time and overtime and takes little or no time off for childbearing or childrearing. Though this ideal-worker norm does not define all jobs today, it defines the good ones: full-time blue-collar jobs in the working-class context, and high level executive and professional jobs for the middle-class and above. When work is structured in this way, caregivers often cannot perform as ideal workers. Their inability to do so gives rise to domesticity's second defining characteristic: its system of providing for caregiving by marginalizing the caregivers, thereby cutting them off from most of the social roles that offer responsibility and authority.

Domesticity introduced not only a new structuring of market work and family work but also a new description of men and women. The ideology of domesticity held that men "naturally" belong in the market because they are competitive and aggressive; women belong in the home because of their "natural" focus on relationships, children, and an ethic of care. In its original context, domesticity's descriptions of men and women served to justify and reproduce its breadwinner/housewife roles by establishing norms that identified successful gender performance with character traits suitable for those roles.

Both the ideology and the practice of domesticity retain their hold. A recent survey found that fully two-thirds of Americans believe it would be best for women to stay home and care for family and children. Domesticity's descriptions of men and women persist in vernacular gender talk such as John Gray's Men Are from Mars, Women Are from Venus, as well as in the strain of feminist theory that associates women with an ethic of care. [For more on the ethic of care, see Chapter 4].

Even more important, market work continues to be structured in ways that perpetuate the economic vulnerability of caregivers. Their vulnerability stems from the way we define the ideal worker, as someone who works at least forty hours a week year round. This ideal worker norm, framed around the traditional life patterns of men, excludes most mothers. Nearly two-thirds of mothers of child-bearing age are not ideal workers even in the minimal sense of working full-time full year. One quarter of mothers of child-bearing age still are home-makers. Single, as well as married mothers are affected: never married mothers are the group of women most likely to be at home.

Moreover, full-time work is no guarantee of avoiding economic vulnerability: even mothers who work full-time often find themselves on the "mommy track." In addition, full-time workers who cannot work overtime often suffer economically because many of the best jobs now require substantial overtime. A rarely recognized, but extraordinarily important fact is that jobs requiring extensive overtime exclude virtually all mothers (93 percent).

Our economy is divided into mothers and others. Having children has a very strong negative effect on women's income, an effect that actually increased in the 1980s despite the fact that women have become better educated. . . . As a result, in an era when women's wages are catching up with men's, mothers' wages lag behind. Given that nearly 90% of women become mothers during their working lives, this pattern is inconsistent with gender equality.

If mothers have failed to achieve equality in market work, equality in the family has proved equally elusive. Buying and cooking food, doing dishes and laundry, caring for children: on average mothers spend thirty-one hours a week on these tasks. Many commentators have noted the contradiction: despite our self-image of gender equality, American women still do 80% of child care and two-thirds of core housework.

In short, the basic elements of domesticity's organization of market work and family work remain intact. . . . Women still specialize in family work. Men still specialize in market work. Market work continues to be framed around the assumption that ideal workers have access to a flow of family work few mothers enjoy. Social and cultural norms still sustain and reproduce this organization of (market and family) work.

Domesticity did not die; it mutated. In the nineteenth century most married women were marginalized outside of the economy. Although women have reentered market work, most remain marginalized today. This is not equality.

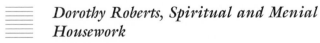

Dorothy Roberts, *Spiritual and Menial Housework*

9 Yale J.L. & Feminism 51, 55-59 (1997)

The "cult of domesticity" legitimized the confinement of women to the private sphere by defining women as suited for motherhood (and unsuited for public life) because of their moral or spiritual nature. Thus, the very idealization of women's spirituality bolstered the opposition between maternal nurturing in the home and masculine work in the cutthroat marketplace.

Household labor, however, is not all spiritual. It involves nasty, tedious physical tasks — standing over a hot stove, cleaning toilets, scrubbing stains off of floors and out of shirts, changing diapers and bedpans. The notion of a purely spiritual domesticity could only be maintained by cleansing housework of its menial parts. The ideological separation of home from market, then, dictated the separation of spiritual and menial housework. Housework's undesirable tasks had to be separated physically and ideologically from the moral aspects of family life.

This dichotomy has two important consequences. First, women may delegate housework's menial tasks to others while retaining their more valuable spiritual duties. Second, this fragmentation fosters a hierarchy among women because the menial aspects of housework are typically delegated by more privileged women to less privileged ones. At the same time, the availability of a class of menial workers, sustained by race and class subordination, makes this division of women's housework possible. Although women's participation in the market is now widely accepted, the assignment of household work to women and the distinction between spiritual and menial housework both persist. In the hit movie *The First Wives' Club*, the character played by Diane Keaton complains to her friends about the work she did for her ex-husband: "I washed his shorts, I ironed them, and I starched them." "You did?" her friends respond in amazement. "Well, I supervised," Keaton clarifies. This scene conveys the spiritual housewife's relationship to menial housework: she supervises the labor of less privileged women.

An early example of the distinction between spiritual and menial housework is embodied in the relationship between Mammy and her mistress. The image of Mammy was that of a rotund, handkerchiefed house servant who humbly nursed her master's children. Mammy was both the perfect mother and the perfect slave; whites saw her as a "passive nurturer, a mother figure who gave all without expectation of return, who not only acknowledged her inferiority to whites but who loved them." It is important to recognize, however, that Mammy did not reflect any virtue in Black motherhood. The ideology of Mammy placed no value in Black women as the mothers of their own children. Rather, whites claimed Mammy's total devotion to the master's children, without regard to the fate of Mammy's own offspring. Moreover, Mammy, while caring for the master's children, remained under the constant supervision of her white mistress. She had no real authority over either the white children she raised or the Black children she bore. Mammy's domestic labor is the perfect illustration of menial housework; her mistress, on the other hand, performed the spiritual work in the house.

One of Mammy's chores was to serve as a wetnurse for her mistress's babies. Delegating breastfeeding to a servant shows how housework's menial features can be detached from even the most intimate of maternal tasks. Today breastfeeding seems emblematic of the spiritual bond between mother and infant, the closest possible connection between two human beings. It is the epitome of maternal nurturing. Yet in the past the physical labor of breastfeeding was disengaged from its spiritual features to permit its performance by a morally inferior slave. When the servant nursed the mistress's baby, this act was not expected to create the sacred bond that existed between the white mother and her child. Thus, the servant could conveniently do the mistress's work without appropriating the mistress's spiritual attributes. In other words, the nature of the work—whether spiritual or menial—depended on the status of the woman performing it.

Today, the spiritual/menial split enables many professional women to go to work without disturbing the sexual division of housework or relinquishing their role as spiritual housekeepers. In her study of domestics and the women who employ them, Judith Rollins found that middle-class women's entry in the workplace did not change their attitudes toward their role in the home. According to Rollins, "The middle-class women I interviewed were not demanding that their husbands play a greater role in housekeeping; they accepted the fact that responsibility for domestic maintenance was theirs, and they solved the problem of their dual responsibilities by hiring other women to assist."[25] Female employers usually view their maids as an extension of the more menial part of themselves rather than as autonomous employees. Hiring a domestic worker leaves the employer free both to work outside the home and to devote herself to the spiritual aspects of being a wife and mother.

The modern household worker's job is defined in a way that prevents its interference with the female employer's spiritual prerogatives. Even if a child spends the entire day with her nanny while her mother is at work, the hour of "quality time" mother and child share at bedtime is considered most important. Of course, the mother expects the nanny to develop a warm and caring relationship with the child. She wants the nanny to treat the child as a special person, and not as a chore. But the mother nevertheless desires her own relationship with her child to be superior to—closer, healthier, and more influential than—the relationship the child has with the nanny.

In her study of working mothers who hire in-home nannies, Cameron Macdonald identified the employers' contradictory impulses:

> [T]he mother's expectation that her nanny care for and love her children as she would herself frequently collides with her own desire to be the primary care giver and with her belief in the ideology of mother-intensive child rearing; it also conflicts with the assumption that the quality of the mother-child relationship should be the same as if she were at home full-time and someone else were not doing the bulk of the actual care.[26]

Macdonald found that the mothers she studied wanted the nanny to operate as a "shadow mother," acting like a mother during the day and then vanishing as soon as the real mother returned, "leaving no trace of her presence in the psychic lives of the children they shared."

These incompatible motives parallel another dilemma mothers face in delegating child care to a less privileged employee. In another study of private child care arrangements, Julia Wrigley discovered that parents were torn between their desire to hire a high-status substitute mother and their preference for a manageable subordinate. "They would like caregivers who share their child-rearing values

25. Judith Rollins, Between Women: Domestics and Their Employers 104 (1985), reprinted in Working in the Service Society (Cameron Lynne Macdonald & Carmen Sirianni eds., 1996).

26. [Cameron Lynne Macdonald, Shadow Mothers: Nannies, Au Pairs, and Invisible Work, in Working in the Service Society 250 (Cameron Lynne Macdonald & Carmen Sirianni eds., 1996).]

and who operate independently," Wrigley explains, "but they also want inexpensive, reliable, controllable employees."[29] Parents often resolve this dilemma by relying on their spiritual supervision of the low-status employees' menial work. For example, one employer commented that "sometimes it was better to accept 'dumb' employees who are under the parents' control rather than deal with cocky ones." In both studies, employers resolved their contradictory desires by distinguishing between their own spiritual and the employees' menial housework.

Thus, the mother's spiritual moments with her child are far more valuable than the long hours the nanny spends caring for the child. Moreover, the working mother might not be able to devote quality time to her child at all if she came home to face the chores that the nanny took care of during the day. Some working mothers also hire another woman, who has even lower status, to clean the house and run errands. By delegating work to a nanny and/or maid, affluent women can fulfill their spiritual calling as mother despite their career in the market.

What is wrong with distinguishing between the roles played by the mother and by the woman she hires to care for her children? Would we not expect to find a difference between a child's relationship with her parents and with the paid household help? My point is not that we should eradicate all distinctions among people who perform housework, but to demonstrate how the distinction made between spiritual and menial housework fosters both a gendered and racialized devaluation of this type of labor. By separating spiritual from menial housework, both the mother and the nanny continue to be undercompensated for their work in the home despite working women's supposed liberation from domestic confinement.

Notes

1. Women's Disproportionate Housework and Caretaking Burdens. Some years ago, sociologist Arlie Hochschild coined the term "second shift" to describe the social norm under which women who work for wages are also expected to take care of the house and the children when they return home. See Hochschild, The Second Shift: Working Parents and the Revolution at Home (1989). Recent studies show that men's share of housework and caretaking has increased, but that women still spend more time in these activities than men, both on workdays and days off work. Eight out of ten working mothers report that they do far more of the household chores than their spouse or partner—results with which surveyed men agreed. See http://mothersandmore. org/press_room/statistics.shtml (last checked September 16, 2005) (citing studies). Employed adult women spend about an hour more per day than employed adult men doing household activities and caring for household members, see http://www.bls.gov/news.release/atus.nr0.htm (last checked September 16, 2005), although men's housework time has almost doubled since 1965. See Suzanne M. Bianchi et al., Is Anyone Doing the Housework? Trends

29. [Julia Wrigley, Other People's Children 5 (1995).]

in the Gender Division of Household Labor, 79 Soc. Forces 191, 196 (Sept. 2000). Men have 30 minutes more of free time per day, and mothers spend more free time alone with children than fathers do. See Marybeth J. Mattingly & Suzanne M. Bianchi, Gender Differences in the Quantity and Quality of Free Time: The U.S. Experience, 81 Social Forces 999, 1014-1015 (March 2003). For other studies, see Julie E. Artis & Elza K. Pavalko, Explaining the Decline in Women's Household Labor: Individual Change and Cohort Differences, 65 J. Marriage & Family 746 (2003); Scott Coltrane, Research on Household Labor: Modeling and Measuring the Social Embeddedness of Routine Family Work, 62 J. Marriage & Fam. 1208 (2000); John P. Robinson & Geoffrey Godbey, Time for Life: The Surprising Ways Americans Use Their Time 100, 334 (1997).

More than a decade ago, studies showed that although working women do more family work than working men, only one-quarter to one-third see this arrangement as unfair. See Mary Clare Lennon & Sarah Rosenfield, Relative Fairness and the Division of Housework: The Importance of Options, 100 Am. J. Soc. 506, 507 (1994). What might explain this fact? See id. (women who have fewer alternatives to marriage and less economic resources are more likely to view uneven division of housework as fair). Is it possible that women just enjoy housework more, or hate it less? See Amy Kroska, Investigating Gender Differences in the Meaning of Household Chores and Child Care, 65 J. Marriage & Family 456, 463, 466 (May 2003) (women attribute more positive, powerful meanings than men to specific household chores such as baby care, meal preparation, and laundry, although women's time in paid labor is negatively related to these positive meanings). Is it simply a matter of expectations? See Rhona Mahony, Kidding Ourselves: Breadwinning, Babies, and Bargaining Power (1995) (using economic game theory to show how negotiations within marriage can produce a traditional division of childcare labor even when both partners are consciously committed to equality); Peggy Orenstein, Flux: Women on Sex, Work, Love, Kids, and Life in a Half-Changed World (2000) (interviewing young career women who reported that they expected to some day marry a man with a high-paying job and leave the workforce to raise children). Drawing on sociological theory, Naomi Cahn suggests that wives take responsibility for a disproportionate share of housework and child care as a way of "performing gender": since women are expected to mother and to take care of the house, doing so gives wives both social approval and interpersonal power. Naomi Cahn, Gendered Identities: Women and Household Work, 44 Vill. L. Rev. 525, 532 (1999); Naomi Cahn, The Power of Caretaking, 12 Yale J.L. & Feminism 177 (2000).

Women provide about 70 percent of all elder care. Peggie R. Smith, Elder Care, Gender, and Work: The Work-Family Issue of the 21st Century, 25 Berkeley J. Emp. & Lab. L. 351, 360 (2004). See also Elizabeth Lehr Essex & Jinkuk Hong, Older Caregiving Parents: Division of Household Labor, Marital Satisfaction, and Caregiver Burden, 54 Fam. Relations 448 (July 2005) (study showing traditional division of household labor for care of adult disabled children).

2. Accommodation vs. Discrimination. As with pregnancy and childbearing (see Section 1, supra), the question arises whether workplace changes for employees with caretaking responsibilities are best viewed as *accommodations* to employees with special needs, or as necessary components of a *non-discriminatory* workplace? Some scholars take a clear accommodation perspective arguing that, like disability or religion, employers have an obligation to undertake some expense and inconvenience if necessary to make it possible for caretakers to be full-fledged members of the work force. See Peggie R. Smith, Accommodating Routine Parental Obligations in an Era of Work-Family Conflict: Lessons from Religious Accommodations, 2001 Wis. L. Rev. 1443; Laura Kessler, The Attachment Gap: Employment Discrimination Law, Women's Cultural Caregiving, and the Limits of the Economic and Liberal Legal Theory, 34 U. Mich. J.L. Reform 371 (2001). Viewed this way, as measures to overcome disadvantages women experience from engaging in gendered activities, workplace accommodations to workers with caretaking responsibilities clearly spring from notions of substantive, rather than formal, equality.

Other scholars have tried to resist the equal treatment/special treatment dichotomy. A critical part of this resistance has been the argument that the workplace is not a neutral structure that needs to be rearranged in women's favor, but rather a set of arrangements already favoring an ideal worker who is male and has no caretaking responsibilities. See Lucinda Finley, Transcending Equality Theory: A Way Out of the Maternity and the Workplace Debate, 86 Colum. L. Rev. 1118 (1986). Restructuring the workplace to assume workers with caretaking responsibilities is not "special treatment" for women, these feminists argue, but rather a recognition of the fundamental reality of women's place in the work force. Joan Williams' call for a "reconstructive feminism" (excerpted in this section) is in this vein. In earlier work Williams argued that the focus of discussion should be not on theories of equality, but on how household work should be allocated within the household, how the cost of childrearing should be shifted from the private to the public arena, and what workplace restructuring should occur. Joan Williams, Do Women Need Special Treatment? Do Feminists Need Equality?, 9 J. Contemp. Legal Issues 279, 285-296 (1998). Does this formulation escape the choice between nondiscrimination and accommodation?

An important part of the case Joan Williams makes for workplace reforms is that a restructured workplace to better accommodate employees with caretaking responsibilities is, in fact, necessary for a more efficient workplace.

> [E]mployers who provide family-friendly workplaces often save money because of decreased attrition and absenteeism, as well as enhancing recruitment and productivity. Practice that employees deem to reflect business necessity may in fact reflect business-irrational practices driven by gender stereotypes. We call this the "discrimination model, linked with the business case."

Joan C. Williams & Nancy Segal, Beyond the Maternal Wall: Relief for Family Caregivers Who Are Discriminated Against on the Job, 26 Harv. Women's L.J. 77, 79 (2003). Is this plausible, i.e., if employers better understood the economics, workplaces would be more family-friendly?

If nondiscrimination is understood to encompass the absence of a disparate impact, one can justify accommodation within a nondiscrimination framework. This is the analysis of Christine Jolls. See Jolls, Antidiscrimination and

Accommodation, 115 Harv. L. Rev. 642, 648 (2001) (defining accommodation to mean incurring special costs in response to distinctive needs). Does this solve the problem? As noted above at p. 224, Williams and Segal, like Jolls, urge greater use of the disparate impact theory. Williams and Segal reject Jolls' accommodation language, however, which they say "sends the unstated message that the woman 'asking for accommodation' is demanding special treatment... [when] the real problem lies with workplace structures rather than with the women"). Id. at 86.

3. Is Caretaking a Public Good? Are work and family conflicts private matters, to be resolved between couples? Workplace issues in which the employer has important responsibilities to reshape the workplace? Family law issues in which the caretaker's contributions to the household are defined in laws governing spousal maintenance, marital property, and marital contracts? Political issues that need to be addressed through social security reform, tax credits, and laws such as the one at issue in *Bachmann*? Government benefits issues that require consideration of more generous welfare programs, such as day-care, vouchers, and wage-replacement grants for caregiving? All of the above? Does the concept of substantive equality point toward any one of these types of measures more than another? What determines which set of results makes the most sense?

Joan Williams attacks the view that work-family conflicts are private issues, arguing that primary caregivers provide the flow of family work that allows "ideal workers" to assume heavily employment responsibilities. See Joan Williams, Unbending Gender: Why Family and Work Conflict and What to Do About It 274 (2000). In this regard, the studies show that men with children work more hours in outside employment than men without children, while the average number of hours worked by women declines when they have children. See http://mothersandmore.org/press_room/statistics.shtml (last checked September 16, 2005) (citing studies). See also Nancy Folbre, The Invisible Heart: Economics and Family Values (2001) (arguing that family life and family values are integral to capitalist markets across a number of domains); Laura T. Kessler, The Attachment Gap: Employment Discrimination Law, Women's Cultural Caregiving, and the Limits of Economic and Liberal Legal Theory, 34 U. Mich. J.L. Reform 371 (2001) (arguing that existing Title VII law relies on a view of women's nurturing work as the result of impaired agency growing out of gender socialization, rather than important and valuable to all of society).

Is the main point to equalize the costs to women of bearing a disproportionate share of caretaking and household tasks? Or is there a more positive, transformative vision of work and family that should inform this discussion? On the latter, and for further development of models of reform emphasizing the affirmative revaluing of women's nurturing work rather than the alleviation of burdens resulting from women's differences, see Chapter 4, pp. 665-677.

Caregiver suits are increasing. In addition to those described in Section 1 (pregnancy) and in Williams & Segal, supra, research directed by Cynthia Calvert at the Worklife Law Program at American University School of Law found 170 verdicts in caregiver discrimination suits between 2000 and 2005. See Dee

McAree, "Sex-Plus" Gender Bias Lawsuits on the Rise, Nat'l L.J., March 7, 2005, at 4.

4. Parenting Leave: The Family and Medical Leave Act. In 1993, Congress passed the federal Family and Medical Leave Act ("FMLA"), 29 U.S.C. §§ 2601-2654 (1999). The FMLA requires employers of more than 50 workers allow up to a three-month, unpaid leave for the care of a new infant or ill family member, with the right to return to the same or an equivalent position without loss of pre-leave benefits. The Act covers employees who have worked for the employer for at least 12 months and for 1,250 hours during the year preceding the start of the leave. At the time of the passage of the FMLA, South Africa was the only other industrialized state without a federal family leave policy.

A 1996 report to Congress found that more than 90 percent of employers said most aspects of the law were "very easy" or "somewhat easy" to administer, more than 89 percent found they incurred "no cost" or "small costs," and more than 86 percent reported "no noticeable effect" on productivity, profitability, and growth. Marc Mory & Lia Pistilli, Note, The Failure of the Family and Medical Leave Act: Alternative Proposals for Contemporary Working Families, 18 Hofstra Lab. & Employment L.J. 689, 697 (2001). As of 1998, however, more than seventy-five percent of working mothers who were eligible to take advantage of rights afforded under the FMLA were unable to do so. "In fact, a recent study by the U.S. Department of Labor found that 88 percent of eligible employees who need time off do not take it because they cannot afford to go without a paycheck." Id. at 689 (quoting 147 Cong. Rec. H188-89 (daily ed. Feb. 6, 2001) (statement of Rep. Woolsey).

Even many who can afford to take leave sometimes do not do so because of resistance by supervisors and colleagues. One study of highly educated individuals found that about a third of women and almost half of men reported that their workplace culture penalized employees for taking advantage of family friendly policies. Sylvia Hewlett & Carolyn Buck Luce, Off Ramps and On Ramps: Keeping Talented Women on the Road to Success, Harv. Bus. Rev., March 2005, at 43. A more specific study of the implementation of the Family and Medical Leave found that many employees did not assert their rights because of well-founded concerns of informal retaliation and blacklisting; they feared being branded as a "troublemaker" or "slacker" and not getting favorable assignments, shifts, or recommendations if they changed jobs. Catherine R. Albiston, Bargaining in the Shadow of Social Institutions: Competing Discourses and Social Change in the Workplace Mobilization of Civil Rights, 39 Law & Soc'y Rev. 11, 23-27, 31-38 (2005). Several studies also have revealed that many employees, when faced with work/family conflicts, prefer alternative solutions to reducing their hours or taking unpaid leave — such as flextime or flexplace. See, e.g., Rosemarie Feuerbach Twomey & Gwen E. Jones, The Family and Medical Leave Act of 1993: A Longitudinal Study of Male and Female Perceptions, 3 Emp. Rts. & Emp. Pol'y J. 229, 249-250 (1999).

The resistance to taking family leave appears to be greater among men than among women. U.S. Department of Labor statistics gathered in 2000 showed that 19.8 percent of female employees take family leave, as compared to only 13.5

percent of male employees. U.S. Dep't of Labor, Balancing the Needs of Families and Employers: The Family and Medical Leave Surveys 2000, at http://www.dol.gov/asp/fmla. This overstates the use men are making of FMLA to address work/family issues. According to the DOL surveys, only seven percent of male employees took leave for care of newborn, ill child, ill spouse, or ill parent — as compared to 12.1 percent of female employees. Men are more likely to take leave for reasons of their own health (7.8 percent) than for these other reasons; while women take leave more often than men for their own health reasons (9.6 percent), fewer take leaves for their own health than take leaves for the care of others. Id. See Chuck Halverson, Note, From Here to Paternity: Why Men Are Not Taking Paternity Leave Under the Family and Medical Leave Act, 18 Wis. Women's L.J. 257 (2003) (surveying DOL and other studies). Why could explain this disparity? See id. at 261-270 (considering factors of social stigma, financial inability to take leave, knowledge of leave options, and resistance by employers). Is it a problem, to which solutions should be sought?

The major recent effort to expand parental leave, The Family Leave Expansion Act, would enlarge the scope of FMLA to cover businesses with over 25 employees, and fund pilot state programs to offer full or partial wage replacement. See S. 282, 109th Cong. (2005); Cong. Rec. S. 984 (Daily Ed., Feb. 3, 2005) (statement of Senator Dodd). The Act has not yet been enacted.

Should the FMLA provide for a *paid* family leave? Who should pay? Gillian Lester, who advocates a comprehensive set of interlocking programs (including day care, antidiscrimination laws, income tax policies and a shorter workweek), argues in favor of the expansion of state insurance programs, like unemployment insurance and temporary disability insurance, to provide wage replacement during parental or family illness leave. Lester, A Defense of State Paid Family Leave, 28 Harv. J.L. & Gender 1, 3-4 (2005). See also Katherine Elizabeth Ulrich, Insuring Family Risks: Suggestions for National Family Policy and Wage Replacement, 14 Yale J.L. & Feminism 1 (2002). In 2002, California became the first state to amend a state disability program to include up to six weeks of compensation for leaves to care for an ill family member, or the birth, adoption, or foster care placement of a new child. Cal. Unemp. Ins. Code § 3301 (Deering 2004), discussed in Jennifer Thompson, Family and Medical Leave for the 21st Century?: A First Glance at California's Paid Family Leave Legislation, 12 U. Miami Bus. L. Rev. 77, 92 (2004); Kathryn Kroggel, Absent Fathers: National Paid Paternity Leave for the United States — Examinations of Foreign and State-Oriented Models, 23 Penn. St. Int'l L. Rev. 439, 462-470 (2004). Twenty-one states have introduced bills to expand their unemployment insurance programs to provide wage replacement for parental leaves. Lester, supra, at 3.

The major recent judicial development has been the U.S. Supreme Court's decision in Nevada v. Hibbs, 538 U.S. 721(2003), upholding the constitutionality of the application of the FMLA to state employees, which Joan Williams uses as an example of a new trend of judicial leniency toward family caregivers. See Joan C. Williams, *Hibbs* as a Federalism Case; *Hibbs* as a Maternal Wall Case, 73 U. Cin. L. Rev. 365 (2004). In *Hibbs*, Nevada argued that a damage remedy was not available against states under the FMLA because of the Eleventh Amendment's guarantee of state sovereign immunity. Chief Justice Rehnquist, writing for a 6-3 majority of the court, held that the FMLA was within the power granted to Congress by the Fourteenth Amendment:

> The FMLA aims to protect the right to be free from gender-based discrimination in the workplace. . . . The history of the many state laws limited women's employment opportunities is chronicled in — and, until relatively recently, was sanctioned by — this Court's own opinions. . . . Congress responded to this history of discrimination by abrogating States' sovereign immunity in Title VII of the Civil Rights Act of 1964. . . . According to the evidence that was before Congress when it enacted the FMLA, States continue to rely on invalid gender stereotypes in the employment context, specifically in the administration of leave benefits. . . . As the FMLA's legislative record reflects, a 1990 Bureau of Labor Statistics survey stated that 37 percent of surveyed private-sector employees were covered by maternity leave policies, while only 18 percent were covered by paternity leave policies. . . . Congress . . . heard testimony that . . . 'Even . . . [w]here child-care leave policies do exist, men, *both in the public and private sectors*, receive notoriously discriminatory treatment in their requests for such leave.' . . . Many States offered women extended 'maternity' leave that far exceeded the typical 4- to 8-week period of physical disability due to pregnancy and childbirth, but very few States granted men a parallel benefit: Fifteen States provided women up to one year of extended maternity leave, while only four provided men with the same. . . . This and other differential leave policies were not attributable to any differential physical needs of men and women, but rather to the pervasive sex-role stereotype that caring for family members is women's work.

538 U.S. at 728-731.

Is Chief Justice Rehnquist correct that differences in leave policies are not attributable to any differential physical needs of men and women? Can the conclusion, based on the failure of states to guarantee equality in employment benefits, be squared with the majority decision also written by Chief Justice Rehnquist, in United States v. Morrison, 529 U.S. 598 (2000) (excerpted in Chapter 3, p. 525), invalidating a federal civil rights remedy for gender-motivated violence which Congress had created to address the failure of states to control violence against women?

5. Parenting Leave: An International Perspective. Three years after the passage of the FMLA, the European Council adopted the European Union Directive on Parental Leave, which provides minimum standards with which the member states must comply. These minimum standards include a right to parental leave for at least three months, protection against dismissal, and the right to return to the same or similar position. For a description of the British paid parental leave program and other European examples, see Kroggel, supra, at 451-462. Most of the Member States of the European Union apply standards that exceed European Union standards for parental leave. Kathryn L. Morris, A Matter of Compliance: How Do U.S. Multinational Corporations Deal with the Discrepancies in the Family and Medical Leave Act of 1993 and the European Union Directive on Parental Leave; Is an International Standard Practical or Appropriate in this Area of Law?, 30 Ga. J. Int'l & Comp. L. 543, 548-553 (2002). Mory and Pistilli observe:

[United States supporters of mandatory paid leave] look to other countries, such as Sweden and Finland, which are among the most benevolent, allowing as much as thirty-eight weeks and thirty-five weeks paid leave, respectively. Moreover, according to the International Labour Organization in Geneva, of the countries that guarantee paid maternity leave for working women "many pay new mothers from a social security fund rather than have women assume the cost of leaving the workplace temporarily[.]" For instance, utilizing its social security fund, Hungary provides a minimum of six months paid leave. Similarly, Brazil offers up to four months maternity leave completely covered by social security. Even third world nations, such as Ghana and Haiti, have implemented paid leave programs.

Mory & Pistilli, supra, at 709.

In many Scandinavian countries, leaves may be split among parents or extended over a number of years. For example, Norway allows parents to spread 29 weeks of childcare over a two-year period following the birth of a child, and Sweden allows a parent to take a 25 percent reduction in working hours until the child is 8 years old. Jan Tormod Dege & Erik Aas, Norway, in Employment Law in Europe 710, 714 (Susan Mayne & Susan Maylon eds., 2001); Steven Erfors, Sweden, in Employment Law in Europe, supra, at 827-830.

The comparative generosity of other countries' family leave policies, however, obscures complex issues about implementation and equity. In some countries, liberal leave policies foster employer hostility against women workers. In Mexico, for example, where women are guaranteed twelve weeks' paid maternity leave, many employers believe they have the right to deny employment if women state an intention to take a leave; others administer illegal pregnancy tests. These infractions are only weakly sanctioned. Id. at 711. Similarly, Japan's Equal Employment Opportunity Law, effective in 1986, provided for equal opportunity and treatment in the job market for men and women. "Unfortunately, the provisions of the law were not mandatory and no enforcement provisions were provided, resulting in minimal effectiveness." Id. at 713.

Moreover, even where family leave policies are both generous and realized in practice as well as theory, problems of gender equality arise. Janet C. Gornick and Marcia K. Meyers observe:

> Although generous leave policies have economic and social benefits for families with very young children, they can create new forms of gender inequality. The total percentage of paid parental leave days taken by fathers amounts to less than 10 percent across the European welfare states.... Because leaves are taken overwhelmingly by mothers, many women pay a price for their long absences from the labor market in the form of lost human capital and career advancement.

Gornick & Meyers, Support for Working Families, 12 Am. Prospect, Jan. 1-15, 2001, at 3.

Some countries have achieved much higher rates of male involvement by a "use it or lose it approach." Sweden, for example, requires that 30 days of paid leave be taken by fathers; it is not transferable to mothers. That requirement, coupled with an extensive public education campaign, has resulted in 70 percent of fathers taking parental leave. Erfors, supra, at 830. Studies of Scandinavian approaches find that when fathers take more leave, it results in shorter leaves by mothers and a smaller loss in their earning potential. Elina Pylkkhanen & Nina Smith, OECD Study, Career Interruptions Due to Parental Leave: A Comparative Study of Denmark and Sweden 11 (2003). For a comprehensive volume discussing parental leaves in many Western European countries, see Parental Leave: Progress or Pitfall? (Peter Moss & Fred Devin eds., 1999).

Drawing on such evidence, several American commentators argue that the FLMA should be amended to reward employers for establishing leave policies that succeed in getting men to take more parental leave. Michael Selmi, Family Leave and the Gender Wage Gap, 78 N.C. L. Rev. 707 (2000) (proposing 6-week paid leave to both men and women that can be claimed only on an all-or-nothing basis); Halverson, supra; Lester, supra, at 80-81 (listing various proposals made by others, including required parental leave for fathers, linking federal contract eligibility of family leave uptake rates by male employees, and public awareness campaigns). Are these proposals worth considering? Is greater male use of parental leaves a sound policy objective?

6. Child Care. Another form of assistance to families is child care assistance. Early in the second wave of feminism, many assumed that the state would step in to provide quality child care for families.

> When Betty Friedan wrote in the '60s [Friedan, The Feminine Mystique (1963)], she assumed that very soon there would be a national system of subsidized child care centers that would be as free, accessible, and high in quality as public libraries. She actually believed this. Not only did she believe this, it was not an implausible vision. After all, that is what has happened in Belgium. That's what happened in France.... Ninety-five percent of nursery school age children in those countries are in government-subsidized child care.

Symposium, Unbending Gender: Why Family and Work Conflict and What to Do About It, 49 Am. U. L. Rev. 901, 904 (2000).

Friedan's vision came nowhere close to realization. Instead, as Joan Williams notes:

> In 1971, when Congress passed a Comprehensive Child Development Act, President Nixon vetoed it under pressure from an intense lobbying campaign that decried the proposal as "a radical piece of social legislation" designed to deliver children to "communal approaches to child-rearing over and against the family-centered approach." A 1975 proposal was also defeated, decried as an effort to "[s]ovietize the family." As a result, the U.S. offers less governmental support for child care than does any other industrialized nation.

Joan Williams, Toward a Reconstructive Feminism: Reconstructing the Relationship of Market Work and Family Work, 19 N. Ill. U. L. Rev. 89, 150-151 (1998).

Current law provides federal funds for various child care assistance programs, including Head Start. The Personal Responsibility and Work Opportunity

Reconciliation Act of 1996, offsetting some of the losses to poor families achieved through "welfare reform," provides a four-billion-dollar increase in child care funding. This Act is discussed in Chapter 5, pp. 942-960. The funding for federal programs, however, has failed to keep up with inflation and many states have reduced their commitment to child care subsidies, even as the number of eligible children has risen from 9.12 million in 2000 to 9.9 million in 2004. For a comprehensive studies of the relevant federal programs, eligibility requirements, funding trends, waiting lists, and differences among the state programs through which federal funds are distributed, see Karen Schulman & Helen Blank, Child Care Assistance Policies 2005: States Fail to Make Up lost Ground, Families Continue to Lack Critical Supports (National Women's Law Center Issue Brief Sept. 2005).

Federal tax laws also allow a tax credit for a percentage of money certain taxpayers spend on child care under the Child and Dependent Care Tax Credit. In dollar terms, the CDCTC is the largest federal government program in the United States aimed at helping families with child care; the Joint Committee on Taxation estimates that in 2005, the CDCTC will cost the federal government $3 billion in foregone tax revenues. Staff of J. Comm. on Taxation, 109th Cong., Estimates of Federal Tax Expenditures for Fiscal Years 2005-2009, at 37 (Comm. Print 2005).

Critics of current federal and state policies continue to advocate a comprehensive national day care system available to all free of charge. See Heather S. Dixon, National Daycare: A Necessary Precursor to Gender Equality with Newfound Promise for Success, 36 Colum. Human Rts. L. Rev. 561 (2005); Sharon C. Nantell, The Tax Paradigm of Child Care: Shifting Attitudes Toward a Private/Parental/Public Alliance, 80 Marq. L. Rev. 879 (1997); Meghan M. Thomsen, The Role of Business and Government in the Provision of Child Care Assistance: A Comparative Analysis of the United States and Canada, 17 U. Pa. J. Int'l. Econ. L. 1209, 1215-1223 (1996).

Most Western countries have gone considerably further in providing government assistance to families with children. Sweden, for example, not only provides paid caretaking leave, discussed in note 4, above, but also a basic child allowance for all families, increased allowances for families with three or more children, and additional allowances to replace support that a non-custodial parent is unable or unwilling to pay. There are additional income supports for post-childbirth leave and for the caretaker parents of handicapped children, as well as an extensive publicly financed child care system. Preferences for child care and housing are available to single parents. The tax system encourages the entry of women into the workforce by taxing the second earner separately, rather than at the marginal rate of the primary wage earner. See Nancy E. Dowd, Envisioning Work and Family: A Critical Perspective on International Models, 26 Harv. J. on Legis. 311, 319-323 (1989). France, like Sweden, has a family allowance system, one that is particularly generous to large families. France also has a nearly universally available child care and preschool education system, regardless of whether the parent or parents are in the paid work force. Id. at 331-335.

Nevertheless, it is not clear that a policy like Sweden's automatically produces gender equality. Women continue to do a disproportionate share of family work and took fifty-two days of leave for every day taken by a man." Joan Williams,

Unbending Gender: Why Family and Work Conflict and What to Do About It 51 (2000); see also Erfors, supra, at 827-830. Indeed, Sweden's level of sex segregation in the workforce is greater than that of the United States. Williams, supra, at 51.

Does subsidized day care make more, or less, sense than paid family leave? How would you evaluate the differences? Who should pay?

Some employers offer significant day care assistance. According to the National Compensation Survey in March of 2005, three percent of all workers receive employer subsidies for child care and five percent have access to on-site or off-site employer-assisted day care. U.S. Bureau of Labor Statistics, National Compensation Survey: Employee Benefits in Private Industry in the United States, March 2005, at 26, Table 22. Workers in white-collar occupations are more than twice as likely to have employer subsidies for child care than blue-collar or service workers. Id. Employers with 100 workers or more are five times more likely to provide child care subsidies, and more than four times more likely to have on-site and off-site child care facilities. Id.

7. Women and Contingent Work. A significant sector of the United States work force is made up of "contingent workers" — i.e., all those workers employed other than on a full-time, permanent basis, including part-time workers, temporary workers, independent contractors, day laborers, and home-based workers. According to Bureau of Labor Statistics data, about 18 percent of the American work force in 2003 worked part-time, with women making up 67.4 percent of the part-time work force. Barry T. Hirsch, Why Do Part-Time Workers Earn Less? The Role of Worker and Job Skills, 58 Indus. & Lab. Rel. Rev. 525, 525-526 (2005). In 2004, approximately 26 percent of employed women usually worked part time, compared with about 11 percent of employed men. U.S. Bureau of Labor Statistics, Women in the Labor Force: A Databook 2 (May 2005).

Part-time workers have lower wages than full-time workers, although studies show that the part-time "penalty" is small especially among younger workers. The gap tends to rise over time as workers who change jobs often, leave the work force for periods at a time, or have part-time work experience only, accumulate less human capital than other workers. Hirsch, supra, at 547-548. Among women, part-time workers are more likely to be married with spouse present and have more children, while the opposite is seen among men. Id. at 532. Part-time workers, unsurprisingly, have much lower rates of employer-provided health insurance and retirement plans. Jeffrey Wenger, Economic Policy Institute, Share of Workers in Nonstandard Jobs Declines; Latest Survey Shows a Narrowing — Though Still Wide — Gap in Pay and Benefits 2, http://www.epinet.org/briefingpapers/bp137.pdf (last visited August 27, 2005).

Contingent work has been thriving, even during spurts in the economy; indeed, some researchers argue that heavy reliance on contingent labor is increasingly necessary to provide businesses with necessary flexibility in a global environment characterized by cheap overseas labor and "just in time" production methods. See Note, Marionettes of Globalization: A Comparative Analysis of Legal Protections for Contingent Workers in the International Community,

27 Syracuse J. Int'l L. & Com. 431, 438 (2000); Katherine M. Forster, Note, Strategic Reform of Contingent Work, 74 S. Cal. L. Rev. 541, 551 (2001).

Beyond the tangible drawbacks of contingent work is also a change in the "psychological contract" between employer and full-time employee.

> It has been widely reported that large corporations no longer offer their employees implicit contracts for lifetime employment. Work has become contingent, not in the sense that it is formally defined as short-term or episodic, but in the sense that the attachment between the firm and the worker has been reduced. The recasualization of work has reportedly become a fact of life both for blue-collar workers and for high-end professionals and managers.

Katherine V.W. Stone, The New Psychological Contract: Implications of the Changing Workplace for Labor and Employment Law, 48 UCLA L. Rev. 519 (2001); see also Gillian Lester, Careers and Contingency, 51 Stan. L. Rev. 73 (1998) (arguing that contingent work is a symptom of "underemployment"). But see Sanford M. Jacoby, Melting Into Air? Downsizing, Job Stability, and the Future of Work, 76 Chi.-Kent L. Rev. 1195 (2000) (arguing that reports of the death of career-type jobs are greatly exaggerated).

Stone notes that the disappearance of "internal labor markets" within corporate firms may help women and minorities, who have traditionally met with barriers to advancement. Stone, supra, at 605. However, other barriers to the advancement of women and people of color in the new "casual" workplace may arise. Stone identifies four such potential problems: (1) white women and employees of color may continue to be given less access to training; (2) the disappearance of formal hierarchies of authority and identifiable "corporate ladders" may make identifying, preventing, and redressing unlawful discrimination more difficult; (3) as employment decisions are increasingly ceded to peers, discrimination may flourish; and (4) as unionization decreases, nepotism and favoritism may flourish as well. Id. at 606-609.

8. Lawyers and the Work/Family Conflict. Lawyers, of course, do not escape the work/family conflict, which is often resolved by cutting back to part-time arrangements. A study of women lawyers in big Pennsylvania law firms by Marina Angel gives a consistent picture of women's work patterns over the past six years. In these firms, women constitute over three-fourths of lawyers in the part-time ranks, slightly under one-third of all lawyers, and between 14 percent and 18 percent of partners. The one significant change over this period is that while in 2000 just under three percent of managing partners were women, in 2005 the figure was just over 16 percent. See Porus P. Cooper, Gender Gap at Law Firms, The Philadelphia Inquirer, July 4, 2005, at C1; Marina Angel, Commission on Women in the Profession 2004 Annual Report Card, 2004 Pa. Bar Ass'n 3 (2004).

The pressures of increasing minimal billing requirements and client expectations of instant responsiveness and total availability have pushed working hours to new and often excessive levels. Do cell phones, e-mails, faxes, and beepers help or hurt?

Consider telecommuting. About 15 percent of women and men reported working at home at least once per week as part of their main job in May 2001. U.S. Bureau of Labor Statistics, Women in the Labor Force: A Databook 2 (May 2005). Working at home is more common for parents than for nonparents, and women are slightly more likely than men to be paid for work they do at home. About 27 percent of women who work at home are self-employed, as compared with 33 percent for men. Id.

Some have urged greater use of telecommuting as one way to restructure the workplace away from male worker norms. See, e.g., Joan Williams, Unbending Gender, supra, at 85; Deborah L. Rhode, Balanced Lives, 102 Colum. L. Rev. 834, 844 (2002). According to a study by the Organization for Economic Cooperation and Development (OECD), which examined the impact of federal and state leave statues, women were more likely to return to the work force and to the same jobs they had before childbirth if they had flexibility in schedules and an ability to do some work at home. Sandra L. Hofferth & Sally C. Curtin, OECD Working Paper, The Impact of Parental Leave on Maternal Return to Work After Childbirth in the United States 9 (2003).

Yet, despite the potential advantages of telecommuting for both men and women, research is showing that (1) employers often use telecommuting to switch women workers to more contingent status employment (see note 6, below); and (2) telecommuting increases the sex-based disparities in domestic work by making women more available at home, while not making men any more willing to do housework and childcare when they are similarly available. See Michelle A. Travis, Telecommuting: The Escher Stairway of Work/Family Conflict, 55 Me. L. Rev. 262, 271, 274 (2002); see also Michelle A. Travis, Equality in the Virtual Workplace, 24 Berkeley J. Emp. & Lab. L. 283 (2003).

How do you plan to cope with the challenges involved in balancing personal and professional commitments? Do you expect to work full-time throughout your career? If so, who will clean your house? Do you plan to have children? If so, who will take care of them? What accommodations do you think are fair to expect from your employer? Further materials on work/family challenges faced by women in law practice are provided in Chapter 4, pp. 697-698.

9. Work, Marriage, and Tax Policy. Edward McCaffery identifies the absence of a range of part-time employment options to accommodate dual-career families as one symptom of market failure and proposes tax-based government intervention to eliminate the inefficiency of current work patterns. His proposal would increase taxes on the primary wage-earner, the man in most two-earner families, and lighten the tax load of secondary workers, primarily women. Edward J. McCaffery, Slouching Towards Equality: Gender Discrimination, Market Efficiency, and Social Change, 103 Yale L.J. 595 (1993). McCaffery argues that this would simultaneously "[throw] some barriers in the way of men's ultra-commitment to the market" and increase women's clout in making the market more accepting of their choices "without having to contort their behavior to fit historically male labor-market participation patterns." McCaffery, supra, at 671. McCaffery also recommends dropping the regulatory prohibition against unequal pay to improve the rational decisionmaking processes of firms by allowing them to take into account the marginal productivity of workers in light of their expected longevity on the job: "[I]f markets work better with women getting paid less, at least in the present, so be it." Id. at 655. Otherwise, McCaffery argues, we penalize firms who "do the right thing" by hiring women, and reward firms who successfully isolate women into certain lower-paying job categories. "In important regards, the means chosen by Title VII to address discrimination might be counterproductive vis-à-vis its own apparent ends." Id.

The McCaffery tax proposal pursues greater efficiency through heavier taxes on inelastic labor supplies (those workers who are least responsive to changes in the tax rate) and lighter taxes on elastic labor supplies (those workers who are most responsive to changes in the tax rate), to encourage women's market work. Anne Alstott identifies some basic conflicts between McCaffery's efficiency objectives and traditional feminist goals such as equal treatment and support to caregivers. See Alstott, Tax Policy and Feminism: Competing Goals and Institutional Choices, 96 Colum. L. Rev. 2001, 2034-2037 (1996). While married women are historically an extremely elastic (responsive) labor supply, Alstott notes that the greatest beneficial effect of McCaffery's proposals would be on nonworking women married to high-earning men, i.e., upper-class housewives who are those most likely to be able to afford child care already. Alstott favors direct assistance to caregivers, because increased incentives to work would not increase the compatibility of working conditions with child care. Id. Along similar lines, Nancy Staudt argues that to adequately value both market and nonmarket work without pushing women into the labor market, housework should be taxed. Nancy C. Staudt, Taxing Housework, 84 Geo. L.J. 1571 (1996). Staudt argues that the burden of the new tax would be shared by the entire household, and that women stand to benefit from it because it would increase their social security benefits and thus their economic security in retirement. Id. at 1640.

The $1.35 trillion tax cut package enacted in 2001 included a phase-out of the "marriage penalty"—the additional income tax burden that most dual income couples bear when they are married. David Cay Johnson, The Tax Bill Up Close: Some Facts, Some Tips, N.Y. Times, June 3, 2001, at C1. Are further middle-income tax breaks likely to improve, or worsen, the ability of women to both work and care for children?

Should law continue to treat "the household" as the taxable unit? Marjorie Kornhauser advocates tax law reforms that abandon the fiction of economic marital partnership and take better account of women's circumstances and priorities toward their children. See Kornhauser, Theory Versus Reality: The Partnership Model of Marriage in Family and Income Tax Law, 69 Temp. L. Rev. 1449 (1996) (favoring treating husbands and wives as separate taxable units and allocating tax preferences according to the parents' likelihood of spending money on their children); Kornhauser, Deconstructing the Taxable Unit: Intrahousehold Allocations and the Dilemma of the Joint Return, 16 N.Y.L. Sch. J. Hum. Rts. 140 (1999) (arguing that a system that treats each person as a separate taxable unit is more equitable, efficient, and more consistent with basic income tax principles than the current system of treating households as a unit).

10. Child Care and the Market in Domestic Workers. As noted above, the primary approach to child care in the United States has been to treat it as a "private" issue to be negotiated by individual women. Government involvement has largely been limited to providing mothers with resources to track down "deadbeat dads." See Ann Laquer Estin, Moving Beyond the Child Support Revolution, 26 Law & Soc. Inquiry 505 (2001). Women who must work but cannot afford high-quality in-home assistance or day care look to their own relatives, to babysitters, or to low-cost, frequently unlicensed family day care centers that feature frequent turnover and poorly trained workers. See Lucie White, Quality Child Care for Low-Income Families: Despair, Impasse, Improvisation, in Hard Labor: Women and Work in the Post-Welfare Era 116, 124-125 (Joel F. Handler and Lucie White eds., 1999).

Those women who can afford it turn to the market in domestic workers for help. Dorothy Roberts argues that the convergence of gender norms, racial norms, and market forces has meant that those who do child care work for wages are often nonwhite. Certainly they are poorly paid; in 2003, full-time child care workers in private households earned, on average, $330 per week. U.S. Bureau of Labor Statistics, Highlights of Women's Earnings in 2003, Report 978 (Sept. 2004). Child care workers are also overwhelmingly female: in 2003, 95.2 percent of family child care providers were women. Id. For the argument that the supply of affordable, quality child care depends upon the improvement of working conditions for child care workers, see Peggie R. Smith, Linking Quality Child Care with Improved Working Conditions, 73 U. Cin. L. Rev. 399 (2004).

Domestic workers are not only poorly paid; they also lack effective legal protections. Domestic work is explicitly excluded from coverage under the National Labor Relations Act (guaranteeing the right to organize and engage in collective bargaining), the Occupational Health and Safety Act, Title VII, and from most state workers compensation acts. The Fair Labor Standards Act, enacted in 1938, originally did not apply to domestic workers; although it was amended in 1974 to provide such coverage, babysitters are explicitly excluded. Domestic workers typically have only limited eligibility for unemployment benefits and are exempt from coverage under civil rights laws in eight states. See generally Peggie R. Smith, Regulating Paid Household Work: Class, Gender, Race, and Agendas of Reform, 48 Am. U. L. Rev. 851 (1999); see also Molly Biklen, Note, Healthcare in the Home: the Companionship Services Exemption to the Fair Labor Standards Act, 35 Colum. Hum Rts. L. Rev. 113, 115-116 (2003) (arguing that the Department of Labor's broad interpretation of the FLSA exemption for personal service providers in private homes "maintains the fiction that caregiving is a service provided between intimates" and not a legitimate form of employment). Collective action is difficult for domestic workers because they are spatially isolated from one another, and enforcement of applicable laws and regulations is a serious problem, particularly when workers are undocumented. See Alan Hyde, A Preliminary Look at the Emerging Tetralogy of Representation of Low-Wage Service Workers, 13 Cornell J.L. & Pub. Pol'y 599, 609-614 (2003) (noting that the small minority of domestic workers in New York who have sought representation have rejected or dismissed unions, receiving assistance instead from advocacy organizations and government entities without a true stake in their well-being); but see Peggie R. Smith, Organizing the Unorganizable: Private Paid Household Workers and Approaches to Employee Representation, 79 N.C. L. Rev. 45 (2000) (arguing that worker-run cooperatives represent a promising strategy for collective action).

11. Immigration and Domestic Work. In December 1992, Zoe Baird became the first woman nominated to the position of United States Attorney General. She subsequently withdrew her nomination when it was discovered that she had failed to pay Social Security taxes for her undocumented live-in childcare worker. The resulting controversy, known as "Nannygate," brought to the surface painful divisions among women. Some working women lambasted Baird as a selfish, "yuppie" mom, while others noted gender bias in the critique of Baird. See Taunya Lovell Banks, Toward a Global Critical Feminist Vision: Domestic Work and the Nanny Tax Debate, 3 J. Gender Race & Just. 1 (1999). In response to this episode, Congress enacted the Social Security Domestic Employment Reform Act of 1994, popularly known as the Nanny Tax law. The new law increases the threshold amount of employee wages required to trigger the tax from $50 quarterly to $1000 annually and requires annual instead of quarterly payments of the tax to ease the reporting burden on employers like Baird. Id. at 3. Banks notes that this reform made it easier for households to hire nannies, but failed to address the problems domestic workers face.

The undocumented status of Baird's nanny was not unusual. Domestic workers from outside the United States can enter the country in one of three ways. First, an American employer can sponsor a foreign worker for temporary employment through the H-2B visa application procedure. However, these visas are limited in number, the application process is long and cumbersome, and domestic workers are classified as "unskilled" labor, the lowest preference category for employment-based visas. Susan L. Brady, Comment, "Female Troubles": The Plight of Foreign Household Workers Seeking Permanent Residency Through Employment-Based Immigration, 27 Hous. J. Int'l L. 609 (2005).

Second, the Exchange Visitor Program provides participants with a J-1 visa for becoming an "au pair." Au pairs are typically young Western European women who enter the United States for one year for the purpose of international cultural exchange. The primary responsibility of an au pair is expected to be childcare and not other domestic work; au pairs are required to receive only the minimum wage. See Linda Kelly, The Fantastic Adventure of Supermom and the Alien: Educating Immigration Policy on the Facts of Life, 31 Conn. L. Rev. 1045, 1059-1060 (1999).

Finally, a domestic worker may enter the United States through illegal means. Thousands of households resort to undocumented workers to meet their childcare needs; these workers are paid lower wages and work longer hours than their legal counterparts. See Melanie Ryan, Swept Under the Carpet: Lack of Legal Protection for Household Workers — A Call for Justice, 20 Women's L. Rep. 159 (1999). They also lack entitlement to overtime or health benefits, and "will be unable to receive social security benefits upon retirement, unemployment benefits if they are suddenly discharged, or disability benefits in case of illness or accident." Debra Cohen-Whelan, Protecting the Hand That Rocks the Cradle: Ensuring the Delivery of Work-Related Benefits to Child Care Workers, 32 Ind. L. Rev. 1187 (1999). Moreover, because of their undocumented status, these domestic workers are especially vulnerable to abuse. See Mary Romero, Immigration, the Servant Problem, and the Legacy of the Domestic Labor Debate: "Where Can You Find Good Help These Days!" 53 U. Miami. L. Rev. 1045 (1999) (describing the exploitation of undocumented child care workers).

What approach to undocumented aliens should feminists favor?

Putting Theory into Practice

2-3. What accommodations should a law firm make to a female associate in a law firm who decides, in her third year of employment, to begin a family? What responses by the law firm to her request for time off should be legally mandated? With which model of equality is your answer most compatible?

2-4. The New York Times notes a trend of women receiving Ivy League educations intending to spend "opt out" of the workforce when they marry and have children. Roughly 60 percent of 138 freshman and senior female Yale students who were surveyed said they planned to cut back on work or stop working entirely when they had children. Louise Story, Many Women at Elite Colleges Set Career Path to Motherhood, N.Y. Times, Sept. 20, 2005, at A1, A18. A survey by the Yale Office of Institutional Research of the classes of 1979, 1984, 1989, and 1994, found that only 56 percent of women graduates still worked, as compared with 90 percent of men. Similarly, a survey of Harvard Business School graduates found that 31 percent of the female graduates of the classes of 1981, 1986, and 1991 who answered the survey worked only part-time, or on contract, and another 31 percent did not work at all. Id. For a more extended treatment of the "opt-out revolution," specifically in regard to women lawyers, see Lisa Belkin, The Opt-Out Revolution, N.Y. Times, Oct. 26, 2003, at 42 (Magazine).

How do you respond to the argument that women should not be taking up spaces in law schools and business schools if they do not plan full-time, full-length careers? For further discussion, see Chapter 4, pp. 673-674.

2-5. A program at the University of Michigan, funded in part by the National Science Foundation to address the acute shortage of female scientists, provides small grants to allow female scientists to hire

> . . . an extra set of hands in the lab or a substitute teacher in the classroom so they can spend more time at home without watching their careers stall. . . . Michigan has even paid for weekend day care so that female scientists have quiet time to write grants and journal articles. . . .
>
> [At Harvard, under a similar program,] the vast majority of the grants have gone to women with children. But [one male doctor] has turned his $25,000 fellowship over to the hospital to hire doctors to cover a portion of his work week in the

emergency room so that he can attend a new clinical-research training program at Harvard . . . and spend more time with his 2-year-old daughter. . . . [The doctor] says he initially felt guilty about taking a fellowship designed for women. "I'm sensitive to the idea that women have it harder than men in making their academic and family careers work, and I didn't want to be competing for an award with women who deserve it," he says. But his wife, who is pregnant with their second child, is a lawyer with the Office of the Massachusetts General. "Her career is just as demanding and high-powered as mine," says [the doctor,] so he felt he qualified for the grant.

Robin Wilson, Family Science, Chron. of Higher Educ., July 22, 2005, at A6, A7-A8. Are government grants to assist scientists manage the tough laboratory hours required of first-rate scientists a good policy? If so, does the acute shortage of women scientists justify limiting such programs to women scientists?

C. RECOGNIZING SEX-LINKED AVERAGE DIFFERENCES

1. Fringe Benefit Plans, Insurance, and Other Actuarially Based Systems

≣ *City of Los Angeles, Department of Water &*
≣ *Power v. Manhart*
435 U.S. 702 (1978)

Mr. Justice STEVENS delivered the opinion of the Court.

As a class, women live longer than men. For this reason, the Los Angeles Department of Water and Power required its female employees to make larger contributions to its pension fund than its male employees. We granted certiorari to decide whether this practice discriminated against individual female employees because of their sex in violation of [Title VII].

For many years the Department has administered retirement, disability, and death-benefit programs for its employees. Upon retirement each employee is eligible for a monthly retirement benefit computed as a fraction of his or her salary multiplied by years of service.[3] The monthly benefits for men and women of the same age, seniority, and salary are equal. Benefits are funded entirely by contributions from the employees and the Department, augmented by the income earned on those contributions. No private insurance company is involved in the administration or payment of benefits.

Based on a study of mortality tables and its own experience, the Department determined that its 2,000 female employees, on the average, will live a few years

---

3. The plan . . . provides for several kinds of pension benefits at the employee's option. . . . [T]he most common is a formula pension equal to 2% of the average monthly salary paid during the last year of employment times the number of years of employment. The benefit is guaranteed for life.

longer than its 10,000 male employees. The cost of a pension for the average retired female is greater than for the average male retiree because more monthly payments must be made to the average woman. The Department therefore required female employees to make monthly contributions to the fund which were 14.84% higher than the contributions required of comparable male employees. Because employee contributions were withheld from paychecks a female employee took home less pay than a male employee earning the same salary.[5] . . .

While this action was pending, the California Legislature enacted a law prohibiting certain municipal agencies from requiring female employees to make higher pension fund contributions than males. The Department therefore amended its plan, effective January 1, 1975. The current plan draws no distinction, either in contributions or in benefits, on the basis of sex. On a motion for summary judgment, the District Court held that the contribution differential [in the old plan] violated [Title VII] and ordered a refund of all excess contributions made before the amendment of the plan. The United States Court of Appeals for the Ninth Circuit affirmed. . . .

I

There are both real and fictional differences between women and men. It is true that the average man is taller than the average woman; it is not true that the average woman driver is more accident prone than the average man. Before [Title VII] was enacted, an employer could fashion his personnel policies on the basis of assumptions about the differences between men and women, whether or not the assumptions were valid.

It is now well recognized that employment decisions cannot be predicated on mere "stereotyped" impressions about the characteristics of males or females. Myths and purely habitual assumptions about a woman's inability to perform certain kinds of work are no longer acceptable reasons for refusing to employ qualified individuals, or for paying them less. This case does not, however, involve a fictional difference between men and women. It involves a generalization that the parties accept as unquestionably true: Women, as a class, do live longer than men. The Department treated its women employees differently from its men employees because the two classes are in fact different. It is equally true, however, that all individuals in the respective classes do not share the characteristic that differentiates the average class representatives. Many women do not live as long as the average man and many men outlive the average woman. The question, therefore, is whether the existence or nonexistence of "discrimination" is to be determined by comparison of class characteristics or individual characteristics. A "stereotyped" answer to that question may not be the same as the answer that the language and purpose of the statute command.

[Title VII] makes it unlawful "to discriminate against any *individual* with respect to his compensation, terms, conditions, or privileges of employment,

5. The significance of the disparity is illustrated by the record of one woman whose contributions to the fund (including interest on the amount withheld each month) amounted to $18,171.40; a similarly situated male would have contributed only $12,843.53.

because of such *individual's* race, color, religion, sex, or national origin."...The statute's focus on the individual is unambiguous. It precludes treatment of individuals as simply components of a racial, religious, sexual, or national class. If height is required for a job, a tall woman may not be refused employment merely because, on the average, women are too short. Even a true generalization about the class is an insufficient reason for disqualifying an individual to whom the generalization does not apply.

That proposition is of critical importance in this case because there is no assurance that any individual woman working for the Department will actually fit the generalization on which the Department's policy is based. Many of those individuals will not live as long as the average man. While they were working, those individuals received smaller paychecks because of their sex, but they will receive no compensating advantage when they retire.

It is true, of course, that while contributions are being collected from the employees, the Department cannot know which individuals will predecease the average woman. Therefore, unless women as a class are assessed an extra charge, they will be subsidized, to some extent, by the class of male employees. It follows, according to the Department, that fairness to its class of male employees justifies the extra assessment against all of its female employees.

But the question of fairness to various classes affected by the statute is essentially a matter of policy for the legislature to address. Congress has decided that classifications based on sex, like those based on national origin or race, are unlawful. Actuarial studies could unquestionably identify differences in life expectancy based on race or national origin, as well as sex.[15] But a statute that was designed to make race irrelevant in the employment market....could not reasonably be construed to permit a take-home-pay differential based on a racial classification.

Even if the statutory language were less clear, the basic policy of the statute requires that we focus on fairness to individuals rather than fairness to classes. Practices that classify employees in terms of religion, race, or sex tend to preserve traditional assumptions about groups rather than thoughtful scrutiny of individuals. The generalization involved in this case illustrates the point. Separate mortality tables are easily interpreted as reflecting innate differences between the sexes; but a significant part of the longevity differential may be explained by the social fact that men are heavier smokers than women.

Finally, there is no reason to believe that Congress intended a special definition of discrimination in the context of employee group insurance coverage. It is true that insurance is concerned with events that are individually unpredictable, but that is characteristic of many employment decisions. Individual risks, like individual performance, may not be predicted by resort to classifications proscribed by Title VII. Indeed, the fact that this case involves a group insurance program highlights a basic flaw in the Department's fairness argument. For when insurance risks are grouped, the better risks always subsidize the poorer risks. Healthy persons subsidize medical benefits for the less healthy; unmarried

15. For example, the life expectancy of a white baby in 1973 was 72.2 years; a nonwhite baby could expect to live 65.9 years, a difference of 6.3 years. See Public Health Service, IIA Vital Statistics of the United States, 1973, Table 5-3.

workers subsidize the pensions of married workers; persons who eat, drink, or smoke to excess may subsidize pension benefits for persons whose habits are more temperate. Treating different classes of risks as though they were the same for purposes of group insurance is a common practice that has never been considered inherently unfair....

An employment practice that requires 2,000 individuals to contribute more money into a fund than 10,000 other employees simply because each of them is a woman, rather than a man, is in direct conflict with both the language and the policy of the Act. Such a practice does not pass the simple test of whether the evidence shows "treatment of a person in a manner which but for that person's sex would be different." It constitutes discrimination and is unlawful unless exempted by the Equal Pay Act of 1963 or some other affirmative justification.

II...

The Equal Pay Act requires employers to pay members of both sexes the same wages for equivalent work, except when the differential is pursuant to one of four specified exceptions. The Department contends that the fourth exception applies here. That exception authorizes a "differential based on any other factor other than sex."

The Department argues that the different contributions exacted from men and women were based on the factor of longevity rather than sex. It is plain, however, that any individual's life expectancy is based on a number of factors, of which sex is only one. The record contains no evidence that any factor other than the employee's sex was taken into account in calculating the 14.84% differential between the respective contributions by men and women....

III

[T]he Department argues that the absence of a discriminatory effect on women as a class justifies an employment practice which, on its face, discriminated against individual employees because of their sex. But even if the Department's actuarial evidence is sufficient to prevent plaintiffs from establishing a prima facie case on the theory that the effect of the practice on women as a class was discriminatory, that evidence does not defeat the claim that the practice, on its face, discriminated against every individual woman employed by the Department.

In essence, the Department is arguing that the prima facie showing of discrimination based on evidence of different contributions for the respective sexes is rebutted by its demonstration that there is a like difference in the cost of providing benefits for the respective classes. That argument might prevail if Title VII contained a cost justification defense comparable to the affirmative defense.... But neither Congress nor the courts have recognized such a defense under Title VII.

Although we conclude that the Department's practice violated Title VII, we do not suggest that the statute was intended to revolutionize the insurance and pension industries. All that is at issue today is a requirement that men and women make unequal contributions to an employer-operated pension fund. Nothing in our holding implies that it would be unlawful for an employer to set aside equal retirement contributions for each employee and let each retiree purchase the largest benefit which his or her accumulated contributions could command in the open market. Nor does it call into question the insurance industry practice of considering the composition of an employer's work force in determining the probable cost of a retirement or death benefit plan....

Mr. Justice BRENNAN took no part in the consideration or decision of this case.

[The opinion of Mr. Justice Blackmun, concurring in part and concurring in the judgment, is omitted.]

Mr. CHIEF JUSTICE BURGER, with whom Mr. Justice REHNQUIST joins, concurring in part and dissenting in part....

Gender-based actuarial tables have been in use since at least 1843, and their statistical validity has been repeatedly verified. The vast life insurance, annuity, and pension plan industry is based on these tables. As the Court recognizes...it is a fact that "women, as a class, do live longer than men." It is equally true that employers cannot know in advance when individual members of the classes will die.... Yet, if they are to operate economically workable group pension programs, it is only rational to permit them to rely on statistically sound and proved disparities in longevity between men and women. Indeed, it seems to me irrational to assume Congress intended to outlaw use of the fact that, for whatever reasons or combination of reasons, women as a class outlive men.

An effect upon pension plans so revolutionary and discriminatory — this time favorable to women at the expense of men — should not be read into the statute without either a clear statement of that intent in the statute, or some reliable indication in the legislative history that this was Congress' purpose....

Here, of course, petitioners are discriminating in take-home pay between men and women.... The practice of petitioners, however, falls squarely under the exemption provided by the Equal Pay Act of 1963 ... [for] a differential based on any other factor other than sex...." The "other factor other than sex" is longevity; sex is the umbrella-constant under which all of the elements leading to differences in longevity are grouped and assimilated, and the only objective feature upon which an employer — or anyone else, including insurance companies — may reliably base a cost differential for the "risk" being insured.

This is in no sense a failure to treat women as "individuals" in violation of the statute, as the Court holds. It is to treat them as individually as it is possible to do in the face of the unknowable length of each individual life. Individually, every woman has the same statistical possibility of outliving men. This is the essence of basing decisions on reliable statistics when individual determinations are infeasible or, as here, impossible.

Of course, women cannot be disqualified from, for example, heavy labor just because the generality of women are thought not as strong as men — a proposition which perhaps may sometime be statistically demonstrable, but will remain individually refutable. When, however, it is impossible to tailor a programichaem such as a pension plan to the individual, nothing should prevent application of reliable statistical facts to the individual, for whom the facts cannot be disproved until long after planning, funding, and operating the program have been undertaken. . . .

Mr. Justice MARSHALL's opinion, concurring in part and dissenting [to the court's holding that the opinion should not be retroactive, is omitted].

Notes

1. Group-Based vs. Individual-Based Equality. What view of equality is reflected in *Manhart*? In an important sense, the case chooses formal equality over a form of "reverse" substantive equality: women and men must be treated alike at the pay-in side, even though as a (substantive) result women, because on average they will live longer, will on average obtain greater pay-out benefits than men. Put another way, the employer may not take account of men's and women's average differences so that the outcomes (again, on average) are the same. Formal equality in these circumstances means that each employee will be treated as an individual rather than as a member of a group, but it also means that women will receive, on average, more benefits than men, unless the employer shifts to a different system. Is that "fair"?

Reconsider Judge Posner's view that disregarding women's greater longevity when fixing pension benefits amounts to a subsidy to women. See pp. 216-219, supra. That view looks at women as a group, instead of the individual woman who may or may not live longer than the average. Is Judge Posner's focus on equalizing the effects of an employment practice on a group, rather than on individuals, consistent with his opinion in American Nurses' Association v. Illinois, set forth at p. 193, where the court found no discrimination in pay differences between sex-segregated job categories, which plaintiffs claimed were of equal worth? Wasn't the claim in *American Nurses'* about unequal, group-based (or average) effects?

For one explanation of why courts apply formal equality in some situations and substantive equality in others, see Leticia M. Saucedo, The Browning of the American Workplace: Protecting Workers in Increasingly Latino-ized Occupations, 80 Notre Dame L. Rev. 303, 323-324 (2004) (suggesting that the "market" defense — the use of information created by or used throughout business or labor markets [discussed more in Chapter 1 on pp. 51-54] — is effective when differential treatment is unclear such as in pay equity cases, but ineffective in cases like *Manhart* in which women clearly are treated differently with respect to the same job.) Is it reasonable or consistent to examine individual-equality in some situations and group-equality in others?

Despite the concern expressed by the defendant in *Manhart* that women as a group receive a disproportionate share of pension benefits, women as a group are less likely to be covered by a pension plan (39 percent, as compared to 46 percent for men), and the average pay out for female retirees is less than half the pension benefits paid out to male retirees. See Dana M. Muir, From *Yuppies* to *Guppies*: Unfunded Mandates and Benefit Plan Regulation, 34 Ga. L. Rev. 195, 1220-1221 (1999). Are these facts relevant to the legal issues in *Manhart*?

2. Efficiency vs. Nondiscrimination in Fringe Benefit and Insurance Plans. Is formal equality compatible with insurance principles? Much has been written about the actuarial assumptions at issue in *Manhart.* One commentator succinctly summarizes the two main philosophic camps that emerged in the 1980s:

> The debate among scholars over more controversial types of insurance classification has polarized into two dominant perspectives: the *efficient discrimination* perspective and the *anti-discrimination* perspective. Under the former, it would be fair to charge Ed, Marie, and Carlos higher insurance rates, because race, sex, and genetic factors are statistically correlated to higher risks of loss. Under the latter, it would not be fair to charge them higher rates, because people do not choose their race, their sex, or their genes: these are noncausal, immutable factors, historically linked to unfair treatment.

Jill Goulding, Note, Race, Sex, and Genetic Discrimination in Insurance: What's Fair?, 80 Cornell L. Rev. 1646, 1647 (1995) (emphasis added).

The "efficient discrimination" critics of *Manhart* have argued that sex is the most efficient proxy for these behaviors and that monitoring these behaviors directly would be too expensive and inefficient. See, e.g., George J. Benston, The Economics of Gender Discrimination in Employee Fringe Benefits: *Manhart* Revisited, 49 U. Chi. L. Rev. 489, 517-519, 530-531 (1982).

The supporters of the result in *Manhart* argue that critics have confused correlation with causation: the biology of sex is not the cause of the actuarial differences but only the most efficient correlate. The correlation between sex and longevity is largely explained by the fact that men engage in more self-destructive behaviors than women. Where efficiency is the only value to be served, pro-*Manhart* advocates argue that the nondiscrimination principles of Title VII should prevail. See, e.g., Lea Brilmayer, Douglas Laycock & Teresa A. Sullivan, The Efficient Use of Group Averages as Nondiscrimination: A Rejoinder to Professor Benston, 50 U. Chi. L. Rev. 222, 223-225 (1983). Brilmayer, Laycock, and Sullivan argue that as long as sex is not the "cause" but only a correlate, using rates and benefits based on sex as a predictor is similar to using race or ethnicity as a selection criterion for credit, college admissions, or hiring. As in these cases, judgments about individuals based on such protected group characteristics are exactly the kind of unfairness civil rights statutes prohibit. Brilmayer et al., supra. Is the result unfair to men?

Is it appropriate to use the regulation of insurance classifications to promote larger social goals? See, e.g., Regina Austin, The Insurance Classification Controversy, 131 U. Pa. L. Rev. 517 (1983). For an examination of this issue in the context of Social Security, see Chapter 5, at pp. 957-958.

This polarized debate over sex discrimination in insurance mainly took place in the 1980s. While the philosophical debate continues today, the efficient discrimination camp has so far won in the policymaking arena as of 1995:

> Only Montana flatly forbids sex discrimination in insurance. California actually requires the use of gender-specific tables for life insurance and annuities. Most states tolerate the use of sex as a classifier as a form of fair discrimination; where regulators have attempted to ban sex discrimination under unfair discrimination statutes, courts

> have rebuffed them, stating that actuarially sound discrimination "cannot be unfair." Ironically for women, the one exception to states' toleration of sex discrimination is in automobile insurance, where statistics support charging women lower premiums. A number of state legislatures have declared that sex discrimination in automobile insurance is unfair, without extending the argument to other types of insurance.

Gaulding, supra, at 1662-1663. Why did the "efficient discrimination" rationale prevail? What variables could possess sufficient explanatory power to serve as an alternative discriminator in insurance classification?

Putting Theory into Practice

2-6. U.S. Department of Transportation data show that men have almost twice as many automobile accidents as women. They also show that men drive on average many more miles per year than women (17,671, as compared to 7,211 miles for women), and that as the number of miles driven per year increases, the accident rate per mile driven decreases. See Karen A. McCluskey, Note, Ending Sex Discrimination in Insurance: The Nondiscrimination in Insurance Act, 11 J. Legis. 457, 470 n.98 (1984). While in recent years women's mileage has increased 135 percent (as compared to 48 percent for men), men still drive more and are still twice as likely to be involved in fatal automobile accidents. Joseph B. Treaster, Deaths of Women in Car Crashes Are Rising, N.Y. Times, Nov. 15, 2001, at C12.

In light of this data, should sex be an appropriate risk factor in setting automobile insurance rates? If so, what are the different ways it could be taken into account? Which is the most "fair"?

2-7. A 1988 survey of insurers indicated that about half of the nation's largest insurers instruct that health, life, and disability insurance be denied to victims of domestic abuse. Deborah S. Hellman, Is Actuarially Fair Insurance Pricing Actually Fair? A Case Study in Insuring Battered Women, 32 Harv. C.R.-C.L. L. Rev. 355, 355-356 (1997). Assume the policy is actuarially sound. Should it be legal?

2. Education

a. Sex-Segregated Schools

≡ *United States v. Virginia*
≡ **518 U.S. 515 (1996)**

GINSBURG, J., delivered the opinion of the court, in which STEVENS, O'CONNOR, KENNEDY, SOUTER, and BREYER, JJ., joined.

Virginia's public institutions of higher learning include an incomparable military college, Virginia Military Institute (VMI). The United States maintains that the Constitution's equal protection guarantee precludes Virginia from reserving exclusively to men the unique educational opportunities VMI affords. We agree. . . .

II

From its establishment in 1839 as one of the Nation's first state military colleges, VMI has remained financially supported by Virginia and "subject to the control of the [Virginia] General Assembly." . . .

VMI today enrolls about 1,300 men as cadets. Its academic offerings in the liberal arts, sciences, and engineering are also available at other public colleges and universities in Virginia. But VMI's mission is special. It is the mission of the school to produce educated and honorable men, prepared for the varied work of civil life, imbued with love of learning, confident in the functions and attitudes of leadership, possessing a high sense of public service, advocates of the American democracy and free enterprise system, and ready as citizen-soldiers to defend their country in time of national peril. . . .

In contrast to the federal service academies, institutions maintained "to prepare cadets for career service in the armed forces," VMI's program "is directed at preparation for both military and civilian life;" "[o]nly about 15% of VMI cadets enter career military service."

VMI produces its "citizen-soldiers" through "an adversative, or doubting, model of education" which features "[p]hysical rigor, mental stress, absolute equality of treatment, absence of privacy, minute regulation of behavior, and indoctrination in desirable values." . . .

VMI cadets live in spartan barracks where surveillance is constant and privacy nonexistent; they wear uniforms, eat together in the mess hall, and regularly participate in drills. Entering students are incessantly exposed to the rat line, "an extreme form of the adversative model," comparable in intensity to Marine Corps boot camp. Tormenting and punishing, the rat line bonds new cadets to their fellow sufferers and, when they have completed the 7-month experience, to their former tormentors.

VMI's "adversative model" is further characterized by a hierarchical "class system" of privileges and responsibilities, a "dyke system" for assigning a senior class mentor to each entering class "rat," and a stringently enforced "honor code," which prescribes that a cadet "'does not lie, cheat, steal nor tolerate those who do.'"

VMI attracts some applicants because of its reputation as an extraordinarily challenging military school, and "because its alumni are exceptionally close to the school." "[W]omen have no opportunity anywhere to gain the benefits of [the system of education at VMI]." . . .

In 1990, prompted by a complaint filed with the Attorney General by a female high-school student seeking admission to VMI, the United States sued the Commonwealth of Virginia and VMI, alleging that VMI's exclusively male admission policy violated the Equal Protection Clause of the Fourteenth Amendment. . . .

In the two years preceding the lawsuit, the District Court noted, VMI had received inquiries from 347 women, but had responded to none of them. "[S]ome women, at least," the court said, "would want to attend the school if they had the opportunity." The court further recognized that, with recruitment, VMI could "achieve at least 10% female enrollment" — "a sufficient 'critical mass' to provide the female cadets with a positive educational experience." And it was also established that "some women are capable of all of the individual activities required of VMI cadets." In addition, experts agreed that if VMI admitted women, "the VMI ROTC experience would become a better training program from the perspective of the armed forces, because it would provide training in dealing with a mixed-gender army."

[The District Court, nonetheless, ruled in favor of VMI, because admission of women would require alterations of some of the distinctive and beneficial aspects of VMI (766 F. Supp. 1407 (1991)); the Fourth Circuit Court of Appeals reversed and remanded, holding that the state could not achieve its purposes by favoring one gender and that VMI had to either admit women, establish a parallel institution or program, or abandon state support (976 F.2d 890 (1992)). In response to the Fourth Circuit's ruling, Virginia proposed a parallel program at Mary Baldwin College, a private liberal arts school for women: Virginia Women's Institute for Leadership (VWIL). The program was to be open, initially, to 25 to 30 students. The District Court decided that the program plan met the requirements of the Equal Protection Clause, (852 F. Supp. 471 (1994)) and a divided Court of Appeals affirmed, at 44 F.3d 1229 (1995).]

III

The cross-petitions in this case present two ultimate issues. First, does Virginia's exclusion of women from the educational opportunities provided by VMI — extraordinary opportunities for military training and civilian leadership development — deny to women "capable of all of the individual activities required of VMI cadets," the equal protection of the laws guaranteed by the Fourteenth Amendment? Second, if VMI's "unique" situation, — as Virginia's sole single-sex public institution of higher education — offends the Constitution's equal protection principle, what is the remedial requirement?

IV...

To summarize the Court's current directions for cases of official classification based on gender: Focusing on the differential treatment or denial of opportunity for which relief is sought, the reviewing court must determine whether the proffered justification is "exceedingly persuasive." The burden of justification is demanding and it rests entirely on the State. [See Mississippi Univ. for Women v. Hogan, 458 U.S. 718, 724 (1982).] The State must show "at least that the [challenged] classification serves 'important governmental objectives and that the discriminatory means employed' are 'substantially related to the achievement of those objectives.'" Id. The justification must be genuine, not hypothesized or invented post hoc in response to litigation. And it must not rely on overbroad generalizations about the different talents, capacities, or preferences of males and females....

The heightened review standard our precedent establishes does not make sex a proscribed classification. Supposed "inherent differences" are no longer accepted as a ground for race or national origin classifications. See Loving v. Virginia, 388 U.S. 1, 87 (1967). Physical differences between men and women, however, are enduring: "[T]he two sexes are not fungible; a community made up exclusively of one [sex] is different from a community composed of both." Ballard v. United States, 329 U.S. 187, 193 (1946).

"Inherent differences" between men and women, we have come to appreciate, remain cause for celebration, but not for denigration of the members of either sex or for artificial constraints on an individual's opportunity. Sex classifications may be used to compensate women "for particular economic disabilities [they have] suffered," Califano v. Webster, 430 U.S. 313, 320 (1977), to "promot[e] equal employment opportunity," see California Federal Sav. & Loan Ass'n v. Guerra, 479 U.S. 272, 289 (1987), to advance full development of the talent and capacities of our Nation's people.[7] But such classifications may not be used, as they once were,...to create or perpetuate the legal, social, and economic inferiority of women.

Measuring the record in this case against the review standard just described, we conclude that Virginia has shown no "exceedingly persuasive justification" for excluding all women from the citizen-soldier training afforded by VMI. We therefore affirm the Fourth Circuit's initial judgment, which held that Virginia had violated the Fourteenth Amendment's Equal Protection Clause. Because the remedy proffered by Virginia — the Mary Baldwin VWIL program — does not cure the constitutional violation, i.e., it does not provide equal opportunity, we reverse the Fourth Circuit's final judgment in this case.

V...

Single-sex education affords pedagogical benefits to at least some students, Virginia emphasizes, and that reality is uncontested in this litigation.[8] Similarly, it is not disputed that diversity among public educational institutions can serve the

---

7. ...We do not question the State's prerogative evenhandedly to support diverse educational opportunities. We address specifically and only an educational opportunity recognized by the District Court and the Court of Appeals as "unique," an opportunity available only at Virginia's premier military institute, the State's sole single-sex public university or college. Cf. Mississippi Univ. for Women v. Hogan, 458 U.S. 718, 720, n.1 (1982) ("Mississippi maintains no other single-sex public university or college. Thus, we are not faced with the question of whether States can provide 'separate but equal' undergraduate institutions for males and females").

8. On this point, the dissent sees fire where there is no flame. "Both men and women can benefit from a single-sex education," the District Court recognized, although "the beneficial effects" of such education, the court added, apparently "are stronger among women than among men." The United States does not challenge that recognition. Cf. C. Jencks & D. Riesman, The Academic Revolution 297-298 (1968): "The pluralistic argument for preserving all-male colleges is uncomfortably similar to the pluralistic argument for preserving all-white colleges.... The all-male college would be relatively easy to defend if it emerged from a world in which women were established as fully equal to men. But it does not. It is therefore likely to be a witting or unwitting device for preserving tacit assumptions of male superiority — assumptions for which women must eventually pay."

public good. But Virginia has not shown that VMI was established, or has been maintained, with a view to diversifying, by its categorical exclusion of women, educational opportunities within the State. In cases of this genre, our precedent instructs that "benign" justifications proffered in defense of categorical exclusions will not be accepted automatically; a tenable justification must describe actual state purposes, not rationalizations for actions in fact differently grounded....

Neither recent nor distant history bears out Virginia's alleged pursuit of diversity through single-sex educational options. In 1839, when the State established VMI, a range of educational opportunities for men and women was scarcely contemplated. Higher education at the time was considered dangerous for women;[9] reflecting widely held views about women's proper place, the Nation's first universities and colleges — for example, Harvard in Massachusetts, William and Mary in Virginia — admitted only men.... VMI was not at all novel in this respect: In admitting no women, VMI followed the lead of the State's flagship school, the University of Virginia, founded in 1819....

Debate concerning women's admission as undergraduates at the main university continued well past the century's midpoint.... If women were admitted, it was feared, they "would encroach on the rights of men; there would be new problems of government, perhaps scandals; the old honor system would have to be changed; standards would be lowered to those of other coeducational schools; and the glorious reputation of the university, as a school for men, would be trailed in the dust."...

Ultimately, in 1970, "the most prestigious institution of higher education in Virginia," the University of Virginia, introduced coeducation and, in 1972 [by court order], began to admit women on an equal basis with men....

Virginia describes the current absence of public single-sex higher education for women as "an historical anomaly." But the historical record indicates action more deliberate than anomalous: First, protection of women against higher education; next, schools for women far from equal in resources and stature to schools for men; finally, conversion of the separate schools to coeducation....

[I]t is uncontested that women's admission would require accommodations, primarily in arranging housing assignments and physical training programs for female cadets. It is also undisputed, however, that "the VMI methodology could be used to educate women." The District Court even allowed that some women may prefer it to the methodology a women's college might pursue. "[S]ome women, at least, would want to attend [VMI] if they had the opportunity,"

9. Dr. Edward H. Clarke of Harvard Medical School, whose influential book, Sex in Education, went through 17 editions, was perhaps the most well-known speaker from the medical community opposing higher education for women. He maintained that the physiological effects of hard study and academic competition with boys would interfere with the development of girls' reproductive organs. See E. Clarke, Sex in Education 38-39, 62-63 (1873); id., at 127 ("identical education of the two sexes is a crime before God and humanity, that physiology protests against, and that experience weeps over"); see also H. Maudsley, Sex in Mind and in Education 17 (1874) ("It is not that girls have not ambition, nor that they fail generally to run the intellectual race [in coeducational settings], but it is asserted that they do it at a cost to their strength and health which entails life-long suffering, and even incapacitates them for the adequate performance of the natural functions of their sex."); C. Meigs, Females and Their Diseases 350 (1848) (after five or six weeks of "mental and educational discipline," a healthy woman would "lose ... the habit of menstruation" and suffer numerous ills as a result of depriving her body for the sake of her mind).

the District Court recognized, and "some women," the expert testimony established, "are capable of all of the individual activities required of VMI cadets." The parties, furthermore, agree that "some women can meet the physical standards [VMI] now impose[s] on men." In sum, as the Court of Appeals stated, "neither the goal of producing citizen soldiers," VMI's *raison d'etre*, "nor VMI's implementing methodology is inherently unsuitable to women."

In support of its initial judgment for Virginia, a judgment rejecting all equal protection objections presented by the United States, the District Court made "findings" on "gender-based developmental differences." These "findings" restate the opinions of Virginia's expert witnesses, opinions about typically male or typically female tendencies." For example, "[m]ales tend to need an atmosphere of adversativeness," while "[f]emales tend to thrive in a cooperative atmosphere." "I'm not saying that some women don't do well under [the] adversative model," VMI's expert on educational institutions testified, "undoubtedly there are some [women] who do"; but educational experiences must be designed "around the rule," this expert maintained, and not "around the exception."

The United States does not challenge any expert witness estimation on average capacities or preferences of men and women. Instead, the United States emphasizes that time and again since this Court's turning point decision in Reed v. Reed, 404 U.S. 71 (1971), we have cautioned reviewing courts to take a "hard look" at generalizations or "tendencies" of the kind pressed by Virginia, and relied upon by the District Court....

It may be assumed, for purposes of this decision, that most women would not choose VMI's adversative method. As Fourth Circuit Judge Motz observed, however, in her dissent from the Court of Appeals' denial of rehearing en banc, it is also probable that "many men would not want to be educated in such an environment." 52 F.3d, at 93. (On that point, even our dissenting colleague might agree.) Education, to be sure, is not a "one size fits all" business. The issue, however, is not whether "women — or men — should be forced to attend VMI"; rather, the question is whether the State can constitutionally deny to women who have the will and capacity, the training and attendant opportunities that VMI uniquely affords.

The notion that admission of women would downgrade VMI's stature, destroy the adversative system and, with it, even the school, is a judgment hardly proved, a prediction hardly different from other "self-fulfilling prophec[ies]," see [*Hogan*], 458 U.S., at 730, once routinely used to deny rights or opportunities. When women first sought admission to the bar and access to legal education, concerns of the same order were expressed....

[Such] fear, according to a 1925 report, accounted for Columbia Law School's resistance to women's admission, although

> [t]he faculty...never maintained that women could not master legal learning....No, its argument has been...more practical. If women were admitted to the Columbia Law School, [the faculty] said, then the choicer, more manly and red-blooded graduates of our great universities would go to the Harvard Law School!

The Nation, Feb. 18, 1925, p. 173....

More recently, women seeking careers in policing encountered resistance based on fears that their presence would "undermine male solidarity," . . . deprive deprive male partners of adequate assistance, and lead to sexual misconduct. . . .

Women's successful entry into the federal military academies,[13] and their participation in the Nation's military forces, indicate that Virginia's fears for the future of VMI may not be solidly grounded. . . . [15]

The State's misunderstanding and, in turn, the District Court's, is apparent from VMI's mission: to produce "citizen-soldiers," individuals "imbued with love of learning, confident in the functions and attitudes of leadership, possessing a high sense of public service, advocates of the American democracy and free enterprise system, and ready . . . to defend their country in time of national peril." . . .

Surely that goal is great enough to accommodate women, who today count as citizens in our American democracy equal in stature to men. Just as surely, the State's great goal is not substantially advanced by women's categorical exclusion, in total disregard of their individual merit, from the State's premier "citizen-soldier" corps.[16] Virginia, in sum, "has fallen far short of establishing the 'exceedingly persuasive justification,'" [*Hogan*], 458 U.S., at 731, that must be the solid base for any gender-defined classification.

VI

In the second phase of the litigation, Virginia presented its remedial plan — maintain VMI as a male-only college and create VWIL as a separate program for women. . . .

The constitutional violation in this case is the categorical exclusion of women from an extraordinary educational opportunity afforded men. A proper remedy for an unconstitutional exclusion, we have explained, aims to "eliminate [so far as possible] the discriminatory effects of the past" and to "bar like discrimination in the future." Louisiana v. United States, 380 U.S. 145, 154 (1965).

Virginia chose not to eliminate, but to leave untouched, VMI's exclusionary policy. For women only, however, Virginia proposed a separate program, different in kind from VMI and unequal in tangible and intangible facilities. . . .

VWIL affords women no opportunity to experience the rigorous military training for which VMI is famed. . . . Instead, the VWIL program "deemphasize[s]"

13. Women cadets have graduated at the top of their class at every federal military academy.

15. Inclusion of women in settings where, traditionally, they were not wanted inevitably entails a period of adjustment. As one West Point cadet squad leader recounted, "[T]he classes of '78 and '79 see the somen as women, but the classes of '80 and '81 see them as classmates." . . .

16. VMI has successfully managed another notable change. The school admitted its first African-American cadets in 1968. See The VMI Story 347-349 (students no longer sing "Dixie," salute the Confederate flag or the tomb of General Robert E. Lee at ceremonies and sports events." As the District Court noted, VMI established a Program on "retention of black cadets" designed to offer academic and social-cultural support to "minority members of a dominantly white and tradition-oriented student body." The school maintains a "special recruitment program for blacks" which, the District Court found, "has had little, if any, effect on VMI's method of accomplishing its mission."

military education, and uses a "cooperative method" of education "which reinforces self-esteem."

VWIL students participate in ROTC and a "largely ceremonial" Virginia Corps of Cadets, but Virginia deliberately did not make VWIL a military institute. The VWIL House is not a military-style residence and VWIL students need not live together throughout the four year program, eat meals together, or wear uniforms during the school day. VWIL students thus do not experience the "barracks" life "crucial to the VMI experience," the spartan living arrangements designed to foster an "egalitarian ethic." "[T]he most important aspects of the VMI educational experience occur in the barracks," the District Court found, yet Virginia deemed that core experience nonessential, indeed inappropriate, for training its female citizen-soldiers.

VWIL students receive their "leadership training" in seminars, externships, and speaker series, episodes and encounters lacking the "[p]hysical rigor, mental stress,...minute regulation of behavior, and indoctrination in desirable values" made hallmarks of VMI's citizen-soldier training. Kept away from the pressures, hazards, and psychological bonding characteristic of VMI's adversative training, VWIL students will not know the "feeling of tremendous accomplishment" commonly experienced by VMI's successful cadets.

Virginia maintains that these methodological differences are "justified pedagogically," based on "important differences between men and women in learning and developmental needs," "psychological and sociological differences" Virginia describes as "real" and "not stereotypes." The Task Force charged with developing the leadership program for women, drawn from the staff and faculty at Mary Baldwin College, "determined that a military model and, especially VMI's adversative method, would be wholly inappropriate for educating and training *most women*"...[and noted that] while some women would be suited to and interested in [a VMI-style experience]," VMI's adversative method "would not be effective for *women as a group*"....

As earlier stated, generalizations about "the way women are," estimates of what is appropriate for *most women*, no longer justify denying opportunity to women whose talent and capacity place them outside the average description. Notably, Virginia never asserted that VMI's method of education suits *most men*. It is also revealing that Virginia accounted for its failure to make the VWIL experience "the entirely militaristic experience of VMI" on the ground that VWIL "is planned for women who do not necessarily expect to pursue military careers." By that reasoning, VMI's "entirely militaristic" program would be inappropriate for men in general or *as a group*, for "[o]nly about 15% of VMI cadets enter career military service."

In contrast to the generalizations about women on which Virginia rests, we note again these dispositive realities: VMI's "implementing methodology" is not "inherently unsuitable to women," "some women...do well under [the] adversative model," "some women, at least, would want to attend [VMI] if they had the opportunity," "some women are capable of all of the individual activities required of VMI cadets," and "can meet the physical standards [VMI] now impose[s] on men."...

In myriad respects other than military training, VWIL does not qualify as VMI's equal. VWIL's student body, faculty, course offerings, and facilities hardly match VMI's. Nor can the VWIL graduate anticipate the benefits associated with VMI's 157-year history, the school's prestige, and its influential alumni network.

Mary Baldwin College, whose degree VWIL students will gain, enrolls first-year women with an average combined SAT score about 100 points lower than the average score for VMI freshmen. The Mary Baldwin faculty holds "significantly fewer Ph.D.'s," and receives substantially lower salaries than the faculty at VMI.

Mary Baldwin does not offer a VWIL student the range of curricular choices available to a VMI cadet. VMI awards baccalaureate degrees in liberal arts, biology, chemistry, civil engineering, electrical and computer engineering, and mechanical engineering. . . . VWIL students attend a school that "does not have a math and science focus," they cannot take at Mary Baldwin any courses in engineering or the advanced math and physics courses VMI offers. . . .

For physical training, Mary Baldwin has "two multi-purpose fields" and "[o]ne gymnasium." VMI has "an NCAA competition level indoor track and field facility; a number of multi-purpose fields; baseball, soccer and lacrosse fields; an obstacle course; large boxing, wrestling and martial arts facilities; an 11-laps-to-the-mile indoor running course; an indoor pool; indoor and outdoor rifle ranges; and a football stadium that also contains a practice field and outdoor track."

Although Virginia has represented that it will provide equal financial support for in-state VWIL students and VMI cadets, and the VMI Foundation has agreed to endow VWIL with $5.4625 million, the difference between the two schools' financial reserves is pronounced. Mary Baldwin's endowment, currently about $19 million, will gain an additional $35 million based on future commitments; VMI's current endowment, $131 million — the largest per-student endowment in the Nation — will gain $220 million.

The VWIL student does not graduate with the advantage of a VMI degree. Her diploma does not unite her with the legions of VMI "graduates [who] have distinguished themselves" in military and civilian life. . . . A VWIL graduate cannot assume that the "network of business owners, corporations, VMI graduates and non-graduate employers . . . interested in hiring VMI graduates," will be equally responsive to her search for employment. . . .

Virginia, in sum, while maintaining VMI for men only, has failed to provide any "comparable single-gender women's institution." Instead, the Commonwealth has created a VWIL program fairly appraised as a "pale shadow" of VMI in terms of the range of curricular choices and faculty stature, funding, prestige, alumni support, and influence.

Virginia's VWIL solution is reminiscent of the remedy Texas proposed 50 years ago, in response to a state trial court's 1946 ruling that, given the equal protection guarantee, African Americans could not be denied a legal education at a state facility. . . . Reluctant to admit African Americans to its flagship University of Texas Law School, the State set up a separate school for Herman Sweatt and other black law students. As originally opened, the new school had no independent faculty or library, and it lacked accreditation. Nevertheless, the state trial and appellate courts were satisfied that the new school offered Sweatt opportunities for the study of law "substantially equivalent to those offered by the State to white students at the University of Texas."

Before this Court considered the case, the new school had gained "a faculty of five full-time professors; a student body of 23; a library of some 16,500 volumes serviced by a full-time staff; a practice court and legal aid association; and one alumnus who ha[d] become a member of the Texas Bar." This Court contrasted resources at the new school with those at the school from which Sweatt had been excluded. The University of Texas Law School had a full-time faculty of 16, a student body of 850, a library containing over 65,000 volumes, scholarship funds, a law review, and moot court facilities. [Sweatt v. Painter, 339 U.S. 629, 632-633 (1950).]

More important than the tangible features, the Court emphasized, are "those qualities which are incapable of objective measurement but which make for greatness" in a school, including "reputation of the faculty, experience of the administration, position and influence of the alumni, standing in the community, traditions and prestige." Facing the marked differences reported in the *Sweatt* opinion, the Court unanimously ruled that Texas had not shown "substantial equality in the [separate] educational opportunities" the State offered. Accordingly, the Court held, the Equal Protection Clause required Texas to admit African Americans to the University of Texas Law School. In line with *Sweatt*, we rule here that Virginia has not shown substantial equality in the separate educational opportunities the State supports at VWIL and VMI.

[Reversed and remanded.]

Justice THOMAS took no part in the consideration or decision of this case.

CHIEF JUSTICE REHNQUIST concurring in judgment. . . .

[U]nlike the majority, I would consider only evidence that postdates our decision in *Hogan*, and would draw no negative inferences from the State's actions before that time. I think that after *Hogan*, the State was entitled to reconsider its policy with respect to VMI, and to not have earlier justifications, or lack thereof, held against it.

Even if diversity in educational opportunity were the State's actual objective, the State's position would still be problematic. The difficulty with its position is that the diversity benefited only one sex; there was single-sex public education available for men at VMI, but no corresponding single-sex public education available for women. . . .

Had Virginia made a genuine effort to devote comparable public resources to a facility for women, and followed through on such a plan, it might well have avoided an equal protection violation. . . .

Justice SCALIA, dissenting.

Today the Court shuts down an institution that has served the people of the Commonwealth of Virginia with pride and distinction for over a century and a half. To achieve that desired result, it rejects (contrary to our established practice) the factual findings of two courts below, sweeps aside the precedents of this

Court, and ignores the history of our people. As to facts: it explicitly rejects the finding that there exist "gender-based developmental differences" supporting Virginia's restriction of the "adversative" method to only a men's institution, and the finding that the all-male composition of the Virginia Military Institute (VMI) is essential to that institution's character. As to precedent: it drastically revises our established standards for reviewing sex-based classifications. And as to history: it counts for nothing the long tradition, enduring down to the present, of men's military colleges supported by both States and the Federal Government.

Much of the Court's opinion is devoted to deprecating the closed-mindedness of our forebears with regard to women's education, and even with regard to the treatment of women in areas that have nothing to do with education. Closed-minded they were — as every age is, including our own, with regard to matters it cannot guess, because it simply does not consider them debatable. The virtue of a democratic system with a First Amendment is that it readily enables the people, over time, to be persuaded that what they took for granted is not so, and to change their laws accordingly. That system is destroyed if the smug assurances of each age are removed from the democratic process and written into the Constitution. So to counterbalance the Court's criticism of our ancestors, let me say a word in their praise: they left us free to change. The same cannot be said of this most illiberal Court, which has embarked on a course of inscribing one after another of the current preferences of the society (and in some cases only the counter-majoritarian preferences of the society's law-trained elite) into our Basic Law. Today it enshrines the notion that no substantial educational value is to be served by an all-men's military academy — so that the decision by the people of Virginia to maintain such an institution denies equal protection to women who cannot attend that institution but can attend others. Since it is entirely clear that the Constitution of the United States — the old one — takes no sides in this educational debate, I dissent.

I...

[I]n my view the function of this Court is to *preserve* our society's values regarding (among other things) equal protection, not to *revise* them; to prevent backsliding from the degree of restriction the Constitution imposed upon democratic government, not to prescribe, on our own authority, progressively higher degrees. For that reason it is my view that, whatever abstract tests we may choose to devise, they cannot supersede — and indeed ought to be crafted *so as to reflect* — those constant and unbroken national traditions that embody the people's understanding of ambiguous constitutional texts. More specifically, it is my view that "when a practice not expressly prohibited by the text of the Bill of Rights bears the endorsement of a long tradition of open, widespread, and unchallenged use that dates back to the beginning of the Republic, we have no proper basis for striking it down." Rutan v. Republican Party of Ill., [497 U.S. 62, 95] (1990) (Scalia, J., dissenting). The same applies, *mutatis mutandis*, to a practice asserted to be in violation of the post-Civil War Fourteenth Amendment....

The all-male constitution of VMI comes squarely within such a governing tradition. Founded by the Commonwealth of Virginia in 1839 and continuously maintained by it since, VMI has always admitted only men. And in that regard it has not been unusual. For almost all of VMI's more than a century and a half of existence, its single-sex status reflected the uniform practice for government-supported military colleges. Another famous Southern institution, The Citadel, has existed as a state-funded school of South Carolina since 1842. And all the federal military colleges — West Point, the Naval Academy at Annapolis, and even the Air Force Academy, which was not established until 1954 — admitted only males for most of their history. Their admission of women in 1976 (upon which the Court today relies), came not by court decree, but because the people, through their elected representatives, decreed a change.... In other words, the tradition of having government-funded military schools for men is as well rooted in the traditions of this country as the tradition of sending only men into military combat. The people may decide to change the one tradition, like the other, through democratic processes; but the assertion that either tradition has been unconstitutional through the centuries is not law, but politics-smuggled-into-law.

And the same applies, more broadly, to single-sex education in general, which, as I shall discuss, is threatened by today's decision with the cut-off of all state and federal support. Government-run *non*military educational institutions for the two sexes have until very recently also been part of our national tradition. "[It is] [c]oeducation, historically, [that] is a novel educational theory. From grade school through high school, college, and graduate and professional training, much of the Nation's population during much of our history has been educated in sexually segregated classrooms." Mississippi Univ. for Women v. Hogan, 458 U.S. 718, 736 (1982) (Powell, J., dissenting). These traditions may of course be changed by the democratic decisions of the people, as they largely have been.

Today, however, change is forced upon Virginia, and reversion to single-sex education is prohibited nationwide, not by democratic processes but by order of this Court. Even while bemoaning the sorry, bygone days of "fixed notions" concerning women's education, the Court favors current notions so fixedly that it is willing to write them into the Constitution of the United States by application of custom-built "tests." This is not the interpretation of a Constitution, but the creation of one.

II

To reject the Court's disposition today, however, it is not necessary to accept my view that the Court's made-up tests cannot displace longstanding national traditions as the primary determinant of what the Constitution means. It is only necessary to apply honestly the test the Court has been applying to sex-based classifications for the past two decades.... We have denominated this standard "intermediate scrutiny" and under it have inquired whether the statutory classification is "substantially related to an important governmental objective."...

Only the amorphous "exceedingly persuasive justification" phrase, and not the standard elaboration of intermediate scrutiny, can be made to yield this conclusion that VMI's single-sex composition is unconstitutional because there exist several women (or, one would have to conclude under the Court's reasoning, a single woman) willing and able to undertake VMI's program. Intermediate scrutiny has never required a least-restrictive-means analysis, but only a "substantial relation" between the classification and the state interests that it serves. . . .

Not content to execute a *de facto* abandonment of the intermediate scrutiny that has been our standard for sex-based classifications for some two decades, the Court purports to reserve the question whether, even in principle, a higher standard (i.e., strict scrutiny) should apply. . . . [The Court's] statements are misleading, insofar as they suggest that we have not already categorically *held* strict scrutiny to be inapplicable to sex-based classifications. . . . And the statements are irresponsible, insofar as they are calculated to destabilize current law. Our task is to clarify the law — not to muddy the waters, and not to exact over-compliance by intimidation. The States and the Federal Government are entitled to know *before they act* the standard to which they will be held, rather than be compelled to guess about the outcome of Supreme Court peek-a-boo.

The Court's intimations are particularly out of place because it is perfectly clear that, if the question of the applicable standard of review for sex-based classifications were to be regarded as an appropriate subject for reconsideration, the stronger argument would be not for elevating the standard to strict scrutiny, but for reducing it to rational-basis review. The latter certainly has a firmer foundation in our past jurisprudence: Whereas no majority of the Court has ever applied strict scrutiny in a case involving sex-based classifications, we routinely applied rational-basis review until the 1970's. . . .

It is hard to consider women a "discrete and insular minorit[y]" unable to employ the "political processes ordinarily to be relied upon," when they constitute a majority of the electorate. And the suggestion that they are incapable of exerting that political power smacks of the same paternalism that the Court so roundly condemns. Moreover, a long list of legislation proves the proposition false. . . .

III . . .

There can be no serious dispute that, as the District Court found, single-sex education and a distinctive educational method "represent legitimate contributions to diversity in the Virginia higher education system." As a theoretical matter, Virginia's educational interest would have been best served (insofar as the two factors we have mentioned are concerned) by six different types of public colleges — an all-men's, an all-women's, and a coeducational college run in the "adversative method," and an all-men's, an all-women's, and a coeducational college run in the "traditional method." But as a practical matter, of course, Virginia's financial resources, like any State's, are not limitless, and the Commonwealth must select among the available options. Virginia thus has decided to fund, in addition to some 14 coeducational 4-year colleges, one college that is run as an all-male school on the adversative model: the Virginia Military Institute.

Virginia did not make this determination regarding the make-up of its public college system on the unrealistic assumption that no other colleges exist. Substantial evidence in the District Court demonstrated that the Commonwealth has long proceeded on the principle that "'[h]igher education resources should be viewed as a whole — public and private'" — because such an approach enhances diversity and because "'it is academic and economic waste to permit unwarranted duplication.'" It is thus significant that, whereas there are "four all-female private [colleges] in Virginia," there is only "one private all-male college," which "indicates that the private sector is providing for th[e] [former] form of education to a much greater extent that it provides for all-male education." In these circumstances, Virginia's election to fund one public all-male institution and one on the adversative model — and to concentrate its resources in a single entity that serves both these interests in diversity — is substantially related to the State's important educational interests....

IV...

Under the constitutional principles announced and applied today, single-sex public education is unconstitutional. By going through the motions of applying a balancing test — asking whether the State has adduced an "exceedingly persuasive justification" for its sex-based classification — the Court creates the illusion that government officials in some future case will have a clear shot at justifying some sort of single-sex public education....

[R]egardless of whether the Court's rationale leaves some small amount of room for lawyers to argue, it ensures that single-sex public education is functionally dead. The costs of litigating the constitutionality of a single-sex education program, and the risks of ultimately losing that litigation, are simply too high to be embraced by public officials....

There are few extant single-sex public educational programs. The potential of today's decision for widespread disruption of existing institutions lies in its application to private single-sex education. Government support is immensely important to private educational institutions. Mary Baldwin College — which designed and runs VWIL — notes that private institutions of higher education in the 1990-1991 school year derived approximately 19 percent of their budgets from federal, state, and local government funds, *not including financial aid to students.* ... [I]t is certainly not beyond the Court that rendered today's decision to hold that a donation to a single-sex college should be deemed contrary to public policy and therefore not deductible if the college discriminates on the basis of sex....

The issue will be not whether government assistance turns private colleges into state actors, but whether the government *itself* would be violating the Constitution by providing state support to single-sex colleges. For example, in Norwood v. Harrison, [413 U.S. 455] (1973), we saw no room to distinguish between state operation of racially segregated schools and state support of privately run segregated schools....

The only hope for state-assisted single-sex private schools is that the Court will not apply in the future the principles of law it has applied today. That is a substantial hope, I am happy and ashamed to say. After all, did not the Court today abandon the principles of law it has applied in our earlier sex-classification cases? And does not the Court positively invite private colleges to rely upon our ad-hocery by assuring them this case is "unique"? I would not advise the foundation of any new single-sex college (especially an all-male one) with the expectation of being allowed to receive any government support; but it is too soon to abandon in despair those single-sex colleges already in existence. It will certainly be possible for this Court to write a future opinion that ignores the broad principles of law set forth today, and that characterizes as utterly dispositive the opinion's perceptions that VMI was a uniquely prestigious all-male institution, conceived in chauvinism, etc., etc. I will not join that opinion....

In an odd sort of way, it is precisely VMI's attachment to such old-fashioned concepts as manly "honor" that has made it, and the system it represents, the target of those who today succeed in abolishing public single-sex education. The record contains a booklet that all first-year VMI students (the so-called "rats") were required to keep in their possession at all times. Near the end there appears the following period-piece, entitled "The Code of a Gentleman":

> Without a strict observance of the fundamental Code of Honor, no man, no matter how "polished," can be considered a gentleman. The honor of a gentleman demands the inviolability of his word, and the incorruptibility of his principles. He is the descendant of the knight, the crusader; he is the defender of the defenseless and the champion of justice . . . or he is not a Gentleman.
>
> A Gentleman . . .
>
> Does not discuss his family affairs in public or with acquaintances.
>
> Does not speak more than casually about his girl friend.
>
> Does not go to a lady's house if he is affected by alcohol. He is temperate in the use of alcohol.
>
> Does not lose his temper; nor exhibit anger, fear, hate, embarrassment, ardor or hilarity in public.
>
> Does not hail a lady from a club window.
>
> A gentleman never discusses the merits or demerits of a lady.
>
> Does not mention names exactly as he avoids the mention of what things cost.
>
> Does not borrow money from a friend, except in dire need. Money borrowed is a debt of honor, and must be repaid as promptly as possible. Debts incurred by a deceased parent, brother, sister or grown child are assumed by honorable men as a debt of honor.
>
> Does not display his wealth, money or possessions.
>
> Does not put his manners on and off, whether in the club or in a ballroom. He treats people with courtesy, no matter what their social position may be.
>
> Does not slap strangers on the back nor so much as lay a finger on a lady.
>
> Does not "lick the boots of those above" nor "kick the face of those below him on the social ladder."
>
> Does not take advantage of another's helplessness or ignorance and assumes that no gentleman will take advantage of him.
>
> A Gentleman respects the reserves of others, but demands that others respect those which are his.
>
> A Gentleman can become what he wills to be. . . .

I do not know whether the men of VMI lived by this Code; perhaps not. But it is powerfully impressive that a public institution of higher education still in existence sought to have them do so. I do not think any of us, women included, will be better off for its destruction.

Notes

1. The End of Single-Sex Colleges? At about the same time that VMI was under constitutional challenge, another military college, The Citadel, which had developed a substitute program for women that was not nearly as well thought out as VWIL, was held to be unconstitutional by the Fourth Circuit Court of Appeals. See Faulkner v. Jones, 66 F.3d 661 (4th Cir. 1995); Valorie K. Vojdik, At War: Narrative Tactics in The Citadel and VMI Litigation, 19 Harv. Women's L.J. 1 (1996) (summarizing tactical choices made in the *Faulkner* and *VMI* cases). The expert testimony in the *VMI* case relating to sex differences in education is reviewed and analyzed in Diane Avery, Institutional Myths, Historical Narratives and Social Science Evidence: Reading the "Record" in the *Virginia Military Institute* Case, 5 S. Cal. Rev. L. & Women's Stud. 189 (1996).

Kimberly Schuld criticizes the *VMI* case for using a "microscopic" perspective, which focuses on the individual level and ignores real sex differences, rather than a "macroscopic" perspective that "would examine the whole of society and the conglomerate of its offerings to determine whether males as a group and females as a group are offered relatively similar opportunities to make individual choices." See Kimberly M. Schuld, Rethinking Educational Equity: Sometimes, Different Can Be an Acceptable Substitute for Equal, 1999 U. Chi. Legal F. 461, 469. Why isn't the "separate but equal" model that is applied to school sports (see section beginning p. 286, infra) just as applicable to the institutions themselves? Can an all-male state school be justified under any circumstances after *VMI*?

Mary Anne Case visited both VMI and VWIL after the *VMI* decision. She found the "rats" at VMI "a sorry lot — terrified, sweating, shaking, and exhausted . . . they were unable to tell their left feet from their right." By contrast nULLS (the VWIL equivalent to rats) were working together, learning the same values of accountability and discipline in a more supporting, encouraging, and non-intimidating environment. See Case, Two Cheers for Cheerleading: The Noisy Integration of VMI and the Quiet Success of Virginia Women in Leadership, 1999 U. Chi. Legal F. 347, 378. She noted, however, that VMI was still the more prestigious, sought-after alternative, even by many women.

> The paradoxes are many: First, the dominant class, men, have selected what appears to be the less attractive standard for themselves. Second, in part because they have selected it, this standard is assumed unquestionably to be desirable; inquiry into it is generally limited only to how far it will be extended to women. Much less attention is paid to whether the separate standard sought to be applied to women might in fact make some sense for women and men alike.

Case, supra, at 349. What do you make of this analysis?

Justice Scalia strongly suggests that *VMI* puts into jeopardy private, as well as public, single-sex education, making it unconstitutional for the government to provide any support to them. Whether he is right may depend, in part, on how close the "exceedingly persuasive justification" standard applied in *VMI* approaches the strict scrutiny test applied to cases of race-based discrimination, since public support of racially discriminatory private schools has been found to be unconstitutional. See Norwood v. Harrison, 413 U.S. 455 (1973). Note that this same "exceedingly persuasive justification" standard was articulated in *Hogan*, a case generally viewed as reaffirming an intermediate standard of review in sex cases. Is Justice Scalia correct that only by the highest level of scrutiny could the Court have found the exclusion of women from *VMI* to be unconstitutional?

The number of all women's colleges have declined from 300 in 1960 to 62 in 2006, despite a small increase in female student interest in the 1990's. Only three percent of college-bound students prefer single-sex institutions, and this has forced many all-women schools to begin to admit men. See, e.g., Lisa Wogan, When Wells Run Dry: Another Women's College Opens the Door to Men, Ms. Magazine, Spring 2005, at 17.

2. The Role of History. What role should history play in the analysis of single-sex schooling? It clearly played an important in the *VMI* decision. For a full and nuanced analysis of this factor, see Jill Elaine Hasday, The Principle and Practice of Women's "Full Citizenship": A Case Study of Sex-Segregated Public Education, 101 Mich. L. Rev. 755 (2002).

History was also a factor in Mississippi University for Women v. Hogan, 458 U.S. 718 (1982), cited in *VMI*. *Hogan* held that a traditionally all-female nursing school could not exclude men, Justice O'Connor reserving for "limited circumstances" the possibility that a gender-based classification favoring one sex might be justified "if it intentionally and directly assists members of the sex that is disproportionately burdened." Id. at 728. *Hogan* rejected the compensatory purpose offered by the state based on the fact that the original mission of the school was not compensatory but rather reflected the stereotyped view of nursing as an exclusively woman's job. An emotional dissent written by Justice Powell and joined by Justice Rehnquist (Chief Justice Burger and Justice Blackmun wrote separate dissents) emphasized the strong and "honored" tradition of single-sex schools in this country, their benefits especially to women, and their contributions to educational diversity. Id. at 744. Justice Powell quoted from the Brief for the MUW Alumnae Association:

> [I]n the aspect of life known as courtship or mate-pairing, the American female remains in the role of the pursued sex, expected to adorn and groom herself to attract the male. . . .
>
> An institution of collegiate higher learning maintained exclusively for women is uniquely able to provide the education atmosphere in which some, but not all, women can best attain maximum learning potential. It can serve to overcome the historic repression of the past and can orient a woman to function and achieve in the still male-dominated economy. It can free its students of the burden of playing the mating game while attending classes, thus giving academic rather than sexual emphasis.

458 U.S. at 739 (Powell, J., dissenting).

Histories of women's education tell a story of the development of collegiate education for women because their "'gentle,' 'unaspiring,' and 'compliant' natures and heightened moral sensibilities rendered them particularly suitable for working with children." See Deborah L. Rhode, Association and Assimilation, 81 Nw. U. L. Rev. 106, 129 (1986). The expansion of educational opportunities for women raised considerable opposition based on doubts about women's physical and mental capacities.

> Critics assembled an array of "scientific" data: women's brains were too light, their foreheads too small, their powers of reasoning too inadequate for rigorous academic programs.

Id. at 130. Damage to women's reproductive capacities from rigorous study, referred to in footnote 9 of the *VMI* opinion, was also felt to be a possibility, perhaps because college-educated women were substantially less likely to marry and had lower reproductive rates than women generally. Rhode, supra, at 130. Rhode reports that even the defenders of higher education for women seemed somewhat ambivalent about its purposes.

> To some advocates of expanded female instruction, such as Catherine Beecher, the primary objective should be "the preparation of woman for her distinctive profession as housekeeper, mother, nurse, and chief educator of infancy and child-hood."...[D]efenders of academic rigor...emphasized that the point of women's instruction in traditional disciplines was both to "enlarge their spheres of thought" and to render them "more interesting companions to men...." Chemistry might be significant in its own right, but its principles were also applicable in the kitchen....[Smith's] first president and early administrators denied that the college would produce competitors with men or diminish the "innate capacities which have even been the glory and charm of true womanhood."

Id. at 131-132 [citations omitted].

To what extent should all-women's schooling be viewed negatively because of this history?

The other part of the history of all-women's schooling is the impressive evidence of the success of its graduates. Frequently cited is the fact that 59 women's colleges in the decades from 1910 to 1950 graduated twice as many women cited in Who's Who of American Women as did 289 co-educational colleges. See M. Elizabeth Tidball, Women's Colleges and Women Achievers Revisited, 5 Signs 505 (1980). Graduates of women's colleges constitute one-third of female board members of Fortune 1,000 companies, over 43 percent of female math doctorates, and over 50 percent of engineering doctorates, even though those colleges contribute less than four percent of total graduates. See Susan Estrich, For Girls' Schools and Women's Colleges: Separate Is Better, N.Y. Times, May 22, 1994, §6, p. 39. It has been noted that studies like Tidball's fail to control for various factors such as socioeconomic status. Had Ivy League Institutions been open to women during the period of the study, critics argue, the percentage of high achievers from co-ed schools would undoubtedly have been greater. See Deborah L. Rhode, Justice and Gender 297 (1989). Still, are there advantages to all-women's schools?

3. Single-Sex Schools at the Elementary and Secondary Level. Recently, interest in single-sex elementary and secondary educational opportunities has risen dramatically. In 2001, Congress passed the No Child Left Behind Act which included a clause stating that "funds made available to local educational agencies . . . shall be used for innovative assistance programs, which may include . . . programs to provide same-gender schools and classrooms (consistent with applicable law)." 20 U.S.C. §7215(a)(23) (Supp. 2002). Even before this legislation, all-female and all-male classrooms and schools had been "slowly infiltrating the country." Laura Fortney, Comment, Public Single-Sex Elementary Schools: "Separate But Equal" in Gender Fifty Years Following *Brown v. Board of Education*, 35 U. Tol. L. Rev. 857, 859 (2004) (listing examples). There were only four public schools in the United States in 1997 offering single-sex educational opportunities. By 2005, there were at least 193. National Ass'n for Single Sex Public Education, Single-Sex Schools, at www.single-sexschools.org/schools.html (last visited August 30, 2005). Most of these schools are co-ed and simply provide students with the option of single-sex classrooms. However, about one-quarter of such schools have been allowed to fully exclude boys. A number of boys' schools have also opened in the last few years. See Fortney, supra, at 859.

That trend gives rise to several concerns. One is that single-sex schooling reinforces gender stereotypes and inadequately trains students for the co-educational world that they will inhabit throughout the rest of their lives. Other concerns relate to potential funding and resource disparities, as well as to the more general notion that separate schools are inherently unequal because segregation itself stigmatizes. See generally Fortney, supra; Rosemary C. Salamone, Feminist Voices in the Debate Over Single-Sex Schooling: Finding Common Grounds, 11 Mich. J. Gender & L. 63, 70 (2004); see also Gary J. Simson, Separate but Equal and Single-Sex Schools, 90 Cornell L. Rev. 443, 455-456 (2005) (suggesting constitutional difficulties with single-sex schools, given the scarcity of evidence that single-sex schools deliver significant academic and developmental benefits that could not be achieved in co-ed schools).

Much of the impetus for the revival of girls-only educational opportunities in the 1990s came from research by the American Association of University Women identifying significant differences between boys and girls as they progress through educational institutions, with girls experiencing a much steeper decline than boys in self-image and in career aspirations, especially those related to math and science:

> Girls, aged eight and nine, are confident, assertive, and feel authoritative about themselves. They emerge from adolescence with a poor self-image, constrained views of their future and their place in society, and much less confidence about themselves and their abilities. Sixty percent of elementary school girls say they are "happy the way I am," a core measure of personal self-esteem. More boys, 67 percent of those surveyed, also strongly agreed with the statement. Over the

next eight years, girls' self-esteem falls 31 percentage points, with only 29 percent of high school girls saying they are happy with themselves. Almost half of the high school boys (46 percent) retain their high self-esteem. By high school, this gender gap increases from 7 points to 17 points.

Survey, Greenberg-Lake Analysis Group, Inc. & American Ass'n of Univ. Women, Shortchanging Girls, Shortchanging America 4 (1991). The survey found a strong relationship between math and science confidence and adolescent self-esteem: students with higher self-esteem liked math and science more. Id. at 12, 16. Most elementary school students had confidence in their ability to do math, with boys having a higher level of confidence (81 percent of girls like math, as compared to 84 percent of boys). The interest of adolescents in math dropped far more precipitously for girls (to 61 percent for girls and 74 percent for boys). Id. at 12. Interestingly, when adjusted for race, black girls and Hispanic girls had higher self-esteem measures in elementary school than white girls, and did not reach as low a level in high school (white girls moved from 55 high self-esteem to 22 percent; black girls from 65 percent to 58 percent; and Hispanic girls from 68 percent to 30 percent). Id. at 9. Peer sexual harassment of girls in schools can also contribute to an environment that is said to undermine self esteem. This issue is discussed in Chapter 3, at pp. 453-466.

Some experts dispute the research showing the relative decline of girls' performance and self-esteem in schools. Psychologist Judith Kleinfeld charges that the AAUW's conclusion that schools shortchange girls is based on "soft and slippery issues, like the 'silencing' of girls in the classroom," rather than on educational achievement tests, college entrance and graduation rates, and earning of advanced degrees. See Judith Kleinfeld, The Myth That Schools Shortchange Girls: Social Science in the Service of Deception (Women's Freedom Network 1998), reported in Kimberly M. Schuld, Rethinking Education Equity: Sometimes, Different Can Be an Acceptable Substitute for Equal, 1999 U. Chi. Legal F. 461, 472-475. See also Kingsley R. Browne, Sex and Temperament in Modern Society: A Darwinian View of the Glass Ceiling and the Gender Gap, 37 Ariz. L. Rev. 972, 1032 (1995) (with respect to the AAUW's conclusion about boys' higher self-esteem, a "plausible explanation . . . is that it was measuring self-deception and braggadocio (and perhaps immaturity) rather than self-esteem").

Kleinfeld argues that from elementary school through college, females receive higher grades, obtain higher class marks, and receive more honors in every field but science and sports. On standardized tests, while boys do better in mathematics, science, and geopolitics, the margins are small; girls do better in reading achievement, and surpass boys in writing skills by a significant amount. Gender differences are more visible in the top 10 percent of self-selected populations taking standardized tests than in the student population as a whole. Schuld, supra, at 475 (citing Kleinfeld).

These conclusions have focused more attention on the educational issues faced disproportionately by boys. Boys are more likely to be at the bottom of their class in schools or assigned to special education classes. Schuld at 475. Recent statistics show that boys are more likely to repeat a grade, have a learning disability, and have their parents called at home to report a problem. They also participate less in extracurricular activities and attend college at lower rates than their girl counterparts, suggesting a "new gender gap." See, e.g., Michelle Conlin, The New Gender Gap: From Kindergarten to Grad School, Boys are Becoming the Second Sex, Business Week Online, May 26, 2003, at http://www.businessweek.com/magazine/content/03_21/b3834001_mz001.htm. Similar conclusions were reached in a large-scale quantitative 1997 study commissioned by the Metropolitan Life Insurance Company Foundation, which measured faculty perceptions as well as students', and linked perceptions to various academic measures, classroom interactions, intentions to complete advanced studies, and interest in extracurricular activities. The study found that girls come out ahead of boys in terms of various self-esteem measures, such as being listened to in class and receiving helpful feedback from their teachers. Like Kleinfeld, the MetLife study found larger gender differences for self-selected high-stakes test-takers than for national representative samples and, like the AAUW study, found that minority girls hold the most optimistic views of the future, while minority boys are the most discouraged about the future and the least interested in getting a good education. Schuld, supra, at 476-477. Further discussion of the gender gap with respect to standardized test scores is on pp. 190-192, supra. Women now make up 56 percent of college enrollments, and as college freshmen they spend more time doing volunteer work and participating in student clubs. See Jodi Wilgoren, Girls Rule: Girls Outperform Boys in High School and in College Enrollment Rates, N.Y. Times Upfront, March 5, 2001, vol. 133, at 8. Is this a problem? Philosopher Christina Hoff Sommers thinks so. See, e.g., Sommers, The War Against Boys: How Misguided Feminism Is Harming Our Young Men (2000).

The benefits of single-sex education are also disputed. On the positive side, one recent British study reports benefits of single-sex classrooms for both boys and girls, improving girls' performance in math and science and boys' passing rates in English and foreign language. Mike Younger et al., Single-Sex Classes and Equal Opportunities for Girls and Boys: Perspectives Through Time from a Mixed Comprehensive School in England, 27 Oxford Rev. Educ. 339 (2005). Other research suggests that students in single-sex classrooms, including boys, are more likely to volunteer to take courses that are traditionally dominated by the opposite sex and such students also maintain more enthusiasm for their courses. Abigail Norfleet James & Herbert Richards, Escaping Stereotypes: Educational Attitudes of Male Alumni of Single-Sex and Coed Schools, 4 Psychol. Men & Masculinity 136, 140 (2003).

On the other hand, a study of six sets of "coordinate schools" (i.e., matched girls schools and boys schools) refuted the expectation that girls and boys face fewer distractions in single-sex schools, with evidence that both boys and girls noted an increase in fighting and disruptive behavior. Amanda Datnow et al., Is Single Gender Schooling Viable in the Public Sector? Lessons from California's Pilot Program 56 (2001). See also Nancy Levit, Separating Equals: Educational Research and the Long-Term Consequences of Sex Segregation, 67 Geo. Wash. L. Rev. 451, 485-492 (1999) (reviewing the literature, much of it conflicting, and concluding that while girls who attend all-girls schools develop, on average, higher self-esteem, they do not benefit from higher achievement levels).

Several have noted that noted gains from single-sex schooling may be due less to the single-sex quality of the school and more to other factors, such as small class size, favorable faculty-student ratio, or special mentoring programs—features that, as Gary Simson points out, could be replicated in co-ed schools. Simson, supra, at 452-453. It should also be noted that even the AAUW believes that, while single-sex education may provide some benefits, "properties of a good education—not a sex segregated environment—make the difference." Position Paper, AAUW Public Policy and Government Relations Department, Single-Sex Education (Mar. 2004), available at http://www.aauw.org/issue_advocacy/actionpages/positionpapers/singlesex. cfm. The AAUW maintains that the focus on single-sex schooling has diverted attention from problems such as lack of funding, shortage of teachers, and inadequate facilities. Id. See also Rosemary Salomone, Feminist Voices in the Debate Over Single-Sex Schooling: Finding Common Ground, 11 Mich. J. Gender & L. 63 (2004) (summarizing disagreements among feminists over single-sex education and arguing that the emphasis should be not on whether single-sex classes or schools are established, but on the quality of the programs).

In evaluating the constitutional and policy considerations entailed in single-sex education, does it matter whether the issue is single-sex schools, or only single-sex classes within co-educational schools? See Note, Single-Sex Classes in Public Secondary Schools: Maximizing the Value of a Public Education for the Nation's Students, 57 Vand. L. Rev. 629, 690 (2004) (favoring single-sex classes, but not single-sex schools, as a way of offering some of the benefits of single-sex education while minimizing constitutional worries).

4. Race and Single-Sex Schooling. Some of the single-sex schooling at issue was designed with the special problems of African-American males in mind. In the 1980s and 1990s, schools for boys in inner-city neighborhoods were established in a number of U.S. cites, including Chicago, Baltimore, Detroit, Milwaukee, Washington, D.C., New York City, and San Diego. See Pamela J. Smith, Comment, All-Male Black Schools and the Equal Protection Clause: A Step Forward Toward Education, 66 Tul. L. Rev. 2003, 2006 n.7 (1992). Between 2000 and 2003, twelve public single-sex schools opened, either as new ventures or as reconstituted formerly co-educational schools, each with student populations over 85 percent non-white; additional schools in various cities are being planned. See Ron Heflin, More States Offer Single-Sex Schools, USA Today, Aug. 24, 2004, available at http://www.usa-today.com/news/nation/2004-08-24-single-sexschools_x.htm. Opinion within the African-American community is mixed, with groups like the the NCAAP opposing segregated schools, and others welcoming the extra help they might bring to at-risk children. Salomone, supra, at 70-73. Proponents of an all-male African-American school in Detroit detail the following "host of ills plaguing Black male teenagers":

> [I]n 1989, the unemployment rate for African-American males living in Detroit was 18.3% compared with 7.1% for all males in the state of Michigan.

The homicide rate for Black males between ages fifteen and twenty-four in Wayne County, Michigan is fourteen times the national rate for all males, twice the rate for African-American males in the State of Michigan, and forty-seven times the homicide rate for white males in Michigan....

Fifty-four percent of Detroit boys eventually drop out of school and over 66% receive suspensions. Boys fall further behind the national average academically in almost every successive year of elementary and secondary school. In the first grade, boys perform at or above grade level on academic achievement tests. By the twelfth grade, boys' achievement is over two grades behind in reading and over three grades behind in mathematics. The report also shows a disparity in academic performance between girls and boys in the Detroit school system. The male dropout rate is approximately 10% higher than the female dropout rate. Boys are suspended three times as often as girls, and boys consistently score lower than girls on standardized reading and math tests....

[E]lementary and adolescent boys often need greater discipline than girls in the same age group. The high suspension rates in Detroit testify to the acute disciplinary problems of Black boys. Some educators argue that young boys misbehave in class to impress young girls and that gender separation might alleviate social pressures that distract both boys and girls from their studies.... In the end, this arrangement would provide a better education for both boys and girls. Many educators also maintain that single-sex schools should employ a high proportion of Black male teachers because Black boys—often abandoned by their fathers—need Black male role models....

[P]rograms designed specifically to address Black male violence might prove more successful in an all-male environment than in a coeducational environment. [E]ducators argue that because it is Black males that are "killing each other," schools should target violence prevention programs at them. Similarly, if disrespect for Black women leads Black men to engage in irresponsible sexual behavior or to eschew family responsibilities, then the schools should implement programs specifically designed to change male behavior.

Note, Inner-City Single-Sex Schools: Educational Reform or Invidious Discrimination? 105 Harv. L. Rev. 1741, 1743-1744 (1992).

One of the supporters of these resegregated schools, Judge Robert Carter, is a former NAACP attorney who worked on Brown v. Board of Education. Judge Carter helped to litigate the concept of equality pursued in *Brown* that depended on the presence of white children, but he has since sought to shift the focus from who attends schools with blacks to the quality of education offered in those schools. Robert Carter, A Reassessment of *Brown v. Board*, in Shades of Brown: New Perspectives on School Desegregation 21 (Derrick Bell ed., 1980). See also Derrick Bell, A Model Alternative Desegregation Plan, in Shades of Brown, supra, at 125 (goal of equal educational opportunity should not be racial balance, but empowerment of black communities that comes with strong black leadership, parental involvement, reinforcement of children's feelings of self-worth, and equal funding and educational standards for schools in black communities).

In Garrett v. Board of Education of School District of Detroit, 775 F. Supp. 1004 (E.D. Mich. 1991), plaintiffs successfully challenged the exclusion of girls from the Detroit all-male academies, which were held to violate both the federal and the state constitutions, as well as Title IX. Critics of the academies focused both on the exclusion of females and on the programmatic focus.

> Such programs are often replete with African-style, sexist "rites of passage" to manhood. By placing an emphasis on racial identity, these programs, such as the one at an all black academy in Los Angeles, encourage black boys to "think black, act black, speak black, buy black, pray black, love black and live black." Such schools are dedicated not to free inquiry and critical thought, but to indoctrination and ideological programming. Some choose to focus on the seven principles of Kwanzaa, which indoctrinate students with such ideological concepts as racial identity and "faith in our [racial and political] leaders." [Michael Meyers, All-Male, Black Schools Unequal, Oregonian, Sept. 30, 1992, at C9.] If such repeat-after-me schooling were designed for white students, one doubts whether educational authorities would tolerate such drivel, much less allow such schools to be subsidized by taxpayers. . . .
>
> The all-male black school is also paternalistic. It stigmatizes boys, ignores girls, and brazenly discounts women as capable teachers of boys. In the minds of all-male black school advocates, only males can teach boys to become men. Shockingly, advocates of this segregation blame black boys' parents, their homelives, and their loose morals for their underachievement. These separatists overgeneralize black males' social problems, using these problems as a scapegoat.

Michael Meyers, The Non-Viability of Single-Race, Single-Sex Schools, 21 N.Y.U. Rev. L. & Soc. Change 663, 665-666 (1994-1995). Is this a fair critique? From the substantive equality viewpoint, what is the response to it? How might the "Afrocentric" focus relate to the tendency for minorities to distance themselves from traditionally minority behaviors when they succeed in majority-controlled environments? How might segregating races affect possible benefits from diversity as discussed in Grutter v. Bollinger, supra, at p. 177ff.?

Some critics of male-only black schools point to the fact that the overall school drop-out rates for African-American females (12 percent) is close to the rate for males (13.5 percent). The homicide rate for young African-American females is four to five times that for young white women, although not as high as the seven to eight times rate differential between African-American and white male youths. African-American girls, in comparison with other girls and African-American boys, have a heightened sensitivity about their bodies and an awareness of their expected participation in domestic and household work. Teachers tend to underestimate their abilities, and they have lower self-esteem than African-American males, despite higher actual performance. Does this mean there should be separate schools for both African-American males, and African-American females? Consider the following:

> Arguments for single-sex education focus on the myriad issues confronting Black male students, such as high rates of incarceration and homicide. The rhetoric suggests that sex segregation addresses these problems because it compensates for the primary deficiency of many Black males: the fact that they are being raised in female-headed households. According to this argument, because Black males are surrounded by women, they lack appropriate role models who "exemplify[] the value of education," or who simply can teach them how to be

men—that is, providers and husbands. Providing these role models thus becomes an imperative, a way to "save families" and communities, which places Black males at the center of the struggle for equal rights in education, and makes Black mothers the locus of the many problems afflicting urban African American communities. . . . [as such] the overarching theme of today's discourse is that single-sex education is necessary to build Black men.With respect to African American girls, the rhetoric focuses on preventing pregnancy. Specifically, advocates have argued that girls in a sex-segregated environment will be less distracted by boys and feel less pressure to become sexually active. . . . [On the other hand] the benefit of a private, predominately white girls' school was that the girls "perceive themselves as more competent, more willing to pursue advanced work in fields such as math and science." So much of the rhetoric regarding Black girls in education is about their sexuality, suggesting that by just sitting in the same classroom with male students, there is a risk of pregnancy. . . . [T]his rhetoric reflects what some have identified as the devaluation of Black motherhood, a related "deep suspicion of black women's sexuality and an intense desire to control their 'excessive' promiscuity and fecundity." While it is certainly true that premature motherhood has serious implications for an uneducated teenager and her child, it is true for white teenagers as well as Black. Yet such concerns typically have not arisen as justifications for all-female schools for white girls. The disparity suggests that underlying this concern is the desire to control Black female reproduction, which Dorothy Roberts has described as "a means of subordinating the entire race." Finally, the rhetoric regarding single-sex education for Black girls is unique in its emphasis on providing safety. For example, the principal of Philadelphia High School for Girls, which is almost eighty percent students of color, has praised the school because there is "'less sexual harassment'" and more "'safety in an urban environment.'" . . . This rhetoric suggests that merely by removing Black males from the environment, these schools become safer even though they remain in urban settings where security is an issue for students and nonstudents alike.

The foregoing suggests that this effort is very much about race. But race is invisible when the players — students, parents, and educators — are people of color, which is the case here. Instead, the discourse centers on sex and the presumably benign nature of separating boys and girls in education, which is not surprising since uttering race and segregation in the same breath is a combustible mix that evokes much higher scrutiny and greater skepticism. However, this single-axis analysis focusing on sex alone is incomplete.

Verna L. Williams, Reform or Retrenchment? Single-Sex Education and the Construction of Race and Gender, 2004 Wis. L. Rev. 15, 21-26 (2004).

All-black academies would be difficult to sustain under existing race discrimination law, which requires the almost impossible task of showing that these schools are a narrowly tailored means to address specific prior intentional discrimination against the group receiving the preference or to achieve a compelling state purpose. City of Richmond v. J.S. Croson Co., 488 U.S. 469 (1989). General societal discrimination will not do. As a practical matter, however, given the absence of white residents in most inner-city schools, it has not been necessary to officially exclude whites in order to achieve the same ends. Those programs that have proceeded, as did the program in Detroit, have had to accept girls. See Daniel Gardenswartz, Public Education: An Inner-City Crisis? 42 Emory L.J. 591, 644 (1993). On balance, are these all-male schools a good idea?

Putting Theory into Practice

2-8. A female Women's Studies professor at a co-educational college does not let men enroll in her feminist ethics course, arguing that, in her experience, male students inhibit the participation of women. As an alternative for male students, she offers one-on-one tutorials, which about two dozen men have taken since she began teaching in 1966. She is sued by a male student under Title IX, and under the Fourteenth Amendment's Equal Protection Clause. Who should win? See Maryam Ahranjani, *Mary Daly v. Boston College*: The Impermissibility of Single-Sex Classrooms Within a Private University, 9 J. Gender, Soc. Pol'y & L. 179 (2001).

2-9. A group of law faculty is considering the formation of a new, all-women's law school based on data about women's comparative performance disadvantage collected at the University of California at Berkeley School of Law (Boalt Hall), Stanford Law School, Yale Law School, and the University of Pennsylvania Law School, described in Chapter 5, pp. 685-690. They seek your advice on whether such an institution would be legal. What do you tell them? Compare Jennifer Gerarda Brown, "To Give Them Countenance": The Case for a Women's Law School, 22 Harv. Women's L.J. 1 (1999) (favoring an all-women's law school), with Jennifer Gerarda Brown, Apostasy?, 75 Chi.-Kent L. Rev. 837 (2000) (citing growing empirical evidence leading her to question her early proposal for a woman's law school and exploring costs to men excluded from all-female schools); Shannan N. Ball, Note, Separate But Equal Is Unequal: The Argument Against an All-Women's Law School, 15 Notre Dame J.L. Ethics & Pub. Pol'y 171 (2001).

2-10. In 1983 the first public school in the United States was established geared specifically to gay and lesbian adolescents and their problems. The New York City Board of Education is operating the school in conjunction with the Institute for the Protection for Lesbian and Gay Youth (since renamed the Hetrick-Martin Institute) — an advocacy and counseling group for gays and lesbians, financed in part by the city and the state of New York. The Harvey Milk School (named after a gay member of the San Francisco board of supervisors who was shot and killed by a political rival) started with 20 students — 14 boys and 6 girls — ranging in age from 14 to 19. All of them are school drop-outs who had difficulty "fitting in at conventional high schools" because of their sexual identity, says the director of clinical programs for the institute. "For the most part, the males are overtly effeminate, some are transvestites, and the girls are all tough," said one teacher. "All of them would be targets for abuse in regular schools." Larry Rohter, New York Offering Public School Geared to Homosexual Students, N.Y. Times, June 6, 1985, at A1. A 2003 report stated that Harvey

Milk was looking to expand to 170 students by September 2004. Michael Bronski, Rethinking the Harvey Milk School: Not-So-Fast Times at Queermont High, The Boston Phoenix, News & Features, Aug. 8-14, 2003, found at http://www.bostonphoenix.com/boston/news_features/other_stories/documents/03073221.asp. For further information about the school, see www.hmi.org.

You have been asked to advise community leaders of another major city whether it should open a school on the Harvey Milk model. Is it legal? Is it a good idea? See Chapter 3, Section E, starting at p. 572, for further discussion of discrimination based on sexual orientation.

2-11. King Abdalaziz University paid Virginia Tech $246,000 to design and operate a faculty development program for teachers from Saudi Arabia. In keeping with the preferences of the University, Virginia Tech created one class for about 30 male faculty members and a separate class for the 30 female faculty members. Eloise Coupey, an associate professor of marketing, filed a sex discrimination complaint. See Virginia: Separate-Sex Classes, N.Y. Times, Aug. 11, 2005, at A19. Should she win?

b. School Athletics

Petrie v. Illinois High School Association
394 N.E.2d 855 (Ill. Ct. App. 1979)

GREEN, Justice.

Plaintiff Trent Petrie by his mother and next friend, Pattsi Petrie challenges (1) a rule of Champaign Central High School (Central) . . . which restricts membership on the sole volleyball team sponsored by the school to girls, and (2) rules of defendant Illinois High School Association (IHSA), a voluntary association of public and private high schools of the state, which restrict membership on the teams participating in the only volleyball tournament sponsored by it to girls. . . .

[Plaintiff is] a 16-year-old junior, 5'11" in height and 170 lbs. in weight, who had reported for the team and had been practicing with it when informed by school officials that he could not play in games with other schools because of defendants' rules. . . .

[In other cases in which rules prohibiting capable girls from playing on boys' teams were struck down on state or federal equal protection grounds, the] exclusion of girls from boys' teams was generally sought on grounds that girls, as a group, were less capable than boys at the sports involved and, in the contact sports, that they were more prone to injury. The courts rejected these arguments reasoning that the blanket prohibition placed a stigma of inferiority on girls as an excluded class and that the obviously better way to determine whether they were capable of playing was to give them a try out and then let the coach make a subjective determination as to whether they were capable of playing. The argument as to the danger of injury was answered by noting that not all girls were of a physique making them excessively injury prone and that, in any event, no objective standards had been set forth to eliminate the more frail boys.

Here, boys were the excluded class and their exclusion was made not because they were not likely to be good enough but because they were likely to be too good to permit adequate opportunities for girls....

The evidence in this case...showed that, in general, high school boys are substantially taller, heavier and stronger than their girl counterparts and have longer extremities. Although we recognize that high school girls have no general disadvantage as to balance, coordination, strategic acumen, or quickness (as distinguished from running speed), we agree that they are generally at a substantial physical disadvantage in playing volleyball. Illustrative of the consequences of such disadvantage as applied to other sports were (1) the indication in [Gomes v. R.I. Interscholastic League, 469 F. Supp. 659 (D.R.I. 1979)] that at the plaintiff's high school the "overwhelming majority" of the positions on teams open to both sexes were held by boys, and (2) testimony in the instant case that in the high school track season previous to the trial, none of the girls' state record holders in track and field "would have qualified in any event for the boys' state track and field meet." Evidence in the instant case of isolated instances of male participation upon girls' teams creating an advantage for those teams indicated the likelihood of similar results if any substantial number of males chose to participate in volleyball.

Classification of a high school volleyball team to limit its membership to girls is consistent with a long-standing tradition in sports of setting up classifications whereby persons having objectively measured characteristics likely to make them more proficient are eliminated from certain classes of competition. Heavier persons are prohibited from competing in lighter weight classes in wrestling and boxing. Persons over a certain age are often prohibited from participating in interscholastic athletics and those under a certain age from competing in events sponsored for senior citizens. Membership in certain interscholastic teams has been limited to those who have not completed their sophomore year. At one time, intercollegiate football between teams whose members weighed no more than 150 lbs. was popular and many high schools and elementary schools have had heavyweight and lightweight football teams. There is no stigma attached to a person eliminated by this system from competing in a class in which that person might have undue advantage.

Suggestion is made that rather than using sex as a classifying factor, teams should be classified on the basis of characteristics mentioned in the last paragraph and done in such a way that in sports where females had a physical disadvantage, they would compete in a class, where the disadvantage would be eliminated. Of course, height might be such a measure for volleyball and a school could have a team whereby most girls would be with boys more nearly their size. However, this would not compensate for the strength differential and would cause great hardship to the taller girls, most of whom would not have the musculature to compete with taller boys. We conclude that a system of measurement to put girls into classes whereby they would be on a physical par with males who would compete in that class would be too difficult to devise. Although systems of handicapping based on measurable prior performance such as golf or bowling scores are used, in those sports and in other individual sports, ratings can be obtained on the basis of prior performance. In team sports, however, any rating of players could only be done on a very subjective basis and would not be practical. Furthermore, even in the individual sports, a system of rating and handicapping places a premium on poor prior performance and is inconsistent with a system of full competition which boys have had for years and which girls are seeking to achieve.

[The court also rejected a quota system for boys, because it would lead to such accommodations as changes in the height of the net, no-spiking rules for boys, or relegating girls to the back court, all changes that work to the detriment of girls.]

The classification of public high school athletic teams upon the basis of gender in sports such as volleyball is itself based on the innate physical differences between the sexes. It is not based on generalizations that are "archaic" (Schlesinger v. Ballard, [419 U.S. 498, 508 (1975)]), nor does it represent an attitude of "romantic paternalism" (Frontiero v. Richardson, [411 U.S. 677, 684 (1973)]. Like all systems of classifications for competition, it is overbroad and underbroad in that it includes females who are athletically superior to many males and excludes males who are less well-endowed athletically than most females. However, we are convinced that it is the only feasible classification to promote the legitimate and substantial state interest of providing for interscholastic athletic opportunity for girls.

Schools could have varsity, subvarsity and lesser levels of varsity squads and no doubt eventually provide the opportunity for a very substantial number of girls to compete in each sport. We must recognize, however, that public institutions have a limited amount of funds and it is common knowledge that many school districts are extremely pressed to maintain their present programs. The extra expense of having this number of squads is obvious. Moreover, to arrange the program in such a way that many girls are denied the chance to be on a team that is described as the school team although with a gender designation, would seem to be a very high price to pay for a complete equality of sexes.

We have no trouble in concluding that having a separate volleyball team and separate tournaments in that sport for girls is substantially related to and serves the achievement of the important governmental objective of maintaining, fostering and promoting athletic opportunities for girls. It, therefore, satisfies the due process requirements of the fourteenth amendment.

[The court also concludes that having separate teams for girls is justified under the "strict scrutiny" standard of the state constitution.]

When a governmental goal is to preserve, foster and promote the opportunities of those of a gender, an element of affirmative action is necessarily involved. . . .

The girls' volleyball season overlaps that of football. In Schlesinger v. Ballard, [419 U.S. 498 (1975)], a statutory provision permitting female naval officers to remain longer in grade than certain male officers was upheld as meeting Federal due process requirements because the female officers had no opportunity to go into combat and thus could not get the promotion enhancements available to males who did so. As the female officers in Ballard were given longer in grade because they could not go into combat, girls here are given volleyball playing opportunities because they have little if any in football....

We conclude that to furnish exactly the same athletic opportunities to boys as to girls would be most difficult and would be detrimental to the compelling governmental interest of equalizing general athletic opportunities between the sexes....

We affirm.

CRAVEN, Justice, dissenting:...

The difficulty with the defendants' position is that they are attempting to achieve a laudable goal ensuring a chance for athletic competition to both large and small, strong and weak students by an impermissible means. While it may in fact be true that most boys are generally larger and stronger than most girls, due process bars classifications based upon such permanent presumptions where individual determinations may, and in fact do, rebut them.... Sex-based generalizations have been discarded in many cases where there was statistical support for the presumption upon which the classifications were based. In [Reed v. Reed, 404 U.S. 71 (1971)], for instance, the court was unwilling to tolerate a mandatory preference for males over females as estate administrators, even while acknowledging that men, as a class, may indeed be more conversant with business....

Defendants here argue that boys must be excluded from the all-girl volleyball team in order to allow the girls a fair chance to compete. In support of their position, they cite statistics on the relative height, strength, and physical development of the average male and the average female of high school age. In short, their position is actually not that they are protecting girls from boys or vice versa, but rather that they are protecting weaker from stronger athletes. The fallacy in their position is revealed by the fact that, although the differences in size and strength within each sex are shown by the evidence to be greater than the differences between the averages for the two sexes, no provision has been made to protect smaller, weaker females from competition with larger, stronger females, or smaller, weaker males from competition with larger, stronger males....

Surely, not even the majority here, nor society generally, would condone the exclusion of blacks from an all-white basketball team on the grounds that blacks generally are more skilled at the game than whites and might tend to dominate it. Nor would we tolerate an exclusion of Catholics from an all-Protestant high school soccer team on the grounds that Catholic elementary schools have traditionally emphasized that sport so as to give their graduates an unfair advantage. Yet the constitutional prohibition against sex discrimination in Illinois is more specific than that against either racial or religious discrimination. There are legally tolerable means of categorizing athletes by size, strength, and ability. To adopt sex as a proxy for more precisely defined means of leveling off competition is both illegal and irrational. It is simply foolish to perpetuate the fear of equality between sexes. It is more than foolish to justify discrimination upon the asserted basis of protection and allowing "catch up" time....

≡ ### O'Connor v. Board of Education of School
≡ ### District 23

645 F.2d 578 (7th Cir. 1981), cert. denied, 454 U.S. 1084 (1981)

BAUER, Circuit Judge.

In this equal protection case, the district court granted a preliminary injunction restraining the Board of Education of Prospect Heights School District No. 23, and other defendants, from refusing to permit plaintiff-appellee Karen O'Connor to try out for the boys' sixth grade basketball team. We stayed enforcement of the preliminary injunction pending appeal and now reverse.

I

Karen O'Connor is an 11-year-old sixth grade student at MacArthur Junior High School in suburban Cook County, Illinois. The school is a member of the Mid-Suburban Junior High School Conference, an association of six junior high schools engaged in interscholastic athletics. Conference rules require separate teams for boys and girls in contact sports, including basketball.

On August 27, 1980, Karen's father asked that she be permitted to try out for the boys' interscholastic basketball team. Karen is a good athlete; a professional basketball coach who observed her play rated her ability as equal to or better than a female high school sophomore and equal to that of a male eighth-grade player. Nonetheless, on October 10, 1980, the Board of Education denied the request, but invited Karen to try out for the girls' interscholastic team. . . .

The district court . . . found that the school's classification violated her fundamental "right to develop" and that "the right to education is a fundamental right and the rights to the constituent elements of an education is a fundamental right (sic)." The court further held that the MacArthur programs for boys' and girls' basketball were unequal because Karen's competition with girls of substantially lesser skill was not as valuable as competition with persons of equal or better skills in the boys' program. The district court also rejected defendants' argument that they would have to open both teams to both sexes and that the boys would dominate. Applying a strict scrutiny analysis, the court held simply that the Board had failed to show that the MacArthur program was the least restrictive alternative. . . .

II

We conclude that the district court abused its discretion in issuing this preliminary injunction. . . .

Neither Judge Marshall nor plaintiff cite any authority to support the proposition that either education or the "right to develop" is a fundamental right. The Supreme Court has expressly rejected the notion that education is a fundamental right. San Antonio Independent School District v. Rodriguez, [411 U.S. 1, 29-39 (1972)].

Viewed under the correct standard, the main issue here is whether Karen O'Connor has demonstrated a reasonable likelihood that the two team approach is not substantially related to the objective of maximizing participation in sports, the avowed objective of the school board. We think she has failed. Unlike some interscholastic athletic programs, the MacArthur program treats the two sexes identically — plaintiff concedes that the teams are equal in terms of funding, facilities, and other "objective" criteria. Both teams are interscholastic. "Separate but equal" teams have received endorsement in many circuits, including this one....

[D]efendants have demonstrated that their program substantially serves the objective of increasing girls' participation in sports.

As Justice Stevens held, in denying the application for a stay,

> In my opinion, the question whether the discrimination is justified cannot depend entirely on whether the girls' program will offer Karen opportunities that are equal in all respects to the advantages she would gain from the higher level of competition in the boys' program. The answer must depend on whether it is permissible for the defendants to structure their athletic programs by using sex as one criterion for eligibility. If the classification is reasonable in substantially all of its applications, I do not believe that the general rule can be said to be unconstitutional simply because it appears arbitrary in an individual case.

O'Connor v. Board of Education, [499 U.S. 1301, 1306 (1980) (denying petition to vacate stay)]....

Reversed and remanded.

Cohen v. Brown University

101 F.3d 155 (1st Cir. 1996), cert. denied, 520 U.S. 1186 (1997)

BOWNES, Senior Circuit Judge.

This is a class action lawsuit charging Brown University, its president, and its athletics director (collectively "Brown") with discrimination against women in the operation of its intercollegiate athletics program, in violation of Title IX of the Education Amendments of 1972, 20 U.S.C. §§ 1681-1688 ("Title IX"), and its implementing regulations, 34 C.F.R. §§ 106.1-106.71. The plaintiff class comprises all present, future, and potential Brown University women students who participate, seek to participate, and/or are deterred from participating in intercollegiate athletics funded by Brown.

This suit was initiated in response to the demotion in May 1991 of Brown's women's gymnastics and volleyball teams from university-funded varsity status to donor-funded varsity status. Contemporaneously, Brown demoted two men's teams, water polo and golf, from university-funded to donor-funded varsity status. As a consequence of these demotions, all four teams lost, not only their university funding, but most of the support and privileges that accompany university-funded varsity status at Brown.

[The District Court granted plaintiffs' request for a preliminary injunction, reinstating the women's gymnastics and volleyball teams to university-funded varsity status and prohibiting Brown from eliminating or reducing the status of any women's varsity team pending the outcome of a trial on the merits. On appeal, a panel of the 1st Circuit affirmed, and remanded for a trial on the merits. Following a bench trial, the District Court found Brown to be in violation of Title IX, and ordered a comprehensive plan for compliance be submitted. The Court found the plan submitted was not comprehensive and did not comply with the opinion. The Court rejected the plan and ordered Brown to elevate and maintain at university-funded varsity status the women's teams.]

...Brown challenges on constitutional and statutory grounds the test employed by the district court in determining whether Brown's intercollegiate athletics program complies with Title IX....

I...

As a Division I institution within the National Collegiate Athletic Association ("NCAA") with respect to all sports but football, Brown participates at the highest level of NCAA competition. Brown operates a two-tiered intercollegiate athletics program with respect to funding: although Brown provides the financial resources required to maintain its university-funded varsity teams, donor-funded varsity athletes must themselves raise the funds necessary to support their teams through private donations. The district court found...that it is difficult for donor-funded varsity athletes to maintain a level of competitiveness commensurate with their abilities and that these athletes operate at a competitive disadvantage in comparison to university-funded varsity athletes....

Brown's decision to demote the women's volleyball and gymnastics teams and the men's water polo and golf teams from university-funded varsity status was apparently made in response to a university-wide cost-cutting directive. The district court found that Brown saved $62,028 by demoting the women's teams and $15,795 by demoting the men's teams, but that the demotions "did not appreciably affect the athletic participation gender ratio."...

Plaintiffs alleged that, at the time of the demotions, the men students at Brown already enjoyed the benefits of a disproportionately large share of both the university resources allocated to athletics and the intercollegiate participation opportunities afforded to student athletes. Thus, plaintiffs contended, what appeared to be the even-handed demotions of two men's and two women's teams, in fact, perpetuated Brown's discriminatory treatment of women in the administration of its intercollegiate athletics program.

The district court...summarized the history of athletics at Brown, finding, *inter alia*, that, while nearly all of the men's varsity teams were established before 1927, virtually all of the women's varsity teams were created between 1971 and 1977, after Brown's merger with Pembroke College. The only women's varsity team created after this period was winter track, in 1982....

[T]he district court found that, in 1993-94, there were 897 students participating in intercollegiate varsity athletics, of which 61.87% (555) were men and 38.13% (342) were women. During the same period, Brown's undergraduate enrollment comprised 5,722 students, of which 48.86% (2,796) were men and 51.14% (2,926) were women....[I]n 1993-94, Brown's intercollegiate athletics program consisted of 32 teams, 16 men's teams and 16 women's teams. Of the university-funded teams, 12 were men's teams and 13 were women's teams; of the donor-funded teams, three were women's teams and four were men's teams. At the time of trial, Brown offered 479 university-funded varsity positions for men, as compared to 312 for women; and 76 donor-funded varsity positions for men, as compared to 30 for women. In 1993-94, then, Brown's varsity program — including both university- and donor-funded sports — afforded over 200 more positions for men than for women. Accordingly, the district court found that Brown maintained a 13.01% disparity between female participation in intercollegiate athletics and female student enrollment, and that "[a]lthough the number of varsity sports offered to men and women are equal, the selection of sports offered to each gender generates far more individual positions for male athletes than for female athletes." . . .

The district court found from extensive testimony that the donor-funded women's gymnastics, women's fencing and women's ski teams, as well as at least one women's club team, the water polo team, had demonstrated the interest and ability to compete at the top varsity level and would benefit from university funding. . . .

The district court did not find that full and effective accommodation of the athletics interests and abilities of Brown's female students would disadvantage Brown's male students.

II

Title IX provides that "[n]o person in the United States shall, on the basis of sex, be excluded from participation in, be denied the benefits of, or be subjected to discrimination under any education program or activity receiving Federal financial assistance." . . . As a private institution that receives federal financial assistance, Brown is required to comply with Title IX.

Title IX also specifies that its prohibition against gender discrimination shall not "be interpreted to require any educational institution to grant preferential or disparate treatment to the members of one sex on account of an imbalance which may exist" between the total number or percentage of persons of that sex participating in any federally supported program or activity, and "the total number or percentage of persons of that sex in any community, State, section, or other area." 20 U.S.C.A. § 1681(b) (West 1990). Subsection (b) also provides, however, that it "shall not be construed to prevent the consideration in any . . . proceeding under this chapter of statistical evidence tending to show that such an imbalance exists with respect to the participation in, or receipt of the benefits of, any such program or activity by the members of one sex." Id.

Applying § 1681(b), the prior panel held that Title IX "does not mandate strict numerical equality between the gender balance of a college's athletic program and the gender balance of its student body." The panel explained that, while evidence of a gender-based disparity in an institution's athletics program is relevant to a determination of noncompliance, "a court assessing Title IX compliance may not find a violation solely because there is a disparity between the gender composition of an educational institution's student constituency, on the one hand, and its athletic programs, on the other hand." . . .

Congress enacted Title IX in response to its finding — after extensive hearings held in 1970 by the House Special Subcommittee on Education — of pervasive discrimination against women with respect to educational opportunities. 118 Cong. Rec. 5804 (1972) (remarks of Sen. Bayh). . . .

The agency responsible for administering Title IX is the United States Department of Education ("DED"), through its Office for Civil Rights ("OCR"). Congress expressly delegated to DED the authority to promulgate regulations for determining whether an athletics program complies with Title IX. Pub. L. No. 93-380, 88 Stat. 612 (1974). The regulations specifically address athletics at 34 C.F.R. §§ 106.37(c) and 106.41. The regulation at issue in this case, 34 C.F.R. § 106.41 (1995), provides:

> (a) *General.* No person shall, on the basis of sex, be excluded from participation in, be denied the benefits of, be treated differently from another person or otherwise be discriminated against in any interscholastic, intercollegiate, club or intramural athletics offered by a recipient, and no recipient shall provide any such athletics separately on such basis.
>
> (b) *Separate teams.* Notwithstanding the requirements of paragraph (a) of this section, a recipient may operate or sponsor separate teams for members of each sex where selection of such teams is based upon competitive skill or the activity involved is a contact sport. However, where a recipient operates or sponsors a team in a particular sport for members of one sex but operates or sponsors no such team for members of the other sex, and athletic opportunities for members of that sex have previously been limited, members of the excluded sex must be allowed to try-out for the team offered unless the sport involved is a contact sport. For the purposes of this part, contact sports include boxing, wrestling, rugby, ice hockey, football, basketball and other sports the purpose or major activity of which involves bodily contact.
>
> (c) *Equal Opportunity.* A recipient which operates or sponsors interscholastic, intercollegiate, club or intramural athletics shall provide equal athletic opportunity for members of both sexes. In determining whether equal opportunities are available the Director will consider, among other factors:
>> (1) Whether the selection of sports and levels of competition effectively accommodate the interests and abilities of members of both sexes;
>> (2) The provision of equipment and supplies;
>> (3) Scheduling of games and practice time;
>> (4) Travel and per diem allowance;
>> (5) Opportunity to receive coaching and academic tutoring;
>> (6) Assignment and compensation for coaches and tutors;
>> (7) Provision of locker rooms, practice and competitive facilities;
>> (8) Provision of medical and training facilities and services;
>> (9) Provision of housing and dining facilities and services;
>> (10) Publicity. . . .

In 1978, several years after the promulgation of the regulations, OCR published a proposed "Policy Interpretation," the purpose of which was to clarify the obligations of federal aid recipients under Title IX to provide equal opportunities in athletics programs.... At issue in this appeal is the proper interpretation of the ... so-called three-part test,[7] which inquires as follows:

> (1) Whether intercollegiate level participation opportunities for male and female students are provided in numbers substantially proportionate to their respective enrollments; or
>
> (2) Where the members of one sex have been and are underrepresented among intercollegiate athletes, whether the institution can show a history and continuing practice of program expansion which is demonstrably responsive to the developing interest and abilities of the members of that sex; or
>
> (3) Where the members of one sex are underrepresented among intercollegiate athletes, and the institution cannot show a continuing practice of program expansion such as that cited above, whether it can be demonstrated that the interests and abilities of the members of that sex have been fully and effectively accommodated by the present program.

44 Fed. Reg. at 71,418.

The district court held that, "because Brown maintains a 13.01% disparity between female participation in intercollegiate athletics and female student enrollment, it cannot gain the protection of prong one." Nor did Brown satisfy prong two. While acknowledging that Brown "has an impressive history of program expansion," the district court found that Brown failed to demonstrate that it has "maintained a *continuing practice* of intercollegiate program expansion for women, the underrepresented sex." The court noted further that, because merely reducing program offerings to the overrepresented gender does not constitute program expansion for the underrepresented gender, the fact that Brown has eliminated or demoted several men's teams does not amount to a continuing practice of program expansion for women. As to prong three, the district court found that Brown had not "fully and effectively accommodated the interest and ability of the underrepresented sex 'to the extent necessary to provide equal opportunity in the selection of sports and levels of competition available to members of both sexes.'" ...

The district court found that Brown predetermines the approximate number of varsity positions available to men and women, and, thus, that "the concept of any measure of unfilled but available athletic slots does not comport with reality." The district court concluded that intercollegiate athletics opportunities "means real opportunities, not illusory ones, and therefore should be measured by counting *actual participants.*" ...

7. For clarification, we note that the cases refer to each part of this three-part test as a "prong" or a "benchmark." Prong one is also called the "substantial proportionality test."

IV

Brown contends that . . . the district court's interpretation and application of the test is irreconcilable with the statute, the regulation, and the agency's interpretation of the law, and effectively renders Title IX an "affirmative action statute" that mandates preferential treatment for women by imposing quotas in excess of women's relative interests and abilities in athletics. Brown asserts, in the alternative, that if the district court properly construed the test, then the test itself violates Title IX and the United States Constitution. . . .

Brown's talismanic incantation of "affirmative action" has no legal application to this case and is not helpful to Brown's cause. While "affirmative action" may have different connotations as a matter of politics, as a matter of law, its meaning is more circumscribed. True affirmative action cases have historically involved a voluntary undertaking to remedy discrimination (as in a program implemented by a governmental body, or by a private employer or institution), by means of specific group-based preferences or numerical goals, and a specific timetable for achieving those goals. See Adarand [Const., Inc. v. Pena], [115 S. Ct. 2097] (1995) (remanding for review under strict scrutiny a challenge to a federal statute establishing a government-wide goal for awarding to minority businesses not less than 5% of the total value of all prime contracts and subcontracts for each fiscal year); . . . Johnson v. Transportation Agency, [480 U.S. 616] (1986) (upholding a temporary program authorizing a county agency to consider sex and race as factors in making promotions in order to achieve a statistically measurable improvement in the representation of women and minorities in major job classifications in which they had been historically underrepresented). . . .

Title IX is not an affirmative action statute; it is an anti-discrimination statute, modeled explicitly after another anti-discrimination statute, Title VI [42 U.S.C. §2000d et seq.]. No aspect of the Title IX regime at issue in this case—inclusive of the statute, the relevant regulation, and the pertinent agency documents—mandates gender-based preferences or quotas, or specific timetables for implementing numerical goals.

Like other anti-discrimination statutory schemes, the Title IX regime *permits* affirmative action. In addition, Title IX, like other anti-discrimination schemes, permits an inference that a significant gender-based statistical disparity may indicate the existence of discrimination. Consistent with the school desegregation cases, the question of substantial proportionality under the Policy Interpretation's three-part test is merely the starting point for analysis, rather than the conclusion; a rebuttable presumption, rather than an inflexible requirement. . . . In short, the substantial proportionality test is but one aspect of the inquiry into whether an institution's athletics program complies with Title IX. . . .

Another important distinction between this case and affirmative action cases is that the district court's remedy requiring Brown to accommodate fully and effectively the athletics interests and abilities of its women students does not raise the concerns underlying the Supreme Court's requirement of a particularized factual predicate to justify voluntary affirmative action plans. In reviewing equal protection challenges to such plans, the Court is concerned that government bodies are reaching out to implement race- or gender-conscious remedial measures that are "ageless in their reach into the past, and timeless in their ability to affect the future,"... on the basis of facts insufficient to support a prima facie case of a constitutional or statutory violation,... to the benefit of unidentified victims of past discrimination....

From a constitutional standpoint, the case before us is altogether different. Here, gender-conscious relief was ordered by an Article III court, constitutionally compelled to have before it litigants with standing to raise the cause of action alleged; for the purpose of providing relief upon a duly adjudicated determination that specific defendants had discriminated against a certified class of women in violation of a federal anti-discrimination statute; based upon findings of fact that were subject to the Federal Rules of Evidence....

From the mere fact that a remedy flowing from a judicial determination of discrimination is gender-conscious, it does not follow that the remedy constitutes "affirmative action." Nor does a "reverse discrimination" claim arise every time an anti-discrimination statute is enforced. While some gender-conscious relief may adversely impact one gender—a fact that has not been demonstrated in this case—that alone would not make the relief "affirmative action" or the consequence of that relief "reverse discrimination."...

Brown maintains that the district court's decision imposes upon universities the obligation to engage in preferential treatment for women by requiring quotas in excess of women's relative interests and abilities. With respect to prong three, Brown asserts that the district court's interpretation of the word "fully" "requires universities to favor women's teams and treat them better than men's [teams]....forces them to eliminate or cap men's teams....[and] forces universities to impose athletic quotas in excess of relative interests and abilities."...

Brown simply ignores the fact that it is required to accommodate fully the interests and abilities of the underrepresented gender, not because the three-part test mandates preferential treatment for women *ab initio*, but because Brown has been found (under prong one) to have allocated its athletics participation opportunities so as to create a significant gender-based disparity with respect to these opportunities, and has failed (under prong two) to show a history and continuing practice of expansion of opportunities for the underrepresented gender....

To adopt [Brown's] relative interests approach would be ...to ...entrench and fix by law the significant gender-based disparity in athletics opportunities found by the district court to exist at Brown.... According to Brown's relative interests interpretation of the equal accommodation principle, the gender-based disparity in athletics participation opportunities at Brown is due to a lack of interest on the part of its female students, rather than to discrimination, and any attempt to remedy the disparity is, by definition, an unlawful quota. This approach is entirely contrary to "Congress's unmistakably clear mandate that educational institutions not use federal monies to perpetuate gender-based discrimination"... and makes it virtually impossible to effectuate Congress's intent to eliminate sex discrimination in intercollegiate athletics.

Brown also claims error in the district court's failure to apply Title VII standards to its analysis of whether Brown's intercollegiate athletics program complies with Title IX. The district court rejected the analogy to Title VII, noting that, while Title VII "seeks to determine whether gender-neutral job openings have been filled without regard to gender[,] Title IX . . . was designed to address the reality that sports teams, unlike the vast majority of jobs, *do* have official gender requirements, and this statute accordingly approaches the concept of discrimination differently from Title VII." . . .

It is imperative to recognize that athletics presents a distinctly different situation from admissions and employment and requires a different analysis in order to determine the existence *vel non* of discrimination. . . . To the extent that Title IX allows institutions to maintain single-sex teams and gender-segregated athletics programs, men and women do not compete against each other for places on team rosters. Accordingly, and notwithstanding Brown's protestations to the contrary, the Title VII concept of the "qualified pool" has no place in a Title IX analysis of equal athletics opportunities for male and female athletes because women are not "qualified" to compete for positions on men's teams, and vice-versa. In addition, the concept of "preference" does not have the same meaning, or raise the same equality concerns, as it does in the employment and admissions contexts. . . .

Interest and ability rarely develop in a vacuum; they evolve as a function of opportunity and experience. The Policy Interpretation recognizes that women's lower rate of participation in athletics reflects women's historical lack of opportunities to participate in sports. . . .

[T]here exists the danger that, rather than providing a true measure of women's interest in sports, statistical evidence purporting to reflect women's interest instead provides only a measure of the very discrimination that is and has been the basis for women's lack of opportunity to participate in sports. Prong three requires some kind of evidence of interest in athletics, and the Title IX framework permits the use of statistical evidence in assessing the level of interest in sports.[15] Nevertheless, to allow a numbers-based lack-of-interest defense to become the instrument of further discrimination against the underrepresented gender would pervert the remedial purpose of Title IX. We conclude that, even if it can be empirically demonstrated that, at a particular time, women have less interest in sports than do men, such evidence, standing alone, cannot justify providing fewer athletics opportunities for women than for men. Furthermore, such evidence is completely irrelevant where, as here, viable and successful women's varsity teams have been demoted or eliminated. . . .

Finally, the tremendous growth in women's participation in sports since Title IX was enacted disproves Brown's argument that women are less interested in sports for reasons unrelated to lack of opportunity. . . .

Had Congress intended to entrench, rather than change, the status quo — with its historical emphasis on men's participation opportunities to the detriment of women's opportunities — it need not have gone to all the trouble of enacting Title IX.

---

15. Under the Policy Interpretation, Institutions may determine the athletic interests and abilities of students by nondiscriminatory methods of their choosing provided:

    a.   The processes take into account the nationally increasing levels of women's interests and abilities;

    b.   The methods of determining interest and ability do not disadvantage the members of an underrepresented sex;

    c.   The methods of determining ability take into account team performance records; and

    d.   The methods are responsive to the expressed interests of students capable of intercollegiate competition who are members of an underrepresented sex.

44 Fed. Reg. at 71,417. . . .

V...

To the extent that Brown challenges the constitutionality of the statutory scheme itself, the challenge rests upon [the assumption that]...*Adarand* ...compels us...to apply strict scrutiny to the analysis....

First,...*Adarand* [applies] to review of legislative affirmative action schemes. This case presents the issue of the legality of a federal district court's determination, based upon adjudicated findings of fact, that a federal anti-discrimination statute has been violated, and of the statutory and constitutional propriety of the judicial remedy ordered to provide redress to plaintiffs with standing who have been injured by the violation.

Second, *Adarand* does not even discuss gender discrimination, and its holding is limited to explicitly race-based classifications. 115 S. Ct. at 2113....

Third, even if *Adarand* did apply, it does not dictate the level of scrutiny to be applied in this case, as Brown concedes. For the last twenty years, the Supreme Court has applied intermediate scrutiny to all cases raising equal protection challenges to gender-based classifications, including the Supreme Court's most recent gender discrimination case, United States v. Virginia, [518 U.S. 515] (1996)....

Under intermediate scrutiny, the burden of demonstrating an exceedingly persuasive justification for a government-imposed, gender-conscious classification is met by showing that the classification serves important governmental objectives, and that the means employed are substantially related to the achievement of those objectives....

We find that the first part of the test is satisfied. The governmental objectives of "avoid[ing] the use of federal resources to support discriminatory practices," and "provid[ing] individual citizens effective protection against those practices," Cannon [v. University of Chicago], 441 U.S. [677] at 704 (1979), are clearly important objectives....

Applying the second prong of the intermediate scrutiny test, we find that the means employed by the district court in fashioning relief for the statutory violation are clearly substantially related to these important objectives. Intermediate scrutiny does not require that there be no other way to accomplish the objectives, but even if that were the standard, it would be satisfied in the unique context presented by the application of Title IX to athletics....

Of course, a remedy that requires an institution to cut, add, or elevate the status of athletes or entire teams may impact the genders differently, but this will be so only if there is a gender-based disparity with respect to athletics opportunities to begin with, which is the only circumstance in which prong three comes into play. Here, however, it has not been shown that Brown's men students will be disadvantaged by the full and effective accommodation of the athletics interests and abilities of its women students....

There can be no doubt that Title IX has changed the face of women's sports as well as our society's interest in and attitude toward women athletes and women's sports.... In addition, there is ample evidence that increased athletics participation opportunities for women and young girls, available as a result of Title IX enforcement, have had salutary effects in other areas of societal concern....

One need look no further than the impressive performances of our country's women athletes in the 1996 Olympic Summer Games to see that Title IX has had a dramatic and positive impact on the capabilities of our women athletes, particularly in team sports. These Olympians represent the first full generation of women to grow up under the aegis of Title IX . . . What stimulated this remarkable change in the quality of women's athletic competition was not a sudden, anomalous upsurge in women's interest in sports, but the enforcement of Title IX's mandate of gender equity in sports. . . .

Affirmed in part, reversed in part, and remanded for further proceedings. . . .

TORRUELLA, Chief Judge (dissenting).

Because I am not persuaded that the majority's view represents the state of the law today, I respectfully dissent. . . .

It is not necessary to equate race and gender to see that the logic of *Adarand* — counseling that we focus on the categories and justifications proffered rather than the labels attached — applies in the context of gender. While cognizant of differences between race-focused and gender-focused Equal Protection precedent, I nevertheless think that *Adarand* compels us to view so-called benign gender-conscious governmental actions under the same lens as any other gender-conscious governmental actions. . . .

In United States v. Virginia, [116 S. Ct. 2264] (1996), the Court faced an Equal Protection challenge to Virginia's practice of maintaining the Virginia Military Institute as an all male institution. Rather than simply apply the traditional test requiring that gender classifications be "substantially related to an important government objective," . . . the Supreme Court applied a more searching "skeptical scrutiny of official action denying rights or opportunities based on sex," [id. at 2274], which requires that "[p]arties who seek to defend gender-based government action must demonstrate an 'exceedingly persuasive justification' for that action." Id. . . .

Virginia "drastically revise[s] our established standards for reviewing sex-based classifications." [116 S. Ct. at 2291] (Scalia, J. dissenting). . . .

I conclude, therefore, that *Adarand* and *Virginia* are irreconcilable with [this court's decision] . . . because it applies a lenient version of intermediate scrutiny that is impermissible following *Adarand* and because it did not apply the "exceedingly persuasive justification" test of *Virginia*. . . .

I believe that the three-prong test, as the district court interprets it, is a quota. I am in square disagreement with the majority, who believe that "[n]o aspect of the Title IX regime at issue in this case . . . mandates gender-based preferences or quotas." . . . Put another way, I agree that "Title IX is not an affirmative action statute" . . . , but I believe that is exactly what the district court has made of it. As interpreted by the district court, the test constitutes an affirmative action, quota-based scheme.

I am less interested in the actual term "quota" than the legally cognizable characteristics that render a quota scheme impermissible. And those characteristics are present here in spades. I am not persuaded by the majority's argument that the three-part test does not constitute a quota because it does not permit an agency or court to find a violation solely on the basis of prong one of the test;

instead, an institution must also fail prongs two and three. As Brown rightly argues, the district court's application of the three-prong test requires Brown to allocate its athletic resources to meet the as-yet-unmet interest of a member of the underrepresented sex, women in this case, while simultaneously neglecting any unmet interest among individuals of the overrepresented sex. To the extent that the rate of interest in athletics diverges between men and women at any institution, the district court's interpretation would require that such an institution treat an individual male student's athletic interest and an individual female student's athletic interest completely differently: one student's reasonable interest would have to be met, by law, while meeting the other student's interest would only aggravate the lack of proportionality giving rise to the legal duty. "The injury in cases of this kind is that a "discriminatory classification prevent[s] . . . competition on an equal footing.'" *Adarand*, [115 S. Ct. at 2104]. As a result, individual male and female students would be precluded from competing against each other for scarce resources; they would instead compete only against members of their own gender. . . .

A pragmatic overview of the effect of the three-prong test leads me to reject the majority's claim that the three-prong test does not amount to a quota because it involves multiple prongs. In my view it is the result of the test, and not the number of steps involved, that should determine if a quota system exists. Regardless of how many steps are involved, the fact remains that the test requires proportionate participation opportunities for both sexes (prong one) unless one sex is simply not interested in participating (prong three). It seems to me that a quota with an exception for situations in which there are insufficient interested students to allow the school to meet it remains a quota. All of the negative effects of a quota remain, and the school can escape the quota under prong three only by offering preferential treatment to the group that has demonstrated less interest in athletics. . . .

The majority is unsympathetic to Brown's claim that the disparity between athletic opportunities for men and women reflect a gender-based difference in interest levels. . . .

If statistical evidence of interest levels is not to be considered by courts, however, there is no way for schools to determine whether they are in compliance. Any studies or surveys they might conduct in order to assess their own compliance would, in the event of litigation, be deemed irrelevant. Regardless of the efforts made by the academic institution, the specter of a lawsuit would be ever-present.

In addition, the majority has put the power to control athletics and the provision of athletic resources in the hands of the underrepresented gender. Virtually every other aspect of college life is entrusted to the institution, but athletics has now been carved out as an exception and the university is no longer in full control of its program. Unless the two genders participate equally in athletics, members of the underrepresented sex would have the ability to demand a varsity level team at any time if they can show sufficient interest. Apparently no weight is given to the sustainability of the interest, the cost of the sport, the university's view on the desirability of the sport, and so on. . . .

Notes

1. Single-Sex Sports Teams. Some courts have held that the Equal Protection Clause prohibits the exclusion of girls from both contact and non-contact sports teams, if no girls' team is offered in the sport. See, e.g., Adams v. Baker, 919 F. Supp. 1496 (D. Kan. 1996) (wrestling); Brenden v. Independent Sch. Dist. 742, 477 F.2d 1292 (8th Cir. 1973) (tennis, cross-country-skiing, and track); Lantz v. Ambach, 570 F. Supp. 1020 (W.D. Mich. 1983) (football); Hoover v. Meikeljohn, 430 F. Supp. 164 (D. Colo. 1977) (soccer); Reed v. Nebraska Sch. Activities Ass'n, 341 F. Supp. 258 (D. Neb. 1972) (golf). Few recent cases succeed on constitutional grounds, however; the prevailing view is that, through the very comprehensive scheme provided by Title IX, Congress intended to foreclose constitutional claims. See Williams v. Sch. Dist. of Bethlehem, 998 F.2d 168, 176 (3d Cir. 1993).

Title IX exempts contact sports from its nondiscrimination provisions, 34 C.F.R. § 106.41(a) (2004), and many courts have assumed that the exemption is reasonable. See, e.g., Kelley v. Board of Trustees, 35 F.3d 265, 270 n.5 (7th Cir. 1994) (stating that "Congress would indeed be surprised to learn that Title IX mandated co-ed football teams"). For one recent analysis of the exemption, see Jamal Greene, Hands Off Policy: Equal Protection and the Contact Sports Exemption of Title IX, 11 Mich. J. Gender & L. 133 (2005). What problems do you see with co-ed teams in, say, wrestling?

Petrie and *O'Connor* represent quite different kinds of claims: Trent Petrie's complaint is that boys, as a group, are denied an opportunity — to play volleyball — that girls have. Karen O'Connor seeks not group-based equality, but the right to be treated as an individual. Both lose. For the same, or for different reasons?

When a school offers a separate team for members of each sex, formal equality is achieved in the group sense, but not in the individual sense. A separate girls' team protects the *average* athletically-talented girl from playing on a team that is not "run over" by boys, but the *exceptional* athletically-talented girl is worse off. Karen O'Connor is limited by generalizations made about members of her sex that are not applicable to her. This is a harm that formal equality ordinarily does not permit. Which version of formal equality is superior — the group-based, separate-but-equal model, or the individual-based model favored by Karen O'Connor?

Karen L. Tokarz argues, in agreement with Judge Craven in *Petrie*, that sex-based teams are highly problematic:

> In addition to depriving individual women of opportunities for physical development, sex segregation in sports adversely affects women economically, socially, and politically. It excludes women from power, fosters the myth of male supremacy, limits occupational choices for women, perpetuates the sex role stereotype of women as passive and weak, and invalidates the expressive/feminine aspect of sports.

Tokarz, Separate but Unequal Educational Sports Programs: The Need for a New Theory of Equality, 1 Berkeley Women's L.J. 201, 239 (1985). Similarly,

Deborah Brake promotes an "affirmative" interpretation of Title IX, arguing that the policy behind Title IX is to eliminate the social structures that devalue women in sport. Under this interpretation, not only should women be able to join men's teams, but men should be able to join women's teams when "the denial of the sport to males rests on cultural assumptions about the sport's femininity." See Deborah Brake, The Struggle for Sex Equality in Sport and the Theory Behind Title IX, 34 U. Mich. J.L. Reform 13, 45 (2001); see also B. Glenn George, Fifty/Fifty: Ending Sex Segregation in School Sports, 63 Ohio St. L.J. 1107 (2002) (arguing against sex-segregated sports).

Others argue that the 14th Amendment requires that women be allowed to compete on men's teams because the opportunities for members of women's teams are not actually equal; men's teams tend to provide more intangible benefits such as television coverage, a higher level of competition, and prestige. See Dana Robinson, A League of Their Own: Do Women Want Segregated Sports? 9 J. Contemp. Legal Issues 321, 328-330 (1998).

Some have argued that separate teams are not justified even on biological terms. Katherine M. Franke, for example, questions the rationality of athletic sex segregation, offering studies showing that

> [b]etween 1964 and 1985 women marathon runners have knocked more than an hour-and-a-half off their running times, while men's times during the same period have decreased by only a few minutes. . . . If the gap between highly trained male and female athletes were to continue to close at the current rate, in thirty to forty years men and women would compete in these sports on an equal basis.

Franke, The Central Mistake of Sex Discrimination Law: The Disaggregation of Sex from Gender, 144 U. Pa. L. Rev. 1, 37-38 (1995). Similar gains have occurred in other sports as a result of women's increased access to coaching, nutrition, fitness, and sports medicine. Franke and others have put into question whether the biological dimorphism assumed by sex-segregated sports, and other things as well, is well-founded. Recent social psychological research supports the theory that expectations and social environment are often more important than predisposition in determining individual's interests and behavior. See, e.g., Jon Hanson & David Yosifon, An Introduction to the Situational Character, Critical Realism, Power Economics, and Deep Capture, 152 U. Pa. L. Rev. 129 (2003). The dimorphism debate continues in Chapter 6 on pp. 1005-1020.

In reasoning that the two-team approach serves the objective of increasing girls' participation in sports, *O'Connor* assumes that if a boys' team was opened to girls, then girls' teams would have to be open to boys. Does this necessarily follow? Even if allowing girls to compete for slots on the boys' team, but not boys to compete for slots on girls' teams, would violate formal equality, is it defensible on substantive equality grounds?

2. Historical Discrimination. While the court in *Petrie* refers vaguely to "past disparity of opportunity," this factor does not play as prominent a role in its analysis as (average) biological differences do. In reaching the same conclusion as the court in *Petrie*, other courts have put greater emphasis on the governmental interest in redressing the effects of past discrimination. See, e.g., Clark v. Arizona Interscholastic Ass'n, 695 F.2d 1126, 1131 (9th Cir. 1982), cert. denied, 464 U.S. 818 (1983) (rejecting challenge to girls' volleyball team). Is this a realistic goal? The brother of the plaintiff in the 1982 *Clark* case, in a later challenge to the same school's girls' volleyball team, argued that since single-sex sports have failed to remedy the effects of past discrimination, and since these effects are due primarily to social attitudes that will not be changed by single-sex sports teams, continued pursuit of the goal through single-sex teams is unconstitutional. The argument was rejected. See Clark v. Arizona Interscholastic Ass'n, 886 F.2d 1191 (9th Cir. 1989).

To what extent was historical discrimination a factor in *Cohen*? Compare the analysis in the employment discrimination context at pp. 172-173.

3. Title IX and Women's Participation in Sports. At one time, strenuous physical activity was thought to be harmful to women's reproductive capacities and competition antithetical to their moral standards. The passage of Title IX reflected the more modern understanding that "girls who play sports have higher self-esteem, less risk of depression, a lower likelihood of engaging in high-risk behaviors, and perform better in school than girls who do not play sports." Deborah Brake, Revisiting Title IX's Legacy: Moving Beyond the Three-Part Test, 12 Am. U. J. Gender Soc. Pol'y & L. 453, 459 (2004). Girls who participate in sports are also less likely to develop osteoporosis and breast cancer, less likely to have an unintended pregnancy, more likely to graduate from high school, and less likely to engage in an array of health-risk behaviors. See Title IX Facts Everyone Should Know, http://www.womenssportsfoundation.org/cgi-bin/iowa/issues/geena/record.html?record=862.

Title IX got off to a slow start. A long delay in its application to institutions as a whole occurred with the 1984 decision of the United States Supreme Court, Grove City College v. Bell, 465 U.S. 555 (1984), which limited the application of Title IX to the specific school program receiving federal funds. This decision was reversed by Congress in the Civil Rights Restoration Act of 1987, 20 U.S.C. §§ 1687-1688 (1994), which extended Title IX to all of the programs of an institution receiving federal funds for any program or activity. Another barrier came down in 1992 when the U.S. Supreme Court allowed individuals to sue for money damages under Title IX, at least for intentional discrimination. See Franklin v. Gwinnett County Public Schools, 503 U.S. 60 (1992).

Despite its limitations and its stalled beginnings, Title IX is widely regarded as having led to substantially increase opportunities for girls and women, especially in sports. Under Title IX, participation in high school sports went from approximately 294,000 girls in 1971 to 2.8 million by the 2002-2003 season. See Brake, Revisiting Title IX's Feminist Legacy, supra, at 458 (citing Women's Sports Foundation 2004 data, available at http://www.womens-sportsfoundation.org/binary-data/WSF_ARTICLE/pdf_file/28.pdf). Participation in intercollegiate sports went from 32,000 before Title IX to over 160,000 in 2004. Id.

Title IX has many exemptions. It excludes participation in contact sports (see 34 C.F.R. § 106.41(b)(2000)), for example; the successful cases in this area are all Equal Protection cases. See note 1, above. It also exempts any institution "that traditionally and continually from its establishments has had a policy of admitting only students of one sex," see 20 U.S.C. § 1681(a)(5) (1994); schools whose primary purpose is to train students for the military services, see § 1681(a)(4); and traditional single-sex groups such as the Boy Scouts and Girl Scouts, YWCAs and YMCAs, sororities and fraternities, mother-daughter or father-son activities, and scholarships for beauty contest winners, see § 1681(a)(6)-(9).

While Title IX does not require that women have the opportunity to participate in a male contact sports team, once a university offers that opportunity, it may be precluded from withdrawing it, under common law principles. In one celebrated case, a jury awarded place-kicker Heather Sue Mercer $2 million in punitive damages after she was permitted by the football coach at Duke University to participate in off-season training and scrimmages and then treated unfairly by the coach, who ultimately removed her from the roster, although he had never cut a male from the team. An account of the case can be found at George, supra, at 1109, 1121-1123. See Mercer v. Duke University, 401 F.3d 199 (4th Cir. 2005) (affirming punitive damages award, even though actual damages were nominal). What is the likely impact of the verdict in *Mercer* on women in contact sports? In one later incident, a female place-kicker who was comfortable kicking from 35 yards was not allowed to try out for the University of Minnesota football team, the University reportedly citing the *Mercer* case. See Dennis Brackin, "U" Says No to Nystrom: Football Team Denies Tryout to Female Place-Kicker, Minneapolis Star Trib., Apr. 18, 2003, at 9C.

4. Allocating Resources Under Title IX. Ordinarily, claims under Title IX do not concern access by women to men's teams, but rather equivalent treatment. Some of the litigated cases address matters of unequal scheduling, access to fields, and equipment. For example, a recent case challenged the school districts of Pelham and Mamaroneck, New York, who scheduled girls' soccer in the spring, and boys' soccer in the fall, in order to stagger use of field space. As a result of the spring schedule, the girls' team was unable to compete in the New York Regional and State Championships, while the boys' team could. The appellate court found that this practice denied equality of athletic opportunity to the female team members, in violation of Title IX. See McCormick v. School Dist. of Mamaroneck, 370 F.3d 275 (2d Cir. 2004).

The most frequent Title IX issue relates to how to allocate resource dollars. Title IX regulations reviewed in *Cohen* make it clear that Title IX does not require that women's sports receive equal expenditures. The allocation of scholarships must match women's participation rates. See 34 C.F.R. § 106.37(c) (1999). With respect to athletic programs more generally, however, equality must be measured by consideration of a variety of open-ended factors relating to the availability of teams and levels of competition, equipment, supplies, scheduling, travel, tutoring, locker rooms, practice facilities, housing, publicity, and the like. See 34 C.F.R. § 106.41(c) (2000).

Forty-four percent of intercollegiate athletes in Division 1 colleges and universities in 2002-2003 were women, as compared to 56 percent men. Scholarship allocations now approach the percentage of women's and men's respective participation in sports. However, Division 1 schools spend twice as much on recruiting expenses for men's teams as for women's teams, and they pay head coaches for women's teams only 61 percent, on average, what they pay coaches of men's teams. See Corey Bray, 2002-03 NCAA Gender-Equity Report 23 (September 2004), found at www.ncaa.org/library/research/gender_equity_study/2002-03_gender-equity-report.pdf. The gap for Division 1-A schools is larger. Women constitute 44 percent of athletes in 1-A schools, but women's teams consume only 30 percent of overall athletics expenses, 30 percent of recruiting expenses, 35 percent of head coach salaries, and 27 percent of assistant coach salaries. Id. at 37.

5. Title IX Compliance. In 2002, college administrators estimated that only 20 percent of athletic programs were in compliance with Title IX. Jerome Solomon, Title IX, 30 Years Later: Sexes Still Unequal in Athletics; Title IX Changed the Playing Field, But It's Not Level, The Houston Chronicle, June 23, 2002, at A1. One study showed that the mean "proportionality gap" in the 2001-2002 academic year was 13.1 — an improvement of only 2.1 since the 1995-1996 year. Less than 20 percent of schools had proportionality gaps under 20. See Deborah J. Anderson et al., Gender Equity in Intercollegiate Athletics: Determinants of Title IX Compliance (July 2004), at Table 2, found at www.ilr.cornell.edu/cheri/WP/cheri_wp45.pdf.

Despite widespread evidence of noncompliance, the Office for Civil Rights has never found an educational institution out of compliance with the athletics regulations of Title IX and has not initiated proceedings to remove federal funds from any institutional, favoring the negotiated settlement route. See Title IX Facts Everyone Should Know, http://www.womenssports foundation.org/cgi-bin/iowa/issues/geena/record.html?record=862. Nor has the U.S. Department of Education investigated widespread evidence of errors in the gender-equity reports filed by colleges and universities. Paula Wasley, Education Dept. Ignores Rife Errors in Gender-Equity Data From College Sports Programs, *USA Today* Reports, Chron. of Higher Educ., Today's News, Oct. 20, 2005.

In 1997, the National Women's Law Center filed complaints with the Office for Civil Rights against 25 colleges and universities for sex discrimination in the awarding of athletic scholarships. Two and one-half years later, eight institutions were found to be in compliance and the other 17 schools agreed to increase scholarship aid to female athletes. See Brake, The Struggle for Sex Equality in Sport, supra, at 75-76.

For discussion of the absence of Title IX compliance reviews by various federal agencies in the areas of science and engineering education, see Catherine Pieronek, Title IX and Gender Equity in Science, Technology, Engineering and Mathematics Education: No Longer an Overlooked Application of the Law, 31 J. College & Univ. L. 291, 328-341 (2005).

6. Title IX and Women's Lack of Interest in Sports. In consolidated lawsuits brought by women against Louisiana State University for discrimination in the provision of facilities and teams for intercollegiate athletics, LSU claimed that its participation rates of 71 percent male and 29 percent female were justified, even though the student population was 51 percent male and 49 percent female, because fewer females were interested in athletics. The Fifth Circuit Court of Appeals, in dismissing the claim with respect to fast-pitch softball, reasoned:

> The heart of [LSU's] contention is that an institution with no coach, no facilities, no varsity team, no scholarships, and no recruiting in a given sport must have on campus enough national-caliber athletes to field a competitive varsity team in that sport before a court can find sufficient interest and abilities to exist. It should go without saying that adopting this criteria would eliminate an effective accommodation claim by any plaintiff, at any time.

Pederson v. Louisiana State University, 213 F.3d 858, 878 (5th Cir. 2000). The court in *Pederson* did not reach the issue of whether lack of interest could be a defense, having concluded that there was sufficient evidence in the record that women did have an interest in fast-pitch softball. Id.

Is the problem in *Pederson* and *Cohen* that women's interests should not be relevant, or that lack of interest cannot be reliably proved? Among the evidence submitted by Brown in the *Cohen* case was:

> (i) admissions data showing greater athletic interest among male applicants than female applicants; (ii) college board data showing greater athletic interest and prior participation rates by prospective male applicants than female applicants; (iii) data from the Cooperative Institutional Research Program at UCLA indicating greater athletic interests among men than women; (iv) an independent telephone survey of 500 randomly selected Brown undergraduates that reveals that Brown offers women participation opportunities in excess of their representation in the pool of interested, qualified students; (v) intramural and club participation rates that demonstrate higher participation rates among men than women; (vi) walk-on and try-out numbers that reflect a greater interest among men than women; (vii) high school participation rates that show a much lower rate of participation among females than among males; (viii) the NCAA Gender Equity Committee data showing that women across the country participate in athletics at a lower rate than men.

Cohen v. Brown University, 101 F.3d 155, 198 n.30 (1st Cir. 1996) (Torruella, C.J., dissenting). If interest was relevant, wouldn't this be enough? What are the reasons for concluding that these factors should not be taken into account?

Once the court determines that Brown's measurements of women's interests in sports are tainted, where does this leave Brown? Can it possibly refute the court's disbelief that women have been given an equal shot at participation in athletics? Does the court's reading of Title IX and the three-part test it endorses makes the empirical debate about women's interests somewhat academic? Is this strict formula fair to Brown? See further discussion in note 8 at p. 310, infra.

While *Cohen* concerned claims by women of discrimination in the inequality of women's opportunities, most of the litigation in this area have been claims men whose teams were eliminated or downgraded as a result of cutbacks necessitated, according to the defendant universities, to create more opportunities for women in sports. From 1981 to 1999, 13 of the 26 men's intercollegiate sports experienced a decline in the number of teams. See Jay Larson, Note, All Sports Are Not Created Equal: College Football and a Proposal to Amend the Title IX Proportionality Prong, 88 Minn. L. Rev. 1598, 1598 (2004). Wrestling experienced the biggest decline, losing 171 intercollegiate teams and 2,648 student-athletes over this period. Id. at 1598 n.5. Faced with this litigation, Courts of Appeal in eight federal circuits adopted the numerical parity approach taken in *Cohen*, setting proportionality of representation of males and females in relation to their enrollment in the school as the goal, or at least as a "safe harbor"; until that goal is met, the rules has been, at least until recently, that a school must demonstrate either a history of expanding opportunities or that all the interests of the underrepresented sex are met. See Nat'l Wrestling Coaches Ass'n v. U.S. Dep't of Educ., 263 F. Supp. 2d 82, 94-95 (D.D.C. 2003) (citing the cases) (further case history below).

Following failures in the courts in individual cases to protest cut-backs in men's athletic programs, in 2002 the National Wrestling Coaches Association filed suit against the Department of Education in 2002, seeking to invalidate the Title IX three-part test set forth in the regulations. The suit failed, largely on standing grounds. See National Wrestling Coaches Association v. Dep't of Educ., 366 F.3d 930 (D.C. Cir. 2004), cert. denied, 125 S. Ct. 2537 (2005). At about the same time, the Bush Administration established the Blue Ribbon Commission on Opportunity in Athletics, which recommended measures that would have substantially changed the three-part test interpreted and enforced in *Cohen*. Following outcry in response to these recommendations, the Department of Education decided not to make any substantive changes. See Deborah Brake, Revisiting Title IX's Feminist Legacy: Moving Beyond the Three-Part Test, 12 Am. U. J. Gender Soc. Pol'y & L. 453, 454-456 (2004). In March 2005, however, the Office for Civil Rights issued a clarification of the three-part test, putting the burden on government regulators and women to prove that an institution is not providing enough opportunities for women to pursue their athletics interests and abilities, and allowing universities to determine the interest level of women in sports through an e-mail survey alone. The NCAA Executive Committee issued a strong statement against the clarification, which it said conflicted with the purpose of encouraging women's interest in sports and eliminating stereotypes that discourage them from participation. The Committee also complained that the clarifications authorized a flawed survey methodology and made no provision for the Department of Education to monitor schools' implementation of the survey or its results. See Gary T. Brown, Executive Committee Urges Against Title IX Compliance Option, NCAA News Online, May 9, 2005, at http://www2. ncaa.org/media_and_events/association_news/ncaa_news_online/2005/05_09.

7. Title IX and Revenue Sports. Should "revenue" sports be treated differently from other sports? Recall that coaches for a revenue sport might be paid more than coaches for a non-revenue sport, since the pressures entailed in generating revenue provide a "factor other than sex" under the Equal Pay Act. See

Chapter 1, p. 43ff. Is it reasonable to claim, further, that the unique function of revenue sports at some schools, in terms of media interest, alumni relations, and publicity, make revenue sports something incomparable to other sports, for Title IX purposes?

Some commentators have argued that revenue sports must be supported at a competitive level because the proceeds from these sports provide the income stream needed to support other athletic programs for both men and women. Accordingly, they argue, the revenue-generating aspect of college sports should be separated from the rest and treated as businesses, rather than as part of the educational mission. See, e.g., Matthew L. Daniel, Title IX and Gender Equity in College Athletics: How Honesty Might Avert a Crisis, 2 Ann. Surv. Am. L. 255, 306-307 (1995). See also Note, Giving the Bat Back to Casey: Suggestions to Reform Title IX's Inequitable Application to Intercollegiate Athletics, 35 Akron L. Rev. 117, 151 (2001) (suggesting that an institution could designate which sports operate as "businesses," and which do not).

One problem with having the rules turn on profitability is the difficulty of calculating whether a sport is operating at a profit or not, which may help to explain why the profitability figures are sometimes hard to reconcile. Compare, e.g., Daniel R. Marburger & Nancy Hogshead-Makar, Is Title IX Really to Blame for the Decline in Intercollegiate Men's Nonrevenue Sports?, 14 Marq. Sports L. Rev. 65, 80 (2003) (citing NCAA data showing that in 2001 in Division 1A schools, 66 percent of men's basketball teams, and 69 percent of football teams had revenues that exceeded expenses, with an average profit in men's basketball of $2,710,000 and an average profit in football of $7,400,000), with Sudha Setty, Leveling the Playing Field: Reforming the Office for Civil Rights to Achieve Better Title IX Enforcement, 32 Colum. J.L. & Soc. Probs. 331, 351 (1999) (citing Women's Sports Foundation data showing that 81 percent of collegiate football programs operate at a deficit, and among Division 1A teams, over one-third of football programs maintain annual deficits in excess of one million dollars). See also John C. Weistart, Can Gender Equity Find a Place in Commercialized College Sports, 3 Duke J. Gender L. & Pol'y 191, 207-208 (1996) (if scholarships, administration, support services, and other overhead items were properly allocated among the individual sports, there are only a small number of schools in which the expensive sports are not subsidized); J. Brad Reich, All the Athletes Are Equal, But Some Are More Equal than Others: An Objective Evaluations of Title IX's Past, Present, and Recommendations for Its Future, 108 Penn. St. L. Rev. 525, 551-553 (2003) (providing additional statistics from various sources, and noting frustration of trying to determine actual profits).

John Weistart points out several other flaws in the case for treating football, or other "revenue sports," differently. He notes, for example, that because of the highly competitive nature of revenue sports, most of the revenues are poured back into those sports, with little diverted to fund non-revenue sports. One study shows that for every additional $1 spent on athletic programs, only between three and seven cents is spent on nonrevenue sports. Weistart, supra, at 213. Weistart argues also that the high expenditures in revenue sports come from the pressures of unrestrained economic competition rather than from any serious concern about the quality or safety of the game; "men's revenue-producing sports have set themselves on a course in which there is no foreseeable relief from the pressure for increased spending." Id. at 248-249. Weistart advocates "mutual disarmament," arguing that an effective uniform cap on expenditures "will not diminish on-the-field competition," but will inevitably improve athletics, as well as allowing more teams to be able to participate on an equal footing. Id. at 249, 253.

8. *Cohen v. Brown*: **Affirmative Action or Remedy for Past Discrimination?** Is the proportionality test adopted in *Cohen* an example of "affirmative action"? This depends, of course, on what one understands as a neutral fact or given, in relation to which some effort might be understood as an "affirmative" intervention.

What if it were determined that affirmative action in this area is necessary to overcome the effect of past discrimination in women's sports? Would this have to be, as Justice O'Connor suggested in the *Grutter* case, a temporary fix, until the effects of discrimination have worn off? Or is there something inherently desirable about having men and women engaged in sports in roughly equal numbers, so that if this "equality" does not come about on its own, it should be encouraged through proportionality measures that "favor" women's participation over men's? Kimberly A. Yuracko examines the difficulties of justifying the proportionality standard under an affirmative action model, and argues for "a more openly perfectionist" or "cultural transformation" justification," based on the positive promotion of the skills and values learned in sports from which women could benefit. See Yuracko, One For You and One For Me: Is Title IX's Sex-Based Proportionality Requirement For College Varsity Athletic Positions Defensible?, 97 Nw. U. L. Rev. 731 (2003).

Cohen rejects Brown's claim about the lack of greater women's interest in athletics based on factors controlled by Brown that historically seemed to contribute to the problem. Scholars have identified numerous ways in which educational institutions have historically contributed to women's lack of interest. These include (1) the dominance of men in leadership positions in college athletics and the relegation of most women to token positions; (2) pay disparities between male and female coaches and in other expenditures for women's sports; (3) the linking of sport with masculinity, which is evidenced in training methods built on norms of masculinity ("you throw like a girl"); (4) hostile talk about women; (5) lesbian-baiting; and (6) the objectification of women in sport (starting with the "quintessentially "feminine' role" of cheerleaders who "[stand] at the periphery, offering unconditional support for the athletes who play the traditionally masculine role of competing in the primary athletic event"). Deborah Brake, The Struggle for Sex Equality in Sport and the Theory Behind Title IX, 34 U. Mich. J.L. Reform 13, 74-122 (2001).

> [N]othing about sports as played in today's educational institutions is "natural"—not even what counts as a "sport." The popularity and revenue-

producing potential of a sport is certain not natural; it is carefully promoted and nurtured by the machinery of college (and professional" athletics. It is a product of countless social and institutional factors, including longstanding and continuing investments in facilities, personnel, programs, recruiting, marketing, and coaching.... These investments contribute to a certain image and status of a sport that greatly affect its marketability. The existence of average differences in male and female bodies in height and upper body strength does not "naturally" translate into inequality in markets and spectatorship.

Brake, Revisiting Title IX's Feminist Legacy, supra, at 481. If Brake is right, what can Brown University do to "affirmatively" reverse the effects of its past practices?

Catharine MacKinnon starts even further back: the problem is not just that women have not been encouraged in sports, she claims; they have been taught to be disinterested:

> Women have learned a lot all these years on the sidelines, watching. Not only have we been excluded from resources, excluded from participation, we have learned actual disability, enforced weakness, lack of spirit/body connection in being and in motion.... It's not *not* learned; it's very specifically learned. ... [M]en, learning to be men, learn not only sports but learn those things that become elevated, extended, measured, valued, and organized in and as sport itself. Women, simply learning to be women, do not learn those things, do learn the opposite of those things. So... being female and being athletic have been socially contradictory and... being male and being athletic have been more or less socially synonymous. Femininity has contradicted, masculinity has been consistent with, being athletic.

Catharine A. MacKinnon, Feminism Unmodified: Discourses on Life and Law 120 (1987). What are the implications of this observation, in terms of the University's obligations?

Does the media contribute to the problem? See Mary Jo Kane, Media Coverage of the Post Title IX Female Athlete: A Feminist Analysis of Sport, Gender, and Power, 3 Duke J. Gender L. & Pol'y 95, 119-120 (1996) (media types female athletes as feminine, or not); see also Note, Cheering on Women and Girls in Sports: Using Title IX To Fight Gender Role Oppression, 110 Harv. L. Rev. 1627, 1632-1633 (1997) (describing self-sexualization of female athletes, to assure their audiences they are not lesbians by wearing their hair long and in ponytails and emphasizing their feminine looks and interests in their off-the-court appearances). Should Brown University be responsible for media-induced attitudes by women about sports? What about women's responsibility for sexualized cheerleading displays?

9. Redefining Sport. Is equality too limited a concept in college sports? Is it really in women's interests to have women's intercollegiate sports follow the road men's sports have taken? Some recognized early on that Title IX reproduced in female sports the same pressure on high visibility and powerhouse teams that is endemic to male sports, rather than on increasing participation in intramural and club programs and the promotion of athletics to improve health and well-being of all students. See, e.g., Mary A. Boutilier & Lucinda SanGiovanni, The Sporting Woman 173-176 (1983). See also Brian Snow & William E. Thro, Still On the Sidelines: Developing the Non-Discrimination Paradigm Under Title IX, 3 Duke J. Gender L. & Pol'y 1, 44 (1996) (greater emphasis should be placed on the vast majority of college students who do not play intercollegiate athletics).

Boutilier and SanGiovanni point out that before Title IX, the Association for Intercollegiate Athletics for Women (AIAW) pursued a less competitive model of sport than the NCAA, one that was dedicated to protecting the "welfare of the student above that of the institution or external interests such as alumni, commercial groups, and the like." Id. at 178. After passage of Title IX, against which the NCAA had first lobbied strongly, the NCAA moved successfully to swallow up the AIAW and take over women's sports. See Murray Sperber, College Sports Inc.: The Athletic Department vs. The University 322-332 (1990); Wendy Olson, Beyond Title IX: Toward an Agenda for Women and Sports in the 1990's, 3 Yale J.L. & Feminism 105, 112 (1990). This takeover, some have contended, imposed a corrupt commercial system on a program that had superior athlete-centered, educationally oriented values. Sperber, supra, at 322-332. Is the takeover of the AIAW by the NCAA a problem under formal equality principles? Is it compelled by these principles?

Many women's advocates have argued that improving athletic opportunities for women does not mean making men's opportunities available to women — the formal equality option — but producing a more process-oriented, cooperative competition mode of sport that better meets women's goals of better health, stress reduction, friendship, and sociability. See Olson, supra, at 145. Catharine MacKinnon associates women's sports not only with the redefinition of sport, but of femininity as well:

> [A]thletics to men is a form of combat. It is a sphere in which one asserts oneself against an object, a person, or a standard. It is a form of coming against and subduing someone who is on the other side, vanquishing enemies. It's competitive. From women's point of view, some rather major elements of the experience appear to be left out.... These include things that men occasionally experience, but that on the whole are not allowed to be the central purpose of male athletics, such as kinesthesis, pleasure in motion, cooperation (and by this I do not mean the male bond), physical self-respect, self-possession, and fun. Because of the history of women's subjection, physicality for women has a different meaning from physicality for men. Physicality for men has meant male dominance; it has meant force, coercion, and the ability to subdue and subject the natural world, one central part of which has been us.
>
> For women, when we have engaged in sport, when we have been physical, it has meant claiming and possessing a physicality that is our own. We have had something to fight and therefore something to gain here, and that is a different relation to our bodies than women are allowed to have in this society. We have had to gain a relation to our bodies *as if they are our own*. This physical self-respect and physical presence that women can get from sport is antithetical to femininity. It is our bodies as acting rather than as acted upon. It is our bodies as

being and presence, our bodies that *we* do things with, that we in fact are and identify with as ourselves, rather than our bodies as things to be looked at or for us to look at in preparation for the crucialness of how we will appear, or even to carry out heads around in the world. In other words, athletics can give us our bodies as a form of being rather than as a form of appearance, or death-likeness.

MacKinnon, Feminism Unmodified: Discourses on Life and Law 121 (1987). What implications does MacKinnon's analysis have for the law?

10. Title IX, Standing, and Retaliation as a Form of Intentional Discrimination. One recent U.S. Supreme Court case involved the question of whether retaliation against a coach who complained about the discriminatory treatment of his female athletes stated a claim under Title IX. The school district claimed that coaches were not among the class of people Title IX was intended to protect, and that Title IX did not impose liability for retaliation. By a 5-4 decision, the Court reversed the dismissal of the coach's complaint. Drawing on analogies to Title VII, Justice O'Connor reasoned that the purpose of Title IX would be undermined if retaliation against coaches, who often were in the best position to identify and report violations, went unpunished, and that "on the basis of sex" did not necessarily refer to the plaintiff's own sex. Jackson v. Birmingham Bd. of Educ., 544 U.S. 167 (2005).

Deborah Brake criticizes the rationales offered in *Jackson*, arguing that they are analytically unsatisfying in light of prior interpretations of Title VII and other anti-discrimination statutes. She argues that a broader understanding of retaliation as a form of intentional discrimination is necessary in interpreting all of the anti-discrimination statutes, based not on a framework of status-based differential treatment, but rather on a conception of discrimination as the maintenance of race and gender privilege. See Brake, Retaliation, 90 Minn. L. Rev. 18 (2005).

Putting Theory into Practice

2-12. It is typical for co-ed intramural teams at colleges and universities to have requirements for participation by women in every game (for example, that at least two women be on the field, or in the batting line-up, at all times). What rules exist at your school for, say, softball, or soccer? Do they make sense from a gender quality perspective? What type of equality do they help to achieve? What is the cost?

2-13. T. was the starting center on the women's basketball team at a small NCAA Division I school in Connecticut. In the summer before her junior year, she became pregnant, as a result of which the coach rescinded her scholarship and dismissed her from the team. Can she prevail in a Title IX suit against the college?

D. SUBSTANTIVE EQUALITY IN THE FAMILY

1. The Traditional View

William Blackstone, 1 Commentaries on the Laws of England
*430-431, 432

By marriage, the husband and wife are one person in law: that is, the very being or legal existence of the woman is suspended during the marriage, or at least is incorporated and consolidated into that of the husband; under whose wing, protection, and cover, she performs everything; and is therefore called in our law-french a *feme-covert, foemina viro co-operta*; it is said to be covert-baron, or under the protection and influence of her husband, her baron, or lord; and her condition during her marriage is called her *coverture*. Upon this principle, of a union of person in husband and wife, depend almost all the legal rights, duties, and disabilities, that either of them acquire by the marriage. I speak not at present of the rights of property, but of such as are merely *personal*. For this reason, a man cannot grant any thing to his wife, or enter into covenant with her; for the grant would be to suppose her separate existence; and to covenant with her would be only to covenant with himself; and therefore it is also generally true, that all compacts made between husband and wife, when single, are voided by the intermarriage. A woman indeed may be attorney for her husband; for that implies no separation from, but is rather a representation of, her lord. And a husband may also bequeath any thing to his wife by will; for that cannot take effect till the coverture is determined by his death. The husband is bound to provide his wife with necessaries by law, as much as himself; and, if she contracts debts for them, he is obliged to pay them; but for anything besides necessaries he is not chargeable. Also if a wife elopes, and lives with another man, the husband is not chargeable even for necessaries; at least if the person who furnishes them is sufficiently apprised of her elopement. If the wife be indebted before marriage, the husband is bound afterwards to pay the debt; for he has adopted her and her circumstances together. If the wife be injured in her person or her property, she can bring no action for redress without her husband's concurrence, and in his name, as well as her own; neither can she be sued without making the husband a defendant.... In criminal prosecutions, it is true, the wife may be indicted and punished separately; for the union is only a civil union. But in trials of any sort they are not allowed to be evidence for, or against, each other: partly because it is impossible their testimony should be indifferent, but principally because of the union of person; and therefore, if they were admitted to be witnesses for each other, they would contradict one maxim of law, "*nemo in propria causa testis esse debet*" [No one ought to be a witness against his own cause.] and if *against* each other, they would contradict another maxim, "*nemo tenetur seipsum accusare*." [No one is bound to accuse himself.]...

But though our law in general considers man and wife as one person, yet there are some instances in which she is separately considered; as inferior to him, and acting by his compulsion. And therefore all deeds executed, and acts done, by her, during her coverture, are void; except it be a fine, or the like matter of record, in which case she must be solely and secretly examined, to learn if her act be voluntary. She cannot by will devise lands to her husband, unless under special circumstances; for at the time of making it she is supposed to be under his coercion. And in some felonies, and other inferior crimes, committed by her, through constraint of her husband, the law excuses her; but this extends not to treason or murder....

Saff v. Saff

402 N.Y.S.2d 690 (App. Div. 1978), appeal dismissed, 415 N.Y.S.2d 829 (N.Y. 1979)

SIMONS, Justice.

Appellant has obtained a divorce from respondent because he abandoned her. She appeals from so much of the judgment as denied her alimony and failed to impose a constructive trust on one half of all respondent's separately owned property....

Appellant and her husband were married in 1936. At the time appellant worked as a maid and respondent was unemployed. Over the next few years both worked at various jobs and gradually they accumulated a small reserve of funds which they held in their joint names. In 1946, after a few false starts, respondent went into partnership with Wallace Dahl and the two men founded Jamestown Fabricated Steel as equal partners. Each man invested $2000 but Dahl was short of cash and respondent loaned him $1000 (later repaid) to purchase his half interest. The money for these payments came from the Saffs' joint funds. In 1950 the company was incorporated and the capital stock was divided between respondent and Dahl. The company...is now estimated to have a net worth exceeding $500,000. In 1975 it grossed $590,000. Appellant has never had any legal interest in the business or in the corporate stock.

A minority of the court would grant appellant relief by imposing a constructive trust on one half of her husband's stock in Jamestown Fabricated Steel, Inc., upon one half of whatever business profits respondent receives from the corporation by way of profit sharing, and upon one half of the annual installments paid to respondent by the corporation to acquire real property formerly owned by him....

Before the court may declare that respondent holds his separately owned property as a trustee for appellant's benefit, appellant must prove that there was (1) a promise by him — express or implied, (2) which caused her to transfer property to him relying on the promise, (3) that a confidential relationship existed between the parties and (4) that respondent has been unjustly enriched at her expense by his conduct.

Marriage is a confidential relationship, of course, and there was a transfer of funds and labor by appellant to respondent. The remedy of constructive trust, however, requires that more be shown. There must be proof that the transfer was made in reliance on a promise that the property transferred would be held for the benefit of appellant, and that respondent was enriched unjustly by retaining the fruits of the transfer.

We find no express promise by respondent. Appellant testified that from 1946 to 1960, apparently after the purchase of the business, respondent told her on various occasions, "Baby girl, what is mine is yours; you're my wife. It's always all half yours, you're my wife." Such representations undoubtedly reflected the emotions of a happier time but they most assuredly did not constitute a promise by respondent that he held one half of his corporate stock as trustee for appellant. The statements meant precisely what most people would interpret them to mean—not that appellant had a proprietary interest in every personal belonging of respondent, be it clothing or corporate stock, but rather that the parties would share their successes equally in raising their family and enjoying their life together.

Failing an express promise, appellant contends there was an implied promise. Unquestionably an implied promise may be sufficient if the evidence otherwise supports a finding that respondent holds property as trustee for another. Such promises may be inferred from the factual circumstances and setting of the parties and they frequently are when the conduct of the injured party is otherwise inexplicable. The fact of the marriage is an important consideration indicating a confidential relationship between the parties, but standing alone it does not provide the basis for an implied promise which will support a constructive trust. Furthermore before a court implies a promise between husband and wife for purposes of a constructive trust, it must be careful to separate those promises going to the marriage relationship and those going to a business relationship. The two may not be mixed together in some sort of salmagundi, as the minority has done, to find an implied promise that the wife will share in the ownership of a specific business because of such unrelated acts as her employment as a maid or drill press operator, her care of the children or her handling of the family finances. The remedy of constructive trust may not be applied randomly to adjust general equities between spouses or as a punitive measure to divvy up a husband's separately owned property because of his past indiscretion.

In this case the marriage relationship cuts against a finding of implied promise to hold one half of respondent's interest in the corporation for the benefit of appellant. Appellant's participation in the business is easily explainable as a normal incident of marriage which was manifestly given as such and for the generous salary she received and without any expectation on her part of any future ownership of the business.

Thus, appellant testified that she worked as a bookkeeper for the company, without pay, from 1946 until 1950. In the beginning the work was minimal for the simple reason that the company had little business. Appellant estimated that during those years the books for a whole month could be done in one day and respondent helped her with the tax returns. The work required more time by 1950, when the business was incorporated, but appellant has never worked more than 20-24 hours per week and she testified that she frequently took the bookkeeping home and completed it there rather than work at the plant. Also, in 1950 the corporation hired an accountant and additional other women employees to do the office work, although appellant continued to do some of the bookkeeping. She has received a salary from the company since 1950. At the time of the divorce her salary from Jamestown Steel was $12,500 per year for this part-time work. During the marriage appellant also worked part-time for a doctor for about two years and she did part-time office work for another two years at Jamestown Plastics, another company then owned by her husband.

If any rebuttal is needed to appellant's claim of implied promise, the proof establishes that respondent consistently refused to give his wife any of the company stock or permit her to be an officer or director of any of his corporations and his wishes were well known to her from the beginning. Appellant has never played a management role in respondent's companies, even in the broadest sense. Her work was always part-time and entirely clerical and she shared in neither the liability, ownership, nor management of the business.

Thus, while there was a transfer of jointly owned funds to acquire the business, the transfer was not induced by the marriage relationship and was not referable to any express or implied promise of ownership. The funds, or at least appellant's share of them, represented a gift, or at best, a loan by appellant, not an investment made as part of her participation in a joint venture.

Further than that, there was no unjust enrichment of respondent. Appellant has been more than adequately compensated for her efforts and in ways fully to be expected in a marriage. Respondent, by his efforts at developing and operating the business, has kept the couple happily circumstanced for 30 years. All of his earnings from the company were deposited in the couple's joint accounts and were used to support appellant. Generous purchases of property and investments were made from these funds for her. The income has been sufficient to enable her to travel, to enjoy the satisfying social and athletic life which she described in her testimony as the routine of "the most beautiful marriage in the world." Appellant will continue to enjoy the support available through respondent's efforts, by the separately owned property accumulated for her or, if her needs require it, by respondent's income for as long as he is able to do so. There is no need for a division of respondent's capital. . . .

[A]ppellant is not penniless. She came to this marriage with few material assets but she has lived a financially secure life for over 30 years since then. The Trial Court granted her exclusive, tax free use of the marital residence and the extensive furnishings in it. She has joint ownership in $100,000 in stocks, several thousand dollars of various stocks in her own name, $15,200 in savings and ownership of a sizeable insurance policy on her husband's life. In addition to this, she receives $12,500 a year income from her part-time employment at Jamestown Steel and she has dividend income of $3,600 per year. Neither the Trial Court nor the majority of this court find alimony justified on these facts. . . .

Judgment affirmed.

CARDAMONE, Justice, dissenting. . . .

From the beginning everything was shared. At the outset of their marriage while Mr. Saff looked unsuccessfully for employment, the Saffs resided in a home where Mrs. Saff worked without pay as a maid for their joint room and board.

Before coming to Jamestown, New York the couple lived and worked in various parts of the country. Sometimes one or the other, occasionally both, would have employment. In those years Mrs. Saff worked at the Lionel Train Corp., General Instruments and Standard Oil Company of New Jersey. She was able to do welding, worked on assembly lines and learned to operate all kinds of machinery, including drill presses. She worked a 58-hour week at sixty cents per hour. Regardless of whether one or both worked, however, the Saffs' savings were always jointly held. They did more than jointly share their earnings. The first home they purchased and their marital home were jointly owned. Most persuasive are the circumstances surrounding Jamestown Plastics. Jamestown Plastics was a business in which Mrs. Saff performed the same duties as she did at Jamestown Steel. Later, it was incorporated. At the time of its sale in 1970, however, the proceeds of this plastics business enterprise were invested by Mr. Saff in jointly owned stock. This act is consistent with his promise concededly made during their marriage that everything was to be shared equally between them despite the fact that Mr. Saff testified that he would never permit Mrs. Saff to hold any stock or serve as an officer or director of any corporation that he had anything to do with. This investment was made in a "happier time"; and, it is only as a result of their marital difficulties that the husband no longer wishes to share half and half with his wife assets held solely in his name. The facts and circumstances of the parties' life together flatly contradict the notion that Mr. Saff's promise was merely a representation made in a "happier time." Rather, this was a promise made by a husband to his wife which he consistently kept until he decided to abandon her.

Mrs. Saff transferred her share of jointly held savings to start Jamestown Steel and rendered valuable services in the early development of this business in reliance on the belief that she shared in the ownership of it. A significant portion of the funds used to launch Jamestown Steel in 1946 was derived from the joint earnings of Mr. and Mrs. Saff and held by them together in a joint account. The business was started in a small, rented garage. The two men spent much of their time selling while Mrs. Saff stayed in the garage next to the telephone. The first load of steel beams the company received were too large to fit into the garage, so Mrs. Saff painted them in order to prevent them from rusting. She ran the office, did the banking, bookkeeping, kept all the books and ledgers, talked to creditors, made out the payroll and other checks, paid the bills, filled out government forms, handled collections and did the tax accounting. She also acted as a secretary. In addition to this work in the family business, Mrs. Saff also worked for a period of time in a doctor's office without pay for three hours per week in order to compensate the doctor for the shots he gave to aid her in becoming pregnant. When the Saffs were unsuccessful in having their own children, they adopted two children. The first adopted child contracted polio and in order for Mrs. Saff to give him the constant care required, she was obliged to bring the company's book work home at night where, her husband concedes, she questioned him endlessly about all transactions in order to keep the business records accurate. Another enterprise called Jamestown Plastics was later launched by the Saffs. Mr. Saff testified that his wife performed full-time duty for this enterprise while also continuing her work for Jamestown Steel. Both parties agreed that Mrs. Saff also handled all of the personal family finances. In brief, it seems an inescapable conclusion that Mrs. Saff was the financial member of this husband-wife team, in business and at home. Mr. Saff himself testified that his wife has been associated with him in business from 1946 to the present. To this very day Mrs. Saff continues to be the steel business bookkeeper. Although the husband testified that she did not begin work until six or eight months after the business had commenced, his testimony is contradicted by the fact that all the business records reflect that the entries from the very first day of business were in Mrs. Saff's handwriting....

Since appellant-wife seeks here an equitable remedy, it is important to note that in granting Mrs. Saff a divorce from her husband on the grounds of abandonment, the Trial Court found that Leonard Saff had left the marital residence in 1972 and has not returned. It further found that Clara Saff had made her husband welcome in their home and never interfered with him or subjected him to any public criticism or ridicule before the separation; and that her complaints, in private, about his drinking were prompted by reason of a warning given by a family doctor. It should also be noted that 12 years prior to this separation Mr. Saff had fathered a child by another woman and that Mrs. Saff forgave him for this and continued their marriage.

2. Gender and Divorce

═══ *Joan Williams, Do Wives Own Half? Winning*
═══ *for Wives After Wendt*
32 Conn. L. Rev. 249, 249-253, 258-261, 265-268 (1999)

Americans are confused about who owns what within the family. One common understanding is that married couples own property jointly — what we can call the joint property theory. Yet this co-exists with the sense of many homemakers that since they "don't work" they "have nothing of their own" — what we can call the "he who earns it, owns it" rule. The resulting confusion affects the economy of gratitude in on-going marriages. "My wife has long been on what we call the Winchester welfare system," a Mr. Winchester told me jocularly, explaining that she still was in graduate school after all these years (punctuated by long stints of caring for the family's children and disruptions as she followed him wherever his job required).

The most profound implications of our confusion occur upon divorce. Consider property division. Statutes typically provide that marital property shall be divided based on each spouse's contributions to the marriage; many states include homemaking either by statute or... by case law. Yet, in applying this law, an interesting pattern emerges. Typically, courts treat property as jointly owned when dealing with modest estates, where splitting the property 50/50 often forces the sale of the family home in order to allow the husband to "get his equity out." Yet, where the estate is large, courts... traditionally use the "he who earns it, owns it" rule, reflecting a sense that wives do not "need" half of, say, a billion dollars. Thus, in Wendt v. Wendt, [No. FA96-0149562-S, 1998 WL 161165 (Conn. Super. Ct. Mar. 31, 1998), aff'd, 757 A.2d 1225 (Conn. App. Ct. 2000)], the husband (CEO of a major subdivision of General Electric) offered his wife $8.3 million of an estate whose worth he estimated at $30 to $40 million, on the grounds that this amount would meet her reasonable needs. His offer reflected established practice... where (according to Professor Mary Moers Wenig) "the more [property] there is, the smaller [the] percentage the non-propertied spouse receives." Professor Wenig found in conversations with experienced divorce lawyers a "glass ceiling" for financial awards for women in Connecticut, reflecting a principle known as "enough is enough." [See Wenig, The Marital Property Law of Connecticut: Past, Present and Future, 1990 Wis. L. Rev. 807.] In this country we do not ordinarily condition ownership on whether owners "need" their property. Why treat wives differently?

This sense is even more explicit in the context of alimony. In [most states], wives' entitlement to alimony is explicitly based on need. "[The] marriage has not continued; why then should [the wife]...continue to share in her former husband's income...?" asks the influential commentator Ira Ellman....The answer of many courts is that she should not. This conclusion is probably inevitable as long as alimony is conceptualized as a sort of privatized welfare system at the expense of the husband. The husband in one executive divorce case was blunt: "The amount of money she'd end up with irrespective is more than enough for anything she would ever want to do. I have a lot of other goals and aspirations and if I were picking places to charitably expend my money, this would not be [one of them]...." Again, the themes of charity and ownership: the Winchester welfare system at work. [There is] cultural confusion about ownership within the family. Traditional approaches justify wives' claims on one of three theories: market replacement value, opportunity costs, or human capital theory. Each has important limitations. The market replacement approach uses the market's depressed valuation of domestic work as the measure of the wife's contributions: what is the value of twenty-seven years of love and devotion when child care workers are among the lowest paid workers in the economy? The opportunity costs approach works well for one narrow category of woman: the wife who trained for, and then gave up, a lucrative professional career. But it leaves out in the cold the 80% of women who do low-paid traditional "women's work," which includes virtually all working-class women as well as middle-class women who trained for traditionally female careers instead of higher-paid traditionally male ones. Because the opportunity costs approach helps only "social males," it will not help most women.

The problems with the human capital approach are subtler. In *Wendt*, for example, human capital theory led to extensive testimony by expert witness Myra Strober about what precisely Mrs. Wendt did during four different periods of the marriage. Strober then testified that "it was very difficult, under the 'human capital' theory, to come up with a dollar amount for the evaluation of the nonmonetary contributions by the plaintiff during those four stages of the marriage." She felt it was easier to come up with a percentage figure applying "equal efforts and equal sacrifice." While the "equal efforts and equal sacrifice" standard is apt, the linkage between the laborious process of enumerating specific contributions and the 50% figure seems obscure.

The *Wendt* court also objected to the human capital approach for another reason. Quoting Professor Ann Estin, it noted that "efforts to value and divide precisely the particular aspects of changes in human capital that have occurred during marriage have the effect of objectifying both husband and wife and their relationship." The human capital approach is "fraught with danger," said the court, because "the attempt to value investments in human capital pushes the institution of marriage from a relationship based on love and obligation toward one based on self-interest." The court quotes the New Jersey Supreme Court: "Marriage is not a business arrangement in which the parties keep track of debits and credits, their accounts to be settled upon divorce."

"A dominant theme of family law scholarship over the past decade has been the search for firm theoretical grounding for financial obligations that survive divorce," and much of this scholarship has imported commercial metaphors into family law. Thus, Cynthia Starnes has argued that ongoing financial obligations to wives should be viewed as the wind-up expenses incident to the dissolution of a partnership. [See Starnes, Divorce and the Displaced Home-maker: A Discourse on Playing with Dolls, Partnership Buyouts and Disasso-ciation Under No-Fault, 60 U. Chi. L. Rev. 67, 122 (1993).] Martha Ertman has argued that the wife should be viewed as a secured creditor, whose claims must be paid off when the marital enterprise is placed under receivership. [Ertman, Commercializing Marriage: A Proposal for Valuing Women?s Work Through Premarital Security Agreements, 77 Tex. L. Rev. 17, 23 (1998).] Ira Ellman analogizes the wife to a real estate investor: "Just as the building owner might have invested in making his building larger than in customizing it for a particular tenant, the wife might have invested in her own market earning capacity rather than in her marriage.... [Yet t]here is no reason why someone else should cover it if she invests in her husband...and he does poorly.... She invested in the wrong building." [Ellman, The Theory of Alimony, 77 Cal. L. Rev. 3, 54, 67 (1989).]

These commercial metaphors are jarring when applied to family life. They send the message that to justify entitlements for wives we must commodify the marital relationship in ways most people find distasteful.... Instead of using com-mercial metaphors, [we need to] revisit the intersection of property law and family life. Once we do, we find the persistence of a gender system historians have called domesticity. An analysis of domesticity provides a new rationale for post-divorce economic obligations that can defuse the kind of commodification anxiety expressed by the *Wendt* court, as well as provide important guidance in child custody cases where the mother is made to suffer because of her work outside the home....

[D]omesticity's peculiar organization of market work and family work first marginalizes mothers from market work, then limits their access to entitlements based on family work. The result is a system that is inconsistent with our commit-ment to gender equality, and leads to the widespread impoverishment of mothers and the children who depend on them.... [W]e need to deconstruct domesticity and develop in its place a new vision of morality in family life....

With the advent of domesticity, two different rationales emerged to justify men's ownership. The first recharacterized women's sewing, cooking, and child-rearing as not "work." "Thus, the responsibilities of wives in their households were generally described in the prescriptive literature less as purposeful activities . . . than as emanations of an abstract but shared Womanhood." . . . If women's work was not work, one did not have to explain why men still owned it.

The second argument that emerged to justify husbands' continued ownership of wives' household work was the view that awarding women entitlements threatened the integrity of family life, by introducing market motivations into the "Home Sweet Home." A staple of domesticity was the notion that women, and their domestic sphere, should not to be sullied by "that bank note world." The anxiety about commodification in the domestic sphere was a way of policing the boundary between home and work.

Both the erasure of household work and the theme of commodification anxiety present important challenges to lawyers representing wives in divorce cases. The erasure of household work creates the sense of mothers at home that the reason that they "own nothing" is that they "don't work."

Clearing up this confusion is the first step in competent representation of a divorcing wife. Attorneys representing wives in large "executive divorce" cases spend large amounts of time getting the wife to enumerate precisely what she did with her time and helping her to see that she did not in fact "do nothing:" she did important family work that freed her husband to devote his attention exclusively to his job. Said one executive's wife, "We've been married eight years and he's always traveled. . . . I've adjusted to it. . . . I've molded my life to his." Said another, "I don't bother him with petty domestic details. He doesn't have time for that. His work is very demanding. . . . He expects me to handle situations as they arise." A third was asked what she thought would have happened if she had objected to her husband's constant travel. She responded without hesitation, "He probably wouldn't be the chairman of the board today." The more successful the husband, sociologists have found, the less likely he is to share domestic work. Reversing the erasure of wife's family work is an important first step in making the wife a confident witness who can testify as to content and the value of her own work.

The erasure of household work also affects judges' attitudes towards alimony, as when one judge opposed alimony on the grounds that he did not believe in keeping women in "a perpetual state of secured indolence." Such "indolence," of course, typically involves full-time child care as well as cooking, laundry, decorating, entertaining, and other tasks that in market contexts are often highly paid and defined as work performed by caterers, decorators, etc. In 1999, one executive husband told his wife he had increased her life insurance. When she asked why, he said he had been thinking about how much he would have to pay people to take care of the house and the children if she were to die, and he realized he was underinsured. Wives' attorneys need to bring the same point home to judges.

An attorney representing the wife in a divorce case also needs to spend considerable time and energy addressing the argument that any decision that awards economic entitlements to the wife sullies the intimacy of family life — for any competent attorney representing the husband will try to use commodification anxiety to ridicule claims that twenty-seven years of love and devotion should have a price.

The key point to be pressed home by the wife's attorney is that awarding family property to the husband does not avoid commodifying it: the issue is not whether the property will be owned, but who will own it. Someone has to own family property: refusing to award it to the wife simply means that it will be a commodity solely owned by the husband.

Nor will awarding sole ownership to the husband avoid strategic behavior within the family. Take the classic "dumping" case in which a rich husband decides to divorce the wife of his youth in order to marry a younger "trophy wife." . . . Wives' attorneys need to point out that, by the time the husband asks for a divorce, he already has commodified the marriage. He now takes a strategic view, and sees the marriage chiefly in terms of how expensive it will be for him to get out of it. The husband already has commodified the marriage; the only issue is whether the court will allow the wife to do so, too, in order to protect her rights.

Again, the issue is not whether the family wage will be owned, but who will own it. In addition, the issue is not whether negotiations will take place, but whether those negotiations will be so one-sided that they will involve overreaching by one of the parties. The effect of decisions that use commodification anxiety to justify awarding family assets to husbands is not to avoid strategic behavior but to strengthen the hand of the husband in on-going marital (and divorce) negotiations. . . .

The joint property theory begins from the principle that ideal workers who are parents are supported by a flow of family work from the primary caregiver of their children. If the ideal worker's performance depends on a flow of family work from his wife, then "his" wage is the product of two adults: his market work, and her family work. If an asset is produced by two family members, it makes no sense to award ownership to only one of them. We should abandon the "he who earns it, owns it" rule as an outdated expression of coverture, and give the wife half the accumulated family wealth based on her family work, without which that wealth would not have been created.

This is true whether or not the children are in child care. In the vast majority of families, the primary caregiver provides much of the child care even when the children are cared for by relatives, a nanny, or a day care center. Recent studies show that mothers spend three times as much time as fathers interacting with children; studies from the late 1980s reported that at that time the average father spent from twelve to twenty-four minutes a day in solo child care. Even when mothers' caregiving consists in part of finding child care and training and supervising child care workers, this, too, is work: managerial work. Studies show that women still do roughly 80% of the management work, even in families where men contribute substantially to the actual caretaking. We do not refuse to pay managers because their employees "really do all the work"; the same principle should apply to mothers.

The joint property theory has implications both for property division and for alimony. In the context of property division, it explains why wives should jointly own the family wealth, eliminating the unexplained jump in human capital theory between joint ownership and an enumeration of the specific contributions of the wife. It also provides the basis for arguing that the household of the custodial parent, often composed of three people, should have a greater share of family wealth than the household of the noncustodial parent, composed of only one. Certainly, in this context, a 50/50 split should be the floor, not the ceiling. In assessing how to split the family assets of a middle class family, the court should take into consideration how such families use their assets: to buy housing that offers a secure home environment and access to good schools, and to send children to college. Children should not lose these entitlements simply because their parents divorce and fathers prefer to found a new family rather than support the old one. In dividing family property, courts should begin from the principle that parents have the duty to share their wealth with their children. They should award more than 50% of family assets if that is necessary to ensure that the life chances of the family's children, to the extent possible, are unaffected by divorce.

In the context of very large estates consisting of more assets than are required to preserve the expectations of the family's children to decent housing and a good education, the joint property theory mandates a 50/50 split.

In most divorces, the key issue is not property division but human capital. This is true because no rule concerning property division makes much difference in most divorces: in our cash flow society, most families have accumulated few assets. Therefore, the key issue is income sharing: who owns the family wage after divorce. The joint property theory offers a new rationale for income sharing that begins from the observation that — after as well as before the divorce — the father can perform as an ideal worker only because the mother's family work allows him to do so. In an economy where ideal workers need to be supported by a flow of family work, a divorced father can continue to perform as an ideal worker only because his ex-wife continues to support his ability to be one by continuing as the primary caregiver of his children. Evidence of this is that divorced fathers with custody often cannot perform as ideal workers because they lack the flow of family work that supports fathers without custody. The joint property theory mandates not a 50/50 split but an equalization of the standard of living in the post-divorce two households.

Because the joint property theory mandates post-divorce sharing on the basis of its analysis of dependence in the modern family, it avoids the language of partnership and other commercial metaphors. . . .

The joint property theory also is quite different from the established theory that wives deserve half because of their contributions, particularly when lawyers focus on wives' direct contributions to husbands' businesses (as when a wife helps decorate the company offices). The joint property theory shifts the focus away from market work onto family work. The point is not that the wife helped the husband in business development, but that the husband could not have performed as an ideal worker without the marginalization of his wife.

If the joint property regime were put into effect, the next question is when it should end. I have proposed that joint property in wages should equalize the standard of living of the two post-divorce households for the period of the children's dependence, followed by a period of years designed to allow the wife to regain her ability to recover her earning potential (if she is young enough) or save for her future (if she is not). This additional period should be set at one additional year of income sharing for each two years of the marriage.... [T]his formula is designed to give the father an incentive to support his former wife's return to nonmarginalized market work: the more she earns, the less income he needs to provide her. The formula also gives the mother herself the incentive to develop a career. Because income sharing does not last for life, mothers who are young enough to do so will have to prepare themselves for a time when income sharing has ended.

≡ *Riehl v. Riehl*
≡ 595 N.W.2d 10 (N.D. 1999)

Opinion by Justice MARING.

Deborah Riehl appeals from a district court judgment dated June 8, 1998, which granted the parties a divorce, divided their marital property, placed the parties' minor children in Deborah's custody, and ordered Andrew to pay rehabilitative spousal and child support. Deborah challenges the award of spousal support. We hold the trial court's decision to award rehabilitative spousal support for only the period of time commensurate with the recipient's period of rehabilitation is clearly erroneous. We reverse and remand the judgment of the district court.

I

At the time of trial, Deborah was age 43 and Andrew was age 45. They had been married for 24 years and had four children. Only the two youngest children were minors at the time of trial. Early in the marriage, Andrew worked as a farm laborer and construction worker. He then attended night school at Bismarck State College (BSC) and after completing a welding program became a boilermaker working both in state and out. Since 1987 Andrew has worked as a boilermaker with Minnkota Power Company in Center, North Dakota. At the time of trial, Andrew was earning $51,352 annually. He is provided with life, disability, health and dental insurance, deferred compensation savings, a medical flex program, and a pension.

Deborah's role during the marriage was primarily that of a homemaker. Over the years, she worked in positions of temporary employment, such as newspaper delivery, janitorial work, telemarketing, teacher's aide, and hotel maid. When the oldest two children entered school, Deborah was able to attend the University of Mary to work toward an elementary education degree. After one year of college, she again became pregnant and, after their fourth child was born, she became a full time homemaker. In the twelve months from the time the parties separated and the trial was Deborah pursued her education and employment options. She worked with the North Dakota Job Service and a private vocational counselor and underwent testing of her aptitudes, interests, and academic proficiency. She also attended adult education classes through the spring and summer of 1997 to prepare for her return to college. At the time of trial, Deborah had almost completed a program at BSC that exposed displaced homemakers to a variety of career options.

The exploratory phase of her rehabilitation efforts directed her to the field of nursing. As a result, Deborah attended BSC in the fall of 1998 to complete basic science related courses which will allow her to enter a full-time college program to earn a bachelor degree in nursing. Deborah will begin the first two years of her nursing education by completing an LPN program through BSC. The program's cost of approximately $7,000 will be funded by a scholarship for which she qualified as a displaced homemaker. Upon completion of the LPN program, she will begin a bachelor of science in nursing (BSN) program at the University of Mary, which requires two to two and a half years to complete depending on course sequencing. The program's approximate cost will be between $18,800 and $23,500.

Deborah commenced this divorce action on February 28, 1997. Shortly before trial, the parties stipulated to the equal division of marital property, allocation of debts, and custody of the minor children to Deborah. The trial court adopted the parties' agreement. Because the parties could agree to neither the amount and duration of spousal support, nor the amount of child support, these issues were presented to the court in a trial held on March 31, 1998. The trial court established child support for the two minor children at $949 per month, required Andrew to provide the children's health insurance and pay the first $210 annually of the children's uncovered medical, dental, optical, or orthodontic expenses, and pay $150 per month toward the children's tuition at a private, parochial school. Deborah requested spousal support in the amount of $1,000 a month for three years, reduced thereafter to $800 a month for six years and then $600 a month for the following six years. At that point, Andrew would be of retirement age and the support would cease. The trial court set spousal support at $800 per month for five years. Deborah appeals that award.

II...

Trial courts in our state must consider the *Ruff-Fischer* guidelines [derived from Ruff v. Ruff, 52 N.W.2d 107 (1952) and Fischer v. Fischer, 139 N.W.2d 845 (N.D. 1966)] in making a determination of spousal support, both as to amount and duration. The factors include:

> the respective ages of the parties, their earning ability, the duration of the marriage and conduct of the parties during the marriage, their station in life, the circumstances and necessities of each, their health and physical condition, their financial circumstances as shown by the property owned at the time, its value at the time, its income-producing capacity, if any, whether accumulated before or after the marriage, and such other matters as may be material.

Although a trial court need not make specific findings as to each factor, we must be able to discern a rationale for its determination.

To be awarded spousal support, the trial court must find the spouse to be "disadvantaged."... A "disadvantaged" spouse is one who has "foregone opportunities or lost advantages as a consequence of the marriage and who has contributed during the marriage to the supporting spouse's increased earning capacity." Van Klootwyk v. Van Klootwyk, 563 N.W.2d 377 (N.D. 1997). Here, the trial court found Deborah to be disadvantaged by the divorce because she "devoted her time and effort throughout the marriage of the parties to maintaining a marital residence and providing child care... [and her] responsibilities have caused her to forego any opportunity for career development, resulting in her present earning capacity at less than one-fourth [of Andrew's]." Without giving a basis for the period of spousal support, the court awarded Deborah $800 per month for five years.

Spousal support is aimed at balancing the burdens and disadvantages created by the divorce. We recognize permanent and rehabilitative spousal support as two distinct remedies. Permanent support is appropriate when the economically disadvantaged spouse cannot be equitably rehabilitated to make up for the opportunities and development she lost during the course of the marriage....

Rehabilitative spousal support, on the other hand, is appropriate when it is possible to restore an economically disadvantaged spouse to independent economic status,... or to equalize the burden of divorce by increasing the disadvantaged spouse's earning capacity.... There are two approaches to awarding rehabilitative spousal support.... One is the "minimalist doctrine" which has as its objective rehabilitating the recipient for minimal self-sufficiency.... We have rejected this doctrine in favor of the more "equitable" approach to determining rehabilitative spousal support, which attempts to provide education, training, or experience that will enable the recipient to achieve "adequate" or "appropriate" self-support while improving her employment skills.... There is no ready formula to determine what amounts to "adequate" or "appropriate" rehabilitative support. In making that determination, however, a trial court should consider the duration of the marriage, the parties' earning capacities, the value of the marital property and other Ruff-Fischer factors.... We have also said in a long-term marriage it is important to consider "continuing a standard of living... [or] balancing the burdens created by the separation when it is impossible to maintain two households at the predivorce standard of living."...

Andrew initially argues the award of spousal support was equitable because Deborah received half of the marital property. Typically, the trial court should consider the marital property division when setting the amount of spousal support.... Here, however, the parties stipulated to an equal division of the marital property. Each party received half the sale proceeds of their home and farmland, Deborah received half of Andrew's pension and 401(k), and the parties had no debt. Any income from these assets will presumably be the same for each party. Andrew's argument ignores the fact that the property division does not adjust the disparate earning capacities of the parties. Under these circumstances, the parties' property division had little bearing on the award of spousal support.

Andrew also argues the award of spousal support was equitable because five years of spousal support adequately rehabilitates Deborah. At the end of five years, he argues, Deborah will be educated, self-supporting and able to "meet her needs." The flaw in his argument is that it endorses the "minimalist doctrine," an approach we have clearly rejected.... "Equitable" rehabilitative support goes further than minimal self-sufficiency; it aims to mitigate marital disadvantage caused by the impact at divorce of an economic role assumed during marriage.

Deborah's BSN program will cost between $18,800 and $23,500, or approximately $315 to $390 per month over the five year period she will be receiving spousal support. After paying for her education, Deborah's rehabilitative spousal support will effectively range from $410 to $485 per month. At the end of five years, assuming all goes as planned, Deborah will have just completed her education and entered the work force as an entry-level registered nurse. During these five years, Deborah will have no other income other than interest income earned on her one-half of the marital assets. She will not be accumulating retirement or pension benefits. She will also have custody of the two younger children during the first three years and custody of the youngest through the fourth year. Meanwhile, Andrew will be earning a salary of at least $52,000 and substantial vested benefits. When Deborah enters the work force at the entry-level she will be 48 years old and earn approximately $27,000, roughly half of Andrew's salary. After deferring meaningful work and education for 24 years to raise her family and support her husband's career, Deborah will be just starting the pursuit of her own career.

As we have said, rehabilitative spousal support aims to make up for the opportunities and development a disadvantaged spouse lost while assuming her economic role in the marriage.... While we have not endorsed the "equalization of income between divorcing spouses,"... we conclude the period of spousal support in this case does not adequately address the burdens of the divorce. Under these facts we are convinced a mistake was made when the trial court awarded spousal support to a homemaker of 24 years for a period commensurate with the length of re-education or rehabilitation at which time the disadvantaged spouse will only be able to earn half of what the payor spouse earns.

III

Deborah argues the trial court's failure to consider permanent spousal support was clearly erroneous. As discussed, permanent spousal support is generally appropriate when the disadvantaged spouse cannot be equitably rehabilitated to make up for the opportunities she lost in the course of the marriage.... Even when the disadvantaged spouse is capable of rehabilitation we have recognized permanent spousal support may be appropriate to equitably share the overall reduction in the parties' separate standard of living....

Because this case involves a long-term marriage and the respective earning capacities and standards of living of the parties will be greatly disparate even after

Deborah receives her RN degree, the trial court should consider whether permanent spousal support would also be equitable to offset the permanent economic disadvantage suffered by Deborah as a consequence of the time she has spent as a homemaker.

IV

The judgment is reversed and remanded to the trial court for consideration of a longer period of spousal support, factoring in Deborah's job-entry process, the parties disparate earning capabilities and standards of living, and Andrew's ability to pay.

[The dissenting opinion by Justice Sandstrom is omitted.]

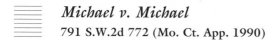

Michael v. Michael
791 S.W.2d 772 (Mo. Ct. App. 1990)

James A. PUDLOWSKI, Presiding Judge.

This is an appeal from a judgment and decree of dissolution which awarded respondent the majority of marital property and awarded appellant $500.00 in attorney's fees and no maintenance.

The evidence adduced at trial established that appellant and respondent were married in August 1972 and separated in April 1987. There were no children born of this marriage. Both appellant and respondent are well educated. Appellant holds a baccalaureate degree in political science and a master's degree in journalism. Respondent holds a baccalaureate degree in journalism and a master's degree in public administration.

In 1972, on the day following the parties' marriage, the couple moved to Little Rock, Arkansas where respondent was going to work for Southwestern Bell Corporation. While living in Little Rock, appellant was employed as a reporter for a local newspaper.

In June 1974, respondent received a promotion and was transferred back to St. Louis. In St. Louis, appellant worked for APC Skills Company and then for Maritz, Inc. In 1978, appellant was fired from Maritz, Inc. Upon appellant being fired, the couple agreed that appellant would not seek outside employment but instead would devote time to writing fiction. In that same year respondent received another transfer and the couple moved to Oklahoma City.

While living in Oklahoma, appellant continued to pursue a writing career, however, later abandoned this endeavor without ever having written a chapter in a book or a scene in a play. After giving up the attempt at writing, appellant worked briefly in a food store and spent 8-9 months working free-lance public relations. When appellant was not employed outside of the home, the couple agreed that appellant would be responsible for the general upkeep of the house and also for the preparation of the evening meal. Appellant spent several hours a day preparing the couple's dinner. Respondent claimed that appellant's other domestic chores were very lax. For two years while the couple was living in

Oklahoma appellant drove respondent to and from work. However, for the rest of the mornings, appellant slept until 10 or 11:00 a.m.

In 1984 respondent was again transferred to St. Louis. After moving to St. Louis, appellant continued to cook the couple's dinner. He also periodically took the respondent to work but did not seek outside employment.

Throughout the marriage, the couple's lifestyle improved and they had a significant amount of disposable income. They were able to purchase homes whenever respondent accepted a job transfer and the couple took many trips including visits to Europe. In addition, respondent generously and gratuitously provided her mother annually with support funds in the sum of $5,000.

At the time of trial, respondent had been working for Southwestern Bell for more than 15 years and was earning over $70,000 per year. Respondent's additional benefits from Southwestern Bell included vested pension benefits through the Southwestern Bell Corporation Management Pension Plan equal to $1,169.58 monthly payable at age sixty-five (65), as of March 1, 1988. Appellant's statement of income and expenses provides that he receives no income from employment, however he receives $75 per month in interest, and his share of the gross income on the previous year's Federal Income Tax Return was $1200.

It is with some interest that we note the gender roles of the parties in this marriage are reversed from the more traditional roles of husband and wife. In the present case the wife is the party who earned the lion's share of the income by working outside of the home during the marriage. The appellant is the party who remained at home throughout the majority of the marriage and did not work outside of the home for several years. However, certainly the sex of the parties should have no bearing on the division of marital property or on the allowance or prohibition of maintenance.

The trial court allocated $51,347 or 75.5% of the parties' marital property to respondent and $14,128 or 21.5% to appellant. The court granted appellant no maintenance but allowed appellant $500 for attorney's fees.

Appellant raises three points on his appeal. Appellant claims that the trial court abused its discretion by its distribution of the parties' marital property, abused its discretion by awarding appellant no maintenance, and abused its discretion by awarding appellant only $500 in attorney's fees....

Mo. Rev. Stat. §452.330 (1988) directs the trial court to divide the marital property in a just manner, after considering all relevant factors including the five factors set out in the statute, as follows:

(1) The economic circumstances of each spouse at the time the division of property is to become effective, including the desirability of awarding the family home or the right to live therein for any reasonable periods to the spouse having custody of any children.

(2) The contribution of each spouse to the acquisition of the marital property, including the contribution of a spouse as a homemaker;

(3) The value of the non-marital property set apart to each spouse;

(4) The conduct of the parties during the marriage; and

(5) Custodial arrangements for minor children.

There are two guiding principles inherent in §452.330: "[F]irst property division should reflect the concept of marriage as a shared enterprise similar to a partnership; and, second property division should be utilized as a means of providing future support for an economically dependent spouse." Krauskopf, A Theory for "Just" Division of Marital Property in Missouri, 41 Mo. L. Rev. 165 (1976).

When applying these guiding principles inherent in §452.330 to the present case we find that the trial court abused its discretion in its division of marital property. We first look at the economic circumstances of each spouse at the time the division of property is to become effective. Throughout the course of the marriage, appellant has become economically dependent on the respondent. At the time of the dissolution of marriage, appellant was unemployed, had not been employed in his chosen field of journalism for fifteen years, and had not been employed full-time since 1978. Conversely, at the time of dissolution of marriage, respondent had elevated herself within the Southwestern Bell organization to a position directing press relations and was earning in excess of $70,000 per year. Additionally, respondent was the recipient of extensive employment benefits including vested pension benefits which equalled $1,169.68 monthly (at age 65) as of March 1, 1988, and a savings plan which at the time of trial had a total vested account balance of $9,968.85.

With regard to the second statutory factor, the contribution of each spouse to the acquisition of marital property, including the contribution of a spouse as homemaker, the trial court found that the respondent, for the greater part of the marriage, had been the sole financial support of the parties and the funds used to acquire the marital property had been earned almost solely by her. Also, the court found that the appellant made no substantial contribution to the marriage as a homemaker because he showed a marked disinclination to undertake the normal domestic duties of a homemaker, engaging only in those duties, such as cooking the evening meal, which he found fulfilling, stimulating and interesting.

Although appellant did not work outside of the home for the majority of the years of the marriage, he did have outside employment for nearly one-third of the marriage. For two additional years appellant drove respondent to work and picked her up from work in the evening. While the appellant's performance of traditional domestic chores was often times lax, he did prepare dinner for himself and respondent throughout the duration of the marriage. We are not finding that appellant's contributions entitled him to an equal division of the marital property, however, we do hold that the trial court's division of property is against the weight of the evidence and therefore an abuse of discretion.

In his second point appellant claims that the trial court erred and abused its discretion in awarding no maintenance to appellant. Appellant argues that although he is educated and possesses a degree in journalism and public administration, the fact that he is 40 years old and has not held employment in either of these fields for the past fifteen (15) years will have a negative effect on his ability to find employment in order to support himself. Appellant does not claim that he is completely unable to support himself. However, due to the extended period of time that appellant has been out of the work force in his field, he requires a period of rehabilitative maintenance during which time he can obtain the necessary education and retraining to allow him to gain satisfactory employment in the field of journalism. Appellant argues that he would require an additional two and one half or three years of education to take course work that would enable him to be self-supporting as a journalist.

We have said that maintenance is awarded when one spouse has detrimentally relied on the other spouse to provide the monetary support during the marriage. If the relying spouse's withdrawal from the marketplace so injures his/her marketable skills that he/she is unable to provide for his/her reasonable needs maintenance may be awarded.... "Rehabilitative maintenance" should be awarded for a term reasonably sufficient to receive job training.... Rehabilitative maintenance is appropriate where there is substantial evidence that the party seeking maintenance will or should become self-supporting....

We have reviewed the record before us and we find that the trial court did err and abuse its discretion in finding that the appellant failed to show that his ten year absence from the journalism field has injured his ability to secure employment therein at this time and earn a sum sufficient to meet his reasonable needs and that appellant wholly failed to establish his entitlement to maintenance under Mo. Rev. Stat. § 452.335 (1986).

Section 452.335 sets out the factors which the court shall consider in ordering maintenance. The second stated factor the court is to consider is the time necessary to acquire sufficient education or training to enable the party seeking maintenance to find appropriate employment.

At trial appellant testified that he intended to enroll for a semester at the University of Texas in a program on Latin American Studies in order to enable him to re-enter journalism as a reporter in Latin America. He indicated that he wrote to several of the major newspapers in Florida and received a response from the Miami Herald which indicated that the appellant's plans for further education would be attractive credentials for a newspaper like the Miami Herald. Appellant further testified that because his most recent articles are fifteen years old, he needs to develop some fresh stories that have been written in the recent past to show editors that he is still able to write and report.

Appellant's need to acquire fresh skills in order to re-enter the field of journalism is reasonable. Journalism is a competitive field. Every year newly graduated students enter the job market with fine skills. If appellant is to be able to compete with these other graduates, it can certainly be expected that additional education would be beneficial. Appellant's plan to return to school in order to increase his marketability as a journalist would ensure that he become self-sufficient. Our disposition of the issues of marital property and maintenance is consistent with the generally accepted principals... that marriage is a shared enterprise and that maintenance should be utilized as a means of providing support for an economically dependent spouse until said spouse is self-reliant...

This matter is remanded for further proceedings consistent with this opinion.

Judge Williams H. CRANDALL, Jr., dissenting....

If we accept the concept of marriage as a shared enterprise similar to a partnership, husband had a negative impact on that partnership. Husband did not sacrifice his career for wife, rather he was a hindrance to her progress. On the issue of maintenance, husband has simply shown that he is unwilling, rather than unable, to support himself through appropriate employment.

For the foregoing reasons I would affirm the decree of dissolution.

Notes

1. The Economic Consequences of Divorce. About half of first marriages end in divorce. Studies have consistently shown that women and children are worse off economically after divorce than men, although the extent of the measured disparity varies by study. One of the most comprehensive studies of married parents who separated in the late 1980s or early 1990s showed that economic well-being, as assessed by income relative to needs, declined for mothers by 36 percent ((10 percent) whereas the financial status of fathers improved by 28 percent ((20 percent). Suzanne M. Bianchi et al., The Gender Gap in the Economic Well-Being of Nonresident Fathers and Custodial Mothers, 36 Demography 195, 197 (May 1999). The average income in husbands' households was about $2,200 per month, compared with $1,600 in wives' households. The difference in per capita income was about $750 per month. The study concluded that nonresident fathers' income was about three times their needs level, on average, in the year after separation, while their former wives and children had income about 1.5 times their household need level. The average level of well-being for mothers and children, in the year after separation, was about 56 percent that of fathers. Wives' well-being exceeded that of their former spouses in about 20 percent of cases, but in 45 percent of cases, the father's financial well-being was more than twice that of the mother's. Id. at 198.

Studies based on more recent data indicate that women's increased labor force participation has reduced their economic vulnerability following a marital breakdown. See Matthew McKeever & Nicholas H. Wolfinger, Shifting Fortunes in a Changing Economy, in Fragile Families and the Marriage Agenda 127 (2005). Divorced women's median per capita income grew by 48 percent from 1980 to 2001 (the increase for married women is 34 percent). Id. at 139. One study based on the National Survey of Families and Households concluded that women who remain single after divorce now have, on average, only a 14 percent drop in median per capital income, and remarried or cohabiting women only a three percent decrease. See Matthew McKeever & Nicholas H. Wolfinger, Reexamining the Economic Costs of Marital Disruption for Women, 82 (1) Soc. Science Q. 202, 207 (March 2001). Contrary to older data, women emerging from longer marriages do not appear to do worse than those emerging from shorter marriages. Id. at 214.

Women are also less dependent on others for economic support than in the past. In 1980, about one-third of a sample from the 1980-2001 Current Population Survey March Demographic Supplement reported receiving child support or spousal maintenance; this figure had declined to 19 percent by 2001. Id. at 149. From 1993 to 2001, participation of custodial parents in public assistance programs fell from 40.7 percent to 28.4 percent. U.S. Dep't of Commerce, U.S.

Census Bureau, Custodial Mothers and Father and Their Child Support: 2001 (Oct. 2003), at 1.

2. The Goals of Divorce Law. What goals should the law be attempting to achieve through its divorce law? Lasting marriages? See Lynn Wardle, No-Fault Divorce and the Divorce Conundrum, 1991 BYU L. Rev. 79 (2001). Equality and/or autonomy for women? See Alicia Brokars Kelly, Rehabilitating Partnership Marriage as A Theory of Wealth Distribution at Divorce: In Recognition of a Shared Life, 19 Wis. Women's L.J. 141 (2004); Susan Moller Okin, Justice, Gender, and the Family (1989); Martha M. Ertman, Marriage as a Trade: Bridging the Private/Public Distinction, 36 Harv. C.R.-C.L. L. Rev. 79 (2001). Basic Fairness? See Ira Ellman, Why Making Family Law Is Hard, 35 Ariz. St. L.J. 699 (2003). Other goals? See Carolyn J. Frantz & Hanoch Dagan, Properties of Marriage, 104 Colum. L. Rev. 75 (2004) (favoring "egalitarian liberal community" as the goal of marriage law).

What would be the implications of each of these different goals, for the appropriate standards for property distribution and spousal support at divorce?

3. Equality and Property Distribution at Divorce. At one time, property was distributed at divorce in accordance with simple property law principles. In common law property states, as illustrated in the *Saff* case, whoever held title to a piece of property left the marriage with that property. The inequities of this approach are illustrated in the case. Community property states worked differently, since their laws were based on a theory of marital partnership and deemed the earnings of each of the marriage partners to be the property of both.

Equitable distribution reform swept the nation in the 1970s and 1980s, leading to statutes that attempted to inject greater fairness into divorce settlements. The principles these reforms attempted to enact, however, were not entirely consistent. Implicit in most equitable distribution statutes was the notion of a marriage partnership, similar to the partnership principle inherent in community property states. This notion assumed the fairness of the division of responsibility during the marriage, and thus the fairness of an equal division of the property at divorce. A competing principle — contribution — invites investigation of how the assets were acquired, and thus tends to favor the spouse whose earnings or efforts produced non-consumed property, although this principle is often modified by giving a wife's (or in *Michael*, the husband's) "homemaker contribution" some recognition. Still another principle — need — emphasizes the spouses' comparative abilities to support themselves after the marriage, and thus favors the more financially dependent spouse.

The strictest equal division rules are found in the community property states of California, Louisiana and New Mexico. See Cal. Fam. Code §2550 (West 2004); La. Rev. Stat. Ann. §9:2801(4)(b) (West Supp. 2004); Ruggles v. Ruggles, 860 P.2d 182, 188 (N.M. 1993). The law in many jurisdictions, including North Dakota where *Michael* was decided, recites the range of factors to consider in dividing property "equitably," including principles of contribution and need. See also Uniform Marriage and Divorce Act 307, 9A U.L.A. (1973) (combining concepts of partnership, contribution, and need).

The presumption applied in some states that marital property should be split 50-50 is, in part, an effort to eliminate some of the gender bias that may be incorporated into notions of what is equitable, especially when the husband made all the money. An equal split certainly represents an improvement for women over the *Saff* approach. The ex-spouse of the GE executive in the *Wendt* case (discussed in the Joan Williams reading) argued that a 50-50 presumption was required both under the state's equitable distribution law and under the state's Equal Rights Amendment. The court rejected the argument, stating that the plaintiff had provided no evidence of either disparate impact, or discriminatory intent. See Wendt v. Wendt, 757 A.2d 1225, 1244 (Conn. App. Ct. 2000).

How should the concept of contribution be applied? Many feminist proposals have sought to capture the value of women's housework and caretaking labor during the marriage, either in the way of property is divided, or in spousal support awards (see note 4, infra, and broader discussion of valuing housework at pp. 665-678). See, e.g., Joan Williams, Unbending Gender, supra, at 124-127 (advocating that wives receive a greater portion of husbands' income after divorce as a way of recognizing women's greater contributions to housework and child care during the marriage).

Martha Fineman argues in favor of a need principle, and then suggests that a 50-50 split is not enough where the earning capacities of the parties are imbalanced. Fineman criticizes formal equality as inadequate to deal with this situation, offering in its place a "substantive" conception of equality based on need. See Martha Albertson Fineman, Societal Factors Affecting the Creation of Legal Rules for Distribution of Property at Divorce, in At the Boundaries of Law: Feminism and Legal Theory 265, 272-273, 278 (Martha Albertson Fineman & Nancy Sweet Thomadsen eds., 1991). Is the need principle compatible with formal equality principles? Mrs. Wendt is not the kind of plaintiff Fineman probably had in mind. Should Mrs. Wendt have obtained an equal split of the marital property? How about Mr. Michael?

What approach makes sense if the purpose of the law is to strengthen marriage as an institution? What if gender equality is the highest goal? Basic fairness between the parties?

4. Equality and Spousal Support. While the rules of equitable distribution address property existing at the time of the divorce, as to which the jurisdiction gives the spouses some claim as a result of the marriage, spousal support (or alimony) concerns continuing claims beyond the marriage, usually on the income of one spouse that has not yet been earned at the time the marriage ended. Traditionally, alimony represented compensation to a dependent wife for her husband's breach of marital duties. With the advent of no-fault divorce, a need rationale supplanted the fault-based rationale, but this rationale begs the question why one spouse should be the insurer of the financial security of the other, when modern marriage law (in most jurisdictions) entitles either spouse to leave the marriage when he or she wants to. Need supplies a standard, but not an explanation for liability that might define the contours of that standard. The analytical confusion is reflected in current law, which (1) disfavors spousal support, preferring to accomplish a "clean break" for the parties through property distribution alone, if possible; (2) if spousal support is ordered, favors term or "rehabilitative" awards designed to get a dependent spouse back on her (or his) feet so that a "clean break" can be accomplished some time in the future (as in *Michael* and *Riehl*); (3) when need comes into play, applies open-ended need and standard-of-living criteria that produce wildly disparate results; and (4) in about half of American jurisdictions, allows or requires consideration of marital fault.

An alternative approach is to treat spousal support as a reflection of non-economic investments in the marital partnership on behalf of the family, necessary to encourage such investments, which would otherwise be irrational or inefficient. In other words, spousal support corrects what would otherwise be distorting financial incentives, assisting parties in making decisions that will be to the benefit of the joint undertaking of marriage. See Ira Ellman, The Theory of Alimony, 77 Cal. L. Rev. 1, 12 (1989). What are the implications of this rationale? The Principles of Family Dissolution adopted by the American Law Institute (ALI), which were written by Ira Ellman as Chief Reporter, provide for "compensatory spousal payments" to close the gap between the parties' earning capacities attributable to lost opportunities by one spouse as a result of investments in the marriage. See American Law Institute, Principles of the Law of Family Dissolution, Chapter 4 (2002).

One potential pitfall of a compensation-based approach is that it would require parties seeking spousal support to prove lost opportunities, which would often be difficult, especially in the case of an individual who did not have career expectations. The ALI Principles obviate this difficulty by using the length of the marriage as a proxy for "lost opportunity," which is then used as the multiplier in the income-gap-closing formula. The rate of increase is also enhanced when the dependent spouse has assumed primary caretaking responsibilities for the couple's offspring. Id. at §5.05. For a more explicitly restitution-based approach to spousal support, see June Carbone, Economics, Feminism and the Reinvention of Alimony: A Reply to Ira Ellman, 43 Vand. L. Rev. 1463 (1990).

The compensation-based approach has been criticized on the grounds that it reflects and reinforces the role specialization in marriage, that is neither efficient, nor fair to women. See Jana Singer, Alimony and Efficiency: The Gendered Costs and Benefits of the Economic Justification for Alimony, 82 Geo. L.J. 2423 (1994). For further exploration of the "efficiency" considerations that are sometimes omitted from consideration of rationales for spousal support and other family law rules, see Ann Laquer Estin, Can Families Be Efficient? A Feminist Appraisal, 4 Mich. J. Gender & L. 1 (1996).

Spouses seeking spousal support after a short marriage are typically treated even less generously than spouses after a long-term marriage. See, e.g., Roginsky v. Blake-Roginsky, 740 A.2d 125 (Md. Ct. App. 1999), cert. denied, 747 A.2d 645 (Md. 2000) (affirming denial of indefinite alimony, even though husband was a nuclear physicist and wife had only worked occasionally as a housekeeper and restaurant server, because marriage had only lasted five years, and wife was only 28 years old at the time of trial). The ALI approach also provides less compensation for shorter marriages, on the theory that there has been less sacrifice on behalf of the marital partnership. Are there circumstances where this would be unjust?

Was *Riehl* correctly decided? What is a fair standard when one spouse leaves the marriage with a much lower earning capacity than the other?

5. Educational Degree as Marital Property? A problem for the law has been how to treat the educational degree or professional license, particularly one earned during the marriage with the economic support of the spouse. What happens when the marriage ends before the non-degree spouse has obtained any of the benefits of that degree? Typically, such families have no appreciable property to distribute, and the supporting spouse is not entitled to support since she has demonstrated self-sufficiency. See Uniform Marriage and Divorce Act 308 (award of "maintenance" requires showing that obligee is "unable to support himself or herself through appropriate employment"). Should the husband be able to "walk away" from the marriage with his degree and owe his ex-wife nothing for her investment in his degree or for her disappointed expectations?

Courts have developed a number of different approaches to deal with this issue. New York courts have gone the furthest, treating a professional degree as marital property, subject to division at divorce at an amount representing the enhanced standard of living allowed by the degree that is attributable to the wife's contribution and efforts toward attainment of the degree. O'Brien v. O'Brien, 489 N.E.2d 712 (N.Y. 1985); see also Grunfeld v. Grunfeld, 731 N.E.2d 142 (N.Y. 2000) (to avoid double-counting, value of spouse's law license could not be distributed as a marital asset without some adjustment in maintenance award that had been based on spouse's future income stream as a lawyer). Most courts have rejected the property theory on the grounds that a degree has none of the transferability attributes of property and that its value depends entirely on the efforts of the degree holder. See, e.g., In re Marriage of Graham, 574 P.2d 75, 77 (Colo. 1978):

> An educational degree, such as an M.B.A., is simply not encompassed even by the broad views of the concepts of "property." It does not have an exchange value or any objective transferable value on an open market. It is personal to the holder. It terminates on death of the holder and is not inheritable. It cannot be assigned, sold, transferred, conveyed, or pledged. An advanced degree is a cumulative product of many years of previous education, combined with diligence and hard work. It may not be acquired by the mere expenditure of money. It is simply an intellectual achievement that may potentially assist in the future acquisition of property.

While the *Graham* case rejected any relief at divorce to the wife, who had contributed 70 percent of the financial support of the family, including educational expenses, during the period her husband was earning his degree, a subsequent case in Colorado extended alimony to the wife on the grounds that her ability to support herself through *appropriate employment* (see the UMDA 308 standard, supra) had to be interpreted in light of the parties' expectations that they would enjoy a higher standard of living after the husband attained his degree. In re Marriage of Alar, 747 P.2d 676 (Colo. 1987).

A growing number of courts have applied theories of contract and equity or other strained theories of spousal support to arrive at awards that often combine features of maintenance and lump-sum property division. See, e.g., Mace v. Mace, 818 So. 2d 1130 (Miss. 2002) (holding that while the husband's advanced degree was not marital property, the wife did have an equitable interest in the husband's medical practice); see also Meyer v. Meyer, 620 N.W.2d 382 (Wis. 2000) (appropriate for trial court to consider pre-marital contributions of one spouse to the medical education of the other in determining spousal maintenance). Is there a problem in appearing to reduce marriage to a balance sheet in which the contributions of each spouse are quantified? See Martinez v. Martinez, 818 P.2d 538, 540-541 (Utah 1991) (disapproving award of "equitable restitution" in professional degree context).

Does the theory for recognizing one spouse's contribution toward the license or degree of the other stop with professional degrees? More common than a spouse who earns a degree during the marriage is the spouse who enhances his or her earning capacity through work experience. Why should the spouse who has invested most heavily in his earning capacity walk away with the benefits of that increase, especially if the other spouse has sacrificed career opportunities in order to invest herself more heavily in home and family? Indeed why not, say some feminist critics of the current system, discussed above. But it is this slippery slope, of course, that has discouraged greater judicial recognition of professional degrees and licenses.

In almost every jurisdiction, earning capacity is not treated as property that is subject to division at divorce. See, e.g., May v. May, 589 S.E.2d 536 (W. Va. 2003). The one state, New York, that explicitly treats degrees and licenses as marital property has also recognized increased earning capacity in some other contexts. See, e.g., Martin v. Martin, 614 N.Y.S.2d 775 (App. Div. 1994) (value of husband's law license earned during marriage was enhanced after twelve-year Congressional career, and thus subject to equitable division as marital property); Elkus v. Elkus, 572 N.Y.S.2d 901 (App. Div. 1991) (husband's involvement in opera singer Frederica von Stade's career, as well as his caring for the children, contributed to career's increase in value, and that increase is marital property). For a review of the New York cases, see Sebastian Weiss, Note, Preventing Inequities in Divorce and Education: The Equitable Distribution of a Career Absent an Advanced Degree or License, 9 Cardozo Women's L.J. 133 (2002).

6. Equality and Child Support. Although the problem of child support is not limited to the divorce context, the difficulties in obtaining realistic child support awards and in enforcing child support orders can exacerbate the economic vulnerability of divorced custodial mothers. In 2001, only 63 percent of the 11.3 million mothers living with children under the age of 21 with the children's fathers had a court decree or agreement for child support. See U.S. Department of Commerce, Bureau of the Census, Child Support for Custodial Mothers and Fathers: 2001, Current Population Reports, Series P-60, No. 225, Table A, at 2 (October 2003). The percentage varied greatly with the custodial mother's race, age, income and marital status: for women with incomes below the poverty level, who had never married, who had less than a high school diploma, or who were black or Hispanic, the child support award rates were below 50 percent; for non-Hispanic white or divorced women, the rates were above two-thirds. Id.

The Child Support Enforcement Amendments of 1984 and the Family Support Act of 1988 and subsequent federal laws condition state receipt of considerable federal monies on state adoption of various measures to improve the quantity, quality, and enforceability of child support orders. Among other things, states must have statewide support guidelines, which act as rebuttable presumptions in all support proceedings. 42 U.S.C. § 667 (2006). States must also implement automatic wage withholding, unless "good cause" exists or the parties have agreed otherwise. 42 U.S.C. §§ 666(a)(8), 666(b)(3) (2006). Other measures provide for the interception of tax refunds (§ 666(a)(3)), garnishment of federal wages (§ 666(a)(1)(4)), and parent locater services (§ 663). The Federal Child Support Recovery Act of 1992 makes it a federal crime to cross state lines to avoid payment of child support. 18 U.S.C. § 228 (2006). A number of federal Courts of Appeal have upheld the Act from the constitutional challenge that it exceeded Congress' authority. See, e.g., U.S. v. Crawford, 115 F.3d 1397 (8th Cir. 1997), cert. denied, 522 U.S. 934 (1997) (child support payments or debts resulting from non-payment are things in, or substantially related to, interstate commerce).

Aggressive state laws have also been added to help improve child support collections. For example, at least 15 states provide for the suspension, revocation, or denial of occupational or business licenses of child support delinquents. See, e.g., Iowa Code § 252J.1 et seq. (West 2004). Fifteen states provide for the suspension or revocation of a delinquent child support obligor's driver's license. See, e.g., N.C. Gen. Stat. § 50-13.12 (West 2004). Other statutes provide for the suspension of permanent license plates or motor vehicle registrations, hunting or fishing licenses, and even marriage licenses. See, e.g., Tex. Fam. Code Ann. § 232.001 et seq. (Vernon Supp. 2002). Such statutes are cited and discussed on the website of the National Conference of State Legislatures at http://www.ncsl.org/programs/cyf/tools.htm.

Also important are the standards for determining the amount of child support liability. Most state guidelines use a formula based either on the percentage of the obligor's income ("percentage formula") or on the parents' relative incomes ("income shares"). Under both formulas, the level of support sought to be captured in a child support order is the marginal expenditure that parent would be expected to pay for the child if the child still lived with the parent. Policymakers aim for this amount so that, theoretically at least, the obligor is paying only the child's expenses and not those of the parent with whom the child primarily lives.

The perceived fairness of child support awards under existing child support formulas depends on the goals one thinks should be achieved and, among other things, the relative earning powers of the two parents. When the parties' incomes are substantially different and the party with whom the child primarily lives is the lower-earning parent (as is typical), the standard of living enjoyed by the child in his or her primary residence is generally lower, sometimes far lower, than the standard of living enjoyed by the nonresidential parent. When the parties' incomes are equivalent, the standards of living in the two households are likely to be equivalent. When the primary residential parent earns more, the child support order may require substantial sacrifice from the obligor parent in order to subsidize a household that is living quite comfortably. States rely increasingly on formulas to achieve consistency and fairness, but it is difficult for formulas to be sensitive to such variations, or to respond to various changes in circumstances that may occur, such as remarriage of one or both parties and the birth of subsequent children by either parent. The issue of retroactivity is also a problem. Retroactive changes in child support awards could create instability, and reduce the incentive of obligors to stay current; for this reason, federal law prohibits the retroactive modification of child support arrearages. What this means, though, is that if the obligor loses his job or becomes disabled and does not immediately move to obtain a judicial modification of his obligation, he will continue to accrue obligations that he will not be able to pay.

These issues can have gender implications of the substantive equality sort — that is, formally neutral rules may produce effects that, given social realities, tend to leave women (and their children) worse off than men. These unequal effects explain the impulse behind income-equalization proposals made by Joan Williams and others. See Marsha Garrison, An Evaluation of Two Models of Parental Obligation, 86 Cal. L. Rev. 41 (1998) (advocating "Community Model" of income-sharing, over a more limited "Autonomy Model" which is based on preventing poverty and enforcing contract-type obligations).

Is equal sharing of post-divorce income justified under formal equality principles, or is it an application of substantive equality principles? Does it matter? What substantive goals should alimony or spousal support accomplish?

The American Law Institute's Principles of Family Dissolution respond to these difficulties with an "enhanced marginal expenditure model" that is more sensitive to income disparities between the parties. The model has two parts, a preliminary assessment and a reduction mechanism. It begins with a base amount, such as one produced under the conventional income shares or percentage formula approaches. It then adds a supplement, representing the diminution in income in the residential household likely to be attributable to the circumstances of being a residential parent. This supplement diminishes as actual income in the residential household approaches the obligor's income. When the parents have equal incomes of sufficient amount, the support payment is limited to the base amount alone. American Law Institute, Principles of the Law of Family Dissolution, § 3.04, at 438-440 (2002). The approach recognizes that the conflict between the nonresidential parent's interest in contributing no more to the child's upbringing than if the family had remained intact, and the child's interest in maintaining the previous standard of living, may never be reconciled. See Ira Mark Ellman, Fudging Failure: The Economic Analysis Used to Construct Child Support Guidelines, 2004 U. Chi. Legal F. 167 (2004). For another effort to achieve complex goals yet consistent results, see Marianne Takas, Improving Child Support Guidelines: Can Simple Formulas Address Complex Families, 26 Fam. L.Q. 171 (1992) (advocating the Melson formula, in effect in Delaware and a couple of other states, which follows a three-step approach producing greater income equalization than either income-shares or percentage-formula methods).

Special problems arise with very high-income and very low-income parents. The problems of poor fathers, who are capable of providing little or no support for their children regardless of how strict the child support system is, are explored in Irwin Garfinkel et al., Fathers Under Fire: The Revolution in Child Support Enforcement (1999); Ann Laquer Estin, Moving Beyond the Child Support Revolution, 26 L. & Soc. Inquiry 505, 517-521 (2001). The self-support reserve included in some proposals, including the American Law Institute Principles described above, attempt to address this set of cases.

As for high-income parents, most jurisdictions set a limit above which child support formulas are not applied. See, e.g., Minn. Stat. Ann. §518.551, subd. 5(b) (West Supp. 2004) (capping income considered for determining child support at $5,000/month). The theory is that over and above a certain income, the amount the formula would yield is simply too far beyond the economic needs of the child and beyond what would have been spent on the child if he or she lived with the obligor. Paying child support based on an extraordinarily high income, it is assumed, will simply be diverted to the support of the residential parent, to whom the obligor's financial obligations, if any, have already been defined. However, can't children of high-income parents ordinarily expect extravagance? Should a child whose expectation for a large inheritance is likely to be frustrated by the obligor's greater loyalty to new children in a subsequent family be entitled to receive, instead, a super-enhanced child support award?

Subsequent families pose especially difficult analytical challenges. Should child support be refigured with each new family obligation, so that the children of an obligor are being supported at an equal level? Or is it to be assumed, when an obligor undertakes new family responsibilities, that the obligor enters those responsibilities with resources reduced by whatever prior obligations have been incurred?

Perhaps the most difficult problem of all is how to handle adjustments in child support in the case of equally shared residential responsibility. Should an obligor's responsibilities be reduced in accordance with the amount of visitation time he or she exercises? It is generally recognized that even when custody is split, the lower earning parent should receive some support to reflect his or her lower capacity to support the child. But how much? And how much visitation, if any, should trigger a set-off? Depending on the answer to such questions, the child support system may create an undesirable incentive to seek primary custody or shared physical custody for the wrong reasons.

Putting Theory into Practice

2-14. State X is considering a proposal providing that a noncustodial parent who does not exercise his or her visitation rights would be required to compensate the custodial parent for the additional economic and psychic costs of the failure to do so. Is this a good proposal? Is it good for women?

2-15. The rule in virtually every state is that child support and visitation are independent rights and obligations: failure to pay child support is not a defense to denial of visitation, and frustration of visitation is not a defense to failure to pay child support. Is this a good rule?

2. Women's "Special Role" as Child-Rearers

Rena K. Uviller, Father's Rights and Feminism: The Maternal Presumption Revisited
1 Harv. Women's L.J. 107, 108-109, 112-114 (1978)

Recognition that women have any claim whatever to custody of their children following divorce was, interestingly, a twentieth century feminist victory. Until this century, fathers had a virtually absolute right to the custody of all children of the marriage. This paternal presumption, essentially irrebuttable, stemmed from English common law which viewed children as the servants of their fathers; the father was entitled to the child's services in return for which the father owed the duty of maintenance and support. "It is a well settled doctrine of common law," wrote the New Hampshire Supreme Court in 1860, "that the father is entitled to the custody of his minor children... that he is bound for their maintenance and nurture, and he has the corresponding right to their obedience and services." [State v. Richardson, 40 N.H. 272, 273 (1860).]...

By the late nineteenth century, nascent theories about the importance of the mother-infant bond occasionally made an inroad on the father's rights. The so-called "tender years doctrine" for the first time gave mothers a slim chance against a fit father. Yet that inroad was tentative indeed, in light of the father's consequent relief from child support duties upon award of children to the mother and because the "tender years" preference was valid only during the child's infancy. Thus, in transferring to the father a four and one-half year old child who had been in its mother's care from birth, a New York court in 1842 observed that the child no longer had need of the mother's "expertise" and noted the father's "natural right" to custody as well as his superior financial resources for the child's education and training. [People ex rel. Barry v. Mercein, 3 Hill 399 (N.Y. 1842).]

Only when the duty was imposed upon fathers to support children not in their custody did the maternal preference, at least for very young children, acquire some force. A father's absolute financial responsibility irrespective of custody was not widely imposed until the 1920's which witnessed the burgeoning influence of psychological theory, particularly Freudian theory, concerning child development and maternal attachment.[16] These factors,

---

16. Anna Freud expressed the child's need for the mother in terms which seem almost obsessive today: "So long as the mother is constant in her role as provider for the child, without undue interruptions through physical absence or undue emotional preoccupation with other persons or matters of interest in her life, there is every chance that the child's attachment to her will remain constant now and that there will be a secure basis for the growth and development of further, similar attachments...." Freud, Some Remarks on Infant Observations, 8 The Psychoanalytic Study of the Child 17 (1953).

together with the entrenched assumptions about woman's role in society, resulted in a marked shift in custodial preference to the mother. In a few states the maternal preference was codified. But for the most part it was judicially imposed....

The maternal presumption in divorce proceedings is anathema to most feminists. The legal presumption that children belong with their mothers absent maternal unfitness reinforces the enduring stereotype of women as instinctive child rearers, inherently unsuited for worldly pursuits. Abjured by those who also reject sex-role assignments in family life, the maternal presumption presupposes a societal order of stay-at-home mothers with fathers as sole economic providers....

Yet giving fathers an equal footing with mothers in custody disputes is a feminist goal that bears reconsideration. Discarding the maternal preference before women as a class have made any substantial headway in the non-domestic world may just be a case of the proverbial cart and horse; under the guise of sex-neutrality, women who want their children may be at a distinct disadvantage in custody disputes due to their inferior earning capacity and an enduring social bias against working mothers.

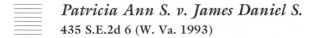

Patricia Ann S. v. James Daniel S.
435 S.E.2d 6 (W. Va. 1993)

Per Curiam...

The parties were married [in] 1967.... Three children were born of the marriage, [who are now ages 14, 11, and 7]. The [mother] was a kindergarten school teacher but left her employment upon the birth of their first child. The [father] is an architect....

The primary issue in this case is the [mother]'s contention that she should be awarded custody of the parties' children.... [S]he cites three points of error committed by the circuit court in granting custody to the [father]: (1) the circuit court erred in failing to find that the [mother] was the primary caretaker; (2) the circuit court erred in utilizing psychological experts prior to the circuit court's determination as to who was entitled to the status of primary caretaker; and, (3) the circuit court erred in granting custody of the children to the [father].

The parties agree that the guidelines for establishing custody are clearly set forth in Garska v. McCoy, [278 S.E.2d 357] (1981). We defined primary caretaker... in *Garska,* as "that natural or adoptive parent who, until the initiation of divorce proceedings, has been primarily responsible for the caring and nurturing of the child." The law presumes that it is in the best interests of young children to be placed in the custody of the primary caretaker....

It is the circuit court's responsibility to determine which parent is the primary caretaker.... In *Garska,* we listed the factors to be considered by the circuit court in making this determination. However,... we pointed out, "[i]f the trial court is unable to establish that one parent has clearly taken primary responsibility for the caring and nurturing duties of a child neither party shall have the benefit of the primary caretaker presumption."

It is clear from the evidence that the parties shared the primary caretaker duties as discussed in *Garska*. While the evidence presented established the fact that the [mother] was the homemaker and the [father] was the wage earner, this Court has recognized that the length of time a parent has alone with a child is not determinative of whether the primary caretaker presumption should attach. . . . The [mother] was at home for the children when they would return from school while the [father] would work throughout the day. However, the [father] was also a substantial participant in the child care duties once he came home from work.

With respect to the child care duties, the [mother] testified that she was a night person, meaning she would stay up late at night and sleep later in the morning. As a result, both parties testified that the [father] would be responsible for getting the boys ready for school and fixing their breakfast. Both parties further testified that the [mother] would primarily plan and prepare the evening meals on the weekdays, but on the weekends the [father] would often prepare the evening meals. The parties also testified that they shared the responsibility for getting the children ready for bed each night.

In terms of school and social activities for the children, the evidence is indicative of the fact that both parties were active in their childrens' social lives. . . . [The mother] participated in PTO (Parent Teacher Organization) meetings and school activities. [A teacher] also testified that the [father] was involved with the childrens' school activities; and, the [father] testified that he was instrumental in helping the children with their homework in the evenings.

Furthermore, each parent organized and participated in social activities with the children. [The mother] would organize birthday parties for the children, and she would often host pool parties for the children and their friends at the parties' home. On the other hand, the [father] would arrange and participate in camping, hiking, and biking trips as well as other sporting events with the children. . . .

Finally, the evidence suggests that the parties shared in the responsibility of disciplining the children. The [father] admitted that he used a belt to whip the boys, but he stated that he used his hand to whip Jennifer. The [mother], however, stated that she no longer uses the belt to whip the children. Rather, the [mother] testified that she had attended parenting classes, and as a result, she employed a new method of discipline such as taking away the childrens' privileges and grounding them for their wrongdoings. . . .

[W]e agree . . . that neither party is entitled to the status of primary caretaker because the child care duties were shared equally by the parties. Therefore, the issue of custody properly rests on the best interests of the child. . . .

With this in mind, we turn to the [mother's] second argument. The [mother] contends that the circuit court erred in utilizing psychological expert witnesses prior to the circuit court's determination as to who was entitled to the status of primary caretaker. . . .

[The father] called psychologist, Mari Sullivan Walker, to testify before the family law master. Ms. Walker met with the [father] and the three children for approximately ninety minutes on September 22, 1990. Ms. Walker was of the opinion that the children perceive their father as the more nurturing person rather than their mother. Ms. Walker testified that all three children told her that the [mother] "beat" them.... Based upon the childrens' responses [to her question how they thought life would be with their father versus life with their mother,] Ms. Walker opined that the children have more faith in their father as opposed to their mother whom they were afraid of and with whom they were angry....

Dr. Charles Yeargan, a child psychologist,... was initially hired by the [mother], but later the parties agreed to use him as a neutral expert to give his opinion regarding the welfare of the children. In October of 1990, Dr. Yeargan interviewed the entire S. family.

In response to questions asked by [father]'s counsel, Dr. Yeargan stated that he didn't ask the children where and with whom they wanted to live; however, based upon the childrens' comments, it was Dr. Yeargan's opinion that the children feel emotionally safer with the [father and that they would prefer to live with him].

Dr. Yeargan stated that the children perceive the [father] as emotional and supportive, and the [mother] is perceived as angry. Further, Dr. Yeargan testified that Jennifer told him that if her brothers live with the [father], then that is where she wants to live. Dr. Yeargan also opined that both parents have behavioral traits that they need to work out in order for them to be able to better cope with and relate to their children.

Ultimately, it was Dr. Yeargan's opinion that it was in the best interests of the two boys, Jason and Justin, that they live with the [father]. With respect to Jennifer, Dr. Yeargan admitted he did not have a lot to go on, but he recommended that Jennifer live with her mother because of "the interests of the two different parties," "the activity levels," "the socialization issues" and "the involvements."

Dr. Carl McGraw... interviewed all three children, the [father], and the [father]'s mother, because she had been helping care for the children. Dr. McGraw stressed the importance of keeping the children together in order to keep the family unit intact. Dr. McGraw noted that he had difficulty understanding Dr. Yeargan's reasoning for splitting the children between each parent. Dr. McGraw testified that the children told him they felt their mother was mean. Dr. McGraw stated he didn't ask the children who they wanted to live with, but he testified that they were adamant about wanting to live with their father. It was Dr. McGraw's opinion that the children would "have a better chance" if all three of them were to live with the [father], considering the rapport [he] has with [them]....

The circuit court determined that the best interests of the children would be served by awarding custody to the [father]. There was an abundance of evidence presented in this case, which included the testimony of the parties, neighbors, teachers, family members, friends, and psychologists.

[In addition to the psychological testimony,] Jessica Halstead Sharp, a neighbor and friend of the parties, testified that she found the [father] to be loving and nurturing towards the children unlike the [mother] who, in Mrs. Sharp's opinion, had a problem dealing with the children. Mrs. Sharp also stated that, on more than one occasion, she overheard the [mother] calling the children vulgar names.

In addition, Nancy Jo S. and Reese and Ron Webb, Jr. testified that the children interact well with the [father]. However, they all felt the [mother] acted hostile with the children, and thus, the children did not respond well to her. All three witnesses further confirmed Mrs. Sharp's testimony that the [mother] called the children vulgar names, and they added, she used bad language around the children as well. . . .

Jason, the eldest son at fourteen years of age, is old enough to make a decision as to which parent he wants to live with, and the record clearly supports the circuit court's finding that Jason should live with his father. . . . Justin, on the other hand, is eleven years of age and not quite capable of making such a decision, but the evidence supports the circuit court's finding that he should live with his father. In addition, the [mother] admits that there is a lot of hostility between the boys and her, and because of this anger she might not be able to manage them. . . .

However, with respect to Jennifer, we do not believe that the record has been adequately developed. . . .

[W]e hold that the circuit court judge did not abuse his discretion by concluding that the best interests of the two boys would be served by awarding custody to the [father]. With respect to Jennifer, we remand the case to the circuit court for further development of the record in order to determine what is in her best interests. . . .

WORKMAN, CHIEF JUSTICE, dissenting.

The majority opinion marks a sharp departure from the primary caretaker rule which has been a viable and working concept in West Virginia for more than a decade. More disturbing, however, is the determination that it is in the best interests of children to place them in the custody of a parent who has abused both the wife and the children. In doing so, the majority implicitly places its stamp of approval on physical and emotional spousal abuse.

Deaths by domestic violence are increasing dramatically every year in West Virginia, and there is much discussion about the inefficacy of the judicial system in dealing with family violence. But until judicial officers on every level come to a better understanding of the phenomenon of family violence in its finer gradations, the response of the court system will continue to fall short. The majority demonstrates a tragic lack of understanding of the true nature of the dynamics that underlie family violence.

Erosion of Primary Caretaker Presumption

The primary caretaker rule as set forth in Garska v. McCoy, [278 S.E. 2d 357] (1981), has been an important part of domestic relations law . . . for more than twelve years. . . .

In setting the child custody law in domestic relations cases we are concerned with three practical considerations. First, we are concerned to prevent the issue of custody from being used in an abusive way as a coercive weapon to affect the level of support payments and the outcome of other issues in the underlying divorce proceeding. Where a custody fight emanates from this reprehensible motive the children inevitably become pawns to be sacrificed in what ultimately becomes a very cynical game. Second, in the average divorce proceeding intelligent determination of relative degrees of fitness requires a precision of measurement which is not possible given the tools available to judges. . . . Third, there is an urgent need in contemporary divorce law for a legal structure upon which a divorcing couple may rely in reaching a settlement.

[278 S.E. 2d at 361-362.] After stating the rationale for implementing the primary caretaker rule, this Court [in *Garska*] ruled that: "in any custody dispute involving children of tender years it is incumbent upon the circuit court to determine as a threshold question which parent was the primary caretaker parent before the domestic strife giving rise to the proceeding began." [278 S.E.2d at 363.]

In the instant case, it was clearly an abuse of discretion for the family law master and the circuit court to deny primary caretaker status to the mother. It is unfathomable that a woman who gives up her career (in this case, that of being a kindergarten teacher) to stay home to raise three children does not qualify as the primary caretaker, when as a full-time stay-at-home mother she breast-fed all three children; was so concerned about unnecessary additives and excess sugar that she processed her own baby food; was responsible for the majority of meal planning and preparation; was primarily responsible for laundering the family's clothing and housecleaning; was a Girl Scout troop leader; was a regular volunteer at her children's school and an active member of the parent-teacher organization; was responsible for scheduling and taking the children to their medical appointments; and was primarily responsible for managing the children's social activities. For some unarticulated reason, both the family law master and the circuit court appear to have been bowled over by the fact that the father helped in the evenings and weekends. Not unlike many modern fathers, the [father] did participate in some of the household and childrearing responsibilities. The mother and father jointly oversaw the bedtime routine of the children. Upon the birth of the third child, the father, by agreement of the parties, awoke the two oldest children and prepared their breakfasts, because the baby (Jennifer) was up a lot at night. As Jennifer grew older and began sleeping all night, the parties continued this routine. Although the mother stayed up late, during those evening hours she cleaned up from dinner, prepared lunches for the children to take to school the next day, and did other household duties. The [father] planned recreational activities such as camping and hiking trips, primarily for the boys. Given the father's admitted ten to twelve-hour work days combined with frequent business trips which took him away from home, it is difficult to conceive how he could ever qualify as having equal caretaking responsibility. The family law master and circuit court's conclusions that neither individual qualified as the primary caretaker has the effect of somehow elevating the father's necessarily limited hours with the children, given his lengthy work days, to accord him the same caretaker status as the full-time stay-at-home mother. The majority in essence places a higher value on a father's time and contribution.

By upholding the circuit court's ruling, the majority begins an erosion of the primary caretaker rule, or at least sends a signal to domestic relations practitioners that it will be situationally ignored when expedient. . . . Sadly, . . . this case boils down to ... one expert versus another [which the primary caretaker presumption was intended to avoid.] We explained the dangers of relying on expert testimony in custody cases in David M. v. Margaret M., [385 S.E.2d 912, 919] (W. Va. 1989):

> Expert witnesses are, after all, very much like lawyers: They are paid to take a set of facts from which different inferences may be drawn and to characterize those facts so that a particular conclusion follows. There are indeed cases in which a mother or father may appear competent on the surface, only to be exposed after perfunctory inquiry as a child abuser. ... When both parents are good parents, the battle of the experts can result only in gibberish.

In this case, the testimony of three expert witnesses was admitted. Only one of the three, Dr. Charles Yeargan, was deemed by the court to be an independent expert. The [father] sought out Dr. Mari Walker, who has since been disciplined by the West Virginia Psychological Association for violation of the ethical principles of the American Psychological Association for her testimony in this case [that is, making a recommendation that the father receive temporary custody of the children on the basis of a single ninety-minute interview]. Later, the [father] sought out another expert, Dr. Carl McGraw, who concurred with the findings of Dr. Walker that custody should be placed with the father. Of primary interest to Dr. McGraw was his concern that the children not be split up among the parents. While this is certainly a laudable concern, it appears that this focus may have totally overshadowed Dr. McGraw's "objectivity" with regard to his ultimate recommendation. ...

The family law master and circuit court ... erred by permitting testimony on the issue of the relative fitness of the parties. Fitness, once it has properly been raised, does not involve a comparison of the parties, but instead requires a showing that the individual designated as the primary caretaker is unfit. ... Because there was no showing of unfitness on the part of the mother, who clearly qualified as the primary caretaker, the majority opinion does great disservice to the primary caretaker rule in addition to exacerbating the pain of this family. ...

Majority Okays Spousal Abuse

This father not only takes a belt to the three children[5] regularly, but he also has taken a belt to his wife. Phenomenally, the family law master did not permit the wife to testify in detail to the physical abuse she endured throughout the marriage, as he apparently concluded it had nothing to do with the children.

---

5. According to the mother's testimony, the father also regularly disciplined Jason (the eldest boy) by grabbing his shoulders and pushing him up against a wall or tree, on one occasion bruising his head. The father admitted overreacting and perhaps using excesssive force, but denied it happened on a regular basis. The mother admitted that she, at one time, also used corporal punishment on the children, but had taken parenting classes in 1989 and learned that there were better ways to handle discipline. She testified that she used time-outs and withdrawal of privileges following her completion of the parenting classes.

In fact, spousal abuse has a tremendous impact on children.

> Children learn several lessons in witnessing the abuse of one of their parents. First, they learn that such behavior appears to be approved by their most important role models and that the violence toward a loved one is acceptable. Children also fail to grasp the full range of negative consequences for the violent behavior and observe, instead, the short term reinforcements, namely compliance by the victim. Thus, they learn the use of coercive power and violence as a way to influence loved ones without being exposed to other more constructive alternatives.
>
> In addition to the effect of the destructive modeling, children who grow up in violent homes experience damaging psychological effects. There is substantial documentation that the spouse abuser's violence causes a variety of psychological problems for children. Children raised in a home in which spouse abuse occurs experience the same fear as do battered children. . . .
>
> Spouse abuse results not only in direct physical and psychological injuries to the children, but, of greatest long-term importance, it breeds a culture of violence in future generations. Up to 80 percent of men who abuse their wives witnessed or experienced abuse in their family of origin. Abused children are at great risk of becoming abusive parents. Thus, the ultimate question in assessing the relative fitness for custody of the abuser and victim is which parent is most likely to provide the children with a healthy, caring and *nonviolent* home.

L. Crites & D. Coker, What Therapists See That Judges May Miss, The Judges' Journal, 9, 11-12, (Spring 1988). . . .

There is yet another aspect of spousal abuse that judges and many others find difficult to understand. These relationships are characterized not only by physical abuse, but also by repeated humiliation and other psychological abuse that "'reaches the level of a campaign to reduce the partner's sense of self-worth and to maintain control'"[;] and "a pattern on the part of the abusive partner to control the victim's daily actions. . . ." Crites & Coker, supra, at 9.

It is clear from Mr. S.'s testimony that he ran this family with an iron hand, a significant trait in abusive relationships being the total power and control of one party. The evidence reflects that for some period of time Mrs. S. was not allowed to have a cent, not even grocery money. She was permitted to write a grocery list, and if her husband was ever-so-gracious, he would include her requests. Once she attempted to take $20 from his wallet and wound up in the emergency room after he wrestled with her over it. Mr. S. testified that he actually found the whole episode rather humorous, likening his wife clinging desperately to the $20 bill by hiding it in her mouth as resembling a lizard with lettuce sticking out of its mouth.

One of the complaints made about this mother is that she lacked the ability to manage the boys, ages twelve and ten at the time of the hearings, and surely the record is clear that it was difficult for her to manage these boys, especially Jason, the older of the two. In her petition for review, she pointed out that for several years, her husband had been "mentally, emotionally, and physically cruel" to her. Studies demonstrate that after ages five or six, children show strong indications of identifying with the aggressor and losing respect for the mother. See Crites & Coker, supra, at 11.

In her personal petition for review to the circuit court, she [the mother] stated:

My two boys in particular identify with their father. Unfortunately, their father has downgraded me for years in front of them and continues to do so. I would become angry in response. The children have seen their father hit me with a belt. My oldest son Jason has bit me and kicked me so hard to have left bruises on me. Jason repeats to me in arguments what his father tells him happens in court. Jason has attacked my mother and caused my father to get a lump on his head by slamming an attic door on his grandfather. Jason is the thirteen year old who has the added problems of puberty on top of this divorce. My second son Justin is ten years old and is having difficulty adjusting. Since he has been with his father, his grades have gone from "A's" and "B's" to some "C's," "D's," and one "F." My six year old daughter, Jennifer is a 4.0 student in first grade. She is also in the gifted program. She has done fine under my care alone this past year.

The evidence reflects that Mr. S. modelled for these children the behavior of demeaning, discrediting, and otherwise disempowering the mother. For example, the father devised a point system to reward good behavior and punish bad behavior. When the mother attempted to participate in the system as a method of encouraging good behavior and managing the children, the children were told that "mommy's points don't count" and "mommy is crazy." The mother testified that the children's response was that "you're not the boss, daddy's the boss. . . ." Furthermore, the father would tally the points and take the children to the toy store for the payoff, which the mother had no financial resources to do.

From Dr. Yeargan's report:

Mr. S. reported that he can't see himself trying to tell the boys to be kinder and gentler to their mother for fear that he'll lose credibility with them. He said, "I'm not too interested in finding a way to help the enemy camp look good or better . . . until all three kids are together and this is resolved. My primary objective is to have the three kids."

Mrs. S. testified that she attended counselling, both in an effort to save the marriage and in an effort to get help in working with the children, and that she read a number of books on parenting and divorce. She admitted that she used bad language (as did the whole family) and that the husband's constant demeaning of her in front of the children made her angry. She acknowledged she had made mistakes and was working to correct them.

Mr. S., however, presents himself as the perfect father as demonstrated by his testimony that his rapport with the children was "exemplary," and "that it would be very difficult to improve upon." He described himself as "nurturing," "kind," "loving," "caring," "understanding," and "patient."

But a look at Dr. Yeargan's report presents a very different picture of this man:

Some of the same parental behaviors that previously contributed to the children feeling torn between parents is continuing; those behaviors are (a) increasing the alienation between the children and their mother and (b) exacerbating the loneliness which the boys feel for their sister and vice versa. In this examiner's opinion the behaviors of Mr. [S.]. . . . are of primary importance in the creation of more alienation and loneliness in the children.

The same report details the control and manipulation of the children by Mr. S.:

> All three children report pain over being split but the two boys report it in a way that reflects their father's opinion. Jason, for example, reports the opinion that the children should not be separated and says that they shouldn't "... because we'll grow up to be total strangers." Justin reports that being "... sad over Jennifer" is his biggest concern. He then goes on to say, "That's really the only problem. Dad says to just tough it out and he's working on it. It's wrong to split up the children cause they'd not grow up together and they'd be total strangers." Two weeks after I talked with the boys Mr. [S.] ... reported to me virtually verbatim the same rationale for why the children should not be split. I infer that (a) the children would naturally express their discomfort in existential terms of the things that they are not now enjoying, (b) their expression of concern for future estrangement indicates how their father is contributing to, not allaying, their fears and (c) the boys, and possibly Jennifer, have been led by their father to hope that he will eventually get the children together under one roof....
>
> All three children report knowledge of complaints which their father has with their mother which should not be told to them. The obvious effect that this knowledge has is to (a) divide their allegiance deeper and (b) alienate them further from their mother. Jennifeer [sic], for example, mentions that her mother does not want to pay the phone bill. Jason reports of his mother, "She'll run up his (father's) credit cards, get new glasses, run up his medical bills, buy vitamins and stuff like that that she doesn't need." When asked how he knew about all of that he replied, "Dad tells us cause there's really nothing he has to hide from us." Justin reports that they "sometimes" still see parents fussing during the times when the parents are picking up or dropping off the children to one another. He goes on to report that his father tells them about various arguments which occur between him and their mother (arguments which occur on the phone, at the office, etc.).
>
> Mr. [S.]. ... arranged for the boys to see a counselor (Michael Sheridan) after the separation and reported to Mrs. [S.]. ... that it was because of their relationship to their mother. According to Mrs. [S.] ... she was excluded by Mr. [S.]. ... from any information or advice by that counselor. Mr. [S.]. ... reported to me that Mr. Sheridan had helped the boys to accept that some of the sanctions being imposed by their mother during visitations were a direct result of their behavior (trashing their mother's Christmas decorations, etc.). However, Mr. [S.] ... did not use that opinion of Mr. Sheridan to support the boys' mother in dealing with the destructive things the boys were doing; he declined to tell her anything about what transpired in Mr. Sheridan's office. Furthermore, in his discussion with me he missed the point that the boys should assume responsibility (i.e. feel some measure of reproach or make amends for misbehaving.) Instead, he assumed that the important lesson that the boys learned from Mr. Sheridan was that "... you can esteem yourselves for coping well with difficulty."

Mr. S. acknowledges that (although less frequently on five-year-old Jennifer), yes, he does use a belt on all three children, and according to unrefuted testimony he also has grabbed Jason by the shoulders and banged Jason's head against a tree. His own description of how he handles physical discipline shows best the kind of fear he uses to exert control over this family:

Normally, the punishment is a smack on the behind with a belt. And I tell them what will happen if they transgress or exceed certain limitations; and, when they, on occasion—not recently, but on occasion—test an adult's authority, which all children are want (sic) to do, I have no choice but to follow through consistently with what I told them would happen.

And when I do that, we discuss it, and I make sure they understand the nature of the discipline. We even negotiate sometimes about how many smacks they want. I will frequently ask them how many smacks that they think that the offense is worth, and frequently they will say four, and I had only planned, maybe, to give them one, maybe two at most, and we will discuss the issue.

Frequently, I will, at the last minute, decide that I can't even spank them anyway, after having gotten them ready to be spanked, decide that I—it's difficult to do, and will let the belt fall aside and smack the bed or the floor and say to them, I'm going to let you go this time, but don't do that again.

On the occasions when I do smack their behinds with a belt, I will always make sure, after I have done it in a controlled and unemotional way—never in anger—that they understand what the punishment was for and why I had to do it, and I will always check their little bottoms to make sure that there is not sufficient force to seriously damage them, say bruising or whatever.

With all of these circumstances, one may wonder why the children were taken from the mother. A close reading of the record reveals that the most damaging things that can be said about Mrs. S. are that 1) she uses bad language; 2) she is very angry; 3) the children told the psychologists that they wanted to live with their father; and 4) one of the psychologists concluded that they "feel safer with their father."

Anger

What judges and indeed many therapists usually fail to understand is the behavior manifestations battered women frequently demonstrate. For example, a battered woman

> may appear in court as unstable, nervous, inarticulate, or angry—a result of her ordeal. The batterer, on the other hand, may appear in command of himself, calm, well spoken, and so forth—and may appear in court as the more fit parent. This may operate to the disadvantage of the victim not only in the eyes of the judge, but also with counselors meeting with one or both of the parents and with psychologists hired to do a psychological evaluation.

Crites & Coker, supra, at 40. It has further been recognized that:

> many women do not present a tearful passive personality to the psychologist. . . . Anger and a new assertiveness are positive characteristics of the recovering abuse victim. She is angry at being abused, and angry at having been blamed by him and by unaware therapists for having caused it. And she is especially angry at his attempts to take the children away.

Crites & Coker, supra, at 41.

Psychologists unfamiliar with all the circumstances and with the unique dynamics of family abuse may make these mistakes:

> 1. They fail to see that the victim's anger is appropriate and normal. . . . 2. They look to the victim's behavior and personality problems to explain the abuse. . . . Such blaming of the victim tends to reinforce the abuser's position that . . . the victim is crazy. 3. They seem to identify with the seemingly sociable, "appropriate" male as a man who has been pushed beyond his limits by an "angry woman." 4. They fail to see beneath the sincere, positive image of the abuser, but look instead for the "typical" abuser personality. . . . 7. Finally, they criticize [the woman] for focusing her anger on her husband. . . .

Crites & Coker, supra, at 42.

It does not appear that any of the psychologists had any information on the domestic abuse and none dealt with the physical abuse; only Dr. Yeargan seems to have had any information on the psychological abuse and domination. If family law masters and judges are to make decisions on the lives of troubled families, they must become sufficiently knowledgeable about physical and emotional domination to enable them to recognize that these factors are just as invidious, and probably more pervasive, than physical abuse alone. And we must begin to see anger on the part of the victim as healthy.

Children's Preference

The children of David Koresh felt safe with him. While this dissent does not seek to compare Mr. S. with David Koresh, it implores judges to see that family relationships wherein one person has all the power (frequently not only through the purse-strings, but also as a result of both learned and socially-imposed help-lessness) are also abusive.

These children learned from their father that their mother did not have even sufficient authority to purchase a package of Oreo cookies for them, that it was okay to demean, disobey, and verbally abuse her, and that physical violence awaited those who did not do as he said. The mother reacted with anger, and the father by word, deed, and dollar delivered the message that mommy's crazy and mommy's contemptible.

Jason was twelve years old at the time of the hearings before the family law master and thirteen by the time of the divorce. Thus, he was only thirteen at the time he last expressed a preference on the record in this case (not fourteen, as the majority indicates). We have said that a child has a right to nominate his own guardian at age fourteen, and that his preference can be accorded deference even before fourteen, depending on his age and maturity. See *David M.*, 385 S.E.2d at 920. Consequently, even though the mother was the primary caretaker, the circuit court cannot be said to have abused its discretion in giving weight to Jason's preference and placing him in the custody of his father. In all likelihood, and by all the evidence, this young man has already demonstrated a propensity to act out anger with violence, and we can only hope we do not see him in court in another generation.

Justin was ten years old and Jennifer six years old at the time their preferences were expressed. Although it could be argued that a ten-year-old's preference could be given some weight, Jennifer at six was too young to express a meaningful preference. Furthermore, a reading of the record makes it quite clear that Jennifer was spirited off to see psychologists by her father and instructed rather specifically on the way by her father and older brother regarding what to say. She related to her mother after-the-fact that she told lies and even Dr. Yeargan discerned that she had been coached.

Justin and Jennifer should have been placed in the custody of their mother. The majority wreaks further havoc on this family (especially Jennifer) by a remand for further evidence. It appears that anxiety and manipulation will again be the order of the day for this little girl, and life's most basic uncertainties will resume as the family is figuratively killed with due process. . . .

Ronald K. Henry, *"Primary Caretaker": Is It a Ruse?*

17 Fam. Advoc. 53, 53-56 (Summer 1994)

"Primary caretaker" is a warm, fuzzy phrase with a superficial appeal. Like all legal terms, however, the substance is in the definition; every definition that has been put forward for this term has systematically counted and recounted the types of tasks mothers most often perform while systematically excluding the ways that fathers most often nurture their children. No effort has been made to hide this bias.

In fact, in some definitions, the very first credit on the list of factors to be considered goes to that parent, regardless of gender, "who has devoted significantly greater time and effort than the other to . . . breast-feeding." The duration of the credit extended to the parent who has performed such services is unlimited according to some definitions, despite the obvious fact that an historic role as breast-feeder has little relevance to the determination of custody of an adolescent who is contemplating the merits of rival street gangs. The more fundamental problem, of course, is the lack of any consideration for the father's efforts on behalf of the child and his involvement throughout the child's life. No one seriously disputes the role of father absence in street gang formation, teenage pregnancy, and other pathologies. Yet, the primary caretaker theory remains fixated on "mothering" and ignores "fathering."

The primary caretaker theory aggressively asserts that traditional "men's work" is irrelevant. The typical definition of the primary caretaker gives credit for shopping but not for earning the money that permits the shopping; for laundering the Little League uniform but not for developing the interest in baseball; for vacuuming the floors but not for cutting the grass; and for chauffeuring the children, but not for driving to work. . . .

Generally, the tasks that count in accumulating primary caretaker points do not involve great skill or invoke debates about hormonal determination. For example, points are usually given for planning and preparing meals. In our house, the 8-year-old loves canned spaghetti in ABC shapes; the 6-year-old hates the ABCs and loves the Ninja Turtles; and the 3-year-old can finger paint equally well with either. To establish a custody preference on the basis of opened-can counts is an affront to all parents and hardly squares with our understanding that many women entered the paid work force precisely because they were stupefied by the mindless tasks of daily child care.

Most unreasonable is the contempt for paid work that is apparent in the primary caretaker theory. Although time spent shopping counts, time spent doing work for pay does not. Often, grocery shopping, clothes shopping, and other shopping are counted separately. A single afternoon of shopping may be counted several times over, yet the paid work that makes the shopping possible is not counted at all. Which parent is really providing for the child's needs?

Going to work requires a parent's devotion and sacrifice. It is obscene to say that spending is nurturing while earning is mere, heartless cash waiting to be transferred under a child support order. I don't know any parent who is incapable of earning. Which is the better care giver?

In any childless, two-adult household, there is a division of the tasks necessary to simply carry on with life. Cooking, cleaning, and shopping are not counted as child care in a childless home any more than paid work, yard maintenance, and home repairs are so counted. The nature of these tasks does not change with the introduction of a child. Instead, all of the tasks—specifically *including* paid work—collectively support the child's environment.

The gender bias that is inherent in the primary caretaker theory is its insistence that the types of tasks most often performed by women—regardless of the presence of children—are more worthy than those most often performed by men. A child may increase the "task burden" in the household, but it does not cause one adult or one subset of tasks to suddenly become more valuable than the other: For every mother who reduces her hours doing paid work because of a "devotion to the child," there is a father who must increase his. . . .

Additionally, with an ever-increasing number of two-career couples, the primary caretaker is likely to be a day-care center. Should the day-care center be awarded custody? . . .

Even if it were possible to remove the gender bias from the selection of "primary care" factors, the theory still suffers from the fact the its "freeze frame" analysis of who-did-what during the marriage ignores the reality that children's needs change. The best breastfeeder may be a lousy soccer coach, math tutor, or spaghetti-can opener.

The historical division of labor during a marriage also says nothing about the abilities of the parents and their actual behavior before or after the marriage. Just as mom and dad had to fend for themselves before the marriage, so also will they be compelled to fend for themselves after the divorce. The "primary caretaker" father will have to get a job. The "wage slave" mother will have to cook more meals and wash her own laundry. Similarly, each will have to provide for the needs of the children during their periods of residence. We know this is necessary and we know that it happens even in cases of the minimalist "standard" visitation order.

The allocation of tasks that existed during the marriage necessarily must change upon divorce. The agreed specialization of labor during the joint enterprise of marriage cannot continue after divorce. Each former spouse will have to perform the full range of tasks, and the difficulties encountered by the former full-time homemaker who must now learn to earn a wage have been a central concern of feminists. The primary caretaker theory, with its imposition of single parent burdens upon the spouse least able to cope with the need for earning a living is thus tangibly damaging to the very class that its bias aims to aid. As growing number of leading feminists have come to understand:

> Shared parenting is not only fair to men and to children, it is the best option for women. After observing women's rights and responsibilities for more than a quarter-century of feminist activism, I conclude that shared parenting is great for women, giving time and opportunity for female parents to pursue education, training, jobs, careers, professions and leisure.
>
> There is nothing scientific, logical or rational to excluding the men, and forever holding the women and children, as if in swaddling clothes themselves, in eternal loving bondage. Most of us have acknowledged that women can do everything that men can do. It is now time to acknowledge that men can do everything women can do.

Karen DeCrow, former president of the National Organization for Women, as reported in the Syracuse News Times, Jan. 5, 1994. . . .

No one will argue that America suffers from an excess of good parenting. Why, then, do we focus on finding easier ways to place children in single parent custody? The focus, instead, should be on developing a structure that demilitarizes divorce, that gets past winner-loser dichotomies, and that encourages the maximum continued involvement of both parents.

Children are born with and need two parents. In all but the small number of cases that involve a pathological parent, courts should strive to strengthen the child's relationship with both. If distance or other factors prevent substantially equal relationships, preference should be given to the parent who shows the greater willingness and ability to cooperate and nurture the child's relationship with the other parent.

Notes

1. Maternal Preference Rules. Once custody evolved from a right of the father to the mother's preference, no language seemed too strong to express the many reasons by mothers were to be favored. See, e.g., Commonwealth v. Addicks, 5 Binn. 520 (Pa. 1813) ("considering [the children's] tender age, they stand in need of that kind of assistance, which can be afforded by none so well as a mother"); Hines v. Hines, 185 N.W. 91, 92 (Iowa 1921) ("other conditions being equal, the mother is God's own institution for the rearing and upbringing of the child. It puts a premium on child culture in the hands of an expert"); Krieger v. Krieger, 81 P.2d 1081, 1083 (Idaho 1938) (the maternal preference "needs no argument to support it because it arises out of the very nature and instincts of motherhood; nature has ordained it").

Mothers continue to have custody of their children the large majority of the time. In 2002, 84.5 percent of custodial parents were mothers, and 15.6 percent were fathers — figures largely unchanged since 1994. See U.S. Census Bureau, Current Population Reports, Custodial Mothers and Their Child Support 1, 2 Table A (October 2003).

Most explicit sex-based custody preferences have been eliminated from the law, courts having found them either unconstitutional, or incompatible with the best-interests-of-the-child test, or both. See, e.g., Pusey v. Pusey, 728 P.2d 117 (Utah 1986) (tender years doctrine both anachronistic and unconstitutional); Ex parte Devine, 398 So. 2d 686 (Ala. 1981) (unconstitutional); Bazemore v. Davis, 394 A.2d 1377 (D.C. Ct. App. 1978) (violates best interests principle). Tennessee applied a tender years presumption until 2000. See Tenn. Code Ann. § 36-6-101(d) (1996), replaced by Tenn. Code Ann. § 36-6-101(d) (Supp. 2000). A preference for the mother of a child born outside a marriage remains in a number of jurisdictions, and the Supreme Court recently upheld distinctions between mothers and fathers of children born out of wedlock. See Section 3, beginning p. 378, infra.

Few feminists today urge a maternal custody preference. But see Mary Ann Mason, Motherhood v. Equal Treatment, 29 J. Fam. L. 1, 24-26 (1990-1991) (favoring maternal preference); Mary Becker, Maternal Feelings: Myth, Taboo, and Child Custody, 1 S. Cal. Rev. L. & Women's Stud. 133, 203-224 (1992) (favoring maternal preference because it recognizes women's greater emotional commitment to their children and better protects women's physical, emotional, and economic interests). Other presumptions or preferences are urged, however, on the grounds that the broad discretion permitted by the open-ended best interests standard leaves room for too much gender bias. See notes 2-6, infra.

2. Preference for Same-Sex Parent. Should the law permit courts to give a preference in custody cases to the parent who is the same sex as the child? The social science evidence is mixed. See Bennett Leventhal et al., Divorce, Custody, and Visitation in Mid-Childhood, in The Scientific Basis of Child Custody Decisions 205, 218-219 (Robert M. Galatzer-Levy & Louis Kraus eds., 1999); K. Alison Clarke-Stewart & Craig Howard, Advantages of Father Custody and Contact for the Psychological Well-Being of School-Age Children, 17 J. App. Dev. Psychol. 239, 257, 264 (1996).

Even if data showed that children benefit from close contact with the parent of the same sex, would this support a rule favoring that parent to have primary custody? How likely is it that any such evidence would, itself, be based on gendered meanings of healthy "sex role identification"? From your own experience, would you expect that successful role modeling depends upon sharing a primary residence with the same-sex parent?

Alabama appears to allow a same-sex parent preference, by statute. See Ala. Code § 30-3-1 (West 2004) ("court may give custody... having regard to... the age and sex of the children"). Other states explicitly prohibit it. See, e.g., Ariz. Rev. Stat. Ann. § 25-403(E) (West 2004) (court "shall not prefer a parent as custodian because of that parent's sex"); Me. Rev. Stat. Ann. tit. 19-A, § 1653(4) (West 2004) ("court may not apply a preference for one parent over the other... because of the parent's gender or the child's age or gender"). In a few jurisdictions, courts have allowed a preference for a parent of the same sex during or right before adolescence on various role-modeling hypotheses. See, e.g., In re Marriage of Arcaute, 632 N.E.2d 1082, 1085 (Ill. App. Ct. 1994) (approving trial court's reasoning that "other things being equal, pre-adolescent children and adolescent young people derive substantial benefits from the close personal relationship with the same sex parents, to whom they look for a model"); Dalin v. Dalin, 512 N.W.2d 685, 689 (N.D. 1994) (in upholding custody award of daughter to mother, appellate court concluded that trial court's questions about who would help teach the child "certain things that a girl should learn that [are] easiest to learn from a woman" were "not motivated by or evidence of gender bias").

The majority rule, however, is that courts may not prefer a parent because he or she is the same sex as the child. See, e.g., Giffin v. Crane, 716 A.2d 1029, 1037 (Md. 1998); Hubbell v. Hubbell, 702 A.2d 129 (Vt. 1997); Seeley v. Jaramillo, 727 P.2d 91, 95 (N.M. 1986); Synakowski v. Synakowski, 594 N.Y.S.2d 852, 853 (App. Div. 1993).

In their longitudinal study of children of divorce in two California counties, Eleanor E. Maccoby and Robert H. Mnookin expected to explain shifts in residential patterns over time from children were shifting to spend more time with the same-sex parent. This hypothesis was not borne out by the data. See Maccoby & Mnookin, Dividing the Child: Social and Legal Dilemmas of Custody 199 (1992).

3. The Best-Interests Test. The prevailing rule in child custody cases is the best-interests-of-the-child test. This test encompasses a wide range of factors: the quality of the "emotional bonds between parent and child," "the ethical, emotional, and intellectual guidance the parent gives to the child throughout his formative years," and how to best provide continuity of care. The criticism of the standard is that such factors are too subjective, leaving room for judges to apply their own instincts and biases and thereby enhancing uncertainty, inconsistency, recriminations among parents, and undesirable strategic behavior. See Katharine T. Bartlett, Preference, Presumption, Predisposition, and Common Sense: From Traditional Custody Doctrines to the American Law Institute's Family Dissolution Project, 36 Fam. L.Q. 11, 11-17 (2002).

Gender bias has been a particular problem. See Susan Beth Jacobs, The Hidden Gender Bias Behind the "Best Interests of the Child" Standard in Custody Decisions, 13 Ga. St. U. L. Rev. 845 (1997). It can work both ways, favoring mothers based on traditional stereotypes and gender role expectations, but also sometimes penalizing them if they fail to conform to the ideal expectations of mothers, or if fathers exceed the minimal expectations traditionally set for them. In one case, for example, a father was awarded custody based on his "slightly more active engagement in their children's lives" even though, according to the dissenting opinion, the undisputed evidence showed that the father spent only nine waking hours per week with the children, as compared with 20 hours by the working mother. According to the dissenting judge, time was credited to the father for activities such as helping with schoolwork in which the mother also engaged but for which she was not given credit. See Hoover v. Hoover, 764 A.2d 1192, 1194 (Vt. 2000). Bias against working mothers and mothers who have had extra-marital affairs has also been apparent in a number of cases. See American Law Institute, Principles of the Law of Family Dissolution: Analysis and Recommendations, §2.12, comment c, at 292-295 (2002).

The best interests test also begs advice of experts who, like judges, may have their own biases and, in any event, who are likely to disagree, especially in close cases in which judges are inclined to rely on them the most. For a critique of both the amorphous nature of the best interests test, and the mental health professionals who are called in to help judges decide cases under it, see Janet M. Bowermaster, Legal Presumptions and the Role of Mental Health Professionals I Child Custody Proceedings, 40 Duq. L. Rev. 265 (2002). Did the experts in *Patricia Ann S.* play a useful role?

4. The Primary Caretaker Presumption. The difficulties with the best interests of the child test have led many commentators to favor adoption of a primary caretaker presumption. See, e.g., Martha Albertson Fineman, The Illusion of Equality: The Rhetoric and Reality of Divorce Reform 180-185 (1991) (for all children); David L. Chambers, Rethinking the Substantive Rules for Custody Disputes in Divorce, 83 Mich. L. Rev. 477 (1985) (for children between six months and five years).

For some years, West Virginia used a primary caretaker presumption, requiring the court to award custody to the primary caretaker parents unless that parent was shown to be unfit. See Garska v. McCoy, 278 S.E.2d 357, 363 (W. Va. 1981). Under this presumption, primary caretaker status was determined by examining which parent provides the day-to-day care of the child, including (1) preparing and planning of meals; (2) bathing, grooming, and dressing; (3) purchasing, cleaning, and care of clothes; (4) medical care, including nursing and trips to physicians; (5) arranging for social interaction among peers after school; (6) arranging alternative care; (7) putting child to bed at night, attending to child in the middle of the night, and waking child in the morning; (8) disciplining, teaching general manners, and toilet training; (9) educating; and (10) teaching elementary skills. *Garska*, supra, 278 S.E.2d at 363.

Is Ronald Henry correct to criticize this test because it favors mothers? What functions are missing that ought to be on the list? What about wage-earning? Note that Henry's charge takes the same form as claims made in favor of affirmative action, accommodations to pregnancy, and initiatives to increase women's opportunities for sports, and other measures intended to achieve substantive goals, beyond formal equality, i.e., a rule cannot be truly neutral if it produces skewed results. Analyze the analytical foundations of this critique. Does a primary caretaker presumption perpetuate gender bias, even if it is not itself discriminatory when applied in specific cases?

The main argument in favor of a primary caretaking presumption is that it is a more determinate standard than the best interests test, thereby reducing the likelihood of experts and prolonged litigation. Insofar as it removes discretion from the judge, proponents also point out that it also reduces the likelihood of gender stereotyping. Another argument in its favor is that, in linking parental rights with parental involvement in childrearing, it encourages that involvement during the marriage. Is that a legitimate goal of the law?

Some have argued that the anticipated advantages of the presumption have not been realized. Based on her review of appellate cases involving the primary caretaker presumption in West Virginia, for example, Mary Becker concludes that the rule increases rather than decreases litigation over child custody, and incorporates the same kind of gender-based stereotypes that disadvantage women under a best-interests-of-the-child test. Becker, Maternal Feelings: Myth, Taboo, and Child Custody, 1 S. Cal. Rev. L. & Women's Stud. 133, 195-200 (1992). Does *Patricia Ann S.* support Becker's thesis? If there is a problem with *Patricia Ann S.*, is it with the primary caretaker presumption, or with the way it is applied?

West Virginia replaced its primary caretaker presumption in 2000. See note 6, p. 363, infra. Two other states experimented with a primary caretaker presumption, but neither retained it. A primary caretaker standard adopted in Minnesota in 1985 by the state's highest court, see Pikula v. Pikula, 374 N.W.2d 705, 712 (Minn. 1985), was overruled by statute four years later. See Minn. Stat. Ann. § 518.17 (subd. 1)(a)(3) (West 2004) (primary caretaker status is one factor to be taken into account, but may not be given presumptive weight). The Minnesota experience is described by Judge Gary Crippen in Stumbling Beyond Best Interests of the Child: Reexamining Child Custody Standard-Setting in the Wake of Minnesota's Four Year Experiment with the Primary Caretaker Preference, 75 Minn. L. Rev. 427, 452-486 (1990) (finding that, contrary to expectations, the primary caretaker preference in Minnesota did not reduce litigation because of broad exceptions carved out of the preference, inappropriate reliance on parental fault and virtue, and gender stereotyping, which the appellate courts failed to correct). Montana also dropped its presumption. See Mont. Code Ann. § 40-4-212(3)(a)(1995) (creating rebuttable presumption that custody should be granted to "the parent who has provided most of the primary care during the child's life"), repealed by 1997 Mont. Laws ch. 15, § 343.

Even without the presumption, primary caretaking is a very significant factor in custody decisions. See, e.g., In re Custody of Kali, 792 N.E.2d 635 (Mass. 2003); In re McBrayer, 83 P.2d 936 (Or. Ct. App. 2004).

5. Joint Custody. Henry argues in favor of a joint physical custody presumption, a legal trend fueled in the 1980s by fathers' rights groups. Every state today permits some form of joint physical custody, but the statutory rules vary widely, both with respect to whether joint custody is ordered, and what it means.

Most commonly, joint custody is simply one among a number of custody alternatives, often joined with a stated policy preference in favor of encouraging parents to share in the rights and responsibilities of raising their children. See, e.g., Colo. Rev. Stat. § 14-10-124(1) (West 2004). A number of states provide some type of presumption or preference in favor of joint custody. In some of these, the presumption is a narrow one that operates only when parents jointly agree. See, e.g., Cal. Fam. Code § 3080 (West 2004). Other states have a presumption in favor of joint custody which can be overcome upon a showing that the child's best interests would not be served by it. See, e.g., D.C. Code Ann. § 16-914(a)(2) (West 2004). Florida has a presumption in favor of shared parental responsibility, which can be overcome only by a showing that it would be detrimental to the child. Fla. Stat. Ann. § 61.13(2)(b)(2) (West 2004). However, Florida law also contemplates that a primary residence be designated (§ 61.13(2)(b)(2)(a) (West 2004)), and Florida courts developed a presumption against awarding rotating or divided custody. See, e.g., Langford v. Ortiz, 654 So. 2d 1237 (Fla. Ct. App. 1995) ("[r]otating custody . . . is presumptively not in the best interests of a child"); but see § 61.13(4)(c)(5) (West 2004) (amending statute to eliminate presumption against rotating custody). Similarly, although Iowa requires the court to order joint custody if either parent requests it unless it cites clear and convincing evidence that it is unreasonable and not in the child's best interests, Iowa Code Ann. § 598.41(2) (West 2004), joint custody in Iowa does not necessary mean joint physical care. Id. at § 598.41(5). In short, it has proved difficult to define a consistent, workable joint-custody standard.

A few states disfavor joint custody awards. Oregon, for example, prohibits an order unless both parents agree. Or. Rev. Stat. § 107.169(3) (1999); see also Vt. Stat. Ann. tit. 15, § 665(a) (1989) (when parents cannot agree, court must order primary or sole custody to one parent).

Is joint custody "good for women"? Arguments in favor of joint custody emphasize the potential it has to express a more egalitarian ideal of parenthood and to break down detrimental gender stereotypes. Joint custody might also offer economic and emotional benefits to women, who would have greater flexibility to pursue their employment objectives and other personal interests than if they had sole custody. See Katharine T. Bartlett & Carol B. Stack, Joint Custody, Feminism and the Dependency Dilemma, 2 Berkeley Women's L.J. 9 (1986); Barbara Stark, Divorce Law, Feminism, and Psychoanalysis: In Dreams Begin Responsibilities, 38 UCLA L. Rev. 1483, 1525 (1991).

The feminist response to rules that favor joint custody, however, has been largely negative. One objection is that to the extent that joint custody exerts any pressure against familiar gender stereotypes, it does so by reducing the custodial rights of mothers who have acted as primary parents in favor of fathers who have not earned those rights. Another concern is that laws that favor joint custody provide additional leverage to men at divorce, who use it to exact concessions from women during divorce or to manipulate or harass women after the divorce, or to prevent them from relocating. See Martha Fineman & Ann Opie, The Uses of Social Science Data in Legal Policymaking: Custody Determinations at Divorce, 1987 Wis. L. Rev. 107, 116-117. This same critique is leveled against what is known as a "friendly parent" custody provision, under which the willingness and ability of a parent to cooperate in contact between the child and the other parent is taken into account in determining custody. See, e.g., Iowa Code Ann. § 598.41(1) (West. 2004) ("court . . . shall order the custody award . . . which will assure the child the opportunity for the maximum continuing physical and emotional contact with both parents"). Florida requires courts to examine both which parent is more likely to "allow the child frequent and continuing contact with the nonresidential parent" and each parent's "willingness and ability" to encourage a close relationship with the other parent. Fla. Stat. Ann. § 61.13(3)a, j (West 2004). Critics of these provisions argue, among other things, that they enhance the opportunities for batterers to abuse and manipulate their victims, and discourage well-intentioned parents—usually mothers—from opposing joint custody for fear that this opposition might be used to label them as a "non-friendly" parent and therefore an inappropriate candidate for primary custodian. See Margaret K. Dore, The "Friendly Parent" Concept: A Flawed Factor for Child Custody, 6 Loy. J. Pub. Int. L. 41 (2004). More particularly on the problem of domestic abuse and child custody, see Chapter 3, pp. 502-505.

Joint custody may also unfairly disadvantage women if courts make unrealistic assumptions about child support. This issue is discussed on pp. 338-341, supra. Child support orders are less common in joint custody cases than in sole custody cases, in part because some courts assume that equal custody ought to mean equal financial responsibility, and in part because mothers in joint residential custody cases tend to have higher incomes than mothers with sole custody. See Jessica Pearson & Nancy Thoennes, Child Custody and Child Support After Divorce, in Joint Custody and Shared Parenting 185, 195 (Jay Folberg ed., 2d ed. 1991). When custody is ordered, child support collection is higher in joint custody cases, id. at 199, but regression analysis of possible indicators of child support compliance has shown that visitation and parental participation variables are not as important in predicting child support compliance as the employment stability of the obligor and the level of parental cooperation. Id. at 199-201. Moreover, to date, no one has been able to demonstrate whether joint custody stimulates greater child support compliance or whether it is simply the case that the kinds of parents involved in joint custody arrangements are also the kinds of parents who take their child support obligations seriously.

Even if there were a causal connection between child support compliance and paternal involvement, would this support greater use of joint custody? What sort of efforts are appropriate to increase the role of fathers in their children's lives? One scholar has argued that the problem with some of these efforts is that they take for granted the interest of mothers in caring for their children (i.e., assume that mothers are volunteers) while providing earned bonuses to fathers who cannot otherwise be counted on to act as responsible parents (i.e., approach fathers as draftees). See Karen Czapanskiy, Volunteers and Draftees: The Struggle for Parental Equality, 38 UCLA L. Rev. 1415 (1991).

The data showing that custodial mothers, generally, are increasingly less dependent upon fathers paying child support are described on pp. 333-334 of this chapter.

The psychological literature evaluating the effects of joint custody on children has been mixed. When parents are able to value each other on behalf of the child, and have good psychological functioning, high self-esteem, and a low level of anger, the child of divorcing parents seems to do well with joint custody; when parents have intense and unremitting anger and hostility, a strong wish to punish the other spouse, low self-esteem, and the tendency to project blame on the other spouse, the arrangement is unlikely to work well and the children suffer. See Muriel Brotsky, Susan Steinman & Steven Zemmelman, Joint Custody Through Mediation: A Longitudinal Assessment of the Children, in Joint Custody and Shared Parenting, supra, at 167. Does the type of custody arrangement affect the level of parental cooperation and hence the ability of children to do well after the divorce of their parents? Some researchers have concluded that the custodial arrangement has little bearing on the amount of cooperation or conflict after divorce; the level of parental hostility at the time of the break-up is a better predictor of the amount of hostility and dissatisfaction thereafter. See id.; Eleanor E. Maccoby & Robert H. Mnookin, Dividing the Child: Social and Legal Dilemmas of Custody 247 (1992).

Despite the dramatic increase in joint custody statutes and the public attention given to the issue, the number of actual equally-shared residential arrangements appears to be modest. In a two-county California study, while joint legal custody (i.e., joint decisionmaking relating to education, medical care, and the like) was awarded in 76 percent of cases, joint physical custody was awarded in only 20 percent of cases. Of the cases in which joint physical custody was awarded, de facto dual residence — where the child spends at least one-third of the time living with each parent — occurred less than half of the time, id. at 152, although 16 percent of families who had not planned to do so ended up with de facto dual residence arrangements. Id. at 168.

6. The Past Caretaking Standard. Given the variety in circumstances in today's families and the importance of the actual custodial arrangements that parents make on their own, Elizabeth S. Scott suggests an alternative to both joint custody and the primary caretaker presumption: Courts should order the custody arrangement at divorce that best approximates parenting patterns while the family was intact. Such an approach, she argues, promotes continuity and stability for children, encourages cooperative rather than adversarial behavior by parents, and provides incentives for both parents to invest in parenting before as well as after divorce. See Scott, Pluralism, Parental Preference, and Child Custody, 80 Cal. L. Rev. 615 (1992).

This approach is reflected in the American Law Institute's Principles on the Law of Family Dissolution, which create a presumption in favor of the division of caretaking responsibility after divorce that approximates the shares of caretaking responsibility each parent assumed before the divorce. See Principles of the Law of Family Dissolution § 2.08, at 178-180 (2002). This approach is followed in the new West Virginia statute. See W. Va. Code Ann. § 48-9-207 (Michie 2004). See also Wash. Rev. Code Ann. § 26.09.187(3)(a)(i) (West 2005) (requiring courts to give "greatest weight" to "[t]he relative strength, nature, and stability of the child's relationship with each parent, including whether a parent has taken greater responsibility for performing caretaking functions relating to the daily needs of the child"). For an explanation and defense of the ALI Principles by the Reporter on the Project, see Katharine T. Bartlett, U.S. Custody Law and Trends in the Context of the ALI Principles of the Law of Family Dissolution, 10 Va. J. Soc. Pol'y & L. 5 (2002).

Is this approach likely to have an effect on gender bias in custody decisions? In which direction? Does it unfairly penalize fathers who are primary breadwinners?

7. Fairness and Custody. To what extent should fairness be a factor in custody rules? In *Patricia Ann S.*, for example, assume that (1) the children are more comfortable with their father and want to live with him; (2) the reason for this is that the father has physically and emotionally abused the mother, eliminating her self-esteem and impairing her parental abilities; and (3) it is a reasonable prediction that the mother will not be able to regain the confidence and trust of her children. In these circumstances (which represent one reading of the case), should fairness to the mother be a factor in her favor?

What about a father who remarries and the stepmother intends to stay at home and care for the child, while the biological mother needs to work full time? If the court decides, in an otherwise close case, that staying at home with the stepmother is better for the child than institutional day care, can it decide the case on this basis, even though this might not be "fair" to the mother?

What about fairness to the non-custodial father when the custodial mother relocates for a better job? To be closer to family? To join her new husband? Are any of these reasons better than the others, in terms of fairness to the father?

8. Comparative Custody Law. A symposium issue of the Family Law Quarterly contains 17 articles addressing the custody law of countries in England and Wales, France, Germany, Greece, Ireland, Russia, Sweden, Nigeria, South Africa, India, Iran, China, Japan, Australia, Mexico, Argentina, and Brazil. The volume explores differences among countries relating to the role of gender in custody decisions and the weight given in custody cases to factors such as domestic violence, remarriage, religious upbringing, and financial stability, as well as customs and laws concerning joint custody and the division of parental authority. See Symposium on Comparative Custody Law, 39 Fam. L.Q. 247 (2005).

Putting Theory into Practice

2-16. Since the birth of her son, David, two years ago, Rhonda quit her job as an assistant office manager to care for her son at home, supported economically by her husband Hugh, who is a high school teacher. They are divorcing. Since Hugh does not make enough money to support two households, Rhonda has agreed that she must return to full-time employment and that David will have to be placed in day care. Rhonda seeks primary custody of David based on her primary caretaking role during the marriage. Hugh argues that he should have primary custody because his mother has agreed to take care of David while he works, whereas if Rhonda has custody she would have to put David in a day care center. By what rule should such a case be decided? What further information should the court have in deciding the case?

Would Hugh's case be any stronger if he remarried, and his new wife is prepared to provide full-time, in-home care for David?

2-17. In the problem above, Hugh presents the testimony of two experts that, although Rhonda was David's primary caretaker during the marriage, she was a disorganized, distant parent who took care of David's physical requirements but did not attend to his emotional and developmental needs. Both experts agree that David responds more positively to Hugh than to Rhonda. Should this evidence be relevant in the resolution of the custody dispute? How important should it be?

In re Marriage of Elser
895 P.2d 619 (Mont. 1995)

Justice Karla M. GRAY delivered the opinion of the Court.

Cindy Ann Ansell...appeals from the findings, conclusions, and order...denying her motion for an order permitting her to remove her minor children to a permanent residence outside of Montana and granting Dan Roy Elser's (Dan) motion to appoint him primary residential custodian if Cindy proceeds with her relocation. We affirm.

The District Court dissolved Cindy's and Dan's marriage via a final decree of dissolution dated November 17, 1993. Pursuant to the terms of a separation agreement incorporated into the final decree, Cindy and Dan were awarded joint custody of Amber and Jaimie, their two minor daughters; Cindy was designated the children's primary residential custodian. Dan was granted visitation rights on alternating weekends and major holidays, residential custody for two months in the winter, and any other visitation agreed to by Cindy and Dan which would not interfere with the children's education and social activities. The separation agreement also provided that "neither party shall remove any of the minor children to a permanent residence outside the State of Montana without the other party's prior written consent or prior approval of a court having proper jurisdiction over the minor children...."

Cindy resided in Hamilton with the children after the dissolution; Dan maintained a residence in Corvallis. Cindy, a radiology assistant, desired to continue her education and applied for admission to the radiology technician program at St. Patrick's Hospital in Missoula. After St. Patrick's denied her application, Cindy notified Dan of her intention to relocate with the children to Kansas and enroll in the University of Kansas' radiology technician program. Dan refused to consent to the relocation.

Cindy moved the District Court for an order permitting her to remove the children to a permanent residence outside of Montana. She included a proposed visitation modification whereby Dan would be allowed to have his two-month custody of the girls during the summer instead of the winter and visitation on alternating major holidays. Dan objected to the children's relocation and moved the court to designate him as their primary residential custodian in the event Cindy relocated out of state. The District Court denied Cindy's motion and ordered that Dan would become the children's primary residential custodian in the event Cindy left Montana. Cindy appeals....

[T]he District Court's ruling on both motions ultimately rested on application of the best interest of the children standard.... [W]e need only review its findings that the move to Kansas is not in the children's best interests. Cindy argues that the record supports findings that spending time with the children was not a priority for Dan and that he could have spent much more time with the children. However, her argument ignores the applicable standards of review.... We review a district court's findings relating to custody modification to determine whether those findings are clearly erroneous....

The District Court first found that the high cost of travel and the impossibility of scheduling a time which coordinated with the children's school schedule and Dan's work schedule would deprive Dan of meaningful custody and visitation. It also found that Dan was committed to being an active parent who was involved with his children as much as possible and that Cindy agreed with Dan that it was important for the children to visit with Dan. Based on these findings, the District Court ultimately found that moving to Kansas was not in the children's best interest.

Ample evidence supports the court's finding that the children's school schedule and Dan's work schedule would make scheduling Dan's two-month extended visitation during the summer impossible. Dan testified that he performs seasonal highway construction work from April through November in Montana and Idaho. He typically works twelve to eighteen hours a day, five or six days a week. He travels home to Corvallis on Friday, arriving sometime early Saturday morning. The remainder of his April through November week-ends are spent doing laundry, catching up on sleep and, on Sunday afternoon, traveling back to the work site. Moreover, although Cindy acknowledged the importance of the children spending time with Dan, she conceded that the right to an extended visitation during the summer months—as she proposed in conjunction with her motion to relocate the children to Kansas—would be meaningless to Dan because of his work schedule. She also acknowledged that extended visitation during the winter months would be impossible from the children's standpoint because of their school schedules and that the relocation effectively would limit Dan's visitation to one week at Christmas.

The court also found that the high cost of travel would contribute to the impact Cindy's proposed move would have on Dan's ability to spend time with his children. Dan and Cindy approximated the airfare between Montana and Kansas at $1,000 and testified that neither of them makes a great deal of money. Dan stated that he could only afford one trip a year for the children to Montana. Cindy speculated that she could purchase one ticket per child per year, but did not commit to paying for any of the children's transportation for visitation.

The evidence also supported the court's determination that Dan is committed to being an active parent. The record reflects both Dan's belief in the importance of spending as much time as possible with his children and that he visited them nearly every other weekend and as often as permitted by his work schedule. Furthermore, Dan's concern about the children's welfare was supported by the fact that, although he has experienced financial difficulty, he continued to make child support payments and, at Cindy's request, paid the entire amount owed to the children's day care and school so they could continue attending.

We conclude that substantial evidence supports the District Court's finding that the proposed relocation to Kansas was not in the children's best interest

Affirmed.

≡ ***Dupre v. Dupre***
≡ 857 A.2d 242 (R.I. 2004)

Justice Paul A. SUTTELL delivered the opinion of the Court.

Of the many emotional consequences attendant upon the dissolution of a marriage, perhaps none is more vexatious than that precipitated by the desire of a parent to relocate with a minor child of the marriage. From the child's perspective, a once-single family has become two, and the relationship and well-being of each of these family units necessarily will have a direct impact on the well-being of the child. Moreover, the desire and right of one parent to move to pursue new opportunities undoubtedly will conflict with the desire and right of the other parent to maintain a close relationship with his or her child. The issue of post-divorce relocation is a complex, but increasingly prevalent, occurrence in today's mobile society....

Robert E. Dupre, Jr., (Robert or plaintiff) and Melanie S. Dupre (Melanie or defendant) were married in 1987 in the south of France. Before their marriage, they had lived together for approximately seven months in 1979 in French Polynesia, both in Papeete, Tahiti, and on the island of Moorea. In September 1979, they moved to Aix-en-Provence in France, where they resided for approximately one year.

In 1980 Robert purchased an apartment building in the Armory District of Providence, and the parties moved to Rhode Island. According to Melanie, Robert told her that if they worked very hard for three or four years renovating the building, they would have a source of income to enable them to return to French Polynesia. After a couple of years, however, Robert purchased a second building. Melanie testified that although she supported Robert in this second project, she "got very frustrated" and told him "time and time again" that she was unhappy living in Providence and wanted to return to French Polynesia.

In 1987 Melanie became pregnant, and the parties decided to marry. They remained living in Providence, and Robert continued to acquire and renovate apartment buildings. At the time of trial, Robert operated a very successful business, the Armory Revival Company, with approximately thirty employees.

Melanie is an artist. She testified that she was able to support herself in Papeete and France by selling her pen and ink drawings and paintings, but that it was a struggle for her in Providence because she did not "feel inspired by the landscape here." She said that she tried to find a niche for herself in the New England area, but "was never able to hook up with either a rep or a gallery where [she] felt [her] work could easily sell." She displayed her work at an average of two art shows a year, but generated very little income therefrom. Sometimes she vacationed in the south of France with the children "just to get some inspiration back because [she] felt so deprived of inspiration." For a year and a half she also worked as a real estate agent, earning approximately $45,000, to help her husband's company and to put some money aside for her trips to Tahiti.

Melanie's discontent and desire to leave the New England area was not lost upon Robert. He did not wish to relocate, however; his business was thriving, and his family, friends, and community were in Rhode Island. According to Robert, Melanie's desire to live somewhere else ultimately led to the dissolution of their marriage. In August 1999, he filed for divorce.

On August 23, 1999, a consent decree was entered by agreement of the parties in which Melanie was permitted to remove the children to Tahiti for the 1999-2000 school year. When they returned to Rhode Island, another order was entered, providing for alternating placement of the children in Rhode Island and also permitting Melanie to take the children to Tahiti for approximately two months. The divorce was scheduled for hearing on April 4, 2001, on which date the parties executed a property settlement agreement. That agreement was incorporated but not merged in the decision pending entry of final judgment that was entered on April 20, 2001. Final judgment was entered on December 31, 2001.

The parties agreed to joint custody and shared physical possession and placement of their two minor children, then nine and thirteen years old, in accordance with a schedule. The schedule provided for placement with Melanie in Rhode Island for the remainder of the school year, then with her in Huahine during the summer until August 19, 2001, after which time they would reside primarily with Robert. Notwithstanding the interlocutory order that the children would reside primarily with Melanie in Rhode Island until the end of the school year, she returned to Huahine on April 29, 2001. Because Robert was out of the country at the time, she left the children separately with a friend and a neighbor until he returned. The property settlement agreement and court order also provided that "if the parties cannot agree as to the primary placement of the children for the academic year 2001-2002 this issue shall be determined by the Providence County Family Court."

The parties indeed could not agree, and submitted the issue of primary placement to the Family Court. In addition, Melanie filed a motion to modify the visitation schedule in light of her desire that the children be placed with her in Huahine. Hearings were held in October and November 2001. Both parties testified, and the trial justice interviewed the children in camera. The defendant also presented as an expert witness Brian Hayden, Ph.D. (Dr. Hayden), a child psychologist who had been asked to do an evaluation and make recommendations with respect to the children's placement for the 2000-2001 academic year. He testified that he interviewed each parent individually, had each complete a psychological questionnaire, spoke to both children, and assessed the interaction between the children and each parent.

Doctor Hayden further testified that Melanie seemed to have a more significant parent/child relationship with the children, and was viewed by them "as their primary caregiver, and the person that provided, at least to them, the greatest sense of psychological security." Although he considered Robert to be a good father, he thought that the children were far more relaxed with their mother and had "a greater exchange of emotion and ideas and play" with her. He said it was clear, however, that they loved their father and enjoyed their time with him.

Doctor Hayden also said that he had seen the children only a week before the trial at a time when they had been living with Robert. Doctor Hayden thought that they were not very happy living with their father. They felt they were not seeing very much of him and were frustrated by their inability to communicate with their mother by e-mail. One complained about his father's disciplinary techniques, and the other "vehemently wanted to be with her mother."

When Dr. Hayden was asked whether he had an opinion about which parent should be the primary caregiver, he responded, "as long as these comments are understood in terms of the children [having] made a clear statement that they would like to live with their mother. I don't know where that would be, but I would support, or at least articulate that their desire is well-founded on their experience with their mother, and they have been consistent over the last thirteen months that the primary parent from their vantage point has been their mother."

He added, "I would be in favor of them living with their mother without any statement as to where that is, but state living with her would be in the best interests of the children." Doctor Hayden also allowed, however, that ideally children thrive on having contact with both parents, that the quality of a child's relationship with a parent can be affected by the frequency and consistency of contact, that it is also important to have relationships with extended family members, and that "what's best for any child[] is for them to have [] consistent and regular contact with both parents."

With respect to the possibility of Melanie's remaining in Rhode Island, Dr. Hayden testified that it was his understanding that she had considered it, but that it was not a viable option for her. He also indicated that he understood her desire to live in Huahine to be not a want but a need, and that "she feels profoundly certain about that need." At the time of the hearing, Melanie was living primarily in Huahine where she had leased a three-bedroom house for three years. In contrast to her life in Huahine, which she described as "blissful," she testified that living in New England made her physically ill, "very depressed and unhappy," "like a plant without water . . . shriveled and dead," and on the edge of a nervous breakdown.

In his decision, the trial justice determined that, by virtue of the property settlement agreement and decision pending entry of final judgment, the court was to address the issues of custody and placement de novo. He undertook a "best interest of the child" analysis, and carefully reviewed the factors enumerated in Pettinato v. Pettinato, 582 A.2d 909 (R.I. 1990). After doing so, he ruled:

> The court finds that the best interests of the children will be served by awarding joint custody to the parents. Additionally, this court is satisfied that the Defendant mother would best serve the emotional and physical needs of the children. These children will need to continue their development in accordance with the manner that was established prior to the divorce. This can only be effectuated by placing the children in the possession of their mother.

He then added:

> The court has concerns regarding the children residing in Huahine. In order for the Defendant to remove the children to Huahine, she must demonstrate (a) a compelling reason and (b) it is [in] the children's best interest. . . . The court finds that insufficient evidence has been provided to warrant a finding that there is a compelling reason for Mrs. Dupre to reside in Huahine. Therefore, the court will not address whether or not such a move is in the child's best interest.

Accordingly, Melanie's request to relocate the children was denied, Robert was awarded placement of the children, and Melanie awarded all reasonable rights of visitation, including "ample visitation for all of the children's school and summer vacations, [if she] chooses to move to Huahine."

[The defendant appealed.] Because we conclude that the trial justice incorrectly applied a compelling-reason standard with respect to the issue of relocation, we vacate.

I...

A survey of our sister states reveals a lack of uniformity and much fluidity in their respective approaches to relocation. Traditional policies disfavored relocation and some courts imposed presumptions in favor of the nonrelocating parent. See, e.g., Pollock v. Pollock, 889 P.2d 633, 635 (Ariz. Ct. App. 1995). . . . Other states have created a presumption in favor of relocation either by statute or decisional law. See, e.g., Minn. Stat. § 518.18(d) (2002) (presumption that court will retain the existing primary placement); Okla. Stat. Ann. tit. 10, § 19 (West 1998) (in absence of a showing of prejudice to the rights or welfare of a child, a custodial parent has a presumptive right to change their child's residence); S.D. Codified Laws § 25-5-13 (Michie 1999) (relocation should be permitted so long as removal does not prejudice the rights or welfare of the child); Wis. Stat. Ann. § 767.327(3)(a)(2)(a) (West 2001) (rebuttable presumption that continuing the current custody arrangement is in the best interests of the child); Hollandsworth v. Knyzewski, 109 S.W.3d 653, 658 (Ark. 2003); In re Marriage of Burgess, 913 P.2d 473, 478 (Cal. 1996). . . .

Some courts have adopted a burden-shifting approach for determining cases in which a parent with primary physical custody seeks to relocate. Under this approach, the initial burden devolves upon the relocating parent to demonstrate a legitimate or good faith reason for the move. Once a prima facie case has been made, the burden shifts to the nonrelocating parent to show that the proposed move is not in the child's best interests. See, e.g., Ireland v. Ireland, 717 A.2d 676, 682 (Conn. 1998); Baures v. Lewis, 770 A.2d 214, 230-231 (N.J. 2001).

Although the several states have taken divergent approaches to the issue of relocation, it is clear that traditional policies that discouraged relocation are increasingly being replaced by a less restrictive view that favors the right of a parent exercising physical custody to relocate the child. . . .

II

We now turn to the status of Rhode Island law as it relates to relocation cases. Other than the general prescription set forth in G.L. 1956 § 15-5-16(d)(1) that "the court shall provide for the reasonable right of visitation by the natural parent not having custody of the children, except upon the showing of cause why the right should not be granted," the Legislature has articulated no presumptions, standards or criteria that apply specifically to relocation issues. Few principles are more firmly established in the law, however, than that in awarding custody, placement, and visitation rights, the "paramount consideration" is the best interests of the child. . . .

III

Numerous law review articles, legal commentators, mental health professionals and social scientists have contributed to the discourse on relocation. Two well-respected legal organizations, the American Law Institute and the American Academy of Matrimonial Lawyers, also have attempted to bring a measure of uniformity to this area of family law.

The American Law Institute (A.L.I.) has addressed the issue of relocation in its Principles of the Law of Family Dissolution (Principles). . . . The A.L.I. Principles reflect "the policy choice that a parent, like any other citizen, should be able to choose his or her place of residence, and that the job of rearing children after divorce should not be made too financially or emotionally burdensome to the parent who has the majority share of custodial responsibility." Principles of the Law of Family Dissolution, A.L.I. ch. 2, §2.17, comment d (2002). The A.L.I. Principles provide that: "The court should allow a parent who has been exercising the clear majority of custodial responsibility to relocate with the child if that parent shows that the relocation is for a valid purpose, in good faith, and to a location that is reasonable in light of the purpose." Id. at §2.17(4)(a).

The American Academy of Matrimonial Lawyers (Academy) has proposed a Model Relocation Act (Model Act) that "is meant to serve as a template for those jurisdictions desiring a statutory solution to the relocation quandary." Perspectives on the Relocation of Children, 15 J. Am. Acad. Matrim. Law. 1, 2 (1998). Among its recommendations, the Model Act identifies seven nonexclusive factors that courts should consider in determining relocation issues.[8]

---

8. The Model Act entitled "Factors to Determine Contested Relocation" provides:

In reaching its decision regarding a proposed relocation, the court shall consider the following factors:

(1) the nature, quality, extent of involvement, and duration of the child's relationship with the person proposing to relocate and with the non-relocating person, siblings, and other significant persons in the child's life;

(2) the age, developmental stage, needs of the child, and the likely impact the relocation will have on the child's physical, educational, and emotional development, taking into consideration any special needs of the child;

(3) the feasibility of preserving the relationship between the non-relocating person and the child through suitable [visitation] arrangements, considering the logistics and financial circumstances of the parties;

(4) the child's preference, taking into consideration the age and maturity of the child;

(5) whether there is an established pattern of conduct of the person seeking the relocation, either to promote or thwart the relationship of the child and the non-relocating person;

(6) whether the relocation of the child will enhance the general quality of life for both the custodial party seeking the relocation and the child, including but not limited to, financial or emotional benefit or educational opportunity;

(7) the reasons of each person for seeking or opposing the relocation; and

(8) any other factor affecting the best interests of the child.

15 J. Am. Acad. Matrim. Law. §405 (1998).

The national trend toward a less restrictive approach toward relocation is fueled in large measure by social studies suggesting that the psychological welfare of a child depends more on the well-being of the family unit with whom the child primarily resides than it does upon maintaining frequent and regular contact with the other parent. See, e.g., Janet M. Bowermaster, Sympathizing with Solomon: Choosing Between Parents in a Mobile Society, 31 U. Louisville J. Fam. L. 791, 884 (1992).... Judith S. Wallerstein & Tony J. Tanke, To Move or Not to Move: Psychological and Legal Considerations in the Relocation of Children Following Divorce, 30 Fam. L.Q. 305, 311, 318 (1996)....

Not surprisingly other social study research suggests that children are better off if they have frequent contact and good relationships with both parents, Marion Gindes, Ph.D., The Psychological Effects of Relocation for Children of Divorce, 10 J. Am. Acad. Matrim. Law. 119, 132 (1998), or that any move, even a relatively short one, is a stressful event for a child, and can have a negative impact on the child's well-being. See, e.g., Joan B. Kelley & Michael E. Lamb, Using Child Development Research to Make Appropriate Custody and Access Decisions for Young Children, 38 Fam. & Conciliation Cts. Rev. 297, 309 (2000)....

This debate among social scientists undoubtedly adds to, or at least explains, the disparate approaches among the various jurisdictions to relocation issues. The appropriate crucible for transforming social theories into jurisprudential policy is the Legislature. In the absence of clearly articulated statutory standards, however, it is the function and prerogative of this Court to provide a measure of guidance to our courts, practitioners and litigants....

We also recognize, however, that a child's "best interests" can be an imprecise and elusive standard, particularly when applied in relocation cases....

It is the trial justice who is in the best position to determine what factors may be relevant on a case-by-case basis, and his or her discretion in this regard should not be unduly constrained. Certain factors, however, can be identified which are of significance whenever a parent seeks to move with his or her children. We hold, therefore, that parties either seeking or opposing the relocation of their minor children should present relevant evidence concerning the following factors so that the court may make appropriate findings:

(1) The nature, quality, extent of involvement, and duration of the child's relationship with the parent proposing to relocate and with the non-relocating parent.... We reject any mechanical or formulaic approach to determining which parent may be acting as a primary caretaker or what may constitute a clear majority of custodial responsibility, but leave that to the sound discretion of the trial justice. It entails more than a simple measurement of the time that the child spends with each parent, and requires an examination of the quality of the relationship that the child enjoys with each parent....

(2) The reasonable likelihood that the relocation will enhance the general quality of life for both the child and the parent seeking the relocation, including, but not limited to, economic and emotional benefits, and educational opportunities....

(3) The probable impact that the relocation will have on the child's physical, educational, and emotional development. Any special needs of the child should also be taken into account in considering this factor. . . .

(4) The feasibility of preserving the relationship between the non-relocating parent and child through suitable visitation arrangements, considering the logistics and financial circumstances of the parties. . . . Certainly, the history and past actions of the relocating parent either to foster the relationship between the child and the other parent, or to frustrate the relationship, would be an important consideration. So, too, would be the failure of the non-relocating parent to avail himself or herself of available opportunities for visitation.

(5) The existence of extended family or other support systems available to the child in both locations. . . .

(6) Each parent's reasons for seeking or opposing the relocation. . . . A parent's desire to relocate with his or her children ought not be predicated upon a whim. On the other hand, . . . a relocating parent need not establish a compelling reason for the move. The motivation for the relocation, however, will be a significant consideration. Clearly, a vindictive desire to interfere in the other parent's relationship with the child would weigh heavily against the parent seeking to relocate. A.L.I. ch. 2, § 2.17(4)(a). The A.L.I. Principles identify the following non-exclusive list of purposes for a relocation as valid:

(1) to be close to significant family or other sources of support, (2) to address significant health problems, (3) to protect the safety of the child or another member of the child's household from a significant risk of harm, (4) to pursue a significant employment or educational opportunity, (5) to be with one's spouse or domestic partner who lives in, or is pursuing a significant employment or educational opportunity in, the new location, (6) to significantly improve the family's quality of life. The relocating parent should have the burden of proving the validity of any other purpose.

Section 2.17(4)(a)(ii).

The A.L.I. Principles further provide that a move for a valid purpose is reasonable unless "its purpose is shown to be substantially achievable without moving, or by moving to a location that is substantially less disruptive of the other parent's relationship to the child." Section 2.17(4)(a)(iii).

The motives of the parent opposing the move also should be considered. A parent may be objecting to the child's relocation to secure a financial advantage or to exercise a measure of control over an ex-spouse, rather than out of a sincere desire to foster a relationship with the child.

(7) In cases of international relocation, the question of whether the country to which the child is to be relocated is a signatory to the Hague Convention on the Civil Aspects of International Child Abduction will be an important consideration.

(8) To the extent that they may be relevant to a relocation inquiry, the *Pettinato* factors also will be significant.[9] We reemphasize that our recitation

9. The factors set forth in Pettinato v. Pettinato, 582 A.2d 909, 913-914 (R.I. 1990) are:

1. The wishes of the child's parent or parents regarding the child's custody.

of factors to be considered is not intended to be exhaustive. Nor is any one factor dispositive. Each case will present its own unique circumstances that a trial justice must balance and weigh as he or she deems appropriate.

IV

With these principles in mind, we turn to the case now before us....

Robert asserts that the [Family Court] erred by awarding physical placement to Melanie without making a concomitant finding that there had been a substantial change of circumstances to warrant a modification of the previous order of joint physical placement. We conclude, however, that the trial justice was correct to treat the issue as an initial determination of placement, rather than as a modification of an existing order.... In essence, when the parties executed the property settlement agreement on April 4, 2001, they agreed to give themselves an additional four and a half months to attempt to resolve the matter on their own, either with or without the assistance of counseling or mediation. The parties having failed to reach an agreement, however, the Family Court had the authority to fashion an order of placement consistent with the children's best interests.

We treat the Family Court proceedings, therefore, as an initial determination of placement, or physical custody, rather than as a modification of an existing order. This is not a distinction without significance. The vast majority of case law to which we previously have alluded, involves post-final judgment relocations. Thus, within the context of this case, we need not delve into such considerations as the allocation of the burden of proof as an appropriate means of advancing the best interests of a child when a parent seeks to move to another geographical location. In post-judgment proceedings, the court already has determined as to what custodial arrangements best serve the child. The child has an interest not only in preserving the stability of those custodial relationships, but also in avoiding the potential trauma of relitigating these issues. Here, however, the issue of primary placement specifically was left open.

In initial custody and placement determinations, the focus is squarely on the best interests of the child, and the parents come before the court on an equal footing, with both "sharing equally the burden of demonstrating with which parent the child's best interests will be served." [citation omitted].... For her part, Melanie argues that the Family Court erred

---

2. The reasonable preference of the child, if the court deems the child to be of sufficient intelligence, understanding, and experience to express a preference.

3. The interaction and interrelationship of the child with the child's parent or parents, the child's siblings, and any other person who may significantly affect the child's best interest.

4. The child's adjustment to the child's home, school, and community.

5. The mental and physical health of all individuals involved.

6. The stability of the child's home environment.

7. The moral fitness of the child's parents.

8. The willingness and ability of each parent to facilitate a close and continuous parent-child relationship between the child and the other parent. (Footnotes omitted.)

by improperly applying a compelling-reason test, and by failing to consider the children's best interests. We agree and accordingly vacate the decision.

In a very real sense, this case cannot properly be characterized as a true relocation case. At the time of the hearing, Melanie, for better or worse, was living in Huahine. The court was not presented with the option of a viable physical custody arrangement in which the children could maintain frequent and regular contact with both parents. That ship already had sailed from port. Melanie had made it abundantly clear to Robert, Dr. Hayden, and the court that she desired and intended to reside in Huahine. Indeed, this was acknowledged in the parties' own agreement. Moreover, it would have been clearly impermissible for the court to deny her request to relocate as a means of attempting to coerce her to remain in Rhode Island.

The question confronting the Family Court, rather, was whether it was in the children's best interests to reside primarily with their mother a half a world away from their father, or with their father a half a world away from their mother. It is a question to which there can be no satisfactory answer. The court did evaluate the children's best interests in a general sense and determined that "mother would best serve the emotional and physical needs of the children" and that their continued development "can only be effectuated by placing the children in the possession of their mother." It failed to evaluate their best interests, however, in light of the then-existing circumstances, including mother's relocation. . . .

This was not a situation in which a parent wished to relocate to an area about which he or she had little information. . . . Clearly, evidence was adduced respecting educational opportunities, health care, and quality of life in Huahine from which the court could make findings of fact relative to the children's best interests.

. . . The defendant chides the trial justice for stating that "the court has concerns regarding the children residing in Huahine, yet not articulating these concerns." We are persuaded, however, that his concerns were self-evident and well-founded. The distance involved virtually precludes any visitation except during school vacation periods, and the time difference makes even electronic communication problematic. There can be little question that the children's relocation to Huahine would likely have a profound impact on Robert's relationship with them.

On the other hand, Melanie's desire to live in Huahine was hardly caprice. . . .

Conclusion . . .

Here, the Family Court was presented with an intractable problem to which there was no satisfactory answer. We vacate not because we are persuaded that the court's decision was inimical to the children's welfare, but because by applying an improper standard, it failed to address their best interests. We remand, therefore, for a new hearing on the issue of placement with directions to evaluate the present best interests of the children in light of current circumstances.

NOTE ON RELOCATION

In 2003, approximately 18 percent of divorced or separated U.S. families reported having changed living quarters within the previous 12 months. Of these, 63 percent relocated within the same county, 20 percent to a different county within the same state, and 16 percent to a different state. See U.S. Census Bureau, Population Division, Current Population Survey, March 2004: Geographic Mobility: 2002-2003. One study of college students from divorced families found that in only 39 percent of cases did neither parent relocate after the divorce. It was equally likely that the child remained with the mother while the father relocated, and that the child relocated with the mother. The study reported "significant disadvantages" on a host of psychological factors for children whose parents had relocated. Sanford L. Braver et al., Relocation of Children After Divorce and Children's Best Interests: New Evidence and Legal Considerations, 17 J. Family Psych. 206, 212 (2003).

The issue of continued custody when the parent with primary custody relocates can arise in many different procedural contexts; the two most common are a petition by the noncustodial parent to modify custody in response to an impending relocation by the parent with primary physical custody, and a petition by the relocating parent in the face of a prior court order or state statute requiring permission to relocate with the child. The issue can also come up before a permanent custody order has been issued, as in the *Dupre* case. While a modification of custody ordinarily requires a threshold showing of changed circumstances as well as an assessment of the best interests of the child, this additional factor is not ordinarily a significant barrier. Whether the focus is only on the child's best interests, or on whether circumstances have changed, what makes the difference is how the jurisdiction balances the conflict between one parent's desire for geographic mobility and continuity in custodial arrangements, as against the other parent's desire to maintain his or her meaningful noncustodial relationship with the child.

The law in this area has been unstable, but the clear trend, articulated in *Dupre*, has been toward increasing deference to the parent with whom the child has been primarily living. The *Dupre* case distinguishes the AAML "laundry list" standards from the ALI approach, which operates with various presumptions. Which is the better approach? Which does the *Dupre* court actually adopt?

Is there an approach to relocation that is truly fair? On the one hand, depriving a custodial parent of the right to move with his or her children is a high price to pay for custody. On the other hand, the non-custodial parent also faces geographic constraints in order to maintain a close relationship to the child. Why not simply prevent both parents from relocating?

Because most children of divorced families are in the physical custody of their mothers, the relocation standard a court applies will have a gender impact. Should that impact be taken into account? If so, how? Is it an appropriate objective of the law to encourage parenting by fathers? What would be the most effective standard to achieve this objective? The interest

some women have expressed in more equal sharing of childrearing responsibilities might suggest more protections for the custodial/visitation rights of
fathers. On the other hand, to the extent women continue to bear the
primary responsibility for children, giving men what may amount to a
veto power over a mother's decision to move weakens the woman's ability
to pursue her own life plans. If the real objective is encouraging joint parenting more generally, proponents of the majority trend and the ALI
approach argue that it would be better to hinge fathers' post-divorce custodial rights on the amount of caretaking they performed *during* the marriage,
not what they say they intend to do thereafter. Is encouraging joint parenting a legitimate goal of the law? See Katharine T. Bartlett, Preference, Presumption, Predisposition, and Common Sense: From Traditional Custody
Doctrines to the American Law Institute's Family Dissolution Project, 36
Fam. L.Q. 11, 19-22 (2002).

In most jurisdictions, whatever deference is given to the custodial parent
disappears if the parents share physical custody equally. See Hoover v. Hoover,
764 A.2d 1192 (Vt. 2000) (while usual rule favors relocating custodial parent,
when childrearing and decisionmaking is jointly shared with active involvement
by both parents, this rule does not apply); Marriage of Frances, 919 P.2d 776
(Colo. 1996) (whereas endangerment test usually applies to modification
actions, best-interests test applies when neither parent is a primary residential
parent).

Whether the parents truly share joint physical custody is determined by
examining the amount of time each parent spends with the child. The ALI
approach favoring custodial parents seeking to relocate applies only in favor of
a parent who is exercising "the clear majority" of custodial responsibility. Principles of the Law of Family Dissolution § 2.17(4)(a), at 354-356 (2002). This
question can be important, since many orders for joint physical custody are joint
in name only. A California study showed that only 52 percent of decrees for joint
physical custody actually resulted in joint residential arrangements, with the bulk
of the remainder involving primary residence with the mother; within a few years
of the divorce, the percentage had slipped to 45 percent. See Eleanor E. Maccoby
& Robert H. Mnookin, Dividing the Child: Social and Legal Dilemmas of Custody 166 (1992).

What judicial review is appropriate, if any, of the relocating parent's reason
for wanting to move? Should any reason be adequate? Are the purposes designated as presumptively legitimate in the ALI standards too broad? Too narrow?
Did the mother in the *Dupre* case meet the ALI standard?

Is there a right to travel implicated in the relocation issue? Technically
not, many courts say, since what is at stake is not a parent's right to relocate,
but to relocate *with the child*. See Maeda v. Maeda, 794 P.2d 268, 270 (Haw.
Ct. App. 1990). But see Wis. Stat. Ann. § 767.327(3)(c)(1) (West 2004)
(courts may prohibit a relocation, without changing the child's physical placement, if it finds that the prohibition is in the best interest of the child).

For discussion of the specific issue of relocation in the context of domestic
violence, see Chapter 4, pp. 502-507.

Putting Theory into Practice

2-18. When Janet and Mark divorced after an eight-year marriage, Janet had no job skills or training. During the marriage, she stayed at home to care for her three children, the first of whom was born almost immediately upon Janet's graduation from high school. At the divorce, Janet decided to give up primary custody of the children, then ages 3, 5, and 8, to Mark, who was planning to remarry, so that Janet would have two years to attend the community college full-time. Still, Janet had custody of the children every weekend and during school vacations, talked to them every night on the telephone, and continued to take primary responsibility for such things as doctor appointments, clothing, haircuts, birthday presents, and the like. Janet missed seeing the children every day, but felt the arrangement was the only way she would be able to make herself economically independent. The children were cared for during the day, when they weren't in school themselves, by their stepmother, who did not work outside the home.

The arrangement seemed to be working well, until one year into the arrangement, Mark announced that he had received a very large promotion and was moving to another state, 1,500 miles away. He intends to take the children with him. Should Janet be able to stop him from moving with the children? Under what general rule?

2-19. The No Child Left Behind Act, 20 U.S.C. § 6316(b)(1)(E)(i) (2002), allows children in "failing" schools to transfer to a non-failing school in the same school district. Eight-year-old Charlie lives with Vivian, his mother, at one end of the school district, served by a very poor elementary school, to which Charlie can walk. His father, George, lives at the other end of the district near a school that the court determines is better educationally. George seeks a change of custody, so that Charlie can live with him and attend the better school. The parents live only 10 miles apart, but the commute by city bus is 45 minutes, George could not do the commute alone, and neither parent's work schedules would allow them to accompany George back and forth to school from Vivian's house.

What else would you want to know, if anything, to decide whether to change custody from Vivian to George? Is there any reason to worry about gender bias? See Steven J. Seem, The Impact of No Child Left Behind on Post-Divorce Custody Modification, 2004 U. Chi. Legal F. 625.

3. Unmarried Parents

▬▬▬
Caban v. Mohammed
▬▬▬ 441 U.S. 380 (1979)
▬▬▬

Mr. Justice POWELL delivered the opinion of the Court.

The appellant, Abdiel Caban, challenges the constitutionality of § 111 of the New York Domestic Relations Law (McKinney 1977), under which two of his natural children were adopted by their natural mother and stepfather without his consent. We find the statute to be unconstitutional, as the distinction it invariably makes between the rights of unmarried mothers and the rights of unmarried fathers has not been shown to be substantially related to an important state interest.

I

Abdiel Caban and appellee Maria Mohammed lived together in New York City from September 1968 until the end of 1973. During this time Caban and Mohammed represented themselves as being husband and wife, although they never legally married. Indeed, until 1974 Caban was married to another woman, from whom he was separated. While living with the appellant, Mohammed gave birth to two children [one born in July 1969 and the other in March 1971]. [Caban] was identified as the father on each child's birth certificate, and lived with the children as their father until the end of 1973. Together with Mohammed, he contributed to the support of the family.

In December 1973, Mohammed took the two children and left the appellant to take up residence with appellee Kazin Mohammed, whom she married on January 30, 1974. For the next nine months, she took [the children] each week-end to visit her mother, Delores Gonzales, who lived one floor above Caban. Because of his friendship with Gonzales, Caban was able to see the children each week when they came to visit their grandmother.

In September 1974, Gonzales left New York to take up residence in her native Puerto Rico. At the Mohammeds' request, the grandmother took [the children] with her. According to appellees, they planned to join the children in Puerto Rico as soon as they had saved enough money to start a business there. During the children's stay with their grandmother, Mrs. Mohammed kept in touch with David and Denise by mail; Caban communicated with the children through his parents, who also resided in Puerto Rico. In November 1975, he went to Puerto Rico, where Gonzales willingly surrendered the children to Caban with the understanding that they would be returned after a few days. Caban, however, returned to New York with the children. When Mrs. Mohammed learned that the children were in Caban's custody, she attempted to retrieve them with the aid of a police officer. After this attempt failed, the appellees instituted custody proceedings in the New York Family Court, which placed the children in the temporary custody of the Mohammeds and gave Caban and his new wife, Nina, visiting rights.

In January 1976, appellees filed a petition under §110 of the New York Domestic Relations Law to adopt [the children]. In March, the Cabans cross petitioned for adoption....

The Surrogate granted the Mohammeds' petition to adopt the children, thereby cutting off all of appellant's parental rights and obligations....

II

Section 111 of the N.Y. Dom. Rel. Law (McKinney 1977) provides in part that

> consent to adoption shall be required as follows:... (b) Of the parents or surviving parent... of a child born in wedlock; [and] (c) Of the mother... of a child born out of wedlock....

[Absent a showing that a parent has abandoned or relinquished his or her rights in the child or has been adjudicated incompetent to care for the child,] an unwed mother has the authority under New York law to block the adoption of her child simply by withholding consent. The unwed father has no similar control over the fate of his child, even when his parental relationship is substantial — as in this case. He may prevent the termination of his parental rights only by showing that the best interests of the child would not permit the child's adoption by the petitioning couple....

III

The question before us... is whether the distinction in §111 between unmarried mothers and unmarried fathers bears a substantial relation to some important state interest....

Contrary to appellees' argument and to the apparent presumption underlying §111, maternal and paternal roles are not invariably different in importance. Even if unwed mothers as a class were closer than unwed fathers to their newborn infants, this generalization concerning parent-child relations would become less acceptable as a basis for legislative distinctions as the age of the child increased. The present case demonstrates that an unwed father may have a relationship with his children fully comparable to that of the mother. [They] lived together as a natural family for several years. As members of this family, both mother and father participated in the care and support of their children. There is no reason to believe that the Caban children — aged 4 and 6 at the time of the adoption proceedings — had a relationship with their mother unrivaled by the affection and concern of their father. We reject, therefore, the claim that the broad, gender-based distinction of §111 is required by any universal difference between maternal and paternal relations at every phase of a child's development.

As an alternative justification for §111, appellees argue that the distinction between unwed fathers and unwed mothers is substantially related to the State's interest in promoting the adoption of illegitimate children....

The State's interest in providing for the well-being of illegitimate children is an important one.... But the unquestioned right of the State to further these desirable ends by legislation is not in itself sufficient to justify the gender-based distinction of §111....

It may be that, given the opportunity, some unwed fathers would prevent the adoption of their illegitimate children. This impediment to adoption usually is the result of a natural parental interest by both genders alike; it is not a manifestation of any profound difference between the affection and concern of mothers and fathers for their children. Neither the State nor the appellees have argued that unwed fathers are more likely to object to the adoption of their children than are unwed mothers; nor is there any self-evident reason why as a class they would be.

Even if the special difficulties attendant upon locating and identifying unwed fathers at birth would justify a legislative distinction between mothers and fathers of newborns,[11] these difficulties need not persist past infancy.... In those cases where the father never has come forward to participate in the rearing of his child, nothing in the Equal Protection Clause precludes the State from withholding from him the privilege of vetoing the adoption of that child.... But in cases such as this, where the father has established a substantial relationship with the child and has admitted his paternity, a State should have no difficulty in identifying the father even of children born out of wedlock....

In sum, we believe that §111 is another example of "overbroad generalizations" in gender-based classifications.... The effect of New York's classification is to discriminate against unwed fathers even when their identity is known and they have manifested a significant paternal interest in the child. The facts of this case illustrate the harshness of classifying unwed fathers as being invariably less qualified and entitled than mothers to exercise a concerned judgment as to the fate of the children. Section 111 both excludes some loving fathers from full participation in the decision whether their children will be adopted and, at the same time, enables some alienated mothers arbitrarily to cut off the paternal rights of fathers. We conclude that this undifferentiated distinction between unwed mothers and unwed fathers, applicable in all circumstances where adoption of a child of theirs is at issue, does not bear a substantial relationship to the State's asserted interests.

The judgment of the New York Court of Appeals is reversed.

[The dissenting opinion of Mr. Justice Stewart is omitted.]

Mr. Justice STEVENS, with whom THE CHIEF JUSTICE and Mr. Justice REHNQUIST join, dissenting....

I

This case concerns the validity of rules affecting the status of the thousands of children who are born out of wedlock every day. All of these children have an interest in acquiring the status of legitimacy; a great many of them have an interest in being adopted by parents who can give them opportunities that would otherwise be denied; for some the basic necessities of life are at stake. The state interest in facilitating adoption in appropriate cases is strong — perhaps even "compelling."

---

11. Because the question is not before us, we express no view whether such difficulties would justify a statute addressed particularly to newborn adoptions, setting forth more stringent requirements concerning the acknowledgment of paternity or a stricter definition of abandonment.

Nevertheless, it is also true that §111(1)(c) gives rights to natural mothers that it withholds from natural fathers. Because it draws this gender-based distinction between two classes of citizens who have an equal right to fair and impartial treatment by their government, it is necessary to determine whether there are differences between the members of the two classes that provide a justification for treating them differently. . . .

Men and women are different, and the difference is relevant to the question whether the mother may be given the exclusive right to consent to the adoption of a child born out of wedlock. Because most adoptions involve newborn infants or very young children, it is appropriate at the outset to focus on the significance of the difference in such cases.

Both parents are equally responsible for the conception of the child out of wedlock. But from that point on through pregnancy and infancy, the differences between the male and the female have an important impact on the child's destiny. Only the mother carries the child; it is she who has the constitutional right to decide whether to bear it or not. In many cases, only the mother knows who sired the child, and it will often be within her power to withhold that fact, and even the fact of her pregnancy, from that person. If during pregnancy the mother should marry a different partner, the child will be legitimate when born, and the natural father may never even know that his "rights" have been affected. On the other hand, only if the natural mother agrees to marry the natural father during that period can the latter's actions have a positive impact on the status of the child; if he instead should marry a different partner during that time, the only effect on the child is negative, for the likelihood of legitimacy will be lessened.

These differences continue at birth and immediately thereafter. During that period, the mother and child are together;[10] the mother's identity is known with certainty. The father, on the other hand, may or may not be present; his identity may be unknown to the world and may even be uncertain to the mother. These natural differences between unmarried fathers and mothers make it probable that the mother, and not the father or both parents, will have custody of the newborn infant.

In short, it is virtually inevitable that from conception through infancy the mother will constantly be faced with decisions about how best to care for the child, whereas it is much less certain that the father will be confronted with comparable problems. There no doubt are cases in which the relationship of the parties at birth makes it appropriate for the State to give the father a voice of some sort in the adoption decision. But as a matter of equal protection analysis, it is perfectly obvious that at the time and immediately after a child is born out of

---

10. In fact, there is some sociological and anthropological research indicating that by virtue of the symbiotic relationship between mother and child during pregnancy and the initial contact between mother and child directly after birth a physical and psychological bond immediately develops between the two that is not then present between the infant and the father or any other person. E.g., 1 & 2 J. Bowlby, Attachment and Loss (1969, 1973); M. Mahler, The Psychological Birth of the Human Infant (1975).

wedlock, differences between men and women justify some differential treatment of the mother and father in the adoption process.

Most particularly, these differences justify a rule that gives the mother of the newborn infant the exclusive right to consent to its adoption. Such a rule gives the mother, in whose sole charge the infant is often placed anyway, the maximum flexibility in deciding how best to care for the child. It also gives the loving father an incentive to marry the mother, and has no adverse impact on the disinterested father. Finally, it facilitates the interests of the adoptive parents, the child, and the public at large by streamlining the often traumatic adoption process and allowing the prompt, complete, and reliable integration of the child into a satisfactory new home at as young an age as is feasible. Put most simply, it permits the maximum participation of interested natural parents without so burdening the adoption process that its attractiveness to potential adoptive parents is destroyed.

This conclusion is borne out by considering the alternative rule proposed by appellant. If the State were to require the consent of both parents, or some kind of hearing to explain why either's consent is unnecessary or unobtainable, it would unquestionably complicate and delay the adoption process. Most importantly, such a rule would remove the mother's freedom of choice in her own and the child's behalf without also relieving her of the unshakable responsibility for the care of the child. Furthermore, questions relating to the adequacy of notice to absent fathers could invade the mother's privacy, cause the adopting parents to doubt the reliability of the new relationship, and add to the expense and time required to conclude what is now usually a simple and certain process. While it might not be irrational for a State to conclude that these costs should be incurred to protect the interest of natural fathers, it is nevertheless plain that those costs, which are largely the result of differences between the mother and the father, establish an imposing justification for some differential treatment of the two sexes in this type of situation. . . .

I have no way of knowing how often disputes between natural parents over adoption of their children arise after the father "has established a substantial relationship with the child and [is willing to admit] his paternity," . . . but has previously been unwilling to take steps to legitimate his relationship. I am inclined to believe that such cases are relatively rare. But whether or not this assumption is valid, the far surer assumption is that in the more common adoption situations, the mother will be the more, and often the only, responsible parent, and that a paternal consent requirement will constitute a hindrance to the adoption process. Because this general rule is amply justified in its normal application, I would therefore require the party challenging its constitutionality to make some demonstration of unfairness in a significant number of situations before concluding that it violates the Equal Protection Clause. That the Court has found a violation without requiring such a showing can only be attributed to its own "stereotyped reaction" to what is unquestionably, but in this case justifiably, a gender-based distinction. . . .

I respectfully dissent.

Nguyen v. Immigration and Naturalization Service

533 U.S. 53 (2001)

Justice KENNEDY delivered the opinion of the Court....

I

Petitioner Tuan Ahn Nguyen was born in Saigon, Vietnam, on September 11, 1969, to copetitioner Joseph Boulais and a Vietnamese citizen. Boulais and Nguyen's mother were not married. Boulais always has been a citizen of the United States, and he was in Vietnam under the employ of a corporation. After he and Nguyen's mother ended their relationship, Nguyen lived for a time with the family of Boulais' new Vietnamese girlfriend. In June 1975, Nguyen, then almost six years of age, came to the United States. He became a lawful permanent resident and was raised in Texas by Boulais.

In 1992, when Nguyen was 22, he pleaded guilty in a Texas state court to two counts of sexual assault on a child. He was sentenced to eight years in prison on each count. Three years later, the United States Immigration and Naturalization Service (INS) initiated deportation proceedings against Nguyen as an alien who had been convicted of two crimes involving moral turpitude, as well as an aggravated felony....

Nguyen appealed to the Board of Immigration of Appeals and, in 1998, while the matter was pending, his father obtained an order of parentage from a state court, based on DNA testing. By this time, Nguyen was 28 years old. The Board dismissed Nguyen's appeal, rejecting his claim to United States citizenship because he had failed to establish compliance with 8 U.S.C. § 1409(a), which sets forth the requirements for one who was born out of wedlock and abroad to a citizen father and a noncitizen mother.

Nguyen and Boulais appealed to the Court of Appeals [which appeal was denied]....

II

The general requirement for acquisition of citizenship by a child born outside the United States and its outlying possessions and to parents who are married, one of whom is a citizen and the other of whom is an alien, is set forth in 8 U.S.C. § 1401(g). The statute provides that the child is also a citizen if, before the birth, the citizen parent had been physically present in the United States for a total of five years, at least two of which were after the parent turned 14 years of age.

As to an individual born under the same circumstances, save that the parents are unwed, § 1409(a) sets forth the following requirements where the father is the citizen parent and the mother is an alien:

> (1) a blood relationship between the person and the father is established by clear and convincing evidence,

(2) the father had the nationality of the United States at the time of the person's birth,

(3) the father (unless deceased) has agreed in writing to provide financial support for the person until the person reaches the age of 18 years, and

(4) while the person is under the age of 18 years —

   (A) the person is legitimated under the law of the person's residence or domicile,

   (B) the father acknowledges paternity of the person in writing under oath, or

   (C) the paternity of the person is established by adjudication of a competent court.

In addition, § 1409(a) incorporates by reference, as to the citizen parent, the residency requirement of § 1401(g).

When the citizen parent of the child born abroad and out of wedlock is the child's mother, the requirements for the transmittal of citizenship are described in § 1409(c):

> (c) Notwithstanding the provision of subsection (a) of this section, a person born, after December 23, 1952, outside the United States and out of wedlock shall be held to have acquired at birth the nationality status of his mother, if the mother had the nationality of the United States at the time of such person's birth, and if the mother had previously been physically present in the United States or one of its outlying possessions for a continuous period of one year.

Section 1409(a) thus imposes a set of requirements on the children of citizen fathers born abroad and out of wedlock to a noncitizen mother that are not imposed under like circumstances when the citizen parent is the mother. All concede the requirements of § 1409(a)(3) and (a)(4), relating to a citizen father's acknowledgment of a child while he is under 18, were not satisfied in this case. . . .

III

For a gender-based classification to withstand equal protection scrutiny, it must be established "at least that the [challenged] classification serves 'important governmental objectives and that the discriminatory means employed' are 'substantially related to the achievement of those objectives.'" United States v. Virginia, 518 U.S. 515, 533 (1996) [internal citation omitted]. For reasons to follow, we conclude § 1409 satisfies this standard. . . .

Before considering the important governmental interests advanced by the statute, [it should be observed that] . . . a citizen mother expecting a child and living abroad has the right to re-enter the United States so the child can be born here and be a 14th Amendment citizen. From one perspective, then, the statute simply ensures equivalence between two expectant mothers who are citizens abroad if one chooses to reenter for the child's birth and the other chooses not to return, or does not have the means to do so. This equivalence is not a factor if the single citizen parent living abroad is the father. For, unlike the unmarried mother, the unmarried father as a general rule cannot control where the child will be born. . . .

Congress' decision to impose requirements on unmarried fathers that differ from those on unmarried mothers is based on the significant difference between their respective relationships to the potential citizen at the time of birth. Specifically, the imposition of the requirement for a paternal relationship, but not a maternal one, is justified by two important governmental objectives. We discuss each in turn. . . .

The first governmental interest to be served is the importance of assuring that a biological parent-child relationship exists. In the case of the mother, the relation is verifiable from the birth itself. The mother's status is documented in most instances by the birth certificate or hospital records and the witnesses who attest to her having given birth.

In the case of the father, the uncontestable fact is that he need not be present at the birth. If he is present, furthermore, that circumstance is not incontrovertible proof of fatherhood. See Lehr v. Robertson, 463 U.S. 248, 260, n.16 (1983). . . . Fathers and mothers are not similarly situated with regard to the proof of biological parenthood. The imposition of a different set of rules for making that legal determination with respect to fathers and mothers is neither surprising nor troublesome from a constitutional perspective. . . . Section 1409(a)(4)'s provision of three options for a father seeking to establish paternity — legitimation, paternity oath, and court order of paternity — is designed to ensure an acceptable documentation of paternity. . . .

. . . As Justice Stevens pointed out in [Miller v. Albright, 523 U.S. 420 (1998)], Congress could have required both mothers and fathers to prove parenthood within 30 days or, for that matter, 18 years, of the child's birth. 523 U.S., at 436. Given that the mother is always present at birth, but that the father need not be, the facially neutral rule would sometimes require fathers to take additional affirmative steps which would not be required of mothers, whose names will appear on the birth certificate as a result of their presence at the birth, and who will have the benefit of witnesses to the birth to call upon. The issue is not the use of gender specific terms instead of neutral ones. Just as neutral terms can mask discrimination that is unlawful, gender specific terms can mark a permissible distinction. The equal protection question is whether the distinction is lawful. Here, the use of gender specific terms takes into account a biological difference between the parents. . . .

The second important governmental interest furthered in a substantial manner by § 1409(a)(4) is the determination to ensure that the child and the citizen parent have some demonstrated opportunity or potential to develop not just a relationship that is recognized, as a formal matter, by the law, but one that consists of the real, everyday ties that provide a connection between child and citizen parent and, in turn, the United States. . . . In the case of a citizen mother and a child born overseas, the opportunity for a meaningful relationship between citizen parent and child inheres in the very event of birth, an event so often critical to our constitutional and statutory understandings of citizenship. The mother knows that the child is in being and is hers and has an initial point of contact with him. There is at least an opportunity for mother and child to develop a real, meaningful relationship.

The same opportunity does not result from the event of birth, as a matter of biological inevitability, in the case of the unwed father. Given the 9-month interval between conception and birth, it is not always certain that a father will know that a child was conceived, nor is it always clear that even the mother will be sure of the father's identity. This fact takes on particular significance in the case of a child born overseas and out of wedlock. One concern in this context has always been with young people, men for the most part, who are on duty with the Armed Forces in foreign countries. . . .

The importance of the governmental interest at issue here is too profound to be satisfied merely by conducting a DNA test. The fact of paternity can be established even without the father's knowledge, not to say his presence. Paternity can be established by taking DNA samples even from a few strands of hair, years after the birth. See Federal Judicial Center, Reference Manual on Scientific Evidence 497 (2d ed. 2000). Yet scientific proof of biological paternity does nothing, by itself, to ensure contact between father and child during the child's minority.

Congress is well within its authority in refusing, absent proof of at least the opportunity for the development of a relationship between citizen parent and child, to commit this country to embracing a child as a citizen entitled as of birth to the full protection of the United States, to the absolute right to enter its borders, and to full participation in the political process. If citizenship is to be conferred by the unwitting means petitioners urge, so that its acquisition abroad bears little relation to the realities of the child's own ties and allegiances, it is for Congress, not this Court, to make that determination. . . .

Having concluded that facilitation of a relationship between parent and child is an important governmental interest, the question remains whether the means Congress chose to further its objective — the imposition of certain additional requirements upon an unwed father — substantially relate to that end. Under this test, the means Congress adopted must be sustained.

First, it should be unsurprising that Congress decided to require that an opportunity for a parent-child relationship occur during the formative years of the child's minority. In furtherance of the desire to ensure some tie between this country and one who seeks citizenship, various other statutory provisions concerning citizenship and naturalization require some act linking the child to the United States to occur before the child reaches 18 years of age. See, e.g., 8 U.S.C. § 1431 (child born abroad to one citizen parent and one noncitizen parent shall become a citizen if, *inter alia*, the noncitizen parent is naturalized before the child reaches 18 years of age and the child begins to reside in the United States before he or she turns 18); § 1432 (imposing same conditions in the case of a child born abroad to two alien parents who are naturalized).

Second, petitioners argue that . . . although a mother will know of her child's birth, "knowledge that one is a parent, no matter how it is acquired, does not guarantee a relationship with one's child." . . . They thus maintain that the imposition of the additional requirements of § 1409(a)(4) only on the children of citizen fathers must reflect a stereotype that women are more likely than men to actually establish a relationship with their children. . . .

. . . Congress would of course be entitled to advance the interest of ensuring an actual, meaningful relationship in every case before citizenship is conferred. Or Congress could excuse compliance with the formal requirements when an actual father-child relationship is proved. It did neither here, perhaps because of the subjectivity, intrusiveness, and difficulties of proof that might attend an inquiry into any particular bond or tie. Instead, Congress enacted an easily administered scheme to promote the different but still substantial interest of ensuring at least an opportunity for a parent-child relationship to develop. Petitioners' argument confuses the means and ends of the equal protection inquiry; § 1409(a)(4) should not be invalidated because Congress elected to advance an interest that is less demanding to satisfy than some other alternative.

Even if one conceives of the interest Congress pursues as the establishment of a real, practical relationship of considerable substance between parent and child in every case, as opposed simply to ensuring the potential for the relationship to begin, petitioners' misconception of the nature of the equal protection inquiry is fatal to their argument. A statute meets the equal protection standard we here apply so long as it is "'substantially related to the achievement of'" the governmental objective in question. [citations omitted] It is almost axiomatic that a policy which seeks to foster the opportunity for meaningful parent-child bonds to develop has a close and substantial bearing on the governmental interest in the actual formation of that bond. None of our gender-based classification equal protection cases have required that the statute under consideration must be capable of achieving its ultimate objective in every instance. . . .

V

To fail to acknowledge even our most basic biological differences — such as the fact that a mother must be present at birth but the father need not be — risks making the guarantee of equal protection superficial, and so disserving it. Mechanistic classification of all our differences as stereotypes would operate to obscure those misconceptions and prejudices that are real. The distinction embodied in the statutory scheme here at issue is not marked by misconception and prejudice, nor does it show disrespect for either class. The difference between men and women in relation to the birth process is a real one, and the principle of equal protection does not forbid Congress to address the problem at hand in a manner specific to each gender.

The judgment of the Court of Appeals is affirmed.

[The opinion of Justice Scalia, with whom Justice Thomas joins, concurring, is omitted.]

Justice O'CONNOR, with whom Justice SOUTER, Justice GINSBURG, and Justice BREYER join, dissenting. . . .

According to the Court, "[t]he first governmental interest to be served is the importance of assuring that a biological parent-child relationship exists." . . . The majority does not elaborate on the importance of this interest, which presumably lies in preventing fraudulent conveyances of citizenship. Nor does the majority demonstrate that this is one of the actual purposes of § 1409(a)(4). Assuming that Congress actually had this purpose in mind in enacting parts of § 1409(a)(4), . . . the INS does not appear to rely on this interest in its effort to sustain § 1409(a)(4)'s sex-based classification. Cf. Brief for Respondent 11 (claiming that § 1409 serves "at least two important interests: first, ensuring that children who are born abroad out of wedlock have, during their minority, attained a sufficiently recognized or formal relationship to their United States citizen parent — and thus to the United States — to justify the conferral of citizenship upon them; and second, preventing such children from being stateless"). In light of the reviewing court's duty to "determine whether the proffered justification is "exceedingly persuasive,'" *Virginia*, 518 U.S., at 533, this disparity between the majority's defense of the statute and the INS' proffered justifications is striking, to say the least.

The gravest defect in the Court's reliance on this interest, however, is the insufficiency of the fit between § 1409(a)(4)'s discriminatory means and the asserted end. . . . It is difficult to see what § 1409(a)(4) accomplishes in furtherance of "assuring that a biological parent-child relationship exists," . . . that § 1409(a)(1) does not achieve on its own. The virtual certainty of a biological link that modern DNA testing affords reinforces the sufficiency of § 1409(a)(1). See *Miller*, supra, at 484-485 (Breyer, J., dissenting).

It is also difficult to see how § 1409(a)(4)'s limitation of the time allowed for obtaining proof of paternity substantially furthers the assurance of a blood relationship. Modern DNA testing, in addition to providing accuracy unmatched by other methods of establishing a biological link, essentially negates the evidentiary significance of the passage of time. Moreover, the application of § 1409(a)(1)'s "clear and convincing evidence" requirement can account for any effect that the passage of time has on the quality of the evidence. . . .

The majority concedes that Congress could achieve the goal of assuring a biological parent-child relationship in a sex-neutral fashion, but then, in a surprising turn, dismisses the availability of sex-neutral alternatives as irrelevant. As the Court suggests, "Congress could have required both mothers and fathers to prove parenthood within 30 days or, for that matter, 18 years, of the child's birth." . . . While the majority trumpets the availability of superior sex-neutral alternatives as confirmation of § 1409(a)(4)'s validity, our precedents demonstrate that this fact is a decided strike *against* the law. Far from being "hollow," the avoidance of gratuitous sex-based distinctions is the hallmark of equal protection. . . .

Assuming, as the majority does, that Congress was actually concerned about ensuring a "demonstrated opportunity" for a relationship, it is questionable whether such an opportunity qualifies as an "important" governmental interest apart from the existence of an actual relationship. By focusing on "opportunity" rather than reality, the majority presumably improves the chances of a sufficient means-end fit. But in doing so, it dilutes significantly the weight of the interest. It is difficult to see how, in this citizenship-conferral context, anyone profits from a "demonstrated opportunity" for a relationship in the absence of the fruition of an actual tie. . . .

[A]vailable sex-neutral alternatives would at least replicate, and could easily exceed, whatever fit there is between § 1409(a)(4)'s discriminatory means and the majority's asserted end. According to the Court, § 1409(a)(4) is designed to ensure that fathers and children have the same "opportunity which the event of birth itself provides for the mother and child." ... Even assuming that this is so, Congress could simply substitute for § 1409(a)(4) a requirement that the parent be present at birth or have knowledge of birth.... Congress could at least allow proof of such presence or knowledge to be one way of demonstrating an opportunity for a relationship. ...

Indeed, the idea that a mother's presence at birth supplies adequate assurance of an opportunity to develop a relationship while a father's presence at birth does not would appear to rest only on an overbroad sex-based generalization.... There is no reason, other than stereotype, to say that fathers who are present at birth lack an opportunity for a relationship on similar terms. The "[p]hysical differences between men and women," *Virginia*, 518 U.S., at 533, therefore do not justify § 1409(a)(4)'s discrimination....

The Court admits that "Congress could excuse compliance with the formal requirements when an actual father-child relationship is proved," but speculates that Congress did not do so "perhaps because of the subjectivity, intrusiveness, and difficulties of proof that might attend an inquiry into any particular bond or tie." ... We have repeatedly rejected efforts to justify sex-based classifications on the ground of administrative convenience.... There is no reason to think that this is a case where administrative convenience concerns are so powerful that they would justify the sex-based discrimination, ... especially where the use of sex as a proxy is so ill fit to the purported ends as it is here. And to the extent Congress might seek simply to ensure an "opportunity" for a relationship, little administrative inconvenience would seem to accompany a sex-neutral requirement of presence at birth, knowledge of birth, or contact between parent and child prior to a certain age....

In denying petitioner's claim that § 1409(a)(4) rests on stereotypes, the majority articulates a misshapen notion of "stereotype" and its significance in our equal protection jurisprudence. The majority asserts that a "stereotype" is "defined as a frame of mind resulting from irrational or uncritical analysis." ... This Court has long recognized, however, that an impermissible stereotype may enjoy empirical support and thus be in a sense "rational." See, e.g., *J.E.B.*, supra, at 139, n.11 ... Indeed, the stereotypes that underlie a sex-based classification "may hold true for many, even most, individuals." *Miller*, 523 U. S., at 460 (Ginsburg, J., dissenting). But in numerous cases where a measure of truth has inhered in the generalization, "the Court has rejected official actions that classify unnecessarily and overbroadly by gender when more accurate and impartial functional lines can be drawn." Id....

Section 1409 was first enacted as § 205 of the Nationality Act of 1940, 54 Stat. 1139-1140. The 1940 Act had been proposed by the President, forwarding a report by a specially convened Committee of Advisors, including the Attorney General. The Committee explained to Congress the rationale for § 205, whose sex-based classification remains in effect today:

> [T]he Department of State has, at least since 1912, uniformly held that an illegitimate child born abroad of an American mother acquires at birth the

nationality of the mother, in the absence of legitimation or adjudication establishing the paternity of the child. This ruling is based...on the ground that the mother in such case stands in the place of the father.... [U]nder American law the mother has a right to custody and control of such child as against the putative father, and *is bound* to maintain it as its *natural guardian*. This rule seems to be in accord with the old Roman law and with the laws of Spain and France." To Revise and Codify the Nationality Laws of the United States, Hearings on H.R. 6127 before the House Committee on Immigration and Naturalization, 76th Cong., 1st Sess., 431 (1945) (reprinting Message from the President, Nationality Laws of the United States (1938)) (emphasis added and internal quotation marks and citations omitted).

Section 1409(a)(4) is thus paradigmatic of a historic regime that left women with responsibility, and freed men from responsibility, for nonmarital children....

It is, of course, true that the failure to recognize relevant differences is out of line with the command of equal protection....But so too do we undermine the promise of equal protection when we try to make our differences carry weight they simply cannot bear. This promise informs the proper application of heightened scrutiny to sex-based classifications and demands our scrupulous adherence to that test.

III...

Today's decision instead represents a deviation from a line of cases in which we have vigilantly applied heightened scrutiny to such classifications to determine whether a constitutional violation has occurred. I trust that the depth and vitality of these precedents will ensure that today's error remains an aberration. I respectfully dissent.

Notes

1. Custodial Preference for Unmarried Mothers. Despite the clear trend in the law against explicit sex-based custody preferences, some states retain a statutory custodial preference for the mother when the parents are unmarried. See, e.g., Okla. Stat. Ann. tit. 10, §6 (2005), interpreted in In re Adoption of Baby Boy D., 742 P.2d 1059, 1068 (Okla. 1985), cert. denied, 484 U.S. 1072 (1988) ("The mother of an illegitimate minor is entitled to its custody"); Vt. Stat. Ann. tit. 14, §2644 (1989) (mother of illegitimate child is child's guardian), interpreted in In re S.A.M., 436 A.2d 736, 738 (Vt. 1981); Ark. Code Ann. §9-10-113 (2006) (legal custody shall be in woman giving birth to the child, unless father petitions and proves his fitness, the fact that he has assumed responsibilities toward the child, and that it is in the child's best interests for him to have custody). Is such a preference consistent with *Caban*? Is this favoritism defensible within formal equality principles? Or is it, as Justice O'Connor states, an "aberration"?

2. Evaluation of the "Substantial Relationship" Test in Step-Parent Adoption Cases. *Caban* extends an earlier case, Stanley v. Illinois, 405 U.S. 645 (1972), which held that the state could not conclusively presume the unfitness of an unmarried father, without notice and a hearing, by making his children wards of the state at the death of the mother. Mr. Stanley had lived with his children for all their lives and with their mother for eighteen years before her death. The pivotal importance of a significant parental relationship evolved further in a subsequent case, Quilloin v. Walcott, 434 U.S. 246 (1978), which upheld a stepparent adoption over the father's objection based on the best interests of the child standard because the father had never lived with the mother and child and had supported and visited the child only irregularly. Moving beyond the procedural rights to notice and a hearing at issue in *Stanley*, *Quilloin*, like *Caban*, concerned the substantive grounds for cutting off the father's rights, establishing that the best interests test was unconstitutional only as applied to fathers who had a significant relationship to their children.

The importance of a significant parental relationship between the unmarried father and the child was further affirmed in the subsequent case of Lehr v. Robertson, 463 U.S. 248 (1983). Mr. Lehr had lived with the mother before the child's birth and visited her in the hospital after the child was born, but after that time, according to Lehr, the mother concealed the child's whereabouts and prevented visitation and other contact through which he might have met New York's statutory requirements entitling him to notice and a hearing relating to a child's proposed adoption. Nevertheless, in an opinion written by Justice Stevens, the Supreme Court held that the father had no constitutional right to challenge the child's adoption by the mother's husband, or even to prior notice and an opportunity to be heard, because he had not "established any custodial, personal, or financial relationship with [the child]," and thus his interests — unlike those of Mr. Caban — were merely "inchoate." 463 U.S. at 267.

The substantial relationship test has appealed to a number of courts in other countries who have also made distinctions in their adoption law between fathers who have been involved in the lives of their children and those who have not. Cases from Canada and the United Kingdom, and from the European Court of Human Rights are summarized in the leading case so holding from the Constitutional Court of South Africa. See Fraser v. The Children's Court, Pretoria North, Case CCT 31/96 (1997).

Does *Lehr* mean that a mother may cut off a biological father's rights without notice to him simply by preventing him from having anything to do with the child? Not exactly. In New York, the one thing Mr. Lehr could have done to protect his rights that did not depend upon the willingness of the mother was to file his name in the putative father registry. *Lehr* is usually read to require that a state must provide some means through which a father may unilaterally protect his rights — if only this little known option. For a detailed discussion of putative father registries, see Rebeca Aizpuru, Note, Protecting the Unwed Father's Opportunity to Parent: A Survey of Paternity Registry Statutes, 18 Rev. Litig. 703 (1999).

States now take a number of different approaches in allocating the burden for notifying an unwed father of his potential parental rights, with some placing the burden on the father using a device such as a putative father registry, some on the mother, whose failure to notify the father may present a valid adoption, and some on the state. For citations, and a full catalog of state statutes relating to unwed fathers, see Cecily L. Helms & Phillis C. Spence, Take Notice Unwed Fathers: An Unwed Mother's Right to Privacy in Adoption Proceedings, 20 Wis. Women's L.J. 1, 10-23, 41-65 (2005). Of particular interest is a Florida case holding that it is a violation of the mother's right to privacy to require disclosure of the sexual relations that led to her pregnancy and the subsequent adoption proceedings. G.P. v. Florida, 842 So. 2d 1059 (Fla. Dist. Ct. App. 2003).

Some of the difficulties raised by unmarried, nonresidential fathers seeking to block the adoption of a child by the man with whom the child and mother actually live could be alleviated if the law was more flexible in recognizing more than one father (and, in other circumstances, more than one mother) at a time. Is this a good idea? What are the problems with this approach? In the context of custody and adoption proceedings involving gay and lesbian couples, see Chapter 3, pp. 594-605.

Caban takes a formal equality approach to the rights of unmarried parents who object to the adoption of their children (at least their older children) by another. Is the Court in *Caban* blind to the gender-based realities involved? Does it ignore reality to assume that unmarried fathers are as motivated to make sound decisions on behalf of their children as unmarried mothers? Does it help improve reality?

Does the Stevens position in *Caban*, reinforced in *Lehr* and followed in *Nguyen*, successfully distinguish between mothers and fathers? Stevens' analysis in both cases turns on the differences between men and women: the mother carries the child and has the constitutional right to decide whether to bear the child or not; in "many cases" only the mother knows who fathered the child, a fact she may choose to hide; the mother may take many steps, such as marrying a different partner before the child is born, that will affect the legal determination of paternity; the mother is present at birth and only her identity is "known with certainty." Do all of these differences bear on the "substantial relationship" test evolved in *Stanley, Quilloin, Caban*, and *Lehr*? Note that some of these factors turn on legal rules, including the rule presuming paternity by the husband of a married mother, the very validity of which is implicitly at issue. Does Justice Stevens' analysis build on precisely those sex-based stereotypes that *Reed, Frontiero, Stanton*, and other equal protection cases meant to preclude? See Caroline Rogus, Conflating Women's Biological and Sociological Roles: The Ideal of Motherhood, Equal Protection, and the Implications of the *Nguyen v. INS* Opinion, 5 U. Pa. J. Const. L. 803 (2003).

Does *Nguyen* effectively overrule *Caban*? If Justice Stevens' dissenting view in *Caban* were to become the new constitutional boundary, for how long should a mother be given the advantage in custodial matters? And what should be sufficient to overcome the presumption that the mother is better situated to make decisions with respect to the child?

New York subsequently adopted different rules for newborns (children under six months) than those upheld in *Lehr*, allowing an adoption without the consent of the unmarried father unless he openly lived with the child, acknowledged his paternity, and paid reasonable pregnancy and birth expenses. N.Y. Dom. Rel. L. §111(1)(e) (1988). In 1990 the state court of appeals held that the New York statute did not give the unmarried father adequate constitutional protection, concluding that "a father who has promptly taken every available avenue to demonstrate that he is willing and able to enter into the fullest possible relationship with his under-six-month old child should have an equally fully protected interest in preventing termination of the relationship by strangers, even if he has not as yet actually been able to form that relationship." Matter of Raquel Marie X., 559 N.Y.S.2d 855 (N.Y. 1990), cert. denied sub nom. Robert C. v. Miguel T., 498 U.S. 984 (1990). In lieu of an actual parental relationship, however, the court specified some criteria that should be applied to determine whether the father of a newborn was entitled to block an adoption. These factors include the father's willingness to assume custody of the child, his public acknowledgment of paternity, his payment of pregnancy and birth expenses, and prompt steps taken to establish legal responsibility for the child. 559 N.Y.S.2d at 865, on remand, 570 N.Y.S.2d 604 (A.D. 2d Dept. 1991).

A similar test proposed by Karen Czapanskiy looks to whether the parent participated "to the fullest extent of his or her capacities in the rearing of the child" and whether the parent has been supportive of the child's other parent. Under these tests, the responsibility displayed toward the fetus by the mother would "count," as would the father's support for the mother throughout her pregnancy, each parent's willingness to take custody and provide for the child soon after the child's birth, and the father's ability to "enter into mutually respectful conversations with the mother about the future of the child before invoking a legal process." Czapanskiy, Volunteers and Draftees: The Struggle for Parental Equality, 38 UCLA L. Rev. 1415, 1477-1478 (1991). Czapanskiy argues that the mother should be required to identify the father and notify him of the birth, "except when the father has made threats or acted violently, or when he consistently has failed to respect her needs or feelings. In such a case, a judicial bypass may be necessary, similar to the judicial bypass available to minors seeking abortions." Id. at 1478-1479. Is this really a gender-neutral standard? See also Katharine K. Baker, Bargaining or Biology? The History and Future of Paternity Law and Parental Status, 14 Cornell J.L. & Pub. Pol'y 1 (2004); Nancy E. Dowd, From Genes, Marriage and Money to Nurture: Redefining Fatherhood, 10 Cardozo Women's L.J. 132 (2003).

Is there a paradox in the state insisting upon support from a nonmarital father, even if he wants no relationship with the child, while denying him all rights to the child if has not perfected his rights, once the mother wants to have the child adopted by another father? So argues Laura Oren, in The Paradox of Unmarried Fathers and The Constitution: Biology "Plus" Defines Relationships; Biology Alone Safeguards the Public Fisc, 11 Wm. & Mary J. Women & L. 47 (2004). Oren uses as an example a case in which two units of a social services department instituted contradictory proceedings, one for support against a recalcitrant father, the other for the child's adoption after the mother had relinquished her rights and the child had been placed in a pre-adoptive home. The father had urged the mother to have an abortion when she was pregnant, and initially denied paternity. After blood tests showed a high probability of his paternity, however, he then sought an order of support, and custody of the child. What should have happened in this case? See Robert S. v. Orange County Dep't of Soc. Servs., 725 N.Y.S.2d 183 (Fam. Ct. 2001) (father's petition dismissed).

3. Adoption by Third-Party Strangers. It is one thing when a mother seeks to have her husband who lives with her and her children obtain legal recognition as the children's father. But should a mother be able to give her child up to strangers over the objection of the biological father? In this situation, courts have tended to be more protective of the fathers' interests. See, e.g., Smith v. Malouf, 772 So. 2d 490 (Miss. 1998) (holding that father had right to withhold his consent to the adoption of his child, in light of his substantial efforts to establish relationship with the child); In re Petition of Doe, 638 N.E.2d 181 (Ill. 1994), cert. denied sub nom. Baby "Richard" by O'Connell v. Kirchner, 513 U.S. 994 (1994) (voiding third-party adoption of Baby Richard three years after placement with adoptive parents when father never consented to adoption and later asserted paternity). Is this increased protection justified?

Does the judicial preference for placement in a two-parent home reflect a realistic or desirable societal goal? Is it relevant that over a third of U.S. births now occur to unmarried mothers and more than a quarter of U.S. children grow up in single parent homes? National Vital Statistics Reports, Births: Final Data for 2002, vol. 52, no. 10 at 8 (December 17, 2003); U.S. Census Bureau, Current Population Survey, March 2002: Children's Living Arrangements and Characteristics: March 2002 (June 2003).

4. The Unmarried Father vs. the Married Mother. What if a child is born to an unmarried father and a mother who is married to someone else? If the biological father establishes a "substantial relationship" with the child, can the mother and her husband nonetheless cut off his involvement with the child, including visitation? Michael H. v. Gerald D., 491 U.S. 110 (1989), involved the constitutionality of a California statute, Cal. Evid. Code §621(a) (West 2004), that created, under some circumstances, an irrebuttable presumption that the father of a child born of a married woman is the woman's husband, precluding the exercise of paternal rights by any other man, including the biological father. Michael H. claimed to have lived off and on with the mother and the child and thus to have satisfied the "substantial relationship" test of *Stanley*, *Quilloin*, *Caban*, and *Lehr*, entitling him to visitation rights when the mother cut off contact. The state, however, denied him standing under the statute to assert his rights as father; the Supreme Court in *Michael H.* upheld the constitutionality of the statute.

Michael H. marked an important doctrinal shift, both for the rights of unmarried fathers and for the recognition of liberty interests under substantive due process analysis more generally. Justice Scalia, writing for the Court, reinterpreted the Court's past rulings in the substantive due process area by insisting "that the asserted liberty interest be rooted in history and tradition." 491 U.S. at 123. Characterizing the father's claim as that of an "adulterous natural father," 491 U.S. at 127 n.6, and construing the Court's previous precedents as ones that recognized the importance of "relationships that develop in the unitary family," 491 U.S. at 123, Justice Scalia reasoned that the father's claim arising from his biological connection to the child could not prevail in the face of an intact marital unit, which the state had chosen to protect.

Tradition had been used in previous cases to limit the state's ability to impose uniformity on families and to restrict their intimate practices. See, e.g., Moore v. City of East Cleveland, 431 U.S. 494, 503 (1977) (invalidating zoning ordinance that prohibited grandmother from living in single-family residence zone with her two grandchildren, based on deeply rooted institution of the extended family in this nation's history and tradition); Griswold v. Connecticut, 381 U.S. 479, 486 (1965) (invalidating ban on contraceptives based on importance of privacy in marital relationship that is "older than the Bill of Rights"). *Michael H.* signalled the use of tradition to restrict, rather than to expand, constitutionally recognized liberty interests. Is it significant that the rights of the mother were superior only because she was attached legally to a man? Does her victory actually reinforce traditional gender role norms? To compare the evolving, and conflicted, role of history and tradition in the Supreme Court's equal protection analysis, see Chapter 3, pp. 613-614.

Putting Theory into Practice

2-20. (a) Jeremiah discovered that his former fiancée was pregnant three weeks before she was ready to give birth, when a Florida adoption-agency lawyer called and asked for his consent to have the baby adopted. Jeremiah refuses to give permission. The mother believes that adoption is in the child's best interests. What is the most appropriate legal standard for handling this dispute?

(b) Eighteen months later, the child is adopted, after Jeremiah's rights are terminated. Jeremiah could have protected his rights by filing with Florida's registry for unwed fathers, but he did not know about the registry until the deadline had passed. Under Florida law, an unmarried biological father has no rights to a child who is younger than six months of age at the time the child is placed for adoption, unless the father has "filed a notarized claim of paternity form with the Florida Putative Father Registry. . . . " Fla. Stat. Ann. § 63.062(2)(b) (2005). In Florida, "an unmarried biological father, by virtue of the fact that he has engaged in a sexual relationship with a woman, is deemed to be on notice that a pregnancy and an adoption proceeding regarding that child may occur and that he has a duty to protect his own rights and interest." Fla. Stat. Ann. § 63.088 (2005).

Jeremiah has never met the child, because the mother would never consent for him to do so. Should Jeremiah be able to set the adoption aside? See Tamar Lewin, Caught in Post-Adoption Trap, Unwed Fathers Fight for Rights, N.Y. Times, March 19, 2006, at 1, 23.

(c) Assume that within six months of the baby's birth Jeremiah filed in the putative registry of Florida, the state in which he and his fiancée had lived, but his fiancée moved to Arizona without his knowledge and placed the child for adoption in that state, which did not have access to Florida's registry. Does that change the outcome in the case? See id. at 23 (describing proposed "Proud Father Act" legislation, which would establish national unwed father registry).

2-21. Indiana law allows for the changing of a child's name, upon petition of a parent, if the change is in the child's best interest. Stephen Warren petitioned the court seeking to change the surname of his four-year old child from his mother's surname to his own surname. Since birth, the child has had the surname of his mother, who was never married to his father. Warren argues that it is in the child's best interests to have his surname because (1) he is a Potowami Indian and it is "relevant to the child's Indian heritage"; and (2) he pays child support, has visitation, and is involved in the child's life. The mother opposes the petition because (1) the child has had her surname since birth and would be confused by the change; (2) all of his records use her surname; and (3) he has siblings with the same surname.

Should the court grant the petition? Explain. See In re Tibbitts, 668 N.E.2d 1266 (Ind. Ct. App. 1996) (petition granted). For a history of surnames and their gendered importance, see Lisa Kelly, Divining the Deep and Inscrutable: Toward a Gender-Neutral, Child-Centered Approach to Child Name Change Proceedings, 99 W. Va. L. Rev. 1 (1996); Merle H. Weiner, "We Are Family": Valuing Associationalism in Disputes over Children's Surnames, 75 N.C. L. Rev. 1625 (1997).

2-22. A state's law requires a parent who is seeking to give a child up for adoption to give notice to the other parent of proceedings to terminate parental rights. For fathers who are unknown or whose whereabouts are unknown, notice must be published in a newspaper and include the name and description of the mother, the name and birth date of the child, a description of the putative father, and the location the mother reasonably believes conception occurred. See Fla. Stat. ch. 63.087 (repealed 2003).

Is this a sensible way to protect the father's right to notice that his parental rights are being terminated?

3

Nonsubordination

The nonsubordination perspective shifts the focus of attention from gender-based difference to the imbalance of power between women and men. This perspective, sometimes referred to as dominance theory, makes the relevant inquiry not whether women are like, or unlike, men, but whether a rule or practice serves to subordinate women to men. Accordingly, similarities and differences between women and men are important not as givens that produce certain expected, rational consequences, but as part of a larger conceptual system designed to make women's subordination seem natural and legitimate. Catharine MacKinnon calls this theory feminism "unmodified," because it analyzes the situation of all women *as women* and abandons the "gender-neutral absolutes, such as difference and sexuality and speech and the state" that, according to MacKinnon, are characteristic of qualified theories such as socialist feminism and liberal feminism. See Catharine A. Mac Kinnon, Feminism Unmodified: Discourses on Life and Law 16 (1987).

This chapter introduces nonsubordination theory by pairing John Stuart Mill's description of women's nineteenth-century "subjection" as a "solitary breach" in the fundamental laws of modern civilization with Catharine MacKinnon's characterization of women's legal subordination as the ability of those with power—men—to identify their own point of view, systematically, as "point-of-viewlessness." The remainder of the chapter explores nonsubordination theory's claim that the law defines sex and sexual difference in ways that mask the universality of men's point of view and naturalize women's relative powerlessness in this society, primarily through legal materials relating to sexual harassment, pornography, domestic violence, and heterosexuality.

It is no accident that most of the topics of this chapter relate to sexual behavior—particularly inside families, workplaces, and educational institutions. This is largely because the sexual realm is where dominance theory has the most to offer in understanding the relationship between gender and law. With respect to access to employment, education, and other public benefits, traditional equality theory has achieved significant improvements in the position of women, although by MacKinnon's lights, these improvements have been marginal exceptions—mostly on behalf of privileged women who fit the male profile. Equality analysis, she argues, is insufficient to address the central inequalities faced by women—sexual harassment, violence against women, poverty, and control of women's sexuality. To address these problems, MacKinnon contends that we must move beyond questions of sameness and difference to the construction of women's sexuality that underpins these more central inequalities. As you study the materials in this chapter, consider what nonsubordination theory contributes to the equality principles studied this far. Is it a supplement, a full replacement, or something else?

A. WOMEN'S RIGHTS AND POWER IN THE LIBERAL STATE

≡≡≡ *John Stuart Mill, The Subjection of Women*
Three Essays by John Stuart Mill 427-428, 443-444, 449-450 (World's Classics edition 1912) (1869)

[T]he principle which regulates the existing social relations between the two sexes—the legal subordination of one sex to the other—is wrong in itself, and now one of the chief hindrances to human improvement;...it ought to be replaced by a principle of perfect equality, admitting no power or privilege on the one side, nor disability on the other.

The...difficulty...is that which exists in all cases in which there is a mass of feeling to be contended against. So long as an opinion is strongly rooted in the feelings, it gains rather than loses in stability by having a preponderating weight of argument against it. For if it were accepted as a result of argument, the refutation of the argument might shake the solidity of the conviction; but when it rests solely on feeling, the worse it fares in argumentative contest, the more persuaded its adherents are that their feeling must have some deeper ground, which the arguments do not reach; and while the feeling remains, it is always throwing up fresh entrenchments of argument to repair any breach made in the old. And there are so many causes tending to make the feelings connected with this subject the most intense and most deeply-rooted of all those which gather round and protect old institutions and customs, that we need not wonder to find them as yet less undermined and loosened than any of the rest by the progress of the great modern spiritual and social transition; nor suppose that the barbarisms to which men cling longest must be less barbarisms than those which they earlier shake off.

All causes, social and natural, combine to make it unlikely that women should be collectively rebellious to the power of men. They are so far in a position different from all other subject classes, that their masters require something more from them than actual service. Men do not want solely the obedience of women, they want their sentiments. All men, except the most brutish, desire to have, in the woman most nearly connected with them, not a forced slave but a willing one; not a slave merely, but a favorite. They have therefore put everything in practice to enslave their minds. The masters of all slaves rely, for maintaining obedience, on fear; either fear of themselves, or religious fears. The masters of women wanted more than simple obedience, and they turned the whole force of education to effect their purpose. All women are brought up from the very earliest years in the belief that their ideal of character is the very opposite to that of men; not self-will, and government by self-control, but submission, and yielding to the control of others. All the moralities tell them that it is their nature, to live for others; to make complete abnegation of themselves, and to have no life but in their affections. And by their affections are meant the only ones they are allowed to have—those to the men with whom they are connected, or to the children who constitute an additional and indefeasible tie between them and a man. When we put together three things—first, the natural attraction between opposite sexes; secondly, the wife's entire dependence on the husband, every privilege or pleasure she has being either his gift, or depending entirely on his will; and lastly, that the principal object of human pursuit, consideration, and all objects of social ambition, can in general be sought or obtained by her only through him—it would be a miracle if the object of being attractive to men had not become the polar star of feminine education and formation of character. And, this great means of influence over the minds of women having been acquired, an instinct of selfishness made men avail themselves of it to the utmost as a means of holding women in subjection, by representing to them meekness, submissiveness, and resignation of all individual will into the hands of a man, as an essential part of sexual attractiveness....

The social subordination of women thus stands out an isolated fact in modern social institutions; a solitary breach of what has become their fundamental law; a single relic of an old world of thought and practice exploded in everything else, but retained in the one thing of most universal interest....

Catharine A. MacKinnon, Feminism Unmodified: Discourses on Life and Law
32-37, 40-43 (1987)

What is a gender question a question of? What is an inequality question a question of? These two questions underlie applications of the equality principle to issues of gender, but they are seldom explicitly asked. I think it speaks to the way gender has structured thought and perception that mainstream legal and moral theory tacitly gives the same answer to them both: these are questions of sameness and difference. The mainstream doctrine of the law of sex discrimination that results is, in my view, largely responsible for the fact that sex equality law has been so utterly ineffective at getting women what we need and are socially prevented from having on the basis of a condition of birth: a chance at productive lives of reasonable physical security, self-expression, individuation, and minimal respect and dignity....

Two alternate paths to equality for women emerge within [the] dominant approach.... The leading one is: be the same as men. This path is termed gender neutrality legally and the single standard philosophically.... To women who want equality yet find that you are different, the doctrine provides an alternate route: be different from men. This equal recognition of difference is termed the special benefit rule or the special protection rule legally, the double standard philosophically....

My concern is not with which of these paths to sex equality is preferable...although most discourse on sex discrimination revolves about these questions as if that were all there is. My point is logically prior: to treat issues of sex equality as issues of sameness and difference *is to take a particular approach*. I call this the difference approach because it is obsessed with the sex difference....

Under the sameness standard, women are measured according to our correspondence with man, our equality judged by our proximity to his measure. Under the difference standard, we are measured according to our lack of correspondence with him, our womanhood judged by our distance from his measure. Gender neutrality is thus simply the male standard, and the special protection rule is simply the female standard, but do not be deceived: masculinity, or maleness, is the referent for both.... As applied, the sameness standard has mostly gotten men the benefit of those few things women historically had—for all the good they did us. Almost every sex discrimination case that has been won at the Supreme Court level has been brought by a man....

In reality, which this approach is not long on because it is liberal idealism talking to itself, virtually every quality that distinguishes men from women is already affirmatively compensated in this society. Men's physiology defines most sports, their needs define auto and health insurance coverage, their socially designed biographies define workplace expectations and successful career patterns, their perspectives and concerns define quality in scholarship, their experiences and obsessions define merit, their objectification of life defines art, their military service defines citizenship, their presence defines family, their inability to get along with each other—their wars and rulerships—defines history, their image defines god, and their genitals define sex. For each of their differences from women, what amounts to an affirmative action plan is in effect, otherwise known as the structure and values of American society. But whenever women are, by this standard, "different" from men and insist on not having it held against us, whenever a difference is used to keep us second class and we refuse to smile about it, equality law has a paradigm trauma and it's crisis time for the doctrine. . . .

The women that gender neutrality benefits, and there are some, show the suppositions of [the difference] approach in highest relief. They are mostly women who have been able to construct a biography that somewhat approximates the male norm, at least on paper. They are the qualified, the least of sex discrimination's victims. When they are denied a man's chance, it looks the most like sex bias. The more unequal society gets, the fewer such women are permitted to exist. Therefore, the more unequal society gets, the less likely the difference doctrine is to be able to do anything about it, because unequal power creates both the appearance and the reality of sex differences along the same lines as it creates its sex inequalities. . . .

There is an alternative approach, one that threads its way through existing law and expresses, I think, the reason equality law exists in the first place. It provides a second answer, a dissident answer in law and philosophy, to both the equality question and the gender question. In this approach, an equality question is a question of the distribution of power. Gender is also a question of power, specifically of male supremacy and female subordination. The question of equality, from the standpoint of what it is going to take to get it, is at root a question of hierarchy, which — as power succeeds in constructing social perception and social reality — derivatively becomes a categorical distinction, a difference. Here, on the first day that matters, dominance was achieved, probably by force. By the second day, division along the same lines had to be relatively firmly in place. On the third day, if not sooner, differences were demarcated, together with social systems to exaggerate them in perception and in fact, because the systematically differential delivery of benefits and deprivations required making no mistake about who was who. Comparatively speaking, man has been resting ever since. Gender might not even code as difference, might not mean distinction epistemologically, were it not for its consequences for social power.

I call this the dominance approach, and it is the ground I have been standing on in criticizing mainstream law. The goal of this dissident approach is not to make legal categories trace and trap the way things are. It is not to make rules that fit reality. It is critical of reality. Its task is not to formulate abstract standards that will produce determinate outcomes in particular cases. Its project is more substantive, more jurisprudential than formulaic, which is why it is difficult for the mainstream discourse to dignify it as an approach to doctrine or to imagine it as a rule of law at all. It proposes to expose that which women have had little choice but to be confined to, in order to change it.

The dominance approach centers on the most sex-differential abuses of women as a gender, abuses that sex equality law in its difference garb could not confront. It is based on a reality about which little of a systematic nature was known before 1970, a reality that calls for a new conception of the problem of sex inequality. This new information includes not only the extent and intractability of sex segregation into poverty, which has been known before, but the range of issues termed violence against women, which has not been. It combines women's material desperation, through being relegated to categories of jobs that pay nil, with the massive amount of rape and attempted rape — 44 percent of all women — about which virtually nothing is done; the sexual assault of children — 38 percent of girls and 10 percent of boys — which is apparently endemic to the patriarchal family; the battery of women that is systematic in one quarter to one third of our homes; prostitution, women's fundamental economic condition, what we do when all else fails, and for many women in this country, all else fails often; and pornography, an industry that traffics in female flesh, making sex inequality into sex to the tune of eight billion dollars a year in profits largely to organized crime.

These experiences have been silenced out of the difference definition of sex equality largely because they happen almost exclusively to women. Understand: for this reason, they are considered not to raise sex equality issues. Because this treatment is done almost uniquely to women, it is implicitly treated as a difference, the sex difference, when in fact it is the socially situated subjection of women. The whole point of women's social relegation to inferiority as a gender is that for the most part these things aren't done to men. . . .

The second approach — which is not abstract, which is at odds with socially imposed reality and therefore does not look like a standard according to the standard for standards — became the implicit model for racial justice applied by the courts during the sixties. It has since eroded with the erosion of judicial commitment to racial equality. It was based on the realization that the condition of Blacks in particular was not fundamentally a matter of rational or irrational differentiation on the basis of race but was fundamentally a matter of white supremacy, under which racial differences became invidious as a consequence. To consider gender in this way, observe again that men are as different from women as women are from men, but socially the sexes are not equally powerful. To be on the top of a hierarchy is certainly different from being on the bottom, but that is an obfuscatingly neutralized way of putting it, as a hierarchy is a great deal more than that. If gender were merely a question of difference, sex inequality would be a problem of mere sexism, of mistaken differentiation, of inaccurate categorization of individuals. This is what the difference approach thinks it is and is therefore sensitive to. But if gender is an inequality first, constructed as a socially relevant differentiation in order to keep that inequality in place, the sex inequality questions are questions of systematic dominance, of male supremacy, which is not at all abstract and is anything but a mistake.

If differentiation into classifications, in itself, is discrimination, as it is in use of law to change group-based social inequalities becomes problematic, even contradictory. This is because the group whose situation is to be changed must necessarily be legally identified and delineated, yet to do so is considered in fundamental tension with the guarantee against legally sanctioned inequality. If differentiation is discrimination, affirmative action, and any legal change in social inequality, is discrimination—but the existing social differentiations which constitute the inequality are not? This is only to say that, in the view that equates differentiation with discrimination, changing an unequal status quo is discrimination, but allowing it to exist is not.

Looking at the difference approach and the dominance approach from each other's point of view clarifies some otherwise confusing tensions in sex equality debates. From the point of view of the dominance approach, it becomes clear that the difference approach adopts the point of view of male supremacy on the status of the sexes. Simply by treating the status quo as "the standard," it invisibly and uncritically accepts the arrangements under male supremacy. In this sense, the difference approach is masculinist, although it can be expressed in a female voice. The dominance approach, in that it sees the inequalities of the social world from the standpoint of the subordination of women to men, is feminist.

NOTE ON DOMINANCE THEORY AND LIBERALISM

John Stuart Mill—the leading spokesman for nineteenth-century liberalism—finds the subordination of women an aberrational blind spot of liberalism. MacKinnon, on the other hand, finds the subordination of women a more or less inevitable consequence of liberalism's emphasis on the individual, its claim to objectivity, and its idealism. As you read the materials in this chapter, consider whether this difference is significant. Try, also, to identify the areas of agreement and disagreement between liberal theory, represented best by the formal equality principles developed in Chapter 2, and the nonsubordination or dominance approach represented in these two readings. In addition to the points of tension MacKinnon identifies, consider the following:

MacKinnon's dominance approach is . . . inconsistent with liberalism's commitment to neutrality with respect to contested conceptions of the good. MacKinnon's approach assumes that equality is the dominant, lexically prior political value. Thus, the fact that anti-pornography laws might result in the suppression of works of serious artistic or literary merit is shrugged off by MacKinnon with the remark, "[I]f a woman is subjected, why should it matter that the work has other value?" [Catharine A. MacKinnon, Feminism Unmodified: Discourses on Life and Law 152-153 (1987).] Similarly, the fact that sweeping judicially-ordered comparable worth reforms might have serious repercussions for the nation's economic health is not seen as a good reason why courts should refrain from treating market-driven pay inequities as actionable forms of sex discrimination. [Id. at 36.] By contrast, current sex discrimination law does not view equality as a sovereign good that invariably trumps such competing values as individual liberty, individual rights, or the common good. It recognizes that there may be "important governmental objectives" [Craig v. Boren, 429 U.S. 190, 199-200 n.7 (1976)] that on occasion override the state's interest in promoting gender equality.

Gregory Bassham, Feminist Legal Theory: A Liberal Response, 6 Notre Dame
J.L. Ethics & Pub. Pol'y 293, 302 (1992). How might MacKinnon respond to
this critique? How much of a challenge does MacKinnon's dominance approach
raise to liberal theory?

B. SEXUAL HARASSMENT

1. Sexual Harassment in the Workplace

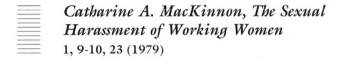

Catharine A. MacKinnon, The Sexual Harassment of Working Women
1, 9-10, 23 (1979)

Intimate violation of women by men is sufficiently pervasive in American society
as to be nearly invisible. Contained by internalized and structural forms of power,
it has been nearly inaudible. Conjoined with men's control over women's material
survival, as in the home or on the job, or over women's learning and educational
advancement in school, it has become institutionalized....

Sexual harassment, most broadly defined, refers to the unwanted imposition
of sexual requirements in the context of a relationship of unequal power. Central
to the concept is the use of power derived from one social sphere to level benefits
or impose deprivations in another. The major dynamic is best expressed as the
reciprocal enforcement of two inequalities.

When one is sexual, the other material, the cumulative sanction is particularly
potent. American society legitimizes male sexual dominance of women and
employer's control of workers....

[T]he sexual harassment of women can occur largely because women occupy
inferior job positions and job roles; at the same time, sexual harassment works to
keep women in such positions. Sexual harassment, then, uses and helps create
women's structurally inferior status....

Catharine A. MacKinnon, Afterword, in Directions in Sexual Harassment Law
672 (Catharine A. MacKinnon and Reva B. Siegel eds., 2004)

In the quarter century since some sex forced by power became illegal in the
United States, has anything changed?

The experience has been named, its injuries afforded the dignity of a civil
rights violation, raising the human status of its survivors. Resentment of
unwanted sex under unequal conditions is expressed more openly and given
more public respect. Women may feel more valid and powerful, less stigmatized
and scared, more like freedom fighters and less like prudes, when they turn down
sex they do not want in unequal settings. Many more people know that a sexual

harasser is a sex bigot and see that the use of power to leverage sexual access as a tool of dominance, whether the perpetrator knows that or not. Where sex equality laws apply — most employment and education, some housing — there is some- place to go to complain. Law is considerably more responsive to survivors than it was before, whether they refuse sexual bargains, resist sexualized environments, or comply with sexual demands they cannot avoid.

But sexual harassment is still not actionable every place it occurs; zero tolerance is the rule virtually nowhere; resistance is far from safe or costless; perpetrators often protect one another, and sometimes victims protect them too. Institutions are often recalcitrant in taking responsibility and are often absolved of liability when they are oblivious. Victims seldom receive the sup- port they deserve. Complaining about sexual harassment can be more injur- ious, if also more self-respecting, than suffering in silence. Forms of power used to force sex other than economic, educational, or governmen- tal...remain exempt from the facial reach of most equality laws. So far as is known, men sexually harass women as often as they did before sexual harassment became illegal.

 ## Kathryn Abrams, Gender Discrimination and the Transformation of Workplace Norms
42 Vand. L. Rev. 1183, 1207-1209 (1989)

[S]exually oriented behavior in the workplace produces at least two responses among women that contribute to their subordination.... One response is a fear of sexual coercion. Sexually oriented behavior brings into the workplace echoes of a context in which men and women often are radically unequal. A woman struggling to establish credibility in a setting in which she may not be, or may not feel, welcome, can be swept off balance by a reminder that she can be raped, fondled, or subjected to repeated sexual demands. Her employment set- ting, already precarious, can be transformed instantly into an unwanted sexual encounter in which she is likely to feel even less control, a transformation that can cast shadows even when demands are not being made. The feelings of anxiety, fear, or vulnerability produced by the spectre of sexual coercion prevent women from feeling, or being viewed as, the equals of their male counterparts in the workplace.

But a woman need not be threatened with sexual coercion to feel, and to be perceived as, unequal in the workplace. Sexual inquiries, jokes, remarks, or innuendoes sometimes can raise the spectre of coercion, but they more predic- tably have the effect of reminding a woman that she is viewed as an object of sexual derision rather than as a credible co-worker. A woman who is continuously queried by male colleagues about her sexual preferences, referred to by co-work- ers as "the fucking flag girl," or depicted on the walls of men's restrooms in sexual poses is being told that she is not, first and foremost, a credible colleague and an equal. This message would be disturbing to any worker, even one who felt com- fortable and secure in the workplace. For a woman worker, who may not have been socialized to feel comfortable in that role, and who may have faced numerous men who have difficulty viewing women as workers rather than wives or dates, this message can be devastating. Treatment that sexualizes women workers prevents them from feeling, and prevents others from perceiving them, as equal in the workplace.

L. Camille Hébert, The Economic Implications of Sexual Harassment for Women
3 Kan. J.L. & Pub. Pol'y 41, 47-50 (Spring 1994)

A common view is that sexual harassment . . . is motivated by sexual desire and that women are targets of sexual harassment because they are sexually attractive to their harasser. . . .

Existing patterns of sexual harassment in the workplace, however, are difficult to explain as caused by only sexual desire — even nonmutual, one-sided sexual desire.

One aspect of the pattern of sexual harassment in the workplace that suggests sexual harassment is motivated, or at least caused, by economic considerations is the profile of the women who are most often subjected to harassment. One characteristic common among women who report sexual harassment is economic vulnerability. . . .

[M]any women who report sexual harassment are very dependent on their jobs, which would make them economically vulnerable to sexual harassment. Women with low seniority and those in low-status and low-skill jobs are more frequently subjected to sexual harassment than women in higher status and higher skill jobs. Women in trainee positions and women on probation are also more frequently subjected to sexual harassment. There is no reason to expect that these women are more sexually attractive or desirable than women who are not in these jobs. . . .

[W]omen who are members of minority groups are more likely to be sexually harassed than nonminority women. . . .

. . . Highly educated women appear to be more likely to be sexually harassed than other women; similarly, women moving into nontraditional jobs — jobs traditionally dominated by men — frequently are subjected to sexual harassment. There is no reason to believe that such women are more sexually attractive than other women.

Nor, however, are these women necessarily more economically vulnerable than other women. In fact, the converse is likely to be true. . . . This does not mean, however, that sexual harassment against these women is not the result of economic factors. In these situations, economic factors other than economic vulnerability appear to be at work, such as the desire of men to ensure continued economic dominance over women in the workplace by discouraging women from entering jobs in which they would compete with men.

Some commentators have argued that sexual harassment is motivated by factors other than power imbalances by pointing to the fact that sexual harassment most often occurs among co-workers rather than between a supervisor and a subordinate. Such a contention, however, fails to recognize that forms of economic power other than supervisory power exist in the workplace. Males may be able to exert economic power over female co-workers by withholding information and training necessary to job performance, particularly when women are moving into jobs that traditionally have been held by men. Men may also be able to assert economic power over female co-workers by threatening to sabotage work or job performance. Finally, men, because of their longer job tenure (and because of their maleness), may simply have more authority with supervisors than newer female employees and thereby be able to influence the supervisor's perception of the women's job performance.

Sexual harassment in the workplace may even be motivated by the frustration some men feel over the loss of economic power in the workplace.... Some men feel threatened, both socially and economically, by the advancement of women; some of these men react to these women with hostility.

It is not surprising that this hostility would manifest itself in abusive sexual activity directed toward women. Because of both biological and social factors, men often have, or believe themselves to have, power over women in their sexual relationships. Some men may resort to sexual harassment in the workplace to assert power in a sexual context, in which they believe they have an advantage over women, and to express frustration over their loss or lack of relative power over women in the workplace context....

A final reason to doubt the sexual attractiveness theory of sexual harassment is that women surveyed in sexual harassment studies report that their harassers also harass others at work. This finding suggests that sexual harassment is more a pattern of abusive behavior than the result of "isolated instances of personal sexual attraction."

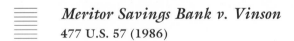

Meritor Savings Bank v. Vinson
477 U.S. 57 (1986)

Justice REHNQUIST delivered the opinion of the court.

This case presents important questions concerning claims of workplace "sexual harassment" brought under Title VII of the Civil Rights Act of 1964....

I

In 1974, respondent Mechelle Vinson met Sidney Taylor, a vice president of what is now petitioner Meritor Savings Bank (bank) and manager of one of its branch offices.... With Taylor as her supervisor, respondent started as a teller-trainee, and thereafter was promoted to teller, head teller, and assistant branch manager. She worked at the same branch for four years, and it is undisputed that her advancement there was based on merit alone. In September 1978, respondent notified Taylor that she was taking sick leave for an indefinite period. On November 1, 1978, the bank discharged her for excessive use of that leave.

Respondent brought this action against Taylor and the bank, claiming that during her four years at the bank she had "constantly been subjected to sexual harassment" by Taylor in violation of Title VII. She sought injunctive relief, compensatory and punitive damages against Taylor and the bank, and attorney's fees.

At the 11-day bench trial, the parties presented conflicting testimony about Taylor's behavior during respondent's employment. Respondent testified that during her probationary period as a teller-trainee, Taylor treated her in a fatherly way and made no sexual advances. Shortly thereafter, however, he invited her out to dinner and, during the course of the meal, suggested that they go to a motel to have sexual relations. At first she refused, but out of what she described as fear of losing her job she eventually agreed. According to respondent, Taylor thereafter made repeated demands upon her for sexual favors, usually at the branch, both during and after business hours; she estimated that over the next several years she had intercourse with him some 40 or 50 times. In addition, respondent testified that Taylor fondled her in front of other employees, followed her into the women's restroom when she went there alone, exposed himself to her, and even forcibly raped her on several occasions. These activities ceased after 1977, respondent stated, when she started going with a steady boyfriend....

Taylor denied respondent's allegations of sexual activity, testifying that he never fondled her, never made suggestive remarks to her, never engaged in sexual intercourse with her, and never asked her to do so. He contended instead that respondent made her accusations in response to a business-related dispute. The bank also denied respondent's allegations and asserted that any sexual harassment by Taylor was unknown to the bank and engaged in without its consent or approval.

The District Court denied relief....

The Court of Appeals for the District of Columbia Circuit reversed. [753 F.2d 141 (D.C. Cir. 1985).]...

II...

Respondent argues ... that unwelcome sexual advances that create an offensive or hostile working environment violate Title VII. Without question, when a supervisor sexually harasses a subordinate because of the subordinate's sex, that supervisor "discriminate[s]" on the basis of sex. Petitioner apparently does not challenge this proposition. It contends instead that in prohibiting discrimination with respect to "compensation, terms, conditions, or privileges" of employment, Congress was concerned with what petitioner describes as "tangible loss" of "an economic character," not "purely psychological aspects of the workplace environment." ... In support of this claim petitioner observes that in both the legislative history of Title VII and this Court's Title VII decisions, the focus has been on tangible, economic barriers erected by discrimination.

We reject petitioner's view. First, the language of Title VII is not limited to "economic" or "tangible" discrimination. The phrase "terms, conditions, or privileges of employment" evinces a congressional intent "'to strike at the entire spectrum of disparate treatment of men and women'" in employment....

Second, in 1980 the EEOC issued Guidelines specifying that "sexual harassment," as there defined, is a form of sex discrimination prohibited by Title VII.... The EEOC Guidelines fully support the view that harassment leading to noneconomic injury can violate Title VII.

In defining "sexual harassment," the Guidelines first describe the kinds of workplace conduct that may be actionable under Title VII. These include "[u]nwelcome sexual advances, requests for sexual favors, and other verbal or physical conduct of a sexual nature." 29 CFR § 1604.11(a) (1985). Relevant to the charges at issue in this case, the Guidelines provide that such sexual misconduct constitutes prohibited "sexual harassment," whether or not it is directly linked to the grant or denial of an economic *quid pro quo*, where "such conduct has the purpose or effect of unreasonably interfering with an individual's work performance or creating an intimidating, hostile, or offensive working environment." § 1604.11(a)(3).

In concluding that so-called "hostile environment" (i.e., non *quid pro quo*) harassment violates Title VII, the EEOC drew upon a substantial body of judicial decisions and EEOC precedent holding that Title VII affords employees the right to work in an environment free from discriminatory intimidation, ridicule, and insult.... Courts applied this principle to harassment based on race, religion, and national origin. Nothing in Title VII suggests that a hostile environment based on discriminatory sexual harassment should not be likewise prohibited. The Guidelines thus appropriately drew from, and were fully consistent with, the existing case law.

Since the Guidelines were issued, courts have uniformly held, and we agree, that a plaintiff may establish a violation of Title VII by proving that discrimination based on sex has created a hostile or abusive work environment. As the Court of Appeals for the Eleventh Circuit wrote in Henson v. Dundee, 682 F.2d 897, 902 (1982): "Sexual harassment which creates a hostile or offensive environment for members of one sex is every bit the arbitrary barrier to sexual equality at the workplace that racial harassment is to racial equality. Surely, a requirement that a man or woman run a gauntlet of sexual abuse in return for the privilege of being allowed to work and make a living can be as demeaning and disconcerting as the harshest of racial epithets."...

Of course, as the courts in both *Rogers* and *Henson* recognized, not all workplace conduct that may be described as "harassment" affects a "term, condition, or privilege" of employment within the meaning of Title VII. See Rogers v. EEOC, [454 F.2d at 238] ("mere utterance of an ethnic or racial epithet which engenders offensive feelings in an employee" would not affect the conditions of employment to sufficiently significant degree to violate Title VII); *Henson*, 682 F.2d, at 904 (quoting same). For sexual harassment to be actionable, it must be sufficiently severe or pervasive "to alter the conditions of [the victim's] employment and create an abusive working environment." Id. Respondent's allegations in this case — which include not only pervasive harassment but also criminal conduct of the most serious nature — are plainly sufficient to state a claim for "hostile environment" sexual harassment....

[T]he District court apparently believed that a claim for sexual harassment will not lie absent an economic effect on the complainant's employment. See id. "It is without question that sexual harassment of female employees in which they are asked or required to submit to sexual demands as a *condition to obtain employment or to maintain employment or to obtain promotions* falls within protection of Title VII") (emphasis added). Since it appears that the District Court made its findings without ever considering the "hostile environment" theory of sexual harassment, the Court of Appeals' decision to remand was correct.

[T]he District Court's conclusion that no actionable harassment occurred might have rested on its earlier "finding" that "[i]f [respondent] and Taylor did engage in an intimate or sexual relationship..., that relationship was a voluntary one." Id. at 42. But the fact that sex-related conduct was "voluntary," in the sense that the complainant was not forced to participate against her will, is not a defense to a sexual harassment suit brought under Title VII. The gravamen of any sexual harassment claim is that the alleged sexual advances were "unwelcome." 29 CFR § 1604.11(a) (1985). While the question whether particular conduct was indeed unwelcome presents difficult problems of proof and turns largely on credibility determinations committed to the trier of fact, the District Court in this case erroneously focused on the "voluntariness" of respondent's participation in the claimed sexual episodes. The correct inquiry is whether respondent by her conduct indicated that the alleged sexual advances were unwelcome, not whether her actual participation in sexual intercourse was voluntary.

Petitioner contends that even if this case must be remanded to the District Court, the Court of Appeals erred in one of the terms of its remand. Specifically, the Court of Appeals stated that testimony about respondent's "dress and personal fantasies," [753 F.2d. at 146 n.36], which the District Court apparently admitted into evidence, "had no place in this litigation." Id. The apparent ground for this conclusion was that respondent's voluntariness vel non in submitting to Taylor's advances was immaterial to her sexual harassment claim. While "voluntariness" in the sense of consent is not a defense to such a claim, it does not follow that a complainant's sexually provocative speech or dress is irrelevant as a matter of law in determining whether he or she found particular sexual advances unwelcome. To the contrary, such evidence is obviously relevant. The EEOC Guidelines emphasize that the trier of fact must determine the existence of sexual harassment in light of "the record as a whole" and "the totality of circumstances, such as the nature of the sexual advances and the context in which the alleged incidents occurred." 29 CFR § 1604.11(b) (1985). Respondent's claim that any marginal relevance of the evidence in question was outweighed by the potential for unfair prejudice is the sort of argument properly addressed to the District Court. In this case the District Court concluded that the evidence should be admitted, and the Court of Appeals' contrary conclusion was based upon the erroneous, categorical view that testimony about provocative dress and publicly expressed sexual fantasies "had no place in this litigation." [753 F.2d at 146 n.36.] While the District Court must carefully weigh the applicable considerations in deciding whether to admit evidence of this kind, there is no *per se* rule against its admissibility....

IV. . . .

Accordingly, the judgement of the Court of Appeals reversing the judgement of the District Court is affirmed, and the case is remanded for further proceedings consistent with this opinion.

It is so ordered.

≣≣ *Harris v. Forklift Systems, Inc.*
≣≣ 510 U.S. 17 (1993)

Justice O'CONNOR delivered the opinion of the Court.

In this case we consider the definition of a discriminatorily "abusive work environment" (also known as a "hostile work environment") under Title VII. . . .

I

Teresa Harris worked as a manager at Forklift Systems, Inc., an equipment rental company, from April 1985 until October 1987. Charles Hardy was Forklift's president.

The Magistrate found that, throughout Harris' time at Forklift, Hardy often insulted her because of her gender and often made her the target of unwanted sexual innuendos. Hardy told Harris on several occasions, in the presence of other employees, "You're a woman, what do you know" and "We need a man as the rental manager"; at least once, he told her she was "a dumb ass woman." . . . Again in front of others, he suggested that the two of them "go to the Holiday Inn to negotiate [Harris'] raise." . . . Hardy occasionally asked Harris and other female employees to get coins from his front pants pocket. He threw objects on the ground in front of Harris and other women, and asked them to pick the objects up. . . . He made sexual innuendos about Harris' and other women's clothing.

In mid-August 1987, Harris complained to Hardy about his conduct. Hardy said he was surprised that Harris was offended, claimed he was only joking, and apologized. . . . He also promised he would stop, and based on this assurance Harris stayed on the job. But in early September, Hardy began anew: While Harris was arranging a deal with one of Forklift's customers, he asked her, again in front of other employees, "What did you do, promise the guy . . . some [sex] Saturday night?" . . . On October 1, Harris collected her paycheck and quit.

Harris then sued Forklift, claiming that Hardy's conduct had created an abusive work environment for her because of her gender. The United States District Court for the Middle District of Tennessee, adopting the report and recommendation of the Magistrate, found this to be "a close case," . . . but held that Hardy's conduct did not create an abusive environment. The court found that some of Hardy's comments "offended [Harris], and would offend the reasonable woman," . . . but that they were not "so severe as to be expected to seriously affect [Harris'] psychological well-being." A reasonable woman manager under like circumstances would have been offended by Hardy, but his conduct would not have risen to the level of interfering with that person's work performance. "Neither do I believe that [Harris] was subjectively so offended that she suffered injury.... Although Hardy may at times have genuinely offended [Harris], I do not believe that he created a working environment so poisoned as to be intimidating or abusive to [Harris]."...

In focusing on the employee's psychological well-being, the District Court was following Circuit precedent. See Rabidue v. Osceola Refining Co., 805 F.2d 611, 620 (6th Cir. 1986), cert. denied, 481 U.S. 1041 (1987). The United States Court of Appeals for the Sixth Circuit affirmed...

II

Title VII...makes it "an unlawful employment practice for an employer ...to discriminate against any individual with respect to his compensation, terms, conditions, or privileges of employment, because of such individual's race, color, religion, sex, or national origin." 42 U.S.C. §2000e-2(a)(1). As we made clear in Meritor Savings Bank v. Vinson, 477 U.S. 57 (1986), this language "is not limited to 'economic' or 'tangible' discrimination. The phrase 'terms, conditions, or privileges of employment' evinces a congressional intent 'to strike at the entire spectrum of disparate treatment of men and women' in employment," which includes requiring people to work in a discriminatorily hostile or abusive environment. Id., at 64, quoting Los Angeles Dept. of Water & Power v. Manhart.... When the workplace is permeated with "discriminatory intimidation, ridicule, and insult," id., at 65, that is "sufficiently severe or pervasive to alter the condition of the victim's employment and create an abusive working environment," id., at 67, Title VII is violated.

This standard, which we reaffirm today, takes a middle path between making actionable any conduct that is merely offensive and requiring the conduct to cause a tangible psychological injury. As we pointed out in *Meritor*, "mere utterance of an...epithet which engenders offensive feelings in an employee,"...does not sufficiently affect the conditions of employment to implicate Title VII. Conduct that is not severe or pervasive enough to create an objectively hostile or abusive work environment — an environment that a reasonable person would find hostile or abusive — is beyond Title VII's purview. Likewise, if the victim does not subjectively perceive the environment to be abusive, the conduct has not actually altered the conditions of the victim's employment, and there is no Title VII violation.

But Title VII comes into play before the harassing conduct leads to a nervous breakdown. A discriminatorily abusive work environment, even one that does not seriously affect employees' psychological well-being, can and often will detract from employees' job performance, discourage employees from remaining on the job, or keep them from advancing in their careers. Moreover, even without regard to these tangible effects, the very fact that the discriminatory conduct was so severe or pervasive that it created a work environment abusive to employees because of their race, gender, religion, or national origin offends Title VII's broad rule of workplace equality. The appalling conduct alleged in *Meritor*, and the reference in that case to environments "'so heavily polluted with discrimination as to destroy completely the emotional and psychological stability of minority group workers,'" [id.] at 66, quoting Rogers v. EEOC, 454 F.2d 234, 238 (5th Cir. 1971), cert. denied, 406 U.S. 957 (1972), merely present some especially egregious examples of harassment. They do not mark the boundary of what is actionable.

We therefore believe the District Court erred in relying on whether the conduct "seriously affect[ed] plaintiff's psychological well-being" or led her to "suffe[r] injury." Such an inquiry may needlessly focus the factfinder's attention on concrete psychological harm, an element Title VII does not require. Certainly Title VII bars conduct that would seriously affect a reasonable person's psychological well-being, but the statute is not limited to such conduct. So long as the environment would reasonably be perceived, and is perceived, as hostile or abusive, *Meritor*, supra, 477 U.S. at 67, there is no need for it also to be psychologically injurious.

This is not, and by its nature cannot be, a mathematically precise test. We need not answer today all the potential questions it raises. . . . But we can say that whether an environment is "hostile" or "abusive" can be determined only by looking at all the circumstances. These may include the frequency of the discriminatory conduct; its severity; whether it is physically threatening or humiliating, or a mere offensive utterance; and whether it unreasonably interferes with an employee's work performance. The effect on the employee's psychological well-being is, of course, relevant to determining whether the plaintiff actually found the environment abusive. But while psychological harm, like any other relevant factor, may be taken into account, no single factor is required. . . .

We therefore reverse the judgment of the Court of Appeals, and remand the case for further proceedings consistent with this opinion.

Justice SCALIA, concurring. . . .

"Abusive" (or "hostile," which in this context I take to mean the same thing) does not seem to me a very clear standard — and I do not think clarity is at all increased by adding the adverb "objectively" or by appealing to a "reasonable person's" notion of what the vague word means. Today's opinion does list a number of factors that contribute to abusiveness, . . . but since it neither says how much of each is necessary (an impossible task) nor identifies any single factor as determinative, it thereby adds little certitude. As a practical matter, today's holding lets virtually unguided juries decide whether sex-related conduct engaged in (or permitted by) an employer is egregious enough to warrant an award of damages. One might say that what constitutes "negligence" (a traditional jury question) is not much more clear and certain than what constitutes "abusiveness." Perhaps so. But the class of plaintiffs seeking to recover for negligence is limited to those who have suffered harm, whereas under this statute "abusiveness" is to be the test of whether legal harm has been suffered, opening more expansive vistas of litigation.

Be that as it may, I know of no alternative to the course the Court today has taken. One of the factors mentioned in the Court's nonexhaustive list—whether the conduct unreasonably interferes with an employee's work performance—would, if it were made an absolute test, provide greater guidance to juries and employers. But I see no basis for such a limitation in the language of the statute. Accepting *Meritor*'s interpretation of the term "conditions of employment" as the law, the test is not whether work has been impaired, but whether working conditions have been discriminatorily altered. I know of no test more faithful to the inherently vague statutory language than the one the Court today adopts. For these reasons, I join the opinion of the Court.

Justice GINSBURG, concurring.

Today the Court reaffirms the holding of Meritor Savings Bank v. Vinson...: "[A] plaintiff may establish a violation of Title VII by proving that discrimination based on sex has created a hostile or abusive work environment." The critical issue, Title VII's text indicates, is whether members of one sex are exposed to disadvantageous terms or conditions of employment to which members of the other sex are not exposed.... As the Equal Employment Opportunity Commission emphasized...the adjudicator's inquiry should center, dominantly, on whether the discriminatory conduct has unreasonably interfered with the plaintiff's work performance. To show such interference, "the plaintiff need not prove that his or her tangible productivity has declined as a result of the harassment." Davis v. Monsanto Chemical Co., 858 F.2d 345, 349 (6th Cir. 1988). It suffices to prove that a reasonable person subjected to the discriminatory conduct would find, as the plaintiff did, that the harassment so altered working conditions as to "ma[k]e it more difficult to do the job."...

The Court's opinion, which I join, seems to me in harmony with the view expressed in this concurring statement.

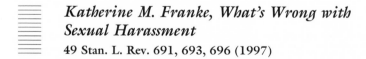

Katherine M. Franke, What's Wrong with Sexual Harassment
49 Stan. L. Rev. 691, 693, 696 (1997)

According to the theory I develop..., the sexual harassment of a woman by a man is an instance of sexism precisely because the act embodies fundamental gender stereotypes: men as sexual conquerors and women as sexually conquered, men as masculine sexual subjects and women as feminine sexual objects.... Sexual harassment is a technology of sexism. It is a disciplinary practice that inscribes, enforces, and polices the identities of both harasser and victim according to a system of gender norms that envisions women as feminine, (hetero)sexual objects, and men as masculine, (hetero)sexual subjects....

On my account, sexual harassment—between any two people of whatever sex—is a form of sex discrimination when it reflects or perpetuates gender stereotypes in the workplace. I suggest a reconceptualization of sexual harassment as gender harassment. Understood in this way, sexual harassment is a kind of sex discrimination not because the conduct would not have been undertaken if the victim had been a different sex, not because it is sexual, and not because men do it to women, but precisely because it is a technology of sexism. That is, it perpetuates, enforces, and polices a set of gender norms that seek to feminize women and masculinize men....

Similarly, sexual harassment operates as a means of policing traditional gender norms particularly in the same-sex context when men who fail to live up to a societal norm of masculinity are punished by their male co-workers through sexual means.

 Kathryn Abrams, The New Jurisprudence of Sexual Harassment
83 Cornell L. Rev. 1169, 1206-1208 (1998)

In some cases, sexual harassment has emerged as a means of preserving male control over the workplace, particularly where the entry of women into a particular workforce appears to call that control into question. A prime example is sexual harassment directed at women who have entered predominantly male fields. Some types of harassment within this category are particularly flagrant, including physical or sexual aggression or persistent, targeted verbal abuse so severe as to serve unequivocal notice that women are not welcome. Women targeted in this way are often compelled to leave the workplace or transfer to a job with different co-workers or another supervisor. Even when they stay, it is clear that they remain at the sufferance of their male co-workers; they have no hope of getting sufficient purchase on the workplace to make it in any sense their own.

Other forms of harassment aimed at preserving male control are slightly subtler. Supervisors or co-workers may sexualize women employees by either propositioning them directly or treating them in a manner that highlights their sexuality, as opposed to other, work related characteristics. Supervisors may demand that women workers conform to dominant feminine stereotypes that operate outside the workplace by making repeated comments or suggestions regarding the employees' physical appearance, or through instructions to behave in a feminine manner. In some cases, it may be applied categorically to signal that women are not taken seriously: that they are considered sex objects or "pets" instead of competent workers. These latter forms of harassment may not be sufficient to compel all women to leave any particular workplace. Yet they make clear—to women and the men who work with them—that mere presence is not equal to influence or control. These forms of harassment suggest that whatever professional goals women pursue, they will continue to be viewed and judged by reference to more traditional female roles and whatever careers they enter, they still will occupy subordinate roles.

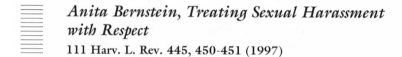

Anita Bernstein, *Treating Sexual Harassment with Respect*
111 Harv. L. Rev. 445, 450-451 (1997)

Hostile environment sexual harassment, I argue, is a type of incivility or — in the locution that I prefer — disrespect. For purposes of doctrine, accordingly, hostile environment complaints should refer to respect; the plaintiff should be required to prove that the defendant — a man, or a woman, or a business entity — did not conform to the standard of a respectful person. This respectful person standard would rightly supplant references to reason and reasonableness; respect is integral to the understanding and remedying of sexual harassment, whereas reason is not.

In giving content to the ideal of equality behind Title VII as well as the ideal of individual autonomy behind dignitary-tort law, this respectful person standard would fit within the two most important legal bases for redressing sexual harassment in the workplace. Focus on respect addresses the concerns of both those who identify with the imperfect humanity of the accused harasser and those who seek foremost to purge sexual coercion from the workplace.

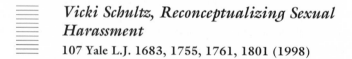

Vicki Schultz, *Reconceptualizing Sexual Harassment*
107 Yale L.J. 1683, 1755, 1761, 1801 (1998)

Contrary to the assumption of the cultural-radical feminist tradition that inspired the development of harassment law, men's desire to exploit or dominate women sexually may not be the exclusive, or even the primary, motivation for harassing women at work. Instead, a drive to maintain the most highly rewarded forms of work as domains of masculine competence underlies many, if not most, forms of sex-based harassment on the job.... [B]y portraying women as less than equal at work, men can secure superior jobs, resources, and influence — all of which afford men leverage over women at home and everyplace else.... [The focus of legal inquiry should be whether the conduct at issue has] the purpose or effect of undermining women's "right to participate in the workplace on [an] equal footing."

Notes

1. **The Problem of Sexual Harassment.** For centuries, women have been subject to behavior now understood to be sexual harassment, but the law offered neither a label nor a remedy for their experiences. Slaves, domestic servants, factory workers, and clerical assistants all were frequently subject to sexual

abuse and unwanted advances. See, e.g., Jacqueline Jones, Labor of Love, Labor of Sorrow: Black Women, Work, and the Family from Slavery to the Present 20, 28-38 (1988); Kerry Seagrave, The Sexual Harassment of Women in the Workplace, 1600-1993, at 23-39 (1994); Helen Campbell, Prisoners of Poverty: Women Wage-Workers, Their Trades, and Their Lives 234 (1887); Faye B. Dudden, Serving Women: Household Service in Nineteenth-Century America 213-219 (1983). The term "sexual harassment" came into use in the mid-1970s. Its origins are generally traced to a consciousness-raising session held by Lin Farley as part of a Cornell University course on women and work. Lin Farley, Sexual Shakedown xi-xiii (1978). Catharine A. MacKinnon's pathbreaking Sexual Harassment of Working Women (1979) provided a theoretical framework for conceptualizing such harassment as a form of sex discrimination actionable under civil rights laws and the equal protection clause of the Fourteenth Amendment.

The frequency of sexual harassment is difficult to gauge with any precision because what constitutes actionable harassment is sometimes unclear and because relatively few individuals make formal complaints. Estimates of women who say they have experienced workplace harassment range between 30 to 80 percent. See Heather Antechol & Deborah Cobb-Clark, The Changing Nature of Employment-Related Sexual Harassment: Evidence from the U.S. Federal Government, 1978-1994, 57 Indus. & Lab. Rel. Rev. 443 (2004) (44 percent of women and 19 percent of men had experienced harassment); Theresa M. Beiner, Gender Myths v. Working Realities: Using Social Science to Reformulate Sexual Harassment Law 1 (2004) (citing studies finding 40 percent to 80 percent); Catalyst, Women in Financial Services: The Word on the Street (2001) (about a third of surveyed Wall Street women report experiencing harassment); Joanna L. Grossman, The First Bite Is Free: Employer Liability for Sexual Harassment, 61 U. Pitt. L. Rev. 671, 673-674 (2000) (citing studies and case histories). Between two-fifths to two-thirds of female lawyers report experiencing sexual harassment, and almost three-quarters believe that it is a problem in their workplaces. See Deborah L. Rhode & Jennifer A. Drobac, Sex-Based Harassment: Workplace Policies for the Legal Profession, Report Prepared for the ABA Commission on Women in the Profession 5 (2002).

Formal complaints have more than doubled over the last decade. Raymond F. Gregory, Unwelcome and Unlawful: Sexual Harassment in the American Workplace 9 (2004); Rhode & Drobac, supra, at 5. The incidence is greatest in male-dominated occupations and, as Hebert indicates, the most common targets are women in subordinate and economically vulnerable positions. Some evidence suggests that women of color are disproportionately likely to be targets. Id.; Tanya K. Hernandez, The Next Challenge in Sexual Harassment Reform: Racial Disparity, 23 Women's Rts. L. Rep. 227 (2002). About 85 percent of formal sexual harassment complaints involve men harassing women; about one percent involve women harassing men, and the remainder involve same-sex harassment. Men account for about 15 percent of claims, up from approximately nine percent of claims in 1992. U.S. Equal Employment Opportunity Comm'n, Sexual Harassment Charges: EEOC & FEPAs Combined: FY 1992–FY 2005, at http://www.eeoc.gov/stats/ harass. html (last visited May 25, 2005).

While many women report having experienced sexual harassment on the job, only about 5 to 15 percent report it, and fewer still can afford the financial and psychological costs of litigation. See Gregory, supra, at 9; Joanna Grossman, The Culture of Compliance: The Final Triumph of Form Over Substance in Sexual Harassment Law, 26 Harv. Women's L.J. 3, 24, n.123 (2003) (citing surveys); Louise Fitzgerald et al., Why Didn't She Just Report Him? The Psychological and Legal Implications of Women's Responses to Sexual Harassment, 51 J. Soc. Issues 117 (1995). Major barriers to reporting include guilt, shame, fear of reprisal or blacklisting, unwillingness to jeopardize working relationships or be known as a humorless whiner, concerns about loss of privacy, and doubts that an effective response to a complaint would be forthcoming. See Gregory, supra, at 134; Fitzgerald et al., supra; Beth A. Quinn, The Paradox of Complaining: Law, Humor, and Harassment in the Everyday Work World, 25 Law & Soc. Inquiry 1151 (2000).

How the law's role in sexual harassment is viewed depends partly on how the phenomenon is understood. When the behaviors in question are viewed as a natural or biological consequence of physical attraction between the sexes, the law may be considered an unwelcome intruder, too "clumsy [a tool] for shaping human behavior." Alex Kozinski, The False Protection of a Gilded Cage, S.F. Recorder, May 27, 1992, at 10. Consider the following argument by defendant president of a company who rubbed his hands up and down plaintiff's sides, touched her breasts, pinched her, patted her buttocks, kissed her, and put his hands up her dress:

> It is important to point out that one of the traditional places where man meets woman is at the work place. Such meetings often result in dating, blossom into love, and eventually into marriage.... If civil liability is implanted on an employer for its employees['] natural interaction between the genders, either the collapse of our commercial system or the end of the human race can be foreseen. No employer could safely employ both males and females, and the number of marriages with children will be substantially decreased. There should be nothing wrong with a man, even a supervisor, telling a female that she looks nice. Nor can there be anything wrong with a man, even a supervisor, asking a female out [on] a date. In doing so the man should not have to gamble on civil liability on her "yes" response.

Jones v. Wesco Investments, Inc., 846 F.2d 1154, 1157 n.6 (8th Cir. 1988) (citing from defendant's brief). See also Barnes v. Costle, 561 F.2d 983, 1001 (D.C. Cir. 1977) (MacKinnon, J., concurring) (sexual advances need not be "intrinsically offensive" in that they may involve "normal and expectable" social behaviors).

Several alternative views of sexual harassment are set forth in the readings above. Which of these feminist accounts is most plausible? What implications does each of them have for how the law should define sexual harassment?

2. Defining Quid Pro Quo Sexual Harassment. As *Meritor* indicates, Title VII prohibits two types of sexual harassment: (1) quid pro quo harassment, in which sexual contact or favor is required as a condition of employment or advancement, and (2) environmental sexual harassment, based on conditions that create an "intimidating, hostile, or offensive" work environment.

A plaintiff establishes a case of quid pro quo harassment if she shows that "submission to the unwanted advances [of a supervisor] was an express or implied condition for receiving job benefits or her refusal to submit resulted in a tangible job detriment." Ogden v. Wax Works, Inc. 214 F. 3d 999, 1006 n.8 (8th Cir. 2000); see also Burlington Industries v. Ellerth, 524 U.S. 742, 751 (1998). Quid pro quo harassment is actionable whether or not the victim submits to the propositions. See Karibian v. Columbia University, 14 F.3d 773, 779 (2d Cir.), cert. denied, 512 U.S. 1213 (1994).

Should co-workers have a qui pro quo claim where an employee acceded to requests for sexual favors and received job benefits that might have gone to other employees? EEOC Guidelines, under a heading diplomatically titled "other related practices," holds that "[w]here employment opportunities or benefits are granted because of an individual's submission to the employer's sexual advances or requests for sexual favors, the employer may be held liable for unlawful sex discrimination against other persons who were qualified for but denied that opportunity or benefit." 45 Fed. Reg. 74,676, 74,677 (1980). However, not all courts have imposed liability under such situations. According to one court, male employees who claimed that they were unfairly passed over for promotion did not have a sex discrimination claim because they were "not prejudiced because of their status as males; rather they were discriminated against because [the program] administrator preferred his [paramour]. Appellees faced exactly the same predicament as that faced by any woman applicant for the promotion." DeCintio v. Westchester County Medical Center, 807 F.2d 304, 308 (2d Cir. 1986), cert. denied, 484 U.S. 825 (1987); see also Candelore v. Clark County Sanitation District, 752 F. Supp. 956 (D. Nev. 1990), aff'd, 975 F.2d 588 (9th Cir. 1992). Which approach to this problem makes sense?

3. Defining Hostile Environment Harassment. Defining a hostile work environment has also presented difficulties. The Court's opinion in *Harris* establishes that "mere utterance" of an "offensive epithet" is not enough, but that "tangible psychological injury" is not required. Justice Ginsburg finds the key in whether the conduct alters the working conditions so as to make it "more difficult to do the job." If Justice Scalia is correct that no basis for such a limitation is apparent in the text or legislative history of Title VII, what follows from that fact?

Consider the following case, in which a plaintiff introduced the following evidence of harassment: (1) her supervisor referred to her as a "pretty girl," as in "There's always a pretty girl giving me something to sign off on." (2) Once when she was wearing a leather skirt, he made a grunting sound like "um um um" as she turned to leave his office. (3) Once when she commented on how hot his office was, he raised his eyebrows and said, "Not until you stepped your foot in here." (4) Once when the announcement "May I have your attention, please" was broadcast over the public-address system, the supervisor stopped at her desk and said, "You know what that means, don't you? All pretty girls run around naked." (5) The supervisor once told her that his wife had told him "I had better clean up my act" and "better think of you as Ms. Anita Hill." (6) When she asked why he had left the office Christmas party early, the supervisor replied that there were so many pretty girls there that he "didn't want to lose control, so I thought I'd better leave." (7) Once when she complained that his office was "smokey" from cigarette smoke, the supervisor replied, "Oh really? Were we dancing, like in a nightclub?" (8) When she asked him whether he had gotten his wife a Valentine's Day card, he responded that he had not but he should because it was lonely in his hotel room, at which point he looked ostentatiously at his hand with a gesture suggesting masturbation. Is this sexual harassment?

Judge Richard Posner analyzed the conduct by considering each incident individually and by noting what it did not include:

> He never touched the plaintiff. He did not invite her, explicitly or by implication, to have sex with him, or to go out on a date with him. He made no threats. He did not expose himself, or show her dirty pictures. He never said anything to her that could not be repeated on prime time television. The comment about Anita Hill was the opposite of solicitation, the implication being that he would get into trouble if he didn't keep his distance.... Some of his repartee, such as "not until you stepped your foot in here," or, "Were we dancing, like in a nightclub?," has the sexual charge of an Abbott and Costello movie. The reference to masturbation completes the impression of a man whose sense of humor took final shape in adolescence. It is no doubt distasteful to a sensitive woman to have such a silly man one's boss, but only a woman of Victorian delicacy — a woman mysteriously aloof from contemporary American popular culture in all its sex-saturated vulgarity — would find [his] patter substantially more distressing than the heat and cigarette smoke of which the plaintiff does not complain.

Baskerville v. Culligan International Co., 50 F.3d 428, 431 (7th Cir. 1995). How would you evaluate this analysis?

Many commentators argue that looking at sexual harassment claims as a series of separate incidents understates their cumulative impact and undermines the policies underlying Title VII. See, e.g., Theresa Beiner, Gender Myths v. Working Realities: Using Social Science to Reformulate Sexual Harassment Law 1, 20-24 (2004); Laura D. Francis, Note, What Part of "Hostile Environment" Don't You Understand? The Need for an Entire-Environment Approach in Sexual Harassment Cases, 72 Geo. Wash. L. Rev. 815 (2004).

That risk may be particularly great where the conduct involves race as well as sex. Women of color account for 16 percent of the female labor force and 33 percent of women's sexual harassment claims. See Tanya K. Hernandez, The Next Challenge in Sexual Harassment Reform: Racial Disparity, 23 Women's Rts. L. Rep. 227, 227 (2002). In one case, the court granted summary judgment against the plaintiff whose claims included an incident where a co-worker dropped his pants and ordered her to "suck my dick, you black bitch." Another co-worker told the woman that he wanted to hang her in a cornfield, and she also encountered a Ku Klux Klan card posted on a factory beam. The court, however, concluded that the behavior was "deplorable, and even offensive, humiliating and threatening," but insufficiently severe and pervasive to alter the terms of employment. EEOC v. Champion Int'l Corp., No. 93 C 20279, 1995 WL 488333, at 2 (N.D. Ill. Aug. 1, 1995).

When an individual is called a "black bitch," is it possible to separate harassment based on gender from harassment based on race? Many commentators have argued that it is not, and some courts have agreed. Andrea L. Dennis, Note, Because I Am Black, Because I Am Woman: Remedying the Sexual Harassment Experience of Black Women, 1996 Ann. Surv. Am. L. 555. For example, in Anthony v. County of Sacramento, 898 F. Supp. 1435 (E.D. Cal. 1995), an African-American woman who was a former sheriff's deputy alleged that she had been subject to "incidents which were offensive on racial grounds and others which targeted her as female, and still others in which she was mistreated as an African-American female." Id. at 1445. The district court agreed with the plaintiff that the incidents should be treated cumulatively and that the jury should also be entitled to consider physical abuse directed at African-American inmates, since such racial hostility created a climate in which the plaintiff "felt not only unwelcome but endangered. . . ." Id. at 1448-1449.

If a supervisory official engages in repeated favoritism toward workers with whom he is having an affair, could that ever constitute a hostile work environment? The EEOC has concluded that "isolated instances of preferential treatment based upon consensual romantic relationships" does not constitute discrimination based on sex. EEOC Notice No. 915-048 (Jan. 12, 1990). What if the conduct is not "isolated"? In Mackey v. Department of Corrections, 130 Cal. Rptr. 2d 57 (Ct. App. 2003), plaintiffs were correctional officers whose supervisor had affairs with three subordinates who were promoted over them. One of these subordinates was also abusive, and her relationship with the supervisor protected her from adverse consequences. A California appellate court rejected the plaintiffs' claim that the conduct created a hostile work environment "by making them believe that they would have to engage in sexual relations with supervisors in order to get ahead." Id. at 65. The California Supreme Court unanimously reversed. It held that an isolated act instance of favoritism would not ordinarily constitute sex harassment. However, it is actionable when it is so widespread that "the demeaning message is conveyed to female employees that they are viewed by management as 'sexual playthings' or that what is required for women to get ahead in the workplace is by engaging in sexual conduct." Miller v. Department of Corrections, 30 Cal. Rptr. 3d 797 (Cal. 2005). Would a better solution be legislation explicitly prohibiting sexual relationships from influencing job opportunities? See Cal. Assembly Bill 1229 (2004).

Does sexually offensive conduct need to be targeted specifically at one sex in order to constitute sexual harassment? In Ocheltree v. Scollon Productions, Inc., 308 F. 3d 351 (4th Cir. 2002), a divided panel of the Fourth Circuit Court of Appeals reversed a jury finding for the plaintiff because most of the sexually explicit conduct at issue was not directed at her because of her gender. 308 F. 3d at 361. Rather, the vulgar language, pictures, and jokes, comments on the sexual habits of staff, and simulations of sexual activity were equally offensive to men and women. "Repulsive" as the conduct was, it was not, in the majority's view, a basis for legal liability; "Title VII was not enacted as a workplace code for 'gentlemanly conduct' or chivalry." Id. at 366. The Fourth Circuit, in en banc review, reversed, and held that the conduct was particularly offensive to women in general and the plaintiff in particular. Ocheltree v. Scollon Productions, Inc., 355 F. 3d 325, 355 (4th Cir. 2003) (en banc). Should courts require evidence of gender-specific motivations or effects? See David S. Schwartz, When is Sex Because of Sex?: The Causation Problem in Sexual Harassment Law, 150 U. Pa. L. Rev. 361 (2002).

4. The Standard for Determining Hostile Work Environment. *Harris* imposes both an objective and a subjective standard for determining a hostile work environment. The plaintiff must have been actually offended, and the offense taken must have been reasonable. A longstanding issue is whether "reasonable" is sex-specific. If the plaintiff is female, should the reasonableness of her reaction be judged from the perspective of a "reasonable person" or from that of a "reasonable woman"? *Harris* refers to the reasonable person standard, which most courts subsequently followed. Only the Ninth Circuit Court of Appeals has applied a reasonable woman standard. See Ellison v. Brady, 924 F.2d 872 (9th Cir. 1991); Fuller v. City of Oakland, 47 F.3d 1522, 1527-1528 (9th Cir. 1995) (using interchangeably "the perspective of a reasonable person with the same fundamental characteristics" and "a reasonable woman"); Steiner v. Showboat Operating Co., 25 F.3d 1459, 1464 (9th Cir. 1994), cert. denied, 513 U.S. 1082 (1995) ("*Ellison* unequivocally directs us to consider what is offensive and hostile to a reasonable woman").

In Oncale v. Sundowner Offshore Services, Inc., 523 U.S. 75 (1998), discussed in *Rene*, infra, p. 443, the U.S. Supreme Court, speaking through Justice Scalia, reaffirmed that the "objective severity of harassment should be judged from the perspective of a reasonable person in the plaintiff's position, considering 'all the circumstances.'" Id. at 81. Does that standard require focusing, as do Justices Ginsburg and Scalia, on how the allegedly harassing conduct in fact affects the performance or opportunities of the plaintiff? Or should courts also consider how the conduct would affect most individuals in the position of the plaintiff? What if, on average, men and women occupying that position would differ in their response?

Some commentators advocate use of the reasonable woman standard based on research finding that women are more likely to perceive certain behaviors, such as unsolicited invitations for sex, as harassing. See Jeremy A. Blumenthal, The Reasonable Woman Standard: A Meta-Analytic Review of Gender Differences in Perceptions of Sexual Harassment, 22 Law & Hum. Behav. 33, 71 (1998); Richard L. Wiener et al., Perceptions of Sexual Harassment: The Effects of Gender, Legal Standard, and Ambivalent Sexism, 21 Law & Hum. Behav. 71 (1997). According to these commentators, a reasonable person standard that ignores the perspectives of women is, in effect, a reasonable man standard that will legitimate, rather than reduce, the incidence of sexual harassment. See, e.g., Caroline A. Forrell & Donna M. Mathews, A Law of Her Own: The Reasonable Woman as a Measure of Man 35-58 (2000).

Other feminists have objected to the reasonable woman standard on the grounds that it fails to recognize the diversity in women's experience, and would be counterproductive to impose a single, uniform standard on a group — women — whose subordination has been made possible by the attribution of uniform, usually condescending, characteristics. Women may be harmed more than they are helped by the assumption that they are all alike and are easily offended victims. See Linda Kelly Hill, The Feminist Misspeak of Sexual Harassment, 57 Fla. L. Rev. 133, 172-180 (2005) (arguing that the reasonable woman standard raises concerns of "victimization, essentialism, and judicial neutrality").

Note that the trial court in *Harris* applied a "reasonable woman" standard and found the circumstances to be a "close case" that did not ultimately justify liability, while the Supreme Court, which used "reasonable person" language, concluded that the facts may have been sufficient to state a case of sexual harassment. This may suggest that the exact contours of the standard are not as important as who is applying them. See Beiner, supra, at 57-59; Stephanie M. Wildman, Ending Male Privilege: Beyond the Reasonable Woman, 98 Mich. L. Rev. 1797, 1812 (2000). Indeed, altering the legal standard from reasonable person to reasonable woman has little affect in mock jury studies; the most comprehensive study, involving five different methods and close to 2000 participants, found that the standard accounted for only about two percent of the variance in perceptions of hostile work environments. Barbara A. Gutek et. al., The Utility of the Reasonable Woman Standard in Hostile Environment Sexual Harassment Cases: A Multimethod Multistudy Examination, 5 Psychol. Pub. Pol'y & L. Rev. 596, 623 (1999). As to who is applying the standard, most recent social science research suggests that men and women do not significantly vary in their interpretations of conduct serious enough to trigger legal liability. Beiner, supra, at 52-54 (reviewing studies); Maria Rotundo et al., A Meta-Analytic Review of Gender Differences in Perceptions of Harassment, 86 J. Applied Psychol. 914, 918-919 (2001); Gutek et al., supra (finding that gender accounted for only six percent of the variance in decisions).

A case history in the difficulties of applying harassment standards involves Paula Jones's complaint concerning William Clinton. Jones alleged that Clinton, when Governor of Arkansas, invited her to his hotel room while she was a state employee, stroked her leg, exposed himself, and invited her to perform oral sex. The district court held that even if the facts were as Jones stated them, they failed to meet the definition of harassment. Clinton had not promised job benefits, and Jones alleged no demonstrable job detriment apart from failure to receive flowers on Secretary's Day and a trivial change in job duties. Nor was this single incident sufficient to show an "abusive environment." Jones v. Clinton, 990 F. Supp. 657, 675 (E.D. Ark. 1998). Jones missed no work following the alleged encounter and made no attempt to avoid daily trips to the Governor's office. She received favorable job evaluations and all available raises. Her only evidence of emotional distress was a belated declaration, filed just before Clinton's summary judgment motion, by a "purported expert with a Ph.D. in education and counseling." After a single meeting with Jones nearly seven years after the alleged incident, he found her to suffer from "severe emotional distress and consequent sexual aversion." Id. at 678 (quoting Patrick Carnes, Jones's expert). According to the trial court, these "vague and conclusory" opinions were unsupported by other evidence. In the court's view, Clinton's alleged conduct, while "boorish and offensive," did not have a demonstrable effect on Jones's job performance, and Clinton was therefore entitled to summary judgment as a matter of law. Id. at 675.

Should the court have allowed the case to go to trial? Consider Catharine MacKinnon's argument that there were triable issues of fact on both the quid pro quo and hostile environment claim. In particular, the record revealed that other women who had sexual relationships with Clinton received job benefits. Catharine A. MacKinnon, Afterword, in Directions in Sexual Harassment Law 672, 688 (Catharine A. MacKinnon & Reva B. Siegel eds., 2004). Should it matter whether Jones knew of such favoritism? For exploration of further issues raised by the Paula Jones case, see note 9, p. 439, infra.

Feminists who did not condemn Clinton's conduct as sex harassment were accused of "tak[ing] a powder on Paula Jones." See Ellen Goodman, Feminists Retreat from Jones Case for Good Reason, Boston Globe, Jan. 16, 1997, at A21 (quoting Human Events magazine). Some feminists responded that Clinton's behavior was offensive, but not harassment, since it was neither pervasive nor severe. See id.; Susan Estrich, Clinton's Conduct Offensive, But Not Sexual Harassment, S.F. Recorder, Nov. 8, 1996, at 5. According to Goodman, "Even in this litigious country, there are still wrongs for which there are no legal remedies. Not every piece of piggish behavior is illegal. You can feel humiliated without being legally sexually harassed." Goodman, What Is Sexual Harassment?, Boston Globe, Feb. 23, 1997, at E7. Estrich agrees: "There's no law saying he can't ask. . . ." Estrich, supra. Should there be?

How should courts determine what acts are sufficiently pervasive and abusive to justify liability? Consider the proposal of Gillian K. Hadfield, who would define sex-based harassment as "sex-based non-job-related workplace conduct that would lead a rational woman to alter her workplace behavior — such as by refusing overtime, projects, or travel that will put her in contact with a harasser, requesting a transfer, or quitting — if she could do so at little or no cost to her." Gillian K. Hadfield, Rational Women: A Test for Sex-Based Harassment, 83 Cal. L. Rev. 1151, 1157 (1995). Hadfield argues that when a woman rationally alters her workplace behavior to eliminate the risk of such conduct, the behavior is discriminatory. Id. at 1174-1181. In her view, this test

> does not privilege women's evaluation of workplace practices over men's. . . . [Nor does it] privilege one particular group of women's preferences about workplace practices over others'. . . . Because Title VII targets sex discrimination . . . the issue is whether a workplace practice has systematically negative consequences for women vis-à-vis men. Even if significant numbers of women enjoy an atmosphere in which sexual jokes abound, if systematically more women than men find this costly, then the practice is discriminatory. . . .

Id. at 1182.

This approach would also eliminate the need to show that the behavior was unwelcome, since "those behaviors that rational women would be willing to pay to avoid are by definition unwelcome." Id. at 1185. See note 5, below. Such a standard, however, would place "the onus on men, employers, and organizations to become educated about what behavior on their subordinates' part would prompt employment changes by a rational female employee. The test rejects the notion that men are entitled to the protection of their misimpressions about how such behavior is interpreted by women." Id. at 1186. Is Hadfield's approach consistent with equality analysis? Would Jones v. Clinton have been decided differently under Hadfield's test? Should it have been?

Kathryn Abrams would place the burden on the defendant to demonstrate that the behavior at issue "was not likely to create a fear of sexual coercion or a sense of devaluative sexualization among women." Abrams, Gender Discrimination and the Transformation of Workplace Norms, 42 Vand. L. Rev. 1183, 1211 (1989). In Abrams' view, it is "normatively desirable to assume that sexual behavior sufficiently offensive to drive a plaintiff to court is harassing and to put the burden on the defendant to show otherwise." Id. at 1248 n.116. Accord, Jane L. Dolkart, Hostile Environment Harassment: Equality, Objectivity, and the Shaping of Legal Standards, 43 Emory L.J. 151, 217 (1994). Is this reasonable?

5. When Is Sexual Conduct "Unwelcome"? What is the purpose of the requirement that the plaintiff in a hostile environment sexual harassment case prove that the conduct was "unwelcome"? The EEOC argued for this standard out of concern that sexual harassment charges not become "a tool by which one party to a consensual sexual relationship may punish the other." Brief for EEOC in *Meritor*, quoted in Ann C. Juliano, Note, Did She Ask for It?: The "Unwelcome" Requirement in Sexual Harassment Cases, 77 Cornell L. Rev. 1558, 1575 (1992). The same rationale, critics argue, has shaped the law of rape: a woman who acts and dresses like she is "asking for it" is often assumed to have consented to whatever follows. Susan Estrich, Sex at Work, 43 Stan. L. Rev. 813, 827 (1991). Louise Fitzgerald, a social psychologist who has spent two decades researching sexual harassment, explains the problem:

> When the EEOC wrote unwelcomeness into sex harassment law and the Supreme Court [Justices] gave it their imprimatur, they were apparently thinking of sex as well, *sex*—sexual attraction, sexual desire, sexual pursuit. But sexual harassment often has little to do with attraction and pursuit and everything to do with power, misogyny, and the crudest form of abuse. The fact that it looks like sex, at least to some, is because men's hostility toward women is so often sexualized.

Fitzgerald, Who Says? Legal Psychological Construction of Women's Resistance to Sexual Harassment, in Directions in Sexual Harassment Law 94, 102 (Catharine A. MacKinnon & Reva B. Siegel eds., 2004).

Fitzgerald and other commentators note that the fundamental problem is that the welcomeness inquiry puts the conduct of the victim on trial, rather than the harasser, and reinforces double standards of morality that treat women's sexual expression more harshly than men's. Such judgmental approaches towards women complainants discourages many from making formal complaints and provides a strategic weapon to force inadequate settlements from those who do come forward. See the discussion of legal ethics in note 9, p. 439, below.

What determines whether sexual advances were "welcome" under the *Meritor* test? Justice Rehnquist finds "sexually provocative speech or dress...obviously relevant." Is this obvious? Consider Juliano's observation: "a woman may dress in order to look attractive to someone. Because a woman is attempting to attract one individual, however, does not mean that she welcomes sexual attention from *all* men." Juliano, supra, at 1585-1586. Does the relevance of sexually provocative speech or dress depend on what drives harassing conduct in a particular workplace context? For example, should it matter what signals Paula Jones sent about her sexual availability in going to the hotel room of a governor whom she had not met and who was widely known as a "womanizer"? Her complaint alleged that she had accepted a state trooper's invitation to meet Clinton in the hope that it might lead to an "enhanced employment opportunity...." Jones v. Clinton, 990 F. Supp. 657, 663 (E.D. Ark. 1998). Should Jones's conduct be relevant in assessing Clinton's?

Under the welcomeness test in *Meritor*, if an employee is required to act in a sexually alluring manner as part of the job description itself, has she consented to being treated as a sexual object? In one case, plaintiffs, while performing their duties as cocktail waitresses, "were required by [Ramada Inn] pursuant to a marketing scheme called the 'confetti concept' to project an air of sexual availability to customers through the use of provocative outfits. [T]hey were required to flirt with customers and to dance, in a sexually provocative and degrading fashion...." Are the sexual proposals and verbal and physical abuse they then received "unwelcome"? When women market their ability to act in a sexual manner, are they assuming the risk of harassment? EEOC v. Newtown Inn Assocs., 647 F. Supp. 957, 958 (E.D. Va. 1986) (not resolving merits of charges); Kelly Ann Cahill, Hooters: Should There Be an Assumption of Risk Defense to Some Hostile Work Environment Sexual Harassment Claims?, 48 Vand. L. Rev. 1107 (1995).

Should a complainant's activities outside of work ever be relevant to her sexual harassment charges? In Burns v. McGregor Electronic Industries, Inc., 955 F.2d 559 (8th Cir. 1992), plaintiff filed charges of sexual harassment on the basis of repeated behavior by at least two employees and the owner of the company, which manufactured stereo speakers. In addition to repeated propositions for dates and oral sex, the owner "showed [plaintiff] advertisements for pornographic films in Penthouse magazine, talked about sex, asked her to watch pornographic movies with him, and made lewd gestures, such as ones imitating masturbation." The harassment escalated after the co-workers learned that the plaintiff had appeared in the nude in two motorcycle magazines. Although the plaintiff did not herself take copies of the magazines to the plant, both the district judge and court of appeals concluded that the pictures were relevant to her claims. According to the appellate panel, "[I]n view of [plaintiff's] willingness to display her nude body to the public in Easy Riders publications, crude magazines at best, her testimony that she was offended by sexually directed comments and Penthouse or Playboy pictures is not credible." Id. at 562. Citing *Meritor*, the court held that the photos "may be relevant to explain the context of some of the comments and actions" and that the plaintiff would have to show that she was "at least as affected as the reasonable person under like circumstances." 955 F. 2d at 565-566. See 989 F.2d 959 (8th Cir. 1993) (reversing the district court finding for the defendant). Is this an appropriate requirement?

Should a plaintiff's participation in the sexual banter of a workplace preclude a claim of sexual harassment based in part on that banter? Courts have found evidence of such participation relevant as to whether the conduct was unwelcome and whether it created a hostile and intimidating environment. In one case, plaintiff admitted at trial that she cursed and used vulgar language while at work. Her co-workers also testified that she often made jokes about sex, including jokes about "screwing her boss," and that she participated in frequent discussions and bantering about sex. Faced with this evidence, the court concluded that "[a]ny harassment plaintiff received . . . was prompted by her own actions, including her tasteless joking. Considering plaintiff's contribution to and apparent enjoyment of the situation, it cannot be said that the defendants created 'an intimidating, hostile, or offensive working environment.'" Loftin-Boggs v. City of Meridian, 633 F. Supp. 1323, 1327 (S.D. Miss. 1986), aff'd, 824 F.2d 971 (5th Cir. 1987), cert. denied, 484 U.S. 1063 (1988). See also Hocevar v. Purdue Frederick Co., 223 F3d 721, 736 (8th Cir. 2000) (denying relief to plaintiff whose use of vulgar language indicated that she did not find workplace conduct unwelcome); but see Swentek v. USAIR, Inc., 830 F.2d 552 (4th Cir. 1987) (trial court held that plaintiff's foul language and conduct, including putting a dildo in her supervisor's mailbox and grabbing the genitals of a pilot with a "frank invitation to a sexual encounter," meant that defendant's conduct, which included reaching under plaintiff's skirt for her genitals, was not unwelcome, even though she asked him to leave her alone; appellate court reversed on grounds that use of foul language or sexual innuendo does not waive plaintiff's legal protections against sexual harassment); Carr v. Allison Gas Turbine Division, General Motors Corp., 32 F. 3d 1007, 1011 (7th Cir. 1994) (plaintiff's vulgar language and dirty jokes could not justify a barrage of derogatory language, pranks, and graffiti); Spencer v. General Elec. Co., 697 F. Supp. 204 (E.D. Va. 1988), aff'd, 894 F.2d 651 (4th Cir. 1990) (joining in milder forms of sexual horseplay that occurred in the office did not waive plaintiff's protection against sexual harassment).

What, besides consent to sexual advances, might explain an employee's participation in such conduct? Such behavior might sometimes serve as a survival technique, or a way to achieve acceptance or defuse a potentially unpleasant situation. See Beth A. Quinn, The Paradox of Complaining: Law, Humor, and Harassment in the Everyday Work World, 25 Law & Soc. Inquiry 1151, 1179-1181 (2000). A similar motive might explain situations in which a plaintiff at some point makes a statement dismissing the significance of the harassment, such as it was "[not] that big of a deal." The Sixth Circuit Court of Appeals found in one case that such a statement should be viewed as a concession that the harassment was not offensive. See Highlander v. K.F.C. Nat'l Management Co., 805 F.2d 644 (6th Cir. 1986). Commenting on that conclusion, Kathryn Abrams writes: "[Plaintiff's] statements that she did not want to raise 'a big stink' may have expressed the discomfort that she felt as a new employee about complaining to management, or the anxiety produced by the entire incident." Abrams, supra, 42 Vand. L. Rev. at 1201.

The continued friendly relations between a plaintiff and the alleged harasser also may serve as proof that the behavior in question did not constitute harassment. See, e.g., Scott v. Sears, Roebuck & Co., 798 F.2d 210, 212-214 (7th Cir. 1986). Does this possible outcome "ignore[] the reality of what women must do to make life bearable in an all-male workplace"? Wendy Pollack, Sexual Harassment: Women's Experience vs. Legal Definitions, 13 Harv. Women's L.J. 35, 72-73 (1990).

The most obvious way for an employee to signal that particular behavior is offensive and unwelcome is to complain about it. Courts have increasingly required such complaints, as note 6 below on employer liability indicates. But when must an employee complain? At the first glimmer of discomfort? When conditions have become intolerable? Is there an in-between? Note, again, the potential catch-22 situation: if the woman complains too early, she is hypersensitive, unreasonable, someone who is "looking for trouble"; if she waits too long, she will be judged to have accepted, or at least to be ambivalent toward, the behavior. See Susan Estrich, Sex at Work, 43 Stan. L. Rev. 813, 826-834, 843-847 (1991); Reed v. Shepard, 939 F.2d 484, 492 (7th Cir. 1991) (female police officer's receptiveness to co-workers' sexually suggestive jokes and activities because she wanted to be accepted by others on the police force was fatal to her sexual harassment claim).

Is there a preferable alternative to the "unwelcome" test? Consider the following possibility:

> [B]urdening the victim with proving that the conduct is unwelcome assumes that sexual advances by any man to any woman are by definition welcome until she proves otherwise. We submit that this is a very odd assumption. Indeed, it seems to us far more reasonable to suggest the opposite: that sexual attention in the workplace should be presumed to be unwelcome, unless the initiator determines otherwise. Thus, the burden falls on the defendant to demonstrate how he knew he was welcome. Shifting the burden of communication in this manner focuses the inquiry where it belongs — on the defendant's behavior, rather than the plaintiff's.

Louise Fitzgerald et al., Why Didn't She Just Report Him? The Psychological and Legal Implications of Women's Responses to Sexual Harassment, 51 J. Soc. Issues 117, 134 (1995). Another possibility is to presume that certain conduct is so offensive that it would not be welcomed by anyone. See Kathryn Abrams, Subordination and Agency in Sexual Harassment Law, in Directions in Sexual Harassment Law, 111, 118 (Catharine A. MacKinnon & Reva B. Siegel eds., 2004) (discussing coercive, insulting, and indecent conduct). See also Fitzgerald, Who Says? Legal Psychological Construction of Women's Resistance to Sexual Harassment, in Directions in Sexual Harassment Law 104 (Catharine A. Mac Kinnon & Reva B. Siegel eds., 2004) (proposing a per se test for certain conduct); Janine Benedet, Hostile Environment Sexual Harassment Claims and Unwelcome Influence of Rape Law, 3 Mich. J. Gender & L. 125, 166, 173-174 (1995) (arguing that welcomeness should not be an issue for conduct such as sexual slurs, physical interference, pornographic photos or objects, or sexual contact not preceded by an expression of interest). Would this approach lead to an unduly sanitized workplace? See Schultz, supra, and the discussion of First Amendment issues in note 7 below.

6. Employer Liability. The Supreme Court in *Meritor* addressed the issue of employer liability for harassment of one of its employees by another employee, but declined to issue "a definitive rule." 477 U.S. at 72. The Court rejected both the "strict liability" rule urged by plaintiff and the employer's position that the existence of a sex harassment policy and grievance procedure that the plaintiff failed to use precluded liability. Rather, *Meritor* interpreted congressional intent as requiring courts to look to general agency principles for guidance. Id. Lower courts divided as to what those principles required, and in 1998, the

Supreme Court issued two companion opinions clarifying the issue, Faragher v. City of Boca Raton, 524 U.S. 775 (1998), and Burlington Industries v. Ellerth, 524 U.S. 742 (1998).

Faragher involved a claim by a college student who worked as a lifeguard for Boca Raton. She alleged that her supervisors had created a "sexually hostile atmosphere" by repeatedly subjecting female lifeguards to "'uninvited and offensive touching,' by making lewd remarks, and by speaking of women in offensive terms." 524 U.S. at 780. One lifeguard allegedly had told Faragher, "Date me or clean the toilets for a year." Id. Although the City had a sexual harassment policy, it was not distributed to her supervisors, and they were unaware of its requirements. While the plaintiff discussed the offensive behavior with a supervisor, she did not consider the discussions to constitute a formal complaint, and the supervisor did not report the problems to any City official. Later, after another female lifeguard made a written complaint to the City's Personnel Director, an investigation was conducted, and the supervisors were sanctioned. The trial court found the City liable under a theory of constructive knowledge, and the court of appeals reversed.

The Supreme Court, speaking through Justice Souter, held:

> [W]e . . . agree with Faragher that in implementing Title VII it makes sense to hold an employer vicariously liable for some tortious conduct of a supervisor made possible by abuse of his supervisory authority. . . .
>
> In order to accommodate the principle of vicarious liability for harm caused by misuse of supervisory authority, as well as Title VII's equally basic policies of encouraging forethought by employers and saving action by objecting employees, we adopt the following holding. . . . An employer is subject to vicarious liability to a victimized employee for an actionable hostile environment created by a supervisor with immediate (or successively higher) authority over the employee. When no tangible employment action is taken, a defending employer may raise an affirmative defense to liability or damages, subject to proof by a preponderance of the evidence. The defense comprises two necessary elements: (a) that the employer exercised reasonable care to prevent and correct promptly any sexually harassing behavior, and (b) that the plaintiff employee unreasonably failed to take advantage of any preventive or corrective opportunities provided by the employer or to avoid harm otherwise. While proof that an employer had promulgated an antiharassment policy with complaint procedure is not necessary in every instance as a matter of law, the need for a stated policy suitable to the employment circumstances may appropriately be addressed in any case when litigating the first element of the defense. And while proof that an employee failed to fulfill the corresponding obligation of reasonable care to avoid harm is not limited to showing an unreasonable failure to use any complaint procedure provided by the employer, a demonstration of such failure will normally suffice to satisfy the employer's burden under the second element of the defense. No affirmative defense is available, however, when the supervisor's harassment culminates in a tangible employment action, such as discharge, demotion, or undesirable reassignment. . . .
>
> The City points to nothing that might justify a conclusion by the District Court on remand that the City had exercised reasonable care. Nor is there any reason to remand for consideration of Faragher's efforts to mitigate her own damages, since the award to her was solely nominal. . . .
>
> [Reversed and remanded for entry of judgment for Faragher.]

524 U.S. at 792, 802, 807-809.

In a further elaboration of the rules on employer liability, the U.S. Supreme Court in Pennsylvania State Police v. Suders, 542 U.S. 129 (2004), held, in a situation in which a constructive discharge was alleged, that while an employer may be held vicariously liable for working conditions that are so intolerable that a reasonable person in the employee's position would feel compelled to resign, the employer must be given the opportunity to prove as an affirmative defense that there was an effective remedial process which the employee unreasonably failed to use. For an analysis of the case, see Megan E. Mowrey & Virginia Ward Vaughn, Employer Liability for Sexual Harassment Culminating in Constructive Discharge: Resolving the Tangible Employment Action Question, 14 S. Cal. Rev. L. & Women's Stud. 25 (2004).

Another key issue involves whether employers will be liable if they make some response to a complaint of harassment, but fail to ensure that the misconduct ceases. Recent cases suggest that employers who wish to avoid accountability must make prompt and thorough investigations and take remedial actions reasonably calculated to prevent further harassment and to protect the complainant. However, failure to stop the abuse is not necessarily essential to an effective defense against liability. See cases cited in Joanna L. Grossman, The First Bite Is Free: Employer Liability for Sexual Harassment, 61 U. Pitt. L. Rev. 671, 699 (2000).

What constitutes a reasonable remedial action? Should employers be able to avoid liability if they transfer complainants out of range of the harasser? In *Suders*, the Court cast some light on this issue by citing with approval a Seventh Circuit case denying an affirmative defense where the employee's transfer involved a less desirable position. Robinson v. Sappington, 351 F.3d 317 (2003), cert. denied, 542 U.S. 937 (2004). However, what if no demotion occurs but complainants or their coworkers object to reassignment? Should innocent parties suffer if it is more convenient to transfer them than their harasser? Compare Sparks v. Regional Medical Center Bd., 792 F. Supp. 735 (N.D. Ala. 1992) (finding no liability for a hospital that transferred a lab technician away from a doctor even though changes in the technician's schedule "created resentment and anger among plaintiff's coworkers who had to carry plaintiff's workload whenever her activities involved direct contact with [the doctor]") with Saxton v. American Telephone & Telegraph Co., 10 F.3d 526, 535-536 (7th Cir. 1993) (after victim declined transfer, company transferred harasser).

How proactive should employers be in attempting to identify and remedy harassment? A survey of some 200 post-*Faragher* and post-*Ellerth* cases found that as long as the employer had a viable anti-harassment policy and a grievance procedure that allows an employee to bypass a harassing supervisor, *Ellerth* and *Faragher* "did little to change employer incentives to reduce the incidence of sexual harassment by supervisors in the workplace." Anne Lawton, Operating in an Empirical Vacuum: The *Ellerth* and *Faragher* Affirmative Defense, 13 Colum. J. Gender & L. 197, 210 (2004). See also David Sherwyn et al., Don't Train Your Employees and Cancel Your "1-800" Harassment Hotline: An Empirical Examination and Correction of the Flaws in the Affirmative Defense to Sexual Harassment Charges, 69 Fordham L. Rev. 1265, 1304 (2001) (survey of 100 federal cases supports conclusion that in order to minimize liability, employers "should not engage in or should eliminate extensive preventive efforts such as expensive sexual harassment sensitivity training, or more particularly, harassment-reporting hotlines"); Amal Bass, Comment, Pennsylvania State Police v. Suders: Turning a Blind Eye to the Reality of Sexual Harassment, 28 Harv. J.L. & Gender 195 (2005).

Surveys suggest that internal complaint mechanisms are often structured in ways that inadvertently discourage their use and diminish their ability to address underlying discrimination issues. For example, because employers cannot promise confidentiality during investigation of a complaint, many victims are unwilling to come forward. See Grossman, Form Over Substance, supra, 26 Harv. Women's L.J. at 61-63; Vicki Schultz, The Sanitized Workplace, 112 Yale L.J. 2061, 2140 (2003). Although the legal standard allows plaintiffs to demonstrate that their failure to complain was reasonable, most judges have been skeptical of those claims. A "generalized fear of retaliation" is insufficient, even if it turns out to be well founded. Martha S. West, Preventing Sex Harassment: The Federal Courts' Wake-Up Call for Women, 68 Brook. L. Rev. 457, 479-486 (2002). As one circuit court put it, "the bringing of a retaliation claim, rather than failing to report harassment, is the proper method for dealing with retaliation." Matvia v. Bald Head Island Management, Inc., 259 F.3d 261, 270 (4th Cir. 2001). The majority of surveyed victims say that complaints make the situation worse. Fitzgerald, supra, at 100. How can the law take account of this reality while providing adequate incentives for employees to provide notice of harassing conditions?

Because internal grievance procedures tend to focus on individual problem solving and preserving harmonious working relationships, experts have noted that they frequently fail to address broader systemic conditions that perpetuate discrimination, such as gender segregation and stratification in the workforce. See West, Preventing Sex Harassment, supra, at 449; Grossman, Form Over Substance, supra, at 42-47; Susan Bisom Rapp, An Ounce of Prevention Is a Poor Substitute for a Pound of Cure: Confronting the Developing Jurisprudence of Education and Prevention in Employment Discrimination Law, 22 Berkeley J. Emp. & Lab. L. 1 (2001); Susan Sturm, Second Generation Employment Discrimination: A Structural Approach, 101 Colum. L. Rev. 458, 483 (2001).

If employers are found liable for sexual harassment, how should damages be assessed in class action contexts? Consider the case involving Astra USA, a drug manufacturer that paid nearly $10 million to settle charges by the EEOC that its top male managers had harassed scores of female sales representatives and subordinates. Rather than adjudicating each employee's claim individually, Astra and the EEOC agreed to a procedure in which a special master would divide claimants into categories, with awards for the categories ranging between $12,000 and $300,000. Individuals were assigned to categories based not only on the severity of the abuse, but also on the alleged harasser's position in the company. Women who complained of continual touching by lower-level supervisors received $150,000, while those who complained of similar behavior by senior managers received $250,000. Does this approach make sense? Mark Maremont, A Case Puts a Value on Touching and Fondling, Wall St. J., May 25, 1999, at B1.

On remand, Harris was awarded $151,435 in damages plus attorney's fees and costs. Harris v. Forklift Systems, Inc., 66 Fair Empl. Prac. Cas. (BNA) 1886 (M.D. Tenn. 1994). How "reasonable" is that result?

7. Harassment Prevention Policies: Do They Go Too Far?   While some believe that harassment prevention policies do not effectively address discriminatory behaviors in the workplace, others argue that the current liability structure gives employers too great an incentive to regulate harmless behaviors, particularly those behaviors involving "trivial" sexual approaches. Consider the following:

> [T]he federal agency and the lower courts charged with interpreting Title VII define[d] harassment primarily in terms of sexual advances and other sexual conduct — an approach I call the sexual model.... [T]his sexual model is too narrow, because the focus on sexual conduct has obscured more fundamental problems of gender-based harassment and discrimination that are not primarily "sexual" in content or design.... [T]he sexual model is also too broad, because the same focus on sexual conduct that has led *courts* to ignore these larger patterns of sexism and discrimination is also leading *companies* to prohibit a broad range of relatively harmless sexual conduct, even when that conduct does not threaten gender equality on the job. In the name of preventing sexual harassment, many companies are proscribing sexual conduct that would not amount to sexual harassment, let alone sex discrimination, under the law. Many firms are banning or discouraging intimate relationships between their employees. Worst of all, companies are disciplining (and even firing) employees for these perceived sexual transgressions without bothering to examine whether they are linked to sex discrimination in purpose or effect.

Schultz, Sanitized Workplace, supra, at 2065.

Eugene Volokh similarly maintains that liability concerns have encouraged employers to promulgate overly broad categorical prohibitions on sexual expression. Eugene Volokh, What Speech Does "Hostile Work Environment" Restrict?, Sexual Harassment: Cases, Case Studies, and Commentary 180, 202 (Paul I. Weizer ed., 2002). Such prohibitions raise obvious First Amendment concerns, discussed on pp. 436-439. In addition, Schultz worries that both employers and employees use trivial examples of sexual conduct as a pretext for other concerns. Employers, for example, have seized on harassment as a convenient cover for discharges that are motivated by age, race, sexual orientation, and performance concerns, while employees have made frivolous harassment claims in an effort to insulate themselves from "retaliation" when there are in fact valid justifications for their demotion or dismissal. Schultz, The Sanitized Workplace, supra, at 2113-2116, 2156.

Schultz is also critical of the growing tendency of employers to become "Cupid Cops." Id. at 2130. See Philip Weiss, Don't Even Think About It: The Cupid Cops Are Watching, N.Y. Times, May 3, 1998 (Magazine), at 43, 45. The limited research available suggests that somewhere between 20 to 40 percent of companies have policies or clear norms on workplace romances, and that the vast majority prohibits or discourages such relationships. Schultz, supra, at 2129. Most prohibitions target relationships between supervisors and their subordinates, and some policies that do not ban these relationships entirely demand that they be disclosed to managers who can monitor the situation.

Underlying these policies are concerns about the coercive potential for those in situations of unequal power, the fact or perception of favoritism, and the problems that can arise if the relationship sours. See Carol Sanger, Consensual Sex and the Limits of the Law, in Directions in Sexual Harassment Law 79-80 (Catharine A. MacKinnon & Reva B. Siegel eds., 2004) (arguing that such relations are not sex harassment but are legitimate subjects for employer regulation).

Critics of prohibitions on workplace romances worry that attempts to enforce them are often ineffective and intrusive, and likely to drive relationships underground. See sources cited in Deborah L. Rhode, Danger or Delight? Is Romance at Work All Bad?, Nat'l L.J., Nov. 23, 1998, at A21. Enforcement is also likely to have gender-biased results; those in subordinate positions, typically women, are the ones typically transferred or dismissed. Moreover, categorical bans on workplace relationships ignore courtship realities. For a growing number of employees, the increasing length of workweeks means that that they have less time to find potential partners outside of the workplace. According to one 2005 survey by Vault, Inc., 58 percent of employees had dated someone at work; 14 percent had dated a supervisor; 19 percent had dated a subordinate. A 2005 study by Careerbuilder.com found that three quarters of employees believed that they should be able to date anyone they wished at work, and almost half (48 percent) preferred to keep their relationships confidential. Mireya Navarro, Love the Job? What About Your Boss?, N.Y. Times, July 24, 2005, at §9, pp. 1, 9.

In an effort to accommodate competing concerns, some organizations allow romantic relationships but ask, or require, the parties to sign a "love contract." For example, the supervisor might send a letter to the subordinate with language such as:

> It is very important to me that our relationship be on an equal footing and that you be fully comfortable that our relationship is at all times voluntary and welcome. I want to assure you that under no circumstances will I allow our relationship or, should it happen, the end of our relationship, to impact on your job or our working relationship.

Schultz, Sanitized Workplace, supra, at 2126. The letter is accompanied by a copy of the organization's sexual harassment policy, and includes a paragraph requesting that the recipient sign and return the document with an acknowledgement that he or she has read it and that the relationship is consensual and welcome.

Is this a reasonable approach? Would you recommend it for the organization where you intend to work? Or should employers drop these "date and tell" requirements and focus instead on prohibiting coercive relationships and favoritism of any form, whether sexually motivated or not. See Schultz, Sanitized Workplace, supra, at 2189.

The potential remedies for sex discrimination under Title VII include injunctive relief as well as damages. In Robinson v. Jacksonville Shipyards, Inc., 760 F. Supp. 1486 (M.D. Fla. 1991), plaintiff established a "hostile environment" case of sexual harassment under Title VII based on the pervasive display at the overwhelmingly male workplace of pornographic pictures and repeated sexual and demeaning remarks and jokes, many of which were directed against the plaintiff. The court found that the employer had condoned this conduct and entered injunctive relief. The decree required the employer to prohibit the display, reading, or viewing of pictures, posters, calendars, graffiti, and other materials that are "sexually suggestive, sexually demeaning, or pornographic." In defining the scope of this prohibition, the decree provided:

> [a] picture will be presumed to be sexually suggestive if it depicts a person of either sex who is not fully clothed or in clothes that are not suited to or ordinarily accepted for the accomplishment of routine work in and around the shipyard and who is posed for the obvious purpose of displaying or drawing attention to private portions of his or her body.

760 F. Supp. at 1542 (Appendix).

Does such an order raise First Amendment issues? The court concluded it did not, because (1) the employer had "no intention to express itself through the sexually-oriented pictures" and had limited other forms of speech (e.g., by banning political campaign literature and buttons); (2) pictures and verbal harassment "are not protected speech [when] they act as discriminatory conduct in the form of a hostile work environment"; (3) "regulation of discriminatory speech in the workplace constitutes nothing more than time, place, and manner regulation of speech"; (4) "female workers were a captive audience in relation to the speech that comprised the hostile work environment"; (5) even if the speech is "treated as fully protected by the First Amendment," the governmental interest in "cleansing the workplace of impediments to the equality of women is . . . a compelling interest that permits [a regulation] . . . narrowly drawn to serve this interest"; and (6) even a governmental employer has the power to enforce workplace rules impinging on free speech rights, in order to maintain discipline and order in the workplace. Id. at 1534-1536.

Can this decision be reconciled with American Booksellers Association v. Hudnut, 771 F.2d 323 (7th Cir. 1985), aff'd mem., 475 U.S. 1001 (1986), excerpted on p. 548 of this chapter? See 760 F. Supp. at 1536 (*Hudnut* distinguishable because the record involving Jacksonville Shipyards demonstrated a concrete harm for identifiable individuals and the remedy "went no further than to regulate the time, place, and manner of the offensive speech"). The constitutionality of the *Robinson* order was raised on appeal, but the employer's bankruptcy precipitated a settlement before the case was decided.

Cases after *Robinson* have frequently found that the pervasive presence of pornography has either provided a context for, or been a form of, sexual harassment. See cases cited in Catharine A. MacKinnon, Sex Equality 1639-1641 (2001). A leading exception is Johnson v. County of Los Angeles Fire Department, 865 F. Supp. 1430 (C.D. Cal. 1994). There, a federal district court struck down a Los Angeles County ban on sexually oriented magazines, particularly those including nude pictures, such as Playboy, Penthouse, and Playgirl, in all fire station work locations, including dormitories, rest rooms, and lockers. Although acknowledging that the prevention of sexual harassment was a compelling government interest, the court held that there was insufficient evidence that the presence of the offending material "directly contributes to a sexually harassing environment. . . ." Id. at 1439. In defending the ordinance, the County introduced expert testimony to the effect that reading magazines such as Playboy may result in "sex-role stereotyping," which in turn may result in "inequitable treatment of women or even sexual harassment." Id. at 1441. Citing *Hudnut*, the trial court held that "it is a fundamental principle of First Amendment law that the government cannot regulate material in order to prevent the readers from developing certain ideas." Id. The court further concluded that the County had not carried its "burden of showing that reading Playboy actually leads to such 'stereotyping' [or] that the existence of 'sex-role stereotyping' leads to an harassing environment." Id. Unlike other cases involving workplace pornography, the women firefighters who were offended by the magazines were not captive audiences: by "averting their eyes," they could avoid exposure to objectionable contents. Id. at 1440. See also Williams v. City of Chicago, 325 F. Supp. 2d 867, 876 (N.D. Ill. 2004) (holding that "while pornography in the workplace likely has a greater negative impact on female employees than on male employees, its mere presence in the workplace affects everyone regardless of sex").

Are *Robinson* and *Johnson* distinguishable? If not, which ruling do you find more persuasive? Should tolerance for sexually explicit expression depend on the nature of the workplace? In Lyle v. Warner Brothers Television, 12 Cal. Rptr. 3d 511 (Ct. App. 2004), rev. granted, 16 Cal. Rptr. 3d 331 (Cal. 2004), a writer's assistant for the television program, *Friends*, argued that she was routinely subject to crude sexual conduct and expression in violation of California employment law. The defendant claimed that such expression was an indispensable means of developing material for the sitcom. The plaintiff, joined by a number of law professors as amici curiae, responded that this objectionable conduct (including simulated masturbation) was not demonstrably connected with anything appearing on *Friends* and that in some cases supervisors ordered her not to record sexually offensive comments. In an editorial supporting the defendant, the L.A. Times maintained that the creative processes needed absolute protection because "nothing is off limits to a creative comedic mind." Found Item: No Room for Delicate Ears, L.A. Times, Feb. 6, 2005, at M6. If you were on the California Supreme Court, which is reviewing the case, what would you decide?

Some commentators have criticized the use of sexual harassment law to regulate workplace speech. Their primary concern is that because the boundaries of sexual harassment are often vague and because employers have no general interest in preserving employee speech, they may adopt overbroad restrictions to minimize their chances of liability for hostile environments. Kingsley Browne, Eugene Volokh, and Vicki Schultz cite multiple examples of sweeping prohibitions against sexually suggestive jokes, banter, and pictures. Kingsley R. Browne, The Silenced Workplace: Employer Censorship Under Title VII, in Directions in Sexual Harassment Law, supra, 399, 400-401, 408; Volokh, supra, at 192-196, 202-203; Schultz, Sanitized Workplace, supra, at 2107-2108. Browne maintains that such regulations are unconstitutional because they are vague and not viewpoint neutral. Browne, supra, at 403-408. Schultz argues that such an effort to sanitize the workplace "induces social stigma and enforces sexual conformity in a way that impoverishes life for everyone." Id. at 2146. In her view, what women need is "sexually open" and "gender egalitarian" workplaces. Id. at 2164.

What, if any, limits would you place on sex harassment prohibitions as applied to workplace expression? Schultz would reform sexual harassment law to eliminate its focus on sexual content; courts under her proposal would prohibit any harassment that occurs because of sex and impose lesser standards of liability on workplaces that were gender-integrated at all levels, because these have been shown to have a lower incidence of offensive conduct. Id. at 2173-2182. For other approaches, see Kelly Cahill Timmons, Sexual Harassment and Disparate Impact: Should Non-Targeted Workplace Sexual Conduct be Actionable Under Title VII?, 81 Neb. L. Rev. 1152, 1186-1187 (2003) (arguing that the test for material not targeted at particularly employees should be whether it has a disparate impact on men and women); Volokh, Freedom of Speech and Workplace Harassment, 39 UCLA L. Rev. 1791 (1992) (contending that harassment law should target only offensive speech directed at a particular employee); Browne, supra (arguing that only individuals, not employers, should be liable for hostile environment harassment in order to prevent overbroad employer regulation); Nadine Strossen, Regulating Workplace Sexual Harassment and Upholding the First Amendment—Avoiding a Collision, 37 Vill. L. Rev. 757 (1992) (overly broad range of prohibited speech in the workplace undermines both free speech and gender equality). For a contrary view, see Jack M. Balkin, Free Speech and Hostile Environments, 99 Colum. L. Rev. 2295, 2307 (1999) (sex harassment law is no more vague than rules of defamation or intentional infliction of emotional distress). For further discussion of First Amendment issues, see pp. 459-466, below, on harassment in educational contexts.

8. Street Hassling. How serious an offense is "street hassling"—i.e., wolf whistles, leers, catcalls, grabs, pinches, crude sexual invitations, and other rude behaviors from strangers, directed at women in public places? Several feminist scholars have argued that the law should reach this conduct. See, e.g., Olatokunbo Olukemi Laniya, Street Smut: Gender, Media, and the Legal Power Dynamics of Street Harassment, or "Hey Sexy" and Other Verbal Ejaculations, 14 Colum. J. Gender & L. 91 (2005) (analyzing deficiencies in prosecutions of 2000 Puerto Rican Day Parade harassments in New York City and concluding that street harassment is a real injury that must be "named, blamed, and claimed"); Cynthia Grant Bowman, Street Harassment and the Informal Ghettoization of Women, 106 Harv. L. Rev. 517 (1993) (advocating redefinition of torts of assault, intentional infliction of emotional distress, and invasion of privacy to encompass street harassment, and a criminal ordinance making street harassment punishable by a $250 fine); Deborah M. Thompson, "The Woman in the Street": Reclaiming the Public Space from Sexual Harassment, 6 Yale J.L. & Feminism 313 (1994) (advocating adoption of complaint procedures by companies that have workers in public places and anti-harassment codes applicable to everyone in public places).

Should street hassling be regulated? If so, how should it be defined? Cynthia Bowman proposes the following:

> Street harassment occurs when one or more unfamiliar men accost one or more women in a public place, on one or more occasions, and intrude or attempt to intrude upon the woman's attention in a manner that is unwelcome to the woman, with language that is explicitly or implicitly sexual. Such language includes, but is not limited to, references to male or female genitalia or to female body parts or

to sexual activities, solicitation of sex, or reference by word or action to the target of the harassment as the object of sexual desire, or similar words that by their very utterance inflict injury or naturally tend to provoke violent resentment, even if the woman did not herself react with violence. The harasser's intent, except his intent to say the words or engage in the conduct, is not an element of this offense. This [definition] does not apply to any peaceable activity intended to express political views or provide public information to others.

Bowman, supra, at 575-576. See also Tiffanie Heben, A Radical Reshaping of the Law: Interpreting and Remedying Street Harassment, 4 S. Cal. Rev. L. & Women's Stud. 183, 213 (1994) (definition should also cover insults related to a person's racial or homosexual identity).

Would you support legislation banning such conduct? If not, is there another approach that you would prefer?

9. Legal Ethics Issues in Sexual Harassment Cases. Sexual harassment cases can often present ethical issues for lawyers on both sides of the litigation. For lawyers representing plaintiffs, the issues include how much evidence is necessary to justify bringing a lawsuit, what to do if the litigation seems motivated by a desire to punish or humiliate the defendant, and how extensively to probe the defendant's background for potentially embarrassing incidents. Consider, for example, the conduct of the lawyers for Paula Jones, discussed above at pp. 425-427. By Jones's account, she initially consulted attorneys not because of adverse consequences at work, but because American Spectator had reported allegations that she had been involved in a sexual relationship with then-Governor Clinton. Jones frequently asserted that all she originally wanted was a retraction from the magazine and an apology from Clinton. When neither was forthcoming, she agreed to file suit. Paula Jones Settlement, Wash. Post, Nov. 15, 1998, at C6; Michael Isikoff, Uncovering Clinton 50-51 (1999). Her legal expenses were subsidized by the Rutherford Institute, a foundation that had funded many right-wing political causes. The Institute also recommended different, more politically connected attorneys, who promptly amended Jones's original complaint to add a claim of sexual assault based on a new allegation: that Clinton had slid his hand up Jones's leg. Under the recently enacted Violence Against Women Act, this claim brought Clinton within the scope of a provision aimed at sexual predators, which entitled lawyers to introduce evidence of his prior sexual history and to obtain broad discovery into prior intimate relationships. Fed. R. Evid. 415(a).

Yet while Jones's lawyers sought information from over 150 individuals concerning Clinton's history, they made almost no effort to discover facts about their client's, such as whether she had suffered adverse job consequences following the hotel incident. They did not even review her employment records before or after she filed suit. See Deborah L. Rhode, Conflicts of Commitment: Legal Ethics in the Impeachment Context, 52 Stan. L. Rev. 269, 295, 313 (2000).

Was the lawyers' behavior unethical? Negligent? Rule 11 of the Federal Rules of Civil Procedure authorizes sanctions if a lawsuit is pursued for "any improper purpose such as to harass" and/or includes claims that lack "evidentiary support" or are unlikely to prove well grounded "after a reasonable opportunity for further investigations or discovery." The Model Rules of Professional Conduct similarly authorize ethical sanctions against lawyers who assert frivolous or harassing claims. Rules 3.1, 3.4. Could Jones's lawyers have been subject to sanctions? Was it ethical for them to seek extensive information about Clinton's prior consensual relationships, including his relationship with Monica Lewinsky, on the theory that such information might have revealed a pattern of rewarding employees for sexual favors? How should attorneys respond when a claim appears extremely unlikely to succeed at trial, but when threats of embarrassing pretrial discovery might serve some other purpose or prompt a substantial settlement? Are cases like *Jones* a harassing use of harassment law? See Rhode, Conflicts of Commitment, supra, at 289-295 (citing observers who believed that the lawyers in *Jones* pursued the claims more out of a desire to humiliate and politically cripple the defendant than to remedy any injury to the plaintiff). Is it relevant that Clinton settled the *Jones* appeal for $850,000, an amount that fell far short of covering the plaintiff's attorney's fees, which totaled over $2 million. Jones ultimately received $200,000 from the settlement. Chuck Bartels, Jones's Lawyers Agree on Settlement, AP Online, Mar. 5, 1999.

Lawyers for defendants often have comparable opportunities to harass their opponents in harassment cases. Rule 412(b)(2) of the Federal Rules of Evidence provides as follows:

> In a civil case, evidence offered to prove the sexual behavior or sexual predisposition of any alleged victim is admissible if . . . its probative value substantially outweighs the danger of harm to any victim and of unfair prejudice to any party. Evidence of an alleged victim's reputation is admissible only if it has been placed in controversy by the alleged victim.

The Rule also provides an in camera proceeding to determine admissibility. However, under Rule 11 of the Federal Rules of Civil Procedure, attorneys may seek not only evidence relevant to their clients' cases, but also information that might reasonably lead to such evidence. Many courts have interpreted this Rule to allow lawyers to ask complainants about intimate sexual matters that might shed light on whether a defendant's conduct was unwelcome or was in fact the cause of the damages alleged. Such questioning has focused on matters including childhood sexual abuse, closeted lesbian experiences, and intimate marital difficulties or infidelities, to mental health treatment, birth control practices, and bra sizes. See Jane H. Aiken, Protecting Plaintiff's Sexual Pasts: Coping With Preconceptions Through Discretion, 51 Emory L.J. 559, 580-581 (2002). The fear of having their personal lives paraded in court proceedings often deters victims from bringing or pursuing harassment claims. Id. at 561, 580-581; Miranda Oshige, What's Sex Got to Do with It?, 47 Stan. L. Rev. 565, 581 (1995). For discussion of similar problems in the context of rape, see Chapter 6, pp. 797-799.

Whose responsibility is it to prevent intrusive questioning of parties in sexual harassment litigation? Trial judges have broad discretion under Rules 26(e) and

45(c) of the Federal Rules of Civil Procedure to limit disclosures to prevent "undue burden" or "embarrassment." Compare Barrenda L. v. Superior Court, 76 Cal. Rptr. 2d 727, 732 (Ct. App. 1998) (holding that plaintiff's right to privacy outweighed defendant's need for information about sexual encounters), with McCleland v. Montgomery Ward & Co., Inc. 1995 WL 571324 (N.D. Ill. Sept 25, 1995) (permitting evidence concerning plaintiff's childhood sex abuse as more probative than prejudicial concerning damages, but excluding evidence that defendant had previously harassed another employee as more prejudicial than probative). To protect parties from needlessly intrusive discovery, should courts require a threshold showing that a plaintiff's claim is well grounded and that there is a clear and convincing need for such evidence? See Rhode, Conflicts of Commitment, supra, at 305; Diane H. Mazur, Sex and Lies: Rules of Ethics, Rules of Evidence, and Our Conflicted Views of the Significance of Honesty, 14 Notre Dame J.L. Ethics & Pub. Pol'y 679, 720 (2000). Alternatively, should the burden be on defendants to make an in camera showing that the prior sexual conduct, not the harassment, was the actual cause of the damages alleged? See Aiken, supra, at 582.

If courts do not limit discovery, do lawyers have an independent obligation to do so? Rule 4.4 of the Model Rules of Professional Conduct provides: "In representing a client, a lawyer shall not use means that have no substantial purpose other than to embarrass, delay, or burden a third person. . . ." Model Rule 1.2 of the Model Rules of Professional Conduct provides that lawyers "shall abide by a client's decisions concerning the objectives of representation," but permits lawyers to forego actions that they consider "repugnant or imprudent." Withdrawal from representation is permissible if it can be accomplished without prejudice when the client insists on pursuing a matter that the lawyer considers "repugnant" or "imprudent." How would these Rules guide your conduct on the issues posed in the problems on pp. 450-453?

In 2002, in response to growing evidence of abusive lawyer conduct, the American Bar Association adopted an amendment to the Model Rules of Professional Conduct. As amended, Rule 1.8j provides that "a lawyer shall not have sexual relations with a client unless a consensual sexual relationship existed between them when the lawyer-client relationship commenced." Some courts and ethical committees have also found that harassment and coercive sexual relations violate general ethical rules prohibiting conduct that adversely reflects on fitness to practice law. See, e.g., Cincinnati Bar Ass'n v. Young, 731 N.E.2d 631 (Ohio 2000) (imposing two-year suspension for harassment of law student). Lawyers may also be liable for malpractice based on such conduct. See Cerrato v. American Home Insurance (D. Conn. No. 3:99CV2355 (RNC), April 2, 2002), discussed in 18 ABA/BNA Lawyers Manual of Professional Conduct (finding that malpractice insurance policy did not cover lawyer's actions in preparing a witness to testify which included lifting her skirt and slapping her buttocks).

10. The Hill-Thomas Hearings. In 1991, the Senate Judiciary Committee convened nationally televised hearings on the confirmation of Clarence Thomas for a seat on the U.S. Supreme Court. One of the witnesses called to testify before the Committee was Anita Hill, a young African-American woman lawyer who had worked under Thomas's supervision first at the Department of Education and then when he moved to head the EEOC. She testified that Thomas had made frequent sexual overtures and that he had described pornographic videos and his own sexual experiences in graphic detail. The Committee called numerous other witnesses in an effort to confirm or contradict this testimony, including other employees of Thomas, friends and acquaintances of Hill, and Thomas himself. The Senate confirmed Thomas by a narrow two-vote margin.

The Hill-Thomas hearings were a defining moment in women's history in this country. Watching an all-male Judiciary Committee grill a woman with no apparent motive to lie on humiliating sexual details mobilized many women who had never before identified with the "women's movement." For many viewers, the hearings called into question certain fundamental assumptions about women's sexuality and workplace opportunities, as well as the capacity of law to cope with sexual harassment.

During the hearings themselves, most Americans did not believe Anita Hill. A New York Times/CBS News poll at the time found that only about a quarter of viewers thought Hill was telling the truth; 58 percent believed Justice Thomas. See Elizabeth Kolbert, The Thomas Nomination: Most in National Survey Say Judge Is the More Believable, N.Y. Times, Oct. 15, 1991, at A1. One year later, however, according to a Wall Street Journal/ NBC News poll, her credibility rating had risen to 44 percent, while his had slipped to 34 percent. See Jill Abramson, Reversal of Fortune: Image of Anita Hill, Brighter in Hindsight, Galvanizes Campaigns, Wall St. J., Oct. 5, 1992, at A1.

Strange Justice: The Selling of Clarence Thomas (1994), an account of the Thomas nomination by Wall Street Journal reporters Jane Mayer and Jill Abramson, concluded that the preponderance of the evidence suggested that Thomas had lied under oath in denying Hill's claims. And a decade after the confirmation process, David Brock, the author of a best-selling book that had attacked Hill, published another book acknowledging that he had previously lied in print in order to protect the reputation of Thomas. In the first book, The Real Anita Hill (1993), Brock repeated his earlier assertions that Hill was "a little bit nutty, a little bit slutty." David Brock, The Real Anita Hill, American Spectator, Mar. 1992, at 18. In Blinded by the Right: The Conscience of an Ex-Conservative (2001), Brock conceded that he had demonized Hill and her supporters without adequate factual basis and that he had falsely stated that there was no evidence that Thomas had rented pornographic videos. See Alex Kuczynski and William Glaberson, Book Author Says He Lied in His Attacks on Anita Hill, N.Y. Times, June 27, 2001, at A12.

Two consequences of the Hill-Thomas hearings were the mobilization of women as a political force and an increase in sexual harassment claims. Female politicians ran for elective office in record numbers in the 1992 elections, some directly in reaction to these events. Women tripled their representation in the Senate (an increase from 2 to 6 seats) and almost doubled it in the House of Representatives (an increase from 28 to 47 seats). AP, Female Ranks in Elected Jobs Get a Big Boost, N.Y. Times, Nov. 8, 1992, at A18. Many of the new successful candidates were women of color; as a result of the 1992 election, one-third of the Democratic women in the House were African-American or Hispanic. A year after the hearings, reports of sexual harassment to the Equal Employment Opportunity Commission were up by over 50 percent. See Jane Gross, Suffering in Silence No More: Fighting Sexual Harassment, N.Y. Times, July 13, 1992, at A1, A16. A growing industry emerged to train employers and employees how to end sexual harassment in the workplace. See id.

Not everyone applauded the increased attention to sexual harassment. Sociologist Orlando Patterson argued in a widely circulated New York Times Opinion editorial that variations in gender, class, ethnicity, and region must be taken into account in determining "what constitutes proper and effective male-female relations." Patterson, Race, Gender and Liberal Fallacies, N.Y. Times, Oct. 10, 1991, at 4-15.

> With his mainstream cultural guard down, Judge Thomas on several misjudged occasions may have done something completely out of the cultural frame of his white, upper-middle-class work world, but immediately recognizable to Professor Hill and most women of Southern working-class backgrounds, white or black, especially the latter.

Id. Is this what it means to take into account differences in race and class? See Chapter 6, pp. 964-978. Patterson also claimed that "[i]f women are to break through the glass ceiling, they must escape the trap of neo-Puritan feminism with its reactionary sacralization of women's bodies." Id. Does he have a point? Is this judgment consistent with anti-subordination theory? Of the extensive writing on the Hill-Thomas hearings, four collections focus specifically on the controversial issues of race and gender politics. See Race, Gender, and Power in America (Anita Faye Hill & Emma Coleman Jordan eds., 1995); Symposium, Gender, Race, and the Politics of Supreme Court Appointments: The Import of the Anita Hill/Clarence Thomas Hearings, 65 S. Cal. L. Rev. 1279 (1992); Race-ing Justice, En-gendering Power: Essays on Anita Hill, Clarence Thomas, and the Construction of Social Reality (Toni Morrison ed., 1992); Court of Appeal: The Black Community Speaks Out on the Racial and Sexual Politics of Thomas v. Hill (Robert Chrisman & Robert L. Allen eds., 1992).

2. Same-Sex Harassment and Men as Victims

Rene v. MGM Grand Hotel, Inc.
305 F.3d 1061 (9th Cir. 2002) (en banc), cert. denied,
538 U.S. 922 (2003)

FLETCHER, Circuit Judge.

This case presents the question of whether an employee who alleges that he was subjected to severe, pervasive, and unwelcome "physical conduct of a sexual nature" in the workplace asserts a viable claim of discrimination based on sex under Title VII of the 1964 Civil Rights Act . . . even if that employee also alleges that the motivation for that discrimination was his sexual orientation. We would hold that an employee's sexual orientation is irrelevant for purposes of Title VII. It neither provides nor precludes a cause of action for sexual harassment. That the harasser is, or may be, motivated by hostility based on sexual orientation is similarly irrelevant, and neither provides nor precludes a cause of action. It is enough that the harasser ha[s] engaged in severe or pervasive unwelcome physical conduct of a sexual nature. We therefore would hold that the plaintiff in this case has stated a cause of action under Title VII.

I

Medina Rene, an openly gay man, appeals from the district court's grant of summary judgment in favor of his employer MGM Grand Hotel in his Title VII action alleging sexual harassment by his male co-workers and supervisor. The relevant facts are not in dispute. Rene worked for the hotel, located in Las Vegas, Nevada, from December 1993 until his termination in June 1996. He worked as a butler on the 29th floor, where his duties involved responding to the requests of the wealthy, high-profile and famous guests for whom that floor was reserved. All of the other butlers on the floor, as well as their supervisor, were also male.

Rene provided extensive evidence that, over the course of a two-year period, his supervisor and several of his fellow butlers subjected him to a hostile work environment on almost a daily basis. The harassers' conduct included whistling and blowing kisses at Rene, calling him "sweetheart" and "muneca" (Spanish for "doll"), telling crude jokes and giving sexually oriented "joke" gifts, and forcing Rene to look at pictures of naked men having sex. On "more times than [Rene said he] could possibly count," the harassment involved offensive physical conduct of a sexual nature. Rene gave deposition testimony that he was caressed and hugged and that his co-workers would "touch [his] body like they would to a woman." On numerous occasions, he said, they grabbed him in the crotch and poked their fingers in his anus through his clothing. When asked what he believed was the motivation behind this harassing behavior, Rene responded that the behavior occurred because he is gay.

On June 20, 1996, Rene filed a charge of discrimination with the Nevada Equal Rights Commission. He alleged that he "was discriminated against because of my sex, male" and indicated "I believe that my sex, male, was a factor in the adverse treatment I received." On April 13, 1997, Rene filed a complaint in federal district court, alleging that he had been unlawfully sexually harassed in violation of Title VII and attaching a copy of his Nevada Equal Rights Commission charge. MGM Grand moved for summary judgment on the grounds that "claims of discrimination based on sexual orientation are not cognizable under Title VII[.]"

The district court agreed that Rene had failed to state a cognizable Title VII claim. In granting summary judgment in favor of MGM Grand, it concluded that "Title VII's prohibition of 'sex' discrimination applies only [to] discrimination on the basis of gender and is not extended to include discrimination based on sexual preference." Rene timely appealed. . . .

III

In granting MGM Grand's motion for summary judgment, the district court did not deny that the sexual assaults alleged by Rene were so objectively offensive that they created a hostile working environment. Rather, it appears to have held that Rene's otherwise viable cause of action was defeated because he believed he was targeted because he is gay. This is not the law. We have surveyed the many cases finding a violation of Title VII based on the offensive touching of the genitalia, buttocks, or breasts of women. In none of those cases has a court denied relief because the victim was, or might have been, a lesbian. The sexual orientation of the victim was simply irrelevant. If sexual orientation is irrelevant for a female victim, we see no reason why it is not also irrelevant for a male victim. . . .

Our opinion today is guided by the principles established by the Supreme Court in Oncale v. Sundowner Offshore Servs., Inc., 523 U.S. 75 (1998). As recounted by the Court, the Title VII plaintiff in *Oncale* had been "forcibly subjected to sex-related, humiliating actions" and had been "physically assaulted . . . in a sexual manner" by other males at his place of employment. Oncale, 523 U.S. at 77. We know from the circuit court's opinion that this physical assault included, among other things, "the use of force by [one co-worker] to push a bar of soap into Oncale's anus while [another co-worker] restrained Oncale as he was showering[.]" 83 F.3d 118, 118-119 (5th Cir. 1996). This behavior occurred, the Court noted, in an all-male workplace. Oncale was a male plaintiff who worked on an all-male off-shore oil drilling rig "as a roustabout on an eight-*man* crew." See 523 U.S. at 77. Oncale's employer, Sundowner, never employed women on any of its drilling rigs. . . . We take two lessons from the Court's decision in *Oncale*.

First, Title VII forbids severe or pervasive same-sex offensive sexual touching. The Court made clear that a plaintiff's action for sexual harassment under Title VII cannot be defeated by a showing that the perpetrator and the victim of an alleged sexual assault are of the same gender. . . .

Second, offensive sexual touching is actionable discrimination even in a same-sex workforce. The Court in *Oncale* made clear that "discrimination" is a necessary predicate to every Title VII claim. That is, a defendant's conduct must not merely be "because of . . . sex"; it must be "'*discrimination* . . . because of . . . sex.'" *Oncale,* 523 U.S. at 81 (emphasis in original). The Court in *Oncale* held that "discrimination . . . because of . . . sex" can occur entirely among men, where some men are subjected to offensive sexual touching and some men are not. There were no women on Oncale's drilling rig; indeed, there were no women on any of his employer's oil rigs. Discrimination is the use of some criterion as a basis for a difference in treatment. In the context of our civil rights laws, including Title VII, discrimination is the use of a *forbidden* criterion as a basis for a *disadvantageous* difference in treatment. "Sex" is the forbidden criterion under Title VII, and discrimination is any disadvantageous difference in treatment "because of . . . sex." The *Oncale* Court's holding that offensive sexual touching in a same-sex workforce is actionable discrimination under Title VII necessarily means that discrimination can take place between members of the same sex, not merely between members of the opposite sex. Thus,

Oncale did not need to show that he was treated worse than members of the opposite sex. It was enough to show that he suffered discrimination *in comparison to other men*.

Viewing the facts, as we must, in the light most favorable to the nonmoving party, we are presented with the tale of a man who was repeatedly grabbed in the crotch and poked in the anus, and who was singled out from his other male co-workers for this treatment. It is clear that the offensive conduct was sexual. It is also clear that the offensive conduct was discriminatory. That is, Rene has alleged that he was treated differently—and disadvantageously—based on sex. This is precisely what Title VII forbids: "discrimination . . . because of . . . sex."

In sum, what we have in this case is a fairly straightforward sexual harassment claim. Title VII prohibits offensive "physical conduct of a sexual nature" when that conduct is sufficiently severe or pervasive. *Meritor*, 477 U.S. at 65. It prohibits such conduct without regard to whether the perpetrator and the victim are of the same or different genders. See *Oncale*, 523 U.S. at 79. And it prohibits such conduct without regard to the sexual orientation—real or perceived—of the victim. . . .

PREGERSON, Circuit Judge, joined by TROTT and BERZON, Circuit Judges, concurring. . . .

I write separately to point out that in my view, this is a case of actionable gender stereotyping harassment.

More than a decade ago, the Supreme Court held that gender stereotyping is actionable under Title VII. See Price Waterhouse v. Hopkins, 490 U.S. 228, 250-251 (1989). More recently, the Supreme Court held that "same-sex sexual harassment is actionable under Title VII." Oncale v. Sundowner Offshore Services, Inc., 523 U.S. 75, 82 (1998). And only last year, we held that same-sex gender stereotyping of the sort suffered by Rene—i.e., gender stereotyping of a male gay employee by his male co-workers— "constituted actionable harassment under . . . Title VII." Nichols v. Azteca Restaurant Enterprises, Inc., 256 F.3d 864, 874-875 (9th Cir. 2001). . . .

The conduct suffered by Rene is indistinguishable from the conduct found actionable in *Nichols*. In that case,

> Male co-workers and a supervisor repeatedly referred to [the male gay plaintiff] in Spanish and English as "she" and "her." Male co-workers mocked [him] for walking and carrying his serving tray "like a woman," and taunted him in Spanish and English as, among other things, a "faggot" and a ". . . female whore."

256 F.3d at 870. We concluded in *Nichols* that "[the] rule that bars discrimination on the basis of sex stereotypes" set in Price Waterhouse "squarely applies to preclude the harassment here." *Nichols*, 256 F.3d at 874-875. More generally, we held that "this verbal abuse was closely related to gender," "occurred because of sex," and therefore "constituted actionable harassment under . . . Title VII." Id.

The similarities between *Nichols* and the present case are striking. . . . For the same reasons that we concluded in *Nichols* that "[the] rule that bars discrimination on the basis of sex stereotypes" set in *Price Waterhouse* "squarely applied to preclude the harassment" at issue there, *Nichols,* 256 F.3d at 874-875, I conclude that this rule also squarely applies to preclude the identical harassment at issue here. Accordingly, this is a case of actionable gender stereotyping harassment.

[The opinions of Circuit Judges Graber and Fisher, concurring, are omitted.]

HUG, Circuit Judge, joined by SCHROEDER, Chief Judge, FERNANDEZ and NELSON, Circuit Judges, dissenting: . . .

The basis for Judge Fletcher's opinion is that harassment of a person in the workplace in the form of severe unwelcome physical conduct of a sexual nature is sufficient to establish a cause of action under Title VII of the Civil Rights Act, regardless of whether that harassment constitutes discrimination *because of* race, color, religion, gender, or national origin. I disagree because this completely eliminates an essential element of that statute, that the harassment be *because of* discrimination against one of the five specified categories of persons named in the statute.

Notes

1. Liability for Same-Sex Harassment.   In the *Oncale* case, on which the court in *Rene* relied, neither Joseph Oncale nor the men who harassed him, by their own accounts, are gay. Oncale is married with two children and does not consider himself a "standard bearer for gay rights," although neither is he a "gay-basher." Joanna Weiss, Same Sex Harassing Illegal Too, Court Says, Times Picayune, Mar. 5, 1998, at A1. Oncale stated in his deposition testimony, however, that he believed that his abusers were homosexuals who "made homosexual advances toward me." See Janet Halley, Sexuality Harassment, in Directions in Sexual Harassment Law 181, 191 (Catharine A. MacKinnon & Reva B. Siegel eds., 2004) (quoting transcript).

Which of the theories set forth on pp. 401-418 best accounts for cases in which men are victims?

According to some researchers, men often harass other men to enforce "the traditional heterosexual male gender role" by encouraging "stereotypical forms of 'masculine' behavior" and punishing "feminine" conduct: "Such behavior can be interpreted as arising from the societal devaluation of femininity and the complementary valorization of male heterosexuality and masculinity." Craig R. Waldo et al., Are Men Sexually Harassed? If So by Whom?, 22 Law & Hum. Behav. 59, 61 (1998). If this theory is right, what would Joseph Oncale need to show on remand to demonstrate that he was harassed "because of sex"? Are there risks that, after *Oncale,* spurious claims of harassment may be used to "out" closeted gays and lesbians or to punish those who are open about their homosexual orientation? See Mary Coombs, Title VII and Homosexual Harassment After *Oncale*: Was It a Victory?, 6 Duke J. of Gender L. & Pol'y 113, 114 (1999). Are there also risks that *Oncale* may be used to repress non-conventional sexual expression? See Halley, supra, at 193-198.

Courts since *Oncale* have diverged on the issue of motive in sexual harassment cases. In the *Rene* case, the Ninth Circuit determined that whether the harasser is "motivated by hostility based on sexual orientation is ... irrelevant." Similarly, in Centola v. Potter, 183 F. Supp. 2d 403, 410 (D. Mass. 2002), the court held that the plaintiff had alleged actionable sex harassment based on coworkers' conduct that vilified him for being effeminate. By contrast, in Spearman v. Ford Motor Co., 231 F.3d 1080 (2000), the Seventh Circuit held that the harassment of a male who was viewed as gay by his co-workers was not actionable sexual harassment because "Congress intended the term 'sex' to mean 'biological male or biological female,' and not one's *sexuality* or sexual orientation."

Which interpretation of the statute is more plausible? Was Medina Rene discriminated against because of his sex or because of his sexual orientation? Can you separate the two? Judge Fletcher reasons that "It is clear that the offensive conduct was sexual. It is also clear that the offensive conduct was discriminatory.... This is precisely what Title VII forbids." Is this reasoning clear to you?

2. Sexual Harassment as an Equality Issue. Is same-sex harassment properly viewed as an issue of sex equality? If so, what kind of equality? Mary Anne C. Case finds an identity between sexual harassment of homosexuals and harassment of women, an identity she establishes through an examination of the harassment of effeminate men:

> By examining the similarity of the taunts typically hurled at both women and gay or effeminate men in hostile environments, taunts that stress feminine sexual passivity of all three groups, [it is apparent] that the sexual harassment inflicted on all three groups may have in common the desire of certain "active" masculine males to drive out of the workplace those they see as contaminating it with the taint of feminine passivity. Such harassment is, therefore, a form of gender discrimination against the feminine, one with serious effects on the job performance and security of its victims, who should have a legal remedy against it regardless of their sex.

Case, Disaggregating Gender from Sex and Sexual Orientation: The Effeminate Man in the Law and Feminist Jurisprudence, 105 Yale L.J. 1, 7 (1995).

Is the disadvantaging of members of one sex in relation to the other the most objectionable feature of sexual harassment? What if a supervisor treats every worker in exactly the same way—abusively, and as a sexual object? Is this sex discrimination? If the conduct is abusive but not sexual, should it be illegal? See Vicki Schultz, Reconceptualizing Sexual Harassment, 107 Yale L.J. 1683 (1998).

A European Union Recommendation on the Protection of Dignity of Women and Men at Work defines the issue in terms of workplace dignity, rather than sex discrimination. See Commission Recommendation 92/131/EEC of 27 November, 1991, 1992 O.J. (L 49) 1-2. Western European countries generally recognize harassment as an offense whether or not it is based on sex. "Mobbing" or "bullying" are actionable torts that include everything from verbal harangues to social ostracism. See Gabrielle S. Friedman, Sexual Harassment Law Should Fight Discrimination, Not Regulate Desire, Legal Affairs, Sept./Oct. 2003, available at http://www.legalaffairs.org/issues/September-October-2003/feature. Would such an approach be preferable to the American model? See generally Susanne Baer, Dignity or Equality?: Responses to Workplace Harassment in European, German, and U.S. Law, in Directions in Sexual Harassment Law 582 (Catharine A. MacKinnon & Reva B. Siegel eds., 2004).

3. Men Harassed by Women.   If sexual harassment is viewed primarily as a means of reinforcing gender subordination in the workplace, what accounts for cases in which women harass male subordinates or co-workers? Although such cases have been rare, they have resulted in some of the largest verdicts in harassment litigation. See Reed Abelson, Men Increasingly Are the Ones Claiming Sex-Harassment by Men, N.Y. Times, June 10, 2001, at A1; Man Wins Sex-Harassment Suit Against a Woman, N.Y. Times, May 21, 1993, at A12 (male manager of spa manufacturing company who sued his former female supervisor for sexual harassment obtained first $1 million verdict in a harassment case). Descriptions of some of these lawsuits can be found in Aimee L. Widor, Comment, Fact or Fiction?: Role-Reversal Sexual Harassment in the Modern Workplace, 58 U. Pitt. L. Rev. 225 (1996); Caroline A. Forell & Donna M. Matthews, A Law of Her Own: The Reasonable Woman as a Measure of Man 71-73 (2000).

Most of these cases involve quid pro quo harassment. See, e.g., Gardinella v. General Electric Co., 833 F. Supp. 617 (W.D. Ky. 1993) (upholding claim brought against supervisor who discriminated against male employee after he refused to continue a sexual relationship with her). Do these cases support the suspicion that sexual harassment charges are sometimes simply an act of revenge following a romantic attraction that ends badly? Or do they indicate that women, no less than men, are capable of abusing power in the workplace? For a critique of the theory underlying role-reversal sexual harassment suits and the ways in which popular culture has reinforced portraits of (1) powerful women as sexually manipulative, and (2) white men as victims of anti-discrimination laws and unjust accusations, see Maria L. Ontiveros, Fictionalizing Harassment—Disclosing the Truth, 93 Mich. L. Rev. 1373 (1995) (book review).

4. Men as Victims of Unjust Accusations.   Should men who are harmed by sexual harassment charges that are not adequately proved have a remedy against their employer or their accuser? Consider the case in which a Milwaukee County jury ordered the Miller Brewing Company and two employees to pay $26 million to an executive fired by the company after repeated charges of sexual harassment. One such charge included the executive's description of a racy episode of *Seinfeld* to an offended female co-worker. The award included $1.5 million in punitive damages against the complaining co-worker. On appeal, the judgment was overturned on the ground that the fired executive had no legal cause of action. Mackenzie v. Miller Brewing Co., 623 N.W.2d 739 (Wis. 2001). At the time of the jury's verdict, the largest known judgment for a single plaintiff victim of sexual harassment was a $7 million punitive damages award against a law firm, Baker & McKenzie, based on its failure to prevent egregious and repeated harassment by a powerful senior partner. That verdict was later cut in half. See Odd Jobs, Wash. Post, Dec. 4, 1994, at H5. What accounts for jurors' apparent willingness to punish an employer's overreaction to harassment charges far more severely than unresponsiveness? In cases where facts are murky, are employers in a no-win situation, at risk of liability for either imposing or not imposing sanctions?

5. The Bisexual "Equal Opportunity" Harasser.   In a celebrated footnote in an early sexual harassment case, the District of Columbia Circuit Court of Appeals discussed a hypothetical case of a bisexual supervisor whose "insistence upon sexual favors would not constitute gender discrimination because it would apply to male and female employees alike." Barnes v. Costle, 561 F.2d 983, 990 n.55 (D.C. Cir. 1977). Most courts that have agreed have done so in cases where the bisexual defense was only hypothetical. See Catharine A. MacKinnon, Sex Equality 928 (2001). In one case involving actual discrimination against both men and women as a defense, the Seventh Circuit Court of Appeals rejected claims by a man and wife who alleged that their supervisor had sexually harassed each of them individually. Holman v. Indiana, 211 F.3d 399 (7th Cir.), cert. denied, 531 U.S. 880 (2000). Under the court's analysis, "Title VII does not cover the 'equal opportunity' or 'bisexual' harasser, then, because such a person is not *discriminating* on the basis of sex. He is not treating one sex better (or worse) than the other; he is treating both sexes the same (albeit badly)." Id. at 403. Compare Judge Posner's observation in dicta in McDonnell v. Cisneros, 84 F.3d 256, 260 (7th Cir. 1996): "It would be exceedingly perverse if a male worker could buy his supervisors and his company immunity from Title VII liability by taking care to harass sexually an occasional male worker, although his preferred targets were female." For an analysis of how the bisexual harasser problem reveals larger problems with the "attraction theory" of sexual harassment, see Martin J. Katz, Reconsidering Attraction in Sexual Harassment, 79 Ind. L.J. 101 (2004).

In a few cases in which the defendant harassed both male and female workers, courts have found that the abuse was not in fact equal. See Steiner v. Showboat Operating Co., 25 F.3d 1459, 1464 (9th Cir. 1994), cert. denied, 513 U.S. 1082 (1995) (defendant's "abuse of men in no way related to their gender, [while] his abuse of female employees . . . centered on the fact that they were females"); Kopp v. Samaritan Health Sys. Inc., 13 F.3d 264, 269 (8th Cir. 1993) (a fact-finder could conclude that the defendant's "treatment of women is worse than his treatment of men").

Do such cases underscore the need for general workplace prohibitions or tort remedies against harassment whether or not it is based on sex? See generally Kenji Yoshino, The Epistemic Contract of Bisexual Erasure, 52 Stan. L. Rev. 353, 432-458 (2000).

Putting Theory into Practice

3-1.   Analyze each of the following situations to determine whether it constitutes a case of "discrimination based on sex." What theories of sex discrimination help you make the determination?

(a) An employee uses obscene language and tells sexually explicit jokes, which are offensive to many co-workers, both male and female.

(b) A supervisor berates all of his subordinate staff, both men and women; he refers to male associates who are insufficiently combative as wimps and pussies, and he refers to assertive women as castrating bitches.

(c) A bisexual employee makes unwanted sexual advances to both male and female workers. After they refuse him twice, he stops, but his presence makes them uncomfortable.

(d) A male employee complains that his female supervisor, over a two-year period, stood close to him, touched him with her hips and thighs, invited him to her apartment, pinched his nipple while supposedly looking for a cigarette in his pocket, and reached into the front pocket of his pants.

(e) Co-workers of a male restaurant waiter call him "she" or "her," or sweetie, and mock him for carrying a tray "like a woman," and ogling male customers.

(f) An employee widely assumed to be gay invites a male co-worker to dance at the office Christmas party, appears to "peep at his privates" in the rest room, and hangs around the co-worker's desk for no obvious work-related reason.

(g) At an all-female mortgage company office, female employees make lewd jokes, ask each other about their sexual experiences, discuss whose breasts are bigger, change clothes in front of one another, and engage in related behavior. One administrative assistant is offended, and claims that it interferes with her work.

(h) Two first-year associates complain to their law firm managing partner that one of their colleagues, an attractive single woman, has consistently received better assignments than they have from the supervising partner in the litigation section. That partner is in the midst of a messy divorce and has made a point of including their colleague in evening strategy sessions and out-of-town depositions on a major case. The managing partner raises the issue with the supervisor, who responds that he is not having an affair with the associate, although he is seeing her "socially." He has channeled assignments to her because she is more available in the evening and for travel than her married colleagues. As long as the relationship is consensual, he views it as "none of the firm's business."

(i) A male construction worker, when he sees a mistake made by a female co-worker, often loudly shares his view that "they should never have allowed women in these jobs." See Kent Greenawalt, Fighting Words 90-91 (1995).

3-2. How would you handle each of the following situations?

(a) You are the ombudsperson for sexual harassment claims at your law firm. You have received several complaints about an informal e-mail distribution list for attorneys and staff who wish to exchange X-rated humor. All members of the list have requested to be on it, and e-mails come with a warning that they should be viewed behind closed doors. The messages mainly involve sexually explicit jokes and graphics. Several female secretaries have walked in on male attorneys while they were viewing the e-mails, and they are now uncomfortable about continuing to work with these attorneys. How should you respond?

(b) You own a grocery store. Several employees complain to you about their exposure in the back room to explicit drawings and conversation by male supervisors and co-workers concerning homosexual activities. No sexual overtures or homophobic comments are made.

(c)   You are the trial judge in a sexual harassment case brought by a female employee who was offended by her supervisor's dumb blonde jokes. The defendant has moved for summary judgment and seeks sanctions against the plaintiff and her lawyer for filing a frivolous claim. See Shramban v. Aetna, Inc., 262 F. Supp. 531, 536 (E.D. Pa. 2003).

3-3.   A Minneapolis woman works as a cashier in a sex-toy shop. Day in, day out, she hears lewd conversations by customers and co-workers in the shop. Does she have a hostile environment claim against her employer, for failing to stop, or protect her from, these conversations? For similar facts, see Gerald D. Skoning, 2000's Ten Wackiest Employment Lawsuits, Nat'l L.J., Apr. 2, 2001, at A21.

3-4.   A police officer works for the same police department as his wife, who is a dispatcher. The wife has had a number of extramarital affairs with other employees of the department, some of them involving open flirting, touching, frequent visits and breaks, and use of department phones for lengthy calls with sexual content. As a result of this behavior, other department employees subject the officer to sexually explicit jokes and comments. Some question the paternity of his children or challenge his masculinity. He believes that his job depends on avoiding a confrontation with those who taunt him or who have had affairs with his wife. Does he have a claim for sexual harassment? How should he proceed? See Mathews v. City of LaVerne, 1997 WL 351073 (C.D. Cal. 1997).

3-5.   If you had been one of Clinton's lawyers, would you have advised questioning Paula Jones concerning her sexual history on the ground that it was relevant to whether she found Clinton's conduct unwelcome and whether she was likely to have suffered emotional distress? What if you believed that Jones's claims were without merit and that her attorneys had committed ethical violations by seeking discovery to harass and politically disable the defendant?

3-6.   Consider the case of an associate who sued her law firm and one of its partners for three years of harassing incidents. This partner's conduct included grabbing the associate's breasts, announcing wet t-shirt contests over the office intercom, and displaying sexual devices on his lap. The law firm defended the claim on the grounds that the conduct was not severe and pervasive and that the associate had worn "short skirts . . . so the conduct wasn't unwelcome." Catherine Brennan, Associate Wins 80K Sex Harassment Verdict, Daily Rec., Dec. 31, 1996, at 2. If you had been a lawyer for the firm, would you have made those arguments? Would you have questioned the associate about her apparel and her own sexual conduct if the client had insisted that you do so?

3-7.   Consider the harassment claim of Andrea Makris, associate producer of the O'Reilly show, against the host Bill O'Reilly, based on telephone conversations that she allegedly recorded. The conversations were said to include vulgarities, sexual propositions, discussion of other sexual liaisons, and threats against any woman who went public with charges. The lawyer for Makris sent a demand letter to O'Reilly seeking $60 million dollars, and engaged in confidential negotiations seeking to settle the claim. When the negotiations failed, O'Reilly's attorneys brought an extortion suit. The lawyer for Makris then filed the harassment complaint and released details to the press. New York law, like that of every other jurisdiction, views statements in demand letters and negotiations as privileged communications, which cannot form the basis of extortion claims. After a nasty public relations war, the parties settled both lawsuits.

How would you evaluate the conduct of the lawyers? What would you have done in their place? Should any of them be subject to sanctions? See Debra S. Katz & Andrew Schroeder, Waging the P.R. Battle, Nat'l L.J., Nov. 8, 2004, at 26.

3-8. A warehouse foreman in a workplace requiring heavy lifting stated repeatedly that he believed women were incapable of performing work in the warehouse and that he would never hire a woman. Although he was not found to have committed any discriminatory personnel action, he was demoted for violating the organization's non-discrimination policy by expressing beliefs that reflected a discriminatory attitude. He challenges that disciplinary action. Should he be reinstated? See Holland v. Dep't of the Air Force, 31 F.3d 1118 (Fed. Cir. 1994).

3. Sexual Harassment in Educational Institutions

a. The Nature of the Problem

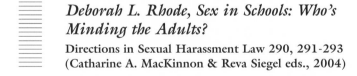

Deborah L. Rhode, Sex in Schools: Who's Minding the Adults?

Directions in Sexual Harassment Law 290, 291-293
(Catharine A. MacKinnon & Reva Siegel eds., 2004)

The prevalence of harassment in [educational settings] is difficult to gauge with precision. The sexes vary in their assessments of what is unwelcome or abusive behavior, and their perceptions depend partly on shifting cultural and legal standards. However, virtually all studies find significant levels of unwanted sexual conduct. In representative studies of college campuses, between 30 to 50% of female students report harassment by professors and 70-80% from peers; the incidents range from insulting comments and propositions to bribes, threats, and assaults. Research on elementary and secondary schools generally finds that between 75 to 85 percent of girls and 75 percent of boys experience harassing conduct ranging from sexual taunts to physical attacks. Over 95 percent of surveyed students observe repeated homophobic behavior.

Such conduct remains common in part because many constituencies deny its significance. These denials take somewhat different form for elementary and secondary schools than for colleges and universities, but common themes emerge. Widespread assumptions are that much harassment is harmless, that victims often invite it, and that overreaction by courts and administrators is a greater problem than the abuse they target.

At the elementary and secondary level, many educators believe that harassment is seldom serious and largely inescapable. As one school principal put it, "children are going to bother each other, tease each other and make each other feel bad. But that is the story of man. That's part of growing up. I really think that calling it sexual harassment is too far out." A mother whose son was suspended for two days complained tearfully that the school was "robbing my boy of his childhood." His childhood included calling a classmate a dyke and shoving her face into a concrete wall.

A related assumption is that victims are responsible either for provoking sexual abuse or for learning to cope with it. Parents and administrators often tell girls who complain about harassment that they "ask for it" by "inappropriate" clothing or conduct. A case in point involves the Los Angeles Spur Posse, a group of high school students who competed with each other for sexual conquests. When some of the teens faced disciplinary action and criminal prosecution for acts including harassment, molestation, and rape, many parents rose to their sons' defense. In their view, the conduct was simply part of any "red blooded American boy's" "testosterone thing." After all, "those girls were trash." Even more demurely behaved victims are told to accept the fact that the "story of man" includes the persecution of woman. As one teacher explained, people will call girls names all their lives and they "have to learn to deal with it."

This willingness to trivialize harassment is encouraged by the media's fixation on trivial examples. Hard cases may make bad law, but bad cases make great press. The infrequent instances of administrative overreaction are grossly overreported. Journalists have a field day with the facts when six- or seven-year-olds are "suspended for a smooch." "Loose Lips," "Kiss and Yell," "Peck of Trouble," chortle the headlines.

From these highly publicized cases, the public receives a highly distorted picture of what the problem is. Conservative critics appear correct in their descriptions of "PC paranoia": "hypersensitive," neopuritan "neurotics" seem to be swamping the system with frivolous complaints. To John Leo, the message of school harassment codes is that "chit-chat about sex can get you brought up on charges," and that the friends who might snitch to authorities should not be trusted. "Better to talk about the weather."

In the equally puritanical environment that Katie Roiphe describes, baseless charges "materialize out of thin air" and even ogling will alert the feminist fanatics now patrolling school corridors. Columnist Debbie Price wonders whether we really should address restroom graffiti in federal lawsuits and turn girls "into sniveling emotional cripples . . . ?" Christina Hoff Sommers worries about the boys who are the real victims — those targeted by the "anti-male influence" of a flourishing "gender bias industry."

Yet if the charge is exaggeration, critics, not complainants, are the worst offenders. Of course, borderline cases do exist, and recent changes in cultural norms have created some genuine confusion about boundaries. But the cases that now reach educational administrators and legal authorities do not involve idle chit-chat or corridor ogling. They generally feature serious repeated abuse. Girls are taunted, threatened, and mauled, and students of color are especially likely to experience physical abuse. Many victims experience fear, depression, insomnia, and loss of self esteem; the result is lower school performance, increased absenteeism, and, in extreme cases, even suicide.

Few of these victims file complaints. Contrary to popular assumptions, the most serious problem with sexual harassment enforcement involves underreporting, not overreaction. The vast majority of students are silenced by humiliation, fear of retaliation, and skepticism about likely remedies. These concerns are well-founded. Formal complaints often yield ineffectual reprimands from administrators and severe retaliation by classmates. The much martyred six-year-old sex criminal received a one day "in school" suspension. He was separated from his class and missed coloring and an ice cream party. Even such minimal punishment for harassment is the exception; "boys will be boys" is still the rule.

Beleaguered administrators are, of course, correct that kids can be cruel in many ways and that no sexual harassment policy is likely to transform educational institutions into Sunnybrook Farms. But we also need better strategies for increasing accountability among those who harass and those best able to prevent it.

b. Legal Liability for Sexual Harassment in Educational Settings

The law with respect to sexual harassment in the educational setting is less developed than that relating to the workplace. Title IX of the Education Amendments of 1972, 20 U.S.C. §1681 et seq. (1994) (discussed more generally in Chapter 2, starting on p. 291) has been held to prohibit both quid pro quo harassment and hostile environment harassment. In Franklin v. Gwinnett County Public Schools, 503 U.S. 60 (1992), a case involving allegations that a teacher had coercive sexual intercourse with a high school student, the United States Supreme Court held that remedies for violations of Title IX are not limited to injunctive relief, but can include damages as well. *Gwinnett*, however, left open the issue of standards of liability, and lower courts divided about the circumstances under which schools could be held accountable for harassment by peers or employees.

The Supreme Court ultimately spoke to those issues in two cases, Gebser v. Lago Vista Independent School District, 524 U.S. 274 (1998), and Davis v. Monroe County Board of Education, 526 U.S. 629 (1999). In *Gebser*, parents of a female student sued the school district after police found that their daughter was having a sexual affair with one of her teachers. By a 5-4 vote, the Court held that schools are not liable for harassment of a student by an employee unless officials had actual notice of the specific misconduct and responded with "deliberate indifference." Id. at 292-293. Under the majority's analysis, it does not matter if the school lacks adequate harassment policies. That decision stands in contrast to other decisions governing workplace harassment from the Court's same 1998 term, discussed at pp. 430-434 above. In both Faragher v. City of Boca Raton, 524 U.S. 775 (1998), and Burlington Industries v. Ellerth, 524 U.S. 742 (1998), the majority held that employers could be liable for a supervisor's harassment even if they lacked specific knowledge of the abuse unless they had adequate policies and procedures that the worker unreasonably failed to use. In effect, the Court has provided more protection from harassment for school employees than for students.

What accounts for this difference in standards? In explaining this result, Justice O'Connor's majority opinion reasoned that any stricter standard would be at odds with the overall compliance scheme of Title IX, which requires federal enforcement agencies to provide notice of any violation of nondiscrimination requirements before initiating enforcement actions. The "central purpose" of this notice is to "avoid diverting education funding from beneficial uses where a recipient was unaware of discrimination in its programs and is willing to institute prompt corrective measures." 524 U.S. at 289. Justice Stevens's dissent noted that the Court's opinion creates incentives to avoid the knowledge that should trigger corrective action. Id. at 299, 300-301 (Stevens, J., dissenting). According to some commentators, the liability standard in *Gebser* may encourage the see-no-evil/hear-no-evil attitudes already in place in many education districts. "When ignorance is bliss, and a defense to legal judgments, why should schools establish effective complaint strategies?" Rhode, Sex in Schools, supra, at 297.

To some, this double standard for educational and employment settings seems perverse. "Students often have fewer options for avoiding an abusive situation than an adult employee, their capacities for resistance are less developed, and their values are more open to influence. Schools are powerful socializing institutions and their failure to address harassment perpetuates the attitudes that perpetuate problems." Id. See also Heather D. Redmond, Davis v. Monroe County Board of Education: Scant Protection for the Student Body, 18 Law & Ineq. 393 (2000).

Harassment by peers adds another layer of problems:

> Sexual harassment in coeducational schools occurs in many contexts. Often, coeducation stifles participation by girls in class discussion. Subtle oppression by boys, who act obviously bored, sighing, groaning and rolling their eyes, sends a powerful message when a girl contributes in class....
>
> Boys verbally abuse girls in and outside the classroom. In addition to the constant attack on the intellectual and academic abilities of girls, boys degrade girls with language that is pejorative of women....
>
> In addition to purposeful abuse, boys oppress girls by monopolizing physical space.... [T]eachers in England ... found that while boys occupy the total area surrounding schools by playing football, girls observe from benches or wander in the periphery of the "boys' space."...
>
> Seven years later, other teachers expanded upon the previous research using photographs of boys and girls in and around the school building. Their research showed that: (1) girls spend their lunch hour clustered in small groups of two to four in inconspicuous areas; (2) girls walk around paths which hug the buildings while boys walk directly across large, open areas; (3) girls often serve as spectators for boys' activities; (4) boys' activities are faster and more violent than girls' activities, and commonly involve large groups; (5) girls use less space than boys when they play active games; and, finally, (6) boys regularly expand their dominion over certain areas by climbing on each other and on structures such as fences and walls....

Contempt for feminine characteristics among adolescent males causes them to emphasize their masculinity to prove that they are as unlike girls as possible. Boys use girls as their negative reference group.... [T]o survive — that is to escape sexual harassment themselves — boys must demonstrate at least an appreciation for sexually predatory heterosexual behavior.

Laurie LeClair, Note, Sexual Harassment Between Peers Under Title VII and Title IX: Why Girls Just Can't Wait to Be Working Women, 16 Vt. L. Rev. 303, 325-327 (1991).

In a 5-4 vote, the Supreme Court in Davis v. Monroe County Board of Education, 526 U.S. 629 (1999), clarified the standards for schools' liability for peer harassment. There, a female student alleged repeated acts of harassment by one of her male classmates, including verbal and physical assaults such as attempts to touch her genital area. Despite several complaints, the school failed to take adequate remedial action. The majority held that a school district's "deliberate indifference to known acts of harassment" by students could give rise to liability, but only when the district "exercises substantial control over the harasser and the context in which the known harassment occurs" and the conduct is so "severe, pervasive, and objectively offensive that it can be said to deprive the victims of access to the educational opportunities or benefits provided by the school." Id. at 633. In assessing the adequacy of remedial responses, courts should not expect that administrators can entirely "purg[e] their schools of actionable peer harassment" and "should refrain from second-guessing [administrators'] disciplinary decisions." Id. at 648.

Critics of the *Gebser* standard generally found *Davis* problematic on the same grounds, in that it creates an incentive for educators to avoid knowledge that might subject them to legal accountability. Could a plaintiff prove "reckless indifference" if she did not complain about harassment because there was no publicized complaint channel? The problem is compounded by lower court rulings that require notice to be given to a school board member or senior supervisor with authority to ensure Title IX compliance. Joan E. Schaffner, Davis v. Monroe County Board of Education: The Unresolved Questions, 21 Women's Rts. L. Rep., 79, 88-90 (2000). See, e.g., Floyd v. Walters, 171 F.3d 1264 (11th Cir. 1999). Given the reluctance of students to complain to anyone, such requirements are said to create an unrealistic limitation on accountability where other, less senior school personnel had knowledge of a problem and failed to take reasonable remedial action. See American Association of University Women Educational Foundation, Hostile Hallways: Bullying, Teasing, and Sexual Harassment in School 4, 7 (2001) (finding that only seven percent of the 81 percent of students who had been sexually harassed had told a teacher).

On the other hand, argues Deborah L. Brake, the deliberate indifference test may be superior to an alternative, discriminatory intent standard insofar as it focuses on and acknowledges the role schools play in exacerbating the harm that results from sexual harassment instead of engaging in the elusive and difficult search for discriminatory intent. See Brake, School Liability for Peer Sexual Harassment After *Davis*: Shifting from Intent to Causation in Discrimination Law, 12 Hastings Women's L.J. 5 (2001).

Would a preferable approach be for state or federal legislation to hold schools to the same standards applicable to employment cases? Justice Ginsburg proposes such standards in her *Gebser* dissent. In essence, her approach would impose liability on school districts even if they lacked specific knowledge of harassment unless they had an effective policy for reporting and redressing such abuse that the complainant failed to use. 524 U.S. at 304 (Ginsburg, J., dissenting). See Doe v. Covington County School Board, 969 F. Supp. 1264 (M.D. Ala. 1997), aff'd, 233 F.3d 1367 (11th Cir. 2000), cert. denied sub nom. Davis v. DeKalb Sch. Dist., 532 U.S. 1066 (2001) (holding that if school fails to develop and publish an adequate grievance system, school officials cannot avoid liability by claiming lack of notice of harassment).

Another alternative are the standards developed by the U.S. Department of Education's Office for Civil Rights (OCR) prior to the Court's decisions in *Gebser* and *Davis*. See Sexual Harassment Guidance: Harassment of Students by School Employees, Other Students, or Third Parties, 62 Fed. Reg. 12034 (March 13, 1997). Under the original Guidelines, a school could be liable for quid pro quo sexual harassment by an "employee in a position of authority, such as teacher or administrator, whether or not it knew or should have known . . . of the harassment at issue." Id. at 12039. In the case of elementary school students, the Guidelines treated any sexual relationship with an adult school employee as nonconsensual and also created a "strong presumption" that such a relationship with a secondary student is nonconsensual. With respect to postsecondary students, the Guidelines set forth a range of factors to determine whether sexual overtures were welcome, including the nature of the relationship, the degree of an employee's influence over the student, and the student's ability to consent. Id. at 12040. According to the Guidelines, strict liability for employee harassment reflects well-established agency law that makes institutions responsible for abuse of their authority. Id. at 12039. The rationale for that accountability in educational contexts is the same as in other workplace settings: employers should bear the costs of harassment because they are in the best position to prevent it.

The OCR Guidelines also authorized institutional liability for sexual harassment by students that creates a hostile environment under two circumstances: if schools lacked effective harassment policies and procedures or if administrators knew or should have known of the abusive conduct and failed to take "immediate and appropriate corrective action." Id. at 12039-12040. The rationale for a negligence rather than a strict liability standard is that students are not agents of a school and peer harassment is more common and more difficult to prevent in the absence of notice than employees' misconduct. However, unlike the Court's approach in *Davis*, this standard would have required school officials to take reasonable steps to investigate and respond to abusive conduct that is plainly visible, serious, and pervasive.

School officials have generally opposed a strict liability standard on the ground that they have limited control over abusive conduct. While other employers can dismiss workers who persist in harassment, administrators believe that they have fewer options in the face of recalcitrant students or faculty who have their own due process rights. Where facts are contested or ambiguous, officials feel "caught in the middle....We weren't doing the harassing. We're the entity with the deep pockets." Guy W. Horsley, quoted in Robin Wilson, William and Mary Seeks to Shift Liability for Damages to Professor in Federal Sexual Harassment Case, Chronicle of Higher Education, June 9, 1995, at A20.

The OCR Guidelines have been revised to conform to *Gebser* and *Davis*. See Office for Civil Rights, U.S. Dep't of Educ., Revised Sexual Harassment Guidance: Harassment of Students by School Employees, Other Students, or Third Parties, Title IX (2001), available at http://www.ed.gov/offices/OCR/archives/pdf/shguide.pdf.

c. Anti-Harassment Policies and Free Speech

One approach to addressing sexual and racial harassment in educational institutions, especially at the college and university level, has been speech codes that prohibit "verbal conduct" or "expression" that interferes with a student's ability to benefit from the educational environment. Advocates of such regulation respond that in a sexist and racist society, "free speech" is available only to those with the power to exercise it, and that anti-harassment codes are critical to protect the dignity and integrity of individuals who cannot effectively "fight back" with counterspeech. In the university setting, it is argued that official tolerance of racist and sexist speech prevents some students from participating fully in the university community and from developing their psychological and intellectual potential. See, e.g., Mari J. Matsuda, Charles R. Lawrence III, Richard Delgado, & Kimberlé Williams Crenshaw, Words That Wound: Critical Race Theory, Assaultive Speech, and the First Amendment (1993). Some proposals relate specifically to the Internet and e-mail systems. See, e.g., Evelyn Oldenkamp, Pornography, the Internet, and Student-to-Student Sexual Harassment: A Dilemma Resolved with Title VII and Title IX, 4 Duke J. Gender L. & Pol'y 159, 162 (1997) (arguing that openly viewing pornography in computer centers constitutes per se hostile environment sexual harassment that should be covered by university conduct codes); David K. McGraw, Note, Sexual Harassment in Cyberspace: The Problem of Unwelcome E-mail, 21 Rutgers Computer & Tech. L.J. 491 (1995) (proposing regulation analogous to current obscene phone call statutes to protect victims of unwanted, harassing e-mail).

These codes have drawn fierce criticism from free speech advocates, who consider them a form of censorship and urge that the appropriate remedy for hurtful speech is not less, but more, speech. See, e.g., Nadine Strossen, Defending Pornography: Free Speech, Sex, and the Fight for Women's Rights (1995); Nadine Strossen, Regulating Racist Speech on Campus: A Modest Proposal?, 1990 Duke L.J. 484.

The tension between schools' interests in both preventing harassment and protecting expression has provoked increasing disputes, but no Supreme Court decision. Speech codes have not fared well, for the most part, in the lower courts. One decision concerned a Michigan regulation prohibiting "[a]ny behavior, verbal or physical, that stigmatizes or victimizes an individual on the basis of race, ethnicity, religion, sex, sexual orientation, creed, national origin, ancestry, age, marital status, handicap or Vietnam-era veteran status, and that . . . [i]nvolves an express or implied threat to . . . or has the purpose or reasonably foreseeable effect of interfering with an individual's academic efforts, employment, participation in University sponsored extra-curricular activities or personal safety." A psychology graduate student challenged the regulation, claiming that his discussion of "controversial theories positing biologically-based differences between sexes and races might be perceived as 'sexist' and 'racist' by some students" and would thus be "chilled" by the regulation. The regulation was invalidated as impermissibly overbroad and vague. Doe v. University of Michigan, 721 F. Supp. 852 (E.D. Mich. 1989). The Third Circuit Court of Appeals reached a similar result in Saxe v. State College Area School District, 240 F.3d 200 (3d Cir. 2001), with respect to a policy defining harassment as "verbal, written or physical conduct which offends, denigrates or belittles an individual . . . [including] unsolicited derogatory remarks, jokes, demeaning comments or behaviors, slurs, mimicking, name calling, graffiti, innuendo, gestures, physical conduct, stalking, [and]threatening [or] bullying [conduct]." Id. at 202, 203. A University of Wisconsin code prohibiting speech and other expressive conduct that intentionally demeans individuals based on certain protected categories and "create[s] an intimidating, hostile, or demeaning environment for education . . . or other university-authorized activity" was also found unconstitutionally vague and overbroad. See UWM Post, Inc. v. Board of Regents of Univ. of Wisconsin, 774 F. Supp. 1163 (E.D. Wis. 1991).

When these codes have been used against classroom behavior by professors, courts have been similarly protective of First Amendment concerns. For example, one federal trial court held that a university could not impose sanctions for sexually related speech under a policy prohibiting "[u]nwelcome sexual advances, requests for sexual favors and other verbal or physical conduct of a sexual nature." The case involved a university writing professor who was suspended without pay for a period of at least one year and required to complete counseling based on the following conduct.

> Silva made the following statement to his technical writing class,

> > I will put focus in terms of sex, so you can better understand it. Focus is like sex. You seek a target. You zero in on your subject. You move from side to side. You close in on the subject. You bracket the subject and center on it. Focus connects experience and language. You and the subject become one. . . .

> Two days later, during the second technical writing class session at issue, Silva employed the following pedagogical approach:

> > I used Little Egypt's definition of belly dancing to illustrate how a good definition combines a general classification (belly dancing) with concrete specifics in a metaphor (like jello shimmying on a plate) to bring home clearly the meaning to one who wishes to learn this form of ethnic dancing.

> Specifically, Silva stated to his class, "Belly dancing is like jello on a plate with a vibrator under the plate." . . . Silva explains,

> > I used the definition to catch the attention of my class to gain their attention when they did not comprehend the explanation. . . .

> Little Egypt's definition of belly dancing is classic in its use of concrete differentia and simple metaphor, i.e., the trembling jello equates to the essential movements necessary to the dance. It is unlike the dance but also its very essence....
>
> The intellectual task was to increase the student's understanding of definition and apply it in her own attempts to define concepts in her technical report, using the simple example as a model....

Silva v. University of New Hampshire, 888 F. Supp. 293, 299 (D.N.H. 1994). Do these statements violate the policy? If so, are they protected by the First Amendment?

Eight formal complaints were submitted to the university, including the following:

> I find Don Silva's constant referrals to sex offensive. He has yet to hold a class in which he did not make a sexually suggestive, or bluntly sexual statement. . . . I am not a prude, but this is not an appropriate way for a writing teacher to communicate with his students. I have three daughters. I would not want this man teaching them.
>
> I felt that [Professor Silva's comments] were disgusting & unnecessary — he assumed all kids present had experience with vibrators, which I find personally insulting, and I felt that the young women, right out of High School, were being seriously degraded.

Professor Silva responded:

> The comparison was on an intellectual plane and the purpose was to relate an abstract comment to everyday experiences most students are familiar with. . . . I used the definition [of belly dancing] to catch the attention of my class. . . .

The trial court was persuaded. The judge held that the school's harassment policy as applied to Silva's classroom speech "is not reasonably related to the legitimate pedagogical purpose of providing a congenial academic environment because it employs an impermissibly subjective standard that fails to take into account the nation's interest in academic freedom." Id. at 314.

A similar anti-harassment policy prohibiting verbal, written, or physical conduct that has the "effect of . . . creating an intimidating, hostile, or offensive learning environment" was found impermissibly vague in another case involving a university writing instructor who discussed subjects such as obscenity, cannibalism, and consensual sex with children in a "devil's advocate" style. Cohen v. San Bernardino Valley College, 92 F.3d 968 (9th Cir. 1996), cert. denied, 520 U.S. 1140 (1997). See also Levin v. Harleston, 770 F. Supp. 895 (S.D.N.Y. 1991), aff'd in part and vacated in part, 966 F.2d 85 (2d Cir. 1992) (absent evidence of harm to students in classroom, public university violated free speech rights of a tenured professor, who advanced views outside the classroom about the intellectual inferiority of blacks, by creating alternative "shadow classes" for his courses).

The law developed in the other direction in Canada, where the Supreme Court of Canada upheld a statute penalizing the communication of statements that willfully promote hatred against any identifiable racial, religious, or ethnic group, in the context of a conviction of a high school teacher for instructing his students in various anti-Semitic views, including the view that the Holocaust was a myth. See Regina v. Keegstra, [1990] 3 S.C.R. 697.

How would you deal with complaints against a law professor who gave as a part of a first-year criminal law exam a hypothetical titled "Revenge of the Big Monkey," consisting of a composite of actual cases involving a victim of a sexual assault who had unsuccessfully sought a late-term abortion? The defendant, following the mandates of a religious cult, attacked the woman and killed her fetus, for which she expressed gratitude. A critique and a defense of the way the complaints over this incident were handled are set forth in Harvey A. Silvergate, Teach at Your Own Risk, Nat'l L.J., Dec. 11, 2000, at A19, and David Leebron, Big Question on Columbia Exam, Nat'l L.J., Jan. 15, 2001, at A21.

Should professors be sanctioned for sexually explicit discussion that is unrelated to the subject under consideration? Should they be subject to training workshops, public meetings, open forums, letters, course evaluations, or collective protests?

d. Faculty-Student Relationships

Faculty-student dating has been another subject of campus concern. The limited available data suggest that such relationships are not uncommon. See Kimberly A. Mango, Comment, Students Versus Professors: Combating Sexual Harassment Under Title IX of the Education Amendments of 1972, 23 Conn. L. Rev. 355, 359-360 (1991) (citing survey findings that a quarter of male faculty at one University of California campus had sexual relationships with a student). Only a small minority of colleges and universities have rules banning sexual relationships between teachers and students under their supervision. See Sherry Young, Getting to Yes: The Case Against Banning Consensual Relationships in Higher Education, 4 Am. U. J. Gender & L., 269, 272-273 (1996); Jerome W.D. Stokes & D. Frank Vinik, Consensual Sexual Relations Between Faculty and Students in Higher Education, 96 Ed. Law Rptr. 899 (1995). The conventional assumption is that broad prohibitions are unnecessary, unenforceable, or unduly paternalistic. For example, opponents of categorical rules maintain:

> "Being sexually propositioned . . . is a normal and healthy part of life. (The real psychological and emotional tragedy probably befalls those who are not)." Edward Greer, What's Wrong with Faculty-Student Sex? Response I, 47 J. Legal Educ. 437, 438 (1997).

> "It is hardly self evident that the 'power imbalance' in such [relationships] favors the teacher. . . . If matters turn out badly, his career is finished." Id.

> "The urge to merge is a powerful one. . . ." Dan Sabotnik, What's Wrong with Faculty-Student Sex? Response II, 47 J. Legal Educ. 441, 443 (1997).

> "You can't legislate love." Dan Blatt, quoted in University of Virginia Considers Wide Ban on Intimate Teacher-Student Ties, N.Y. Times, Apr. 14, 1993, at A22.

A prohibition on faculty-student sexual relations "portrays students as timid and in need of protection." "It's like saying I can't make choices about who I want to date." Sara Rimer, Love on Campus: Trying to Set Rules for the Emotions, N.Y. Times Oct. 1, 2003, at A21 (quoting Berkeley student news paper editorial and Berkeley student journalist Virginia Griffey).

"It would take cult-like reprogramming to stop professors and students from dating. 'From everything we know sociologically, anthropologically, and biologically, males tend to be attracted to nubile potential mates, and women tend to be attracted to older men who...are successful and represent symbols of power.'" Tanya Shevitz, Dating Rule Was Defined at Cal, S.F. Chronicle, Dec. 3, 1001, at A 25 (quoting Barry Dan, Professor of Sociology).

Feminist literary critic Jane Gallop argues that women are at a "disadvantage" in a faculty-student relationship, but believes that "denying women the right to consent further infantilizes us." Jane Gallop, Feminism and Harassment Policy, Academe, Sept.-Oct. 1994, at 16, 22. See also Jane Gallop, Feminist Accused of Sexual Harassment 41-43 (1997).

Law professor Sherry Young similarly maintains that

[f]eminists should not be in the business of reducing the range of choice available to women, no matter how much they may question the wisdom of some of the choices that are made....Feminists should not promote an image of women as helpless victims incapable of functioning under conditions of inequality of power....The most pernicious idea to emerge from the debate on consensual relationship policies is the notion that feminists should be in the business of questioning the capacity of women, limiting the choices available to women, or urging institutions to disregard the testimony of women about their lives, their aspirations, and their emotional commitments.

Young, supra, at 298, 302.

Compare Robin West's analysis:

Smart male students view themselves as all sorts of things, including young intellectuals. A good male student will often attach himself to a brilliant professor, and will aspire to *be like* him.... Unlike the male student, [the good female student] is more likely to be attracted to the brilliant professor, and aspire not to be like him, but to give herself *to* him. In her own way the "giving" female student will seek the recognition and praise which all students crave, by offering her sexuality. She may be intellectually gifted and she may perceive herself as such. But to the extent that the female student...tries to define herself as an intellectual, she does so at the cost of internal war. For the definition of "self" as a sexually giving self rather than an academically demanding self is always there, always in competition, always available. For the female student, the intellectual self must fight the giving self, both in external and internal reality. The women who lose this battle have lost far more than the women who lost the A to which they were entitled, and so has the world....

...."Falling-in-love" with high school teachers, college professors, or research assistants really does destroy the productivity, the careers, the earning potential, and eventually the self respect of many gifted women. Smart women drop out of high school, college and graduate school (and pretty women are at the highest risk) to date, marry, to help, and to serve those they perceive as intellectual giants. Eventually they learn boredom, the weariness of inactivity, and the self-contempt of nonproductivity. But in spite of its incredible familiarity, most academic men and many academic women do not see this worth discussing. This ignorance must be ideological. My guess is that we cannot see the harm of these consensual relationships to precisely the degree to which we have adopted the blinders of liberalism. It is a harm caused not by coercive, occasional acts, but by the way we have defined the self that consents to the non-coercive relationship in which we engage. It is a harm that a liberal legal regime which resolutely regards the giving of consent as the infallible proxy of an increase in self-regarded and self-assessed value cannot possibly address.

Robin L. West, The Difference in Women's Hedonic Lives: A Phenomenological Critique of Feminist Legal Theory, 3 Wis. Women's L.J. 81, 109-111 (1987).

Other feminists agree. In part, their concerns are based on students' own accounts of sexual overtures by faculty. In one representative study, almost three-quarters of those who rejected a professor's advances considered them coercive and about half of those who had sexual relationships believed that some degree of coercion was involved. See surveys discussed in Caroline Forell, What's Wrong with Faculty-Student Sex? The Law School Context, 47 J. Legal Educ. 47 (1997). Moreover, "faculty whose self-image and self-interest are at stake may underestimate the pressures that students experience. Regardless of the teacher's own intentions, students may believe that their acceptance or rejection of sexual overtures will have academic consequences. Given the power disparities involved, even relationships that appear consensual at the outset may become less so over time." Rhode, Sex in Schools, supra, at 296.

Some feminists also doubt that power differentials can be offset by students' theoretical remedies for harassment. Except in egregious cases, few students have been willing to file complaints, and few institutions have been willing to impose serious sanctions. Some campus codes lack adequate authorization for such sanctions, and even where the rules are clear, the evidence often is not. Moreover, most campus enforcement structures address only those faculty-student sexual relationships that meet conventional definitions of sexual harassment. Some believe that the harms to both individuals and institutions can be significant even in the absence of an explicit quid pro quo or a pervasive hostile environment. In relationships where the professor has any advisory or supervisory authority over the student, both the fact and the appearance of academic integrity are at risk. Even when the relationship is fully consensual, the potential for unconscious bias in evaluation, recommendations, and mentoring is inescapable. And even if the professor does not in fact offer or deliver special advantages, others may suspect favoritism, and the reputation of both parties to the relationship may be compromised. Neither the student nor others whose opinions matter can trust the objectivity of the professor's assessment. Forell, supra; see also Carol Sanger, Consensual Sex and the Limits of the Law, in Directions in Sexual Harassment Law 86-87 (Catharine A. MacKinnon & Reva B. Siegel eds., 2004); Carol Sanger, The Erotics of Torts, 96 Mich. L. Rev. 1852 (1998) (reviewing Jane Gallop, Feminist Accused of Sexual Harassment, supra).

A growing number of institutions attempt to discourage faculty-student relationships. A few, such as William &, Mary ban all "amorous relations between faculty and undergraduates," or between graduate students and their supervisors. Diana Jean Schemo, William & Mary: Not if She's His Student, N.Y. Times, Dec. 2, 2001, at A34. Other schools counsel against such relationships and place a heavy burden on the faculty member to establish that they were consensual if a student complains. See Young, supra, at 273. Some institutions prohibit faculty-student relationships where the professor has direct academic responsibility for the student. If a relationship arises, the faculty member must make other arrangements for supervision of the student's work. Id. at 273-275; Rimer, supra, at A21. For a case involving the resignation of the dean of the University of California at Berkeley (Boalt Hall) following charges that he made unwelcome sexual advances to an intoxicated student whom he drove home from a party, see Deborah L. Rhode, Professor of Desire, Nat'l L.J., Jan. 27, 2003, at A17.

What is the best approach for dealing with "consensual" relationships between professors and students? Robin West, though she believes these relationships have many bad consequences for women, believes that prohibition is the wrong answer because "it is hard to say whether and when they are harmful." Moreover, she reasons, attempting to do so risks reinforcing repressive conservative agendas and deflects attention from the feminist challenge to consensual sex. Robin West, Unwelcome Sex: Toward a Harm-Based Analysis, in Directions in Sex Harassment Law, supra, at 130, 151. By contrast, Carol Sanger believes that "policies based on fairness differ in kind from those rooted in incapacity," and that academic institutions have legitimate interests in preventing the fact or appearance of bias. Sanger, Consensual Sex, supra, at 87. What would you recommend for your own school?

Putting Theory into Practice

3-9. For each of the following problems, consider (1) whether the conduct constitutes sexual harassment; (2) whether it would be appropriate for a university to attempt to prohibit the conduct through rules and regulations; and (3) if the conduct is undesirable, what types of nonregulatory strategies a university might wisely engage in.

(a) A male college student pursues a female student for a date. He calls her frequently on the phone, and when he sees her on campus, he approaches her and asks her to go out with him. She repeatedly refuses and asks him to leave her alone and stop calling. He persists. He has never touched her.

(b) One fraternity on campus has an annual "red light district" party. All female students who attend are required to dress as prostitutes. At the party, the male students simulate "pick-ups" of the prostitutes. Invariably, some "mock" solicitations develop during that evening into actual seductions. Another fraternity invites a stripper to perform on campus the routine she offers at a local club.

(c) A university professor finds himself attracted to one of his students, whom he feels is also attracted to him. Aware of the problems that can arise with faculty-student dating, he attempts to put his feelings of attraction aside.

After picking up more and more "signals" that the student would welcome some initiative on his part, however, he finally asks her out for coffee one afternoon. This leads to an invitation to attend university events such as lectures and to come as his guest to dinners for visiting professors.

(d) Students post anatomically explicit and derogatory remarks on a male-only computer bulletin board. Other students circulate a poster with a nude caricature of a woman candidate for office of a student organization and send to an e-mail list of 20 friends a parody titled "Top 75 Reasons Why Women [Bitches] Should Not Have Freedom of Speech."

(e) Male students claim that an openly gay male professor has come on to them sexually by leering at them after class and by including favorable references to same-sex relationships in his lectures on ancient Greece. One student claims that the professor brushed his buttocks when leaving class in a crowded corridor.

3-10. Twenty years after graduating from Yale College, journalist Naomi Wolf published a widely circulated article detailing an incident of sexual harassment that she had experienced as a student. A famous English professor allegedly placed a hand on her inner thigh. When Wolf was recently invited to join a Yale development campaign, she asked about the effectiveness of current harassment procedures. When, after repeated requests for information, she received none, she recounted both experiences. Naomi Wolf, The Silent Treatment, http://www.ny-metro.com/nymetro/news/features/n_9932/index.html, March 1, 2004. How would you evaluate her conduct? Would it affect your answer if the faculty member was one of the university's most celebrated professors, and someone long known for making sexual advances to students?

C. DOMESTIC VIOLENCE

1. Domestic Violence: The Problem

State v. Norman
378 S.E.2d 8 (N.C. 1989)

MITCHELL, Justice.

. . . At trial, the State presented the testimony of Deputy Sheriff R.H. Epley of the Rutherford County Sheriff's Department, who was called to the Norman residence on the night of 12 June 1985. Inside the home, Epley found the defendant's husband, John Thomas Norman, lying on a bed in a rear bedroom with his face toward the wall and his back toward the middle of the room. He was dead. . . . A later autopsy revealed three gunshot wounds to the head, two of which caused fatal brain injury. The autopsy also revealed a .12 percent blood alcohol level in the victim's body.

Later that night, the defendant related an account of the events leading to the killing. . . . The defendant told Epley that her husband had been beating her all day and had made her lie down on the floor while he slept on the bed. After her husband fell asleep, the defendant carried her grandchild to the defendant's mother's house. The defendant took a pistol from her mother's purse and walked the short distance back to her home. She pointed the pistol at the back of her sleeping husband's head, but it jammed the first time she tried to shoot him. She fixed the gun and then shot her husband in the back of the head as he lay sleeping. After one shot, she felt her husband's chest and determined that he was still breathing and making sounds. She then shot him twice more in the back of the head. The defendant told Epley that she killed her husband because "she took all she was going to take from him so she shot him."

The defendant presented evidence tending to show a long history of physical and mental abuse by her husband due to his alcoholism. At the time of the killing, the thirty-nine-year-old defendant and her husband had been married almost twenty-five years and had several children. The defendant testified that her husband had started drinking and abusing her about five years after they were married. His physical abuse of her consisted of frequent assaults that included slapping, punching and kicking her, striking her with various objects, and throwing glasses, beer bottles and other objects at her. The defendant described other specific incidents of abuse, such as her husband putting her cigarettes out on her, throwing hot coffee on her, breaking glass against her face and crushing food on her face. Although the defendant did not present evidence of ever having received medical treatment for any physical injuries inflicted by her husband, she displayed several scars about her face which she attributed to her husband's assaults.

The defendant's evidence also tended to show other indignities inflicted upon her by her husband. Her evidence tended to show that her husband did not work and forced her to make money by prostitution, and that he made humor of that fact to family and friends. He would beat her if she resisted going out to prostitute herself or if he was unsatisfied with the amounts of money she made. He routinely called the defendant "dog," "bitch" and "whore," and on a few occasions made her eat pet food out of the pets' bowls and bark like a dog. He often made her sleep on the floor. At times, he deprived her of food and refused to let her get food for the family. During those years of abuse, the defendant's husband threatened numerous times to kill her and to maim her in various ways.

The defendant said her husband's abuse occurred only when he was intoxicated, but that he would not give up drinking. She said she and her husband "got along very well when he was sober," and that he was "a good guy" when he was not drunk. She had accompanied her husband to the local mental health center for sporadic counseling sessions for his problem, but he continued to drink.

In the early morning hours on the day before his death, the defendant's husband, who was intoxicated, went to a rest area off I-85 near Kings Mountain where the defendant was engaging in prostitution and assaulted her. While driving home, he was stopped by a patrolman and jailed on a charge of driving while impaired. After the defendant's mother got him out of jail at the defendant's request later that morning, he resumed his drinking and abuse of the defendant.

The defendant's evidence also tended to show that her husband seemed angrier than ever after he was released from jail and that his abuse of the defendant was more frequent. That evening, sheriff's deputies were called to the Norman residence, and the defendant complained that her husband had been beating her all day and she could not take it anymore. The defendant was advised to file a complaint, but she said she was afraid her husband would kill her if she had him arrested. The deputies told her they needed a warrant before they could arrest her husband, and they left the scene.

The deputies were called back less than an hour later after the defendant had taken a bottle of pills. The defendant's husband cursed her and called her names as she was attended by paramedics, and he told them to let her die. A sheriff's deputy finally chased him back into his house as the defendant was put into an ambulance. The defendant's stomach was pumped at the local hospital, and she was sent home with her mother.

While in the hospital, the defendant was visited by a therapist with whom she discussed filing charges against her husband and having him committed for treatment. Before the therapist left, the defendant agreed to go to the mental health center the next day to discuss those possibilities. The therapist testified at trial that the defendant seemed depressed in the hospital, and that she expressed considerable anger toward her husband. He testified that the defendant threatened a number of times that night to kill her husband and that she said she should kill him "because of the things he had done to her."

The next day, the day she shot her husband, the defendant went to the mental health center to talk about charges and possible commitment, and she confronted her husband with that possibility. She testified that she told her husband later that day: "J.T., straighten up. Quit drinking. I'm going to have you committed to help you." She said her husband then told her he would "see them coming" and would cut her throat before they got to him.

The defendant also went to the social services office that day to seek welfare benefits, but her husband followed her there, interrupted her interview and made her go home with him. He continued his abuse of her, threatening to kill and to maim her, slapping her, kicking her, and throwing objects at her. At one point, he took her cigarette and put it out on her, causing a small burn on her upper torso. He would not let her eat or bring food into the house for their children.

That evening, the defendant and her husband went into their bedroom to lie down, and he called her a "dog" and made her lie on the floor when he lay down on the bed. Their daughter brought in her baby to leave with the defendant, and the defendant's husband agreed to let her baby-sit. After the defendant's husband fell asleep, the baby started crying and the defendant took it to her mother's house so it would not wake up her husband. She returned shortly with the pistol and killed her husband.

The defendant testified at trial that she was too afraid of her husband to press charges against him or to leave him. She said that she had temporarily left their home on several previous occasions, but he had always found her, brought her home and beaten her. Asked why she killed her husband, the defendant replied: "Because I was scared of him and I knowed when he woke up, it was going to be the same thing, and I was scared when he took me to the truck stop that night it was going to be worse then he had ever been. I just couldn't take it no more. There ain't no way, even if it means going to prison. It's better than living in that. That's worse hell than anything."

The defendant and other witnesses testified that for years her husband had frequently threatened to kill her and to maim her. When asked if she believed those threats, the defendant replied: "Yes. I believed him; he would, he would kill me if he got a chance. If he thought he wouldn't a had to went to jail, he would a done it."

[The Norman case is continued on p. 513, below.]

Karla Fischer, Neil Vidmar & René Ellis, *The Culture of Battering and the Role of Mediation in Domestic Violence Cases*
46 SMU L. Rev. 2117 *passim* (1993)

The culture of battering refers to the relationship context of an abusive relationship. The first of the three elements of the culture of battering is the abuse, which includes at least one of the following types: physical, emotional, sexual, familial, and property. Professionals have increasingly recognized non-physical forms of abuse as harmful to domestic violence victims. The second element is the systematic pattern of domination and control that the batterer exerts over his victim. This pattern may be initiated by the batterer's gradual imposition of a series of rules that his victim must follow or be punished for violating. Over time, victims may censor their own behavior in anticipation of yet-unexpressed rules. The abuser's rein on the members of the household is enhanced by the use of emotional abuse and financial and social isolation, all of which help keep the victim in fear of impending abuse. Victims may engage in episodes of rebellion or resistance to the rules, which are nearly always met with more serious violence. Even separating from the abuser, an act of rebellion by itself, does not secure the end of the abuse; rather, it frequently escalates it. The third element, hiding, denying, and minimizing the abuse, refers to typical coping strategies that battered women use to reduce the psychological impact of the abuse. Each of these elements to some degree must be present in order for a culture of battering to be established....

As sociologist Liz Kelly has noted, the prevailing stereotype about domestic violence is that assaults are "physical, frequent, and life threatening." Yet, the reality of battered women's lives does not conform solely to this image. Advocates for battered women have long noted that financial abuse and property abuse are forms of emotional abuse inflicted upon women. Abusers frequently restrict women's access to money and destroy their personal property in an effort to gain control over them or keep them in a state of fear. Emotional and sexual abuse may be even more common. Forms of emotional abuse include acts that do not constitute overt threats of injury or violence, such as constant humiliation, insults, degradation, and ridicule. Of course, explicit threats to harm or kill, including those attached to vivid descriptions of the method the abuser would use to carry it out, also have emotional consequences. The abuser may extend threats of harm to the victim's extended family or her children....

Battered women have frequently reported that abusers are extremely controlling of the everyday activities of the family. This domination can be all encompassing: as one of the batterers from Angela Browne's study was fond of stating, "[y]ou're going to dance to my music . . . be the kind of wife I want you to be." Charlotte Fedders' account of the escalating rules imposed by her husband over the course of their seventeen year, extremely violent marriage is particularly illuminating about the range of control that abusers can exert. Her husband insisted that no one (including guests and their toddler children) wear shoes in the house, that the furniture be in the same indentations in the carpet, that the vacuum marks in the carpet be parallel, and that any sand spilled from the children's sandbox during their play be removed from the surrounding grass. Charlotte was not allowed to write checks from their joint checking account. Any real or perceived infraction of these rules could result in her husband beating her, or at the very least, the expression of his irritation that was frequently a harbinger to a beating.

Typically, battered women talk to the men about the abuse, partly as an attempt to concretize the rules that are connected to the absence of abuse. In turn, many abusers promise to stop the abuse. One abuser in Browne's study formalized such discussions into a written document, where he set forth a list of conditions that his victim was to agree to in exchange for cessation of his violence. These conditions were: (1) the children were to keep their rooms clean without being told; (2) the children could not argue with each other; (3) he was to have absolute freedom to come and go as he wished, and could have a girlfriend if he wanted one; (4) she would perform oral sex on him anytime he requested; and (5) she would have anal sex with him. He enforced this document shortly after she "agreed" to it and continued to sexually assault her until his death. This abuser simply made explicit the rules in the relationship and made it obvious that abuse was the punishment for violating the rules.

In many abusive relationships, however, the rules do not need to be verbally expressed to create a family atmosphere controlled by the batterer. Charlotte Fedders' story is a prototype of a battered woman who becomes very good at reading nonverbal messages from her abuser. She writes of how she restricted the play of her four young boys in order to avoid her husband's increasingly subtle signs of displeasure:

> Eventually . . . we just stopped using the living room and the family room because little things out of place would make him angry. . . . If [the boys'] rooms were a mess, he'd complain to me, so I was reluctant to let them play there. So they pretty much played in the basement. . . . I'd let them play only in the backyard, not the front, because John was so proud and particular about it. He wanted it perfectly green, and orderly. . . . He didn't like my putting a swing set up for the kids in the backyard, so it had to go all the way in the back, where no one would see it.

[Charlotte Fedders & Laura Eliott, Shattered Dreams 140-141 (1987).]

As time goes on in a battering relationship, as in the Fedders' case, specific rules and their attached consequences give way to a general climate of increasingly subtle control, where the batterer needs to do less and less to structure his family's behavior. Caught up in the day to day fight for survival, the victims may not even be aware of this censorship process. . . .

What fuels this self censorship process is the responsibility the victim feels, both as a woman socialized into believing that making relationships work is her job, and the responsibility added by the abuser, who blames her for the "failure" of the relationship, as evidenced by the occurrence of abuse. Women are taught in our society to care for others, to make decisions around what is best for other people, even if it denigrates their own needs. Batterers reinforce this societal message by consistently blaming women for everything that goes awry in their lives. The end result is manifested in frantic attempts by the woman to be the perfect wife, mother, and homemaker....

The pattern of rule-making and rule-enforcing, nested within the control and domination exerted by the batterer over his family, is frequently interspersed with episodes of rebellion by the victims.... These resistance incidents are not initiated with ignorance on the part of victims, and they are very much aware that any type of challenge to the batterer is likely to result in further, perhaps escalating, violence....

...Fischer specifically asked the battered women in her study who had obtained court protective orders about the methods they had employed in attempting to stop the violence. Of the thirty-one strategies described, the women in her sample had tried an average of thirteen different strategies, including talking to the abuser about the abuse, consulting family and friends, calling the police, leaving him, and seeking counseling or legal advice. Fischer concluded that the number and variety of strategies tried suggests that battered women continue over time to increase their helpseeking rather than to decrease it and become passive....

Our argument that abuse occurs within a relationship context of control and domination is an explicit rejection of the popular belief that abuse is simply a logical extension of a heated argument or disagreement....

Battered women's narratives of the context of abuse suggests quite the opposite of conflict. Women are typically beaten in a variety of situations that could hardly be classified as conflict: while sleeping, while using the toilet, and while in another room that the batterer suddenly entered to begin his beating. The usual scenario women describe is that at one moment all is calm and in the next, there is a major, seemingly untriggered explosion:

> I remember walking in, got undressed, and put my robe on, and I was going to get a glass of milk. At one moment we were laying together and kissing and everything seemed fine. And, it was like a second later, he was saying that I stayed out too late, and asked who was there and stuff, and then just ... everything blew up. I know he threw me off the bed. And he told me he was going to beat me to death. And, then he said, "I'm going to set the trailer on fire with you and your daughter in it." And then he goes, "well, first, bitch, you are going to get me a glass of ice water."

In addition to the information about context, batterers' behavior during abusive incidents does not support an image that these men are out of control with anger. Women have reported deliberate, calculating behavior, ranging from searching for and destroying a treasured object of hers to striking her in areas of her body that do not show bruises (e.g. her scalp) or in areas where she would be embarrassed to show others her bruises.

Anger and conflict may be frequently confused with violence because both can be a proxy for abuse. The abuser may in fact be angry when he beats his victim or a conflict over what she has served for dinner may have developed before the incident of violence. But this simple coexistence in time does not mean that the anger or conflict has caused the violence. Lurking underneath the surface anger or conflict is the batterer's need to express his power over his victim. Even if the anger is controlled and all sources of conflict are removed from the relationship, violence still occurs. After all, batterers are usually involved in other social relationships, at work or elsewhere, where they become angry or have conflicts with others that they do not abuse. Their ability to cope with anger in some situations but not at home suggests that conflict and anger are not at the root of domestic violence. Perhaps the best evidence, however, that abuse is not about anger or conflict is that violence continues to occur, frequently escalating, after women leave their abusers.

Martha R. Mahoney, Legal Images of Battered Women: Redefining the Issue of Separation
90 Mich. L. Rev. 1, 2-3, 5-7 (1991)

The courtroom is the theater in which the dramas of battered women have been brought to public attention. Trials like that of Francine Hughes, whose story became the book and movie The Burning Bed, create a cultural and legal spotlight that has in some ways benefited women by increasing public knowledge of the existence of domestic violence. However, the press has emphasized sensational cases that have a high level of terrorism against women and a grotesque quality of abuse. These cases come to define a cultural image of domestic violence, and the women in these cases define an image of battered women.

These images disguise the commonality of violence against women. Up to one half of all American women — and approximately two thirds of women who are separated or divorced — report having experienced physical assault in their relationships. However, litigation and judicial decisionmaking in cases of severe violence reflect implicit or explicit assumptions that domestic violence is rare or exceptional.... [The fiction that such violence is exceptional] limits the help we may seek when we encounter trouble, the charges we are willing to file, our votes as jurors when charges have been filed by or against others, and our consciousness of the meaning of the struggles and dangers of our own experience....

The question "why didn't she leave?" shapes both social and legal inquiry on battering; much of the legal reliance on academic expertise on battered women has developed in order to address this question. At the moment of separation or attempted separation — for many women, the first encounter with the authority of law — the batterer's quest for control often becomes most acutely violent and potentially lethal. Ironically, although the proliferation of shelters and the elaboration of statutory structures facilitating the grant of protective orders vividly demonstrate both socially and legally the dangers attendant on separation, a woman's "failure" to permanently separate from a violent relationship is still widely held to be mysterious and in need of explanation, an indicator of her pathology rather than her batterer's. We have had neither cultural names nor legal doctrines specifically tailored to the particular assault on a woman's body and volition that seeks to block her from leaving, retaliate for her departure, or forcibly end the separation. I propose that we name this attack "separation assault."

Separation assault is the common though invisible thread that unites the equal protection suits on enforcement of temporary restraining orders, the cases with dead women that appear in many doctrinal categories, and the cases with dead men—the self-defense cases. As with other assaults on women that were not cognizable until the feminist movement named and explained them, separation assault must be identified before women can recognize our own experience and before we can develop legal rules to deal with this particular sort of violence. Naming one particular aspect of the violence then illuminates the rest: for example, the very concept of "acquaintance rape" moves consciousness away from the stereotype of rape (assault by a stranger) and toward a focus on the woman's volition (violation of her will, "consent"). Similarly, by emphasizing the urgent control moves that seek to prevent the woman from ending the relationship, the concept of separation assault raises questions that inevitably focus additional attention on the ongoing struggle for power and control in the relationship. . . .

Notes

1. Defining Domestic Violence. The language used to describe physical and verbal attacks against intimate partners continues to evolve. Battered women's advocates initially introduced the term "domestic violence" to replace more colloquial terms such as "wife beating." More recently, the terms "intimate violence" or "intimate partner violence" serve to encompass the abuse of elders, children, and siblings. Mahoney's proposed term "separation assault" highlights the heightened danger the victims of intimate violence face when they attempt to leave the relationship.

Descriptions of the essential nature of intimate partner violence have also evolved. Domestic violence workers introduced the word "battering" to replace "beating." However, the popular meaning of "battering" is physical abuse, and many researchers now argue that the quest for control, and not physical violence per se, best captures an abusive relationship. "Battering" can be a problematic term to the extent that it invites focus on broken bones rather than the sometimes subtle forms of abuse that violence workers document, such as threats, isolation, and control over necessities. These incidents may not appear in studies of physical violence or in reported cases. Evan Stark, Re-Presenting Woman Battering: From Battered Woman Syndrome to Coercive Control, 58 Alb. L. Rev. 973, 983 (1995); Deborah Tuerkeimer,

Recognizing and Remedying the Harm of Battering: A Call To Criminalize Domestic Violence, 94 J. Crim. L. & Criminology 959 (2004). Do Fischer, Vidmar, and Ellis distinguish the relationships they consider pathological from ordinary conflict in intimate relationships?

2. Incidence of Domestic Violence. Determining the frequency and severity of intimate violence is difficult both because varying criteria are used to define it and because such abuse is underreported. One of the most comprehensive studies is the National Violence Against Women Survey (NVAWS), conducted by the Center for Policy Research and co-sponsored by the National Institute of Justice and the Centers for Disease Control and Prevention. The survey consisted of telephone interviews with a nationally representative sample of 8,000 U.S. men and 8,000 U.S. women; the participants were asked about their experiences as victims of various kinds of violence, including intimate partner violence. Patricia Tjaden & Nancy Thoennes, Full Report of the Prevalence, Incidence, and Consequences of Violence Against Women, Findings from the National Violence Against Women Survey (NCJ 183781), Nov. 2000, available at http://www.ncjrs.org; see also Patricia Tjaden & Nancy Thoennes, Extent, Nature, and Consequences of Intimate Partner Violence, Findings from the National Violence Against Women Survey (NCJ 181867), July 2000. The July 2000 report analyzing survey results concluded:

> Intimate partner violence is pervasive in U.S. society. Nearly 25 percent of surveyed women and 7.6 percent of surveyed men said they were raped and/or physically assaulted by a current or former spouse, cohabiting partner, or date at some time in their lifetime; 1.5 percent of surveyed women and 0.9 percent of surveyed men said they were raped and/or physically assaulted by a partner in the previous 12 months. According to these estimates, approximately 1.5 million women and 834,732 men are raped and/or physically assaulted by an intimate partner annually in the United States. Because many victims are victimized more than once, the number of intimate partner victimizations exceeds the number of intimate partner victims annually. Thus, approximately 4.8 million intimate partner rapes and physical assaults are perpetrated against U.S. women annually, and approximately 2.9 million intimate partner physical assaults are committed against U.S. men annually.

Id. at iii. Only about a quarter of physical assaults by intimates are reported; a majority of survivors believe that the "police would not or could not do anything for them." Id.

Researchers have come to no consensus about whether women or men are more likely to be victimized by domestic violence. The NVAWS concluded that women are significantly more likely to be the victim of intimate violence than men. This conclusion is consistent with the finding of the Bureau of Justice Statistics' National Crime Victimization Survey (NCVS) that intimate violence is primarily a crime against women. See Callie Marie Rennison & Sarah Welchans, Bureau of Justice Statistics, Special Report: Intimate Partner Violence (NCJ 178247), May 2000, at 1, available at http://www.ojp.usdoj.gov/bjs/pub/pdf/ipv.pdf (in 1998, females were the victims in 72 percent of intimate murders and the victims in about 85 percent of the non-lethal intimate violence).

Other research suggests that women are at least as physically aggressive as men, but less likely to inflict serious injury. See Martin Fiebert, References Examining Assaults by Women on their Spouses or Male Partners: An Annotated Bibliography (2001), available at http://www.menweb.org/ fiebert.htm (reviewing over 100 national and international studies). The NVAWS report found that 39 percent of female intimate violence victims, compared with 24.8 percent of male intimate violence victims, reported being injured during their most recent physical assault. Tjaden & Thoennes, Full Report, supra, at iv; see also Tjaden & Thoennes, Extent, Nature, and Consequences, supra, at iv (finding that women experience more chronic and more injurious physical assaults at the hands of intimate partners than do men). But see Daniel G. Saunders, Are Physical Assaults by Wives and Girlfriends a Major Social Problem?: A Review of the Literature, 8 Violence Against Women 1424, 1439 (2002) (criticizing Fiebert's study).

It would appear that men are less likely to report intimate abuse. See Fiebert, supra. For an overview of barriers that men encounter in reporting abuse and in seeking social services, see Alexander Deushelt, Recognizing Domestic Violence Directed Towards Men: Overcoming Societal Perceptions, Conducting Accurate Studies, and Enacting Responsible Legislation, 12 Kan. J.L. & Pub. Pol'y 249 (2003).

The NCVS reports a 21 percent decrease in violence against women by intimate partners during the late 1990s. The most common explanations for the decline are: (1) the increased provision of legal services for victims of intimate partner abuse, (2) improvements in women's economic status, and (3) demographic trends, most notably the aging of the population. Amy Farmer & Jill Tiefenthaler, Explaining the Recent Decline in Domestic Violence, 21 Contemp. Econ. Pol'y 158 (April 2003). Between the late 1970s and late 1990s, the number of men killed by intimate partners declined by two-thirds; the number of women killed declined only slightly. Researchers attribute the decline in male deaths to the fact that domestic violence programs enable many women to leave relationships before they feel that they need to use deadly force in self-protection. Laura Dugan, Explaining the Decline in Intimate Partner Homicide: The Effects of Changing Domesticity, Women's Status, and Domestic Violence Resources, 3 Homicide Stud. 187 (1999).

Almost five percent of surveyed women and 0.6 percent of surveyed men reported being stalked by a current or former spouse, cohabiting partner, or date during their lifetime, and 0.5 percent of surveyed women and 0.2 percent of surveyed men reported having been stalked within the past 12 months. Tjaden & Thoennes, Extent, Nature, and Consequences, supra, at iii. If these numbers are representative, 503,485 women and 185,496 men are stalked by an intimate partner annually in the United States. Id.

3. Characteristics of Domestic Violence. Early empirical studies identified a connection between domestic violence and traditionally patriarchal heterosexual families. Murray A. Straus et al., Behind Closed Doors: Violence in the American Family 194 (1980). Some evidence also suggests that family violence rates are highest in states where women have the lowest economic and educational status. See Kersti A. Yllo & Murray A. Straus, Patriarchy and Violence Against Wives: The Impact of Structural and Normative Factors, in Physical Violence in American Families: Risk Factors and Adaptations to Violence in 8,145 Families 383, 397 (Murray A. Straus & Richard Gelles eds., 1990).

In an effort to include same-sex and opposite-sex intimate partner violence in the same analysis, some theorists have backed away from the "patriarchal" model of domestic violence and adopted a "nongendered" model that stresses psychological rather than sociological explanations. See Ryiah Lilith, Reconsidering the Abuse That Dare Not Speak Its Name: A Criticism of Recent Legal Scholarship Regarding Same-Gender Domestic Violence, 7 Mich. J. Gender & L. 181, 189 (2001).

As Mahoney's excerpt above suggests, women are most likely to be injured in an intimate relationship in the course of trying to end it. The NVAWS report found that married women who lived apart from their husbands were nearly four times more likely to report that their husbands had raped, physically assaulted, and/or stalked them than women who lived with their husbands (20 percent and 5.4 percent, respectively). Tjaden & Thoennes, Extent, Nature, and Consequences, supra, at 37. Another study found that up to three-fourths of reported domestic assaults occur after the victim has left the batterer.

Since domestic violence characteristically takes place in the home, children in the family are also affected. Several million children witness violence each year and often suffer "internalizing" effects such as depression, anxiety, and withdrawal, as well as "externalizing" effects such as aggression, "acting out" behaviors, and delinquency. See Stephen Doyne et al., Custody Disputes Involving Domestic Violence: Making Children's Needs a Priority, 50 Juv. & Fam. Ct. J. 1 (Spring 1999); Amy B. Levin, Comment, Child Witnesses of Domestic Violence: How Should Judges Apply the Best Interests of the Child Standard in Custody and Visitation Cases Involving Domestic Violence?, 47 UCLA L. Rev. 813, 833 (2000). Children of battered women also run the risk of being abused themselves. Developments in the Law—Legal Responses to Domestic Violence, 106 Harv. L. Rev. 1597, 1608-1609 (1993) (reporting that children who witness domestic violence are abused at a rate 15 times higher than the national average).

4. Domestic Violence in Population Subgroups. The NVAWS survey found that 37.5 percent of American Indian and Alaska Native women are victims of rape, physical assault, or stalking in their lifetimes by an intimate partner, as compared to 29.1 percent of African-American women, 24.8 percent of white women, and 15 percent of Asian/Pacific Islander women. See Tjaden & Thoennes, Full Report, supra, at 26. African-American women are about three times as likely as white women to be murdered by a spouse or ex-spouse, and twice as likely to be murdered by a boyfriend. See Bureau of Justice Statistics, Homicide Trends in the U.S., available at http://www.ojp.usdoj.gov/bjs/homicide/tables/intgreltab.htm (citing statistics from the FBI, Supplementary Homicide Reports, 1976-2002). Probably as a result of negative perceptions or experiences involving law enforcement and social service agencies, African-American women are also more reluctant to report violence to these institutions than are white woman. See Robert Hampton et al., 9 Violence Against Women 533, 534 (2003); Zanita E. Fenton, Silence Compounded—The Conjunction of Race and Gender Violence, 11 Am. U. J. Gender Soc. Pol'y & L. 271 (2003).

Studies that have investigated the incidence of domestic violence across class consistently find a link between poverty and abuse. Angelo M. Moe & Mytal Bell, Abject Economics: The Effects of Battering and Violence on Women's Work and Employability, 10 Violence Against Women 29, 35-36 (2004) (citing surveys such as those finding that between one- and two-thirds of women on welfare experience violence). Poor women are particularly vulnerable to abuse because their lack of financial resources and employment skills traps them in violent relationships. See Shelby A.D. Moore, Understanding the Connection Between Domestic Violence, Crime, and Poverty: How Welfare Reform May Keep Battered Women From Leaving Abusive Relationships, 12 Tex. J. Women & L. 451, 475-476 (2003). By the same token, as discussion in on pp. 499-501 below indicates, violence impairs individuals' ability to find and retain work, which perpetuates economic dependence. Id.; Moe & Bell, supra, at 35. Some research indicates that when the violence rates are controlled for class-related variables, such as family income and occupation, the incidence of abuse is lower for African Americans than whites, and equivalent for Hispanics. See Noel A. Caznave & Murray A. Straus, Race, Class, Network Embeddedness, and Family Violence: A Search for Potent Support Systems, in Physical Violence, supra, at 336; Murray A. Straus & Christine Smith, Violence in Hispanic Families in the United States: Incidence Rates and Structural Interpretations, in Physical Violence, supra, at 341, 364.

Research on lesbian and gay domestic violence has been limited and conflicting. Compare Office of Justice Programs, U.S. Dep't of Justice, Full Report of the Prevalence, Incidence, and Consequences of Violence Against Women (NCJ-18781) (2000) (finding a higher incidence of violence among lesbian couples than gay couples or heterosexual couples); Nancy J. Knauer, Same-Sex Domestic Violence: Claiming a Domestic Sphere While Risking Negative Stereotypes, 8 Temp. Pol. & Civ. Rts. L. Rev. 325, 330 (1999) (same-sex intimate partner violence occurs at about the same rate as cross-sex intimate partner violence); Lilith, supra, at 188-189 (evidence of same-sex abuse is exaggerated). Some survey data indicates that the incidence of domestic violence among lesbians is lower than the incidence among heterosexual women and gay men. The NVAWS study, for example, found that among same-sex cohabiting couples (who were not asked their sexual orientation), women were nearly three times more likely to report being victimized by a male partner than by a female partner (30.4 percent versus 11.4 percent). Tjaden & Thoennes, Extent, Nature, and Consequences, supra, at 30. Women who were cohabiting with men were nearly twice as likely to report victimization as were women cohabiting with women. (20.3 percent versus 11.4 percent). Same-sex cohabiting men were nearly twice as likely to report being victimized by their male partners as were opposite-sex cohabiting men by their female partners (15.4 percent and 7.7 percent). Id. at 31. The authors of the NVAWS report conclude that intimate partner violence is perpetrated primarily by men, whether against male or female partners. Id.

What might account for these different findings? What are the implications for public policy?

5. Barriers Unique to Battered Immigrant Women. The government keeps no national data on the incidence of domestic violence among immigrants to the United States, although information available from organizations working with battered immigrants reflects a serious problem. See Felicia E. Franco, Unconditional Safety for Conditional Immigrant Women, 11 Berkeley Women's L.J. 99, 102 (1996); Maurice Goldman, The Violence Against Women Act: Meeting Its Goal in Protecting Battered Immigrant Women?, 37 Fam. & Conciliation Cts. Rev. 375, 377 n.14 (1999) (reporting that, according to one survey conducted by a Washington, D.C., organization that assists battered immigrants, 77 percent of Latina immigrants reported being subject to abuse).

Lack of language ability, cultural differences, unfamiliarity with the U.S. legal system and local social services, and economic dependence on the abuser are all factors that may combine to trap battered immigrant women in violent relationships. See Linda Kelly, Stories from the Front: Seeking Refuge for Battered Immigrants in the Violence Against Women Act, 92 Nw. U. L. Rev. 665 (1998). These women also face a maze of complex legal problems arising from their immigration status; their ability to seek protection against intimate violence is often compromised by the possibility of deportation and spousal threats to block efforts at naturalization. See Tien-li Loke, Note, Trapped in Domestic Violence: The Impact of United States Immigration Laws on Battered Immigrant Women, 6 B.U. Pub. Int. L.J. 589 (1997). To address this issue, the 1994 Violence Against Women Act included provisions explicitly designed to enable a battered wife to seek permanent resident status without requiring her husband to petition on her behalf. To attain this status, the woman must establish by credible evidence that she entered into a good faith marriage, that she has good moral character, that she or her children have experienced battery or cruelty from the abusive spouse, and that the husband is a legal permanent resident or citizen with whom she lived in the United States. For many battered women, these requirements proved impossible to meet in practice due to a lack of evidence, knowledge, and legal assistance, as well as language barriers. So too, the moral character requirement often excluded those who had been arrested for domestic violence offenses committed in self-defense or whose husbands had filed custody claims alleging maternal deficiencies. Deanna Kwong, Removing Barriers for Battered Immigrant Women: A Comparison of Immigrant Protections Under VAWA I & II, 17 Berkeley Women's L.J. 137 (2002); Hannah R. Shapiro, Battered Immigrant Women Caught in the Intersection of U.S. Criminal and Immigration Laws: Consequences and Remedies, 16 Temp. Int'l & Comp. L.J. 27 (2002); Sarah M. Wood, VAWA's Unfinished Business: The Immigrant Women Who Fall Through the Cracks, 11 Duke J. Gender L. & Pol'y 141 (2004).

A reauthorization of VAWA, including the Battered Immigrant Women Protection Act of 2000 (BIWPA), attempted to remedy some of the problems with VAWA in its original form. The new legislation removed restrictive evidentiary requirements for VAWA petitions, broadened the categories of who could be eligible for VAWA protection, increased access to basic services and legal representation, and gave the government authority to find good moral character despite charges related to abuse. VAWA II also enabled battered women to apply for a U visa if a qualifying legal official certifies their cooperation in prosecutions of batterers. To qualify for a U visa, an applicant must obtain a certification from a qualifying official, such as a police officer, prosecutor or judge, that the immigrant victim, "has been helpful, is being helpful, or is likely to be helpful" in the investigation of certain criminal activity set forth in the statute. 8 U.S.C. §1101(a)(15)(U) (2000). Further VAWA modifications in 2005 stop the deportation of immigrant victims of domestic violence, sexual assault, or trafficking, allows the children and other designated family members of U visa recipients to stay with the victims, strengthens VAWA confidentiality enforcement, guarantees access to legal services for immigrant victims, and authorizes employment of certain abused immigrant spouses, among other things. See Pub. L. No 109-162 (Jan. 5, 2006) (explored further at pp. 534-535, infra). For further detail about the 2005 legislation, see www.vawa2005.org.

2. Legal Responses to Domestic Violence

≣ *William Blackstone, 1 Commentaries on the
Laws of England*
*432-433

The husband ..., by the old law, might give his wife moderate correction. For, as he is to answer for her misbehaviour, the law thought it reasonable to intrust him with this power of restraining her, by domestic chastisement, in the same moderation that a man is allowed to correct his apprentices or children; for whom the master or parent is also liable in some cases to answer. But this power of correction was confined within reasonable bounds, and the husband was prohibited from using any violence to his wife.... The civil law gave the husband the same, or a larger, authority over his wife.... But with us, in the politer reign of Charles the Second, this power of correction began to be doubted; and a wife may now have security of the peace against her husband; or, in return, a husband against his wife. Yet the lower rank of people, who were always fond of the old common law, still claim and exert their ancient privilege; and the courts of law will still permit a husband to restrain a wife of her liberty, in case of any gross misbehaviour.

≣ *State v. Rhodes*
61 N.C. 453 (1868)

The defendant was indicted for an assault and battery upon his 'wife, Elizabeth Rhodes. Upon the evidence submitted to them the jury returned the following special verdict:

"We find that the defendant struck Elizabeth Rhodes, his wife, three licks, with a switch about the size of one of his fingers (but not as large as a man's thumb), without any provocation except some words uttered by her and not recollected by the witness."

His Honor was of opinion that the defendant had a right to whip his wife with a switch no larger than his thumb, and that upon the facts found in the special verdict he was not guilty in law. Judgment in favor of the defendant was accordingly entered and the State appealed.

READE, J. The violence complained of would without question have constituted a battery if the subject of it had not been the defendant's wife. The question is how far that fact affects the case.

The courts have been loath to take cognizance of trivial complaints arising out of the domestic relations — such as master and apprentice, teacher and pupil, parent and child, husband and wife. Not because those relations are not subject to the law, but because the evil of publicity would be greater than the evil involved in the trifles complained of; and because they ought to be left to family government. . . .

In this case no provocation worth the name was proved. The fact found was that it was "without any provocation except some words which were not recollected by the witness." The words must have been of the slightest import to have made no impression on the memory. We must therefore consider the violence as unprovoked. The question is therefore plainly presented, whether the court will allow a conviction of the husband for moderate correction of the wife without provocation. . . .

We have sought the aid of the experience and wisdom of other times and of other countries.

Blackstone says "that the husband, by the old law, might give the wife moderate correction, for as he was to answer for her misbehavior, he ought to have the power to control her; but that in the polite reign of Charles the Second, this power of correction began to be doubted." 1 Black., 444. Wharton says, that by the ancient common law the husband possessed the power to chastise his wife; but that the tendency of criminal courts in the present day is to regard the marital relation as no defense to a battery. . . . Chancellor Walworth says of such correction, that it is not authorized by the law of any civilized country; not indeed meaning that England is not civilized, but referring to the anomalous relics of barbarism which cleave to her jurisprudence. . . . The old law of moderate correction has been questioned even in England, and has been repudiated in Ireland and Scotland. The old rule is approved in Mississippi, but it has met with but little favor elsewhere in the United States. . . . In looking into the discussions of the other States we find but little uniformity.

From what has been said it will be seen how much the subject is at sea. And, probably, it will ever be so: for it will always be influenced by the habits, manners and condition of every community. Yet it is necessary that we should lay down something as precise and practical as the nature of the subject will admit of, for the guidance of our courts.

Our conclusion is that family government is recognized by law as being as complete in itself as the State government is in itself, and yet subordinate to it; and that we will not interfere with or attempt to control it, in favor of either husband or wife, unless in cases where permanent or malicious injury is inflicted or threatened, or the condition of the party is intolerable. For, however great are the evils of ill temper, quarrels, and even personal conflicts inflicting only temporary pain, they are not comparable with the evils which would result from raising the curtain, and exposing to public curiosity and criticism, the nursery and the bed chamber. Every household has and must have, a government of its own, modeled to suit the temper, disposition and condition of its inmates. Mere ebullitions of passion, impulsive violence, and temporary pain, affection will soon forget and forgive, and each member will find excuse for the other in his own frailties. But when trifles are taken hold of by the public, and the parties are exposed and disgraced, and each endeavors to justify himself or herself by criminating the other, that which ought to be forgotten in a day, will be remembered for life.

It is urged in this case that as there was no provocation the violence was of course excessive and malicious; that everyone in whatever relation of life should be able to purchase immunity from pain, by obedience to authority and faithfulness in duty. And it is insisted that in S. v. Pendergrass, 2 D. & B., 365, which was the case of schoolmistress whipping a child, that doctrine is laid down. It is true that it is there said, that the master may be punishable even when he does not transcend the powers granted; i.e., when he does not inflict permanent injury, if he grossly abuse his powers, and use them as a cover for his malice. But observe, the language is, if he grossly abuse his powers. So that every one would say at once, there was no cause for it, and it was purely malicious and cruel. If this be not the rule then every violence which would amount to an assault upon a stranger, would have to be investigated to see whether there was any provocation. And that would contravene what we have said, that we will punish no case of trifling importance. If in every such case we are to hunt for the provocation, how will the proof be supplied? Take the case before us. The witness said there was no provocation except some slight words. But then who can tell what significance the trifling words may have had to the husband? Who can tell what had happened an hour before, and every hour for a week? To him they may have been sharper than a sword. And so in every case, it might be impossible for the court to appreciate what might be offered as an excuse, or no excuse might appear at all, when a complete justification exists. Or, suppose the provocation could in every case be known, and the court should undertake to weigh the provocation in every trifling family broil, what would be the standard? Suppose a case coming up to us from a hovel, where neither delicacy of sentiment nor refinement of manners is appreciated or known. The parties themselves would be amazed, if they were to be held responsible for rudeness or trifling violence. What do they care for insults and indignities? In such cases what end would be gained by investigation or punishment? Take a case from the middle class, where modesty and purity have their abode, but nevertheless have not immunity from the frailties of nature, and are sometimes moved by the mysteries of passion. What could be more harassing to them, or injurious to society, than to draw a crowd around their seclusion? Or take a case from the higher ranks, where education and culture have so refined nature, that a look cuts like a knife, and a word strikes like a hammer; where the most delicate attention gives pleasure, and the slightest neglect pain; where an indignity is disgrace and exposure is ruin. Bring all these cases into court side by side, with the same offense charged and the same proof made; and what conceivable charge of the court to the jury would be alike appropriate to all the cases, except that they all have domestic government, which they have formed for themselves, suited to their own peculiar conditions, and that those governments are supreme, and from them there is no appeal except in cases of great importance requiring the strong arm of the law, and that to those governments they must submit themselves.

It will be observed that the ground upon which we have put this decision is not that the husband has the right to whip his wife much or little; but that we will not interfere with family government in trifling cases. We will no more interfere where the husband whips the wife than where the wife whips the husband; and yet we would hardly be supposed to hold that a wife has a right to whip her husband. We will not inflict upon society the greater evil of raising the curtain upon domestic privacy, to punish the lesser evil of trifling violence. Two boys under fourteen years of age fight upon the playground, and yet the courts will take no notice of it, not for the reason that boys have the right to fight, but because the interests of society require that they should be left to the more appropriate discipline of the school room and of home. It is not true that boys have a right to fight; nor is it true that a husband has a right to whip his wife. And if he had, it is not easily seen how the thumb is the standard of size for the instrument which he may use, as some of the old authorities have said; and in deference to which was his Honor's charge. A light blow, or many light blows, with a stick larger than the thumb, might produce no injury; but a switch half the size might be so used as to produce death. The standard is the effect produced, and not the manner of producing it, or the instrument used....

No error.

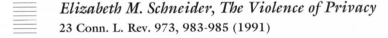

Elizabeth M. Schneider, *The Violence of Privacy*
23 Conn. L. Rev. 973, 983-985 (1991)

Battering is deeply threatening. It goes to our most fundamental assumptions about the nature of intimate relations and the safeness of family life. The concept of male battering of women as a "private" issue exerts a powerful ideological pull on our consciousness because, in some sense, it is something that we would like to believe. By seeing woman-abuse as "private," we affirm it as a problem that is individual, that only involves a particular male-female relationship, and for which there is no social responsibility to remedy.... Focusing on the woman, not the man, perpetuates the power of patriarchy. Denial supports and legitimates this power; the concept of privacy is a key aspect of this denial.

Denial takes many forms and operates on many levels. Men deny battering in order to protect their own privilege. Women need to deny the pervasiveness of the problem so as not to link it to their own life situations. Individual women who are battered tend to minimize the violence in order to distance themselves from some internalized negative concept of "battered woman." I see denial in the attitudes of jurors, who try to remove themselves and say that it could never happen to me; if it did, I would handle it differently.... The findings of many state task force reports on gender bias in the courts have painstakingly recorded judicial attitudes of denial. Clearly, there is serious denial on the part of state legislators, members of Congress and the Executive Branch who never mention battering as an important public issue. In battering, we see both the power of denial and the denial of power. The concept of privacy is an ideological rationale for this denial and serves to maintain it....

[A]s Martha Minow has suggested, [the] social failure to intervene in male battering of women on grounds of privacy should not be seen as separate from violence, but as a part of the violence.

> When clerks in a local court harass a woman who applies for a restraining order against the violence in her home, they are part of the violence. Society is organized to permit violence in the home; it is organized through images in mass media and through broadly based social attitudes that condone violence. Society permits such violence to go unchallenged through the isolation of families and the failures of police to respond. Public, rather than private patterns of conduct and morals are implicated. Some police officers refuse to respond to domestic violence; some officers themselves abuse their spouses. Some clerks and judges think domestic violence matters do not belong in court. These failures to respond to domestic violence are public, not private, actions.

[Martha Minow, Words and the Door to the Land of Change: Law, Language, and Family Violence, 43 Vand. L. Rev. 1665, 1671-1672 (1990)]. Although social failure to respond to problems of battered women has been justified on grounds of privacy, this failure to respond is an affirmative political decision that has serious public consequences. The rationale of privacy masks the political nature of the decision. Privacy thus plays a particularly subtle and pernicious ideological role in supporting, encouraging, and legitimating violence against women....

══ ### *Stevenson v. Stevenson*
══ **714 A.2d 986 (N.J. Super. Ct. 1998)**

COOK, J.S.C....

In what appears as a matter of first impression in New Jersey, this case presents the question whether a final restraining order issued under the

Prevention of Domestic Violence Act, N.J.S.A. § 2C:25-17-33, must be dissolved in all cases where the plaintiff so requests. For the reasons expressed below, this court determines that dissolution of a final restraining order at the request of plaintiff is not mandatory. Rather, dissolution in such cases is at the court's discretion, and should depend upon a showing of good cause, with an independent finding by the court based upon the facts presented in each case....

On November 6, 1997, the parties appeared before this court for a hearing on plaintiff's complaint charging defendant with numerous violations of the Prevention of Domestic Violence Act (the Act). The testimony of plaintiff, the photographic exhibits offered by her counsel, and the graphic appearance at the hearing of the residual effects of the severe physical injuries she suffered, established by a clear preponderance of the evidence that defendant was guilty of attempted criminal homicide, aggravated assault, terroristic threats, criminal restraint and burglary, all in violation of the Act. These violations arose from a brutal, sadistic and prolonged attack by defendant on his wife during the late evening and early morning hours of October 29-30, 1997.

Plaintiff, who appeared at the hearing with two black and severely swollen eyes, testified that on the late evening of October 29, 1997, defendant came into the marital bedroom, went into a total rage, punched plaintiff with both fists, held her down with his knees, kicked her in the back and ribs, and continued beating her there for approximately 25 minutes. Defendant then dragged her by her hair down the stairs and out of the house, and shoved her into his van, saying that they were going to go to a friend's house. Plaintiff was bleeding from her ears, nose and mouth. She got out of the van, ran to a neighbor's house and banged on the door. Defendant chased her, screaming he would kill her, and that he should have killed her before. She was "petrified". He caught up to her outside the neighbor's house, and choked her with both hands around her throat. He then dragged her down the street and pushed her back into the van. She escaped again and ran to another neighbor's house. At that point, defendant's vicious attack on his wife had been going on for 45 minutes. She went inside the neighbor's house and asked her neighbor to call the police, while she went into a powder room, closed the door, and tried to hide from defendant. Defendant went into the neighbor's house and proceeded to rip the powder room door off its hinges. The door landed on plaintiff. He dragged her out of the house, and back towards their house. Plaintiff grabbed onto trees along the way, trying to resist. He was furious because she had asked her neighbor to call the police. Finally, he let go of her, got into the van and left. She was badly injured and very scared. A neighbor came with a blanket and rendered first aid. She was rushed by ambulance to the Emergency Room of West Jersey Hospital. She had three large lumps on her head, two black eyes, blood running from her ears, and abrasions and lacerations all over her body. She also had trouble breathing. At the West Jersey Hospital Emergency Room, she was diagnosed as having head and lung injuries, and was in such critical condition that she had to be medevac'd by helicopter to the Cooper Hospital Trauma Center. She had a fractured skull, a concussion, four broken ribs, and a punctured lung (pneumothorax), in addition to the injuries noted above. She remained hospitalized at Cooper for several days, and was still under medical care at the time of the hearing on November 6, 1997.

At the hearing, the court had the opportunity not only to hear the testimony of plaintiff, but to observe her injuries and review the photographic exhibits submitted by her counsel as well. Plaintiff's eyes were severely swollen, black and blue, and almost closed. She was in obvious physical pain and distress. The photographic exhibits submitted by plaintiff's counsel depicted her injuries, as well as the powder room door that defendant ripped off its hinges in the neighbor's home where plaintiff sought refuge. The photos, including those of plaintiff's facial and head injuries, and the hole in her chest where a tube was inserted to re-inflate her punctured lung, depicted a severally beaten and battered woman.

Plaintiff testified she was in fear of defendant. She related a prior history of domestic violence on his part, including previous assaults. She was afraid he would take their ten year-old son and leave the area, noting that he would do anything and everything to get physical custody and keep their son away from her. She added that their ten year-old son was in the house throughout the forty-five minute period that the beating of his mother took place.

Defendant, who was represented by counsel at the hearing, did not testify. No evidence was presented to controvert plaintiff's testimony, or the domestic violence charges she made against him. . . .

Because of (1) the barbaric conduct of the defendant during the nightmarish incident of October 29-30, 1997; (2) the evidence of his drunkenness that night and in the past; (3) his prior history of domestic violence; and (4) plaintiff's clearly expressed fear that defendant would take her son away if not restrained, a final restraining order was entered. The order prohibited any further acts of domestic violence, and barred him from having any contact or communication with the plaintiff and from harassing or stalking her. The order also required defendant to undergo substance abuse and psychological evaluations, and restricted him to supervised visitation only. He was also ordered to pay plaintiff's attorneys' fees of $2,400 by December 12, 1997; child and spousal support; all household expenses; and other expenses enumerated in the order. The deadline for payment of plaintiff's counsel fees was modified by an order of December 23, 1997 [to allow for monthly payments]. . . .

At the hearing on plaintiff's request that the court dissolve the final restraining order, several violations of the order came to light. For example, it appeared that the defendant has engaged in *unsupervised visitation* with the child, including trips out-of-state. He has continually attempted to contact plaintiff. He has not abided by the psychotherapy recommendations of the Steininger Center, nor with the substance abuse recommendations of Segaloff. Both of those reports are discussed below. He has not paid any of the attorney's fees he was ordered to pay. In short, the defendant has flouted and violated the final restraining order. . . .

At the hearing on March 13, 1998, plaintiff asked the court to dissolve the final restraining order. She claimed she had reconsidered her relationship with the defendant and wanted him to be involved with their son's life. She requested that the restraints be dissolved, but only on the condition that he commit no future violence.

The final restraining order permitted *supervised visitation only*, pending a risk assessment and further order of the court. Risk assessment evaluations, substance abuse evaluations, and psychological evaluations of defendant were received by the court. At the request of and by agreement of both parties, through their counsel, copies of those evaluation reports were provided to the parties and their counsel. Plaintiff testified she had read the reports....

Those reports include (1) a psychological evaluation of defendant by Dr. Stuart Kurlansik, Chief Psychologist, The Steininger Center; and (2) a drug and alcohol abuse evaluation of defendant by Patricia Thurman, a substance abuse counsellor at the Substance Abuse Center in Southern New Jersey, Inc., t/a Segaloff Counseling and Treatment Center....

The report of Dr. Kurlansik of The Steininger Center is extensive, and covers eight pages. Dr. Kurlansik conducted two testing and interview sessions with defendant, each a week apart. Dr. Karlansik reported inter alia that:

> When asked to describe the events which resulted in his referral to this office, Mr. Stevenson reported that "I assaulted my wife. I beat her up very badly."...
>
> He reported prior fights with his wife, but "nothing to this degree." He claimed that *every time they fought, he was drunk*. He stated that she never had to go to the hospital in previous fights. He stated that the previous fights involved punching, although not to the face. He stated that he bruised her in prior fights, but then claimed that she bruises easily. He reported that he had been in fights with other people during the period of his marriage as well. He stated that he boxes and plays hockey, and fought during the course of a game. He stated that he has had a few fights outside of the sport events, however. He then said there had been a handful, the most recent occurring [a year ago] at a roller rink [when] the other coach had been a poor sport, and "we ended up in a physical confrontation."... Another time, four years ago, he stated that he was a spectator at an ice hockey [game] in which his son was playing. He stated that a parent of one of his teams' children became involved in a fight with three of the opposing team's parents, and he "intervened." *He reported having a fight five years ago in a bar, and stated that he was intoxicated at the time*. He stated that he had played a game of pool for twenty dollars and the other person lost the game, and did not want to pay, "so I hit him."...
>
> He denied any arrests as a result of fighting as an adult. As a juvenile, he stated that he was incarcerated at Glen Mills for a total of three years, and stated that "we could go on for hours" regarding juvenile incidents. He stated that he was at Glen Mills twice — once at age thirteen for assault, and the second time at age fourteen for robbery.
>
> His current marriage has been his only marriage. He married on December 28, 1986. The most recent separation occurred October 29, 1997. He reported one other separation, two years ago. He stated that "things just weren't working well." This separation lasted about three months.
>
> Mr. Stevenson reported no [Dep't of Youth and Family Services] involvement in his family of origin, but stated that he left home when he was about twelve years old. He stated that he ran away to California, and knew no one there. He was arrested for trying to rob a restaurant, was held for sixty days, and was sent to Glen Mills.... He was later arrested for fighting, and was again sent to Glen Mills for fourteen months.... He left Glen Mills when he turned seventeen....

He reported that he has a *short temper*, although "not now." He claimed that the experience which brought him here has changed his life and a short temper is "not gonna be a trait for me anymore." . . .

An objective measure of personality functioning, the Million Clinical Multiaxial Inventory—III, was administered. . . . [T]he interpretive report stated that "on the basis of the test data (assuming denial is not present), it may be reasonable to assume that the patient is exhibiting psychological dysfunction of mild to moderate severity." An Axis I (an "acute" disorder) diagnosis of Generalized Anxiety Disorder is suggested, while Axis II (enduring features of an individual's personality, and therefore more "chronic") diagnosis of: "*Antisocial Personality Traits,*" "*Passive-Aggressive Personality Traits,*" "*Avoidant Personality Traits,*" and "*Sadistic Personality Features*" are suggested. The NCS report hypothesizes . . . that he may manifest (among other things) a lack of empathy, intolerance, and display "impulsive and quixotic emotionality." It goes on to state that *individuals with his profile can "be easily provoked into sudden and unpredictable reactions," which "may be punctuated periodically by angry outbursts."*

Recommendations:

It is strongly urged that Mr. Stevenson participate in psychotherapy, to help him learn to control his anger (and to find more appropriate ways of expressing it), as well as to reduce his anxiety. Psychotherapy might also address what appears to be an issue with *excessive use of alcohol at times.*

In her substance abuse evaluation of defendant, Ms. Thurman, a substance abuse counsellor at the Substance Abuse Center of Southern New Jersey, t/a Segaloff Counseling and Treatment Center, reported that: . . .

Robert, a 34 year-old white male, was interviewed on November 29, 1997, at 8:30 a.m. Eye contact was fair, affect closed, guarded and *very accusatory toward his estranged wife, Melody.*

When asked about his use of drugs and alcoholic beverages, Mr. Stevenson states he's never used drugs of any kind and attempts to portray himself as a modest drinker, however, says the day he was charged "*I had a little too much to drink*" . . . . But, Robert was quick to defend his actions by blaming the problem on "I caught my wife trying to buy drugs on the phone" and sees no relationship between his drinking and his current family problems. . . .

Concluding, based upon the limited information available to us, *we strongly suspect Mr. Stevenson is drinking more than he reports and we feel he would greatly benefit from outpatient counseling to enable him to cease drinking and evaluate his family problems in a drug free state. The fact the client admits he was under the influence at the time of the altercation with his wife prompts us to question the severity of his drinking and its relationship to his family problems.* . . . If Mr. Stevenson is not already in treatment for substance abuse, *we would then recommend he be mandated to complete at least 3 months in substance abuse treatment.* . . .

At a risk assessment conference with a Family Court staff therapist, plaintiff expressed concern over defendant's "*need for control,*" and again said she feared he would flee with their son, perhaps to Arizona. . . . She also said that on more than one occasion, defendant has threatened that he "will do anything and everything he has to" in order to gain custody of his son. Plaintiff requested that supervised visitation continue.

There remain several criminal charges pending against defendant as a result of his sadistic attack on his wife, including criminal attempt — murder; aggravated assault; burglary; criminal mischief; threatened violence; and criminal restraint. He is reportedly free on $75,000 cash bail, and is awaiting further proceedings in the criminal case.

When considering a plaintiff's request to dissolve the Final Restraining Order, a court must not forget that it is the public policy of the State of New Jersey, expressed by the Legislature in the Act, N.J.S.A. § 2C:25-18, *that victims of domestic violence must be assured the maximum protection from abuse the law can provide; that the official response to domestic violence, including that of the courts, shall communicate the attitude that domestic violent behavior will not be excused or tolerated; and that it is the responsibility of the courts to protect victims of domestic violence* by ordering those remedies and sanctions that are *available to assure the safety of the victims* and the public. . . .

In addition, the Legislature has mandated that a final restraining order cannot be dissolved [or modified], *unless good cause is shown.* . . . Even where good cause is shown, the language of the statute, N.J.S.A. § 2C:25-29d., expressly makes dissolution *discretionary*, not mandatory (". . . final order *may* be dissolved").

Plaintiff's dissolution request, made despite the latest brutal beating she suffered at the hands of a drunken husband who has a past history of wife-beating and an alcohol abuse problem, is consistent with phase three of "the battered woman's syndrome." That phase of the battering cycle is characterized by a period of loving behavior by the batterer, during which pleas for forgiveness and protestations of devotion are often mixed with promises to seek counselling, stop drinking and refrain from further violence. A period of relative calm may last as long as several months, but in a battering relationship the affection and contrition of the batterer will eventually fade, and phases one and two, the "tension-building" phase and the "acute battering incident" phase, will start anew. State v. Kelly, [478 A.2d 364 (N.J. 1984)]. Plaintiff has gone through the battering cycle with defendant at least twice. Through this dissolution request she seeks to remain in the situation. She thus meets the definition of a "battered woman." Id., quoting from L. Walker, The Battered Woman at xv (1979). The New Jersey Legislature recognized the plight of battered women when it enacted the Act and provided battered women with the remedy of *permanent* restraining orders against wife-beaters and other batterers of women. Id. . . .

Obviously, if there were no basis at all for plaintiff to fear further violence — as most certainly there is, given the nature and extent of this attack and defendant's past history of violence, including domestic violence against plaintiff; then there would be no need to condition dissolution on the absence of further violence. But there is that inherent fear, a fear that this court and any reasonable person viewing this situation would certainly share.

[Because fear is vital to the continuance of power and control in a domestic violence relationship, and this fear can impact the victim's ability to act in the best interests of her child, it is important to consider the victim's fear of the defendant.

Carfagno v. Carfagno, 672 A.2d 751 (N.J. Ch. Div. 1995).] When considering the question of fear of defendant, *Carfagno* notes that the test should not be the victim's subjective fear. Rather, the test is one of objective fear, i.e., that fear which a reasonable victim similarly situated would have under the circumstances....

When considering a victim's application to dissolve, and whether there is good cause to do so, a court must determine whether objective fear can be said to continue to exist, and also whether there is a real danger of domestic violence recurring, in the event the restraining order is dissolved....Whether or not this plaintiff would agree, it is clear that *from the standpoint of objective fear*, that a reasonable victim of such a brutal beating by a husband, who has assaulted her in the past and has a history of other violent behavior, and is the subject of experts' findings of uncontrolled anger and excessive use of alcohol, would have a reasonable fear that future violence by her husband would occur, were the restraining order dissolved.

Even in cases of reconciliation, the court must still make *an independent finding* that continued protection is unnecessary before vacating a restraining order. Torres v. Lancelloti, [607 A.2d 1375 (N.J. Ch. Div. 1992)]. The "good cause" proviso of N.J.S.A. § 2C:25-29d requires no less. Without making an independent finding based on the objective evidence, a court does not meet the public policy dictates of the Act...N.J.S.A. § 2C:25-18....

In this case, given the uncontroverted evidence of defendant's brutality against his wife, his history of violence both within and without the domestic arena, his alcohol abuse and uncontrolled assaultive behavior when under the influence, and the reports before the court, including those of The Steininger Center and Segaloff, a reasonable, objective and independent determination of the facts leads to the inescapable conclusion that a real threat of recurrence of domestic violence by defendant upon his battered wife will exist, if the Final Restraining Order is dissolved. This court will not be an accomplice to further violence by this defendant, by wholly dissolving at this point the restraints that have been entered against him. Accordingly, and for lack of good cause shown, plaintiff's application to dissolve the Final Restraining Order is denied.

The court does find cause to modify the Final Restraining Order with respect to certain matters concerning the child of the parties, as follows. The final restraining order shall remain in full force and effect, except that contact or communication between plaintiff and defendant relating to supervised visitation, and to the safety, health, education, welfare, status or activities of the minor child of the parties, shall be permitted. There shall be no further modification of the final restraining order, without application to and with the express approval of the court.

Defendant shall promptly undergo psychotherapy as recommended in the report of Dr. Kurlansik of The Steininger Center. He shall also promptly undergo at least three months of substance abuse treatment at the Camden County Division of Alcoholism and Substance Abuse, as recommended by Patricia Thurman of the Segaloff Counseling and Treatment Center. Upon completion of psychotherapy and substance abuse treatment, the court will consider unsupervised visitation.

Notes

1. Legal Responses to Domestic Violence: An Historical Perspective. As Reva Siegel reports, "The Anglo-American common law originally provided that a husband, as master of his household, could subject his wife to corporal punishment or 'chastisement' so long as he did not inflict permanent injury upon her." Reva B. Siegel, "The Rule of Love": Wife Beating as Prerogative and Privacy, 105 Yale L.J. 2117, 2118 (1996). Although as early as 1641 the Massachusetts Bay Colony had moved away from this rule — proclaiming in its "Body of Liberties" that "[e]verie marryied woeman shall be free from bodilie correction or stripes by her husband, unless it be in his owwn defence upon her assault" — it was not until the nineteenth century that feminist agitation successfully brought "wife beating" to the attention of law reformers in the United States and Britain. See Evan Stark, Re-Presenting Woman Battering: From Battered Woman Syndrome to Coercive Control, 58 Alb. L. Rev. 973, 987-988 (1995).

By the end of the Civil War, the American legal system had repudiated the doctrine of chastisement. However, during the Reconstruction Era, a new body of common law emerged under which judges, instead of recognizing a husband's right to beat his wife, concluded that "the legal system should not interfere in cases of wife beating, in order to protect the privacy of the marriage relationship and to promote domestic harmony." Siegel, supra, at 2120.

> These changes in the rule structure of marital status law were justified in a distinctive rhetoric: one that diverged from the traditional idiom of chastisement doctrine. Instead of reasoning about marriage in the older, hierarchy-based norms of the common law, jurists began to justify the regulation of domestic violence in the language of privacy and love associated with companionate marriage in the industrial era.

Id.

Meanwhile, wife beating was quickly transformed from a women's rights issue to a "law and order" issue. By the end of the nineteenth century, wife beating was viewed as a crime, but increasingly characterized as solely the practice of "lawless or unruly men of the 'dangerous classes,'" particularly African-American men and men from low-status immigrant ethnic groups such as German and Irish Americans. Id. at 2139. A particularly popular punishment for such men in the imagination of law reformers was the whipping post: between 1876 and 1906, 12 states and the District of Columbia considered legislation that would enable wife beaters to be flogged, and several prominent members of the American Bar Association campaigned for such legislation. Id. at 2137. Thus, according to Siegel, wife beating was used as an excuse for stigmatizing and disciplining racially "other" men; as a corollary, domestic violence among the economically and racially privileged classes disappeared from view.

Legal reformers made significant distinctions among the victims of domestic violence as well as the perpetrators. For example, English reformers were careful to distinguish between "good women," who deserved protection from domestic violence, and "the naggy harpy" who brought beatings upon herself. See Stark, supra, at 989.

By the 1920s, the victims of child abuse and woman battering had been transferred from "protection societies," which sought to provide women and children a safe haven from abusive men, to "child welfare agencies," which attempted to regulate domestic life more broadly. In the process, mothers were increasingly seen as part of the problem. For example, Stark notes that "[i]n 1899, the new Illinois juvenile courts replaced the term 'child abuse' with the term 'neglect,' while 'family' or 'domestic relations' courts sought to decriminalize woman battering by taking 'domestic trouble cases' as an occasion to help the wives master the habits of cleanliness, nutrition, and child care." Id. at 991. By the New Deal, child abuse was commonly attributed to mothers who were overly "domineering," and male violence against women faded from public view. Id. at 992. The goal of the new family court system was to keep the family intact; accordingly, judges encouraged battered women to accept responsibility for their role in provoking the violence and discouraged them from filing criminal charges. Siegel, supra, at 2170. Those views, and the perception of domestic violence as a private matter, lasted well into the 1970s.

Throughout the 1960s and 1970s, the underenforcement of crimes involving family members was notorious. A study of thousands of incidents in Boston, Chicago, and Washington, D.C., found that in cases where both victim and offender were present when police arrived, fewer than half of all felonies involving family members resulted in arrest. See Lawrence W. Sherman, The Influence of Criminology on Criminal Law: Evaluating Arrests for Misdemeanor Domestic Violence, 83 J. Crim. L. & Criminology 1, 11 (1992) (citing sources); see also Sarah Mausolff Buel, Note, Mandatory Arrest for Domestic Violence, 11 Harv. Women's L.J. 213, 217 (1988) (citing surveys showing arrest rates from three to 10 percent). For further historical accounts of violence against women in Anglo-American social life and efforts to control it, see Linda Gordon, Heroes of Their Own Lives: The Politics and History of Family Violence (1988); A. James Hammerton, Cruelty and Companionship: Conflict in Nineteenth-Century Married Life (1992); Elizabeth Pleck, Domestic Tyranny: The Making of Social Policy Against Family Violence from Colonial Times to the Present (1987).

2. Contemporary Legal Responses to Domestic Violence: Mandatory Arrest, Prosecution, and Reporting Policies. Beginning in the 1960s, the women's movement sought to make "private" violence a public issue. Feminists created shelters to protect the health and safety of battered women and children. Activists also undertook public education campaigns to call attention to male violence and state inaction, and to change attitudes about the victims of abuse. So too, advocates began using legal strategies "to reform how the police officers, prosecutors, health workers, and judges who compose the front line of the criminal justice system respond to cases of intimate abuse." Linda G. Mills, Killing Her Softly: Intimate Abuse and the Violence of State Intervention, 113 Harv. L. Rev. 550, 557 (1999). To improve law enforcement efforts, reformers have pursued mandatory arrest, mandatory prosecution, and mandatory reporting policies.

Mandatory or pro-arrest policies require police officers to arrest a suspect if there is probable cause to believe that an assault or battery has occurred, without regard to the victim's consent or objection. Id. at 558. These policies began to appear in the wake of a landmark Minneapolis study of the relationship between arrest and recidivism in domestic violence cases, published in 1984 by Lawrence Sherman and Richard Berk. Lawrence W. Sherman & Richard A. Berk, The Specific Deterrent Effects of Arrest for Domestic Assault, 49 Am. Soc. Rev. 261 (1984). The Minneapolis experiment — along with several high-profile lawsuits against police departments — stimulated a wave of mandatory arrest statutes. As of June 2003, twenty-one states and the District of Columbia had passed such legislation. Emily J. Sack, Battered Women and the State: The Struggle for the Future of Domestic Violence Policy, 2004 Wis. L. Rev. 1657, 1670, citing Neal Miller, Inst. for Law & Justice, A Law Enforcement and Prosecution Perspective 7 & n.74 (2003) (listing mandatory arrest statutes), available at http://www.il-j.org/dv/dvvawa2000.htm. By 2005, 19 states also required arrests for violations of domestic restraining orders. Castle Rock v. Gonzales, 125 S. Ct. 2796, 2818 & n.10 (2005) (Stevens, J., dissenting), discussed in note 5, p. 497, infra. Other changes in police procedure complemented and strengthened mandatory arrest policies, such as required documentation of domestic violence incidents, the institution of domestic violence databases, and the creation of trained domestic violence officers and investigators. Sack, supra, at 1671. In New York City, from 1993, when the mandatory arrest policy was instituted, to 1999, felony domestic violence arrests increased by 33 percent, misdemeanor domestic violence arrests by 114 percent, and arrests for violation of orders of protection by 76 percent. Id. at 1672. See also C.D. Maxwell et al., Nat'l Inst. of Justice, The Effects of Arrest on Intimate Partner Violence: New Evidence from the Spouse Abuse Replication Program (NCJ-188199) (2001) (analyzing over 4000 incidents from multiple sites and finding that arrests reduced subsequent violence).

Mandatory or no-drop prosecution policies require prosecutors to prosecute domestic violence cases regardless of the victim's wishes. Jurisdictions with aggressive prosecution or no-drop policies are cited in Cheryl Hanna, The Paradox of Hope: The Crime and Punishment of Domestic Violence, 39 Wm. & Mary L. Rev. 1505, 1520 n.52 (1998). There is some evidence that no-drop policies have had a role not only in increasing domestic violence prosecutions, but in lowering recidivism, and raising the rate of victim involvement in cases, particularly where the no-drop policy is part of a wider range of prosecutorial innovations, including victim support services. Sack, supra, at 1674; Angela Corsilles, Note, No-Drop Policies in the Prosecution of Domestic Violence Cases: Guarantee to Action or Dangerous Solution?, 63 Fordham L. Rev. 853, 873-874 (1994).

When battered women are reluctant to testify against their batterers, prosecutors may use strategies similar to those used in murder cases: introducing spontaneous statements made by the victim at the time of arrest, police officers' testimony, and videos or photographs taken at the time of the injury in lieu of the victim's testimony. See Mills, supra, at 561. The future of prosecutions for domestic violence when the victim cannot be located, or does not wish to testify, have been put in question by Crawford v. Washington, 541 U.S. 36 (2004). The Supreme Court in *Crawford* held that testimonial evidence is not admissible against a criminal defendant unless the witness who made the statements at issue is unavailable and the defendant had a prior opportunity for cross-examination. The U.S. Supreme Court granted certiorari in two cases involving challenges to convictions for charges related to domestic violence where the convictions were based, in part, on statements by the victim at the time of the abuse, or in the course of police investigation thereafter. In Washington v. Davis, 111 P.3d 844 (Wash. 2005), cert. granted sub nom. Davis v. Washington, 126 S. Ct. 552 (2005), the defendant challenged the trial court's admission of a 911 call as an excited utterance after his conviction for violation of a domestic no-contact order. The Washington Supreme Court held that the statement was not "testimonial," but rather a response to immediate danger and cry for for help; it also found that the conviction was supported by overwhelming other evidence, and thus that any error was harmless. See also People v. Moscat, 777 N.Y.S.2d 875 (N.Y. Crim. Ct. 2004) (911 call is not testimonial for purposes of the *Crawford* rule). In Hammon v. Indiana, 829 N.E.2d 444 (Ind. 2005), cert. granted, 126 S. Ct. 547 (2005), defendant challenged his conviction for domestic battery and violation of his probation, following the admission into evidence of the victim's statements to the police in the course of their investigation. The Indiana Supreme Court held that the initial statements made by the victim were not testimonial because they were gathered by the police to find out what had happened rather than for the purpose of preserving testimony. The same court found, however, that a formal affidavit by the victim that was also entered into evidence was testimonial and, had the trial been before a jury, its admission might have been sufficient to reverse the conviction. Because the trial was tried to the bench, the court held that the error was harmless. For analysis of the various issues raised by these types of cases, see Tom Liniger, Prosecuting Batterers After Crawford, 91 Va. L. Rev. 747 (2005); Myrna S. Raeder, Remember the Ladies and Children Too: *Crawford*'s Impact on Domestic Violence and Child Sexual Abuse Cases, 71 Brook L. Rev. 411 (2005); Robert P. Mosteller, *Crawford*'s Impact on Hearsay Statements in Domestic Violence and Child Sexual Abuse Cases, 71 Brook. L. Rev. 411 (2005).

Mandatory medical reporting laws are another form of intervention. Over four-fifths of the states require reporting by health care providers if the patient has an injury that appears to have resulted from a deadly weapon. Linda K. Bledsoe et al., Understanding the Impact of Intimate Partner Violence Mandatory Reporting Law, 10 Violence Against Women 536, 544 (2004). A few states have laws that specifically address intimate partner violence. Id. Advocates of these laws see them as a way to insure early law enforcement intervention when women's lives and health are at risk, and note that women are more likely to visit doctors than call the police. Such statutes are also thought to provide accountability for health services providers and encourage better responses to violence-related injuries. Id. at 538; Shelby A.D. Moore, Understanding the Connection Between Domestic Violence, Crime, and Poverty: How Welfare Reform May Keep Battered Women From Leaving Abusive Relationships, 12 Tex. J. Women & L. 451, 473 n.132 (2003).

3. Feminist Critics of Aggressive Prosecution Measures. Proponents argue that mandatory arrest and prosecution strategies are the best way to force law enforcement officials to take domestic violence seriously and to minimize the possibility of invidious discrimination. By taking the decision to proceed away from victims, they contend, a mandatory approach also can reduce the exposure of victims to pressure and retaliation from the abuser. See, e.g., Jeffrey Fagan, Nat'l Inst. of Justice, The Criminalization of Domestic Violence: Promises and Limits 1, 6-11 (1996); Joan Zorza, Must We Stop Arresting Batterers?: Analysis and Policy Implications of New Police Domestic Violence Studies, 28 New Eng. L. Rev. 929 (1994) (arguing that the published studies, correctly interpreted, show that arrest is generally the superior method of deterring future violence).

Despite the claimed advantages of mandatory prosecution and no-drop policies for victims of domestic violence, however, these policies have faced many criticisms from within the battered women's advocacy community. One set of criticisms concerns the effectiveness of the policies, based in part on a second landmark study led by Lawrence Sherman finding that, over the long term, violence increased in cases where the perpetrator was arrested, and that the frequency of repeat violence increased when the persons arrested were unemployed, unmarried, high school dropouts, or African-American. Lawrence W. Sherman et al., The Variable Effects of Arrest on Criminal Careers: The Milwaukee Domestic Violence Experiment, 83 J. Crim. L. & Criminology 137, 158-163 (1992). Among other studies finding little or no deterrent effect, see Robert C. Davis et al., The Deterrent Effect of Prosecuting Domestic Violence Misdemeanors, 44 Crime & Delinq. 434, 441 (1998).

Critics also worry that mandatory interventions put victims in jeopardy of retaliation and further violence. Deborah Epstein et al., Transforming Aggressive Prosecution Policies: Prioritizing Victims' Long-Term Safety in the Prosecution of Domestic Violence Cases, 12 Am. U. J. Gender Soc. Pol'y & L. 465, 476-477 (2003) (reviewing findings of risks to women). These interventions also are said to compound victims' trauma and erode their sense of efficacy, autonomy, and self-esteem. Linda Mills argues that mandatory policies "visit upon these victims an entirely distinct violent interaction, one that contains many of the emotionally abusive elements of the victim's relationship with the batterer." Mills, Killing Her Softly, supra, at 568. The failure to prioritize victims' needs and concerns, in turn, is said to decrease their perceptions of the legitimacy of the process and their willingness to turn to law enforcement and social services agencies in the future. Epstein et al., supra, at 460-470. For a critical feminist view of mandatory arrest policies on the grounds that they sacrifice women's autonomy, see G. Kristian Miccio, A House Divided: Mandatory Arrest, Domestic Violence, and the Conservatization of the Battered Women's Movement, 42 Hous. L. Rev. 237 (2005).

Critics also stress the likelihood that arrest and prosecution will remain more frequent in African-American and Latino communities. Some note that minority communities are disproportionately targeted by law enforcement officials, who often share racial stereotypes about the violent nature of African-American and Latino men. See Barbara Fedders, Lobbying for Mandatory-Arrest Policies: Race, Class, and the Politics of the Battered Women's Movement, 23 N.Y.U. Rev. L. & Soc. Change 281 (1997).

Other commentators cite research indicating that when police officers see evidence of aggression by both parties to a dispute, they often end up arresting both, although more thorough investigation would reveal that women's aggression was in self-defense. See David Hirshel & Eve Buzwa, Understanding the Context of Dual Arrest with Directions for Future Research, 8 Violence Against Women 1449 (2002); Sue Osthoff, But Gertrude, I Beg To Differ, a Hit Is Not a Hit: When Battered Women Are Arrested for Assaulting Their Partners, 8 Violence Against Women 1521, 1533-1535 (2002). When women are arrested under these procedures, they often face substantial problems in getting charges dismissed; some end up accepting diversion to programs targeted at male batterers. Osthoff, supra, at 1535-1537. In some jurisdictions, victims have even been jailed for refusing to testify after filing an abuse complaint. Sack, supra, at 1681-1682. Other issues relating to civil orders of protection that may backfire against the victims of domestic violence, as well as consequences of abuse related to child custody, employment, and housing, are explored in the notes below.

As to medical interventions, critics worry that women whose history of abuse makes them aware of reporting requirements may be deterred from seeking treatment. Bledsoe et al., at 538; Ariella Hyman & Ronald A. Chez, Mandatory Reporting of Domestic Violence by Health Care Providers: A Misguided Approach, 5 Women's Health Issues 208, 209 (1995); Michael A. Rodriguez et al., Mandatory Reporting of Intimate Violence to Police: Views of Physicians in California, 89 Am. J. Pub. Health 575, 577 (1999) (reporting that 60 percent of physicians would not report if the patient objected because notification could worsen the violence). The American Medical Association opposes mandatory reporting out of concerns for patients' safety, confidentiality, and autonomy. Bledsoe et al., supra at 539. What little evidence is available on the impact of mandatory reporting laws suggests that much depends on what happens with the report. Kentucky is unique in designating social service providers as the recipients, and they respect women's decisions to refuse assistance or cooperate with prosecutions. Some evidence indicates that this law has proved beneficial in increasing social services to battered women and children, particularly those in rural areas. Id. at 555. See also Mia M. McFarlane, Mandatory Reporting of Domestic Violence: An Inappropriate Response for New York Health Care Professionals, 17 Buff. Pub. Int. L.J. 1 (1998-1999).

Given these problems, some feminists conclude that strategies providing women with material resources such as housing, food, clothing, or money should take priority over policies that merely seek greater accountability by batterers. Donna Coker, Shifting Power for Battered Women: Law, Material Resources, and Poor Women of Color, 33 U.C. Davis L. Rev. 1009 (2000). They also argue that law enforcement agencies should make victims' long-term safety the preeminent concern. That may argue for dropping charges where victims are at high risk for retaliation and abusers are unlikely to get lengthy sentences. Epstein et al., supra, at 493-494. Efforts to connect victims with intensive advocacy and social services programs, and more flexibility in criminal dispositions to respond to victims' needs (such as requirements that the batterer complete a substance abuse program), are also suggested reforms. The limited available evidence suggests that focusing on women's needs increases their willingness to cooperate with prosecutors and reduces their exposure to repeated abuse. Id. at 486-498.

Emily Sack argues that rather than eliminating aggressive arrest, prosecution, and reporting policies, they should be improved, through better training and education of police officers, and limits on the use of the criminal justice system to coerce or punish victims. Sack, supra, at 1722.

The most systematic recent attempt to determine the preferences of battered women surveyed some 240 women in shelters, finding that about three-quarters supported mandatory arrest and medical reporting laws, and about two-thirds favored no-drop policies. Between 15 and 20 percent believed that these policies would not benefit them and that they personally would be less likely to seek medical or law enforcement assistance in communities that had such requirements. Alisa Smith, It's My Decision, Isn't It?, 6 Violence Against Women 1384, 1395-1396 (2000).

4. Contemporary Legal Responses to Intimate Violence: New Crimes and Civil Enforcement. Domestic violence reform efforts have centered not only on promoting greater compliance with existing laws, but also on enacting new criminal laws and expanding civil enforcement strategies. Some states, for example, have separate criminal prohibitions on violence occurring among intimates. See Minn. Stat. §518B.01 (West 2005). In 1990, California was the first state to enact an anti-stalking law, after actress Rebecca Schaeffer was killed there by an obsessed fan in 1989. Within two years of the passage of the California statute, over half the states had passed laws to criminalize stalking; by 1998, all 50 states had stalking laws. Carol E. Jordan et al., Stalking: Cultural, Clinical and Legal Considerations, 38 Brandeis L.J. 513, 516 (2000). The first wave of such statutes was plagued with constitutional problems of vagueness and overbreadth, but later statutes were more narrowly written, tracking the model code developed by the Justice Department in conjunction with the National Criminal Justice Administration and the National Institute of Justice and released in October 1993. See Nat'l Inst. of Justice, Domestic Violence, Stalking, and Antistalking Legislation: An Annual Report to Congress Under the Violence Against Women Act 4 (1996). For an overview of the statutes and case law, see Jordan et al., supra. The federal Violence Against Women Act, enacted in 1994, extends funding to states to address problems of stalking and domestic violence. See 42 U.S.C. §§14031-14042 (West 2005). The Act is discussed in more detail in starting on p. 525, infra.

All 50 states, as well as the District of Columbia and Puerto Rico, now have procedures for civil restraining orders, which can enjoin individuals from harassing, threatening, or abusing a victim. As a practical matter, these orders are only as effective as the willingness of the abuser to obey them and the ability of the state to enforce them. The effectiveness of these legal avenues depends as well on the resources of law enforcement agencies, and the ability of victims to access the legal process and stand up to the actual or potential retaliation that use of the legal process may stimulate. Thirty-four states have adopted criminal contempt laws to help enforce protection orders, and 45 jurisdictions have criminal statutes that make violating a protection order a criminal offense. Deborah Epstein, Effective Intervention in Domestic Violence Cases: Rethinking the Roles of Prosecutors, Judges, and the Court System, 11 Yale J.L. & Feminism 3, 12 (1999).

What about the approach of the court in *Stephenson*: keeping a protective order in effect, even over the objection of the victim? Review the criticisms of mandatory arrest, prosecution, and reporting laws in note 3, p. 493, supra. Are mandatory policies the natural consequence of viewing domestic violence as a public problem rather than a private one? What are the costs? See Cathleen A. Booth, No-Drop Policies: Effective Legislation or Protectionist Attitude? 30 U. Tol. L. Rev. 621, 644-645 (1999) (noting both the advantages and disadvantages of *Stephenson*, including the possible loss of leverage for women in divorce nego-tiations, and their additional exposure to violence).

Should victims of abuse ever be held accountable for violating a restraining order? Some judges have imposed fines or jail sentences for a battered woman's contempt of a civil protection order. For example, Kentucky Judge Megan Lake Thornton fined an impoverished woman $100 for reconciling with her husband a few days after she had obtained a protective order. Thornton explained, "I find that offensive. It drives me nuts when people just decide to do whatever they want." Id. (quoting Thornton). Like a vocal minority of family court judges, she has made it clear that no contact orders apply equally to abusers and targets of abuse. "People are ordered to follow them and I don't care which side you are on." Francis X. Clines, Judge's Domestic Violence Ruling Creates an Outcry in Kentucky, N.Y. Times, Jan. 8, 2002, at A14 (quoting Thornton). Domestic violence advocates view that kind of formalistic egalitarian approach as unrealistic, unjust, and "a barrier that stops abused women from seeking protection of the court." Clines, supra, at A14 (quoting Carol Jordan, director of the Kentucky Governor's Office of Child Abuse and Domestic Violence). When parties have children, financial difficulties, or continuing love for their abusers, "[i]t's pretty hard to say, 'Never speak again.'" Clines, supra, at A14 (quoting Sherry Currens, Executive Director of the Kentucky Domestic Violence Association). See Sandy Chesnut, The Practice of Dual Arrests in Domestic Violence Situations: Does It Accomplish Anything?, 70 Miss. L.J. 971 (2001).

If you were a domestic violence advocate whose client was sanctioned by Judge Thornton, how would you proceed? Would you advise your client to appeal? Start a recall election petition drive? Call a press conference? All, or none of the above?

5. Civil Damage Claims. Another legal resource for survivors of intimate violence is the civil damages suit. Tort claims brought by women against their spouses face the barrier of interspousal immunity, a holdover from the days of coverture. See Clare Dalton, Domestic Violence, Domestic Torts and Divorce: Constraints and Possibilities, 31 New Eng. L. Rev. 319 (1997). For evaluation of the usefulness of expanding tort remedies against abusers, see Merle H. Weiner, Domestic Violence and the Per Se Standard of Outrage, 54 Md. L. Rev. 183 (1995).

Survivors of domestic violence have also sought to hold the state itself accountable for its failure to protect them. During the 1980s, a number of leading decisions allowed federal civil rights actions under § 1983 of the Civil Rights Act against municipalities whose police failed to respond to domestic violence com-plaints or who applied special arrest policies that discriminated against the victims of domestic violence. See, e.g., Hynson v. City of Chester, 864 F.2d 1026 (3d Cir. 1988) (mother and children of woman killed by her abusive boyfriend allowed to sue police who refused to arrest the boyfriend the day before the murder because the woman's restraining order had expired); Watson v. Kansas City, 857 F.2d 690 (10th Cir. 1988) (wife whose abusive husband was a police officer was told when reporting incidents never to call the police again or they would have her arrested and take away her children; the police department took no disciplinary action against the husband, whose behavior culminated in a brutal rape of his wife and attack on his children); Thurman v. City of Torrington, 595 F. Supp. 1521 (D. Conn. 1984) (police repeatedly ignored woman's complaints about estranged husband and even stood by as abusive incidents occurred). The *Thurman* case led to a consent judgment against the city for $2.3 million. See George P. Choundas, Neither Equal nor Protected: The Invisible Law of Equal Protection, the Legal Invisibility of Its Gender-Based Victims, 44 Emory L.J. 1069 (1995).

In 1989, the Supreme Court ruled in DeShaney v. Winnebago County Department of Social Services, 489 U.S. 189 (1989), that the state was not liable under § 1983 of the 1964 Civil Rights Act for the failure of local child protection officials to protect a young boy from beatings by his father that resulted in permanent brain damage. In the majority's view, the Due Process Clause does not "require the state to protect the life, liberty, and property of its citizens against invasion by private actors" over which it had no control. Id. at. 195. *DeShaney*, however, did not foreclose the possibility of a § 1983 claim for discriminatory enforcement of laws protecting victims of domestic violence under the equal protection clause — the theory pursued in *Thurman*, *Watson*, and *Hynson*. See, e.g., Culbertson v. Doan, 65 F. Supp. 2d 702 (S.D. Ohio 1999) (denying motion to dismiss for failure to state a claim when the chief of police failed to act on the decedent's reports of her boyfriend's abuse and beatings, asking, "Why does she keep going back to it?"; the decedent was eventually murdered by the boyfriend). After *DeShaney*, some courts also found that certain circumstances might create a "special relationship" requiring the state to protect a citizen from private violence. See, e.g., Mastroianni v. County of Suffolk, 691 N.E.2d 613 (N.Y. 1997) (special relationship arose when the police failed to arrest a husband despite their knowledge of his violent history and their knowledge that he had violated an order of protection; minutes after the police left, the husband stabbed the wife to death).

However in 2005, in Castle Rock v. Gonzales, 125 S. Ct. 2796 (2005), the Court made clear that a jurisdiction's mandatory arrest policy does not create such a special relationship, or an entitlement under the Due Process Clause giving rise to possible § 1983 liability. In *Castle Rock*, the respondent, Jessica Gonzales, repeatedly requested the local police to arrest her ex-husband for violation of a civil restraining order after he abducted their three daughters who were playing in the family's front yard. According to the facts in the complaint, which the Court accepted for purposes of the decision, the respondent contacted the police six times between 7:30 p.m. and 1:00 a.m. the next morning. She even went to the police station to file an incident report and begged the officers to look for her husband, who had a history of instability and violence. The officer who took the report made "no reasonable effort to enforce the TRO or locate the three children.

Instead he went to dinner." Shortly after 3:00 a.m., the husband arrived at the police station and opened fire. Officers shot back, killing him in the exchange, and then discovered the dead bodies of his daughters in his pick up truck.

Colorado, like 18 other states, has a mandatory arrest law for violations of restraining orders. It provides that:

> (a) Whenever a protection order is issued, the protected person shall be provided with a copy of such order. A peace officer shall use every reasonable means to enforce a protection order.
> (b) A peace officer shall arrest, or, if an arrest would be impractical under the circumstances, seek a warrant for the arrest of a restrained person when the peace officer has information amounting to probable cause that [the order has been violated] . . .

Colo. Rev. Stat. §18-6-803.5(3) (2005).

Speaking for the majority, Justice Scalia reasoned that these statutory provisions have not "truly made enforcement of restraining orders mandatory. A well-established tradition of police discretion has coexisted with apparently mandatory arrest statutes." *Castle Rock*, 125 S. Ct. at 2805-2806. Even if it were otherwise, and the respondent was entitled to enforcement, the majority concluded that such an entitlement would not constitute a property interest protected by the Due Process Clause. Id. at 2810. Justice Souter, joined by Justice Breyer, concurred in the judgment but wrote separately to emphasize the concern that finding a property right to enforcement would in effect "federalize every mandatory state-law direction to executive officers whose performance on the job can be vitally significant to individuals affected." Id. at 2812-2813 (Souter, J., concurring). Justice Stevens, joined by Justice Ginsburg, dissented. As he read the statute, in light of its legislative history, "the police were required to provide enforcement. They lacked the discretion to do nothing." Id. at 2819-2820 (Stevens, J., dissenting). This, in the dissent's view, gave the respondent a property interest in enforcement, which the state could not abridge without observing fair procedures. And, the dissent concluded, such procedures were clearly lacking under the facts alleged.

Which view do you find most convincing?

6. Domestic Violence in the Workplace. Over the past decade, the impact of domestic violence on the workplace has attracted increasing recognition. Estimates suggest that anywhere between 75 to 95 percent of those who are subject to domestic violence experience related problems at work. See Family Violence Prevention Fund, The Facts on the Workplace and Domestic Violence, available at http://endabuse.org/resources/facts/Workplace .pdf. Marie Tessier, More States Give Abuse Victims Right to Time Off, Jan. 18, 2005, available at www.womensenews.org (quoting Robin Runge, director of the ABA's Commission on Domestic Violence). Problems include assaults, stalking, harassing or threatening phone calls; destruction of work products; and lateness or absenteeism due to physical injuries, legal proceedings, and disruption of childcare and transportation arrangements. American companies are losing an estimated three to five billion dollars annually in absenteeism, lost productivity, turnover, and medical expenses. Julie Leopold, Execs Aware of Domestic Violence Costs, Feb. 3, 2003, available at www.womensenews.org; Angelo M. Moe & Mytal Bell, Abject Economics: The Effects of Battering and Violence on Women's Work and Employability, 10 Violence Against Women 29, 34 (2004); see also Jody Raphael, Battering Through the Lens of Class, 11 Am. U. J. Gender Soc. Pol'y & L. 367, 369 (2003). All too often, it is charged, employers respond by penalizing or terminating employees who are victims, which compounds their problems and reinforces economic dependence on abusers. See Tessier, supra. Workplaces that do not provide adequate security force many women to leave their jobs out of safety concerns. Moe & Bell, Abject Economics, supra, at 45-47.

When employees leave or are terminated due to violence-related issues, they have generally been considered ineligible for unemployment insurance benefits. To address the economic hardships and vulnerabilities that result, about half the states have enacted laws explicitly granting benefits in some circumstances. For example, workers may be eligible for compensation where separation from employment reflects their reasonable actions to protect themselves or their families from domestic violence. See Rep. Roybal-Allard Introduces Legislation to Assist Victims of Domestic Violence to Maintain Employment, Economic Stability, U.S. Fed. News, June 30, 2005. However, claims under these statutory schemes have been infrequent. Nat'l Employment Law Project, Unemployment Insurance for Survivors of Domestic Violence (Feb. 2001) (reporting annual state claims ranging from five to 20). The same is true for workers' compensation benefits, which are available for accidental injuries that arise out of employment. Although most workplace violence would not qualify, some state law is broad enough to cover certain forms of intentional abuse by co-workers or non-employees.

In some instances, employees may also be able to sue their employers for wrongful termination. Employees have won or settled a number of such cases. In one Oregon proceeding, the plaintiff and her abusive partner worked at the same company. After he began harassing her at work, vandalizing her car, and threatening to kill her if the employer did not fire her, the employer gave into the threat without taking any disciplinary action against the abuser. The woman sued under Title VII and Oregon's antidiscrimination statute, and the case settled. See In Brief, NOW Legal Defense and Education Fund, Winter 2000. In another Massachusetts case, a woman who was terminated for taking time off from work to enforce a civil protection order successfully settled a suit for wrongful termination. See Apessos v. Memorial Press Group, 15 Mass. L. Rptr. 322, 2002 WL 31324115 (Mass. Super. 2002) (rejecting defendant's motion to dismiss a claim for wrongful termination).

Some employees have also sued for their employers' failure to take reasonable measures in response to foreseeable violence. These cases include tort claims for negligence in security, hiring, retention, and supervision. These are difficult cases to win. In Carroll v. Shoney's, 775 So. 2d 753 (Ala. 2000), for example, the court denied relief to the estate of a murdered woman who sued her restaurant employer for negligence. The woman was a counter worker on the evening shift who had been beaten by her husband. She informed her assistant manager about the abuse and asked him to call the police if her husband came to the restaurant. When the husband arrived and made threats, the police escorted him from the premises, but released him after the restaurant did not press charges. The following day, management rejected the woman's requests to be excused from work and promised to call the police if the man showed up. He did, and shot her in the head before law enforcement officials could be alerted. The majority of the Alabama Supreme Court held that the restaurant was not liable because the murder was not foreseeable. Id. at 757. The dissent, by contrast, claimed that the standard under prior cases was not "that the particular consequences should have been anticipated, but rather that some general harm or consequence could have been anticipated." Id. Such a harm was "expectable" as the dissent viewed the facts, and the defendant had amplified the risks by placing the woman at the front counter. Id. at 758.

Strategies to address workplace violence are proceeding on several fronts. The Corporate Alliance to End Partner Violence brings together companies across the country to collaborate on ways to increase awareness among employers and to support policy initiatives. See Laila Karamally, Companies Try to Bring Domestic Violence Issues into the Open, 83 Workforce Mgmt. 60 (Sept. 2004). These initiatives include laws that ban discrimination based on domestic violence and provide unpaid leave for employees to deal with violence-related concerns. A small, but growing number of states and localities have such legislation. Leopold, supra. Congress has also considered federal legislation such as the Victims' Economic Security and Safety Act, proposed in the 107th, 108th, and 109th Congresses, which would prohibit discrimination based on domestic violence, guarantee eligible employees up to 30 days of leave to address domestic violence issues, and ensure unemployment compensation for those separated from employment due to domestic violence. These provisions were included in a 2005 proposed bill reauthorizing the Violence Against Women Act, see H.R. 2876, 109th Cong. (2005); S. 1197, 109th Cong. (2005), and the website of the National Taskforce to End Sexual & Domestic Violence Against Women, http://www.vawa2005.org (providing up-to-date news and information on the current VAWA legislation); however, they were not contained in the final reauthorization. See Pub. L. No 109-162 (Jan. 5, 2006).

What strategies do you believe are most essential to deal with workplace violence? What stands in the way?

7. Domestic Violence and Housing Discrimination. A related issue involves housing discrimination based on domestic violence, which has only recently gained attention. A typical case involved Tiffani Alvera, who obtained a temporary restraining order against her husband after a brutal beating. She presented a copy of the order to the manager of her apartment complex, a federally subsidized cluster of residences for low-income tenants. Instead of sympathy, she received a notice of eviction. The management company for the complex maintained a policy of "zero tolerance for violence" that required eviction of any household with a member who posed a risk to the safety and well being of other tenants. Alvera filed a complaint with the federal Department of Housing and Urban Development (HUD), which then brought a sex discrimination suit on her behalf under state and federal fair housing law. Because women constituted the majority of victims subject to eviction for domestic violence, the complaint alleged that "no-violence" policies had a disparate impact. The case ultimately settled under a consent decree requiring the management company to cease evicting or otherwise discriminating against victims of domestic violence and to provide training to its employees concerning the policy. United States ex rel. Tiffani Alvera v. C.B.M. Group, Inc. No. 01-857-PA (D. Or. June 8, 2001), discussed in Tamar Lewin, Zero Tolerance Policy is Challenged, N.Y. Times, July 11, 2001, at A10; see also Lenora M. Lapidus, Doubly Victimized: Housing Discrimination Against Victims of Domestic Violence, 11 Am. U. J. Gender Soc. Pol'y & L. 377, 378-382 (2003). A 2005 Vermont case reached a similar result. See Bouley v. Young-Sabourin, discussed in Vivian Berger, Don't Evict Victims, Nat'l L.J. June 6, 2005, at B3.

Battered women face other forms of housing discrimination in addition to evictions. For example, landlords often conduct criminal record checks of potential renters, and exclude both complainants and victims charged with domestic violence under mandatory arrest policies. See Lapidus, supra, at 384-385; Susan A. Reif & Lisa Krisher, Subsidized Housing and the Unique Needs of Domestic Violence Victims, 34 Clearinghouse Rev. 20, 28 (2000). In some instances, only the batterer's name appears on the lease agreement, which causes landlords to assert that it cannot evict the abuser and allow the victim to continue occupancy. Id. at 27. Public housing authorities often lack procedures allowing battered women to transfer to another residence to escape a batterer. Id. at 31; Lapidus, supra, at 385-386. For an overview of problems and strategies, see Nat'l Housing Law Project, Responding to Congressional Directive to Protect Victims of Domestic Violence, 33 Housing L. Bull. 43 (2002).

8. Domestic Violence and Child Custody. Battered women often have young children, and they often provide additional ways for men to exercise domination and abuse. A battered mother is all the more reluctant to leave her batterer if by doing so she jeopardizes the economic support of her children. Moreover, custody and visitation law was not developed with intimate violence in mind: a battered mother's psychological profile or her reluctance to cooperate with the batterer may work against her in her efforts to secure permanent custody of the children, and she may even be blamed for her failure to protect them from abuse. Visitation rights and joint custody arrangements may also give batterers the ability to continue their abuse. Finally, battered mothers who escape a relationship and leave children behind may jeopardize their safety and their own future ability to regain custody.

In principle, if not always in practice, custody and visitation law has recognized the problem of domestic violence. At least 17 states have a rebuttable presumption of some form against awarding custody to a parent who has perpetrated domestic violence. Nancy K.D. Lemon, Statutes Creating Rebuttable Presumptions Against Custody to Batterers: How Effective Are They?, 28 Wm. Mitchell L. Rev. 601 (2001), and many other states direct the court to take domestic violence into account in making custody and visitation decisions. For a set of strict rules proposed by the American Law Institute relating to domestic violence and child custody, as well as citations to many of the relevant statutes, see American Law Institute, Principles of the Law of Family Dissolution: Analysis and Recommendations, §2.11, and Comment c to §2.11, at 255-256, 261-267 (2002). On the issue of supervised visitation, see Maureen Sheeran & Scott Hampton, Supervised Visitation in Cases of Domestic Violence, 50 Juv. & Fam. Ct. J. 13 (1999), reprinted in Lemon, Domestic Violence Law, supra, at 353-356. Critics say that, in spite of statutes protective of the victims of domestic violence in custody cases, many judges and experts who make custody evaluations fail to accord significant weight to evidence of domestic violence. Stephen E. Doyne et al., Custody Disputes Involving Domestic Violence: Making Children's Needs a Priority, 50 Juv. & Fam. Ct. J. 1 (1999). One survey of battered women and domestic violence advocates found that most believed that courts as well as family services officers had ignored or minimized their claims of abuse; women who alleged violence were frequently treated as "unreasonable" or "hysterical." Wellesley Ctrs. for Women, Battered Mothers Speak Out: A Human Rights Report on Domestic Violence and Child Custody in the Massachusetts Family Courts (2002) available at http://www.wcwonline. org/wrn/batteredreport.html. On issues related to judges' lack of knowledge about the effects of domestic violence on families, as well as their resistance to applying the law, see Lundy Bancroft & Jay G. Silverman, The Batterer as Parent: Addressing the Impact of Domestic Violence on Family Dynamics 115-128 (2002); Joan S. Meier, Domestic Violence, Child Custody, and Child Protection: Understanding Judicial Resistance and Imagining the Solutions, 11 Am. U. J. Gender Soc. Pol'y & L. 657, 673-674 & n.50 (2003) (citing cases discounting spousal assaults as unlikely to recur, inadequately corroborated by independent evidence, or provoked by the wife's conduct; merely "occasional incidents").

The existence of "friendly parent" provisions, discussed in Chapter 2, pp. 361-362, can further complicate the matter. One survey found that over three-quarters of custody evaluators recommended denying sole or joint custody to a parent who "alienates the child from the other parent by negatively interpreting the other parent's behavior." Lemon, supra, at 346. Joan Zorza reports that because of evaluators' negative reactions to women who raise the issue of abuse, "[b]atterers who physically or sexually abuse their children are more likely to win full or joint custody than abusive fathers who have never physically or sexually abused a child." Zorza, Protecting the Children, in Lemon, Domestic Violence Law, supra, at 335. Another difficult issue in battering relationships is allocating culpability when the children themselves are abused. If children are present when police arrive at the home of a domestic violence incident, in some jurisdictions "the officers, as mandated reporters of child maltreatment, will routinely report not only the perpetrator, but also the victim to the child protection agency," who may then "charge a victim with 'failure to protect' her children by permitting domestic violence to occur while they are living in the home." Sack, supra, at 1684. See also The "Failure to Protect" Working Group, Charging Battered Mothers with "Failure to Protect": Still Blaming the Victim, 27 Fordham Urb. L.J. 849, 849-857 (2000); Effective Intervention in Domestic

Violence Cases: Rethinking the Roles of Prosecutors, Judges, and the Court System, 11 Yale J.L. & Feminism 3, 34-38 (1999); Bryan A. Liang & Wendy L. Macfarlane, Murder by Omission; Child Abuse and the Passive Parent, 36 Harv. J. on Legis. 397, 409-410 (1999); Shelby A.D. Moore, Understanding the Connection Between Domestic Violence, Crime, and Poverty: How Welfare Reform May Keep Battered Women From Leaving Abusive Relationships, 12 Tex. J. Women & L. 451, 457-459 (2003); Lesley E. Daigle, Empowering Women to Protect: Improving Intervention with Victims of Domestic Violence in Cases of Child Abuse and Neglect; A Study of Travis County, Texas, 7 Tex. J. Women & L. 287, 313 (1998) (exploring programmatic initiatives to protect children in dangerous situations); G. Kristian Miccio, A Reasonable Battered Mother? Redefining, Reconstructing, and Recreating the Battered Mother in Child Protective Proceedings, 22 Harv. Women's L.J. 89 (1999) (arguing for a "reasonable battered mother test").

A tragic case raising the issue whether fathers are held to the same standard as mothers concerning child neglect concerns Andrea Yates, a woman with a history of serious mental health difficulties and suicidal tendencies, who drowned her five children in a bathtub. Shortly before the killings, her husband recognized that she was no longer taking medication, and was exhibiting signs of serious dysfunction. He contacted a mental health facility to request her admission and asked his mother to stay at the family home to minimize his wife's time alone with the children. He did not, however, take other measures to prevent abuse. After the killings, prosecutors concluded that there was insufficient evidence to press charges against the husband. Moore, supra, at 484; Nation in Brief, Wash. Post, June 15, 2002, at A24. Shelby Moore disagrees, and argues that the case reflects the double standards underpinning the abuse and neglect system, faulting abused mothers for failure to intervene when they have fewer and more dangerous options than fathers in cases like *Yates*. Moore, supra, at 485. As Moore and other scholars note, men also are not held liable for neglecting children whom they abandon to the care of the mother. The *Yates* case is discussed further in Chapter 4, pp. 745-746.

Should the law require less or more of both parents? Should there be an affirmative defense to abuse and neglect statutes for domestic violence victims who reasonably believe that intervention would not be effective in preventing injury to a child. See Tex. Penal Code Ann. § 22.04(k)(2) (Vernon 2005), discussed in Moore, supra, at 260 n.39.

Deborah Epstein suggests:

> [C]hildren's rights advocates, in their fight to protect young children from injury and death, too often fail to consider the dynamics of spousal abuse. However, domestic violence activists, desperate to bring the problem of woman abuse into public awareness and engender concern, have felt compelled to insist that all battered women are completely innocent victims. They have resisted recognizing that some victims belong to families where each member relates to one another through violence and threats of violence.

Epstein, Effective Intervention, supra, at 36-37. For a thoughtful exploration of the difficulty of avoiding either demonizing or sentimentalizing mothers of abused children, see Dorothy E. Roberts, Mothers Who Fail to Protect Their Children: Accounting for Private and Public Responsibility, in Mother Troubles: Rethinking Contemporary Maternal Dilemmas 31 (Julia E. Hanigsberg & Sara Ruddick eds., 1999). For a landmark decision finding that that child welfare authorities had violated mothers' constitutional rights by removing children without sufficiently investigating what they could have done or could do to protect children from abusive partners, see Nicholson v. Scoppetta, 203 F. Supp. 2d 153 (E.D.N.Y. 2002), vacated in part and remanded on other grounds, 116 Fed. Appx. 313 (2d Cir. 2004).

Finally, how should the law respond when a battered woman flees with the children—or when an abuser does? See Janet M. Bowermaster, Relocation Custody Disputes Involving Domestic Violence, 46 U. Kan. L. Rev. 433 (1998). The Uniform Child Custody Jurisdiction and Enforcement Act (UCCJEA) seeks to protect victims and to promote coordination and cooperation among courts in various jurisdictions. For an explanation of the UCCJEA, and the problems, see Billie Lee Dunford-Jackson, The Uniform Child Custody Jurisdiction and Enforcement Act: Affording Enhanced Protection for Victims of Domestic Violence and Their Children, 50 Juv. & Fam. Ct. J. 55 (1999), reprinted in Lemon, Domestic Violence Law, supra, at 366. Other relevant statutes are the Parental Kidnapping Prevention Act (PKPA), 28 U.S.C. § 1738A (2005), and the full faith and credit requirements of the Violence Against Women Act (VAWA), 18 U.S.C. § 2265 (2005). When parent abductors flee the United States altogether, the Hague Child Abduction Convention mandates the return of children to their place of "habitual residence" for a custody determination. The drafters of the Convention created an exception for cases where there is a grave risk of danger to the child if he or she is returned. For the claim that American courts have not interpreted this exception to include victims of domestic violence, see Regan Fordice Grilli, Domestic Violence: Is It Being Sanctioned by the Hague Convention?, 4 Sw. J.L. & Trade Am. 71 (1997), reprinted in Lemon, Domestic Violence Law, supra, at 372.

Under the Hague Convention, a state is not required to return a child if "there is a grave risk that his or her return would expose the child to physical or psychological harm or otherwise place the child in an intolerable situation." Hague Convention of October 25, 1980 on the Civil Aspects of International Child Abduction, Article 13(b). In other circumstances, courts are using judicial remedies known as "undertakings" to return mothers and their children back to the country of origin for local courts to arrange custody. See Roxanne Hoegger, What If She Leaves? Domestic Violence Cases Under the Hague Convention and the Insufficiency of the Undertakings Remedy, 18 Berkeley Women's L.J. 181 (2003) (suggesting that what is needed is "an explicit domestic violence defense to claims of child abduction.")

9. Alternative Dispute Resolution for Domestic Violence Cases: Mediation, Domestic Violence Courts, and "Peacemaking." About one-quarter of states mandate mediation for custody and visitation issues. See American Law Institute, Principles, supra, § 2.07, Comment b, at 171 (listing many statutes). Somewhat fewer than half the states explicitly allow the court to use its discretion in whether to mandate mediation, and a few states have voluntary mediation systems, sometimes in combination with involuntary components. Id. (citing statutes). In most jurisdictions, mediation is prohibited when domestic violence has occurred, unless the victim requests it. Id. California alone does not provide a complete exemption, but rather permits the mediator to meet separately with the parties where there has been a history of domestic violence. See Cal. Fam. Code § 3181 (West 2005); Kerry Loomis, Domestic Violence and Mediation: A Tragic Combination for Victims in California Family Court, 35 Cal. W. L. Rev. 355 (1999).

Whether mediation is appropriate in cases involving domestic violence has been a matter of dispute. Advocates of mediation argue that it "can provide a supportive, empowering environment for women who in many cases have been stripped of their identity, dignity, and self-esteem." Holly Joyce, Mediation and Domestic Violence: Legislative Responses, 14 J. Am. Acad. Matrimonial Law. 447, 458 (1997). Mediation is less adversarial than the judicial system; it also encourages the parties to take responsibility for structuring solutions rather than depending on lawyers. Mediation procedures can be structured to minimize contact between the spouses, and a trained mediator can sometimes help "break the cycle of abuse" by forcing focus on underlying problems. As advocates freely acknowledge, mediation is not appropriate for all situations, particularly those involving continuing coercion and large imbalances in power. But, proponents emphasize, not all domestic violence cases are alike and it may be suitable for many. Id. at 456-458.

By contrast, battered women's advocates often reject mediation as an acceptable approach to disputes involving domestic violence. As Donna Coker describes some of the objections:

> In family court mediation, the ideal mediator is supposed to be neutral, with the sole purpose of effectuating the desires of the parties. As Trina Grillo writes, this ideal of neutrality frequently masks mediation's informal rules of behavior: Focus on the future and not the past, do not be too emotional, and especially do not be too angry. Sara Cobb similarly notes the manner in which mediation "domesticates" stories of violence by moving the focus from the victim's rights to the victim's needs. In part, this is a result of a mediation methodology that eschews factfinding and blame. For battered women, this creates the risk that mediation will reinforce the batterer's belief in the rightness of his behavior, minimize the harm of his violence and control, and undermine the victim's belief in her right not to be beaten. The insistence on a purportedly neutral mediator fails to identify the immorality of the batterer's (past, present, ongoing) behavior and limits the support a mediator can give a battered woman.

Donna Coker, Enhancing Autonomy for Battered Women: Lessons from Navajo Peacemaking, 47 UCLA L. Rev. 1, 88-89 (1999). In recognition of such problems, the statute authorizing funding under VAWA specifically prohibits "mediation or counseling involving offenders and victims physically together, in cases where sexual assault, domestic violence, dating violence, or child sexual abuse is an issue." See 42 U.S.C. § 3796gg-6(d)(4) (2000); Dep't of Justice, Legal Assistance for Victims Grant Recipients Policy Guidebook 5 (2002), available at http://www.ojp.usdoj.gov/vawo/docs/lavgbook02.pdf.

Is it odd, given the criticisms that some feminists have levied against the formal legal system as a tool of male dominance, that most battered women's advocates nevertheless prefer formal, legalized mechanisms over less formal, non-adversarial alternatives? Is such a categorical preference warranted or should each case be considered in light of its own circumstances and victims' preferences? Consider this question again in light of the materials in Chapter 4.

The process of ending an abusive relationship, particularly when marriage and/or children are involved, can be prolonged and complicated. Multiple legal proceedings in both criminal and civil courts may be necessary. Domestic violence victims generally have multiple needs, such as those involving safety, medical care, housing, counseling, custody, childcare, financial assistance, employment, education, job training, immigration, and relocation resources. To address these cross-cutting concerns, experts generally support the creation of unified, specialized domestic violence courts and holistic legal and social services. Deborah Epstein explains:

> Integrated domestic violence courts typically aim to achieve at least three fundamental goals. First, they try to provide victims with a "one-stop shopping" intake center that provides comprehensive assistance with the full range of intimate violence litigation and related social services. Second, they try to coordinate civil protection order, family law, and criminal dockets so that the court can handle cases, to the greatest extent possible, on a "one family, one judge" basis. Finally, they ensure that the court itself is located in a place that provides victims with security and protection from physical assault.

Deborah Epstein, Effective Intervention in Domestic Violence Cases: Rethinking the Roles of Prosecutors, Judges, and the Court System, 11 Yale J.L. & Feminism 3, 28 (1999). In unified court systems, one judge and resource coordinator work on solving all of the legal issues arising from the violence, and enlisting the support of relevant social service agencies. Assigning a single, expert judge who has responsibility for actively monitoring the case, some say, is the most effective strategy for reducing recidivism and ensuring a just resolution that will meet victims' needs. See id.; Center for Court Innovation, What Makes a Domestic Violence Court Work 4-6 (2002); Epstein et al., supra, at 491-495; Juliette Terzieff, New York Courts Untangle Domestic Violence, June 6, 2005, available at www.womensenews.org.

The premise of holistic domestic violence services is similar. Rather than shuttling between multiple service providers, including non-profit and government agencies, the concept is that victims should have access to "one stop" multidisciplinary organizations. See Deborah L. Rhode, Access to Justice 107, 120 (2004); Stacy L. Brustin, Legal Services Provision Through Multidisciplinary Practice-Encouraging Holistic Advocacy While Protecting Ethical Interests, 73 U. Colo. L. Rev. 787, 788 (2002).

Donna Coker argues that the Navajo practice of Peacemaking also may hold useful lessons for dispute resolution in cases of domestic violence. Under this process,

> parties meet with a peacemaker and others who have either a special relationship to the parties (e.g., family and friends) or relevant expertise (e.g., alcohol treatment

counselors and hospital social workers). Each participant is given a chance to describe the problem that the petitioner has identified as the reason for the session. The peacemaker then leads the group in developing recommendations and agreements designed to ameliorate or solve the problem.

Coker, Enhancing Autonomy, supra, at 34-35. In the Navajo legal system, criminal cases may be referred to Peacemaking under judicial diversion programs or as a condition of probation. Civil courts also have the authority to refer cases to Peacemaking, and litigants may initiate such proceedings themselves. Id. at 37. Do you agree with Coker that Peacemaking may be useful in some intimate partner abuse cases?

3. Domestic Violence and Substantive Criminal Law

People v. Berry
556 P.2d 777 (Cal. 1976)

SULLIVAN, Justice.

Defendant Albert Joseph Berry was charged by indictment with one count of murder and one count of assault by means of force likely to produce great bodily injury. . . . The assault was allegedly committed on July 23, 1974, and the murder on July 26, 1974. In each count, the alleged victim was defendant's wife, Rachel Pessah Berry. A jury found defendant guilty as charged and determined that the murder was of the first degree. Defendant was sentenced to state prison for the term prescribed by law. He appeals from the judgment of conviction.

Defendant contends that there is sufficient evidence in the record to show that he committed the homicide while in a state of uncontrollable rage caused by provocation and flowing from a condition of diminished capacity and therefore that it was error for the trial court to fail to instruct the injury on voluntary manslaughter as indeed he had requested. . . .

Defendant, a cook, 46 years old, and Rachel Pessah, a 20-year-old girl from Israel, were married on May 27, 1974. Three days later Rachel went to Israel by herself, returning on July 13, 1974. On July 23, 1974, defendant choked Rachel into unconsciousness. She was treated at a hospital where she reported her strangulation by defendant to an officer of the San Francisco Police Department. On July 25, Inspector Sammon, who had been assigned to the case, met with Rachel and as a result of the interview a warrant was issued for defendant's arrest.

While Rachel was at the hospital, defendant removed his clothes from their apartment and stored them in a Greyhound Bus Depot locker. He stayed overnight at the home of a friend, Mrs. Jean Berk, admitting to her that he had choked his wife. On July 26, he telephoned Mrs. Berk and informed her that he had killed Rachel with a telephone cord on that morning at their apartment. . . .

At trial defendant did not deny strangling his wife, but claimed through his own testimony and the testimony of a psychiatrist, Dr. Martin Blinder, that he was provoked into killing her because of a sudden and uncontrollable rage so as to reduce the offense to one of voluntary manslaughter. He testified that upon her return from Israel, Rachel announced to him that while there she had fallen in love with another man, one Yako, and had enjoyed his sexual favors, that he was coming to this country to claim her and that she wished a divorce. Thus commenced a tormenting two weeks in which Rachel alternately taunted defendant with her involvement with Yako and at the same time sexually excited defendant, indicating her desire to remain with him. Defendant's detailed testimony, summarized below, chronicles this strange course of events.

After their marriage, Rachel lived with defendant for only three days and then left for Israel. Immediately upon her return to San Francisco she told defendant about her relationship with and love for Yako. This brought about further argument and a brawl that evening in which defendant choked Rachel and she responded by scratching him deeply many times. Nonetheless they continued to live together. Rachel kept taunting defendant with Yako and demanding a divorce. She claimed she thought she might be pregnant by Yako. She showed defendant pictures of herself with Yako. Nevertheless, during a return trip from Santa Rosa, Rachel demanded immediate sexual intercourse with defendant in the car, which was achieved; however upon reaching their apartment, she again stated that she loved Yako and that she would not have intercourse with defendant in the future.

On the evening of July 22d defendant and Rachel went to a movie where they engaged in heavy petting. When they returned home and got into bed, Rachel announced that she had intended to make love with defendant, "But I am saving myself for this man Yako, so I don't think I will." Defendant got out of bed and prepared to leave the apartment, whereupon Rachel screamed and yelled at him. Defendant choked her into unconsciousness.

Two hours later defendant called a taxi for his wife to take her to the hospital. He put his clothes in the Greyhound bus station and went to the home of his friend Mrs. Berk for the night. The next day he went to Reno and returned the day after. Rachel informed him by telephone that there was a warrant for his arrest as a result of her report to the police about the choking incident. On July 25th defendant returned to the apartment to talk to Rachel, but she was out. He slept there overnight. Rachel returned around 11 a.m. the next day. Upon seeing defendant there, she said, "I suppose you have come here to kill me." Defendant responded, "yes," changed his response to "no," and then again to "yes," and finally stated "I have really come to talk to you." Rachel began screaming. Defendant grabbed her by the shoulder and tried to stop her screaming. She continued. They struggled and finally defendant strangled her with a telephone cord.

Dr. Martin Blinder, a physician and psychiatrist, called by the defense, testified that Rachel was a depressed, suicidally inclined girl and that this suicidal impulse led her to involve herself ever more deeply in a dangerous situation with defendant. She did this by sexually arousing him and taunting him into jealous rages in an unconscious desire to provoke him into killing her and thus consummating her desire for suicide. Throughout the period commencing with her return from Israel until her death, that is from July 13 to July 26, Rachel continually provoked defendant with sexual taunts and incitements, alternating acceptance and rejection of him. This conduct was accompanied by repeated references to her involvement with another man; it led defendant to choke her on two occasions, until finally she achieved her unconscious desire and was strangled. Dr. Blinder testified that as a result of this cumulative series of provocations, defendant at the time he fatally strangled Rachel, was in a state of uncontrollable rage, completely under the sway of passion.

We first take up defendant's claim that on the basis of the foregoing evidence he was entitled to an instruction on voluntary manslaughter as defined by statute which is "the unlawful killing of a human being, without malice . . . upon a sudden quarrel or heat of passion. " [In an earlier case the court approved the following quotation of the law:] "[T]he fundamental of the inquiry is whether or not the defendant's reason was, at the time of his act, so disturbed or obscured by some passion — not necessarily fear and never, of course, the passion for revenge — to such an extent as would render ordinary men of average disposition liable to act rashly or without due deliberation and reflection, and from this passion rather than judgment."

We further held . . . that there is no specific type of provocation required by section 192 and that verbal provocation may be sufficient. [In a previous case] in the course of explaining the phrase "heat of passion" used in the statute defining manslaughter we pointed out that " 'passion' need not mean 'rage' or 'anger' " but may be any "[v]iolent, intense, high-wrought or enthusiastic emotion" and concluded there 'that defendant was aroused to a heat of 'passion' by a series of events over a considerable period of time. . . ." Accordingly we there declared that evidence of admissions of infidelity by the defendant's paramour, taunts directed to him and other conduct, "supports a finding that defendant killed in wild desperation induced by [the woman's] long continued provocatory conduct." We find this reasoning persuasive in the case now before us. Defendant's testimony chronicles a two-week period of provocatory conduct by his wife Rachel that could arouse a passion of jealousy, pain and sexual rage in an ordinary man of average disposition such as to cause him to act rashly from this passion. It is significant that both defendant and Dr. Blinder testified that the former was in the heat of passion under an uncontrollable rage when he killed Rachel.

The Attorney General contends that the killing could not have been done in the heat of passion because there was a cooling period, defendant having waited in the apartment for 20 hours. However, the long course of provocatory conduct, which had resulted in intermittent outbreaks of rage under specific provocation in the past, reached its final culmination in the apartment when Rachel began screaming. . . .

. . . There was no clear direction to the jury to consider the evidence of Rachel's course of provocatory conduct so as to determine whether defendant, as an ordinary man of average disposition, having been exposed to such conduct, was provoked into committing the homicide under a heat of passion. Therefore we conclude that the jury's determination that defendant was guilty of murder of the first degree under the instructions given did not necessarily indicate that "the factual question posed by the omitted instruction was necessarily resolved adversely to the defendant under other, properly given instructions" — in other words that the jury had found that defendant had not killed Rachel under a heat of passion. Since this theory of provocation constituted defendant's entire defense to the first count, we have no difficulty concluding that the failure to give such instruction was prejudicial error and requires us to reverse the conviction of murder of the first degree.

Donna K. Coker, *Heat of Passion and Wife Killing: Men Who Batter/Men Who Kill*
2 S. Cal. Rev. L. & Women's Stud. 71, 93-94, 116, 117-120, 123, 128 (1992)

[H]omicide law divides sane individuals who intentionally kill into two major categories: those who premeditate murder and those who act in the heat of passion. Social stereotypes of wife-killing that characterize the killer as a previously non-violent man who "snapped" under pressure, roughly parallel the understandings which underlie heat-of-passion doctrine. However, this social stereotype is grossly inaccurate when applied to men who are identified as "batterers" and when applied to the general category of husband-wife killings. Violence perpetrated by abusive men is purposeful, not spontaneous; the majority of men who kill their wives have a documented history of violent assaults. Furthermore, one would expect to find empirical evidence of wife-killers who fit the stereotype of the heat-of-passion killer in those reports of forensic psychiatrists whose job it is to aid defense counsel, yet these reports seem to confirm that men who kill and men who batter have remarkably similar personality traits and similar motivations. While further research is needed before we can determine whether or not the "impassioned" wife-killer exists, if he does exist, he is apparently part of a very small group of wife-killers. . . .

. . . The case of People v. Berry appears in many criminal law textbooks as well as legal treatises, generally for the proposition that the question of "cooling off" is a jury question. . . .

[Coker reviews the facts of the case and Dr. Blinder's testimony.]

The defense needed Blinder's testimony for two different, but equally critical, reasons. First, the fact that Berry had a prior conviction for stabbing and injuring his second wife had already been ruled admissible. Blinder's testimony was required to neutralize this damaging fact, but, in fact, Blinder went one step better by explaining that Berry's past violence resulted from his repeated emotional victimization at the hands of women. Second, Blinder's testimony was needed most obviously in order to cast the killing as a heat of passion killing and, in particular, to explain the 20-hour wait in Rachel's apartment as a result of cumulative passion and not premeditation and lying-in-wait. The result was psychiatric testimony that brilliantly — if tautologically — turned facts about Berry that suggested the antithesis of a "heat of passion killer" — i.e., a proclivity for violence, a history of serious prior assaults on the victim identical in kind to the fatal assault, Berry's stabbing of his ex-wife under remarkably similar circumstances, and a psychological profile fitting that of an abuser — into evidence of Berry's increasing provocation as the result of Rachel's relentless "taunting." . . .

In essence, Berry's defense was that he was the sort of man who abused women — but the twist was Blinder's psychiatric explanation that Berry's violence was a result of his choosing women who enraged him and provoked him to violence. The fact that Berry had a prior conviction for assaulting his ex-wife with a butcher knife, that in past relationships with other women he had destroyed their property, forcing former girlfriends to "put him out of the house, locking the door," indicated to Blinder the personality of the women with whom Berry involved himself, more than it demonstrated Berry's dangerous and abusive nature. Blinder testified that these women "offer[ed] him the promise of comfort but ultimately deliver[ed] emotional pain." Yet Blinder's testimony provides a classic portrait of an abuser. Berry was most dangerous when women threatened to leave him. Berry was "emotionally dependent" on wives and girlfriends; he threatened physical violence in order to control women; he destroyed women's property; and he had a history of violent relationships with wives and lovers. The Supreme Court's opinion read Dr. Blinder's testimony to focus narrowly on the effect of Rachel's "provocative" behavior on Berry's mental state. Dr. Blinder's testimony, however, refers to a cumulative rage resulting from the provocation of all the women in Berry's entire life:

> Q: ... How would you characterize [Berry's] state of mind ... [at the time of the homicide]?
>
> A: ... I would say that he was in a state of uncontrollable rage which was a product of having to contend with what seems to me an incredibly provacative [sic] situation, an incredibly provacative [sic] young woman, and that this immediate situation was superimposed upon Mr. Berry having encountered the situation time and time again. So that we have a cumulative effect dating back to the way his mother dealt with him. . . .
>
> Q: ... [Y]ou say that the situation involving Rachel Berry and Albert Berry ... was the product of ... cumulative ... provocations. Now, specifically, what would you base your opinion as to provocations on? . . .
>
> A: ... We have two factors here. . . . The past history, that is, the history of this man well in advance of his meeting the deceased. And then the history of his relationship with her. And I think the two go together. . . . After 15 years [of marriage to his second wife] and five children, his wife leaves him for ... another another man. . . . They continued to live together, during which time his wife taunted him about her boyfriend. . . .
>
> One night while they were having sex, his wife [called him by the name of her boyfriend]. Despondent and enraged at the same time, he went into the kitchen, obtained a knife, and stabbed his wife in the abdomen. And she was not serious [sic]. He only got to spend a year in jail for that. . . .
>
> So we have this pattern of enormous dependency on these women and then rupture of the relationship with tremendous rage, almost uncontrollable. I think in one instance he put his foot through the stereo ... he had purchased for one of these girls [sic]. . . .
>
> So we see a succession of women, beginning with his mother, who offer the promise of comfort but ultimately deliver indifference and emotional pain.

The irony of this defense testimony is found in its confirmation that Berry had a propensity to assault wives and lovers under circumstances in which he claimed the woman's infidelity provoked him. Rachel, then, became the recipient of Berry's cumulative rage against all the past women in his life. In a tautological way, Berry's past abuse of other women was used to strengthen his claim of

Rachel's provocative nature: Berry had a pattern of involvement with emotionally abusive women; his violence was in response to their "abuse" — never the other way around. Rachel was involved with Berry; therefore, it is more than likely that Rachel emotionally abused Berry and that his violence was the result of provocation occasioned by her abuse....

...The California Supreme Court opinion repeatedly echoes the tenor of Blinder's words — using terms such as "the result" or "culmination" — terms that diffuse responsibility and make Berry's violence seem inevitable and uncontrollable....

Though Blinder's testimony focused on Rachel's "provocative" sexual behavior, the truth is that Berry didn't kill Rachel until it appeared that she might make good on her threat to leave him.... Blinder's testimony completely ignores this fact. Not surprisingly, perhaps, Blinder's testimony is completely from Berry's perspective: the relationship dynamics continue, even though Rachel has rejected attempts at reconciliation and has filed a police report. Of course, a defense witness tells it from the perspective of the accused, but in this circumstance, the defendant's perspective is largely that of the Court and that of the Law, as well. That perspective, as identified in this article, suggests that a woman's "abandonment" of a husband is provocative — and that a woman's preference of another lover is provocation of the worst sort.

State v. Norman
378 S.E.2d 8 (N.C. 1989)

[The facts of the case are given on p. 466, above.]

Two expert witnesses in forensic psychology and psychiatry who examined the defendant after the shooting, Dr. William Tyson and Dr. Robert Rollins, testified that the defendant fit the profile of battered wife syndrome. This condition, they testified, is characterized by such abuse and degradation that the battered wife comes to believe she is unable to help herself and cannot expect help from anyone else. She believes that she cannot escape the complete control of her husband and that he is invulnerable to law enforcement and other sources of help.

Dr. Tyson, a psychologist, was asked his opinion as to whether, on 12 June 1985, "it appeared reasonably necessary for Judy Norman to shoot J.T. Norman?" He replied: "I believe that...Mrs. Norman believed herself to be doomed...to a life of the worst kind of torture and abuse, degradation that she had experienced over the years in a progressive way; that it would only get worse, and that death was inevitable...." Dr. Tyson later added: "I think Judy Norman felt that she had no choice, both in the protection of herself and her family, but to engage, exhibit deadly force against Mr. Norman, and that in so doing, she was sacrificing herself, both for herself and for her family."

Dr. Rollins, who was the defendant's attending physician at Dorothea Dix Hospital when she was sent there for evaluation, testified that in his opinion the defendant was a typical abused spouse and that "[s]he saw herself as powerless to deal with the situation, that there was no alternative, no way she could escape it."

Dr. Rollins was asked his opinion as to whether "on June 12th, 1985, it appeared reasonably necessary that Judy Norman would take the life of J.T. Norman?" Dr. Rollins replied that in his opinion, "that course of action did appear necessary to Mrs. Norman."

Based on the evidence that the defendant exhibited battered wife syndrome, that she believed she could not escape her husband nor expect help from others, that her husband had threatened her, and that her husband's abuse of her had worsened in the two days preceding his death, the Court of Appeals concluded that a jury reasonably could have found that her killing of her husband was justified as an act of perfect self-defense. The Court of Appeals reasoned that the nature of battered wife syndrome is such that a jury could not be precluded from finding the defendant killed her husband lawfully in perfect self-defense, even though he was asleep when she killed him. We disagree.

The right to kill in self-defense is based on the necessity, real or reasonably apparent, of killing an unlawful aggressor to save oneself from *imminent* death or great bodily harm at his hands. . . . Our law has recognized that self-preservation under such circumstances springs from a primal impulse and is an inherent right of natural law. . . .

The killing of another human being is the most extreme recourse to our inherent right of self-preservation and can be justified in law only by the utmost real or apparent necessity brought about by the decedent. For that reason, our law of self-defense has required that a defendant claiming that a homicide was justified and, as a result, inherently lawful by reason of perfect self-defense must establish that she reasonably believed at the time of the killing she otherwise would have immediately suffered death or great bodily harm. Only if defendants are required to show that they killed due to a reasonable belief that death or great bodily harm was imminent can the justification for homicide remain clearly and firmly rooted in necessity. The imminence requirement ensures that deadly force will be used only where it is necessary as a last resort in the exercise of the inherent right of self-preservation. . . .

The term "imminent," as used to describe such perceived threats of death or great bodily harm as will justify a homicide by reason of perfect self-defense, has been defined as "immediate danger, such as must be instantly met, such as cannot be guarded against by calling for the assistance of others or the protection of the law." Black's Law Dictionary 676 (5th ed. 1979). . . .

The evidence in this case did not tend to show that the defendant reasonably believed that she was confronted by a threat of imminent death or great bodily harm. The evidence tended to show that no harm was "imminent" or about to happen to the defendant when she shot her husband. The uncontroverted evidence was that her husband had been asleep for some time when she walked to her mother's house, returned with the pistol, fixed the pistol after it jammed and then shot her husband three times in the back of the head. The defendant was not faced with an instantaneous choice between killing her husband or being killed or seriously injured. Instead, *all* of the evidence tended to show that the defendant had ample time and opportunity to resort to other means of preventing further abuse by her husband. . . .

Dr. Tyson...testified that the defendant "believed herself to be doomed...to a life of the worst kind of torture and abuse, degradation that she had experienced over the years in a progressive way; that it would only get worse, and that death was inevitable." Such evidence of the defendant's speculative beliefs concerning her remote and indefinite future, while indicating she had felt generally threatened, did not tend to show that she killed in the belief — reasonable or otherwise — that her husband presented a threat of imminent death or great bodily harm....

The reasoning of our Court of Appeals in this case...proposes justifying the taking of human life not upon the reasonable belief it is necessary to prevent death or great bodily harm — which the imminence requirement ensures — but upon purely subjective speculation that the decedent probably would present a threat to life at a future time and that the defendant would not be able to avoid the predicted threat....

...The relaxed requirements for perfect self-defense proposed by our Court of Appeals would tend to categorically legalize the opportune killing of abusive husbands by their wives solely on the basis of the wives' testimony concerning their subjective speculation as to the probability of future felonious assaults by their husbands. Homicidal self-help would then become a lawful solution, and perhaps the easiest and most effective solution, to this problem....It has even been suggested that the relaxed requirements of self-defense found in what is often called the "battered woman's defense" could be extended in *principle to any type of case* in which a defendant testified that he or she subjectively believed that killing was necessary and proportionate to any perceived threat....

In conclusion, we decline to expand our law of self-defense beyond the limits of immediacy and necessity which have heretofore provided an appropriately narrow but firm basis upon which homicide may be justified....

Reversed.

MARTIN, Justice, dissenting.

At the outset it is to be noted that the peril of fabricated evidence is not unique to the trials of battered wives who kill. The possibility of invented evidence arises in all cases in which a party is seeking the benefit of self-defense. Moreover, in this case there were a number of witnesses other than defendant who testified as to the actual presence of circumstances supporting a claim of self-defense. This record contains no reasonable basis to attack the credibility of evidence for the defendant....

Evidence presented by defendant described a twenty-year history of beatings and other dehumanizing and degrading treatment by her husband. In his expert testimony a clinical psychologist concluded that defendant fit "and exceed[ed]" the profile of an abused or battered spouse, analogizing this treatment to the dehumanization process suffered by prisoners of war under the Nazis during the Second World War and the brainwashing techniques of the Korean War. The psychologist described the defendant as a woman incarcerated by abuse, by fear, and by her conviction that her husband was invincible and inescapable:

Mrs. Norman didn't leave because she believed, fully believed that escape was totally impossible. There was no place to go. He, she had left before; he had come and gotten her. She had gone to the Department of Social Services. He had come and gotten her. The law, she believed the law could not protect her; no one could protect her, and I must admit, looking over the records, that there was nothing done that would contradict that belief. . . .

. . . For the battered wife, if there is no escape, if there is no window of relief or momentary sense of safety, then the next attack, which could be the fatal one, is imminent. In the context of the doctrine of self-defense, "imminent" is a term the meaning of which must be grasped from the defendant's point of view. Properly stated, the second prong of the question is not whether the threat was in fact *imminent*, but whether defendant's belief in the impending nature of the threat, given the circumstances as she saw them, was reasonable in the mind of a person of ordinary firmness.

Defendant's intense fear, based on her belief that her husband intended not only to maim or deface her, as he had in the past, but to kill her, was evident in the testimony of witnesses who recounted events of the last three days of the decedent's life. This testimony could have led a juror to conclude that defendant reasonably perceived a threat to her life as "imminent," even while her husband slept. . . .

From this evidence of the exacerbated nature of the last three days of twenty years of provocation, a juror could conclude that defendant believed that her husband's threats to her life were viable, that serious bodily harm was imminent, and that it was necessary to kill her husband to escape that harm. And from this evidence a juror could find defendant's belief in the necessity to kill her husband not merely reasonable but compelling. . . .

Notes

1. "Heat of Passion" Manslaughter and the Reasonable "Man." A feature of Anglo-American law since the early English common law has been that a killing in the "sudden heat of passion" is not murder, but rather the lesser crime of voluntary manslaughter, and that "adequate provocation" by the victim may cause a reasonable man to lose his reason and act in the heat of passion. See Joshua Dressler, Understanding Criminal Law § 31.07[A], [B], at 527-528 (3d ed. 2001). Catching one's spouse in the act of adultery traditionally has been described as the quintessential example of adequate provocation. See id. § 31.07[C], at 535 (adultery is "the highest invasion of [a husband's] property"). Sexual taunting, as in People v. Berry, provides a contemporary exemplar.

The heat of passion doctrine is not the only means by which the law has affirmed male sexual jealousy. In some southern and western states in the early twentieth century, juries recognized an "unwritten law" of "honor defense" that allowed a defendant to be acquitted entirely when he killed his wife or his wife's lover out of sexual jealousy. See Laurie J. Taylor, Comment, Provoked Reason in Men and Women: Heat-of-Passion Manslaughter and Imperfect Self Defense, 33 UCLA L. Rev. 1679, 1694 (1986). Indeed, until the 1960s and 1970s, statutes in four states — Georgia, New Mexico, Texas, and Utah — made it justifiable homicide for a husband to kill his wife's lover. Id.

Some jurisdictions that have codified the common law doctrine of heat of passion have relaxed the most stringent conditions on which a voluntary manslaughter instruction is available. For example, the judge no longer decides which behaviors are or are not adequate provocation as a matter of law. Rather, the question of whether a "reasonable man" would be put into the heat of passion by the victim's behavior is a question for the jury. In addition, the traditional requirement of "cooling time" has been relaxed, as in *Berry*. Instead, courts have begun to reason that provocation and passion may build up over a long period of time.

The Model Penal Code (MPC) represents the furthest edge of this liberalizing trend. Under the MPC, a homicide that would otherwise be murder may be reduced to manslaughter if the defendant can show that he acted under the influence of "extreme mental or emotional disturbance for which there is reasonable explanation or excuse." Whether there is a reasonable explanation or excuse for the disturbance is to be judged from the point of view of "a person in the actor's situation under the circumstances as he believes them to be." MPC §210.3(1)(b). The intention of the MPC drafters was to focus on the defendant's disturbed state of mind, rather than the existence of justifying circumstances, and to eliminate the older categorical approach to finding "adequate provocation." See MPC §210(3) cmt. at 61.

Which version of the law — the older common law approach, the newer common law approach, or the MPC approach — best serves women? Victoria Nourse compiled heat of passion cases from each of these three types of jurisdictions and reported two interesting findings. First, she found that a woman's attempt to leave the relationship, or the man's belief in her infidelity, was the most common "provocation" when men killed women and sought reduction of their crime to manslaughter. Nourse also found that the behavior identified as "infidelity" varied considerably in MPC jurisdictions:

> Claims of "discovered infidelity" appear quite rarely in my MPC data set, whether the claim arises in the context of a former or a current relationship. Far more frequent are claims based on confessions or allegations of infidelity. Less frequent, but also present, are cases involving lesser breaches, such as "dancing with [an]other man," "receiv[ing] a phone call from a former boyfriend," or seeing the victim with another.

Victoria Nourse, Passion's Progress: Modern Law Reform and the Provocation Defense, 106 Yale L.J. 1331, 1363-1364 (1997).

Second, Nourse's study demonstrated that claims of infidelity in which the relationship had ended were much more likely to go to the jury in MPC states than in states following the common law:

In MPC jurisdictions, unlike traditional ones, I found three times as many infidelity cases reporting separation (thirty-seven percent) as cases of infidelity in a continuing relationship (twelve percent). Indeed, cases of "separation and infidelity" are the single largest category in reform jurisdictions. In all of these cases, the relationship was ending or was over. Consider, for example, [a case in which the] victim moved, sought to end her marriage, filed for divorce, notified the police, and obtained a restraining order. Testimony at trial suggested that the victim told the defendant that she would not return and may have "mentioned another man," or told the defendant that "he could believe what he wanted to believe about the rumors" about another man. Clearly, this case is not simply about a rival (even if we assume that there is another man, as my methodology requires). One party has sought to end the relationship, and the other refuses to accede to that choice, killing the party who seeks to leave.

Id. at 1359-1360. Nourse asks: "If intimate homicide frequently involves separated couples why does our canonical legal image still revolve around sexual infidelity?" Id. at 1345. It would appear that ending the relationship does not end some men's concerns about infidelity. In one study of separation assaults, jealousy was a major factor; male partners frequently warned women whom they later killed, "If I can't have you, nobody can." Ruth E. Fleury et al., When Ending the Relationship Does Not End the Violence, 6 Violence Against Women 1363, 1365 (2000). The result of doctrines such as "heat of passion" can be, then, a lesser sentence for wife killers. Myrna Raeder cites statistics published by the Bureau of Justice Statistics of the Department of Justice in a 1995 study finding that only a fifth of female spousal murders resulted in a conviction for first-degree murder and only 13 percent of those convicted received life imprisonment; only two percent were sentenced to death. Myrna S. Raeder, The Admissibility of Prior Acts of Domestic Violence: Simpson and Beyond, 69 S. Cal. L. Rev. 1463, 1477 (1996) (citing Patrick A. Langan & John M. Dawson, Spouse Murder Defendants in Large Urban Counties (U.S. Dep't of Justice 1995)).

Should law reform move back in the direction of the traditional common law approach, under which "words alone" are never adequate provocation and infidelity must be witnessed? See Emily L. Miller, Comment, (Wo)manslaughter: Voluntary Manslaughter, Gender, and the Model Penal Code, 50 Emory L.J. 665, 666 (2001) (arguing that "the MPC formulation of voluntary manslaughter has rendered an untenable expansion of the doctrine," one that has been "particularly disastrous for women").

For three centuries, English courts reserved the heat of passion defense to men, and early American law followed suit. Before the 1960s, many states retained laws that allowed a husband to kill his wife's lover, but made no concession for the wife who killed her husband or lover. Although the current heat of passion doctrine is gender neutral in form, women rarely assert the defense, perhaps because women are socialized to respond less aggressively than men to most provoking behavior, including infidelity. See Christine R. Harris, A Review of Sex Differences in Sexual Jealousy, Including Self-Report Data, Psychosociological Responses, Interpersonal Violence, and Morbid Jealousy, 2 Personality & Soc. Psychol. Rev. 102 (2003).

Are juries likely to react the same way to women and men who invoke the heat of passion defense? No statistical evidence is available, but some experts cite representative cases to suggest gender bias. A case in point is that of Houston dentist Clara Harris, who killed her husband after he failed to keep his promise to end his extramarital affair with his office's receptionist. Harris confronted her husband and his mistress at a hotel, and the two women became involved in a violent fight. Hotel employees separated them, and Harris, still enraged, got in her car and ran over her husband twice in the parking lot. She was convicted of murder, despite her testimony that she was "in a fog" at the time, and that it was a "blackout," period, a "crazy time." Eye witnesses reported that after she had hit her husband, she jumped from the car, asked him repeatedly whether he was "okay" and screamed, "I am sorry." See Nick Madigan, Wife Testifies She Was "In a Fog" Just Before Her Car Struck Husband, N.Y. Times, Feb. 8, 2003, at A11; Ruth Rendon, Harris Witness Testifies Death Scene "Like Movie," Houston Chron., Jan. 14, 2003, at A1. The jury convicted her of murder, and of using a deadly weapon, which enhanced the offense. During the sentencing phase, the jury also found that she had acted in the heat of passion, but imposed the maximum sentence of twenty years. Ron Nissamov, Parham Shares Views on Harris, Houston Chron., Feb. 16, 2003, at 33. During the trial, both sides capitalized on gender stereotypes. The prosecution painted Harris as a wife who ignored her husband's needs and who was a selfish spendthrift. The defense painted the mistress as an unscrupulous and promiscuous woman with a history of "abnormal relationships," including an alleged lesbian affair. Lucas Wall, Common Link in Uncommon Lives: Clara Harris: Mother of Twins Kept to Herself, Houston Chron., Aug. 4, 2002, at 37; Ruth Rendon, "I Could Kill Him," Harris Told Teen: Defense Says Words Taken Out of Context, Houston Chron., Jan. 17, 2003, at 36.

Compare the result in *Harris* with Maryland v. Peacock, No. 94-CR-0943 (Balt. Cty. Ct, Oct 17, 1994), quoted in Catharine A. MacKinnon, Sex Equality 753-754 (2001). There, the defendant shot and killed his wife when he discovered her having sex with another man. He pleaded guilty to manslaughter and was sentenced for three years, with immediate eligibility for work release and possible home detention. In justifying the sentence, the judge explained that the "betrayal" was "almost unmanageable." "I seriously wonder how many married men would have the strength to walk away, but without inflicting some corporeal punishment. I shudder to think what I would do. . . . I have no question in my mind that no judge of this circuit and probably no judge of this state will ever see Kenneth Peacock again."

What message do sentences like that in *Harris* and *Peacock* send? What sentences would you impose?

Should "hot-blooded" separation murders and assaults be seen as deserving of more punishment than cold-blooded killings? For example, Minnesota authorizes a finding of first-degree murder based on repeated abuse. See Minn. Stat. Ann §609.185(6) (West 2005) (defining murder in the first degree as, among other things, causing "death of a human being while committing domestic abuse, when the perpetrator has engaged in a past pattern of domestic abuse upon the victim or upon another family or household member and the death occurs under circumstances manifesting an extreme indifference to human life")? Or should the law treat defendants who act in the extremes of emotion as less culpable? Should legal doctrine also acknowledge the unfortunate, but inescapable, truth that threats to end a relationship, particularly when entwined with sexual jealousy, in fact enrage men? Is equality best achieved by restricting the heat of passion doctrine or by enlarging it to mitigate women's killings, such as those described below?

2. The Battered Woman's Syndrome. Battered woman's syndrome (BWS) is a subcategory of post-traumatic stress disorder involving "thoughts, feelings, and actions that logically follow a frightening experience that one expects could be repeated." Lenore E.A. Walker, Battered Women Syndrome and Self-Defense, 6 Notre Dame J.L. Ethics & Pub. Pol'y 321, 327 (1992). The syndrome is associated with three major symptom clusters, each of which can be accompanied by neurochemical and other physical changes. These clusters are (1) cognitive disturbances, including repetitive intrusive memories and flashbacks that cause battered women to reexperience fragments of previous abusive incidents and that increase their perception of danger; (2) high arousal symptoms that cause battered women to be nervous, jumpy, and hypervigilant to cues of potential danger; and (3) avoidance symptoms, including depression, denial, minimization, and repression, often leading to isolation as the batterer exerts his power and control needs over the woman. Id. at 327-328.

BWS researchers offer two psychological theories to help juries understand the syndrome: learned helplessness and the cycle theory of violence. The theory of learned helplessness is an effort to explain how a woman in an abusive relationship might lose the ability to respond to various situations "rationally," that is, to respond as others viewing the situation from the outside would have acted. The theory was first developed by experimental psychologist Marvin Seligman to explain the fact that dogs and other animals subjected to electric shocks that they are powerless to control will soon stop trying to escape or to avert the shocks. In the context of battered women, the theory of learned helplessness explains a woman's failure to leave an abusive relationship in the context of a recognizable cycle. That cycle includes a tension-building phase, an acute battering incident, and a period of loving-contrition or absence of tension. The pattern leads the battered woman to believe that she is unable to help herself, that others cannot help her, and that the batterer might in fact reform. Walker, supra, at 330.

In this state of learned helplessness, what causes a battered woman to turn on her batterer? Many abused women do not, but others at some point experience a "turning point." Charles Patrick Ewing, Battered Women Who Kill: Psychological Self-Defense as Legal Justification 65 (1987). The turning point may come when there is a marked increase in the severity of the abuse, when the abuse becomes visible to others who question the woman's denial or rationalizations, or when the "loving-contrition" phase becomes increasingly short or disappears altogether. Id. at 65. At that point, the victim moves from the state of learned helplessness to a state of the "victimized self," who concludes that she must either assert herself or be killed. Id. at 65-66. For some victims, this means finally being able to leave their batterers; others stay and suffer various forms of "psychological death"; a few kill their batterers. Id. at 66.

Lenore Walker describes the three distinct phases that typify the battering relationship:

> [V]iolence does not constantly occur in most battering relationships, nor does it occur randomly. Rather, there are three predictable phases: a phase of tension building, leading up to a second phase which is the acute battering incident, followed by a third phase, which is a period of loving contrition or at least a cessation of the violent behavior.
>
> The third phase provides positive reinforcement for women to remain in the relationship. This periodic reinforcement provides a powerful incentive to remain in a battering relationship: the woman hopes that the undesirable behavior of phases I and II will not recur and that the phase III behavior will continue. Unfortunately, according to our results, the tension building period actually becomes more pronounced, and the periods of loving contrition shorten and become less reinforcing over time. Many of the battered women we interviewed terminated the relationship when the ratio between abusive and loving behavior changed in this manner.

Lenore E. Walker et al., Beyond the Juror's Ken: Battered Women, 7 Vt. L. Rev. 1, 9 (1982).

3. The Battered Woman in Self-Defense Law: Substantive and Procedural Proposals. The most common criticism of the law of self-defense in the battered woman context is that it reflects patterns of male aggression: a "fair fight" between physical equals meeting in a single, discrete confrontation. This approach fails to take into account the realities of battered women. Its "objective" standard of reasonableness ignores the special circumstances facing women in abusive relationships that men believe that they could leave. See Walter Steele & Christine Sigman, Reexamining the Doctrine of Self Defense to Accommodate Battered Women, 18 Am. J. Crim. L. 169, 175-176 (1991). So too, the law's failure to consider verbal threats to be an adequate provocation may fail to account for the genuine risk that they convey in light of the history of battering. Id. at 177-178. The "imminence" standard, in assuming that "a threat of attack may be withdrawn at the last minute, implicitly adopts bluff and counterbluff as a norm of social interaction between two equal aggressors." Id. at 178. The rule that only proportionate force be used in self-defense also assumes a "confrontation . . . between two equal males." Id. at 180. Do these criticisms seem justified in the context of *Norman*?

Some proposals for reform, corresponding to the criticisms described above, call for the substitution of a "reasonable woman" standard or even a "reasonable battered woman" standard. Phyllis L. Crocker, The Meaning of Equality for Battered Womwn Who Kill Men in Self-Defense, 8 Harv. Women's L.J. 121, 123, 126 (1985). Some commentators, however, argue that the problem is not so much the substantive law, but how it is applied. For example, Holly Maguigan's survey of appellate cases involving abused women who killed their abusers suggests that the "real problem" is not the doctrine of self-defense, but the restrictive way that courts interpret it and fail to give appropriate instructions to the jury.

Holly Maguigan, Battered Women and Self-Defense: Myths and Misconceptions in Current Reform Proposals, 140 U. Pa. L. Rev. 379, 382-387, 457-458 (1991). See also Richard A. Rosen, On Self-Defense, Imminence, and Women Who Kill Their Batterers, 71 N.C. L. Rev. 371 (1993) (arguing for a modification of the "imminence" requirement to shift to the jury the determination whether the use of deadly force was "necessary").

Assuming that expert testimony on battered woman's syndrome should have gone to the jury in *Norman*, should the defendant's circumstances (once understood in that light) constitute a justification, exonerating her from guilt, or merely an excuse or mitigating factor affecting the degree of crime or the sentence? Most reformers have assumed the former. For the argument that excuse or mitigation is the better approach, see Cathryn J. Rosen, The Excuse of Self-Defense: Correcting a Historical Accident on Behalf of Battered Women Who Kill, 36 Am. U. L. Rev. 11 (1986); see also State v. Koss, 551 N.E.2d 970 (Ohio 1990) (Holmes, J., concurring opinion) (battered woman syndrome is excuse rather than justification); State v. Torres, 393 S.E.2d 535 (N.C. Ct. App. 1990) (battered woman's syndrome may be a mitigating factor affecting sentence, but failure to find it a mitigating factor in this case not an error).

4. Concerns About the Battered Woman's Syndrome. Uneasiness about use of the battered woman's syndrome reflects various concerns. The *Norman* court's objection was that such evidence could be too easily manipulated, and might encourage opportunistic premeditated killings by scheming wives. In an effort to test the validity of this concern, one scholar collected the data from numerous studies comparing battered women who killed their husbands to those who did not. He concluded that women who kill their husbands suffer from far more frequent, more severe, and more prolonged abuse than other battered women; they have less ability to support themselves and thus to escape from their situations; they are more likely to have children who are also being abused by the batterer; and they are more likely to live in an environment where a gun is present and where the batterer abuses alcohol or other drugs. See Ewing, supra, at 23-40. What are the reform implications of these conclusions?

David L. Faigman and Amy J. Wright assert that "[t]he battered woman syndrome illustrates all that is wrong with the law's use of science." David L. Faigman & Amy J. Wright, The Battered Woman's Syndrome in the Age of Science, 39 Ariz. L. Rev. 67, 68 (1997). With respect to the "cycle theory" of violence, Faigman and Wright point out several flaws in Walker's original method. For example, her interview technique allowed the subjects to guess what answer the researchers were looking for and relied on the interviewers' interpretation of the subjects' answers rather than their actual responses. In addition, Walker did not offer any data as to the duration of the "cycle of violence." Nor did her research demonstrate that all or even most subjects experienced all three stages of the cycle. Id. at 77-78. With respect to the theory of learned helplessness, Faigman and Wright join other social scientists in doubting the applicability of data based on animals to battered women. The dogs in the original experiments exhibited total passivity in response to repeated abuse. Research involving battered women, however, finds that they resist in multiple ways. Most obviously, learned helplessness fails to explain cases in which women fight back by killing their batters. Id. at 79.

As to the use of BWS evidence in the courts, Faigman and Wright point out that the learned helplessness theory implies an excuse through mitigation based on the woman's passivity and the lasting effects of psychological trauma. By contrast, self-defense involves justification based on the reasonableness of the defendant's behavior. That asymmetry may help explain why BWS evidence seldom produces an acquittal. Id. at 113. See Donald Alexander, More Than Victims: Battered Women, the Syndrome Society, and the Law (1996).

Battered women's advocates have also raised concerns about the use of the battered women's syndrome. Although acknowledging that this explanation is an improvement on the traditional view that women who kill are crazy or irrational, these feminists express concern that widespread use will create a single standard that all battered women will be expected to meet. A woman who fails to match the BWS profile may be assumed (by herself as well as others) to be not really battered, and her self defense not really justified:

> An ironic twist to the increased public awareness [of battered woman's syndrome] is that it has informed the ignorant as well as the enlightened. Those who previously responded to the case of a battered woman with prejudice now pretend to accept the legitimacy of a true battered woman's self-defense, as well as the accompanying expert testimony, but structure their opposition to the defense by asserting that the woman in question "does not fit the mold." This skewed perception has given rise to distinctions between "good" and "bad" battered women....
>
> "Good" battered women are passive, loyal housewives, acting as loving companions to their abusers. These women must have flawless characters and continually appeal to the police and courts for help, regardless of the futility of their efforts. By contrast, the "bad" battered woman is one who [demonstrates independence and efforts at control].... Infidelity or abuse of drugs is equally discrediting.

Michael Dowd, Dispelling the Myths About the "Battered Woman's Defense": Towards a New Understanding, 19 Fordham Urb. L.J. 567, 581 (1992); see Alafair S. Burke, Rational Actors, Self-Dense and Duress: Making Sense, Not Syndrome Out of the Battered Woman, 81 N.C. L. Rev. 212, 230-247 (2002).

The risk Dowd describes may be highest for African-American women because they are subject to racial stereotypes that suggest they may be acting out of revenge and anger rather than fear. See Linda L. Ammons, Mules, Madonnas, Babies, Bathwater, Racial Imagery, and Stereotypes: The African-American Woman and the Battered Woman Syndrome, 1995 Wis. L. Rev. 1003. Compare this general problem to that of using the rappe trauma syndrome to defend against a rape charge, explored on p. 794. Lesbian and gay victims of battering also may fail to fit the profile of a "battered woman." See Phyllis Goldfarb, Describing Without Circumscribing: Questioning the Construction of Gender in the Discourse of Intimate Violence, 64 Geo. Wash. L. Rev. 582 (1996) (describing how, in a sample of petitioners seeking commutation of their sentences, the lesbian who had killed her female partner "faced the longest odds in her struggle to be seen and heard").

Another risk is that the syndrome will reinforce the view of woman as passive, sick, powerless, and victimized, a view from which so many negative consequences flow. See Anne M. Coughlin, Excusing Women, 82 Cal. L. Rev. 1 (1994). One of these consequences is loss of child custody, discussed above. In the view of some commentators, "learned helplessness" is a term less descriptive of the typical battered woman than of the "helping" professions that have responded so inadequately to her needs. Professionals in law, medicine, politics, and social services have directed too much attention to *her* responses, not *his* abuses, to *her* psychological dysfunction, not *our* societal failures." Deborah L. Rhode, Speaking of Sex: The Denial of Gender Equality 116 (1997).

Most women's rights advocates argue that we need to shift the focus of domestic violence evidence from the particular violent acts of the batterer and the psychology of the victim to the overall pattern of coercion and control that characterizes a battering relationship and to the social support structures necessary to enable victims to escape. See Karla Fischer et al., The Culture of Battering and the Role of Mediation in Domestic Violence Cases, 46 SMU L. Rev. 2117 (1993); Evan Stark, Re-Presenting Woman Battering: From Battered Woman Syndrome to Coercive Control, 58 Alb. L. Rev. 973 (1995). Myrna Raeder suggests that the problem of stereotyping that currently arises from BWS evidence stems from overreliance on "syndromes" and "profiles" as the only way to introduce expert testimony. She argues that experts should be permitted to give more general "social framework" testimony about domestic violence. Myrna S. Raeder, The Better Way: The Role of Batterers' Profiles and Expert "Social Framework" Background in Cases Implicating Domestic Violence, 68 U. Colo. L. Rev. 147, 151-152 (1997). Elizabeth Schneider, too, criticizes the tendency to view battered women simplistically, as either victims or agents, and argues for a more complex notion of "situated agency" that recognizes abused women's capacities and constraints. Elizabeth Schneider, Resistance to Equality, 57 U. Pitt. L. Rev. 477, 499 (1996).

5. Post-Conviction Strategies for Battered Women. After serving four years of her six-year sentence, Judy Norman's sentence was commuted to time served by Governor James Martin. No reasons were given. See Elizabeth Leland, Abused Wife's Sentence Commuted, Charlotte Observer, July 8, 1989, at B1.

Systematic efforts for clemency on behalf of convicted women in over 20 other states have also yielded some results. Estimates suggest that about 125 women convicted of killing an abuser have been freed since 1978. However, the trend toward clemency has slowed. Almost all the petitions were granted during the 1980s and early 1990s. In some states, no requests have ever been successful, even in cases where they were convicted before expert testimony on battered women was available at trial. See Burke, supra; Schneider, Particularity and Generality, supra, at 519.

Men's rights groups generally oppose efforts to mitigate penalties for battered women. According to Warren Farrell, feminists argue "'there's never an excuse for violence against women.' Now they [are] saying 'but there's always an excuse for violence against men.'" Rhode, supra, at 115 (quoting Farrell). How would you respond? What criteria would you advise governors to apply in considering clemency requests by battered women convicted of killing their abusers? See Linda L. Ammons, Discretionary Justice: A Legal and Policy Analysis of a Governor's Use of the Clemency Power in the Cases of Incarcerated Battered Women, 3 J.L. & Pol'y 1 (1994); see also Linda L. Ammons, Dealing with the Nastiness: Mixing Feminism and Criminal Law in the Review of Cases of Battered Incarcerated Women — A Tenth-Year Reflection, 4 Buff. Crim. L. Rev 891 (2001); Linda L. Ammons, Why Do You Do the Things You Do? Clemency for Battered Incarcerated Women: A Decade's Review, 11 Am. U.J. Gender Soc. Pol'y & L. 533 (2003).

4. Domestic Violence and the State

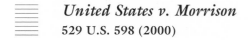

United States v. Morrison
529 U.S. 598 (2000)

Chief Justice REHNQUIST delivered the opinion of the Court.

In these cases we consider the constitutionality of 42 U.S.C. § 13981, which provides a federal civil remedy for the victims of gender-motivated violence. The United States Court of Appeals for the Fourth Circuit, sitting en banc, struck down § 13981 because it concluded that Congress lacked constitutional authority to enact the section's civil remedy. Believing that these cases are controlled by our decisions in United States v. Lopez, 514 U.S. 549 (1995), United States v. Harris, 106 U.S. 629 (1883), and the In re Civil Rights Cases, 109 U.S. 3 (1883), we affirm.

I

Petitioner Christy Brzonkala enrolled at Virginia Polytechnic Institute (Virginia Tech) in the fall of 1994. In September of that year, Brzonkala met respondents Antonio Morrison and James Crawford, who were both students at Virginia Tech and members of its varsity football team. Brzonkala alleges that, within 30 minutes of meeting Morrison and Crawford, they assaulted and repeatedly raped her. After the attack, Morrison allegedly told Brzonkala, "You better not have any...diseases." In the months following the rape, Morrison also allegedly announced in the dormitory's dining room that he "like[d] to get girls drunk and...." The omitted portions, quoted verbatim in the briefs on file with this Court, consist of boasting, debased remarks about what Morrison would do to women, vulgar remarks that cannot fail to shock and offend.[1]

Brzonkala alleges that this attack caused her to become severely emotionally disturbed and depressed. She sought assistance from a university psychiatrist, who prescribed antidepressant medication. Shortly after the rape Brzonkala stopped attending classes and withdrew from the university.

---

1. [The comments to which Justice Rehnquist alludes include Morrison's remark, immediately after raping Brzonkala, that "You better not have any fucking diseases"; his public announcement some months later that "I like to get girls drunk and fuck the shit out of them"; and a remark made later to Crawford by another male student athlete that he "should have killed the bitch."]

In early 1995, Brzonkala filed a complaint against respondents under Virginia Tech's Sexual Assault Policy. During the school-conducted hearing on her complaint, Morrison admitted having sexual contact with her despite the fact that she had twice told him "no." [The school initially found Morrison guilty of sexual assault and suspended him. However, Morrison subsequently challenged the conviction in court, alleging the policy under which he was convicted had not been widely circulated to students. But Morrison again was convicted under a separate policy and suspended for "using abusive language." Morrison then appealed and his sentence was set aside; the university senior vice president and provost found it excessive when compared to similar cases.] . . .

After learning from a newspaper that Morrison would be returning to Virginia Tech for the fall 1995 semester, she dropped out of the university.

In December 1995, Brzonkala sued Morrison, Crawford, and Virginia Tech in the United States District Court for the Western District of Virginia. Her complaint alleged that Morrison's and Crawford's attack violated § 13981 and that Virginia Tech's handling of her complaint violated Title IX of the Education Amendments of 1972. . . .

The District Court dismissed Brzonkala's Title IX claims against Virginia Tech for failure to state a claim upon which relief can be granted. It then held that Brzonkala's complaint stated a claim against Morrison and Crawford under § 13981, but dismissed the complaint because it concluded that Congress lacked authority to enact the section under either the Commerce Clause or § 5 of the Fourteenth Amendment. . . .

[An en banc panel of the Court of Appeals], by a divided vote, affirmed the District Court's conclusion that Congress lacked constitutional authority to enact § 13981's civil remedy. Because the Court of Appeals invalidated a federal statute on constitutional grounds, we granted certiorari. . . .

Section 13981 was part of the Violence Against Women Act of 1994, § 40302, 108 Stat. 1941-1942. It states that "[a]ll persons within the United States shall have the right to be free from crimes of violence motivated by gender." 42 U.S.C. § 13981(b). To enforce that right, subsection (c) declares:

> A person (including a person who acts under color of any statute, ordinance, regulation, custom, or usage of any State) who commits a crime of violence motivated by gender and thus deprives another of the right declared in subsection (b) of this section shall be liable to the party injured, in an action for the recovery of compensatory and punitive damages, injunctive and declaratory relief, and such other relief as a court may deem appropriate.

Section 13981 defines a "crim[e] of violence motivated by gender" as "a crime of violence committed because of gender or on the basis of gender, and due, at least in part, to an animus based on the victim's gender." § 13981(d)(1). It also provides that the term "crime of violence" includes any

> (A) . . . act or series of acts that would constitute a felony against the person or that would constitute a felony against property if the conduct presents a serious risk of physical injury to another, and that would come within the meaning of

State or Federal offenses described in section 16 of Title 18, whether or not those acts have actually resulted in criminal charges, prosecution, or conviction and whether or not those acts were committed in the special maritime, territorial, or prison jurisdiction of the United States;" and "(B) includes an act or series of acts that would constitute a felony described in subparagraph (A) but for the relationship between the person who takes such action and the individual against whom such action is taken." § 13981(d)(2).

Further clarifying the broad scope of § 13981's civil remedy, subsection (e)(2) states that "[n]othing in this section requires a prior criminal complaint, prosecution, or conviction to establish the elements of a cause of action under subsection (c) of this section." And subsection (e)(3) provides a § 13981 litigant with a choice of forums: Federal and state courts "shall have concurrent jurisdiction" over complaints brought under the section.

Although the foregoing language of § 13981 covers a wide swath of criminal conduct, Congress placed some limitations on the section's federal civil remedy. Subsection (e)(1) states that "[n]othing in this section entitles a person to a cause of action under subsection (c) of this section for random acts of violence unrelated to gender or for acts that cannot be demonstrated, by a preponderance of the evidence, to be motivated by gender." Subsection (e)(4) further states that § 13981 shall not be construed "to confer on the courts of the United States jurisdiction over any State law claim seeking the establishment of a divorce, alimony, equitable distribution of marital property, or child custody decree."

Every law enacted by Congress must be based on one or more of its powers enumerated in the Constitution. . . . Congress explicitly identified the sources of federal authority on which it relied in enacting § 13981. It said that a "federal civil rights cause of action" is established "[p]ursuant to the affirmative power of Congress . . . under section 5 of the Fourteenth Amendment to the Constitution, as well as under section 8 of Article I of the Constitution." 42 U.S.C. § 13981(a). We address Congress' authority to enact this remedy under each of these constitutional provisions in turn.

II . . .

As we observed in *Lopez*, modern Commerce Clause jurisprudence has "identified three broad categories of activity that Congress may regulate under its commerce power." . . .

Petitioners . . . seek to sustain § 13981 as a regulation of activity that substantially affects interstate commerce. Given § 13981's focus on gender-motivated violence wherever it occurs . . . we agree that this is the proper inquiry. . . .

[T]he proper resolution of the present cases is clear. Gender-motivated crimes of violence are not, in any sense of the phrase, economic activity. While we need not adopt a categorical rule against aggregating the effects of any noneconomic activity in order to decide these cases, thus far in our Nation's history our cases have upheld Commerce Clause regulation of intrastate activity only where that activity is economic in nature. . . .

In contrast with the lack of congressional findings that we faced in *Lopez*, § 13981 is supported by numerous findings regarding the serious impact that gender-motivated violence has on victims and their families. But the existence of congressional findings is not sufficient, by itself, to sustain the constitutionality of Commerce Clause legislation.... Rather, "[w]hether particular operations affect interstate commerce sufficiently to come under the constitutional power of Congress to regulate them is ultimately a judicial rather than a legislative question, and can be settled finally only by this Court."...

In these cases, Congress' findings are substantially weakened by the fact that they rely so heavily on a method of reasoning that we have already rejected as unworkable if we are to maintain the Constitution's enumeration of powers. Congress found that gender-motivated violence affects interstate commerce

> "by deterring potential victims from traveling interstate, from engaging in employment in interstate business, and from transacting with business, and in places involved in interstate commerce; ... by diminishing national productivity, increasing medical and other costs, and decreasing the supply of and the demand for interstate products."...

Given these findings and petitioners' arguments, the concern that we expressed in *Lopez* that Congress might use the Commerce Clause to completely obliterate the Constitution's distinction between national and local authority seems well founded. The reasoning that petitioners advance seeks to follow the but-for causal chain from the initial occurrence of violent crime (the suppression of which has always been the prime object of the States' police power) to every attenuated effect upon interstate commerce. If accepted, petitioners' reasoning would allow Congress to regulate any crime as long as the nationwide, aggregated impact of that crime has substantial effects on employment, production, transit, or consumption. Indeed, if Congress may regulate gender-motivated violence, it would be able to regulate murder or any other type of violence since gender-motivated violence, as a subset of all violent crime, is certain to have lesser economic impacts than the larger class of which it is a part.

Petitioners' reasoning, moreover, will not limit Congress to regulating violence but may, as we suggested in *Lopez*, be applied equally as well to family law and other areas of traditional state regulation since the aggregate effect of marriage, divorce, and childrearing on the national economy is undoubtedly significant. Congress may have recognized this specter when it expressly precluded § 13981 from being used in the family law context. See 42 U.S.C. § 13981(e)(4). Under our written Constitution, however, the limitation of congressional authority is not solely a matter of legislative grace....

We accordingly reject the argument that Congress may regulate non-economic, violent criminal conduct based solely on that conduct's aggregate effect on interstate commerce. The Constitution requires a distinction between what is truly national and what is truly local.... The regulation and punishment of intrastate violence that is not directed at the instrumentalities, channels, or goods involved in interstate commerce has always been the province of the States....

III

Because we conclude that the Commerce Clause does not provide Congress with authority to enact § 13981, we address petitioners' alternative argument that the section's civil remedy should be upheld as an exercise of Congress' remedial power under § 5 of the Fourteenth Amendment....

Petitioners' § 5 argument is founded on an assertion that there is pervasive bias in various state justice systems against victims of gender-motivated violence. This assertion is supported by a voluminous congressional record. Specifically, Congress received evidence that many participants in state justice systems are perpetuating an array of erroneous stereotypes and assumptions. Congress concluded that these discriminatory stereotypes often result in insufficient investigation and prosecution of gender-motivated crime, inappropriate focus on the behavior and credibility of the victims of that crime, and unacceptably lenient punishments for those who are actually convicted of gender-motivated violence.... Petitioners contend that this bias denies victims of gender-motivated violence the equal protection of the laws and that Congress therefore acted appropriately in enacting a private civil remedy against the perpetrators of gender-motivated violence to both remedy the States' bias and deter future instances of discrimination in the state courts.

As our cases have established, state-sponsored gender discrimination violates equal protection unless it "serves important governmental objectives and . . . the discriminatory means employed" are "substantially related to the achievement of those objectives." United States v. Virginia, 518 U.S. 515, 533 (1996).... However, the language and purpose of the Fourteenth Amendment place certain limitations on the manner in which Congress may attack discriminatory conduct. These limitations are necessary to prevent the Fourteenth Amendment from obliterating the Framers' carefully crafted balance of power between the States and the National Government.... Foremost among these limitations is the time-honored principle that the Fourteenth Amendment, by its very terms, prohibits only state action....

[The Court elucidates its view that the Fourteenth Amendment prohibits only discriminatory state action, not discriminatory private conduct—and that the statute at hand deals with private conduct, not state action. The Court further states that the statute's remedy also fails to offend the Amendment, as it visits no consequences on state actors.]

Section 13981 is also different from these previously upheld remedies in that it applies uniformly throughout the Nation. Congress' findings indicate that the problem of discrimination against the victims of gender-motivated crimes does not exist in all States, or even most States....

For these reasons, we conclude that Congress' power under § 5 does not extend to the enactment of § 13981.

IV

... If the allegations here are true, no civilized system of justice could fail to provide her a remedy for the conduct of respondent Morrison. But under our federal system that remedy must be provided by the Commonwealth of Virginia, and not by the United States. The judgment of the Court of Appeals is Affirmed.

[The concurring opinion of Justice Thomas is omitted.]

Justice SOUTER, with whom Justice STEVENS, Justice GINSBURG, and Justice BREYER join, dissenting....

I...

One obvious difference from United States v. Lopez is the mountain of data assembled by Congress, here showing the effects of violence against women on interstate commerce. Passage of the Act in 1994 was preceded by four years of hearings, which included testimony from physicians and law professors; from survivors of rape and domestic violence; and from representatives of state law enforcement and private business. The record includes reports on gender bias from task forces in 21 States, and we have the benefit of specific factual findings in the eight separate Reports issued by Congress and its committees over the long course leading to enactment....

With respect to domestic violence, Congress received evidence for the following findings:

"Three out of four American women will be victims of violent crimes sometime during their life." H.R. Rep. No. 103-395, p. 25 (1993) (citing U.S. Dep't of Justice, Report to the Nation on Crime and Justice 29 (2d ed. 1988)).

"Violence is the leading cause of injuries to women ages 15 to 44...." S. Rep. No. 103-138, p. 38 (1993) (citing Surgeon General Antonia Novello, From the Surgeon General, U.S. Public Health Services, 267 JAMA 3132 (1992)).

"[A]s many as 50 percent of homeless women and children are fleeing domestic violence." S. Rep. No. 101-545, p. 37 (1990) (citing E. Schneider, Legal Reform Efforts for Battered Women: Past, Present, and Future (July 1990)).

"Since 1974, the assault rate against women has outstripped the rate for men by at least twice for some age groups and far more for others." S. Rep. No. 101-545, at 30 (citing Bureau of Justice Statistics, Criminal Victimization in the United States (1974) (Table 5)).

"[B]attering 'is the single largest cause of injury to women in the United States.'" S. Rep. No. 101-545, at 37 (quoting Van Hightower & McManus, Limits of State Constitutional Guarantees: Lessons from Efforts to Implement Domestic Violence Policies, 49 Pub. Admin. Rev. 269 (May/June 1989)). "An estimated 4 million American women are battered each year by their husbands or partners." H.R. Rep. No. 103-395, at 26 (citing Council on Scientific Affairs, American Medical Assn., Violence Against Women: Relevance for Medical Practitioners, 267 JAMA 3184, 3185 (1992)).

"Over 1 million women in the United States seek medical assistance each year for injuries sustained [from] their husbands or other partners." S. Rep. No. 101-545, at 37 (citing Stark & Flitcraft, Medical Therapy as Repression: The Case of the Battered Woman, Health & Medicine (Summer/Fall 1982)).

"Between 2,000 and 4,000 women die every year from [domestic] abuse." S. Rep. No. 101-545, at 36 (citing Schneider, supra).

"[A]rrest rates may be as low as 1 for every 100 domestic assaults." S. Rep. No. 101-545, at 38 (citing Dutton, Profiling of Wife Assaulters: Preliminary Evidence for Trimodal Analysis, 3 Violence and Victims 5-30 (1988)).

"Partial estimates show that violent crime against women costs this country at least 3 billion — not million, but billion — dollars a year." S. Rep. No. 101-545, at 33 (citing Schneider, supra, at 4).

"[E]stimates suggest that we spend $5 to $10 billion a year on health care, criminal justice, and other social costs of domestic violence." S. Rep. No. 103-138, at 41 (citing Biden, Domestic Violence: A Crime, Not a Quarrel, Trial 56 (June 1993)).

The evidence as to rape was similarly extensive, supporting these conclusions:

"[The incidence of] rape rose four times as fast as the total national crime rate over the past 10 years." S. Rep. No. 101-545, at 30 (citing Federal Bureau of Investigation Uniform Crime Reports (1988)).

"According to one study, close to half a million girls now in high school will be raped before they graduate." S. Rep. No. 101-545, at 31 (citing R. Warshaw, I Never Called It Rape 117 (1988)).

"[One hundred twenty-five thousand] college women can expect to be raped during this — or any — year." S. Rep. No. 101-545, at 43 (citing testimony of Dr. Mary Koss before the Senate Judiciary Committee, Aug. 29, 1990).

"[T]hree-quarters of women never go to the movies alone after dark because of the fear of rape and nearly 50 percent do not use public transit alone after dark for the same reason." S. Rep. No. 102-197, p. 38 (1991) (citing M. Gordon & S. Riger, The Female Fear 15 (1989)).

"[Forty-one] percent of judges surveyed believed that juries give sexual assault victims less credibility than other crime victims." S. Rep. No. 102-197, at 47 (citing Colorado Supreme Court Task Force on Gender Bias in the Courts, Gender Justice in the Colorado Courts 91 (1990)).

"Less than 1 percent of all [rape] victims have collected damages." S. Rep. No. 102-197, at 44 (citing report by Jury Verdict Research, Inc.).

" '[A]n individual who commits rape has only about 4 chances in 100 of being arrested, prosecuted, and found guilty of any offense.' " S. Rep. No. 101-545, at 33, n.30 (quoting H. Field & L. Bienen, Jurors and Rape: A Study in Psychology and Law 95 (1980)).

"Almost one-quarter of convicted rapists never go to prison and another quarter received sentences in local jails where the average sentence is 11 months." S. Rep. No. 103-138, at 38 (citing Majority Staff Report of Senate Committee on the Judiciary, The Response to Rape: Detours on the Road to Equal Justice, 103d Cong., 1st Sess., 2 (Comm. Print 1993)).

"[A]lmost 50 percent of rape victims lose their jobs or are forced to quit because of the crime's severity." S. Rep. No. 102-197, at 53 (citing Ellis, Atkeson, & Calhoun, An Assessment of Long-Term Reaction to Rape, 90 J. Abnormal Psych., No. 3, p.264 (1981)).

Based on the data thus partially summarized, Congress found that

"crimes of violence motivated by gender have a substantial adverse effect on interstate commerce, by deterring potential victims from traveling interstate, from engaging in employment in interstate business, and from transacting with business, and in places involved, in interstate commerce . . . [,] by diminishing national productivity, increasing medical and other costs, and decreasing the supply of and the demand for interstate products. . . ." H.R. Conf. Rep. No. 103- 711, p. 385 (1994), U.S. Code Cong. & Admin. News 1994, pp. 1803, 1853.

Congress thereby explicitly stated the predicate for the exercise of its Commerce Clause power. Is its conclusion irrational in view of the data amassed? True, the methodology of particular studies may be challenged, and some of the figures arrived at may be disputed. But the sufficiency of the evidence before Congress to provide a rational basis for the finding cannot seriously be questioned. . . .

Indeed, the legislative record here is far more voluminous than the record compiled by Congress and found sufficient in two prior cases upholding Title II of the Civil Rights Act of 1964 against Commerce Clause challenges. . . .

II . . .

The premise that the enumeration of powers implies that other powers are withheld is sound; the conclusion that some particular categories of subject matter are therefore presumptively beyond the reach of the commerce power is, however, a non sequitur. From the fact that Art. I, § 8, cl. 3 grants an authority limited to regulating commerce, it follows only that Congress may claim no authority under that section to address any subject that does not affect commerce. It does not at all follow that an activity affecting commerce nonetheless falls outside the commerce power, depending on the specific character of the activity, or the authority of a State to regulate it along with Congress. My disagreement with the majority is not, however, confined to logic, for history has shown that categorical exclusions have proven as unworkable in practice as they are unsupportable in theory. . . .

Justice BREYER, with whom Justice STEVENS joins, and with whom Justice SOUTER and Justice GINSBURG join as to Part I-A, dissenting. . . .

[Justice Breyer reasons that the economic/non-economic distinction is difficult to apply, that it requires awkward exceptions, and that "[n]othing in the Constitution's language, or that of earlier cases prior to *Lopez*, explains why the Court should ignore one highly relevant characteristic of an interstate-commerce-affecting cause (how "local" it is), while placing critical constitutional weight upon a different, less obviously relevant, feature (how "economic" it is)."] . . .

To determine the lawfulness of statutes simply by asking whether Congress could reasonably have found that aggregated local instances significantly affect interstate commerce will allow Congress to regulate almost anything. . . .

This consideration, however, while serious, does not reflect a jurisprudential defect, so much as it reflects a practical reality. We live in a Nation knit together by two centuries of scientific, technological, commercial and environmental change. Those changes, taken together, mean that virtually every kind of activity, no matter how local, genuinely can affect commerce, or its conditions, outside the State...at least when considered in the aggregate....

Since judges cannot change the world, the "defect" means that, within the bounds of the rational, Congress, not the courts, must remain primarily responsible for striking the appropriate state/federal balance....

Moreover, as Justice Souter has pointed out, Congress compiled a "mountain of data" explicitly documenting the interstate commercial effects of gender-motivated crimes of violence....After considering alternatives, it focused the federal law upon documented deficiencies in state legal systems. And it tailored the law to prevent its use in certain areas of traditional state concern, such as divorce, alimony, or child custody. 42 U.S.C. §13981(e)(4). Consequently, the law before us seems to represent an instance, not of state/federal conflict, but of state/federal efforts to cooperate in order to help solve a mutually acknowledged national problem. Cf. §§300w-10, 3796gg, 3796hh, 10409, 13931 (providing federal moneys to encourage state and local initiatives to combat gender-motivated violence)....

II

Given my conclusion on the Commerce Clause question, I need not consider Congress' authority under §5 of the Fourteenth Amendment. Nonetheless, I doubt the Court's reasoning rejecting that source of authority....

[W]hy can Congress not provide a remedy against private actors? Those private actors, of course, did not themselves violate the Constitution. But this Court has held that Congress at least sometimes can enact remedial "[l]egislation...[that] prohibits conduct which is not itself unconstitutional." The statutory remedy does not in any sense purport to "determine what constitutes a constitutional violation." It intrudes little upon either States or private parties. It may lead state actors to improve their own remedial systems, primarily through example. It restricts private actors only by imposing liability for private conduct that is, in the main, already forbidden by state law. Why is the remedy "disproportionate"? And given the relation between remedy and violation — the creation of a federal remedy to substitute for constitutionally inadequate state remedies — where is the lack of "congruence"?

The majority adds that Congress found that the problem of inadequacy of state remedies "does not exist in all States, or even most States." But Congress had before it the task force reports of at least 21 States documenting constitutional violations. And it made its own findings about pervasive gender-based stereotypes hampering many state legal systems, sometimes unconstitutionally so....The record nowhere reveals a congressional finding that the problem "does not exist" elsewhere. Why can Congress not take the evidence before it as evidence of a national problem? This Court has not previously held that Congress must document the existence of a problem in every State prior to proposing a national solution. And the deference this Court gives to Congress' chosen remedy under §5,...suggests that any such requirement would be inappropriate.

Notes

1. The Violence Against Women Act.   The Violence Against Women Act (VAWA) committed the federal government to fighting domestic violence through a number of different mechanisms. Passed as part of the Violent Crime Control and Law Enforcement Act of 1994, Pub. L. No. 103-322, 108 Stat. 1796 (codified as amended in scattered sections of 8 U.S.C., 16 U.S.C., 18 U.S.C., 28 U.S.C., and 42 U.S.C.), a massive omnibus crime bill, VAWA links child abuse with violence against women and focuses on the criminal justice system as the key to addressing both. See generally George B. Stevenson, Federal Antiviolence and Abuse Legislation: Toward Elimination of Disparate Justice for Women and Children, 33 Willamette L. Rev. 855 (1997).

The larger crime bill of which VAWA was a part, for example, tightens the controls over domestic violence offenders in probation or post-prison status and limits offenders' opportunities for probation. Courts are required to sentence all first-time offenders to prison or probation, rather than deferred or diverted prosecution as under previous practice. One condition of first-time offender probation is participation in a nonprofit rehabilitation program approved by the court in consultation with a State Coalition Against Domestic Violence. Stevenson, supra, at 860. Assault with intent to rape, sexual abuse, and attempt, conspiracy, or solicitation to commit these offenses qualify as "serious violent felonies" under the federal "three strikes and you're out" sentencing program (requiring life imprisonment for persons convicted in federal court of a serious violent felony after prior conviction in a state or federal court of two serious felonies or a serious violent offense and a serious drug offense). Id. at 859.

The Safe Homes for Women Act, created under VAWA, provides law enforcement personnel with the authority to enforce civil protection orders from other states. Id. at 872. It also requires every state or Indian tribe to give full faith and credit to protection orders issued by any other state or tribe. Id. VAWA authorizes funding for entering data on stalking and domestic violence into local, state, and national databases and authorizes technical assistance to state and tribal judges handling stalking and domestic violence cases. Id. at 873.

VAWA also expanded the State Justice Institute's authority and mission to study and eliminate gender bias in all criminal justice and court systems, requiring each federal circuit judicial council to form gender bias task forces to study gender bias and implement reforms. "The Institute has the authority to award grants to develop model programs to be used in training state and Indian tribal judges and court personnel on dealing with rape, sexual assault, domestic violence, and other crimes of gender-motivated violence." Id. at 881-882.

Feminist commentators hailed VAWA as a historic moment in the struggle to have the law recognize the unique experiences of women of color. Jenny Rivera notes:

> The VAWA recognizes that within communities of color there are different issues and discrete culturally-based concerns. For example, law enforcement and prosecution federal grants are available for, inter alia, purposes of "developing or improving delivery of victim services to racial, cultural, ethnic, and language minorities...."

Further, states must set forth in their grant applications the demographics of the service population, including information on "race, ethnicity and language background..." in order to qualify for a grant. Applicants for the National Domestic Violence Hotline grant had to provide a plan for servicing "non-English speaking callers," such as by employing Spanish-speaking hotline personnel, and had to demonstrate a commitment to "diversity, and to the provision of services to ethnic, racial, and non-English speaking minorities...."

Jenny Rivera, The Violence Against Women Act and the Construction of Multiple Consciousness in the Civil Rights and Feminist Movements, 4 J.L. & Pol'y 464, 494-495 (1996). The Act also expanded the remedies available to battered immigrant women, see 8 U.S.C. §1154(a)(1)(A)(iii)(I) (2000), and the protections for these women were extended even further in the 2005 VAWA reauthorization legislation. See Pub. L. No. 109-162 (Jan. 5, 2006), discussed in on pp. 478-479, supra.

Finally, VAWA created new substantive law, making it a federal crime to cross state lines for the purpose of or in the course of "harassing, intimidating, or injuring a spouse or intimate partner," And creating a civil rights remedy for "crimes of violence motivated by gender." Under this latter provision, any person, including a person who acts under color of state law, who commits a crime of violence "because of gender or on the basis of gender and due, at least in part, to an animus based on the victim's gender" shall be liable for "compensatory and punitive damages, injunctive and declaratory relief, and such other relief as a court may deem appropriate." 42 U.S.C. §13981 (1994). It was this aspect of the VAWA that was held to be without constitutional foundation in *Morrison*. If the Court had sustained this provision, how significant a strategy do you think it would have been in challenging domestic violence. Based on her extensive experience in doing public education and outreach on the civil rights remedy in VAWA, Julie Goldscheid concluded that such provisions would have been of limited use. For the same reasons domestic violence victims seldom bring tort suits, they would be reluctant to file civil rights claims; they want to minimize interaction with abusers, and they would often be unable to collect significant damages. See Julie Goldscheid, Advancing Equality in Domestic Violence Reform, 11 Am. U. J. Gender, Soc. Pol'y & L. 417, 422-423 (2003). By contrast, Sally Goldfarb argues that civil rights remedies could have served important objectives by challenging assumptions that domestic violence is personal and private, and by holding government officials accountable for addressing it. Sally Goldfarb, Applying the Discrimination Model to Violence Against Women: Some Reflections on Theory and Practice, 11 Am. U. J. Gender, Soc. Pol'y & L. 251, 255 (2003). Who is right? Should the women's movement invest significant effort in campaigning for state and local civil rights remedies to address gender-based violence?

2. Domestic Violence and the Public/Private Dichotomy. American law's traditional boundaries between public and private realms has often left domestic violence unchallenged and unchanged. Feminists have observed that much conduct that would be considered criminal if it occurred between strangers is considered acceptable if it occurs between intimates, particularly if it does not lead to serious injury. The euphemisms that batterers and judges use to describe such behavior often reflect this "domestic discount" (e.g., "getting physical," an "unfortunate incident," only a "whack"). See Deborah L. Rhode, Speaking of Sex: The Denial of Gender Equality 109-110 (1997). Viewing domestic violence in terms of this public/private dichotomy has helped explain how the personal experience of battering is politically structured: in short, how "the personal is political." Both the abuse, and the conditions that perpetuate it — lack of income, family and cultural expectations, and so forth are experienced on the personal level. So is treatment for a batterer. See Carolyn Puzella, Social Scientists' Perspectives on the Causes of Spousal Abuse, 11 J. Contemp. Legal Issues 37 (2000) (reviewing personal and sociocultural causes). Yet what resources are available to the battered woman and how others expect her, and her batterer, to act, reflect broader social and political forces. Even the fact that abuse is experienced as personal, as Schneider argues in the reading on p. 482, is not a "given," but a choice structured by the larger society. MacKinnon puts it this way:

> The *Morrison* majority does not simply respect a preexisting line between what is private and what is public. It draws that line by abandoning women wherever violence against them takes place. *Morrison* effectively defines the private as the location where effective redress for sex-based violence is unavailable, ignoring the destruction of women's freedom and equality in private by the lack of public limits on male violence. The private is thus constructed of public impunity.

Catharine A. MacKinnon, Disputing Male Sovereignty: On United States v. Morrison, 114 Harv. L. Rev. 135, 170 (2002).

What follows from the feminist critique of the public/private distinction? Is there any realm that the law should not reach? In her comprehensive study of the different forms the critique of the public/private dichotomy has taken, Ruth Gavison argues that the real question is not whether there is to be a division between public and private; the division is inevitable and necessary to women as well as to men. The question is, rather, whether or not the line between the two, in particular concrete circumstances, is drawn in ways that subordinate women. See Ruth Gavison, Feminism and the Public/Private Distinction, 45 Stan. L. Rev. 1, 36-37 (1992). See also Tracy E. Higgins, Reviving the Public/Private Distinction in Feminist Theorizing, 75 Chi.-Kent L. Rev. 847 (2000) (arguing that feminists have much to gain in preserving the public/private line and the right of privacy). Consider that claim in light of the other ways that privacy has functioned in the law, including pornography (pp. 540-572), reproductive rights (pp. 844-942), and same-sex relationships (pp. 572-626).

3. The Nonsubordination Approach and the Dilemma of Criminalization. If the state is not neutral, but rather amplifies and protects male power over women, can we expect the law, particularly the criminal justice system, to adequately challenge domestic violence? Naomi Cahn suggests grounds for skepticism.

...To the extent that the law is based on community and public norms developed through public consensus, it does not and cannot reflect the needs of outsider groups. Where social groups are unequal, regardless of the existence of legal discrimination, it is difficult for those groups to influence policy.

The criminal route also serves to give control to the state. Where sensitivity to women is not a real priority, women can sacrifice control, getting little support in return....Thus, instead of the criminal justice system alone, we need to use more affirmative and civil supports for women.

Naomi Cahn, Policing Women: Moral Arguments and the Dilemmas of Criminalization, 49 DePaul L. Rev. 817, 821 (2000). See also Donna Coker, Crime Control and Feminist Law Reform in Domestic Violence Law: A Critical Review, 4 Buff. Crim. L. Rev. 801, 805 (2000) ("Not only does a focus on crime control deflect attention from other anti-domestic violence strategies, crime control policies result in greater state control of women, particularly poor women."); Machaela M. Hoctor, Comment, Domestic Violence as a Crime Against the State: The Need for Mandatory Arrest in California, 85 Cal. L. Rev. 643, 691 (1997) (questioning the use of the criminal justice system to challenge domestic violence, given the stigmatized status of gay men and lesbians); Jenny Rivera, Domestic Violence Against Latinas by Latino Males: An Analysis of Race, National Origin, and Gender Differentials, 14 B.C. Third World L.J. 231, 248 (1994) (noting that for women of color, using the criminal justice state to combat domestic violence will only intensify the racist criminalization of men of color).

How should this dilemma be addressed?

How might we diminish the risk that increasing state intervention against domestic violence will increase state control of women? First, we must organize for more material assistance for battered women. Crime control policies are costly, but lawmakers continue to be willing to allocate funds for purpose that sound like "fighting crime." We must begin to articulate that economic justice for women and children is part of domestic violence prevention. Bundling services within crime control programs does not adequately address this need. This is true both because of the limitations of the programs and because many battered women do not come to the attention of the criminal justice system. A focus on economic justice requires that battered women's advocates work to strengthen coalitions with activists and organizations that attend to the broader picture of violence against women in inner cities and the broader picture of women's economic status.

Second, we must recognize that universal policies are unlikely to be successful. Rather, effective policies must derive from local struggles and local organizing efforts.

Third, we must explore alternatives to mandatory policies for establishing control of the state's response to domestic violence.

Coker, supra, at 859-860.

4. Domestic Violence as an International Human Rights Issue. Isabel Marcus argues that the very term "domestic violence" plays into the public/private distinction and domesticates the problem. She proposes that domestic violence be viewed as an international human rights issue.

> I am persuaded that the value of this broader perspective lies in its inclusive "bottom line." As international human rights theory and practice moves beyond the limitations and constraints of traditional, Western, liberal, political theory, they articulate an expansive vision which substitutes a global "our" for a narrower "my" rights. We know that family violence, especially wife abuse, is a widespread phenomenon; the global "our" is clearly applicable to it, despite the fact that "some acts of violation are not crimes in law, others are legitimized in custom or court opinion, and most are blamed on the victims themselves."

Isabel Marcus, Reframing "Domestic Violence": Terrorism in the Home, in Martha Albertson Fineman & Roxanne Mykitiuk, The Public Nature of Domestic Violence: The Discovery of Domestic Abuse 11, 28 (1994). See also Rhonda Copelon, Recognizing the Egregious in the Everyday: Domestic Violence as Torture, 25 Colum. Hum. Rts. L. Rev. 291 (1994); Dorothy Q. Thomas & Michele E. Beasley, Domestic Violence as a Human Rights Issue, 58 Alb. L. Rev. 1119 (1995).

The issue was brought to the fore in June 1999, when a federal immigration appeals panel overturned a grant of asylum to Rodi Alvarado Pena, a Guatemalan woman seeking refuge in the United States because the Guatemalan legal system had failed to protect her from her abusive husband. In re R-A, 22 I & N Dec. 906 (A.G. 2001; B.I.A. 1999). The decision created a public outcry and seemingly flew in the face of Immigration and Naturalization Service guidelines promulgated in 1995 that recognized rape, domestic abuse, and other forms of violence against women as possible grounds for asylum. See Amanda Blanck, Domestic Violence as a Basis for Asylum Status: A Human Rights Based Approach, 22 Women's Rts. L. Rep. 47 (2000); Karen Musalo, Matter of R-A: An Analysis of the Decision and Its Implications, 76 Interpreter Releases 1177 (Aug. 9, 1999). The opinion was later vacated by former Attorney General Janet Reno in 2001, 22 I & N Dec. at 906, and finally settled by then-Attorney General John Ashcroft on January 25, 2005. See In re R-A, 23 I & N Dec. 694 (A.G. 2005) (remanding the case "to the Board of Immigration Appeals for reconsideration following final publication of the proposed rule published at 65 Fed. Reg. 76,588 (Dec. 7, 2000)"). See also Aguirre-Cervantes v. INS, 242 F.3d 1169 (9th Cir. 2001) (overturning Board of Immigration Appeals and granting asylum to a woman who, along with other members of her immediate family, had been abused by her father), remanded to the BIA for stipulated reopening of administrative proceedings, 273 F.3d 1220 (9th Cir. 2001).

In the United States, the right to asylum is governed by the international definition of a "refugee." The United Nations Convention Relating to the Status of Refugees defines a refugee in part as any person who "owing to a well-founded fear of being persecuted for reasons of race, religion, national origin, membership in a particular social group or political opinion, is outside the country of his nationality and is unable or, owing to such fear, is unwilling to avail himself of the protection of that country." 1951 Convention Relating to the Status of

Refugees, July 28, 1951, 19 U.S.T. 6259, 189 U.N.T.S. 137. Victims of domestic violence have generally based their claims for asylum on the "membership in a particular social group [or political opinion]" category. For an analysis of this requirement and discussion of many of the relevant cases, see Andrea Binder, Gender and the "Membership in a Particular Social Group" Category of the 1951 Refugee Convention, 10 Colum. J. Gender & L. 167 (2001).

Canada and Australia, as well as the United States, have adopted nonbinding guidelines for asylum inspectors that call on them to consider claims of domestic violence in assessing asylum claims. See Andrew N. Langham, Comment, The Erosion of Refugee Rights in Australia: Two Proposed Amendments to the Migration Act, 8 Pac. Rim L. & Pol'y J. 651, 662 (1999) (describing the process for reviewing asylum applications in Australia). The British House of Lords and the Canadian Supreme Court have interpreted the U.N. Convention to allow gender to be the defining characteristic of a particular social group where a pattern of discriminatory treatment exists. See Ex parte Shah v. Sec'y of State for Home Dep't, [1999] 2 All E.R. 545; Canada v. Ward, [1993] 2 S.C.R. 689. These cases are analyzed in Deborah Anker, Refugee Status and Violence Against Women in the "Domestic" Sphere: The Non-State Actor Question, 15 Geo. Immigr. L.J. 391 (2001). See also Khawar v. Minister for Immigr. & Multicultural Affairs [HCA 14 (Australian High Court 2002) (approving a domestic violence asylum claim from Pakistan).

Other international documents also provide support for treating domestic violence as a human rights issue. The Declaration on the Elimination of Violence Against Women and the UNHCR Guidelines on the Protection of Refugee Women recognize domestic violence as a form of gender discrimination, and thus a human rights violation. Blanck, supra, at 47-48. The UN Convention Against Torture is another possible foundation for asylum claims when women flee domestic violence; Blanck reports that "the United Nations Special Rapporteur on Violence Against Women has recommended that bodies that report on human rights abuses and violence against women and treaty bodies consider treating domestic violence as an internationally proscribed form of torture." Id. at 72; see Barbara Cochrane Alexander, Note, Convention Against Torture: A Viable Alternative Legal Remedy for Domestic Violence Victims, 15 Am. U. Int'l L. Rev. 895 (2000). Should women fleeing domestic violence in their home countries be entitled to claim asylum in the United States? How would you assess the arguments for such protection? See, e.g., Joan Fitzpatrick, The Gender Dimension of U.S. Immigration Policy, 9 Yale J.L. & Feminism 23, 47 (1997).

Could international law have provided the basis for a different result in *Morrison*? An amicus brief filed by feminist international law scholars argued that it could. As their brief noted, both customary international law and international human right covenants recognize a right to be free from gender-based violence. The United States is a party to several of these agreements. Accordingly, the brief maintained, the federal government is permitted, and even arguably required, to protect women from such violence. Because international law is part of the law of the United States, and the Constitution grants Congress the authority to pass laws defining and punishing offenses under the law of nations, the Violence Against Woman Act could be deemed an appropriate exercise of federal power. See Brief of Amici Curiae International Law Scholars and Human Rights experts in Support of Petitions, Brzonkala v. Morrison, 529 U.S. 598 (2000); Rosa Ehrenreich Brooks, Feminism and International Law: An Opportunity for Transformation, 14 Yale J.L. & Feminism 345, 358 (2002). The majority did not mention this argument in striking down the Act.

Putting Theory into Practice

3-11. Child welfare authorities removed Sharon's three children from her home based on findings that her husband had subjected them to repeated abuse, such as beating them with a stick, throwing things at them, and swearing at them. A mental health evaluation of Sharon showed that she did not always put the needs of the children first, that her parenting skills were weak, and that she was a battered wife who had a history of relationships with batterers. Her social profile and personality type suggested that she was particularly vulnerable to abuse. The child welfare authorities now seek to terminate Sharon's parental rights to her children on the theory that even if she leaves her current husband, she is likely to enter into another relationship that will be dangerous to the children.

Under your state's abuse and neglect law, parental rights can be terminated on a showing that a parent has failed to prevent another person from abusing a child and that it is reasonably likely that the child will be abused if returned to the parent.

As Sharon's lawyers, what arguments would you make against termination of her parental rights? Should you win?

3-12. Debra and Terrance are cocaine addicts, arrested for the commission of several armed robberies. Debra admits the crimes, but claims a defense of duress, on the ground that she participated in the robberies out of fear that Terrance would kill her if she did not. In support of her defense, Debra seeks to present expert testimony indicating that she suffers from battered woman's syndrome; she has a history of physical and emotional abuse that escalated every time she tried to leave Terrance. Evidence of battered woman's syndrome has been admitted in the jurisdiction in cases in which a battered woman has killed her batterer and claims self-defense. What arguments do you anticipate in opposition to Debra's offer to produce expert testimony in support of her duress defense? As Debra's lawyer, how would you answer those arguments? For related issues in the context of criminal sentencing, see Chapter 4, pp. 738-748.

D. PORNOGRAPHY

Sex sells. That has always been true, but increased technological innovations have created increased opportunities for private consumption of pornography. Adult theaters, rental videos, pay-per-view movies on cable and world-sites, phone sex, and Internet websites are estimated to generate somewhere between $10 billion and $14 billion annually. Americans spend more on pornography than on all other movies, performing arts, and professional football, basketball, and baseball combined. Frank Rich, Naked Capitalists, N.Y. Times Magazine, May 20, 2001, at 51; Hearings on Protecting Children from Inappropriate Materials on the Internet, Before the Subcomm. on Telecommunications, Trade, and Consumer Protection of the House Comm. on Commerce, 105th Cong. 1, 22 (Sept. 11, 1998) [hereinafter Hearings] (testimony of Congressman Ernest J. Istook, Jr.).

1. Pornography and Nonsubordination Theory

≡ *Deborah L. Rhode, Speaking of Sex:*
≡ *The Denial of Gender Equality*
≡ 130-135 (1997)

Our current controversy [over pornography] builds on longstanding difficulties in legal doctrine. Until quite recently, "pornography" was not a term that figured in American law. Legal standards have referred to "obscenity," and they have been vaguely defined and idiosyncratically enforced. At the height of censorship, government authorities prosecuted everything from nudity on playing cards to classics by Tolstoy. Contemporary Supreme Court doctrine holds that the government can ban material if, under contemporary community standards, the work as a whole appeals to the "prurient interest," depicts sex in a "patently offensive" way, and lacks serious literary, artistic, political, or scientific value.

This obscenity standard is problematic both in theory and in practice. A threshold difficulty is the odd psychological state that judges and juries must reach in order to find a work legally obscene. They must admit that the material is both sexually arousing *and* patently offensive.... Since this is a state that few individuals are happy to admit, the threshold standard for censorship is rarely met. Even when it is, the material often is exempt from regulation based on its socially redeeming value.

Moreover, the cost of item-by-item enforcement is far too great to contain a mushrooming industry. Once sexually degrading materials begin to saturate a local market, it becomes increasingly difficult to prove that they are offensive under contemporary community standards. As a consequence, American pornography suppliers have become solidly entrenched, with estimated annual profits exceeding $10 billion. Consumers rent more than 400 million X-rated videos each year, and computer technology is expanding opportunities for interactive sadism.... Bulletin board systems on the Internet also are competing to be "the nastiest place on earth," complete with images of parents forcing children to have sex with animals.

Not only is current obscenity law unable to stem industry growth; it also cannot prevent harassing prosecutions. Law enforcement officials often bring charges that have little chance of prevailing, particularly against works by gay, lesbian, and minority artists. Among the most highly publicized examples have been the prosecutions of Two Live Crew for offensive song lyrics and of the

Cleveland Art Museum for showing homoerotic photographs by Robert Map-plethorpe. Many schools, libraries, and arts organizations also have banned or denied funding for "dirty" materials. Frequently suppressed "smut" includes books by William Faulkner, J.D. Salinger, and Alice Walker....

The harms that feminists associate with pornography are not the ones that lawmakers traditionally associate with obscenity: the corruption of morals, the offense to public sensibilities, and the erosion of family values. Rather, what many feminists stress are injuries to women both as individuals and as a group. Accord-ing to these feminists, pornography eroticizes inequality. It degrades, dehuma-nizes, and objectifies women, legitimates men's brutality, and perpetrates racist stereotypes.

The most obvious harms involve models who are coerced and abused in the creation of pornographic material. In theory, these individuals have reme-dies under existing criminal and civil law; in practice, such remedies are almost never available. Rarely do women want to compound their injuries by initiat-ing litigation that usually involves considerable financial costs, personal humi-liation, fear of retaliation, and difficulties of proof. Yet while it is clear that some models have experienced barbaric treatment, it is less clear how often this happens, and what would effectively prevent it. We lack any systematic research on the frequency of exploitation, and many sex workers claim that it is not a widespread problem. Nor is it obvious that bans on pornography would lessen the risk. As America's history with alcohol prohibition indicates, forcing a highly profitable industry underground is unlikely to protect parti-cipants. Even with laws like the Indianapolis ordinance, [which provides a civil rights remedy against those who traffic in pornography] victims would con-front most of the same deterrents to reporting abuse that make current legal provisions so ineffectual.

A second category of harms involves the use of pornography as a blue-print for sexual violence and degradation. The testimony of injured victims, particularly when coupled with police reports and psychiatric records, leaves no doubt about the brutality that pornographic materials sometimes inspire. But again, the difficulty is that we have no gauge of frequency. Nor do we know whether pornography actually *causes* abuse, or only influences its form. Even if we could link sexual violence to certain pornographic works, suppression would not necessarily be an appropriate response. "Copycat" crimes are com-mon, and pornography is by no means the only or even the most common source of inspiration. Dramatizations of *The Brothers Karamazov*, *Roots*, *The Ten Commandments*, and *The Burning Bed* (a feminist account of domestic violence) are among the culprits. Comprehensive research also finds that no literary work equals the Bible as a reported factor in inspiring and justifying sexual abuse.

A more indirect harm, but in many feminists' view the most pervasive one, involves pornography's effects on attitudes toward sexual violence and sexual subordination. Most boys first learn about sex through pornography, and the messages it sends scarcely encourage relationships of mutual respect, caring, and intimacy. Selections like "Cheerleader Gang Bang," "Black Bitch," "Teen Twits and Twats," and "Jap Sadists' Virgin Slave" link sexual pleasure with female degradation and racial domination. Because such messages work at the noncognitive level, the usual remedy for offensive speech — more speech — may not be effective. . . .

Two decades of laboratory research provide concrete evidence of harmful effects. Studies have consistently found that exposure to sexually violent material increases viewers' expressed willingness to commit rape and decreases their sensitivity to its damage. Yet such research cannot adequately demonstrate the duration or degree of pornography's effect on behavior in the outside world. Most experts believe that the change in viewers' attitudes following laboratory experience with pornography reflects the violence more than the sex. Although this distinction can be difficult to draw, many experts estimate that violent materials account for well under 10 percent of the pornography market. Sex offenders do not differ significantly from other individuals in their exposure or response to pornography. These offenders are more likely to be readers of *Field and Stream* than of sexually explicit material.

Other efforts to measure the harms of pornography by comparing changes over time or across cultures have been even more inconclusive. Although reported rapes have increased in some countries when pornography laws have grown more liberal, reported crimes are a highly imperfect index of sexual violence. Moreover, correlation does not prove causation. Other factors may account for the increase both in pornography and in reported assaults, and not all studies even find such correlations. Cross-cultural research also raises doubts about direct causal relationships. Some countries with high pornography consumption have low rates of reported violence against women. Other countries that heavily censor sexual expression are scarcely feminist meccas; middle-eastern Muslim societies have little pornography *or* gender equality.

Yet it is a mistake to conclude, as do many civil libertarians, that there is *no* demonstrable link between sexual expression, sexual attitudes, and sexual violence. In a nation that spends some $130 billion each year in advertising, it should not be necessary to belabor the point that images matter. A quarter-century's research leaves no doubt that aggression is in large part learned behavior, and that at least part of the learning process involves words and images. In short, the real question is not whether there is *some* link between pornography and social harms, but whether it is strong enough to justify the risks of regulation.

[One risk is that the vagueness of terms like "subordination" and "degradation" will lead to overbroad or biased enforcement.] Experience in Canada bears this out. There, recently modified prohibitions authorize the suppression of sexually explicit material that is violent, degrading, or dehumanizing. Prominent targets of Canadian censorship have not been brutal misogynist works . . . but gay and lesbian publications. These feminist-inspired changes may not have created the problem, but neither have they prevented it. Ironically enough, border patrols have seized two books by antipornography crusader Andrea Dworkin. . . .

A related concern is the absence of any logical limiting principle for legislation targeting subordination. Women are not the only, or necessarily the most, subordinate group in American society — and sexually explicit images are not necessarily the most harmful ones. As social science experts like Edward

Donnerstein and Daniel Linz note, materials "outside of the pornographic or the X-rated market may in fact be of more concern, since they are imbued with a certain legitimacy, and tend to have much wider acceptance." So too, if the government can suppress sexually explicit expression that degrades women, what about hate speech that contributes to racial violence, or homophobic parodies that encourage gay-bashing? Though some restrictions may be justifiable, the risks of overly broad control are substantial. Once regulation starts down this road, logical stopping points might be hard to find.

A further concern is that provisions distinguishing between "good" and "bad" forms of sexual pleasure will reinforce sexist stereotypes. Some recent studies suggest that women rent 40 percent of hard-core videos, and almost half of surveyed women report watching pornographic films regularly. Many of these viewers find some images of female subordination arousing, as is obvious from any stroll into the world of [paperback romance novels]. Even if such enjoyment is the product of sexist conditioning, it does not follow that women need more "sexual shame, guilt, and hypocrisy—this time served up as feminism."...For many individuals, nonviolent erotica can provide a safe outlet for channeling sexual domination, treating sexual dysfunctions, and fantasizing about practices that they would not attempt in real life. In that sense, pornography provides some of the "safest sex" available.

Even if our society's ultimate goal is to reduce the prevalence of pornographic material, censorship has never been adequate to the task. Suppression generally increases the appeal of sexually arousing materials....

Yet it does not follow that all the line drawing is futile, or that all anti-pornography regulation would carry the same risks as recent initiatives. For example, some First Amendment scholars propose banning only sexually explicit visual portrayals of force or violence that lack redeeming literary, artistic, political, or scientific value. Such a standard would sweep far less broadly than either prevailing obscenity laws or alternatives focused on subordination, and would target only material that is most clearly harmful. While such narrow prohibitions will be difficult to enforce, our experience with child pornography legislation suggests that limited restrictions can somewhat reduce the availability and acceptability of targeted material. At the very least, a narrowly drawn prohibition would make an important symbolic statement with relatively little cost to core First Amendment values. Films like "Dorothy: Slave to Pain" and "Pussy on a Stick" are not cornerstones of democratic discourse.

Yet neither should we overstate the importance of such pornography prohibitions or place them at the top of women's agenda. Given the limited reach and barriers to enforcement of proposed legislation, any effect on cultural norms is likely to be quite small. Moreover, while censorship strategies may look like the "cheapest items on [women's] shopping list," they carry hidden costs. Suppression requires political coalitions that strengthen antifeminist organizations and deflect energy from strategies that are less sexy but ultimately more critical.

Catharine A. MacKinnon, Feminism Unmodified: Discourses on Life and Law
171-172 (1987)

Pornography sexualizes rape, battery, sexual harassment, prostitution, and child sexual abuse; it thereby celebrates, promotes, authorizes and legitimizes them. More generally, it eroticizes the dominance and submission that is the dynamic common to them all. It makes hierarchy sexy and calls that "the truth about sex" or just a mirror of reality. Through this process pornography constructs what a woman is as what men want from sex....

Pornography constructs what a woman is in terms of its view of what men want sexually, such that acts of rape, battery, sexual harassment, prostitution, and sexual abuse of children become acts of sexual equality. Pornography's world of equality is a harmonious and balanced place. Men and women are perfectly complementary and perfectly bipolar. Women's desire to be fucked by men is equal to men's desire to fuck women. All the ways men love to take and violate women, women love to be taken and violated. The women who most love this are most men's equals, the most liberated; the most participatory child is the most grown-up, the most equal to an adult. Their consent merely expresses or ratifies these preexisting facts.

The content of pornography is one thing. There, women substantively desire dispossession and cruelty. We desperately want to be bound, battered, tortured, humiliated, and killed....What pornography does goes beyond its content: it eroticizes hierarchy, it sexualizes inequality. It makes dominance and submission into sex. Inequality is its central dynamic; the illusion of freedom coming together with the reality of force is central to its working....

From this perspective, pornography is neither harmless fantasy nor a corrupt and confused misrepresentation of an otherwise natural and healthy sexual situation. It institutionalizes the sexuality of male supremacy, fusing the erotization of dominance and submission with the social construction of male and female. To the extent that gender is sexual, pornography is part of constituting the meaning of that sexuality.

Catharine A. MacKinnon, Pornography as Defamation and Discrimination
71 B.U. L. Rev. 793, 799-803, 809-810 (1991)

Pornography has a central role in actualizing...[a] system of subordination in the contemporary West, beginning with the conditions of its production. Women in pornography are bound, battered, tortured, harassed, raped, and sometimes killed; or in the glossy men's entertainment magazines, "merely" humiliated, molested, objectified, and used. In all pornography, women are prostituted. This is done because it means sexual pleasure to pornography's consumers and profits to its providers, largely organized crime. But to those who are exploited, it means being bound, battered, tortured, harassed, raped, and sometimes killed, or merely humiliated, molested, objectified, and used. It is done because someone who has more power than they do, someone who matters, someone with rights, a full human being and a full citizen, gets pleasure from seeing it, or doing it, or seeing it as a form of doing it. In order to produce what the consumer wants to see, it must first be done to someone, usually a woman, a woman with few real choices. Because he wants to see it done, it is done to her. . . .

Over time, the evidence on the harm of pornography has only become stronger. When explicit sex and express violence against women are combined, particularly when rape is portrayed as pleasurable or positive for the victim, the risk of violence against women increases as a result of exposure. It is uncontroversial that exposure to such materials increases aggression against women in laboratory settings, increases attitudes which are related to violence against women in the real world, and increases self-reported likelihood to rape. As a result of exposure, a significant percentage of men, many not otherwise predisposed, as well as the twenty-five to thirty-five percent who report some proclivity to rape a woman, come to believe that violence against women is acceptable. Materials which combine sex with aggression also have perceptual effects which desensitize consumers to rape trauma and to sexual violence. In one study, simulated juries who had been exposed to such material were less able than real juries to perceive that an account of a rape was an account of a rape, through which the victim was harmed.

The most advanced research in this area studies the effects of materials which degrade and dehumanize women without showing violence, as that term is defined in the research. Such material has been shown to lower inhibitions on aggression by men against women, increase acceptance on women's sexual servitude, increase sexual callousness toward women, decrease the desire of both sexes to have female children, increase reported willingness to rape, and increase the belief in male dominance in intimate relationships. For high-frequency consumers, these materials also increase self-reported sexually aggressive behavior.

Men who use pornography often believe that they do not think or do these things. But the evidence shows that the use of pornography makes it impossible for men to tell when sex is forced, that women are human, and that rape is rape. Pornography makes men hostile and aggressive toward women, and it makes women silent. While these effects are not invariant or always immediate, and do not affect all men to the same degree, there is no reason to think they are not acted upon and every reason and overwhelming evidence to think that they are — if not right then, then sometime, if not violently, then through some other kind of discrimination. . . .

[P]ornography, through its production, is revealed as a traffic in sexual slavery. Through its consumption, it further institutionalizes a subhuman, victimized, second class status for women by conditioning men's orgasm to sexual inequality. When men use pornography, they experience in their bodies, not just their minds, that one-sided sex — sex between a person (them) and a thing (it) — is sex, that sexual use is sex, sexual abuse is sex, sexual domination is sex. This is the sexuality that they then demand, practice, purchase, and live out in their everyday social relations with others. Pornography works by making sexism sexy. As a primal experience of gender hierarchy, pornography is a major way in which sexism is enjoyed and practiced, as well as learned. It is one way that male supremacy is spread and made socially real. Through the use of pornography for masturbation . . . power and powerlessness are experienced and inculcated as sexual excitement and release. Inequality between women and men is what is sexy about pornography — the more unequal the sexier. In other words, pornography makes sexuality into a key dynamic in gender inequality by viscerally defining gender through the experience of hierarchical sexuality. On the way, it exploits inequalities of race, class, age, religion, sexual identity, and disability by sexualizing them through gender.

Seen in this way, pornography is at once a concrete practice and an ideological statement. The concrete practices are discriminatory; the ideological statements are defamatory. Construed as defamation in the conventional sense, pornography says that women are a lower form of human life defined by their availability for sexual use. Women are dehumanized through the conditioning of male sexuality to their use and abuse, which sexualizes, hence lowers, women across the culture, not only in express sexual interactions. . . .

A discrimination theory of defamation would center on its harm to subordinate groups. Group libel is an equality issue when its promotion undermines the social equality of a target group that is traditionally and systematically disadvantaged. Group defamation promotes the disadvantage of disadvantaged groups. Group-based enmity, ill-will, intolerance, and prejudice are the attitudinal engines of the exclusion, denigration, and subordination that comprise social inequality. Without bigotry, social systems of enforced separation and apartheid would be unnecessary, impossible, and unthinkable. Stereotyping and stigmatization of historically disadvantaged groups through group hate propaganda shape their social image and reputation, arguably controlling the opportunities of individual members more powerfully than their individual abilities do. It is impossible for an individual to receive equality of opportunity when surrounded by an atmosphere of group hatred or contempt.

In this light, group defamation can be seen as a specific kind of discriminatory practice, a verbal form inequality takes. Anti-Semitism promotes the inequality of Jews on the basis of religion and ethnicity. White supremacy promotes inequality on the basis of race, color, and sometimes ethnic origin. Group defamation in this sense is not the mere expression of anti-Semitic or white supremacist opinion but a practice of discrimination similar to sexual harassment and other discriminatory acts that take verbal form. It is arguably an integral link in systemic discrimination which keeps target groups in subordinated positions through the promotion of terror, intolerance, degradation, segregation, exclusion, vilification, violence, and genocide. The nature of the practice can be seen and proven from the damage it does, from immediate psychic wounding to consequent physical aggression. Where advocacy of genocide is part of group defamation, an equality approach to its regulation would observe that to be liquidated because of the group you belong to is the ultimate inequality.

2. Efforts to Define Pornography as Sex-Based Discrimination: The Legal Response

American Booksellers Association, Inc. v. Hudnut
771 F.2d 323 (7th Cir. 1985), aff'd mem., 475 U.S. 1001, reh'g denied, 475 U.S. 1132 (1986)

EASTERBROOK, Circuit Judge.

Indianapolis enacted an ordinance defining "pornography" as a practice that discriminates against women. "Pornography" is to be redressed through the administrative and judicial methods used for other discrimination. The City's definition of "pornography" is considerably different from "obscenity," which the Supreme Court has held is not protected by the First Amendment.

To be "obscene" under Miller v. California, [413 U.S. 15 (1973)], "a publication must, taken as a whole, appeal to the prurient interest, must contain patently offensive depictions or descriptions of specified sexual conduct, and on the whole have no serious literary, artistic, political, or scientific value." Brockett v. Spokane Arcades, Inc., [472 U.S. 491, 501 (1985)]. Offensiveness must be assessed under the standards of the community. Both offensiveness and an appeal to something other than "normal, healthy sexual desires" (Brockett, supra, 472 U.S. at 498) are essential elements of "obscenity."

"Pornography" under the ordinance is "the graphic sexually explicit subordination of women, whether in pictures or in words, that also includes one or more of the following: (1) Women are presented as sexual objects who enjoy pain or humiliation; or (2) Women are presented as sexual objects who experience sexual pleasure in being raped; or (3) Women are presented as sexual objects tied up or cut up or mutilated or bruised or physically hurt, or as dismembered or truncated or fragmented or severed into body parts; or (4) Women are presented as being penetrated by objects or animals; or (5) Women are presented in scenarios of degradation, injury, abasement, torture, shown as filthy or inferior, bleeding, bruised, or hurt in a context that makes these conditions sexual; or (6) Women are presented as sexual objects for domination, conquest, violation, exploitation, possession, or use, or through postures or positions of servility or submission or display." Indianapolis Code §16-3(q). The statute provides that the "use of men, children, or transsexuals in the place of women in paragraphs (1) through (6) above shall also constitute pornography under this section." The ordinance as passed in April 1984 defined "sexually explicit" to mean actual or simulated intercourse or the uncovered exhibition of the genitals, buttocks or anus. An amendment in June 1984 deleted this provision, leaving the term undefined.

The Indianapolis ordinance does not refer to the prurient interest, to offensiveness, or to the standards of the community. It demands attention to particular depictions, not to the work judged as a whole. It is irrelevant under the ordinance whether the work has literary, artistic, political, or scientific value. The City and many amici point to these omissions as virtues. They maintain that pornography influences attitudes, and the statute is a way to alter the socialization of men and women rather than to vindicate community standards of offensiveness. And as one of the principal drafters of the ordinance has asserted, "if a woman is subjected, why should it matter that the work has other value?" Catharine A. MacKinnon, Pornography, Civil Rights, and Speech, 20 Harv. C.R.-C.L. L. Rev. 1, 21 (1985).

Civil rights groups and feminists have entered this case as amici on both sides. Those supporting the ordinance say that it will play an important role in reducing the tendency of men to view women as sexual objects, a tendency that leads to both unacceptable attitudes and discrimination in the workplace and violence away from it. Those opposing the ordinance point out that much radical feminist literature is explicit and depicts women in ways forbidden by the ordinance and that the ordinance would reopen old battles. It is unclear how Indianapolis would treat works from James Joyce's Ulysses to Homer's Iliad; both depict women as submissive objects for conquest and domination.

We do not try to balance the arguments for and against an ordinance such as this. The ordinance discriminates on the ground of the content of the speech. Speech treating women in the approved way — in sexual encounters "premised on equality" (MacKinnon, supra, at 22) — is lawful no matter how sexually explicit. Speech treating women in the disapproved way — as submissive in matters sexual or as enjoying humiliation — is unlawful no matter how significant the literary, artistic, or political qualities of the work taken as a whole. The state may not ordain preferred viewpoints in this way. The Constitution forbids the state to declare one perspective right and silence opponents.

I

The ordinance contains four prohibitions. People may not "traffic" in pornography, "coerce" others into performing in pornographic works, or "force" pornography on anyone. Anyone injured by someone who has seen or read pornography has a right of action against the maker or seller.

Trafficking is defined in § 16-3(g)(4) as the "production, sale, exhibition, or distribution of pornography." The offense excludes exhibition in a public or educational library, but a "special display" in a library may be sex discrimination. Section 16-3(g)(4)(C) provides that the trafficking paragraph "shall not be construed to make isolated passages or isolated parts actionable."

"Coercion into pornographic performance" is defined in § 16-3(g)(5) as "[c]oercing, intimidating or fraudulently inducing any person . . . into performing for pornography. . . ." The ordinance specifies that proof of any of the following "shall not constitute a defense: I. That the person is a woman; . . . VI. That the person has previously posed for sexually explicit pictures . . . with anyone . . . ; . . . VIII. That the person actually consented to a use of the performance that is changed into pornography; . . . IX. That the person knew that the purpose of the acts or events in question was to make pornography; . . . XI. That the person signed a contract, or made statements affirming a willingness to cooperate in the production of pornography; XII. That no physical force, threats, or weapons were used in the making of the pornography; or XIII. That the person was paid or otherwise compensated."

"Forcing pornography on a person," according to § 16-3(g)(5), is the "forcing of pornography on any woman, man, child, or transsexual in any place of employment, in education, in a home, or in any public place." The statute does not define forcing, but one of its authors states that the definition reaches pornography shown to medical students as part of their education or given to language students for translation. MacKinnon, supra, at 40-41.

Section 16-3(g)(7) defines as a prohibited practice the "assault, physical attack, or injury of any woman, man, child, or transsexual in a way that is directly caused by specific pornography."

For purposes of all four offenses, it is generally "not . . . a defense that the respondent did not know or intend that the materials were pornography. . . ." Section 16-3(g)(8). But the ordinance provides that damages are unavailable in trafficking cases unless the complainant proves "that the respondent knew or had reason to know that the materials were pornography." It is a complete defense to a trafficking case that all of the materials in question were pornography only by virtue of category (6) of the definition of pornography. In cases of assault caused by pornography, those who seek damages from "a seller, exhibitor or distributor" must show that the defendant knew or had reason to know of the material's status as pornography. By implication, those who seek damages from an author need not show this. A woman aggrieved by trafficking in pornography may file a complaint "as a woman acting against the subordination of women" with the office of equal opportunity. Section 16-17(b). A man, child, or transsexual also may protest trafficking "but must prove injury in the same way that a woman is injured. . . ." " Id. Subsection (a) also provides, however, that "any person claiming to be aggrieved" by trafficking, coercion, forcing, or assault may complain against the "perpetrators." . . .

The office investigates and within 30 days makes a recommendation to a panel of the equal opportunity advisory board. The panel then decides whether there is reasonable cause to proceed (§ 16-24(2)) and may refer the dispute to a conciliation conference or to a complaint adjudication committee for a hearing (§§ 16-24(3), 16-26(a)). The committee uses the same procedures ordinarily associated with civil rights litigation. It may make findings and enter orders, including both orders to cease and desist and orders "to take further affirmative action . . . including but not limited to the power to restore complainant's losses. . . ." Section 16-26(d). Either party may appeal the committee's decision to the board, which reviews the record before the committee and may modify its decision. . . . The board's decisions are subject to review in the ordinary course. Ind. Stat. 4-22-1-14. . . .

The district court held the ordinance unconstitutional. 598 F. Supp. 1316 (S.D. Ind. 1984). . . .

II

The plaintiffs are a congeries of distributors and readers of books, magazines, and films. The American Booksellers Association comprises about 5,200 bookstores and chains. The Association for American Publishers includes most of the country's publishers. Video Shack, Inc., sells and rents video cassettes in Indianapolis. Kelly Bentley, a resident of Indianapolis, reads books and watches films. There are many more plaintiffs. Collectively the plaintiffs (or their members, whose interests they represent) make, sell, or read just about every kind of material that could be affected by the ordinance, from hard-core films to W.B. Yeats's poem "Leda and the Swan" (from the myth of Zeus in the form of a swan impregnating an apparently subordinate Leda), to the collected works of James Joyce, D.H. Lawrence, and John Cleland....

III

"If there is any fixed star in our constitutional constellation, it is that no official, high or petty, can prescribe what shall be orthodox in politics, nationalism, religion, or other matters of opinion or force citizens to confess by word or act their faith therein." West Virginia State Board of Education v. Barnette, [319 U.S. 624, 642 (1943)]. Under the First Amendment the government must leave to the people the evaluation of ideas. Bald or subtle, an idea is as powerful as the audience allows it to be. A belief may be pernicious—the beliefs of Nazis led to the death of millions, those of the Klan to the repression of millions. A pernicious belief may prevail. Totalitarian governments today rule much of the planet, practicing suppression of billions and spreading dogma that may enslave others. One of the things that separates our society from theirs is our absolute right to propagate opinions that the government finds wrong or even hateful....

Under the ordinance graphic sexually explicit speech is "pornography" or not depending on the perspective the author adopts. Speech that "subordinates" women and also, for example, presents women as enjoying pain, humiliation, or rape, or even simply presents women in "positions of servility or submission or display" is forbidden, no matter how great the literary or political value of the work taken as a whole. Speech that portrays women in positions of equality is lawful, no matter how graphic the sexual content. This is thought control. It establishes an "approved" view of women, of how they may react to sexual encounters, of how the sexes may relate to each other. Those who espouse the approved view may use sexual images; those who do not, may not.

Indianapolis justifies the ordinance on the ground that pornography affects thoughts. Men who see women depicted as subordinate are more likely to treat them so. Pornography is an aspect of dominance. It does not persuade people so much as change them. It works by socializing, by establishing the expected and the permissible. In this view pornography is not an idea; pornography is the injury.

There is much to this perspective. Beliefs are also facts. People often act in accordance with the images and patterns they find around them. People raised in a religion tend to accept the tenets of that religion, often without independent examination. People taught from birth that black people are fit only for slavery rarely rebelled against that creed; beliefs coupled with the self-interest of the masters established a social structure that inflicted great harm while enduring for centuries. Words and images act at the level of the subconscious before they persuade at the level of the conscious. Even the truth has little chance unless a statement fits within the framework of beliefs that may never have been subjected to rational study.

Therefore we accept the premises of this legislation. Depictions of subordination tend to perpetuate subordination. The subordinate status of women in turn leads to affront and lower pay at work, insult and injury at home, battery and rape on the streets.[2] In the language of the legislature, "[p]ornography is central in creating and maintaining sex as a basis of discrimination. Pornography is a systematic practice of exploitation and subordination based on sex which differentially harms women. The bigotry and contempt it produces, with the acts of aggression it fosters, harm women's opportunities for equality and rights [of all kinds]." Indianapolis Code § 16-1(a)(2).

Yet this simply demonstrates the power of pornography as speech. All of these unhappy effects depend on mental intermediation. Pornography affects how people see the world, their fellows, and social relations. If pornography is what pornography does, so is other speech. Hitler's orations affected how some Germans saw Jews. Communism is a world view, not simply a Manifesto by Marx and Engels or a set of speeches. Efforts to suppress communist speech in the United States were based on the belief that the public acceptability of such ideas would increase the likelihood of totalitarian government. Religions affect socialization in the most pervasive way. The opinion in Wisconsin v. Yoder, [406 U.S. 205 (1972)], shows how a religion can dominate an entire approach to life, governing much more than the relation between the sexes. Many people believe that the existence of television, apart from the content of specific programs, leads to intellectual laziness, to a penchant for violence, to many other ills. The Alien and Sedition Acts passed during the administration of John Adams rested on a sincerely held belief that disrespect for the government leads to social collapse and revolution — a belief with support in the history of many nations. Most governments of the world act on this empirical regularity, suppressing critical speech. In the United States, however, the strength of the support for this belief is irrelevant. Seditious libel is protected speech unless the danger is not only grave but also imminent. See New York Times Co. v. Sullivan, [376 U.S. 254 (1964)]; cf. Brandenburg v. Ohio, supra; New York Times Co. v. United States, [403 U.S. 713 (1971)].

Racial bigotry, anti-semitism, violence on television, reporters' biases — these and many more influence the culture and shape our socialization. None is directly answerable by more speech, unless that speech too finds its place in the popular culture. Yet all is protected as speech, however insidious. Any other

---

2. MacKinnon's article collects empirical work that supports this proposition. The social science studies are very difficult to interpret, however, and they conflict. Because much of the effect of speech comes through a process of socialization, it is difficult to measure incremental benefits and injuries caused by particular speech. Several psychologists have found, for example, that those who see violent, sexually explicit films tend to have more violent thoughts. But how often does this lead to actual violence? National commissions on obscenity here, in the United Kingdom, and in Canada have found that it is not possible to demonstrate a direct link between obscenity and rape or exhibitionism. . . . The several opinions in Miller v. California discuss the U.S. commission.

answer leaves the government in control of all of the institutions of culture, the great censor and director of which thoughts are good for us.

Sexual responses often are unthinking responses, and the association of sexual arousal with the subordination of women therefore may have a substantial effect. But almost all cultural stimuli provoke unconscious responses. Religious ceremonies condition their participants. Teachers convey messages by selecting what not to cover; the implicit message about what is off limits or unthinkable may be more powerful than the messages for which they present rational argument. Television scripts contain unarticulated assumptions. People may be conditioned in subtle ways. If the fact that speech plays a role in a process of conditioning were enough to permit governmental regulation, that would be the end of freedom of speech. . . .

The more immediate point, however, is that the image of pain is not necessarily pain. In Body Double, a suspense film directed by Brian DePalma, a woman who has disrobed and presented a sexually explicit display is murdered by an intruder with a drill. The drill runs through the woman's body. The film is sexually explicit and a murder occurs—yet no one believes that the actress suffered pain or died. . . . In Carnal Knowledge a woman grovels to please the sexual whims of a character played by Jack Nicholson; no one believes that there was a real sexual submission, and the Supreme Court held the film protected by the First Amendment. Jenkins v. Georgia, [418 U.S. 153 (1974)]. And this works both ways. The description of women's sexual domination of men in Lysistrata was not real dominance. Depictions may affect slavery, war, or sexual roles, but a book about slavery is not itself slavery, or a book about death by poison a murder.

Much of Indianapolis's argument rests on the belief that when speech is "unanswerable," and the metaphor that there is a "marketplace of ideas" does not apply, the First Amendment does not apply either. The metaphor is honored; Milton's Areopagitica and John Stewart [sic] Mill's On Liberty defend freedom of speech on the ground that the truth will prevail, and many of the most important cases under the First Amendment recite this position. The Framers undoubtedly believed it. As a general matter it is true. But the Constitution does not make the dominance of truth a necessary condition of freedom of speech. To say that it does would be to confuse an outcome of free speech with a necessary condition for the application of the amendment.

A power to limit speech on the ground that truth has not yet prevailed and is not likely to prevail implies the power to declare truth. At some point the government must be able to say (as Indianapolis has said): "We know what the truth is, yet a free exchange of speech has not driven out falsity, so that we must now prohibit falsity." If the government may declare the truth, why wait for the failure of speech? Under the First Amendment, however, there is no such thing as a false idea, Gertz v. Robert Welch, Inc., [418 U.S. 323, 339 (1974)], so the government may not restrict speech on the ground that in a free exchange truth is not yet dominant.

At any time, some speech is ahead in the game; the more numerous speakers prevail. Supporters of minority candidates may be forever "excluded" from the political process because their candidates never win, because few people believe their positions. This does not mean that freedom of speech has failed. . . .

We come, finally, to the argument that pornography is "low value" speech, that it is enough like obscenity that Indianapolis may prohibit it. Some cases hold that speech far removed from politics and other subjects at the core of the Framers' concerns may be subjected to special regulation. E.g., FCC v. Pacifica Foundation, [438 U.S. 726 (1978)]; Young v. American Mini Theatres, Inc., [427 U.S. 50, 67-70 (1976)] (plurality opinion); Chaplinsky v. New Hampshire, [315 U.S. 568, 571-572 (1942)]. These cases do not sustain statutes that select among viewpoints, however. In *Pacifica* the FCC sought to keep vile language off the air during certain times. The Court held that it may; but the Court would not have sustained a regulation prohibiting scatological descriptions of Republicans but not scatological descriptions of Democrats, or any other form of selection among viewpoints. See Planned Parenthood Ass'n v. Chicago Transit Authority, 767 F.2d 1225, 1232-1233 (7th Cir. 1985).

At all events, "pornography" is not low value speech within the meaning of these cases. Indianapolis seeks to prohibit certain speech because it believes this speech influences social relations and politics on a grand scale, that it controls attitudes at home and in the legislature. This precludes a characterization of the speech as low value. True, pornography and obscenity have sex in common. But Indianapolis left out of its definition any reference to literary, artistic, political, or scientific value. The ordinance applies to graphic sexually explicit subordination in works great and small. The Court sometimes balances the value of speech against the costs of its restriction, but it does this by category of speech and not by the content of particular works. . . . Indianapolis has created an approved point of view and so loses the support of these cases.

Any rationale we could imagine in support of this ordinance could not be limited to sex discrimination. Free speech has been on balance an ally of those seeking change. Governments that want stasis start by restricting speech. Culture is a powerful force of continuity; Indianapolis paints pornography as part of the culture of power. Change in any complex system ultimately depends on the ability of outsiders to challenge accepted views and the reigning institutions. Without a strong guarantee of freedom of speech, there is no effective right to challenge what is.

IV

. . . The offense of coercion to engage in a pornographic performance . . . has elements that might be constitutional. Without question a state may prohibit fraud, trickery, or the use of force to induce people to perform — in pornographic films or in any other films. Such a statute may be written without regard to the viewpoint depicted in the work. New York v. Ferber, [458 U.S. 747 (1982)], suggests that when a state has a strong interest in forbidding the conduct that makes up a film (in *Ferber* sexual acts involving minors), it may restrict or forbid dissemination of the film in order to reinforce the prohibition of the conduct. A state may apply such a rule to non-sexual coercion (although it need not)....

But the Indianapolis ordinance, unlike our hypothetical statute, is not neutral with respect to viewpoint. The ban on distribution of works containing coerced performances is limited to pornography; coercion is irrelevant if the work is not "pornography," and we have held the definition of "pornography" to be defective root and branch. A legislature might replace "pornography" in § 16-3(g)(4) with "any film containing explicit sex" or some similar expression, but even the broadest severability clause does not permit a federal court to rewrite as opposed to excise. Rewriting is work for the legislature of Indianapolis....

Much speech is dangerous. Chemists whose work might help someone build a bomb, political theorists whose papers might start political movements that lead to riots, speakers whose ideas attract violent protesters, all these and more leave loss in their wake. Unless the remedy is very closely confined, it could be more dangerous to speech than all the libel judgments in history. The constitutional requirements for a valid recovery for assault caused by speech might turn out to be too rigorous for any plaintiff to meet. But the Indianapolis ordinance requires the complainant to show that the attack was "directly caused by specific pornography" (§ 16-3(g)(7)), and it is not beyond the realm of possibility that a state court could construe this limitation in a way that would make the statute constitutional. We are not authorized to prevent the state from trying.

Again, however, the assault statute is tied to "pornography," and we cannot find a sensible way to repair the defect without seizing power that belongs elsewhere. Indianapolis might choose to have no ordinance if it cannot be limited to viewpoint-specific harms, or it might choose to extend the scope to all speech, just as the law of libel applies to all speech. An attempt to repair this ordinance would be nothing but a blind guess.

No amount of struggle with particular words and phrases in this ordinance can leave anything in effect. The district court came to the same conclusion. Its judgment is therefore Affirmed.

[A concurring opinion by Swygert, Senior Circuit Judge, is omitted.]

3. Feminist Responses to Feminist Anti-Pornography Initiatives

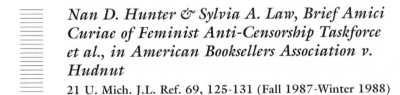

Nan D. Hunter & Sylvia A. Law, Brief Amici Curiae of Feminist Anti-Censorship Taskforce et al., in American Booksellers Association v. Hudnut
21 U. Mich. J.L. Ref. 69, 125-131 (Fall 1987-Winter 1988)

The [Indianapolis] ordinance defines pornography in gender specific terms as "the graphic sexually explicit subordination of women" that also presents "women" in particular ways proscribed by the law.... The heart of the ordinance is the suppression of sexually explicit images of women, based on a finding of "subordination," a term which is not defined. The ordinance implies that sexually explicit images of women necessarily subordinate and degrade women and perpetuates stereotypes of women as helpless victims and people who could not seek or enjoy sex.

The ordinance also reinforces sexist stereotypes of men. It denies the possibility that graphic sexually explicit images of a man could ever subordinate or degrade him. It provides no remedy for sexually explicit images showing men as "dismembered, truncated or fragmented" or "shown as filthy or inferior, bleeding, bruised or hurt."...

The ordinance reinforces yet another sexist stereotype of men as aggressive beasts. Appellants assert:

> By conditioning the male orgasm to female subordination, pornography... makes the subordination of women pleasurable and seemingly legitimate. Each time men are sexually aroused by pornography, they learn to connect a woman's sexual pleasure to abuse and a woman's sexual nature to inferiority. They learn this in their bodies, not just their minds, so that it becomes a natural physiological response. At this point pornography leaves no more room for further debate than does shouting "kill" to an attack dog.

Men are not attack dogs, but morally responsible human beings. The ordinance reinforces a destructive sexist stereotype of men as irresponsible beasts, with "natural physiological responses" which can be triggered by sexually explicit images of women, and for which the men cannot be held accountable. Thus, men are conditioned into violent acts or negative beliefs by sexual images; women are not. Further, the ordinance is wholly blind to the possibility that men could be hurt and degraded by images presenting them as violent or sadistic.

The ordinance also reinforces sexist images of woman as incapable of consent. It creates a remedy for people "coerced" to participate in the production of pornography....

In effect, the ordinance creates a strong presumption that women who participate in the creation of sexually explicit material are coerced. A woman's manifestation of consent—no matter how plain, informed, or even self-initiated—does not constitute a defense to her subsequent claim of coercion. Women are judged incompetent to consent to participate in the creation of sexually explicit material and condemned as "bad" if they do so....

This provision does far more than simply provide a remedy to women who are pressured into the creation of pornography which they subsequently seek to suppress. It functions to make all women incompetent to enter into legally binding contracts for the production of sexually explicit material. When women are legally disabled from making binding agreements, they are denied power to negotiate for fair treatment and decent pay. Enforcement of the ordinance would drive production of sexually explicit material even further into an underground economy, where the working conditions of women in the sex industry would worsen, not improve....

The ordinance damages individuals who do not fit the stereotypes it embodies. It delegitimates and makes socially invisible women who find sexually explicit images of women "in positions of display" or "penetrated by objects" to be erotic, liberating, or educational. These women are told that their perceptions are a product of "false consciousness" and that such images are so inherently degrading that they may be suppressed by the state. At the same time, it stamps the imprimatur of state approval on the belief that men are attack dogs triggered to violence by the sight of a sexually explicit image of a woman. It delegitimates and makes socially invisible those men who consider themselves gentle, respectful of women, or inhibited about expressing their sexuality.

Even worse, the stereotypes of the ordinance perpetuate traditional social views of sex-based difference. By defining sexually explicit images of women as subordinating and degrading to them, the ordinance reinforces the stereotypical view that "good" women do not seek and enjoy sex. As applied, it would deny women access to sexually explicit material at a time in our history when women have just begun to acquire the social and economic power to develop our own images of sexuality. Stereotypes of hair-trigger male susceptibility to violent imagery can be invoked as an excuse to avoid directly blaming the men who commit violent acts.

Finally, the ordinance perpetuates a stereotype of women as helpless victims, incapable of consent, and in need of protection. . . . We have learned through hard experience that gender-based classifications protecting women from their own presumed innate vulnerability reflect "an attitude of 'romantic paternalism' which, in practical effect, puts women not on a pedestal but in a cage." Frontiero v. Richardson, 411 U.S. 677, 684 (1973). . . .

Women were, and continue to be, in a position of social and economic vulnerability that inhibits their ability to negotiate fair terms and conditions of wage labor. Further, the pervasive sexism and violence of our culture make women vulnerable to exploitation and inhibit their ability to enter into sexual or other relationships on a free and voluntary basis. . . .

But even accurate generalizations about women's need for help do not justify sex-based classifications such as those in this ordinance. It is also true that women generally are still the ones who nurture young children. Yet we understand that laws giving mothers an irrebuttable "tender years" presumption for custody, or offering child rearing leaves only to mothers but not to fathers, ultimately hurt women and are unconstitutional.

Carlin Meyer, *Sex, Sin, and Women's Liberation: Against Porn-Suppression*
72 Tex. L. Rev. 1097, 1136, 1138-1141, 1155-1156, 1184-1185, 1187-1189, 1192-1193 (1994)

The subject matters of much porn are complex and contradictory and may, depending on the manner in which they are presented, absorbed, or understood, contribute to feminist goals. Pornography breaks the boundaries of traditionally confined sex and sexual depiction.... Precisely because pornography is so outrageous, it can be explosively subversive, challenging social strictures that keep women oppressed....

Women who dare to admit that they enjoy porn note that its images are "many and varied"—some "fragmented and idealized," others "crude and unflattering," others "dreamy, psychedelic," and still others "violent, reptilian." They emphasize that their responses to it are "layered and complex and multiple." For young women, porn not only offers otherwise unavailable information about sex, but by providing imaginary transgressions of traditionally restrictive sexual parameters, it provides reassurance and permission to be sexual. And the same porn imagery that shows women on display often also portrays them as sexually powerful. The very power of sexual imagery to objectify women may be—and often is—subversively employed to reverse or at least question the process or basis of objectification.

Moreover, literal subject matter does not capture meaning or import. Contemporary scholarship in fields ranging from semiotics to cultural critique have taught us that within the "language" of depiction, images vary according to subtle, cloaked signs and symbols; references, pre-conceptions, "understood" vocabulary, gaze, and perspective all affect meaning....

Indeed, it is not content alone, but also context and audience reception that determine whether a portrayal degrades women. Porn gains its meaning because of sexual "taboos" that confine viewing to secrecy; because of the predispositions of its largely male audience concerning what it ought to mean and how they ought to react to it; because it is shown in "stag" contexts—often in association with military and sports conquest; and because it is used as a ritual of male bonding, of Oedipal rebellion against the authority of mothers, of growth towards manhood, and hence is linked to exclusion and vanquishment of the female. Disassociated from some or all of these contexts and meanings, its import may change.

By treating "subordination" as residing in the image itself rather than in the engagement between image and audience, anti-porn advocates ignore the "play" between the two. Point of view, presentation, medium, and, most importantly, the pre-existing understandings, beliefs, cultural discourses, and language of the audience invest an image with meaning. Significance arises not from the images alone, but from their place within the artistic, cultural, moral, and sexual discourse that changes over time and according to the audience and the particular context....

Some, like Barbara Omolade, bell hooks, and Angela Harris argue that the lens of race is at least as important as that of sex in understanding patriarchal sexuality. Omolade points to European men's "cultural definitions of sex, nudity, and blackness as base, foul and bestial," [Omolade, Hearts of Darkness in Powers of Desire: The Politics of Sexuality 350, 351 (Ann Snitow et al. eds., 1983)] and hooks describes the contemporary commodification of "race and ethnicity" as "resources for pleasure" such that "the culture of specific groups, as well as the bodies of individuals, can be seen as constituting an alternative playground where members of dominating races, genders, [and] sexual practices affirm their power-over in intimate relations with the Other." [bell hooks, Black Looks: Race and

Representation 23 (1992).] Harris notes that "[f]or black women, rape is . . . an experience as deeply rooted in color as in gender." [Angela P. Harris, Race and Essentialism in Feminist Legal Theory, 42 Stan. L. Rev. 581, 598 (1990).] Still other writers point to the importance of class, noting the sexual stigmatization of lower classes — such as prostitutes, "foreigners," slaves, and minorities — and arguing that the creation of the category "pornography" may itself be a product of dominant groups' desire to maintain power. To require that debate over these issues eschew evocative sexual depiction and take place only in arid scholarly form is to deny feminism one of the most powerful tools of exploration and change. . . .

Most pornography, because of its exaggerated and unrealistic portrayal, invites the viewer or reader to suspend belief rather than to take its portrayals as "true." The manner in which it is typically "consumed" — in secret, "stag" arenas, or specially zoned theaters — heightens its unreal quality. Unlike television's serials, soaps, and even, sometimes, advertisements, which purport to portray "real life" by situating themselves in "real" time and space and wresting with true life problems, porn is suspended in time and space, presenting a fantasy world of endless sex uninterrupted by daily tasks and unmarred by mundane detail or real-life responsibilities. Thus, although it may be "at the pinnacle of the sexist iconography of insatiable male sexual activity and ubiquitous female sexual availability," and may even be "the 'truest' form of patriarchal ideology," it represents a fantasy world that neither creates nor expresses men's "straightforwardly conscious wishes and intentions." [Lynne Segal, Slow Motion: Changing Masculinities, Changing Men 222 (1990).] . . .

Porn's shallow world of insatiable women and unflaggingly erect men is hardly the stuff from which the complex web of Western sexuality could be woven. Rather, contrasting notions of "acceptable male emotions associated with the approved discourses on male sexuality" — for example "[s]ex restrained by love and marriage, sex which is 'protective,' 'respectable' and 'faithful' " — are essential to and give meaning to porn's contrary world of "sex greedy for immediate, unlimited, self-centered gratification." Empedestaled, chaste, and virtuous women are central to constituting other women as sexually "debased" and therefore available for sexual domination or abuse. Men are induced to find pleasure in fantasies of sexual domination not only by treating women as sex objects, but also by treating them as too pure to touch, or too stupid, flutter-brained, or frigid to be sexual at all. Aggression is "eroticized" not simply by treating women as objects of male lust, but by placing them in the contradictory roles of virgins and whores; of mothers, wives, servants, and lovers; of guardians of morality who impel men to sin and then punish them for their "Fall." Male domination is sexualized not merely when women are pictured as enjoying rape, but also when a boy's growth towards manhood is associated with conquest and vanquishment — of nature, of enemies, and of women.

To reduce Western erotica to a pornographic picture is to understate the power and depth of patriarchal conditioning, which could not be captured within porn's one-sided, shallow, and repetitive imagery. Porn is meant, like the popular mystery genre, to allow escape into shallow plots and fantasies of quick and easy satisfaction, not to foster conversion. . . .

Nor is it likely that porn's blatant show of force against women increases its effectiveness in persuading its audience to view women as objects or to use force against them. . . . In other words, porn's graphic display of male sexual power over and violence toward women, as well as the similar portrayals in mainstream advertising, television, and film, are the likely symptoms of and reactions to weakening male power, rather than indications of porn's centrality to establishing male power in the first instance. . . .

[E]ven were it the case that bodily arousal or the repeat viewing that porn seems to spawn enhances audience absorption of an ideological subtext, suppression would not be a viable strategy. For it would be impossible to suppress all imagery that is arousing at the expense of women. One would have to get rid of depictions ranging from Alfred Hitchcock's *Psycho*, in which the protagonist's unnatural attachment to his own mother drives him to murder women to whom he is attracted, to slasher and other horror films, to large segments of popular music and music videos. Indeed, one might even have to suppress advertising imagery, for much of it aims to persuade by arousal, and expresses the same views of women as are found in porn. . . .

[W]omen do not seem to be as silenced as anti-porn advocates claim: Across class, race, occupation, ethnicity, and geographic locale, women are speaking out and being listened to as never before. Advocates of suppression answer that porn is proliferating precisely because women's voices have begun to emerge, and porn is part of society's way of shutting women back up. Though the evidence of backlash against women's changing roles and newly emergent power is plentiful, and though porn proliferation is very likely part of it, it is but a minor part and has not, so far, seemed to silence women. Indeed, "it is precisely since the 1970s, and the explosion of pornography in the West, that women have been most vociferously — and successfully — objecting to men's violence against them." [Segal, *supra*, at 227.]

In sum, porn simply is not the powerful force that anti-porn advocates imagine. It may often be sexist, vulgar, violent, and horrific. The wish to be rid of it is surely understandable. But there are no easy ways to be rid of imagery that portrays women in ways we might wish women not be portrayed — nor, especially, be treated — and suppressionist quick-fix strategies do more harm than good.

Mary C. Dunlap, Sexual Speech and the State: Putting Pornography in Its Place
17 Golden Gate U. L. Rev. 359, 365-369 (1987)

The need for "sexually explicit" expression, and for more and clearer communication about sexual matters, seems to multiply with every day's revelations of new relationships, possibilities between people, and phenomena. . . . [B]efore any further restrictions on sexual speech are urged, the proponents of such restrictions [should] consider the following list of priorities of the feminist and human rights movements, and the concrete implications of restrictions upon "sexually explicit" expression upon each priority:

1. The effort to give children better, more effective tools to combat sexual abuse, including familial sexual abuse and incest;

2. Enablement/empowerment of both minors and adults to know more about their own developing sexualities (including the pro's and con's of being gay, lesbian, bisexual, heterosexual, celibate or otherwise); the methods and effects of particular forms of contraception; pregnancy in and out of marriage; surrogate motherhood; venereal disease; abortion choice; AIDS/ARC causes, modes of prevention and treatment; rape and sexual assault; the sex industry (including prostitution, pornography, commercialization of sex);

3. Improvement of intimate relationships, by people learning to say what they do and do not like, want or need in the way of sex;

4. Breaking down sex-stereotyping and sex-role stereotyping in all realms of life, in work, play, economics, sexual activity;

5. Expanding the possibilities of aesthetic and artistic adventuring about sex (viewing sexual activity as a frontier, in which fantasy, imagination and art need to be free to develop, alongside "safe sex" and auto-erotic practices) and developing rich and satisfying sources of erotica (that is, non-violent and egalitarian sexual media);

6. Working to overcome the dichotomization and polarization of "women" versus "ladies," and of sexually active women including "promiscuous" women, prostitutes, single mothers and teenage females versus virtuous females, virgins, and monogamous, virtuous wives;

7. Elevating and enriching the level of public media about sexual activity (from the "dirty secrets" approach common in current media to something at once loftier and deeper) with attention to preserving fun as well as dignity and to respecting the need for privacy as well as public education in sexual matters;

8. Getting the government out of the bedroom where the activities occurring there are both "victimless" and essentially private while getting the government to act to prevent and remedy forms of serious and damaging violence against women that have been historically legally neglected or insulated from legal scrutiny by assertions of male, paternal privilege and authority (e.g. marital rape; child abuse and incest; sexual harassment);

9. Distinguishing between sex and violence.

[E]ach of the above listed items cuts against the approach of the "anti-pornography" ordinance, literally (in terms of a conflict between serving that priority and enforcing the ordinance), in policy terms, and in terms of constitutional and political development of "free speech."

Notes

1. Pornography and the First Amendment. *Hudnut* reflects the conventional First Amendment response to legal restrictions on pornography. Nadine Strossen, president of the ACLU, presents a fuller statement of objections to pornography regulation based on the First Amendment, which she believes is fully consistent with women's interests in free speech, in Defending Pornography: Free Speech, Sex, and the Fight for Women's Rights (1995).

Some defenses of pornography regulation have focused on reconciling such regulation with existing First Amendment doctrine. They note that

> free expression is not the only value that we value, and courts have long tolerated many content-based restrictions on speech. Obvious examples include prohibitions on libel, bribery, fraud, workplace harassment, and employers' threats concerning unions. The harms associated with some of this restricted speech are not self-evidently greater than those traceable to certain pornography, such as sexually violent material.

Rhode, Speaking of Sex, supra at 53. See Cass Sunstein, Pornography and the First Amendment, 1986 Duke L.J. 589 (arguing that pornography is "low value" expression, which produces sufficient harm to justify regulation). Other commentators argue that anti-pornography statutes like the Indianapolis ordinance are no more vague than existing obscenity law and may in fact be less subject to inconsistent, idiosyncratic enforcement. See, e.g., James Lindgren, Defining Pornography 141 U. Pa. L. Rev. 1153, 1214-1215 (1993) (finding that law students were better able to apply the ordinance's concept of subordination than the *Miller* obscenity standard).

In challenging the conventional First Amendment approach to pornography, MacKinnon maintains:

> Laissez-faire might be an adequate theory . . . in a nonhierarchical society. In a society of gender inequality, the speech of the powerful impresses its view upon the world, concealing the truth of powerlessness under a despairing acquiescence that provides the appearance of consent and makes protest inaudible as well as rare. Pornography can invent women because it has the power to make its vision into reality, which then passes, objectively, for truth. So while the First Amendment supports pornography on the belief that consensus and progress are facilitated by allowing all views, however divergent and unorthodox, it fails to notice that pornography . . . is not at all divergent or unorthodox. It is the ruling ideology. Feminism, the dissenting view, is suppressed by pornography. Thus, while defenders of pornography argue that allowing all speech, including pornography, frees the mind to fulfill itself, pornography freely enslaves women's minds and bodies inseparably, normalizing the terror that enforces silence on women's point of view.

Catharine A. MacKinnon, Toward a Feminist Theory of the State 205 (1989). See also In Harm's Way: The Pornography Civil Rights Hearings (Catharine A. MacKinnon & Andrea Dworkin eds., 1997); Catharine A. MacKinnon, Only Words (1993); Catharine A. MacKinnon, Feminism Unmodified: Discourses on Life and Law 127-138 (1987); Andrea Dworkin, Against the Male Flood: Censorship, Pornography, and Equality, 8 Harv. Women's L.J. 1 (1985).

Legislation somewhat similar to the Indianapolis ordinance has been upheld by the Canadian Supreme Court. In Regina v. Butler, 89 D.L.R.4th 449 (S.C.C. 1992), the court sustained a statute that criminalizes "any publication a dominant characteristic of which is the undue exploitation of sex, or of sex and any one or more of the following subjects, namely crime, horror, cruelty and violence," interpreting the statute to prohibit any "materials that subordinate, degrade or dehumanize women." Cf. Regina v. Keegstra, [1990] 3 S.C.R. 697 (upholding statute penalizing communication of statements that willfully promote hatred against any identifiable racial, religious, or ethnic group). See Justin A. Giordano, The United States Constitution's First Amendment vs. the Canadian Charter of Rights and Freedoms: A Comparative Analysis of Obscenity and Pornography as Forms of Expression, 26 N.C. Cent. L.J. 71 (2004) (comparing pornography regulation in Canada and the United States). Whether *Butler* has been effective in challenging pornography and whether it has been selectively applied to gay and lesbian publications remain a matter of controversy. See Brenda Cossman, Feminist Fashion or Morality in Drag? The Sexual Subject of the *Butler* Decision, in Bad Attitudes on Trial: Pornography, Feminism and the *Butler* Decision (Lisa Botell & Becki L. Ross eds., 1997); Joan Kennedy Taylor, Does Sexual Speech Harm Women? The Split Within Feminism, 5 Stan. L. & Pol'y Rev. 49, 52 (1994) (discussing selective enforcement). But see Ann Scales, Avoiding Constitutional Depression: Bad Attitudes and the Fate of *Butler*, 7 Can. J. of Women & Law 349 (1994) (defending *Butler* and arguing that it was misapplied in the high-profile case against lesbian literature, which critics use as an example of the dangers of anti-pornography regulation).

2. Evaluating the Harm of Pornography. Evidence concerning the harms of pornography remains conflicting and contested. In 2004, the Subcommittee on Science, Technology, and Space of the Senate Committee on Commerce held a hearing on The Science Behind Pornography Addiction, Hearing on S. 2056, 108th Cong. 253 (2004). At the hearing, James B. Weaver, III summarized the findings of studies documenting harms from pornography, reviewed in James B. Weaver, III, Pornography and Sexual Callousness: The Perceptual and Behavioral Consequences of Exposure to Pornography, in Media, Children and the Family: Social, Scientific, Psychodynamic, and Clinical Perspectives 215, 219-221 (Dolf Zillmann et al. eds., 1994), and John S. Lyons et al., A Systematic Review of the Effects of Aggressive and Nonaggressive Pornography, in id., 271, 302-311. According to this research, prolonged exposure to pornography promotes sexual callousness, increases proclivity to rape, promotes adverse perceptions of women, and erodes trust and honesty in intimate relationships. (See statement of James B. Weaver III, available at http://commerce.senate.gov/hearings/testimony.cfm?id=1343&wit_id=3911.

Other experts have similarly argued that frequent viewing of pornography leads to unrealistic expectations concerning women's appearance and behavior, and difficulties in forming sexually satisfying relationships. See Pamela Paul, The Porn Factor, Time, Jan. 19, 2004, at 99. In a Kaiser Family Foundation study, about half of the fifteen- to twenty-four-year olds surveyed believed that adolescents who see pornography on the Internet are more likely to have sex before they are ready and that such material promotes bad attitudes toward women. Id. A study of battered women also found that pornography use by the batterer was correlated with an increased likelihood of sexual as well as physical abuse. Janet Hinson Shope, When Words Are Not Enough: The Search for the Effect of Pornography on Abused Women, 10 Violence Against Women 56, 67-68 (2004).

By contrast, other experts maintain that the vast majority of pornography viewers are occasional, recreational users, not addicts, that such use can be beneficial in sparking desire and enhancing satisfaction. Paul, supra, at 99. Many researchers also believe that the causal relationships between pornography and sexual violence have not been established and that the 2004 Hearings were stacked to exclude researchers who would have provided more credible evidence than the pornography opponents who testified. See Paul, supra, at 9; Clay Calvert, The First Amendment, the Media, and Cultural Wars: Eight Important Lessons from 2004 about Speech, Censorship, Science, and Public Policy, 41. Cal. W. L. Rev. 325, 344 (2005).

An equally contested issue is what kinds of explicit sexual imagery are most damaging. The premise of an Indianapolis-style ordinance is that violent pornography is more harmful and therefore more appropriate for regulation than nonviolent pornography. By contrast, some feminists, including Carlin Meyer, contend that the most adverse affects on women's self-image come from nonviolent mainstream images that appear acceptable and normal. In one sense, Meyer's point is fully consistent with one principle of dominance theory, which is that legal rules proscribing only the most severe forms of certain behaviors thereby legitimize the remainder. See Katharine T. Bartlett, Porno-Symbolism: A Response to Professor McConahay, 51 Law & Contemp. Probs. 71, 73 (Winter 1988). Wouldn't MacKinnon's own dominance theory also suggest that tighter controls on violent pornography would further eroticize violence against women? Is the answer to regulate more, or less?

Meyer argues for less regulation, both because she does not believe that violent pornography causes the harms that opponents cite, and because, even if it did, trying to prevent it through legal regulation would be counterproductive. On the latter point, David Cole agrees.

> Sexual expression . . . inevitably confounds society's attempts to regulate it. It subverts every taboo by making it a fetish. The forbidden is simultaneously eroticized. As a result, attempts to regulate sexual expression are doomed to failure; by creating taboos to transgress, regulation only adds to sexual expression's appeal.

David Cole, Playing by Pornography's Rules: The Regulation of Sexual Expression, 143 U. Pa. L. Rev. 111, 116 (1994). See also Jeffrey G. Sherman, Love Speech: The Social Utility of Pornography, 47 Stan. L. Rev. 661 (1995) (arguing that gay male pornography is valuable both because it affirms the sexual lives of gay men and because it undercuts homophobia, the eradication of which means the eradication of misogyny); Amy Adler, What's Left?: Hate Speech, Pornography, and the Problem for Artistic Expression, 84 Cal. L. Rev. 1499 (1997) (restrictions on pornography and hate speech sacrifice vital interests of protest and criticism from within the left).

Another area of controversy involves the use of zoning regulations to curtail certain adverse community affects associated with adult entertainment businesses. In City of Los Angeles v. Alameda Books, Inc, 535 U.S. 425 (2002), the Court sustained a municipal ordinance that prohibited multiple adult businesses from operating under the same roof. In so ruling, the Court accepted the city's argument that this prohibition was a justifiable response to increases in prostitution, robbery, assaults, and thefts in areas where adult entertainment establishments centered. Free-speech advocates have criticized such uses of zoning on two primary grounds. The first is that the evidence for ordinances like Los Angeles' is weak. A second claim is that restricting adult businesses to central depressed city areas while banning them from more affluent communities stigmatizes erotic materials and limits' the rights of individuals to construct their own sexualities. See Stephanie Lasker, Comment, Sex and the City: Zoning Pornography Peddlers and Live Nude Shows, 49 UCLA L. Rev. 1139, 1158-1159, 1181-1184 (2002). If you were a city leader, how would you balance these competing concerns?

3. Pornography and Agency. At the heart of the debate over pornography regulation is the extent to which women, or men, are capable of defining their own sexuality. Those favoring regulation of pornography assume that its proliferation prevents women from being independent agents in their own sexuality. From this perspective, women's choices appear constrained by the ways in which sex has been defined in *men's* interests. Those opposing regulation assume that women have the capacity to think and act for themselves, and to know what they want. For a thorough examination of the history of this battle within feminism and of the tension between agency and coercion views of women, see Kathryn Abrams, Sex Wars Redux: Agency and Coercion in Feminist Legal Theory, 95 Colum. L. Rev. 304 (1995). Abrams argues that neither extreme view is convincing and that a more adequate theory would recognize both women's capacity for self-direction and the constraints within which this capacity must often be exercised. Id. at 350-376. See also Susan H. Williams, Truth, Autonomy, and Speech, Feminist Theory and the First Amendment 277-278 (2004) (discussing the limits on individuals' ability to escape the influence of representations of their group); Mary Joe Frug, Postmodern Legal Feminism 151-152 (1992) (arguing that opponents of pornography should attempt to deconstruct rather than repress it and should focus their efforts on exploring alternative visions of sexuality); Lasker, supra, at 1144 (arguing that pornography zoning undermines women's agency); Meyer, supra, at 1194-1199 (arguing for largely nonlegal strategies to create alternative media images — in a word, counterspeech.)

Is pornography similarly damaging to men's sexual agency? Consider Harry Brod's argument:

> I shall be claiming that pornography has a negative impact on men's own sexuality. This is a claim that an aspect of an oppressive system, patriarchy, operates, at least in part, to the disadvantage of the group it privileges, men. This claim does not deny that the overall effect of the system is to operate in men's advantage, nor does it deny that the same aspect of the system under consideration, that is, male sexuality and pornography under patriarchy, might not also contribute to the expansion and maintenance of male power even as it also works to men's disadvantage.... I view raising consciousness of the prices of male power as part of a strategy through which we could at least potentially mobilize men against pornography's destructive effects on both women and men....

In terms of both its manifest image of and its effects on male sexuality, that is, in both intrinsic and consequentialist terms, pornography restricts male sensuality in favor of a genital, performance oriented male sexuality. Men become sexual acrobats endowed with oversized and overused organs. . . . The predominant image of women in pornography presents women as always sexually ready, willing, able, and eager. The necessary corollary to pornography's myth of female perpetual availability is its myth of male perpetual readiness. Just as the former fuels male misogyny when real-life women fail to perform to pornographic standards, so do men's failures to similarly perform fuel male insecurities. . . . Men [feel] needs for intimacy, but are trained to deny them, and are encouraged further to see physical affection and intimacy primarily if not exclusively in sexual terms. This leads to the familiar syndrome wherein, as one man put it:

> Although what most men want is physical affection, what they end up thinking they want is to be laid by a Playboy bunny.

This puts a strain on male sexuality. Looking to sex to fulfill what are really non-sexual needs, men end up disappointed and frustrated. Sometimes they feel an unfilled void, and blame it on their or their partner's sexual inadequacy.

Harry Brod, Pornography and the Alienation of Male Sexuality, in Rethinking Masculinity: Philosophical Explorations in Light of Feminism 149, 151-154 (Larry May & Robert A. Strikwerda eds., 1992).

Is Brod's claim convincing? If so, why has it been so difficult to enlist men in the campaign to restrict pornography or to challenge mainstream images of male sexuality? Compare Brod's analysis with Brad Armstrong's autobiographical account of his work as a porn star:

> I'm just very happy with what I've done. On a social level, I think these movies are helping people's lives. A lot of our crowd, our audience, is made up of guys who maybe aren't the best-looking dudes in town. Maybe they're dorks or disabled or something like that, and there's no chance they're ever going to get laid. And I think the adult business definitely gives those guys an outlet. Otherwise, they'll explode.
>
> And lately, a lot of couples are benefitting from our films as well. . . . There are so many people who are so unhappy sexually. But now, because of the way sex has become so important in the media and so open, and people are finally talking about stuff and showing stuff sexually, people are realizing how unhappy they are and doing something about it. For the guys to bring these movies home to their spouses or girlfriends, sometimes it can really stimulate their relationship. Sometimes it works, sometimes it doesn't. But at least if a guy is unhappy with the way his wife is performing, he can watch porno and jerk off maybe, rather than have an affair. Everyone can disagree, but I think it's definitely at least an outlet for guys.

Brad Armstrong, Porn Star, in Gig: Americans Talk About Their Jobs at the Turn of the Millennium 359, 364 (John Bowe et al. eds., 2000).

If Armstrong is right, does it follow that pornography will serve men's sexual interests?

If pornography, advertising, law, and other social influences do not define sexuality and sex-based roles, what does? Is there some "natural" set of sexual drives and desires that these other influences distort? Or is it a question of which forces should be allowed to influence the formation of choice and intent and which ones should not?

First Amendment doctrine strives for "neutrality" on this issue, but as Cass Sunstein argues, prevailing views of neutrality assume as baselines the naturalness and justice of existing sexual practices, including ones that subordinate women to men. See Sunstein, Neutrality in Constitutional Law (with Special Reference to Pornography, Abortion, and Surrogacy), 92 Colum. L. Rev. 1, 49 (1992) (arguing that a better view of neutrality would seek to identify and prohibit practices that make women's sexuality into an object to be controlled and used by others). Drucilla Cornell argues that the best way to think about autonomy in this context is as an "imaginary domain" that the law should protect but not limit. In her view, "no woman should be forced to see her 'sex' as it is stereotypically presented in hardcore porn." This view leads her to support zoning ordinances to channel pornography's possible encroachment, but no more. See Cornell, The Imaginary Domain; Abortion, Pornography and Sexual Harassment 103 (1995). For further explanation of the meaning of autonomy and choice in sexual matters, see Chapter 5.

Is there a danger that the feminist campaign against pornography will "strengthen[] the political power of the Right to censor sexual and oppressive discourse and to pass measures aimed at controlling women's bodies and sexuality"? Meyer, supra, at 1101. Some have accused MacKinnon of making alliances with "traditional political and religious conservatives who staunchly oppose women's rights, but who also seek to suppress pornography." Strossen, supra, at 13. MacKinnon has refuted such charges, pointing out in detail the misrepresentations giving rise to them, as well as the lack of conservative advocates or politicians supporting the feminist civil rights ordinance. See Catharine A. MacKinnon, The Roar on the Other Side of Silence, in In Harm's Way: The Pornography Civil Rights Hearings 3, 10 (Catharine A. MacKinnon & Andrea Dworkin eds., 1997). What about the fact that those opposing the feminist anti-pornography civil rights ordinance range from conservative judges such as Judge Frank Easterbrook (author of *Hudnut*) and liberal members of the ACLU such as Nadine Strossen? See Catharine A. MacKinnon, Pornography Left and Right, 30 Harv. C.R.-C.L. L. Rev. 143, 147-148 (1995) (questioning why convergence of the left and right against feminist civil rights ordinance is not viewed as an "unholy alliance").

4. Pornography, the Internet, and Children. The increasingly accessible Internet has expanded opportunities for the creation and distribution of pornography. The adult on-line industry is estimated to generate about a billion dollars annually and to grow at an exponential pace over the next few years. National Research Council, Youth, Pornography, and the Internet (2002); Kevin F. Ryan, All the Decent Drapery of Life, Rudely Torn Off, Vt. B.J. 7, 8 (June 2002).

The Internet poses special challenges for regulation. The first problem is detection. The sheer size of cyberspace makes it difficult to police. A second problem is accountability. Even if illegal content is discovered online, the responsible party may be impossible to track. Both of these difficulties are exacerbated by encryption technology, which allows parties to disguise their identities. A third problem is jurisdictional. If pornographers are located outside the state's territory, the state cannot enforce an action against them. Within the United States, this may be partially resolved by recent decisions finding personal jurisdiction anywhere that individuals can foresee their Web content being viewed. See, e.g., Inset Systems, Inc. v. Instruction Set, Inc., 937 F. Supp. 161 (D. Conn. 1996). However, no such jurisdiction is available for pornography originating outside the United States, and efforts to deal with the problems posed by the international nature of cyberspace have yielded inadequate results. See, e.g., The International Convention of Crime by the Council of Europe (1999), at http://conventions.coe.int/treaty/en/projects/cybercrime.htm [hereinafter Treaty] (including provisions aimed at creating greater uniformity in cyberjurisdiction).

There are, moreover, other problems in applying existing obscenity law to cyberporn. Which community's "community standards" are to be imposed when on-line materials can be downloaded anywhere? See Ashcroft v. American Civil Liberties Union, 535 U.S. 564 (2002), discussed infra, and Sean J. Petrie, Note, Indecent Proposals: How Each Branch of the Federal Government Overstepped Its Institutional Authority in the Development of Internet Obscenity Law, 49 Stan. L. Rev. 637 (1997). The Internet's decentralized structure also resists regulation by permitting users to reroute access around "blocks." In addition, users can post messages anonymously through the use of remailers, making it difficult to suspend privileges or identify senders. There are also costs of overly broad efforts to restrict sexual expression. As Meyer notes, "[c]ybersex offers us a chance to oust the dominant masculinist and misogynist pornographers from their control over sexual territory and to begin reclaiming and reconstructing sexuality in the relative safety of cyberspace." Carlin Meyer, Reclaiming Sex from the Pornographers: Cybersexual Possibilities, 83 Geo. L.J. 1969, 1979-1994 (1995) (discussing enforcement barriers and risks). See Keth A. Ditthavong, Note, Paving the Way for Women on the Information Superhighway: Curbing Sexism Not Freedoms, 4 Am. U. J. Gender & L. 455 (1996).

A related problem involves enforcement of laws attempting to restrict minors' access to pornography. The same technologies that make it easy for individuals to disguise their identity make it equally easy to disguise their age. The first congressional attempt to cope with this problem borrowed from dial-a-porn, criminalized transmissions of "obscene or indecent" and "patently offensive" messages to a minor. See Communications Decency Act, 47 U.S.C. §223(a), (d) (Supp. 1997) (also known as the "Exon Bill"). In reviewing the constitutionality of the Act, the Supreme Court rejected the analogy to the heavily regulated broadcast media, on the ground that the Internet is neither a "scarce" resource nor an "invasive" medium; the majority accordingly struck down the "indecent" and "patently offensive" provisions as overly broad restrictions on speech. Reno v. ACLU, 521 U.S. 844 (1997).

A subsequent act, the Child Online Protection Act, 47 U.S.C. §§231a-e (Supp. IV 1998) (COPA), imposes criminal penalties on those who knowingly make available to minors through the World Wide Web commercial materials "harmful to minors." Commercial websites that include such material must use age verification mechanisms such as credit cards or adult identification numbers. Harm is defined in terms modeled on the *Miller* obscenity standard; the statute exempts material that has "serious literary, artistic, political or scientific value for minors" and defines indecency in terms of "contemporary community standards." The Third Circuit enjoined the statute. In its view, the use of those standards would mean that "communication available to a nationwide audience will be judged by the community most likely to be offended by the message." ACLU v. Reno, 217 F.3d 162, 174 (3rd Cir. 2000). The Supreme Court reversed and remanded the case for further proceedings. In essence, the Court determined that a publisher has a responsibility to abide by community standards even if it chooses to use a vehicle like the Internet, which potentially reaches every community across the globe. Ashcroft v. American Civil Liberties Union, 535 U.S. 564, 583 (2002). On remand, the Third Circuit again enjoined enforcement of the statute, and on appeal the Supreme Court affirmed the injunction and remanded the case for trial on the merits. The Court accepted the argument that plausible, less restrictive alternatives to COPA might be available, such as filtering and blocking software. Ashcroft v. American Civil Liberties Union, 542 U.S. 656 (2004).

A related case involved the constitutionality of the Children's Internet Protection Act (CIPA) (now codified as 20 U.S.C. § 6777 (2006)). It requires publicly funded elementary schools, secondary schools, and libraries that provide Internet access to (1) block or filter adults' access to visual depictions of obscenity or child pornography and (2) block or filter children's access to obscenity, child pornography, or other material that is "harmful to minors." The American Library Association challenged the act on the grounds that filtering systems were under and over inclusive. Other free speech advocates have similarly argued that filters build in political, social and cultural biases that restrict the right of local communities to enforce their own standards. Statement of Will Doherty, Executive Director, Online Policy Group, February 10, 2003, available at http://www.sethf.com/infothought/blog/archives/000184.html. By contrast, support of CIPA argued that libraries deserved no special shield from statutes prohibiting distribution of sexual materials harmful to minors, and that Congress was entitled to determine conditions under which tax dollars should be spent. Gregory K. Laughlin, Sex, Lies, and Library Cards: The First Amendment Implications of the Use of Software Filters to Control Access to Internet Pornography in Public Libraries, 51 Drake L. Rev. 213, 262 (2003); Michael Janofsky, What Would Dewey Do? Libraries Grapple with Internet, N.Y. Times, Dec. 2, 2002, at A13.

In United States v. American Library Association, Inc., 539 U.S. 194 (2003), a divided Court held that CIPA was not on its face unconstitutional. The majority ruled that Internet access was not a public forum, and that just as decisions to exclude pornographic materials from written collections did not warrant heightened scrutiny, exclusions resulting from software filters required no such scrutiny. Even if that software erroneously blocked some constitutionally protected material, patrons had an easy remedy: they could request librarians to unblock the material or disable the filters. Such a system created no unconstitutional conditions; Congress was not denying a benefit but insuring that public funds be spent for authorized purposes. Justice Kennedy, who concurred in the judgment, wrote separately to emphasize that if some libraries lacked capacity to unblock protected material and if patrons' access to that material was burdened in a substantial way, they could challenge the statute as applied. 539 U.S., at 235 (Kennedy, J., concurring). For a general discussion of the problem and the need for better technological responses, see Lillian Edwards, Pornography and the Internet, in Law and the Internet: A Framework for Electronic Commerce 275, 280 (Lillian Edwards & Charlotte Waelde eds., 2000).

Libraries have taken a range of approaches to monitoring Internet usage. Some place monitor screens where they are visible from a librarian's desk and will alert parents to inappropriate use. Other libraries require parents to be present at Internet stations or to sign waivers allowing their children to have access. Almost all libraries have written guidelines and many provide training programs. See generally Library Research Center, University of Illinois, Survey of Internet Access Management in Public Libraries, prepared for the American Library Association (2000). Despite such efforts, libraries continue to receive large numbers of complaints about inappropriate Internet use. Laughlin, supra, at 269. Some have been sued by their own workers for maintaining a hostile work environment by allowing display of sexually explicit materials. See Gary Young, No Smut at Work, Please, Nat'l L.J., Sept. 15, 2003, at A1, A32 (describing payment of $435,000 to twelve employees of Minneapolis Public Library).

The Child Pornography Prevention Act, 18 U.S.C. § 2251 et seq. (CPPA), marks the latest congressional effort to deal with the proliferation of pornography featuring children. A March 2000 report of President Clinton's working group on Internet crime summarizes this legislation:

> Child pornography offenses are covered by 18 U.S.C. § 2251 et seq. These laws specifically include computers within the proscribed means of distribution and possession of child pornography. They specifically prohibit the production, transportation, receipt, or distribution of visual depictions that involve the use of a minor (any person under the age of 18) engaged in sexually explicit conduct, where the producer or distributor knows or has reason to know, that the depiction was or will be transported in interstate commerce or was created using a camera (or the like) that had traveled in interstate commerce. Computer graphic images — including computer or computer-generated images or pictures of a minor engaged in sexually explicit conduct; "morphed" images that appear to be (through computer manipulation) of a minor engaged in sexually explicit conduct; and images that are adults promoted as children engaged in sexually explicit conduct — are included within the definition of "visual depictions." 18 U.S.C. § 2256(5) and (8).

The Electronic Frontier: The Challenge of Unlawful Conduct Involving the Use of the Internet, Report of the President's Working Group (2000), at http://www.usdoj.gov/criminal/cybercrime/unlawful.htm.

CPPA came under attack for its provisions criminalizing visual depictions involving no actual child. Critics of these provisions claimed that they were overbroad, especially in those situations where the child is a digitally simulated creation. By contrast, supporters argued that these images are flooding the market and present just as great a risk of harm to children as pornography using live models. See Jisuk Woo, The Concept of "Harm" in Computer-Generated Images of

Child Pornography, 22 J. Marshall J. Computer & Info. L. 717 (2004). After the circuits had divided on the constitutionality of the legislation, the Supreme Court granted certiorari to resolve the conflict.

At oral argument on the statute, a central issue involved the adequacy of the statute's affirmative defense for movies produced using adult actors for scenes that appear to involve sexual conduct by minors. Films like Lolita, Traffic, and Titanic all involve such scenes. Justice Scalia questioned whether there would in fact be "radical tragic consequences" for First Amendment jurisprudence if such scenes could not be shown. "What great works could be taken away from us if we were unable to show minors copulating?" When counsel for the plaintiffs mentioned Traffic, the Tin Drum, and several films with Brooke Shields, Justice Scalia responded, "This is not, you know, the Mona Lisa or Venus De Milo or anything that has lasted more than thirty years." When Justice Stevens smilingly interjected a reference to Romeo and Juliet, Justice Scalia responded, "you've seen a different version of that play than I have." Tony Mauro, Virtual Reality Check, American Lawyer, Dec. 2001, at 70 (quoting Justice Scalia).

In Ashcroft v. Free Speech Coalition, 535 U.S. 234 (2002), the Court held that the statute proscribed material that was neither obscene nor child pornography, and therefore could not withstand First Amendment challenge. In so ruling, the Court rejected the government's argument that such works could be banned because they contributed to child abuse when pedophiles used them to stimulate an appetite for sexual contact or to lure children into criminal acts. In the Court's view, child pornography had not been demonstrated to be "intrinsically related" to child abuse and the link between abuse and virtual child pornography was only "contingent and indirect." In addition, the Court held that the affirmative defense allowed under the statute did not adequately protect those who created or distributed virtual child pornography from facing felony conviction for innocent acts.

If you had been counsel for the plaintiff in *Ashcroft,* how would you have responded to Justice Scalia at oral argument? If you had been on the Court, how would you have weighed the free speech interests of the public against the harms to children? According to Congressional findings, even where minors are not involved in making scenes involving sexual activity, the resulting images may desensitize the viewer to the sexual exploitation of children. Is this risk sufficient to sustain the statute? What is the relevance of studies indicating that child pornography is involved in most convictions for child molestation? See Candice Kim, From Fantasy to Reality: The Link Between Viewing Child Pornography and Molesting Children, Prosecutor, Mar.-Apr. 2005, at 17.

Putting Theory into Practice

3-13. You are a staff attorney for a local women's organization. Your organization is approached by both sides in the *Hudnut* case and asked to file an amicus brief. What would you do, and how would you make your decision?

3-14. Your organization is contacted by a women students' organization of a nearby state university. The group is offended by the practices of several fraternities, which show porn films and invite strippers to perform on campus at all-male parties. The students believe that these practices encourage date rape. When they approached the university administration, they were advised that the male students were entitled to exercise their First Amendment rights. How would you respond? What strategies would you propose?

3-15. You are the Dean of Humanities at a university that offers a student-devised course on "Male Sexuality." The course includes a field trip to a gay strip club, class discussion of photographs of the students' genitals, and a requirement that each student produce a work of pornography. Adverse publicity has led to demands that the university cease offering the course. How should this be handled? See Cathy Young, Skin Flicks 101: What Porn Studies Profs Don't Get About Sex, 35 Reason 20 (May 2003).

E. SEXUAL IDENTITY DISCRIMINATION

The term "homosexual" emerged in the nineteenth century to describe same-sex orientation activity. The term "gay," which has been traced to medieval Europe, came into broader use in the 1960s, as a reference for both individuals and a political movement. Although the term historically was gender neutral, in contemporary usage gay often refers to men, and lesbians is the preferred term for women.

Estimates of the number of individuals who are gay or lesbian are difficult to come by, especially given that an individual's sexual preference for members of one sex or the other is best understood as a continuous rather than a binary variable. See Richard A. Posner, Sex and Reason 294 (1992). Most studies, depending on methodology and definitions used, place the figures between 6 and 13 percent of men and 2 and 6 percent of women. Id. (estimating that 6 percent of adult men and 2 percent of adult women are more or less exclusively homosexual in their sexual preferences); Richard Schneider, "The People Gay" and the 10% Debate, 7 Harv. Gay & Lesbian Rev. 4 (March 22, 2000, available at 2000 WL 25098410) (estimating that 6 percent of men and 4 percent of women "self-identify" as gay or lesbian); Gay and Lesbian Stats: A Pocket Guide of Facts and Figures 10-12 (Bennet L. Singer & David Deschamps eds., 1994).

1. Gay Marriage Is Not Marriage

≡ *Jones v. Hallahan*
≡ 501 S.W.2d 588 (Ky. 1973)

VANCE, Commissioner.

The appellants, each of whom is a female person, seek review of a judgment of the Jefferson Circuit Court which held that they were not entitled to have issued to them a license to marry each other.

Appellants contend that the failure of the clerk to issue the license deprived them of three basic constitutional rights, namely, the right to marry; the right of association; and the right to free exercise of religion. They also contend that the refusal subjects them to cruel and unusual punishment.

The sections of Kentucky statutes relating to marriage do not include a definition of that term. It must therefore be defined according to common usage.

Webster's New International Dictionary, Second Edition, defines marriage as follows:

> A state of being married, or being united to a person or persons of the opposite sex as husband or wife; also, the mutual relation of husband and wife; wedlock; abstractly, the institution whereby men and women are joined in a special kind of social and legal dependence, for the purpose of founding and maintaining a family.

The Century Dictionary and Encyclopedia defines marriage as:

> The legal union of a man with a woman for life; the state or condition of being married; the legal relation of spouses to each other; wedlock; the formal declaration or contract by which a man and a woman join in wedlock.

Black's Law Dictionary, Fourth Edition, defines marriage as:

> The civil status, condition or relation of one man and one woman united in law for life, for the discharge to each other and the community of the duties legally incumbent upon those whose association is founded on the distinction of sex.

Kentucky statutes do not specifically prohibit marriage between persons of the same sex nor do they authorize the issuance of a marriage license to such persons.

Marriage was a custom long before the state commenced to issue licenses for that purpose. For a time the records of marriage were kept by the church. Some states even now recognize a common-law marriage which has neither the benefit of license nor clergy. In all cases, however, marriage has always been considered as the union of a man and a woman and we have been presented with no authority to the contrary.

It appears to us that appellants are prevented from marrying, not by the statutes of Kentucky or the refusal of the County Court Clerk of Jefferson County to issue them a license, but rather by their own incapability of entering into a marriage as that term is defined.

A license to enter into a status or a relationship which the parties are incapable of achieving is a nullity. If the appellants had concealed from the clerk the fact that they were of the same sex and he had issued a license to them and a ceremony had been performed, the resulting relationship would not constitute a marriage.

This is a case of first impression in Kentucky. To our knowledge, only two other states have considered the question and both of them have reached the same result that we reach in this opinion. Baker v. Nelson, [191 N.W.2d 185 (Minn. 1971), appeal dismissed for want of a substantial federal question, 409 U.S. 810

(1972)]; Anonymous v. Anonymous, [325 N.Y.S.2d 499 (Sup. Ct., Queens Co. 1971)].

Baker v. Nelson considered many of the constitutional issues raised by the appellants here and decided them adversely to appellants. In our view, however, no constitutional issue is involved. We find no constitutional sanction or protection of the right of marriage between persons of the same sex.

The claim of religious freedom cannot be extended to make the professed doctrines superior to the law of the land and in effect to permit every citizen to become a law unto himself. Reynolds v. United States, [98 U.S. 145 (1878)]. We do not consider the refusal to issue the license a punishment.

In substance, the relationship proposed by the appellants does not authorize the issuance of a marriage license because what they propose is not a marriage.

The judgment is affirmed.

All concur.

Goodridge v. Department of Health
798 N.E.2d 941 (Mass. 2003)

MARSHALL, C.J.

Marriage is a vital social institution. The exclusive commitment of two individuals to each other nurtures love and mutual support; it brings stability to our society. For those who choose to marry, and for their children, marriage provides an abundance of legal, financial, and social benefits. In return it imposes weighty legal, financial, and social obligations. The question before us is whether, consistent with the Massachusetts Constitution, the Commonwealth may deny the protections, benefits, and obligations conferred by civil marriage to two individuals of the same sex who wish to marry. We conclude that it may not....

I

The plaintiffs are fourteen individuals from five Massachusetts counties. As of April 11, 2001, the date they filed their complaint, the plaintiffs Gloria Bailey, sixty years old, and Linda Davies, fifty-five years old, had been in a committed relationship for thirty years; ... the plaintiffs Hillary Goodridge, forty-four years old, and Julie Goodridge, forty-three years old, had been in a committed relationship for thirteen years and lived with their five year old daughter; the plaintiffs Gary Chalmers, thirty-five years old, and Richard Linnell, thirty-seven years old, had been in a committed relationship for thirteen years and lived with their eight year old daughter and Richard's mother....

Each plaintiff attests a desire to marry his or her partner in order to affirm publicly their commitment to each other and to secure the legal protections and benefits afforded to married couples and their children....

In March and April, 2001, each of the plaintiff couples attempted to obtain a marriage license from a city or town clerk's office.... In each case, the clerk either refused to accept the notice of intention to marry or denied a marriage license to the couple on the ground that Massachusetts does not recognize same-sex marriage....

On April 11, 2001, the plaintiffs filed suit in the Superior Court.... The department...admitted to a policy and practice of denying marriage licenses to same-sex couples.... A Superior Court judge ruled for the department [based on the plain wording of the statute....

III...

The plaintiffs' claim that the marriage restriction violates the Massachusetts Constitution can be analyzed in two ways. Does it offend the Constitution's guarantees of equality before the law? Or do the liberty and due process provisions of the Massachusetts Constitution secure the plaintiffs' right to marry their chosen partner? In matters implicating marriage, family life, and the upbringing of children, the two constitutional concepts frequently overlap, as they do here....

We begin by considering the nature of civil marriage itself.... Civil marriage is created and regulated through exercise of the police power.... In broad terms, [the police power] is the Legislature's power to enact rules to regulate conduct, to the extent that such laws are "necessary to secure the health, safety, good order, comfort, or general welfare of the community."...

Without question, civil marriage enhances the "welfare of the community."...Civil marriage anchors an ordered society by encouraging stable relationships over transient ones. It is central to the way the Commonwealth identifies individuals, provides for the orderly distribution of property, ensures that children and adults are cared for and supported whenever possible from private rather than public funds, and tracks important epidemiological and demographic data.

Marriage also bestows enormous private and social advantages on those who choose to marry. Civil marriage is at once a deeply personal commitment to another human being and a highly public celebration of the ideals of mutuality, companionship, intimacy, fidelity, and family. "It is an association that promotes a way of life, not causes; a harmony in living, not political faiths; a bilateral loyalty, not commercial or social projects." Griswold v. Connecticut, 381 U.S. 479, 486 (1965). Because it fulfils yearnings for security, safe haven, and connection that express our common humanity, civil marriage is an esteemed institution, and the decision whether and whom to marry is among life's momentous acts of self-definition....

The benefits accessible only by way of a marriage license are enormous, touching nearly every aspect of life and death. The department states that "hundreds of statutes" are related to marriage and to marital benefits. With no attempt to be comprehensive, we note that some of the statutory benefits conferred by the Legislature on those who enter into civil marriage include, as to property: joint Massachusetts income tax filing; tenancy by the entirety (a form of ownership that provides certain protections against creditors and allows for the automatic descent of property to the surviving spouse without probate); extension of the benefit of the homestead protection (securing up to $300,000 in equity from creditors) to one's spouse and children; automatic rights to inherit the property of a deceased spouse who does not leave a will; the rights of elective share and of dower (which allow surviving spouses certain property rights where the decedent spouse has not made adequate provision for the survivor in a will); entitlement to wages owed to a deceased employee; eligibility to continue certain businesses of a deceased spouse; the right to share the medical policy of one's spouse; thirty-nine week continuation of health coverage for the spouse of a person who is laid off or dies; preferential options under the Commonwealth's pension system; preferential benefits in the Commonwealth's medical program, MassHealth; access to veterans' spousal benefits and preferences; financial protections for spouses of certain Commonwealth employees (fire fighters, police officers, prosecutors, among others) killed in the performance of duty; the equitable division of marital property on divorce; temporary and permanent alimony rights; the right to separate support on separation of the parties that does not result in divorce; and the right to bring claims for wrongful death and loss of consortium, and for funeral and burial expenses and punitive damages resulting from tort actions (citations omitted)....

Exclusive marital benefits that are not directly tied to property rights include the presumptions of legitimacy and parentage of children born to a married couple; and evidentiary rights, such as the prohibition against spouses testifying against one another about their private conversations, applicable in both civil and criminal cases.... Other statutory benefits of a personal nature available only to married individuals include qualification for bereavement or medical leave to care for individuals related by blood or marriage; an automatic "family member" preference to make medical decisions for an incompetent or disabled spouse who does not have a contrary health care proxy; the application of predictable rules of child custody, visitation, support, and removal out-of-State when married parents divorce; priority rights to administer the estate of a deceased spouse who dies without a will, and requirement that surviving spouse must consent to the appointment of any other person as administrator; and the right to interment in the lot or tomb owned by one's deceased spouse (citations omitted)....

Where a married couple has children, their children are also directly or indirectly, but no less auspiciously, the recipients of the special legal and economic protections obtained by civil marriage. Notwithstanding the Commonwealth's strong public policy to abolish legal distinctions between marital and nonmarital children in providing for the support and care of minors, . . . the fact remains that marital children reap a measure of family stability and economic security based on their parents' legally privileged status that is largely inaccessible, or not as readily accessible, to nonmarital children. Some of these benefits are social, such as the enhanced approval that still attends the status of being a marital child. Others are material, such as the greater ease of access to family-based State and Federal benefits that attend the presumptions of one's parentage.

It is undoubtedly for these concrete reasons, as well as for its intimately personal significance, that civil marriage has long been termed a "civil right." See, e.g., Loving v. Virginia, 388 U.S. 1, 12 (1967) ("Marriage is one of the 'basic civil rights of man,' fundamental to our very existence and survival"), quoting Skinner v. Oklahoma, 316 U.S. 535, 541 (1942).... The United States Supreme Court has described the right to marry as "of fundamental importance for all individuals" and as "part of the fundamental 'right of privacy' implicit in the

Fourteenth Amendment's Due Process Clause." Zablocki v. Redhail, 434 U.S. 374, 384 (1978). See Loving v. Virginia, supra ("The freedom to marry has long been recognized as one of the vital personal rights essential to the orderly pursuit of happiness by free men").

Without the right to marry — or more properly, the right to choose to marry — one is excluded from the full range of human experience and denied full protection of the laws for one's "avowed commitment to an intimate and lasting human relationship." Baker v. State, 744 A.2d 864, 889 (Vt. 1999). Because civil marriage is central to the lives of individuals and the welfare of the community, our laws assiduously protect the individual's right to marry against undue government incursion. Laws may not "interfere directly and substantially with the right to marry." Zablocki v. Redhail, supra at 387....

Unquestionably, the regulatory power of the Commonwealth over civil marriage is broad, as is the Commonwealth's discretion to award public benefits.... Individuals who have the choice to marry each other and nevertheless choose not to may properly be denied the legal benefits of marriage.... But that same logic cannot hold for a qualified individual who would marry if she or he only could....

For decades, indeed centuries, in much of this country (including Massachusetts) no lawful marriage was possible between white and black Americans. That long history availed not when the Supreme Court of California held in 1948 that a legislative prohibition against interracial marriage violated the due process and equality guarantees of the Fourteenth Amendment, Perez v. Sharp, 198 P.2d 17 (Cal.1948), or when, nineteen years later, the United States Supreme Court also held that a statutory bar to interracial marriage violated the Fourteenth Amendment, Loving v. Virginia, 388 U.S. 1 (1967). As both *Perez* and *Loving* make clear, the right to marry means little if it does not include the right to marry the person of one's choice, subject to appropriate government restrictions in the interests of public health, safety, and welfare.... In this case, as in *Perez* and *Loving*, a statute deprives individuals of access to an institution of fundamental legal, personal, and social significance — the institution of marriage — because of a single trait: skin color in *Perez* and *Loving*, sexual orientation here. As it did in *Perez* and *Loving*, history must yield to a more fully developed understanding of the invidious quality of the discrimination.

The Massachusetts Constitution protects matters of personal liberty against government incursion as zealously, and often more so, than does the Federal Constitution, even where both Constitutions employ essentially the same language....

The plaintiffs challenge the marriage statute on both equal protection and due process grounds.... The department argues that no fundamental right or "suspect" class is at issue here, and rational basis is the appropriate standard of review. For the reasons we explain below, we conclude that the marriage ban does not meet the rational basis test for either due process or equal protection. Because the statute does not survive rational basis review, we do not consider the plaintiffs' arguments that this case merits strict judicial scrutiny.

The department posits three legislative rationales for prohibiting same-sex couples from marrying: (1) providing a "favorable setting for procreation"; (2) ensuring the optimal setting for child rearing, which the department defines as "a two-parent family with one parent of each sex"; and (3) preserving scarce State and private financial resources. We consider each in turn.

The judge in the Superior Court endorsed the first rationale, holding that "the state's interest in regulating marriage is based on the traditional concept that marriage's primary purpose is procreation." This is incorrect. Our laws of civil marriage do not privilege procreative heterosexual intercourse between married people above every other form of adult intimacy and every other means of creating a family. General Laws c. 207 contains no requirement that the applicants for a marriage license attest to their ability or intention to conceive children by coitus. Fertility is not a condition of marriage, nor is it grounds for divorce. People who have never consummated their marriage, and never plan to, may be and stay married.... People who cannot stir from their deathbed may marry.... While it is certainly true that many, perhaps most, married couples have children together (assisted or unassisted), it is the exclusive and permanent commitment of the marriage partners to one another, not the begetting of children, that is the sine qua non of civil marriage.

Moreover, the Commonwealth affirmatively facilitates bringing children into a family regardless of whether the intended parent is married or unmarried, whether the child is adopted or born into a family, whether assistive technology was used to conceive the child, and whether the parent or her partner is heterosexual, homosexual, or bisexual. If procreation were a necessary component of civil marriage, our statutes would draw a tighter circle around the permissible bounds of nonmarital child bearing and the creation of families by noncoital means. The attempt to isolate procreation as "the source of a fundamental right to marry"... overlooks the integrated way in which courts have examined the complex and overlapping realms of personal autonomy, marriage, family life, and child rearing. Our jurisprudence recognizes that, in these nuanced and fundamentally private areas of life, such a narrow focus is inappropriate.

The "marriage is procreation" argument singles out the one unbridgeable difference between same-sex and opposite-sex couples, and transforms that difference into the essence of legal marriage. Like "Amendment 2" to the Constitution of Colorado, which effectively denied homosexual persons equality under the law and full access to the political process, the marriage restriction impermissibly "identifies persons by a single trait and then denies them protection across the board." Romer v. Evans, 517 U.S. 620, 633 (1996). In so doing, the State's action confers an official stamp of approval on the destructive stereotype that same-sex relationships are inherently unstable and inferior to opposite-sex relationships and are not worthy of respect.

The department's first stated rationale, equating marriage with unassisted heterosexual procreation, shades imperceptibly into its second: that confining marriage to opposite-sex couples ensures that children are raised in the "optimal" setting. Protecting the welfare of children is a paramount State policy. Restricting marriage to opposite-sex couples, however, cannot plausibly further this policy. "The demographic changes of the past century make it difficult to speak of an average American family. The composition of families varies greatly from household to household." Troxel v. Granville, 530 U.S. 57, 63 (2000). Massachusetts has responded supportively to "the changing realities of the American family," id. at 64, and has moved vigorously to strengthen the modern family in its many variations. See, e.g., G. L. c. 209C (paternity statute); G. L. c. 119, § 39D (grandparent visitation statute); Blixt v. Blixt, 774 N.E.2d 1052 (2002), cert. denied, 537 U.S. 1189 (2003) (same); E.N.O. v. L.M.M., 711 N.E.2d 886 (Mass. 1999), cert. denied, 528 U.S. 1005 (1999) (de facto parent);...and Adoption of Tammy, 619 N.E.2d 315 (Mass. 1993) (co-parent adoption). Moreover, we have repudiated the common-law power of the State to provide varying levels of protection to children based on the circumstances of birth.... The "best interests of the child" standard does not turn on a parent's sexual orientation or marital status....

The department has offered no evidence that forbidding marriage to people of the same sex will increase the number of couples choosing to enter into opposite-sex marriages in order to have and raise children. There is thus no rational relationship between the marriage statute and the Commonwealth's proffered goal of protecting the "optimal" child rearing unit. Moreover, the department readily concedes that people in same-sex couples may be "excellent" parents. These couples (including four of the plaintiff couples) have children for the reasons others do — to love them, to care for them, to nurture them. But the task of child rearing for same-sex couples is made infinitely harder by their status as outliers to the marriage laws. While establishing the parentage of children as soon as possible is crucial to the safety and welfare of children,...same-sex couples must undergo the sometimes lengthy and intrusive process of second-parent adoption to establish their joint parentage. While the enhanced income provided by marital benefits is an important source of security and stability for married couples and their children, those benefits are denied to families headed by same-sex couples.... While the laws of divorce provide clear and reasonably predictable guidelines for child support, child custody, and property division on dissolution of a marriage, same-sex couples who dissolve their relationships find themselves and their children in the highly unpredictable terrain of equity jurisdiction. See E.N.O. v. L.M.M., supra. Given the wide range of public benefits reserved only for married couples, we do not credit the department's contention that the absence of access to civil marriage amounts to little more than an inconvenience to same-sex couples and their children. Excluding same-sex couples from civil marriage will not make children of opposite-sex marriages more secure, but it does prevent children of same-sex couples from enjoying the immeasurable advantages that flow from the assurance of "a stable family structure in which children will be reared, educated, and socialized." [See Cordy, J., dissenting.]

In this case, we are confronted with an entire, sizeable class of parents raising children who have absolutely no access to civil marriage and its protections because they are forbidden from procuring a marriage license. It cannot be rational under our laws, and indeed it is not permitted, to penalize children by depriving them of State benefits because the State disapproves of their parents' sexual orientation.

The third rationale advanced by the department is that limiting marriage to opposite-sex couples furthers the Legislature's interest in conserving scarce State and private financial resources. The marriage restriction is rational, it argues, because the General Court logically could assume that same-sex couples are more financially independent than married couples and thus less needy of public marital benefits, such as tax advantages, or private marital benefits, such as employer-financed health plans that include spouses in their coverage.

An absolute statutory ban on same-sex marriage bears no rational relationship to the goal of economy. First, the department's conclusory generalization — that same-sex couples are less financially dependent on each other than opposite-sex couples — ignores that many same-sex couples, such as many of the plaintiffs in this case, have children and other dependents (here, aged parents) in their care. The department does not contend, nor could it, that these dependents are less needy or deserving than the dependents of married couples. Second, Massachusetts marriage laws do not condition receipt of public and private financial benefits to married individuals on a demonstration of financial dependence on each other; the benefits are available to married couples regardless of whether they mingle their finances or actually depend on each other for support.

The department suggests additional rationales for prohibiting same-sex couples from marrying, which are developed by some amici. It argues that broadening civil marriage to include same-sex couples will trivialize or destroy the institution of marriage as it has historically been fashioned. Certainly our decision today marks a significant change in the definition of marriage as it has been inherited from the common law, and understood by many societies for centuries. But it does not disturb the fundamental value of marriage in our society....

It has been argued that, due to the State's strong interest in the institution of marriage as a stabilizing social structure, only the Legislature can control and define its boundaries. Accordingly, our elected representatives legitimately may choose to exclude same-sex couples from civil marriage in order to assure all citizens of the Commonwealth that (1) the benefits of our marriage laws are available explicitly to create and support a family setting that is, in the Legislature's view, optimal for child rearing, and (2) the State does not endorse gay and lesbian parenthood as the equivalent of being raised by one's married biological parents. These arguments miss the point. The Massachusetts Constitution requires that legislation meet certain criteria and not extend beyond certain limits. It is the function of courts to determine whether these criteria are met and whether these limits are exceeded.... We owe great deference to the Legislature to decide social and policy issues, but it is the traditional and settled role of courts to decide constitutional issues.

Indeed, every State court that has recently considered the issue we decide today has exercised its duty in the same way, by carefully scrutinizing the statutory ban on same-sex marriages in light of relevant State constitutional provisions. See Brause v. Bureau of Vital Statistics, No. 3AN-95-6562CJ (Alaska Super. Ct., Feb. 27, 1998) (concluding marriage statute violated right to privacy provision in Alaska Constitution) (superseded by constitutional amendment, art. I, §25 of the Constitution of Alaska); Baehr v. Lewin, 852 P.2d 44 (Haw. 1993) (concluding marriage statute implicated Hawaii Constitution's equal protection clause; remanding case to lower court for further proceedings); Baker v. State, 744 A.2d 864 (Vt. 1999) (concluding marriage statute violated Vermont Constitution's common benefits clause). But see Standhardt v. Superior Court, 77 P.3d 451 (Ariz. Ct. App. 2003) (marriage statute does not violate liberty interests under either Federal or Arizona Constitution). See also Halpern v. Toronto (City), 172 O.A.C. 276 (2003) (concluding marriage statute violated equal protection provisions of Canada's Charter of Rights and Freedoms); Eagle Canada, Inc. v. Canada (Attorney Gen.), 13 B.C.L.R. (4th) 1 (2003) (same)....

As a public institution and a right of fundamental importance, civil marriage is an evolving paradigm. The common law was exceptionally harsh toward women who became wives: a woman's legal identity all but evaporated into that of her husband.... Alarms about the imminent erosion of the "natural" order of marriage were sounded over the demise of antimiscegenation laws, the expansion of the rights of married women, and the introduction of "no-fault" divorce. Marriage has survived all of these transformations, and we have no doubt that marriage will continue to be a vibrant and revered institution.

We also reject the argument suggested by the department, and elaborated by some amici, that expanding the institution of civil marriage in Massachusetts to include same-sex couples will lead to interstate conflict. We would not presume to dictate how another State should respond to today's decision. But neither should considerations of comity prevent us from according Massachusetts residents the full measure of protection available under the Massachusetts Constitution. The genius of our Federal system is that each State's Constitution has vitality specific to its own traditions, and that, subject to the minimum requirements of the Fourteenth Amendment, each State is free to address difficult issues of individual liberty in the manner its own Constitution demands....

IV

We consider next the plaintiffs' request for relief.... We face a problem similar to one that recently confronted the Court of Appeal for Ontario, the highest court of that Canadian province, when it considered the constitutionality of the same-sex marriage ban under Canada's Federal Constitution, the Charter of Rights and Freedoms (Charter). See Halpern v. Toronto (City), 172 O.A.C. 276 (2003).... In holding that the limitation of civil marriage to opposite-sex couples violated the Charter, the Court of Appeal refined the common-law meaning of marriage. We concur with this remedy, which is entirely consonant with established principles of jurisprudence empowering a court to refine a common-law principle in light of evolving constitutional standards....

We construe civil marriage to mean the voluntary union of two persons as spouses, to the exclusion of all others. This reformulation redresses the plaintiffs' constitutional injury and furthers the aim of marriage to promote stable, exclusive relationships. It advances the two legitimate State interests the department has identified: providing a stable setting for child rearing and conserving State resources. It leaves intact the Legislature's broad discretion to regulate marriage....

We declare that barring an individual from the protections, benefits, and obligations of civil marriage solely because that person would marry a person of the same sex violates the Massachusetts Constitution. We vacate the summary judgment for the department. We remand this case to the Superior Court for entry of judgment consistent with this opinion. Entry of judgment shall be stayed for 180 days to permit the Legislature to take such action as it may deem appropriate in light of this opinion. . . .

So ordered.

[The opinion of Greaney, J., concurring, is omitted.]

SPINA, J., joined by SOSMAN and CORDY, JJ., dissenting.

What is at stake in this case is not the unequal treatment of individuals or whether individual rights have been impermissibly burdened, but the power of the Legislature to effectuate social change without interference from the courts, pursuant to art. 30 of the Massachusetts Declaration of Rights. The power to regulate marriage lies with the Legislature, not with the judiciary. . . . Today, the court has transformed its role as protector of individual rights into the role of creator of rights, and I respectfully dissent.

1. *Equal protection.* Although the court did not address the plaintiffs' gender discrimination claim, G. L. c. 207 does not unconstitutionally discriminate on the basis of gender. A claim of gender discrimination will lie where it is shown that differential treatment disadvantages one sex over the other. . . . General Laws c. 207 enumerates certain qualifications for obtaining a marriage license. It creates no distinction between the sexes, but applies to men and women in precisely the same way. It does not create any disadvantage identified with gender, as both men and women are similarly limited to marrying a person of the opposite sex. See Commonwealth v. King, 372 N.E.2d 196 (Mass. 1977) (law prohibiting prostitution not discriminatory based on gender because of equal application to men and women).

Similarly, the marriage statutes do not discriminate on the basis of sexual orientation. As the court correctly recognizes, constitutional protections are extended to individuals, not couples. . . . The marriage statutes do not disqualify individuals on the basis of sexual orientation from entering into marriage. All individuals, with certain exceptions not relevant here, are free to marry. Whether an individual chooses not to marry because of sexual orientation or any other reason should be of no concern to the court.

The court concludes, however, that G. L. c. 207 unconstitutionally discriminates against the individual plaintiffs because it denies them the "right to marry the person of one's choice" where that person is of the same sex. . . . To reach this result the court relies on Loving v. Virginia, 388 U.S. 1, 12 (1967), and transforms "choice" into the essential element of the institution of marriage. The *Loving* case did not use the word "choice" in this manner, and it did not point to the result that the court reaches today. In *Loving*, the Supreme Court struck down as unconstitutional a statute that prohibited Caucasians from marrying non-Caucasians. It concluded that the statute was intended to preserve white supremacy and invidiously discriminated against non-Caucasians because of their race. . . . The "choice" to which the Supreme Court referred was the "choice to marry," and it concluded that with respect to the institution of marriage, the State had no compelling interest in limiting the choice to marry along racial lines. . . .

Unlike the *Loving* and *Sharp* cases, the Massachusetts Legislature has erected no barrier to marriage that intentionally discriminates against anyone. Within the institution of marriage, anyone is free to marry, with certain exceptions that are not challenged. In the absence of any discriminatory purpose, the State's marriage statutes do not violate principles of equal protection.... This court should not have invoked even the most deferential standard of review within equal protection analysis because no individual was denied access to the institution of marriage.

2. Due process. The marriage statutes do not impermissibly burden a right protected by our constitutional guarantee of due process implicit in art. 10 of our Declaration of Rights. There is no restriction on the right of any plaintiff to enter into marriage. Each is free to marry a willing person of the opposite sex....

Substantive due process protects individual rights against unwarranted government intrusion.... However, today the court does not fashion a remedy that affords greater protection of a right. Instead, using the rubric of due process, it has redefined marriage....

Before applying any level of constitutional analysis there must be a recognized right at stake. Same-sex marriage, or the "right to marry the person of one's choice" as the court today defines that right, does not fall within the fundamental right to marry. Same-sex marriage is not "deeply rooted in this Nation's history," and the court does not suggest that it is. Except for the occasional isolated decision in recent years, see, e.g., Baker v. State, 744 A.2d 864 (Vt. 1999), same-sex marriage is not a right, fundamental or otherwise, recognized in this country. Just one example of the Legislature's refusal to recognize same-sex marriage can be found in a section of the legislation amending G. L. c. 151B to prohibit discrimination in the workplace on the basis of sexual orientation, which states: "Nothing in this act shall be construed so as to legitimize or validate a 'homosexual marriage'...." St. 1989, c. 516, § 19. In this Commonwealth and in this country, the roots of the institution of marriage are deeply set in history as a civil union between a single man and a single woman. There is no basis for the court to recognize same-sex marriage as a constitutionally protected right.

3. Remedy. The remedy that the court has fashioned both in the name of equal protection and due process exceeds the bounds of judicial restraint mandated by art. 30. The remedy that construes gender-specific language as gender-neutral amounts to a statutory revision that replaces the intent of the Legislature with that of the court. Article 30 permits the court to apply principles of equal protection and to modify statutory language only if legislative intent is preserved.... Here, the alteration of the gender-specific language alters precisely what the Legislature unambiguously intended to preserve, the marital rights of single men and women. Such a dramatic change in social institutions must remain at the behest of the people through the democratic process....

SOSMAN, J., joined by SPINA and CORDY, JJ., dissenting.

... Reduced to its essence, the court's opinion concludes that, because same-sex couples are now raising children, and withholding the benefits of civil marriage from their union makes it harder for them to raise those children, the State must therefore provide the benefits of civil marriage to same-sex couples just as it does to opposite-sex couples. Of course, many people are raising children outside the confines of traditional marriage, and, by definition, those children are being deprived of the various benefits that would flow if they were being raised in a household with married parents. That does not mean that the Legislature must accord the full benefits of marital status on every household raising children. Rather, the Legislature need only have some rational basis for concluding that, at present, those alternate family structures have not yet been conclusively shown to be the equivalent of the marital family structure that has established itself as a successful one over a period of centuries. People are of course at liberty to raise their children in various family structures, as long as they are not literally harming their children by doing so.... That does not mean that the State is required to provide identical forms of encouragement, endorsement, and support to all of the infinite variety of household structures that a free society permits....

...To reach the result it does, the court has tortured the rational basis test beyond recognition.... Applying that deferential test in the manner it is customarily applied, the exclusion of gay and lesbian couples from the institution of civil marriage passes constitutional muster. I respectfully dissent.

[The opinion of Justice Cordy, dissenting, is omitted.]

Notes

1. Same-Sex Marriage Litigation: An Overview. *Goodridge* was decided in the context of a contentious national struggle involving every layer and branch of government. In Baehr v. Lewin, the Supreme Court of Hawaii became the first court to embrace the sex discrimination argument in addressing same-sex marriage. 852 P.2d 44 (Haw. 1993), reconsideration and clarification granted in part, 875 P.2d 225 (Haw. 1993), rev'd, and remanded sub nom. Baehr v. Miike, 994 P.2d 566 (Haw. 1999) (mem.) (after constitutional amendment overruling earlier decision). The court held that under state equal protection analysis the state would have to show a compelling interest to justify denying marriage licenses to same-sex couples. 852 P.2d at 59-68. However, before the case could reach the Hawaii Supreme Court after remand and an extensive trial on the compelling state interest question, the people of Hawaii in 1998 approved an amendment to the state constitution that mooted the issue by providing that "The legislature shall have the power to reserve marriage to opposite-sex couples." Haw. Const., art. 1, § 23.

The constitutional amendment in Hawaii was, in some measure, at the invitation of the U.S. Congress which, in 1996, passed the Defense of Marriage Act (DOMA), permitting states to choose not to recognize same-sex marriages performed in another state. See 1 U.S.C. § 7 (1996), and 28 U.S.C. § 1738C (1996). DOMA provides, in relevant part:

> No State, territory, or possession of the United States, or Indian tribe, shall be required to give effect to any public act, record, or judicial proceeding of any other State, territory, possession, or tribe respecting a relationship between persons of the same sex that is treated as a marriage under the laws of such other State, territory, possession, or tribe, or a right or claim arising from such relationship.

28 U.S.C. §1738C (1996). DOMA also defines "marriage" for the purposes of federal law as the legal union between one man and one woman as husband and wife. 1 U.S.C. §7 (1996). DOMA is further discussed in note 2, below.

In other jurisdictions, as in Hawaii, same-sex marriage has had its ups and downs. A state court decision in Alaska finding that the state's ban on same-sex marriage violated the state constitutional right to privacy provisions, Brause v. Bureau of Vital Statistics, No. 3AN-95-6562CJ (Alaska Super. Ct. Feb. 27, 1998), was also superseded by constitutional amendment. Constitution of Alaska, art. I, §25. In Baker v. State, 744 A.2d 864 (Vt. 1999), the Vermont Supreme Court found that prohibiting same-sex marriages violated the common benefits provision of the Vermont Constitution; the problem was cured in Vermont with a civil union alternative, rather than a marriage option. See note 3, below.

In San Francisco, Mayor Gavin Newsome decided to allow the issuance of marriage licenses to same-sex couples, on the grounds that the denial of these licenses discriminatory and unconstitutional. Approximately 4,000 same-sex marriages were performed in San Francisco between Feburary 12, 2004, and March 11, 2004, when the California Supreme Court ordered the city to stop issuing marriage licenses, and voided the marriages. See Lockyer v. City and County of San Francisco, 17 Cal. Rptr. 3d 225 (Cal. 2004). In a subsequent action in California, a San Francisco Superior Court determined, in six consolidated cases, that the state law limiting marriage to heterosexual couples violated state's guarantee of equal protection. See, e.g., Coordination Proceeding, Special Title [Rule 1550(c)] (Marriage Cases), Cal. Super. Ct., No. 4365, 31 Fam. L. Rep. 1219 (March 22, 2005).

In Oregon, on the initiative of some members of the Multnomah County Board of Commissions, the county counsel stated that the Oregon ban on same-sex marriages was unconstitutional, whereupon the county began issuing marriage licenses to same-sex couples. After 3,000 marriages licenses were issued, the Governor directed the State Registrar not to file or register any same-sex marriage records forwarded from Multnomah County, and some of the same-sex couples sued, seeking declaratory and injunctive relief. The trial court agreed with plaintiffs that the ban on same-sex marriage was unconstitutional, but instead of extending the right of marriage to same-sex couples, fashioned a remedy extending to them the benefits of marriage, without altering the statute limited marriage to opposite-sex couples. While the case was pending on appeal, the Oregon voters adopted a state constitutional amendment defining marriage as a relationship between one man and one woman. The Oregon supreme court then invalidated the marriages on statutory grounds, holding that it did not need to consider the independent effect of the constitutional amendment. See Li v. State of Oregon, 110 P.3d 91 (Ore. 2005).

New York has also seen a number of challenges to its marriage law which does not explicitly ban same-sex marriages but, in using the words "wife," "husband," "bride," and "groom," has been construed to intend traditional heterosexual marriage only. See, e.g., Hernandez v. Robles, 794 N.Y.S.2d 579 (N.Y. Misc. 2005) (ordering New York's City Clerk not to deny any couple a marriage license solely on the ground that the two people are of the same sex), reversed and vacated, 805 N.Y.S.2d 354 (N.Y. App. Div. 2005) (New York's reservation of marriage to heterosexual couples is rationally related to multiple legitimate state purposes); Hebel v. West, 803 N.Y.S.2d 242 (N.Y. App. Div. 2005) (affirming trial court injunction against a village mayor and two marriage officers from solemnizing same-sex marriages without duly issued marriage licenses); Seymour v. Holcomb, 790 N.Y.S.2d 858 (N.Y. Misc. 2005) (same-sex couples failed to show that New York law not authorizing marriage licenses to same-sex couples denied them equal protection or due process).

In the midst of this context of court challenges, legislative responses, and executive initiatives, in February 2004 President George W. Bush called for a federal constitutional amendment to ban same-sex marriage in February 2004. President George W. Bush, President Calls for Constitutional Amendment Protecting Marriage, Remarks by the President, The Roosevelt Room (Feb. 24, 2004), available at http://www.whitehouse.gov/news/releases/2004/02/20040224-2.html. U.S. Senate Resolution 1 proposed:

> Marriage in the United States shall consist only of the union between a man and a woman. Neither this Constitution, nor the Constitution of any State, nor State or Federal Law, shall be construed to require that marriage or the legal incidents thereof be conferred upon any union other than the union of a man and a woman.

S.J. Res. 1, 109th Cong. (2005). Similarly, U.S. House Resolution 56 proposed:

> Section 1. Marriage in the United States shall consist only of the union of a man and a woman. Neither this Constitution or the constitution of any State, nor state or federal law, shall be construed to require that marital status or the legal incidents thereof be conferred upon unmarried couples or groups.

H.R.J. Res. 56, 108th Cong. 1 (2004).

The Senate proposal failed to pass a cloture vote on July 14, 2004, S.J. Res. 40, 108th Cong. (2004), and the House proposal failed to pass the House with the required two-third majority on September 30, 2004, H.R.J. Res. 106, 108th Cong. (2004). On January 24, 2005, the Senate proposed the amendment again with minor changes to language. S.J. Res. 1, 109th Cong. (2005).

2. Defense of Marriage Acts. By last count, forty-two states currently have Defense of Marriage Acts. Three of those states have statutory language that pre-dates the federal DOMA. Eighteen states have defined marriage in their constitutions, 11 of them as a result of referenda in the November 2004 elections. Voters Approve State Constitutional Bans on Same-Sex Marriage in Eleven States, Lesbian/Gay Law Notes (December 2004), found at http://www.qrd.org/qrd/www/usa/legal/lgln. Only seven states have neither statutes nor constitutional language defining marriage explicitly to exclude same-sex marriage. These states include Connecticut, Massachusetts, New Jersey, New Mexico, New York, Rhode Island, and Wisconsin. Same Sex Marriage, National Conference of State Legislatures, April 2005, available at http://www.ncsl.org/programs/cyf/samesex.htm.

It is unclear how much DOMA adds to the law. Although there is not a "roving" public policy exception to the full faith and credit clause, see Baker v. General Motors Corp., 522 U.S. 222, 233 (1998), even without DOMA, the forum's "public policy" remains relevant to which state's law is applicable to controversies involving a marriage–that is, if marriage is covered by the full faith and credit clause, which is also a question. See Brian H. Bix, State of the Union: The States' Interest in the Marital Status of Their Citizens, 55 U. Miami L. Rev. 1, 25 (2000); Troy King, Marriage Between a Man and a Woman: A Fight to Save the Traditional Family One Case at a Time, 16 Stan. L. & Pol'y Rev. 57, 66-67 (2005); see also Restatement (Second) of Conflict of Laws, §283 (1971).

Some commentators have questioned the constitutionality of DOMA, and state laws passed pursuant to the Act. See, e.g., Mark P. Strasser, "Defending" Marriage in Light of the Moreno-Cleburne-Romer-Lawrence Jurisprudence: Why DOMA Cannot Pass Muster After *Lawrence*, 38 Creighton L. Rev. 421 (2005); Litigating the Defense of Marriage Act: The Next Battleground for Same-Sex Marriage, 117 Harv. L. Rev. 2684 (2004); and Larry Kramer, Same-Sex Marriage, Conflict of Laws and the Unconstitutional Public Policy Exception, 106 Yale L.J. 1965 (1997). One scholar argues that not only does DOMA violate the full faith and credit clause, but the public policy exception to the rule requiring recognition of out-of-state marriages does as well. See Kramer, supra.

So far, most courts have upheld legislation passed under DOMA. See, e.g., Smelt v. Orange County, C.D. Cal., No. 04-1042-GLT, June 16, 2005 (holding that the federal DOMA does not violate a same-sex couple's due process and equal protection rights under the federal constitution); Wilson v. Ake, 354 F. Supp. 2d 1298 (M.D. Fla. 2005) (Florida not required to recognize Massachusetts marriage of lesbian couple, under full faith and credit, due process, or equal protection provisions). State courts have also upheld the constitutionality of state Defense of Marriage Acts. See, e.g., Forum for Equal. PAC v. McKeithen, 893 So. 2d 715 (La. 2005); Morrison v. Sadler, 821 N.E.2d 15 (Ind. App. 2005). But cf. Citizens for Equal Protection Inc. v. Bruning, 368 F. Supp. 2d 980 (D. Neb. 2005) (on First Amendment, equal protection and due process grounds, invalidating broad state constitutional ban same-sex marriages, domestic partnerships, and civil unions).

3. The Civil Union Alternative. In December 1999, the Supreme Court of Vermont declared in Baker v. State, 744 A.2d 864, 867 (Vt. 1999), that the Vermont Constitution's Common Benefits Clause prohibits the exclusion of same-sex couples from the benefits and protections of marriage. Unlike *Goodridge*, in which the Supreme Judicial Court of Massachusetts held that same-sex couples must be included within civil marriage laws, the *Baker* court ruled that the Vermont Legislature had the choice whether to provide these benefits and protections by including same-sex couples within civil marriage laws, or by establishing an alternative system. Id.

In April 2000, the Vermont Legislature created a parallel system of "civil unions" for same-sex couples that went beyond the "domestic partnership" and "reciprocal beneficiaries" laws existing at the time in California, Hawaii, and many other U.S. localities. The Vermont civil union statute entitles the parties of civil unions to "all the same benefits, protections and responsibilities under law, whether they derive from statute, administrative or court rule, policy, common law or any other source of civil law, as are granted to spouses in a marriage." Vt. Stat. Ann. tit. 15, § 1204(a) (2004). The requisites of a valid civil union are the same as those for marriage in Vermont, except that the persons do not need to be of the opposite sex. Id. at §§ 1202, 1203. Couples who do not qualify for either a marriage or a civil union may still qualify as reciprocal beneficiaries, which entitles the parties to make legal decisions for one another, such as those relating to hospital visitation and medical care, anatomical gifts, disposition of remains, and nursing home care. See Vt. Stat. Ann. tit. 15, §§ 1301-1306 (2004).

In the first five years after Vermont's recognition of same-sex civil unions, 7,464 civil unions were performed in that state. Of those, 1,118 were to Vermont residents. There have been 68 dissolutions, which mirror divorces. Adrienne Mand Lewin, Vermont Marks Five Years of Civil Unions, ABC News, April 26, 2005, available at http://abcnews.go.com/US/LegalCenter/story?-id=695367.

In April 2005, Connecticut became the first state to legalize civil unions without prompting from the courts. The Connecticut civil union law provides, in pertinent part:

> Parties to a civil union shall have all the same benefits, protections and responsibilities under law, whether derived from the general statutes, administrative regulations or court rules, policy, common law or any other source of civil law, as are granted to spouses in a marriage, which is defined as the union of one man and one woman.

2005 Ct. P.A. 10, § 14. Shortly before passage of this statute, a Connecticut trial court would not annul the marriage of a lesbian couple because it found that the marriage between Connecticut residents was not valid under the law of Massachusetts and thus that there was no marriage to annul. Lane v. Albanese, 2005 Conn. Super. LEXIS 759, No. FA 04-4002128-S, March 18, 2005.

4. Domestic Partnership Benefits. As of June 2005, 11 state governments, 129 city and county governments, 295 colleges and universities, 234 Fortune 500 companies, and 7,599 other private sector companies offered domestic partner health benefits. For a continually updated count provided by the Human Rights Campaign, see http://www.hrc.org/worknet.

Taxpayer challenges have sought to invalidate the domestic partnership benefit ordinances of some local governments. With mixed results, the lawsuits have commonly focused on two primary allegations: (1) that the policies are outside the scope of municipal authority granted by state law, and (2) that they infringe upon the exclusively state legislative authority over domestic relations law. Joshua K. Baker, Status, Benefits, and Recognition: Current Controversies in the Marriage Debate, 18 BYU J. Pub. L. 569, 600 (2004). See, e.g., Arlington County v. White, 528 S.E.2d 706 (Va. 2000) (invalidating ordinance); Irizarry v. Bd. of Educ., 251 F.3d 604 (7th Cir. 2001) (affirming ordinance); Tyma v. Montgomery County, 801 A.2d 148 (Md. 2002) (affirming ordinance); Devlin v. City of Philadelphia, 809 A.2d 980 (Pa. Commw. Ct. 2002) (invalidating ordinance).

Cases seeking domestic partner benefits in the absence of clear statutory authority have also had mixed results. Compare Raum v. Restaurant Associates, Inc., 675 N.Y.S.2d 343 (App. Div. 1st Dept. 1998), appeal dismissed, 704 N.E.2d 229 (N.Y. 1998) (dismissing wrongful death action by same-sex partner); University of Alaska v. Tumeo, 933 P.2d 1147 (Alaska 1997) (denial of health insurance benefits to domestic partners of university employees is not a violation of state human rights act); Cornell v. Hamilton, 791 N.E.2d 214, 215 (Ind. Ct. App. 2003) (failure to extend three-day paid bereavement leave to gay partner does not violate Indiana's privileges and immunities clause); Rutgers Council of AAUP Chapters v. Rutgers, 689 A.2d 828 (N.J. Super. Ct. App. Div. 1997) (denial of employee health insurance benefits to same-sex domestic partners does not violate state's law against discrimination, right to equal protection under state constitution, or order prohibiting executive branch agencies from discrimination on basis of sexual orientation), with Snetsinger v. Mont. Univ. System, 104 P.3d 445 (Mont. 2004) (failure of state university to extend dependency benefits to same-sex partners that are available to unmarried opposite-sex couples violates Montana's equal protection clause); Levin v. Yeshiva University, 730 N.Y.S.2d 15 (N.Y. 2001) (lesbian couple raised a question of fact about whether policy of excluding same-sex couples from Yeshiva University's family housing violated New York City human rights law, because it creates a disparate impact based on sexual orientation; dismissal of claim against University reversed by unanimous court); Braschi v. Stahl Assocs., 543 N.E.2d 49 (N.Y. 1989) (construing rent control statute to include surviving partner of the leaseholder); Tanner v. Oregon Health Sciences University, 971 P.2d 435 (Or. Ct. App. 1998) (university's failure to extend eligibility for life and medical insurance benefits to domestic partners violates the Oregon Constitution's privileges or immunities clause).

Goodridge captures a wide array of privileges and benefits of marriage. Are legal benefits all that is at stake in the controversy over same-sex marriage? See Mary Becker, Family Law in the Secular State and Restrictions on Same-Sex Marriage: Two Are Better than One, 2001 U. Ill. L. Rev. 1, 31-44 (stressing importance of availability of marriage as a source of emotional support to its participants, and describing research showing that, even controlling for differences between cohabitors and those who marry, cohabitors are less happy and more depressed than their married counterparts).

5. The Comparative Context. A number of European countries have been leaders in recognizing same-sex marriage. Same-sex marriage became legal in the Netherlands in 2001, when the official definition of marriage was expanded to include "two persons of different sex or of the same sex." This change established complete parity between same-sex and opposite-sex couples, including the right to adopt children. The Belgian Parliament approved similar legislation permitting same-sex marriages in early 2003, though without accompanying rights of adoption. Developments in the Law II, Inching Down the Aisle: Differing Paths Toward the Legalization of Same-Sex Marriage in the United States and Europe, 116 Harv. L. Rev. 2004, 2007-2008 (2004). The South African Supreme Court of Appeals in November 2004 ruled that the country's definition of marriage should be changed from the union of one man and one woman to "the union of two persons to the exclusion of all others for life." SA Ruling May Allow Gay Unions, BBC News, November 30, 2004, available at http://news.bbc.co.uk/2/hi/africa/4055549.stm. In 2005, Canada and Spain also legalized same-sex marriage. Canada Legalizes Gay Marriage, CNN News, July 20, 2005, available at http://www.cnn.com/2005/WORLD/americas/07/20/marriage.canada.ap; Spain Legislates Marriage Parity, Canada Soon to Follow, Lesbian/Gay Notes, Summer 2005, available at http://www.qrd.org/qrd/www/use/lgln.

Several other countries recognize "registered partnerships," which entail most, but not all, of the same rights and responsibilities as those associated with opposite-sex marriage. These countries include Denmark (1989), Norway (1993), Sweden (1995), in Iceland in 1996, and Finland (2002). Less expansive forms of same-sex unions were legalized in Hungary (1998), France (1999), Germany (2000), and Portugal (2001). Inching Down the Aisle, supra, at 2007-2008.

In November 2004, the United Kingdom passed the Civil Partnership Bill. Effective December 21, 2005, gay and lesbian couples who register will receive some of the same rights as married couples, including accident compensation, life insurance, immigration, inheritance, spouse and child support and workplace benefits. Timeline: Fight for Gay Equality, BBC News, May, 9, 2005, available at http://news.bbc.co.uk/1/hi/uk/4530803.stm.

In June 2005, voters in Switzerland passed a referendum allowing same-sex partnership registration. Under the law, homosexual couples have the same rights as heterosexual married couples with regard to pensions, insurance, and taxation. However, child adoption is still legally excluded. World/Election Watch – Switzerland, CNN News, June 5, 2005, available at http://edition.cnn.com/WORLD/election.watch/europe/switzerland11.html.

In December 2004, Israel announced it will give limited rights to same-sex couples. Dan Izenberg, Mazuz Backs Rights of Same-sex Couples, Jerusalem Post, Dec. 9, 2004, at 5, available at http://pqasb.pqarchiver.com/jpost/index.html?ts=1118016159. And since December 2004, gay and lesbian couples in New Zealand have been able to register their unions and receive many of the same rights as heterosexual married couples. The law allows couples to have a ceremony and claim next-of-kin status when a partner dies and to have control over a partner's medical treatment. New Zealand Recognizes Same-sex Unions, BBC News, December 9, 2004, available at http://news.bbc.co.uk/2/hi/asia-pacific/4081089.stm. Limited rights for same-sex couples have also been created in New South Wales, Argentina, and Brazil. Id. at 49. See also William N. Eskridge, Jr., Comparative Law and the Same-Sex Marriage Debate: A Step-by-Step Approach Toward State Recognition, 31 McGeorge L. Rev. 641 (2000) (listing laws and cases of other countries); Nancy D. Polikoff, Recognizing Partners but Not Parents/Recognizing Parents but Not Partners: Gay and Lesbian Family Law in Europe and the United States, 17 N.Y.L. Sch. J. Hum. Rts. 711 (2000) (comparing rights afforded by domestic partnership laws in different countries, including parental rights).

In countries with domestic registration procedures, relatively few same-sex couples have taken advantage of registration procedures that allow them to receive available benefits. See Eskridge, supra, at 653-654, 661 (only 2,372 Danish couples after nine years of registered partnership law, 674 couples after four years of the Norwegian law, 749 after four years of the Swedish law, 45 after two years of the Icelandic law, and 5,217 after one year of the Dutch law). Male couples take advantage of partnership registration at much higher rates than female couples, "in some years at double or triple the rates," although the ratio falls off over time. Id. at 661. What might explain this disparity?

6. Resistance to Gay Marriage. What is the source of resistance to gay marriage? One commentator, advocating the disaggregation of the religious from the secular licensing of marriage, offers the following:

> In my view, the following is the best explanation of the opposition to legal recognition of same-sex marriage on the part of evangelical Protestant religious conservatives who claim such recognition would undercut their own marriages: Unlike observant Jews and Roman Catholics, who clearly understand that civil marriage and marriage within their faith are not the same, such that one can be married in the eyes of the state and not the faith and vice versa, Protestant denominations in the United States have essentially abdicated the definition, creation and, above all the dissolution of marriage to the state. There is, for example, nothing like the get or annulment available to or required of Protestants. This leaves religiously conservative Protestants far more dependent on the state's regulation of marriage, far less able to distinguish conceptually between marriage as their religion defines it and as state law does and, unsurprisingly, far more opposed on a percentage basis to same-sex marriage than conservative Catholics and Jews who otherwise, according to poll data, share their opposition to homosexuality. According to a representative poll taken in July 2003, for example, while 64% of Protestants oppose "gay marriage," Catholics also oppose it, but by a smaller margin than the entire population," 50% of Catholics as compared to 55% of the population as a whole. And according to survey results released by the Pew forum in October 2004, 55% of Jews supported same-sex marriage, while opposition reached 48% among white Roman Catholics, 52% among Latino Catholics, 71% among Latino Protestants, 72% among Black Protestants and 75% among white evangelical Protestants.

Mary Anne Case, Marriage Licenses, 89 Minn. L. Rev. 1758, 1795-1796 (2005). Case concludes that "marriage licenses in the plural . . . may be at least a useful, if not a necessary, precondition to settling the question of the civil licensing of marriages . . . if not 'under God' then in 'one nation, with liberty and justice for all.'" Id. at 1797.

Would a plural licensing system satisfy those who object to same-sex marriage?

7. Gay and Lesbian Marriage: Dominance or Freedom? The gay and lesbian community has not universally supported the campaign for same-sex marriage. On the one hand, gay and lesbian marriage would permit homosexual couples to obtain some of the legal benefits of marriage—many of these summarized in *Goodridge*—on the same basis as heterosexual couples. In addition, recognition of same-sex marriage would help to "normalize" the status of gays and lesbians, thus both stabilizing those relationships themselves and potentially eliminating some of the fears and prejudice surrounding homosexuality in society at large. The fullest analyses of same-sex marriage from a positive perspective include William Eskridge, The Case for Same-Sex Marriage (1996); David L. Chambers, What If? The Legal Consequences of Marriage and the Legal Needs of Lesbian and Gay Male Couples, 95 Mich. L. Rev. 447 (1996). One of the classics on why gays and lesbians should work to make marriage legal for themselves and their partners is Thomas Stoddard, Why Gay People Should Seek the Right to Marry, 2 Out/Look, Nat'l Gay & Lesbian Q. 9 (Fall 1989).

On the other hand, some commentators have argued out that gays and lesbians should be suspicious of gaining access to social forms that have historically defined and controlled women in oppressive ways. Perhaps not surprisingly, this argument has been pursued less by gay men than by lesbians, who worry that importing the trappings of heterosexual relationships into lesbian relations ("hetero-relationizing") will weaken the broader, extended relationships within lesbian communities; encourage possessive, patriarchal-style patterns of submission and dominance; and cultivate unacceptable distinctions between married and unmarried lesbians. Consider the following:

> [M]arriage will not liberate us as lesbians and gay men. In fact, it will constrain us, make us more invisible, force our assimilation into the mainstream, and undermine the goals of gay liberation. [A]ttaining the right to marry will not transform our society from one that makes narrow, but dramatic, distinctions between those who are married and those who are not married to one that respects and encourages choice of relationships and family diversity. Marriage runs contrary to two of the primary goals of the lesbian and gay movement: the affirmation of gay identity and culture; and the validation of many forms of relationships. . . .
>
> Justice for gay men and lesbians will be achieved only when we are accepted and supported in this society *despite* our differences from the dominant culture and the choices we make regarding our relationships. Being queer is more than setting up house, sleeping with a person of the same gender, and seeking state approval for doing so. It is an identity, a culture with many variations. It is a way of dealing with the world by diminishing the constraints of gender roles which have for so long kept women and gay people oppressed and invisible. Being queer means pushing the parameters of sex, sexuality, and family, and in the process transforming the very fabric of society. . . .
>
> The moment we argue, as some among us insist on doing, that we should be treated as equals because we are really just like married couples and hold the same values to be true, we undermine the very purpose of our movement and begin the dangerous process of silencing our different voices. As a lesbian, I am fundamentally different from non-lesbian women. That's the point. Marriage, as it exists today, is antithetical to my liberation as a lesbian and as a woman because it mainstreams my life and voice. I do not want [to] be known as "Mrs. Attached-To-Somebody-Else." Nor do I want to give the state the power to regulate my primary relationship.

Paula L. Ettelbrick, Since When Is Marriage a Path to Liberation, 2 Out/Look, Nat'l Gay & Lesbian Q. 9, 14 (Fall 1989). For related views, see Nancy D. Polikoff,

We Will Get What We Ask For: Why Legalizing Gay and Lesbian Marriage Will Not "Dismantle the Legal Structure of Gender in Every Marriage," 79 Val. U.L. Rev. 1535 (1993); Paula L. Ettelbrick, Wedlock Alert: A Comment on Lesbian and Gay Family Recognition, 5 J.L. & Pol'y 107 (1996); see also Katha Pollitt, Gay Marriage? Don't Say I Didn't Warn You, in Subject to Debate: Sense and Dissents on Women, Politics, and Culture 109 (Katha Pollitt ed., 2001) ("Marriage will not only open up to gay men and lesbians whole new vistas of guilt, frustration, claustrophobia, bewilderment, unfairness and sorrow, it will offer them the opportunity to prolong this misery by tormenting each other in court."); Same-Sex Marriage: Pro and Con, A Reader (Andrew Sullivan ed., 1997) (essays for and against same-sex marriage).

Putting Theory into Practice

3-16. Roberta, who was born with male genitalia, has a successful operation to align his biological sex with his psychological sex, which is female. He then marries George. Ten years later, Roberta files for divorce and seeks spousal support against George. George challenges the validity of the marriage on the grounds that the state does not recognize marriage between two men. Who should win? Compare In re Estate of Gardiner, 22 P.3d 1086 (Kan. Ct. App. 2001) and M.T. v. J.T., 355 A.2d 204 (N.J. Super. Ct. App. Div. 1976) (transsexual marriage valid) with Littleton v. Prange, 9 S.W.3d 223 (Tex. Ct. App. 1999) and In re Ladrach, 513 N.E.2d 828 (Ohio Misc. 2d Ct. 1987) (transsexual marriage not valid). Legal issues raised by transsexualism are explored in Section 3, pp. 605-618, infra (employment), and in Chapter 6, pp. 1005-1020, Section 3 (marriage, employment, and other issues).

3-17. Assume the following two cases. The first involves a man and a woman who were married for one year, during which time the man, a pro basketball player, earned almost $3 million, $2 million of which he saved. Under state law, at divorce the woman is entitled to half of that amount as her share of the community property. The second involves the break-up of two gay men who lived together for over 20 years, during which time one of them encouraged the economic dependence of the other. At the time of the break-up, the dependent partner sought a share of the $2 million in assets held by the other partner that were accumulated during their relationship. Because the parties are not married, he is not entitled to any of these assets.

Can you justify these outcomes? See American Law Institute, Principles of the Law of Family Dissolution: Analysis and Recommendation, Part I, Chapter 5 (2000), and American Law Institute, Principles of the Law of Family Dissolution: Analysis and Recommendation, Chapter 6 (2000) (comprehensive recommendations for equalizing treatment of support issues at family dissolution between family relationships based on marriage and those based on domestic partnerships).

2. Lesbian Parent Is Not a Parent

In the Matter of Alison D. v. Virginia M.
569 N.Y.S.2d 586 (N.Y. 1991)

PER CURIAM.

At issue in this case is whether petitioner, a biological stranger to a child who is properly in the custody of his biological mother, has standing to seek visitation with the child under Domestic Relations Law §70. Petitioner relies on both her established relationship with the child and her alleged agreement with the biological mother to support her claim that she has standing. We agree with the Appellate Division . . . that, although petitioner apparently nurtured a close and loving relationship with the child, she is not a parent within the meaning of Domestic Relations Law §70. Accordingly, we affirm.

I

Petitioner Alison D. and respondent Virginia M. established a relationship in September 1977 and began living together in March 1978. In March 1980, they decided to have a child and agreed that respondent would be artificially inseminated. Together, they planned for the conception and birth of the child and agreed to share jointly all rights and responsibilities of child-rearing. In July 1981, respondent gave birth to a baby boy, A.D.M., who was given petitioner's last name as his middle name and respondent's last name became his last name. Petitioner shared in all birthing expenses and, after A.D.M.'s birth, continued to provide for his support. During A.D.M.'s first two years, petitioner and respondent jointly cared for and made decisions regarding the child.

In November 1983, when the child was 2 years and 4 months old, petitioner and respondent terminated their relationship and petitioner moved out of the home they jointly owned. Petitioner and respondent agreed to a visitation schedule whereby petitioner continued to see the child a few times a week. Petitioner also agreed to continue to pay one half of the mortgage and major household expenses. By this time, the child had referred to both respondent and petitioner as "mommy." Petitioner's visitation with the child continued until 1986, at which time respondent bought out petitioner's interest in the house and then began to restrict petitioner's visitation with the child. In 1987 petitioner moved to Ireland to pursue career opportunities, but continued her attempts to communicate with the child. Thereafter, respondent terminated all contact between petitioner and the child, returning all of petitioner's gifts and letters. No dispute exists that respondent is a fit parent. Petitioner commenced this proceeding seeking visitation rights pursuant to Domestic Relations Law §70. . . .

II

Pursuant to Domestic Relations Law §70 "either parent may apply to the supreme court for a writ of habeas corpus to have such minor child brought before such court; and [the court] may award the natural guardianship, charge and custody of such child to either parent . . . as the case may require." Although the Court is mindful of petitioner's understandable concern for and interest in the child and of her expectation and desire that her contact with the child would continue, she has no right under Domestic Relations Law § 70 to seek visitation and, thereby, limit or diminish the right of the concededly fit biological parent to choose with whom her child associates. She is not a "parent" within the meaning of § 70.

Petitioner concedes that she is not the child's "parent"; that is, she is not the biological mother of the child nor is she a legal parent by virtue of an adoption. Rather she claims to have acted as a "de facto" parent or that she should be viewed as a parent "by estoppel." Therefore, she claims she has standing to seek visitation rights. These claims, however, are insufficient under § 70. Traditionally, in this State it is the child's mother and father who, assuming fitness, have the right to the care and custody of their child, even in situations where the nonparent has exercised some control over the child with the parents' consent. . . . To allow the courts to award visitation — a limited form of custody — to a third person would necessarily impair the parents' right to custody and control. . . . Petitioner concedes that respondent is a fit parent. Therefore she has no right to petition the court to displace the choice made by this fit parent in deciding what is in the child's best interests.

Section 70 gives parents the right to bring proceedings to ensure their proper exercise of their care, custody and control. . . . Where the Legislature deemed it appropriate, it gave other categories of persons standing to seek visitation and it gave the courts the power to determine whether an award of visitation would be in the child's best interests (see, e.g., Domestic Relations Law § 71 [special proceeding or habeas corpus to obtain visitation rights for siblings]; § 72 [special proceeding or habeas corpus to obtain visitation rights for grandparents]. . . . We decline petitioner's invitation to read the term parent in § 70 to include categories of nonparents who have developed a relationship with a child or who have had prior relationships with a child's parents and who wish to continue visitation with the child (accord, Nancy S. v. Michele G., 279 Cal. Rptr. 212 (Ct. App. 1991)). While one may dispute in an individual case whether it would be beneficial to a child to have continued contact with a nonparent, the Legislature did not in § 70 give such nonparent the opportunity to compel a fit parent to allow them to do so. . . .

KAYE, Judge (dissenting).

The Court's decision, fixing biology as the key to visitation rights, has impact far beyond this particular controversy, one that may affect a wide spectrum of relationships — including those of longtime heterosexual stepparents, "common-law" and nonheterosexual partners such as involved here, and even participants in scientific reproduction procedures. Estimates that more than 15.5 million children do not live with two biological parents, and that as many as 8 to 10 million children are born into families with a gay or lesbian parent, suggest just how widespread the impact may be (see, Polikoff, This Child Does Have Two Mothers: Redefining Parenthood to Meet the Needs of Children in Lesbian-

Mother and Other Nontraditional Families, 78 Geo. L.J. 459, 461, n.2 (1990); Bartlett, Rethinking Parenthood as an Exclusive Status: The Need for Legal Alternatives When the Premise of the Nuclear Family Has Failed, 70 Va. L. Rev. 879, 880-881 (1984) . . .).

But the impact of today's decision falls hardest on the children of those relationships, limiting their opportunity to maintain bonds that may be crucial to their development. The majority's retreat from the courts' proper role — its tightening of rules that should in visitation petitions, above all, retain the capacity to take the children's interests into account — compels this dissent.

In focusing the difference, it is perhaps helpful to begin with what is not at issue. This is not a custody case, but solely a visitation petition. The issue on this appeal is not whether petitioner should actually have visitation rights. Nor is the issue the relationship between Alison D. and Virginia M. Rather, the sole issue is the relationship between Alison D. and A.D.M., in particular whether Alison D.'s petition for visitation should even be considered on its merits. I would conclude that the trial court had jurisdiction to hear the merits of this petition.

The relevant facts are amply described in the Court's opinion. Most significantly, Virginia M. agrees that, after long cohabitation with Alison D. and before A.D.M.'s conception, it was "explicitly planned that the child would be theirs to raise together." It is also uncontested that the two shared "financial and emotional preparations" for the birth, and that for several years Alison D. actually filled the role of coparent to A.D.M., both tangibly and intangibly. In all, a parent-child relationship — encouraged or at least condoned by Virginia M. — apparently existed between A.D.M. and Alison D. during the first six years of the child's life.

While acknowledging that relationship, the Court nonetheless proclaims powerlessness to consider the child's interest at all, because the word "parent" in the statute imposes an absolute barrier to Alison D.'s petition for visitation. That same conclusion would follow, as the Appellate Division dissenter noted, were the coparenting relationship one of 10 or more years, and irrespective of how close or deep the emotional ties might be between petitioner and child, or how devastating isolation might be to the child. I cannot agree that such a result is mandated by §70, or any other law.

Domestic Relations Law §70 provides a mechanism for "either parent" to bring a habeas corpus proceeding to determine a child's custody. Other State Legislatures, in comparable statutes, have defined "parent" specifically (see, e.g., Cal. Civ. Code §7001 [defining parent-child relationship as between "a child and his natural or adoptive parents"]), and that definition has of course bound the courts (see Nancy S. v. Michele G., [279 Cal. Rptr. 212 (Cal. App. 1991) (applying the statutory definition)]). Significantly, the Domestic Relations Law contains no such limitation. Indeed, it does not define the term "parent" at all. That remains for the courts to do, as often happens when statutory terms are undefined.

The majority insists, however, that the word "parent" in this case can only be read to mean biological parent; the response "one fit parent" now forecloses all inquiry into the child's best interest, even in visitation proceedings. We have not previously taken such a hard line in these matters, but in the absence of express legislative direction have attempted to read otherwise undefined words of the statute so as to effectuate the legislative purposes. The Legislature has made plain an objective in § 70 to promote "the best interest of the child" and the child's "welfare and happiness." (Domestic Relations Law § 70.) Those words should not be ignored by us in defining standing for visitation purposes — they have not been in prior case law. . . .

As the Court wrote in Matter of Bennett v. Jeffreys, [356 N.E.2d 277 (N.Y. 1976)] — even in recognizing the superior right of a biological parent to the custody of her child — "when there is a conflict, the best interest of the child has always been regarded as superior to the right of parental custody. Indeed, analysis of the cases reveals a shifting of emphasis rather than a remaking of substance. This shifting reflects more the modern principle that a child is a person, and not a subperson over whom the parent has an absolute possessory interest."

Apart from imposing upon itself an unnecessarily restrictive definition of "parent," and apart from turning its back on a tradition of reading § 70 so as to promote the welfare of the children, in accord with the parens patriae power, the Court also overlooks the significant distinction between visitation and custody proceedings.

While both are of special concern to the State, custody and visitation are significantly different. . . . Custody disputes implicate a parent's right to rear a child — with the child's corresponding right to be raised by a parent. . . . Infringement of that right must be based on the fitness — more precisely the lack of fitness — of the custodial parent.

Visitation rights also implicate a right of the custodial parent, but it is the right to choose with whom the child associates. . . . Any burden on the exercise of that right must be based on the child's overriding need to maintain a particular relationship. . . . Logically, the fitness concern present in custody disputes is irrelevant in visitation petitions, where continuing contact with the child rather than severing of a parental tie is in issue. For that reason, we refused to extend the Bennett "extraordinary circumstances" doctrine — which relates to the fitness of the custodial parent — to visitation petitions (Matter of Ronald FF. v. Cindy GG., [511 N.E.2d 75 (N.Y. 1987)].

The Court now takes the law a step beyond *Ronald FF.* by establishing the Bennett "extraordinary circumstances" test as the only way to reach the child's best interest in a § 70 proceeding. In that *Ronald FF.* determined that extraordinary circumstances are irrelevant in the visitation context, our holding today thus firmly closes the door on all consideration of the child's best interest in visitation proceedings such as the one before us, unless petitioner is a biological parent.

Of course there must be some limitation on who can petition for visitation. Domestic Relations Law § 70 specifies that the person must be the child's "parent," and the law additionally recognizes certain rights of biological and legal parents. Arguments that every dedicated caretaker could sue for visitation if the term "parent" were broadened, or that such action would necessarily effect sweeping change throughout the law, overlook and misportray the Court's role in defining otherwise undefined statutory terms to effect particular statutory purposes, and to do so narrowly, for those purposes only.

Countless examples of that process may be found in our case law, the Court looking to modern-day realities in giving definition to statutory concepts.... Only recently, we defined the term "family" in the eviction provisions of the rent stabilization laws so as to advance the legislative objective, making abundantly clear that the definition was limited to the statute in issue and did not effect a wholesale change in the law (see Braschi v. Stahl Assocs. Co., [543 N.E.2d 49 (N.Y. 1989)]).

In discharging this responsibility, recent decisions from other jurisdictions, for the most part concerning visitation rights of stepparents, are instructive (see, e.g., Gribble v. Gribble, [583 P.2d 64 (Utah 1978)]; Spells v. Spells, [378 A.2d 879 (Pa. Super. 1977)]). For example in *Spells*, [378 A.2d at 881-882], the court fashioned a test for "parental status" or "in loco parentis" requiring that the petitioner demonstrate actual assumption of the parental role and discharge of parental responsibilities. It should be required that the relationship with the child came into being with the consent of the biological or legal parent, and that the petitioner at least have had joint custody of the child for a significant period of time (see, Rethinking Parenthood as an Exclusive Status, supra, 70 Va. L. Rev. at 945-946). Other factors likely should be added to constitute a test that protects all relevant interests — much as we did in *Braschi*....

It is not my intention to spell out a definition but only to point out that it is surely within our competence to do so. It is indeed regrettable that we decline to exercise that authority in this visitation matter, given the explicit statutory objectives, the court's power, and the fact that all consideration of the child's interest is, for the future, otherwise absolutely foreclosed.

I would remand the case to Supreme Court for an exercise of its discretion in determining whether Alison D. stands *in loco parentis* to A.D.M. and, if so, whether it is in the child's best interest to allow her the visitation rights she claims.

Notes

1. Custody Disputes Involving Gay and Lesbian Parents. Biological parents may face difficult custody issues if they are gay or lesbian. For some time, some courts employed a per se approach, whereby homosexuality was deemed to render a parent per se unfit to have custody of a child. The leading case for some years was Roe v. Roe, 324 S.E.2d 691, 694 (Va. 1985) (holding that a parent's homosexual relationship renders the parent unfit and an improper custodian), although the Virginia rule was modified a decade later by Bottoms v. Bottoms, 457 S.E.2d 102 (Va. 1995). While no court currently claims to use a per se approach, the possibility still exists in modified form. Lynn Wardle, for example, proposes a rebuttable presumption that "ongoing homosexual relations by an adult seeking or exercising parental rights is not in the best interests of the child." See Lynn D. Wardle, The

Potential Impact of Homosexual Parenting on Children, 1997 U. Ill. L. Rev. 833, 894.

Approximately thirteen states follow an approach that permits the fact-finder to draw an inference that a parent's homosexual conduct is harmful to a child but does not require it. Jovana Vujovic, Child Custody and Visitation, 5 Geo J. Gender & L. 477, 493 (2004). Although courts in these states have ostensibly abandoned the per se rule, the inference approach often amounts to the same result given the assumptions many judges make about the effects of homosexuality on children. See, e.g., Pulliam v. Smith, 501 S.E.2d 898 (N.C. 1998) (affirming trial court's assumption that homosexual activity within the home, including kissing in the presence of the child and being in bed together, is detrimental to a child's best interests). See also Ex parte J.M.F., 730 So. 2d 1190, 1194-1196 (Ala. 1998) (upholding modification of custody from mother to father, based on court finding that a change in the mother's lesbian relationship from a discreet affair to one that was "openly homosexual" is a change of circumstances and that the trial court did not abuse its discretion in determining on the basis of "scientific studies" that a change in custody would materially promote the child's best interests); Scott v. Scott, 665 So. 2d 760, 766 (La. Ct. App. 1995) (affirming change of custody from lesbian mother to heterosexual father when primary custody with the homosexual parent would embarrass the child, in this case due to the child's enrollment at a private religious school which advocates Christian fundamentalist beliefs).

A growing number of courts now refuse to take homosexual behavior or orientation into account in custody matters unless harm to the child is affirmatively demonstrated. See, e.g., McGriff v. McGriff, 99 P.3d 111, 117 (Idaho 2004) (holding that only when there is a nexus between harm to the child and a parent's homosexuality can that parent's sexual orientation be a factor in modifying custody of a child; custody denied to homosexual father on other grounds); Damron v. Damron, 670 N.W.2d 871 (N.D. 2003) (holding that custodial parent's homosexual household was not grounds for modifying custody absent evidence of actual or potential harm to the children's physical or emotional health or impairment of their emotional development); Berry v. Berry, 2005 Tenn. App. LEXIS 320 (holding that custody by a mother could not be modified when there was no credible evidence to support a finding that her sexual orientation would have an adverse impact on the child).

The harm standard was adopted by the American Law Institute in its Principles of Family Dissolution: Analysis and Recommendations, see Part I, §§ 2.12(1)(d), (e) (2000) (prohibiting in custody cases consideration of sexual orientation and consideration of sexual conduct of a parent except when harm to the child is shown). At least half of the states now require a showing of harm before homosexuality can be a factor in a custody suit. See Vujovic, supra, at 491-492.

Generally, under the harm standard, real or imagined stigma from having a homosexual parent is insufficient. In Blew v. Verta, 617 A.2d 31, 35-36 (Pa. Super. Ct. 1992), for example, an appellate court reversed a trial court's limitations on the ability of a lesbian mother to visit with her son in the presence of her lover on the grounds that the child had to learn to accept his parent's homosexuality.

[O]ne of life's realities is that one of his parents is homosexual. In the absence of evidence that the homosexuality in some way harms the boy, limiting [his] relationship with that parent fails to permit him to confront his life situation, however unconventional it may be.... [The child's] best interest is served by exposing him to reality and not fostering in him shame or abhorrence for his mother's non-traditional commitment.

Id. at 36. See also Jacoby v. Jacoby, 763 So. 2d 410, 413 (Fla. Dist. Ct. App. 2000) (law cannot give effect to private biases, which in any event "flow not from the fact that the children were living with a homosexual mother, but from the fact that she is a homosexual").

Ordinarily, courts find that the harm standard is not satisfied. In some cases, however, courts have found that homosexual conduct by a parent is detrimental to the child. See, e.g., J.A.D. v. F.J.D., 978 S.W.2d 336, 339 (Mo. 1998) (lesbian mother denied custody because, while a homosexual parent is not ipso facto unfit for custody, the impact of homosexual or heterosexual misconduct on the children may be considered in making a custody determination). Other cases in which the harm standard was satisfied include Marlow v. Marlow, 702 N.E.2d 733 (Ind. Ct. App. 1998) (upholding restrictions on visitation by gay father of three young sons who were being raised by their mother in a conservative Christian setting in which homosexuality was considered a sin and who had exhibited behavior consistent with emotional distress while visiting with their father, including bed-wetting, difficulty sleeping, and nightmares); Piatt v. Piatt, 499 S.E.2d 567, 570 (Va. Ct. App. 1998) (upholding award of primary physical custody to the father based on findings that the mother's post-separation sexual relationships with other women and her "experimentation" with her sexual orientation had manifested her inner "turmoil" and "lack of control," which had a direct bearing on her ability to provide a stable home environment); In re Marriage of Martins, 645 N.E.2d 567 (Ill. App. Ct. 1995) (mother failed to give adequate time and attention to the children after announcement that she was a lesbian and had multiple female roommates whose moving in and out of the home the children did not like; also, children had behavioral problems and emotional struggles, requiring counseling).

The District of Columbia is the only jurisdiction that explicitly forbids by statute the use of a parent's sexual orientation as the sole basis for denying child custody or visitation rights. See D.C. Code Ann. § 16-914(a)(1)(A) ("In any proceeding between parents in which the custody of a child is raised as an issue, the best interest of the child shall be the primary consideration. The race, color, national origin, political affiliation, sex, or sexual orientation of a party, in and of itself, shall not be a conclusive consideration.").

Some scholars argue that the Supreme Court's opinion in Lawrence v. Texas, 539 U.S. 558 (2003), broadly announces a principle of constitutional respect for gay people and same-sex relationships that may eventually reverse most or all of the anti-gay reasoning in areas of law outside the bedroom, including child custody. See, e.g., Matt Larsen, *Lawrence v. Texas* and Family Law: Gay Parents' Constitutional Rights in Child Custody Proceedings, 60 N.Y.U. Ann. Surv. Am. L. 53, 54-55 (2004). Focusing on the rights of a "person" rather than those of a "gay person," the Court explicitly found that the liberty protected by the Due Process Clause includes the freedom to engage in "certain intimate conduct." 539 U.S. at 562. How are courts likely to respond to this reasoning in the custody context, where the best-interests-of-the-child test prevails? Arguing that Lawrence v. Texas will have little if any bearing on custody cases, see Martin R. Gardner, Adoption by Homosexuals in the Wake of *Lawrence v. Texas*, 6 J.L. & Fam. Stud. 19 (2004).

2. Lesbian De Facto Parents. In its time, *Alison D.* represented the clear majority approach to lesbian co-parent cases. Almost all courts denied visitation and custody rights to lesbians who were de facto, nonbiological parents, either because they lacked standing or because they failed to meet the substantive criteria for parenthood under the state's custody statute. See also West v. Sacramento County, 69 Cal. Rptr. 2d 160 (Cal. Ct. App. 1997); McGuffin v. Overton, 542 N.W.2d 288 (Mich. Ct. App. 1995), appeal denied, 546 N.W.2d 256 (Mich. 1996).

In 1995, a Wisconsin case provided a framework for awarding custody to a lesbian co-parent. See In re Marriage of H.S.H.-K., 533 N.W.2d 419 (Wis. 1995). This case concluded that the court had equitable power to determine visitation in an action brought by a lesbian co-parent, upon her separation from the mother. Courts since *H.S.H.-K.* have applied equitable doctrines such as equitable parenthood, parent by estoppel, or *in loco parentis* to extend rights to visitation or, in some cases, custody, to lesbian co-parents. See, e.g., Clifford K. v. Paul S. ex rel. Z.B.S., 619 S.E.2d 138 (W. Va. 2005) (lesbian domestic partner, who had raised child with since deceased biological mother, has standing to pursue custody of child in action against child's grandfather); King v. S.B. (In re A.B.), 818 N.E.2d 126 (Ind. Ct. App. 2004) (both members of a couple that participated in a commitment ceremony and agreed jointly to bear and raise a child together have legal status as parents, after couple's relationship dissolves); T.B. v. L.R.M., 786 A.2d 913, 918-19 (Pa. 2001) (establishing the right of a former same-sex partner to bring an action for child visitation and partial custody despite her legal inability to adopt the child); Rubano v. DiCenzo, 759 A.2d 959, 966 (R.I. 2000) (lesbian co-parent entitled to bring action to enforce visitation agreement); V.C. v. M.J.B., 748 A.2d 539, 555 (N.J. 2000) (holding that a former same-sex partner was a "psychological parent" whose child-visitation rights could not be unilaterally terminated by the biological mother); E.N.O. v. L.M.M., 711 N.E.2d 886, 892 (Mass. 1999), cert. denied, 528 U.S. 1005 (1999) (holding that a same-sex partner with whom biological mother had made a co-parenting agreement was a de facto parent. and that the evidence supported a grant of visitation). In the right case, a lesbian co-parent may even obtain primary custody, over the claim of the biological mother. See, e.g., Jones v. Jones, A25041/05, No. 271 EDA 2005 (Pa. Super Ct.) ("non- precedential decision"), reported in Lesbian/Gay Law Notes, Oct. 2005, at 1.

Several cases (e.g., *Clifford K.*, supra; King v. S.B., supra; *Jones*, supra) involve children conceived through artificial insemination, after the co-parents agreed to bear and raise a child together. In a custody dispute still not resolved at the time this book went to press, former partners in a Vermont civil union disagreed about the impact of the state's civil union laws on the custody of a child. A Vermont court determined that the child born to a woman via artificial insemination in a civil union, with the consent of both parties, was presumed to be the child of both parties, and thus that both partners had all of the rights and duties of parents. The birth mother then took the child to a Virginia court, which issued an order declaring that Vermont's civil union was null and void in Virginia, and that the birth mother was the child's sole parent. See Miller-Jenkins v. Miller-Jenkins, Vt. Fam. Ct., No. 454-11-03, November 17, 2004, at http://pub/bna/com/fl/4541103.htm; Miller-Jenkins v. Miller-Jenkins, Va. Cir. Ct., No. CH04-280, October 15, 2004, at http://pub.bna.com/fl/04280.htm. For further discussion of parenthood issues raised by artificial insemination and other non-traditional means, see Chapter 5, pp. 920-921.

In a few lesbian co-parent cases, the main issue has not been custody or visitation, but the co-parent's obligation to pay child support. See, e.g., Elisa B. v. Superior Court, 117 P.3d 660 (Cal. 2005) (in suit filed by welfare agency after couple split up and birth mother became dependent upon public support, co-parent liable for support based on fact that she had actively participated in plan to use donor insemination and raise twins as co-parents).

The safest avenue for lesbian co-parents seeking to establish a legal parental status is second parent, or co-parent, adoption, which is allowed in a growing number of jurisdictions including New York, the state in which *Alison D.* was decided. Second-parent adoption, where allowed, permits an individual to adopt the child of his or her partner, either marital or non-marital, without the usual requirement of termination of that partner's parental rights and responsibilities. As of 2005, second-parent adoptions are now allowed by statute or court decision in California, Connecticut, the District of Columbia, Illinois, Indiana, Massachusetts, New York, New Jersey, Pennsylvania, Vermont, and some counties of 15 other states. Courtney G. Joslin, The Legal Parentage of Children Born to Same-Sex Couples, 39 Fam. L. Q. 683, 691 (2005). In some states, this can be accomplished before the birth of the child, by petitioning the court for a "stipulated judgment" providing that both names be entered on the child's birth certificate and be recognized as the legal parents of the child. This practice survived a recent challenge in California in Kristine H. v. Lisa R., 37 Cal. 4th 156 (Cal. 2005); see also In re J.D.M., 2004 Ohio App. LEXIS 5166, Cases No. CA2003-11-113, CA2004-04-035, CA2004-04-040 (Oct. 11, 2004); Steven H. Snyder & Mary Patricia Bryan, The Use of Prebirth Parentage Orders in Surrogacy Proceedings, 39 Family L. Q. 633 (2005).

Florida law expressly prohibits gay and lesbian adoptions. Fla. Stat. Ann. §63.042(3) (2005). See Lofton v. Sec'y of the Dep't of Children & Family Servs., 358 F.3d 804 (11th Cir. 2004), cert. denied, 543 U.S. 1081 (2005) (upholding statute from constitutional challenge). Gay parent adoption also remains unavailable in jurisdictions that prevent any adoption by a person of the same sex as the biological parent who wishes to retain parental rights. See, e.g., In the Interest of Adoption of Baby Z., 724 A.2d 1035 (Conn. 1999); Matter of Adoption of T.K.J., 931 P.2d 488 (Colo. App. Ct. 1996), cert. denied, 1997 Colo. LEXIS 70 (Colo. Jan. 21, 1997). Should the law grant status as mother to more than one woman?

3. The Resistance to Gay and Lesbian Parenting. What exactly is the nature of the opposition to lesbian and gay custody of children? Among the most deeply held rationales is that lesbian and gay parents are bad role models and that their children are not well adjusted. One specific concern is that children raised by gay and lesbian parents are exposed to premature sexualization or inappropriate sexual practices. See Lynn D. Wardle, Adult Sexuality, The Best Interests of Children, and Placement Liability of Foster-Care and Adoption Agencies, 6 J.L. & Fam. Studies 59, 97-99 (2004). Most experts agree, however, that children of homosexuals do not differ significantly in their psychosocial development from children in heterosexual families. Four of the most recent studies are described in William Meezan & Jonathan Rauch, Gay Marriage, Same-Sex Parenting, and America's Children, in Marriage and Child Wellbeing, 15 The Future of Children 97, 105-106 (Fall 2005). The two most recent of these are Jennifer L. Wainwright et al., Psychosocial Adjustment, School Outcomes, and Romantic Relationships of Adolescents with Same-Sex Parents, 75 Child Dev. 1886 (Dec. 2004), and Susan Golombok et al., Children with Lesbian Parents: A Community Study, 39 Dev. Psychol. 20 (Jan. 2003). See also Judith Stacey & Timothy J. Biblarz, (How) Does the Sexual Orientation of Parents Matter, 66 Am. Soc. Rev. 159, 170-171 (2001) (concluding that "[b]ecause every relevant study to date shows that parental sexual orientation per se has no measurable effect on the quality of parent child relationships or on children's mental health or social adjustment, there is no evidentiary basis for considering parental sexual orientation is decisions about children's 'best interest'"); Raymond W. Chan, Barbara Raboy, & Charlotte J. Patterson, Psychosocial Adjustment Among Children Conceived via Donor Insemination by Lesbian and Heterosexual Mothers, 69 Child Dev. 443, 453-455 (1998) (concluding, based on study of 80 families who had conceived children through artificial insemination, 55 headed by lesbians and 25 by heterosexual parents, that child's psychosocial adjustment was not affected by either sexual orientation of parents or number of parents in household). Reviews of the literature also produce no reliable support that gay or lesbian adults are more likely to molest children than heterosexual adults. See, e.g., Carole Jenny et al., Are Children at Risk for Sexual Abuse by Homosexuals?, 94 Pediatrics 41, 44 (July 1994); see also Susan J. Becker, Child Sexual Abuse Allegations Against a Lesbian or Gay Parent in a Custody or Visitation Dispute: Battling the Overt and Insidious Bias of Experts and Judges, 74 Denv. U. L. Rev. 75, 77 (1996) (describing studies).

Critics of custody by gay and lesbian parents argue that the studies purporting to show no harm are methodologically flawed. See Lynn D. Wardle, Considering the Impacts on Children and Society of "Lesbigay" Parenting, 23 Quinnipiac L. Rev. 541, 550 (2004); Lynn D. Wardle, The Potential Impact of Homosexual Parenting on Children, 1997 U. Ill. L. Rev. 833. Among the criticisms are small sample sizes; overreliance on convenience rather than random samples; inappropriate comparison groups; failure to control for such variables as income, education, employment, health, age, religion, and existence of family and other support systems; absence of longitudinal data; and "social desirability" bias in the analysis and collection of data. Id. at 844-852. See also Diana Baumrind, Commentary on Sexual Orientation: Research and Social Policy Implications, 31

Dev. Psychol. 130 (1995) (reviewing literature and criticizing methodology of some of the studies); Paul Cameron & Kirk Cameron, Did the APA Misrepresent the Scientific Literature to Courts in Support of Homosexual Custody?, 131 J. Psychol. 313 (1997) (criticizing American Psychological Association and others for misreading studies and ignoring evidence of influence of homosexual parents on sexual orientation of children). For a response to Professor Wardle, see Carlos A. Ball & Janice Farrell Pea, Warring with Wardle: Morality, Social Science, and Gay and Lesbian Parents, 1998 U. Ill. L. Rev. 253, 279-308.

What if it *is* established that being raised by a homosexual parent makes a child more likely to be a homosexual? Should that be considered a harm? Susan Golombok and Fiona Tasker have concluded, from a comparative longitudinal study, that while there is no significant difference in sexual attraction to someone of the same gender between those raised by lesbian single mothers and those raised by heterosexual single mothers, children raised in lesbian families are more likely to consider, and to have, homosexual involvement than are their peers raised by heterosexual mothers. See Golombok & Tasker, Do Parents Influence the Sexual Orientation of Their Children? Findings from a Longitudinal Study of Lesbian Families, 32 Dev. Psychol. 3, 7 (1996); Tasker & Golombok, Growing Up in a Lesbian Family: Effects on Child Development 102-114 (1997). What role should these findings play in custody decisions? What about evidence that young people from lesbian families report more positive relationships with their mother's female partner, both as adolescents and as adults, than children of heterosexual mothers report with their mother's male partners? See Golombok & Tasker, supra, at 53.

Putting Theory into Practice

3-18. At a custody trial between parents, evidence is offered to show that a lesbian mother snuggles with her children and her female companion in bed, has her the children march with her in a gay and lesbian rights parade, and has her children participate in a "commitment ceremony" with her companion? Her children also have an "astonishing grasp of anatomical terminology." Should this evidence be admissible? What are the arguments on each side? See Hertzler v. Hertzler, 908 P.2d 946 (Wyo. 1995).

3-19. Thomas orally agreed with a lesbian couple that his sperm would be used to inseminate one of them and that he would forego all parental rights to any child born as a result. They also agreed that Thomas would be available to meet the child if she became curious about her origins. A child was born and when she was about five years old, the couple contacted Thomas so that she could meet him. For the next five or six years, Thomas visited with the child several times and developed a relationship with her, with the permission of the child's mothers. The parties eventually began to disagree, however, about the length and terms of the visits. Thomas files an action seeking court-ordered visitation. Should he succeed?

Should advocates of the custodial rights of gay and lesbian parents favor Thomas's claim or not? If so, what access to the child should Thomas be allowed?

See Nancy D. Polikoff, Breaking the Link Between Biology and Parental Rights in Planned Lesbian Families: When Semen Donors Are Not Fathers, 2 Geo. J. Gender & L. 57 (2000) (rights of sperm donor should be defined, and limited, by the agreement between the donor and the mother, which should be enforceable); Fred A. Bernstein, This Child Does Have Two Mothers...and a Sperm Donor with Visitation, 22 N.Y.U. Rev. L. & Soc. Change 1 (1996) (advocating court-ordered maintenance of sperm donor-child relationship at approximate level permitted by mothers prior to litigation).

3-20. A woman helps raise the child of her lesbian partner for six years, and provides the majority of the financial support for the child while the child's mother is more involved in the child's daily activities. When their relationship ends, the mother refuses to allow her partner to have contact with the child, who then files a petition for de facto custodian status. Should this petition be granted? See B.F. v. T.D., Ky. Ct. App., No. 2004-CA-000083-ME, April 15, 2005.

3. Employment Discrimination Based on Sexual Orientation

≡≡≡ *DeSantis v. Pacific Telephone &*
≡≡≡ *Telegraph Co., Inc.*
≡≡≡ 608 F.2d 327 (9th Cir. 1979)

CHOY, Circuit Judge....

[Appellants,] all males, claimed that Pacific Telephone & Telegraph Co. (PT & T) impermissibly discriminated against them because of their homosexuality.... The district court dismissed their complaint....

[W]e conclude that Title VII's prohibition of "sex" discrimination applies only to discrimination on the basis of gender and should not be judicially extended to include sexual preference such as homosexuality....

Appellants argue...that in a trial they could establish that discrimination against homosexuals disproportionately effects men and that this disproportionate impact and correlation between discrimination on the basis of sexual preference and discrimination on the basis of "sex" requires that sexual preference be considered a subcategory of the "sex" category of Title VII.... Adoption of this bootstrap device...would achieve by judicial "construction" what Congress did not do....

Appellants next contend that...an employer generally may not use different employment criteria for men and women. They claim that if a male employee prefers males as sexual partners, he will be treated differently from a female who prefers male partners.... We must again reject appellants' efforts to "bootstrap" Title VII protection for homosexuals.... [W]e note that whether dealing with men or women the employer is using the same criterion: it will not hire or promote a person who prefers sexual partners of the same sex....

Appellants argue that the EEOC has held that discrimination against an employee because of the race of the employee's friends may constitute discrimination based on race in violation of Title VII. . . . They contend that analogously discrimination because of the sex of the employees' sexual partner should constitute discrimination based on sex.

Appellants, however, have not alleged that appellees have policies of discriminating against employees because of the gender of their friends. That is, they do not claim that the appellees will terminate anyone with a male (or female) friend. They claim instead that the appellees discriminate against employees who have a certain type of relationship, i.e., homosexual relationship with certain friends. As noted earlier, that relationship is not protected by Title VII. . . .

Affirmed.

[The opinion of Judge Sneed, concurring and dissenting, is omitted.]

≡≡≡ *Padula v. Webster*
≡≡≡ 822 F.2d 97 (D.C. Cir. 1987)

SILBERMAN, Circuit Judge.

Appellant Margaret A. Padula alleges that the Federal Bureau of Investigation ("FBI" or "Bureau") refused to employ her as a special agent because of her homosexuality, in violation of both Bureau policy and the equal protection guarantee of the Constitution. Ruling on a motion for summary judgment, the district court rejected both these challenges, concluding that the hiring decision was committed to the FBI's discretion by law and did not infringe upon appellant's constitutional rights. We affirm. . . .

Padula alleges that the FBI refused to hire her solely because of her homosexuality and that this action denied her the equal protection of the law guaranteed by the fourteenth amendment. She urges us to recognize homosexuality as a suspect or quasi-suspect classification. A suspect classification is subjected to strict scrutiny and will be sustained only if "suitably tailored to serve a compelling state interest" . . . whereas under heightened scrutiny given to a quasi-suspect class, the challenged classification must be "substantially related to a legitimate state interest." . . .

We perceive ostensible disagreement between the parties as to the description of the class in question. The government insists the FBI's hiring policy focuses only on homosexual conduct, not homosexual status. By that, we understand the government to be saying that it would not consider relevant for employment purposes homosexual orientation that did not result in homosexual conduct. Plaintiff rejects that distinction, suggesting that "homosexual status is accorded to people who engage in homosexual conduct, and people who engage in homosexual conduct are accorded homosexual status." But whether or not homosexual status attaches to someone who does not — for whatever reason — engage in homosexual conduct, appellant does not claim those circumstances apply to her. The parties' definitional disagreement is therefore irrelevant to this case. The issue presented us is only whether homosexuals, when defined as persons who engage in homosexual conduct, constitute a suspect or quasi-suspect classification and accordingly whether the FBI's hiring decision is subject to strict or heightened scrutiny.

The Supreme Court has used several explicit criteria to identify suspect and quasi-suspect classifications. In San Antonio School Dist. v. Rodriguez, [411 U.S. 1 (1973)], the Court stated that a suspect class is one "saddled with such disabilities, or subjected to such a history of purposeful unequal treatment, or relegated to such a position of political powerlessness as to command extraordinary protection from the majoritarian political process." [Id. at 28.] The immutability of the group's identifying trait is also a factor to be considered. See Frontiero v. Richardson, [411 U.S. 677, 686 (1973)]. However, the Supreme Court has recognized only three classifications as suspect: race...alienage...and national origin...and two others as quasi-suspect: gender...and illegitimacy.... Appellant, asserting that homosexuals meet all the requisite criteria, would have us add homosexuality to that list. Appellees, on the other hand, contend that two recent cases, Bowers v. Hardwick, [478 U.S. 186 (1986),] and Dronenburg v. Zech, 741 F.2d 1388 (D.C. Cir. 1984), are insurmountable barriers to appellant's claim. We agree.

In *Dronenburg*, a naval petty officer claimed violation of his constitutional rights to privacy and to equal protection of the laws because he was discharged from the Navy for engaging in homosexual conduct. A panel of this court rejected the claim, holding that "we can find no constitutional right to engage in homosexual conduct and,...as judges, we have no warrant to create one." Id. at 1397....

Dronenburg anticipated by two years the Supreme Court's decision in *Hardwick*, in which the Court upheld a Georgia law criminalizing sodomy against a challenge that it violated the due process clause. In *Hardwick*, the Court explained that the right to privacy as defined in its previous decisions inheres only in family relationships, marriage and procreation and does not extend more broadly to all kinds of private sexual conduct between consenting adults. 478 U.S. at 191. Putting the privacy precedent aside, the Court further concluded that a right to engage in consensual sodomy is not constitutionally protected as a fundamental right since it is neither "implicit in the concept of ordered liberty," id. at 191-192 (quoting Palko v. Connecticut, [302 U.S. 319, 325-326 (1937)]), nor "deeply rooted in this Nation's history and tradition." Id. at 192 (quoting Moore v. East Cleveland, [431 U.S. 494 (1977)] (opinion of Powell, J.)). Accordingly, the Court's review of the Georgia statute inquired only whether a rational basis for the law existed. And the Court determined that the presumed beliefs of the Georgia electorate that sodomy is immoral provide an adequate rationale for criminalizing such conduct. Id. at 196....

We...think the courts' reasoning in *Hardwick* and *Dronenburg* forecloses appellant's efforts to gain suspect class status for practicing homosexuals. It would be quite anomalous, on its face, to declare status defined by conduct that states may constitutionally criminalize as deserving of strict scrutiny under the equal protection clause. More importantly, in all those cases in which the Supreme Court has accorded suspect or quasi-suspect status to a class, the

Court's holding was predicated on an unarticulated, but necessarily implicit, notion that it is plainly unjustifiable (in accordance with standards not altogether clear to us) to discriminate invidiously against the particular class.... If the Court was unwilling to object to state laws that criminalize the behavior that defines the class, it is hardly open to a lower court to conclude that state sponsored discrimination against the class is invidious. After all, there can hardly be more palpable discrimination against a class than making the conduct that defines the class criminal....

That does not mean, however, that any kind of negative state action against homosexuals would be constitutionally authorized. Laws or government practices must still, if challenged, pass the rational basis test of the equal protection clause. A governmental agency that discriminates against homosexuals must justify that discrimination in terms of some government purpose.... In *Dronenburg*, the court held that it was rational for the Navy to conclude that homosexual conduct was detrimental to the maintenance of morale and discipline. 741 F.2d at 1398. The court observed that homosexuality "generate[s] dislike and disapproval among many...who find it morally offensive," and, moreover, is criminalized in many states. Id.

The FBI, as the Bureau points out, is a national law enforcement agency whose agents must be able to work in all the states of the nation. To have agents who engage in conduct criminalized in roughly one-half of the states would undermine the law enforcement credibility of the Bureau. Perhaps more important, FBI agents perform counterintelligence duties that involve highly classified matters relating to national security. It is not irrational for the Bureau to conclude that the criminalization of homosexual conduct coupled with the general public opprobrium toward homosexuality exposes many homosexuals, even "open" homosexuals, to the risk of possible blackmail to protect their partners, if not themselves. We therefore conclude the Bureau's specialized functions, like the Navy's in *Dronenburg*, rationally justify consideration of homosexual conduct that could adversely affect that agency's responsibilities. The judgment of the district court is hereby Affirmed.

≡≡≡ ### *Shahar v. Bowers*
≡ 114 F.3d 1097 (11th Cir. 1997) (en banc), cert. denied,
≡ 522 U.S. 1049 (1998)

EDMONDSON, Circuit Judge....

Plaintiff Robin Joy Shahar is a woman who has "married" another woman in a ceremony performed by a rabbi within the Reconstructionist Movement of Judaism. According to Shahar, though the State of Georgia does not recognize her "marriage" and she does not claim that the "marriage" has legal effect, she and her partner consider themselves to be "married."

Since August 1981, Defendant-Appellee Michael J. Bowers has been the Attorney General of the State of Georgia, a statewide elective office. He has been elected to the office four times. As the Attorney General, Bowers is the chief legal officer of the State of Georgia and head of the Georgia Department of Law (the "Department"). His responsibilities include enforcing the laws of the State by acting as a prosecutor in certain criminal actions....

[After hearing of her "marriage," the Attorney General withdrew an employment offer to Shahar.] Shahar brought the present action against the Attorney General, individually and in his official capacity, seeking both damages and injunctive relief (including "reinstatement"). She said revoking her offer violated her free exercise and free association rights and her rights to equal protection and substantive due process. Bowers moved for summary judgment on all causes of action....

Even when we assume, for argument's sake, that either the right to intimate association or the right to expressive association or both are present, we know they are not absolute.... We conclude that the appropriate test for evaluating the constitutional implications of the State of Georgia's decision — as an employer — to withdraw Shahar's job offer based on her "marriage" is the same test as the test for evaluating the constitutional implications of a government employer's decision based on an employee's exercise of her right to free speech, that is, the balancing test [of Pickering v. Board of Educ., 391 U.S. 563 (1968)].... [G]overnment employees who have access to their employer's confidences or who act as spokespersons for their employers, as well as those employees with some policy-making role, are in a special class of employees and . . . seldom prevail under the First Amendment in keeping their jobs when they conflict with their employers.

As both parties acknowledge, this case arises against the backdrop of an ongoing controversy in Georgia about homosexual sodomy, homosexual marriages, and other related issues, including a sodomy prosecution — in which the Attorney General's staff was engaged — resulting in the well-known Supreme Court decision in Bowers v. Hardwick, [478 U.S. 186] (1986) (criminal prosecution of homosexual sodomy does not violate substantive due process). When the Attorney General viewed Shahar's decision to "wed" openly — complete with changing her name — another woman (in a large "wedding") against this background of ongoing controversy, he saw her acts as having a realistic likelihood to affect her (and, therefore, the Department's) credibility, to interfere with the Department's ability to handle certain kinds of controversial matters (such as claims to same-sex marriage licenses, homosexual parental rights, employee benefits, insurance coverage of "domestic partners"), to interfere with the Department's efforts to enforce Georgia's laws against homosexual sodomy, and to create other difficulties within the Department which would be likely to harm the public perception of the Department....

In addition, because of Shahar's decision to participate in such a controversial same-sex "wedding" and "marriage" and the fact that she seemingly did not appreciate the importance of appearances and the need to avoid bringing "controversy" to the Department, the Attorney General lost confidence in her ability to make good judgments for the Department....

Shahar says that by taking into account . . . concerns about public reaction, the Attorney General impermissibly discriminated against homosexuals; and she refers us to the Supreme Court's recent decision in Romer v. Evans, [517 U.S.

620] (1996). In *Romer*, the Supreme Court struck down an amendment to a state constitution as irrational because the amendment's sole purpose was to disadvantage a particular class of people (to "den[y] them protection across the board," [id. at 1628]) and because the government engaged in "classification of persons undertaken for its own sake, something the Equal Protection Clause does not permit." [Id. at 1629.]

Romer is about people's condition; this case is about a person's conduct. And, *Romer* is no employment case. Considering (in deciding to revoke a job offer) public reaction to a future Staff Attorney's conduct in taking part in a same-sex "wedding" and subsequent "marriage" is not the same kind of decision as an across-the-board denial of legal protection to a group because of their condition, that is, sexual orientation or preference. . . .

We do not decide today that the Attorney General did or did not do the right thing when he withdrew the pertinent employment offer. That decision is properly not ours to make. What we decide is much different and less: . . . the Law Department's . . . Attorney General has made a personnel decision which none of the asserted federal constitutional provisions prohibited him from making.

Affirmed.

TJOFLAT, Circuit Judge, specially concurring. . . .

[I]n order to find that Shahar's relationship is protected as an intimate association, we must find that homosexual relationships have "played a critical role in the culture and traditions of the Nation by cultivating and transmitting shared ideals and beliefs." I conclude that this simply is not the case. Shahar has pointed to nothing to suggest that homosexual relationships have played a critical role in our history and tradition. On the contrary, the Supreme Court's decision in Bowers v. Hardwick, [478 U.S. 186] (1986), suggests that homosexual relationships have not played such a role. . . . [A] court cannot engage in *Pickering* balancing without identifying the constitutional source of the employee's right and assigning the right a weight or constitutional value. . . .

GODBOLD, Senior Circuit Judge, joined by BARKETT, Circuit Judge, and KRAVITCH, Senior Circuit Judge, dissenting.

The court en banc has pretermitted decision of whether Shahar has constitutional rights of intimate association or expressive association. Instead it assumes that she enjoyed such rights and decides that these presumed rights have not been violated because the Attorney General acted reasonably in "revoking [Shahar's] employment offer."

I would grasp the nettle and hold that in the particular circumstances of this case Shahar enjoyed rights of intimate association and expressive association and that the Attorney General violated those rights because he did not act reasonably in revoking the agreement made with Shahar.

Shahar does not assert a right to be married as provided by the laws of Georgia (statutory or common law), or to be issued a marriage license, or to inherit from her spouse, or to be entitled to social security benefits through her spouse. She does not question the constitutionality of the Georgia marriage license statute or any provisions of Georgia law that speak in terms of marriage as a ceremony, or as a status, between persons of different sexes. Nor does she question the validity of Georgia principles of common law marriages. As the panel of this Court held in its now-vacated opinion:

> What Shahar claims is that she proposed to—and did—engage in a Jewish religious ceremony that is recognized as a marriage ceremony by the branch of Judaism to which she adheres; that this conferred upon her and her partner a religious-based status that is apart from and independent of civil marriage as provided by Georgia law; and that she can accept, describe, and hold out both the ceremonial event and the status created by it by using the term "marriage."

The religious and historical roots of the associational rights that Shahar defends were spelled out in the panel opinion. Because that opinion has now been vacated, they deserve to be repeated.

> The intimate association Shahar asserts is not based upon false or sham assertions of religious belief, or hasty decision, of overnight conversion. She and her partner grew up in traditional Jewish families. Shahar attended Hebrew school from the third grade. She was bat mitzvahed at age 13 and continued in Hebrew school until she was confirmed at age 16. Greenfield grew up in a conservative, kosher, Jewish home. She went through Jewish training through high school, attended Jewish summer camps, and was involved in Jewish youth groups.
>
> Shahar and Greenfield have been significant participants in the life of their synagogue, located in Atlanta. It is affiliated with the Reconstructionist Movement, one of several movements within Judaism....

The evidence demonstrates without dispute that same-sex marriage is accepted within the Reconstructionist Movement of Judaism, that Shahar and her partner are committed to that belief, and that, in keeping with their Jewish principles, they carefully and thoughtfully prepared for marriage. The Attorney General did not act reasonably.... Respectfully, I dissent.

BIRCH, Circuit Judge, joined by BARKETT, Circuit Judge, GODBOLD and KRAVITCH, Senior Circuit Judges, dissenting....

The inferences from Shahar's acknowledged homosexuality that she is likely to violate Georgia's sodomy law, or would be unable or unwilling to enforce Georgia's sodomy or marriage laws, is no more justified on behalf of Bowers or his employees than it is on behalf of the public. Moreover, it is important to note that Bowers' speculation regarding Shahar's ability to handle certain types of cases is just that: speculation. Bowers has emphatically refused to meet with Shahar to discuss any of his concerns. Compounding this deficiency in Bowers' assertion that his prediction is "reasonable" is the fact that Bowers does not make the same assumption with respect to any of his other employees: He does not assume, for instance, that an unmarried employee who is openly dating an individual of the opposite sex has likely committed fornication....

In short, Bowers' asserted interests in taking adverse action against Shahar are based on inferences from her status as a homosexual which Bowers claims that he, the public, and department staff are entitled to make. In light of the Supreme

Court's decision in *Romer*, these status-based inferences, unsupported by any facts in the record and explained only by animosity toward and stereotyping of homosexuals, do not constitute a legitimate interest that outweighs Shahar's First Amendment right of intimate association. . . .

[The separate dissenting opinions of Judge Kravitch and Judge Barkett are omitted.]

Notes

1. Discrimination Based on Sexual Orientation Is Not Discrimination Based on Sex. *DeSantis* is an old case, but not out of date. It states what remains the standard view of Title VII: discrimination against gays and lesbians does not constitute discrimination based on sex. Likewise, *Padula* and *Shahar* state the prevailing law that the U.S. Constitution is not violated by state discrimination against gays and lesbians in the employment context. Further discussion of the constitutional dimensions of sexual orientation discrimination are explored in the notes below. Efforts to enact federal legislation prohibiting discrimination based on sexual orientation have been largely unsuccessful. The Employment Non-Discrimination Act (ENDA) has been proposed in different forms on multiple occasions since 1993. In its most common version, ENDA would "forbid[ ] employers from discriminating on the basis of sexual orientation with regard to hiring, firing, or terms of employment; [and] forbid[ ] retaliatory conduct." Although similar to Title VII, the statute would not apply to military and religious organizations or disparate impact claims. It would not permit affirmative action based on sexual orientation and would not require benefits for domestic partners. ENDA failed to pass the Senate by one vote in 1996, and subsequent versions have not come up for a vote in either house. S. 932, 104th Cong. (1996); H.R. 3285, 108th Cong. (2003); S. 1705, 108th Cong. (2003).

On the other hand, seventeen states — California, Connecticut, Hawaii, Illinois, Maine, Maryland, Massachusetts, Minnesota, Nevada, New Hampshire, New Jersey, New Mexico, New York, Oregon, Rhode Island, Vermont, and Wisconsin — and the District of Columbia have general laws protecting gay and lesbian employees, and five states also prohibit discrimination based on gender identity. See http://www.lambdalegal.org, last visited June 2005. In addition, a growing number of businesses have begun to add sexual orientation to their anti-discrimination policies, with 49 of the Fortune 50 companies including sexual orientation in their non-discrimination policies, and 410 companies in the Fortune 500 at the end of 2004. A total of 51 Fortune 500 companies include transgender people in their policies. See www.hrc.org, last visited June 2005.

Two legal developments may serve to add weight to pressure to creates legal rights based on sexual orientation in the employment context. First, in Rene v. MGM Grand Hotel, Inc., 305 F.3d 1061 (9th Cir. 2002), cert. denied, 538 U.S. 922 (2003), the Ninth Circuit Court of Appeals held that sexual harassment against an openly gay man was actionable under Title VII even if motivated by the victim's sexual orientation, based on the U.S. Supreme Court's stereotyping analysis in Price Waterhouse v. Hopkins, 490 U.S. 228, 250-251 (1989). *Rene* is set forth and discussed on p. 443 of this chapter, supra. *Price Waterhouse* is set forth and analyzed in Chapter 1, p. 59, supra. Second, recent cases involving transsexuals have also applied the *Price Waterhouse* stereotyping analysis to hold that discrimination against transsexuals in the employment context can violate Title VII. The lead case in this area is Smith v. Salem, 378 F.3d 566 (6th Cir. 2004), set forth and discussed in Chapter 6, p. 1009, along with other cases relating to the rights of transsexuals. Should *Price Waterhouse* be equally applicable to gays and lesbians?

2. Sexual Orientation and Strict Scrutiny. Gay rights advocates have frequently attempted to establish that homosexuals as a class have the characteristics required for special constitutional protection: (1) a history of discrimination; (2) exhibition of obvious, immutable, or distinguishing characteristics that define them as members of a discrete group; and (3) political powerlessness, or the burdening of a fundamental right. See Bowen v. Gilliard, 483 U.S. 587 (1987). Do gays and lesbians meet these criteria?

(a) *History of Discrimination.* Many judges, including those in Ben-Shalom v. Marsh, 881 F.2d 454 (7th Cir. 1989), cert. denied, 494 U.S. 1004 (1990), have reasoned that while gays and lesbians have suffered a history of discrimination, they seem to have enough political power today such that discrimination against them is not "invidious." Id. at 465-466. Is this reasoning persuasive? On this reasoning, how would you account for the persistence of discrimination and the lack of legal remedies in areas such as employment, housing, and family law?

In Lawrence v. Texas, 539 U.S. 558 (2003), the Supreme Court found no longstanding history of discrimination against homosexuals.

> [T]here is no longstanding history in this country of laws directed at homosexual conduct as a distinct matter. Early American sodomy laws were not directed at homosexuals as such but instead sought to prohibit nonprocreative sexual activity more generally, whether between men and women or men and men. Moreover, early sodomy laws seem not to have been enforced against consenting adults acting in private.... Far from possessing "ancient roots," American laws targeting same-sex couples did not develop until the last third of the 20th century. Even now, only nine States have singled out same-sex relations for criminal prosecution....

Yet, in Bowers v. Hardwick, 478 U.S. 186 (1986), the Court previously found an extended history of criminal prohibitions of homosexual conduct.

> Proscriptions against that conduct have ancient roots.... Sodomy was a criminal offense at common law and was forbidden by the laws of the original thirteen States when they ratified the Bill of Rights. In 1868 when the Fourteenth Amendment was ratified, all but 5 of the 37 States in the Union had criminal sodomy laws. In fact, until 1961, all 50 States outlawed sodomy, and today, 24 States and the District of Columbia continue to provide criminal penalties for sodomy performed in private and between consenting adults.

Id. at 192-194.

Can you explain the different analyses of history reflected in these two cases?

How does the concurring opinion of Judge Tjoflat in the *Shahar* case, 114 F.3d 1097 (11th Cir. 1997), differ from these two statements? If Judge Tjoflat is right and homosexual relationships have not "played a critical role in the culture and traditions of this Nation," 114 F.3d at 1115, what follows?

Consider an alternative view of historical discrimination in a case involving exclusionary policies by the military: "In all probability, homosexuality is not considered a deeply-rooted part of our traditions *precisely because* homosexuals have historically been subjected to invidious discrimination." Watkins v. United States Army, 875 F.2d 699, 719 (9th Cir. 1989) (Norris, J., concurring), cert. denied, 498 U.S. 957 (1990).

Which view of history do you find most persuasive? For a history of persecution of homosexuals dating from the third century, see Able v. United States, 968 F. Supp. 850, 852-855 (E.D.N.Y. 1997). For a focus on the criminalization of lesbian conduct, see Ruthann Robson, Lesbianism in Anglo-American Legal History, 5 Wis. Women's L.J. 1, 21-41 (1990).

(b) *"Exhibition" of "Obvious" or "Immutable" Characteristics.* For gays and lesbians, a standard requiring "exhibition" of "obvious" characteristics often poses a no-win situation. Individuals who do not "exhibit" their homosexuality are not entitled to special constitutional review. See Steffan v. Cheney, 780 F. Supp. 1, 5-6 (D.D.C. 1991), aff'd sub nom. Steffan v. Perry, 41 F.3d 677 (D.C. Cir. 1994). On the other hand, the more overt the "exhibition" of sexual orientation, the stronger the argument that gays or lesbians threaten legitimate concerns of order and morale in the workplace. See Steffan v. Perry, 41 F.3d 677 (D.C. Cir. 1994) (en banc). The other catch is that gays and lesbians are penalized both for exhibiting their sexual orientation, and for hiding it. See, e.g., Doe v. Gates, 981 F.2d 1316 (D.C. Cir.), cert. denied, 510 U.S. 928 (1993) (upholding discharge of CIA employee not because he was gay, but because he had hidden information about his involvement in same-sex activity that the agency viewed as relevant for security reasons).

The issue of "immutability" poses a related dilemma for gays and lesbians. On the one hand, part of the harm of discrimination is the pressure it creates to suppress, and thereby alter, same-sex orientation. On the other hand, if sexual orientation is alterable, gays and lesbians have the ability to avoid discrimination. The costs of such alteration might be clearer to heterosexuals if they imagined the tables turned:

> Would heterosexuals living in a city that passed an ordinance banning those who engaged in or desired to engage in sex with persons of the *opposite* sex find it easy not only to abstain from heterosexual activity but also to shift the object of their sexual desires to persons of the same sex?

Watkins v. United States Army, 847 F.2d 1329, 1347-1348 (9th Cir. 1988), after reh'g, 875 F.2d 699 (9th Cir.), cert. denied, 498 U.S. 957 (1990).

Should the immutability requirement be redefined? Consider Judge Norris's observation in a case involving military policy:

> It is clear that by "immutability" the Court has never meant strict immutability in the sense that members of the class must be physically unable to change or mask the trait defining their class. People can have operations to change their sex. Aliens can ordinarily become naturalized citizens. The status of illegitimate children can be changed. People can frequently hide their national origin by changing their customs, their names, or their associations. Lighter skinned blacks can sometimes "pass" for white, as can Latinos for Anglos, and some people can even change their racial appearance with pigment injections. See J. Griffin, Black Like Me (1977). At a minimum, then, the Supreme Court is willing to treat a trait as effectively immutable if changing it would involve great difficulty, such as requiring a major physical change or a traumatic change of identity. Reading the case law in a more capacious manner, "immutability" may describe those traits that are so central to a person's identity that it would be abhorrent for government to penalize a person for refusing to change them, regardless of how easy that change might be physically. Racial discrimination, for example, would not suddenly become constitutional if medical science developed an easy, cheap, and painless method of changing one's skin pigment.

Watkins, 875 F.2d at 726 (Norris, J., concurring). See also Able v. United States, 968 F. Supp. 850, 863-864 (E.D.N.Y. 1997) (whether or not homosexuality is genetic and immutable, it forms a significant part of a person's identity justifying heightened scrutiny).

Should the criterion of immutability be eliminated altogether? Recall the discussion of the issue of immutability as it related to appearance and weight requirements in Chapter 1, pp. 95-100. Weight is mutable in one sense and immutable in another, but in either case, weight restrictions systematically subordinate women. According to Janet E. Halley, immutability analysis misrepresents the complex way in which sexual identity develops and the harmful effects of discrimination on that identity. The invidiousness of discrimination does not depend on the immutability of homosexuality. Rather,

> [a]ntihomosexuality discrimination encourages people to manipulate the identity they attach to themselves, both in the secrecy of their own minds and on the public stage, in...their subjective and their public identities. It ensures that personal desires, sexual behavior, subjective identity and public identity will frequently get out of sync with each other. However carefully an individual disposes these elements, they are all subject to sudden, either joyous or catastrophic, rearrangement. That is to say, they are mutable....

Janet E. Halley, The Politics of the Closet: Towards Equal Protection for Gay, Lesbian, and Bisexual Identity, 36 UCLA L. Rev. 915, 933 (1989). See also Janet E. Halley, Sexual Orientation and the Politics of Biology: A Critique of the Argument from Immutability, 46 Stan. L. Rev. 503 (1994).

Halley argues that it is a group's "acute vulnerability in the political process" rather than the immutability of any trait uniting or defining the group that gives rise to the need for stringent constitutional review:

> [I]mmutability is not required by the Court's equal protection precedents, which focus instead on process implications often associated with apparently immutable traits. A proper reading of these precedents demonstrates that the equal protection clause vigilantly protects not monolithic groups but rather the dialogue that generates group identity and suggests that gay rights advocates and courts attend not to product but to process, not to the class but to the classification of homosexuals. . . .

Halley, Politics of the Closet, supra, at 923, 926-927.

Halley's analysis leads to a distinction between discrimination that interferes with public debate and disclosure of sexual orientation, which deserves constitutional protection, and other legislative decisions to deter homosexuality, which do not warrant special constitutional scrutiny. Id. at 923. She finds an analogy to this distinction in First Amendment law that protects speech, but not conduct. Id. at 967. Yet Halley is also critical of the way the speech/conduct distinction has been invoked in contexts such as discrimination by the military. See note 6, pp. 624-626, below.

The focus on political vulnerability received some indirect support from the Supreme Court's decision in Romer v. Evans, 517 U.S. 620 (1996). There, for the first time, the Court found that a law penalizing same-sex orientation was unconstitutional. At issue was a Colorado constitutional amendment (Proposition 2) repealing and prohibiting all state and local anti-discrimination policies with respect to homosexuals. In the majority's view, this amendment failed to meet the rational relationship standard under the equal protection clause because it arbitrarily prevented a group from protecting its interests through the normal political process. This discrimination, the Court stated, could not be justified by a "bare desire to harm a politically unpopular group" (quoting Dept. of Agriculture v. Moreno, 413 U.S. 528, 534 (1973)). For discussion of the *Romer* case, see symposia at 68 U. Colo. L. Rev. 285 (1997), and at 50 Vand. L. Rev. 361 (1997); see also Andrew M. Jacobs, *Romer* Wasn't Built in a Day: The Subtle Transformation in Judicial Argument over Gay Rights, 1996 Wis. L. Rev. 893 (1996) (tracing the shift of the gay rights debate from questions about the morality of homosexuality to questions about the consequences and wisdom of penalizing it.)

Legal theories emphasizing the importance of both mutable and immutable forces in the formation of gay identity draw on a wide array of social science research. Some research suggests that sexuality is not solely a result of physiological or cultural influences, but rather is shaped through "a complex interaction of biological, psychological, and social forces." See, e.g., Gregory M. Herek, Myths About Sexual Orientation: A Lawyer's Guide to Social Science Research, 1 Law & Sexuality 133, 151 (1991). Such work reinforces concerns about the usefulness of the immutability standard in cases involving sexual orientation. Steffan v. Cheney, supra, 780 F. Supp. at 6-7.

Still, some scientific studies point to a physiological, and perhaps immutable, basis for sexual orientation. In one such study, Swedish scientists exposed heterosexual men and women and homosexual men to chemicals found in male and female sex hormones. One chemical is a testosterone derivative produced in men's sweat. The other chemical is an estrogen-like compound in women's urine. These chemicals have long been suspected of being pheromones, molecules emitted by one individual that evoke some behavior in another of the same species. Pheromones trigger basic responses, such as sexual attraction, in many animals. The researchers found that the testosterone compound activated the hypothalamus in homosexual men and heterosexual women, but not heterosexual men. Conversely, the estrogen compound activated the hypothalamus only in heterosexual men. Ivanka Savic et al., Brain Response to Putative Pheromones in Homosexual Men, 102 Proc. of the Nat'l Acad. of Sci. 7356-7361 (May 17, 2005).

The finding is similar to a report by Dr. Simon LeVay at the Salk Institute in San Diego, California. LeVay examined the brains of 41 cadavers: 19 allegedly homosexual men, 16 allegedly heterosexual men, and 6 allegedly heterosexual women. His study focused on a group of neurons in the hypothalamus structure called the interstitial nuclei of the anterior hypothalamus, or the INAH3, finding that this region is twice as large in straight men as in women or gay men. Simon LeVay, A Difference in Hypothalamic Structure Between Heterosexual and Homosexual Men, 253 Science 253 1034-1037 (August 1991). The brain scanning technique used by the Swedish researchers lacks the resolution to see the region studied by LeVay, which is a mere millimeter or so across, but both findings suggest that the hypothalamus is organized in a way related to sexual orientation.

Another study recruited heterosexuals and homosexuals that had twins, either identical or non-identical. The study found found that within 56 gay men who had an identical twin brother, 52 percent of them were both gay. But among 54 gay men with a non-identical twin brother, only 22 percent of them were both gay. Two years later, this study was done on lesbians. The findings correspond to those of the earlier research done on gay men. Within 71 lesbians who had an identical twin sister, 48 percent were both lesbians. And of the 37 lesbians that had a non-identical twin sister, only 16 percent were both lesbians. Michael Bailey and Richard Pillard, A Genetic Study of Male Sexual Orientation, 48 Arch. Gen. Psychiatry 1089-1096 (1991); Bailey et al., Heritable Factors Influence Sexual Orientation in Women, 50 Arch. Gen. Psychiatry 217-223 (March 1993).

Of what relevance is this data to the legal claims? Is it possible that sexual orientation is, indeed, immutable but that in the legal context the claim is not worth making?

(c) *Political Powerlessness.* The issue of political powerlessness is equally problematic. One court has observed:

> Even *if* it were proven that homosexual orientation was immutable, or indeed, not subject to individual choice, it is still very clear that homosexuals as a class enjoy a good deal of political power in our society, not only with respect to themselves, but also with respect to issues of the day that affect them.
>
> It is beyond doubt that the homosexual community has been able to reach out and gain the attention of politicians of all sorts. One need only remember

St. Patrick's Day 1991 in New York City to see Mayor David Dinkins marching in the traditionally Irish-Catholic parade with homosexual groups and activists who were important supporters during his tough mayoral campaign. There are many other important and high visibility issues which have brought the homosexual community into the political landscape in this country and in the states, not the least of which is the AIDS epidemic and the related issues of funding for research and drugs, school attendance for children who are HIV-positive, and insurance coverage for victims.

Assuming arguendo that there is continuing antipathy and prejudice exhibited towards the plaintiff's class, it cannot successfully be maintained that the political branches are not paying attention to homosexuals or to those who advocate legislation favorable to them. Just because there are only a few members of Congress who are openly homosexual does not mean that homosexuals are a class without influence. There are not many medical doctors in Congress either, and yet that profession is exceptionally well represented on Capitol Hill. It is far more important to notice that references to sexual orientation, sexual preference and AIDS show up from time to time in the law of the various states, localities, and in the federal law.

Steffan v. Cheney, supra, 780 F. Supp. at 7-9.

How would you try to measure the political influence of gays and lesbians? How does it compare with the influence of other groups that enjoy special constitutional protection? Would it strengthen the argument for stricter scrutiny of sexual orientation cases if Mayor Dinkins had not marched with homosexuals in the St. Patrick's Day parade, if the AIDS epidemic had never occurred, or if references to sexual orientation did not "show up from time to time in the law"?

3. The "Rational Basis" for Discrimination Based on Sexual Orientation. As the court in *Padula* concedes, even if gays and lesbians are not entitled to special protection under the equal protection clause, discrimination against them must pass the rationality standard. A growing number of commentators claim that challenging the rationality of discrimination based on sexual orientation is legally and politically the best line of attack for gay rights advocates. See, e.g., Toni M. Massaro, Gay Rights, Thick and Thin, 49 Stan. L. Rev. 45, 55 (1996). Do you agree? A few courts have found exclusion of homosexuals from the military irrational, only to be reversed on appeal. See, e.g., Steffan v. Aspin, 8 F.3d 57 (D.C. App. 1993), rev'd en banc, Steffan v. Perry, 41 F.3d 677 (D.C. Cir. 1994); Meinhold v. United States Dep't of Defense, 808 F. Supp. 1455 (C.D. Cal. 1993), rev'd, 34 F.3d 1469 (9th Cir. 1994).

How sound are the rationales in support of the exclusion of Margaret Padula from the FBI? In what sense is law enforcement credibility undermined? How about the "possible blackmail" issue? Is this rational in a case in which the plaintiff "is unembarrassed and open about [her sexual orientation] and it is a fact well known to her family, friends and co-workers"? How significant is the concern that even if the plaintiff does not need to protect herself from exposure as a homosexual, she may need to "protect [her] partners"? Padula v. Webster, supra, 822 F.2d at 99, 104.

4. Discrimination on the Basis of Sexual Orientation by "Private" Associations. A divided United States Supreme Court in Boy Scouts of America v.

Dale, 530 U.S. 640 (2000), upheld the right of the Boy Scouts to exclude members based on sexual orientation. The case involved James Dale, who joined the Scouts at age eight and for the next 12 years was an exemplary member. He earned 25 merit badges and the honored status of Eagle Scout. Shortly after being appointed an assistant troop leader, Dale enrolled at Rutgers University, where he became co-president of the Lesbian and Gay Alliance. His membership in the Scouts was revoked after a Newark newspaper identified him as president and quoted comments that he made in connection with a seminar on health needs of gay and lesbian teens.

Dale then filed a complaint under New Jersey public accommodation law, which bars discrimination based on characteristics such as race, ethnicity, and sexual orientation. The New Jersey Supreme Court upheld his claim, and in a 5-4 decision, the U. S. Supreme Court reversed. Writing for the majority, Chief Justice Rehnquist concluded that the New Jersey law violated the Boy Scouts' rights of speech and association. Under the Court's analysis, "the presence of a gay rights activist would force the organization to send a message that the Boy Scouts accepts homosexual conduct." According to Scout leadership, such a message would be inconsistent with its oath and laws requiring Scouts to be "morally straight" and "clean" in body and mind.

In upholding the Scouts' policy, the majority relied heavily on its prior decision in Hurley v. Irish-American Gay, Lesbian and Bisexual Group of Boston, Inc., 515 U.S. 557 (1995). In *Hurley*, the Court ruled that organizers of a St. Patrick's Day parade could not be compelled by Massachusetts public accommodation law to let gays and lesbians march behind a GLBT banner. Just as those parade organizers had the right "not to propound a particular point of view," the Boy Scouts had a right not to convey the message of legitimacy that Dale's membership would imply.

> The Boy Scouts asserts that it "teach[es] that homosexual conduct is not morally straight" . . . and that it does "not want to promote homosexual conduct as a legitimate form of behavior. . . . " We need not inquire further to determine the nature of the Boy Scouts' expression with respect to homosexuality. . . .
>
> As we give deference to an association's assertions regarding the nature of its expression, we must also give deference to an association's view of what would impair its expression. . . .
>
> The Boy Scouts takes an official position with respect to homosexual conduct, and that is sufficient for First Amendment purposes. In this same vein, Dale makes much of the claim that the Boy Scouts does not revoke the membership of heterosexual Scout leaders that openly disagree with the Boy Scouts' policy on sexual orientation. But if this is true, it is irrelevant. The presence of an avowed homosexual and gay rights activist in an assistant scoutmaster's uniform sends a distinctly different message from the presence of a heterosexual assistant scoutmaster who is on record as disagreeing with Boy Scouts policy.

530 U.S. at 651, 653, 655-656.

Justice Stevens, writing for himself and three other Justices, took issue with the majority's analysis of both the facts and the law.

[N]either one of [the Scouts' guiding] principles — "morally straight" and "clean" — says the slightest thing about homosexuality. Indeed, neither term in the Boy Scouts' Law and Oath expresses any position whatsoever on sexual matters.

BSA's published guidance on that topic underscores this point. Scouts, for example, are directed to receive their sex education at home or in school, but not from the organization. . . .

Several principles are made perfectly clear by [the Court's past cases in this area]. First, to prevail on a claim of expressive association in the face of a State's antidiscrimination law, it is not enough simply to engage in *some kind* of expressive activity. . . . Second, it is not enough to adopt an openly avowed exclusionary membership policy. . . . Third, it is not sufficient merely to articulate *some* connection between the group's expressive activities and its exclusionary policy. . . .

Rather, [the question is whether an anti-discrimination law] "impose[s] any *serious burdens*" on the group's "collective effort on behalf of [its] shared *goals*. . . . "

The evidence before this Court makes it exceptionally clear that BSA has, at most, simply adopted an exclusionary membership policy and has no shared goal of disapproving of homosexuality.

530 U.S. at 668-669, 682-684.

The *Dale* holding has been controversial among constitutional scholars, policymakers, and the general public. Some commentators have viewed the decision as inconsistent with prior cases involving discrimination by private associations. In upholding state bans on exclusion of women from groups like the Rotary Club and Jaycees (see Chapter 1, p. 137), the Court has concluded that any incidental burden on expression is more than outweighed by compelling government interests in minimizing prejudice. See Darren Lenard Hutchinson, "Closet Case": Boy Scouts of America v. Dale and the Reinforcement of Gay, Lesbian, Bisexual, and Transgender Invisibility, 75 Tul. L. Rev. 81, 86 (2001) (*Dale* represents "a withering of the standard set forth in Roberts v. Jaycees, discussed in Chapter 1, pp. 139-140). The contrary view of *Dale* is that it is a reaffirmation of the "sovereignty of the individual, enshrined in the First Amendment's freedom of speech, thought, and association." Fred Chou, Good Cases Make Bad Law, N.Y. Times, Apr. 27, 2000, at A31.

Following the *Dale* decision, related disputes surfaced about whether public entities like schools and police departments should eliminate their support of Boy Scout activities. According to gay rights advocates, taxpayer funds should not assist an organization that claims in its recruiting material that "any boy is welcome," but decides otherwise in practice. Given the high incidence of physical violence, harassment, isolation, depression, and school-related difficulties suffered by gay youths, child development experts similarly argue that public support should go only to organizations that inculcate values of tolerance and mutual respect. See Brief of Amicus Curiae American Psychological Association in Boy Scouts v. Dale, 199 U.S. Briefs 699 (2000).

Supporters of Boy Scouts respond that public funds for Scout activities primarily benefit poor communities.

Defunding the Scouts would be a tragic loss for inner-city youths and for the country. Gay pride that comes at the expense of poor children is bought at too high a price. If gay activists are so convinced that boys need gay role models, they can start alternative organizations with just that goal. But they should leave the Scouts alone.

Heather MacDonald, Boy Scout Battle Pits Gay Activists vs. Minority Kids, Wall St. J., July 6, 2000, at A26. If you were a member of a school board or city council in a poor community, would you favor cutting all ties with the Boy Scouts?

In relying on the First Amendment's freedom of association, does *Dale* give support to the right of private law schools to pursue their affirmative action plans? See David P. Gearey, Comment, New Protections After Boy Scouts of America v. Dale: A Private University's First Amendment Right to Pursue Diversity, 71 U. Chi. L. Rev. 1583 (2004). Does it support law schools in their challenge to the Solomon Amendments conditioning receipt of federal funds to universities on the availabiliy of their on-campus interview program to the military, when law schools strongly object to the discriminatory policies of the military? This is the theory in FAIR v. Rumsfeld, discussed in note 7, p. 625, infra.

5. Sexual Orientation and Military Policy.   Some of the law concerning discrimination on the basis of sexual orientation has developed in the context of military policy. The military has long excluded or discharged individuals who are found to be gay or lesbian or who have engaged in homosexual acts. What began as an effort by the Clinton administration to eliminate such discrimination led instead to the enactment of congressional legislation codifying a "Don't Ask, Don't Tell" policy. Under this policy, codified in the National Defense Authorization Act of 1994, military authorities may not expressly ask service members if they are homosexual, but may exclude or discharge them from the military if they acknowledge being a homosexual or if they have engaged, or have a "propensity to engage," in homosexual acts. Although the statute appears to focus on conduct rather than status, identification as a homosexual gives rise to a presumption of propensity to engage in homosexual acts. Once service members acknowledge being homosexual, they can remain in military service only upon disproving the propensity to engage in homosexual conduct. 10 U.S.C. §§654(b)(1), (2) (1994). Service members who have engaged in homosexual conduct may avoid discharge only by showing such conduct is a departure from their usual behavior or unlikely to recur. Id.

Section 654(a) of the Act sets forth congressional findings that combat effectiveness requires "high morale, good order and discipline, and unit cohesion"; that the ban on open homosexuals continues to be imperative because of "the unique circumstances of military service"; and that open homosexuals would pose an unacceptable threat to the necessary "high morale, good order and discipline." 10 U.S.C. §§654(a)(6), (13)-(15) (1998). Those claims have been largely accepted by courts in challenges brought to the military's exclusion of gays and lesbians (in cases cited in these notes). A representative conclusion is this:

> Homosexuality is incompatible with military service. The presence in the military environment of persons who engage in homosexual conduct or who, by their statements, demonstrate a propensity to engage in homosexual conduct, seriously impairs

the accomplishment of the military mission. The presence of such members adversely affects the ability of the Military Services to maintain discipline, good order, and morale; to foster mutual trust and confidence among service members[;] to ensure the integrity of the system of rank and command; to facilitate assignment and world-wide deployment of service members who frequently must live and work under close conditions affording minimal privacy; to recruit and retain members of the Military Services; to maintain the public acceptability of military service; and to prevent breaches of security.

Steffan v. Cheney, supra, 780 F. Supp. at 10. Is the concern expressed here frivolous? A self-fulfilling prophecy? Can it be proved? Could the same point have been made about racial integration?

What is the relevance, if any, of a 2004 survey finding that 42 percent of the military believed that gays and lesbians should be allowed to serve openly, and that 50 percent thought that they should not? Max Boot, Gay or Female: Uncle Sam Should Want You, L.A. Times, May 26, 2005, at B15.

The court in Dronenberg v. Zech, 741 F.2d 1388 (D.C. Cir. 1984), reasons:

> The Navy is not required to produce social science data or the results of controlled experiments to prove what common sense and common experience demonstrate. This very case illustrates dangers of the sort the Navy is entitled to consider. A 27-year-old petty officer had repeated sexual relations with a 19-year-old seaman recruit. The latter then chose to break off the relationship. Episodes of this sort are certain to be deleterious to morale and discipline, to call into question the even-handedness of superiors' dealings with lower ranks, to make personal dealings uncomfortable where the relationship is sexually ambiguous, to generate dislike and disapproval among many who find homosexuality morally offensive, and it must be said, given the powers of military superiors over their inferiors, to enhance the possibility of homosexual seduction.

Id. at 1398.

Is the court describing a feature unique to same-sex relationships? Is there something about these relationships that increases the risks of sexual misconduct? Is it appropriate for the court to rest its decision on "common sense and common experience" rather than evidence? If the problem is that gay or lesbian members of the armed services cannot command the respect of others, should the military permit discriminatory attitudes to justify continued discrimination? Is this constitutionally acceptable? Consider Judge Abner Mikva's observation in Steffan v. Aspin:

> [A] cardinal principle of equal protection law holds that the government cannot discriminate against a certain class in order to give effect to the prejudice of others. Even if the government does not itself act out of prejudice, it cannot discriminate in an effort to avoid the effects of others' prejudice. Such discrimination plays directly into the hands of the bigots; it intensifies and encourages their prejudice.

8 F.3d, 57, 68 (D.C. Cir. 1993), rev'd en banc sub nom. Steffan v. Perry, 41 F.3d 677 (D.C. Cir. 1994) (en banc).

Prior to the announcement of the 1993 "Don't Ask, Don't Tell" policy, Secretary of Defense Les Aspin requested from the National Defense Research Institute (NDRI) information and analysis that would be useful in helping to formulate a policy. The NDRI reviewed analogous institutions and experiences, finding that in countries that allow homosexuals to serve in the military, including Canada, France, Germany, Israel, the Netherlands, and Norway, (1) the number of openly homosexual service members is small and is believed to represent only a minority of homosexuals actually serving, (2) service members who acknowledge their homosexuality were "appropriately circumspect" in their behavior and did not call attention to themselves, and (3) few problems were reported that were caused by the presence of homosexual service members, and those that did arise were resolved satisfactorily on a case-by-case basis. NDRI, Sexual Orientation and U.S. Military Personnel Policy: Options and Assessment 11-15 (1993). The NDRI study made similar findings with respect to fire and police departments in the United States that have policies of nondiscrimination, including Chicago, Houston, Los Angeles, New York, San Diego, and Seattle. The findings showed that acknowledged homosexuals are sensitive to the overall norms and customs of their organizations and try to avoid causing trouble. Anti-gay prejudice does not disappear, but negative behavior is more moderate than commonly predicted. With respect to the unit cohesion rationale, the study concluded that many factors work to promote the norms of cohesion and performance, even in the face of hostility based on sexual orientation. As a result, the inability of some individuals to accept the presence of an acknowledged gay or lesbian generally results in a degree of ostracism rather than a breakdown of the unit. Id. at 28-31.

The study further found that implementation of nondiscrimination policies is most successful where the message is unambiguous, consistently delivered, and uniformly enforced. Id. at 15-20. These findings correspond to the lessons learned from the history of racial integration in the U.S. military in the late 1940s. Id. at 20-22. How significant is this kind of information under a rationality standard of review? Consider General Colin Powell's response to analogies based on racial integration:

> [O]pen homosexuality . . . is something quite different than the acceptance of benign characteristics such as color or race or background. . . . It involves matters of privacy and human sexuality that, in our judgment, if allowed to openly exist within the force, will create serious issues having to do with cohesion and having to do with the well-being of the force.

Assessment of the Plan to Lift the Ban on Homosexuals in the Military: Hearings Before the Military Forces and Personnel Subcomm. of the Comm. on Armed Servs., House of Representatives, 103d Cong. 32 (1994) (testimony of Gen. Colin Powell, Chairman, Joint Chiefs of Staff). How would you respond to General Powell?

In Smith & Grady v. United Kingdom, 29 Eur. Ct. H.R. 493 (1999), the European Court of Human Rights struck down the United Kingdom's prohibition on homosexuals in the military. Under the court's analysis, the prohibition violated service members' right to privacy guaranteed by Article 8(1) of the

European Convention for the Protection of Human Rights and Fundamental Freedoms, Nov. 4 1950, 312 U.N.T.S. 221. In so ruling, the court rejected the UK's claim that "negative attitudes" toward homosexual service members made the policy necessary for military morale and "fighting power," and therefore "necessary in a democratic society" under Article 8(2), which authorizes exceptions to individual privacy rights. According to the court, the existence of prejudice should not justify its perpetuation. Negative attitudes toward gays and lesbians were no more acceptable than "similar negative attitudes toward those of a different race, origin, or color." Id. at ¶97. By all accounts, implementation of the *Grady* decision proceeded without significant difficulty. Raymond A. Psonak, Don't Ask, Don't Tell, Don't Discharge, At Least in Europe: A Comparison of the Policies on Homosexuals in the Military in the United States and Europe After Grady v. United Kingdom, 33 Conn. L. Rev. 337, 346 (2000); Scott Morris, Europe Enters a New Millennium While the United States Drowns in Don't Ask, Don't Tell: Twin Decisions by the European Court of Human Rights, 9 Am. U. J. Gender Soc. Pol'y & L. 423 (2001). The *Grady* ruling leaves the United States with the most restrictive military policy toward sexual orientation among Western industrialized countries. Id. Should the experience of other nations be relevant in assessing the rationality of U.S. policy?

Although sponsors of the "Don't Ask, Don't Tell" policy intended it to reduce harassment and exclusion of gay and lesbian soldiers, the results have been otherwise. The military discharged over 10,000 service members between 1994 and 2003. See Servicemembers Legal Defense Network, Conduct Unbecoming: The Tenth Annual Report on "Don't Ask, Don't Tell, Don't Pursue, Don't Harass" 1 (2004), found at http://dont.stanford.edu. Of those discharged due to sexual orientation in 2003, 33 percent were women, although women make up only 15 percent of the active force. Id. at 18. The number of discharges has dropped since the wars in Afghanistan and Iraq, and public opinion has also become more opposed to the policy. In a December 2003 Gallup poll, 79 percent of Americans said they support allowing lesbian, gay, and bisexual Americans to serve openly in the armed services. A Fox News survey put the figure at 64 percent. In 1993, the number was 57 percent. Id. at 2.

6. First Amendment Challenges to Discrimination in the Military: Distinguishing Conduct from Status. In rejecting First Amendment challenges to military policies on sexual orientation, courts have distinguished between homosexual status, which is protected by the First Amendment, and homosexual conduct, which is not. See, e.g., Ben-Shalom v. Marsh, 881 F.2d 454, 464 (7th Cir. 1989), cert. denied, 494 U.S. 1004 (1990). Janet Halley criticizes this distinction on the ground that status is penalized when homosexual conduct or propensity is presumed from homosexual status and when individuals who have engaged in homosexual conduct can disprove propensity by establishing their status as a heterosexual. See Janet E. Halley, Don't: A Readers' Guide to the Military's Anti-Gay Policy (1999); Janet E. Halley, The Status/Conduct Distinction in the 1993 Revisions to Military Anti-Gay Policy: A Legal Archaeology, 3 GLQ: J. Lesbian & Gay Stud. 159, 183-188 (1996). In Halley's view, this "actuarial model of propensity" is even worse for gays and lesbians than an outright exclusion based on homosexual identity. "Every moving part of the new policy is designed to *look like* conduct regulation in order *to hide* the fact that it turns decisively on status. At least the old policy was as bad as it looked; problems of deceptive appearance, ruse, tautology, and outright misrepresentation make the new policy a regulatory Trojan Horse." Halley, Don't, supra, at 2 (emphasis in original). See also Francisco Valdes, Queers, Sissies, Dykes, and Tomboys: Deconstructing the Conflation of "Sex," "Gender," and "Sexual Orientation" in Euro-American Law and Society, 83 Cal. L. Rev. 1, 22-23 (1995) (arguing that gays and lesbians should resist the "conflation" between homosexual identity and conduct). Cf. Diane H. Mazur, The Unknown Soldier: A Critique of "Gays in the Military" Scholarship and Litigation, 29 U.C. Davis L. Rev. 223 (1996) (arguing that both sides in debate could more rationally discuss pros and cons of military policy).

For further consideration of the special issues relating to lesbians in the military, see Section F, pp. 626-635, below.

7. Solomon Amendments. Following the implementation of "Don't Ask, Don't Tell," colleges and universities increasingly began to prohibit the military from recruiting on campus. Momentum grew also for preventing campus access to ROTC programs. In response, Congress enacted the Solomon Amendment — actually a series of amendments to various budget appropriations acts by Congress — requiring all institutions of higher education that receive federal funding to provide military recruiters with equal access to students during the hiring season.

The first incarnation of the Solomon Amendment (Solomon I) was enacted in 1995 as part of the National Defense Authorization Act. National Defense Authorization Act for Fiscal Year 1995, Pub. L. No. 103-337, 558, 108 Stat. 2663, 2776 (1994). This legislation denied Department of Defense funding to colleges and universities that barred ROTC or military recruitment access. The second (Solomon II) was enacted in 1997 as part of the Omnibus Appropriation Act. Omnibus Consolidated Appropriations Act of 1997, Pub. L. No. 104-208, 514(b), 110 Stat. 3009, 3009-271 (1996). This legislation dramatically extended the reach of Solomon by including in the list of at-risk funds all monies from the Departments of Labor, Health and Human Services, and Education. This change added most federal research and financial aid subsidies into the pool of threatened funds.

The Solomon legislation was also recodified and consolidated in 1999, and in that process the subunit rule was eliminated. National Defense Authorization Act for Fiscal Year 2000, Pub. L. No. 106-65, 549, 113 Stat. 512, 609 (1999). Previously, if a law school denied the military access, only the subunit of the law school was at risk of losing funds. After recodification, if the law school denied the military access, the entire university could lose federal funding. Recodification also extended the affected funds to subsidies from the Department of Transportation.

In November 2004, a lawsuit brought by an association of 30 law schools and law faculties challenged the Solomon Amendments. In FAIR

v. Rumsfeld, 390 F.3d 219 (3rd Cir. 2004), the U.S. Third Circuit Court of Appeals ruled that law schools could ban the military from campus on First Amendment grounds. Writing for the court, Judge Thomas Ambro stated that the Solomon Amendment forced law schools to "propagate, accommodate, and subsidize the military's message" to which they did not agree. Id. at 236. The ruling cited the Supreme Court's decision in Boy Scouts of America v. Dale, 530 U.S. 640 (2000), discussed in note 4, supra. "Just as the Boy Scouts believed that 'homosexual conduct is inconsistent with the Scout Oath,'...the law schools believe that employment discrimination is inconsistent with their commitment to justice and fairness," wrote Judge Ambro. In January 2005, in response to a lawsuit by Yale Law School, a federal district court in Connecticut also declared the Solomon Amendment unconstitutional under the First Amendment. See in Burt v. Rumsfeld, 354 F. Supp. 2d 156 (D. Conn. 2005).

In March 2006, the U.S. Supreme Court reversed the Third Circuit ruling in an 8-0 decision holding that the Solomon Amendment affects conduct, not speech. "It affects what law schools must *do*—afford equal access to military recruiters—not what they may or may not *say*." Rumsfeld v. Forum for Academic & Institutional Rights, 2006 Lexis 2025 (March 6, 2006).

Putting Theory into Practice

3-21. The Federal Sentencing Guideline § 3A1.1 permits increased penalties if the victim of the crime was "unusually vulnerable due to age, physical or mental condition, or...otherwise particularly susceptible to the criminal conduct." A defendant is convicted of extortion after having attempted to blackmail a married man who had had a homosexual affair. Under the Guidelines, should the victim's homosexuality be a factor in considering whether he was unusually vulnerable to blackmail? See U.S. v. Lallemand, 989 F.2d 936 (7th Cir. 1993).

F. WOMEN IN THE MILITARY

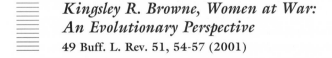

Kingsley R. Browne, Women at War:
An Evolutionary Perspective
49 Buff. L. Rev. 51, 54-57 (2001)

To date, the argument in favor of including women in [combat and close combat support] positions has proceeded under three fundamental assumptions: (1) that warfare in this modern age is fundamentally different from the warfare experienced by our fathers and our more distant ancestors; thus prior experience is no guide to future conduct; (2) that men and women are essentially identical in combat-relevant ways, other than (most would agree) in physical strength, a trait they view as largely irrelevant; thus, men and women are for the most part interchangeable in military positions; and (3) that the primary impediments to integration of women are male "attitudes" operating at a cognitive level; thus, only the lack of proper leadership stands in the way of overcoming this "ideology of masculinism."

All three of these assumptions are subject to serious question and have led to an under-appreciation of the costs and difficulty of sexual integration. The first assumption . . . is based upon a misunderstanding of modern warfare, a misunderstanding made considerably more acute by the lopsided experience of the allies in the Gulf War and the even more lopsided NATO air assault against the Serbs. Yet the business of war is still killing and risking being killed, often at short ranges. Many combat tasks, even in this technological age, have not changed that much from earlier times, and many continue to require physical strength, a trait that virtually everyone agrees is differentially distributed between the sexes.

The second assumption . . . overlooks a vast literature on temperamental and cognitive sex differences. Traits that are important to combat personnel include physical aggressiveness; willingness to kill strangers; willingness to expose oneself to physical risk; and cognitive skills, such as the three-dimensional spatial ability that is so critical to the "situational awareness" of fighter pilots. The questions raised by sex differences in these attributes are primarily whether they can be efficiently tested in advance of actual combat and whether there is enough overlap between the sexes to warrant considering women as well as men for combat positions.

The third assumption . . . overlooks the possibility of predispositions rooted deep in the psyches of both males and females that may stand as an obstacle to integration. Thus, even though some women as individuals possess as much strength, aggressiveness, and inclination to take risks as many men, there may still be reasons for excluding them from combat service. The relevant issue is "femaleness qua femaleness" rather than the individualized attributes of the women in question. Some of the questions that must be answered are whether men have an innate predisposition to resist introduction of women into certain all-male groups; whether introduction of women will disrupt cohesion by creating competition among men for the attentions of women; whether introduction of women will impair effectives by causing men to be overprotective of women; whether women can elicit following behavior in men to the same extent that other men can; and whether introduction of women will diminish the willingness of men to risk their lives and make the military less attractive to potential male "warriors." These questions involve not the capacity of women as individuals to be soldiers but rather the social dynamic that results from mixing men and women under what are often very trying conditions. This set of issues is more difficult to analyze than the former, because it is generally easier to measure traits of individuals than it is to measure social interactions between them. . . .

Is it really true that warfare has changed so much as to reverse the almost unanimous conclusion of human history that defense of the community and external projects of force should rest with men?

Notes

1. Historical Background. Throughout the nation's history, cultural expectations and legal restrictions have severely limited female involvement in the armed forces. Until the early 1970s, women constituted less than two percent of the American military and discrimination in placement and promotion was widespread, particularly for women of color. Enrollment was limited through quotas on female applicants; exclusion from combat positions, military academies, and training programs; and disqualification of women who became pregnant or had minor children. The prevailing view was apparent in one 1968 federal district court opinion: "In providing for involuntary service for men and voluntary service for women, Congress followed the teachings of history that if a nation is to survive, men must provide the first line of defense while women keep the home fires burning." United States v. St. Clair, 291 F. Supp. 122, 125 (S.D.N.Y. 1968).

In the mid-1970s, many of these restrictions were modified or withdrawn, without judicial intervention. As a result, female participation in the armed forces substantially increased, reaching 10 percent by the late 1980s, 13 percent by the turn of the century, and 15 percent by 2005.

Women's military participation has also increased in most other nations, although there have been considerable variations across time and culture. What accounts for these differences? Social scientists have stressed interrelated cultural, political, international, and military factors. At the cultural level, the greater a society's emphasis on authoritariarianism, hierarchy, and conformity, and the greater its occupational segregation by gender, the more limited women's military participation is likely to be. At the political level, women's participation is generally lower in states that lack stable, legitimate civilian governments, and in which the military exercises significant influence over the political process. At the military level, women's participation tends to be lower in armed forces that are elitist and aggressive (rather than defensive and deterrent), and reliant on conventional forces rather than sophisticated technologies. At the international level, the greater the threat to national security and need for military personnel, the greater the opportunities for women. See Darlene Iskra et. al, Women's Participation in Armed Forces Cross-Nationally; Expanding Segal's Model, 50 Current Soc. 771, 787-792 (2002); Gerhard Kummel, When Boy Meets Girl: The "Feminization" of the Military: An Introduction Also to be Read as Postscript, 50 Current Soc. 615, 627-631 (2002).

2. Legal Challenges. The first case to reach the Supreme Court concerning sex discrimination in the military was Rostker v. Golberg, 453 U.S. 57 (1981). At issue was a claim by a male plaintiff that the military's compulsory draft registration system, which included only men, constituted a violation of the equal protection clause. Speaking for the majority, Justice Rehnquist rejected that claim.

> No one could deny that under Craig [v. Boren], the Government's interest in raising and supporting armies is an "important governmental interest." Congress

and its Committees carefully considered and debated...alternative means of furthering that interest....

Congress was fully aware not merely of the many facts and figures presented to it by witnesses who testified before its Committees, but [also] of the current thinking as to the place of women in the Armed Services....

This case is quite different from several of the gender-based discrimination cases we have considered in that, despite appellees' assertions, Congress did not act "unthinkingly" or "reflexively and not for any considered reason."...The question of registering women for the draft not only received considerable national attention and was the subject of wide-ranging public debate, but also was extensively considered by Congress in hearings, floor debate, and in committee....

[T]he decision to exempt women from registration was not the "'accidental by-product of a traditional way of thinking about females.'"...

The purpose of registration [historically], therefore was to prepare for a draft of *combat troops.*

Women as a group, however, unlike men as a group, are not eligible for combat.... Congress specifically recognized and endorsed the exclusion of women from combat in exempting women from registration. In the words of the Senate Report:

> The principle that women should not intentionally and routinely engage in combat is fundamental, and enjoys wide support among our people. It is universally supported by military leaders who have testified before the Committee.... Current law and policy exclude women from being assigned to combat in our military forces, and the Committee reaffirms this policy....

The Senate Report specifically found that "[w]omen should not be intentionally or routinely placed in combat positions in our military services."...The President expressed his intent to continue the current military policy precluding women from combat....

The existence of combat restrictions clearly indicates the basis for Congress' decision to exempt women from registration. The purpose of registration was to prepare for a draft of combat troops. Since women are excluded from combat, Congress concluded that they would not be needed in the event of a draft, and therefore decided not to register them.

453 U.S. at 70-72, 74, 76-77.

Since the plaintiff in *Rostker* had not challenged the constitutionality of the combat exemption, the Court found it unnecessary to resolve that issue, although the tenor of the decision left little doubt that a majority of Justices were prepared to defer to Congress on this matter. Justice Marshall, joined by Justice Brennan, dissented. As they read the record, the government had not sustained the burden of showing that a gender-based classification substantially furthered the goal of military preparedness. Even assuming the legitimacy of excluding women from combat, their exclusion from registration did not follow. According to government estimates, about a third of those drafted during a national mobilization would not need combat skills. The registration system at issue included non-combat-eligible males, and the Joint Chiefs of Staff had been united in their desire to include females as well. Although some cost would be involved in registering more women than necessary in a system that precluded their combat service, the dissent noted that Supreme Court decisions had often rejected administrative expense as a rationale for gender classifications. 453 U.S. at 85 (Marshall, J., dissenting).

Justice Rehnquist's opinion emphasized that the exclusion of women was not an accidental by-product "of a traditional way of thinking about females." What if it was a deliberate byproduct of traditional gender stereotypes? See discussion in Chapter 1, pp. 41-42.

3. Women in Combat. Legislative debates about women's participation in the military, particularly in combat positions, reflect an extended array of assumptions about women's physical and psychological unfitness for fighting and the cultural costs of seeing the nation's nurturers as "cannon fodder." Many military and congressional leaders remain convinced that actual "fighting is a man's job" and that most female soldiers lack sufficient strength, endurance, aggressiveness, or ability to "kill impersonally" in combat. Some maintain that aggression is "an intrinsic male" quality, and one author concludes that regardless of whether women are "innately less aggressive and combative than men" or "victims of cultural conditioning that represses their natural warlike instincts to levels below those typical of males," women are less aggressive than men and should thusly be excluded from combat missions. For these and other arguments, see sources quoted in Arnulfo Urias, The Politics of Biology: Evolutionary Biology and the Exclusion of Women from Combat, 14 S. Cal. Rev. L. & Women's Stud. 83, 101-102 (2004); Linda Bird Francke, Ground Zero: The Gender Wars in the Military 130-151 (1997).

Other popular commentary echoes similar themes and warns that American national security has been threatened by the "feminization" of the military. See Stephanie Gutman, The Kinder, Gentler Military: Can America's Gender-Neutral Fighting Force Still Win Wars? (2000); Brian Mitchell, Women in the Military: Flirting with Disaster (1998). According to Mitchell, the integration of women "threatens to leave the American military no more disciplined, no more efficient, no more fearsome, no more military than the United States Postal Service." Id. at xvii.

Rush Limbaugh summarizes a widespread view:

> What will feminists seek in the military, first and foremost? Equality. Fairness. Gender quotas. Well, the military's chief goal is excellence. We shouldn't emasculate (pun intended) by shackling it with the demands of every silly social movement that is currently fashionable in society. The military has a job to do.... Its success will always be measured by its ability to destroy and decimate; not by whether it has a requisite percentage of women in foxholes, in daycare centers, or flying F-16s. I know this sounds harsh, but that's the way war is. Frankly, I don't believe that women should be in combat roles even if they can do the job. Why? You ask. Simple. Women have a civilizing role in society. War is that cruel last option in human relations. It isn't about career opportunities. Women have definite societal roles that are crucial to the continuation of mankind. They establish enduring values that are handed down from generation to generation. Women are the ones who give birth, without which the propagation of the species would not be perpetuated.
>
> I just don't believe that we have to subject women to the horrors and rigors of war.... [I]t's bad enough that men come home in body bags. Why do we need to put women in them as well?

Rush Limbaugh III, The Way Things Ought to Be 200-201 (1992).

Opponents of women in combat also raise a host of concerns about pregnancy, promiscuity, and "gender-norming" — the practice of adjusting strength and fitness standards to reflect sex-based differences. According to these commentators, the military's effort to accommodate women is fostering resentment, diluting performance requirements, creating double standards, inspiring inappropriate chivalry, compromising morale, impairing recruitment, and diverting attention from more central goals of combat preparedness. Underlying these concerns were a host of symbolic issues about masculinity, manhood, and dominance. General William Westmoreland expressed a common attitude with uncommon candor. "No man with any gumption wants a woman to fight his nation's battles." William Westmoreland, quoted in Judith Wagner Decrew, The Combat Exclusion and the Role of Women in the Military, Hypatia, Winter 1995, at 62.

Proponents of equality of opportunity for women point out that, with respect to physical capabilities, the most comprehensive studies conclude that with appropriate training the vast majority of women can meet the physical demands of combat. See, e.g., J. Michael Brower, Undermining Old Taboos: U.S. Studies Say Women Can Meet Physical Demands of Combat, Armed Forces J. Int'l, May 1996, at 13 (reporting on studies sponored by the Army Research Institute and the British Ministry of Defense); Francke, supra, at 248; Mark Hagar, GI Jane and the Limits of Liberalism, 10 Transnat'l J.L. & Contemp. Probs. 219 (2000); Blythe Leszkay, Feminism on the Front Lines, 14 Hastings Women's L.J. 133, 161 (2003). Supporters of women in combat also argue that that aggression levels, like size, overlap between men and women, and that while "[male] hormones produce a male mind oriented more toward risk, aggression, and competition, just as they produce a male anatomy that is larger, hairier, and more muscular," maleness only approximates aggression. See Urias, supra, at 105-106.

As in civilian contexts, military positions requiring particular levels of strength, endurance, or agility can be allocated under gender-neutral guidelines that match individual capabilities with job requirements. Moreover, as many experts have noted, technological changes in warfare have reduced the relevance of physical strength in combat and eroded the distinctions between combat and combat-related positions. Federal judge Richard Posner puts it this way: "We live in an age of push-button warfare. Women can push buttons as well as men." Richard Posner, Overcoming Law 55 (1995).

Definitions of combat have changed over time, and many combat exclusions have been lifted, including the exclusion from flying combat missions and service on combatant naval vessels. Michael J. Frevola, Damn the Torpedoes, Full Speed Ahead: The Argument for Total Sex Integration in the Armed Services, 28 Conn. L. Rev. 621, 626 (1996). The Department of Defense's official policy is still to ban women from serving in front-line combat positions, but in the Iraq War, the lack of a defined front line and insurgents' guerrilla tactics expose female troops in many support positions to deadly situations. Of the approximately 10,780 female Marines (officer and enlisted) serving on active duty in 2005, nearly 3,000 serve in combat support fields, including engineering, military police, ordinance and

motor transport. Marine Corps Concepts and Programs 2005, available at http://
hqinet001.hqmc.usmc.mil/p&r/concepts/2005/TOC1.htm. As one Army Lt.
Colonel put it, in Iraq, every soldier is "in harm's way." Mona Iskander, Female
Troops in Iraq Redefine Combat Roles, www.womensenews.org, July 5, 2004.

An amendment to the 2006 Defense Authorization Bill introduced on May
11, 2005, by Rep. John McHugh (R-NY), chairman of the House Armed Services
Committee's Military Personnel Subcommittee, would prohibit female service-
members from serving in combat support units. National Defense Authorization
Act for Fiscal Year 2006, H.R. 1815, 109th Cong. (2005). On the other side, the
Marine Corps says that female Marines in combat support roles are helping the
military respect cultural sensitivities in Iraq by searching female Iraqi citizens
moving through checkpoints, for example. Female Troops in Iraq Exposed to
Combat, CNN, June 28, 2005, available at http://www.cnn.com/2005/
WORLD/meast/06/25/women.combat. Whether to challenge sex-based policies, particularly those that exclude women from combat and draft registration
systems, has been a matter of long-standing dispute within the feminist community. Advocates of equal treatment argue that protective policies disserve women's
interests by protecting women out of positions of greatest power, status, and
reward. Lack of combat eligibility restricts women's job opportunities, credibility,
and career advancement in the military and limits their ability to capitalize on
wartime service in other political and employment contexts. Double standards in
the military also carry other costs in reinforcing traditional gender roles and
stereotypes. In this vein, Mary Becker notes:

> Exclusion of women from militia service in combat denies women the obliga-
> tions of full citizenship. This denial inevitably translates into disadvantaging women
> as citizens by depriving them of power they would otherwise share more equally with
> men. . . .
> [K]eeping women out of combat maintains the image of the male warrior, who
> is superior to physically passive women who need his protection and cannot resist his
> violence. . . . The military trains men to operate within a macho culture with the
> belief that they are superior to women. . . .
> [K]eeping women out of combat positions . . . supports the taboo against
> women using force, especially lethal force. . . . Maintaining male control of lethal
> force clearly preserves male interests both with respect to control of the military itself
> (a powerful institution in its own right) and with respect to men's power over
> women through physical intimidation throughout society. . . .

Mary E. Becker, The Politics of Women's Wrongs and the Bill of "Rights": A
Bicentennial Perspective, 59 U. Chi. L. Rev. 453, 496-498 (1992). See also
Karst, The Pursuit of Motherhood and the Desegregation of the Armed Forces,
38 UCLA L. Rev. 499, 579 (1991) ("The exclusion of women from combat
positions does not keep women out of harm's way; it keeps women in their
place. [Exclusion of women, like exclusion of gays, serves] to maintain the gender
line, and thus to maintain for the services a traditionally masculine image: power
and weapons in the hands of 'real men.'").

If service in the military is an incidence of citizenship, is it simply a matter of
whether women should be allowed to participate in the military? Shouldn't they

feel obligated to do so? See Diane H. Mazur, A Call to Arms, 22 Harv. Women's L.J. 39 (1999) (arguing that feminists are not in a position to criticize the military's treatment of servicewomen until they accept responsibility of participation in the military).

Other feminists argue that women should seek to challenge military culture, not to assimilate within it. Following President Carter's 1980 proposal for gender-neutral draft registration, a New Haven women's group issued the following response:

> —Women have traditionally fought for peace, and there is no reason for us to abandon that position now.
> —Our quest for equality must not lead us to embrace blindly all the standards and values of male institutions.
> —We reject the war reflex as an instance of male hysteria; in its essence, feminism is opposed to violence.
> Women's experience leads us firmly to reject the claim that might makes right.... Anything that legitimates violence is inherently a threat to women, who are disproportionately the victims of violent acts. It is impossible to separate America's use of violence abroad from the use of violence against women in the American home and on American streets....
> ...The conscription of women will not change the structure of power in the military or in this country. Why should we bide by a decision over which we have had no say? Once we are drafted, who will decide where we will serve? ... These decisions will be made as they have always been made, by the *men* in the Pentagon and the White House, men who have refused to fight for equal rights for women, men who have on countless occasions demonstrated their disregard for the legitimate grievances and sovereign rights of oppressed people all over the world....

Feminist Opposition to the Draft, quoted in Catharine A. MacKinnon, Sex Equality 270-271 (2001). For similar points in the context of the Gulf War, see Ellen Goodman, Value Judgments 158-159 (1993) (Gulf War shows the lopsidedness of gender change, with "[m]ore women...on the front lines than in the inner circle").

A slim majority of Americans favor assigning women to ground combat positions. Mollie M. Ginty, Record Number of Female Soldier Fall, www.womensenews.org, March 20, 2005. Can women have it both ways — that is, have the right to serve in combat without the obligation? If not, which way should they try to have it? What formulation of gender equality is most consistent with your answer?

4. Sexual Abuse in the Armed Forces. Another long-standing concern involving women and the military is sexual abuse. Certain characteristics of military life increase the risks of sexual misconduct: a highly masculine culture that reinforces aggression; strict hierarchies and limited opportunities for subordinates to escape abusive circumstances; stresses caused by lack of privacy and dangerous or onerous living conditions; separation from spouses or partners; and traditions of hazing for new or "deviant" recruits. The result has been a high level of domestic violence, sexual harassment, and rape during wartime.

A steady succession of scandals concerning sexual assault in the military has prompted studies, hearings, and reports — 18 in the last 15 years. Lara Friedrich & Ann Decleene, Scandal Patrol, Ms., Fall 2004, at 14. Although the reluctance of victims to report abuse makes the full extent of the underlying problem difficult to gauge, according to a Department of Defense task force, there were approximately 70 alleged sexual assaults per 100,000 uniformed service members in 2002, and again in 2003. Nine percent of the identified victims were male. Department of Defense, Task Force Report on Care for Victims of Sexual Assault, April 2004, at 19-20, available at www.globalsecurity.org/military/library/report/2004/d20040513satfreport.pdf. It is estimated that a quarter of women in the military report experiencing a sexual assault during their service. Marie Tessier, Sexual Assault Pervasive in the Military, Experts Say, www.womensenews.org, March 31, 2003. Rates of domestic violence are estimated as three to five times higher among military couples than civilian couples. Cathleen Lutz, Living Room Terrorists, Women's Rev. of Books, Feb. 2004, at 17-18. See also Jacquelyn C. Campbell et al., Intimate Partner Violence and Abuse Among Active Duty Military Women, 9 Violence Against Women 1072 (2003). Responses to both domestic violence and sexual assault have been strongly criticized, on grounds that the armed forces have often failed to investigate complaints, protect complainants, and impose serious sanctions. Lutz, supra, 17-18; Tessier, supra. The problem is mirrored in the persistent and pervasive incidents of sexual abuse in military academies. See Report of the Defense Task Force on Sexual Harassment and Violence at the Military Service Academies (2005).

Since the early 1990s, the Uniform Code of Military Justice has declared zero tolerance for sexual harassment, but it is not clear what percentage of incidents are reported. The reasons were well illustrated by a recent case in which Lt. General Claudia Kennedy, the Army's highest-ranking woman, revealed that she had beeen harassed four years earlier by an officer subsequently chosen for the position of deputy inspector general, whose responsibilities would have included the investigation of sexual harassment. The appointment was withdrawn, but coverage of the incident suggested that women are reluctant to open their personal lives to investigation for fear of being blamed for inviting a sexual advance. Elizabeth Becker, Women in Military Say Silence on Harassment Protects Careers, N.Y. Times, May 12, 2000, at A1. In commenting on Lt. General Kennedy's dilemma, one female officer noted, "Now instead of being remembered as the first woman to earn three stars in the Army, she is going to be remembered as that woman with the sex complaint." Id.

Strategies for improving the military's responsiveness to sexual abuse include more training and accountability of officers and service providers; more information and outreach to victims; greater representation of women, particularly in supervisory positions; more protection and remedies for soldiers who report misconduct; redefinition of rules prohibiting "fraternization" to focus on nonconsensual conduct and relationships presenting conflicts of interest. Department of Defense, Task Force Report on Care for Victims of Sexual Assault (April 2004), at 21-35; Michael F. Noone, Chimera or Jackalope? Department of Defense Efforts to Apply Civilian Harassment Criteria to the Military, 6 Duke J. Gender L. &

Pol'y 151 (1999); Martha Chamallas, The New Gender Panic: Reflections on Sex Scandals in the Military, 83 Minn. L. Rev. 305, 374-375 (1999).

What strategies strike you as most promising? In the final analysis, Diane Mazur notes:

> The reason the chain of command has been ineffective in controlling sexual mis-conduct in the military is that no one, at any level, has truly considered it a priority. The "zero tolerance" slogan is just a slogan, unconnected to serious consequences for those who fail to change behavior. The military is quite talented at changing behavior; it has to want to change that behavior.

Diane Mazur, The Beginning of the End for Women in the Military, 48 Fla. L. Rev. 461, 469-470 (1996). How can the military become more motivated? For discussion of comprehensive new initiatives governing investigation, prosecution, preventive education, and victim support, see Department of Defense Policy on Prevention and Response to Sexual Assault (Jan. 2005).

4

Difference Theory

In this chapter, concern for women's equality is filtered through a commitment to revaluing characteristics that are typically associated with women, rather than eliminating them or minimizing their effects. Within difference theory (also referred to as cultural feminism, relational feminism, or an ethic of care), women's differences are viewed less as problems to be overcome than as potentially valuable resources that might serve as a better model of law and social organization than existing "male" characteristics and values. These differences are said to include a greater sense of interconnectedness, a priority on relationships over rights, and a preference for more contextualized, less abstract forms of reasoning. This chapter investigates the nature of these claimed differences and their implications for the legal system.

A majority of feminist theorists view difference theory with suspicion because of the risk that attributing certain traditional virtues to women will reinforce the ideologies of subordination that those theories are intended to dispel. At the same time, almost everyone assumes that the increasing presence of women in law schools, in law practice, in elected office, on juries, and on the bench will affect how law is taught, practiced, applied, and made. Is there a contradiction here? Does it matter whether the purported differences between women and men are based in biology or are a result of cultural conditioning?

Difference theory provides the occasion for exploring the impact of women in all roles in the legal system. It also provides an occasion for further examination of the relationship between theory and practice: Is the insistence that women are like men a truth upon which theory should be built or a strategy to achieve a form of justice that must be justified on other premises?

A. THE CONNECTION THESIS

≡ *Robin West, Jurisprudence and Gender*
≡ 55 U. Chi. L. Rev. 1, 1-3, 14-15, 58-60 (1988)

[V]irtually all modern American legal theorists, like most modern moral and political philosophers, either explicitly or implicitly embrace what I will call the "separation thesis" about what it means to be a human being: a "human being," whatever else he is, is physically separate from all other human beings. I am one human being and you are another, and that distinction between you and me is central to the meaning of the phrase "human being." . . .

By virtue of their shared embrace of the separation thesis, all of our modern legal theory . . . is essentially and irretrievably masculine. . . . [T]he cluster of claims that jointly constitute the "separation thesis" — the claim that human beings are, definitionally, distinct from one another, the claim that the referent of "I" is singular and unambiguous, the claim that the word "individual" has an uncontested biological meaning, namely that we are each physically individuated from every other, the claim that we are individuals "first," and the claim that what separates us is epistemologically and morally prior to what connects us — while "trivially true" of men, [is] patently untrue of women. Women are not essentially, necessarily, inevitably, invariably, always, and forever separate from other human beings: women, distinctively, are quite clearly "connected" to another human life when pregnant. In fact, women are in some sense "connected" to life and to other human beings during at least four recurrent and critical material experiences: the experience of pregnancy itself; the invasive and "connecting" experience of heterosexual penetration, which may lead to pregnancy; the monthly experience of menstruation, which represents the potential for pregnancy; and the post-pregnancy experience of breast-feeding. Indeed, perhaps the central insight of feminist theory of the last decade has been that women are "essentially connected," not "essentially separate," from the rest of human life, both materially, through pregnancy, intercourse, and breast-feeding, and existentially, through the moral and practical life. . . .

The "connection thesis" is simply this: Women are actually or potentially materially connected to other human life. Men aren't. This material fact has existential consequences. While it may be true for men that the individual is "epistemologically and morally prior to the collectivity," it is not true for women. The potential for material connection with the other defines women's subjective, phenomenological and existential state, just as surely as the inevitability of material separation from the other defines men's existential state. Our potential for material connection engenders pleasures and pains, values and dangers, and attractions and fears, which are entirely different from those which follow, *for men*, from the necessity of separation. Indeed, it is the rediscovery of the multitude of implications from this material difference between men and women which has enlivened (and divided) both cultural and radical feminism in this decade. . . . As Carol Gilligan notes, this development is somewhat paradoxical: during the same decade that liberal feminist political activists and lawyers pressed for equal (meaning same) treatment by the law, feminist theorists in the non-legal disciplines rediscovered women's differences from men....

If both cultural and radical feminists hold some version of the connection thesis, then one way of understanding the issues that divide [them]...[is to examine their] contrasting accounts of the subjective experience of the material and existential state of connection. According to cultural feminist accounts of women's subjectivity, women value intimacy, develop a capacity for nurturance, and an ethic of care for the "other" with which we are connected, just as we learn to dread and fear separation from the other. Radical feminists tell a very different story. According to radical feminism, women's connection with the "other" is above all else invasive and intrusive: women's potential for material "connection" invites invasion into the physical integrity of our bodies, and intrusion into the existential integrity of our lives. Although women may "officially" value the intimacy of connection, we "unofficially" dread the intrusion it inevitably entails, and long for the individuation and independence that deliverance from that state of connection would permit....

By the claim that modern jurisprudence is "masculine," I mean two things. First, I mean that the values [and] the dangers that characterize women's lives are not reflected at any level whatsoever in contracts, torts, constitutional law, or any other field of legal doctrine. The values that flow from women's material potential for physical connection are not recognized as values by the Rule of Law, and the dangers attendant to that state are not recognized as dangers by the Rule of Law.

First, the Rule of Law does not value intimacy—its official value is autonomy. The material consequence of this theoretical undervaluation of women's values...is that women are economically *impoverished*....Nurturant, intimate labor is neither valued by liberal legalism nor compensated by the market economy. It is not compensated in the home and it is not compensated in the workplace—wherever intimacy is, there is no compensation. Similarly, separation of the individual from his or her family, community, or children is not understood to be a harm, and we are not protected against it....

Nor does the Rule of Law recognize . . . the contradiction which characterizes women's, but not men's, lives: while we value the intimacy we find so natural, we are endangered by the invasion and dread the intrusion in our lives which intimacy entails, and we long for individuation and independence. Neither sexual nor fetal invasion of the self by the other is recognized to be a harm worth bothering about. Sexual invasion through rape is understood to be a harm, and is criminalized as such, only when it involves some other harm: today, when it is accomplished by violence that appears in a form men understand (meaning a plausible threat of annihilation); in earlier times, when it was understood as theft of another man's property. But marital rape, date rape, acquaintance rape...are either not criminalized, or if they are, they are not punished—to do so would force a recognition of the concrete, experiential harm to identity formation that sexual invasion accomplishes.

Similarly, fetal invasion is not understood to be harmful....[T]he danger an unwanted fetus poses is not to the body's security at all, but rather to the body's integrity. [T]he woman's fear is not that she will die, but that she will cease to be or never become a self. The danger of unwanted pregnancy is the danger of invasion by the other, not of annihilation by the other. In sum, the Rule of Law does not recognize the danger of invasion, nor does it recognize the individual's need for, much less entitlement to, individuation and independence from the intrusion which heterosexual penetration and fetal invasion entails. The material consequence of this lack of recognition in the real world is that women are *objectified*—regarded as creatures who can't be harmed.

Leslie Bender, From Gender Difference to Feminist Solidarity: Using Carol Gilligan and an Ethic of Care in Law
15 Vt. L. Rev. 1, 36-37, 39-42 (1990)

[Psychologist Carol] Gilligan noted two distinct, although not mutually exclusive, perspectives in her analysis of people's orientations in solving moral dilemmas. One perspective, which she denominated an ethic of justice, closely parallels the dominant rationality and methodology of Anglo-American law. This justice ethic is based on a rights model, where problem-solving consists of the application of abstract, generalized principles to arbitrate rights disputes between separate individuals (conflicting rights-holders) and to privilege one right over another. The justice-oriented problem-solver seeks a distanced stance from which to make objective decisions by applying formal rules of equality and other general principles of justice. Traditionally, this perspective was deemed the highest stage of moral development, and it has monopolized legal reasoning.

Gilligan observed, however, that some people solve moral dilemmas using a different, but equally adequate, methodology. This second distinctive perspective, which Gilligan called an ethic of care, focuses attention on the unique context of the dispute and the parties' on-going relationships and interdependencies. The care-oriented problem-solver examines the connections between and among people, looking at their interpersonal responsibilities and needs. Preventing hurt, preserving relationships, and developing cooperative solutions rooted in the concrete particulars of the conflict are objectives of a care-oriented ethical analysis. A care-based problem-solver often "questions the hypothetical" to gather more relevant information in order to better understand the full scope of the problem and the practical, material consequences of any decision. By considering the specific needs of all the parties, as articulated from those parties' own perspectives, and by attending to particularized contexts rather than abstract rights and universalizable rules, care-oriented problem-solvers frequently design creative, alternative solutions that may never occur to their justice-oriented counterparts.

Gilligan's thesis is that care concerns are a largely unacknowledged or unprivileged way of analyzing moral dilemmas, and that while they are used by both men and women, women focus on care and relationships considerably more than men do....

Some feminist theories reject Gilligan's gender-linked analysis of ethical orientations because they fear that it will reinscribe women with characteristics that are a consequence of, or have been the fodder for, gender domination. This is a very serious concern. Carol Gilligan's work has been critiqued for burdening women with continuing tasks of caregiving, pleasing others, and self-sacrifice....

A second, related criticism of Gilligan's ethic of care is that caregiving itself is draining and self-sacrificing. If women are expected to maintain our caregiving work, particularly in our workplaces, we will not have time and energy left to fulfill our own needs, to care for our families, or to promote our personal and political advancement. This is especially true, since women are still responsible for the majority of housekeeping, caregiving, and emotional work in the home. If we advertise ourselves as caregivers, we will be forced to continue our extra work at home and in the workplace.

Finally, there is an equally strong criticism that these caregiving traits do not apply to all women, that many women do not exhibit them, and that many women do not even want to be associated with them. The truth of this last criticism is self-evident. All of the above critiques are searing, and each has a strong ring of truth. Those of us who advocate that gender differences be acknowledged need to worry about them....

Acknowledging the possible link between care and gender, [Catharine] MacKinnon and others suggest that care is a voice of oppression or subordination. If that is how this ethic of care and responsibility is created, she argues, we should not celebrate its link to women....

That the origins of an ethic of care are in part suspect advises especial caution, but not necessarily rejection. Caring and cooperation are quintessential values and should be promoted and nurtured in our society, even if historically their work has been unduly, unfairly, and disproportionately foisted upon women. Rather than reject caring as lesser because of its association with women and women's work, or its correlation with oppressed statuses, we can decide that care, cooperation and interpersonal responsibility are so vital to human progress and happiness that they ought to be done by everyone. If we truly value caregiving, we should reward the people who do it with our society's traditional indicia of respect — prestige and economic advantages. Society's positive reinforcement of its important values encourages more people to excel at those tasks, master those skills, and adopt those orientations.

Caregiving, cooperation and an orientation toward interpersonal responsibility can be socially and legally promoted as easily as economic efficiency, competitive hierarchies, and self-interest have been. If, in fact, these traits do correlate with being men or women, they are not sex-linked, but gender-linked. Because gender is a process of socialization, men can be socialized to be caregivers and to assume an orientation of interpersonal responsibility and cooperation, just as easily as women have been. Certainly some men are already extremely competent caregivers. Cooperation, caregiving, and interpersonal responsibility orientations need not be taught through subordination, exclusion, marginalization, and fear. If an ethic of care is an orientation that we want reproduced and promoted in everyone, we need to discover ways to inculcate it without oppression....

≡
≡
≡
≡

Mary Becker, Patriarchy and Inequality: Toward a Substantive Feminism
1999 U. Chi. Legal F. 21, 21-22, 48-49

As we reach the turn of the century, feminism seems to be at an impasse. Young women agree that women should receive equal pay and equal treatment as workers, but many insist that they are not feminists. Women have made strides in educational institutions and as workers during the current wave of the feminist movement, yet progress now seems to be at a snail's pace. Most women continue to do most caretaking and domestic work at home and now also work for wages. Most men are aware of women's second shift and its unfairness, but are uninterested in change. Media treat women better in some ways, but continue to focus primarily on men and on women in relationship to men. Most heroines are thin and beautiful. Women, particularly young women, are more obsessed than in earlier eras with weight and physical appearance as measures of merit. Real equality appears to be an ever-receding chimera.

I suggest that part of the problem is the failure of feminists, particularly feminists working for legal change, to look at the big picture: a social structure that is male-centered, male-identified, male-dominated, and which valorizes qualities narrowly defined as masculine. Neither of the approaches to change dominant in legal circles — liberal feminism and dominance feminism — has the potential to seriously threaten this structure because both are empty at their core, offering no values inconsistent with patriarchal values. Cultural feminism does offer values inconsistent with patriarchal values, but has been widely discredited in legal circles.

In this essay, ["relational feminism"] offers benefits to all members of society, not just women. Human beings, whether men, women, or children, do not flourish when hyper-masculinity is glorified and traditionally feminine qualities (such as care, caretaking, and valuing relationships) are denigrated. Nor do human beings flourish when all males are pressured to adopt hyper-masculine attributes and repress feminine ones, and all females are pressured to adopt traditionally feminine attributes and repress masculine ones. Relational feminism has the potential to improve life for many people, not just women. . . .

Relational feminism does not reject either the equal treatment of similarly-situated women and men (formal equality's focus) nor more power as it is currently defined (dominance feminism's focus). But relational equality has a different focus: working for human happiness and fulfillment for women (and men). Similar treatment of similarly-situated women and men is often appropriate from this perspective. And giving more power, as it is currently described, to women is often appropriate. All else being equal, it is good (conducive to human happiness and fulfillment) for similar individuals to be treated similarly regardless of sex and good for women to have as much power, as it is currently defined, as men.

Sometimes, however, all is not otherwise equal, and other goods may be more important for women than either of these. If, for example, individual decisionmakers unconsciously prefer men because of patriarchal biases, a rule mandating formally equal treatment of women and men may be inappropriate. Or there may be instances in which something may be more important than power for women's happiness and fulfillment.

More importantly, one's focuses determine one's agenda and priorities. A focus on formal equality will produce a quite different agenda with quite different priorities from an anti-subordination focus. Similarly, a relational feminism focus will produce a quite different agenda with quite different priorities from either of the others. For example, the need to value caretaking and relationships, particularly with dependents, will be high on a relational feminism agenda, and might not even appear on a formal equality or anti-subordination agenda.

To date, cultural feminism is the only strand of feminist theory with values that are incompatible with patriarchal values. Cultural feminism has, therefore, the potential to challenge patriarchy.

NOTE ON THE CONNECTION THESIS

Lawrence Kohlberg's six-stage model of moral development associates progression in moral thinking with increasingly abstract levels of reasoning. In her highly influential work published in 1982, In a Different Voice: Psychological Theory and Women's Development, Carol Gilligan demonstrated that this model reflected the stages through which boys typically progressed better than it did the stages followed by girls. In one of her most well known studies, Gilligan compared how boys and girls responded to "Heinz's dilemma," in which Heinz's wife is dying of cancer and requires a drug that Heinz cannot afford to purchase from the local pharmacist. The children are asked whether Heinz should steal the drug. Summarizing Gilligan's findings, Carrie Menkel-Meadow explains:

> Jake, an eleven-year-old boy, sees the problem as one of "balancing rights," like a judge who must make a decision or a mathematician who must solve an algebraic equation. Life is worth more than property, therefore Heinz should steal the drug. For Amy, an eleven-year-old girl, the problem is different. Like a "bad" law student who "fights the hypo" she wants to know more facts. Have Heinz and the druggist explored other possibilities, like a loan or credit transaction? Why couldn't Heinz and the druggist simply sit down and talk it out so that the druggist would come to see the importance of Heinz's wife's life? In Gilligan's terms, Jake explores the Heinz dilemma with the "logic of justice" while Amy uses the "ethic of care." Amy scores lower on the Kohlberg scale because she sees the problem rooted in the persons involved rather than in the larger universal issues posed by the dilemma.

Carrie Menkel-Meadow, Portia in a Different Voice: Speculations on a Women's Lawyering Process, 1 Berkeley Women's L.J. 39, 46 (1985).

Is it clear that Jake's mode of analysis is closer to the legal paradigm of reasoning? What does it mean for problems to be "rooted in the persons involved rather than in the larger universal issues"? For a recent overview of the "connection thesis" literature, see Patricia W. Hatamyar & Kevin M. Simmons, Are

Women More Ethical Lawyers? An Empirical Study, 31 Fla. St. L. Rev. 785, 839-841 (2004).

Those who are critical of cultural feminism tend to see it as supporting rather than challenging patriarchy because it takes stereotypical gender associations as true. Even cultural feminists like Sara Ruddick, for example, observe that the association of men with war, women with peace is romantic rather than realistic: many men abhor war, and many women are excited by it. Sara Ruddick, Maternal Thinking: Toward a Politics of Peace at 154-155 (1989). Moreover, images that stem from this association—such as the image of women "keeping the home fires burning" while their men go to war—can be used to perpetuate warrior culture rather than challenge it. Linking "war" to men and "peace" to women suggests that both war and maleness itself are part of the natural order. Id. at 156-157. In this way, the ethic of care can be understood as socially conservative rather than progressive. These and other critiques of cultural feminism are explored throughout the chapter.

B. THE CONNECTION THESIS: A BIOLOGICAL BASIS?

Richard A. Epstein, Gender Is for Nouns
41 DePaul L. Rev. 981, 989-990 (1992)

[B]iological differences must be taken into account in dealing with all forms of human behavior, however far removed they may appear to be from biological roots.

[C]onsider the question of differences in spatial perception. Here, the traditional account of its origins is quite persuasive. So long as there is any division of labor between the two sexes, it must be decided who will stay with the newborn child and who will venture forth to explore, to fight, and to hunt. This is true because there are clear losses to the family unit if both parents have identical tasks. In economic terms, the potential gains from specialization and trade are too large to be ignored, especially under conditions of extreme scarcity. The mere fact that the mother carries with her a supply of milk makes it clear that she is the better candidate for staying with the child, consequently leaving the male of the species to engage in a broad class of explorative activities. The nurturing instincts usually attributable to women are a set of attitudinal adaptations that reduce the cost of doing activities that help promote the survival of both her and her offspring. Although modern women operate in settings far different from those of their ancient mothers, the initial tendency still remains: If nurturing brings greater pleasure or requires lower cost for women than for men, then we should expect to see women devote a greater percentage of their resources to it than men. This specialization will endure in the aggregate and should be accepted for what it is: a healthy adaptation that works for the benefit of all concerned, and not as a sign of inferiority or disrespect.

There are offsetting adjustments in the male, for the devotion of greater mental resources to spatial arrangements at the cost of other advantages carries with it a strong reproductive payoff. The ability to give this characteristic selectively to one sex to the exclusion of the other also carries with it a strong reproductive advantage in that it is possible to leave superior endowments in all offspring. The alternative strategy, which gives the same cognitive skills and basic attitudes to all offspring, will leave both males and females at a relative disadvantage for their biologically specialized tasks, especially since there is no gain from reversing the sex roles in parenting. The other gains from specialization are still too great to be overcome. This explanation involves the interaction of social function with biological fitness. Is there any purely social explanation that can account for these differences?

Kathryn Abrams, *Social Construction, Roving Biologism, and Reasonable Women: A Response to Professor Epstein*
41 DePaul L. Rev. 1021, 1024-1028 (1992)

[O]f all the possible influences over the division of labor within the family, Professor [Richard] Epstein begins from a biological capacity that is no longer inexorably linked to differentiation. Breast milk is not, nor has it in memory been, the only alternative for nourishing infants.... To enshrine this difference as central, at a time when we have the technological capacity to generate adequate substitutes is a bit like describing the structure of contemporary society as arising from the human inability to master air travel. However, Professor Epstein argues that despite the changes wrought by contemporary technology, the critical seeds of differentiation have already been sown: Once the adaptations described "become embedded in the brain, the glacial pace of evolutionary change means that they cannot be undone in an age when infant formula is a tolerable sub-stitute for mother's milk." So it seems that these adaptations also require scrutiny.

The male adaptation is arguably more plausible, though it might still be challenged as insufficiently empirically grounded or as inadequately explained.... [I]t is not clear... why the initial division of labor arising from breastfeeding would necessarily reinforce [his explorative and spatial perception advantages]. Why should the male adventurer have more opportunity to develop these capacities than the female, who is constantly balancing and shifting her infants, or cannily judging the distance between her children and danger?

The female adaptation — the development of a gender-wide capacity for nurturance — is even more problematic. Nurturance is an attitude, an attribute of personality. Only the most extreme proponents of sociobiology... would assert that nurturance is or comes to be embodied in a particular portion of the brain....[I]t may be useful to juxtapose a countervailing explanation offered by proponents of social construction, one that reflects not only greater plausibility but the analytic complexity of such efforts.

Nurturance is an attitudinal characteristic that arises in response to certain circumstances and is passed on — to the extent that it is not a function of continuing adaptation to changing circumstances — by women watching and mothering each other. It thus becomes important to ask: To what is nurturing a necessary adaptation? It seems plausible that it was a response, at one time, to the evidently restrictive need to feed an infant, from one's own body, every few hours. But to describe it simply, and contemporarily, in this way is to overlook the numerous social and attitudinal structures that grew up to reinforce women's restriction to these tasks. These include the convictions of husbands, which may have emerged originally to protect their access to the "broad class of explorative activities" that women's childrearing labor permitted them, but continued in response to solidifying social convictions that childcare is "women's work" or that it is a sign of a husband's weakness or failure to provide if a wife with children "has to work." Nurturance may also have been an adaptation to limited opportunities for women outside the home, which began with workplaces that excluded women entirely, excluded pregnant women as unseemly or unfit, or regulated the hours of working women in deference to their "first task" in the home. In more contemporary times, women's decision to develop this aspect of their personalities may have responded to employers' failure to accommodate workers who are also parents, or spouses' failure to share the domestic tasks that fall disproportionately to mothers who continue to work. This explanation should not be understood to undercut the value of nurturance, or to deny that there are many attributes of small children that are attractive, lovable, or inducing of nurturant impulses. It is intended simply to suggest that to describe nurturance as an adaptation to the capacity to breastfeed, passed on through some variant of Lamarckian evolution is to miss many features of the social world in which human beings have evolved.

[Another] point of controversy is Professor Epstein's conclusion that because nurturance brings more pleasure or lower cost to women than men, it should be accepted as a "healthy adaptation that works to the benefit of all concerned." Setting aside the doubts previously raised about the origins of this development, this assertion makes the further error of confusing results that have some biological basis with results that are socially or normatively acceptable....The lower cost of nurturance to women...is attributable largely to the fact that, given the rigidity of familial patterns and workplace structures, many men have never been given the opportunity to develop it. Moreover, lower cost (in relation to men) should not automatically be associated with greater pleasure in nurturing for women. The increasingly audible discontent of women with the current division of labor in the family belies this conclusion, as the low pay and low social valuation of those who perform childcare in place of biological mothers belies the conclusion that the current specialization is no "sign of inferiority or disrespect."

Kingsley R. Browne, Sex and Temperament in Modern Society: A Darwinian View of the Glass Ceiling and the Gender Gap
37 Ariz. L. Rev. 971 (1995)

It is my central thesis that much of what we call the glass ceiling and gender gap is the product of basic biological sex differences in personality and temperament. These differences have resulted from differential reproductive strategies that have been adopted by the two sexes during human history and are every bit as much a product of natural selection as our bipedal locomotion and opposable thumbs. Although these temperamental traits evolved in our hunting-and-gathering ancestral environment, they remain with us today whether or not they remain adaptive....

Evolutionary theory predicts that men will tend to exhibit greater status-seeking, competitiveness, and risk-taking than women, and that women will exhibit more nurturance and affiliative behavior. These predictions are borne out in every known human society. With respect to all of these traits, the differences are statistical, in the sense that they are generalizations that do not hold true for all individuals. However, even relatively small between-group differences can have a dramatic effect on the sex ratio at the extremes. Moreover, since the glass ceiling and the gender gap in compensation are themselves both group-based phenomena, it seems appropriate to seek an explanation for them in terms of group-based traits....

It is a common observation — sometimes a complaint — that in order for women to attain the highest levels of success in the working world they must "be like men." Prominent among the qualities of successful female executives are the "male" traits of aggressiveness, ambition and drive, strong career orientation ("a passion for success"), and risk-taking. Women are consistently perceived to have a lesser level of these traits than men. Even apart from commitment to children, women as a class differ in important temperamental ways from men. Combined with women's greater commitment to families these temperamental differences have a powerful effect....

If a substantial contributor to the "glass ceiling" is the fact that women tend not to display, to the same degree that men do, the temperamental traits and accompanying behaviors that result in achieving the highest levels, then in order for women to achieve parity, something must change: either the job requirements or women themselves. Many students of the glass ceiling have advocated both changes: employers should stop rewarding driven and ambitious people, and girls should be socialized to manifest the same drive and ambition as males. For a whole host of reasons, both of these suggestions are unlikely to bear fruit.

It seems unlikely in the extreme that employers will cease rewarding employees who exhibit a high degree of commitment to the employer. All else being equal — and in the absence of some prohibition — an employer will generally prefer a worker who puts in more hours to one who puts in fewer; it will prefer a worker who will travel or relocate to one who will not; and it will prefer a worker whose career is not interrupted by lengthy absences from the labor market to one whose is. Those employees are simply more valuable. Moreover, it is a fact of life in modern America that men work more hours, are more willing to travel and relocate, and are less likely to leave the labor force for extended periods....

[T]he simplistic observation that men and women have different average earnings tells one very little, but the fact that earnings are easier to quantify and compare than other important job attributes has led to an undue focus on wage disparities. To the extent that compensation differences are due to the kinds of differences described above, it is not clear why there should be societal intervention. The studies described above suggest that if women make the same kinds of human-capital investments and occupational choices as men, their compensation will be much more similar to men's than it is now. If they choose to work fewer hours, seek less job-related training, and select jobs that have advantages that for them outweigh the lower pay, it is difficult to see why there is any need for correction. Preventing employers from giving higher pay to employees who work more hours, have greater job-related training, or occupy riskier jobs seems foolish.

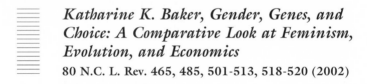

Katharine K. Baker, Gender, Genes, and Choice: A Comparative Look at Feminism, Evolution, and Economics
80 N.C. L. Rev. 465, 485, 501-513, 518-520 (2002)

Both economics and biology rely on the idea that actors, be they individuals or genes, maximize their self-interest. For an economist, this maximization process is about people choosing courses that will best accommodate their needs and desires. For a biologist, this maximization process is about genes leading people to demonstrate certain behaviors. Those behaviors will come to dominate if they end up reproducing more offspring than other kinds of behaviors. Economists explain their maximization process as one in which individuals choose to maximize their own utility. Biologists explain their maximization process as one in which genes produce certain reproductively successful behaviors. Both systems are considered rational in that the actor adopts the best means of achieving its ends. Both systems also rely on unitary metrics to determine whether those ends have been achieved....

[T]he conventional economic model of maximization requires a boundaried, self-interested, rational actor, while the biological model requires a gene, temporarily housed in a human shell, whose only goal is to perpetuate itself in other shells. The economic model also requires individuals to exercise their own agency and actively choose life courses, while in the biological model, individuals barely act at all; they react to the dictates of the genes within them. Despite the different, almost opposite, emphasis that economics and biology place on the roles of self and choice, both retain the core principle of maximization. Selves maximize utility. Behavior choices (and the genes that produce them) maximize reproductive success....

[E]volutionary biology and the economic approach to law . . . also draw critical assumptions about the meaning of stability. For both biology and economics, stability suggests equilibria. More important, . . . equilibria suggest optimality. . . .

[T]he inference of optimality from stability is pernicious. First, this inference ignores the role that the law can play in shaping preferences. . . .

The law helps shape preferences by reinforcing and/or creating and/or undermining social norms. Law and economics scholarship has recognized the importance of norms for some time, but often this scholarship has focused on norms that exist to supplant law, not norms that the law itself helps to create. The New Palgrave Dictionary of Economics and the Law describes three kinds of norms: equilibrium-selection norms, rationality-limiting norms, and preference-changing norms. The social norms of driving on the right side of the road in the United States and on the left in Britain are examples of equilibrium-selection norms. These are norms that develop in response to situations in which some equilibria are necessary for efficiency reasons, but no rational reason exists for people to prefer one norm over another. Conforming to an equilibrium-selection norm is perfectly compatible with self-interest. Rationality-limiting norms, on the other hand, are norms that keep people from doing what would be in their interest simply because society tells us that "it is not done." Norms setting expectations of politeness or norms requiring men to wear neckties would be examples of rationality-limiting norms. Preference-changing norms are norms that actually change people's preferences. One can start getting to work at 8:00 a.m. merely because everyone else does so, but then come to prefer the 8:00 a.m. arrival time.

The economic account of human interaction suggests that most norms are equilibrium-selection norms. They are norms that develop to facilitate interaction or overall welfare-maximization. Thus, an economist might well suggest that the norms surrounding gender are equilibrium-selection norms. Social norms may encourage women to be intuitive, relationship-oriented, and communitarian, while they encourage men to be rational, independent, and hierarchical, because this division of behavioral characteristics facilitates many aspects of social interaction, including (probably most importantly, but not exclusively) mating behavior. According to this account, women are better off acting feminine and doing the work that women are supposed to do and then getting rewarded by men (with resources), while men are better off competing with each other and establishing their own autonomy so that they can garner maximum resources and get the most desirable women. Conforming to gender norms is thus perfectly compatible with each individual's self-interest.

A feminist account of patriarchy, though, suggests that many gender norms are rationality-limiting norms. They are norms enforced by those that benefit from them, and they are not necessarily compatible with everyone's self-interest. Thus, a feminist would argue that those who have a stake in the status quo of gender prefer adherence to gender norms. Gender norms give men more access to social power, resources, and even reproductive opportunity. Women who try to transgress these norms by being assertive, autonomous, or "malelike" in any way are often scorned because those with social power try to ensure that everyone comes to internalize an allegiance to gender norms, even if those norms are rationality-limiting for some.

Meanwhile, the feminist normative agenda suggests that the law's role is to encourage preference-changing norms. Norms of equality and attempts to implement those norms legally, with laws like Title VII of the Civil Rights Act of 1964 and Title IX of the Education Amendments of 1970, are examples of preference-changing norms. . . .

Admittedly, on average women have traditionally expressed less of a taste for athletics than have men, just as, on average, women have demonstrated less of a taste for military training than have men. Biology explains why this would be so. Economics provides the graphs of expressed preferences that demonstrate why we therefore have the sports and military institutions that we have. But the Title IX evidence strongly suggests that whatever biological reason explains the differential in men's and women's tastes, and however our existing institutions reflect those preferences, preferences can change. Once one acknowledges the role that the law can play in changing preferences, the importance of the equilibria modeled by existing preferences and the inferences that one can draw from those equilibria decline significantly.

Jonathan Gruber's study of mandatory childbirth benefits provides another example of how legal mandates may generate preference-changing norms. Gruber's study showed that the imposition of mandatory maternity benefits terms in labor contracts did not lead (as traditional economic theory would predict that it would) to decreased employment or lower wages. As Jolls, Sunstein, and Thaler point out, these findings suggest that mandatory labor terms may do more than simply shift the labor demand curve in (because the cost of labor rises); they may simultaneously shift the labor supply curve out. In other words, without fully realizing this before the preference-changing norm was mandated, more people were willing to work if they got maternity benefits. Thus, the data suggests that women's preference for maternity benefits, like their preference for sports programs, can be affected by their sense of entitlement.

Men's preferences also can be changed. By failing to incorporate normative programs to alter preferences, those using biology to influence law tend to offer policy suggestions that accept, as given, male demand or preference for perverse behaviors. Thus, Randy Thornhill and Craig Palmer, two leading biological researchers on rape, suggest educational programs that teach young women about how "clothing and makeup . . . may influence the likelihood of rape." Owen Jones, who has written on the legal implications of evolutionary analysis for both rape and child abuse, suggests a series of preventative strategies for child abuse, all of which involve subjecting stepparents to special scrutiny. Kingsley Browne argues that sexual harassment law must accept as given the fact that men see situations as "more sexually oriented than women do" because they see the world "through sexual glasses." All of these proposals demonstrate a disturbing willingness to accept men's current inclinations to rape and abuse women and children. By focusing on genetic inclinations as given, biologists methodologically ignore the extent to which the law is capable of changing internalized norms and hence preferences.

Such a focus is too narrow. If the only goal is reducing abuse, then anyone familiar with statistics on child abuse will readily conclude that we should simply keep men away from children. Reducing abuse isn't the only goal, however. Women and children (and probably more than a few men) want to encourage men to be responsible, loving caretakers for children. Similarly, if the only goal is reducing rape, then restricting or regulating men's access to women might be a logical strategy, but the feminist goal to reduce rape is not just rooted in protecting women against potential danger and unwanted offspring. It is also rooted in getting men to respect women's physical and sexual integrity. Feminists do not want to just punish men who are inclined to rape or abuse; they want to alter those inclinations. Feminist legal reformers, like most people alive, have multiple ends. Some of these ends involve changing preferences as given, even if these preferences have a biological origin. . . .

The second reason why modeling the equilibria produced by demonstrated behavior is of little use to feminist law reform is that these models tend to discount the potential role of path dependence. Path dependence is the tendency to follow a path, not because it is a more efficient or more desirable or a more rewarding means of getting from point A to point B, but because it exists. Mark Roe uses the example of a path formed by a fur trader who pioneers a circuitous route in order to avoid wolves' dens and other natural dangers. Future travelers follow the trader's path with wagons and carriages because taking the worn path is easier. The more the path gets worn, the greater its advantage, relative to a never-worn route. Eventually, factories, homes, and towns grow up along the path even though the dangers that originally determined its route have long since disappeared.

A circuitous fur-trade-path-turned-highway suggests that the paths we take may not be optimally efficient. Instead of presuming, therefore, that given the opportunity to choose, individuals will gravitate toward optimally efficient behavior, it behooves us to analyze the potential for path dependence. According to Roe, there are three reasons why path dependence often withstands competitive pressure. The first problem is one of "imagination, of which we never have enough." The second reason is that the path taken simply did not matter that much to success, so sufficient incentive to change paths never emerged, even if an alternative might be marginally more successful. Energies were better spent elsewhere. The third reason is that various laws prohibit deviation from the standard path. All three of these explanations could explain why various women's movements and the simple evolutionary course have failed to significantly undermine our system of gender. . . .

The strong potential for path dependence with regard to gender suggests that although genetics may be able to explain our gender preferences, it does not necessarily do so. Much of evolutionary biology and neoclassical economics, and particularly the disciplines' claims with regard to gender, are unfalsifiable. Path dependence explanations are comparably unfalsifiable, but that just means that one must be careful to explore all potential explanations before relying too much on either economics or biology. . . .

In the biologist's world, women's sacrifice is normal, if not chosen. Embracing vulnerability will often mean reproductive success for women. Thus, the old legal model assumed women's vulnerability in a way that squelched women's potential autonomy. In the economist's world, women's vulnerability is chosen and therefore legitimate, outside the scope of the law's concern. Thus, the new legal model simply lets women continually choose conditions of dependence. In a feminist world, the law helps eradicate women's vulnerability for at least two reasons. First, women may put themselves in positions of dependence mostly because path restrictions and rationality-limiting norms take away any realistic options they have to choose otherwise. Second, regardless of whether women have meaningful opportunities to avoid dependence, women's investment in others creates value for which they should be compensated. The law must be concerned with women's vulnerability because we have strong reasons to question whether that vulnerability is "normal" or "chosen." But even if it is "normal" or "chosen," the failure to compensate for the contributions women make to others is normatively unacceptable.

If women sacrifice their own potential independence because sex discrimination makes that independence seem like a distant dream and everyone's imagination is limited, or because rationality-limiting norms ridicule them for defying gender stereotypes, or because by asserting their independence they put too much else in jeopardy, then they are making choices that they would not make in a world with different norms and laws. As discussed above, the law can play a role in changing those norms so that women have alternatives to self-sacrifice. To the extent that norms scorn the woman who may preference her job over her family, but scorn the man who takes paternity leave or sacrifices his own career opportunities, we encourage women's dependence. Biologists may say that social norms now just replicate what was a matter of evolutionary necessity, but the important point is that social norms are malleable. At present, social constructions of gender give different social meaning to the same acts of parental and marital sacrifice. For women, sacrificing their marketability is an expression of love. For men, enhancing their marketability (and thereby providing better for their families) is an expression of love. Social norms give women an incentive to be vulnerable and men an incentive not to be, even though women have no biological reason to render themselves vulnerable anymore. The law's job is to undermine those social norms if they reinforce undesired inequality.

The second reason why the law must be concerned with why women choose conditions of dependence is that often these conditions of dependence are absolutely essential to the institutions societies tend to hold dear, most significantly, parenting and marriage. If women are disproportionately responsible for holding these institutions together, it is only fair to compensate them for doing so. Biologist Robert Trivers' "cruel bind" analysis suggests that human females may have had to make familial investments once because if they did not, their children would perish. Because men could force women to shoulder a disproportionate share of the burden of parenting, they did. More recent feminist analysis suggests that those evolutionary conditions now replicate themselves through social norms and gender. As Joan Williams writes, "Women know that if they do not sacrifice no one will, whereas men assume that if they do not, women will." Medical advances now ensure that a child can survive just as easily with male parental investment as with female, but women continually make the sacrifices that men do not. Women may do this because, as a matter of evolutionary adaptation, it was advantageous for them to do so, but there is no reason for their role to now stay static. As Trivers himself acknowledges, the disproportionate burden placed on the investing parent is "cruel."

To be sure, women serve their own ends when they invest in the relationships that they nurture. This is why the radically subjective economists often ignore or deem acceptable women's disproportionate investment. If a woman's familial investment increases her utility (regardless of what her investment is relative to a man's), then the investment is not problematic to the economist. But women generate significant positive communal benefits when they invest in marriage and children. Society in general and families in particular benefit from women's familial investments. These benefits often get lost, however, in the economic and biological accounts that focus on individual, not collective, well-being, and they get subordinated, if not undermined, in analyses that rely on unitary metrics.

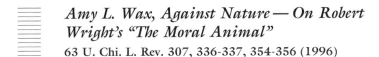

Amy L. Wax, *Against Nature — On Robert Wright's "The Moral Animal"*
63 U. Chi. L. Rev. 307, 336-337, 354-356 (1996)

Lessons of sociobiology align with fundamental precepts of social conservatism for three reasons. First, although an evolutionary approach does not require denying the efficacy of concerted social intervention to influence behavior — indeed, it explains why such social intervention is a common feature of communal life — it identifies the main obstacles to radical social change as lying within the individual rather than outside of him. It posits unavoidable trade-offs ultimately grounded in biological nature — between freedom and order, desire and well-being, and stability and equality — that confront every melioristic or utopian project. Second, sociobiology suggests that the observed superiority of some traditional institutions (such as the two-parent family) in performing certain functions (such as raising children) does not stem from the arbitrary decision to "privilege" those institutions (although they have indeed been privileged in law and custom). Rather, the functional superiority is the product of features inherent to the institutions as they respond to our biological endowments. Third, sociobiology points to the importance of moral climate and "cultural values" in fostering behaviors that make for a peaceful and prosperous society. . . .

The picture of human psychology that emerges from the study of evolution suggests that projects for social change have the greatest chance of success if framed as attempts to create norms of acceptable or commendable behavior. Changing norms will likely prove more important than effecting purely external or structural changes in institutions on the one hand, or transforming individual personality or fundamental preference structures on the other. Rather than justifying the ends to which the techniques of social control can be applied, these insights invite us to view the "moralization" of conduct as a method that can be put to many uses.

These observations are applicable to a range of social issues from drunk driving to parenting to teen pregnancy. They also have implications for the common feminist aspiration of greater equality for the sexes inside and outside of marriage. If conventional monogamy can be enforced "against nature," why not the feminist ideal? If civilization exists to frustrate natural preferences, it could as well be feminist civilization as any other. . . .

[T]he most efficacious approach to the quest for greater sexual equality would not be one primarily directed at working a fundamental change in men's "primary" tastes and preferences. It would not necessarily have to await the emergence of a greater impulse for "nurturing" or a diminished attraction to competition in the male population. Rather than focusing on such transformations of feelings or attitudes, the focus should be on cultivating social expectations that play to the sense of moral duty and social obligation. . . . The most effective "nonsexist" upbringing may not consist of getting boys to play with dolls, but in defining proper conduct as fulfilling the duties of helpfulness, caring, and fairness, and in instilling egalitarian expectations concerning compliance with those duties.

Notes

1. Cultural Feminist Explanations for Women's Ethic of Care. There are a number of sociological and psychological theories to explain the apparent association between women and an ethic of care, touching all points along the spectrum from purely biological to purely cultural explanations. In emphasizing the role of pregnancy and breast-feeding and the "invasive" aspects of sexual intercourse for women, Robin West seems to share Richard Epstein's reliance on biological foundations. Do these two theorists use "biology" in the same way?

Other feminist theorists combine socialization theories with psychological theories, surmising that women's ethic of care is deeply imprinted in their psyches by childhood experience. One decades-old version of this hypothesis is that because mothers raise children in this society, boys develop by separating from their differently gendered mothers, thus reinforcing values of separation and individual identity; girls, on the other hand, develop by identifying with their mothers to whom they remain connected, thus reinforcing values of relationship and communal identity. See Nancy Chodorow, The Reproduction of Mothering: Psychoanalysis and the Sociology of Gender (1978); see also Patrice DiQuinzio, The Impossibility of Motherhood: Feminism, Individualism, and the Problem of Mothering xiii (1999). Philosopher Sara Ruddick acknowledges an identifiably "female" perspective on the world, but locates its source in the social practice of "mothering," which she argues is potentially gender-neutral. Sara Ruddick, Maternal Thinking: Toward a Politics of Peace (1989). In Ruddick's view, both men and women can be mothers, and not all women are mothers (although she recognizes that most women have at least considered mothering as a likely part of their lives).

Is there a specifically "female" experience of the world? If so, what is its source? Does it matter whether the source is biological, cultural, or a combination of the two? Robin West suggests that what matters most is that the difference between male and female experience, values, and commitments is real:

> It truly would be extremely odd, as [Gilligan] argued, if it turned out that the vastly greater amount of child raising and homekeeping, the world over and throughout history, in which women engage — a fact apparently conceded by all — has *no impact whatsoever* on the moral orientations of the two sexes. Similarly it really would be extremely odd if it turned out that our shared experience as infants and children under the protection and tutelage and love of *women* — our shared experiences derived from the fact that we are all *to woman* born — also has *no* differentiating effect or impact on the way the two sexes view relational ethics. It would be odd if it turned out that the experiences of pregnancy and childbirth, shared by the majority of all women everywhere, have no effect, and lend to women's perspectives no unifying and distinguishing threads. The null hypothesis, if we are questioning sameness or difference, might more defensibly be identified as the claim of difference, rather than the claim of sameness, in the face of these quite different early experiences of the world.

Robin West, Caring for Justice 18-19 (1997). Does this raise problems of essentialism, raised in Chapter 6?

2. The Normative Implications of the Evolutionary Thesis. The controversial question of whether and to what extent differences between men and women are rooted in biology has produced an extensive scientific literature — too extensive to permit even a representative sampling. Without the opportunity to fully explore the research, the question for this chapter will have to be not *whether* the premises of evolutionary biology (also called "developmental biology" and "sociobiology") are true, but rather *what follows* if they are true.

To Richard Epstein, different personality types and social roles are a matter of efficiency — nature's efficiency. Efforts to change the instincts that have emerged as adaptive behaviors are simply inefficient. Kingsley Browne, while he states that there are no "necessary" implications, makes it clear that once the "glass ceiling" or the gender gap in women's earnings is explained as a product of natural selection processes, there is no longer sex discrimination for which a legal remedy is necessary. Elsewhere he states that efforts to prohibit sexual harassment are doomed, insofar as they go "against the grain" of human psychology. See Browne, An Evolutionary Perspective of Sexual Harassment: Seeking Roots in Biology Rather than Ideology, 8 J. Contemp. Legal Issues 5 (1997); see also Kingsley R. Browne, Women at War: An Evolutionary Perspective, 49 Buff. L. Rev. 51, 56 (2001) (using evolutionary psychology and the literature of sex-linked cognitive and behavioral differences to challenge the assumption that "all it will take to integrate women into combat roles is educating men out of their ideology of masculinism") (excerpt set forth in Chapter 3, p. 626.)

To George Gilder, the traditional two-parent nuclear family is the answer, for it is the only way women can channel men's roving sexual impulses toward the good of the family and, by extension, the good of society as a whole.

A man without a woman has a deep inner sense of dispensability, perhaps evolved during the millennia of service in the front lines of tribal defense. He is sexually optional. Several dominant males could impregnate all the women and perpetuate the tribe. It is this sense of dispensability that makes young men good fighters, good crusaders, good martyrs. But it also weakens the male ability to care deeply and long and stunts young men's sense of the preciousness of human beings. Because the woman has always been directly responsible for infants and almost always exclusively responsible, she is dubious about the dying and killing that have surrounded male activities.

Once the man marries he can change. He has to change, for his wife will not long have him if he remains in spirit a single man. He must settle his life, and commit it to the needs of raising a family. He must exchange the moral and spiritual rhythms of the hunt for a higher, more extended mode of sexual life. He must submit, ethically and sexually, to the values of maternal morality and futurity.

Gilder, Men and Marriage 15-16 (1986). To Gilder, the problem with women pursuing employment outside the home is not only that children need their mothers' care but also that unless men's energies are directed toward the long-term goal of providing for their families, their sexual energies and aggressions will necessarily be turned against society. Id. at 153.

In opposing an evolutionary perspective, Catharine MacKinnon seems to agree with the premise of some of its advocates that the perspective would justify the status quo:

> The point of human nature theories . . . is to attribute a fixed bottom line, an unchangeability that we must live within and keep in view, a baseline that no choice or policy can alter. These theories set limits, telling us that "there have always been" certain things, as if no further explanation is needed, certainly not a social one; as if the fact that "there have always been" certain things necessarily points to biology. This assumption, while not justified, does not in itself make such theories false, but the variability of sexual facts across and within cultures and times, as well as the fact that the particular limits thus asserted reinscribed the unequal gendered social status quo, tends to undermine their claim to being prior to society. In other words, theories that attempt to explain facts of women's inequality to men — say, rape or prostitution or sexual harassment or pornography — in terms of human nature are first and last theories of what women must put up with.

Catharine A. MacKinnon, Pornography Left and Right, 30 Harv. C.R.-C.L. L. Rev. 143, 151-152 (1995).

Other feminists agree with Amy Wax in the reading above that the characteristics directly produced (according to sociobiology) by the sexually dimorphic scramble to keep one's genes alive are not givens that must be accepted, but rather potential threats to the moral order that society has the power to harness and control. The view that "description" is not "prescription" and that what "is" is not the same as what "ought to be" is the prevailing one among a growing school of legal scholars who have insisted that knowledge of behavioral biology is essential for the law to operate effectively and efficiently. See, e.g., Owen D. Jones & Timothy H. Goldsmith, Law and Behavioral Biology, 105 Colum. L. Rev. 405 (2005); Owen D. Jones, Law and the Biology of Rape: Reflections on

Transitions, 11 Hastings Women's L.J. 151 (2000); Owen D. Jones, Sex, Culture, and the Biology of Rape: Toward Explanation and Prevention, 87 Cal. L. Rev. 827 (1999); see also Symposia, Biology and Sexual Aggression, 39 Jurimetrics 133, 243 (Fall & Winter 1999).

Most feminists agree with Wax that even if evolutionary theory explains some behaviors, it does not define appropriate social norms.

> The most critical development in our evolutionary past may be not so much the development of any particular behavior or trait, but the ability to reshape our behavior with others. As our biological knowledge grows, we are almost certain to find that our genes create the capacity for various behaviors and virtues, with love, loyalty, and commitment among them, but that these values do not happen automatically. Instead, the right conditions in childhood, including parent-child attachment, family stability, appropriate role models, and education, prime the neural pathways that allow[] some behavior to develop and become deeply ingrained. Over longer periods of time, the prevalence of certain norms within a group can favor the passing on of the genes associated with that behavior, so that these genes, whether they are the genes that control the ability to learn, the discipline to conform behavior to norms, or the tendency to [do] so with a minimum of external coercion, become more common over time.

June Carbone & Naomi Cahn, The Biological Basis of Commitment: Does One Size Fit All?, 25 Women's Rts. L. Rep. 223, 247-248 (2004). See also Katharine K. Baker, Biology for Feminists, 75 Chi.-Kent L. Rev. 805, 806-807 (2000) (biology forces feminist to "embrace our normative convictions"); Wax, supra, at 329-330 ("[M]an does indeed have tendencies, some stronger, more pervasive, and more 'hard wired' than others. To say that, however, is not to say that the tendencies cannot be curbed or overcome by the forces of culture or morality.").

One could differ, of course, about what the moral principles should be that should guide society's response to the biological givens—i.e., whether they should be guided by Gilder's sense of gender role order, Wax's "feminist ideal," Carbone's and Cahn's "virtues" or love, loyalty, and commitment, or some other set of principles. Does sociobiological analysis add anything to the choice between social ideals?

3. Evolutionary Biology: The Feminist Critique. Although some feminists have been willing to work within the basic premises of evolutionary biology, others—as exemplified by the Abrams reading—have been negative. Formal equality feminists tend to downplay differences, biological or otherwise, and to emphasize similarities and thus the need for equal treatment. Biological differences are harder to deny than other differences. Nevertheless, formal equality advocates conclude that many characteristics that appear as differences—even pregnancy—are similar enough to a common human condition not unique to women (e.g., disability). Thus, even biological differences are not assumed to justify different treatment.

Substantive equality theorists highlight sex-based differences, but treat them as handicaps rather than as strengths, and insist that the law has the obligation to make accommodations so that their differences do not result in unequal outcomes for women.

The dominance theory account of these differences is one of social construction, not biological determinism, and their objective is not to "accommodate" women's differences, biological or otherwise, but to eliminate the subordination that results when these differences are manipulated to legitimize and perpetuate male power over women.

Relational feminists approach the issue of biology with some ambivalence. Unlike formal equality theorists, they highlight rather than minimize difference, even biological difference, as a source of strength and diversity. But while substantive equality theorists are concerned about how ignoring difference perpetuates sexual subordination, relational feminists are concerned about the loss to society of devaluing perspectives that would improve community and its moral integrity and cohesion. That some of these perspectives may be biologically based helps relational theorists establish the actual existence of differences that formal equality advocates want to deny. But insofar as these theorists seek a blueprint for a less combative and more interconnected and caring world, proving that gender difference is biologically based can be, if anything, an impediment, since it would seem to require working—in Amy Wax's terms—"against nature."

Can evolutionary theory support feminist purposes? See also Julie A. Seaman, Form and (Dys)Function in Sexual Harassment Law: Biology, Culture, and the Spandrels of Title VII, 37 Ariz. St. L.J. 321 (2005) (evolutionary theories mean that sexual harassment is "because of" the victim's sex, and that employers should be held responsible for allowing workplace conditions that are likely to give rise to typical harassment behaviors).

C. THE LEGAL IMPLICATIONS OF THE "ETHIC OF CARE"

1. Relational Values in Substantive Law

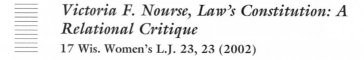

Victoria F. Nourse, Law's Constitution: A Relational Critique
17 Wis. Women's L.J. 23, 23 (2002)

It is a simple fact: we begin from others. Without others we, quite literally, could not live, feel, be born. Every mother, every mother's partner, every father, every child, knows this. But law sees these relations as something lesser, as foreign. Mention the word "relationship" to the average lawyer and she will likely assume that you are talking about sex, dating, or perhaps marriage. She may even wonder what "relationship" has to do with the law at all.

. . . I wonder whether it is possible to flip that equation, to think of the relational as central, rather than peripheral, to law's most ambitious public projects.

Leslie Bender, A Lawyer's Primer on Feminist Theory and Tort
38 J. Legal Educ. 3, 31-36 (1988)

Negligence law could begin with Gilligan's articulation of the feminine voice's ethic of care — a premise that no one should be hurt. We could convert the present standard of "care of a reasonable person under the same or similar circumstances" to a standard of "conscious care and concern of a responsible neighbor or social acquaintance for another under the same or similar circumstances."...

The recognition that we are all interdependent and connected and that we are by nature social beings who must interact with one another should lead us to judge conduct as tortious when it does not evidence responsible care or concern for another's safety, welfare, or health. Tort law should begin with a premise of responsibility rather than rights, of interconnectedness rather than separation, and a priority of safety rather than profit or efficiency. The masculine voice of rights, autonomy, and abstraction has led to a standard that protects efficiency and profit; the feminine voice can design a tort system that encourages behavior that is caring about others' safety and responsive to others' needs or hurts, and that attends to human contexts and consequences....

One of the most difficult areas in which questions of duty and the standard of care arise is the "no duty to rescue" case. The problem is traditionally illustrated by the drowning-stranger hypothetical and the infamous case of Yania v. Bigan.[117]...

Each year that I teach torts I watch again as a majority of my students initially find this legal "no duty" rule reprehensible. After the rationale is explained and the students become immersed in the "reasoned" analysis, and after they take a distanced, objective posture informed by liberalism's concerns for autonomy and liberty, many come to accept the legal rule that intuitively had seemed so wrong to them. They are taught to reject their emotions, instincts, and ethics, and to view accidents and tragedies abstractly, removed from their social and particularized contexts, and to apply instead rationally-derived universal principles and a vision of human nature as atomistic, self-interested, and as free from constraint as possible. They are also taught that there are legally relevant distinctions between acts and omissions.

How would this drowning-stranger hypothetical look from a new legal perspective informed by a feminist ethic based upon notions of caring, responsibility, interconnectedness, and cooperation? If we put abstract reasoning and autonomy aside momentarily, we can see what else matters. In defining duty, what matters is that someone, a human being, a part of us, is drowning and will die without some

---

117. [155 A.2d 343 (1959)]. Yania was a business competitor of Bigan and had gone onto Bigan's land to speak with him. Both men were involved in strip-mining, and Bigan was working at a deep trench partially filled with water. Although the facts are ambiguous, there was testimony that Bigan dared or cajoled Yania to jump into the pit, in which he drowned as Bigan looked on. It is equally possible that Yania jumped into the pit to demonstrate to Bigan his expertise in solving the problem there. In either case, Yania drowned and Yania's widow sued Bigan. She lost. The Pennsylvania Supreme Court refused to impose an affirmative duty on one party to rescue or aid another.

affirmative action. That seems more urgent, more imperative, more important than any possible infringement of individual autonomy by the imposition of an affirmative duty. If we think about the stranger as a human being for a moment, we may realize that much more is involved than balancing one person's interest in having his life saved and another's interest in not having affirmative duties imposed upon him in the absence of a special relationship, although even then the balance seems to me to weigh in favor of imposing a duty or standard of care that requires action. The drowning stranger is not the only person affected by the lack of care. He is not detached from everyone else. He no doubt has people who care about him — parents, spouse, children, friends, colleagues; groups he participates in — religious, social, athletic, artistic, political, educational, work-related; he may even have people who depend upon him for emotional or financial support. He is interconnected with others. If the stranger drowns, many will be harmed. It is not an isolated event with one person's interests balanced against another's. When our legal system trains us to understand the drowning-stranger story as a limited event between two people, both of whom have interests at least equally worth protecting, and when the social ramifications we credit most are the impositions on personal liberty of action, we take a human situation and translate it into a cold, dehumanized algebraic equation. We forget that we are talking about human death or grave physical harms and their reverberating consequences when we equate the consequences with such things as one person's momentary freedom not to act. People are decontextualized for the analysis, yet no one really lives an acontextual life. . . .

If instead we impose a duty of acting responsibly with the same self-conscious care for the safety of others that we would give our neighbors or people we know, we require the actor to consider the human consequences of her failure to rescue. . . .

The duty to act with care for another's safety, which under appropriate circumstances would include an affirmative duty to act to protect or prevent harm to another, would be shaped by the particular context. One's ability to aid and one's proximity to the need would be relevant considerations. Whether one met that duty would not be determined by how a reasonable person would have acted under the circumstances but by whether one acted out of a conscious care and concern for the safety, health, and well-being of the victim in the way one would act out of care for a neighbor or friend. . . . This seemingly minor change would transform the core of negligence law to a human, responsive system.

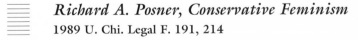

Richard A. Posner, Conservative Feminism
1989 U. Chi. Legal F. 191, 214

[M]ost people are what they are; most neighbors are not caring, and most accident victims are not neighbors. Human nature will not be altered by holding injurers liable for having failed to take the care that a caring neighbor would have taken. The only effect of adopting Bender's proposal would be to shift negligence liability in the direction of strict liability. Her "caring neighbor" is an unnecessary step in the analysis. Bender might as well argue directly for strict liability on the ground that it is the more altruistic regime than negligence.

Is it? Strict liability is sometimes defended on the ground that it provides more compensation to more accident victims. This is a partial analysis. Strict liability can also result in higher prices, and the burden may be borne by consumers. The net distributive impact is unclear. If these complications are ignored, maybe a feminine outlook on law could be expected to stress compensation — obviously Bender associates altruism with women. On the other hand, strict liability is more rule-like, less standard-like, less contextualist, less sensitive to the particulars of the individual accident, than negligence is; in that respect it is the more masculine standard.

Notes

1. "Mainstreaming" the Ethic of Care in the Law. Difference theory has been deployed both as a critique that existing law ignores women-associated values, and as the basis for the affirmative case for making women-associated values more present in the law. As critique and as substantive reform agenda, difference theory has been applied to virtually every area of the law.

For example, feminist critiques have examined procedural and evidentiary issues and argued that procedural rules often incorporate gendered priorities into the legal system. Judith Resnik examines judicial tasks denoted by the gendered term "housekeeping" (as in "mere housekeeping"), which are reassigned from Article III judges to Article I judges or to state courts, refused appellate review, and in other ways given less attention and status in the judicial system. Housekeeping matters tend to involve more fact-finding rather than abstract legal analysis, as well as "the complex and messy activity of interacting with litigants, witnesses, and lawyers." They also include a disproportionate number of cases such as prisoner petitions and social security cases that are tedious and mundane. See Resnik, Housekeeping: The Nature and Allocation of Work in Federal Trial Courts, 24 Ga. L. Rev. 909, 945, 960-961 (1990). Resnik advocates "[r]etrieving — without romanticizing — the importance of 'humble' activities, acknowledging the power in the work of maintenance and of the organization of daily structures, and reallocating obligations for caretaking," id. at 957, a process that entails "identifying, understanding, reassessing, and reallocating 'housekeeping' — the daily, sometimes powerful, poignant, and compelling, sometimes repetitive and non-engaging, activities that nourish oneself and others." Id. at 964. See also Resnik, "Naturally" Without Gender: Women, Jurisdiction, and the Federal Courts, 66 N.Y.U. L. Rev. 1682, 1698-1699 (1991) (arguing that many jurisdictional rules assumed (wrongly) to be "natural," including the "domestic relations" exception to federal jurisdiction in diversity cases, reflect an official hierarchy of legal issues in which women's concerns come last). Related critiques concerning the practices of judging, dispute resolution, criminal sentencing, civil remedies, and legal reasoning are explored later in this chapter.

Among those using difference theory to propose changes to the law of evidence, see Aviva Orenstein, Apology Excepted: Incorporating a Feminist Analysis

Into Evidence Policy Where You Would Least Expect It, 28 Sw. U. L. Rev. 113 (1999) (proposing new "apology exception" to evidentiary rule relating to admissions by party-opponents, based on feminist relational values); Kit Kinports, Evidence Engendered, 1991 U. Ill. L. Rev. 413 (criticizing evidence law for characteristics, such as abstractness, formality, hierarchy, and adversarialness, that tend both to institutionalize female disadvantage in concrete cases and to reinforce values that are not congenial to many women); Rosemary C. Hunter, Gender in Evidence: Masculine Norms vs. Feminist Reforms, 19 Harv. Women's L.J. 127, 129 (1996) (criticizing rules of evidence for, among other things, privileging "fact over value, reason over emotion, presence over absence, physical over psychological, perception over intuition").

Tax law has been a particularly lively area for exploration of relational justice themes. Marjorie Kornhauser defends progressive income tax rules from a "female voice" perspective that emphasizes interdependence and altruism. See Kornhauser, The Rhetoric of the Anti-Progressive Income Tax Movement: A Typical Male Reaction, 86 Mich. L. Rev. 465 (1987); see also Edward McCaffery, Taxing Women (1997) (proposing tax reforms to facilitate women's choices to both work and bear family responsibilities) (discussed in Chapter 2, pp. 248-249).

In a pioneering article in business law, Kathleen A. Lahey and Sarah W. Salter challenge the "patriarchal nature of the dominations upon which corporate culture depends" and urge legal reforms in corporate law that reflect "the ethics of care, responsibility, connection and sharing" and that are organized about "the values of contextuality, continuity, and holistic participation." See Kathleen A. Lahey & Sarah W. Salter, Corporate Law in Legal Theory and Legal Scholarship: From Classicism to Feminism, 23 Osgoode Hall L.J. 543, 555-556, 570 (1985); see also Kellye Y. Testy, Capitalism and Freedom — For Whom?: Feminist Legal Theory and Progressive Corporate Law, 67 L. & Contemp. Probs. 87, 99 (2004) (urging union of progressive corporate law and feminist legal theory, which articulates "a normative vision of the relationship between life and law, one that prescribes a moral vision for social ordering, based upon the principles of equality and human flourishing"); Theresa A. Gabaldon, Assumptions About Relationships Reflected in the Federal Securities Laws, 17 Wis. Women's L.J. 215 (2002) (examining role of relationships in the context of federal securities laws); Barbara Ann White, Feminist Foundations for the Law of Business: One Law and Economics Scholar's Survey and (Re)View, 10 UCLA Women's L.J. 39 (1999) (urging feminist methods of recognizing the excluded voice and the feminist ethic of care in business law, which she finds consistent with law and economics principles).

International law scholars attempt to bring women's values into the processes of international lawmaking and practice. See, e.g., Rosa Ehrenreich Brooks, Feminism and International Law: An Opportunity for Transformation, 14 Yale J.L. & Feminism 345 (2002); Hilary Charlesworth & Christine Chinkin, The Boundaries of International Law (2000); Karen Engle, International Human Rights and Feminism: When Discourses Meet, 13 Mich. J. Int'l L. 517 (1992).

Other proposals abound. In labor law, Marion Crain advocates "feminized" labor unions to achieve collective empowerment for working women based on values of connection and community rather than separation and autonomy. See Marion Crain, Feminizing Unions: Challenging the Gendered Structure of Wage Labor, 89 Mich. L. Rev. 1155, 1198 (1991); Marion Crain, Images of Power in Labor Law: A Feminist Deconstruction, 33 B.C. L. Rev. 481, 486 (1992). Debora L. Threedy draws on relational feminism to promote the notion of relational contract. Threedy, Feminists and Contract Doctrine, 32 Ind. L. Rev. 1247 (1999). Ann Hubbard invokes the ethic of care in proposing how best to interpret provisions of the American with Disabilities Act. See Hubbard, The Myth of Independence and the Major Life Activity of Caring, 8 J. Gender, Race & Justice 327 (2004). Susan Stefan urges that the law of competence applied in cases involving such matters as guardianships, medical treatment decisions, and the validity of divorce separation agreements move beyond current assumptions about rational decision making that better reflect men's concepts of rationality and positions of autonomy than women's. See Stefan, Silencing the Different Voice: Competence, Feminist Theory and Law, 47 U. Miami L. Rev. 763 (1993). Others use ethic of care principles to promote various agendas sometimes associated through the umbrella term of "ecofeminism," including environmental justice, animal rights, and international world peace. See, e.g., Robert R.M. Verchick, In a Greener Voice: Feminist Theory and Environmental Justice, 19 Harv. Women's L.J. 23 (1996); Beyond Animal Rights: A Feminist Caring Ethic for the Treatment of Animals (Josephine Donovan & Carol J. Adams eds., 1996); Bringing Peace Home: Feminism, Violence, and Nature (Karen J. Warren & Duane L. Cady eds., 1996).

Updating Leslie Bender's case for the duty to rescue, see Nancy Levit, The Kindness of Strangers: Interdisciplinary Foundations of a Duty to Act, 40 Washburn L.J. 463 (2001).

2. The Feminist Critique of Relational Justice Theory. Linda C. McClain catalogs the major feminist objections to legal theories based on an ethic of care. Most of these criticisms fall into one of two categories: (1) an ethic of care is an impractical and unworkable foundation for law, and (2) an ethic of care is bad for women. See McClain, "Atomistic Man" Revisited: Liberalism, Connection, and Feminist Jurisprudence, 65 S. Cal. L. Rev. 1171, 1196-1202 (1992). McClain concludes that the voice of care is important, but is better attributed to liberal humanist values than specifically "female" values. Her point is that there is room within liberal theory for debate about these values and that rather than forcing a "stark pick between mothering and contract, or care and justice, or connection and separation," feminists should engage in dialogue about how their insights about interdependency, connection, and responsibility can be incorporated within the liberal legal system. "[P]rinciples of justice, equality, and autonomy can coexist with and inform care and responsibility, just as care and connection, for both liberals and feminists, aid in the pursuit of justice." McClain, supra, at 1263.

Joan Tronto echoes this theme, arguing that "we need to stop talking about 'women's morality' and start talking instead about a care ethic that includes the values traditionally associated with women." Joan C. Tronto, Moral Boundaries: A Political Argument for an Ethic of Care 3 (1993).

Is this gender-neutral approach appealing? Consider the following:

[S]ome who have been attracted by the advantages of an ethic of care have argued that it has non-gender-based sources and could be adopted as a "humanist" approach to law, that is, one that promotes the value of caring apart from any language of gender relations. Frankly, while I am sympathetic to feminists who make this argument, I believe it is politically, theoretically, and factually unsound to move women from center stage in this proposed reconstruction of legal and ethical discourse based on an ethic of care. Interpersonal caregiving is something that women have specialized in for years. We have special knowledge and insights to offer. After many, many years of being submerged, we have finally come above the surface and caught our long-awaited breath. The air tastes good. A change to "humanism," I fear, will ultimately press us under water again. While we clearly must be very cautious about perpetuating disempowering or disadvantaging stereotypes, the move from "women" to "human" seems to dupe us into an even worse co-optation of being reabsorbed, resilenced, and resubmerged into a newly invisible system of male dominance. Consequently, I reject critiques of a gender-based ethic of care that locate the ethic of care in a humanist approach.

Leslie Bender, From Gender Difference to Feminist Solidarity: Using Carol Gilligan and an Ethic of Care in Law, 15 Vt. L. Rev. 1, 40 (1990). For agreement on this point, see Linda J. Lacey, Mimicking the Words, but Missing the Message: The Misuse of Cultural Feminist Themes in Religion and Family Law Jurisprudence, 35 B.C. L. Rev. 1, 46 (1993) (argues that the problem is not that cultural feminism is bad for women or that it but that it is often misapplied — for example, as a basis for opposing abortion rights or for reimposing fault standards in divorce law). Is there middle ground? See Robin West, Caring for Justice 20 (1997) (arguing that it is true both that "the experiences that inform an ethic of care are largely the caregiving experiences of women" and that "men as well as women can and should employ such an ethic").

3. Are Women More Ethical Lawyers than Men? Patricia Hatamyar and Kevin M. Simmons examined the imposition of disciplinary sanctions against lawyers. The sample for the study included attorney discipline cases in all fifty states and the District of Columbia that actually resulted in some kind of adverse public sanction in the calendar year 2000. Hatamyar & Simmons, Are Women More Ethical Lawyers?, 31 Fla. St. U. L. Rev. 785 (2004). The study found a highly significant difference in the overall rates at which male and female attorneys were disciplined. Based on the proportions of men and women in the attorney population as a whole, one would expect that about 76.4 percent of the disciplined attorneys would be male and 23.6 percent would be female. In fact, the study found 88.3 percent of the disciplined attorneys were male and 11.7 percent were female. In other words, less than half the number of female attorneys who would be expected to be disciplined based on their representation in the profession were actually sanctioned. Male lawyers had disproportionately high rates of discipline in all but four states, and for almost every category of violation.

The authors explore possible reasons for the differences, including that: (1) that the year 2000 might not have been representative; (2) disciplinary agencies might treat women differently than men; (3) men may be more likely to engage in the types of legal practice that have high rates of grievances; (4) the average age of female attorneys is less than that of male attorneys and age might correlate positively with the incidence of discipline; (5) women might have a lower substance abuse rate and might be more likely to seek professional help for depression; (6) female attorneys may be less motivated by monetary gain than male attorneys; (7) women may be more cautious as a result of perceived discrimination; and (8) due to innate and/or socialized differences, women may be less likely than men to do things that make clients and peers angry enough to file a grievance. According to the authors, research in other disciplines suggests biological and social gender differences (such as women's better communication skills) that might lead clients to be more satisfied, or at least less aggravated, with female attorneys.

Based on your experience, is any of this plausible? Which hypotheses seem most worth testing? For other claimed differences, see pp. 698-701.

Some have argued that the feminist ethic of care would support changes to the professional code of ethics for lawyers. See, e.g., Rachel Vogelstein, Confidentiality vs. Care: Re-evaluating the Duty to Self, Client, and Others, 92 Geo. L.J. 153 (2003). What do you suppose those changes would be?

2. Taking Women's Work Seriously

≡≡≡≡
≡≡≡≡ *Martha Albertson Fineman, Cracking the*
≡≡≡≡ *Foundational Myths: Independence,*
≡≡≡≡ *Autonomy, and Self-Sufficiency*
≡≡≡≡ 8 Am. U. J. Gender Soc. Pol'y & L. 13, 16-27 (1999)

It is puzzling, as well as paradoxical, that the term dependency has such negative connotations [in political discourse]. Its very existence prompts and justifies mean spirited and ill-conceived political responses, such as the recent welfare "reform." Far from being pathological, avoidable, and the result of individual failings, dependency is a universal and inevitable part of the human development. It is inherent in the human condition.

All of us were dependent as children, and many of us will be dependent as we age, become ill, or suffer disabilities. In this sense, dependency is "inevitable" and not deserving of condemnation or stigma. Note that the examples I have chosen to illustrate this category of inevitable dependency are biological or physical in nature. Biological dependencies, however, do not exhaust the potential range of situations of dependence. For example, in addition to biological dependence, one may be psychologically or emotionally dependent on others. In fact, these other forms of dependence may even accompany the physiological or biological dependence, which I have labeled inevitable. But economic, psychological, and emotional dependency are not generally understood to be universally experienced. As a result, assertions about their inevitability in each individual's life would be controversial. It is the characteristic of universality (which indisputably accompanies inevitable dependence) that is central to my argument for societal or collective responsibility. In other words, the realization that biological dependency is both inevitable and universal is theoretically important. Upon this foundational realization is built my claim for justice — the demand that society value and accommodate the labor done by the caretakers of inevitable dependants.

I argue that the caretaking work creates a collective or societal debt. Each and every member of society is obligated by this debt. Furthermore, this debt transcends individual circumstances. In other words, we need not be elderly, ill, or children any longer to be held individually responsible. Nor can we satisfy or discharge our collective responsibility within our individual, private families. Merely being financially generous with our own mothers or duly supporting our own wives will not suffice to satisfy our share of the societal debt generally owed to all caretakers.

My argument that the caretaking debt is a collective one is based on the fact that biological dependency is inherent to the human condition, and therefore, of necessity of collective or societal concern. Just as individual dependency needs must be met if an individual is to survive, collective dependency needs must be met if a society is to survive and perpetuate itself. The mandate that the state (collective society) respond to dependency, therefore, is not a matter of altruism or empathy (which are individual responses often resulting in charity), but one that is primary and essential because such a response is fundamentally society-preserving.

If infants or ill persons are not cared for, nurtured, nourished, and perhaps loved, they will perish. We can say, therefore, that they owe an individual debt to their individual caretakers. But the obligation is not theirs alone — nor is their obligation confined only to their own caretakers. A sense of social justice demands a broader sense of obligation. Without aggregate caretaking, there could be no society, so we might say that it is caretaking labor that produces and reproduces society. Caretaking labor provides the citizens, the workers, the voters, the consumers, the students, and others who populate society and its institutions. The uncompensated labor of caretakers is an unrecognized subsidy, not only to the individuals who directly receive it, but more significantly, to the entire society....

The assignment of responsibility for the burdens of dependency to the family in the first instance, and within the family to women, operates in an unjust manner because this arrangement has significant negative material consequences for the caretaker. This obvious observation allows me to introduce an additional, but often overlooked, form of dependency into the argument — "derivative dependency." Derivative dependency arises on the part of the person who assumes responsibility for the care of the inevitable dependent person. I refer to this form of dependency as derivative to capture the very simple point that those who care for others are themselves dependent on resources in order to undertake that care. Caretakers have a need for monetary or material resources. They also need recourse to institutional supports and accommodation, a need for structural arrangements that facilitate caretaking.

Currently, neither the economic nor the structural supports for caretaking are adequate. Many caretakers and their dependents find themselves impoverished or severely economically compromised. Some of their economic problems stem from the fact that within families, caretaking work is unpaid and not considered worthy of social subsidies. There are also, however, direct costs associated with caretaking. Caretaking labor interferes with the pursuit and development of wage labor options. Caretaking labor saps energy and efforts from investment in career or market activities, those things that produce economic rewards. There are foregone opportunities and costs associated with caretaking, and even caretakers who work in the paid labor force typically have more tenuous ties to the public sphere because they must also accommodate caretaking demands in the private. These costs are not distributed among all beneficiaries of caretaking (institutional or individual). Unjustly, the major economic and career costs associated with caretaking are typically borne by the caretaker alone.

Further, most institutions in society remain relatively unresponsive to innovations that would lessen the costs of caretaking. Caretaking occurs in a larger context and caretakers often need accommodation in order to fulfill multiple responsibilities. For example, many caretakers also engage in market work. Far from structurally accommodating or facilitating caretaking, however, workplaces operate in modes incompatible with the idea that workers also have obligations for dependency. Workplace expectations compete with the demands of caretaking—we assume that workers are those independent and autonomous individuals who are free to work long and regimented hours.

In discussing the costs and impediments associated with undertaking the tasks of caretaking, it is important to emphasize that, unlike inevitable dependency, derivative dependency is not a universal experience. In fact, many people in our society totally escape the burdens and costs that arise from assuming a caretaking role, perhaps even freed for other pursuits by the caretaking labor of others. The status of derivative dependency is structured by and through existing societal institutions, culturally and socially assigned according to a script rooted in ideologies, particularly those of capitalism and patriarchy. These scripts function at an unconscious (and therefore, unexamined) level, and channel our beliefs and feelings about what is considered natural and what are appropriate institutional arrangements. When individuals act according to these scripts, consistent with prevailing ideology and institutional arrangements, we say they have chosen their path from the available options. The construction of this notion of individual choice allows us to avoid general responsibility for the inequity and justify the maintenance of the status quo. We ignore the fact that individual choice occurs within the constraints of social conditions. These constraints include ideology, history, and tradition, all of which funnel decisions into prescribed channels and often operate in a practical and symbolic manner to limit options.

As it now stands in this society, derivative dependents are expected to get both economic and structural resources within the family. The market is unresponsive and uninvolved, and the state is perceived as a last resort for financial resources, the refuge of the failed family. A caretaker who must resort to governmental assistance may do so only if she can demonstrate that she is needy in a highly stigmatized process. . . .

In order to move from our current situation to a more just resolution for the dilemma of caretaking and dependency, we will need more than a responsive state. The state will also have to be an active participant in shaping and monitoring other societal institutions. One fundamental task will be monitoring and preventing the exploitation and appropriation of the labor of some citizens through institutional and ideological arrangements. This must be prevented even when the justification for the labor's appropriation and exploitation is that it is used for the good of the majority. Further, it must be prevented even in contexts where social constraints and conventions coerce consent from the laborer.

In this endeavor, the state must use its regulatory and redistributive authority to ensure that those things that are not valued or are undervalued in market or marriage are, nonetheless, publicly and politically recognized as socially productive and given value. Conferral of value requires the transfer of some economic resources from the collective society to caretakers through the establishment of mechanisms that tax those who receive the benefits of caretaking in order to compensate those who do the caretaking. Other societies do this in a variety of ways, such as using tax revenues to provide childcare allowances and universal benefits that assist caretakers, or through a basic income guarantee. Money, however, is not enough. The active state must also structure accommodation of the needs of caretaking into society's institutions.

[Additional portions of this article are set forth on pp. 949-950.]

≡
≡ *Vicki Schultz, Life's Work*
≡ 100 Colum. L. Rev. 1881, 1883-1886, 1900-1905 (2000)

[T]he concept of a "life's work" [describes] some of the central elements of a utopian vision in which women and men from all walks of life can stand alongside each other as equals, pursuing our chosen projects and forging connected lives. In the process, we come to view each other as equal citizens and human beings, each entitled to equal respect and a claim on society's resources because of our shared commitments and contributions. As individuals, our work provides us with a forum to realize at least some of our aspirations, to form bonds with others, to serve society, and to project ourselves into the larger world beyond our own families and friends. It also provides us with the wherewithal to sustain ourselves, economically and socially, so that we may enter into intimate relationships with the security that permits us to love (and leave) freely, without need of recompense. This world of equal citizenship, stable community, and a strong, secure selfhood for everyone is the world I believe feminism was born to bring into being.

Recently, however, a number of feminists and liberals have begun to move away from such a vision; some even associate an emphasis on equal work with conservatism. Some feminist legal scholars now advocate paying women to care for their own families in their own households; many seem to have given up on achieving genuine gender integration of the work done in both households and workplaces. Some liberal thinkers urge that we provide everyone a guaranteed income or capital allotment; they believe tying the distribution of social goods to work interferes with individual freedom and choice. The presence of these discourses has moved me to articulate a feminist vision of the significance of paid work to the good life, to equality, and to women. I agree that it is vitally important to create society-wide mechanisms for allocating the costs of household labor and for allowing people to realize their preferences. But, unless we pay attention to the institutional contexts through which housework is valued and individual choice realized, stubborn patterns of gender inequality will continue to reassert themselves—including the gender-based distribution of work that is at the root of women's disadvantage. In the search for social justice, separatism simply won't suffice....

In my view, a robust conception of equality can be best achieved through paid work, rather than despite it. Work is a site of deep self-formation that offers rich opportunities for human flourishing (or devastation). To a large extent, it is through our work—how it is defined, distributed, characterized, and controlled—that we develop into the "men" and "women" we see ourselves and others see us as being. Because law's domain includes work and its connection to other spheres of existence, the prospect of who we become as a society, and as individuals, is shaped profoundly by the laws that create and control the institutions that govern our experiences as workers. I believe that it is only by recognizing the formative power of such forces that we can imagine and invent ourselves as full human agents....

Paid work has the potential to become the universal platform for equal citizenship it has been imagined to be, but only if we ensure meaningful participation in the workforce by attending to the specific needs of various social groups and individuals. In the past, legal efforts to achieve equality focused on protecting people from identity-based discrimination; we have tended to take the number and quality of jobs, job-holding services, wages, and working conditions produced by the market as a neutral baseline to which no one is to be denied access because of group status. But in order to make paid work the basis for equal citizenship, we will have to take steps to ensure that what the market produces is both substantively adequate and universally available for everyone. This means that, in the future, we will have to supplement employment discrimination law with measures like job-creation programs, wage subsidies, universal child care and health care programs, enhanced employee representation, and a reduced workweek for everyone. To achieve such reforms, feminists must move beyond an identity politics that presses for cultural recognition and revaluation of "women's experience." We must join forces with a broad array of groups—including the labor movement—not simply to advance each other's interests, but to fashion a shared interest in creating a social order in which work is consistent with egalitarian conceptions of citizenship and care....

It is vitally important to acknowledge the hidden labor that is performed in households, and to create society-wide mechanisms for allocating its costs rather than continuing to impose them on individual family members (too often, women). One method of doing so is already being implemented on a massive scale: collectivizing housework by converting it into employment. A great deal of work once performed in private households has been handed over to day-care providers, cleaning services, home health aides, landscapers, and the like. Feminists could think creatively about how to capitalize on this trend by supporting efforts to upgrade the pay, promotional prospects, and working conditions associated with work once performed by at-home spouses. Compared to marriage and intimate relationships, labor markets and workplaces are spaces in which it is easier for workers to mobilize to obtain public accountability and protection. By transforming at least some forms of household work into paid employment, we could more easily protect those who do the work from discrimination, unfair labor practices, wage and hour violations, adverse working conditions, health and safety threats, and other problems on the job. We could also make it easier for those who perform household labor to engage in collective action to improve their situation. The recent victory of 70,000 California home health care workers in organizing a union, for example, holds promise for highlighting—and upgrading—the value of service work. Such victories continue the work started by the comparable worth campaigns of the 1980s.

Converting household work into paid employment not only provides jobs for many people who need them, it also frees those who provide unpaid family labor to pursue more fully for pay the work that suits them best. Countless middle- and working-class families buy time or convenience by purchasing such things as child care, cleaning services, dinners from McDonald's, lawn mowing, haircuts, car repair, and other services that should count as commercialized forms of household labor. There may, of course, be some forms of household labor that cannot or should not be commodified. There may also be some services that average- or low-income people cannot afford. But, there is no reason why a commercialization strategy must be limited to pure market forces. Some services could be subsidized for those who cannot afford them, or even made available for free to everyone (like public schooling, a now universal service that was once provided exclusively within the family setting).

Despite the fact that converting household labor into paid work collectivizes it and renders it more visible and publicly accountable, feminists in the movement to value housework tend to shun this approach. Instead, these feminists are proposing schemes to compensate women for performing household labor in private homes. Some legal feminists argue that (heterosexual) women's household labor provides their male partners with the time and resources to specialize in market work, and thus the men should compensate the women. These feminists propose marriage-based "joint property" schemes that redistribute income from husbands (or sometimes higher wage-earners, assumed to be husbands) to wives (or lower wage-earners, assumed to be wives) at divorce. Other feminists promote state-based "welfare" strategies in which the government pays caregiver stipends that are not tied to paid employment, but are instead intended to permit women to choose full-time or near full-time homemaking and child care. In joint property proposals the source of funding is the husband, while in welfare approaches it is the state. But both strategies channel funds through the family unit to pay women to keep house and care for our own kin.

Wittingly or unwittingly, advocates of these family-based approaches replicate some of the same conservative assumptions that have been used traditionally to justify women's disadvantage. Indeed, feminists in this movement tend to rely on the human capital literature to assert that it is women's disproportionate responsibility for housework and child care that accounts for our lower wages and our inferior position in the workforce. Unfortunately, many of these feminists seem unaware of (or uninformed about) the body of sociological work that casts doubt on the validity of human capital theory. Within the social sciences, the debate is between conventional economists—who pin women's plight on our family roles—and feminist sociologists (and sociologically-inclined economists)—who have produced evidence that discriminatory workplace dynamics are a more fundamental cause. The sociological literature points toward a more contextual approach that rejects static family-based conceptions of women's difference; it shows instead that socially-constructed features of the workworld help create the very gender differences (manifested in work aspirations, employment patterns, and familial divisions of labor) that human capital theory attributes to women themselves. Such an approach creates greater possibilities for change. If the sources of women's disadvantage lie not in sociobiological forces that commit women more heavily to child care and housework but instead in the political economy of paid work, we can challenge the sex bias in allegedly gender-neutral forces in labor markets and work places. We can create more empowering gender arrangements by demanding work and working conditions that will give women more economic security, more political clout, more household bargaining power, and perhaps even more personal strength with which to pursue our dreams.

[Additional portions of this article are set forth on pp. 950-952.]

Notes

1. Substantive Equality vs. Difference Theory as a Basis for Legal Reform. The program for workplace reform generated by relational theory overlaps considerably the agenda of those urging the "special treatment" substantive equality approach discussed in Chapter 2. Both include such items as greater public responsibility for children, family leave policies, and more expansive employer policies for flex-time and part-time work possibilities.

Compare the justifications for these reforms offered by the different theoretical approaches. Within substantive equality models, measures to equalize the sexes' legal and economic status are woman-centered and justified as a means of eliminating some of the disadvantages women would otherwise experience—i.e., making the best of a bad world. In contrast, difference theory, or cultural feminism, justifies such measures as part of the blueprint for a more ideal world for everyone. See Laura T. Kessler, The Attachment Gap: Employment Discrimination Law, Women's Cultural Caregiving, and the Limits of Economic and Liberal Legal Theory, 34 U. Mich. J.L. Reform 371 (2001) (comparing characterization of women's experiences of caregiving as a condition of impaired agency growing out of gender socialization, with a focus on the fundamental importance and value of women's caregiving labor). Is there an advantage to characterizing these measures as a positive, societal ideal, rather than as an accommodation to women?

2. Furthering "Family Values": What Needs to Change? Fineman's assertion that caretaking is a public good, and therefore a collective social responsibility, accords with the arguments of other feminist thinkers. Economist Nancy Folbre, for example, argues that the "invisible hand" of the market cannot function without the "invisible heart" of care: "Markets cannot function effectively outside the framework of families and communities built on values of love, obligation, and reciprocity." Nancy Folbre, The Invisible Heart: Economics and Family Values xi (2001); see also Mona Harrington, Care and Equality: Inventing a New Family Politics (1999) (arguing for a public conversation on rethinking the family); Maxine Eichner, Square Peg in a Round Hole: Parenting Policies and Liberal Theory, 59 Ohio St. L.J. 133 (1998) (arguing for a "community-oriented treatment of parenting" that "actively promotes the welfare of parents, children, and the relationships between them as collective societal goals"). Fineman, Folbre, and Harrington all reason that caretaking has traditionally been performed without pay by women but, now that women are flooding into paid work, societies must find some other equitable way to provide caretaking services. See also Joan Williams, Unbending Gender: Why Family and Work Conflict and What to Do About It (2000).

What might greater state support for caretaking look like? Income supplements for families with dependents, greater subsidies through the tax code for child care expenses, and mandatory paid leave are examples of state strategies that have been followed in other countries, and to a lesser extent in the United States. See Chapter 2, at pp. 222-228, 232-251. These reforms leave existing employment and family patterns relatively intact, with government subsidies to lessen burdens on women and families.

For some feminists, involving the government in subsidizing care work requires rethinking "the family" entirely. Martha Fineman, for example, argues that the state has a legitimate interest in caring for dependents, but no legitimate interest in the kinds of intimate relationships adults form with one another. Therefore, she concludes, marriage should be abolished as a legal category, or at least as the unit through which state supports for caregiving should flow. Fineman argues that the paradigm of the caregiving family should be the dyad of Mother/Child rather than Husband/Wife, and that state support should flow accordingly to "caregiving families," understood as dependents and the people who nurture them. Martha Albertson Fineman, The Neutered Mother, the Sexual Family, and Other Twentieth Century Tragedies 228-236 (1995).

Vicki Schultz, who favors decent work for all, believes that only participation in the paid work force can bring women full citizenship. Her approach points toward reforms of the workplace rather than the family or government programs. But not all feminists agree. In a symposium responding to Schultz's article, one commentator noted:

> [W]hile I share the goal of making opportunities for paid employment opportunities universally available, I reject the premise that such employment is always necessary or sufficient to a life well lived. Many women, and an increasing number of men, do not define themselves exclusively or even primarily in terms of what they do for a living. . . .
>
> At the most general level, what makes people satisfied is a sense of having met life's challenges. Work is a central part of what can yield such fulfillment and provide individuals with meaning, structure, identity, and self-esteem. But it is *only* a part, and pay is less critical than other aspects of the work experience in creating satisfaction. Opportunities for challenge, control, achievement, agency, and mastery of skills are generally rated as more important than compensation. Indeed, unpaid labor

often provides greater satisfaction in these respects than paid labor . . . because individuals can choose projects that develop their skills and enriches their experience in the service of causes that they find valuable.

[Accordingly,] [w]e need first to redesign our workplaces to foster balanced lives. All employees benefit from time for substantial family and civic activities, and their labor-force participation should be structured accordingly. Shorter workweeks, alternative schedules, elimination of mandatory overtime, and paid family leaves for both sexes are obvious priorities. All employees should have opportunities for part-time work that carries proportional wages and benefits and that does not permanently threaten career advancement. Education and incentive programs should be designed to encourage men to take advantage of such options and to assume a fair share of family responsibilities.

A second cluster of reforms should focus on making care-giving services and opportunities more widely available and socially rewarded. Quality child- and elder-care should be accessible to all families. Reforms in tax, social security, and divorce law should seek to ensure that those who engage in substantial unpaid care-taking do not pay an inequitable price. And finally, we should do more to make volunteer activities a rewarding and rewarded part of every American's life.

Deborah L. Rhode, Balanced Lives, 102 Colum. L. Rev. 834, 836, 846 (2002). Do you agree? What would be necessary to achieve these reforms? What stands in the way?

Is it the desire for "balance" that explains the substantial number of professional women who "opt out" of the paid work force for substantial periods? See Chapter 2, Problem 2-4, p. 252, for discussion of this pattern and its impact on the income of lawyers and other upper level workers. The "opt out revolution" has gained increasing attention from the popular media and has sparked considerable controversy. In one widely discussed cover story in the New York Times Magazine, journalist Lisa Belkin attributes the phenomenon to women's different choices. In essence, her analysis is that women are underrepresented in leadership positions, including law firm partnerships, less because "the workplace has failed women" than because "women are rejecting the workplace." "Why don't women run the world?," asks Belkin. "Maybe it's because they don't want to." The Opt Out Revolution, N.Y. Times, Oct. 26, 2003, at 42, 44, 45 (Magazine). See also Louise Story, Many Women at Elite Colleges Set Career Path to Motherhood, N.Y. Times, Sept. 20, 2005, at A1, A18, also discussed in Problem 2-4, Chapter 2 (60 percent of sample of Yale female seniors expect to cut back or leave the work force when they have children, and over 60 percent of female graduates of classes of Harvard Business School in 1981, 1986, and 1991, either didn't work, or worked part-time or did contract work).

The article, like similar accounts on Sixty Minutes and in other popular magazines and news programs, has sparked considerable controversy. According to many feminists, what is missing or marginal in these stories is the extent to which women's choices are socially constructed and constrained. What drops out of the "opt-out" narrative are the complex forces that drive women's decisions. Missing also is attention to the choices that men make, as parents, policy leaders, and managers, that also limit the choices available to women.

Belkin's sample was an Atlanta book group of full time homemakers with Princeton degrees, a San Francisco mother's group of MBAs, and "countless" readers with whom she has corresponded over recent years. It was, by her own acknowledgment, a group of economically privileged women, who chose to leave the paid workforce because they had high earning partners who chose differently. As Belkin's profiles suggest, and more rigorous studies confirm, when women drop off the leadership track, it is not necessarily because full-time motherhood is what they want. Rather, it is because no semblance of a balanced life is available in the jobs that they leave behind, and because their husbands are unwilling to assume a substantial share of family responsibilities. As one response to Belkin put it, "If women are 'choosing' not to 'run the world,' it is partly because men are choosing not to run the washer/dryer." Deborah L. Rhode, Women and Work Nat'l L.J., Dec. 8, 2003, at A22. For other discussions, see Sylvia Ann Hewlett & Carolyn Bush Luce, Off Ramps and On Ramps, 83 Harv. Bus. Rev., March 2005, at 43.

If opting out is becoming a more common choice, is this primarily a matter of continued structure of discrimination within which women's choices are made, or do younger women want a different relationship to their world than the one available under the equality model so hard fought for by the women of their mothers' generation? For a provocative view of the subject, again from the New York Times, see Maureen Dowd, What's a Modern Girl to Do?, N.Y. Times, October 30, 2005, at 50 (Magazine) (describing a new generation of young women who expect their dates to pick up the check at dinner, play hard to get, and take their husbands' surnames when they marry). Are women turning their back on the gains won by feminism? Or are they exercising the freedom of choice earned on their behalf?

3. The "Delegation" Strategy. In the absence of government institutions and programs to support caretaking, American women who work turn to the market to purchase caretaking services. Joan Williams refers to this strategy as "full commodification." Adrienne Davis calls it "delegation." Symposium, supra, at 903. Dorothy E. Roberts observes that the delegation strategy relies on a labor force that is overwhelmingly female, poorly paid, and disproportionately populated by immigrant women and native-born women of color. Roberts, Spiritual and Menial Housework, 9 Yale J.L. & Feminism 51, 51 (1997). Many policymakers also worry that delegation to the market produces either inferior care or no care for those without money to pay for it, as well as an across-the-board industry focus on cost-cutting and efficiency at the expense of quality. See, e.g., Folbre, supra, at 60-64. For a critique of full commodification and a suggestion that "reconstructive feminism" provides a way forward, see Williams, Unbending Gender: Why Family and Work Conflict and What to Do About It (2000).

Domesticity also has its critics.

> Underlying domesticity's romantic description of mothers selflessly devoted to children's needs are class aspirations acknowledged today only in accepted codes (parents want their children to be "successful" and "productive"). To quote Lillian

Rubin, "professional middle-class parents... assum[e] that their children are destined to do work like theirs — work that calls for innovation, initiative, flexibility, creativity, sensitivity to others, and a well-developed set of interpersonal skills...." [Lillian Rubin, Worlds of Pain 128 (1976).] Mothers stay home to develop these skills in their children. Barbara Ehrenreich is one of the few writers who recognize the link between gender roles and class formation:

> The concern was expressed in various ways: "I don't want to miss the early years"; or "I don't want to leave my children with just anyone." But the real issue was the old middle-class dilemma of whether "anyone" such as a Jamaican housekeeper or a Hispanic day-care worker was equipped to instill such middle-class virtues as concentration and intellectual discipline. For many young middle-class couples the choice was stark: Have the mother work and risk retarding the child's intellectual development, or have the mother stay home, build up the child's I.Q., and risk being unable to pay for a pricey nursery school or, later, private college. [Barbara Ehrenreich, Fear of Falling 221 (1989).]

"It is one thing to have children," Ehrenreich notes, "and another thing... to have children who will be disciplined enough to devote the first twenty or thirty years of their lives to scaling the educational obstacles to a middle-class career." [Id. at 83.] Much of what mothers do is designed to preserve and pass on what has been called the family's social capital: their style of life, religious and ethnic rituals, and social position.

Joan Williams, Toward a Reconstructive Feminism: Reconstructing the Relationship of Market Work and Family Work, 19 N. Ill. U. L. Rev. 89, 131-132 (1998).

Ehrenreich seems to attach a negative connotation to these mothers' efforts. Other commentators note the cultural pressures that cause women to believe that time-intensive involvement in parenting is necessary for their children's ultimate well-being. As one of the full-time mothers interviewed in Judith Warner's 2005 study put it, "We want only the best for our kids, but unfortunately, the definition of 'the best for our kids' is interpreted very narrowly by society...." Judith Warner, Perfect Madness: Motherhood in the Age of Anxiety 220 (2005).

4. Feminist Critiques of Caretaking as a Public Good. A number of feminist theorists resist the notion of caretaking as a public good. Katherine Franke's primary concern is the further reinforcement of the normativity of reproduction, along with its various cultural associations and a sexual division of labor that oppresses women.

> Reproduction has been so taken for granted that only women who are not parents are regarded as having made a choice — a choice that is constructed as nontraditional, nonconventional, and for some, non-natural....
>
> Reproduction raises numerous sticky normative questions, yet underexplored within feminism, with respect to choice, coercion, and policies that incentivize and disincentivize reproductive uses of women's sexual bodies.

Franke, Theorizing Yes: An Essay on Feminism, Law, and Desire, 101 Colum. L. Rev. 181, 186-187 (2001).

Franke also raises fairness issues about the public support for an activity over which the public retains so little control.

> [E]ven though there is an enormous public interest in the labor performed by mothers... children remain the private property of their parents, which is an arrangement most feminists do not find troubling. The politics of public value, public subsidy, but private accountability with respect to raising children is revealed to be quite paradoxical under close examination.... [For example, a] large number of home schoolers are fundamentalist christian families who... "are no longer fighting against the mainstream — they're 'dropping out' and creating their own private American." Many families... are heeding the call of Paul Weyrich, a founder of the Christian Right, to "drop out of this culture, and find places... where we can live godly, righteous, and sober lives." Not coincidentally, these families, and many others like them, are also making the loudest demands for public subsidies or vouchers that will finance home-schooling as well as private, parochial school tuition for families that seek to remove their children from the public school system. It must be worth at least thinking about the carte blanche we give the privatized family to refuse to teach "our" future citizens public norms of tolerance, equality, and humanity — or worse. The freedom to indulge such non-public, if not anti-public, preferences in the raising of children can be quite alarming — especially when the public is called upon to finance the raising of these future christian soldiers. We have delegated to private parties the task of producing and raising the next generation, and we have done so in the absence of any public accountability for what kinds of people this public service produces.
>
> What also strikes me as worthy of examination is the degree to which parenting is described as productive society activity while, in many regards, parenting has become as much or more about consumption than production. Sylvia Anne Hewlett, the founder of the National Parenting Association, mused in a recent op-ed piece... about how the public fails to recognize the financial sacrifices that mothers make to raise children. What with "therapy, summer camp, computer equipment and so on," kids are just darn expensive, she argued. The "and so on" explicitly entails Pokemon accessories, My Little Pony dolls, Barbies, fancy sneakers, and other expensive articles of consumption that are aggressively marketed to children these days. While I don't think that children of any economic class should be deprived of the toys and other items that bring joy into their lives, I am concerned about the bourgeois framing of an issue that gives the larger public the tab for the marketing-induced "needs" of children. And all in the name of "society-preserving work." That children want things, or their parents wish to provide them to their children, is an insufficient justification for shifting the costs of those needs to the public.

Id. at 191-192.

Another critic, Mary Anne Case, focuses on the unfairness of shifting the burden of caretaking to those who choose not to have children.

> The difficulty I have experienced goes beyond privileging certain kinds of family over others, and more broadly extends to a privileging of family matters over an employee's other life concerns.
>
> [I]f the premise of some parents' advocates really is one of strong equality of result (i.e., that parent should, in effect, be held harmless in time and money from their decision to have children; that their decision to have children should be made as

close as possible to costless), then we really are talking, if not quite about a zero-sum game, then at least about a massive redistribution from nonparents to parents, one which, on grounds, *inter alia*, of inequity to people like myself, I would strongly oppose.

Case, How High the Apple Pie? A Few Troubling Questions About Where, Why, and How the Burden of Care for Children Should Be Shifted, 76 Chi.-Kent L. Rev. 1753, 1767, 1771 (2001). For a rich historical analysis of how feminism came to "abandon" the interests of single women, see Rachel F. Moran, How Second-Wave Feminism Forgot the Single Woman, 33 Hofstra L. Rev. 223 (2004).

For a direct response to these critiques from the relational feminism point of view, see Mary Becker, Care and Feminists, 17 Wis. Women's L.J. 57, 64 (2002) (better public support for caretakers is important not just because raising children creates a public good, but because autonomy, connection, and competence, which are not consistent with poverty, are important for human well-being).

Even if caretaking is a public good, is there a reason why it should be singled out for coordinated social policy over other public goods such as the arts, the environment, or health and safety? Are babies more important than paintings, wildlife preservation, clean water, or cures for cancer?

Putting Theory into Practice

4-1. From among the courses in which you are currently enrolled, identify some legal reforms that might better reflect "woman's voice" than does current law. Try to justify these initiatives in terms of one of the approaches featured in the previous chapters of this book. Which is the better framework for advancing the proposal?

4-2. Consistent with her emphasis on connection and responsibility, Robin West proposes that women's reproductive freedoms rest on responsibility as well as rights:

[S]upport for expanded reproductive freedom should rest on the claim that only by accepting the responsibility to make these judgments do women manifest their freedom to pursue their authentically chosen and desired life goals....Women need the freedom to make reproductive decisions not merely to vindicate a right to be left alone but often to strengthen their ties to others: to plan responsibly and have a family for which they can provide, to pursue professional or work commitments made to the outside world, or to continue supporting their families or communities. At other times the decision to abort is necessitated not by a murderous urge to end life, but by the harsh reality of a financially irresponsible partner, a society indifferent to the care of children, and a workplace incapable of accommodating or supporting the needs of working parents. At many other times the need to abort follows directly from a violent sexual assault. When made for any of these reasons, the decision to abort is not one made in an egoistic private vacuum. Whatever the reason, the decision to abort is almost invariably made within a web of interlocking, competing, and often irreconcilable responsibilities and commitments.

Robin West, Foreword, Taking Freedom Seriously, 104 Harv. L. Rev. 43, 83-85 (1990) (further portions appear in Chapter 5 at p. 900). What are the consequences of tying the abortion right to the concept of responsibility? Does West's position have any implications, for example, with respect to what restrictions the law ought to impose on drug-abusing pregnant women? (See Chapter 5, pp. 926-942.) Does the concept of responsibility support the right to abortion, or undermine it?

4-3. The following case is described in David Margolick, At the Bar, N.Y. Times, July 10, 1992, at B8. Michael Mattioli is a 66-year-old retired psychologist. For over 30 years, he lived in a Manhattan apartment complex owned by New York University. He then moved "temporarily" to Rochester to care for his mother, age 95, and his father, age 99, so that they would be spared the "indignity of dying in a nursing home." His mother died four years later, but his father lived on. New York University sought to evict Mattioli from his Manhattan apartment on the basis of a statute allowing eviction of tenants who do not use the premises as their primary residence. Mattioli believed he should be able to keep his apartment, since he intended to return there as soon as his father no longer needed him. "I'm sure that at N.Y.U.'s medical school and law school and nursing school, they're teaching about the problems of the elderly," he said. "I don't think they're teaching that people who are taking responsibility for their own parents should be driven out of their apartments." Id.

Should the circumstances of Mattioli's departure from his apartment and his intention to return sometime in the indefinite future provide a defense to the eviction action? How, if at all, can difference theory be relevant? Is the theory helpful only to Mattioli, or can New York University appeal to it as well?

4-4. What are the implications of the ethic of care when a "surrogate mother" wants to change her mind once the child is born and, instead of giving the child up to the biological father, retain primary custody of the child herself? (This issue is addressed in Chapter 5, at pp. 907-925.)

D. GENDER AND THE LEGAL PROFESSION

1. Historical Background

Bradwell v. Illinois
83 U.S. (16 Wall.) 130 (1872)

Mrs. Myra Bradwell, residing in the State of Illinois, made application to the judges of the Supreme Court of that State for a license to practice law....

The statute of Illinois on [this] subject...enacts that no person shall be permitted to practice as an attorney or counsellor-at-law...without having previously obtained a license for that purpose from some two of the justices of the Supreme Court....

[The Supreme Court of Illinois denied the application because she was a married woman.]

[Mr. Justice Miller delivered the opinion of the court, affirming the denial, on grounds that "the right to control and regulate the granting of license to practice law in the courts of a State is one of those powers which are not transferred for its protection to the Federal government, and its exercise is in no manner governed or controlled by citizenship of the United States in the party seeking such license...."]

Mr. Justice BRADLEY, concurring:

I concur in the judgment of the court in this case, by which the judgment of the Supreme Court of Illinois is affirmed, but not for the reasons specified in the opinion just read.

The claim of the plaintiff, who is a married woman, to be admitted to practice as an attorney and counsellor-at-law, is based upon the supposed right of every person, man or woman, to engage in any lawful employment for a livelihood. The Supreme Court of Illinois denied the application on the ground that, by the common law, which is the basis of the laws of Illinois, only men were admitted to the bar, and the legislature had not made any change in this respect....

The claim that, under the fourteenth amendment of the Constitution, which declares that no State shall make or enforce any law which shall abridge the privileges and immunities of citizens of the United States, the statute law of Illinois, or the common law prevailing in that State, can no longer be set up as a barrier against the right of females to pursue any lawful employment for a livelihood (the practice of law included), assumes that it is one of the privileges and immunities of women as citizens to engage in any and every profession, occupation, or employment in civil life.

It certainly cannot be affirmed, as an historical fact, that this has ever been established as one of the fundamental privileges and immunities of the sex. On the contrary, the civil law, as well as nature herself, has always recognized a wide difference in the respective spheres and destinies of man and woman. Man is, or should be, woman's protector and defender. The natural and proper timidity and delicacy which belongs to the female sex evidently unfits it for many of the occupations of civil life. The constitution of the family organization, which is founded in the divine ordinance, as well as in the nature of things, indicates the domestic sphere as that which properly belongs to the domain and functions of womanhood. The harmony, not to say identity, of interests and views which belong, or should belong, to the family institution is repugnant to the idea of a woman adopting a distinct and independent career from that of her husband. So firmly fixed was this sentiment in the founders of the common law that it became a maxim of that system of jurisprudence that a woman had no legal existence separate from her husband, who was regarded as her head and representative in the social state;

and, notwithstanding some recent modifications of this civil status, many of the special rules of law flowing from and dependent upon this cardinal principle still exist in full force in most States. One of these is, that a married woman is incapable, without her husband's consent, of making contracts which shall be binding on her or him. This very incapacity was one circumstance which the Supreme Court of Illinois deemed important in rendering a married woman incompetent fully to perform the duties and trusts that belong to the office of an attorney and counsellor.

It is true that many women are unmarried and not affected by any of the duties, complications, and incapacities arising out of the married state, but these are exceptions to the general rule. The paramount destiny and mission of woman are to fulfil the noble and benign offices of wife and mother. This is the law of the Creator. And the rules of civil society must be adapted to the general constitution of things, and cannot be based upon exceptional cases.

The humane movements of modern society, which have for their object the multiplication of avenues for woman's advancement, and of occupations adapted to her condition and sex, have my heartiest concurrence. But I am not prepared to say that it is one of her fundamental rights and privileges to be admitted into every office and position, including those which require highly special qualifications and demanding special responsibilities. In the nature of things it is not every citizen of every age, sex, and condition that is qualified for every calling and position. It is the prerogative of the legislator to prescribe regulations founded on nature, reason, and experience for the due admission of qualified persons to professions and callings demanding special skill and confidence. This fairly belongs to the police power of the State; and, in my opinion, in view of the peculiar characteristics, destiny, and mission of woman, it is within the province of the legislature to ordain what offices, positions, and callings shall be filled and discharged by men, and shall receive the benefit of those energies and responsibilities, and that decision and firmness which are presumed to predominate in the sterner sex.

For these reasons I think that the laws of Illinois now complained of are not obnoxious to the charge of abridging any of the privileges and immunities of citizens of the United States.

Mr. Justice SWAYNE and Mr. Justice FIELD concurred in the foregoing opinion of Mr. Justice BRADLEY.

THE CHIEF JUSTICE dissented from the judgment of the court, and from all the opinions.

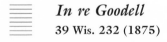

In re Goodell
39 Wis. 232 (1875)

RYAN, C.J....

This is the first application for admission of a female to the bar of this court. And it is just matter for congratulation that it is made in favor of a lady whose character raises no personal objection: something perhaps not always to be looked for in women who forsake the ways of their sex for the ways of ours. . . .

[We] find no statutory authority for the admission of females to the bar of any court of this state. And, with all the respect and sympathy for this lady which all men owe to all good women, we cannot regret that we do not. We cannot but think the common law wise in excluding women from the profession of the law. The profession enters largely into the well being of society; and, to be honorably filled and safely to society, exacts the devotion of life. The law of nature destines and qualifies the female sex for the bearing and nurture of children of our race and for the custody of the homes of the world and their maintenance in love and honor. And all life-long callings of women, inconsistent with these radical and sacred duties of their sex, as is the profession of the law, are departures from the order of nature; and when voluntary, treason against it. The cruel chances of life sometimes baffle both sexes, and may leave women free from the peculiar duties of their sex. These may need employment, and should be welcome to any not derogatory to their sex and its proprieties, or inconsistent with the good order of society. But it is public policy to provide for the sex, not for its superfluous members; and not to tempt women from the proper duties of their sex by opening to them duties peculiar to ours. There are many employments in life not unfit for female character. The profession of the law is surely not one of these. The peculiar qualities of womanhood, its gentle graces, its quick sensibility, its emotional impulses, its subordination of hard reason to sympathetic feeling, are surely not qualifications for forensic strife. Nature has tempered woman as little for the juridical conflicts of the court room, as for the physical conflicts of the battle field. Womanhood is moulded for gentler and better things. And it is not the saints of the world who chiefly give employment to our profession. It has essentially and habitually to do with all that is selfish and malicious, knavish and criminal, coarse and brutal, repulsive and obscene, in human life. It would be revolting to all female sense of the innocence and sanctity of their sex, shocking to man's reverence for womanhood and faith in woman, on which hinge all the better affections and humanities of life, that woman should be permitted to mix professionally in all the nastiness of the world which finds its way into courts of justice; all the unclean issues, all the collateral questions, of sodomy, incest, rape, seduction, fornication, adultery, pregnancy, bastardy, legitimacy, prostitution, lascivious cohabitation, abortion, infanticide, obscene publications, libel and slander of sex, impotence, divorce: all nameless catalogue of indecencies, *la chronique scandaleuse* of all the vices and all the infirmities of all society, with which the profession has to deal, and which go towards filling judicial reports which must be read for accurate knowledge of the law. This is bad enough for men. . . . Reverence for all womanhood would suffer in the public spectacle of woman so instructed and so engaged. . . . Discussions [in cases such as rape and paternity] are habitually necessary in courts of justice, which are unfit for female ears. The habitual presence of women at these would tend to relax the public sense of decency and propriety. If, as counsel threatened, these things are to come, we will take no voluntary part in bringing them about.

By the Court. — The motion is denied.

NOTE ON THE BACKGROUND OF WOMEN
IN THE PRACTICE OF LAW

If it is true that women have a "different voice," one might expect the participation of women in the legal system to have a distinctive impact on that system. For most of this nation's history, the conventional view was that women's "difference" made women unfit for law and law unfit for women. In the colonial era, when labor was scarce and relatively few occupations required formal licenses, a few women did manage to participate in legal transactions either by acting as their husband's representative or by obtaining special authorization to proceed independently. During the late eighteenth century, however, the gradual formalization of bar admission criteria made it increasingly difficult for women to act as lawyers. The inability of married women to make contracts reinforced the barriers to any independent career. And, of course, African-American women under slavery had no capacity to assert legal rights.

After the Civil War, the rise in women's educational and political activism contributed to a growing stream of female applicants to the bar. In 1867, Iowa became the first state to license a woman attorney, Belle Babb Mansfield, and the following decades witnessed a gradual increase in female candidates from largely white middle- and upper-middle-class backgrounds. Women's initial reception as lawyers in most jurisdictions was less than enthusiastic. Many nineteenth-century lawmakers invested the sexes' "separate spheres" with both spiritual and constitutional significance, including Justice Bradley's invocation of women's domesticity as "the divine ordinance."

In addition to concerns over women's proper role and peculiar sensibilities and susceptibilities expressed in Justice Bradley's opinion in *Bradwell* were notions linking women's exposure to professional disputes to such ills as infertility, frigidity, and "race suicide." "Theories about the deadly 'brain-womb' conflict warned that women who diverted their scarce energies to cognitive rather than reproductive pursuits risked permanent physical and psychological damage." Deborah L. Rhode, Midcourse Corrections: Women in Legal Education, 53 J. Legal Educ. 475, 477 (2003).

By the turn of the twentieth century, various political, legal, and social forces had coalesced to secure women's rights to admission to the bar in about half the states, and by 1920, formal barriers were largely removed. Informal obstacles remained, however, reflecting earlier views. "Bring on as many women lawyers as you choose," predicted one District of Columbia judge. "I do not believe they will be a success." Belva Lockwood, My Efforts to Become a Lawyer, in Women and the American Economy: A Documentary History 1675-1929, at 297-301 (W. Elliot Brownlee & Mary M. Brownlee eds., 1976).

Many bar associations and law schools denied female applicants or limited their admission, using a broad array of excuses: law books were too heavy for women students; men would be distracted by their presence; or separate lavatory facilities were unavailable. Legal educators were also reluctant to squander scarce places on female applicants who would lack the same opportunities as their male counterparts to take advantage of legal training. For a good history of this period, see Cynthia Fuchs Epstein, Women in the Legal Profession at the Turn of the Twenty-First Century: Assessing Glass Ceilings and Open Doors, 49 Kan. L. Rev. 733 (2001). The first woman was admitted into an American law school in 1868. Admission to the other elite law schools did not come until much later. Columbia did not enroll women law students until 1927, and Harvard remained all male until 1950. Not until 1972 did all accredited law schools eliminate explicit sex-based restrictions.

Until the 1960s, women constituted about three percent of enrollment in law schools, less than three percent of the profession, and one-half percent of law professors. For the facts and figures, see Karen Berger Morello, The Invisible Bar: The Woman Lawyer in America 1638 to the Present 11, 44, 96, 100 (1986); Donna Fossum, Women in the Legal Profession: A Progress Report, 67 Women's L.J. 1 (1981); Cynthia Epstein, Women in Law 61-67 (1981); Marina Angel, The Modern University and its Law School: Hierarchical, Bureaucratic Structures Replace Coarchical, Collegial Ones: Women Disappear from Tenure Track and Reemerge as Caregivers: Tenure Disappears or Becomes Unrecognizable, 38 Akron L. Rev. 789 (2005).

Similar patterns were apparent in most other western industrialized nations. The first women were generally admitted to the legal profession between 1900 and 1925, but remained a small proportion of the profession until the 1970s. See Ulrike Schultz, Introduction: Women in the World's Legal Professions: Overview and Synthesis, in Women in the World's Legal Profession xxv, xxxv (Ulrike Schultz & Gisela Shaw eds., 2003).

Discrimination against racial, ethnic, and religious minorities was also pervasive. Throughout the nineteenth and early twentieth centuries, many employers, law schools, and bar associations excluded Jews, Eastern European immigrants, and applicants of color. Jerold Auerbach, Unequal Justice: Lawyers and Social Change in Modern America (1976). Not until the mid-1960s were all members of the Association of American Law Schools able to report that they did not officially discriminate on the basis of race or ethnicity. Lack of financial resources and educational preparation also restricted access by minorities to law school. Once admitted to the bar, minority lawyers faced continued resistance from potential employers and clients. Barriers to women of color were especially great because the few institutions that did not discriminate on the basis of race often did so on the basis of sex. Charlotte Ray, one of the first black women to graduate from law school (Howard, 1873), gained admittance by using her initials rather than her first name on application papers. After an unsuccessful struggle to obtain legal work, she returned to her earlier career of teaching in public schools. Between 1875 and 1925, no more than 25 black women were reported to be practicing law. By 1940, the number had only doubled. Geraldine Segal, Blacks in the Law 1, 4, 215, 240 (1983); Morello, supra, at 143-147.

Until women began entering law schools in substantial numbers during the 1970s, a common practice was to ignore their classroom presence as much as possible except for special issues or ceremonial occasions. For example, some professors observed Ladies Days, on which they called only on women students for selected cases or hypotheticals involving "women's concerns." Rape and

needlework were favored topics. Epstein, supra, at 66-67. Schools had no organizations for women law students, although, as Justice Ruth Bader Ginsburg
and Dean Barbara Black later noted, associations were often available for wives
of law students; activities included, teas, bake sales, fashion shows, and speaker
series with topics such as the importance of the well-informed spouse ("educated
but not equal"). Barbara Aronstein Black, Something to Remember, Something
to Celebrate: Women at Columbia Law School, 102 Colum. L. Rev. 1451,
1454 (2002); Ruth Bader Ginsburg, Women at the Bar: A Generation of
Change, 2 Puget Sound L. Rev. 1, 6 (1978). During this era, formal complaint
channels for matters like sexual harassment were nonexistent. When harassment
happened, it had neither a label nor a remedy. Women spoke of having a "problem" with a professor, and the problem was always theirs, never his. Rhode,
supra, at 480.

Discrimination in the placement process was less the exception than the rule:

> Many interviewers candidly acknowledged that their firms "did not and would not
> hire a woman." Some partners offered a secretarial position, provided that the
> woman law graduate could pass a typing test; Supreme Court Justice Sandra
> Day O'Connor had that experience. Others were simply apologetic. As one put
> it to an early Stanford law student: "You are highly qualified for the position, but
> what do you plan to do about being a woman?" A Harvard women applicant was
> told that "[u]nfortunately we hired a woman lawyer several moths ago and I'm
> sure you can understand how we would feel about having two at the same time."-
> ...Placement directors who learned of such incidents generally just passed the
> information along to women applicants to save them the time and frustration of
> fruitless interviews. It apparently did not occur to law school administrators that
> they might actually do something to discourage such discrimination by denying
> interview facilities to employers who engaged in it.

Rhode, Midcourse Corrections, supra at 479. See Judith Richards Hope, Pin-
stripes and Pearls 155-162 (2004).

Sol Linowitz, a prominent Washington practitioner, summarized men's
response to these patterns:

> There were only two women in my class at Cornell Law School, and to tell the
> truth we felt somewhat uncomfortable when they were around. It never occurred to
> us to wonder whether *they* felt uncomfortable.
> Nobody in those days thought of bigoted exclusion from the higher levels of
> legal practice as an ethical problem. For those who were excluded, it would have
> been pretentious; for others, with few exceptions, it was the way of the world —
> unfair, perhaps, but manageable. After all, you couldn't ask lawyers to be partners
> with people with whom they did not feel "comfortable."

Sol M. Linowitz with Martin Mayer, The Betrayed Profession 6 (1994).

During the late 1960s and 1970s, the climate for both white women and
women of color improved substantially. The women's rights and civil rights
movements encouraged more women, including racial and ethnic minorities,
to apply to law schools and to challenge discriminatory practices. During the

Vietnam War, a reduction in the pool of qualified male law school applicants also helped to boost women's admission. By the mid-1980s, over a third of new entrants to law school were women. By the turn of the century, women constituted at least half of law students. The growth of affirmative action and financial aid programs also increased the representation of women of color. Similar progress occurred in most European and Anglo-American countries. Women now typically account for a quarter to a third of the legal profession and about half of new entrants to the profession. Schultz, supra, at xxxvii.

2. Legal Education

During the 1980s, American law schools also became the subject of growing critiques. One concern was that their authoritarian, teacher-centered methods fostered alienation and hierarchy. See, e.g., Duncan Kennedy, Legal Education as Training for Hierarchy, in The Politics of Law: A Progressive Critique 38-58 (David Kairys ed., 2d ed. 1990) (orig. pub. 1982). Another criticism was that that this process systematically disadvantaged women. Studies at the University of California at Berkeley School of Law (Boalt Hall), Stanford, and a number of other law schools in the 1980s and 1990s found that female students performed less well than their male classmates, given predictions based on test scores and college performance, and were less likely to graduate at the top of the class or to hold other key positions such as membership on law review. The gap was widest for women of color. The basic studies are Linda F. Wightman, Law School Admission Council Research Report Series, Women in Legal Education: A Comparison of the Law School Performance and Law School Experience of Women and Men 25 (1996); Lani Guinier et al., Becoming Gentlemen 41 (1997); Lorraine Dutsky, Still Unequal: The Shameful Truth About Women and Justice in America 29 (1996); Suzanne Homer & Lois Schwartz, Admitted but Not Accepted: Outsiders Take an Inside Look at Law School, 5 Berkeley Women's Law (1989-1990). In most studies, women had substantially lower rates of class participation than men. See research summarized in Wightman, supra, at 25, 36, 72-74; Nancy Levit, Keeping Feminism in Its Place: Sex Segregation and the Domestication of Female Academics, 49 Kan. L. Rev. 775, 780 (2001); Deborah L. Rhode, Whistling Vivaldi: Legal Education and the Politics of Progress, 23 N.Y.U. Rev. L. & Soc. Change 217, 219-223 (1997); Elizabeth Mertz et al., What Difference Does Difference Make: The Challenge for Legal Education, 48 J. Legal Educ. 1 (1998). Many of these studies also found that women had higher levels of alienation and lower levels of self-esteem than men; problems of harassment and devaluation were greatest for lesbian and gay students and students of color. Wightman, supra; Homer & Schwartz, supra, at 52; Catherine Weiss & Louise Melling, The Legal Education of Twenty Women, 40 Stan. L. Rev. 1299, 1300-1302, 1363 (1988); Janice L. Austin et al., Results from a Survey: Gay, Lesbian, and Bisexual Students' Attitudes About Law School, 48 J. Legal Educ. 157 (1998); Scott N. Ihrig, Sexual Orientation in Law School:

Experiences of Gay, Lesbian, and Bisexual Law Students, 14 Law & Ineq. 555 (1996).

Other, more recent research paints a more complicated picture. Studies at some, but not all, schools find that women are performing academically at least as well as men and are overrepresented on law reviews. Shannan N. Ball, Separate but Equal Is Unequal: The Argument Against an All-Women's Law School, 15 Notre Dame J.L. Ethics & Pub. Pol'y 171 (2001); Jennifer Brown, To Give Them Countenance: The Case for a Women's Law School, 22 Harv. Women's L.J. 1 (1999). Surveys at leading law schools such as Harvard and Yale still indicate that women speak less often in class, are less likely to have their comments validated and pursued, and less likely to be mentored. See The Study on Women's Experiences at Harvard Law School (2004), discussed in "Women's Experience" Raises Concerns, Harvard L.S. Record, Feb. 26, 2004, at 1 (noting that male students were 50 percent more likely to speak voluntarily at least once during a class meeting than female students, and that female students constituted a significantly smaller proportion of "frequent talkers"); Yale Law Women, Yale Law School Faculty, and Students Speak About Gender (2002), available at http://www.yale.edu/ylw, discussed in Sari Bashi & Maryana Iskander, Methodology Matters, 53 J. Legal Educ. 505, 505-506 (2003).

The most comprehensive study of classroom participation finds that gender differences are complicated by other factors such as the sex, race, and teaching style of the professor and the male/female class ratio. Mertz et al., supra, at 75-77. Women — particularly women of color — express less satisfaction with their law school experience than men. See Wightman, supra, at 25, 36, 72-74; ABA Commission on Women in the Profession, The Unfinished Agenda: Women and the Legal Profession 29 (2001). However, some research also suggests that preexisting ideological commitments and career goals also affect response to the educational experience. For example, in a study of Harvard students, women who entered law school primarily for reasons such as status, income, and job security were generally satisfied with their training, while women who entered with predominantly social justice motivations found the institution sexist and dehumanizing. Robert Granville, The Making of Elite Lawyers, 104-106 (1992).

What implications should be drawn from these findings? Which descriptions are most consistent with your experience? To what extent are women responsible for the gender disparities that persist? In commenting on the Harvard Law School study on class participation rates, an editorial in the student newspaper faulted women for "consciously choosing to let their male peers do most the talking" and asserted female students had a "duty" to speak up. Women's Experience, supra, at 1. Another commentator, in response to feminists' arguments that the aggressive, competitive atmosphere of law school classrooms silences women, claims that such assertions revive nineteenth century stereotypes about women's inability to engage in the "hot strifes of the bar." John O. McGinnis, At Law School, Unstrict Scrutiny, Wall St. J., July 27, 2005, at D10 (discussing Dan Subotnik, Toxic Diversity (2005)). How would you respond?

Which of the following strategies seem most likely to be effective in addressing gender-related problems:

- More affirmative action efforts in faculty hiring, particularly for women of color;
- More participatory and less competitive learning techniques, such as cooperative problem-solving exercises, simulations, student-run discussions, narratives from film and literature, and experiential reflections in journals and short assignments;
- More curricular integration of materials involving gender, race, ethnicity, class, and sexual orientation;
- More efforts to promote tolerance and to curb harassing or demeaning conduct;
- More mentoring and feedback on student performance;
- More efforts to hold faculty accountable on diversity-related issues through student course evaluations and peer review;
- More efforts to hold schools accountable through institutionalized oversight structures in each institution and in accreditation and membership review bodies like the American Bar Association and the Association of American Law Schools [AALS].

See Rhode, Midcourse Corrections, supra, at 487-488, and Whistling Vivaldi, supra, at 223-224; Susan Sturn & Lani Guinier, Learning from Conflict: Reflections on Teaching About Race and Gender, 53 J. Legal Educ. 515, 531-545 (2003) (discussing alternative classroom pedagogy). For a broad range of critiques of legal education and proposals for reform, see Mary Jane Mossman, Gender Equality Education and the Legal Profession, 12 Sup. Ct. Rev. (2d) 187 (Spring 2000).

Women faculty have made substantial progress in legal education, but remain substantially underrepresented in positions of greatest status, influence, and job security. AALS data indicate that over the last twelve years surveyed, women have been hired at higher rates than men for all but one of those years; their cumulative success rate is 14 percent compared with 11 percent for men. Women of color have also been more successful than other applicants over the same period; their cumulative success rate is 17 percent compared with 12 percent for non-minority applicants. However, while women constitute slightly over a third of all law faculty, they account for only a quarter of full professors and 15 percent of deans. Women of color constitute seven percent of the faculty but only four percent of professors and one percent of deans. Richard A. White, AALS Statistical Report on Law School Faculty 2 (2003); see also Herma Hill Kay, Women Law School Deans: A Different Breed, Or Just One of the Boys? 14 Yale J.L. & Feminism 219 (2002) (providing history of women deans, and many statistics). As the report of the ABA Commission on Women in the Profession notes:

> Women faculty are still clustered in the least prestigious academic specialties and positions, such as librarians, research and writing instructors, and non-tenured clinicians. Gender inequalities persist within as well as across these specialties. For example, women account for two-thirds of legal writing instructors, but are only half as likely as their male counterparts to hold tenured positions or to direct writing

programs. At many schools, women students are also underrepresented in the most prestigious positions such as law review editors, class officers, and members of academic honor societies. The limited research available finds that these gender and racial disparities cannot be entirely explained by objective factors such as academic credentials or experience. Some evidence also suggests that women of color are underrepresented in student bodies relative to their undergraduate performance and academic potential.

ABA Commission on Women in the Profession, The Unfinished Agenda, supra, at 27. See Angel, supra, at 791. For similar data, see Richard K. Neumann, Jr., Women in Legal Education: A Statistical Update, 73 UMKC L. Rev. 419 (2004); Levitt, supra, at 778-783.

What accounts for these disparities has been subject to dispute. The most comprehensive effort to explain women's underrepresentation is Deborah Merritt's study of some 1,100 faculty who began teaching between 1986 and 1991. Deborah Jones Merritt, Are Women Stuck on the Academic Ladder? An Empirical Perspective, 10 UCLA Women's L.J. 249 (2000). Merritt found that differences in experience, credentials, and geographic mobility explained some gender differences, but not others. For example, controlling for relevant variables accounted for women's greater likelihood to take non-tenure-track positions and men's greater likelihood to obtain positions at the most prestigious schools. Id. at 250-252. However, differences in credentials and geographic constraints did not explain why men were hired at higher ranks and ended up teaching more prestigious subjects (such as constitutional law rather than legal writing). Nor was it entirely clear why white men were considerably more likely to obtain tenure, hold chairs, or serve as deans. Id. at 252-253. Some of the difference may have been attributable to the fact that white men published more scholarly articles (particularly in prestigious journals) than white women and women of color. Id. White men also attached less value than women to public service and to addressing non-academic audiences. However, women did match men in serving as associate deans, and women of color were even more likely than white men (or women) to hold such positions. Id.

In analyzing these results, Merritt suggests that unconscious discrimination, unequal family commitments, and different career priorities are all at work. Women appear less willing to relocate in pursuit of the most prestigious jobs and clerkships, and less focused on obtaining deanships or publishing articles in the most elite academic journals. Merritt, supra, at 245-247. "If women want different career paths than men," Merritt concludes, "then we shouldn't measure their advancement along traditional lines." Id. at 247. How do Merritt's conclusions differ from Kingsley Browne's, on p. 647 ? For the argument in this context that women's different biological makeup and different choices concerning family and career priorities largely explain their underrepresentation and call for no institutional remedies, see Dan Subotnik, Bah, Humbug to the Bleak Story of Women Law Faculty: A Response to Professor Newmann, 51 J. Legal Educ. 141, 143-148 (2001).

What constitutes equal opportunity in the law school context? Should we assume that women's different priorities are always freely chosen or that they are the primary explanation for different levels of advancement? Consider the following account of largely unconscious forms of gender bias:

> [Women professors are] subject to the same double standards and double binds that women encounter in other professional settings. Their competence is subject to heightened scrutiny and they risk criticism for being too assertive or not assertive enough. Multiple studies document unconscious bias in scholarly evaluations; for example, the same resumes or publications are rated higher when they are assumed to belong to men rather than women. Given the subjectivity of academic hiring and promotion standards, such biases are extremely difficulty to identify or remedy. The same is true of biases in student course evaluations. Comments like "she's too liberated for me" are still depressingly common. Even more frequent are the assessments that reflect such biases but are not candid in expressing them.
>
> Women also assume a disproportionate share of academic "housekeeping" work that interferes with the time available for scholarly research, which is, of course, what matters most in law school reward structures. Substantial gender disparities are reported in time spent on advising students and student organizations, attending law school events, and serving on committees. At most institutions, the small number of women of color further increases their burdens. And the devaluation of such service in the academic pecking order reinforces gender inequalities.
>
> Women's disproportionate family responsibilities also carry a cost when pitted against substantial research, teaching, and committee obligations. Although academics' work schedules generally permit more flexibility than those in other professional contexts, performance pressures and time demands can be even more unbounded. The problem is exacerbated by the overlap between women's biological and tenure clocks. About two-thirds of surveyed women law professors cite work/ family conflicts as a significant problem.
>
> Women's unequal domestic and academic service burdens also reduce the time available for the informal networking and mentoring that are often critical for career advancement. The relatively small number of senior women, particularly women of color, in many institutions and substantive specialities also lead to professional isolation and marginalization. There are still too many "good old boys" and too few "good old girls" to create level playing fields in most academic settings.
>
> The devaluation of teaching and scholarship that focuses on gender, race, ethnicity, and sexual orientation also discourages junior faculty from pursuing such interests and disadvantages those who persist. In short, too many women, particularly women who are "different" along other dimensions, still feel uncomfortable in the educational environment; too few have advanced to positions where they can significantly affect it.

Rhode, Midcourse Corrections, supra, at 482-483, 487. See also Martha Chamallis, The Shadow of Professor Kingsfield; Contemporary Dilemmas Facing Women Law Professors, 11 Wm. & Mary J. Women & L. 195, 200-202 (2005) (discussing unconscious biases and the accumulation of small disadvantages); Marjorie E. Kornhauser, Rooms of Their Own: An Empirical Study of Occupational Segregation by Gender Among Law Professors, 73 UMKC L. Rev. 293 (2004) (finding that four-fifths of law school courses have a gender identity, in that they are taught largely by members of one sex or the other, and that the courses disproportionately taught by women, such as family law, juvenile law,

poverty law, and legal research and writing, have less prestige than those disproportionately taught by men, such as constitutional law, corporations, federal tax,
and law and economics); Marjorie E. Kornhauser, Why a Duck? Are Feminist
Legal Journals An Endangered Species, and If So, Are They Worth Saving, 12
Hastings Women's L.J. 478 (2003) (documenting the bias against publishing
feminist articles by leading law journals).

Considerable evidence suggests that all of these problems are greater for
women of color, who lack the presumption of competence accorded to other
academics, and are subject to less respect, more hostile evaluations, and more
exclusion from informal networks. See Katherine L. Vaughns, Women of Color in
Law Teaching: Shared Identities, Different Experiences, 53 J. Legal Educ. 496
(2003); Anne B. Onyekwuluje, Guess Who's Coming to Class: Teaching
Through the Politics of Race, Class, and Gender, in Women Faculty of Color
in the White Classroom: Narratives on the Pedagogical Implications of Teacher
Diversity 247 (Lucila Vargas ed., 2002); Annette Koldodny, Raising Standards
While Lowering Anxieties: Rethinking the Promotion and Tenure Process, in
Power Race, and Gender in Academe: Strangers in the Tower? 9 (Shirley
Geok-lin Lim & Maria Herrera-Sobek eds., 2000); Pamela J. Smith, The Tyr-
annies of Silence of the Untenured Professors of Color, 33 U.C. Davis L. Rev.
1105 (2000).

If these are the barriers that impede women's advance, how should law
schools respond? Alternatively, if Subotnik is correct that women's family commitments explain their underrepresentation in the most demanding academic
positions, does it follow that they "lack the psychological makeup for success"?
Subotnik, supra, at 147.

Putting Theory into Practice

4-5. The ABA Commission on Women in the Profession, like many commentators in this field, has recommended that law schools establish committees to
identify and address gender-related concerns. ABA Commission, Don't Just Hear
It Through the Grapevine: Studying Gender Questions at Your Law School
(1998). Does your school have such a committee? What might such a committee
accomplish? What are its potential pitfalls?

4-6. Have there been any gender patterns in class participation in the
course for which you have been reading this book? Analyze these dynamics.
How does one get recognition in your class? What factors seem to affect who
gets called on, who asks questions, and who stays after class to ask questions? Is
this class typical? How would you assess the climate for women in your law
school? What about women of color?

To the extent that female students participate less in class and feel more
alienated from the educational process, what strategies should law professors
consider to address these disparities? How would you evaluate these strategies
in terms of the different perspectives examined in this course?

3. Legal Practice

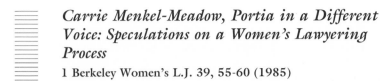

Carrie Menkel-Meadow, Portia in a Different Voice: Speculations on a Women's Lawyering Process

1 Berkeley Women's L.J. 39, 55-60 (1985)

Does the female voice of relationships, care and connection lead to a different form of law practice? Although the present adversarial system may limit the ways in which concern for others may be expressed toward adversaries, the values of relationship and care may be expressed with one's work partners. In this area at least, we have some evidence that Portia's voice has had an influence. As [Cynthia] Epstein has documented [in Women in Law, ch. 9 (1981)] early attempts to form a separate feminist practice focused on establishing non-hierarchical organizations with participatory decision-making. This was a political expression of the psychological qualities observed by Gilligan in the relationships and connections that women lawyers sought to forge with each other while engaged in practices that pitted them against the traditional models. Some of these women lawyers were explicit in their rejection of male principles in the ordering of legal work. . . .

While hierarchy produces efficiency and individual achievement, as lawyers, [women] . . . might choose to emphasize other values such as collectivity and interpersonal connection. This attempt to work in a different way not only affects relationships within the working unit, but is also apparent in the work of feminists who seek to demystify law and the legal profession by working with clients on lay advocacy projects or self-representation.

To illustrate the issues involved in a woman's way of practicing law, consider the following example. My colleague Grace Blumberg, an expert in marital property law, was asked to write the first draft of an amicus brief in a case involving the legal treatment of a professional degree in a community property regime. She describes the work on this effort with a group of California women lawyers as follows:

> The effort to transform a generally literate coherent brief into "proper form" took some 100 person hours, more than eight times the amount of time it took the author to write the brief. . . . The participants, leaving the author aside, seemed to get some substantial psychic rewards from this 100 hours spent mostly in conferences of two and three persons. They created an atmosphere of social intimacy between relative strangers. Although at least 90 percent of the time was spent hard at work, the atmosphere was of a social event. Food was always served even though it was not any discernible meal time. . . . Personal information and confidences were exchanged in the interstices of work. I was struck by the incongruity of my product (female) and my process (male) and in contrast, their product (male) and process (female). My product was revealing, tentative and dialectic. In contrast my process was individualistic and individual, highly concerned with the goal of efficiency and not at all interested in collaboration as an end in itself. In contrast, their product was extremely formal, authoritarian, con-

cealing and impersonal. Their process was communitarian and communicative, full of feeling and interpersonal experience.

The story of this brief-writing exercise also reveals another aspect of the women's lawyering process — concern for the interconnection of personal and professional life. In the "interstices of work," the lawyers engaged in this project shared information about their personal lives and brought sustenance to each other (intellectually, emotionally and nutritionally). Virtually every report of women lawyers discusses the impact of personal lives on professional lives and vice versa, where one finds almost no such reports in the descriptions and ethnographies of male lawyers. The concern for the quality of life and the relation between one's work and one's personal life is consistent with the ethic of care and relationship exhibited by Gilligan's female subjects....

Perhaps the most salient feature of Portia's different voice is in the lawyer-client relationship, where the values of care and responsibility for others seem most directly applicable. [Women]...with their ability to "take the part of the other and submerge the self," may be able to enter the world of the client, thereby understanding more fully what the client desires and why, without the domination of what the lawyer perceives to be "in the client's best interest." More fully developed sensitivities to empathy and altruism...may enable women lawyers to understand a fuller range of client needs and objectives.... [Where male lawyers] may make assumptions about the primacy of economic and efficiency considerations of their cases,...[female lawyers] may see a greater number of issues in the social, psychological and moral aspects. Of course, in a fully mature and integrated vision of lawyering all of these aspects of the case would be considered important....

[T]he tendency to personalize and contextualize problems may incline women lawyers to ask for more information on a broader range of subjects and thereby develop a fuller understanding of the context of the client's life. This, in turn, may make women better lawyers, especially in their relationships with clients and in their ability to see the human complexities of some legal problems.... If women are more concerned with the context in which the dispute is embedded, would they not search for more facts and be less concerned about creation of a precedent of universal applicability?...

If [women] use different considerations in their moral reasoning, would they create different ethical codes for the profession based on their different ways of engaging in moral reasoning?...Would [women] create rules about relationships between lawyers, based on mutual affiliation in the same profession, and requiring greater candor and fairness in dealing with each other? Would the conflict of interest rules or withdrawal from representation rules be different because of an ethic of care and affiliation that would lead to a different conception of client loyalty? Might a broader conception of the legal problem and its causes lead to less concern about the unauthorized practice of law and more toleration, if not encouragement, of work with other professionals and lay persons to solve those problems?

Katharine T. Bartlett, *Feminist Legal Methods*
103 Harv. L. Rev. 829, 836-837, 843-847, 862-863 (1990)

When feminists "do law," they do what other lawyers do: they examine the facts of a legal issue or dispute, they identify the essential features of those facts, they determine what legal principles should guide the resolution of the dispute, and they apply those principles to the facts. This process unfolds not in a linear, sequential, or strictly logical manner, but rather in a pragmatic, interactive manner. Facts determine which rules are appropriate, and rules determine which facts are relevant. In doing law, feminists like other lawyers use a full range of methods of legal reasoning—deduction, induction, analogy, and use of hypotheticals, policy, and other general principles.

In addition to these conventional methods of doing law, however, feminists use other methods. These methods, though not all unique to feminists, attempt to reveal features of a legal issue which more traditional methods tend to overlook or suppress. One method, asking the woman question, is designed to expose how the substance of law may silently and without justification submerge the perspectives of women and other excluded groups. Another method, feminist practical reasoning, expands traditional notions of legal relevance to make legal decisionmaking more sensitive to the features of a case not already reflected in legal doctrine. A third method, consciousness-raising, offers a means of testing the validity of accepted legal principles through the lens of the personal experience of those directly affected by those principles....

Is asking the woman question really a method at all, or it is a mask for something else, such as legal substance, or politics? The [United States] legal system has assumed that method and substance have different functions, and that method cannot serve its purpose unless it remains separate from, and independent of, substantive "bias." Rules of legal method, like rules of legal procedure, are supposed to insulate substantive rules from arbitrary application....Within this conventional view, it might be charged that the method of asking the woman question fails to respect the necessary separation between method and substance. Indeed, asking the woman question seems to be a "loaded," overtly political activity, which reaches far beyond the "neutral" tasks of ascertaining law and facts and applying one to the other.

Of course, not only feminist legal methods but *all* legal methods shape substance; the difference is that feminists have been called on it....

The real question is...[not] whether [a method has substantive consequences] but whether the relationship between method and substance is "proper."... A purely result-oriented method in which decisionmakers may decide every case in order to reach the result they think most desirable ...improperly exerts no meaningful constraints on the decisionmaker. Also improper is a method that imposes arbitrary or unjustified constraints, such as one that requires a decisionmaker to decide in favor of all female claimants or against all employers.

In contrast, the method of asking the woman question...demands ...special attention to a set of interests and concerns that otherwise may be, and historically have been, overlooked. The substance of asking the woman question lies in *what* it asks to uncover: disadvantage based upon gender. The political nature of this method arises only because it seeks information that is not supposed to exist. The claim that this information may exist — and that the woman question is therefore necessary — is political, but only to the extent that the stated or implied claim that it does not exist is *also* political.

Asking the woman question confronts the assumption of legal neutrality, and has substantive consequences only if the law is not gender-neutral. The bias of the method is the bias toward uncovering a certain kind of bias. The bias disadvantages those who are otherwise benefited by law and legal methods whose gender implications are *not* revealed. If this is "bias," feminists must insist that it is "good" (or "proper") bias, not "bad."...

[As for more contextualized methods of legal reasoning,] feminists' substantive analyses of legal decisionmaking have revealed to them that so-called neutral means of deciding cases tend to mask, not eliminate, political and social considerations from legal decisionmaking. Feminists have found that neutral rules and procedures tend to drive underground the ideologies of the decisionmaker, and that these ideologies do not serve women's interests well. Disadvantaged by hidden bias, feminists see the value of modes of legal reasoning that expose and open up debate concerning the underlying political and moral considerations. By forcing articulation and understanding of those considerations, practical reasoning forces justification of results based upon what interests are actually at stake.

The "substance" of feminist practical reasoning consists of an alertness to certain forms of injustice that otherwise go unnoticed and unaddressed. Feminists turn to contextualized methods of reasoning to allow greater understanding and exposure of that injustice. Reasoning from context can change perceptions about the world, which may then further expand the contexts within which such reasoning seems appropriate, which in turn may lead to still further changes in perceptions. The expansion of existing boundaries of relevance based upon changed perceptions of the world is familiar to the process of legal reform. The shift from Plessy v. Ferguson to Brown v. Board of Education, for example, rested upon the expansion of the "legally relevant" in race discrimination cases to include the actual experiences of black Americans and the inferiority implicit in segregation. Much of the judicial reform that has been beneficial to women, as well, has come about through expanding the lens of legal relevance to encompass the missing perspectives of women and to accommodate perceptions about the nature and role of women. Feminist practical reasoning compels continued expansion of such perceptions.

Notes

1. A Profile of Women in the Legal Profession. A statistical profile of women in the American bar reflects both dramatic progress and continued constraints. Since the 1960s, the representation of women in the American legal profession has increased from about three percent to 30 percent, and at the turn of the century, they constituted a majority of entering law students. Yet female practitioners remain underrepresented at the top and overrepresented at the bottom in terms of status, power, and financial reward. Women account for only 17 percent of law firm partners, 16 percent of federal district court judges, and 15 percent of law school deans and general counsels. The gap widens for women of color, who account for only three percent of the profession, and one percent of deans, general counsels, and law firm partners. See Paula A. Patton, Women Lawyers: Their Status, Influence, and Retention in the Legal Profession, 11 Wm. & Mary J. Women & L. 173, 174 (2005); ABA Commission on Women in the Profession, Current Glance of Women and the Law 1 (2003); Richard A. White, AALS Statistical Report on Law School Faculty 2 (2003); Elizabeth Chambliss, Miles to Go: Progress of Minorities in the Legal Profession (ABA Commission on Racial and Ethnic Diversity in the Legal Profession, 2005). See also National Association of Law Placement [NALP], Women and Attorneys of Color at Law Firms (2004). Minority representation in the bar lags behind that in most other professions, as well as in the labor force generally. According to the most recent available data, minorities constituted about 25 percent of the civilian labor force, 25 percent of physicians, 23 percent of computer scientists, 20 percent of accountants, and 18 percent of academics, compared to 10 percent of lawyers. Chambliss, supra, at 6. Women account for a higher percentage of minority lawyers than white lawyers (44 percent compared to 30 percent). Id.

The main challenge in achieving gender equity in the legal profession involves retention and promotion. The problem is not simply that women have not been in the pipeline long enough to achieve substantial representation at the highest levels. Rather, even studies that control for age and experience find persistent gender disparities. In a study by the Equal Employment Opportunity Commission [EEOC] of large firms, men were five times as likely to become partners as women. EEOC, Diversity in Law Firms 9 (2003), available at www.eeoc.gov/stats/reports/diversity/law/index.html. In the New York Bar glass ceiling study, women were three times less likely to become partners as men, and in the ABF study, less than half as likely as men. See also Nancy Reichman & Joyce S. Sterling, Gender Penalties Revisited 12, 13 (2004), available at http://www.cwba.org. The disparities are most pronounced at the highest levels, such as managing partners and senior government officials. See ABA Commission on Women in the Profession, The Unfinished Agenda: A Report on the Status of Women in the Legal Profession 14 (2001) (noting that only five percent of managing partners are women); Vanessa Blum, Report Offers Detailed Look at DOJ Lawyers; Many Women, Minorities Find Jobs in Lower Ranks, But Not at Top, Legal Times, Oct. 27, 2003, at 1 (of some 9000 lawyers working for U.S. Justice Department, men are 50 percent more likely to be in the most senior posts than women, and white men are more than three times as likely to be in such than minority women). Similar gender disparities are apparent in most other European and Anglo-American nations. See Ulrike Schultz, Introduction: Women in the World's Legal Professions: Overview and Synthesis, in Women in the World's Legal Profession xxv, xliv (Ulrike Schultz & Gisela Shaw eds., 2003) (noting that even when women achieve partnership, they lack the same degree of power, independence and decision-making authority as men). The proportion of women of color who are equity partners remains stuck at around 1 percent, and almost none remain at the firm at which they began. National Association of Law Placement Foundation, Beyond the Bidding Wars: A Survey of Associate Attrition, Departure, Destinations, and Workplace Initiatives 23 (2000)(describing attrition rates); Molly McDonough, No Easy Path to Diversity, ABA J. Report, Dec. 17, 2004 (noting that 75 percent of women of color leave within first five years).

Men and women are now similarly distributed in most legal settings, although women are disproportionately underrepresented in business (which accounts for nine percent of female lawyers and 11 percent of male lawyers) and overrepresented in public interest positions (which account for four percent of female lawyers and two percent of male lawyers). In private practice, the ratio of female to male lawyers is 58 percent to 61 percent. In government, men and women are evenly represented (12 percent).

Studies of career change reflect some gender disparities. For example, in the recent Colorado bar study, virtually all men moved up in status over the course of the twelve years surveyed. That was true of only about half of women. Reichman & Sterling, supra, at 14-15. Male lawyers' primary explanation for leaving their last job is "new opportunities in law" (46 percent); the second most common reason is unhappiness with compensation (23 percent). Women are slightly more likely to cite dissatisfaction with compensation (26 percent), and far less likely to cite new opportunities in law (27 percent). Women also give reasons that no men offer: lifestyle concerns (10 percent), unhappiness with legal practice (six percent), and opportunities outside of law (4 percent). Id. at 25. These findings are consistent with a number of earlier studies and with patterns in most European nations, where women move "sideways not up." Schultz, supra, at xlv. See also Reichman & Sterling, supra, at 25-26 (men find it less socially acceptable to cite lifestyle or family reasons, or disaffection, as reasons for career change).

What implications do you draw from these differences? Again, is Kingsley Browne right in his article excerpted on p. 647 above: there is no glass ceiling, only different career paths? Should women's lower status and traditional career paths be of concern? Consider Carrie Menkel-Meadow's observation:

> Achievement of high-status and lucrative positions in large law firms represents the liberal feminist achievement of the American Dream. But is it a dream or a nightmare? Monetary and prestige measures of success, drawn from conventional male-constructed sociology, all too often are taken as the measure of women's progress in the profession, even where there is some evidence women themselves look to other measures, like doing socially useful work or having meaningful relationships at work with clients and co-workers. Both cultural and more radical feminist critiques remind us that becoming surrogate males is not the feminist-humanist transformative vision. Committing many hours to routinized tasks, within a highly stratified hierarchy, on cases and transactions with debatable social utility, while leaving one's children in the care of low-income women is hardly the feminist vision of a more humane world. . . . Women want to be in the workforce but may want to reconstruct what it means to be a productive worker.

Carrie Menkel-Meadow, Exploring a Research Agenda of the Feminization of the Legal Profession: Theories of Gender and Social Change, 14 Law & Soc. Inquiry 289, 307-308 (1989).

2. Work/Family Conflicts. Work/family conflicts have long been a barrier to women in the legal profession. In hearings before the ABA Commission on Women in the Profession, the primary obstacle identified by those testifying was legal employers' failure to accommodate family responsibilities. ABA, Hearings to Identify Current Obstacles, Opportunities Facing Women Lawyers (May 7, 2003), available at http://abanet.org/lpm/lpt/articles/mgt05041.html. Two central problems are the excessive hours in many practice settings, and the inadequacy of part-time options, parental leave, and flexible schedule arrangements.

Over the past quarter century, the number of hours expected of lawyers has risen substantially. In private practice, current norms are close to 2000 billable hours per year, and to charge honestly at those levels often requires 60-hour work weeks. The norms in many corporate and public sector organizations are similar. See Deborah L. Rhode, Balanced Lives: Changing the Culture of Workplace Practice (ABA Commission on Women in the Profession, 2002). A related problem is the inadequacy of part-time arrangements. Although about 95 percent of surveyed firms permit part-time schedules, only about four percent of lawyers actually take them. Patton, supra, at 189. About three-quarters of surveyed women believe that taking an alternative schedule would jeopardize their prospects for partnership. Catalyst, Women in Law: Making the Case 19 (2001). There is ample basis for such concern. Associates in many practice settings report that "no time . . . is the right time" to get pregnant. Patton, supra, at 180. Lawyers at all stages of their careers find that taking time off, even for a brief parental leave, results in the loss of challenging work and career development opportunities. As one Wall Street associate put it, being pregnant was like being "a leper in a public square." Vivia Chen, Cracks in the Ceiling, Am. Law., June 2003, at 81. See Patton, supra at 180; Deborah L. Rhode, Balanced Lives for Lawyers, 70 Fordham L. Rev. 2207, 2213 (2002); Reichman & Sterling, supra, at 35, 43. In addition to isolation and marginalization, many part-time lawyers report "schedule creep. . . . Reduced hours are not respected, 'unexpected emergencies' become expected events, and attorneys can often end up with full-time work for part-time pay." Rhode, Balanced Lives, supra, at 2213. See Patti Giglio, Rethinking the Hours, Legal Times, Nov. 8, 2004, at 1; Joan Williams, Canaries in the Mine: Work/Family Conflict and the Law, 70 Fordham L. Rev. 2221, 2224 (2002).

The lack of parental leave and caretaking assistance pose similar obstacles. Although the vast majority of legal employers provide paid maternity leave, the duration is often inadequate and only about 10 to 15 percent of surveyed employers provide the same opportunities for men. See sources cited in Rhode, Balanced Lives, supra, at 2214. Few law firms have followed the lead of major corporations and accounting firms in providing help to employees in securing affordable, quality childcare and elder care, particularly for emergencies, weekends, and evenings. Id. Such failures carry significant costs in recruitment, retention, absenteeism, and job-related stress. See American Bar Association Commission on Women in the

Profession, Legal Progeny: A Guide to Providing Child Care Benefits for Legal Employers, Lawyers, and Bar Associations 2-3 (2003).

For examples of model workplace policies, see Rhode, Balanced Lives: Changing the Culture, supra; ABA Commission on Women in the Profession, Legal Progeny, supra; Angela Cheng, Part-Time Culture Grows at Firms, Nat'l L.J., Oct. 26, 2004, at A1; Joan Williams et al., Better on Balance? The Corporate Counsel Work/Life Report, 10 Wm. & Mary J. Women & L. 367 (2004).

3. When Does Gender Difference Make a Difference? Do women bring special qualities to the practice of law? Matthew Hale Carpenter, in unsuccessfully defending the right of Myra Bradwell to become a member of the Illinois Bar, argued that while some cases may require the "rough qualities possessed by men,... [t]here are many causes in which the silver voice of a woman would accomplish more than the severity and sternness of man could achieve." Bradwell v. Illinois, 83 U.S. 130, 137 (1872).

Among contemporary lawyers, perceptions of gender differences are widely shared. In a representative ABA Journal poll, only eight percent of women lawyers believed that male and female lawyers had the same strengths, and only 18 percent believed that they had the same weaknesses. Terry Carter, Paths Need Paving, ABA J., Sept. 2000, at 34. Slightly under half of male lawyers believed that men and women had the same strengths and weaknesses. Id. Women lawyers were thought to have greater empathy and "better people skills," but insufficient assertiveness and aggressiveness. Id. Lawyers in other nations often hold similar views. See Hilary Sommerlad & Peter Sanderson, Gender, Choice, and Commitment (1998) (describing male barristers' perception of male colleagues as powerful, aggressive, logical, tough, strong, and dominant and female colleagues as vulnerable, intuitive, empathetic, emotional, and subjective, and barristers' belief that male characteristics were more professionally desirable); Schultz, supra, at lvii (describing small scale studies that find differences in women's working styles, such as being more generous with their time and more concerned with client relations than their male counterparts).

Many commentators, like Menkel-Meadow in the excerpted reading, have argued that women lawyers practice in a "different voice," more sensitive to values of care, compassion, and cooperation than prevailing legal norms. See, e.g., Rand Jack & Dana Crowley Jack, Moral Vision and Professional Decisions: The Changing Values of Women and Men Lawyers (1989); Susan P. Sturm, From Gladiators to Problem-Solvers: Connecting Conversations About Women, the Academy, and the Legal Profession, 4 Duke J. Gender L. & Pol'y 119 (1997).

Such differences are assumed to account for sex-linked differences in choice of specialties, such as women's disproportionate representation among family lawyers, family court judges, and teachers of family law. See Schultz, supra, at xxxvii (practitioners and judges); Lynn Mather, Gender in Context: Women in Family Law 33, in Women in the World's Legal Professions: Overview and Synthesis, in Women in the World's Legal Professions, supra, 33, 35 (lawyers); Marjorie E. Kornhauser, Rooms of Their Own: An Empirical Study of Occupational Segregation by Gender Among Law Professors, 73 UMKC L. Rev. 293 (2004) (law professors); Deborah Jones Merritt & Barbara F. Reskin, Sex, Race, and

Credentials: The Truth About Affirmative Action in Law Faculty Hiring, 97 Colum. L. Rev. 199, 258-259 (1997) (law professors). Is there a plausible "different voice" explanation for these disparities?

The evidence for most presumed differences between male and female lawyers is weaker than commonly supposed. None of the early work claiming such gender differences drew on large-scale, methodologically adequate empirical surveys. See, e.g., Jack & Jack, supra (relying on interviews with 36 attorneys in one county). More recent social science research does not reveal the sharp gender-linked variations that many commentators and practitioners assume. For example, a sophisticated survey by William Felstiner and colleagues finds no measurable differences in clients' perception of male and female lawyers; both sexes are seen as friendly, polite, organized, confident, and trustworthy. Nor does the sex of lawyers matter in terms of whether a client would be willing to recommend them or use them again. William Felstiner et al., The Effect of Lawyers' Gender on Client Perceptions of Lawyers, in Women in the World's Legal Professions, supra, at 23, 26. Similarly, Lynn Mather's empirical study of divorce attorneys in three New England states finds that male and female lawyers both prefer amicable settlements. The gender differences were generally minor and often ran contrary to conventional stereotypes. Women tended to place slightly more value than men on being sensitive listener (4.5 on scale of 5, compared to 4.18). However, female lawyers were also more likely than their male colleagues to say that they discouraged clients from talking about emotional and personal problems. And female lawyers were also more likely to be seen as unreasonable, aggressive, hard-nosed advocates, who were willing to pursue unreasonable client objectives. In interpreting such findings, Mather notes that women attorneys were disproportionately likely to represent women clients, and may have been willing to fight harder on "small points" because they realized the importance that financial concessions might have for their clients' well-being. Mather, like other contemporary commentators, stresses the importance of context, and concludes that gender is only one of the factors that influence lawyers' working styles. Mather, supra, at 39-40; Schultz, supra, at lvii.

Surveys of leadership styles and decision-making behavior also have reached mixed results that underscore the contextual variations in gender difference. Some research based on laboratory experiments and individuals' self-descriptions finds that women display greater interpersonal skills and adopt more participatory, democratic styles, while men rely on more directive and task-oriented approaches. Jeanette Cleveland et al., Women and Men in Management 307 (1999); Alice H. Eagly & Blair T. Johnson, Gender and Leadership Style: A Meta-Analysis, 108 Psychol. Bull. 233, 233-256 (1990); Alice H. Eagly et al., Gender and the Effectiveness of Leaders: A Meta-Analysis, 117 Psychol. Bull. 125, 125-145 (1995). Yet other large-scale studies based on self-reports find no such gender differences. Radcliffe Public Policy Institute & The Boston Club, Suiting Themselves: Women's Leadership Styles in Today's Workplace (1999). Nor do these differences emerge in most research involving evaluations of leaders by supervisors, subordinates, and peers in real-world settings; Karin Klenke, Women and Leadership: A Contextual Perspective 160 (1996); Eagly & Johnson, supra, at 246-247; Cheryl Simrell King, Sex Role Identity and Decision

Styles: How Gender Helps Explain the Paucity of Women at the Top, in Gender Power, Leadership and Governance 67, 71 (Georgia Duerst-Lahti & Rita Mae Kelly eds., 1995). For an overview, see Deborah L. Rhode, The Difference "Difference" Makes, in The Difference "Difference" Makes: Women and Leadership 3, 18-20 (Deborah L. Rhode ed., 2003).

Gender stereotypes may help to explain these divergent results. Sex stereotypes are particularly likely to influence lab studies and self-descriptions. In experimental situations where participants have relatively little information about each other, they are more likely to fall back on conventional assumptions about appropriate masculine and feminine behavior. Such assumptions may also skew individuals' willingness to behave or to describe their behavior in ways that deviate from stereotypical norms. Klenke, supra, at 151. Since women do not enjoy the same presumption of competence, the same latitude for assertiveness, and the same access to power as their male colleagues, a less autocratic style may seem necessary. Eagly & Johnson, supra, at 247-248. By contrast, the force of conventional stereotypes is weaker in actual organizational settings than in lab studies or self-assessments. Women who have achieved decisionmaking positions in traditionally male-dominated professions generally have been socialized to follow prevailing practices. Joanne Martin & Debra Meyerson, Women and Power: Confronting Resistance and Disorganized Action, in Power and Influence in Organizations 311, 313 (Roderick M. Kramer & Margaret A. Neale eds., 1998); Cleveland et al., supra, at 293-299.

Another context in which gender differences have been extensively researched involves negotiating behavior. Over the past two decades, a large body of theoretical and empirical research has attempted to determine whether men and women have different negotiating styles and effectiveness. A recent summary of this work finds

> conflicting claims and widely disparate results — such as the most recent studies' conclusions that "men negotiate significantly better outcomes than women" . . . ; "women behave more cooperatively than men" . . . ; "women may obtain lower joint outcomes in integrative bargaining because of a higher level of concern for the other" . . . , but also that "there are no statistically significant differences in negotiation outcomes and performance between men and women". . . .

Carrie Menkel-Meadow, Teaching About Gender and Negotiation: Sex, Truths, and Videotape, 16 Negotiation J. 357 (Oct. 2000).

In accounting for these conflicting results, it may be significant that gender is mediated by other aspects of the negotiating context that vary across research settings. These other aspects include the relative social status, perceived power, and attitudes toward conflict of the participants. Whether negotiators are the same sex, whether they have ongoing relationships, and whether they are acting for themselves or as representatives for someone else also matters. For reviews of multiple studies, see id.; Sandra R. Farber & Monica Rickenberg, Under-Confident Women and Over-Confident Men: Gender and a Sense of Competence in a Simulated Negotiation, 11 Yale J.L. & Feminism 271, 286, 301 (1999).

One of the few findings of gender difference that holds up across multiple studies is that women seem to feel less confident than men even when there are no objective differences in outcome. Farber & Rickenberg, supra, at 301. Another common finding is that male and female negotiators are expected to perform differently even where there is little actual difference in goals, orientation, or outcomes. See studies cited in Carrie Menkel-Meadow, Portia Redux: Another Look at Gender, Feminism and Legal Ethics, 2 Va. J. Soc. Pol'y & L. 75 (1994).

It is possible, of course, to argue for more caring and cooperative approaches to legal practice on the basis of feminist commitments, not feminine characteristics. Much recent work by feminists as well as other commentators concludes that non-adversarial collaborative and problem-solving techniques may be more effective than more conventional adversarial methods and that more participatory, less hierarchical lawyering styles can improve representation of clients. See Carrie Menkel-Meadow, The Limits of Adversarial Ethics, in Ethics in Practice: Lawyers' Roles, Responsibilities, and Regulation (Deborah L. Rhode ed., 2000); Deborah L. Rhode, In the Interests of Justice 49-115 (2001); Sturm, supra, at 127-128, 135-137.

For a discussion of a study showing that woman lawyers receive fewer disciplinary sanctions than male lawyers, see pp. 664-665.

4. Women Supporting Women. American women lawyers' collective efforts on behalf of women have taken a variety of forms. Some feminist attorneys have formed public interest women's rights organizations that have spearheaded reforms on a wide array of issues including employment, education, families, reproductive choice, and sex-linked violence. A small number of practitioners have formed private law firms that focus on women's issues or target women clients in areas such as matrimonial law and personal injury litigation. See Leigh Jones, Women to Women, Nat'l L.J. July 12, 2004, at 1, 7. Many cities and states have separate women's bar associations, or active women's sections within existing bar organizations. A number of these groups have launched "No Glass Ceiling Initiatives" in which firms commit to specific goals concerning the representation of women in partnership and top management positions. See Jane Di Renzo Pigat & Sharon Jones, Walking the Talk: Creating a Law Firm Culture Where Women Succeed 11 (ABA Commission on Women in the Profession, 2004). Many law firms and corporations have women's associations that promote mentoring, networking, and professional development. See Rhode, The Difference "Difference" Makes, supra, at 29-30; Emily Barker, Engendering Change, American Lawyer, June, 2003, at 82-84. Some large corporate clients have assisted these efforts by signing pledges that commit them to consider the diversity of law firms when selecting outside counsel. See Pigat & Jones, supra, at 2 (noting that by 2003, 500 CEOs had signed the pledge, Diversity in the Workplace: A Statement of Principle). How effective client pressures will prove in practice remains unclear. In one recent study of in-house counsel at 200 Fortune 1000 firms, diversity rated 4.1 in importance on a 10-point scale. The study concluded that cost and quality are dominant concerns and diversity is at best a tie-breaker. Elizabeth Chambliss, Miles to Go: Progress of Minorities in the

Legal Profession 35 (ABA Commission on Racial and Ethnic Diversity in the Legal Profession, 2005).

Not all women lawyers have wanted to be associated with such initiatives. Some have been wary of being viewed as activists on women's issues, given the charges of favoritism and negative stereotypes that such involvement may evoke. In conservative practice contexts, women worry about labels such as "oversensitive, abrasive, difficult, self serving, [or] whiner." Rhode, The Difference "Difference" Makes, supra, at 24. (Recall the facts of the *Ezold* case, at p. 63.) Attorneys who rose to senior positions in an earlier era sometimes feel that if they "made it" without special help, so can other women. Id.

What can be done to challenge these stereotypes? Do they affect women law students as well as practitioners? Leila Robinson, the first woman lawyer in Massachusetts, counseled her female colleagues: "Do not take sex into the practice. Don't be 'lady lawyers'. Simply be lawyers and recognize no distinction between yourselves and the other members of the bar." Letter from Lelia J. Robinson [Sawtelle] to the Equity Club (Apr. 9, 1887), reprinted in Women Lawyers and the Origins of Professional Identity in America: The Letters of the Equity Club, 1887 to 1890, 66 (Virginia G. Drachman ed., 1993) Is that still good advice? Why or why not? What strategies would be most effective in building coalitions for change within the legal profession?

5. Feminist Legal Method? The readings in this section suggest that feminist legal analysis is more contextualized than more traditional forms of analysis. Others have similarly advocated "pragmatic" or "situated" forms of decisionmaking, or "practical reasoning," not necessarily under the "feminist" label. See, e.g., Margaret Jane Radin, The Pragmatist and the Feminist, 63 S. Cal. L. Rev. 1699 (1990); Martha Minow, Foreword: Justice Engendered, 101 Harv. L. Rev. 10 (1987). What difference does feminist method make? Will it help women? Is it biased? How does it compare, for example, to the law and economics method?

> It is important to note that the feminist hypothesis that the law is not as neutral and objective as it claims to be when it comes to women is just that — a hypothesis. As a hypothesis, that judgment only kicks off the method. There is no impact (political or otherwise) from feminist method until it is proved. If the hypothesis is proved, this means that gender bias does (or did) exist, in which case it is not the scholar who . . . is partisan, but the law itself. . . .
>
> [A]lthough feminist method looks to women's experiences for its evidence, it must establish what it purports to show. Factual assertions need to be proven, even if feminist inquiry results in altering what constitutes proof. Material must be relevant, even if feminists, applying feminist method, succeed in redrawing the boundaries of relevance. Normative claims must be persuasive, even if what is deemed persuasive is changed by feminist questioning of underlying assumptions and paradigms.
>
> In important respects, feminist method has had much in common with the methods of law and economics scholarship. Law and economics scholars begin with a hypothesis — that individuals act in self-interested, profit-maximizing ways and that the law can best serve its goals if it takes account of these motivations. This hypothesis, based on prior discoveries that individuals act in self-interested, profit-

maximizing ways, directs the inquiry of law and economics scholars in specific legal contexts to determine how the law operates, and how it might be improved to enhance desirable and efficient behavior. And like feminist scholarship, the hypothesis has no effect, other than to give direction to the research, until some proposition is shown through evidence and argument that is persuasive to those whom the scholars would like to persuade.

Katharine T. Bartlett, Cracking Foundations as Feminist Method, 8 Am. U. J. Gender Soc. Pol'y & L. 31, 39-41 (2000). Why does feminist method appear, to some, so political? Is it sometimes, simply put, unpersuasive (as law and economics analysis can also be unpersuasive)? Is it that its critics are too interested (or "political") to accept it? Id. at 41-42. What difference does feminist method make in analyzing the *Lamb* case on p. 753 of this chapter?

Some have argued that the law's need for stability, predictability, and impartiality "would be seriously undermined by a jurisprudence that strongly privileges responsibility over rights, relationships over fairness, and context-specific judgment over rule-based decision-making." Gregory Bassham, Feminist Legal Theory: A Liberal Response, 6 Notre Dame J.L. & Pub. Pol'y 293, 310 (1992). Is this a fair criticism of feminist method? Or does it suggest too sharp a dichotomy between context-specific and rule-based analysis?

4. Women Judges

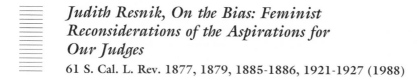

Judith Resnik, On the Bias: Feminist Reconsiderations of the Aspirations for Our Judges
61 S. Cal. L. Rev. 1877, 1879, 1885-1886, 1921-1927 (1988)

I have two central questions: First, what are the contemporary aspirations for those who judge? Second, how do feminist theories inform or challenge these aspirations?

At one level, the answer to the first question is so easy that some might suggest it is a "straw person." A vast body of legal literature addresses the question of what qualifies a person to be a judge. We speak about seeking individuals who will be "impartial," "disengaged," "independent," and who will hear both sides and judge fairly....

One can also understand the impulse towards seeking judges who lack self-interest. Judges hold awesome powers in this society. Their judgments change lives, transfer assets, imprison individuals, and even determine life and death. How tremendously frightening it would be to think that judgments were motivated by personal gain, that the interests of others were routinely sacrificed to advance judges' self-serving goals. Statements of the requirement of disengagement assuage our anxiety about judicial promotion of self.

Two other aspects of disengagement might be understood from the differing vantage points of the judges and the judged. Disengagement may free judges to act. Psychologically, the distance between judges and their judgments may enable judges to render the decisions that so profoundly affect the lives of others. If freed from having to engage personally with what occurs subsequent to their judgments, judges may be enabled to impose rulings that would otherwise be too painful to pronounce. And, psychologically, those who are judged may wish for a judge who is, at some level, a mystical "Other," not like ourselves but endowed with special wisdom and insight.

The imagery of Justice is emblematic of many of these hopes. The judicial icon is a goddess-like figure, frequently shown with scales, sword, and, after the sixteenth century, with a blindfold. First a goddess within the Greek and Roman traditions, Justitia evolved into Justice, one of the cardinal virtues endorsed by Christianity. And the power to judge shifted from kings, in the name of gods, to kings in their own right, and then from kings to judges, governing bodies continued to adorn their buildings with scenes of the Last Judgment and with images of Justice. Not simply a relic of the past, Justice still appears in courthouses and other civic buildings throughout the country. How ironic, in a world in which all judges were men, that sovereigns continued to display Justitia as the paradigm judge. Yet, given the magnitude of the power that resides in judges, how appropriate to seek an Other, some mythical figure, quintessentially nonpartisan, who would have the wisdom of the divine.

Impartiality, freedom from bias or prejudgment, independence, disengagement. These are terms that are culturally dependent. Anthropologists remind us that other systems of justice do not require such attributes for their judges. But taken in the context of the exercise of judgment by state officials rather than by elders known to the community, in the context of the history of ongoing struggles between judges and sovereigns, and in the context of the immense power that judges possess, the quest for such qualities in judges can be readily appreciated. . . .

The language of the law of judges and the language of feminism have virtually no convergences. . . . A touchstone of feminism is connection; over and over again, feminist theories speak about our interrelatedness, our interdependencies, our selves and others as impossible of comprehension in isolation. . . .

The case law and commentary on the role of judges have none of these qualities. Instead one finds that fiat: "No man is permitted to try cases where he has an interest in the outcome." Such a statement is not accompanied by an acknowledgment that we are all interested, that not all interests are equal nor equally bad, and that the kind of interest intended to be banned is a particular form of self-aggrandizement. Rather, the traditional aspirations for judges assume a single kind of undesirable interest, a connection linked to corruption. The terms of the world of the judge — disinterest, disengagement, impartiality, independence — are words that are deeply suspicious of relationship. . . .

At one level, what is missing is evident: We do not, but we could, demand that those who hold power do so with attentive love, with care, with nurturance, with a responsible sense of one's self as connected to and dependent upon those who are being judged. . . . But there are (at least) three difficulties. The first is one of domination. Assuming that we could alter the aspirations for judging, what would happen if the list of judicial qualifications were simply enlarged by adding the qualities feminist theories have helped us learn to value? Here, we must heed Rosemary Ruether's warning to reject an androgynous Judg/ess because, under conditions of patriarchy, the addition of traits associated with the female only ratifies their second class status.... Ruether's point may also be echoed in legal doctrine about the relationship between the law and equity. Law is the starting place. Equity is the cabined, secondary response — appended, ad hoc, supplementary and suspect. Stirring a bit of connection and responsible nurturance in the pot of powerful disengagement of our judges is hardly the kind of transformative response that feminist insights demand. A revised, rather than an expanded, list of attributes, is required.

A second problem is one of enthusiasm. How sure can we be that connection and care are qualities we want for our judges? Women's experience of connection and care have not been uniformly uplifting. As Robin West so well summarizes, radical feminists remind us that with connection can come debasement, the experience of intimacy as paralysis, of interdependence as moments when one loses a sense of self, all accompanied by what Sara Ruddick describes as "cheery denial." Judges, like women, may well fear intimacy. Isolating judges by calls for distance and disengagement and by fragmentation of responsibility could, in one sense, have been understood as enabling. How, one might ask, could an empathic judge sentence another-in-whom-one-sees-oneself to years of incarceration? How could judges impose economic burdens on struggling individuals or entities? For those of us who might applaud a possible reduction in criminal penalties which such intimacy and empathy might foster, we must recognize that our empathic judges would not simply experience connection with defendants, but also with victims. Might such judges respond with too harsh condemnations? Or with paralysis from being torn in too many directions?

I think paralysis-by-connection to be no more likely than paralysis-by intellectualization. In our current world, in which we do not ask judges to recognize their connectedness to those before them, some judges impose harsh sentences and some more lenient ones; some judges impose obligations upon litigants without much apparent stress while others appear reluctant to sanction. The length of judicial opinions and the energy of some dissents bear testimony to the tugs and pulls of contemporary judging, complete with its claims of dispassion and disinterest.

But then, one might ask if feminist revision is needed, and (not surprisingly), my answer is yes. Recognition of the tugs, the pulls, and the burdens of judging would be beneficial.... Perhaps if we learned to speak of judging as a terrible and terrifying job, as a burden of inflicting pain by virtue of judgment, we might develop modes of resolution different from those so readily accepted today. We might seek more communal modes of decision-making, insisting upon groups of two, three, or four judges to share the honor, the obligation, and the pain of decision. When we recognize the burden and the pain of judging, we might uncover one element of adjudication that exists but is relatively unacknowledged: Much "adjudication" is not a win/lose proposition but an effort at accommodation, with judges and juries responding to both sides but currently without vocabulary or permission to express empathy with competing claims. Many verdicts allocate victory to both sides, but our tradition is to mask that allocation rather than to endorse the practice of seeing multiple claims of right. Feminism may help bolster our trust in practice and permit us to remove the facades of total victory and defeat.

A third problem with revising the list of aspirations for our judges is one of meaning and application. Care, connection, nurturance, identification are distinct qualities, each in need of contextual examination. If we simply stipulate to an expanded list of qualities for judges, we slip back into the universalism that feminist vantage points have taught us to suspect. Moreover, courts have claimed to be nurturant in the past; the juvenile court and intermediate sentencing were both based upon arguments of an obligation to be responsive to the needs of the populations presumably being served. Maternal thinking is appealing as a model, but many accounts of juvenile court and intermediate sentencing suggest that parenting modes are profoundly disabling to those parented. Where does "attentive love" come from in a society as heterogeneous as ours? Communitarianism is a popular word in legal academe today, but the word is used without much attention paid to the fact of a multitude of extant communities, with competing modes of being....

One might then return to the argument . . . [t]hat . . . feminism and adjudication may simply be incompatible. [But] I am suspicious of a response in the name of feminism, that declines to accept power, authority and responsibility. Sara Ruddick is instructive here; maternal thinking is predicated upon the practice of adults caring for children. The fact of power, and an acceptance of the obligation to exercise it, comes from the social practice of caretaking. Because current social practice demands ongoing relationships between mother and child, the power is tempered with compassion, the authority with affection.

Notes

1. Gender Differences in Judging.   One of the first legal scholars to bring feminist theory to bear on judging was Suzanna Sherry. Sherry argued that there is a "feminine" jurisprudence that is apparent even among relatively conservative female judges such as Justice Sandra Day O'Connor. This assertedly feminine jurisprudence bears some similarity to civic republicanism, which is characterized by a focus on responsibility and human interdependence rather than abstract universal principles. See Suzanna Sherry, Civil Virtue and the Feminine Voice in Constitutional Adjudication, 72 Va. L. Rev. 543 (1986). See also Brenda Kruse, Comment, Women of the Highest Court: Does Gender Bias or Personal Life Experience Influence Their Opinions, 36 U. Tol. L. Rev. 995 (2005) (arguing that the experience of being a woman has shaped Justice O'Connor's and Justice Ginsburg's decisions in employment discrimination cases). Many critics have questioned Sherry's analysis. See, e.g., Tony Mauro, O'Connor & Ginsburg, Together and Apart, Legal Times, June 9, 2003, at 14 (quoting Deborah Merritt); Mary Joe Frug, Progressive Feminist Legal Scholarship: Can We Claim "A Different Voice"?, 15 Harv. Women's L.J. 37, 44-46 (1992). Consider Justice O'Connor's opinions in *J.E.B.*, in Section 6, p. 722, below, and Harris v. Forklift Systems, Inc., in Chapter 3, p. 413. Compare those decisions with Justice Ginsburg's opinion in cases such as United States v. Virginia, set forth in Chapter 2, p. 260. Do these Justices speak with the same voice? They have often been called by each other's name, even by experienced Supreme Court advocates (including an Acting Solicitor General) and occasionally by their own colleagues. Ruth Bader Ginsburg, A Place for Women, Vital Speeches, May 1, 2001. Do you think it is similarity in judicial style that accounts for such mistakes?

A comparison in 2003 revealed that Justice O'Connor and Justice Ginsburg voted for the same result approximately 75 percent of the time. In the 2003 term, Justice O'Connor agreed with Justice Kennedy 83 percent of the time, while Justice Ginsburg agreed with Justices Breyer and Souter 94 percent. Mauro, supra, at 15.

Consider Justice O'Connor's response when asked whether "being a female justice has ever made a difference" in how she views a particular issue or case: "as another woman ... state court judge once said, ... at the end of the day, a wise old woman and a wise old man are going to reach the same decision." Sandra Day O'Connor, NewsHour with Jim Lehrer, June 9, 2003. In reference to Suzanna Sherry's claim that she has a distinctly "feminine approach," O'Connor responds, "I would guess that my colleagues on the Court would be as surprised as I am by these conclusions." Mauro, supra, at 15 (quoting O'Connor). Justice Ginsburg agrees, and has stated that she can detect "no reliable indicator of distinctly male or ... female thinking — or even penmanship." Id., quoting Ginsburg. That is not to imply that the experience of being a woman is entirely irrelevant to the world views that affect their judgments. As one of Justice O'Connor's former clerks put it,

> I think Justice O'Connor's life as a woman ... in [a male-dominated legal culture] couldn't help but have an effect on her views in cases involving women. That said, I'm not certain that impacted her any more strongly than having been a state legislator, or having grown up on a rural ranch in Arizona ... or having been a mother of three children, or any other life experiences. They were a piece. She is who she is.

Linda Feldmann & Warren Richey, Will Bush Nominate a Woman?, Christian Science Monitor, July 6, 2005, at 1 (quoting Ron Nell Andersen Jones). Anna Quindlen makes a similar point:

> O'Connor, the first female Supreme Court justice, was never known as a feminist firebrand. But she had what I think of as transformative experience, something that can't help but suffuse your life and your mind. She carried within her the memory of what it was like to be reflexively devalued despite being smart and capable. I think it's probably a good thing for a judge to have faced down that sort of organized systemic injustice.

Quindlen, Remembrance of Things Past, Newsweek, March 6, 2006, at 69.

The hypothesis that women judges reason differently than their male colleagues is a difficult one to test. Studies of voting behavior of women judges have come at the problem in different ways, depending on the methodology. See, e.g., Sean Farhang & Gregory Wawro, Institutional Dynamics on the U. S. Courts of

Appeals: Minority Representation under Panel Decision Making, 20 J.L. Econ. & Org. 209, 301 (2004) (finding that the presence of a female or minority judge on an appellate panel increased the likelihood that a white male judge would vote in favor of plaintiffs alleging employment discrimination); Jennifer A. Segal, Representative Decision Making on the Federal Bench, Clinton's District Court Appointees, 53 Pol. Res. Q. 137, 142-146 (2000) (finding few gender differences but noting that male judges were somewhat more supportive of women's issues than female judges). For overviews of such studies, see Theresa Beiner, Female Judging, 36 U. Tol. L. Rev. 821, 821-829 (2005); Fred O. Smith, Jr., Gendered Justice: Do Male and Female Judges Rule Differently on Questions of Gay Rights? Stan. L. Rev. 2087, 2089-2091 (2005).

One of the most careful studies, using a sample of 556 sexual harassment cases consisting of 1666 votes by individual judges and controlling for ideology, race, prior employment, federal appellate experience, and age, concluded that (1) being female increased the probability that a judge found for the plaintiff by 86 percent (from 22 percent to 41 percent) in sexual harassment cases and by 65 percent (from 17 percent to 28 percent) in sex discrimination cases, and (2) having a female on the panel more than doubled the probability that a male judge, regardless of his ideology, rules for the plaintiff in sexual harassment cases (increasing the probability from 16 percent to 35 percent) and nearly tripled the probability in sex discrimination cases (increasing it from 11 percent to 30 percent). Jennifer L. Peresie, Female Judges Matter: Gender and Collegial Decisionmaking in the Federal Appellate Courts, 114 Yale L.J. 1759, 1776, 1778 (2005). What could explain these results? The author of the study explores four possible explanations: (1) that female judges influence male judges through simple deliberation; (2) that male judges defer to female judges in sex discrimination cases; (3) that male judges make implicit strategic bargains with female judges for their votes in future cases; and (4) that female judges cause male judges to moderate their anti-plaintiff preferences. Id. at 1781-1786. Which explanation(s), if any, seem plausible to you?

Studies of women judges in other countries have found "isolated cases of gender-specific approaches to the judicial task." Ulrike Schultz, Introduction: Women in the World's Legal Professions: Overview and Synthesis, in Women in the World's Legal Profession xxv, li (Ulrike Schultz & Gisela Shaw eds., 2003). Even in these cases, the results are not always consistent with gender stereotypes. For example in divorce cases involving spousal maintenance, women judges in some countries are less likely than their male colleagues to favor housewives, perhaps because these women "apply their own personal professional standards." Id. However, studies of state supreme court decisions in American divorce cases found that female judges were more supportive of women after controlling for political party affiliation. See Elaine Martin & Barry Pyle, State High Courts and Divorce: The Impact of Judicial Gender, 36 U. Toledo L. Rev. 923 (2005).

A recent survey of federal and state appellate decisions found that female judges were significantly more likely than male judges to rule in favor of gay rights. The difference was significant when controlling for factors including age and party affiliation. Smith, supra, at 1097, 2111. By contrast, no significant gender differences emerged in Congressional votes on the Defense of Marriage

Act, which asserts that states are not required to recognize same-sex marriages performed in other states. Id. at 2114. Similarly, public opinion research finds no significant differences in men's and women's attitudes on the morality of same-sex relationships, although highly educated women are much more likely than highly educated men to believe that same-sex couples should have the right to marry. Id. at 2116. Female law students are also more liberal than male students on gay rights issues. See id. at 2120; J.D. Droddy & C. Scott Peters, The Effect of Law School on Political Attitudes: Some Evidence From the Class of 2000, 53 J. Legal Educ. 33 (2003). Extrapolating from such findings, Fred Smith argues that the women who attend law school and become eligible for judgeships are more highly educated and have less traditional views of gender roles than the general public, which helps account for later differences in judicial voting behavior on gay rights issues. Smith, supra, at 2097. If Smith is right, why do the studies not reflect stronger gender differences on related women's issues? What might account for the current patterns?

2. Diversity on the Bench. Currently, women are estimated to account for about 20 percent of the American judiciary; they hold 19 percent of federal appellate judgeships, 18 percent of federal district court judgeships, and 28 percent of judgeships on the highest state courts. Alliance for Justice, Demographic Overview of the Federal Judiciary, available at http://allianceforjustice.org/judicial_selection_rersources/selection_database/byCourtRaceGender.asp; Lynn Hecht Schafran, Not From Central Casting: The Amazing Rise of Women in the American Judiciary, 36 U. Tol. L. Rev. 953, 973 (2005). Women of color constitute about five percent of federal judges; figures for the state judiciary are not available. Id. at 955; Chambliss, supra, at 54. Women's representation in other countries averages about 25 percent, but the proportion varies considerably by country, ranging from 63 percent in Poland to five percent in Japan. Schultz, supra, at li.

How important is increasing women's representation on the federal bench if the women likely to be appointed are unlikely to identify as feminists?

Resnik assumes that greater female representation of women on the judiciary will make a difference, although she does not claim a "feminine" style of judging. Rather, she appears to be making a normative claim about feminist judging. Robin West makes a similar assumption and argues that "[j]udges should aim for justice, but if they hope to achieve it, then they must *also* aim for care." Robin West, Caring for Justice 24 (1997). Does the preceding evidence suggest that the values of women judges are sufficiently different from men's to justify affirmative action in the appointment process? Is it possible that women judges bring different priorities to their work, and make a difference in how the courts function apart from the outcomes in particular cases? See Judith S. Kaye, Women Chiefs: Shaping the Third Branch, 36 U. Tol. L. Rev. 899 (2005) (discussing initiatives such as family, domestic violence, and drug courts); Mary M. Schroeder, Judging With a Difference, 14 Yale J.L. & Feminism 255, 256-261 (2002) (citing initiatives such as improving treatment of immigrant trainees and support for judges with disabilities); Beiner, supra, at 831, 843, 847 (describing involvement in women judges organizations and gender bias task forces). Are there symbolic values to having a judiciary that is representative of the public irrespective the extent to which women or minority judges have an identifiable, group-linked perspective? See id. at 823 (describing value of diversity and legitimacy). How would you describe these values?

Suppose that a candidate for a high judicial office had a history of strongly supporting women in cases involving gender issues. Would this suggest bias if the candidate was female? Would it support disqualification in such cases? What if the judge was on the board of a gender bias organization supported by a women's rights group that argued cases before the court? See David G. Savage & Richard A. Serrano, Ginsburg Stands by Involvement with Group, L.A. Times, March 13, 2004, at A14 (discussing Justice Ginsburg's ties with NOW Legal Defense Fund).

In Black v. Sullivan & Cromwell, 418 F. Supp. 1 (1975), Judge Constance Baker Motley denied a motion seeking her recusal on grounds that her sex and prior experience as a civil rights attorney would bias her in favor of the plaintiff in a gender discrimination case. In rejecting that motion, the court ruled that if the "background or sex or race of each judge were, by definition, sufficient grounds for removal, no judge on this court could hear this case, or many others, by virtue of the fact that all of them were attorneys, often with distinguished law firms or public service backgrounds." Id. at 4. Consider also a 2003 case in which an attorney requested recusal of a female judge in a case involving allegations that the defendant had groped a female nurse and used vulgar language. The attorney could not see how a woman judge "would be fair because of the nature of the allegations." Schafran, supra, at 959 (quoting the attorney). Can you? Would a male judge necessarily be more "fair"? To what extent do we want judges to build on their experience of group membership in deciding cases? Where is the line between empathy and partiality? Is it coherent to claim both that women have a "different voice" and that they bring no bias to their own decisionmaking?

3. Women in Arbitration. Should the underrepresentation of women in arbitration be of concern? Only about six percent of some 50,000 American Arbitration Association (AAA) arbiters are female. Victoria J. Craine, Note, The Mandatory Arbitration Clause: Forum Selection or Employee Coercion?, 8 B.U. Pub. Int. L.J. 537, 550 (1999). In Smith v. American Arbitration Association, 233 F.3d 502, 508 (7th Cir. 2000), a woman required by contract to arbitrate a securities dispute sued the AAA and her opponent based on the lack of diversity in the arbitration panel. The AAA had sent the parties a list of 15 possible arbiters, and the opponent corporation struck the only woman, whom the plaintiff had identified as her first choice. Plaintiff alleged a violation of the equal protection clause and a breach of contract due to the absence of women on the panel chosen and the process of selection. In rejecting her claim, Judge Posner observed:

No effort to substantiate the suggestion that male judges or arbitrators are prejudiced against wealthy women who have purely commercial disputes with corporations has been made; nor has Smith pointed to any issue in this litigation to which a man might be insensitive. The relief sought, which seems premised on the belief that a female litigant is entitled to be judged by a panel that includes at least one woman, borders on the fantastic.

Id. at 504. How would you have responded to Judge Posner if you had been the attorney for the plaintiff?

5. Women as Parties, Witnesses, and Litigators

≡ *In re Marriage of Iverson*
≡ 15 Cal. Rptr. 2d 70 (Ct. App. 1992)

SILLS, P.J.

Cheryl Iverson appeals from a judgment dissolving her marriage of 15 years to George Chick Iverson. Primarily she challenges the trial court's finding that a premarital agreement signed by the parties was valid.

The oral statement of decision of the judge who presided over the trial of the validity of the premarital agreement — and who acted as trier of fact in that proceeding — is so replete with gender bias that we are forced to conclude Cheryl could not have received a fair trial. Accordingly, we must reverse and direct the matter be retried before a different judge.

. . . During the trial, Chick testified he did not want to get married, told Cheryl he did not want to get married, and made it clear to his associates he was perfectly happy not getting married.

Cheryl told a somewhat different story. Chick first brought up the subject of marriage. He asked her to marry him in front of the late actor John Wayne, just after Chick had asked Wayne to be his best man. Marriage was the reason she moved in with Chick. He told her he wanted the couple to live together and be married.

The testimony also differed on the circumstances surrounding Cheryl's signing of the agreement. Chick presented the testimony of Rita Cruikshank, wife of the late William Cruikshank, Chick's attorney. She testified that in June 1972, Cheryl and Chick met on her husband's boat. William Cruikshank read the agreement to them. He asked if they understood what he was reading to them. They answered yes. This happened several times while he was reading the agreement. After he finished, he turned to Cheryl and told her, "Cheryl, I think maybe it's advisable you see another attorney, make sure this is what you want to do." Cheryl said, "No, no, no. Whatever Chick wants." He then handed Cheryl a pen. She signed.

Cheryl testified she never discussed the contents of the agreement with an attorney before she signed it. Nor could she recall even being advised by any attorney about her rights to property that might be acquired during her marriage to Chick. She had no recollection of ever signing the agreement (though she acknowledged signing it, because her name was on it).

After the testimony was finished, the trial judge noted there was "too much money" involved in the case "for it not to be appealed." He then said, "I want whoever reviews this to be able to have the benefit of my reasoning for how I get to where I got." He then elaborated:

> One of the things that struck me, first of all, was that the petitioner in this case, Cheryl Iverson, only had five or six luncheon dates with Chick Iverson before she decided to move into his home. Now, he sure as heck does not look like John Wayne and he doesn't look like John Derek. And even if we take 17 years off him, I don't think he looks like Adonis.
>
> And, so, we have a situation in the beginning where we have a girl who has been testified to [sic] was lovely, and is lovely, but who did not have much of an education, and did not have much of a background in business, and did not have much by way of material wealth. Had nothing going for her except for her physical attractiveness. Who, somehow or other, comes to the attention of Mr. Iverson and, after five or six luncheon dates, is invited to move into his home.
>
> It seems to me that the process of marrying is one in which there is some mutual advantages from the act of getting married, maybe different ones from the act of establishing a relationship, a live-in type, spousal-type relationship.
>
> But, in light of the testimony that Mr. Iverson had come out of a very unpleasant, very unhappy marriage, his statement that he was reluctant to get married again adds some dimension here. "Once burned, twice cautious." He had just gone through a divorce which cost him a million dollars. He does not want to get in one of those things again. He has talked to his important friends in the film industry and other areas, where living together is the common situation rather than marriage. And, so, decides that's the best thing for him. He makes an offer to petitioner, who thinks it's good. And then she moves in.
>
> I cannot accept the fact that, as she said, he was the one that proposed marriage to her. That would be the last thing that would be on his mind. And why, in heaven's name, do you buy the cow when you get the milk free, as we used to say. And, so, he's getting the milk free. And Cheryl is living with him in his home.
>
> And the impetus for marriage must be coming from her side, because there's nothing Mr. Iverson is going to get out of it. Marriage is a drag on the market. It's a deprivation of his freedom. He's got everything that he would want out of a relationship with none of the obligations. Now, I am of the opinion that the impetus for the marriage in the home, prior to the incident of the birthday party for John Wayne, came almost entirely from the petitioner in this case, resisted by respondent.

≣≣
≣≣ *Catchpole v. Brannon*
≣≣ **42 Cal. Rptr. 2d 440 (Ct. App. 1995)**

KLINE, P.J.

This case presents the unusual question whether the alleged gender bias of the trial judge requires us to set aside his judgment.

Appellant, Marie Catchpole, commenced this litigation in the Superior Court of Humboldt County, asserting claims of sexual harassment, assault and battery, and intentional and negligent infliction of emotional distress against respondents [who were her employers at Burger King (EBK)].... Judgment against appellant was rendered by a superior court judge sitting without a jury....

Appellant testified she was subjected to a hostile work environment at EBK, in which supervisors, particularly Brannon, encouraged employees to discuss sexual matters, to touch each other, and to "rate" customers' attractiveness. Several former employees also testified that Brannon flirted with female employees, talked about their bodies, showed them lingerie magazines and ads for X-rated strip shows, offered unsolicited "advice" about sexual matters, and touched them inappropriately. In addition, a former employee and two female friends testified that they had gone to Brannon's home on numerous occasions, where Brannon and his wife provided alcohol and marijuana and showed them pornographic movies. EBK had a nonfraternization policy, which prohibited managers from associating with employees away from EBK. Brannon had earlier been reprimanded for inviting employees to his house in violation of that policy. Melody Rane, Greenhalgh, and several EBK employees testified that appellant was difficult to get along with and rude to other employees.

Appellant testified that in the early morning of December 11, 1987, at Brannon's insistence, she went to his home after work to discuss her problems with coworkers. Brannon forcibly removed her clothes and performed an act of oral sex on her, after which he forced her to orally copulate him.

Nearly two months later, on February 2, 1988, appellant mentioned the assault to another EBK employee, who then reported it to the assistant manager on duty.... Brannon was fired the next day....

After appellant reported Brannon's assault, she was allegedly subjected to retaliatory harassment by numerous employees at EBK who blamed her for his dismissal. These acts of retaliation, about which she complained repeatedly, were assertedly never adequately addressed by management....

The trial judge's lengthy interrogation of [the plaintiff] differed markedly from the treatment he accorded others who testified, most of whom, including respondent Brannon, were asked no questions. The court's initial questions set the tone for what was to follow:

> THE COURT: Okay. No doubt this particular lawsuit has been difficult for you, and embarrassing for you, and I assume a lot of people in your position would have chosen to not go forward with a lawsuit of this sort. Can you tell me why you decided to do it?
>
> THE WITNESS [appellant]: Yes. Because I felt I needed to do something to get in control of the situation. I felt so humiliated and so down trodden, that I needed a way to overcome this. Um, I wanted to set right what was wrong. I — I wanted to, um, be able to have a chance to say what I felt was wrong; what had been done to me, and the injustices I felt at the time. I — I felt they were never addressed, and now is my chance to address them. Whether I win or not, I'm still going to win in my heart, because I was able to sit here and address the people that wronged me.
>
> THE COURT: Okay. You indicated in your testimony...that your father, to this day, feels that you shouldn't have been where you were on December the 11th. He somehow blames you for what happened; is that right?

THE WITNESS: Did I say that in my testimony?

THE COURT: I thought you did.

THE WITNESS: Um—

THE COURT: At least that's what I got out of what you said.

THE WITNESS: My—my father felt—um, he—he didn't understand how I had gotten into this mess. And—and, um, he is very upset about it. And I don't know whether he thinks I should have been or should not have been.

THE COURT: Okay. Um, maybe I assumed something that a father might feel that way. . . . Is this suit in any way connected with how your father feels about the situation? You want to prove something to him?

THE WITNESS: I—I never thought of that.

THE COURT: Okay. Fine. You understand that regardless of what the motivations are within yourself, that the allegations that you made against these people are very serious allegations?

THE WITNESS: Yes.

THE COURT: Okay. Fine. And you understand that if Mr. Brannon's opening statement is correct, he has already lost, I guess, quite a bit of money, and been subject to certain trials and tribulations as a result of those allegations, correct?

THE WITNESS: Yes.

THE COURT: Okay. Likewise, I assume that you understand that Ken and the Ranes and the other crew members have been subjected to the claims of harassment; um, that they either harassed you or failed to prevent the harassment, and I assume you understand that in many ways it's going to be your word against all of those other people?

THE WITNESS: No.

THE COURT: You don't understand that?

THE WITNESS: No, I—

THE COURT: Okay. Go ahead.

THE WITNESS: Um, I have corroboration.

THE COURT: Okay. I'm not saying you don't, I'm just saying that you need—I assume that you understand that the Brannons are going to say you weren't at their house on December 11th; that Kent's going to say that most of what you said about him is incorrect, and probably a lot of these crew members are going to come in here and say they didn't do anything wrong, either. So in some ways, um, absent—I don't know what corroboration you have, but absent that corroboration, it's still a lot of your word against their word. Do you understand that?

THE WITNESS: Yes.

THE COURT: Okay. So you understand that your testimony is going to be looked at very carefully, and that you can't simply tell me that the conversation on November 19th, 1987 was A, B, C and D. If you can't remember that conversation, in total—in other words, you can't just paraphrase a conversation. Do you understand that?

THE WITNESS: Yes. . . .

[I]mmediately following the opening statements of counsel, the judge asked appellant's counsel how long the trial was going to take.

MR. ZIGLER: I think we're going to have trouble finishing next week, Your Honor.

THE COURT: Well, how many witnesses do you have?

MR. ZIGLER: Potentially twenty-two, Your Honor.

THE COURT: Jesus Christ. Well, there is a limited amount of judicial resource here. If you think it's worth it, Mr. Zigler, you may proceed. . . .

. . . The following exchange . . . pertains to appellant's acceptance of Brannon's invitation to come to his house to discuss the problems she was having at work. . . .

THE COURT: Um, as I understand your testimony, even though you liked to work [Brannon's] shift, you didn't like his sexualization of the work place; is that right?

THE WITNESS: Yes.

THE COURT: Why did you go to his house?

THE WITNESS: I just — I have said previously that I had gone to him about that, and had [sic] apologized.

THE COURT: But I don't understand. If you were —

THE WITNESS: I had forgiven him. I didn't hold a grudge. And then he told me he had a wife. I mean, all fear's [sic] flew out of my head then. To me, a wife and kids meant a complete family, um, safety, and he was just inviting me over to —

THE COURT: But couldn't you have easily said, "No, not tonight. I'm tired. I have got to go to school tomorrow. I'll talk about it later." Why not? Why didn't you say that?

THE WITNESS: I —

THE COURT: You don't know?

THE WITNESS: I didn't feel that I could.

THE COURT: Okay. How about —

THE WITNESS: I didn't want to offend him.

THE COURT: When you went back to Burger King that night, and whatever he did in there, he was doing, um, why didn't you just get in your car at that point and drive home, and say, "I'll see you to [sic] tomorrow. I don't have time to wait around here while you do that for your wife."

THE WITNESS: My car wasn't there. It was at his house.

THE COURT: What I'm saying is, why didn't you say, "Sorry, Rudy. I can't go back with you. I'm too tired. I'm going now."

THE WITNESS: Well, we were at the store, and then we drove back to his house.

THE COURT: I understand you went to his house. What I'm saying is, before you went back to the store to get whatever he got, why didn't you just say, you know, "It's too late. I can't wait around here any more."

THE WITNESS: He said he really wanted to discuss it with me that night, and that I needed to stay. I said I would listen.

THE COURT: When his wife went to bed at 2:30 that morning, you were still concerned about school the next day, correct?

THE WITNESS: Yes.

THE COURT: Why didn't you leave then?

THE WITNESS: He began — he said that he hadn't really gotten a chance to talk to me. He was going to stay up and do his paperwork.

THE COURT: I understand that. But, you know, when do you assert yourself? Why didn't you just say, "Hey, I don't care whether you talked to me or not, I'm tired."

THE WITNESS: I couldn't assert myself.

THE COURT: You couldn't?

THE WITNESS: No, he—he was a—he was my manager. I didn't—if he said I had to discuss something with him, I needed to. That didn't mean that I wanted to stay and have sex with him.

THE COURT: Do you think—well, I'm not saying it meant anything. Do you think he could have fired you if you had walked out at that point?

THE WITNESS: Yes.

THE COURT: Okay. Why did you take a second drink when you were tired and wanted to go home?

THE WITNESS: A second drink of juice?

THE COURT: Whatever it was. I don't know what it was. Why did you take one if you wanted to go home? Why didn't you just say, "No, I'm tired. I have got to go home."

THE WITNESS: I said I was tired; I said, "I want to go home." And he said, "I'm just"—like I said, he said he wanted to talk to me about this, and he was going to be doing his paperwork, and he went and got me a drink. I mean, I didn't refuse. I just said, "Sure."

THE COURT: Um, somehow he managed to hold you and take your clothes off. How did that happen; do you recall?

THE WITNESS: Yeah.

THE COURT: Okay. How?

THE WITNESS: He had a steal [sic] grip on my arm. Um, the blouse was snapped. He took and unsnapped it. Um, he—he was scaring me with the tone of his voice, and, um, at that point he shook me. Um—

THE COURT: Okay.

THE WITNESS: He unsnapped my pants. He still had a steal [sic] grip on me, and unbuttoned his shirt.

THE COURT: There was no time between this entire process that he didn't have his—a steal [sic] grip? You—

THE WITNESS: Exactly.

THE COURT: What about the time you testified to when he was performing oral sex on you, and had his hands on your breasts?

THE WITNESS: His arms were very large and he—he had them very heavily on me.

THE COURT: Okay.

THE WITNESS: I felt I had no choice. And if I made a move, his wife would come out.

THE COURT: I guess I understand that, that you were afraid that his wife would just add to your problems, but why didn't you tell him, "Okay. I'm going to scream loud enough to wake up your kids." That would sort of put him in a pickle, wouldn't it?

THE WITNESS: I didn't think about that.

THE COURT: Okay. Where was the phone?

THE WITNESS: I don't know. In the kitchen, I guess. I—I didn't see a phone.

THE COURT: You didn't see a phone in the living room?

THE WITNESS: No.

THE COURT: You stated at one point, and I don't know where this was, during the events of that morning, that once he had taken your clothes off, that you were constantly trying to get them on and leave. Did you ever consider just leaving without your clothes?

THE WITNESS: No.

THE COURT: That wouldn't be something that you would want to do?

THE WITNESS: No.

THE COURT: Okay. Um, another thing you mentioned, that at some point during the course of the assault upon you, that you said, "I don't want to do this. I don't want to get pregnant." Was pregnancy really something that crossed your mind at this point?

THE WITNESS: Yes, it was, because he said he wanted to get into my cherry. I was trying to —

THE COURT: You weren't worried about your — your physical safety at this point?

THE WITNESS: Yes, I was worried about my physical safety. I was trying to deter him. I was trying to give him a reason not to.

THE COURT: Okay. How long, once he inserted his penis into your mouth, was that in your mouth?

THE WITNESS: A few minutes.

THE COURT: After all of this happened, and you left about 6:30, did you go to class that day?

THE WITNESS: Well, I — I went to the dorms and slept for a few hours. And then I did, yes.

THE COURT: After you had a chance to think about what had happened to you that morning, did you blame yourself for letting this happen?

THE WITNESS: I didn't blame myself. I — I was angry for — um, with myself for not, um, getting out of it. That I couldn't get out of it. I — I was in a — that I was in a bind. That — a bind that humiliated me so much.

THE COURT: So you were concerned that you weren't in control, is that right?

THE WITNESS: In control of Rudy?

THE COURT: Of the event.

THE WITNESS: No, I certainly wasn't in control.

THE COURT: Well, isn't that what you just said, you were angry with yourself for letting — putting yourself in the position where you didn't have control?

THE WITNESS: I was angry with myself that it happened; I was angry with my body; I was angry that I even agreed to go over there.

THE COURT: Well, I can understand that. And the reason you brought this lawsuit was to gain some control, right?

THE WITNESS: Yes. To gain some control in my life, and not falsely. [...]

In his Notice of Tentative Decision, the trial judge rejected out of hand "the basic scenario of an alleged sexual assault away from the work place, where the victim waits for an hour to accompany her alleged attacker, and then allows a four hour attack to occur in a residence with the attacker's family at home...." For this reason, the court rhetorically inquired, " 'Why was it necessary to use up the court system with a case which was, so obviously, one which could only be detrimental to everyone concerned?' Attorneys have a duty to evaluate their cases and present claims which have at least marginal merit. This case was clearly not one which should have been filed or tried. If sanctions could be imposed for this misuse of resource they would be imposed here."

While we cannot say as a matter of law that appellant was entitled to judgment in her favor, the court's characterization of the case distorts the record.... The implication that appellant invited Brannon's sexual attention or consented to his advances was never advanced by respondents; nor did respondents seriously dispute that the assault, which was corroborated by Officer Parris, actually took place; their chief contention was simply that it was not work related. Nor does the record suggest appellant "sought the attention of Mr. Brannon." Among other things, Dr. Berg's testimony that appellant was "passive" and usually avoided "personal interactions" was never contradicted. The emphasis the court placed on appellant's failure to "scream" at the time of the assault so as to alert Brannon's wife ignores appellant's uncontradicted testimony that Brannon had told her that if his wife woke she "wouldn't be mad at all, and wouldn't help me at all. That she — she would, in fact, like to join in. And I took that as a threat, because if she came out there, then I would have two against me. Two big people against me instead of one." Though, as we have said, many of appellant's factual claims were contested, the court appears to have been almost entirely indifferent to evidence corroborating her fundamental contentions regarding the sexualization of her workplace, the harassment she experienced there, and the assault itself. Among other things, the court completely brushed aside Brannon's failure on the stand to explicitly deny the assault and the sexual harassment attributed to him and others by appellant. In short, the court's treatment of the evidence does not appear to have been even-handed.

[T]he judgment seems to have improperly turned on stereotypes about women rather than a realistic evaluation of the facts . . . , a problem apparently all too common in sexual harassment cases. The court's disparagement of appellant's credibility on the grounds that she accepted Brannon's invitation to come to his house, remained alone with him, and did not resist his assault more forcibly is based on an unrealistic and gender-biased standard of reasonableness. Among other things, the court appears oblivious to appellant's dependence on her assailant for her job and scholarship and the need to placate him for those reasons. The court was equally indifferent to the intimidation a woman in appellant's position would likely experience. . . .

NOTE ON BIAS IN THE COURTROOM

Do *Iverson* and *Catchpole* exhibit judicial bias? Were the responses by the appellate court adequate?

The kinds of explicit gender stereotypes in these excerpts are unusual, but they have not vanished entirely, and other forms of gender bias are more common. See Joan Dempsey Klein, Remarks, 36 U. Toledo L. Rev. 918 (2005) (describing recent case of New York Judge Robert Hamley who resigned after stating that domestic violence cases were a "waste of the court's time" and that most women asked to get "smacked around.") Beginning in 1982, courts began establishing gender bias task forces. Some jurisdictions also established separate commissions on racial and ethnic bias or gave one commission responsibility to consider all diversity-related issues. By the turn of the twenty-first century, some 65 state and federal courts had issued reports on bias in the justice system. ABA Commission on Women in the Profession, The Unfinished Agenda, supra, at 20.

Published reports of gender bias in the courts have relied on some mix of quantitative and qualitative approaches, and have considered issues such as the demographics of the bench, bar, and court personnel; the outcomes for male and female litigants in areas like bail, sentencing, and custody awards; and the perceptions of participants in the justice system. The ABA Commission on Women in the Profession summarizes the problems exemplified by these studies and the reforms necessary to address them.

Between two-thirds and three-quarters of women report experiencing bias, while only a quarter to a third of men report observing it and far fewer report experiencing it. Women are also more likely than men to believe that bias is a significant problem and that female attorneys are treated less favorably than male attorneys by judges and opposing counsel. Two-thirds of African American lawyers, but less than a fifth of white lawyers, report witnessing racial bias in the justice system in the last three years. About forty percent of surveyed lawyers report witnessing or experiencing sexual orientation bias in professional settings, even in jurisdictions that have ordinances prohibiting it. Between about a quarter to a half of lawyers with disabilities also experience various forms of bias in the legal system....

Demeaning conduct takes a variety of forms. To be sure, gender bias rules and educational programs have reduced the most egregious problems. Female lawyers no longer routinely cope with labels such as "pretty girl," "little lady," "lawyerette," "baby doll," "sweetie" and "attorney generalette." Nor do women frequently encounter questions such as whether they "really understand all the economics involved in this [antitrust] case," or whether their clients are "satisfied with the representation [they] had at trial even though [the lawyer] was a woman."

However, some of these problems persist, particularly those involving disrespectful forms of address. Female lawyers, administrative personnel, and witnesses are still addressed by their first names, while male counterparts are not....

Women also report recurring instances of being ignored, interrupted, or mistaken for nonprofessional support staff. And support staff, for their part, often experience similarly demeaning comments and have been expected to perform menial personal services, such as making coffee or running non-work related errands.

Such problems persist partly because they are not acknowledged as problems. Many white men, who have not been on the receiving end of systematic bias, tend to discount its significance. The gender gap in experience is striking. For example, in the District of Columbia Circuit survey of lawyers, only 3 percent of white men, but over a third of white women and half of women of color, had been mistaken for non-lawyers by other counsel.

When men observe such incidents, they often seem like isolated, idiosyncratic, or inadvertent slights. A common reaction is that women should just "grow up and stop whining." Such reactions both silence and stigmatize complainants. Many women are unwilling to jeopardize a client's case or their own career prospects by antagonizing decision makers or earning a reputation as "humorless," "oversensitive," or a "troublemaker."...

A common finding of gender bias studies is that the credibility of female lawyers, litigants, and witnesses is often discounted. Examples range from the occasional overt comment, such as "Shut up. Let's hear what the men have to say," to the much more common and subtle patterns of devaluation, such as openly ignoring or trivializing claims.

In some instances, judicial attitudes are tied to perceptions about the substantive rights or injuries at issue. Claims involving violence, acquaintance rape, sexual harassment, and employment discrimination face special skepticism. In New Jersey's recent follow-up survey of gender bias, about 60 to 70 percent of women (compared with about a quarter of men) reported that victims of domestic violence and sex harassment had less credibility than other victims.

ABA Commission on Women in the Profession, The Unfinished Agenda, supra, at 20-21. How serious are the reported complaints? For a comprehensive bibliography, see National Center for State Courts, Racial and Ethnic Bias in the Courts: Bibliography, prepared for the National Consortium of Task Forces and Commissions on Racial and Ethnic Bias in the Courts (2002). For further discussion of the gender bias studies, see Lynn Hecht Schafran & Norma J. Wikler, National Judicial Education Program, Gender Fairness in the Courts: Action in the New Millennium (2001).

Since the Commission issued its report, a number of studies have documented the persistence of bias. A survey of over 700 female attorneys by DRI — The Voice of the Defense Bar, the nation's largest association of defense lawyers, found that over 70 percent of practitioners reported experiencing gender bias in the courtroom. Tresa Baldas, Gender Bias, Still a Problem, Nat'l L.J. Feb. 14, 2005, at A6. In another survey of some 4600 litigators, about three-quarters of women and half of men had experienced some form of incivility, including gender related disparagement or unwanted sexual attention, in the preceding five years in federal courts. Women encountered more frequent and more serious incidents. Lilia Cortina et al., What's Gender Got to Do with It? Incivility in the Federal Courts, 27 Law & Soc. Inquiry, 235, 245-246 (2002).

The ABA has taken some steps to attempt to address these issues, amending both the ABA Model Code of Judicial Conduct, Section 3B(6), and the Model Rules of Professional Conduct, Rule 8.4, to include prohibitions on gender bias in the courtroom. The Model Code for Judicial Conduct was revised in 1990 to provide:

A judge shall perform judicial duties without bias or prejudice ... and shall not permit staff, court officials and others subject to the judge's direction and control to do so. (Canon 3B, 5).

A judge shall require lawyers in proceedings before the judge to refrain from manifesting, by words or conduct, bias or prejudice ... against parties, witnesses, counsel or others. This Section does not preclude legitimate advocacy when race, sex, religion national origin, disability, age, sexual orientation, or socioeconomic status, or other similar factors, are issues in the proceeding. (Canon 3B, 6).

In 1998, the ABA added the following Comment to Rule 8.4:

A lawyer who, in the course of representing a client, knowingly manifests by words or conduct, bias or prejudice based upon race, sex, religion, national origin, disability, age, sexual orientation or socioeconomic status violates [this rule] when such actions are prejudicial to the administration of justice. Legitimate advocacy respecting the foregoing factors does not violate [this rule].

Although the vast majority of surveyed judges and lawyers believe that judges should always or usually intervene to remedy bias, such intervention is rare. Kimberly A. Lonsway, Understanding the Judicial Role in Addressing Gender Bias: A View from the Eighth Circuit Federal Court System, 27 Law & Soc. Inquiry 205, 209-210, 216 (2002) (summarizing studies). In a survey of federal judges from the Eighth Circuit, 70 percent had never intervened to address gender bias. Id. Several factors may account for the low incidence of correctives. One is that most objectionable behavior occurs outside the presence of judges and attorneys rarely report it. Id. at 226. In recent surveys, only about 10-13 percent of attorneys indicated that they had made informal reports of bias, and less than one to two percent had filed formal reports. Id. at 227; Cortina et al., supra, at 249. Explanations for the failure to report included a belief that the conduct was not sufficiently serious or unusual to warrant correctives; that reports would be futile, or that complaints might subject the lawyer to reprisals or unfavorable stereotypes (e.g., "feminazi"). Id. at 251; Lonsway et al., supra, at 210.

A second explanation is that some, usually male, judges fail to perceive biased conduct, including their own, as objectionable or as important enough to warrant responses. Lonsway et al., supra, at 214-218. Other factors inhibiting judicial responses are concerns about impartiality and the absence of clear guidance about appropriate remedies. Id. at 212, 227.

Putting Theory into Practice

4-7. In France, 80 percent of new judges are female. As in other civil law countries, the judiciary is a separate career track. To become a member of the bench, individuals apply for positions at a special college either directly from law school or from positions in the bar. Applicants are selected based on performance on an exam. In recent years, about three-quarters of the applicants have been women and they do slightly better on the exam; their pass rate has been 11 percent compared to eight percent for men. Part of the explanation for the disparities in applications is that judges average three times less income than lawyers, and occupy a relatively low status in the profession.

The current concern is that men, who are 80 percent of defendants in the courts, might lose confidence in a system dominated by women judges. According to the French Justice Minister, quotas might be necessary if the current trends continue. Women judges have been highly critical of the suggestion. As the vice president of the Magistrates Union noted, "No one ever talked about quotas when the judiciary was dominated by men...." Adam Sage, Women on Top in Race to Sit on the Bench, London Times, June 3, 2003, at 3 (quoting Veronique Imbert).

Should quotas be imposed?

4-8. A Ugandan woman with the first name Jane came before a Massachusetts immigration judge seeking asylum. Her claim was based on incidents of torture and rape in her homeland. Before denying her request, the judge quipped, "Jane Come Here. Me Tarzan." And as Cheetah, Nat'l L.J. Aug. 11, 2003, at 3.

In a hearing in Orange County, the judge opened the proceedings by asking the female lawyer of record for her business card to substantiate the fact that she was an attorney. The court then inquired of the woman, who was wearing maternity clothes, "Are you ready to have your baby? Is it momentarily?" He then added, "Well, your appearance, Ms. Roberson, leaves a lot to be desired, as far as your clothing is concerned." Anthony P. Capozzi, Gender Bias Is Alive and Well, Cal. Bar J., June 2004, at 9.

If you had been the lawyer in either of these cases, how would you have responded? If you had a filed a formal complaint, how should either of the judges have been subject to sanctions?

4-9. Defense attorney Dennis Scheib filed a motion in a criminal case asking the judge to order prosecutor Nancy Grace not to wear scoop necks, skirts shorter than one inch above the knee, or dresses slit up the sides, on the grounds such dress would be distracting to the jury and would give her an unfair advantage in court. See Martha Ezzard, And No Scoop Necks, Please: Courtroom Sexism: The "Southern Belle" Charge, Atlanta Const., Nov. 6, 1995, at 12A.

Should he prevail? Is his motion an example of gender bias? What about judicial orders directing women lawyers not to wear pants in open court on the ground that they fail to show sufficient respect for the dignity of judicial proceedings?

6. Gender and Juries

J.E.B. v. Alabama ex rel. T.B.
511 U.S. 127 (1994)

Justice BLACKMUN delivered the opinion of the Court[, in which STEVENS, O'CONNOR, SOUTER, and GINSBURG, JJ., joined].

I

On behalf of [the mother of a minor child], respondent State of Alabama filed a complaint for paternity and child support against petitioner J.E.B. in the District Court of Jackson County, Alabama.... The trial court assembled a panel of 36 potential jurors, 12 males and 24 females. After the court excused three jurors for cause, only 10 of the remaining 33 jurors were male. The State then used 9 of its 10 peremptory strikes to remove male jurors; petitioner used all but one of his strikes to remove female jurors. As a result, all the selected jurors were female.

Before the jury was empaneled, petitioner objected to the State's peremptory challenges on the ground that they were exercised against male jurors solely on the basis of gender, in violation of the Equal Protection Clause.... Petitioner argued that the logic and reasoning of Batson v. Kentucky, [476 U.S. 79 (1986),] which prohibits peremptory strikes solely on the basis of race, similarly forbids intentional discrimination on the basis of gender. The court rejected petitioner's claim and empaneled the all-female jury. The jury found petitioner to be the father of the child and the court entered an order directing him to pay child support....

...Today we reaffirm what, by now, should be axiomatic: Intentional discrimination on the basis of gender by state actors violates the Equal Protection Clause, particularly where, as here, the discrimination serves to ratify and perpetuate invidious, archaic, and overbroad stereotypes about the relative abilities of men and women.

II

Discrimination on the basis of gender in the exercise of peremptory challenges is a relatively recent phenomenon. Gender-based peremptory strikes were hardly practicable for most of our country's existence, since, until the 19th century, women were completely excluded from jury service. So well-entrenched was this exclusion of women that in 1880 this Court, while finding that the exclusion of African-American men from juries violated the Fourteenth Amendment, expressed no doubt that a State "may confine the selection [of jurors] to males." Strauder v. West Virginia, [100 U.S. 303, 310 (1880)].

Many States continued to exclude women from jury service well into the present century, despite the fact that women attained suffrage upon ratification of the Nineteenth Amendment in 1920. States that did permit women to serve on juries often erected other barriers, such as registration requirements and automatic exemptions, designed to deter women from exercising their right to jury service....

...In this country, supporters of the exclusion of women from juries tended to couch their objections in terms of the ostensible need to protect women from the ugliness and depravity of trials. Women were thought to be too fragile and virginal to withstand the polluted courtroom atmosphere....

This Court in Ballard v. United States, [329 U.S. 187 (1946)], first questioned the fundamental fairness of denying women the right to serve on juries. Relying on its supervisory powers over the federal courts, it held that women may not be excluded from the venire in federal trials in States where women were eligible for jury service under local law. In response to the argument that women have no superior or unique perspective, such that defendants are denied a fair trial by virtue of their exclusion from jury panels, the Court explained:

> It is said . . . that an all male panel drawn from the various groups within a community will be as truly representative as if women were included. The thought is that the factors which tend to influence the action of women are the same as those which influence the action of men — personality, background, economic status — and not sex. Yet it is not enough to say that women when sitting as jurors neither act nor tend to act as a class. Men likewise do not act like a class.... The truth is that the two sexes are not fungible; a community made up exclusively of one is different from a

community composed of both; the subtle interplay of influence one on the other is among the imponderables. To insulate the courtroom from either may not in a given case make an iota of difference. Yet a flavor, a distinct quality is lost if either sex is excluded.

[Id. at 193-194.]

Fifteen years later, however, the Court still was unwilling to translate its appreciation for the value of women's contribution to civic life into an enforceable right to equal treatment under state laws governing jury service. In Hoyt v. Florida, [368 U.S. 57, 61 (1961)], the Court found it reasonable, "despite the enlightened emancipation of women," to exempt women from mandatory jury service by statute, allowing women to serve on juries only if they volunteered to serve. The Court justified the differential exemption policy on the ground that women, unlike men, occupied a unique position "as the center of home and family life." [Id. at 62].

In 1975, the Court finally repudiated the reasoning of *Hoyt* and struck down, under the Sixth Amendment, an affirmative registration statute nearly identical to the one at issue in *Hoyt*. See Taylor v. Louisiana, [419 U.S. 522 (1975)]. We explained: "Restricting jury service to only special groups or excluding identifiable segments playing major roles in the community cannot be squared with the constitutional concept of jury trial." [Id. at 530]. The diverse and representative character of the jury must be maintained "'partly as assurance of a diffused impartiality and partly because sharing in the administration of justice is a phase of civic responsibility.'" [Id. at 530-531].

III

Taylor relied on Sixth Amendment principles, but the opinion's approach is consistent with the heightened equal protection scrutiny afforded gender-based classifications. . . .

While the prejudicial attitudes toward women in this country have not been identical to those held toward racial minorities, the similarities between the experiences of racial minorities and women, in some contexts, "overpower those differences." Note, Beyond *Batson*: Eliminating Gender-Based Peremptory Challenges, 105 Harv. L. Rev. 1920, 1921 (1992). . . .

Certainly, with respect to jury service, African-Americans and women share a history of total exclusion, a history which came to an end for women many years after the embarrassing chapter in our history came to an end for African-Americans.

We need not determine, however, whether women or racial minorities have suffered more at the hands of discriminatory state actors during the decades of our Nation's history. It is necessary only to acknowledge that "our Nation has had a long and unfortunate history of sex discrimination," [id. at 684], a history which warrants the heightened scrutiny we afford all gender-based classifications today. Under our equal protection jurisprudence, gender-based classifications require "an exceedingly persuasive justification" in order to survive constitutional scrutiny. See Personnel Administrator of Massachusetts v. Feeney, [442

U.S. 256, 273 (1979)]. . . . Thus, the only question is whether discrimination on the basis of gender in jury selection substantially furthers the State's legitimate interest in achieving a fair and impartial trial. In making this assessment, we do not weigh the value of peremptory challenges as an institution against our asserted commitment to eradicate invidious discrimination from the courtroom. Instead, we consider whether peremptory challenges based on gender stereotypes provide substantial aid to a litigant's effort to secure a fair and impartial jury.

Far from proffering an exceptionally persuasive justification for its gender-based peremptory challenges, respondent maintains that its decision to strike virtually all the males from the jury in this case "may reasonably have been based upon the perception, supported by history, that men otherwise totally qualified to serve upon a jury might be more sympathetic and receptive to the arguments of a man alleged in a paternity action to be the father of an out-of-wedlock child, while women equally qualified to serve upon a jury might be more sympathetic and receptive to the arguments of the complaining witness who bore the child." Brief for Respondent.[9]

We shall not accept as a defense to gender-based peremptory challenges "the very stereotype the law condemns." Powers v. Ohio, [499 U.S. 400, 410 (1991)]. Respondent's rationale, not unlike those regularly expressed for gender-based strikes, is reminiscent of the arguments advanced to justify the total exclusion of women from juries.[10] Respondent offers virtually no support for the conclusion that gender alone is an accurate predictor of juror's attitudes; yet it urges this Court to condone the same stereotypes that justified the wholesale exclusion of women from juries and the ballot box. Respondent seems to assume that gross generalizations that would be deemed impermissible if made on the basis of race are somehow permissible when made on the basis of gender.

9. Respondent cites one study in support of its quasi-empirical claim that women and men may have different attitudes about certain issues justifying the use of gender as a proxy for bias. See R. Hastie, S. Penrod & N. Pennington, Inside the Jury 140 (1983). The authors conclude: "Neither student nor citizen judgments for typical criminal case material have revealed differences between male and female verdict preferences. . . . The picture differs [only] for rape cases, where female jurors appear to be somewhat more conviction-prone than male jurors." The majority of students suggest that gender plays no identifiable role in juror attitudes. See, e.g., V. Hans & N. Vidmar, Judging the Jury 76 (1986). . . .

10. A manual formerly used to instruct prosecutors in Dallas, Texas, provided the following advice: "I don't like women jurors because I can't trust them. They do, however, make the best jurors in cases involving crimes against children. It is possible that their 'women's intuition' can help you if you can't win your case with the facts." Alschuler, The Supreme Court and the Jury: Voir Dire, Peremptory Challenges, and the Review of Jury Verdicts, 56 U. Chi. L. Rev. 153, 210 (1989). Another widely circulated trial manual speculated:

> If counsel is depending upon a clearly applicable rule of law and if he wants to avoid a verdict of "intuition" or "sympathy," if his verdict in amount is to be proved by clearly demonstrated blackboard figures for example, generally he would want a male juror. . . .
> [But women] are desired jurors when the plaintiff is a man. A woman juror may see a man impeached from the beginning of the case to the end, but there is at least the chance with the woman juror (particularly if the man happens to be handsome or appealing) [that] the plaintiff's derelictions in and out of court will be overlooked. A woman is inclined to forgive sin in the opposite sex; but definitely not her own. . . . 3 M. Belli, Modern Trials 51.67 and 51.68, pp. 446-447 (2d ed. 1982).

Discrimination in jury selection, whether based on race or on gender, causes harm to the litigants, the community, and the individual jurors who are wrongfully excluded from participation in the judicial process. The litigants are harmed by the risk that the prejudice which motivated the discriminatory selection of the jury will infect the entire proceedings. . . . The community is harmed by the State's participation in the perpetuation of invidious group stereotypes and the inevitable loss of confidence in our judicial system that state-sanctioned discrimination in the courtroom engenders.

When state actors exercise peremptory challenges in reliance on gender stereotypes, they ratify and reinforce prejudicial views of the relative abilities of men and women. Because these stereotypes have wreaked injustice in so many other spheres of our country's public life, active discrimination by litigants on the basis of gender during jury selection "invites cynicism respecting the jury's neutrality and its obligation to adhere to the law." Powers v. Ohio, [499 U.S. at 412]. The potential for cynicism is particularly acute in cases where gender-related issues are prominent, such as cases involving rape, sexual harassment, or paternity. . . .

In recent cases we have emphasized that individual jurors themselves have a right to nondiscriminatory jury selection procedures. . . . Contrary to respondent's suggestion, this right extends to both men and women. . . . All persons, when granted the opportunity to serve on a jury, have the right not to be excluded summarily because of discriminatory and stereotypical presumptions that reflect and reinforce patterns of historical discrimination. Striking individual jurors on the assumption that they hold particular views simply because of their gender is "practically a brand upon them, affixed by law, an assertion of their inferiority." Strauder v. West Virginia, [100 U.S. at 308]. It denigrates the dignity of the excluded juror, and, for a woman, reinvokes a history of exclusion from political participation.[14] The message it sends to all those in the courtroom, and all those who may later learn of the discriminatory act, is that certain individuals, for no reason other than gender, are presumed unqualified by state actors to decide important questions upon which reasonable persons could disagree.[15]

IV

Our conclusion that litigants may not strike potential jurors solely on the basis of gender does not imply the elimination of all peremptory challenges. . . . Parties still may remove jurors whom they feel might be less acceptable

14. The popular refrain is that all peremptory challenges are based on stereotypes of some kind, expressing various intuitive and frequently erroneous biases. But where peremptory challenges are made on the basis of group characteristics other than race or gender (like occupation, for example), they do not reinforce the same stereotypes about the group's competence or predispositions that have been used to prevent them from voting, participating on juries, pursuing their chosen professions, or otherwise contributing to civic life. . . .

15. Justice Scalia argues that there is no "discrimination and dishonor" in being subject to a race- or gender-based peremptory strike. . . . The only support Justice Scalia offers for his conclusion is the fact that race-and gender-based peremptory challenges have a long history in this country. . . . We do not dispute that this Court long has tolerated the discriminatory use of peremptory challenges, but this is not a reason to continue to do so. Many of "our people's traditions," such as de jure segregation and the total exclusion of women from juries, are now unconstitutional even though they once co-existed with the Equal Protection Clause.

than others on the panel; gender simply may not serve as a proxy for bias. Parties may also exercise their peremptory challenges to remove from the venire any group or class of individuals normally subject to "rational basis" review. . . . Even strikes based on characteristics that are disproportionately associated with one gender could be appropriate, absent a showing of pretext.[16]

If conducted properly, voir dire can inform litigants about potential jurors, making reliance upon stereotypical and pejorative notions about a particular gender or race both unnecessary and unwise. Voir dire provides a means of discovering actual or implied bias and a firmer basis upon which the parties may exercise their peremptory challenges intelligently. . . .

Failing to provide jurors the same protection against gender discrimination as race discrimination could frustrate the purpose of *Batson* itself. Because gender and race are overlapping categories, gender can be used as a pretext for racial discrimination.[18] Allowing parties to remove racial minorities from the jury not because of their race, but because of their gender, contravenes well-established equal protection principles and could insulate effectively racial discrimination from judicial scrutiny.

V

Equal opportunity to participate in the fair administration of justice is fundamental to our democratic system.[19] It not only furthers the goals of the jury system. It reaffirms the promise of equality under the law — that all citizens, regardless of race, ethnicity, or gender, have the chance to take part directly in our democracy. . . .

Justice O'CONNOR, concurring.

I agree with the Court that the Equal Protection Clause prohibits the government from excluding a person from jury service on account of that person's

---

16. For example, challenging all persons who have had military experience would disproportionately affect men at this time, while challenging all persons employed as nurses would disproportionately affect women. Without a showing of pretext, however, these challenges may well not be unconstitutional, since they are not gender- or race-based. . . .

18. The temptation to use gender as a pretext for racial discrimination may explain why the majority of the lower court decisions extending *Batson* to gender involve the use of peremptory challenges to remove minority women. All four of the gender-based peremptory cases to reach the federal courts of appeals . . . involved the striking of minority women.

19. This Court almost a half century ago stated:

> The American tradition of trial by jury, considered in connection with either criminal or civil proceedings, necessarily contemplates an impartial jury drawn from a cross-section of the community. . . . This does not mean, of course, that every jury must contain representatives of all the economic, social, religious, racial, political and geographical groups of the community; frequently such complete representation would be impossible. But it does mean that prospective jurors shall be selected by court officials without systematic and intentional exclusion of any of these groups. Recognition must be given to the fact that those eligible for jury service are to be found in every stratum of society. Jury competence is an individual rather than a group or class matter. That fact lies at the very heart of the jury system. To disregard it is to open the door to class distinctions and discriminations which are abhorrent to the democratic ideals of trial by jury.

Thiel v. Southern Pacific Co., [328 U.S. 217, 220 (1946)].

gender.... But today's important blow against gender discrimination is not cost-less. I write separately to discuss some of these costs, and to express my belief that today's holding should be limited to the government's use of gender-based per-emptory strikes.

Batson v. Kentucky... itself was a significant intrusion into the jury selection process. *Batson* mini-hearings are now routine in state and federal trial courts, and *Batson* appeals have proliferated as well.... In further constitutionalizing jury selection procedures, the Court increases the number of cases in which jury selection — once a sideshow — will become part of the main event.

For this same reason, today's decision further erodes the role of the peremptory challenge. The peremptory challenge is "a practice of ancient origin" and is "part of our common law heritage." Edmonson v. Leesville Concrete Co., [500 U.S. 614, 639 (1991)] (O'Connor, J., dissenting). The principal value of the peremptory is that it helps produce fair and impartial juries. Swain v. Alabama, [380 U.S. 202, 218-219 (1965)]....

Moreover, "[t]he essential nature of the peremptory challenge is that it is one exercised without a reason stated, without inquiry and without being subject to the court's control." [*Swain*, 380 U.S. at 220]. Indeed, often a reason for it cannot be stated, for a trial lawyer's judgments about a juror's sympathies are sometimes based on experienced hunches and educated guesses, derived from a juror's responses at voir dire or a juror's "'bare looks and gestures.'" [Id.] That a trial lawyer's instinctive assessment of a juror's predisposition cannot meet the high standards of a challenge for cause does not mean that the lawyer's instinct is erroneous.... Our belief that experienced lawyers will often correctly intuit which jurors are likely to be the least sympathetic, and our understanding that the lawyer will often be unable to explain the intuition, are the very reason we cherish the peremptory challenge. But, as we add, layer by layer, additional constitutional restraints on the use of the peremptory, we force lawyers to articulate what we know is often inarticulable.

In so doing we make the peremptory challenge less discretionary and more like a challenge for cause. We also increase the possibility that biased jurors will be allowed onto the jury, because sometimes a lawyer will be unable to provide an acceptable gender-neutral explanation even though the lawyer is in fact correct that the juror is unsympathetic. Similarly, in jurisdictions where lawyers exercise their strikes in open court, lawyers may be deterred from using their peremptories, out of the fear that if they are unable to justify the strike the court will seat a juror who knows that the striking party thought him unfit. Because I believe the peremptory remains an important litigator's tool and a fundamental part of the process of selecting impartial juries, our increasing limitation of it gives me pause.

Nor is the value of the peremptory challenge to the litigant diminished when the peremptory is exercised in a gender-based manner. We know that like race, gender matters. A plethora of studies make clear that in rape cases, for example, female jurors are somewhat more likely to vote to convict than male jurors. See R. Hastie, S. Penrod & N. Pennington, Inside the Jury 140-141 (1983).... Moreover, though there have been no similarly definitive studies regarding, for example, sexual harassment, child custody, or spousal or child abuse, one need not be a sexist to share the intuition that in certain cases a person's gender and resulting life experience will be relevant to his or her view of the case. "'Jurors are not expected to come into the jury box and leave behind all that their human experience has taught them.'" Beck v. Alabama, [447 U.S. 625, 642 (1980)]. Individuals are not expected to ignore as jurors what they know as men — or women.

Today's decision severely limits a litigant's ability to act on this intuition, for the import of our holding is that any correlation between a juror's gender and attitudes is irrelevant as a matter of constitutional law. But to say that gender makes no difference as a matter of law is not to say that gender makes no difference as a matter of fact. I previously have said with regard to *Batson*: "That the Court will not tolerate prosecutors' racially discriminatory use of the peremptory challenge, in effect, is a special rule of relevance, a statement about what this Nation stands for, rather than a statement of fact." Brown v. North Carolina, [479 U.S. 940, 941-942 (1986)] (O'Connor, J., concurring in denial of certiorari). Today's decision is a statement that, in an effort to eliminate the potential discriminatory use of the peremptory, . . . gender is now governed by the special rule of relevance formerly reserved for race. Though we gain much from this statement, we cannot ignore what we lose. In extending *Batson* to gender we have added an additional burden to the state and federal trial process, taken a step closer to eliminating the peremptory challenge, and diminished the ability of litigants to act on sometimes accurate gender-based assumptions about juror attitudes.

These concerns reinforce my conviction that today's decision should be limited to a prohibition on the government's use of gender-based peremptory challenges. The Equal Protection Clause prohibits only discrimination by state actors. . . .

Accordingly, I adhere to my position that the Equal Protection Clause does not limit the exercise of peremptory challenges by private civil litigants and criminal defendants. This case itself presents no state action dilemma, for here the State of Alabama itself filed the paternity suit on behalf of petitioner. But what of the next case? Will we, in the name of fighting gender discrimination, hold that the battered wife — on trial for wounding her abusive husband — is a state actor? Will we preclude her from using her peremptory challenges to ensure that the jury of her peers contains as many women members as possible? I assume we will, but I hope we will not.

Justice KENNEDY, concurring in the judgment.

I am in full agreement with the Court. . . .

The importance of individual rights to our analysis prompts a further observation concerning what I conceive to be the intended effect of today's decision. We do not prohibit racial and gender bias in jury selection only to encourage it in jury deliberations. Once seated, a juror should not give free rein to some racial or gender bias of his or her own. The jury system is a kind of compact by which power is transferred from the judge to jury, the jury in turn deciding the case in accord with the instructions defining the relevant issues for consideration. The wise limitation on the authority of courts to inquire into the reasons underlying a jury's verdict does not mean that a jury ought to disregard the court's instructions. A juror who allows racial or gender bias to influence assessment of the case breaches the compact and renounces his or her oath.

In this regard, it is important to recognize that a juror sits not as a representative of a racial or sexual group but as an individual citizen. Nothing would be more pernicious to the jury system than for society to presume that persons of different backgrounds go to the jury room to voice prejudice.... The jury pool must be representative of the community, but that is a structural mechanism for preventing bias, not enfranchising it.... Thus, the Constitution guarantees a right only to an impartial jury, not to a jury composed of members of a particular race or gender....

Justice SCALIA, with whom THE CHIEF JUSTICE and Justice THOMAS join, dissenting.

Today's opinion is an inspiring demonstration of how thoroughly up-to-date and right-thinking we Justices are in matters pertaining to the sexes (or as the Court would have it, the genders), and how sternly we disapprove the male chauvinist attitudes of our predecessors.... The parties do not contest that discrimination on the basis of sex[1] is subject to what our cases call "heightened scrutiny," and the citation of one of those cases (preferably one involving men rather than women, see, e.g., Mississippi Univ. for Women v. Hogan, [458 U.S. 718, 723-724 (1982),] is all that was needed....

The core of the Court's reasoning is that peremptory challenges on the basis of any group characteristic subject to heightened scrutiny are inconsistent with the guarantee of the Equal Protection Clause. That conclusion can be reached only by focusing unrealistically upon individual exercises of the peremptory challenge, and ignoring the totality of the practice. Since all groups are subject to the peremptory challenge (and will be made the object of it, depending upon the nature of the particular case) it is hard to see how any group is denied equal protection.... That explains why peremptory challenges coexisted with the Equal Protection Clause for 120 years. This case is a perfect example of how the system as a whole is even-handed. While the only claim before the Court is petitioner's complaint that the prosecutor struck male jurors, for every man struck by the government petitioner's own lawyer struck a woman. To say that men were singled out for discriminatory treatment in this process is preposterous. The situation would be different if both sides systematically struck individuals of one group, so that the strikes evinced group-based animus and served as a proxy for segregated venire lists. See Swain v. Alabama, [80 U.S. 202, 223-224 (1965)]. The pattern here, however, displays not a systemic sex-based animus but each side's desire to get a jury favorably disposed to its case. That is why the Court's characterization of respondent's argument as "reminiscent of the

---

1. Throughout this opinion, I shall refer to the issue as sex discrimination rather than (as the Court does) gender discrimination. The word "gender" has acquired the new and useful connotation of cultural or attitudinal characteristics (as opposed to physical characteristics) distinctive to the sexes. That is to say, gender is to sex as feminine is to female and masculine to male. The present case does not involve peremptory strikes exercised on the basis of femininity or masculinity (as far as it appears, effeminate men did not survive the prosecution's peremptories). The case involves, therefore, sex discrimination plain and simple.

arguments advanced to justify the total exclusion of women from juries" is patently false. Women were categorically excluded from juries because of doubt that they were competent; women are stricken from juries by peremptory challenge because of doubt that they are well disposed to the striking party's case.... There is discrimination and dishonor in the former, and not in the latter — which explains the 106-year interlude between our holding that exclusion from juries on the basis of race was unconstitutional, Strauder v. West Virginia, [supra], and our holding that peremptory challenges on the basis of race were unconstitutional, Batson v. Kentucky, supra.

Although the Court's legal reasoning in this case is largely obscured by anti-male-chauvinist oratory, to the extent such reasoning is discernible it invalidates much more than sex-based strikes.... [The Court's analysis] places all peremptory strikes based on any group characteristic at risk, since they can all be denominated "stereotypes." Perhaps, however (though I do not see why it should be so), only the stereotyping of groups entitled to heightened or strict scrutiny constitutes "the very stereotype the law condemns" — so that other stereotyping (e.g., wide-eyed blondes and football players are dumb) remains OK. Or perhaps when the Court refers to "impermissible stereotypes," it means the adjective to be limiting rather than descriptive — so that we can expect to learn from the Court's peremptory/stereotyping jurisprudence in the future which stereotypes the Constitution frowns upon and which it does not....

[M]ake no mistake about it: there really is no substitute for the peremptory. Voir dire (though it can be expected to expand as a consequence of today's decision) cannot fill the gap. The biases that go along with group characteristics tend to be biases that the juror himself does not perceive, so that it is no use asking about them. It is fruitless to inquire of a male juror whether he harbors any subliminal prejudice in favor of unwed fathers....

In order, it seems to me, not to eliminate any real denial of equal protection, but simply to pay conspicuous obeisance to the equality of the sexes, the Court imperils a practice that has been considered an essential part of fair jury trial since the dawn of the common law. The Constitution of the United States neither requires nor permits this vandalizing of our people's traditions.

For these reasons, I dissent.

Carol Weisbrod, Images of the Woman Juror
9 Harv. Women's L.J. 59, 70-76 (1986)

Proponents of women's suffrage and jury service argued that giving political responsibility to women would allow them to contribute to the public world the special beneficial influence they wielded in the home. Believing that the benefits women gave to the home could readily be transferred to the public world, their goal was, as Frances Willard put it in 1888, "to make the whole world homelike".... A suffragist at the turn of the century perhaps best summarized the point by saying that "the feminine heart, the maternal influence, are needed in the court-room as well as in the home."

The perceptive capacities of women were sometimes seen as superior to men's in a way particularly relevant to jury service. Supporters of women's jury service thought domestic virtue gave women a heightened ability to sense the truth. A state official in 1884 offered the following in favor of women jurors: "They do not reason like men upon the evidence, but, being possessed of a higher quality of intellectuality, i.e., keen perceptions, they see the truth of the thing at a glance." Proponents also argued that, once having determined the truth, women would hold fast to their positions, ensuring a just verdict.

Supporters of women's jury service also argued that women's heightened perceptions included the ability to understand other women, whether as witnesses or defendants, better than men could. Thus, one author claimed that in most criminal cases where women are involved, women could "be of immense service in clearing up evidence, and showing to the male jurors on the panel the absurdity or impossibility of some of the statements." . . .

Inherent in some of these arguments is not only the idea that women could better understand and therefore better judge other women, but also the assumption that women may judge each other according to a different standard than men would use. The 1917 Susan Glaspell story, A Jury of Her Peers [reprinted in The Best Short Stories of 1917, at 256-282 (E.J. O'Brien ed., 1918)] illustrates both of these ideas. The story describes a visit to a farm in which a man has been found strangled. His wife, Minnie, is in jail, accused of the murder. Three men, including the sheriff and the county attorney, visit the couple's home, accompanied by two women: one, the sheriff's wife, a woman "married to the law," the other, a neighbor of Minnie. The men are looking for evidence of motive but are unsuccessful. The women look at various domestic items and discover the motive. . . . The facts noticed by the women relate to exclusively female and domestic matters, such as housekeeping and sewing. Thus, tiny domestic hints discovered by other women's unique perceptive abilities provide the critical missing evidentiary link relating to motive. The motive relates broadly to Minnie's unhappiness with her husband, a cold man whose temperament is suggested by the fact that he broke open the bird cage and strangled Minnie's songbird. Minnie, like the canary, had sung when she was a young girl — "He killed that too."

The "judgment of her peers" is to keep silent about the evidence they uncovered. Since the men pay little attention to Minnie's domestic items — and would probably not have recognized their meaning even if they had — the effect of the women's silence is to keep the men ignorant of the motive. Without such evidence, the men fear that the jury will tend to acquit ("you know how these juries are with women"). The men are identified with the law, and the story assumes that the (presumably male) jury of the outside world would have judged the wife guilty of her husband's murder despite any amount of provocation or derangement. The women are identified as love or forgiveness, but also perhaps as a kind of higher law or higher justice.

The story thus contains both of the assumptions found in the historical literature: that women see things that men do not see, at least in relation to other women, and that women and men evaluate those discoveries differently. Although the murder is excused by the female jury of peers, the story suggests that it would not be justified in the actual judicial system. The women are not merely more sensitive than men in what they see about the woman defendant; they also seem to operate under a different moral code. As the story is told, the crimes of neglecting Minnie, destroying her spirit and happiness, and killing her songbird are all related to her crime of killing her husband. These crimes by her husband are offered as moral justification when the jury of women decides, in effect, to acquit a murderess.

 Cristina M. Rodriguez, Note, Clearing the Smoke-Filled Room: Women Jurors and the Disruption of an Old-Boys' Network in Nineteenth-Century America
108 Yale L.J. 1805, 1806-1807, 1812-1814, 1816-1819 (1999)

To comprehend why jury service had a social significance distinct from suffrage, rather than consider nineteenth-century women jurors as variations on women voters, the former should be seen in the same context as women who sought access to the bar. Both women lawyers and women jurors can be understood as outsiders who invaded the space of the courtroom and challenged the masculinist legal culture that operated according to the internal logic of an "old-boys" or insiders' network. Opposition to women jurors did flow in part from traditional objections to changes in the legal status of women; not only would women be distracted from their domestic duties, but the status of juror did not befit feminine nature. The primary opposition, however, emanated from a desire to preserve a particular legal culture. The mixed jury experiments in the Wyoming and Washington Territories suggest that women jurors introduced into the fluid legal culture of post-Civil War America a concept of a "gendered justice," or the belief that women as women would perform their duties as jurors differently from their male counterparts. By disrupting the status quo of the male-dominated legal profession, the possibility of a gendered justice fueled opposition to female jury service, even as female suffrage remained grudgingly accepted....

Proponents of the experiments projected that if women could be persuaded to sit on juries, they would operate unconstrained by the same external conditions that beset male jurors and would act as their judgment and consciences dictated. Justice Howe [presiding over the mixed juries] concluded that by serving on juries, women would have the best possible opportunity to "aid in suppressing the dens of infamy which curse the country."....

[By contrast, critics] argued that women in the courtroom would distract men by changing the legal discussion into "a charming tete-a-tete with the best looking young man on the jury.... Session[s]... would witness a delightful but wicked flirtation between good-looking juryman and the volatile wife." Unable to focus on the "legal harangue," women jurors would instead introduce frivolous conversation, emblematic of their domestic sphere, into the sober proceedings....

Across the country, journalists and concerned citizens,...pondered what "female justice" meant. The *New Orleans Times*... charged that the jury experiment was premised on a fictitious female "masculinity," concluding that the mixed jury would actually yield beneficial results by proving women to be incapable of sitting "as the peers of men without setting at defiance all the laws of delicacy and propriety."

The *Philadelphia Press* offered an alternative view.... The paper asserted that women, by nature, moralized excessively and therefore did not belong as decisionmakers in a legal system that depended on discovering nuances and gradations in responsibility. "Is it possible for a jury of women, carrying with them all their sensitiveness, sympathies, predilections, jealousies, prejudices, hatreds, to reach an impartial verdict?" Regardless of whether opponents believed the woman juror to be "too soft" or "too hard," a consistent argument ran through all of the criticism: The woman juror, by defying the separate spheres construct, dangerously conflated gender roles in a manner incompatible with prevailing legal culture....

In the end, media accounts abounded with five predictable conclusions: (1) women's exalted moral natures rendered them ill-suited for the dirty world of the courtroom; (2) the characteristic emotions that made women good mothers would operate to cloud their judgment; (3) incapable of apprehending abstractions, women would be unable to decipher the technicalities of the law and intricacies of evidence; (4) inherently frivolous, women jurors would be too distracted to perform their duties, distracting male jurors in the process; and (5) the demands of women's domestic responsibilities made jury service a logistical impossibility....

Notes

1. Equality and Impartiality in Jury Selection. The jury system reflects a tension between the right to be judged by one's peers, and the right to an impartial tribunal. When Gwendolyn Hoyt unsuccessfully challenged a jury selection system that gave automatic exemptions to women, she was seeking to obtain a jury of her peers under circumstances in which the sex of jurors might matter: the murder of her abusive husband.

> [T]he affair occurred in the context of a marital upheaval involving, among other things, the suspected infidelity of the appellant's husband, and culminating in the husband's final rejection of his wife's efforts at reconciliation. It is claimed, in substance, that women jurors would have been more understanding or compassionate than men in assessing the quality of appellant's act and her defense of "temporary insanity."

Hoyt v. Florida, 368 U.S. 57, 58 (1961). The Court, however, held that a broad statutory exemption was justifiable, "whether born of the State's historic public policy or of a determination that it would not be administratively feasible to decide in each individual instance whether the family responsibilities of a prospective female juror were serious enough to warrant an exemption." Id. at 63.

Fifteen years later, *Hoyt* was overruled in Taylor v. Louisiana, 419 U.S. 522 (1975), primarily on the basis of defendants' Sixth Amendment right to an impartial jury of their peers. However, the Court also recognized women's equal protection interests in "sharing in the administration of justice [as] a phase of civil responsibility." Id at 530-531. These dual rationales rested on competing assumptions. The concern for the fairness of the defendant's trial assumes that women and men may offer different perspectives; the concern for the right of prospective jurors to be treated as equals assumes that there are no significant sex-based differences.

This tension is also apparent in *J.E.B.* As Justice O'Connor notes, there are some cases in which gender does make a difference. Does pretending otherwise improve the accuracy of the jury system? How broad is the ruling? For the extensions of *Batson* beyond its original facts, see Edmonson v. Leesville Concrete Co., 500 U.S. 614 (1991) (*Batson* applied to civil cases); Georgia v. McCollum, 505 U.S. 42 (1992) (*Batson* applied to criminal defendants).

What exactly does impartiality mean in the context of a jury of peers? Is it that a potential juror should have no views on any relevant subject? Or that jury perspectives in some sense should be drawn from a cross-section of the community, and "not arbitrarily skewed for or against any particular group or characteristic"? See Holland v. Illinois, 493 U.S. 474, 515 (1990) (Stevens, J., dissenting). Should the goal be proportional representation on juries? See Kenneth S. Klein & Theodore D. Klastorin, Do Diverse Juries Aid or Impede Justice?, 1999 Wis. L. Rev. 553 (1999).

Although *J.E.B.* has met with considerable support in theory, it has proven more problematic in practice. Part of the difficulty, Charles Ogletree notes, is that while gender may be an imperfect proxy for relevant attitudes, it is not an entirely irrational one when other more accurate information is unavailable. The stereotypes that influence lawyers in jury selection may also be ones that "affect the behavior of men and women in the jury box." Charles Ogletree, Just Say No! A Proposal to Eliminate Racially Discriminatory Uses of Peremptory Challenges, 31 Am. Crim. L. Rev. 1099, 1104 (1994).

The point, according to Ogletree, is not that *J.E.B.* was wrongly decided. It is rather that the Court appeared to underestimate the difficulties in enforcing its ruling. Inventive lawyers can always summon nondiscriminatory reasons for a challenge, and most trial courts are reluctant to reject them as pretextual unless they are patently implausible or clearly incorporate impermissible stereotypes. Appellate courts are similarly reluctant to reverse lower court rulings, which often turn on factual determinations of credibility. And lawyers who feel ethically obligated to gain sympathetic hearings for their clients may be equally reluctant to acknowledge — even to themselves — the role that impermissible stereotypes play in their juror selections. See Leonard Post, A Loaded Box of Stereotypes, Nat'l L.J. April 25, 2005, at A1, A18 (noting that lawyers and jury consultants believe that concerns such as sex, race, ethnicity, and religion routinely figure in juror exclusions and citing examples from litigation training programs); Pam Karlan, Race, Rights, and Remedies in Constitutional Adjudication, 96 Mich. L. Rev.

2001, 2014-2016 (1998) (noting the difficulties of identifying the cases in which racial discrimination actually prejudiced the defendant).

Given these evidentiary hurdles, it is perhaps unsurprising that claims of gender discrimination in peremptory challenges are relatively rare. A survey by Susan Hightower found that in the first five years under *J.E.B.*, there had been only 127 reported complaints and 23 reversals in all state and federal systems. Susan Hightower, Sex and the Peremptory Strike: An Empirical Analysis of J.E.B. v. Alabama's First Five Years, 52 Stan. L. Rev. 895 (2000). Clearly the ruling has not been as burdensome as critics predicted. But neither has it been as effective as supporters hoped. Surveyed cases include numerous examples of peremptories that have been sustained despite the stereotypes underlying them. Women have been struck for being "timid," "not assertive," "weak," "vacillating," overweight, and single mothers. Id. 924-926. One particularly striking case, Talley v. State, 687 So. 2d 1261 (Ala. Crim. App. 1996), involved a battered woman on trial for murder of her husband. The state used all 13 of its strikes against women, and the court upheld the exclusions. Among the reasons that the prosecutor offered were that a female prospective juror had "heard of the battered woman syndrome," "agree[d] with feminists ideals and goals," or had read romance novels, "indicating that she did not look as life as it is." Id. at 1267.

Do the practical problems in enforcing prohibitions on bias in jury selection argue for abolition or reduction of peremptory challenges? Commentators are divided. Some suggest that if trial judges are insufficiently willing to enforce prohibitions on bias, the response should be more judicial education and less deference by appellate courts. If lawyers are reluctant to disregard gender as a proxy for predisposition, the best strategy is to provide more accurate information and more disincentives for biased challenges. Expanded use of detailed voir dires, confidential questionnaires, and exclusions for cause would be steps in that direction. If part of the problem now is courts' reluctance to police bias, would we be better off in a system that eliminated peremptory challenges and gave judges more control over jury selection? Under what circumstances might you use gender as a proxy in jury selection?

How should courts deal with strikes based on an individual's sexual orientation? Should lawyers be entitled to ask jurors questions about their living arrangements and about conduct that might suggest a lesbian or gay identity? See Vanessa H. Eisemann, Striking a Balance of Fairness: Sexual Orientation and Voir Dire, 13 Yale J.L. & Feminism 1 (2001) (arguing that sexual orientation should be treated like race, religion, ethnicity, and gender for the purposes of what is a permissible basis for a peremptory strike).

2. Juror Discretion. Does feminist theory provide a rationale for giving juries more or less discretion? Is there room for emotion in jury deliberations? See Joan W. Howarth, Deciding to Kill: Revealing the Gender in the Task Handed to Capital Jurors, 1994 Wis. L. Rev. 1345 (capital sentence is fundamentally about values and conscience, not just facts).

Would greater jury discretion favor women? It may depend upon the crime and the circumstances. See Andrea Shapiro, Unequal Before the Law: Men,

Women and the Death Penalty, 8 Am. U. J. Gender Soc. Pol'y & L. 427, 469 (2000) (women who maintain "the image of a 'real' woman will be spared from the ultimate sentence of death," while those who "blatantly and explicitly disturb society's notions of the 'real' woman will not"); Victor L. Streib, Death Penalty for Female Offenders, 58 U. Cin. L. Rev. 845, 868, 877-878 (1990) (while juries and judges are more lenient toward most female offenders, those who are poor and uneducated, and who exhibit shockingly "unladylike" behavior, are subject to especially punitive sentences). Elizabeth Rapaport shows that women tend to benefit more from proportionality review because they are less severe aggravators and have fewer prior crimes. See Elizabeth Rapaport, Staying Alive: Executive Clemency, Equal Protection, and the Politics of Gender in Women's Capital Cases, 4 Buff. Crim. L. Rev. 967, 968, 979 (2001). Women also benefit from a higher rate of clemency; of 44 cases, seven have been women. Id. at 981.

The Supreme Court in 1991, reversing its prior decisions in the area, held that victim impact statements are constitutionally allowed in capital murder proceedings as a means of showing the "uniqueness" of each individual and the specific harm caused by the crime. See Payne v. Tennessee, 501 U.S. 808 (1991). By the turn of the twenty-first century, a majority of states had added victims' rights amendments to their constitutions. See Jennifer J. Stearman, An Amendment to the Constitution of the United States to Protect the Rights of Crime Victims: Exploring the Effectiveness of State Efforts, 30 U. Balt. L.F. 43 (1999). What are the likely results of such contextualized focus on victims? Are women likely to benefit? Minorities? What about the context of the defendant? See Abbe Smith, Criminal Responsibility, Social Responsibility, and Angry Young Men: Reflections of a Feminist Criminal Defense Lawyer, 21 N.Y.U. Rev. L. & Soc. Change 433, 489 (1994-1995) (need for juries "to hear about the social misery that underlies crime," including "the conditions under which deprived inner-city youth and battered women live").

Further discussion of issues of criminal sentencing, including the appropriate role of compassion, are discussed in Section 7, p. 738, below.

Putting Theory into Practice

4-10. In the trial of O.J. Simpson for murder of his battered wife, jury consultants for both sides found that black women were the group most likely to vote for acquittal; they were least likely to credit the domestic violence evidence, or to respond favorably to Marcia Clark, the white woman lead prosecutor. Albert W. Alshuler, How to Win the Trial of the Century: The Ethics of Lord Brougham and the O.J. Simpson Defense Team, 29 McGeorge L. Rev. 311, 312 (1998). Although the judge submitted a detailed 79-page questionnaire to prospective jurors concerning possible sources of bias, defense counsel still believed that it was in their interest to use peremptory challenges to increase black women's representation on the jury.

If you had been one of the defense lawyers in the *Simpson* case, what would you have done? If your team had used its peremptory challenges to exclude men and white women, is it likely that the prosecution could have established a constitutional violation?

7. Women and the Criminal Justice System

United States v. Handy
752 F. Supp. 561 (E.D.N.Y. 1990)

GLASSER, District Judge:

Ms. Handy pleaded guilty to a single count indictment charging her with conspiring with William Johnson to distribute and possess with intent to distribute cocaine. The events leading up to her arrest describe a reverse buy—that is to say—the defendants were not selling cocaine to an undercover officer or to a confidential informant, but were negotiating to buy cocaine for a stated price. The money with which to consummate the purchase was in a handbag on the floor near Ms. Handy and totaled $75,000. Also in her handbag were a diluent used to "cut" cocaine and glassine envelopes.

Johnson was, for the preceding five years, Handy's boyfriend. On the day prior to her arrest, he requested her to accompany him to New York City to buy narcotics. She agreed to accompany him and to carry the purchase money. She denied ever having done so before. She admitted to knowing for at least two years of Johnson's involvement in illegal activity based upon the inconsistency between his lifestyle and his earnings as a meat cutter and she suspected that the illegal activity was drug related.

The facts which identify this defendant as Nadine Handy, a person, rather than an objective manifestation of discrete criteria to which are assigned numbers which, when added together yield a sentencing result, are as follows:

She was born in Baltimore, Maryland, thirty-six years ago. She was one of ten children whose father died when she was three and whose mother died at the age of forty when the defendant was fifteen years old. She is the mother of three out-of-wedlock children. She gave birth to her first child when she was seventeen and still in high school. He is now nineteen years old and is a strong candidate for a basketball scholarship to college with aspirations of playing professional basketball thereafter. She gave birth to her second child, a daughter, two years later and left high school. This child is now sixteen, is enrolled in the "gifted and talented" class in her local high school and is the likely recipient of a $1,000 annual college scholarship. She gave birth to her second daughter who is now eight years old and in the third grade. All the children live with her. She has no prior criminal record.

Ms. Handy has been gainfully employed for the past thirteen years. For the past eight years she has been employed by the same firm, Farm Fresh Food, Inc. in Baltimore to which she returned to resume her work when released on bail. She has borne the sole responsibility for rearing her three children and supporting them without public assistance. She also undertook to care for the two children of her boyfriend, Johnson, when they came to Baltimore from California. Letters written on behalf of Ms. Handy describe her selflessness in that regard and the positive influence she has had on their lives.

The picture of Ms. Handy portrayed by the salient facts I summarized and by the many letters on her behalf, is of a young woman born into and reared in poverty in an urban environment which is a socio-economic minefield through which she threaded her way and emerged unscathed, relatively speaking. That is to say, she abjured the suffocating effects of the world of welfare for the independence and dignity-reinforcing world of work and has been steadily and gainfully employed for thirteen years. She has single-handedly and successfully guided three children through the socio-economic minefield of a not atypically treacherous urban environment. Letters addressed to the court attest to the high regard in which she is held at work and in her community. What then brings her before the court? The explanation which is all but inescapable is that this single parent fell in love with the co-defendant, William Johnson and despite her many other strengths did not have the strength to say "no" to him. The story is as old as the story of civilization — he offered her an apple and she did eat. That the government did not view her as a sophisticated, knowledgeable drug dealer is indicated by its stipulation at the time of her plea not to oppose a four point guideline reduction for her minimal role in the offense. There is no indication that the defendant was drawn to trafficking in drugs by the lure of the huge sums of money incident to such traffic. Were that the case it would be reasonable to assume that she would not persist in working as a meat wrapper at an average salary of approximately $250 per week.

Is a downward modification appropriate and justified by the statutes and the guidelines promulgated pursuant thereto? I believe it is. I believe that the conclusion I reach is one a sentencing judge is permitted to reach within the framework of the guidelines. I do not depart as an expression of general dissatisfaction with the guidelines. It is rather late in the day for that and would be tilting at windmills. . . .

I find the circumstances related to family ties and relationships and to previous and current employment record to be sufficiently extraordinary to warrant a downward departure for the following reasons. Although ordinarily an employment record is not relevant in determining whether a sentence should be outside the guidelines, U.S.S.G. §5H1.5, the continuous employment for thirteen years of this single parent of three teenage children is extraordinary. That factor, coupled with the fact that an exceptionally promising future of the older two children would be threatened by the prolonged incarceration of this mother drives the court to conclude that a downward departure is warranted. . . .

Lest the decision in this case is sought to be regarded as authority for a downward departure in every case of a single parent, or in every case in which a defendant has been gainfully employed, I emphasize that it is not so intended. The decision in this case is intensely fact specific. I also wish to emphasize that although passing references have been made in the course of this opinion to the socio-economic background of the defendant and to the fact that she is a first offender, those factors were not regarded as factors warranting a downward departure. . . .

Notes

1. Gender and Sentencing Reform. Before the promulgation of sentencing guidelines, the individual circumstances of the defendant were regularly considered by judges when determining punishment, and women generally received more lenient sentences than men who committed similar crimes. See, e.g., Nancy Gertner, Women, Justice and Authority: How Justice Affects Women: Women Offenders and the Sentencing Guidelines, 14 Yale J.L. & Feminism 291, 292 (2002).

In an effort to eliminate unwarranted sentencing disparity, Congress passed the Sentencing Reform Act of 1984, Pub. L. No. 98-473, tit. 11, ch. 2, 98 Stat. 1987 (1984) (codified at 18 U.S.C. §§ 3551-3673; 28 U.S.C. §§ 991-998). The Act was meant to promote the goals of honesty, uniformity, and proportionality in sentencing by mandating "real time," uniform sentences for similar conduct. The Federal Sentencing Commission established the Federal Sentencing Guidelines in order to shift the focus of punishment away from the characteristics of the defendant to the characteristics of the crime. The Guidelines prohibited consideration of traditional "individualizing" factors, except in "extraordinary" situations, and specified that family ties and responsibilities were not ordinarily relevant. See U.S. Sentencing Guidelines Manual § 5H1.10 (1997).

Studies of Guideline sentencing showed that women still received more lenient sentencing than men, with judges having to justify downward judicial departures from the Sentencing Guidelines. See, e.g., David B. Mustard, Racial, Ethnic, and Gender Disparities in Sentencing: Evidence from the U.S. Federal Courts, 44 J.L. & Econ. 285 (2001). Some argue that the disparity was due to a paternalistic stereotyping of women as either weaker and less able to withstand imprisonment, or more submissive and thus less responsible for their crimes. See Monica Pa, Towards a Feminist Theory of Violence, 9 U. Chi. L. Sch. Roundtable 45, 72 (2002) (quoting judge as stating, "I am more lenient toward women, and I've just not been able to grasp why that is, except I love my mother very much."). Others charge that Mustard's and similar studies failed to control for various factors, including the effects of minimum mandatory sentences and departures. See, e.g., Panel 1: Disparity in Sentencing—Race and Gender, 15 Fed. Sent'g Rep. 160 (2003) (paper by Kevin Blackwell, developed with Paul Hofer).

A series of Supreme Court cases beginning with Blakely v. Washington, 542 U.S. 296 (2004), which struck down Washington state's sentencing guidelines, has transformed the use of sentencing guidelines. Following on the heels of *Blakely*, the Supreme Court in early 2005 ruled that because the guidelines required judges to increase sentences based on factors that had not been proven to a jury beyond a reasonable doubt, the system violated defendants' Sixth Amendment rights. United States v. Booker, 125 S. Ct. 738 (2005). The Court allowed the guidelines to remain as an advisory—though not mandatory—sentencing instruction, and held that sentences outside the range would be subject to a "reasonableness" test on appeal. Id.

It remains to be seen what effect the Guidelines will have now that they are only advisory. For a discussion of potential ramifications for female offenders post-*Booker*, see Myrna S. Raeder, A Primer on Gender-Related Issues that Affect Female Offenders, 20 Crim. Just. 4 (Spring 2005).

Handy demonstrates the difficulties of staying within the boundaries set by the sentencing guideline reforms. For example, the judge in *Handy* makes four references to the defendant's background, six to her status as a single parent, six to the defendant being gainfully employed and/or not on welfare, four to the defendant's "exceptionally promising" children, and three to the defendant's relationship with the co-defendant. It would seem the judge was impressed by the defendant's life choices, choices made despite being "reared in poverty in an urban environment which is a socio-economic minefield." Are these the kind of "extraordinary" contextual considerations allowed under the Federal Sentencing Guidelines or the kind of information about family ties and responsibility that should not be relevant? Do you think the outcome of the case would have been different had all else been the same, except that the defendant had no children? What if she had been a man? Should the result be the same?

As for sentencing of women in state courts, some debate has focused on whether women receive higher sentences than men for violent crimes against their spouses. Debate was fueled by two Baltimore County, Maryland, sentences handed down on the same day in 1994. In one case, a judge sentenced a man to 18 months in prison for killing his wife, whom he found in bed with another man; in the other case, a woman was sentenced to three years in prison for killing her abusive husband. These cases, and the conflicting studies on disparate sentencing, are reviewed in Wendy Keller, Disparate Treatment of Spouse Murder Defendants, 6 S. Cal. Rev. L. & Women's Stud. 255 (1996).

Criticism of sentencing reform has also focused on its detrimental impact on members of racial minority groups. See Leadership Conference on Civil Rights, Justice on Trial: Racial Disparities in the American Criminal Justice System (2000). Specifically on the impact of sentencing reform on African-American women, see Paula C. Johnson, At the Intersection of Injustice: Experiences of African-American Women in Crime and Sentencing, 4 Am. U. J. Gender & L. 1, 9 (1995) (arguing that the "progression toward mandatory sentencing . . . perpetuates the historically devalued status of African-American women, construing them as undeserving of social benefits and as intrinsically incorrigible," and also violates the Eighth Amendment).

2. Motherhood and Criminal Justice. In 1999, an estimated 721,500 state and federal prisoners were parents to nearly 1.5 million children under age 18. 5 JCPR Policy Briefs (4), Where Children Live When Parents Are Incarcerated (2003). The majority (77 percent) of children whose fathers are incarcerated live with their mothers, while 15 percent live with a grandparent or other relative. Children of mothers who are incarcerated most often live with grandparents or other relatives; only 17 percent live with their fathers. Id. Thus, although incarceration obviously takes men away from their children, "neutral" sentencing has a different impact on women (and their children) than on men (and their children). See Lanette P. Dalley, Imprisoned Mothers and Their Children: Their Often

742 ≡≡≡ *4. Difference Theory*

Conflicting Legal Rights, 22 Hamline J. Pub. L. & Pol'y 1 (2000). Does the failure of the Sentencing Guidelines to take parental responsibility into account therefore constitute gender bias against women offenders?

Consider the following:

> The purpose of just punishment emphasizes consistency in sentencing. If the "same" sentence has an inconsistent impact on two different defendants, then considering the two sentences as equivalent is unjust. An incarcerative sentence may have a distinctly different impact on a parent than it has on a non-parent. For example, in many states incarceration constitutes a ground for termination of parental rights. A two year prison sentence does not equal two years in prison accompanied by permanent loss of child custody. . . .

Eleanor Bush, Considering the Defendant's Children at Sentencing, 2 Fed. Sent'g Rep. 194, 194 (1990); see also Myrna Raeder, Gender and Sentencing: Single Moms, Battered Women, and other Sex-Based Anomalies in the Gender-Free World of the Federal Sentencing Guidelines, 20 Pepp. L. Rev. 905, 961 (1993) (blindly imposing equal treatment on parents at sentencing when the rest of society does not "makes a mockery of so-called gender neutrality in sentencing").

Senior United States District Court Judge Jack Weinstein agrees, suggesting that, while the motivation behind gender-neutral sentencing guidelines may have been commendable, the results have often been nonsensical. "[O]stensibly gender-neutral provisions do not lead to gender-neutral results in a society in which many male and female experiences with crime, family life, and community differ." Jack Weinstein, The Effect of Sentencing on Women, Men, the Family, and the Community, 5 Colum. J. Gender & L. 169, 181 (1996). Weinstein advocates an approach to sentencing that incorporates consideration of the effect of a parent's incarceration on her children.

> The lack of parental supervision resulting from incarceration of heads of households can lead into a vicious downward spiral of criminal activity, jail sentences, and possible death for [children of incarcerated parents] at a young age. . . . Avoiding punitive solutions based solely on incarceration for defendants who are heads of households may prevent the children from being victimized because of their parents' acts while at the same time it may guarantee a certain degree of stability that can encourage a home environment where the children can pursue alternatives beyond criminal activity.

Id. at 179.

Would a categorical policy of mitigation of sentences for offenders with primary child care responsibilities reinforce gender stereotypes? Or recognize gendered realities?

> Such a policy would effectively use the criminal law to reward women for their status as mothers (or, alternatively, to punish women for not having children). It would say in effect, "you have violated the criminal law, but we'll overlook that so you can do what you are supposed to do — care for your children." This denies single-mother

offenders the status of full moral agents and disregards the social contributions of childless women, whose employment and community ties are not given the same consideration in sentencing.

Ilene H. Nagel & Barry L. Johnson, Gender Issues and the Criminal Law: The Role of Gender in a Structured Sentencing System: Equal Treatment, Policy Choices, and the Sentencing of Female Offenders Under the United States Sentencing Guidelines, 85 J. Crim. L. & Criminology 181, 208 (1994).

Courts that have specifically addressed the issue of parental responsibility at sentencing have generally decided that motherhood itself is not an extraordinary circumstance and thus, without more, is not a valid basis for a downward departure.

> A sole, custodial parent is not a rarity in today's society, and imprisoning such a parent will by definition separate the parent from the children. It is apparent that in many cases the other parent may be unable or unwilling to care for the children, and that the children will have to live with relatives, friends, or even in foster homes. . . . This situation, though unfortunate, is simply not out of the ordinary.

United States v. Brand, 907 F.2d 31, 33 (4th Cir.), cert. denied, 498 U.S. 1014 (1990). In practice under sentencing guidelines, however, research indicates that judges take into account the extralegal factor of motherhood in determining sentences. For example, one federal judge noted that the defendant "does not have a spouse who can care for her children," and the burden upon relatives of caring for the defendant's newborn child. United States v. Mateo, 299 F. Supp. 2d 201, 212-213 (S.D.N.Y. 2004). See also Sean B. Berberian, Protecting Children: Explaining Disparities in the Female Offender's Pretrial Process, and Policy Issues Surrounding Lenient Treatment of Mothers, 10 Hastings Women's L.J. 369 (1999) (finding that women with children were significantly more likely to receive pretrial release and lower bail/bond amounts).

On June 27, 1994, President Nelson Mandela of the Republic of South Africa signed a Presidential Act providing an early release from prison for certain categories of prisoners, including "all mothers in prison on 10 May 1994, with minor children under the age of twelve (12) years." Fathers were not included. In his statement in support of the Act, President Mandela stated that he was motivated predominantly by a concern for children who had been deprived of the nurturing and care that their mothers would ordinarily have provided.

> Having spent many years in prison myself, I am well aware of the hardship which flows from incarceration. I am also well aware that imprisonment inevitably has harsh consequences for the family of the prisoner.
>
> Account was taken of the special role I believe that mothers play in the care and nurturing of younger children. . . .
>
> I have had an on-going concern about the general plight of young children in South Africa. . . . In my experience there are only a minority of fathers who are actively involved in nurturing and caring for their children. . . .

President of the Republic of South Africa v. Hugo, 1997 (4) SA 1 (CC).

A father with a child under the age of 12 who was not entitled to early release under the order challenged his exclusion under the anti-discrimination provisions of the interim South African Constitution. Is there any question about how this case would be decided in the United States? A majority of the South African Constitutional Court rejected the challenge on the grounds that the early release order was not "unfair discrimination." One justice dissented, and another determined that although the Act constituted "unfair discrimination," it was justified. See id.

A related problem is that the relatively small number of women offenders means they are concentrated in a few facilities, often at great distances from their families. In California, for example, three-quarters of women prisoners are housed in two facilities in a remote rural town. As a consequence, over half of their children never visit them during their incarceration. Jennifer Warren, System Fails Women, Study Says, L.A. Times, Dec. 16, 2004, at B1 (discussing Little Hoover Commission report). See Carla Thompson, Alabama Moves Female Prisoners Away from Children, www.womensenews.org, July 18, 2003. Most states remove infants from their mothers almost immediately after birth, and women do not have the opportunity to nurse or bond with their newborns. Lori B. Girshick, No Safe Haven: Stories of Women in Prison 115 (1999). Children of imprisoned parents are five to six times as likely as their peers to end up behind bars, and 10 percent land in foster care. Warren, supra, at B1. For an overview of problems, see Susan F. Sharp and M. Elaine Eriksen, Imprisoned Mothers and Their Children, in Women in Prison: Gender and Social Control (Barbara H. Zaitzow & Jim Thomas eds., 2003).

3. Pregnancy. Case law under the federal Guidelines concerning downward departures for pregnancy is limited. In United States v. Pozzy, 902 F.2d 133, 138-139 (1st Cir.), cert. denied, 498 U.S. 943 (1990), the court noted that "pregnancy of convicted female felons is neither atypical nor unusual." Myrna Raeder calls this conclusion "suspect," pointing out that while pregnant *female* felons may not be unusual, pregnant *felons* are, and that by confining the sample to women, the First Circuit violated the Sentencing Commission's ban on consideration based on sex. Raeder, Gender and Sentencing, supra, at 947. Is this sound analysis?

The Court in *Pozzy* also expressed concern that giving a downward departure for pregnancy would send "an obvious message to all female defendants that pregnancy is 'a way out.' " 902 F.2d at 139. The D.C. Circuit vacated a sentence based on a downward departure given to a pregnant woman who conceived after her arrest. United States v. Dyce, 91 F.3d 1462 (D.C. Cir. 1996), cert. denied, 519 U.S. 1018 (1996). But see United States v. Arize, 792 F. Supp. 920 (E.D.N.Y. 1992) (defendant's unknown pregnancy at time of offense a valid basis for downward departure because of the potential that defendant would permanently lose custody of the child); United States v. Pokuaa, 782 F. Supp. 747 (E.D.N.Y. 1992) (downward departure given to defendant who was in seventh month of pregnancy at time of sentencing and who was experiencing complications with the pregnancy).

4. Sentencing, Prior Abuse, and Postpartum Depression. Nearly 50 percent of female federal inmates and 60 percent of female state inmates report having been a victim of physical or sexual abuse. Caroline Wolf Harlow, Prior Abuse Reported by Inmates and Probationers 2, Bureau Just. Stat. (April 1999). One of the factors "not ordinarily relevant" to determining whether to depart from the federal Sentencing Guidelines is a defendant's mental or emotional condition. U.S. Sentencing Guidelines Manual §5H1.3 (1997). This provision has been considered by some courts to be an extraordinary condition justifying a downward sentencing departure for abused female offenders, provided the defendant can establish a nexus between the abuse and the offense. In this regard, the Guidelines are in line with traditional sentencing assessments of an individual defendant's blameworthiness. What about when the abuse isn't current, but may have affected, at least indirectly, defendant's ability to control her behavior?

In October of 1994, only two weeks after being granted custody of her two children, Susan Smith of Union, South Carolina, loaded her young sons into her car, drove to a nearby lake, pointed the car toward the lake, and then released the hand brake and jumped out. After a nine-day search for the African-American carjacker who Smith told police drove off with her children, Smith admitted she had killed her sons. Her capital murder trial was short, and during the penalty phase, her attorneys argued for leniency based on a history of depression brought on in large part by sexual abuse she suffered as a child. The jury sentenced her to life imprisonment, sparing her the death penalty. See Chris Burritt & Jack Warner, The Susan Smith Trial, Atlanta Const., July 22, 1995, at C8; Jurors in Susan Smith Trial Say They Don't Have Any Regrets, Atlanta Const., Aug. 28, 1995, at C6.

In a more recent, well-publicized case, Andrea Yates, who suffered from severe postpartum depression, drowned her five children, ages six months to seven years, in the family bathtub. She was convicted for the murders of three of the children. A jury deliberated for forty minutes before sentencing her to life in prison instead of the death penalty. What facts would you need before deciding on guilt, and sentencing, in this case?

One commentator explains:

> The "baby blues," or "blues," occurs in fifty to seventy percent of women in the first six to eight weeks after birth; symptoms include crying, general depression, and fatigue. The "blues" does not impair a mother's judgment and is probably not a disorder or disease. Postpartum depression occurs in ten to twenty percent of women and may persist for one year. It is categorized as a type of reaction depression and involves feelings of hopelessness, inadequacy, anxiety, and moodiness. Although studies are few, the level of support that the mother receives from the father and family is more determinative of the depression than are demographic and biological factors. Postpartum psychosis occurs in one to two of every one thousand births and can lead to suicide or infanticide. It involves a major deviation from the normal processes of thinking, behavior, and emotion. Emotional reactions may be inappropriate to the circumstances, and actions may not be related to facts. For example, a mother may say that she sees the room upside down, express concern that a small pimple on her child's face is a

misplaced testis, or fear that the hospital staff is part of a conspiracy to kill the baby. Anxiety can lead to panic attacks; a mother often has obsessive thoughts about harming the baby by putting it in the oven, drowning it, cutting off its body parts, or dropping it from an elevated surface. Hospitalization is necessary for the protection of both the mother and the child.

Michele Connell, The Postpartum Psychosis Defense and Feminism: More or Less Justice For Women?, 63 Case W. Res. L. Rev. 143, 146-147 (2002). Is compassion appropriate in the Andrea Yates case? Does it matter that postpartum depression is a female-specific defense? One study of the 24 cases in which postpartum psychosis was employed as a defense showed that of those cases, eight women were acquitted, four were given probation (for a total of half of he cases with no prison time), while ten were sentenced to between three and twenty years and two received life sentences. Connell, supra, at 147-148.

For an argument that compassion is more appropriate reaction than disgust in this particular case, see Elizabeth T. Bangs, Disgust and the Drownings in Texas: The Law Must Tackle Emotion When Women Kill Their Children, 12 UCLA Women's L.J. 87 (2001) (Book Review). See also Michelle Oberman, Mothers Who Kill: Coming to Terms with Modern American Infanticide, 8 DePaul J. Health Care L. 3 (2004) (explaining ambivalence in approach to mothers who kill, and justifications for partially excusing infanticide); Joan W. Howarth, Executing White Masculinities: Learning from Karla Faye Tucker, 81 Or. L. Rev. 183, 226-227 (2002) (exploring conflicting and perverse messages and tensions created by the highly public transformation of Karla Faye Tucker from a brutal murderer, "to a super-feminine, likeable, attractive woman").

Prior abuse was not presented as a factor in the Yates case but, as noted above, it was an important part of Susan Smith's sentencing hearing. Past victimization has been found as a basis for downward departure from the Federal Sentencing Guidelines as well. In United States v. Roe, 976 F.2d 1216, 1218 (9th Cir. 1992), the court found that a history of abuse so severe that the defendant was 'virtually a mind puppet" was extraordinary and that a downward departure was not forbidden by the Guidelines. Similarly, in United States v. Gaviria, 804 F. Supp. 476, 477 (E.D.N.Y. 1992), the sentencing judge granted a downward departure to a woman who, according to a psychiatrist, "reflect[ed] the stigmata of an abused person." See also United States v. Delgado, 994 F. Supp. 143 (E.D.N.Y. 1998) (granting a downward departure in part because of the childhood abuse suffered by the female defendant and because of her "difficult" life). Several federal courts have insisted that a causal link or nexus between the defendant's condition and the crime be found. See, e.g., United States v. Perkins, 963 F.2d 1523, 1528 (D.C. Cir. 1992) (reversing and remanding a downward departure from the Guidelines for a woman diagnosed with "dependent personality disorder" because the sentencing judge failed to find a nexus between the defendant's condition and the crime she committed). Nagel and Johnson assert that this nexus requirement is essential to the preservation of women's autonomy: "If the defendant's victimization did not influence the offense behavior, any departure is merely a 'victim' discount, imposed out of pity for the defendant, rather than out of a sense that a lesser sentence is deserved.

Such departures would undermine the moral agency of their recipients. . . ." Nagel & Johnson, supra, at 211.

Should sentencing be affected by a woman's involvement in a controlling relationship? This issue arises most often in the context of drug conspiracies; indeed, the number of women incarcerated for drug trafficking reached 6.8 percent of all offenders in 2002. Paige M. Harrison & Allen J. Beck, Prisoners in 2002, Bureau of Justice Statistics, July 2003, at 1. It is thought that a significant number of these women—what one commentator calls "women of circumstance," are "wives, mothers, sisters, daughters, girlfriends, and nieces, who become involved in crime because of their financial dependence on, fear of, or romantic attachment to a male drug trafficker." Shimica Gaskins, Note, "Women of Circumstance"—The Effects of Mandatory Minimum Sentencing on Women Minimally Involved in Drug Crimes, 41 Am. Crim. L. Rev. 1533, 1534 (2004). They are "desperate, unsuspecting or coerced women who often have no prior criminal history and serve as the sole caretakers of young children," caught up in the criminal justice by way of conspiracy laws, and subject to high sentences as a result of tough sentencing laws. Id. at 1536 (written before *Booker*, described in note 1 on p. 740). Furthermore, women may be more likely to receive harsher sentences for their participation in drug rings, either because of their refusal to snitch, out of either loyalty or fear, on their drug-dealing boyfriends, or because they do not know enough valuable information to obtain a reduced sentence as a cooperating witness. See Gaskins, supra, at 1544. Even the "safety value" of §80001 of the Violent Crime Control and Drug Enforcement Act of 1994, 18 U.S.C. §3553, intended to provide relief to non-violent, low-level drug offenders, may not help these women if they are fearful of cooperating, or weren't involved in the conspiracy to have information wanted by the authorities. Gaskins, supra, at 1547. For another critique, see Haneefah A. Jackson, Note, When Love Is Not a Crime: Why the Drug Prosecutions and Punishments of Female Non-Conspirators Cannot Be Justified by Retributive Principles, 46 How. L.J. 517 (2003).

Kemba Smith was a student at Hampton University with no prior criminal record. She got involved with a man eight years older, who was the ringleader of a cocaine enterprise. By the time Kemba realized her boyfriend was a drug dealer, he was abusing her, and she was fearful of him (and he eventually killed his best friend for informing on him). Kemba never handled any of the drugs, but she obtained a 24-year prison sentence. President Clinton pardoned her after six years of incarceration and a mass media campaign. See Gaskins, supra, at 1535.

The Guidelines do not specifically consider the possibility that a defendant's conduct may be the result of some form of dominance that falls short of physical abuse or duress. Courts have occasionally granted downward departures based on a perceived subservience in a female defendant. For instance, in United States v. Naylor, 735 F. Supp. 928 (D. Minn. 1990), the court found the defendant deserving of a downward departure because of her romantic relationship with a manipulative, much older co-defendant. The court determined that while Naylor's co-defendant did not physically abuse her, he used his relationship with her purposefully to exploit her and manipulate her into involvement in a cocaine distribution conspiracy. Compare United States v. Guiro, 887 F. Supp. 66, 67

(E.D.N.Y. 1995) (defendant "drawn into the drug conspiracy through her romantic attachment to a drug dealer"), with United States v. Thomas, 181 F.3d 870 (7th Cir. 1999) (denying a downward departure for a female defendant who claimed she committed tax fraud because of the abuse she suffered at the hands of her husband and because of her dependent personality). Is allowing leniency for subservience paternalistic, or a realistic and humane recognition of gender difference? At least one study reports that increasing the number of female judges in a district is associated with lower sex disparity in sentencing for serious crimes, in part because female offenders benefit from paternalistic biases of male judges. See Max Schanzenbach, Racial and Sex Disparities in Prison Sentences: The Effect of District-Level Judicial Demographics, 24 J. Legal Stud. 57 (2005). For further discussion of gender differences in judging, see pp. 703-711, supra.

Will recognition of the control of women by their boyfriends or husbands reinforce stereotypical assumptions that women are led astray by men? The case of the "Miss America Bandit" illustrates the potential danger of allowing departures based on an individual judge's paternalistic instincts. In United States v. Mast, No. CR-88-0720-AAH-1 (C.D. Cal. 1989), rev'd on other grounds, 925 F.2d. 1472 (9th Cir. 1991), a young woman was convicted of a string of bank robberies. At sentencing, the judge ordered a downward departure based on the defendant's domination by her boyfriend, even though there were no indications of physical abuse. The judge's comments during the sentencing hearing included: "men have exercised traditional control over the activities of women, and I'm not going to ignore that, no matter how much flak I get from women's lib"; and "I think it's a fact of life that men can exercise a Svengali influence over women"; and "women are a soft touch, particularly if sex is involved." See John Griffith, Woman Faces Counts in Bank Case, Oregonian, Feb. 4, 1992, at C8; Kim Murphy, "Soft Touch" Bandit Gets a Break from Judge on Term, L.A. Times, May 13, 1989. Is this judge really taking the social reality of the defendant into consideration, or is he instead imposing his own views of reality on the situation? How much of a factor did the defendant's relationship with her boyfriend appear to be in the *Handy* sentence?

8. Women and Civil Remedies

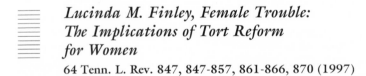

Lucinda M. Finley, Female Trouble:
The Implications of Tort Reform
for Women
64 Tenn. L. Rev. 847, 847-857, 861-866, 870 (1997)

Tort reform, particularly in products liability actions, has been on the federal legislative burner for over a decade. Its latest incarnation, the Common Sense Product Liability Legal Reform Act of 1996, came within a presidential veto of enactment during the recently concluded 104th Congress. Legislatures in various states have also passed or proposed reform measures, including limitations on nonpecuniary loss and punitive damages. . . .

This article analyzes these proposals and their possible adverse impact on women and women's health....

[C]riticisms leveled at nonpecuniary loss damages and their underlying value judgem[]ents are seriously questionable, if not fundamentally flawed....It is hardly value neutral to privilege those activities or types of loss that have a market price over those that are seriously undervalued or not readily valued by the market. Money is not the measure of all human value; activities or losses that are not easily fungible with money are not, therefore, unimportant or unreal....

How many people would give up their fertility, sexual functioning, ability to relate to people and enjoy human interaction, and their favorite activities in exchange for a guaranteed income stream to cover wages and medical bills?...[Arguing that the tort system which trades in money should only try to replace lost funds] ignores or underestimates the social function of tort law — signaling and reinforcing messages about the aspects of human life and types of people that our society values and deems worth protecting....

There are several prevalent types of injuries that disproportionately happen to women, and cause harms considered to be nonpecuniary loss. These injuries include: hostile environment sexual harassment; sexual assault or coercive sexual abuse from teachers, parents, and health care providers; reproductive harm, such as infertility caused by a drug or contraceptive, like DES or Dalkon Shield, used only by women in connection with sex or reproduction; and the painful disfigurement of capsular contracture of the breasts caused by a highly gendered product like breast implants. All of these injuries can certainly adversely impact a woman's earnings potential and cause her to incur medical expenses. However, the primary impact of these injuries is in eviscerating self-esteem, dignity, or a sense of security; causing physical and psychic pain; or impairing sexual or relationship fulfillment. Reproductive or sexual harm caused by drugs and medical devices has a highly disproportionate impact on women, because far more drugs and devices have been devised to control women's fertility or bodily functions associated with sex and childbearing than have been devised for men. These drugs and devices have harmed women by rendering them infertile, causing malformed reproductive organs, causing miscarriages or septic abortions, or causing menstrual chaos.

These harms represent aspects of life and human wholeness that either have little or no value in the marketplace or that society feels most uncomfortable about commodifying by assigning a market value....

Another reason why nonpecuniary loss damages remain particularly important for women is that the pecuniary harm caused by many types of injuries that disproportionately affect women is not readily appreciated or is easily overlooked by lawyers, judges, and juries. For example, when a woman has to endure a sexually hostile environment at work, and suffers the accompanying elevated stress and erosion of dignity and self-esteem, her productivity, work performance, career aspirations, and promotion or relocation prospects will all be adversely affected....

The disparate impact of market-based damage measurement is derived from two principal sources: (1) the generally lower value the market assigns to women's work and to women wage earners and (2) the market's failure to recognize or value many productive activities in which women engage when those activities, such as household management and caretaking, are performed in the private realm. Damages for past lost income simply replicate the unequal wage rates of the market, and thus make assessments about the relative worth of human lives that many people would find distasteful. . . .

Courts often calculate damages for projected future income or lost earning capacity by using gender and race based earnings tables. These tables lock tort damages into the assumptions that past inequities will continue unabated into the future, and that no woman or person of color will ever break out of stereotypical patterns for her gender or race. In addition, courts frequently discount projections of women's future earning capacity by incorporating gender-biased assumptions about the effect of marriage and childbearing on women's work force participation, advancement, and earnings.

Pecuniary loss calculations usually fail to recognize or assess adequately the productive economic value of women's household and caretaking activities. For example, if a woman wage earner is injured, the calculation of pecuniary loss damages rarely includes the lost value of her ability to clean and manage the home or to care for family members, despite the productiveness and economic importance of these services. Similarly, if a family member requires extensive caretaking services, that person will be able to recover something for the market value of such services. However, if another family member, more often a female, leaves or curtails her job to provide this care, neither she nor the injured person will be able to recover the caretaker's lost market income, even though the economic unit of which the injured person is a part has undoubtedly suffered a pecuniary loss. Even when courts do acknowledge the economic value of household services, as they are not likely to do when calculating pecuniary loss damages for the wrongful death or disability of a homemaker, the market assigns much lower values to these activities than their true social importance or value, precisely because they are "women's work." . . .

Several empirical studies and evaluations of case reports have demonstrated that women's tort recoveries, particularly for pecuniary loss, are on average well below recoveries for men. These studies magnify the importance of the nonpecuniary loss category of damages for women. . . . Any limitation that focuses on health care liability will disproportionately affect women simply because, overall, women consume more health care services than men and women comprise the majority of malpractice plaintiffs. . . .

Proposals that would link punitive damages only to economic loss . . . are particularly problematic from the perspective of gender equity. . . . If only the economic loss component of damages counts towards assessing punitive damages, then higher wage earners injured primarily in ways that affect their earning capacity will be able to recover significant punitive damages, without regard to the gravity of the defendant's conduct. . . . Those who are injured primarily in nonpecuniary ways, such as women who have suffered reproductive or sexual injuries, will rarely be able to recover more than the amount of the cap, no matter how egregious the defendant's disregard of health and safety. . . . The incentives to take women's sexual and reproductive health more seriously will be seriously undermined if a potential injurer knows that the punitive damages . . . will rarely exceed a readily manageable amount such as $250,000.

For example, A.H. Robins continued to market the Dalkon Shield IUD, despite mounting reports of pelvic inflammatory disease, perforated uteruses, infertility, septic abortions and internal corporate reports acknowledging that the infection causing propensity of the product could be greatly reduced for a cost of a few cents per device. . . . A.H. Robins did not urge physicians and women to remove the Dalkon Shields, until the company was assessed punitive damage awards in excess of one million dollars in cases that otherwise had low compensatory damages that averaged $11,000 to $40,000. . . .

An FDA-approval defense from punitive damages should be of particular concern to women. An unusually high number of the drugs and devices that have gone wrong and become alarming public health problems have been gender-specific products for use in women's bodies [including DES, the early versions of birth control pills, IUDs such as the Dalkon Shield and Copper-7, Parlodel, Ritodine, and silicone gel breast implants.]

Notes

1. The Relationship between Tort Remedies and Earnings. A significant component of the undervaluation of women's claims in tort law is their lower assumed, and actual, level of earnings. As tort reform efforts continue on both the federal and state levels, a cap on noneconomic damages is increasingly seen as the most effective way to provide relief from skyrocketing insurance premiums. As discussed above, caps on noneconomic damages disproportionately affect women. On the whole, though men tend to receive larger damage awards overall, women and the elderly receive a significantly larger portion of their awards as noneconomic damages. Lucinda Finley, The Hidden Victims of Tort Reform: Women, Children and the Elderly, 53 Emory L.J. 1263 (2004). In California, where a $250,000 cap on noneconomic damages has been in place since 1975, a review of verdicts over 10 years revealed that women's pre-cap median injury award was 94 percent of the men's median award; after the noneconomic damages were reduced by the cap, the women's median went down to 58.6 percent of the men's. Id. at 1285-1286. This factor also affects members of other groups, such as racial minorities. For an analysis of the race and gender effects of using the standard economic data in setting tort recovery awards, see Martha Chamallas, The Architecture of Bias: Deep Structures in Tort Law, 146 U. Pa. L. Rev. 463 (1998). Other sources on gender bias in tort recovery awards include Thomas Koenig & Michael Rustad, His and Her Tort Reform: Gender Injustice in Disguise, 70 Wash. & Lee L. Rev. 1 (1995); Jane Goodman et al., Money, Sex, and Death: Gender Bias in Wrongful Death Damage Awards, 25 Law & Soc'y Rev. 263 (1991).

Another component is the devaluation of what women do outside of paid employment. For an exhaustive analysis of the ways in which the law devalues household labor, see Katharine Silbaugh, Turning Labor into Love: Housework and the Law, 91 Nw. U. L. Rev. 1 (1996); see also Nancy C. Staudt, Taxing

Housework, 84 Geo. L.J. 1571 (1996) (considering appropriate treatment of home labor in tax law). For a more detailed analysis of the extent to which women's labor is devalued, see Chapter 2, p. 228ff.

There is some tension between those seeking realistic valuation of household work and those seeking to bring nonmarket understandings to bear on market activities. See, e.g., Margaret Jane Radin, Contested Commodities (1996). Will efforts to quantify homemaking and childrearing awards actually cheapen, by commodifying, these activities? Is this to women's advantage? Katharine Silbaugh answers this challenge by arguing that economic understandings of housework supplement rather than supplant other understandings. Silbaugh, Commodification and Women's Household Labor, 9 Yale J.L. & Feminism 81, 95 (1997). In any event, she argues, recognition of the value of household work is urgent with respect to how the public welfare system and its beneficiaries are perceived, how much domestic workers are paid, whether they are covered by various labor laws and workers' compensation programs, how the Social Security system deals with women's work, and how courts treat divorce settlements and contracts related to homemaking. Id. at 110-119.

2. Bias and Remedies. In addition to the disparity in men's and women's earnings and the undervaluation of women's services, Finley points to the failure of judges and juries to understand the kinds of non-economic losses that women experience. Is the problem that women value non-economic loss more than men? See Elizabeth Handsley, Mental Injury Occasioned by Harm to Another: A Feminist Critique, 14 Law & Ineq. 391 (1996) (tort law should recognize greater value women tend to place on relationships, caring, and connection by giving greater recognition to mental injury suffered when others are injured or killed). Or is it instead (or also) that women experience non-economic losses that men simply do not experience?

Bias may also come into play in evaluating defenses to tort actions. For example, many tort actions by women have been dismissed, or no damages found, on the grounds that the injuries alleged by the plaintiff, such as nervous symptoms, pain, emotional distress, and sexual dysfunction, were the result of menopause rather than the wrongful conduct of the defendant. These cases are summarized in Phyllis T. Bookspan & Maxine Kline, On Mirrors and Gavels: A Chronicle of How Menopause Was Used as a Legal Defense Against Women, 32 Ind. L. Rev. 1267 (1999).

Putting Theory into Practice

4-11. The following case is not a sex discrimination case in the ordinary sense, nor are either of the opinions written by a woman judge. Do the opinions reflect any of the characteristics associated with women's "different voice"? Do any of the legal arguments used or legal precedents distinguished mask assumptions that are biased against women?

Note especially the different factual summaries in the two opinions. What accounts for the different choice of facts? Different decisions about relevance?

Different methods of legal reasoning? Are these differences ones of "substance" or "method"? How might you rewrite the opinion to better reflect what is meant in this chapter by women's "different voice"?

In re Lamb
776 P.2d 765 (Cal. 1989)

BY THE COURT:

Petitioner Laura Beth Lamb was admitted to practice in December 1983. She has no prior record of discipline. On November 13, 1986, she pled nolo contendere to two felony counts of false personation to obtain a benefit. (Pen. Code, § 529, subd. 3.) The charges arose from allegations that petitioner took the July 1985 bar examination for her husband.

Upon receiving the record of conviction, we referred the matter to the State Bar for a determination whether the misconduct involved moral turpitude and, if so, what discipline should be imposed. Among other things, the parties stipulated before the State Bar Court that moral turpitude was involved. The hearing officer proposed disbarment, and the review department concurred. Petitioner sought review.

Petitioner's case has sympathetic aspects, and her expressions of contrition seem genuine. Nonetheless, her deceitful crime was exceptionally serious. Considering the public danger inherent in bar exam cheating, and the criminal dishonesty and moral turpitude involved, "[o]nly . . . the most compelling mitigating circumstances" could prevent disbarment. (See Rules Proc. of State Bar, div. V, Stds. for Atty. Sanctions for Prof. Misconduct, std. 3.2 ["Standards"].) Moreover, despite her intellectual promise, the psychological problems which led to petitioner's moral misjudgment cast continuing doubt upon her fitness to practice law. Under the circumstances, we adopt the State Bar Court's proposal and disbar petitioner.

Facts

Before the State Bar Court, the parties stipulated as follows: Petitioner posed as her husband Morgan Lamb in a photograph submitted to the State Bar as identification for the July 1985 bar examination. She later appeared at the examination and represented herself as her husband. To avoid detection, she deliberately smeared her thumbprint and forged her husband's signature on the admission card. Petitioner then took the examination in her husband's place, signing his name on the examination booklets. She passed the examination. An anonymous telephone tip to the State Bar in November 1985 triggered an investigation which led to the current proceeding. The stipulation concedes that petitioner's misconduct involved moral turpitude and constituted a willful violation of her oath and duties as an attorney. . . .

[D]ocumentary evidence originally presented to the criminal court on the issue of sentence was introduced in the State Bar disciplinary proceeding for purposes of mitigation. These documents indicate that petitioner's troubled background led her to value family life and marital harmony at all costs. From 1983 to 1985, after their graduation from law school, petitioner's husband suffered a series of professional setbacks, including loss of employment and bar exam failures in both Texas and California. He reacted with violent rage and depression, and the marriage deteriorated rapidly. Meanwhile, petitioner became pregnant in late 1984. Her pregnancy and general health were endangered by serious complications of her chronic diabetes. The confluence of emotional and physical stress caused petitioner to conclude that her only hope for her unborn child was to accede to her husband's pleas that she take the July 1985 exam in his place.[2]

After her arrest in April 1986, petitioner was fired from her position as an enforcement attorney for the Securities and Exchange Commission. Petitioner initially sought a new job as a lawyer, but ultimately refrained from law practice after her arrest. Petitioner works as a legal secretary. She and her husband are now divorced.

After petitioner's arrest, her criminal counsel referred her to a psychiatrist, Dr. Faerstein, for evaluation and treatment. Dr. Faerstein saw her on three occasions, for a total of five and one-half hours, between May and July 1986. In a February 1987 letter to the superior court, he opined that petitioner's immature personality and physical illness led her to have unrealistic goals, deny her marital problems, and make irrational life judgments. According to Dr. Faerstein, petitioner's misconduct stemmed from "a misguided and psychologically pathological attempt" at saving her marriage.

Dr. Faerstein found petitioner genuinely contrite and "amenable to therapy" for her "long-term psychological problems." With an "adequate course of psychotherapy," he concluded, "she may be able to function with sufficient social judgment, restraint and appropriateness as to be able to function as a member of the bar. Such a decision would clearly depend on future opinions from her treating therapist."

In a letter to the court dated February 17, 1987, Francine Bartfield, a licensed clinical social worker, stated that she had been treating petitioner since December 2, 1986. Bartfield confirmed that petitioner was "a confused, socially naive, immature young woman, who [exercised] poor judgment, and acted [not from antisocial motives but from] a distorted notion that she could save her marriage." According to Bartfield, petitioner was contrite, understood her misconduct was "seriously pathological," and was unlikely to "do anything remotely like this again." Petitioner's "prognosis for the future is good," Bartfield wrote, "provided she remains in therapy long enough to develop the psychic structures that have not, yet, matured.... This will require a long term commitment...."

Finally, the stipulated record includes letters from relatives, friends, classmates, and professional colleagues. These attest to petitioner's exceptional character, her legal ability, and her life difficulties.

The State Bar Court hearing occurred on November 9, 1987. The parties stipulated to petitioner's completion of 132 community-service hours during the

---

2. Though seven months pregnant and seriously ill when she took the exam, petitioner managed to receive the ninth highest score in the state for July 1985. She entered the hospital immediately after completing the exam. When her condition became life-threatening, labor was induced, and a healthy daughter was born prematurely.

first six months of her probation.... In a brief statement, petitioner declared, "I just want to assure you that I'm sorry for what happened, and I wish I could have thought of a better way to handle my problems, but at the time, I just couldn't, and I'm so sorry."

The hearing officer issued his decision on January 25, 1988. In recommending disbarment, the hearing officer reasoned as follows: Because petitioner had committed crimes involving moral turpitude, disbarment was required unless "the most compelling mitigating circumstances clearly predominate...." (Std. 3.2.) In aggravation, the case involved multiple acts of wrongdoing or demonstrated a pattern of misconduct (std. 1.2(b)(ii)), involved dishonesty and concealment (std. 1.2(b)(iii)), and significantly harmed the public and the administration of justice (std. 1.2(b)(iv)). While petitioner's "predicament" was "extreme," her emotional inability to see "ethical options" endangered the public.[3] Despite petitioner's need for long-term treatment to overcome her emotional problems, there was no evidence she had committed "voluntarily" to therapy or had continued it after termination of her probation condition. Hence, mere suspension with a therapy condition would not adequately protect the public.

On February 8, 1988, petitioner moved to reopen proceedings before the hearing officer and to submit additional evidence of her commitment to therapy. (Rules Proc. of State Bar, rule 562.) The motion was denied....

On August 2, 1988, the review department unanimously adopted the hearing officer's disbarment recommendation. This petition followed....

Discussion ...

Petitioner's deceitful acts were of exceptional gravity. Her conduct threatened innumerable clients with significant injury through unknowing exposure to an unqualified practitioner. It undermined the integrity of the State Bar's admission system, on which public confidence in the competence of attorneys is founded. Substantial harm to "the public [and] the administration of justice" (std. 1.2(b)(iv)) was averted only by an anonymous tip. And, though it did not directly occur in petitioner's "practice" of law, her misconduct evidenced her disregard of the State Bar's admission rules and directly "relate[d]" to her obligations as an attorney. (Cf. std. 2.3.)

As the State Bar suggests on review, because petitioner's criminal breach of professional standards was so morally serious and so dangerous, only the most overwhelming evidence of mitigation could prevent her disbarment in the public interest. Petitioner fails to sustain that heavy burden.

Petitioner urges that her misconduct stemmed from overwhelming physical and psychological pressures. The Standards provide that "extreme emotional

---

3. In the hearing officer's view, "She could have gone to a battered women's shelter or to any of the persons who wrote letters on her behalf, including her mother, her father, or her sister, for advice, shelter, and, if necessary, for protection against her husband. Her expressed motivation for the impersonation, the protection of her unborn child, is most noble, but placing herself under the stress of the impersonation actually endangered the health of the fetus, as she admits...."

difficulties or physical disabilities" at the time of the misconduct may sometimes serve as mitigating circumstances. However, because of the need for public protection against unfit practitioners, a member subject to discipline must first establish "through clear and convincing evidence that he or she no longer suffers from such difficulties or disabilities." (Std. 1.2(e)(iv).) Considering the magnitude of petitioner's misconduct, and its pertinence to her fitness as an attorney, proof of her complete and sustained recovery and rehabilitation must be exceptionally strong. (See std. 1.2(e)(viii).)

We find no such proof here. Petitioner claims the State Bar Court ignored up-to-date evidence of her sincerity and continuing progress in therapy.[5] However, professional evaluations conducted the previous year uniformly found a guarded prognosis dependent on a long-term treatment program. Though replete with testimonials to her talent and general character, the record contains, and petitioner submitted, no "clear and convincing" indication of petitioner's *sustained and complete* rehabilitation from chronic personal problems which led to her catastrophic misjudgment. (See In re Conflenti, [624 P.2d 253 (Cal. 1981)].) Thus we, like the State Bar Court, cannot be sure of petitioner's ability to avoid comparable mistakes in her future practice.[6]

Petitioner emphasizes that she has ended the marriage which contributed to her acute stress. She also points out that diabetes, though sometimes controllable, cannot be cured. Thus, she urges, she has done everything possible to eliminate the causes of her misconduct.

However, the consensus of mental health professionals was that petitioner suffered a *chronic emotional disability, independent* of her marital and physical problems, which contributed substantially to her disastrous misjudgment. As noted, we have no convincing evidence that her susceptibility in this regard has ended.

Petitioner appends to her reply brief *in this court* a letter *to us*, dated December 10, 1988, from Francine Bartfield. Bartfield reports that she continued to treat petitioner weekly until July 1988, when loss of insurance coverage forced petitioner to seek less expensive psychological counseling. Bartfield's letter claims petitioner participated sincerely in therapy, gained insight, made personality changes which ensure her misconduct will not recur, has an "excellent"

---

5. As noted above, the hearing officer denied petitioner's post hearing motion to submit additional evidence of commitment to therapy. Petitioner's counsel claims no documentary evidence "updating" petitioner's progress was presented at the hearing itself because it was assumed that the oral "stipulation" to that effect . . . would suffice. However, it appears that documentary evidence was omitted by the oversight of petitioner's counsel; in the oral stipulation, counsel referred merely to a "letter" or "letters" which "your Honor will read." . . .

6. Petitioner notes cases in which we have considered personal, psychological, or physical problems in mitigation without requiring complete recovery or rehabilitation. . . . The only *criminal-conviction* case cited, however, In re Nadrich, [747 P.2d 1146 (Cal. 1988)], involved circumstances not present here. In 1982, Nadrich sustained a federal conviction for distributing LSD in interstate commerce. While serious, Nadrich's conduct was thus less closely related to his honesty, oath, and duties as an attorney than petitioner's here. Moreover, evidence showed that Nadrich became a drug courier to subsidize his involuntary, medically-induced Percodan addiction. He had continued in psychotherapy since 1982, and had abstained from drugs for the intervening six years. Our case law generally supports the view that physical, mental, or emotional problems do not excuse, and may indeed require, discipline necessary for the protection of the public. . . .

prognosis, and appears fit to practice law "in an ethical and lawful manner." Bartfield states her understanding that petitioner remains in counseling and has no plans to terminate her treatment.

In general, this court does not consider evidence other than that which was before the State Bar Court. "...We are particularly wary of extrinsic evidence consisting of 'opinions about petitioner's mental attitude [that are] based largely on petitioner's own out-of-court statements. Such evidence is virtually impossible to evaluate in the absence of cross-examination.' (In re Possino, [689 P.2d 115 (Cal. 1984)].) [Bartfield's December 1988 letter is] inherently unreliable under this test. The [letter merely reflects] personal beliefs in petitioner's ... recovery, and [is] based exclusively upon conversations or interviews with [her]...." [quoting Rosenthal v. State Bar, 738 P.2d 740, 742 (Cal. 1987)].

In any event, considering the magnitude of petitioner's transgression, the 1988 Bartfield letter is insufficient evidence of her recovery. The legal, ethical, and moral pressures of daily practice come in many forms. Besides raw avarice and self-aggrandizement, they may include the sincere but misguided desire to please a persuasive or overbearing client.... Petitioner's proffered evidence fails to demonstrate the sustained recovery which would satisfy us of her ability to withstand such stresses.

Petitioner appears to exhibit genuine remorse, and she presents numerous testimonials to her integrity. The parties stipulate to her candor and cooperation in the State Bar investigation. These factors may be deemed mitigating in appropriate circumstances. (See std. 1.2(e)(v), (vi), (vii).) Her youth and her apparent absence of antisocial motive also weigh in her favor.[7] Considering the seriousness of petitioner's misconduct, however, this evidence is not sufficient to overturn the disbarment recommendation absent a showing of complete and sustained rehabilitation....

Despite our sympathetic feelings, our paramount duty is to protect the public, the courts, and the profession. Accordingly we, like the State Bar Court, believe that reinstatement proceedings are the means by which petitioner should demonstrate her clear rehabilitation after "the passage of considerable time." (Std. 1.2(e)(viii).) We therefore adopt the State Bar Court's recommendation that petitioner be disbarred....

The Rules of Procedure of the State Bar specify that a petition for reinstatement may not be filed "within five years after the effective date of interim suspension or disbarment or resignation whichever first occurred...."

KAUFMAN, Justice, dissenting.

I dissent.

There was public danger inherent in petitioner's serious misconduct, but the circumstances that gave rise to that misconduct were unique and no longer exist. Contrary to the majority's premise, there is no danger to the public or anyone else

---

7. On the other hand, the absence of a prior disciplinary record counts for little where, as here, the attorney has been in practice only a short time and the current misconduct is serious. (E.g., In re Schwartz, [644 P.2d 833 (Cal. 1982)]; std. 1.2(e)(i).) Nor is petitioner's community service, imposed as a condition of probation, a substantial mitigating factor.

from petitioner's one-time, aberrational conduct stemming from circumstances that no longer exist and as to which there is not the slightest possibility of recurrence. Thus, while disbarment in this case will doubtlessly be applauded in some circles, it is wholly unwarranted. It serves only to punish an apparently talented lawyer whose misconduct resulted from the most desperate, life-threatening circumstances. Indeed, such drastic discipline serves the public interest less well than would a long period of probation on appropriate conditions, including proof of fitness before returning to the practice of law.

The record discloses the following uncontroverted facts: After adamantly refusing several times her then-husband's insistent demands that she take the bar examination for him, petitioner eventually did so only when she was so desperately physically ill and overwhelmingly mentally intimidated by his barbaric threats and conduct that she felt she had no alternative but to do so, or lose the unborn child with which she was then many months pregnant. The child has long since been born and petitioner's marriage to her former husband has been dissolved. The circumstances were absolutely unique and could not possibly recur.

Petitioner is an insulin-dependent diabetic. When she became pregnant, her physician advised her the pregnancy and its anticipated complications would be life threatening and recommended that she have the pregnancy aborted. She refused. What ensued was nightmarish.

The physician's predictions proved all too true. Petitioner's pregnancy was extremely difficult and provoked severe complications of her diabetes, resulting in substantial, even life-threatening risks to her and her unborn child.

Hormonal changes because of the pregnancy made petitioner's diabetes difficult to control. Yet the doctors told petitioner that inadequate control could result in an overly large baby or render the mother unable to properly nourish the baby. Petitioner was compelled to maintain a strict dietary regimen and to undergo multiple blood tests and insulin injections each day; still, she was unable to achieve control of her diabetic condition. The unstable diabetes produced a toxic substance, acetone, in petitioner's body. She became so weak and dizzy she could hardly hold her head up. Petitioner's physicians told her that the heavy levels of acetone in her body could cause severe spinal deformities or other handicapping or fatal defects in the baby.

Petitioner developed toxemia and proteinuria, both kidney malfunctions, early in her pregnancy. Toxemia raises the blood pressure and can kill the mother, or the fetus, or both. Petitioner's blood pressure was elevated to dangerous levels for both her and her child.

Proteinuria caused her kidneys to over-eliminate protein from the body, depriving it of needed nourishment for herself and the fetus. Petitioner was required to lie still and not to exert herself to avoid expending her slender protein resources. The proteinuria also resulted in massive edema (swelling). Petitioner's legs became so swollen that her skin was split and bleeding. Her attending physicians feared the swelling would enter the womb and threaten the life of the fetus. The proteinuria further exacerbated petitioner's already dangerously high blood pressure. To alleviate the proteinuria, petitioner entered the hospital to receive intravenous blood protein. She also required two blood transfusions.

Petitioner was also hospitalized numerous times during her pregnancy because of uncontrollable vomiting and a dangerous insulin reaction.

In addition, petitioner suffered from proliferative diabetic retinopathy, a condition which causes hemorrhaging of blood vessels in the eyes and can result in blindness. The pregnancy further weakened the blood vessels in petitioner's eyes and increased the risk of blindness.

The complications of the pregnancy not only stripped petitioner of her physical resources, but the extreme stress of the pregnancy, her inability to control her diabetes, and the effects of the acetone, high blood pressure and protein deficiency fundamentally affected petitioner's mental and emotional health as well. She lived in fear that as a result of the pregnancy there was a good chance that she would become blind, the baby would be severely handicapped, or that death would result for either petitioner, the baby, or both. In short, petitioner was mentally and emotionally distraught and confused.

In addition to the overwhelming physical and emotional problems of her pregnancy, petitioner's marriage and home life had become nothing short of a disaster.

Petitioner had met Morgan Lamb in law school. In 1983, after their graduation from law school, Morgan accepted employment at a prestigious law firm in Houston. Petitioner joined Morgan in Houston and they were married in October 1983. After passing the California bar examination, petitioner was hired as an attorney in the Houston office of the Securities and Exchange Commission (SEC). Soon after, however, things began to fall apart.

Morgan failed the Texas bar examination. He began to act depressed and moody. He would cry, hide in bed, or watch television. He also became violently argumentative.

Morgan retook the Texas bar examination. He was so convinced he would fail again that he became hysterical. Although he did pass, he was fired by his law firm. His reactions became more extreme, violent and unpredictable. He would shout and throw things, and even abused petitioner physically.

After these setbacks, petitioner and her husband attempted a new start. They moved to Los Angeles where Morgan had secured a position with a prominent law firm. Petitioner was able to transfer to the Los Angeles office of the SEC.

Morgan sat for the February 1985 California bar examination. By this time, petitioner was pregnant and already so ill she had to take a leave of absence from her job. Then, within a short space of time, Morgan was fired from his position with the Los Angeles law firm and he received a letter notifying him that he had failed the California bar examination. After that, he lost any semblance of self-control. He threw heavy objects and furniture. He smashed large lamps and tore down the curtain rods. He screamed at petitioner and pushed her violently. He threatened to kill himself. He threatened to kill petitioner and the baby. Petitioner was so frightened she removed a gun he kept near the bed. Members of petitioner's family who visited her saw broken glass on the floor, smashed lamps, holes in the wall and bits of food plastered on the wall. Petitioner lived in fear of her husband's violent tantrums.

Petitioner desperately wanted to save her marriage and the lives of herself and her baby. The stress of her home situation placed an intolerable stress on the unborn baby because of petitioner's extremely high blood pressure and physical illnesses. Her doctors told her she had to alleviate the stress or risk the life of her baby or herself. Petitioner was required to lie still because of her dangerous protein deficiency. At times, however, Morgan would shake her and force her to get up and do housework and take care of him.

Morgan became convinced he could not pass the bar examination and repeatedly importuned petitioner to take it for him. She refused numerous times, although she was afraid of what he might do to her or to himself if she did not relent. Each time she refused he would fly into a rage. Finally, in her weak and confused state, petitioner gave in to her husband's demands that she take the exam for him because she could not think of any way to refuse without endangering herself or the baby. She submitted her photograph with his application to take the July 1985 bar examination. Even thereafter, she attempted to convince her husband to take the examination himself and studied with him so that he would be prepared for the examination. For a short time, that plan seemed to be working, but then Morgan began to find more and more excuses not to study. Ultimately, petitioner succumbed to the overwhelming pressures and took the examination posing as her husband.

Immediately upon completing the bar examination, petitioner entered the hospital, where her doctors urged her to have the baby delivered at once or risk the death of both herself and her baby. Petitioner refused because the baby's lungs were too underdeveloped for it to survive outside her body. Petitioner underwent experimental treatments to help the baby's lungs develop. She herself was on the verge of death and required intensive care. After ten days, labor was induced and a healthy baby girl was born, two months prematurely.

Petitioner does not claim that her conduct was justified or legally excused by these circumstances. She in fact stipulated her conduct involved moral turpitude and accepts responsibility for it. Rather, the issue is what discipline is appropriate for petitioner's conduct.

In fastening upon disbarment as the appropriate discipline the majority give insufficient consideration to the mitigating circumstances in this case. The majority discount petitioner's evidence in mitigation because they do not find it "clear and convincing" that she no longer suffers from the extreme emotional and physical difficulties which contributed to her misconduct. (Rules Proc. of State Bar, div. V, Stds. for Atty. Sanctions for Prof. Misconduct, std. 1.2(e)(iv).) They, like the hearing officer and the review department, reach this conclusion on the basis that petitioner's problems require long-term ongoing psychological therapy, and that she has failed to demonstrate a commitment to such counseling.

Petitioner's "long-term" psychological problems relate to her childhood in a dysfunctional family where one parent abused drugs and all the family members became withdrawn and isolated. Yet it is uncontroverted that, despite the psychological shortcomings attributable to her past, petitioner had always been able to conform her conduct to the highest ethical standards. The record shows that the conduct leading to this offense was completely aberrational and out of character. It was only in the unique combination of situational circumstances here, in which she was on the verge of complete physical, mental and emotional collapse, that she engaged in these bizarre acts.

Petitioner has shown, not only clearly and convincingly, but beyond question, that she has done everything possible to eliminate the extreme emotional and physical difficulties that led to the misconduct. She is, of course, no longer pregnant and no longer suffers the dire complications brought on by the combination of pregnancy and her diabetes. She has ended her marriage to Morgan Lamb. Though she cannot change the fact of her diabetes, she has brought it under control. And she has committed to voluntary, long-term therapy to overcome her problems. A fair reading of the record shows that the hearing officer had before him significant evidence that, despite her need for therapy to overcome her past problems, her therapist was of the opinion that it was extremely unlikely that petitioner "will do anything remotely like this again." In addition, petitioner's probation after her criminal conviction was terminated early, based in part on her success in ongoing therapy. The hearing officer's concern that petitioner would not continue in therapy absent the compulsion of probation has been answered. Petitioner has voluntarily continued in therapy after termination of her probation, and she has submitted a letter to this court from her therapist documenting her continued progress in therapy.[1]

The circumstances established by the record are clearly overwhelmingly mitigating and demand a discipline less severe than disbarment. This court has imposed less severe discipline in cases where the mitigating circumstances were far less compelling and where the misconduct was at least as egregious.

In the recent case of In re Mostman, [765 P.2d 448 (Cal. 1989)], an attorney solicited another person to kill or do bodily injury to a former client. The mitigating circumstances included initial refusals to engage in misconduct, the conduct did not stem from the attorney's practice of law, the attorney was in great emotional distress because he believed the former client had engaged in a campaign of intimidation and harassment against him, and he had been remorseful and cooperative concerning his conviction. Although the attorney had been twice disciplined before, we imposed five years' probation and an actual suspension of two years. In In re Nadrich, [747 P.2d 1146 (Cal. 1988)], an attorney was convicted of possessing, with intent to distribute, 30 grams of LSD. In mitigation, the attorney's addiction to an opiate-based prescription medication, the abrupt cutting-off of his prescription and his withdrawal from law practice had "create[d] an overwhelming financial pressure." We ordered five years' probation with one-year actual suspension. In In re Higbie, [493 P.2d 97 (Cal. 1972)], an attorney conspired to smuggle marijuana into the country. We ordered a two-year suspension with one-year actual suspension, rather than disbarment, because the primary motivation for the wrongful behavior was not personal profit (the attorney acted at the insistence of a friend—a pilot—that the attorney help him find employment, but the pilot was really "setting him up" to claim a bounty) and

1. The majority's rejection of this letter is improvident, indeed, inexplicable, in view of the fact the hearing officer's recommendation of disbarment was based almost solely on the alleged lack of demonstrated commitment to therapy, yet he denied petitioner's motion to reopen to submit further evidence on the question.

because of the attorney's prior good record. In In re Kreamer, [535 P.2d 728 (Cal. 1975)], an attorney was convicted of illegal possession of marijuana and of conspiracy to distribute the marijuana. Chronic depression brought on by a breakup with his fiancee led the attorney to use marijuana and to withdraw from his law practice. He turned to drug dealing when faced with mounting debts. We ordered three years' probation and no actual suspension. In In re Jones, [487 P.2d 1016 (Cal. 1971)], an attorney was convicted of subornation of perjury and submission of false evidence. In mitigation he offered his lack of prior disciplinary record, his previous good reputation, his age (66), his difficulty in securing employment to support his 10-year-old twins, and financial difficulties resulting from his criminal and bar proceedings. We imposed three years' probation with one-year actual suspension. (See also Frazer v. State Bar, [737 P.2d 1338 (Cal. 1987),] in which an attorney committed multiple acts of willful misconduct, abandoning clients to their prejudice, obtaining substantial loans under unfair terms and pursuant to misrepresentations, and ultimately losing the money without making any repayment. On the basis of the attorney's agoraphobia as a mitigating factor we ordered five years' probation with actual suspension for eighteen months and until restitution had been made. In Maltaman v. State Bar, [741 P.2d 185 (Cal. 1987)], an attorney willfully disobeyed important court orders and attempted deliberately to mislead a judicial officer. He also lied on several occasions during his disciplinary proceedings. We imposed five years' probation with one-year actual suspension.)

The failure of this court to accord petitioner in this case at least as favorable consideration is to me inexplicable. Petitioner's conduct here was highly situational and a complete departure from her normal conduct. It resulted from an unfortunate and unique coincidence of circumstances, as to which there is virtually no chance of recurrence. Her actions were devoid of any motivation of venality or baseness.

We have often reiterated that the primary purpose of discipline is the protection of the public, the profession and the courts rather than punishment of the attorney. (In re Severo, [714 P.2d 1244 (Cal. 1986)].) Disbarment here serves only to punish petitioner. An alternative is available which would, in my view, far better serve the public, the profession and the courts. To the extent necessary, we may impose conditions of probation which will ensure that the attorney is rehabilitated and the public is protected. I would impose a lengthy probation, with a substantial term of actual suspension and with appropriate probationary conditions, including continued therapy and a demonstration of fitness before returning to the practice of law.

Postscript. In responding to the court's decision in *Lamb,* one California columnist concluded:

> Over the years, I've written about lawyers who bilked senile clients of their last dollars, lawyers who deceived old people into making them beneficiaries of large estates, lawyers who grabbed fees so large that their clients received almost nothing. And they're still practicing.... Laura Beth Lamb, who behaved honorably after her deception came to light, is now working as a legal secretary in Los Angeles while she

performs what amounts to more than 62 40-hour weeks of community service. . . . I hope she gets back in [the bar]. California could use more lawyers like Laura Lamb.

Bill Mandel, "State Bar Persecutes a Victim," San Francisco Examiner, Aug. 14, 1989, at A4.

In light of *Lamb*, consider the implications of a study showing that female attorneys are disciplined for ethical violations at only half the rate of male lawyers. See Patricia W. Hatamyar & Kevin M. Simmons, Are Women More Ethical Lawyers? An Empirical Study, 31 Fla. St. U. L. Rev. 785 (2004), discussed on pp. 664-665 of this chapter. The findings could not be explained by differences in length of service, type of practice, or age. Id. What do you make of that?

Ten years after her disbarment, Laura Beth Salant (formerly Lamb) was reinstated by the California Supreme Court over the objection of state bar disciplinary prosecutors. During the intervening decade, Salant worked as a paralegal for the IRS, and according to the State Bar court review department, compiled "a most impressive record of employment, outstanding character and psychological rehabilitation." After the bar court recommended reinstatement, prosecutors asked the California Supreme Court for review. They claimed that Salant had falsely represented that she had obtained a restraining order against her ex-husband and that she had failed to file a required affidavit informing clients of her disbarment. Salant maintained that her former attorney had agreed to file the affidavit and that, after eight years of psychotherapy, she had turned her life around. The California Supreme Court ordered reinstatement. Woman Who Impersonated Husband Ordered Reinstated, California Bar Journal, 1999, at 27, 28.

5

Autonomy

Legal standards typically assume that the individual is capable of formulating a specific "intent" to act, exercising free "choice" or "consent," behaving as a "reasonable" person, or coming to a "meeting of the minds." Women's rights advocates make similar assumptions when they argue that women should have greater personal autonomy, more freedom to make their own choices, and sufficient power to control their own lives.

Most contemporary social theory, however, does not fully accept the Enlightenment view of the self as stable, self-apparent, autonomous, or capable of acting, intending, agreeing, and consenting independently of external influence. Today, the individual is more often understood by social and critical theorists as constituted through multiple sources of identity which overlap, intersect, and sometimes contradict. Under this view, an individual's experience of identity and autonomy is conceded to be often self-deceiving, insofar as it masks social, institutional, and ideological forces that construct and constrain the individual's desires, choices, and perceptions of reality.

Like the challenges to the ability of law to be neutral, objective, or, in any meaningful way, universal, explored in Chapter 3, challenges to the capacity of individuals to act autonomously can be a paralyzing insight: if true consent and choice are not possible, how can law and freedom both exist? For advocates of women's rights, however, critical perspectives on the concept of individual autonomy have had some productive effects in better identifying sources of constraint and generating pragmatic strategies for challenging them. Feminist theorists and activists have been able to accept that choice is a relative concept — not always what it seems — while refining an agenda built on the notion that, in most matters at least, more choice is still better than less. In so doing, feminists have expanded traditional understandings of autonomy, both those relating to freedom from interference by others, and those concerned with the ability to flourish in a more positive sense.

This chapter explores these themes in the context of issues in which standards of autonomy, choice, and consent are most often associated — rape, prostitution, pregnancy, abortion, and welfare.

A. SEX AND CONSENT

1. "Statutory" Rape: The (Ir)relevance of Consent

≡≡≡ *Michael M. v. Superior Court of Sonoma*
County
450 U.S. 464 (1981)

Justice REHNQUIST announced the judgment of the Court and delivered an opinion, in which THE CHIEF JUSTICE, Justice STEWART, and Justice POWELL joined.

The question presented in this case is whether California's "statutory rape" law, § 261.5 of the Cal. Penal Code Ann. (West Supp. 1981), violates the Equal Protection Clause of the Fourteenth Amendment. Section 261.5 defines unlawful sexual intercourse as "an act of sexual intercourse accomplished with a female not the wife of the perpetrator, where the female is under the age of 18 years." The statute thus makes men alone criminally liable for the act of sexual intercourse.

In July 1978, a complaint was filed in the Municipal Court of Sonoma County, Cal., alleging that petitioner, then a 17-year-old male, had had unlawful sexual intercourse with a female under the age of 18, in violation of § 261.5. The evidence, adduced at a preliminary hearing showed that at approximately midnight on June 3, 1978, petitioner and two friends approached Sharon, a 16-year-old female, and her sister as they waited at a bus stop. Petitioner and Sharon, who had already been drinking, moved away from the others and began to kiss. After being struck in the face for rebuffing petitioner's initial advances, Sharon submitted to sexual intercourse with petitioner. Prior to trial, petitioner sought to set aside the information on both state and federal constitutional grounds, asserting that § 261.5 unlawfully discriminated on the basis of gender. The trial court and the California Court of Appeal denied petitioner's request for relief and petitioner sought review in the Supreme Court of California.

The Supreme Court held that "section 261.5 discriminates on the basis of sex because only females may be victims, and only males may violate the section." [601 P.2d 572, 574 (Cal. 1979).] The court then subjected the classification to "strict scrutiny," stating that it must be justified by a compelling state interest. It found that the classification was "supported not by mere social convention but by the immutable physiological fact that it is the female exclusively who can become pregnant." [Id.] Canvassing "the tragic human costs of illegitimate teenage pregnancies," including the large number of teenage abortions, the increased medical risk associated with teenage pregnancies, and the social consequences of teenage childbearing, the court concluded that the State has a compelling interest in preventing such pregnancies. Because males alone can "physiologically cause the result which the law properly seeks to avoid," the court further held that the gender classification was readily justified as a means of identifying offender and victim. For the reasons stated below, we affirm the judgment of the California Supreme Court.

As is evident from our opinions, the Court has had some difficulty in agreeing upon the proper approach and analysis in cases involving challenges to gender-based classifications....

Underlying these decisions is the principle that a legislature may not "make overbroad generalizations based on sex which are entirely unrelated to any differences between men and women or which demean the ability or social status of the affected class."...But because the Equal Protection Clause does not "demand that a statute necessarily apply equally to all persons" or require "'things which are different in fact...to be treated in law as though they were the same,'"... this Court has consistently upheld statutes where the gender classification is not invidious, but rather realistically reflects the fact that the sexes are not similarly situated in certain circumstances....As the Court has stated, a legislature may "provide for the special problems of women." Weinberger v. Wiesenfeld, [420 U.S. 636, 653 (1975)].

Applying those principles to this case, the fact that the California Legislature criminalized the act of illicit sexual intercourse with a minor female is a sure indication of its intent or purpose to discourage that conduct. Precisely why the legislature desired that result is of course somewhat less clear. This Court has long recognized that "[i]nquiries into congressional motives or purposes are a hazardous matter,"...and the search for the "actual" or "primary" purpose of a statute is likely to be elusive.... Here, for example, the individual legislators may have voted for the statute for a variety of reasons. Some legislators may have been concerned about preventing teenage pregnancies, others about protecting young females from physical injury or from the loss of "chastity," and still others about promoting various religious and moral attitudes towards premarital sex.

The justification for the statute offered by the State, and accepted by the Supreme Court of California, is that the legislature sought to prevent illegitimate teenage pregnancies. That finding, of course, is entitled to great deference.... And although our cases establish that the State's asserted reason for the enactment of a statute may be rejected, if it "could not have been a goal of the legislation,"...this is not such a case.

We are satisfied not only that the prevention of illegitimate pregnancy is at least one of the "purposes" of the statute, but also that the State has a strong interest in preventing such pregnancy. At the risk of stating the obvious, teenage pregnancies, which have increased dramatically over the last two decades, have significant social, medical, and economic consequences for both the mother and her child, and the State. Of particular concern to the State is that approximately half of all teenage pregnancies end in abortion. And of those children who are born, their illegitimacy makes them likely candidates to become wards of the State.[6]

---

6. The policy and intent of the California Legislature evinced in other legislation buttresses our view that the prevention of teenage pregnancy is a purpose of the statute. The preamble to the

We need not be medical doctors to discern that young men and young women are not similarly situated with respect to the problems and the risks of sexual intercourse. Only women may become pregnant, and they suffer disproportionately the profound physical, emotional and psychological consequences of sexual activity. The statute at issue here protects women from sexual intercourse at an age when those consequences are particularly severe.

The question thus boils down to whether a State may attack the problem of sexual intercourse and teenage pregnancy directly by prohibiting a male from having sexual intercourse with a minor female.[8] We hold that such a statute is sufficiently related to the State's objectives to pass constitutional muster.

Because virtually all of the significant harmful and inescapably identifiable consequences of teenage pregnancy fall on the young female, a legislature acts well within its authority when it elects to punish only the participant who, by nature, suffers few of the consequences of his conduct. It is hardly unreasonable for a legislature acting to protect minor females to exclude them from punishment. Moreover, the risk of pregnancy itself constitutes a substantial deterrence to young females. No similar natural sanctions deter males. A criminal sanction imposed solely on males thus serves to roughly "equalize" the deterrents on the sexes.

We are unable to accept petitioner's contention that the statute is impermissibly under-inclusive and must, in order to pass judicial scrutiny, be *broadened* so as to hold the female as criminally liable as the male. It is argued that this statute is not *necessary* to deter teenage pregnancy because a gender-neutral statute, where both male and female would be subject to prosecution, would serve that goal equally well. The relevant inquiry, however, is not whether the statute is drawn as precisely as it might have been, but whether the line chosen by the California Legislature is within constitutional limitations.

In any event, we cannot say that a gender-neutral statute would be as effective as the statute California has chosen to enact. The State persuasively contends that a gender-neutral statute would frustrate its interest in effective enforcement. Its view is that a female is surely less likely to report violations of the statute if she herself would be subject to criminal prosecution. In an area already fraught with prosecutorial difficulties, we decline to hold that the Equal Protection Clause requires a legislature to enact a statute so broad that it may well be incapable of enforcement.

Pregnancy Freedom of Choice Act, for example, states: "The legislature finds that pregnancy among unmarried persons under 21 years of age constitutes an increasing social problem in the State of California." Cal. Welf. & Inst. Code Ann. § 16145 (West 1980).

Subsequent to the decision below, the California Legislature considered and rejected proposals to render § 261.5 gender neutral, thereby ratifying the judgment of the California Supreme Court. That is enough to answer petitioner's contention that the statute was the "'accidental by-product of a traditional way of thinking about females.'" Califano v. Webster, [430 U.S. 313, 320 (1977)] (quoting Califano v. Goldfarb, [430 U.S. 199, 223 (1977)] (Stevens, J., concurring in judgment)). Certainly this decision of the California Legislature is as good a source as is this Court in deciding what is "current" and what is "outmoded" in the perception of women.

8. We do not understand petitioner to question a State's authority to make sexual intercourse among teenagers a criminal act, at least on a gender-neutral basis. In Carey v. Population Services International, [431 U.S. 678, 694, n.17 (1977)] (plurality opinion of Brennan, J.), four Members of the Court assumed for the purposes of that case that a State may regulate the sexual behavior of minors, while four other Members of the Court more emphatically stated that such regulation would be permissible. . . .

We similarly reject petitioner's argument that § 261.5 is impermissibly over-broad because it makes unlawful sexual intercourse with prepubescent females, who are, by definition, incapable of becoming pregnant. Quite apart from the fact that the statute could well be justified on the grounds that very young females are particularly susceptible to physical injury from sexual intercourse, . . . it is ludicrous to suggest that the Constitution requires the California Legislature to limit the scope of its rape statute to older teenagers and exclude young girls.

There remains only petitioner's contention that the statute is unconstitutional as it is applied to him because he, like Sharon, was under 18 at the time of sexual intercourse. Petitioner argues that the statute is flawed because it presumes that as between two persons under 18, the male is the culpable aggressor. We find petitioner's contentions unpersuasive. Contrary to his assertions, the statute does not rest on the assumption that males are generally the aggressors. It is instead an attempt by a legislature to prevent illegitimate teenage pregnancy by providing an additional deterrent for men. The age of the man is irrelevant since young men are as capable as older men of inflicting the harm sought to be prevented.

In upholding the California statute we also recognize that this is not a case where a statute is being challenged on the grounds that it "invidiously discriminates" against females. To the contrary, the statute places a burden on males which is not shared by females. But we find nothing to suggest that men, because of past discrimination or peculiar disadvantages, are in need of the special solicitude of the courts. Nor is this a case where the gender classification is made "solely for . . . administrative convenience," . . . or rests on "the baggage of sexual stereotypes." . . . As we have held, the statute instead reasonably reflects the fact that the consequences of sexual intercourse and pregnancy fall more heavily on the female than on the male.

Accordingly, the judgment of the California Supreme Court is Affirmed.

[The concurring opinion of Justice Stewart is omitted.]

Justice BLACKMUN, concurring in the judgment.

It is gratifying that the plurality recognizes that "[a]t the risk of stating the obvious, teenage pregnancies . . . have increased dramatically over the last two decades" and "have significant social, medical, and economic consequences for both the mother and her child, and the State." . . . There have been times when I have wondered whether the Court was capable of this perception, particularly when it has struggled with the different but not unrelated problems that attend abortion issues. . . .

Some might conclude that the two uses of the criminal sanction — here flatly to forbid intercourse in order to forestall teenage pregnancies, and in *Matheson* to prohibit a physician's abortion procedure except upon notice to the parents of the pregnant minor — are vastly different proscriptions. But the basic social and privacy problems are much the same. Both Utah's statute in *Matheson* and California's statute in this case are legislatively created tools intended to achieve similar ends and addressed to the same societal concerns: the control and direction of young people's sexual activities. . . .

I, however, cannot vote to strike down the California statutory rape law, for I think it is a sufficiently reasoned and constitutional effort to control the problem at its inception. For me, there is an important difference between this state action and a State's adamant and rigid refusal to face, or even to recognize, the "significant . . . consequences" — to the woman — of a forced or unwanted conception. I have found it difficult to rule constitutional, for example, state efforts to block, at that later point, a woman's attempt to deal with the enormity of the problem confronting her, just as I have rejected state efforts to prevent women from rationally taking steps to prevent that problem from arising. See, e.g., Carey v. Population Services International, [431 U.S. 678 (1977)]. See also Griswold v. Connecticut, [381 U.S. 479 (1965)]. In contrast, I am persuaded that, although a minor has substantial privacy rights in intimate affairs connected with procreation, California's efforts to prevent teenage pregnancy are to be viewed differently from Utah's efforts to inhibit a woman from dealing with pregnancy once it has become an inevitability. . . .

I think, too, that it is only fair, with respect to this particular petitioner, to point out that his partner, Sharon, appears not to have been an unwilling participant in at least the initial stages of the intimacies that took place the night of June 3, 1978.* Petitioner's and Sharon's nonacquaintance with each other before the incident; their drinking; their withdrawal from the others of the group; their

___

*Sharon at the preliminary hearing testified as follows: "Q. [by the Deputy District Attorney]. On June the 4th, at approximately midnight — midnight of June the 3rd, were you in Rohnert Park?" A. [by Sharon]. Yes. "Q. Is that in Sonoma County?" A. Yes. "Q. Did anything unusual happen to you that night in Rohnert Park?" A. Yes. "Q. Would you briefly describe what happened that night? Did you see the defendant that night in Rohnert Park?" A. Yes. "Q. Where did you first meet him?" A. At a bus stop. "Q. Was anyone with you?" A. My sister. "Q. Was anyone with the defendant?" A. Yes. "Q. How many people were with the defendant?" A. Two. "Q. Now, after you met the defendant, what happened?" A. We walked down to the railroad tracks. "Q. What happened at the railroad tracks?" A. We were drinking at the railroad tracks and we walked over to this bush and he started kissing me and stuff, and I was kissing him back, too, at first. Then, I was telling him to stop — "Q. Yes." A. — and I was telling him to slow down and stop. He said, "Okay, okay." But then he just kept doing it. He just kept doing it and then my sister and two other guys came over to where we were and my sister said — told me to get up and come home. And then I didn't — "Q. Yes." A. — and then my sister and — "Q. All right." A. — David, one of the boys that were there, started walking home and we stayed there and then later — "Q. All right." A. — Bruce left Michael, you know. "The Court: Michael being the defendant?" The Witness: Yeah. We was lying there and we were kissing each other, and then he asked me if I wanted to walk him over to the park; so we walked over to the park and we sat down on a bench and then he started kissing me again and we were laying on the bench. And he told me to take my pants off. I said, "No," and I was trying to get up and he hit me back down on the bench and then I just said to myself, "Forget it," and I let him do what he wanted to do and he took my pants off and he was telling me to put my legs around him and stuff—

"Q. Did you have sexual intercourse with the defendant?" A. Yeah. "Q. He did put his penis into your vagina?" A. Yes. "Q. You said that he hit you?" A. Yeah. "Q. How did he hit you?" A. He slugged me in the face. "Q. With what did he slug you?" A. His fist. "Q. Where abouts in the face?" A. On my chin. "Q. As a result of that, did you have any bruises or any kind of an injury?" A. Yeah. "Q. What happened?" A. I had bruises. "The Court: Did he hit you one time or did he hit you more than once?" The Witness: He hit me about two or three times.

"Q. Now, during the course of that evening, did the defendant ask you your age?" A. Yeah. "Q. And what did you tell him?" A. Sixteen. "Q. Did you tell him you were sixteen?" A. Yes. "Q. Now, you said you had been drinking, is that correct?" A. Yes. "Q. Would you describe your condition as a result of the drinking?" A. I was a little drunk." App. 20-23.

CROSS-EXAMINATION "Q. Did you go off with Mr. M. away from the others?" A. Yeah. "Q. Why did you do that?" A. I don't know. I guess I wanted to. "Q. Did you have any need to go to the bathroom when you were there." A. Yes. "Q. And what did you do?" A. Me and my sister walked foreplay, in which she willingly participated and seems to have encouraged; and the closeness of their ages (a difference of only one year and 18 days) are factors that should make this case an unattractive one to prosecute at all, and especially to prosecute as a felony, rather than as a misdemeanor chargeable under § 261.5. But the State has chosen to prosecute in that manner, and the facts, I reluctantly conclude, may fit the crime.

Justice BRENNAN, with whom Justices WHITE and MARSHALL join, dissenting. . . .

I fear that the plurality opinion and Justices Stewart and Blackmun reach the opposite result by placing too much emphasis on the desirability of achieving the State's asserted statutory goal — prevention of teenage pregnancy — and not enough emphasis on the fundamental question of whether the sex-based discrimination in the California statute is substantially related to the achievement of that goal. . . .

[E]ven assuming that prevention of teenage pregnancy is an important governmental objective and that it is in fact an objective of § 261.5 . . . , California still has the burden of proving that there are fewer teenage pregnancies under its gender-based statutory rape law than there would be if the law were gender neutral. To meet this burden, the State must show that because its statutory rape law punishes only males, and not females, it more effectively deters minor females from having sexual intercourse. [5]

---

down the railroad tracks to some bushes and went to the bathroom. "Q. Now, you and Mr. M., as I understand it, went off into the bushes, is that correct?" A. Yes. "Q. Okay. And what did you do when you and Mr. M. were there in the bushes?" A. We were kissing and hugging. "Q. Were you sitting up?" A. We were laying down. "Q. You were lying down. This was in the bushes?" A. Yes. "Q. How far away from the rest of them were you?" A. They were just bushes right next to the railroad tracks. We just walked off into the bushes; not very far.

"Q. So your sister and the other two boys came over to where you were, you and Michael were, is that right?" A. Yeah. "Q. What did they say to you, if you remember?" A. My sister didn't say anything. She said, "Come on, Sharon, let's go home." "Q. She asked you to go home with her?" A. (Affirmative nod.) "Q. Did you go home with her?" A. No. "Q. You wanted to stay with Mr. M.?" A. I don't know. "Q. Was this before or after he hit you?" A. Before.

"Q. What happened in the five minutes that Bruce stayed there with you and Michael?" A. I don't remember. "Q. You don't remember at all?" A. (Negative head shake.) "Q. Did you have occasion at that time to kiss Bruce?" A. Yeah. "Q. You did? You were kissing Bruce at that time?" A. (Affirmative nod.) "Q. Was Bruce kissing you?" A. Yes. "Q. And were you standing up at this time?" A. No, we were sitting down.

"Q. Okay. So at this point in time you had left Mr. M. and you were hugging and kissing with Bruce, is that right?" A. Yeah. "Q. And you were sitting up." A. Yes. "Q. Was your sister still there then?" A. No. Yeah, she was at first. "Q. What was she doing?" A. She was standing up with Michael and David. "Q. Yes. Was she doing anything with Michael and David?" A. No, I don't think so. "Q. Whose idea was it for you and Bruce to kiss? Did you initiate that?" A. Yes. "Q. What happened after Bruce left?" A. Michael asked me if I wanted to go walk to the park. "Q. And what did you say?" A. I said, "Yes." "Q. And then what happened?" A. We walked to the park.

"Q. How long did it take you to get to the park?" A. About ten or fifteen minutes. "Q. And did you walk there?" A. Yes. "Q. Did Mr. M. ever mention his name?" A. Yes. Id., at 27-32.

5. Petitioner has not questioned the State's constitutional power to achieve its asserted objective by criminalizing consensual sexual activity. However, I note that our cases would not foreclose such a privacy challenge. The State is attempting to reduce the incidence of teenage pregnancy by imposing criminal sanctions on those who engage in consensual sexual activity with minor females. We have stressed, however, that "[i]f the right of privacy means anything, it is the right of the individual, married or single, to be free from unwarranted governmental intrusion into matters so fundamentally

The plurality assumes that a gender-neutral statute would be less effective than § 261.5 in deterring sexual activity because a gender-neutral statute would create significant enforcement problems. . . . However, a State's bare assertion that its gender-based statutory classification substantially furthers an important governmental interest is not enough to meet its burden of proof under Craig v. Boren, [429 U.S. 190 (1976)]. . . .

The State has not produced such evidence in this case. Moreover, there are at least two serious flaws in the State's assertion that law enforcement problems created by a gender-neutral statutory rape law would make such a statute less effective than a gender-based statute in deterring sexual activity.

First, the experience of other jurisdictions, and California itself, belies the plurality's conclusion that a gender-neutral statutory rape law "may well be incapable of enforcement." There are now at least 37 States that have enacted gender-neutral statutory rape laws. Although most of these laws protect young persons (of either sex) from the sexual exploitation of older individuals, the laws of Arizona, Florida, and Illinois permit prosecution of both minor females and minor males for engaging in mutual sexual conduct. California has introduced no evidence that those States have been handicapped by the enforcement problems the plurality finds so persuasive.[7] Surely, if those States could provide such evidence, we might expect that California would have introduced it.

In addition, the California Legislature in recent years has revised other sections of the Penal Code to make them gender-neutral. For example, Cal. Penal Code Ann. § 286(b)(1) and § 288a(b)(1) (West Supp. 1981), prohibiting sodomy and oral copulation with a "person who is under 18 years of age," could cause two minor homosexuals to be subjected to criminal sanctions for engaging in mutually consensual conduct. Again, the State has introduced no evidence to explain why a gender-neutral statutory rape law would be any more difficult to enforce than those statutes.

The second flaw in the State's assertion is that even assuming that a gender-neutral statute would be more difficult to enforce, the State has still not shown that those enforcement problems would make such a statute less effective than a gender-based statute in deterring minor females from engaging in sexual intercourse.[8] Common sense, however, suggests that a gender-neutral statutory rape law is potentially a greater deterrent of sexual activity than a gender-based law, for the simple reason that a gender-neutral law subjects both men and women to

---

affecting a person as the decision whether to bear or beget a child." Eisenstadt v. Baird, [405 U.S. 438, 453 (1972)] (footnote omitted). Minors, too, enjoy a right of privacy in connection with decisions affecting procreation. Carey v. Population Services International, [431 U.S. 678, 693 (1977)]. Thus, despite the suggestion of the plurality to the contrary . . . , it is not settled that a State may rely on a pregnancy-prevention justification to make consensual sexual intercourse among minors a criminal act.

7. There is a logical reason for this. In contrast to laws governing forcible rape, statutory rape laws apply to consensual sexual activity. Force is not an element of the crime. Since a woman who consents to an act of sexual intercourse is unlikely to report her partner to the police — whether or not she is subject to criminal sanctions — enforcement would not be undermined if the statute were to be made gender neutral. . . .

8. As it is, § 261.5 seems to be an ineffective deterrent of sexual activity. . . . According to statistics provided by the State, an average of only 61 juvenile males and 352 adult males were arrested for statutory rape each year between 1975 and 1978. . . . During each of those years there were approximately one million Californian girls between the ages of 13-17. . . . Although the record in this case does not indicate the incidence of sexual intercourse involving those girls during that period, the California State Department of Health estimates that there were almost 50,000 pregnancies among 13-to-17-year-old girls during 1976. . . . I think it is fair to speculate from this evidence that a

criminal sanctions and thus arguably has a deterrent effect on twice as many potential violators. Even if fewer persons were prosecuted under the gender-neutral law, as the State suggests, it would still be true that twice as many persons would be subject to arrest. The State's failure to prove that a gender-neutral law would be a less effective deterrent than a gender-based law, like the State's failure to prove that a gender-neutral law would be difficult to enforce, should have led this Court to invalidate §261.5.

III

Until very recently, no California court or commentator had suggested that the purpose of California's statutory rape law was to protect young women from the risk of pregnancy. Indeed, the historical development of §261.5 demonstrates that the law was initially enacted on the premise that young women, in contrast to young men, were to be deemed legally incapable of consenting to an act of sexual intercourse.[9] Because their chastity was considered particularly precious, those young women were felt to be uniquely in need of the State's protection.[10] In contrast, young men were assumed to be capable of making such

---

comparison of the number of arrests for statutory rape in California with the number of acts of sexual intercourse involving minor females in that State would likely demonstrate to a male contemplating sexual activity with a minor female that his chances of being arrested are reassuringly low. I seriously question, therefore, whether §261.5 as enforced has a substantial deterrent effect....

9. California's statutory rape law had its origins in the Statutes of Westminster enacted during the reign of Edward I at the close of the 13th century.... The age of consent at that time was 12 years, reduced to 10 years in 1576.... This statute was part of the common law brought to the United States. Thus, when the first California penal statute was enacted, it contained a provision (1850 Cal. Stats., ch. 99, §47, p. 234) that proscribed sexual intercourse with females under the age of 10. In 1889, the California statute was amended to make the age of consent 14.... In 1897, the age was advanced to 16.... In 1913 it was fixed at 18, where it now remains....

Because females generally have not reached puberty by the age of 10, it is inconceivable that a statute designed to prevent pregnancy would be directed at acts of sexual intercourse with females under that age.

The only legislative history available, the draftsmen's notes to the Penal Code of 1872, supports the view that the purpose of California's statutory rape law was to protect those who were too young to give consent. The draftsmen explained that the "[statutory rape] provision embodies the well settled rule of the existing law; that a girl under ten years of age is incapable of giving any consent to an act of intercourse which can reduce it below the grade of rape."... There was no mention whatever of pregnancy prevention....

10. Past decisions of the California courts confirm that the law was designed to protect the State's young females from their own uninformed decisionmaking. In People v. Verdegreen, 106 Cal. 211, 214-215, 39 P. 607, 608-609 (1895), for example, the California Supreme Court stated: "The obvious purpose of [the statutory rape law] is the protection of society by protecting from violation the virtue of young and unsophisticated girls.... It is the insidious approach and vile tampering with their persons that primarily undermines the virtue of young girls, and eventually destroys it; and the prevention of this, as much as the principal act, must undoubtedly have been the intent of the legislature." As recently as 1964, the California Supreme Court decided People v. Hernandez, [393 P.2d 674], in which it stated that the under-age female "is presumed too innocent and naive to understand the implications and nature of her act.... The law's concern with her capacity or lack thereof to so understand is explained in part by a popular conception of the social, moral and personal values which are preserved by the abstinence from sexual indulgence on the part of a young woman. An unwise disposition of her sexual favor is deemed to do harm both to herself and the social mores by which the community's conduct patterns are established. Hence the law of statutory rape intervenes in an effort to avoid such a disposition."

It was only in deciding *Michael M.* that the California Supreme Court decided for the first time in the 130-year history of the statute, that pregnancy prevention had become one of the purposes of the statute.

decisions for themselves; the law therefore did not offer them any special protection.

It is perhaps because the gender classification in California's statutory rape law was initially designed to further these outmoded sexual stereotypes, rather than to reduce the incidence of teenage pregnancies, that the State has been unable to demonstrate a substantial relationship between the classification and its newly asserted goal. . . .

I would hold that § 261.5 violates the Equal Protection Clause of the Fourteenth Amendment, and I would reverse the judgment of the California Supreme Court.

Justice STEVENS, dissenting.

Local custom and belief — rather than statutory laws of venerable but doubtful ancestry — will determine the volume of sexual activity among unmarried teenagers. The empirical evidence cited by the plurality demonstrates the futility of the notion that a statutory prohibition will significantly affect the volume of that activity or provide a meaningful solution to the problems created by it. Nevertheless, as a matter of constitutional power, unlike my Brother Brennan . . . , I would have no doubt about the validity of a state law prohibiting all unmarried teenagers from engaging in sexual intercourse. The societal interests in reducing the incidence of venereal disease and teenage pregnancy are sufficient, in my judgment, to justify a prohibition of conduct that increases the risk of those harms.

My conclusion that a nondiscriminatory prohibition would be constitutional does not help me answer the question whether a prohibition applicable to only half of the joint participants in the risk-creating conduct is also valid. It cannot be true that the validity of a total ban is an adequate justification for a selective prohibition; otherwise, the constitutional objection to discriminatory rules would be meaningless. The question in this case is whether the difference between males and females justifies this statutory discrimination based entirely on sex. . . .

In my judgment, the fact that a class of persons is especially vulnerable to a risk that a statute is designed to avoid is a reason for making the statute applicable to that class. The argument that a special need for protection provides a rational explanation for an exemption is one I simply do not comprehend.[6] . . .

If pregnancy or some other special harm is suffered by one of the two participants in the prohibited act, that special harm no doubt would constitute a legitimate mitigating factor in deciding what, if any, punishment might be appropriate in a given case. But from the standpoint of fashioning a general preventive

---

6. A hypothetical racial classification will illustrate my point. Assume that skin pigmentation provides some measure of protection against cancer caused by exposure to certain chemicals in the atmosphere and, therefore, that white employees confront a greater risk than black employees in certain industrial settings. Would it be rational to require black employees to wear protective clothing but to exempt whites from that requirement? It seems to me that the greater risk of harm to white workers would be a reason for including them in the requirement — not for granting them an exemption.

rule — or, indeed, in determining appropriate punishment when neither party in fact has suffered any special harm — I regard a total exemption for the members of the more endangered class as utterly irrational.

In my opinion, the only acceptable justification for a general rule requiring disparate treatment of the two participants in a joint act must be a legislative judgment that one is more guilty than the other. The risk-creating conduct that this statute is designed to prevent requires the participation of two persons — one male and one female.[7] In many situations it is probably true that one is the aggressor and the other is either an unwilling, or at least a less willing, participant in the joint act. If a statute authorized punishment of only one participant and required the prosecutor to prove that that participant had been the aggressor, I assume that the discrimination would be valid. Although the question is less clear, I also assume, for the purpose of deciding this case, that it would be permissible to punish only the male participant, if one element of the offense were proof that he had been the aggressor, or at least in some respects the more responsible participant in the joint act. The statute at issue in this case, however, requires no such proof. The question raised by this statute is whether the State, consistently with the Federal Constitution, may always punish the male and never the female when they are equally responsible or when the female is the more responsible of the two.

It would seem to me that an impartial lawmaker could give only one answer to that question. The fact that the California Legislature has decided to apply its prohibition only to the male may reflect a legislative judgment that in the typical case the male is actually the more guilty party. Any such judgment must, in turn, assume that the decision to engage in the risk-creating conduct is always — or at least typically — a male decision. If that assumption is valid, the statutory classification should also be valid. But what is the support for the assumption? It is not contained in the record of this case or in any legislative history or scholarly study that has been called to our attention. I think it is supported to some extent by traditional attitudes toward male-female relationships. But the possibility that such a habitual attitude may reflect nothing more than an irrational prejudice makes it an insufficient justification for discriminatory treatment that is otherwise blatantly unfair. For, as I read this statute, it requires that one, and only one, of two equally guilty wrongdoers be stigmatized by a criminal conviction. . . .

[I do not] find at all persuasive the suggestion that this discrimination is adequately justified by the desire to encourage females to inform against their male partners. Even if the concept of a wholesale informant's exemption were an acceptable enforcement device, what is the justification for defining the exempt class entirely by reference to sex rather than by reference to a more neutral criter-

---

7. In light of this indisputable biological fact, I find somewhat puzzling the California Supreme Court's conclusion, quoted by the plurality . . . that males "are the *only* persons who may physiologically cause the result which the law properly seeks to avoid." [601 P.2d 572, 575 (1979)] (emphasis in original). Presumably, the California Supreme Court was referring to the equally indisputable biological fact that only females may become pregnant. However, if pregnancy results from sexual intercourse between two willing participants — and the California statute is directed at such conduct — I would find it difficult to conclude that the pregnancy was "caused" solely by the male participant.

ion such as relative innocence? Indeed, if the exempt class is to be composed entirely of members of one sex, what is there to support the view that the statutory purpose will be better served by granting the informing license to females rather than to males? If a discarded male partner informs on a promiscuous female, a timely threat of prosecution might well prevent the precise harm the statute is intended to minimize.

Finally, even if my logic is faulty and there actually is some speculative basis for treating equally guilty males and females differently, I still believe that any such speculative justification would be outweighed by the paramount interest in even-handed enforcement of the law. A rule that authorizes punishment of only one of two equally guilty wrongdoers violates the essence of the constitutional requirement that the sovereign must govern impartially.

I respectfully dissent.

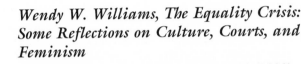

Wendy W. Williams, *The Equality Crisis: Some Reflections on Culture, Courts, and Feminism*
7 Women's Rts. L. Rep. 175, 185-187, 200 (1982)

The original statutory rape laws were quite explicitly based on [a view of the man as aggressor in sex]. Then, as is true even today, men were considered the natural and proper initiators of sex. In the face of male sexual initiative, women could do one of two things, yield or veto, "consent" or decline. What normal women did not, *should* not, do was to initiate sexual contact, to be the sexual aggressor. The premise underlying statutory rape laws was that young women's chastity was precious and their naivete enormous. Their inability knowingly to consent to sexual intercourse meant that they required protection by laws which made their consent irrelevant but punished and deterred the "aggressive" male. . . .

Statutory rape is, in criminal law terms, a clear instance of a victimless crime, since all parties are, by definition, voluntary participants. In what sense, then, can Rehnquist assert that the woman is victim and the man offender? One begins to get an inkling when, later, the Justice explains that the statutory rape law is "protective" legislation: "The statute here protects women from sexual intercourse at an age when those consequences are particularly severe." [*Michael M.*, 450 U.S. 464, 471-472 (1981).] His preconceptions become manifest when, finally, Rehnquist on one occasion calls the statute a "rape" statute [id. at 475]—by omitting the word "statutory" inadvertently exposing his hidden assumptions and underlining the belief structure which the very title of the crime, "statutory rape," lays bare. . . .

The notion that men are frequently the sexual aggressors and that the law ought to be able to take that reality into account in very concrete ways is hardly one that feminists could reject out of hand (I'm thinking here of sexual harassment and forcible rape, among other things); it is therefore an area . . . in which we need to pay special attention to our impulses lest we inadvertently support and give credence to the very social constructs and behaviors we so earnestly mean to oppose. . . . At this point, we need to think as deeply as we can about what we want the future of women and men to be. Do we want equality of the sexes — or do we want justice for two kinds of human beings who are fundamentally different?

Notes

1. Consent and Statutory Rape. Technically, consent is not an element of statutory rape. Does it follow, however, as Williams maintains, that the offense is "a clear instance of a victimless crime since all parties are, by definition, voluntary participants"? Do the facts presented in Justice Rehnquist's and Justice Blackmun's opinions suggest that the willingness of the victim's participation in the events giving rise to the prosecution might have had some relevance to the case? Notice that these two Justices reach the same conclusion in the case, but apparently based on different views about Sharon's level of consent. From Justice Rehnquist, all we know is that Sharon was "struck in the face" for "rebuffing" Michael's advances and then she "submitted" to sexual intercourse. Such factual situations support a common justification for statutory rape law: that underage girls "consent" to sexual relationships that we, as a society, can and should recognize as exploitative. Michelle Oberman, Statutory Rape Laws, A.B.A. J., Aug. 1996, at 86. However, the Court does not defend the result on this ground. Would such a rationale be convincing?

Under Justice Blackmun's reading of the facts, Sharon's "not unwilling" participation in the incident suggests that it wasn't *real* rape but a lesser, "statutory" version. Do you agree with Justice Blackmun's interpretation that Sharon was not an unwilling participant? What consequences should follow from your answer?

If Sharon was "willing," what does this say about the majority's justification for the sex-based statute — that the fear of pregnancy is an effective deterrent?

What role should the victim's conduct play in a statutory rape prosecutions? Michelle Oberman reports:

> [A]t common law, the accused was permitted a complete defense if he could demonstrate credible evidence of prior promiscuous behavior on the part of the minor. The Model Penal Code's statutory rape provision preserves this defense, noting in the commentary that prior sexual promiscuity "rebuts the presumption of naivete and inexperience" that justifies the criminal nature of statutory rape. . . .
>
> Not all jurisdictions maintain the promiscuity defense, and among those that do, not all equate promiscuity with non-virginity. Yet even in those cases which attempt to differentiate promiscuity from non-virginity, the ambiguous nature of the term "promiscuous" results in an intrusive and value-laden inquiry into the victim's sexual past.

Michelle Oberman, Turning Girls into Women: Re-Evaluating Modern Statutory Rape Law, 85 J. Crim. L. & Criminology 15, 32-33 (1994). Oberman argues that the promiscuity defense introduces the issue of consent into statutory rape law:

when the girl has had previous sexual experience, prosecutors do not press charges, juries do not convict, or sentences are light. Id. at 53. See also Deborah W. Denno, Why the Model Penal Code's Sexual Offense Provisions Should Be Pulled and Replaced, Ohio St. J. Crim. L. 207, 215 (2003) (noting absence of promiscuity defense in recently enacted legislation).

Does it follow that an underage girl's willingness to engage in sexual conduct should play no role in statutory rape prosecutions? What is the nature of the "consent" to sex in cases like *Michael M.*? Oberman argues:

> [E]ven assuming that girls do experience sexual pleasure and desire, these are only two of a multiplicity of factors which induce their consent to sex.
>
> The stories girls tell about the "consensual" sex in which they engage reflect a poignant subtext of hope and pain. Girls express longing for emotional attachment, romance, and respect. At the same time, they suffer enormous insecurity and diminished self-image. These two factors are clearly interrelated—the worse girls feel about themselves, the more they look to males for ratification of the women that they are becoming. The importance of being attractive to males takes on a central role in many girls' lives.... Girls want boyfriends, relationships, or somebody who will hold them and tell them that they are wanted.
>
> Girls negotiate access to the fulfillment of these emotional needs by way of sex. A girl who wants males to find her attractive, who wants acceptance and popularity, might reasonably consent to sex with a popular boy, to multiple popular boys, or with any partner who can persuade her that she is attractive and desirable. Males recognize, and occasionally exploit, girls' insecurity.

Id. at 65-66. Oberman concludes:

> Modern statutory rape law ... classifies intercourse as either consensual sex or rape. However, from the girl's vantage point, her consent may have been so fraught with ambivalence that it was meaningless....
>
> If girls' autonomy is to be taken seriously, the law must evaluate the sexual decisions they make, and formulate a legal response which enhances the likelihood that those decisions are autonomous ones.

Id. at 70. See also Michelle Oberman, Girls in the Master's House: Of Protection, Patriarchy and the Potential for Using the Master's Tools to Reconfigure Statutory Rape Law, 50 DePaul L. Rev. 799, 824-825 (2001). What would such a legal response look like?

2. Statutory Rape Laws. The age of consent for sexual intercourse ranges from 12 to 18 under various state laws, the most common age of consent being 16. Kate Sutherland, From Jailbird to Jailbait: Age of Consent Laws and the Construction of Teenage Sexualities, 9 Wm. & Mary J. Women & L. 313, 314 (2003). The statutory rape laws of all states except Idaho are now sex-neutral. One commentator contends that the legislative motivation behind the change is not recognition of female sexual autonomy, but instead recognition of changing societal attitudes toward male sexuality and realization that boys, as well as girls, are vulnerable to sexual exploitation by older people. Susannah Miller, Note, The Overturning of *Michael M.*: Statutory Rape Law Becomes Gender-Neutral in California, 5 U.C.L.A. Women's L.J. 289, 297 (1994).

Many states now focus on the number of years that separate the parties, either ignoring relationships between adolescents of similar ages, or making these interactions less serious. California, for example, imposes criminal liability for consensual sex only if there is a gap in age between the parties and the victim is under the statutory age of consent. Any person who engages in unlawful sexual intercourse with a minor who is not more than three years older or three years younger than the perpetrator is guilty of a misdemeanor, whereas any person over the age of 21 years who engages in unlawful sexual intercourse with a minor under 16 years of age may be guilty of either a misdemeanor or a felony. Cal. Penal Code § 261.5 (West 2005).

Laws that treat sexual acts between teenagers more leniently, or ignore them altogether, are sometimes called "Romeo and Juliet Laws." One issue under these laws is whether they apply to sexual conduct between persons of the same sex. One Kansas case involved an 18-year-old young man who was charged with sodomy against a 15-year-old boy. If the younger boy had been a girl, the longest prison sentence the Kansas Romeo and Juliet Law allowed would have been 15 months. Because the law was expressly limited to opposite-sex cases, the defendant was sentenced to more than 17 years in prison. The sentence was reversed on appeal, on state and federal equal protection grounds. See State v. Limon, 122 P.3d 22 (Kan. 2005).

3. Statutory Rape Enforcement. Beginning in the mid-1990s, California and several other states, in order to reduce teenage pregnancy and welfare costs, launched a campaign to toughen enforcement of statutory rape laws and to publicize the illegality of sex with minors. Congress encouraged such policies under the Personal Responsibility and Work Opportunity Act of 1996. This Act, discussed more fully in Section C of this chapter, advises criminal and welfare agencies to "aggressively enforce statutory rape laws." 42 U.S.C. § 14016 (2005). The 1996 Amendments to the Federal Child Abuse Prevention and Treatment Act authorized grants to states for programs relating to investigation and prosecution of statutory rape that involve caretakers or family members. 42 U.S.C. § 5106(g) (2005).

How should prosecutors decide whether to pursue statutory rape violations? How important is the apparent consent of the victim, the ages of the parties, or the fact that sexual intercourse led to pregnancy? Should adults in special trust relationships such as teachers or athletic coaches be especially targeted? What about men who father children who end up on welfare? Should the reluctance of teenage girls to seek reproductive health care out of fear it may lead to the prosecution of someone for rape be a concern? On the last factor, see Abigail English & Catherine Teare, Statutory Rape Enforcement and Child Abuse Reporting: Effects on Health Care Access for Adolescents, 50 DePaul L. Rev. 827 (2001).

How should courts and/or legislatures respond to a practice of allowing men arrested for statutory rape to marry their pregnant partners in lieu of jail time? In

Orange County, California, it is reported that "young teenage girls, some even at the age of thirteen, have been permitted to marry the adult men who statutorily raped or molested them. The permission to engage in these marriages comes from juvenile court judges on the advice of welfare agency officials, and provides the statutory rapist with an affirmative defense to any possible pending statutory rape charge." Kelly C. Connerton, The Resurgance of the Marital Rape Exemption: The Victimization of Teens By Their Statutory Rapists, 61 Alb. L. Rev. 237, 256 (1997).

The issue was brought to greater public attention when, in May 2005, 22-year-old Matthew Koso married his 14-year-old pregnant girlfriend, whom he began dating when she was 12. The couple lived in Nebraska, but were able to cross state lines and marry in Kansas, which allows boys as young as 14 to marry girls as young as 12, as long as the parents of the minor permit. Should the case be prosecuted as statutory rape in Nebraska? The editorial staff of the New York Times thought so, arguing that "neither parental nor state approval makes it right to tie a girl as young as 12 to another person in what is supposed to be a lifetime commitment." See What's the Matter with Kansas?, N.Y. Times, Aug. 31, 2005, at A18. Are they right? Consider the following:

> [D]o not get caught up in the notion that the [New York] Times has taken a principled stand on the inability of underage girls to properly decide what is right for themselves even with parental consultation. For more than a decade, the Times has assumed the strong editorial position that parental notification laws for underage girls getting abortions — even for those who cross state lines — are wrong.

Mark E. Hyman, The Times Crosses State Lines, The American Spectator, Sept. 9, 2005. Is this point well taken?

Prosecutions of women who have had sex with boys are gaining more attention. One of the most well-known cases was a Seattle grade school teacher, Mary Kay Letourneau, who at age 35 had sex with her 13-year-old student, for which she received a 7-1/2 year prison sentence. All but six months of the sentence was suspended conditional upon her entering a sex-offender treatment programming and refraining from contact with the boy. Shortly thereafter her sentence was reinstated after she was found in his company. She had one child with the boy prior to sentencing, and conceived another during her brief release. Sutherland, supra, at 320. The couple married once the boy became of age. Other cases include female teachers in Tennessee and Florida. Lisa Lynette Clark of Georgia was impregnated by her son's 15-year-old friend, whom she married a day before she was arrested. Another woman was sentenced to 30 years in 2005 for having sex with teenagers, to whom she provided drugs and alcohol. Kate Zernike, The Siren Song of Sex With Boys, N.Y. Times, Dec. 11, 2005, at WK3 (Sunday Week in Review). Are these cases any different from the more traditional statutory rape of girls by men?

4. Statutory Rape: A Violent Crime? United States v. Shannon, 110 F.3d 382, 389 (7th Cir. 1996), cert. denied, 522 U.S. 888 (1997), held that the defendant's prior conviction for nonforcible statutory rape of a thirteen-year-old girl was a crime of violence within the meaning of the Federal Sentencing Guidelines discussed previously at pp. 738–748. The Guidelines define a crime of violence as a felony that either involves force, attempted force, or threat of force, or involves conduct that presents a serious potential risk of physical injury to the victim. U.S.S.G. §4B1.2(1). The statute at issue criminalizes "sexual contact or sexual intercourse with a person who has not attained the age of 16." Wis. Stat. Ann. §948.02(2) (West 2005). Writing for the majority, Judge Richard Posner explained:

> The Wisconsin statute covers a lot of ground, and some of it may not be crime of violence ground. But sexual intercourse with a 13-year-old is in our view a crime of violence within the meaning of the guidelines, because it does present a serious risk of physical injury. A 13-year-old is unlikely to have a full appreciation of the disease and fertility risks of intercourse, and accurate knowledge of contraceptive and disease-preventive measures, and the maturity to make a rational comparison of the costs and benefits of premarital intercourse.... Furthermore, a very young girl who becomes pregnant is quite likely not to take good care of herself and her fetus, making the pregnancy more dangerous to both....
>
> To the extent that a 13-year-old is incapable of appreciating the full risk and consequences of sexual intercourse, her ensuing pregnancy and parturition (or abortion) must be considered at least quasi-involuntary and could be considered, therefore, a physical injury even if the pregnancy is normal.... The pregnancy of a 13-year-old is arguably a physical injury in itself and clearly creates a substantial risk of secondary physical injury to mother or fetus from complications of the pregnancy.

110 F.3d at 387-388.

Judge Posner's opinion leaves open the question of whether sexual contact short of intercourse, or sexual intercourse with a 15-year-old, would also necessarily constitute a crime of violence. What should be the result on those facts? What if the victim was a boy, and the relationship was consensual?

Putting Theory into Practice

5-1. A law in State X defines statutory rape as sexual intercourse with a child under the age of 16. Colleen, age 20, gives birth to a baby fathered by 16-year-old Shane, who at the time of conception was 15. Colleen was, for several years, Shane's babysitter, and Shane never complained to his parents about the sexual liaison with Colleen. Colleen is charged with statutory rape, but pleads to the lesser crime of contributing to a child's misconduct. Colleen applies for public assistance, and the Department of Social Services petitions the court to order Shane to contribute to the child's financial support. The Parentage Act of State X, which mandates that parents provide support for their children, makes no exception for parents who are minors. What should be the result? See State ex rel. Hermesmann v. Speyer, 847 P.2d 1273 (Kan. 1993) (minor parent is liable for child support despite status as victim of statutory rape); Ruth Jones, Inequality From Gender-Neutral Laws: Why Must Male Victims of Statutory Rape Pay Child Support for Children Resulting From Their Victimization? 36 Ga. L. Rev. 411 (2002).

2. Rape: Distinguishing Consent and Nonconsent

Catharine A. MacKinnon, Toward a Feminist Theory of the State
172-178 (1989)

Under law, rape is a sex crime that is not regarded as a crime when it looks like sex. The law, speaking generally, defines rape as intercourse with force or coercion and without consent....

Rape cases finding insufficient evidence of force reveal that acceptable sex, in the legal perspective, can entail a lot of force. This is both a result of the way specific facts are perceived and interpreted within the legal system and the way the injury is defined by law. The level of acceptable force is adjudicated starting just above the level set by what is seen as normal male sexual behavior, including the normal level of force, rather than at the victim's, or women's, point of violation. In this context, to seek to define rape as violent not sexual is as understandable as it is futile....

The point of defining rape as "violence not sex" has been to claim an ungendered and nonsexual ground for affirming sex (heterosexuality) while rejecting violence (rape). The problem remains what it has always been: telling the difference. The convergence of sexuality with violence, long used at law to deny the reality of women's violation, is recognized by rape survivors with a difference: where the legal system has seen the intercourse in rape, victims see the rape in intercourse.... To know what is wrong with rape, [we must] know what is right about sex. If this, in turn, proves difficult, the difficulty is as instructive as the difficulty men have in telling the difference when women see one. Perhaps the wrong of rape has proved so difficult to define because the unquestionable starting point has been that rape is defined as distinct from intercourse, while for women it is difficult to distinguish the two under conditions of male dominance....

The law of rape divides women into spheres of consent according to indices of relationship to men. Which category of presumed consent a woman is in depends upon who she is relative to a man who wants her, not what she says or does. These categories tell men whom they can legally fuck, who is open season and who is off limits, not how to listen to women. The paradigm categories are the virginal daughter and other young girls, with whom all sex is proscribed, and the whorelike wives and prostitutes, with whom no sex is proscribed. Daughters may not consent; wives and prostitutes are assumed to, and cannot. Actual consent or nonconsent, far less actual desire, is comparatively irrelevant. If rape laws existed to enforce women's control over access to their sexuality, as the consent defense implies, no would mean no, marital rape would not be a widespread exception, and it would not be effectively legal to rape a prostitute....

The adjudicated line between rape and intercourse commonly centers on some assessment of the woman's "will." But how should the law or the accused know a woman's will?...

The deeper problem is that women are socialized to passive receptivity; may have or perceive no alternative to acquiescence; may prefer it to the escalated risk of injury and the humiliation of a lost fight; submit to survive. Also, force and desire are not mutually exclusive under male supremacy. So long as dominance is eroticized, they never will be. Some women eroticize dominance and submission; it beats feeling forced. Sexual intercourse may be deeply unwanted, the woman would never have initiated it, yet no force may be present. So much force may have been used that the woman never risked saying no. Force may be used, yet the woman may prefer the sex — to avoid more force or because she, too, eroticizes dominance. Women and men know this. Considering rape as violence not sex evades, at the moment it most seems to confront, the issue of who controls women's sexuality and the dominance/submission dynamic that has defined it. When sex is violent, women may have lost control over what is done to them, but absence of force does not ensure the presence of that control. Nor, under conditions of male dominance, does the presence of force make an interaction non-sexual. If sex is normally something men do to women, the issue is less whether there was force than whether consent is a meaningful concept.

Federal Rule of Evidence 412

(a) Evidence generally inadmissible. — The following evidence is not admissible in any civil or criminal proceeding involving alleged sexual misconduct except as provided in subdivisions (b) and (c):

(1) Evidence offered to prove that any alleged victim engaged in other sexual behavior.

(2) Evidence offered to prove any alleged victim's sexual predisposition.

(b) Exceptions. —

(1) In a criminal case, the following evidence is admissible, if otherwise admissible under these rules:

(A) evidence of specific instances of sexual behavior by the alleged victim offered to prove that a person other than the accused was the source of semen, injury or other physical evidence;

(B) evidence of specific instances of sexual behavior by the alleged victim with respect to the person accused of the sexual misconduct offered by the accused to prove consent or by the prosecution; and

(C) evidence the exclusion of which would violate the constitutional rights of the defendant.

State v. Colbath

540 A.2d 1212 (N.H. 1988)

SOUTER, Justice. . . .

During the noon hour of June 28, 1985, the defendant, Richard Colbath, went with some companions to the Smokey Lantern tavern in Farmington, where he became acquainted with the female complainant. There was evidence that she directed sexually provocative attention toward several men in the bar, with whom she associated during the ensuing afternoon, the defendant among them. He testified that he had engaged in "feeling [the complainant's] breasts [and] bottom [and that she had been] rubbing his crotch" before the two of them eventually left the tavern and went to the defendant's trailer. It is undisputed that sexual intercourse followed; forcible according to the complainant, consensual according to the defendant. In any case, before they left the trailer the two of them were joined unexpectedly by a young woman who lived with the defendant, who came home at an unusual hour suspecting that the defendant was indulging in faithless behavior. With her suspicion confirmed, she became enraged, kicked the trailer door open and went for the complainant, whom she assaulted violently and dragged outside by the hair. It took the intervention of the defendant and a third woman to bring the melee to an end.

As soon as the complainant returned to town she accused the defendant of rape, and the police promptly arrested and charged him accordingly. During the initial investigation on the evening of June 28, Candice Lepene, the daughter of the tavern's owner, told the police that she had seen the complainant leave the tavern with the defendant during the afternoon. In a subsequent written statement, however, she said that she did not know whether the complainant had left with a companion or alone, but she described the complainant prior to her departure as "a girl with dark hair hanging all over everyone and making out with Richard Colbath and a few others." The police did not disclose this statement to the defense prior to trial, although defense counsel knew that Lepene had given a statement and subpoenaed her to testify at trial. . . .

The trial itself focused on the defense of consent, which the defendant addressed by his own testimony about the complainant's behavior with him at the bar and at the trailer, and by seeking to elicit exculpatory evidence that the complainant had appeared to invite sexual advances from other men as well as from himself in the hours preceding the incident. Some of this evidence was excluded and some admitted. During the charge, however, the judge instructed the jury, subject to the defendant's objection, that evidence of the complainant's behavior with other men was irrelevant to the issues before them. This appeal followed the verdict of guilty. . . .

[The issue in this appeal is] raised by the defendant's objection to the jury instruction that evidence of the complainant's behavior with men other than the defendant in the hours preceding the incident was immaterial, or irrelevant, to the question of the defendant's guilt or innocence. . . .

The trial judge first allowed the defense to elicit testimony from the complainant that at one point during the afternoon she had been sitting in the lap of one of the defendant's companions named Gillis. Shortly after that testimony, and before the defendant had called any witnesses, the State moved for a ruling *in limine* to prohibit defense witnesses from testifying about the complainant's behavior in the tavern with any other men than the defendant. . . . [The court issued] a ruling granting the prosecution's motion, for the stated reason that the complainant's "conduct with others is not material on the issue of whether or not she consented to have sexual intercourse with" the defendant. The court later supplemented this reason with the alternative grounds that the testimony in question was inadmissible as evidence of character, and inadmissible as well under the rape shield law, [N.H. Rev. Stat. Ann. 632-A:6 (1988)], which bars evidence of "[p]rior consensual sexual activity between the victim and any person other than" the defendant, when offered to prove an offense under . . . chapter 632-A.

This ruling did not end the matter, however. Although the court had ordered defense counsel not to ask his own witnesses about the complainant's behavior with third parties, further evidence of such activity did come in through the State's next witness, Candice Lepene. She testified on direct examination that the complainant had left the tavern in the company of various men several times during the afternoon, and the court admitted her statement to the police, quoted above, that she had seen "a girl with dark hair hanging all over everyone and making out with Richard Colbath and a few others." On cross-examination Lepene was permitted to testify further about her earlier statement.

When it came time for jury instructions, however, the court's charge reflected its earlier ruling on the motion *in limine*. First, the judge reminded the jurors that he had received evidence of the complainant's public activities with various men on the afternoon of the 28th, including her own admission that she had engaged in close physical contact with at least one man besides the defendant. Then the judge explained that he had allowed the jury to hear this testimony only to provide background information, and he went on to instruct the jurors plainly that the complainant's "conduct with other individuals is not relevant on the issue of whether or not she gave consent to sexual intercourse." . . .

The defendant has suggested that we address this issue simply as one of statutory construction [of the rape shield law's bar against admitting evidence of "prior consensual sexual activity between the victim and any person other than the defendant," N.H. Rev. Stat. Ann. §632-A:6 (1988)], by holding that the shield law's mandate to exclude evidence of "consensual sexual activity" with others can have no application to overt sexual activity of the complainant in a bar open to the public. . . .

Despite the absolute terms of the shield law's prohibition, our cases have consistently reflected the common recognition that such a statute's reach has to be limited by a defendant's State and national constitutional rights to confront the witnesses against him and to present his own exculpatory evidence. . . . Thus, this court has held that a rape defendant must be given an opportunity to demonstrate that the "probative value [of the statutorily inadmissible evidence] in the context of that particular case outweighs its prejudicial effect on the prosecutrix." State v. Howard, [426 A.2d 457, 461 (1981)].

As soon as we address this process of assigning relative weight to prejudicial and probative force, it becomes apparent that the public character of the complainant's behavior is significant. On the one hand, describing a complainant's open, sexually suggestive conduct in the presence of patrons of a public bar obviously has far less potential for damaging the sensibilities than revealing what the same person may have done in the company of another behind a closed door. On the other hand, evidence of public displays of general interest in sexual activity can be taken to indicate a contemporaneous receptiveness to sexual advances that cannot be inferred from evidence of private behavior with chosen sex partners. . . .

In this case, for example, the jury could have taken evidence of the complainant's openly sexually provocative behavior toward a group of men as evidence of her probable attitude toward an individual within the group. Evidence that the publicly inviting acts occurred closely in time to the alleged sexual assault by one such man could have been viewed as indicating the complainant's likely attitude at the time of the sexual activity in question. It would, in fact, understate the importance of such evidence in this case to speak of it merely as relevant. We should recall that the fact of intercourse was not denied, and that the evidence of assault was subject to the explanation that the defendant's jealous living companion had inflicted the visible injuries. The companion's furious behavior had a further bearing on the case, as well, for the jury could have regarded her attack as a reason for the complainant to regret a voluntary liaison with the defendant, and as a motive for the complainant to allege rape as a way to explain her injuries and excuse her undignified predicament. With the sex act thus admitted, with the evidence of violence subject to exculpatory explanation, and with a motive for the complainant to make a false accusation, the outcome of the prosecution could well have turned on a very close judgment about the complainant's attitude of resistance or consent.

Because little significance can be assigned here either to the privacy interest or to a fear of misleading the jury, the trial court was bound to recognize the defendant's interest in presenting probably crucial evidence of the complainant's behavior closely preceding the alleged rape. Thus, the facts of this case well illustrate the court's previous observation that the sexual activities of a complainant immediately prior to an alleged rape may well be subject to a defendant's constitutional right to present evidence. . . . The demand of the Constitution is all the clearer when those activities were carried on in a public setting. Because the jury instruction effectively excluded the evidence in question, the conviction must be reversed and the case remanded for a new trial.

Reversed and remanded.

Redmond v. Kingston
240 F.3d 590 (7th Cir. 2001)

POSNER, Circuit Judge . . .

The petitioner, Redmond, a counselor at an institution for drug- and alcohol-abusing minors, was convicted of statutory rape of Heather, a 15-year-old resident of the institution. The specific charge was that he had traded cocaine to her for sex. The state acknowledged at argument that the principal evidence of the offense was Heather's testimony and that of another resident, Michelle, who, however, merely repeated what Heather had told her had happened. There was also evidence that Heather had tested positive for cocaine after the alleged offense but that she had a long history of using cocaine and might have gotten it from someone other than Redmond or for something other than sex.

Eleven months before the alleged offense, Heather had told her mother that she had been forcibly raped, and she had offered her torn clothes as evidence. She had repeated the story of the rape, with many circumstantial details, to a hospital nurse and to a police officer investigating the incident, but later had admitted making up the story (and ripping her clothes herself) in order to get her mother's attention. Her new story was that she had had sex with the man she had accused of forcible rape, but that it had been with her consent. Since she was underage, the police continued to investigate the incident as a crime. The man was never found, and there is no evidence other than Heather's say-so that the incident actually occurred. There is no serious doubt that her recantation of the forcible-rape story was truthful. Redmond offered more than thirty police reports of the investigation of Heather's claim that she had been forcibly raped, convincingly demonstrating its falsity, and in addition the district attorney had instituted contempt charges against Heather. . . .

Redmond wanted to bring out her lie on cross-examination in order to show that Heather would lie about a sexual assault in order to get attention, and thus had a motive to accuse him falsely. The trial judge, seconded by the Wisconsin court of appeals, refused to permit this cross-examination. The court of appeals held that although the state's rape-shield law makes an exception for a prior false charge of a sexual assault, Wis. Stat. §972.11(2)(b)3, Heather's false charge did not have "sufficient probative value to outweigh its inflammatory and prejudicial nature," and therefore, under another section of the statute, §971.31(11), it was inadmissible. The court thought the false charge merely "cumulative of other evidence which went to Heather's credibility," namely that she had begun using drugs at the age of 12, had stolen and occasionally danced(!) to obtain money for cocaine, had run away from the institution, had skipped school, and had told lies in the past. Furthermore, the court thought the evidence of the false charge might have "confused the issue" since "the initial recantation involved consent which was not an element of the current charges," and also that it might have misled the jury "into focusing on Heather's willingness to have sexual intercourse with a complete stranger, instead of on the charges against Redmond." . . .

With all due respect, we believe that the court of appeals' analysis and conclusion cannot be considered a reasonable application of the Supreme Court's confrontation doctrine. . . . The evidence of the false charge of forcible rape was not cumulative of other evidence bearing on Heather's credibility, because none of the other evidence either involved a false charge of being sexually assaulted or furnished a motive for such a charge. The fact that a teenage girl has a disordered past and lies a lot (who doesn't?) does not predict that she will make up stories about having sex. To indulge such an assumption would be to place such persons largely beyond the protection of the law. But the fact that the girl had led her mother, a nurse, and the police on a wild goose chase for a rapist merely to get her mother's attention supplied a powerful reason for disbelieving her testimony eleven months later about having sex with another man, by showing that she had a motive for what would otherwise be an unusual fabrication. . . .

And thus the court's ruling, though ostensibly based on the rape-shield statute, derives no support from that statute. The statute protects complaining witnesses in rape cases (including statutory-rape cases) from being questioned about their sexual conduct, but a false charge of rape is not sexual conduct. . . . The false-charge "exception" to the rape-shield statute is not really an exception, but rather a reminder of the limited meaning of "sexual conduct" as defined in the statute. The only basis for the court's ruling was the general principle of the law of evidence, which is codified for federal trials in Fed. R. Evid. 403 but is equally a principle of Wisconsin's law of evidence, see Wis. Stat. § 904.03, that relevant evidence may be excluded if its probative value is substantially outweighed by its prejudicial (confusing, or cumulative) effect. When that unexceptionable rule is applied as it was here to exclude highly probative, noncumulative, nonconfusing, nonprejudicial evidence tendered by a criminal defendant that is vital to the central issue in the case (Heather's credibility), the defendant's constitutional right of confrontation has been infringed....

The judgment is reversed with directions to order the petitioner released unless the state retries him within 120 days of the date of this decision.

Reversed.

▬▬▬
Susan Estrich, Rape
▬▬▬ 95 Yale L.J. 1087, 1102-1105 (1986)

My view is that...a "negligent rapist" should be punished, albeit—as in murder—less severely than the man who acts with purpose or knowledge, or even knowledge of the risk. First, he is sufficiently blame-worthy for it to be just to punish him. Second, the injury he inflicts is sufficiently grave to deserve the law's prohibition.

The traditional argument against negligence liability is that punishment should be limited to cases of choice, because to punish a man for his stupidity is unjust and, in deterrence terms, ineffective. Under this view, a man should only be held responsible for what he does knowingly or purposely or at least while aware of the risks involved....

If inaccuracy or indifference to consent is [the best that a man can do] because he lacks the capacity to act reasonably, then it might well be unjust and ineffective to punish him for it. But such men will be rare...at least as long as voluntary drunkenness is not equated with inherent lack of capacity. More common is the case of the man who could have done better but didn't; could have paid attention, but didn't; heard her say no, or saw her tears, but decided to ignore them. Neither justice nor deterrence argues against punishing this man.

Certainly, if the "reasonable" attitude to which a male defendant is held is defined according to a "no means yes" philosophy that celebrates male aggressiveness and female passivity, there is little potential for unfairness in holding men who fall below *that* standard criminally liable. Under such a low standard of reasonableness, only a very drunk man could honestly be mistaken as to a woman's consent, and a man who voluntarily sheds his capacity to act and perceive reasonably should not be heard to complain here—any more than with respect to other crimes—that he is being punished in the absence of choice.

But even if reasonableness is defined—as I argue it should be—according to a rule that "no means no," it is not unfair to hold those men who violate the rule criminally responsible, provided that there is fair warning of the rule. I understand that some men in our society have honestly believed in a different reality of sexual relations, and that many may honestly view such situations differently than women. But, it is precisely because men and women may perceive these situations differently, and because the injury to women stemming from the different male perception may be grave, that it is necessary and appropriate for the law to impose a duty upon men to act with reason, and to punish them when they violate that duty.

In holding a man to such a standard of reasonableness, the law signifies that it considers a woman's consent to sex to be significant enough to merit a man's reasoned attention. In effect, the law imposes a duty on men to open their eyes and use their heads before engaging in sex — not to read a woman's mind, but to give her credit for knowing her own mind when she speaks it. The man who has the inherent capacity to act reasonably, but fails to do so, has made the blame-worthy choice to violate this duty. While the injury caused by purposeful conduct may be greater than that caused by negligent acts, being negligently sexually penetrated without one's consent remains a grave harm, and being treated like an object whose words or actions are not even worthy of consideration adds insult to injury. This dehumanization exacerbates the denial of dignity and autonomy which is so much a part of the injury of rape, and it is equally present in both the purposeful and negligent rape.

By holding out the prospect of punishment for negligence, the law provides an additional motive for men to "take care before acting, to use their faculties and draw on their experience in gauging the potentialities of contemplated conduct." We may not yet have reached the point where men are required to ask verbally. But if silence does not negate consent, at least the word "no" should, and those who ignore such an explicit sign of non-consent should be subject to criminal liability.

Notes

1. Rape in the United States. According to governmental and crime center research, one out of every six U.S. women and one out of 33 U.S. men have experienced an attempted or completed rape as a child and/or adult. About eight percent of U.S. adolescents have been victims of at least one sexual assault, and slightly over half of sexual assault victims are females younger than 25. http://www.ojp.usdoj.gov/ovc/assist/nvaa2002/chapter10.html.

Explanations for rape fall along three main dimensions: individual, sociobiological, and cultural. At the individual level:

> Profiles of rapists indicate that many are primarily attracted to power; they want the feeling of domination, adventure, and self-esteem that comes from coercive sex. Other men emphasize anger; rape is a means to punish or avenge some wrong by a particular woman, women in general, or another adversary. Most rapists blame their victims, and some stress situational influences such as peer pressure or drug and alcohol abuse. Exposure to family violence during childhood increases the likelihood that men will engage in sexually violent activities as adults.

Deborah L. Rhode, Speaking of Sex: The Denial of Gender Equality 121 (1997). See also Diana Scully, Understanding Sexual Violence: A Study of Convicted Rapists (1990).

The sociobiological explanation is that, at an evolutionary level, men having intercourse with a large number of fertile females has "favorable reproductive consequences." For men who have difficulty attracting willing partners, coercive sex is "adaptive" and likely to be favored by natural selection. Recent scholarship about the importance and relevance of an evolutionary perspective to law and policy relating to rape is cited in Chapter 4, pp. 655-657. See especially Owen D. Jones & Timothy H. Goldsmith, Law and Behavioral Biology, 105 Colum. L. Rev. 405 (2005); Randy Thornhill & Craig T. Palmer, A Natural History of Rape: Biological Bases of Sexual Coercion 182-183 (2000).

One question feminists have raised in response to sociobiological claims is why, if rape is adaptive and genetically hardwired, there is so much cultural variation in attitudes toward rape, and why are there societies in which rape is so rare? See Peggy Reeves Sanday, Female Power and Male Dominance: On the Origins of Sexual Inequality (1981) (comparative anthropological study of male and female power in various cultures). Another question is why, if rape is primarily a reproductive strategy, about a third of victims are too young or old to reproduce, and why nonvaginal assaults are so common? And, if rape is predominantly about sex, not power, and sexually alluring dress is such a significant contributing factor, what accounts for the massive rape of women in wartime?

On the cultural dimension, some commentators stress the role of the eroticization of male aggression in popular films, television, fiction, and video games, as well as gender stereotypes in media coverage of sexual assault. See Rhode, Speaking of Sex, supra, at 83-85, 128; Helen Benedict, Virgin or Vamp: How the Press Covers Sex Crimes (1992). For further exploration of cultural themes relating to rape, see note 4, p. 792, below.

2. Rape Law Reform. To date, rape law reform in this country has come in two waves: (1) the Model Penal Code (MPC) revision of the 1950s, and (2) laws responding to the feminist critique of rape laws, which began in the 1970s. The MPC, which stimulated statutory reform in many states, abolished a common provision requiring the victim to offer the "utmost" or "reasonable" resistance. This reform refocused the crime from the consent of the woman to the conduct of the defendant. To increase the likelihood of convictions and to reduce the scope for idiosyncratic or biased judgments, the MPC also divided rape into three categories. First-degree felony rape was reserved for life-threatening conduct where the parties were strangers or where the defendant inflicted serious bodily harm. Life-threatening rape between acquaintances was a second-degree felony. Less serious abuses were grouped under a new third-degree felony of "gross sexual imposition." See Stephen J. Schulhofer, Taking Sexual Autonomy Seriously, 11 Law & Phil. 35, 36-38 (1992).

In the next wave of law reform, new legislation, such as rape shield statutes, was designed to protect the victims as well as to obtain convictions. By the close of the 1990s, all states had such provisions. In addition, in 1994, Congress enacted Federal Rules of Evidence 413 and 415, which make evidence of the defendant's prior instances of sexual violence admissible in federal cases, even if relevant only to the defendant's disposition or propensity to engage in such conduct. The rules have been controversial, because they carve out an exception to the usual doctrine that prior similar acts are inadmissible to show propensity, and because they have been used to generate broad discovery in cases where evidence of the claimed assault is dubious. See Mark A. Sheft, Federal Rule of Evidence 413: A Dangerous New Frontier, 33 Am. Crim. L. Rev. 57 (1995).

Other reforms spurred by women's rights advocates included further refinements in the grading systems for sexual offenses, reformulation of statutory provisions with gender-neutral language, elimination or relaxation of the marital rape exemption, and alterations in the substantive requirements of force and nonconsent to facilitate convictions. Schulhofer, supra, at 38-39.

Evidence on the effect of these reforms is mixed. See Stacy Futter & Walter Mebane, The Effects of Rape Law Reform on Rape Case Processing, 16 Berkeley Women's L.J. 72 (2001) (finding that changes increased the changes that a rape would lead to an arrest and reduced the variability of arrest outcomes across police agencies); Cassia Spohn & Julie Horney, The Impact of Rape Law Reform on the Processing of Simple and Aggravated Rape Cases, 86 J. Crim. L. 861 (1996) (finding little or no change in rape reports, arrests, or convictions, but some improvement in the treatment of complaints); Gregory Matoesian, Reproducing Rape: Domination Through Talk in the Courtroom 17 (1993) (rape reform has had only a symbolic effect on society); see also Andrew Taslitz, Rape and the Culture Of the Courtroom 154-155 (1999) (discussing the failure of rape reform to address rape myths).

3. Consent. Nowhere, perhaps, are views about the meaning of consent as divided as in the context of rape. Perspectives range from Justice Souter's assumption that consent can be determined by "evidence of public displays of general interest in sexual activity" to Catharine MacKinnon's claim that consent is merely a label that the law places on the kind of sex acceptable under conditions of gender inequality. Note that Justice Souter's view presupposes the greatest amount of female self-control, MacKinnon's the least. Which understanding is likely to lead to rules giving women greater sexual autonomy?

Much of the contemporary debate on rape law has centered on how or whether to redefine consent. Susan Estrich, for example, proposes that the law should focus on the reasonableness of the defendant's intent and should assume that a reasonable man understands "no" to mean "no." Does it go too far? Far enough? Some feminists worry that such a reformulation would fail to protect a woman frightened into passivity. They would focus on the coerciveness of the man's conduct or require an affirmative yes. See, e.g., Lynne Henderson, What Makes Rape a Crime, 3 Berkeley Women's L.J. 193, 216-217 (1988); Lani Anne Remick, Read Her Lips: An Argument for a Verbal Consent Standard on Rape, 141 U. Pa. L. Rev. 1103 (1993).

Stephen Schulhofer argues that the focus of criminal prohibitions should be protecting women's autonomy—her physical integrity and her capacity to choose, unconstrained by impermissible pressures and limitations. Schulhofer, supra, at 71-72; Schulhofer, Unwanted Sex: The Culture of Intimidation and the Failure of Law (2000). To that end, Schulhofer proposes a crime of nonviolent sexual misconduct for invading women's bodily integrity in the face of ambivalence, objection, or silence. Such a statute would encompass economic pressure or other coercive behavior to obtain sex. See also Linda R. Hirshman & Jane E. Larson, Hard Bargains: The Politics of Sex 268-272 (1998) (arguing that by forcing the stronger partner to bargain with the weaker for explicit consent, we begin to ensure mutuality in adult sexual relationships).

4. Cultural Attitudes and "Rape Myths." What assumptions underlie the courts' analysis in *Colbath* and *Redmond*? Experts identify four categories of "rape myths" which they say help to explain the requirements of rape laws and their interpretation by judges, juries, and law enforcement personnel: (1) only certain women (i.e., those with "bad" reputations) are raped; (2) only certain men (i.e., psychopaths) rape; (3) women invite or deserve rape by their appearance and behavior; and (4) women fantasize or fabricate rape, motivated by desire, revenge, blackmail, jealousy, guilt, or embarrassment. Rhode, Speaking of Sex, supra, at 120-121; Mary Koss et al., No Safe Haven: Male Violence Against Women at Home, at Work, and in the Community 7-17, 185-187 (1994); Morrison Torrey, When Will We Be Believed? Rape Myths and the Idea of a Fair Trial in Rape Prosecutions, 24 U.C. Davis L. Rev. 1013, 1025 (1991).

On the powerful influence of popular attitudes about rape on the attitudes of offenders, complainants, police, prosecutors, jurors, and judges, shaping decisions about whether to report or prosecute a crime, whether to convict or acquit a defendant, how to treat a complainant, and how to sentence a defendant, see Andrew E. Taslitz, Patriarchal Stories I: Cultural Rape Narratives in the Courtroom, 5 S. Cal. Rev. L. & Women's Stud. 387, 393 (1996); Lisa A. Binder, "With More Than Admiration He Admired": Images of Beauty and Defilement in Judicial Narratives of Rape, 18 Harv. Women's L.J. 265 (1995); Susan F. Hirsch, Interpreting Media Representations of a "Right of Madness": Law and Culture in the Construction of Rape Identities, 19 Law & Soc. Inquiry 1023 (1994).

Consider the following examples:

- In 2002, Harvard University adopted a new policy requiring victims of sexual assault by peers to produce "sufficient independent corroboration," as a requirement for the investigation of the complaint. After substantial protest and a complaint by a student alleging that the policy constituted sex discrimination in violation of Title IX of the Civil Rights Act, the University altered the policy to require the student victim to provide "as much information as possible," which the federal Office of Civil Rights found acceptable. Eric Hoover, Harvard's Sexual Assault Policy Does Not Violate Students' Rights, U.S. Inquiry Finds, Chron. of Higher Ed., April 3, 2003, at A1. For the policy, see http://www. registrar.fas.harvard.edu/handbooks/student.2003-2004/chapter4/ adboard.html. See also Michelle J. Anderson, The Legacy of the Prompt Complaint Requirement, Corroboration Requirement, and Cautionary Instructions on Campus Sexual Assault, 84 B.U. L. Rev. 945, 994 (2004); Stephanie Schmid, A Perfunctory Change? Harvard

University's New Sexual Misconduct Complaint Procedure: Lessons from the Frontlines of Campus Adjudication Systems, 18 Berkeley Women's L.J. 165 (2005).

- A survey of public allegations of sexual assault against 168 prominent athletes found that a third resulted in no charges and another fifth in charges that were dismissed. Sports Figures, Cases Involving Athletes and Sexual Assault, USA Today, Dec. 22, 2003, at A1, A5. Women who accuse stars like Kobe Bryant and Mike Tyson receive death threats and harassment for being "gold diggers" who needlessly destroy revered role models for conduct that they invite by going to his hotel room alone. Bill Saporito, Kobe Rebounds, Time, Sept. 13, 2004, at 72.
- Parents who shrugged off the rapes of high school girls by the Los Angeles "Spur Posse" (whose members competed with each other for sexual conquests) on the ground that "those girls were trash." Emily Jaffe, Girls Who Go Too Far, Newsweek, July 22, 1991, at 58.
- A juror who voted to acquit William Kennedy Smith of the rape of a woman he picked up in a bar because "he's too charming and too good-looking to have to resort to violence for a night out." Lynn Hecht Schafran, The Importance of Voir Dire in Rape Trials, Trial, Aug. 1992, at 26.
- A juror who voted to acquit three St. John's University fraternity brothers of a widely publicized gang rape on the assumption that "Hell hath no fury like a woman scorned." Peggy Reeves Sanday, A Woman Scorned: Acquaintance Rape on Trial 238 (1996).
- A judge who voted to overturn a rape conviction on the theory that "when an adult woman goes to a man's room, [she certainly has] to realize that they [are] not going upstairs to play Scrabble." State v. Rusk, 424 A.2d 720, 733-734 (Md. 1981) (Cole, J., dissenting).

Many experts have concluded that rape law reforms are unlikely to be effective without challenging these public attitudes. Andrew Taslitz, Rape and the Culture of the Courtroom 154-155 (1999); Lisa Frohmann & Elizabeth Mertz, Legal Reform and Social Construction: Violence, Gender, and the Law, 19 Law & Soc. Inquiry 829, 835 (1995). If these experts are correct, what strategies will work best, and how can lawyers and scholars assist the process?

5. Rape Trauma Syndrome. To what extent can experts be helpful in resolving issues of consent? In the course of improving clinical treatment for rape victims, researchers have developed a profile of rape victims known as the "rape trauma syndrome." The syndrome is characterized by two phases: Phase I or the "acute phase" is a period of disorganization in which the victim is either emotionally out of control—crying, sobbing, restless, or tense—or extraordinarily controlled—calm, composed, or subdued. Headaches, fatigue, and gastrointestinal, and genitourinary, and sleep disturbances are common during this period. Phase II or the "long-term reorganization process" is a period of nightmares, phobic reactions, sexual fears, and changes in routine. See Ann Wolbert Burgess & Lynda Lytle Holmstrom, Rape Trauma Syndrome, in Forcible Rape:

The Crime, the Victim, and the Offender 315 (Duncan Chappell et al. eds., 1977).

Some courts have approved use of expert testimony about rape trauma syndrome to help prove that a forcible assault, rather than consensual sex, occurred. See, e.g., Street v. United States, 602 A.2d 141 (D.C. App. 1992). Typically, however, admissibility of this testimony is limited to rehabilitating the victim's credibility rather than proving the prosecution's case-in-chief. In both contexts, expert testimony regarding rape trauma syndrome may be effective in dispelling rape myths regarding victim's behavior after the rape. In one New York case, the court noted:

> [T]he reaction of a rape victim in the hours following her attack is not something within the common understanding of the average lay juror. Indeed, the defense would clearly want the jury to infer that because the victim was not upset following the attack, she must not have been raped. This inference runs contrary to the studies cited earlier, which suggest that half of all women who have been forcibly raped are controlled and subdued following the attack.... Thus, we conclude that evidence of this type is relevant to dispel misconceptions that jurors might possess regarding the ordinary responses of rape victims in the first hours after their attack.

People v. Taylor, 552 N.E.2d 131, 138 (N.Y. 1990).

If evidence of rape trauma syndrome is admissible to show lack of consent, should it also be admissible to show that an alleged victim's behavior was atypical, and thus inconsistent with her account of rape? The Indiana Supreme Court held that it was an abuse of discretion to exclude expert testimony that the victim's conduct in returning to the bar where the rape allegedly had taken place was inconsistent with that of a person who had been forcibly raped. Henson v. State, 535 N.E.2d 1189 (Ind. 1989).

Like battered women's syndrome, rape trauma syndrome has come under fire by some commentators, who charge that the science is not adequate to support it under the standards for admitting scientific evidence under the U.S. Supreme Court's decision in Daubert v. Merrell Dow Pharm., Inc., 509 U.S. 579, 590 (1993) (to qualify as scientific evidence under Federal Rules of Evidence 702, trial judge must determine that proposed testimony is supported by appropriate scientific validation based on what is known). See, e.g., Mark S. Brodin, Behavioral Science Evidence in the Age of Daubert: Reflections of a Skeptic, 73 U. Cin. L. Rev. 867, 891-892 (2005) ("Researchers in the fields may have failed to critically test their hypotheses for fear of being labeled politically correct"); David Faigman, The Law's Scientific Revolution: Reflections and Ruminations of the Law's Use of Experts in Year Seven of the Revolution, 57 Wash. & Lee L. Rev. 661, 674 (2000) ("[i]n our time, the rape trauma syndrome, the battered woman syndrome, repressed memories, posttraumatic stress disorder, and child abuse accommodation syndrome all represent accession to holy writ"). Some feminists also contend that the syndrome has been used to re-pathologize women. Susan Stefan argues, for example, that labeling rape survivors as victims of a "syndrome" encourages juries and judges to think of them as crazy and helpless, and their responses to having been raped as symptoms of mental disorder rather as normal reactions to violence.

> Focusing on rape trauma syndrome in a criminal trial shifts attention from the defendant's actions to the victim's reactions. The use of rape trauma syndrome to explain "counterintuitive" reactions — such as a woman's delay in reporting rape — in terms of her pathology, precludes explaining these reactions as sensible behavior in the context of endemic male violence against women. The use of rape trauma syndrome evidence also threatens to reintroduce the parade of horribles women worked so hard to eliminate for the last twenty years: psychiatric examination of the rape victim, defendants' access to the woman's medical and psychiatric records, admission of evidence of the victim's past sexual behavior, and even corroboration requirements. It is understandable that prosecutors use rape trauma syndrome evidence in court because it may increase the chance of conviction, but its use is no feminist victory.

Susan Stefan, The Protection Racket: Rape Trauma Syndrome, Psychiatric Labeling, and Law, 88 Nw. U. L. Rev. 1271, 1274-1275 (1994).

3. Rape and Lawyers' Ethical Responsibilities

American Bar Association Standards for Criminal Justice: Prosecution Function and Defense Function
Standard 4-7.6(b) (3d ed. 1993)

(b) Defense counsel's belief or knowledge that the witness is telling the truth does not preclude cross-examination.

Model Code of Professional Responsibility
DR 7-106(c) (1980)

(c) In appearing in his professional capacity before a tribunal, a lawyer shall not: . . .

(2) Ask any question that he has no reasonable basis to believe is relevant to the case and that is intended to degrade a witness or other person.

Model Rules of Professional Conduct
Rule 4.4: Respect for Rights of Third Persons (1983)

In representing a client, a lawyer shall not use means that have no substantial purpose other than to embarrass, delay, or burden a third person, or use methods of obtaining evidence that violate the legal rights of such a person.

Cookie Ridolfi, Statement on Representing Rape Defendants
(July 26, 1989) (unpublished manuscript, on file with author at Santa Clara Law School)

I have never felt conflicted about what side I stand on in a criminal trial. My political sensibilities keep me firmly planted on the side of the defendant. As a public defender for nearly seven years, I have seen that my clients are victims of poverty, racism, and a criminal justice system that, despite its lofty ideals, presumes guilt, not innocence. My experience has shown me that the system is stacked against an accused and doubly stacked against those who are not white or are poor....

However, my role as a defender in sexual assault cases is not clear or simple. These cases frequently require that I, a feminist who rejects harmful stereotypes of women, exploit those same stereotypes in defense of my client. In the majority of sexual assault cases, the complainant and defendant know one another and fabrication or consent is raised as a defense.... As a consequence, in most sex cases, my role is to charge the complainant with having agreed to the sexual encounter, or having asked for it, or of being a woman scorned whose feelings of rejection caused her to cry rape as an act of revenge.

Some defense attorneys believe that effective cross-examination can be done in a way that does not demean the complainant. I disagree. No matter what tone of voice is used or how politely the questions are put, a good cross-examination must still ultimately demonstrate that the complaining witness is a liar.... An attorney who is concerned about a complainant's feelings necessarily compromises her client's right to an advocate with exclusive loyalty.

In the conflict between my commitment to defender work and my increasing distress over what is required of me in a sex case, the fact that my own gender is also an issue at trial weighs heavily. Last year I defended a man charged with assault and rape. He and the complainant were dance partners in a club featuring provocative "live dancing." She testified that the defendant appeared at her door late one night, forced his way inside, then dragged her into the basement where he viciously raped and beat her. The client said that he had been invited into the house for sex which was interrupted when the complainant's husband came home; it was her husband who beat her, not him.

After more than a week of trial where emotions ran high for everyone, the jury acquitted him. Afterwards, I met with jurors. One woman juror told me that she believed in his innocence because she was certain that I could not have fought for him in the way that I did had he committed that crime.... I later learned that he was arrested and convicted in two new rape/assault cases similar to the one I had tried.... [T]hat trial and that complainant still haunt me. I think of the horror described from the witness stand and I believe now that it is true. I think about the fact that the defendant left the courthouse a free man and returned to a community that pitied him as a victim and despised her as the victimizer. I think about the two women that were beaten and raped by him just a few months later. Finally, I think about my role in that.

Despite this experience and my growing discomfort with my own participation in the defense of rape cases, I remain firm in my belief that every person, no matter what the charge or circumstances of the case, deserves dedicated and competent counsel. I also know that some men are victims of a woman's false charges of rape and agree strongly that this defense must be pursued when a defendant makes this claim. I am not critical of any other woman who chooses to defend a man charged with rape. But for all of the reasons I have given, I would find it difficult to again be in the position where I would have to challenge a woman's claim of rape knowing that what she claims may be true.

Notes

1. The Scope of Rape Shield Statutes. In *Colbath*, the defendant sought evidence of the victim's previous behavior with other men on the same day the alleged crime took place. Without ruling directly on the defendant's construction of the rape shield statute, Justice Souter states that there are other constitutional principles that control the case, namely, the defendant's right to "confront the witnesses against him and to present his own exculpatory evidence." These principles give the defendant "an opportunity to demonstrate that the "probative value [of the statutorily inadmissible evidence] in the context of that particular case outweighs its prejudicial effect on the prosecutrix.'" Under what standards is the court to balance these interests? Does this approach adequately take into account the purpose of the rape shield statute?

Starting with Michigan in 1974, all states except Arizona have enacted rape shield laws. Michelle A. Anderson, From Chastity Requirement to Sexuality License: Sexual Consent and a New Rape Shield Law, 70 Geo. Wash. L. Rev. 51, 81 (2002). Half of these laws contain general prohibitions on evidence of prior sexual conduct subject to one or more legislated exceptions, such as prior sexual conduct between the complainant and the accused; an alternative source of semen, pregnancy or injury; a pattern of prior sexual conduct by the complainant; bias or motive to fabricate; a mistaken belief by the accused in the complainant's consent; and prior false accusations of sexual assault by the complainant. For a listing of all statutes and the exceptions they allow, see id. at 81-83. Eleven states and the District of Columbia apply a constitutional catch-all provision. Id. at 83-84. Nine states allow judicial discretion. Id. at 84-85. Four states determine the admissibility of a woman's sexual history based on the purpose for which the evidence is offered. In California and Delaware, sexual history offered to prove the complainant's consent to sexual intercourse is prohibited, but sexual history offered to attack her credibility is admissible. Just the reverse is the standard in Nevada and Washington. Id. at 85.

Rape shield statutes have drawn criticism from all sides. Civil libertarians and criminal defense counsel often claim that the protections compromise defendants' rights to a fair trial. As stated by one defense counsel:

> Now a public-policy decision designed to correct vestiges of Victorian-era morality has stacked the deck against every citizen accused of a sex crime. . . .

Our justice system depends on the belief that a randomly drawn jury, culled only for prejudice and partiality, can detect truth and falsity. But if a jury is given a skewed presentation of the facts, or if important facts are withheld from a jury, we cannot expect it to do justice.

Most rape cases that turn on whether a sex act was consensual . . . [will] ultimately come down to a "he said/she said" contest between the accused and the accuser. But how can a jury accurately judge the credibility of the two parties if the accused has been presented in the worst possible light while the accuser is enshrouded in a cloak of purity?

Barry Tarlow, Criminal Justice: Rape Suspects' Uphill Road, L.A. Times, Aug. 17, 2003, at M3.

By contrast, many feminists claim that the exemptions compromise complainants' rights to privacy and deter other victims from reporting the crime. One commentator, reviewing many cases, suggests that rape shield laws have not been effective in undermining the unofficial but pervasive "chastity requirement," imbedded in traditional rules of credibility and consent. Anderson, supra, at 74-75, 94-95. See also James B. Johnston, How the Confrontation Clause Defeated the Rape Shield Statute: Acquaintance Rape, the Consent Defense and the New Jersey Supreme Court's Ruling in *State v. Barron*, 14 S. Cal. Rev. L. & Soc. Change 197 (2005) (arguing that a New Jersey case "ignored" rape shield statute in the face of confrontation clause claims by the accused).

Another potential difficulty, illustrated especially in celebrity trials, is that the media is able, through leaks and paid investigators, to publish compromising information that would be inadmissible in trial. A 2003 case involving a Los Angeles Lakers basketball star, Kobe Bryant, illustrates some of the difficulties surrounding current shield provisions. A hotel clerk whom Bryant invited to his room claimed that he threw her over a chair, put his hands around her neck, and raped her. Bryant claimed that they had consensual sex, that the "strangling thing" was something that he did during consensual sex (as a girlfriend would confirm), and that the complainant's vaginal bruising could have occurred during consensual sex that she had with other partners around the time in question. The transcript of preliminary hearing is available at http://www.thesmokinggun.com/archive/0924041kobea1.html. Media coverage of the case was extensive. The victim's name, address, and telephone number as well as details about her sex life quickly surfaced, as did a prom picture of her raising her dress to show a garter. She was the target of several death threats and frequent harassment.

In applying Colorado's shield law, the trial judge determined that the complainant's sexual activity around the time of the assault (within approximately 72 hours preceding the assault and her physical examination) could be admitted as evidence. On three occasions, court clerks mistakenly released transcripts of closed hearings to the press, and the defense attorney inadvertently referred to the complainant by name in open court, in violation of court order. In response to the harassment, threats, and humiliating coverage, the victim indicated that she would not testify and the prosecutor subsequently dropped the charges. She filed a civil suit instead, and Bryant issued a carefully crafted apology. Kirk Johnson, As

Accuser Balks, Prosecutors Drop Bryant Rape Case, N.Y. Times, Sept. 2, 2004; Bill Saporito, Kobe Rebounds, Time, Sept. 13, 2004, at 72.

The Bryant case intensified longstanding controversies regarding sexual privacy, fair trials, and a free press. Some commentators argued that the restrictions by the court on publishing the complainant's name or picture, and comparable self-imposed limitations by major media publications, were ineffectual, counterproductive, and an infringement of the public's right to know. From their perspective, such bans perpetuated the stigma and shame that the shield statutes were designed to prevent. One columnist, Geneva Overholser, resigned when the Poynter Institute, a respected journalism education organization, excised the complainant's name from her column. Nat Ives, Online Columnist Quits, Citing Excessive Editing, N.Y. Times, Sept. 20, 2004, at C9. Other observers responded that publicizing complainants' names would deter them from reporting assaults that would subject them to a second victimization in the press. As to the public's "right to know," communications professor Mark Crispin Miller summarized widespread views that the information at issue in cases like Kobe Bryant had less to do with legitimate First Amendment interests than "garden variety voyeurism." Kate Zernike, What Privacy? Everything Else But the Name, N.Y. Times, Aug. 3, 2003, at E4 (quoting Miller).

Does Federal Rule of Evidence 412 strike the right balance? To justify admission, should evidence of prior sexual history be not just "relevant" but "highly relevant" *and* have probative value that "substantially outweighs" its potential prejudice or invasion of privacy? One proposal would allow evidence of a complainant's sexual history only to show an alternate source for the semen, pregnancy, disease, or injury; to convent consent "in a specific way or to engage in a specific sexual act at issue," or to show bias or motive to fabricate the rape charge. Anderson, supra, at 147. Is this reasonable?

What balance should law and journalistic ethics strike in these cases? What would best serve the interests of justice? Or, is columnist Dahlia Lithwick right that justice is simply impossible in a case like Kobe Bryant's, where "everyone emerges so damaged that it hardly matters who won." Dahlia Lithwick, The Shield That Failed, N.Y. Times, Aug. 8, 2004, at WK11.

2. Ethical Responsibilities in Criminal Defense. The role of defense counsel in rape cases often raises fundamental questions of legal ethics:

- What are lawyers' responsibilities when they believe that their clients are guilty or wish to assert positions that are factually untrue?
- Are clients entitled to a defense that includes impeaching a witness whom the lawyer believes is telling the truth?
- Should lawyers' obligations take into account the costs to potential witnesses? If so, does rape stand on a different footing from other civil or criminal proceedings? Alternatively, does any matter involving particularly vulnerable victims present similar considerations?
- Should the lawyer's sex affect resolution of these issues? Does a defendant gain an extra and unwarranted advantage from representation by a female attorney in a case where the sexual history of a female complainant is

relevant? Might a juror assume that no woman would zealously attack another woman's credibility without a belief that she was testifying untruthfully?

Do the bar's ethical rules provide adequate guidance on these questions?

The American bar's prevailing view is that a lawyer's belief that a client is guilty or that an opposing witness is truthful should not prevent efforts to present the most persuasive possible case, which may include impeaching that witness's testimony. In essence, the justification for a vigorous defense in criminal contexts is that the system cannot guarantee due process if attorneys deny adequate representation to any clients they assume are guilty. The only way to ensure that the state has met its burden of proof is for lawyers to put questions that might raise a reasonable doubt, irrespective of their personal beliefs in the truth of the witnesses' account. So, too, the only way to ensure trust and candor in attorney-client relationships is to avoid penalizing clients for inculpating disclosures. Many commentators take the position that criminal defense entails special obligations of zealous advocacy, both because of the potential for abusive state power and because of the special stakes for the defendant whose liberty, reputation, and sometimes life may be at risk. See Deborah L. Rhode, In the Interests of Justice 54-56, 73-74 (2001); David Luban, Are Criminal Defenders Different?, 91 Mich. L. Rev. 1729 (1993).

To some commentators, however, impeachment of truthful witnesses is especially problematic in rape cases. Zealous advocacy in that context may carry special costs because of the particularly grave potential for humiliation; the risk that invasive cross-examination will deter victims from reporting rapes; and the societal impact of sanctioning "rape myths," suggesting that complainants provoke, desire, or deserve what they get. Lawyers' appeals to such myths are often effective. Jurors are less likely to convict a defendant if evidence suggests that the victim engaged in nonmarital sex, drank, used drugs, dressed "provocatively," or knew the defendant, however brief their acquaintance. The same information affects judicial decisionmaking, and racial bias amplifies these effects when the complainant is a woman of color. Rhode, Speaking of Sex, supra, at 121-127. In addition, rape victims often suffer from rape trauma syndrome, which may lead them to suppress details of an assault. Zealous cross-examination on such details may unduly discredit a victim's basically accurate account.

Exploitation of rape complainants' special vulnerability can have a corrosive impact on the entire law enforcement system. Rape is the most underreported felony, in part because of a further victimization of victims that rape shield statutes have only partially addressed. To commentators such as David Luban, such considerations suggest limits on lawyers' roles:

> Matters would be different if rape were rare and false accusations of rape occurred regularly. Then the advocate's role would properly focus on the vulnerability of men, not of women. Suffice it to say that the world is not this way. . . . In my view, then, the advocate's role should stop well short of an all-out assault. . . . The lawyer can ask the victim whether she consented. The lawyer can also argue reasonable doubt to the jury. What she cannot do is cross-examine her to make her look like a whore.

David Luban, Partisanship, Betrayal, and Autonomy: A Reply to Stephen Ellman, 90 Colum. L. Rev. 1004, 1029-1031 (1990).

Does Luban sufficiently consider the costs to male defendants who may misjudge consent? Should defendants be entitled to have the jury see the case from their perspective? Compare the view of one public defender:

> The effect of the women's movement on me has been as strong as on anyone else, but I'm no one special; I try to win my cases. If I could get my client off by appealing to the jury's sexism I probably would because I'd be more concerned with this one guy and his freedom than the ethical issue of sexism.

Timothy Beneke, Men on Rape 104-105 (1982). Is this responsible? Is it unethical? Would it be ethical to do otherwise?

Do, or should, women criminal defense attorneys practice law differently than their male colleagues, particularly in cases involving female victims of sexual abuse? In Emotional Trials: The Moral Dilemma of Women Criminal Defense Attorneys (2004), Cynthia Siemsen draws on interviews with women defense attorneys who have grappled with legal ethics issues in cases involving sexual abuse: rape, domestic violence, and child molestation. These women had encountered endless variations on the same question: "How can you defend him?" And they hated having to repeat endless variations on the same response: "everyone is entitled to representation," "it's not our role to judge them," "I'm not defending the act . . . I'm defending the right to a fair proceeding." Cookie Ridolfi's statement fits this pattern.

Siemsen found that many lawyers developed strategies that took them beyond these ritualistic responses. For example, many women defenders worked hard to empathize with their client, regardless of the heinousness of the act. Sometimes there was reason to doubt the prosecution's case: "victims lie, police lie." Often factors in defendants' own life histories helped to explain or mitigate the offense; they were victims of child sexual abuse or domestic violence; they had drug or mental health disabilities that called for institutionalized treatment not extended incarceration. In many cases, excessive penalty structures, particularly California's three-strikes law, created incentives to provide the best possible defense. Many of these lawyers found special satisfaction in the "social work" aspect of their work: they looked for opportunities to help turn someone's life around. Is this an appropriate role for defense counsel? Should women defense counsel be more "sensitive" in cross-examining rape victims?

The vast majority of defenders in the Siemsen study reported that their work was not in tension with their feminism. Rather, they saw defending the "poorest of the poor" as an extension of feminist values, reflecting a commitment to individual rights, a respect for human dignity, and a compassion for those who had been victims as well as victimizers. Id. at 107. Do you agree?

3. The Rape Crisis Counselor Privilege. A related issue is whether a rape complainant should have the right to shield disclosures made to rape crisis counselors. About half the states and the District of Columbia have enacted privilege statutes that protect such information. The Federal Rules of Evidence do not provide such a privilege. The state statutes are listed in Jennifer Bruno, Pitfalls for the Unwary: How Sexual Assault Counselor-Victim Privileges May Fall Short of Their Intended Protections, 2002 U. Ill. L. Rev. 1373, 1381 n. 52. In 14 states and the District of Columbia the privilege is absolute, and in nine states, the privilege is qualified. Id. at 1384-1385.

The justifications for the privilege are obvious. Victims of sexual assault are likely to obtain higher quality counseling if confidentiality can be protected, and without that protection, the injuries of a sexual assault may be compounded by public disclosure of intimate details from therapeutic sessions. Id. at 1381. Rape crisis centers are often the primary source of assistance for victims, and failure to protect confidential disclosures to counselors at these centers whether or not they are licensed physicians would compromise treatment and reporting, particularly for individuals who cannot afford to pay for assistance from psychiatrists who can assert the privilege. Id. at 1382; Anna Y. Joo, Broadening the Scope of Counselor Patience Privilege to Protect the Privacy of the Sexual Assault Survivor, 32 Harv. J. Legis. 255, 264-266 (1995); Jaffee v. Redmond, 518 U.S. 1, 17 (1996).

The justifications for allowing defendants access to therapeutic records are equally obvious. In some rape cases, the boundaries of consent and coercion are blurred at best, and subtle, even unintended, encouragement by rape counselors to define an interaction as rape may affect how a complainant later recalls the event. See Rachel Capoccia, Piercing the Veil of Tears: The Admission of Rape Crisis Counselors' Records in Acquaintance Rape Trials, 68 S. Cal. L.J. 1335, 1342 (1995). Other relevant details in therapeutic records may include the complainant's prior involvement with the accused and a history of mental health problems. Given the enormous costs to the defendant of an unjust conviction, some relinquishment of the complainant's privacy interests may appear reasonable.

How would you strike the balance? Would a justifiable compromise be to allow the judge to review the materials in camera to determine if their probative value is sufficient to outweigh the complainant's interest in confidentiality? Or would this solution compromise both competing principles, particularly since the judge must typically make the determination without knowing the nature of the case? If counselors refuse to turn over records in violation of a court order, what sanctions should follow? See Adam Liptak, Privacy of Rape Victim Clashes With Trial Rights, N.Y. Times, Jan. 26, 2003, at A16 (describing Massachusetts Resource Center's offer to have 500 women volunteers serve a day in jail to satisfy a sanction, rather than pay a $500 a day fine that would preempt assistance for hundreds of women); see also Cadet Rape Case Halted Over Refusal on Files, N.Y. Times, June 25, 2005, at A10 (describing military judge's suspension of trial as a result of a civilian counselor's refusal to turn over records).

If a privilege exists, should it be waived if the counselor accompanies the victim into interviews with police officers or prosecutors, or if the victim intends to, or does, tell others the same information? This issue is explored in Bruno, supra, at 1393-1399 (proposing that the statutory privilege provide that "the confidential communication between a victim and a sexual assault counselor is available to a third person only when the *victim reasonably* believes the disclosure is in *furtherance* of the desired result of counseling").

4. Racial Bias. At one time, rape of a nonwhite woman was not a crime. See George v. State, 37 Miss. 316 (1859). See also A. Leon Higginbotham, Jr., & Anne F. Jacobs, The "Law Only as an Enemy": The Legitimization of Racial Powerlessness Through the Colonial Laws of Virginia, 70 N.C. L. Rev. 969, 1056 (1992) (rape of black slave women not a crime in Mississippi, Missouri, and Virginia before the Civil War). By contrast, the rape of a white woman by a black man was long considered the most horrific offense and provided the most common justification for lynching. At various times, the law required that blacks convicted of raping white women be castrated. Higginbotham & Jacobs, at 1055-1060.

Although most rapes, like most other crimes, are intraracial rather than interracial, rapes in which black men are the perpetrators and white women the victims continue to receive the greatest attention and the most serious sanctions. One study of Indianapolis rape cases found that "most of the reported rapes involved Black suspects and Black victims. The second largest category involved white suspects on white victims, while Black on white rapes constituted the smallest group of reported rapes. As these cases progressed through the system, however, the percentage of cases involving Black suspects and white victims steadily increased, the percentage of Black intraracial assaults steadily decreased, and the percentage of white on white rapes remained relatively constant." Elizabeth Iglesias, Rape, Race, and Representation: The Power of Discourse, Discourses of Power, and the Reconstruction of Heterosexuality, 49 Vand. L. Rev. 869, 881 (1996) (citing study). A Texas study similarly found that the median sentence for a black man who raped a white woman was 19 years. For a white man who raped a white woman, it was five years. Ray F. Herndon, Race Tilts the Scales of Social Justice, Dallas Times Herald, Aug. 9, 1990, at A1.

4. Rape in Wartime: Violence against Women as a Human Rights Issue

Women have long been targets of mass rape during wartime. Accounts of brutalization are common in the literature of ancient Greece and Rome. The Old Testament similarly chronicles the invasion of Canaan by Hebrew tribes, whose spoils of war included "sheep, cattle, asses, and thirty-two thousand girls who had had no intercourse with a man." Early prohibitions on this practice were largely unenforced. A 14th century English Ordinances of War made rape a capital offense, but it did not apply to sieges, the most common form of warfare at the time. In the United States, initial prohibitions on rape in wartime appeared in the 1863 military code for the Union Army, which codified early humanitarian law protecting non-combatants. Catherine Niarchos, Women, War, and Rape: Challenges Facing the International Tribunal for the Former Yugoslavia, Hum. Rts. Q. 647, 660-661 (Nov. 1995). At the international level, Article 46 of the Hague Convention of 1907 outlawed rape during occupations, and the Geneva Convention of 1929, which governed treatment of prisoners of war, guaranteed female prisoners all the regard "due their sex." Patricia Viseur Sellers, Sexual

Violence and Peremptory Norms: The Legal Value of Rape, 34 Case W. Res. J. Int'l L. 287, 289 (2002).

These prohibitions did little to deter massive rapes during World War II. The most notorious cases involved Japanese soldiers' "comfort facilities" staffed by women, especially disfavored ethnicities such as Koreans and Filipinos, who were abducted or otherwise coerced into sexual slavery. An estimated 200,000 women were involved, often listed in official military documents as "military supplies"; almost three-quarters died from their treatment. Most of those who survived the camps were murdered or abandoned in dangerous areas at the close of the war. Angela M. Higgins, "Else We Are Condemned to Go From Darkness to Darkness": Victims of Gender-Based War Crimes and the Need for Civil Redress in U.S. Courts, 70 UMKC L. Rev. 677, 681 (2002); Shellie K. Park, Broken Silence: Redressing the Mass Rape and Sexual Enslavement of Asian Women by the Japanese Government in an Appropriate Forum, 3 Asian-Pacific L. & Pol'y J. 2, 28 (2002). Although the International Military Tribunal of the Far East gathered evidence on these abuses, its charter did not include sexual offenses and its proceedings (the Tokyo Trials) largely ignored them except when they were coupled with other offenses. Kelly D. Askin, A Decade of the Development of Gender Crimes in International Courts and Tribunals: 1993 to 2003, 11 (No. 3) Hum. Rts. Brief 16, 16 (2004). In Germany, rape was subsumed under crimes against humanity but was not included in a single indictment. A Woman Scorned for the "Least Condemned" War Crime: Precedent and Problems with Prosecuting Rape as a Serious War Crime in the International Criminal Tribunal for Rwanda, 13 Colum. J. Gender & L. 274, 281-282 (2004). Because the Allies ran the Nuremberg Tribunal, they ignored atrocities committed by their own soldiers, including an estimated rape of some 100,000 to 800,000 women in the Soviet capture of Berlin. Niarchos, supra, at 665-666.

After World War II, international law began to include explicit prohibitions on rape during wartime. Article 27 of the 1949 Geneva Conventions, and subsequent Protocols of 1977 protect women against "rape, enforced prostitution, or any form of indecent assault. Fourth Geneva Convention relative to the Protection of Civilian Persons in Times of War, 6 U.S.T. 3516 (1956) (hereinafter Fourth Geneva Convention); Protection of Victims of International Armed Conflicts (Protocol I), Art. 76(1), 16 ILM 1391 (1977). More recently, the 1998 Rome Statute, which defines the jurisdiction of the International Criminal Court (ICC), defines "rape, sexual slavery, enforced prostitution, forced pregnancy, enforced sterilization, or any other form of sexual violence of comparable gravity" as crimes against humanity, war crimes, and potentially part of genocide. Rome Statute of the International Criminal Court, July 17, 1998, Art. 7(1)(g), U.N. Doc. A/CONF. 183/9 (1998). Although the United States is not currently a signatory to the Rome Statute, U.S. courts have provided civil relief to victims of wartime rape under the Alien Torts Claim Act. In 1995, for example, the Second Circuit Court of Appeals held that Radovan Karadzic, leader of the Bosnian-Serb territory, could be held accountable for rape as an act of genocide and other war crimes committed during the Yugoslav conflict. A jury subsequently awarded the plaintiffs $745 million in compensatory and punitive damages. Kadik v. Karadzic, discussed in Catharine MacKinnon, Sex Equality: Rape Law 897 (2001).

The international community first began to prosecute rape as a human rights violation largely in response to the atrocities committed in Rwanda and Yugoslavia in the early 1990s. Estimates of the number of rapes that occurred during the Yugoslavian conflict range from 20,000 to 50,000. This magnitude of sexual violence is not unprecedented; Pakistani soldiers raped an estimated 200,000 women during the war over Bangladesh's independence, and Japanese soldiers raped at least 20,000 Chinese women in the "rape of Nanking" from 1937-1938. Joshua S. Goldstein, War and Gender 363 (2001). However, what is distinctive about rape in the former Yugoslavia was its role in ethnic cleansing. For example, Muslim and Croatian women were raped in order to make women tainted and therefore unmarriageable within their cultures as well as to produce Serbian babies. Lynda E. Boose, Crossing the River Drina: Bosnian Rape Camps, Turkish Impalement, and Serb Cultural Memory, 28 Signs 71, 73-74 (Autumn 2002). Many women were murdered after rape, or held in camps where they were raped repeatedly, often until they died. In Rwanda, an estimated 250,000 to 535,000 Tutsi women were raped, and some 200,000 murdered. Most of those who survived are now HIV positive. Jennifer M. Hentz, The Impact of HIV on the Rape Crisis in the African Great Lakes Region, 12 (No. 2) Hum. Rts. Brief 12, 13 (2005); Sharon Frederick, Rape: Weapon of Terror 89 (2001).

What also distinguishes these mass rapes is the response of the international community, prompted by the emergence of a feminist voice. Supporters of women's rights have played a critical role in chronicling such atrocities, serving on tribunals challenging the inadequacy of legal remedies, and educating the international community about the cultural contexts that license such abuse. Cynthia Enloe, Afterword: Have the Bosnian Rapes Opened a New Era of Feminist Consciousness?, in Mass Rape: The War Against Women in Bosnia-Herzegovina 220 (Alexandra Stiglmayer ed., Marion Faber trans., 1994). The efforts of the international women's rights community were instrumental in the development of the International Criminal Tribunal for the former Yugoslavia (ICTY) and the International Criminal Tribunal for Rwanda (ICTR) and in the explicit inclusion of rape as a crime against humanity within these Tribunals' jurisdiction. The ICTY also contributed significantly to setting precedent for prosecuting rape as a war crime. For the first time, an international tribunal recognized rape as a tool of genocide and a crime against humanity, and indicted a former head of government, Slobodan Milosevic, for mass rapes constituting such a crime. Adrienne Kalosieh, Consent to Genocide?: The ICTY's Improper Use of the Consent Paradigm to Prosecute Genocidal Rape in FOCA, 24 Women's Rts. L. Rep. 121, 129 (2003); Jared Olanoff, Holding a Head of State Liable for War Crimes, 27 Suffolk Transnat'l L. Rev. 327, 331-334 (2004); Patricia H. Davis, The Politics of Prosecuting Rape as a War Crime, 34 Int'l L. 1223 (Winter 2000).

After unsuccessful attempts to seek redress in the Japanese courts, advocates for comfort women convened a Women's International War Crimes Tribunal. Comprised of legal scholars, the tribunal heard testimony and passed judgment on high-ranking Japanese military and political leaders for their role in authorizing sexual slavery. Although the judgment carried no binding force, it has served an important role in clarifying international law and in pressuring the

Japanese government to contribute to the Asian Women's Fund. The Fund has also raised $4 million in non-governmental funds to compensate former comfort women, although some refuse to accept such reparations on the grounds that this approach allows Japan to continue to avoid issuing a formal apology. Afreen R. Ahmed, The Shame of Hwang v. Japan: How the International Community Has Failed Asia's "Comfort Women," 14 Tex. J. Women & L. 121, 147 (2004); Christine Wawrynek, World War II Comfort Women: Japan's Sex Slaves or Former Prostitutes?, 19 N.Y.L. Sch. J. Hum. Rts. 913, 920 (2003). See also Hwang Geum Joo v. Japan, 332 F.3d 679, 681 (2003) (dismissing complaints against Japan by surviving comfort women on grounds of sovereign immunity), vacated and remanded, 542 U.S. 901(2004) (remanding on the basis of Republic of Austria v. Altmann, 541 U.S. 677 (2004), which held that sovereign immunity is not a bar to damages recovery by victims of Nazi confiscations based on statute enacted after the confiscations).

Other efforts on the international front have centered on preventing gender violence from occurring in future conflicts. One involves implementation of command responsibility, which is now codified in Article 28 of the Rome Statute. Article 28 establishes that military and non-military leaders can be held responsible for crimes under the ICC's jurisdiction. To be held liable, an individual must (1) be in a command relationship to the subordinate who committed the crime in question, (2) have "knowledge" that the subordinates either committed or were about to commit the crime in question, and (3) have failed to prevent or punish the crime in question. While some commentators have argued that strict liability for superior officers is the best way to deter abuse, others have claimed that it does not focus blame on those who actually commit the crime. Compare Sherrie L. Russell-Brown, The Last Line of Defense: The Doctrine of Command Responsibility and Gender Crimes in Armed Conflict, 22 Wis. Int'l L.J. 125, 130-131 (2004) (arguing for strict liability), with Mirjan Damaska, The Shadow Side of Command Responsibility, 49 Am. J. Comp. L. 455 (2001) (raising concerns about such liability).

Despite these efforts, gender violence is still pervasive in armed conflict, most visibly in the Democratic Republic of the Congo (DRC). Amnesty International estimates that more women have been raped in the DRC than in any other conflict, though the exact number still remains unknown. Each armed band of soldiers has developed a "signature" manner of raping a woman: the local defense forces (known as Mai Mai) use branches or bayonets to commit the rapes and then mutilate their victims, the Burundians rape both men and women, and the Rwandans gang rape their victims. It is estimated that sixty percent of the combatants are HIV positive, and approximately thirty percent of women raped during the conflict now have the disease. Jennifer M. Hentz, The Impact of HIV on the Rape Crisis in the African Great Lakes Region, 12 (No. 2) Hum. Rts. Brief 12, 13 (2005); Tsjeard Bouta, Georg Frerks & Ian Bannon, Gender, Conflict, and Development 35 (2005). In many other African conflicts, rape victims also die from attempted abortions in the bush and lack of medical care during childbirth. Susan McKay, Reconstructing Fragile Lives: Girls' Social Reintegration in Northern Uganda and Sierra Leone, in Gender, Peacebuilding, and Reconstruction 21-22 (Caroline Sweetman ed., 2005).

United Nations peacekeeping forces have not only been often ineffective in preventing such abuse, but it has been reported that they have been perpetrators as well. In the U.N. mission in the Congo, soldiers have coerced sex, often with minors, by offering money, food, or employment. Going rates are said to be as little as $1 or $2. Victims rarely report abuse, due to concerns of ostracism by their families and communities. Marc Lacey, In Congo War, Even Peacekeepers Add to Horror, N.Y. Times, Dec. 18, 2004, at A1; Russell-Brown, supra, at 127. In Bosnia, U.N. peacekeepers reportedly patronized sex clubs and assisted sex traffickers in purchasing women and falsifying their documents. Colum Lynch, Ex-U.N. Officer Sues U.S. Firm Over Dismissal: Lawsuit Alleges Retaliation for Reporting Co-Worker's Sexual Misconduct in Bosnia, Wash. Post, June 23, 2001, at A20. Concerned by the high incidence of HIV/AIDS among peacekeeping forces in the Congo and Sierra Leone, U.N. officials decided to issue each soldier one condom per day and provide warnings in U.N. Manuals such as: "Like many of the troops in your unit, you probably feel that having 'casual sex' is a big part of 'off-duty' time to help you relax and unwind. You could easily get infected by having sex with a person you just met." Colum Lynch, U.N. Plans to Give Condoms to the Troops, N.Y. Times, Mar. 18, 2000, at A13.

These failures in the international community's response to rape in war time raise broader issues about the culture of violence. How are sexual assaults related to the masculinist ideology of the military? How do we explain the role of women, such as Pauline Nyiramusuhuko, Rwanda's former minister of women's affairs, who is being prosecuted for inciting Hutus to rape and brutalize thousands of female Tutsis? To what extent do wartime rapes mirror, or dwarf, the everyday "private," domestic rapes of women and children?

5. Marital Rape

Kizer v. Commonwealth of Virginia
321 S.E.2d 291 (Va. 1984)

COMPTON, Justice.
Indicted for the rape of his wife in violation of Code § 18.2-61, Edward Alan Kizer was found guilty in a bench trial and sentenced on September 9, 1983 to confinement in the penitentiary for a term of 20 years. Execution of 15 years of the sentence was suspended and the defendant was placed on probation for life.... [We reverse the conviction.]

The facts mainly are undisputed. Defendant and his wife, Jeri, were married in June of 1981 in Texas. The couple moved to Norfolk where defendant, age 20, was stationed aboard ship as an enlisted man in the Navy. They occupied rented quarters ashore that were leased in both names. Following the birth of a child, the couple began having marital difficulties. In September of 1982, about six months before the incident in question, the wife returned to Texas briefly. According to her testimony, the purpose of the trip was "to visit" her parents for two weeks; the visit was not "a separation" from her husband.

During the "middle of February" 1983, about three weeks before the alleged offense, the defendant "moved back to the ship." The wife continued to reside in the apartment with the child. According to the wife's testimony, the separation occurred because "[t]he marriage was over and I did not want the marriage to be any longer...." The wife added that she "wanted to be separated and in the process to file for divorce after the legal separation in Virginia." The defendant testified that the parties were not "legally separated" and that he moved to the ship "to avoid any other arguing with my wife...in front of our son because we did not want to subject him to arguing between me and my wife, Jeri."

Previously, the wife had left the husband from "about the first of January to about the middle of February" 1983. After the parties "had talked to each other," she returned to the marital home, saying to the husband, "I want to make it work but I do not love you." The defendant had suspected his wife of "fooling around" while he was on duty at sea, but testified that he "still loved the girl" and wanted the marriage "to work."

During the three-week period from the middle of February to the date of the incident, the defendant came to the apartment to visit the child pursuant to an oral agreement with the wife. She estimated he made "a couple" visits. The defendant testified that he "tried" to visit the boy "seven or eight times." The parties had agreed that the defendant would notify the wife in advance of a planned visit so that she would not be in the apartment when he arrived.

On March 5, the day before the incident in question, the defendant came to the apartment without notifying the wife. She refused to allow him to enter the premises during the morning and again during the afternoon. Still later in the day, she permitted him to see the child as the wife, accompanied by a male friend, left the apartment on the friend's motorcycle. She returned to the apartment about five hours later, at 11:30 p.m., but did not remain. The defendant told her he was staying at the marital abode because he did not want to return to the ship due to the lateness of the hour.

The evidence showed that the parties did not engage in sexual intercourse during the period from September 1982, when she visited her parents in Texas, until the date of the incident in question. During a portion of this time, the defendant was aboard ship at sea.

Prior to the alleged offense, the defendant filed a petition in court seeking an award of custody of his child. In addition, the parties decided in February to consult a lawyer "about getting a legal separation." As the parties were en route to an attorney's office, the wife told defendant that she had changed her mind and that she did not want to separate "right now." He said, "Are you sure?" and she responded, "Yes." They returned to their apartment. The wife testified that she decided to discontinue the trip to the attorney because the defendant had just received notification that his father was very ill and she did not want to put more "pressure" on him at that time.

The evidence showed that before the day of the alleged offense, the defendant discussed "the rape laws of Virginia" with a friend. The defendant had said that "he [the defendant] was kind of hard up for sex" and that he thought he "ought to go over there and rip her clothes off of her and take it."

On the day in question, March 6, the defendant had been visiting friends in an apartment "across the hall" from the marital home. He knocked on the door to his apartment about 6:00 p.m. and asked his wife to allow him to use the shower. She refused because she was afraid to be in the premises alone with him. The defendant insisted on gaining entry and, as the wife tried to lock the front door to the apartment, he kicked the door twice. The door "came open and the frame came off the door," according to the wife's testimony. The defendant took the child from the mother's arms and placed him on the floor. The defendant picked up the wife, carried her to the bedroom, ripped off her clothing, and forcibly had sexual intercourse with her. During this time, she was screaming, scratching, kicking, and pulling defendant's hair. At one point during the 45-minute episode, the wife broke away from the defendant and rushed to the bedroom window, screaming for help. After the assault, the wife ran from the apartment and reported the incident to a police officer who was in the area.

The defendant was arrested on a warrant that day about 9:45 p.m., after earlier having confessed to the acts essentially as related by the wife. About three weeks after the incident, and before the rape trial, the defendant was awarded custody of his son following a hearing.

On appeal, the question presented is whether, under this evidence, the Commonwealth established beyond a reasonable doubt the elements necessary to sustain a conviction for marital rape. In such a case, under [Weishaupt v. Commonwealth, 315 S.E.2d 847 (Va. 1984)], the prosecution, in addition to establishing a violation of the general rape statute, Code 18.2-61, must prove beyond a reasonable doubt that the wife unilaterally had revoked her implied consent to marital intercourse. [315 S.E.2d at 855.] The wife's revocation of consent must be demonstrated by a manifest intent "to terminate the marital relationship." [Id.] The facts necessary to show this intention to terminate must reveal that the wife: has lived separate and apart from the husband; has refrained from voluntary sexual intercourse with her husband; and, "in light of all the circumstances," has conducted herself "in a manner that establishes a de facto end to the marriage." [Id.]...

In the present case, the evidence shows, first, a violation of the rape statute sufficient to sustain a conviction of the defendant for the rape of a female not his wife. Second, the evidence establishes that the parties lived separate and apart. Third, the proof shows that the wife refrained from voluntary sexual intercourse with the defendant. The evidence fails, however, to show beyond a reasonable doubt the wife conducted herself in a manner that established an actual end to the marriage, in light of all the circumstances.

Significantly, the wife's marital conduct during the six-month period before the assault was equivocal, ambivalent, and ambiguous. Prior to September 1982, the parties had been having domestic difficulties but apparently had been living together as husband and wife. She left Norfolk and went to Texas to "visit" her parents. But she testified that this was not a "separation" in the divorce sense. She returned from Texas and during part of the September-January period, the husband was on shipboard duty at sea. In January, the wife left again but returned after the parties "talked." She stated at the time that she wanted to make the marriage "work." In February, she terminated a planned trip with her husband to a divorce lawyer, advising the husband that she had changed her mind and did not wish to separate "right now." Finally, about three weeks before the alleged offense, the husband began living aboard ship in port. At the time, the wife considered the marriage to be "over."

Evaluating the foregoing circumstances in the light most favorable to the Commonwealth, we think it is apparent that the wife subjectively considered the marriage fractured beyond repair when the parties separated in February. Nevertheless, we cannot say that this subjective intent was manifested objectively to the husband, in view of the wife's vacillating conduct, so that he perceived, or reasonably should have perceived, that the marriage actually was ended.

The facts in *Weishaupt*, upon which the Attorney General relies in urging affirmance, are in sharp contrast to the circumstances of the present case. There, the wife moved out of the marital abode, taking with her the infant child of the parties. At the time of the offense, the parties had been separated continuously for 11 months and had not engaged in sexual relations during the period. There was no contact between the parties during the separation except telephone conversations concerning the child and chance meetings in public. During the period, the wife had consulted a divorce attorney who advised waiting until the parties were separated for a full year before filing suit for divorce. In sum, unlike the present case, the wife's marital conduct in *Weishaupt* during the pertinent period, viewed objectively, was unequivocal, definite, and certain; her conduct manifestly demonstrated that the marriage was in fact at an end and evidenced that the wife unilaterally had revoked her implied consent to marital intercourse. In *Weishaupt*, unlike this case, the Commonwealth proved beyond a reasonable doubt that the husband knew, or reasonably should have known, that the marriage was terminated de facto.

Accordingly, the judgment of conviction in this case will be reversed and the indictment will be dismissed.

THOMAS, Justice, dissenting.

The victim in this case took a horrible beating. The integrity of her body was brutally invaded by her estranged husband. The facts in this appeal are such that the majority concedes that had the victim not been married to the assailant, the assailant would have been guilty of rape. Nevertheless, in an opinion which fails to give due precedential weight to the Court's recent decision in Weishaupt v. Commonwealth, [315 S.E.2d 847 (Va. 1984)], the majority concludes, in essence, that Edward Kizer had a right to do what he did. The majority opinion marks a retreat from the principles announced in *Weishaupt*. . . .

According to the majority, before a husband can be found guilty of raping his wife, the wife must make "manifest objectively to the husband" the wife's view that the marriage is at an end. *Weishaupt* nowhere requires that the wife make manifest to her husband that the marriage is at an end. *Weishaupt* requires only that the wife make manifest to an objective observer "her intent to terminate the marital relationship." The difference is that, under the majority view, the trial court must place itself in the position of the estranged husband to determine whether the husband should have known that his wife considered the marriage over. Under *Weishaupt*, the court was not required to place itself in the husband's shoes; instead, it was called upon to occupy the more traditional posture of looking at the facts from the perspective of an objective observer to determine whether from that perspective the wife conducted herself in a manner that showed the marriage to be over. . . .

Prior to the attack, the husband filed suit to secure custody of the couple's child. . . . The majority mentions this fact but makes nothing of it, thus glossing over a very critical point.

In the normal course of events, husbands do not file custody suits unless they consider their marriages to be over. It is unrealistic to believe that the husband in this case would have sued for the custody of his child unless he thought the relationship with his wife was at an end. . . . The pendency of the custody suit added to the six-month absence of sexual relations and the one-month separation would lead any objective husband or impartial observer to conclude that the marriage in question was at an end.

Thus, in my opinion, the conviction for rape should be affirmed.

CARRICO, C.J., joins in this dissent.

NOTE ON THE MARITAL RAPE EXEMPTION

The common law marital rape exemption is credited to Sir Matthew Hale, 1 History of the Pleas of the Crown 628 (1st American ed. 1847). It was based on the assumption that in marriage the wife gave her irrevocable consent to intercourse with her husband. The notion of irrevocable consent appears to have been a euphemism for the deeper underlying notion that a woman is the property of a man—first her father and then her husband. See People v. Liberta, 474 N.E.2d 567, 576 (N.Y. 1984), cert. denied, 471 U.S. 1020 (1985). Moreover, at common law, the concept of marital unity viewed husband and wife as one, and a married man, therefore, could not be liable for raping himself.

As those rationales grew increasingly anachronistic, commentators replaced them with various, sometimes inconsistent, policy arguments. One commentator assumed that marital rape occurred so infrequently that legal remedies were unnecessary. Others assumed that it occurred so frequently that any remedial structure would be overwhelmed by complaints, as women seeking divorces would file complaints to blackmail their husbands in order to obtain better settlements in divorce. Deborah L. Rhode, Justice and Gender 250 (1988). The Model Penal Code commentary to §213.1 reasons that courts should not intrude on the "privacy" of the family relationship, that a husband's use of force against his wife is not as harmful as other kinds of forced sex, and that spousal rape presents greater evidentiary problems than other rapes.

As of 2003, 24 states and the District of Columbia had abolished marital immunity for sexual offenses, either by judicial decision or by statute. The 26 other states have retained some form of marital immunity; in some of these immunity for forcible rape has been eliminated, but in 20 states marriage is a defense for lesser degrees of sexual assault. For example, 20 states grant marital immunity for sex with a spouse who is incapacitated or unconscious, and 15 states grant immunity unless requirements such as prompt complaint, extra force, separation, or divorce are met. For a listing of all statutes, see Michelle J. Anderson, Marital Immunity, Intimate Relationships, and Improper Inferences: A New Law on Sexual Offenses by Intimates, 54 Hastings L.J. 1465, 1468-1473, nn.8-12, 1557-1574 (2003).

Is there a convincing argument that marital rape should be treated as a more, not a less, serious crime? Empirical research indicates that the greatest adverse psychological effects on women who have been raped are those resulting from sexual assaults by a husband or a relative. In one study, 52 percent of women raped by a husband and 52 percent of women raped by a relative reported long-term effects on their lives. For women raped by a stranger, the figure was 39 percent; for women raped by an acquaintance, 25 percent; and for women raped by a friend, date, or lover, 22 percent. Diana E. H. Russell, Rape in Marriage 192-193 (rev. ed. 1990). See also research cited in Rhode, Justice and Gender, supra, at 251, and in David Finkelhor & Kersti Yllo, License to Rape: Sexual Abuse of Wives 137, 140 (1985) (finding long-term injury to self-confidence and self-esteem). A few courts have specifically rejected the rationale that marital rape is less traumatic than stranger rape. See, e.g., People v. M.D., 595 N.E.2d 702, 712 (Ill. App. Ct.), appeal denied, 602 N.E.2d 467 (Ill. 1992).

What assumptions underlie the requirement in some states that a wife file a complaint of rape within a shortened period of time? See, e.g., S.C. Code Ann. §16-3-658 (2004) (must file within 30 days); Cal. Penal Code §262 (West Supp. 2004) (must file within one year unless independent admissible evidence exists).

Some legislative reforms have actually broadened, rather than narrowed, the marital rape exemption. A few states, for example, recognize an exemption for parties living together who are not legally married to one another. See, e.g., Conn. Gen. Stat. Ann. §53(a)-67(b) (West 2004).

Kizer illustrates just one of the possible loopholes in such "liberalized" approaches to marital rape. What is the purpose of the requirement that the wife objectively manifest an unequivocal intent that the marriage is over? If you disagree with the reversal of the conviction, is it because you object to the standard or to the way it was applied in the case?

Since *Kizer*, Virginia law has been amended to eliminate the marital rape exemption. The current law, however, provides discretion to the court to suspend a sentence upon the defendant's completion of counseling or therapy "if, after consideration of the views of the complaining witness and such other evidence as may be relevant, the court finds such action will promote maintenance of the family unit and will be in the best interest of the complaining witness." Va. Code Ann. §18.2-61 (2005).

Comprehensive histories of the marital rape exemption can be found at Jill Elaine Hasday, Contest and Consent: A Legal History of Marital Rape, 88 Cal. L. Rev. 1373 (2000); Rebecca M. Ryan, The Sex Right: A Legal History of the Marital Rape Exemption, 20 Law & Soc. Inquiry 941 (1995).

6. Acquaintance Rape: The Social and Legal Meaning of Consent

Karen M. Kramer, Note, Rule by Myth: The Social and Legal Dynamics Governing Alcohol-Related Acquaintance Rapes
47 Stan. L. Rev. 115, 141-143 (1994)

[The following account is taken from a supplemental report prepared by Detective Tim Frecceri in the case of State v. Thomas, No. B9198729, Palo Alto Mun. Ct. Preliminary Examination, Nov. 13, 1991; see also Cal. Super. Ct. Sentencing Proceedings, Jan. 31, 1992, State v. Thomas, No. 151643.]

Anne had arrived as a freshman at [Stanford] University a few days before the incident. While meeting other residents in her dorm, Anne stopped in Thomas's room because she heard him playing music she liked. After visiting other people, she returned to his room later that evening and Thomas offered her a beer. Although Anne had only drunk alcohol once before, she accepted the beer. Other students who had been in Thomas's room when Anne arrived left for a different party. In the period of two hours, Thomas gave Anne half a beer and eight drinks of peppermint schnapps, all of which she drank. Anne asked Thomas, "if he was trying to get her drunk, but he told her he was not, and assured her that everything was O.K."

After consuming the alcohol, Anne "didn't feel too good, so she laid down ...on his bed." When asked if she had any intention of teasing or seducing Thomas, she emphatically said, "no." To the contrary, "because of alcohol's effect on her, she had to lay down and didn't do a lot of talking." After a while, she and Thomas began to kiss; soon he had completely undressed her.

In her conversation with the detective, Anne explained that she didn't feel any pressure from the suspect, and that he didn't make any verbal threats to her as he undressed her. However, she said, she felt a certain coercion from [Thomas's] presence, coupled with the fact that her condition and judgment had been impaired by alcohol. She mentioned [Thomas's] physical size as part of this coercion, estimating that he is at least 6'04" or more, and has a muscular build. She also mentioned the manner in which [Thomas] spoke to her as part of this coercion, recalling that from when he began providing her with alcohol to when they were having sexual intercourse, he kept saying to her in a calm, soothing voice, statements like, "It's O.K. You can do what you want, no one has to know, I won't hurt you," among other things. . . . When she became aware that things were going beyond holding and kissing, she indicated to [Thomas] that he should stop. . . . [Anne] told him, "I can't do this, I have a boyfriend." [Thomas] responded by saying, "It's O.K., he doesn't have to know." [Anne] then told [Thomas] that she was a virgin and that she was only seventeen years old. [Thomas] responded by saying something similar to, "It's O.K. No one has to know, your family doesn't have to find out, this can be between you and me. If you want it, it's O.K. I won't hurt you." [Anne] recalled that she protested more than once; she is certain that she told [Thomas] several times that she couldn't do it because she was a virgin and because she was only seventeen years old. [However, Thomas] proceeded to have sexual intercourse with [her]. . . . [Anne] felt sharp vaginal pain and said, "Ow, stop." [Thomas] stopped for a minute or so and continued to lay next to [Anne], kissing and touching her. As she became aware that he was preparing to have sexual intercourse again, she again told the suspect, "I can't, I'm a virgin." . . . Nevertheless, [Thomas] positioned himself above [Anne], as she lay on her back, and again inserted his erect penis into her vagina. Once again, after a few moments of [Thomas] pushing his penis into [Anne's] vagina, she felt a sharp vagina[l] pain, so she said, "Ow, stop." [Anne] thinks she might have told [Thomas], "that hurts," as well. . . . [Thomas] then asked her, "If you don't want it in you, will you at least kiss it?" [Anne] complied. . . . She could not recall her frame of mind at this time, though she did feel somewhat obligated to do this to the suspect. She indicated that because she was intoxicated and had impaired judgment, because [Thomas] was unable to continue intercourse with her, due to her vagina[l] pain, and because of his physical presence, she was aware of implied coercion.

After Thomas had an orgasm, Anne dressed and left the room, leaving behind several personal items, including her wallet, glasses, and shoes.

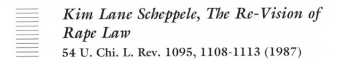

Kim Lane Scheppele, *The Re-Vision of Rape Law*

54 U. Chi. L. Rev. 1095, 1108-1113 (1987)

Social psychological research shows that men often tend to read sexual intent into women's behavior when that intent is not there, but women do not seem to do the same with men. Men see women's friendliness as evidence of seductiveness and promiscuity when the women themselves think they're merely being polite. When given the same cues in a story about a friendship or a dating context, men are more likely than women to see the relationship as potentially sexual and to expect more sexual activity to be forthcoming. Men seem to sexualize their descriptions of women and of social situations, seeing women as being sexually receptive and as leading men on even with the most meager evidence.

And these attitudes are not just harmless pictures of the world, but frames within which men act. A study of a small number of convicted rapists indicates that they were very confused by women's signals in social or sexual situations and that they did not perceive what, to the women, were clear rejections of sexual advances as negative cues. After examining a group of studies in which men have been asked to report their likelihood of raping, Malamuth reports that about 35 percent of men indicated some chance that they would rape a woman if they could be assured that they would not be caught and punished. And those men who reported a higher likelihood of raping women were more accepting of a series of rape myths, such as the views that women want to be raped, that they ask for rape by the way they dress and act, that they are indicating they want to have sex if they invite men to their apartments or engage in kissing or touching of any sort. Studies of the sexual activity of college students conducted periodically since the 1950s indicate that between one-fourth and one-fifth of college women reported that they have been forced into sexual activity and recent studies show that between one-quarter and one-third of college men admit to using coercive methods to force women into sex. Men who engage in such coercive sexual activity are more likely to see women as adversaries and to have a value system that legitimizes aggression, particularly toward women.

The social psychological evidence reveals that, where men and women have a chance to interact and exchange cues about their intentions, men are frequently likely to be wrong about what the woman thinks is going on. Where perceptions diverge in this way, a woman may experience a rape that a man thought was just the normal aggression needed to overcome what he saw was the "no" that meant "yes." The social psychological evidence gives us reason to believe that these perceptual fault lines are deep, enduring, and of enormous consequence in daily life.

What is the law to do? The situation that confronts courts is not just the difficult matter of separating truth from falsehood, determining whether someone in the rape case is lying or whether there is enough evidence to sustain a conviction. Both judges and juries must face the fact that there often will be conflicting true versions of the same event and that what is true for one of the parties may not be true for the other. The only evidence we have consists of perceptions, whether they are the reports of the victim and defendant (filtered through the perceptions of judge and jury) or the ways judges' and juries' first-hand perceptions lead them to interpret the physical evidence and testimony available. There is no such thing as a value-neutral fact. All facts are made meaningful and "real" against a backdrop of expectations and interpretive conventions. Given the current state of divergent perceptions of men and women, the more troubling question for law is not the question of truth and falsehood, but instead the question of which true version of a particular story should be adopted as the official version of what happened.

Here, the obvious solutions of farming factual problems out to juries or putting more women on the bench are unlikely to settle the question satisfactorily, but not for the obvious reason. One might think that with the evidence presented here, it will be impossible for juries composed of men and women ever to agree on anything or that female judges necessarily will reach different conclusions from male judges, destroying whatever coherence exists in law. But we know from experience, at least with juries, that this is not so. In addition, surveys of the general public indicate that men and women are not significantly different in many of their attitudes toward the appropriate legal standards for judging rape. When asked about whether the degree of a woman's resistance should be the major factor determining whether a rape has occurred, whether a delay in reporting means a rape probably didn't happen, and whether convicted rapists should get long sentences, men and women reveal almost identical attitudes. Other questions, such as whether it would do some women good to be raped or whether a woman provokes a rapist by her appearance, do provoke different responses from women and men, but it is significant that in most of the questions where the subject is the correct legal standard there is substantial agreement. It is not impossible or even difficult to get agreement about the relevant legal standards against which particular cases should be judged and there seems to be substantial agreement about the correct legal result in particular cases. The perceptual fault lines between women and men do not seem to carry over into the context of law.

That is exactly the problem. Women and men do have very different perceptions of experience, but in the context of law one set of perceptions is hidden. Michel Foucault speaks of subjugated knowledge to describe such buried views. What remains — the perceptions acknowledged, recognized, and seen in law — is the socially constructed "objective" point of view against which both men's and women's actions are judged by both men and women.

Notes

1. The Frequency of Acquaintance Rape. In 2004, about seven in ten rapes or sexual assaults against women were by a relative, a friend, or an acquaintance, Bureau of Justice Crime Statistics, found at http://www.ojp.usdoj.gov/bjs/cvict_c.htm, last revised April 2, 2006. The National Crime Victimization Survey — Violent Victimization of College Students (1995-2002) found that the average annual rate of rape/sexual assault was 3.8 per 1000 college students (6 of 1000 female students and 1.4 of 1000 male students). About four fifths of the rapes/sexual assaults involved acquaintances and almost 90 percent involved no weapon. See http://www.ojp.usdoj.gov/bjs/pub/pdf/vvcs02.pdf. Over a quarter of some 4,000 surveyed college-age women had experienced rape, attempted rape, unwanted sexual contact, or stalking during the seven-month period preceding the survey. Almost half the women who were identified by the researcher as having been raped did not consider it to be a rape. Over 40 percent did not report it because they did not think it was serious and were not sure a crime had been committed. Over 13 percent did not know how to make a report. Another 20 percent who were raped did not report it because they anticipated harsh or dismissive treatment by others in the justice system. Women had been taking drugs or alcohol in about 40 percent of the rape cases. Id.

2. Consent and Responsibility. Not all research finds as stark a difference in male and female perceptions as Scheppele describes. One study, for example, asked students to interpret various scenarios found that men and women had similar interpretations of conduct suggesting refusal and coercion. The main difference was that men were likely to interpret nonresistance as consent, while women viewed it as somewhere between consent and refusal. Jodee M. McCaw and Charlene Y. Senn, Perception of Cues in Conflictual Dating Situations, 4 Violence Against Women 609 (1998).

Surveys of college students find that neither men nor women have complete confidence that a woman's "no" means "no" in a sexual situation. Karen Kramer reports that in a survey by the Stanford University Rape Education Project, "[t]he 1,190 male and female students who responded overwhelmingly reported that when they say 'no' in a sexual situation, they mean it.

Yet both men and women rated a 'no' from others as less meaningful than their own. Particularly striking was the belief among women that they mean no when they say 'no,' but that other women often do not." Kramer, supra, 47 Stan. L. Rev. at 118. Indeed, some college women admit to engaging in "token resistance," defined as "saying 'no' when they mean 'yes.' In another study, about a third of the women admitted to having said "no" when they meant "yes," largely out of a desire to avoid appearing promiscuous. Charlene L. Muehlenhard & Lisa C. Hollabaugh, Do Women Sometimes Say No When They Mean Yes?: The Prevalence and Correlates of Women's Token Resistance to Sex, 54 J. Personality & Soc. Psychol. 872, 872 (1988). See also Andrew E. Taslitz, Patriarchal Stories I: Cultural Rape: Narratives in the Courtroom 5 S. Cal. Rev. L. & Women's Stud. 389, 468 (1996) (reporting 1991 study in which one-third of surveyed college students believed that women who say no often mean maybe or yes). Do you think studies today would yield similar findings?

John Leo reflects widespread concerns when he objects to the "no means no" formula in consent on the ground that "no can mean 'maybe', 'convince me', 'back off a while', or 'get lost'. The mating game does not proceed by words alone." John Leo, Two Steps Ahead of the Thought Police 247 (1994). In Leo's view, the "demonization" of men that is common in feminists' writing on date rape is profoundly unjust. If women cannot be clear about their preferences, men should not pay the price. Id.

Some feminists, too, object to the broadened definitions of rape on the grounds that they reinforce traditional views of women as dependent and passive.

> By protecting women against verbal coercion, [rape-crisis] feminists are promoting the view of women as weak-willed, alabaster bodies, whose virtue must be protected from the cunning encroachments of the outside world. The idea that women can't withstand verbal or emotional pressure infantilizes them. The suggestion lurking behind this definition of rape is that men are not just physically but intellectually and emotionally more powerful than women. Printing pamphlets about verbal coercion institutionalizes an unacceptable female position. . . .
>
> Allowing verbal coercion to constitute rape is a sign of tolerance toward the ultra feminine stance of passivity. The brand of "low self-esteem" [described by these feminists] should not be tolerated, it should be changed. Whether or not we feel pressured, regardless of our level of self-esteem, the responsibility for our actions is still our own.

Katherine Roiphe, The Morning After: Fear, Sex, and Feminism on College Campuses 66-68 (1993).

Another complaint is that overly aggressive definitions of rape give women unreasonable control to define, after the fact, what is or is not acceptable, consensual sex. See Neil Gilbert, The Phantom Epidemic of Sexual Assault, The Public Interest 54 (1991). Whose perspective should prevail about what constitutes non-consensual sex? What rape rules would put men and women on an "equal" footing? Given the enormous costs on both sides, who should bear the risk of misunderstood signals? How much responsibility should women have to prevent such misunderstandings?

In one study, 42 percent of the women who were raped said they had sex again with the men who assaulted them. What explains this?

> Because the rape victim doesn't believe that what has happened to her is rape, she sometimes decides to give her attacker another chance. After all, he's nice-looking, has a good job, or belongs to the right fraternity, and everyone else seems to think he's a great guy.
>
> What happens? Often, the same thing: He rapes her again. That's when most women bail out of continuing to see the men involved. In the Ms. survey, women who were raped had a mean average of 2.02 episodes.... Sometimes a woman sees the man who raped her again in order to turn the rape into an experience of sexual intercourse that happened in the context of an ongoing relationship and, therefore, to make it acceptable. For example, after being raped by a man she had dated for three weeks, Bonnie then had intercourse with him (she had been a virgin at the time of the rape). She explains her action as an attempt to "sort of legitimize what happened."

Robin Warshaw, I Never Called It Rape 63 (1988). If an adult woman doesn't realize she has been raped, to what extent is there a harm the law should recognize? As one commentator puts it,

> Never is the murky nature of consent more evident than when a woman indicates that she agreed to some sexual activity on the occasion of an alleged rape. How does "yes" on such occasions — to foreplay, to oral sex, or even initially to sexual intercourse — affect an objective determination of consent to an alleged act of rape? How does this "yes" affect the objective reasonableness of a man's belief in consent to an alleged act of rape — the crux of the mistake-of-fact defense?
>
> After having spent so much time establishing the basic premise that "no" means "no," what is now being witnessed is the beginning of a shift in attention to more complex issues of rape — issues surrounding the presence, rather than the absence, of consent.... A woman must be able to consent to sexual contact without creating the presumption that she has consented to sexual intercourse. Similarly, a woman must be able to consent to sexual intercourse while retaining the right to revoke that consent for any reason. Rape law, in acknowledging a woman's right to say "no," must also respect her right to say "yes."

Acquaintance Rape and Degrees of Consent: "No" Means "No," But What Does "Yes" Mean?, 117 Harv. L. Rev. 2341 (2004).

Stephen J. Schulhofer similarly argues that intercourse, without a clear declaration of consent by the woman, should be punishable as "nonviolent sexual misconduct." Schulhofer, Taking Sexual Autonomy Seriously, 11 Law & Phil. 35, 77 (1992). Would this new criminal prohibition solve or compound the problems that Gilbert, Roiphe, and Scheppele discuss? Would women feel under pressure to give explicit consent to sex that they did not desire? How should the law deal with misunderstandings, mistakes of fact, or the ambivalence noted in the surveys above?

Was the Stanford student in Kramer's article raped? What do you make of the "coercion" she says she experienced? Kramer reports that the police detective investigating the case recommended that the district attorney prosecute Thomas on several charges, including statutory rape and a violation of California Penal Code § 261.3, which defines an act as rape when "a person is prevented from resisting by any intoxicating or anesthetic substance, or any controlled substance, administered by or with the privity of the accused." The district attorney concluded that there was insufficient evidence to charge forcible rape and decided to charge Thomas only with statutory rape. Kramer, supra, 47 Stan. L. Rev. at 143. Would Thomas have been charged and convicted under Schulhofer's proposal? If so, what penalties would be appropriate?

Do the issues of consent and coercion in acquaintance rape mask other cultural dynamics? Kramer argues that cases of acquaintance rape are complicated by social expectations about alcohol: it is widely believed in our society that "alcohol increases sexual arousal, loosens women's sexual inhibitions, and increases men's feelings of power and dominance." Kramer, supra, at 120; see also Caroline Knapp, Drinking: A Love Story (1996) (arguing that for many women, drinking is a way to engage in sexual behavior without taking responsibility for it). Should alcohol abuse be a mitigating factor for the perpetrator (he wasn't fully in control of his actions) and/or an aggravating factor for the complainant (she shouldn't have put herself in that position)? In some cases women students who have reported rapes have been charged with violations of school drinking and drug policies. Is this sensible? See Michelle J. Anderson, The Legacy of the Prompt Complaint Requirement, Corroboration Requirement, and Cautionary Instructions on Campus Sexual Assault, 84 B.U. L. Rev. 945, 1010 (2004).

Could the explanation for date rape be "male self-deception"?

> The common thread in all the relevant types of self-deception is that semiconscious or unconscious processes, motivated by serving an overriding self-interest, suppress from the conscious mind certain thoughts and feelings that might work against that interest, thereby permitting us to act contrary to our sincerely professed conscious principles.

Andrew E. Taslitz, Willfully Blinded: On Date Rape and Self-Deception, 28 Harv. J.L. & Gender 381, 394 (2005). Taslitz explores a variety of forms of semiconscious and unconscious self-deceptions in date rape, ranging from willful ignorance, systematic ignoring, emotional detachment, and rationalization (semiconscious), to various heuristic devices and biases which are reinforced by (unconscious) self-interest. Id. at 413-420. Taslitz's work builds on the work of Deborah W. Denno. See Denno, Crime and Consciousness: Science and Involuntary Acts, 87 Minn. L. Rev. 269 (2002).

What are the implications of Taslitz's analysis? Does the semiconscious/unconscious nature of the act make it more, or less, blameworthy?

> Self-deception can be overcome by sustained efforts. . . . A "reasonableness" standard that is defined by jurors as a duty of reasonable inquiry to determine an intended sexual partner's desires is an effective way to combat male self-deception. . . . Because self-deception is this area is morally worse than the simple ignorance involved in ordinary criminal negligence, self-deceptive negligence as a proxy for actual

self-deception merits more severe punishment than is generally accorded to crimes of negligence.

Taslitz, supra, at 434, 446. If Taslitz's diagnosis is correct, is more punishment the right prescription?

The search for viable standards continues. Michelle Anderson proposes an alternative to both the "no means no" approach (which she calls the "No Model") and the "yes means yes" approach (which she calls the "Yes Model"). She calls the new model the "Negotiation Model."

> [T]he law should define "rape" as engaging in an act of sexual penetration with another person when the actor fails to negotiate the penetration with the partner before it occurs. The law should define "negotiation" as an open discussion in which partners come to a free and autonomous agreement about the act of penetration. Negotiations would have to be verbal unless the partners had established a context in which they could reliably read one another's nonverbal behavior to indicate free and autonomous agreement. Force, coercion, or misrepresentations by the actor would be evidence of a failure to negotiate.

Michelle J. Anderson, Negotiating Sex, 78 S. Cal. L. Rev. 1401, 1407 (2005). Is this a workable solution? Does it take account of the difficulties of multiple interpretations discussed by Schlepple and others?

The Canadian Criminal Code, Section 273(b) provides that the accused's belief that the complainant consented is not a defense if it involved "recklessness or willful blindness," or the accused did not take "reasonable steps . . . to ascertain that the complainant was consenting." Is this a satisfactory solution?

3. Institutional Responsibilities. What are the responsibilities of educational institutions to prevent and remedy sexual assault? In 1990, as part of an effort to increase accountability for student safety, Congress passed the Campus Security Act. It requires all colleges and universities receiving federal funds to report campus crime statistics, including all forcible or nonforcible sexual offenses. 20 U.S.C § 1092(f)(1)(F)(i)(II) (2004). Failure to report can result in fines up to $25,000 or other enforcement action by the U.S. Department of Education.

Despite this requirement, many sexual assaults are said to go unreported, partly because institutions are reluctant to disclose anything that would alarm prospective students and their families. Anderson, Legacy of the Prompt Complaint Requirement, supra, at 1010-1012. Schools have an additional reason to avoid reporting when an incident of sexual assault involves a star athlete whose eligibility might be compromised or when the defendant threatens to sue for violation of his own due process rights. Id. at 1013; Deborah Reed, Where's the Penalty Flag: A Call for the NCAA to Promulgate an Eligibility Rule Revokinga Male Student-Athlete's Eligibility to Participate in Intercollegiate Athletics for Committing Violent Acts Against Women, 21 Women's Rts. L. Rep. 41 (1999). A case in point involved Christy Brzonkala, the student whose claim under the Violence Against Women Act resulted in Supreme Court review. See United States v. Morrison, excerpted on p. 525 in Chapter 3. Virginia Tech failed to disclose her complaint of rape by two prominent football players and attempted to dissuade her from making any public disclosures. See also United States v. Miami University, 91 F. Supp. 2d 1132 (S.D. Ohio 2000) (student disciplinary records are "education records" protected by the Family Educational Rights and Privacy Act, and thus may not be released to media).

Should Congress amend the Campus Security Act to include a private right of action for monetary damages if a school negligently fails to report abuse? If the rapes occur in connection with official athletic events, such as recruiting parties, could the institution be liable for sex harassment under Title IX for creating a hostile environment? See Erik Brady, Colorado Scandal Fallout, USA Today, May 26, 2004, at C1, C2. Should rape complainants be protected from disciplinary charges based on their own misconduct involving drugs or alcohol? See Anderson, Legacy of the Prompt Complaint Requirement, supra, at 1019. What other prevention and remedial measures might be appropriate? Are women ever justified in resorting to "self-help?" Consider, for example, the widely criticized practice of students who, frustrated by administrative inaction, responded by naming their alleged assailants on bathroom walls. See William Celis, Date Rape and a List at Brown, N.Y. Times, Nov. 18, 1990, at 26. Are rape education programs the preferable alternative? Do your believe that your institution has effective rape education programs?

Putting Theory into Practice

5-2. Might sexual intercourse under the following circumstances be viewed as nonconsensual? Should it constitute a crime? Are there additional facts that you would need to answer that question?

(a) A welfare-dependent mother of three young children who can't make ends meet has unwanted sex with her landlord in order to prevent eviction.
(b) A struggling law student has unwanted sex with a fellow student so that she will have his assistance in publishing an acceptable law review note and in running for an officer position on the review.
(c) A woman has sex with her boyfriend to keep him from leaving her.

7. Prostitution: Consent Under Conditions of Constraint

Margaret Jane Radin, The Pragmatist and the Feminist
63 S. Cal. L. Rev. 1699, 1699-1701 (1990)

If the social regime permits buying and selling of sexuality . . . , thereby treating [it] as a fungible market commodit[y] given the capitalistic understandings of monetary exchange, there is a threat to the personhood of women, who are the "owners" of these "commodities." The threat to personhood from commodification arises because essential attributes are treated as severable fungible objects, and this denies the integrity and uniqueness of the self. But if the social regime prohibits this kind of commodification it denies women the choice to market their sexual . . . services, and given the current feminization of poverty and lack of avenues for free choice for women, this also poses a threat to the personhood of women. The threat from enforced noncommodification arises because narrowing women's choices is a threat to liberation, and because their choices to market sexual . . . services, even if nonideal, may represent the best alternatives available to those who would choose them.

Thus the double bind: both commodification and noncommodification may be harmful. Harmful, that is, under our current social conditions. Neither one need be harmful in an ideal world. The fact that money changes hands need not necessarily contaminate human interactions of sharing, nor must the fact that a social order makes nonmonetary sharing its norm necessarily deprive or subordinate anyone. That commodification now tends toward fungibility of women and noncommodification now tends toward their domination and continued subordination are artifacts of the current social hierarchy. In other words, the fact of oppression is what gives rise to the double bind.

Thus, it appears that the solution to the double bind is not to solve but to dissolve it: remove the oppressive circumstances. But in the meantime, if we are practically limited to those two choices, which are we to choose? I think that the answer must be pragmatic. We must look carefully at the nonideal circumstances in each case and decide which horn of the dilemma is better (or less bad), and we must keep re-deciding as time goes on.

To generalize a bit, it seems that there are two ways to think about justice. One is to think about justice in an ideal world, the best world that we can now conceive. The other is to think about nonideal justice; given where we now find ourselves, what is the better decision? In making this decision, we think about what actions can bring us closer to ideal justice. For example, if we allow commodification, we may push further away any ideal of a less commodified future. But if we enforce noncommodification, we may push further away any ideal of a less dominated future. In making our decisions of nonideal justice, we must also realize that these decisions will help to reconstitute our ideals. For example, if we commodify all attributes of personhood, the ideal of personhood we now know will evolve into another one that does not conceive fungibility as bad. The double bind, then, is a problem involving nonideal justice, and I think its only solution can be pragmatic. There is no general solution; there are only piecemeal, temporary solutions.

≡≡≡≡≡ *Holly B. Fechner, Three Stories of Prostitution*
≡≡≡≡≡ *in the West: Prostitutes' Groups, Law, and*
≡≡≡≡≡ *Feminist "Truth"*
4 Colum. J. Gender & L. 26, 33, 34, 37, 40-45, 47-50 (1994)

The Red Thread (De Rode Draad), founded in the Netherlands in 1985 by prostitutes and ex-prostitutes, organizes women in prostitution to assert their civil rights. It educates the public, provides legal and health education to prostitutes, acts as a community center for women in prostitution, and advocates for decriminalization of prostitution for all parties.

The English Collective of Prostitutes [ECP] argues that poverty is the cause of prostitution and that women need other economic options. It was founded in 1975 by prostitutes and ex-prostitutes. . . . The ECP concentrates on public education through numerous campaigns for decriminalization of prostitution and improved social services for women.

Women Hurt in Systems of Prostitution Engaged in Revolt [WHISPER], begun in 1985 by survivors of prostitution and women's advocates, views prostitution as violence against women and children that constitutes an integral part of a pervasive system of sex discrimination. WHISPER educates the public and women in prostitution and advocates for social services for women attempting to escape sexual exploitation. It supports strengthened legal penalties against pimps and tricks and expanded civil rights remedies for women and children. . . .

Women of color disproportionately comprise the clientele of each group, mirroring their overrepresentation in lesser paid forms of prostitution in each country. . . .

The Red Thread employs a liberal feminist analysis of prostitution. It is affiliated with the International Committee for Prostitutes' Rights (ICPR) and various sister organizations in the United States, particularly COYOTE in San Francisco. Four themes pervade the Red Thread's materials and campaigns: prostitution as work, improving prostitutes' working conditions, maximizing and validating women's choices, and eradicating the social stigma of prostitution through such methods as public education and decriminalization of prostitution. Consistent with fundamental principles of liberalism, the Red Thread's story describes prostitution in terms of rights, independence, autonomy and self-fulfillment. The Red Thread's vision of equality insists that prostitution is work and that prostitutes deserve the same rights as other workers. . . . The Red Thread attempts to convey a sense of dignity and sophistication about the "profession" of prostitution to the world and to women working in prostitution. . . .

The [ECP] represents prostitutes' interests based on social feminist theories. . . . It advocates economic justice for all women and abolition of all laws against prostitution. . . . Three themes pervade its materials and organizing efforts: poverty is the cause of prostitution, women (particularly women of color and lesbians) are often poor, and the government supports these conditions by its inaction. Poverty forces women into the sex industry, argues the ECP. "This is what prostitution is about — money and the lack of it," its leaders exclaim. "That lack, that poverty, is what is immoral and criminal." By positing poverty as the cause of prostitution, the ECP argues that women are not free to choose prostitution as a work option: "Sex is supposed to be personal, always a free choice, different from work. But it's not a free choice when we are dependent on men for money." Poverty turns sex into work out of necessity.

The ECP offers a feminist critique of capitalism that views sexuality as merely one more commodity to be sold on the market. "[S]exuality is a commodity all women are forced to 'sell' in one way or another. Our poverty as women leaves us little choice." . . . Prostitutes refuse to accept their poverty by making money from what most women give to men for free. . . .

In this way, prostitution is a form of protest. . . . In the view of the ECP, the government is implicated in the oppression of women by failing to provide adequate social services and failing to value women's contributions to society. The government, the ECP claims, is the biggest pimp of all by taking advantage of women's labor (in the form of emotional and sexual services to men and physical and emotional care of families) and failing to compensate them for it as other services are compensated within a social welfare state. . . .

Increased social welfare benefits, increased wages for work by women, and wages for housework so that no woman is forced into prostitution form the basis for the ECP's solution. . . .

The ECP favors decriminalization — the compete abolition of all laws against prostitution. It perceives prostitution laws as punishing women for their refusal to be poor. . . .

WHISPER . . . asserts that prostitution is a system of exploitation and violence that differentially harms women. Because women suffer the harms of prostitution, WHISPER proposes social and legal reforms to shift the burden to men who benefit from it, particularly pimps and tricks. It endorses the abolition of all laws that penalize women and children in prostitution and supports enhanced penalties for pimps and tricks, including new civil rights causes of action for women and children used in prostitution. It opposes what it views as the sexual liberals' promotion of, and apology for, the commercial exploitation of women. . . .

"The real harm of prostitution," its leaders claim, "is that it allows men to use women as sexual objects, [in] a rape-like mentality." Prostitution makes all women objects for men's use and abuse. . . . Prostitution allows men unconditional sexual access to women and children limited solely by their ability to pay for it.

The mere exchange of money, claims WHISPER, cannot change acts of violence against women into work. . . . WHISPER argues that addressing prostitution as if it were an occupation buys into the myth perpetuated by men that women are available to serve men's sexual desires.

> By documenting the violence and manipulation used to recruit and trap women in the sex industry, we've come to realize that prostitution is not a "career choice" or a "victimless crime," but rather prostitution creates an environment in which crimes against women and children are defined as a commercial enterprise.

Women cannot choose or consent to prostitution under current conditions of sex inequality, claims WHISPER. . . .

Notes

1. Historical Background. Prostitution has long been a focus of feminist concern:

> During most of its first century, the American women's movement viewed prostitution as the preeminent metaphor for sexual oppression. The "social evil," variously defined, became the symbol of female subordination.

In explaining that focus, historians have identified a complex set of forces. Until the antebellum period, prostitution remained an unobtrusive presence on the social and legal landscape. Early-nineteenth-century common law did not criminalize prostitution per se, although it could be prosecuted under other offenses such as lewdness, fornication, adultery, or disorderly conduct. The shortage of women and the tight-knit character of American communities worked against commercial vice. Much of the adult sexual exploitation that occurred involved slaves and domestic servants rather than an independent class of prostitutes. With industrialization, urbanization, and western migration, prostitution became more visible. As single men moved to the frontier, they decreased the supply of eligible bachelors in established communities and increased the demand for sexual outlets in unsettled regions. Markets also emerged near military camps and seaports. Women, particularly immigrants and women of color, who could find neither husbands nor adequate employment, were increasingly likely to conclude that the "wages of sin" were better than any available alternative. The relative anonymity of urban areas, the growing secularization of American society, and the tacit tolerance of law-enforcement officials accelerated such trends. Despite occasional "whorehouse riots," in which an aroused citizenry torched local brothels, the tendency was toward peaceful coexistence as long as prostitutes kept within accepted geographic and social bounds.

Deborah L. Rhode, Justice and Gender 253 (1989).

The first major challenges to prostitution, variously characterized as "moral reform" and "social purity" campaigns, began in the 1830s and resurfaced in the late nineteenth and early twentieth centuries. At the outset, the leaders of these initiatives were mainly male clergy and philanthropists, but women's organizations soon joined the crusade. Their goals were to reform prostitutes and to discourage men from employing or recruiting them. Id. at 254-255; Elizabeth Pleck, Feminist Responses to "Crimes Against Women," 1868-1896, 8 Signs 451 (1983). These efforts led to expanded criminal prohibitions and enforcement strategies.

The criminalization of prostitution has been justified on multiple grounds: promoting conventional morality, protecting public health, avoiding public nuisance, and preventing sexual exploitation and abuse. Class, race, and ethnic prejudice also underpinned many of the early "antivice" campaigns. Many moral reformers were particularly concerned by the vision of husbands of white women consorting with lower-class immigrants and women of color. Rhode, Justice and Gender, supra, at 256; see also Mark Thomas Connelly, The Response to Prostitution in the Progressive Era 50-69, 97 (1980).

In 1908, the U.S. Supreme Court articulated the central moral argument for criminal sanctions:

> The lives and example of such persons are in hostility to "the idea of the family, as consisting in the springing from the union for life of one man and one woman in the holy estate of matrimony; the sure foundation of all that is stable and noble in our civilization, the best guaranty of that reverent morality which is the source of all beneficent progress in social and political improvement."

United States v. Bitty, 208 U.S. 393, 401 (1908) (quoting Murphy v. Ramsey, 114 U.S. 15, 45 (1885)). Should this view inform current policy?

2. The Legal Status of Prostitution. The legal status of prostitution varies widely. Most countries either prohibit or regulate the sale of sex, but the scope of permissible behavior, the severity of penalties, and the practices of enforcement agencies differ considerably. In this nation, every state but Nevada prohibits engaging in sexual intercourse for money or offering to do so. Every state but Nevada also makes it a crime knowingly to encourage or compel a person to sell sex for money (pandering) or to receive "something of value" knowing that it was earned through an act of prostitution (pimping). Sylvia Law, Commercial Sex: Beyond Decriminalization, 73 S. Cal. L. Rev. 523, 530 (2000). Most jurisdictions classify first-time offenses as misdemeanors, but typically punish repeat behavior as a felony. Joann Miller, Prostitution in Contemporary American Society, in Sexual Coercion: A Sourcebook on Its Nature, Causes and Prevention 45, 53 (Elizabeth Grauerholz & Mary Koralewski eds., 1991). About half of all states have a "patron clause," which subjects customers to the same penalty as prostitutes. Id. at 53, 57 n.9. Other jurisdictions classify patronizing a prostitute as a less serious offense.

Nevada permits prostitution in counties with populations under 200,000 persons, subject to highly restrictive licensing conditions. Prostitutes must be registered and fingerprinted by the police and must work in brothels where they typically have no control over their hours or customers. County police have broad discretion to regulate the conditions under which commercial sex is permissible. For example, prostitutes generally may not have their children live in the same community in which they work, drive a car in city limits, or be on the streets after 5 p.m. Law, supra, at 560. In the areas surrounding brothels, this system has effectively reduced street solicitation and incidental crime, and has largely eliminated the risks of sexually transmitted diseases. However, it has failed to curtail illegal prostitution elsewhere in the state. About a thousand women work in 33 licensed brothels and account for only a small percentage of those estimated to be working in Nevada. Id.

Most European countries, following the United Nations recommendations, have repealed prohibitions on engaging in prostitution but have retained laws against soliciting, pimping, pandering, running a disorderly house, or transporting a woman across national boundaries for purposes of prostitution. See Nanette J. Davis, Prostitution: An International Handbook on Trends, Problems, and Policies (1993). Other restrictions range from fairly laissez-faire approaches in countries like Denmark and the Netherlands, to tightly controlled zoning systems for licensed brothels in many German cities. See Law, supra, at 552-554; see also Priscilla Alexander, Prostitution: A Difficult Issue for Feminists, in Sex Work: Writings by Women in the Sex Industry 184 (Frédérique Delacoste & Priscilla Alexander eds., 2d ed. 1987). Even where commercial sex is legal and taxable, workers often lack basic rights and benefits, such as pensions, health insurance, and unemployment benefits. "Jasmin," Prostitution Is Work, 37 Soc. Text 33 (1993). The same is true in Nevada, where prostitutes are classified as independent contractors rather than employees. Law, supra, at 543.

In other countries, particularly those in Asia, South America, and the Mideast, prostitution remains a criminal offense. The prohibitions in some tradition-oriented societies are quite severe. In other nations, a de facto licensing system has evolved despite formal prohibitions. Through de facto or de jure licensing structures, a growing number of Asian and European countries are also developing sex tourism industries. See notes 5 and 6, infra, pp. 835–843.

Tolerance for prostitution has been especially common in areas around military installations and other predominantly male work sites. In some countries, the United States armed forces traditionally worked with local authorities to promote "safe" but accessible sex for overseas servicemen. United States bases have attracted large concentrations of "bar girls" or "hospitality women," sometimes 10,000 to 20,000 per base. Women not complying with registration requirements (including periodic medical exams) were subject to arrest, and employers with a specified percentage of unregistered workers could be declared off-limits to servicemen. Cynthia Enloe, The Morning After 118-120, 142-160 (1993); Saundra Pollock Sturdevant & Brenda Stoltzfus, Olongopo: The Bar System, in Let the Good Times Roll: Prostitution and the United States Military in Asia 45 (Saundra Pollock Sturdevant & Brenda Stoltzfus eds., 1992); Tong du Chun: The Bar System, in Let the Good Times Roll, supra, at 176. In response to growing concerns about the global sex trade, the Department of Defense proposed an addition to its Manual for Courts Martial that would make patronizing a prostitute a chargeable offense under the Uniform Code of Military Justice, effective in late 2005. U.S. Dep't of State, Trafficking in Persons Report 11 (June 2005).

In this country, traditionally the common law defined prostitution in sex specific terms, as the act of a "female . . . offering her body to an indiscriminate intercourse with men for money or the equivalent." Black's Law Dictionary 1386 (4th ed. 1968). Legal challenges led to conflicting results. See, e.g., Plas v. State, 598 P.2d 966 (Alaska 1979) (striking down sex-specific prostitution statute on equal protection grounds); Flute v. State, 282 S.E.2d 112, 113 (Ga. 1981) (upholding pandering law applicable only to male pandering of females).

Although most statutes are now gender-neutral in form, law enforcement officials rarely prosecute customers or pimps. For example, over a two-year period in New York, which has a statute punishing both parties who engage in commercial sex, customers accounted for only about one percent of all arrests. The percentage of pimps among those arrested was even lower. Miller, supra at 52. A Boston survey reveals similar patterns. See Minouche Kandel, Whores in Court: Judicial Processing of Prostitutes in the Boston Municipal Court in 1990, 4 Yale J.L. & Feminism 333 (1992) (finding 263 arrests of female prostitutes and 8 of male pimps; half of the 8 were dismissed).

Efforts to challenge such discriminatory enforcement patterns have been largely unsuccessful. In some jurisdictions, the reasoning has been that no impermissible discrimination occurs as long as male and female prostitutes are treated alike. People v. Superior Court of Alameda County, 562 P.2d 1315, 1321 (Cal. 1977). In other jurisdictions, the rationale has been that sellers of sex constitute a "greater danger to society" than buyers. State v. Tookes, 699 P.2d 983, 988 (Haw. 1985); People v. Nelson, 427 N.Y.S.2d 194, 197 (N.Y. City Ct. 1980) In addition, courts have often concluded that "concentrating . . . enforcement effort on the 'profiteer,' rather than the customer, of commercial vice" is a way for a police department "to efficiently utilize its limited resources...." People v. Superior Court of Alameda County, supra, 562 P.2d at 1320, 1321.

In Commonwealth v. An Unnamed Defendant, 492 N.E.2d 1184 (Mass. App. Ct. 1986), a Massachusetts appellate court held that a local police department policy to arrest female but not male streetwalkers or male customers failed to satisfy strict scrutiny under the state's Equal Rights Amendment. One stated reason for the policy was that the citizens complained only about the women, and they were more recognizable to the officers. Is this a more plausible explanation for selective enforcement policies? If patrons faced a substantial risk of arrest, could the resulting stigma have a significant deterrent effect on the trade? Consider the experience of the Oakland Police Department during the mid-1970s, when it was briefly compelled by court order to employ female decoys and arrest male customers. This practice reportedly resulted in a "devastating" reduction in prostitution-related offenses. People v. Superior Court of Alameda County, supra, 562 P.2d at 1325 (Tobriner, J., dissenting). See also Julie Lefler, Shining the Spotlight on Johns: Moving Toward Equal Treatment of Male Customers and Female Prostitutes, 10 Hastings L.J. 11 (1999).

Current policies are costly. The largest cities spend over $100 million yearly in prostitution arrests. Ronald Weitzer, Prostitution Control in America: Rethinking Public Policy, 32 Crime, L. & Soc. Change 83 (1999). It costs over $2,000 to prosecute a single woman offender, who typically returns almost immediately to the streets. San Francisco Task Force on Prostitution, Final Report Submitted to the Board of Supervisors of the City and County of San Francisco (1996). In one study, almost two thirds of incarcerated prostitutes reported at least five arrests. Maureen A. Norton-Hawk, The Counterproductivity of Incarcerating Female Street Prostitutes, 22 Deviant Behav. 403, 405 (2001). Although some evidence suggests that most streetwalkers would like to quit, a variety of forces make exit difficult: lack of education and employment skills, the stigma of an arrest record, substance abuse and mental health problems, and control by pimps. C. Aaron McNeece & Elizabeth Mayfield Arnold, Program Closure: The Impact on Participants in a Program for Female Prostitutes, 12 Res. Soc. Work Prac. 159, 168 (2002) (reporting that 90 percent of interviewees expressed desire to leave); Robert Victor Wolf, New Strategies for an Old Profession: A Court and a Community Combat a Streetwalking Epidemic, 22 Just. Sys. J. 347, 353 (2001) (describing barriers to exit). Jail time increases the intensity and duration of women's involvement in streetwalking. Norton-Hawk, supra, at 404-408.

3. Alternative Regulatory Structures. Few, if any, feminists support America's current approach to prostitution. One criticism is that the system stigmatizes and degrades certain women, predominantly poor women and women of color, for doing overtly what many women have always done covertly: trade sex for material advantages. Women of color account for an estimated 40 percent of street prostitutes in the United States, 50 percent of those who are arrested, and 85 percent of those who receive jail sentences. Women of color also pay higher fines and serve longer jail times than their white counterparts. Ann M. Lucas,

Class, Gender and Deviancy: The Criminalization of Prostitution, 10 Berkeley Women's L.J. 47, 49 (1995); Bednita Nelson, Prostitution: Where Racism and Sexism Intersect, 1 Mich. J. Gender & L. 81, 85 (1993).

Criminalizing commercial sex increases women's vulnerability to physical abuse and economic coercion. Studies of streetwalkers typically find that about two-thirds to four-fifths are subject to physical assault and to extremely high rates of rape and murder. See sources cited in Alexander, supra, at 184; Law, supra, at 533; MacKinnon, Sex Equality, supra, at 1410-1419. Women are reluctant to report activities that could lead to prosecution, and police systematically fail to pursue complaints by sex workers. Law, supra, at 533. Arrest records heighten women's difficulties in moving to alternative work and often force them to rely on pimps and middlemen to screen customers or provide money for bail and fines. Deborah L. Rhode, Justice and Gender 260-261 (1997).

The most commonly proposed alternatives to the current system, described in the Fechner reading, are:

- full decriminalization, i.e., removal of penalties from all consensual sexual activities and related commercial practices;
- partial decriminalization, i.e., removal of penalties from the sale of sexual services but not from other related activities such as purchasing, pimping, pandering, soliciting, or advertising; and
- regulation, i.e., removal of penalties from activities that meet state-imposed requirements, such as zoning restrictions, licensing regulations, and health exams.

For more about the decriminalization approach and measures to allow women to exert greater control over the conditions of work, see Jody Freeman, The Feminist Debate over Prostitution Reform: Prostitutes' Rights Groups, Radical Feminists, and the (Im)possibility of Consent, 5 Berkeley Women's L.J. 75, 90 (1989-1990). For further elaboration of a criminalization approach that focuses on greater use of criminal sanctions against "pimps" and "johns," including publishing of names and pictures of prostitutes' patrons in local newspapers, see Courtney Guyton Persons, Sex in the Sunlight: The Effectiveness, Efficiency, Constitutionality, and Advisability of Publishing Names and Pictures of Prostitutes' Patrons, 49 Vand. L. Rev. 1525 (1996) (concluding that the practice is not likely to be effective and, when occurring before conviction, violates defendants' fair trial rights).

Minnesota and Florida create civil remedies, including compensatory and punitive damages and attorney's fees, for women and girls compelled to participate in prostitution through such means as threats, extortion, promise of legal benefit or rewards such as an acting or modeling contract, promise of marriage, threat of legal interference with the woman's relationship with her children, and exploitation of a developmental disability or substance dependency or of a woman's need for food, shelter, safety, or affection. Fla. Stat. Ann. §796.09 (West 2005); Minn. Stat. Ann. §611A.81 (West 2005). For discussion of the Florida statute by one of its drafters, see Margaret A. Baldwin, Strategies of Connection: Prostitution and Feminist Politics, 1 Mich. J. Gender & L. 65

(1993). One action under the statute was brought against a car salesman and his dealership when the salesman allegedly coerced the plaintiff, whose credit was said not to be good enough to get a car loan, into having sex as a condition of obtaining a car. Reported decisions under such statutes are extremely rare. MacKinnon, Sex Equality, supra, 1497 (noting only one decision, but indicating that several actions had been settled). Would you expect sex workers' organizations to support civil liability actions?

Most feminists and sex workers agree on two points: criminal penalties for workers are not appropriate, and more strategies are necessary to ensure their safety. From this perspective, the best way for society to minimize the harms associated with prostitution is to maximize women's other employment choices, increase their access to social services, and minimize the safety risks and social stigma associated with consensual commercial sex. See Carlin Meyer, Decriminalizing Prostitution: Liberation or Dehumanization?, 1 Cardozo Women's L.J. 105, 108 (1993); see also Catharine A. MacKinnon, Prostitution and Civil Rights, 1 Mich. J. Gender & L. 13, 20 (1996) (claiming that criminal laws against prostitution are a form of sex discrimination, in that they represent "legal victimization piled on top of social victimization," which legitimates women's subordination).

Most feminists and sex workers are also united in opposing regulation as an alternative to decriminalization. Workers generally object to the highly restrictive conditions imposed by licensing structures and to the large share of profits taken by brothel owners (typically 50 percent). Law, supra, at 561; Rebecca Mead, American Pimp, New Yorker, Apr. 23 & 30, 2001, at 74, 78. Only a small percentage of Nevada's prostitutes work in licensed brothels despite the relatively substantial incomes available. Women in small establishments can net up to $1,500 a week after room and board, while women in large establishments make substantially more. As independent contractors, prostitutes generally set their own prices for different services, and customers at establishments like the Moonlight Bunnyranch pay from $100 to several thousand dollars for their experience. Mead, supra, at 82. Is the profitability of such forms of prostitution part of the problem, or a solution? To what extent would legalization of prostitution represent state collaboration in the exploitation and commodification of female sexuality?

The only recent law reform effort in this area, a ballot initiative in Berkeley, California, would have made prostitution the city's lowest law enforcement priority, along with marijuana possession, and would have redirected much of the municipal enforcement budget to services for sex workers. Most city leaders opposed the measure, in part because it would have insulated pimps, along with prostitutes, from prosecution. It was defeated by a two-to-one margin. See Chip Johnson, A Look Back at the Year's Newstories, San Francisco Chron., Dec. 31, 2004, at B1.

More politically acceptable are diversion programs pioneered by a number of problem-solving courts, such as Hartford Connecticut's Community Court and New York City's Midtown Community Court. These programs allow defendants who plead guilty to prostitution to avoid incarceration if they participate in individualized treatment plans. Such plans include social services designed to address underlying problems, such as substance abuse or lack of education and employment skills. These programs have substantially reduced recidivism rates, as have some similar efforts targeted at juvenile offenders. See Wolf, supra, at 352-353; Bernice Yeung, Throw Away Girls, Cal. Law., Nov. 2003, at 59. Why do you think more communities have not adopted such approaches? What are the barriers to legislative and legal reform?

4. Prostitution and the Autonomy of Women. At issue in debates over prostitution are fundamental issues about the meaning of consent and the nature of sexual expression under circumstances of true equality. Among the most divisive issues are whether women who engage in commercial sex have made truly free choices to do so and whether sex work is work like any other and preferable along some dimensions. What complicates the debate are the diversity of experiences among women engaged in commercial sex and the inadequate or conflicting data concerning their experiences.

The objective conditions and subjective perceptions of prostitutes vary considerably. As one worker put it, "[s]ome [women] feel they are victims. Some *are* victims. And then there are others who have made that choice and celebrate that choice." Sex Trade Workers and Feminists: Myths and Illusions, in Good Girls/ Bad Girls: Feminists and Sex Trade Workers Face to Face 202 (Laurie Bell ed., 1987). As another commentator notes:

> Some prostitutes may find the work emotionally taxing or disagreeable. They may have violent confrontations with their clients or pimps. However, some of these lamentable conditions are also shared by women who are in violent noncommercial relationships. Many women are forced to work in sweatshops...are sexually exploited by their bosses or are in abusive marriages. There is potential for coercion in any relationship. Nevertheless, it would be imprudent to suggest that such unpleasantness be resolved by prohibiting these relationships altogether.

Norma Jean Almodovar, For Their Own Good: The Results of the Prostitution Laws as Enforced by Cops, Politicians and Judges, 10 Hastings Women's L.J. 119, 123 (1999); see also Yeung, supra, at 24 (describing abusive situations of underage streetwalkers both before and during prostitution).

Some prostitutes claim that the first time they felt powerful was the first time they turned a trick. Alexander, supra, at 188; Gail McPherson, The Whore Stigma: Female Disorder and Male UnWorthiness, 37 Soc. Text 39, 54 (1993). According to one worker:

> [B]eing able to earn [a substantial income] is a blessing...I have no regret for my experiences. Prostitution brought me social life, money, sex and entertainment....I was alone in college, on welfare with a son. He wanted football clothes. He got them.

Anonymous, Prostitution: A Narrative by a Former "Call Girl," 1 Mich. J. Gender & L. 105 (1993). One prostitute who had previously worked in a male-dominated occupation servicing telephone lines recalled that "I came home exhausted every day plus I was harassed by guys on the job. Working as a prostitute in a massage parlor is far less draining and I still get that kick of being an assertive woman." McPherson, supra, at 57.

For at least some women, generally independent call girls, sex work can carry substantial economic rewards with relatively little risk of prosecution or disease. The prominent Hollywood Madame, Heidi Fleiss, "wouldn't recommend prostitution as a career because it doesn't have great long-term prospects." But in the short term, the money can help someone finish school, start a business, or do something else "positive with her life." Heidi Fleiss, as told to Nadya Labi, In Defense of Prostitution, Legal Affairs, Sept./Oct. 2003, available at http://www.legalaffairs.org/issues/September-October-2003/feature_fleiss_sepoct03.msp.

One Stanford law school graduate, Cristina Schultz, appears to have pursued such a strategy by working as an escort during her legal education. Her Internet site featured topless photos and listed rates ranging from $1250 for two hours to $3000 for six hours. According to one posting on the site, "I have paid off 100 percent of my student loans and I have tried to send a positive message to SF escorts re: assumptions about the nature and social status of women in the business." Dan Reed, Stanford Law Grad, U.S. Clash over Cache of Cash, San Jose Mercury News, Oct. 6, 2004, at B1. In another posting, Schultz states, "During my education, I was continually taught to question paradigms and assumptions. I never understood, however, why this questioning had to stop when it bumped up against accepted social and sexual norms. I never understood why you had to be a down-to-earth educated chaste career-girl or a sexual, sensual adventuress or temptress." John Roemer, Degree of Flexibility: Stanford Law Grad Turned Escort Says Her Legal Training Taught Her to Question Assumptions, San Francisco Daily J., Oct. 25, 2004, at A1. Federal prosecutors, however, never understood how Schultz could have sustained her life style legally. Although she declared only $28,000 in income over a five-year period, her living expenses during this time totaled over $3000 a month and she paid off loans of over $300,000. On a confidential escort rating site, some 82 men claimed to have had sex with her. Although law enforcement officials did not press charges, they seized some $61,000 in assets under civil forfeiture laws. Id.; She Works Hard for the Money, Playboy, Feb. 1, 2005, at 49. Was this an appropriate result? If Schultz applies to the bar, should she be found morally fit to practice law?

Even for well-compensated sex workers, however, many feminists question whether prostitution represents the kind of free, informed, individual choice that is worthy of respect. Consider the position as set forth by Dorchen Leidholdt, Associate Director of the Coalition Against Traffic in Women, a nongovernmental organization with consultative status to the United Nations Economic and Social Council:

> Prostitution is not about women making money. It is about other people — usually men — making money off women's bodies. Pimps, brothel owners, club owners, hotel chains, travel agencies, pornographers, organized crime syndicates, and governments are the real economic beneficiaries of the sex trade in women. . . .

Prostitution is not about individuals. It is an institution of male dominance, and it is also a global industry in which the prostituting of women is constantly being packaged in new ways, using new forms of technology, tapping new markets: sex-tourism, mail-order bride selling, sex entertainment, sex immigration, dial-a-porn, computer pornography.

Just as prostitution isn't about individuals, it isn't about choice. Instead, prostitution is about the absence of meaningful choices; about having alternative routes to survival cut off or being in a situation where you don't have options to begin with.... [T]he majority of women in prostitution in the country—most studies estimate 60-70 percent—have histories of sexual abuse in childhood.... Add to this the reality that the population targeted by pimps and traffickers is teenagers. It becomes clear that the majority of prostitutes are socialized into "sex work" in childhood and adolescence when consent is meaningless and choice an illusion.

Then there are the related factors of poverty, lack of education, and homelessness. Women in prostitution, with few exceptions, are not people who debated between the advantages of going to law school or working at the X-tasy Massage Parlor. The average education level of a sample of Portland, Oregon [prostitutes] was tenth grade....

Choice vanishes when, in order to endure the prostitution, women become addicted to alcohol or drugs, or become prostitutes to support their addiction. In the Portland, Oregon, study, 85% of the women were drug or alcohol abusers.

Nor is choice present when a woman is so traumatized by having stranger after stranger use her body as a seminal spittoon that she accepts prostitution as her destiny.

Just as prostitution is not about choice, it's not about work. Or if it is, it is work in the same way that slavery or bonded labor is work—work that violates human dignity and every other human right. What other kind of work has as job training years of being sexually abused in childhood? What other job has as its working conditions: rape...beatings...and premature death and murder....

Dorchen Liedholdt, Prostitution: A Violation of Women's Human Rights, 1 Cardozo Women's L.J. 133, 136-141 (1993). Catharine MacKinnon adds:

Women's precluded options in societies that discriminate on the basis of sex, including in employment, are fundamental to the prostitution context. If prostitution is a free choice, why are the women with the fewest choices the ones most often found doing it?

Catharine MacKinnon, Prostitution and Civil Rights, 1 Mich. J. Gender & L. 13, 27-28 (1996).

According to some sociologists, when prostitutes give favorable accounts of their experience, they are engaging in "neutralizing techniques":

Sociologists use the term to describe the way in which socially despised and marginalized groups survive their marginal condition. Such techniques may be employed because the only alternative available may be the painful one of self-contempt. The idea that prostitution is freely chosen is such a technique.

Sheila Jeffreys, The Idea of Prostitution 137 (1997); see also Beverly Balos, The Wrong Way to Equality: Privileging Consent in the Trafficking of Women for Sexual Exploitation, 27 Harv. Women's L.J. 137 (2004).

In response to such claims, defenders of sex work often note that survey research on abuse is usually based on street workers and prostitutes serving prison sentences, which overrepresent particularly vulnerable groups such as teenagers and drug users. According to these commentators, generalizations based on such groups are a "gross distortion." McPherson, supra, at 53. Many sex workers are also offended by the dismissal of their own perceptions as false consciousness. As members of one Canadian organization of sex workers put it:

> When you are a prostitute that says, "Well, I don't agree with the way you're inter-preting my life, I don't feel oppressed or I don't feel exploited in the way that you're saying," they say things like "she's too blinded to her own oppression to see her experience for what it really is, and it really is the patriarchy." They find it necessary to interpret prostitutes' experience of their lives and then feed it back to the pros-titutes to tell them what's really happening, whereas they wouldn't dare be so con-descending or patronizing with any other group of women.

Realistic Feminists: An Interview with Valerie Scott, Peggy Miller, and Ryan Hotchkiss of the Canadian Organization for the Rights of Prostitutes, in Good Girls/Bad Girls, supra, at 204, 213.

In a world of true equality, would commercial sex be inherently exploitative? Are the degrading aspects of current prostitution largely attributable to its social and legal status rather than to its intrinsic nature? Consider these views:

> Anonymous sex has validity in its own right. Since when is sex only acceptable and valid and good sex if it's linked to love or linked to someone that they have invested in, in terms of a relationship? There are a lot of people who feel unwilling or reluctant or unable to express a lot of pockets of their sexuality and their sexual needs unless it is with someone they don't have to look at afterwards. There's an excitement that goes with a new person, a novelty. Needing novelty is perfectly acceptable around other needs that we have. . . . Humanity benefits from giving legitimacy to all kinds of needs as long as they're consensual. . . . [Prostitutes'] ideal situation is like anybody else's — that we have control over our work environment. . . .

Realistic Feminists, in Good Girls/Bad Girls, supra, at 206, 209.

> We need to reflect on whether romantic love is really the only valid foundation for sexual interaction; to question the view that "legitimate" sexual intimacy must be tied to spiritual connection. All too many of us seem to have swallowed wholesale this ideology: we abhor . . . "impersonal" sex; we yearn for intimate "pillow talk"; we disdain the prostitute for engaging in sex without "real connection." (Which of us hasn't engaged in sex without connection? It wasn't prostitutes who told their daughters to "close your eyes and think . . . [of the Empire]"). . . .
>
> [Andrea] Dworkin suggests that men's incapacity to see sex partners as "whole" is necessarily — in her words — a "paralyzation of individuality." Must we all learn to see the subjects of our sexual desire as whole, equal, non-partial, and unsegmented? Even were it desirable, *can* we eliminate inequality in the realm of the intimate? Can we do so before we eliminate pervasive economic and social inequality? And if not, what do we do in the meantime?

Carlin Meyer, Decriminalizing Prostitution: Liberation or Dehumanization?, 1 Cardozo Women's L.J. 105, 117 (1993).

5. Prostitution, Capitalism, and the International Traffic in Women. After drugs and guns, sex trafficking is the most profitable activity of organized crime with annual profits approaching $7 billion. Abigail Schwarz, Sex Trafficking in Cambodia, 17 Colum. J. Asian L. 371, 374 (2004). Most governmental and non governmental organizations estimate that between one and four million people are trafficked globally. Between 600,000 and 800,000 are transported across national borders. Four-fifths are women and children. An estimated 50,000 are brought into the United States each year, largely from Southeast Asia, Eastern Europe, Latin America, and the newly independent states of the former Soviet Union, including Russia. Michelle R. Adelman, International Sex Trafficking: Dismantling the Demand, 13 S. Cal. Rev. L & Women's Stud. 387, 388 (2004); see also U.S. Dep't of State, Trafficking in Persons Report 6 (June 2005); Mohamed Y. Mattar, Trafficking in Persons: An Annotated Legal Bibliography, 96 Law Libr. J. 669 (2004); Symposium on Sexual Slavery, 13 Hastings Women L.J. 1 (2002).

Trafficking encompasses a range of crimes, including sex tourism, debt bondage, involuntary servitude, forced prostitution, and rape. The 2000 United Nations Convention Against Transnational Organized Crime; Protocol to Prevent, Suppress, and Punish Trafficking in Persons, Especially Women and Children, includes as trafficking "the recruitment, transportation, transfer, harboring or receipt of persons, by means of the threat or use of force or other forms of coercion, of abduction, of fraud, of deception, of the abuse of power or of a position of vulnerability or of the giving or receiving of payments or benefits to achieve the consent of a person having control over another person, for the purposes of exploitation." Exploitation includes "the prostitution of others or other forms of sexual exploitation, forced labor or services, slavery, or practices similar to slavery, servitude, or the removal of organs." See also The United Nations Convention for the Suppression of the Traffic in Persons and of the Exploitation of the Prostitution of Others (1949). The United States has adopted a similar definition in the Victims of Trafficking and Violence Protection Act of 2000, which prohibits:

> (A) sex trafficking in which a commercial sex is induced by force, fraud, or coercion, or in which the person induced to perform such an act has not attained 18 years of age; or
>
> (B) the recruitment, harboring, transportation, provision, or obtaining a person for labor or services, through the use of force, fraud, or coercion for the purpose of subjection to involuntary servitude, peonage, debt bondage, or slavery."

Pub. L. No. 106-386, 114 Stat. 1464, § 103(8) (2000) (codified as amended at 22 U.S.C. § 7102 (2005)). The 2003 reauthorization of this statute established a private right of action for persons who are trafficked to the United States. The civil remedies provision is analyzed in Kathleen Kim & Kusia Hreshchyshyn,

Human Trafficking Private Right of Action: Civil Rights for Trafficked Persons in the United States, 16 Hastings Women's L.J. 1 (2004).

Much of the current trafficking industry involves deception, kidnapping, or outright purchase of women and girls for work in the sex trade. Some women or their families are duped by advertisements or agents promising jobs such as waitresses, au pairs, sales clerks, actresses, and exotic dancers. Other women voluntarily accompany a new husband or a boyfriend to another country where they are sold into bondage. U.S. Dep't of State, Trafficking in Persons Report, supra, at 6-11; see also Alexandra V. Orlova, Trafficking of Women and Children for Exploitation in the Commerical Sex Trade: The Case of the Russian Federation, 6 Geo. J. Gender & Law 157 (2005); Jo Doezema & Kamala Kempadoo, Global Sex Workers: Rights, Resistance and Redefinition 69 (1998); Peter Landsman, The Girls Next Door, N.Y. Times, Jan. 25, 2004, at 32 (Magazine). Women and children are also drugged or kidnapped and smuggled across state lines. Many are then resold to brothels and kept against their will by a variety of methods. Typically, they are taken to a city or foreign country where they lack marketable skills and familiarity with the language and legal culture. Their passports and other forms of identification are removed, and they are threatened with assault, murder, or prosecution by local authorities if they try to escape. Some are told that if they do manage to leave, their family members will suffer retaliation. Once women have entered the sex trade, the social stigma they encounter further restricts their employment and marriage options; many face ostracism if they return to their original communities. See U.S. Dep't of State, Trafficking in Persons Report, supra, at 6-11; see also Louise Brown, Sex Slaves: The Trafficking of Women in Asia 61-97 (2000); Francis T. Miko, Trafficking in Women and Children: The U.S. and International Response (1999); Somini Sengupta, Child Traffickers Prey on Bangladesh, N.Y. Times, April 29, 2002, at A6.

Some women are promised freedom after they have earned enough to repay their travel, purchase price, room and board, and interest on these debts. Often, however, such promises are not kept or the costs remain prohibitive. Pasuk Phongpaichit, Trafficking in People in Thailand, in Illegal Immigration and Commercial Sex: The New Slave Trade 84-85 (Phil Williams ed., 1999). Women who refuse to work may be raped, physically assaulted, denied food, or forcibly restrained from leaving houses of prostitution. U.S. Dep't of State, Trafficking in Persons Report, supra, at 8-9 (reporting rates of rape between 60-75 percent, and rates of physical assault between 70-95 percent). In one notorious case, sex workers chained to their beds died in a Thailand brothel fire. Charlotte Bunch, Women's Rights as Human Rights: Toward a Re-Vision of Human Rights, in Gender Violence: A Development and Human Rights Issue 8 (Charlotte Bunch & Roxanna Carrillo eds., 1991).

Many prostitutes have 10- to 18-hour shifts in squalid conditions with no choice of customers and little birth control or health care. Siripon Sakhrobanek et al., The Traffic in Women: Human Realities of the International Sex Trade 4-5 (1997). The rising rate of sexually transmitted disease, coupled with long-standing beliefs about the value of intercourse with virgins, has heightened demand for ever younger partners of both sexes, and purchase of preteens and adolescents has become increasingly common. Ngo Vinh Long, Vietnam, in Prostitution: An International Handbook on Trends, Problems and Policies (Nanette J. Davis ed., 1993); Trafficking of Women and Children in the International Sex Trade: Hearing Before the House Subcomm. on International Operations and Human Rights of the Comm. on International Relations, 106th Cong. 10 (1999); see also Janie Chuang, Redirecting the Debate over Trafficking in Women: Definitions, Paradigms, and Contexts, 11 Harv. Hum. Rts. J. 69 (1998) (discussing the dynamics of poverty that encourage sales of daughters). Another all too representative account appears in the State Department's 2005 Trafficking Report:

> Neary grew up in rural Cambodia. Her parents died when she was a child, and, in an effort to give her a better life, her sister married her off when she was 17. Three months later they went to visit a fishing village. Her husband rented a room in what Neary thought was a guest house. But when she woke the next morning, her husband was gone. The owner of the house told her she had been sold by her husband for $300 and that she was actually in a brothel.
>
> For five years, Neary was raped by five to seven men every day. In addition to brutal physical abuse, Neary was infected with HIV and contracted AIDS. The brothel threw her out when she became sick, and she eventually found her way to a local shelter. She died of HIV/AIDS at the age of 23.

U.S. Dep't of State, Trafficking in Persons Report, supra, at 6.

A related and rapidly increasing industry involves sex tourism. By the late 1990s, some two dozen companies were offering "sex tours" to countries such as Thailand and the Philippines, where purchasers have ready access to bars and brothels. Luchina Fisher, Judge to Rule on Ground-Breaking Sex Tourism Case, Sept. 22, 2003, available at http://womensenewstoday.org; see also Lynn L. Lim, The Sex Trade (1998). A representative California travel agency ad reads: "Sex Tours to Thailand, Real Girls, Real Sex, Real Cheap. These women are the most sexually available in the world. Did you know you can actually buy a virgin girl for as little as $200? You could fuck a different girl for the rest of your life." The agency offers a prize to the man who has sex with the most girls on the tour.

To what extent is such prostitution a reflection of racist as well as sexist dynamics? Laurie Shrage observes that "when we look at sex commerce cross-culturally and historically, one thing that stands out but stands unexplained is that a large percentage of sex customers seek (or sought) sex workers whose racial, ethnic, national, or class identities are (or were) different from their own." Laurie Shrage, Moral Dilemmas of Feminism: Prostitution, Adultery, and Abortion 142 (1994); see also Vednita Nelson, Prostitution: Where Racism and Sexism Intersect, 1 Mich. J. Gender & L. 81 (1993). Shrage continues:

> [I]f we do not assume that racism and xenophobia have diminished, then we might wonder how inter-ethnic "sex tourism" manages to be compatible with the ongoing existence of racial and national hatreds and fears — especially when such sentiments create barriers to intermarriage and, in general, to greater social cohesion in most areas of our lives. How does sex trading overcome these hostile sentiments? Or, if it

does not, does interracial prostitution reflect an interracial rape mentality more than one of interracial respect?

Shrage, supra, at 144.

Several scholars have made the case for treating forced prostitution as a form of slavery. See, e.g., Kathleen Barry, Female Sexual Slavery (1979); Neal Devins, Men Who Own Women: A Thirteenth Amendment Critique of Forced Prostitution, 103 Yale L.J. 791 (1993). Here again, however, the line between "voluntary" and "forced" prostitution is complex and at times contested. When prostitution appears to be the only way a woman can support her family, has she made a free and rational choice to become a prostitute, or should it be said that she was coerced? See Balos, supra, at 137; Joan Fitzpatrick, Trafficking as a Human Rights Violation: The Complex Intersection of Legal Frameworks for Conceptualizing and Combating Trafficking, 24 Mich. J. Int'l L. 1143, 1167 (2003).

What other strategies might be most effective in curbing sex trafficking and tourism? The U.S. State Department, as well as most experts in the field, has advocated a three-pronged approach: prevention, punishment, and protection. U.S. State Dep't, Trafficking in Persons Report, supra, at 20-25; see also Miko, Trafficking in Women and Children, supra. Prevention approaches would focus on challenging the cultural devaluation of women, expanding their education and employment opportunities, providing shelters and services for victims, reducing poverty in the countries that supply the global trade, and providing better information to vulnerable groups about the strategies of traffickers and the legal remedies available. Coalition Against Trafficking in Women, Declaration of Rights for Women in Conditions of Sex Trafficking and Prostitution (Jan. 19, 1999); Miko, Trafficking in Women and Children, supra; U.S. State Dep't, Trafficking in Persons Report, supra, at 20-36.

Travel agencies could better adhere to the global Code of Conduct for the Protection of Children from Sexual Exploitation in Travel and Tourism (1999), available at http://www.thecode.org. About a hundred agencies from 18 countries have signed the Code, which requires ethical policies and contract clauses repudiating the sexual exploitation of children, training for personnel, and annual reporting on compliance. More consumer pressure, including airport protests against sex tour participants, might discourage some of the most egregious conduct. Coalition Against Trafficking in Women, Holding Men Accountable in Los Angeles (Apr. 18, 1998).

From the standpoint of punishment, part of the reason that the global sex trade has become such an expanding vehicle for international crime, second only to drugs and guns, is that the penalties have been lighter. For example, in the United States, the maximum federal penalty for dealing in a kilogram of heroin is life in prison; the mandatory minimum for crack cocaine is five years. By contrast, sex traffickers, who procure women for compulsory sex and assist their imprisonment, have received sentences as light as one to four years. See United States v. Casteneda, 239 F.3d 978 (9th Cir. 2001). In many foreign countries, enforcement of anti-trafficking laws remains grossly inadequate due to lack of resources and training, corruption of police and immigration officials, and governmental ambivalence about curtailing profitable sex tourism activities. See Landsman, supra, at 37; Lim, supra, at 136-139; see also Kelly E. Hyland, The Impact of the Protocol to Prevent, Suppress, and Punish Trafficking in Persons, Especially Women and Children, 8 Hum. Rts. Brief 30, 30-31 (2001).

The Victims of Trafficking and Violence Protection Act (TVPA) of 2000 attempts to respond to these problems by increasing the maximum penalties for trafficking to 20 years, providing a civil damages remedy for victims, increasing assistance to international law enforcement efforts, and giving the President discretionary power to impose sanctions on nations that fail to meet minimum standards for enforcement of anti-trafficking prohibitions. Pub. L. No. 106-386, 114 Stat. 1464, §§ 109, 110(d), 112(a), and 112(a)(2) (2000) (codified as amended at 22 U.S.C. § 2152d, 22 U.S.C. § 7107, 18 U.S.C. § 1589-1594 (2005), respectively). In addition, the TVPA establishes an annual Trafficking in Persons (TIP) Report, published by the State Department, that separates countries into Tier 1 countries, which meet the minimum standards set by the U.S. government for eliminating trafficking; Tier 2 countries, which do not comply with the minimum standards but are making "significant efforts to bring themselves into compliance"; and Tier 3 countries, which do not comply with the minimum standards and are not making "significant efforts to bring themselves into compliance." 22 U.C.S. § 7107(b)(1) (2005). The United States will not provide "nonhumanitarian, nontrade-related foreign assistance" to Tier 3 countries and will also direct the International Monetary Fund to vote against "any loan or other utilization of the funds of the respective institution to that country." 22 U.S.C. § 7107(d)(1) (2005).

To combat child sexual tourism, Congress in 2003 passed the Prosecutorial Remedies and Other Tools to End the Exploitation of Children Today (PROTECT) Act, and the Trafficking Victims Reauthorization Act, which increase penalties to a maximum of 30 years imprisonment for engaging in child sexual trafficking. As of 2005, there had been about a dozen convictions of child sexual tourists. U.S. Dep't of State, Trafficking in Persons, supra, at 23. In the first action against a United State tourist agency, the New York attorney general obtained a restraining order against Big Apple Oriental Tours, which allegedly employed tour guides to negotiate sexual services for American customers in the Philippines. Fisher, supra.

The 2000 Trafficking Act also addresses the third area in which increased efforts are necessary: protection of victims. Traditionally, the targets of trafficking have often been punished more harshly than the traffickers themselves. Id. at §§ 112(a), 14, 17. Women have been subject to immediate deportation, which deters reporting and cooperation with enforcement efforts. Under the new Act, some 5,000 "T" visas will now be available each year for women who are assisting investigators or who would "suffer extreme hardship" if deported. Id. at § 107(e). So too, the recently adopted U.N. Protocol to Prevent, Suppress, and Punish Trafficking in Persons, Especially Women and Children (supplementing the United Nations Convention against Transnational Organized Crime), contained in Annex II of the Report of the Ad Hoc Committee on the Elaboration of a Convention Against Transnational Organized Crime on the Work of its First to Eleventh Sessions, U.N. Doc. A/55/383 (2000), directs signatory nations to consider implementing measures to assist victims, such as medical, psychological, and counseling services, and employment, education, and training opportunities.

To that end, in 2003, the United States pledged some $50 million to groups that work against trafficking and provide assistance to its victims. However, controversy has arisen over the government's decision to target the funds only to domestic and international groups that oppose prostitution. Some women's rights activists see that decision as analogous to the administration's global gag rule, which denies United States assistance to groups that provide abortion-related information or services. The New York-based women's rights organization, Equality Now, opposes the policy on the grounds that it interferes with legitimate advocacy and support service on behalf of women involved in the sex trade. Jennifer Friedlin, Debate Roars Over Anti-Trafficking Funds, April 16, 2004, available at http://womensenewstoday.org. The administration defends its position on the ground that it is more effective to support organizations that "see trafficking and prostitution as both inextricably mixed and socially harmful." Id. (quoting Kent Hill, assistant administrator for U.S. Agency for International Development). Who is right?

6. Mail-Order Brides. The last quarter century has witnessed the growth of a "mail-order bride" industry that sells addresses of eligible women to men seeking companions or wives. The World Association of Introduction Agencies recognizes some 2,700 agencies worldwide, which broker an estimated 4,000 American marriages annually. U.S. Citizenship & Immigr. Servs., International Matchmaking Organizations: A Report to Congress (1999), available at http:// uscis.gov/graphics/aboutus/repsstudies/Mobrept.htm; Kate O'Rourke, To Have and to Hold: A Postmodern Feminist Response to the Mail-Order Bride Industry, 30 Denv. J. Int'l L. & Pol'y 475, 476 (2002).

This industry represents a modern variation on an earlier tradition of picture brides, a system in which individual families arranged marriages between their daughters and men of the same racial or ethnic groups abroad. That practice was encouraged by restrictive immigration laws, such as U.S. anti-Asian immigrant exclusion acts, which largely restricted legal immigration status to male laborers and prevented them from traveling back and forth to their native lands to arrange their own marriages. Once a picture bride was selected, the marriage would be legalized in Asia, and the wife would be eligible to immigrate to the United States. Christine S.Y. Chun, The Mail-order Bride Industry: The Perpetuation of Transnational Economic Inequalities and Stereotypes, 17 U. Pa. J. Int'l Econ. L. 1155, 1157-1158 (1996). The practice died out in the mid-20th century as a result of the repeal of the exclusion acts and the growth of the Asian population in the United States. However, a superficially similar practice resurfaced in the 1970s in the form of a mail-order bride industry. Part of the impetus for the contemporary business was the Vietnam War, and the experience of American soldiers with Asian prostitutes. Former military personnel are prominent founders of modern bridal agencies and constitute a large percentage of their customers. Donna R. Lee, Mail Fantasy: Global Sexual Exploitation in the Mail-Order Bride Industry and Proposed Legal Solutions, 5 Asian L.J. 139, 160 (1998).

International matchmaking involves two primary forms. The more innocuous type is penpal clubs. Matchmaking organizations offer information to and about men and women for free. An estimated 10,000 foreign women looking for marriage or a relationship belong. Vanessa Brocato, Profitable Proposals: Explaining and Addressing the Mail-Order Bride Industry Through International Human Rights Law, 5 San Diego Int'l. L.J. 225, 230 (2004).

The second type of organization is the mail-order bride agency, which generally recruits and screens potential candidates from economically disadvantaged countries through newspaper and magazine advertisements. These agencies market catalogues to men that include women's names, pictures, and biographical data including physical measurements and personal interests.

Women from the Philippines and Latin America account for a large percentage of the prospective brides because many speak English, are familiar with American culture, live in poverty, and know that marriage is the easiest way to obtain U.S. citizenship. An increasing number of women are from the former Soviet Union and Eastern Europe. Vanessa B.M. Vergara, Abusive Mail-Order Bride Marriage and the Thirteenth Amendment, 94 Nw. U. L. Rev. 1547, 1560 (2000).

Mail-order bride catalogues are highly salable in and of themselves, as they feature very attractive women and provide "a fantasy for American men who have been unlucky in love." The women are typically portrayed as exotic, dutiful, and accommodating. A typical entry reads: "Maria Claire (19) Philippines/5'3"; 105; hospital attendant (nursing aide grad). Catholic. 'I'm kind, honest, and humble to everybody and most of all loving and caring. Never been touch and never been kiss except to the one I'm looking to. In shorts, single and still negotiable.'" Cherry Blossoms, Nov./Dec. 1995. The website of Chance for Love maintains: "The Russian woman has not been exposed to the world of rampant feminism that asserts its rights in America. She is the weaker gender and knows it." David Crary, Protecting Mail-Order Brides, Ariz. Rep., July 6, 2003, A2. Another catalog features candidates "docile, exotic, and available as bed partners and domestic help at the same time." Eddy Meng, Mail-Order Brides: Gilded Prostitution and the Legal Response, 28 U. Mich. J.L. Reform 197, 205 (1995). Each of these women is painted as an "eternal treasure . . . whose main objective in life is to please her husband." Id.

The catalogs are targeted to men from industrialized countries such as the United States, Australia, and Canada. The typical client is white, older than the potential bride, financially well off, and politically conservative. Most have at least two years of college and have been divorced at least once. U.S. Citizenship & Immigr. Servs., International Matchmaking Organizations, supra. Many consider American women too independent, selfish, and career oriented. For a fee, men buy the addresses of the women they select from the catalogs. Some agencies also offer video presentations, services such as private investigators and clinical psychologists. Customers then mail letters to potential brides or join a group tour that allows members to interview potential applicants. Typically the man travels to the home country of the potential bride, often through arrangements made by the agency. If, after meeting, the couples agree to marry, the wedding occurs in the woman's home country or the husband-to-be applies for a fiancée visa, which allows the prospective bride to travel to the man's country. United States immigration law requires the couple to marry within 90 days. Once they are married, the bride obtains resident status on a two-year conditional basis. Ninety days before the expiration of the two-year period, the couple must jointly petition for unrestricted permanent residency status for the wife. The burden of proof is on the couple to establish that the marriage is viable and was not fraudulently arranged to evade immigration restrictions. Immigration Marriage Fraud Amendments of 1986, Pub. L. No. 99-639, 100 Stat. 3537 (codified at 8 U.S.C. § 1186a (2005)).

The total cost to the men typically ranges from $5,000 to $15,000. Vergara, supra, at 1558. The agencies do not screen their male customers or provide any assistance to brides once they reach their new home country, and no governmental or nongovernmental organizations monitor the experience of these women. Lee, supra, at 144.

Expectations are frequently disappointed. Although the practice appeals to men seeking submissive wives, the women who participate are sufficiently independent and resourceful to leave their culture and often do not fit the stereotype of the docile helpmate. So too, many women's knowledge of American society comes from romanticized media portrayals and they believe that American husbands treat their wives better than husbands in their home countries. Chun, supra, at 1176; Beverly Encarguez Perez, Woman Warrior Meets Mail-Order Bride: Finding an Asian American Voice in the Women's Movement, 18 Berkeley Women's L.J. 211, 221 (2003). However, the men seeking foreign brides frequently have negative attitudes toward women. Many have experienced a bitter divorce or break-up, and a substantial number become physically and emotionally abusive toward new wives who do not fulfill their fantasies.

The extent of domestic violence in mail-order marriages is impossible to estimate with any accuracy, since police records do not reveal this information and women have well-documented reasons not to report abuse. They frequently fear further retaliation against themselves or their children, and loss of economic support. These concerns are common in any violent relationship, but are especially prominent among mail-order wives for multiple reasons. These women typically have no family or support network on which they can rely and lack the language and employment skills for financial independence. Few have funds to seek legal assistance or to return to their native country. Many fear deportation, and the cultural stigma of divorce. Those who come from nations with a tradition of gender subordination may also see some abuse as a standard feature of marital relationships. Chun, supra, at 1186-1187; Perez, supra, at 228-229. In one recent study, mail-order brides were six times more likely to experience domestic violence than other women. Peter Clough, Mail-Order Bride Phenomenon — Conclusion of a Series: Internet Brides Roll the Dice for Love or Misery, Vancouver Province (Canada), Oct. 31, 2004, available at 2004 WLNR 11829049; see also Linda Kelly, Marriage for Sale: The Mail-Order Bride Industry and the Changing Value of Marriage, 5 J. Gender Race & Just. 175, 186-187 (2001) (citing studies).

In response to these problems, the U.S. Immigration and Nationality Act, the Violence Against Women Act, and the Battered Immigrant Women Protection Act provide for a waiver of the joint petition requirement for permanent residency in certain circumstances, including spousal abuse. See Lisa C. Ikemoto, Mail Fraud, 3 J. Gender Race & Just. 511, 541 (2000). The Illegal Immigration Reform and Immigrant Responsibility Act of 1996 requires international matchmaking agencies to provide potential brides information in their native language about U.S. permanent residence status, the battered spouse waiver, and the unregulated nature of the industry, 8 U.S.C. § 1375 (2005), and more recent federal legislation in the Violence Against Women and Dep't of Justice Reauth. Act of 2005 provides prospective brides with information about their prospective husband's prior marriages and criminal records, and limits customers to one fiancée visa each year in order to prevent serial abuse. See Pub. L. No. 109-162 (signed into law on Jan. 5, 2006).

Among additional reforms that have been proposed are a ban on citizens with a history of domestic violence obtaining fiancée visas for a prescribed number of years, a shorter period of conditional residency, and a civil liability cause of action against marriage brokers. In the first successful matchmaker lawsuit, Nataliya Fox obtained a $430,000 award against Encounters International for failing to screen customers for violence, misstating deportation risks, and omitting required disclosures about the legal rights of domestic violence victims. She suffered severe physical abuse from her husband, who had a prior history of battering. He eventually divorced Nataliya, paid her $110,000 in a settlement, and obtained a new mail-order bride. Mail-Order Brides Beware, Asia Intelligence Wire, Dec. 6, 2004, available at 2004 WLNR 13401738.

Although the Philippines makes operation of a mail-order bridal agency a criminal offense, that statute has proven largely ineffective; a lack of resources and jurisdiction over international agencies permit the matchmaking industry to thrive. Chun, supra, at 1190; Perez, supra, at 232-233.

Putting Theory into Practice

5-3. After defeat of the Berkeley ordinance, discussed in note 3, p. 830 — an initiative which would have made prostitution the city's lowest law enforcement priority — a women's rights organization seeks your assistance in drafting a new initiative that might be more palatable to voters. What is your advice?

5-4. A group of women students at a state law school decide to organize a conference to draw attention to the harmful effects of prostitution and the extent to which it perpetuates gender subordination. The organizers have lined up a number of highly prominent participants, all of whom oppose decriminalization of most prostitution-related activities. The students also intend to ask some well-known scholars to present alternative points of view on prostitution, including support of decriminalization. The leading anti-prostitution speakers refuse to participate if "pro-prostitution" advocates are present. How should the students proceed? What legal, moral, or policy considerations are relevant?

5-5. Conference organizers in problem 5-4, above, agree not to invite the activists favoring decriminalization. However, the students arrange with a local artist to present an exhibit expressing their views. The exhibit includes a videotape featuring works by and about prostitutes, and footage from sexually explicit films in which sex workers appear. Two of the conference speakers demand that the videotape be removed because they feel, "based on their experiences at other events, that the tape would be a threat to their safety." Tamar Lewin, Furor on Exhibit at Law School Splits Feminists, N.Y. Times, Nov. 13, 1992, at B9. Students remove the tape, at which point the artist withdraws the entire exhibit.

Complaints are then made that the conference organizers' action constitutes censorship of speech in violation of the First Amendment. One professor, who was not involved in the decision to remove the tape, responds: "I don't see this as a fight within feminism but a fight between those who wish to end male supremacy and those who wish to do better under it." Id.

How would you have handled the incident if you had been one of the student leaders? How should the dean and university legal counsel respond to the First Amendment claims?

B. PREGNANCY AND AUTONOMY

1. Control of Conception and Other Aspects of Women's Health

≡ *Griswold v. Connecticut*
≡ 381 U.S. 479 (1965)
≡

Mr. Justice DOUGLAS delivered the opinion of the court.

[Appellants, Planned Parenthood personnel who prescribed contraceptives for "married persons," were charged as accessories to the violation of the Connecticut statute prohibiting the use of contraceptives. The Court first held that they had standing to assert their patients' privacy rights.]

[W]e are met with a wide range of questions that implicate the Due Process Clause of the Fourteenth Amendment. Overtones of some arguments suggest that Lochner v. New York, 198 U.S. 45 [(1905)], should be our guide. But we decline that invitation. . . . We do not sit as a super-legislature to determine the wisdom, need, and propriety of laws that touch economic problems, business affairs, or social conditions. This law, however, operates directly on an intimate relation of husband and wife and their physician's role in one aspect of that relation.

The association of people is not mentioned in the Constitution nor in the Bill of Rights. The right to educate a child in a school of the parents' choice — whether public or private or parochial — is also not mentioned. Nor is the right to study any particular subject or any foreign language. Yet the First Amendment has been construed to include certain of those rights. . . .

By Pierce v. Society of Sisters, [268 U.S. 510 (1925)], the right to educate one's children as one chooses is made applicable to the States by the force of the First and Fourteenth Amendments. By Meyer v. Nebraska, [262 U.S. 390 (1923)], the same dignity is given the right to study the German language in a private school. In other words, the State may not, consistently with the spirit of the First Amendment, contract the spectrum of available knowledge. . . .

In NAACP v. Alabama, 357 U.S. 449, 462 [(1958)], we protected the "freedom to associate and privacy in one's associations," noting that freedom of association was a peripheral First Amendment right. Disclosure of membership lists of a constitutionally valid association, we held, was invalid "as entailing the likelihood of a substantial restraint upon the exercise by petitioner's members of their right to freedom of association." Ibid. In other words, the First Amendment has a penumbra where privacy is protected from governmental intrusion. In like context, we have protected forms of "association" that are not political in the customary sense but pertain to the social, legal, and economic benefit of the members. In Schware v. Board of Bar Examiners, 353 U.S. 232 [(1957)], we held it not permissible to bar a lawyer from practice, because he had once been a member of the Communist Party. The man's "association with that Party" was not shown to be "anything more than a political faith in a political party" (id., at 244) and was not action of a kind proving bad moral character. Id. at 245-246. . . .

The foregoing cases suggest that specific guarantees in the Bill of Rights have penumbras, formed by emanations from those guarantees that help give them life and substance. Various guarantees create zones of privacy. The right of association contained in the penumbra of the First Amendment is one, as we have seen. The Third Amendment in its prohibitions against the quartering of soldiers "in any house" in time of peace without the consent of the owner is another facet of that privacy. The Fourth Amendment explicitly affirms the "right of the people to be secure in their persons, houses, papers, and effects, against unreasonable searches and seizures." The Fifth Amendment in its Self-Incrimination Clause enables the citizen to create a zone of privacy which government may not force him to surrender to his detriment. The Ninth Amendment provides: "The enumeration in the constitution, of certain rights, shall not be construed to deny or disparage others retained by the people."

The Fourth and Fifth Amendments were described in Boyd v. United States, 116 U.S. 616, 630 [(1886)], as protection against all governmental invasions "of the sanctity of a man's home and the privacies of life." We recently referred in Mapp v. Ohio, 367 U.S. 643, 656 [(1961)], to the Fourth Amendment as creating a "right to privacy, no less important than any other right carefully and particularly reserved to the people."

We have had many controversies over these penumbral rights of "privacy and repose." These cases bear witness that the right of privacy which presses for recognition here is a legitimate one.

The present case, then, concerns a relationship lying within the zone of privacy which, in forbidding the use of contraceptives rather than regulating their manufacture or sale, seeks to achieve its goals by...having a maximum destructive impact upon that relationship. Such a law cannot stand in light of the familiar principle, so often applied by the Court, that a "governmental purpose to control or prevent activities constitutionally subject to state regulation may not be achieved by means which sweep unnecessarily broadly and thereby invade the area of protected freedoms." NAACP v. Alabama, [377 U.S. 288, 307 (1964)]. Would we allow the police to search the sacred precincts of marital bedrooms for telltale signs of the use of contraceptives? The very idea is repulsive to the notions of privacy surrounding the marriage relationship.

We deal with a right of privacy older than the Bill of Rights—older than our political parties, older than our school system. Marriage is a coming together for better or worse, hopefully enduring, and intimate to the degree of being sacred. It is an association that promotes a way of life, not causes; a harmony in living, not political faiths; a bilateral loyalty, not commercial or social projects. Yet it is an association for as noble a purpose as any involved in our prior decisions.

Reversed.

Mr. Justice GOLDBERG, whom THE CHIEF JUSTICE and Mr. Justice BRENNAN join, concurring....

[I]t should be said of the Court's holding today that it in no way interferes with a State's proper regulation of sexual promiscuity or misconduct. As my Brother Harlan so well stated in his dissenting opinion in Poe v. Ullman, [361 U.S. 497, 553 (1961)]:

Adultery, homosexuality and the like are sexual intimacies which the State forbids...but the intimacy of husband and wife is necessarily an essential and accepted feature of the institution of marriage, an institution which the State not only must allow, but which always and in every age it has fostered and protected. It is one thing when the State exerts its power either to forbid extra-marital sexuality...or to say who may marry, but it is quite another when, having acknowledged a marriage and the intimacies inherent in it, it undertakes to regulate by means of the criminal law the details of that intimacy.

In sum, I believe that the right of privacy in the marital relation is fundamental and basic—a personal right "retained by the people" within the meaning of the Ninth Amendment. Connecticut cannot constitutionally abridge this fundamental right, which is protected by the Fourteenth Amendment from infringement by the States. I agree with the Court that petitioners' convictions must therefore be reversed.

═══ ### *Eisenstadt v. Baird*
═══ 405 U.S. 438 (1972)

Mr. Justice BRENNAN delivered the opinion of the Court.

Appellee William Baird was convicted at a bench trial in the Massachusetts Superior Court under Massachusetts General Laws Ann., c.272, §21, first, for exhibiting contraceptive articles in the course of delivering a lecture on contraception to a group of students at Boston University and, second, for giving a young woman a package of Emko vaginal foam at the close of his address. The Massachusetts Supreme Judicial Court unanimously set aside the conviction for exhibiting contraceptives . . . but . . . sustained the conviction for giving away the foam. [Baird then obtained a writ of habeas corpus in federal court, and the state appealed.] We affirm.

Massachusetts General Laws Ann., c.272, §21, under which Baird was convicted, provides a maximum five-year term of imprisonment for "whoever . . . gives away . . . any drug, medicine, instrument or article whatever for the prevention of conception," except as authorized in §21A. Under §21A, "[a] registered physician may administer to or prescribe for any married person drugs or articles intended for the prevention of pregnancy or conception. [And a] registered pharmacist actually engaged in the business of pharmacy may furnish such drugs or articles to any married person presenting a prescription from a registered physician." As interpreted by the State Supreme Judicial Court, these provisions make it a felony for anyone, other than a registered physician or pharmacist acting in accordance with the terms of §21A, to dispense any article with the intention that it be used for the prevention of conception. The statutory scheme distinguishes among three distinct classes of distributees — first, married persons may obtain contraceptives to prevent pregnancy, but only from doctors or druggists on prescription; second, single persons may not obtain contraceptives from anyone to prevent pregnancy; and, third, married or single persons may obtain contraceptives from anyone to prevent, not pregnancy, but the spread of disease. This construction of state law is, of course, binding on us.

The legislative purposes that the statute is meant to serve are not altogether clear. In Commonwealth v. Baird, [247 N.E.2d 574 (1969)], the Supreme Judicial Court noted only the State's interest in protecting the health of its citizens: "(T)he prohibition in §21," the court declared, "is directly related to" the State's goal of "preventing the distribution of articles designed to prevent conception which may have undesirable, if not dangerous, physical consequences," [247 N.E.2d at 578]. In a subsequent decision, Sturgis v. Attorney General, [260 N.E.2d 687, 690 (Mass. 1970)], the court, however, found "a second and more compelling ground for upholding the statute" — namely, to protect morals through "regulating the private sexual lives of single persons." The Court of Appeals, for reasons that will appear, did not consider the promotion of health or the protection of morals through the deterrence of fornication to be the legislative aim. Instead, the court concluded that the statutory goal was to limit contraception in and of itself — a purpose that the court held conflicted "with fundamental human rights" under Griswold v. Connecticut, [381 U.S. 479 (1965)], where this Court struck down Connecticut's prohibition against the use of contraceptives as an unconstitutional infringement of the right of marital privacy. [Baird v. Eisenstadt, 429 F.2d 1398, 1401-1402 (1st Cir. 1970).]

We agree that the goals of deterring premarital sex and regulating the distribution of potentially harmful articles cannot reasonably be regarded as legislative aims of §21 and §21A. And we hold that the statute, viewed as a prohibition on contraception per se, violates the rights of single persons under the Equal Protection Clause of the Fourteenth Amendment. . . .

II

The basic principles governing application of the Equal Protection Clause of the Fourteenth Amendment are familiar.... The question for our determination in this case is whether there is some ground of difference that rationally explains the different treatment accorded married and unmarried persons.... For the reasons that follow, we conclude that no such ground exists.

First.... Conceding that the State could, consistently with the Equal Protection Clause, regard the problems of extramarital and premarital sexual relations as "[e]vils...of different dimensions and proportions, requiring different remedies," Williamson v. Lee Optical Co., [348 U.S. 483, 489 (1955)], we cannot agree that the deterrence of premarital sex may reasonably be regarded as the purpose of the Massachusetts law.

It would be plainly unreasonable to assume that Massachusetts has prescribed pregnancy and the birth of an unwanted child as punishment for fornication, which is a misdemeanor under Massachusetts [law]. Aside from the scheme of values that assumption would attribute to the State, it is abundantly clear that the effect of the ban on distribution of contraceptives to unmarried persons has at best a marginal relation to the proffered objective. What Mr. Justice Goldberg said in Griswold v. Connecticut, supra, at 498 (concurring opinion), ... is equally applicable here. "The rationality of this justification is dubious, particularly in light of the admitted widespread availability to all persons in the State of Connecticut, unmarried as well as married, of birth-control devices for the prevention of disease, as distinguished from the prevention of conception." Like Connecticut's laws, § 21 and § 21A do not at all regulate the distribution of contraceptives when they are to be used to prevent, not pregnancy, but the spread of disease. Nor, in making contraceptives available to married persons without regard to their intended use, does Massachusetts attempt to deter married persons from engaging in illicit sexual relations with unmarried persons. Even on the assumption that the fear of pregnancy operates as a deterrent to fornication, the Massachusetts statute is thus so riddled with exceptions that deterrence of premarital sex cannot reasonably be regarded as its aim.

Moreover, § 21 and § 21A on their face have a dubious relation to the State's criminal prohibition on fornication. As the Court of Appeals explained, "Fornication is a misdemeanor [in Massachusetts], entailing a thirty dollar fine, or three months in jail. Violation of the present statute is a felony, punishable by five years in prison...." 429 F.2d at 1401. Even conceding the legislature a full measure of discretion in fashioning means to prevent fornication, and recognizing that the State may seek to deter prohibited conduct by punishing more severely those who facilitate than those who actually engage in its commission, we, like the Court of Appeals, cannot believe that in this instance Massachusetts has chosen to expose the aider and abetter who simply gives away a contraceptive to 20 times the 90-day sentence of the offender himself....

Second.... The Supreme Judicial Court in Commonwealth v. Baird, supra, held that the purpose of the [law in question] was to serve the health needs of the community by regulating the distribution of potentially harmful articles.

[The Court here concludes that it would be irrational for a law grounded on health needs to distinguish between married and unmarried persons, since their health needs would be identical.]

Third. If the Massachusetts statute cannot be upheld as a deterrent to fornication or as a health measure, may it, nevertheless, be sustained simply as a prohibition on contraception? . . . We need not and do not, however, decide that important question in this case because, whatever the rights of the individual to access to contraceptives may be, the rights must be the same for the unmarried and the married alike.

If under *Griswold* the distribution of contraceptives to married persons cannot be prohibited, a ban on distribution to unmarried persons would be equally impermissible. It is true that in *Griswold* the right of privacy in question inhered in the marital relationship. Yet the marital couple is not an independent entity with a mind and heart of its own, but an association of two individuals each with a separate intellectual and emotional makeup. If the right of privacy means anything, it is the right of the individual, married or single, to be free from unwarranted governmental intrusion into matters so fundamentally affecting a person as the decision whether to bear or beget a child.

On the other hand, if *Griswold* is no bar to a prohibition on the distribution of contraceptives, the State could not, consistently with the Equal Protection Clause, outlaw distribution to unmarried but not to married persons. In each case the evil, as perceived by the State, would be identical, and the underinclusion would be invidious. . . . The judgment of the Court of Appeals is affirmed.

Mr. Justice POWELL and Mr. Justice REHNQUIST took no part in the consideration or decision of this case.

[The concurring opinion of Mr. Justice Douglas is omitted.]

[The concurring opinion of Mr. Justice White, with whom Mr. Justice Blackmun joined, is omitted.]

[The dissenting opinion of Mr. Chief Justice Burger is omitted.]

≡ *Erickson v. Bartell Drug Co.*
≡ **141 F. Supp. 2d 1266 (W.D. Wash. 2001)**

Robert S. LASNIK, Judge.

The parties' cross-motions for summary judgment in this case raise an issue of first impression in the federal courts whether the selective exclusion of prescription contraceptives from defendant's generally comprehensive prescription plan constitutes discrimination on the basis of sex.[1] In particular, plaintiffs assert

---

1. Bartell's benefit plan is self-insured and covers all prescription drugs, including a number of preventative drugs and devices, such as blood-pressure and cholesterol-lowering drugs, hormone replacement therapies, prenatal vitamins, and drugs to prevent allergic reactions, breast cancer, and

that Bartell's decision not to cover prescription contraceptives such as birth control pills, Norplant, Depo-Provera, intra-uterine devices, and diaphragms under its Prescription Benefit Plan for non-union employees violates Title VII . . .

This matter is proceeding as a class action on behalf of "all female employees of Bartell who at any time after December 29, 1997, were enrolled in Bartell's Prescription Benefit Plan for non-union employees while using prescription contraceptives."

A. Application of Title VII. . .

In 1978, Congress had the opportunity to expound on its view of sex discrimination by amending Title VII to make clear that discrimination because of "pregnancy, childbirth, or related medical conditions" is discrimination on the basis of sex. . . . The amendment, known as the Pregnancy Discrimination Act ("PDA"), was not meant to alter the contours of Title VII: rather, Congress intended to correct what it felt was an erroneous interpretation of Title VII by the United States Supreme Court in General Elec. Co. v Gilbert, 429 U.S. 125 (1976). In *Gilbert*, the Supreme Court held that an otherwise comprehensive short-term disability policy that excluded pregnancy-related disabilities from coverage did not discriminate on the basis of sex. . . .

Although this litigation involves an exclusion for prescription contraceptives rather than an exclusion for pregnancy-related disability costs, the legal principles established by *Gilbert* and its legislative reversal govern the outcome of this case. An employer has chosen to offer an employment benefit which excludes from its scope of coverage services which are available only to women. All of the services covered by the policy are available to both men and women, so, as was the case in *Gilbert*, "there is no risk from which men are protected and women are not. Likewise, there is no risk from which women are protected and men are not." *Gilbert*, 429 U.S. at 135 (quoting Geduldig v. Aiello, 417 U.S. 484, 496-97 (1974). Nevertheless, the intent of Congress in enacting the PDA, even if not the exact language used in the amendment, shows that mere facial parity of coverage does not excuse or justify an exclusion which carves out benefits that are uniquely designed for women. . . .

The PDA is not a begrudging recognition of a limited grant of rights to a strictly defined group of women who happen to be pregnant. Read in the context of Title VII as a whole, it is a broad acknowledgment of the intent of Congress to outlaw any and all discrimination against any and all women in the terms and conditions of their employment, including the benefits an employer provides to its employees. Male and female employees have different, sex-based disability and healthcare needs, and the law is no longer blind to the fact that only women can get pregnant, bear children, or use prescription contraception. The special or increased healthcare needs associated with a woman's unique sex-based characteristics must be met to the same extent, and on the same terms, as other

---

blood clotting. The plan specifically excludes from coverage a handful of products, including contraceptive devices, drugs prescribed for weight reduction, infertility drugs, smoking cessation drugs, dermatologicals for cosmetic purposes, growth hormones, and experimental drugs.

healthcare needs. Even if one were to assume that Bartell's prescription plan was not the result of intentional discrimination,[7] the exclusion of women-only benefits from a generally comprehensive prescription plan is sex discrimination under Title VII.

Title VII does not require employers to offer any particular type or category of benefit. However, when an employer decides to offer a prescription plan covering everything except a few specifically excluded drugs and devices, it has a legal obligation to make sure that the resulting plan does not discriminate based on sex-based characteristics and that it provides equally comprehensive coverage for both sexes. . . . In light of the fact that prescription contraceptives are used only by women, Bartell's choice to exclude that particular benefit from its generally applicable benefit plan is discriminatory.

B. Specific Arguments Raised by Defendant-Employer . . .

An underlying theme in Bartell's argument is that a woman's ability to control her fertility differs from the type of illness and disease normally treated with prescription drugs in such significant respects that it is permissible to treat prescription contraceptives differently than all other prescription medicines. The evidence submitted by plaintiffs shows, however, that the availability of affordable and effective contraceptives is of great importance to the health of women and children because it can help to prevent a litany of physical, emotional, economic, and social consequences. See Sylvia A. Law, Sex Discrimination and Insurance for Contraception, 73 Wash. L. Rev. 363, 364-68 (1998).

[T]he adverse economic and social consequences of unintended pregnancies fall most harshly on women and interfere with their choice to participate fully and equally in the "marketplace and the world of ideas." Stanton v. Stanton, 421 U.S. 7, 14-15 (1975). See also Planned Parenthood v. Casey, 505 U.S. 833, 856 (1992) ("The ability of women to participate equally in the economic and social life of the nation has been facilitated by their ability to control their reproductive lives."). . . .

The fact that prescription contraceptives are preventative appears to be an irrelevant distinction in this case: Bartell covers a number of preventative drugs under its plan. The fact that pregnancy is a "natural" state and is not considered a disease or illness is also a distinction without a difference. Being pregnant, though natural, is not a state that is desired by all women or at all points in a woman's life. Prescription contraceptives, like all other preventative drugs, help the recipient avoid unwanted physical changes. As discussed above, identifying and obtaining an effective method of contraception is a primary healthcare issue throughout

---

7. There is no evidence or indication that Bartell's coverage decisions were intended to hinder women in their ability to participate in the workforce or to deprive them of equal treatment in employment or benefits. The most reasonable explanation for the current state of affairs is that the exclusion of women-only benefits is merely an unquestioned holdover from a time when employment-related benefits were doled out less equitably than they are today. The lack of evidence of bad faith or malice toward women does not affect the validity of plaintiffs' Title VII claim. Where a benefit plan is discriminatory on its face, no inquiry into subjective intent is necessary. . . .

much of a woman's life and is, in many instances, of more immediate importance to her daily healthcare situation than most other medical needs.... Although there are some distinctions that can be drawn between prescription contraceptives and the other prescription drugs covered by Bartell's plan, none of them is substantive or otherwise justifies the exclusion of contraceptives from a generally comprehensive healthcare plan....

Bartell also suggests that it should be permitted to limit the scope of its employee benefit programs in order to control costs. Cost is not, however, a defense to allegations of discrimination under Title VII. See Los Angeles Dept. of Water & Power v. Manhart, 435 U.S. 702, 716-17 (1978).... While it is undoubtedly true that employers may cut benefits, raise deductibles, or otherwise alter coverage options to comply with budgetary constraints, the method by which the employer seeks to curb costs must not be discriminatory. Bartell offers its employees an admittedly generous package of healthcare benefits, including both third-party healthcare plans and an in-house prescription program. It cannot, however, penalize female employees in an effort to keep its benefit costs low. The cost savings Bartell realizes by excluding prescription contraceptives from its healthcare plans are being directly borne by only one sex in violation of Title VII....

Prescription contraceptives are not the only drugs or devices excluded from coverage under Bartell's benefit plan. Bartell argues that it has chosen to exclude from coverage all drugs for "family planning," and that this exclusion is neutral and non-discriminatory. There is no "family planning" exclusion in the benefit plan, however, and the contours of such a theoretical exclusion are not clear. On the list of excluded drugs and devices, contraceptive devices and infertility drugs are the two categories which might be considered "family planning" measures. Contrary to defendant's explanation, there appear to be some drugs which fall under the "family planning" rubric which are covered by the plan. Prenatal vitamins, for example, are frequently prescribed in anticipation of a woman becoming pregnant and are expressly covered under the plan. And although both parties agree that Bartell's plan excludes coverage for Viagra, an impotency drug, it is not clear that it falls into any of the excluded categories....

Plaintiffs' motion for summary judgment on their disparate treatment claim is granted. Bartell is hereby ordered to cover each of the available options for prescription contraception to the same extent, and on the same terms, that it covers other drugs, devices, and preventative care for non-union employees. It is further ordered that Bartell shall offer coverage for contraception-related services, including the initial visit to the prescribing physician and any follow-up visits or outpatient services, to the same extent, and on the same terms, as it offers coverage for other outpatient services for its non-union employees....

Notes

1. The Constitutional Right to Contraception. The Court in *Griswold* attempts to distinguish its decision from Lochner v. New York and other discredited early-twentieth-century cases overturning economic legislation on grounds such legislation infringed upon the freedom of contract of property owners and their employees. The distinction the Court offers is that *Griswold* "operates directly on an intimate relation of husband and wife and their physician's role in one aspect of that relation," rather than "economic problems, business affairs, or social conditions." Is the distinction successful? Whether it is or not, the principle of *Griswold* has been reaffirmed numerous times since, and is now so well established that, since the defeat of Judge Robert Bork's nomination to the U.S. Supreme Court in 1987, it would appear a Supreme Court nominee cannot now be confirmed to the Court unless he or she accepts *Griswold* and other "super-precedents." See Federal News Service, Press Conference with Senator Arlen Specter (R-PA), Chairman of the Senate Judiciary Committee, Nomination of Judge Samuel A. Alito to Be Associate Justice of the Supreme Court, Senate Radio/TV Gallery, The Capitol, Washington D.C., October 31, 2005.

The right in *Griswold* was based squarely on the special status of marriage in this society. How could it follow, then, as the Court in Eisenstadt v. Baird concludes, that the right protected covers unmarried as well as married persons? Could it also follow that the right to contraception extends to minors? In invalidating a New York law criminalizing the distribution of contraceptives by anyone other than a licensed pharmacist, and the distribution, advertisement, or display of contraceptives by anyone to minors, the Supreme Court sidestepped this question. Carey v. Population Serv. Int'l, 431 U.S. 678, 694 n.17 (1977) (plurality opinion). Justice Powell in his concurring opinion argued, however, that "there is . . . no justification for subjecting restrictions on the sexual activity of the young to heightened judicial review." Id. at 705 (Powell, J., concurring).

If there is a right to contraceptives, is there also a constitutional right to have sex? In striking down a Texas statute prohibiting same-sex sodomy, the Supreme Court cited Eisenstadt and Carey for the proposition that the liberty interest protected sexual decisions by unmarried persons, but stopped short of declaring a fundamental right to sexual activity between consenting adults. See Lawrence v. Texas, 539 U.S. 558 (2003), discussed on pp. 600–601.

2. Contraception and Women's Autonomy. Do women benefit from being the ones primarily responsible for birth control? On the one hand, of course, female contraception allows women to maintain greater control over their reproductive decisions. On the other hand, what is the broader impact of viewing contraception as a "woman's responsibility"?

Consider the following:

> So long as women do not control access to our sexuality, abortion facilitates women's heterosexual availability. In other words, under conditions of gender inequality, sexual liberation in this sense does not free women; it frees male sexual aggression. The availability of abortion removes the one remaining legitimized reason that women have had for refusing sex besides the headache.

MacKinnon, Feminism Unmodified: Discourses on Life and Law 99 (1987). Is MacKinnon suggesting that contraception reduces women's autonomy? If so, is she right?

Does the practice of contraception reproduce, or at least reflect, underlying class and gender ideologies? Historian Linda Gordon underlines the class dimensions of birth control, explaining how men, particularly those of lower socio-economic status, tend to associate masculinity with sexual images of virility. This identity is undercut by the use of contraception "because it introduces calculation and negotiation with women into sexual relations," while among the prosperous, masculinity is associated to a greater extent with earning power, responsibility, children's high achievement, and other goals that tend to be served by contraceptive use. Gordon, Woman's Body, Woman's Right: Birth Control in America 480 (updated ed. 1990). Among women in lower socioeconomic classes, raising children can be drudgery, but "less alienat[ing] and more creative than most alternatives; it offers many others at least a semblance of control over their working conditions and goals." Id. Race is a further complicating factor. At various times and circumstances, racial pride might stimulate fertility or it might stimulate greater use of contraception. Race also affects the availability of competing opportunities to motherhood and thus the motivation to reproduce. Id. at 481. For an historical analysis of how the different stages of the birth control movement in this country reflected the interests of different classes of women, whose autonomy was articulated in quite different terms, see id. at xix-xxi.

Significantly, female contraceptive alternatives do not protect against AIDS and other sexually transmitted diseases. Male condom use has increased dramatically, relied upon by 11 percent of women of reproductive age in 2002, as compared to 16.7 percent of women relying on female sterilization, 18.9 percent using birth control pills, 5.7 percent using male sterilization, 3.3 percent using injectable contraceptives, .2 percent using diaphragms, and 1.3 percent using IUDs. See National Center for Health Statistics, Use of Contraception and Use of Family Planning Services in the United States: 1982-2002, Advance Data from Vital and Health Statistics, No. 350 (Dec. 2004).

3. Emergency Contraception. The most recent controversy in the reproductive rights area concerns the availability of the "morning-after pill" as a form of emergency contraception. The FDA approved the pill for sale by prescription in 1999. In 2003, the manufacturer of one morning-after product, Plan B, sought permission to sell the drug over the counter. One reason in support of the switch is that the pill must be taken within 120 hours of unprotected intercourse, and the sooner it is taken, the better it works. An FDA expert advisory panel recommended the change in status, by a vote of 23 to 4, and the change was also supported by the American College of Obstetricians and Gynecologists. On May 6, 2004, however, the FDA rejected the request, on the grounds that Plan B had not been proved safe for teenagers under the age of 16. After Congress asked the Government Accountability Office to investigate, the GAO found that the reasons for rejecting nonprescription sales were contrary to the FDA's standard practice, and that the rejection was the first of the 67 proposals of the last decade to change from prescription-only to over-the-counter availability that had been turned down over the advice of the expert, advisory panels. Conservative political pressures were blamed. David Goldstein, Battle Over "Morning-After Pill" Another Collision of Politics, Religion, The Kansas City Star, Nov. 21,

2005; U.S. Conservative Pressures Could Sideline Medical Advances, Says Ex-FDA Official, Pharma Marketletter, Nov. 22, 2005.

By one estimate, as much as 43 percent of the decline in abortion between 1994 and 2000 can be attributed to emergency contraception. See Rachel K. Jones, Jacqueline E. Darroch & Stanley K. Henshaw, Contraceptive Use Among U.S. Women Having Abortions in 2000-2001, 34 Perspectives on Sexual & Reproductive Health 226 (2002).

For discussion of the refusal of some Catholic hospitals to provide emergency contraception (as well as abortion and other reproductive health services), see pp. 890-891, and problems 5-8 and 5-9 on pp. 894-895 of this chapter.

4. Contraception and Women's Health Risks. Contraceptives have posed numerous health risks to women. These risks have led to successful lawsuits against manufacturers for inadequate warnings about the risks of birth control pills, see, e.g., MacDonald v. Ortho Pharmaceutical Corp., 475 N.E.2d 65 (Mass.), cert. denied, 474 U.S. 920 (1985), and for failure to give proper instructions for use of diaphragms, see, e.g., Baroldy v. Ortho Pharmaceutical Corp., 760 P.2d 574 (Ariz. Ct. App. 1988), and spermicidal jelly, see, e.g., Wells v. Ortho Pharmaceutical Corp., 788 F.2d 741 (11th Cir.), cert. denied, 479 U.S. 950 (1986).

The most widespread damage to women as a result of dangerous contraceptives related to the negligent design and manufacturing problems of some intrauterine contraceptive devices (IUDs). Litigation over injuries caused by the Dalkon Shield device, including ectopic pregnancy, septic abortion, birth defects, infant death, infertility, and pelvic inflammatory disease, began in the 1970s, and by 1985, the sole manufacturer, A.H. Robins Co., had disposed of more than 9,000 claims and faced an additional 5,000. Robins filed for bankruptcy and had all claims consolidated in federal court, which established a fund of over $2.4 billion out of which all claims were to be paid. See In re A.H. Robins, Inc., 880 F.2d 694 (4th Cir.), cert. denied, 493 U.S. 959 (1989). For a history of the Dalkon Shield litigation, see Karen M. Hicks, Surviving the Dalkon Shield IUD: Women v. The Pharmaceutical Industry (1994). For criticism of the unethical conduct of corporate officials and lawyers in suppressing information about the risks of the Dalkon Shield, and subjecting victims to hard ball litigation tactics (including an invasive "dirty questions" list for cross examination), see In re A.H. Robbins, Co., 107 F.R.D. 2, 14-15 (D. Kan. 1985); Deborah L. Rhode & David Luban, Legal Ethics 146 (2004); Ronald A. Bacigal, The Limits of Litigation: The Dalkon Shield Controversy 19-20 (1990).

The Dalkon Shield litigation and high damages awards in other contraceptive cases have been blamed for a narrowing of reproductive choices for American women, on the theory that they have made drug manufacturers reluctant to pursue alternatives available widely in other countries. Ironically, new forms of the IUD have been developed, and extensive studies have demonstrated that they are safe and effective, but memories of the Dalkon Shield cause women, physicians, and sex educators to avoid them. Sylvia A. Law, Tort Liability and the Availability of Contraceptive Drugs and Devices in the United States, 23 N.Y.U. Rev. L. & Soc. Change 339, 383-385 (1997).

The great promise of the Dalkon Shield was that it located responsibility for contraception in medical technology rather than in women, who might forget or misuse other forms of reproductive control. Does such a reliance on technology rather than on women themselves represent a step forward or backward for women's autonomy? For a history and critique of the development and marketing of the Dalkon Shield, which argues in favor of woman-centered methods for reproductive choice, see Nicole J. Grant, The Selling of Contraception: The Dalkon Shield Case, Sexuality, and Women's Autonomy (1992).

Another issue relating to long-term contraceptive devices is that they present possibilities of control over, rather than by, women. Worries have surfaced that forms of contraception like Depo-Provera, which is injected into the arm every three months to suppress ovulation, will be too easily imposed on women, turning a source of woman's autonomy into a means of control over her. See Philip J. Hilts, Panel Urges Contraceptive's Approval, N.Y. Times, June 20, 1992, at A6. Before its removal from the U.S. market in 2002, similar concerns surrounded the hormonal implant device Norplant. Leslie Berger, After Long Hiatus, New Contraceptives Emerge, N.Y. Times, Dec. 10, 2002, at F5. For consideration of contraception or sterilization as a condition of probation, see pp. 937-939 and problem 5-13 on p. 940.

5. Gender Bias in Health Care. The health concerns about female contraception is part of a broader set of complaints about gender bias in health care. Some of these complaints concern the failure to take seriously, and treat, certain conditions in women, such as heart disease, renal disease, and lung cancer, for which men receive better health care. See Mary Crossley, Infected Judgment: Legal Responses to Physician Bias, 48 Vill. L. Rev. 195, 225, 227-229 (2003) (citing studies); Sandra C. Gan et al., Treatment of Acute Myocardial Infarction Among Men and Women, 343 New Eng. J. Med. 8 (July 2000) (reporting on study of 139,000 Medicare patients, showing that women were seven percent less likely to receive clot-dissolving drugs in the first hour of treatment for heart attacks; had fewer catheterizations, which determine if angioplasty or heart-bypass operations are needed; and in other ways received a lesser level of care); Council on Ethical and Judicial Affairs, Gender Disparities in Clinical Decision Making, 266 JAMA 559, 560 (1991); Diane E. Hoffman & Anita J. Tarzian, The Girl Who Cried Pain: A Bias Against Women in the Treatment of Pain, 29 J.L. Med. & Ethics 13 (2001).

These complaints parallel even more significant documentation of racial disparities in the delivery of health care. See, e.g., Crossley, supra, at 211-223; Lisa C. Ikemoto, Racial Disparities in Health Care and Cultural Competency, 48 St. Louis U. L.J. 75 (2003); see also J. Hector Pope et al., Missed Diagnoses of Acute Cardiac Ischemia in the Emergency Department, 342 New Eng. J. Med. 1163 (Apr. 2000) (study concluding that emergency rooms incorrectly sent home a disproportionate number of women and blacks with the warning signs of heart attacks).

Other complaints concern the overuse of certain invasive procedures or restrictive instructions. See, e.g., Crossley, supra, at 226-227; Dana G. Safran et al., Gender Differences in Medical Treatment: The Case of Physician-Prescribed Activity Restrictions, 45 Soc. Sci. & Med. 711, 715 (1997) (finding that odds of physician directing a woman to restrict her activity was 3.6 times higher than for a man); Margaret M. Donohoe, Our Epidemic of Unnecessary Caesarean Sections: The Role of the Law in Creating It, The Role of the Law in Stopping It, 11 Wis. Women's L.J. 197 (1996) (discussing evidence that Cesarean sections are overused); Van Wijk et al., Gender Perspectives and Quality of Care: Towards Appropriate and Adequate Health Care for Women, 43 Soc. Sci. & Med. 707, 708 (1996) (more health care is not necessarily better, especially with respect to women's reproductive health).

Both the under-treatment, and over-treatment, of women may be related to the fact that, until the most recent decade, women were disproportionately excluded from medical research and drug test trials. See Crossley, supra, at 224 (citing studies); Terri D. Keville, The Invisible Woman: Gender Bias in Medical Research, 15 Women's Rts. L. Rep. 123 (1994); Karen H. Rothenberg, Gender Matters: Implications for Clinical Research and Women's Health Care, 32 Hous. L. Rev. 1210 (1996). The NIH Revitalization Act of 1993, 42 U.S.C. § 289a-2 (1994), requires the National Institutes of Heath of the Department of Heath and Human Services to include women and minorities as subjects of clinical research. For criticism of the guidelines issued under this legislation, see Jonathan M. Eisenberg, NIH Promulgates New Guidelines for the Inclusion of Women and Minorities in Medical Research, 10 Berkeley Women's L.J. 183 (1995).

Concerns about the general regard for women's health have been fueled by the discovery of numerous drugs and other products for women that, as in the case of some contraceptives have turned out to be medically unsafe. One of the most injurious was DES, a synthetic estrogen hormone prescribed between 1940 and 1970 to prevent miscarriages and later linked to cancer and birth defects that become increasingly severe with each new generation. Compare Brown v. Superior Court, 751 P.2d 470 (Cal. 1988) (under circumstances in which women not aware of which manufacturer made the DES they were prescribed, court upheld "market share" liability among all companies that manufactured the drug) with Payton v. Abbott Labs, 437 N.E.2d 171 (Mass. 1982) (rejecting market share liability theory) and O'Brien v. Eli Lilly & Co., 668 F.2d 704 (3d Cir. 1981) (holding that two-year statute of limitations for claim against DES manufacturer began running from date plaintiff daughter read magazine article describing connections between drug and cancer, after which if she had exercised due diligence, she would have determined that her mother had taken the drug that arguably caused her subsequent cancer). For a history of DES and its physical and psychological effects, see Roberta J. Apfel & Susan M. Fisher, To Do No Harm: DES and the Dilemmas of Modern Medicine (1984). See also O'Gilvie v. International Playtex, Inc., 821 F.2d 1438 (10th Cir. 1987), cert. denied, 486 U.S. 1032 (1988) (upholding jury verdict for over $1.5 million in actual damages and $10 million in punitive damages for death from toxic shock syndrome caused by tampons); Dralle v. Ruder, 500 N.E.2d 514 (Ill. Ct. App. 1986) (upholding strict liability and negligence action against manufacturer of Bendectin, an anti-nausea medication prescribed during pregnancy that was found to cause birth defects), judgment rev'd, 529 N.E.2d 209 (Ill. 1988) (no loss of companionship damages); Oxendine v. Merrell Dow Pharmaceuticals, Inc., 506 A.2d 1100 (D.C. 1986) (reversing j.n.o.v. for defendant after jury awarded $750,000 in compensatory damages for birth defects caused by Bendectin, and remanding for trial on punitive damages).

Another example of medical technology for women that may not have been adequately tested is silicone gel-filled breast implants, used by women cancer patients who have had mastectomies and by hundreds of thousands more women who have sought to attain the perfect breast size. While the harm of breast implants is highly disputed, the rupture and leakage of silicone from implants have been associated with very serious arthritic and auto-immune disorders. With a number of cases in the early 1990s yielding multi-million-dollar verdicts (one for $25 million, including $20 million in punitive damages), in late 1992 the Food and Drug Administration (FDA) withdrew approval for silicone breast implants except for "urgent need" patients who had had mastectomies. See 21 C.F.R. pt. 821; David E. Bernstein, The Breast Implant Fiasco (Review Essay), 87 Cal. L. Rev. 457, 479 (1999); Laurel L. Hooper et al., Assessing Causation in Breast Implant Litigation: The Role of Science Panels, 64 Law & Contemp. Probs. 139 (2001). Silicone implant makers have spent more than $6 billion to settle about 370,000 claims. Greg Gordon, Debate on Breast Implants Focusing on Different Toxin: Some Scientists Say Platinum Poses More Risks Than Silicone, Star Trib. (Minneapolis), Dec. 18, 2000, at 1A. Since this time, saline implants have dominated the North American market. In 2005, however, a new type of silicone breast implant became available which is claimed to have a low complication rate (3.4 percent, with follow-up in the range of 16 to 36 months). The FDA approved the new implants, subject to certain conditions. Further study will be necessary to ascertain longer-term risk. See Reconstructive Surgery: Study Finds New Type of Silicone Implant Offers More Natural Looking Breasts, Low Complication Rate, Medical Devices & Surgical Technology Week, via News-Rx.com & NewsRx.net, Nov. 6, 2005.

6. Insurance and Women's Health. Other issues raising suggestions of discriminatory health treatment for women concern the coverage of health care insurance. Is *Bartell* correctly decided? Where, exactly, is the discrimination? Is it because the exclusion of contraceptives (oral contraceptives cost about $300 per year) means that women's out-of-pocket costs for prescription drugs average 68 percent more than men's? Lila Arzua, Why Cover Contraceptives, Wash. Post, Aug. 2, 2000, at A31; Julie F. Kay, Prescription Drug Plans Discriminate Against Women, Reproductive Freedom News, Oct. 2000, at 3. Is it because other drugs used only by men, such as Viagra, which promotes male sexual performance, often (although apparently not under the facts in *Bartell*) are covered by insurance? See EEOC v. UPS, 141 F. Supp. 2d 1216 (D. Minn. 2001) (a plan that covered drugs for male hormonal disorders but not the birth control pill, which can be an important treatment for female hormonal disorders, constitute a facial disparate treatment and disparate impact claim under Title VII).

Since 1998, health plans participating in the Federal Employees Health Benefit Program have been required to provide prescription contraceptive coverage if other prescription drugs are covered. See P.L. 108-7, 117 Stat. 474 (Feb. 20, 2003). A growing number of states mandate that insurance companies offer contraceptive coverage in their prescription drug plans. Cheryl terHorst, Law Group Takes Aim at Insurers' Snub of the Pill, Chi. Trib., Nov. 2, 2002, at C3 (reporting 20 states in 2002). Should the court in *Bartell* have waited for other states to act? What about the specificity of the court's order? Is it an indication that the court is legislating, rather than acting in a proper judicial role? Or is it the only way to correct the discrimination in this case?

Does it follow from *Bartell* that infertility treatments should also be covered? Previous to *Bartell*, courts had not compelled such coverage. See, e.g., Krauel v. Iowa Methodist Med. Ctr., 95 F.3d 674, 679-680 (8th Cir. 1996); Saks v. Franklin Covey Co., 117 F. Supp. 2d 318, 328-329 (S.D.N.Y. 2000). Bartell explicitly recognizes the decisions, without disapproval. 141 F. Supp. 2d at 1275 n.14. Fourteen states have laws regulating coverage of infertility benefits, although the degree of mandated coverage varies significantly between jurisdictions and between plans. For a discussion of this issue, see Brietta R. Clark, *Erickson v. Bartell Drug Co.*: A Roadmap for Gender Equality in Reproductive Health Care of An Empty Promise?, 23 Law & Ineq. J. 299, 317-318 & n.121 (2005). Relevant cases are discussed in id. at 342-347.

Whether various medical procedures are "standard" treatments, covered by health plans, or "experimental or investigational," and thus not covered, may also raise issues of sex discrimination, although in litigation the cases tend to focus on how to interpret insurance policies rather than whether the policies are discriminatory. For an analysis of various issues relating to insurance coverage for treatment of breast cancer, see Julia Anastasio, Legislative Developments in the Regulation of Insurance Coverage: Will These New Regulations Benefit Women with Breast Cancer?, 7 Am. U. J. Gender, Soc. Pol'y & L. 56 (1998-1999) (summarizing and analyzing proposed legislation).

7. Sterilization. As stated in note 2, p. 854, above, sterilization is currently the second-most widely used birth control technique. Almost 17 percent of women rely on female sterilization for contraception, and nearly six percent rely on male sterilization.

Sterilization, traditionally, has been associated with compulsory sterilization and the well-known statement by Justice Holmes that "Three generations of embeciles is enough." Buck v. Bell, 274 U.S. 200, 207 (1927). For a history, see Michael G. Silver, Note, Eugenics and Compulsory Sterilization Laws: Providing Redress for the Victims of a Shameful Era in United States History, 72 Geo. Wash. L. Rev. 862 (2004).

The view of the Supreme Court toward compulsory sterilization changed in Skinner v. Oklahoma ex rel. Williamson, 316 U.S. 535 (1942), which held that it was a violation of equal protection for the state to sterilize a man convicted of some specific felonies (grand larceny and larceny by trespass) but not others (embezzlement). However, some states continue to authorize compulsory sterilization under some circumstances. See, e.g., Cal. Penal Code § 645 (West 2005) (authorizing hormone suppression treatment for parolees convicted of certain sexual offenses); Wash. Rev. Code § 9.92.100 (2005) (authorizing sterilization for persons convicted of sex with female under age ten).

Sterilization abuse has been well documented, impacting disproportionately on poor and minority women whose welfare benefits in some cases have been conditioned on "consenting" to sterilization. See, e.g., Relf v. Weinberger, 372 F. Supp. 1196, 1199 (D.D.C. 1974), on remand sub nom. Relf v. Mathews, 403 F. Supp. 1235 (D.D.C. 1975), vacated sub nom. Relf v. Weinberger, 565 F.2d 722 (D.C. Cir. 1977) (two black girls, ages 12 and 14, were sterilized at a federally funded clinic in Alabama without their knowledge or the knowledge of their parents); Stump v. Sparkman, 435 U.S. 349 (1978) (judge ordered sterilization of 15-year-old girl who was told only that her appendix was being removed, pursuant to petition by girl's mother that she was mildly retarded; judge held absolutely immune from liability); Harris v. Karam, No. CIV 78-601 (D. Ariz. 1979), described in Dick Grosboll, Sterilization Abuse: Current State of the Law and Remedies for Abuse, 10 Golden Gate U. L. Rev. 1147, 1155-1156 (1980) (county officials conditioned medical services on the patient's consent to birth control, sterilization, or abortion). Federal regulations and state laws are designed to protect against such abuses. See, e.g., Utah Code Ann. §62A-6-108 (2005).

The issue of "forced" sterilization in the context of conditions of probation in connection with criminal charges of child abuse or neglect is explored on pp. 937-939 of this chapter.

As forced sterilization laws tightened, it became more difficult for parents and guardians to obtain sterilization for developmentally disabled women whose best interests—including their autonomy—might benefit from sterilization. Attention then shifted to how sterilization standards should both protect women, but also enable them to live more autonomous, richer lives. The shift in emphasis from "disabling" to "enabling" laws is analyzed in James C. Dugan, Note, The Conflict Between "Disabling" and "Enabling" Paradigms in Law: Sterilization, the Developmentally Disabled, and the Americans With Disabilities Act of 1990, 78 Cornell L. Rev. 507 (1993). Among the statutes reflecting this shift, see Conn. Gen. Stat. §45a-699(b) (2006) (court may consent to sterilization if presented with clear and convincing evidence that it is in the best interests of the individual); Vt. Stat. Ann. tit. 18, §8712(c) (2005) (court may order sterilization of an incompetent person if it is in the best interests of the person). Compare In re Romero, 790 P.2d 819 (Colo. 1990) (to sterilize woman without her consent, need to prove incompetency by clear and convincing evidence), with In re Wirsing, 573 N.W.2d 51, 55 (Mich. 1998) (no "clear and convincing" requirement; court can exercise discretion in applying "best interests" standard).

Many states require the appointment of a special guardian ad litem for the incompetent individual to represent that individual's interests before sterilization will be allowed. See, e.g., In re Sterilization of Moore, 221 S.E.2d 307; In re Grady, 426 A.2d 467 (N.J. 1981). What should be the role of that guardian? One scholar argues that the guardian always should oppose sterilization. See George Annas, Sterilization of the Mentally Retarded: A Decision for the Courts, 1981 Hastings Cent. Rep. 19 (Aug.). Does this position attach too great an importance to procreative "autonomy"? Or too little? See Conservatorship of Valerie N., 707

P.2d 760, 772 (Cal. 1985) (statutory prohibition on elective sterilization of developmentally disabled persons on whose behalf sterilization is sought by a parent or guardian violates "privacy and liberty interests protected by the Fourteenth Amendment").

Putting Theory into Practice

5-6. In 1995, an estimated 85,000 women underwent a mastectomy as part of their treatment for breast cancer. About half of them opted for breast reconstruction. The availability of breast reconstruction after a mastectomy, studies have shown, encourages women to obtain early treatment because it makes the prospect of breast cancer less frightening and mutilating than it would otherwise be. A recent survey found that over 100 health insurance companies nationwide have either denied or restricted coverage for breast reconstruction. For example, some companies do not cover reconstruction of the second breast that the woman may choose to have removed as a preventative measure.

Is this an equality issue? See Cristine Nardi, Comment, When Health Insurers Deny Coverage for Breast Reconstructive Surgery: Gender Meets Disability, 1997 Wis. L. Rev. 777 (summarizing relevant state legislation and federal legislative proposals, and urging a national standard).

2. Abortion

a. The Legal Framework

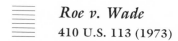

Roe v. Wade
410 U.S. 113 (1973)

Justice BLACKMUN delivered the opinion of the Court....

I

[Texas law makes] it a crime to "procure an abortion," as therein defined, or to attempt one, except with respect to "an abortion procured or attempted by medical advice for the purpose of saving the life of the mother." Similar statutes are in existence in a majority of the States....

II

Jane Roe, a single woman who was residing in Dallas County, Texas, instituted this federal action in March 1970 [seeking] a declaratory judgment that the Texas criminal abortion statutes were unconstitutional on their face, and an injunction restraining the defendant from enforcing the statutes....

V

The principal thrust of appellant's attack on the Texas statutes is that they improperly invade a right, said to be possessed by the pregnant woman, to choose to terminate her pregnancy....

VII

Three reasons have been advanced to explain historically the enactment of criminal abortion laws in the 19th century and to justify their continued existence.

It has been argued occasionally that these laws were the product of a Victorian social concern to discourage illicit sexual conduct. Texas, however, does not advance this justification in the present case....

A second reason is concerned with abortion as a medical procedure. When most criminal abortion laws were first enacted, the procedure was a hazardous one for the woman.... Modern medical techniques have altered this situation....

The third reason is the State's interest — some phrase it in terms of duty — in protecting prenatal life. Some of the argument for this justification rests on the theory that a new human life is present from the moment of conception. The State's interest and general obligation to protect life then extends, it is argued, to prenatal life. Only when the life of the pregnant mother herself is at stake, balanced against the life she carries within her, should the interest of the embryo or fetus not prevail. Logically, of course, a legitimate state interest in this area need not stand or fall on acceptance of the belief that life begins at conception or at some other point prior to live birth. In assessing the State's interest, recognition may be given to the less rigid claim that as long as at least *potential* life is involved, the State may assert interests beyond the protection of the pregnant woman alone....

VIII

The Constitution does not explicitly mention any right of privacy. In a line of decisions, however, going back perhaps as far as Union Pacific R. Co. v. Botsford, 141 U.S. 250, 251 (1891), the Court has recognized that a right of personal privacy, or a guarantee of certain areas or zones of privacy, does exist under the Constitution. In varying contexts, the Court or individual Justices have, indeed, found at least the roots of that right in the First Amendment...; in the Fourth and Fifth Amendments...; in the penumbras of the Bill of Rights...; or in the concept of liberty guaranteed by the first section of the Fourteenth Amendment.... These decisions make it clear that only personal rights that can be deemed "fundamental" or "implicit in the concept of ordered liberty," Palko v. Connecticut, 302 U.S. 319, 325 (1937), are included in this guarantee of personal privacy. They also make it clear that the right has some extension to activities relating to marriage, Loving v. Virginia, 388 U.S. 1, 12 (1967); procreation, Skinner v. Oklahoma, 316 U.S. 535, 541-542 (1942); contraception, Eisenstadt v. Baird, 405 U.S., at 453-454; id., at 460, 463-465 (White, J., concurring in result); family relationships, Prince v. Massachusetts, 321 U.S. 158,

166 (1944); and child rearing and education, Pierce v. Society of Sisters, 268 U.S. 510, 535 (1925), Meyer v. Nebraska, supra.

This right of privacy, whether it be founded in the Fourteenth Amendment's concept of personal liberty and restrictions upon state action, as we feel it is, or, as the District Court determined, in the Ninth Amendment's reservation of rights to the people, is broad enough to encompass a woman's decision whether or not to terminate her pregnancy. The detriment that the State would impose upon the pregnant woman by denying this choice altogether is apparent. Specific and direct harm medically diagnosable even in early pregnancy may be involved. Maternity, or additional offspring, may force upon the woman a distressful life and future. Psychological harm may be imminent. Mental and physical health may be taxed by child care. There is also the distress, for all concerned, associated with the unwanted child, and there is the problem of bringing a child into a family already unable, psychologically and otherwise, to care for it. In other cases, as in this one, the additional difficulties and continuing stigma of unwed motherhood may be involved. All these are factors the woman and her responsible physician necessarily will consider in consultation.

On the basis of elements such as these, appellant and some *amici* argue that the woman's right is absolute and that she is entitled to terminate her pregnancy at whatever time, in whatever way, and for whatever reason she alone chooses. With this we do not agree. Appellant's arguments that Texas either has no valid interest at all in regulating the abortion decision, or no interest strong enough to support any limitation upon the woman's sole determination, are unpersuasive. The Court's decisions recognizing a right of privacy also acknowledge that some state regulation in areas protected by that right is appropriate. As noted above, a State may properly assert important interests in safeguarding health, in maintaining medical standards, and in protecting potential life. At some point in pregnancy, these respective interests become sufficiently compelling to sustain regulation of the factors that govern the abortion decision. The privacy right involved, therefore, cannot be said to be absolute. . . .

We, therefore, conclude that the right of personal privacy includes the abortion decision, but that this right is not unqualified and must be considered against important state interests in regulation. . . .

IX. . .

A

The appellee and certain *amici* argue that the fetus is a "person" within the language and meaning of the Fourteenth Amendment. In support of this, they outline at length and in detail the well-known facts of fetal development. If this suggestion of personhood is established, the appellant's case, of course, collapses, for the fetus' right to life would then be guaranteed specifically by the Amendment. . . .

The Constitution does not define "person" in so many words. Section 1 of the Fourteenth Amendment contains three references to "person." The first, in defining "citizens," speaks of "persons born or naturalized in the United States."

The word also appears both in the Due Process Clause and in the Equal Protection Clause. "Person" is used in other places in the Constitution.... [I]n nearly all these instances, the use of the word is such that it has application only postnatally. None indicates, with any assurance, that it has any possible pre-natal application.

All this, together with our observation ... that throughout the major portion of the 19th century prevailing legal abortion practices were far freer than they are today, persuades us that the word "person," as used in the Fourteenth Amendment, does not include the unborn....

B ...

Texas urges that, apart from the Fourteenth Amendment, life begins at conception and is present throughout pregnancy, and that, therefore, the State has a compelling interest in protecting that life from and after conception. We need not resolve the difficult question of when life begins. When those trained in the respective disciplines of medicine, philosophy, and theology are unable to arrive at any consensus, the judiciary, at this point in the development of man's knowledge, is not in a position to speculate as to the answer....

In areas other than criminal abortion, the law has been reluctant to endorse any theory that life, as we recognize it, begins before live birth or to accord legal rights to the unborn except in narrowly defined situations and except when the rights are contingent upon live birth. For example, the traditional rule of tort law denied recovery for prenatal injuries even though the child was born alive. That rule has been changed in almost every jurisdiction. In most States, recovery is said to be permitted only if the fetus was viable, or at least quick, when the injuries were sustained, though few courts have squarely so held. In a recent development, generally opposed by the commentators, some States permit the parents of a still-born child to maintain an action for wrongful death because of prenatal injuries. Such an action, however, would appear to be one to vindicate the parents' interest and is thus consistent with the view that the fetus, at most, represents only the potentiality of life. Similarly, unborn children have been recognized as acquiring rights or interests by way of inheritance or other devolution of property, and have been represented by guardians *ad litem*. Perfection of the interests involved, again, has generally been contingent upon live birth. In short, the unborn have never been recognized in the law as persons in the whole sense.

X

In view of all this, we do not agree that, by adopting one theory of life, Texas may override the rights of the pregnant woman that are at stake. We repeat, however, that the State does have an important and legitimate interest in preserving and protecting the health of the pregnant woman, whether she be a resident of the State or a nonresident who seeks medical consultation and treatment there, and that it has still *another* important and legitimate interest in protecting the potentiality of human life. These interests are separate and distinct. Each grows in substantiality as the woman approaches term and, at a point during pregnancy, each becomes "compelling."

With respect to the State's important and legitimate interest in the health of the mother, the "compelling" point, in the light of present medical knowledge, is at approximately the end of the first trimester. This is so because of the now-established medical fact . . . that until the end of the first trimester mortality in abortion may be less than mortality in normal childbirth. It follows that, from and after this point, a State may regulate the abortion procedure to the extent that the regulation reasonably relates to the preservation and protection of maternal health. Examples of permissible state regulation in this area are requirements as to the qualifications of the person who is to perform the abortion; as to the licensure of that person; as to the facility in which the procedure is to be performed, that is, whether it must be a hospital or may be a clinic or some other place of less-than-hospital status; as to the licensing of the facility; and the like.

This means, on the other hand, that, for the period of pregnancy prior to this "compelling" point, the attending physician, in consultation with his patient, is free to determine, without regulation by the State, that, in his medical judgment, the patient's pregnancy should be terminated. If that decision is reached, the judgment may be effectuated by an abortion free of interference by the State.

With respect to the State's important and legitimate interest in potential life, the "compelling" point is at viability. This is so because the fetus then presumably has the capability of meaningful life outside the mother's womb. State regulation protective of fetal life after viability thus has both logical and biological justifications. If the State is interested in protecting fetal life after viability, it may go so far as to proscribe abortion during that period, except when it is necessary to preserve the life or health of the mother.

Measured against these standards, [Texas law], in restricting legal abortions to those "procured or attempted by medical advice for the purpose of saving the life of the mother," sweeps too broadly. The statute makes no distinction between abortions performed early in pregnancy and those performed later, and it limits to a single reason, "saving" the mother's life, the legal justification for the procedure. The statute, therefore, cannot survive the constitutional attack made upon it here. . . .

[The concurring opinion of Justice Stewart is omitted.]

[The dissenting opinion of Justice Rehnquist is omitted.]

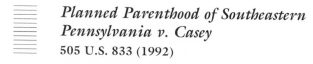

Planned Parenthood of Southeastern Pennsylvania v. Casey
505 U.S. 833 (1992)

Justice O'CONNOR, Justice KENNEDY, and Justice SOUTER announced the judgment of the Court and delivered the opinion of the Court with respect to Parts I, II, III, V-A, V-C, and VI, in which Justice BLACKMUN and Justice STEVENS join, an opinion with respect to Part V-E, in which Justice STEVENS joins, and an opinion with respect to Parts IV, V-B, and V-D.

I

Liberty finds no refuge in a jurisprudence of doubt. Yet 19 years after our holding that the Constitution protects a woman's right to terminate her pregnancy in its early stages, Roe v. Wade, 410 U.S. 113 (1973), that definition of liberty is still questioned. Joining the respondents as amicus curiae, the United States, as it has done in five other cases in the last decade, again asks us to overrule *Roe.* . . .

At issue in these cases are five provisions of the Pennsylvania Abortion Control Act of 1982 as amended in 1988 and 1989. 18 Pa. Cons. Stat. §§ 3203-3220 (1990). . . . The Act requires that a woman seeking an abortion give her informed consent prior to the abortion procedure, and specifies that she be provided with certain information at least 24 hours before the abortion is performed. § 3205. For a minor to obtain an abortion, the Act requires the informed consent of one of her parents, but provides for a judicial bypass option if the minor does not wish to or cannot obtain a parent's consent. § 3206. Another provision of the Act requires that, unless certain exceptions apply, a married woman seeking an abortion must sign a statement indicating that she has notified her husband of her intended abortion. § 3209. The Act exempts compliance with these three requirements in the event of a "medical emergency," which is defined in § 3203 of the Act. See §§ 3203, 3205(a), 3206(a), 3209(c). In addition to the above provisions regulating the performance of abortions, the Act imposes certain reporting requirements on facilities that provide abortion services. §§ 3207(b), 3214(a), 3214(f). . . .

After considering the fundamental constitutional questions resolved by Roe, principles of institutional integrity, and the rule of *stare decisis*, we are led to conclude this: the essential holding of Roe v. Wade should be retained and once again reaffirmed.

It must be stated at the outset and with clarity that *Roe*'s essential holding, the holding we reaffirm, has three parts. First is a recognition of the right of the woman to choose to have an abortion before viability and to obtain it without undue interference from the State. Before viability, the State's interests are not strong enough to support a prohibition of abortion or the imposition of a substantial obstacle to the woman's effective right to elect the procedure. Second is a confirmation of the State's power to restrict abortions after fetal viability, if the law contains exceptions for pregnancies which endanger a woman's life or health. And third is the principle that the State has legitimate interests from the outset of the pregnancy in protecting the health of the woman and the life of the fetus that may become a child. These principles do not contradict one another; and we adhere to each.

II

Constitutional protection of the woman's decision to terminate her pregnancy derives from the Due Process Clause of the Fourteenth Amendment. It declares that no State shall "deprive any person of life, liberty, or property, without due process of law." . . .

Neither the Bill of Rights nor the specific practices of States at the time of the adoption of the Fourteenth Amendment marks the outer limits of the substantive sphere of liberty which the Fourteenth Amendment protects. See U.S. Const., Amend. 9. As the second Justice Harlan recognized: "[T]he full scope of the liberty guaranteed by the Due Process Clause cannot be found in or limited by the precise terms of the specific guarantees elsewhere provided in the Constitution. This 'liberty' is not a series of isolated points pricked out in terms of the taking of property; the freedom of speech, press, and religion; the right to keep and bear arms; the freedom from unreasonable searches and seizures; and so on. It is a rational continuum which, broadly speaking, includes a freedom from all substantial arbitrary impositions and purposeless restraints,... and which also recognizes, what a reasonable and sensitive judgment must, that certain interests require particularly careful scrutiny of the state needs asserted to justify their abridgment." Poe v. Ullman, [367 U.S. 497, 543 (1961) (Harlan, J., dissenting)]....

Our law affords constitutional protection to personal decisions relating to marriage, procreation, contraception, family relationships, child rearing, and education.... These matters, involving the most intimate and personal choices a person may make in a lifetime, choices central to personal dignity and autonomy, are central to the liberty protected by the Fourteenth Amendment. At the heart of liberty is the right to define one's own concept of existence, of meaning, of the universe, and of the mystery of human life. Beliefs about these matters could not define the attributes of personhood were they formed under compulsion of the State.

These considerations begin our analysis of the woman's interest in terminating her pregnancy but cannot end it, for this reason: though the abortion decision may originate within the zone of conscience and belief, it is more than a philosophic exercise. Abortion is a unique act. It is an act fraught with consequences for others: for the woman who must live with the implications of her decision; for the persons who perform and assist in the procedure; for the spouse, family, and society which must confront the knowledge that these procedures exist, procedures some deem nothing short of an act of violence against innocent human life; and, depending on one's beliefs, for the life or potential life that is aborted. Though abortion is conduct, it does not follow that the State is entitled to proscribe it in all instances. That is because the liberty of the woman is at stake in a sense unique to the human condition and so unique to the law. The mother who carries a child to full term is subject to anxieties, to physical constraints, to pain that only she must bear. That these sacrifices have from the beginning of the human race been endured by woman with a pride that ennobles her in the eyes of others and gives to the infant a bond of love cannot alone be grounds for the State to insist she make the sacrifice. Her suffering is too intimate and personal for the State to insist, without more, upon its own vision of the woman's role, however dominant that vision has been in the course of our history and our culture. The destiny of the woman must be shaped to a large extent on her own conception of her spiritual imperatives and her place in society.

It should be recognized, moreover, that in some critical respects the abortion decision is of the same character as the decision to use contraception, to which Griswold v. Connecticut, [381 U.S. 479 (1965),] Eisenstadt v. Baird, [405 U.S. 438 (1972),] and Carey v. Population Services International, [431 U.S. 678 (1977),] afford constitutional protection. We have no doubt as to the correctness of those decisions. They support the reasoning in *Roe* relating to the woman's liberty because they involve personal decisions concerning not only the meaning of procreation but also human responsibility and respect for it. As with abortion, reasonable people will have differences of opinion about these matters. One view is based on such reverence for the wonder of creation that any pregnancy ought to be welcomed and carried to full term no matter how difficult it will be to provide for the child and ensure its well-being. Another is that the inability to provide for the nurture and care of the infant is a cruelty to the child and an anguish to the parent. These are intimate views with infinite variations, and their deep, personal character underlay our decisions in *Griswold*, *Eisenstadt*, and *Carey*. The same concerns are present when the woman confronts the reality that, perhaps despite her attempts to avoid it, she has become pregnant.

It was this dimension of personal liberty that *Roe* sought to protect. . . .

[T]he reservations any of us may have in reaffirming the central holding of *Roe* are outweighed by the explication of individual liberty we have given combined with the force of *stare decisis*. . . .

III

A

[W]hen this Court reexamines a prior holding, its judgment is customarily informed by a series of prudential and pragmatic considerations designed to test the consistency of overruling a prior decision with the ideal of the rule of law, and to gauge the respective costs of reaffirming and overruling a prior case. Thus, for example, we may ask whether the rule has proved to be intolerable simply in defying practical workability . . . ; whether the rule is subject to a kind of reliance that would lend a special hardship to the consequences of overruling and add inequity to the cost of repudiation . . . ; whether related principles of law have so far developed as to have left the old rule no more than a remnant of abandoned doctrine . . . ; or whether facts have so changed or come to be seen so differently, as to have robbed the old rule of significant application or justification. . . .

Although *Roe* has engendered opposition, it has in no sense proven "unworkable," . . . representing as it does a simple limitation beyond which a state law is unenforceable. . . .

The inquiry into reliance counts the cost of a rule's repudiation as it would fall on those who have relied reasonably on the rule's continued application. Since the classic case for weighing reliance heavily in favor of following the earlier rule occurs in the commercial context, see Payne v. Tennessee, [501 U.S. 808 (1991)], where advance planning of great precision is most obviously a necessity, it is no cause for surprise that some would find no reliance worthy of consideration in support of *Roe*.

...Abortion is customarily chosen as an unplanned response to the consequence of unplanned activity or to the failure of conventional birth control, and except on the assumption that no intercourse would have occurred but for *Roe*'s holding, such behavior may appear to justify no reliance claim. Even if reliance could be claimed on that unrealistic assumption, the argument might run, any reliance interest would be *de minimis*. This argument would be premised on the hypothesis that reproductive planning could take virtually immediate account of any sudden restoration of state authority to ban abortions.

To eliminate the issue of reliance that easily, however, one would need to limit cognizable reliance to specific instances of sexual activity. But to do this would be simply to refuse to face the fact that for two decades of economic and social developments, people have organized intimate relationships and made choices that define their views of themselves and their places in society, in reliance on the availability of abortion in the event that contraception should fail. The ability of women to participate equally in the economic and social life of the Nation has been facilitated by their ability to control their reproductive lives.... The Constitution serves human values, and while the effect of reliance on *Roe* cannot be exactly measured, neither can the certain cost of overruling *Roe* for people who have ordered their thinking and living around that case be dismissed.

No evolution of legal principle has left *Roe*'s doctrinal footings weaker than they were in 1973. No development of constitutional law since the case was decided has implicitly or explicitly left *Roe* behind as a mere survivor of obsolete constitutional thinking.

It will be recognized, of course, that *Roe* stands at an intersection of two lines of decisions, but in whichever doctrinal category one reads the case, the result for present purposes will be the same. The *Roe* Court itself placed its holding in the succession of cases most prominently exemplified by *Griswold*...see *Roe*, 410 U.S., at 152-153. When it is so seen, *Roe* is clearly in no jeopardy....

Roe...may be seen [also]...as a rule (whether or not mistaken) of personal autonomy and bodily integrity, with doctrinal affinity to cases recognizing limits on governmental power to mandate medical treatment or to bar its rejection. If so, our cases since *Roe* accord with *Roe*'s view that a State's interest in the protection of life falls short of justifying any plenary override of individual liberty claims....

If indeed the woman's interest in deciding whether to bear and beget a child had not been recognized as in *Roe*, the State might as readily restrict a woman's right to choose to carry a pregnancy to term as to terminate it, to further asserted state interests in population control, or eugenics, for example. Yet *Roe* has been sensibly relied upon to counter any such suggestions. E.g., Arnold v. Board of Education of Escambia County, Ala., 880 F.2d 305, 311 (11th Cir. 1989) (relying upon *Roe* and concluding that government officials violate the Constitution by coercing a minor to have an abortion); Avery v. County of Burke, 660 F.2d 111, 115 (4th Cir. 1981) (county agency inducing teenage girl to undergo unwanted sterilization on the basis of misrepresentation that she had sickle cell trait)....

We have seen how time has overtaken some of *Roe*'s factual assumptions: advances in maternal health care allow for abortions safe to the mother later in pregnancy than was true in 1973, see *Akron I*, [462 U.S.] at 429, n.11, and advances in neonatal care have advanced viability to a point somewhat earlier.... But these facts go only to the scheme of time limits on the realization of competing interests, and the divergences from the factual premises of 1973 have no bearing on the validity of *Roe*'s central holding, that viability marks the earliest point at which the State's interest in fetal life is constitutionally adequate to justify a legislative ban on nontherapeutic abortions. The soundness or unsoundness of that constitutional judgment in no sense turns on whether viability occurs at approximately 28 weeks, as was usual at the time of *Roe*, at 23 to 24 weeks, as it sometimes does today, or at some moment even slightly earlier in pregnancy, as it may if fetal respiratory capacity can somehow be enhanced in the future. Whenever it may occur, the attainment of viability may continue to serve as the critical fact, just as it has done since *Roe* was decided; which is to say that no change in *Roe*'s factual underpinning has left its central holding obsolete, and none supports an argument for overruling it....

Within the bounds of normal *stare decisis* analysis, then, and subject to the considerations on which it customarily turns, the stronger argument is for affirming *Roe*'s central holding, with whatever degree of personal reluctance any of us may have, not for overruling it....

C . . .

The Court's power lies . . . in its legitimacy, a product of substance and perception that shows itself in the people's acceptance of the Judiciary as fit to determine what the Nation's law means and to declare what it demands....

The Court must take care to speak and act in ways that allow people to accept its decisions on the terms the Court claims for them, as grounded truly in principle, not as compromises with social and political pressures having, as such, no bearing on the principled choices that the Court is obliged to make....

Where, in the performance of its judicial duties, the Court decides a case in such a way as to resolve the sort of intensely divisive controversy reflected in *Roe* and those rare, comparable cases, its decision has a dimension that the resolution of the normal case does not carry. It is the dimension present whenever the Court's interpretation of the Constitution calls the contending sides of a national controversy to end their national division by accepting a common mandate rooted in the Constitution.

The Court is not asked to do this very often, having thus addressed the Nation only twice in our lifetime, in the decisions of Brown v. Board of Education, 347 U.S. 483 (1954) and *Roe*. But when the Court does act in this way, its decision requires an equally rare precedential force to counter the inevitable efforts to overturn it and to thwart its implementation. Some of those efforts may be mere unprincipled emotional reactions; others may proceed from principles worthy of profound respect. But whatever the premises of opposition may be, only the most convincing justification under accepted standards of precedent could suffice to demonstrate that a later decision overruling the first was anything but a surrender to political pressure, and an unjustified repudiation of the principle on which the Court staked its authority in the first instance. So to overrule under fire in the absence of the most compelling reason to reexamine a watershed decision would subvert the Court's legitimacy beyond any serious question....

Some cost will be paid by anyone who approves or implements a constitutional decision where it is unpopular, or who refuses to work to undermine the decision or to force its reversal. The price may be criticism or ostracism, or it may be violence. An extra price will be paid by those who themselves disapprove of the decision's results when viewed outside of constitutional terms, but who nevertheless struggle to accept it, because they respect the rule of law. To all those who will be so tested by following, the Court implicitly undertakes to remain steadfast, lest in the end a price be paid for nothing. The promise of constancy, once given, binds its maker for as long as the power to stand by the decision survives and the understanding of the issue has not changed so fundamentally as to render the commitment obsolete....

A decision to overrule *Roe*'s essential holding under the existing circumstances would address error, if error there was, at the cost of both profound and unnecessary damage to the Court's legitimacy, and to the Nation's commitment to the rule of law. It is therefore imperative to adhere to the essence of *Roe*'s original decision, and we do so today.

IV . . .

. . . The woman's right to terminate her pregnancy before viability is the most central principle of Roe v. Wade. It is a rule of law and a component of liberty we cannot renounce.

On the other side of the equation is the interest of the State in the protection of potential life. The *Roe* Court recognized the State's "important and legitimate interest in protecting the potentiality of human life." *Roe*, supra, at 162....

That portion of the decision in *Roe* has been given too little acknowledgment and implementation by the Court in its subsequent cases. Those cases decided that any regulation touching upon the abortion decision must survive strict scrutiny, to be sustained only if drawn in narrow terms to further a compelling state interest. See, e.g., *Akron I*, 462 U.S. at 427. Not all of the cases decided under that formulation can be reconciled with the holding in *Roe* itself....

Roe established a trimester framework to govern abortion regulations....

The trimester framework no doubt was erected to ensure that the woman's right to choose not become so subordinate to the State's interest in promoting fetal life that her choice exists in theory but not in fact. We do not agree, however, that the trimester approach is necessary to accomplish this objective. A framework of this rigidity was unnecessary and in its later interpretation sometimes contradicted the State's permissible exercise of its powers.

Though the woman has a right to choose to terminate or continue her pregnancy before viability, it does not at all follow that the State is prohibited from taking steps to ensure that this choice is thoughtful and informed. Even in the earliest stages of pregnancy, the State may enact rules and regulations designed to encourage her to know that there are philosophic and social arguments of great weight that can be brought to bear in favor of continuing the pregnancy to full term and that there are procedures and institutions to allow adoption of unwanted children as well as a certain degree of state assistance if the mother chooses to raise the child herself. "[T]he Constitution does not forbid a State or city, pursuant to democratic processes, from expressing a preference for 'normal childbirth.'" Webster v. Reproductive Health Services, 492 U.S. at 511. . . . It follows that States are free to enact laws to provide a reasonable framework for a woman to make a decision that has such profound and lasting meaning. This, too, we find consistent with *Roe*'s central premises, and indeed the inevitable consequence of our holding that the State has an interest in protecting the life of the unborn. . . .

Numerous forms of state regulation might have the incidental effect of increasing the cost or decreasing the availability of medical care, whether for abortion or any other medical procedure. The fact that a law which serves a valid purpose, one not designed to strike at the right itself, has the incidental effect of making it more difficult or more expensive to procure an abortion cannot be enough to invalidate it. Only where state regulation imposes an undue burden on a woman's ability to make this decision does the power of the State reach into the heart of the liberty protected by the Due Process Clause. . . .

A finding of an undue burden is a shorthand for the conclusion that a state regulation has the purpose or effect of placing a substantial obstacle in the path of a woman seeking an abortion of a nonviable fetus. A statute with this purpose is invalid because the means chosen by the State to further the interest in potential life must be calculated to inform the woman's free choice, not hinder it. . . .

Some guiding principles should emerge. What is at stake is the woman's right to make the ultimate decision, not a right to be insulated from all others in doing so. Regulations which do no more than create a structural mechanism by which the State, or the parent or guardian of a minor, may express profound respect for the life of the unborn are permitted, if they are not a substantial obstacle to the woman's exercise of the right to choose. . . . Unless it has that effect on her right of choice, a state measure designed to persuade her to choose childbirth over abortion will be upheld if reasonably related to that goal. Regulations designed to foster the health of a woman seeking an abortion are valid if they do not constitute an undue burden. . . .

These principles control our assessment of the Pennsylvania statute, and we now turn to the issue of the validity of its challenged provisions.

V . . .

A

[The Court upholds the medical emergency definition, as construed by the court of appeals to include three conditions — preeclampsia, inevitable abortion, and premature ruptured membrane — that the district court had found were not covered by the statute.]

B . . .

Except in a medical emergency, the statute requires that at least 24 hours before performing an abortion a physician inform the woman of the nature of the procedure, the health risks of the abortion and of childbirth, and the "probable gestational age of the unborn child." The physician or a qualified nonphysician must inform the woman of the availability of printed materials published by the State describing the fetus and providing information about medical assistance for childbirth, information about child support from the father, and a list of agencies which provide adoption and other services as alternatives to abortion. An abortion may not be performed unless the woman certifies in writing that she has been informed of the availability of these printed materials and has been provided them if she chooses to view them. . . .

To the extent *Akron I* [, 462 U.S. 416 (1983),] and *Thornburgh* [, 476 U.S. at 762,] find a constitutional violation when the government requires, as it does here, the giving of truthful, nonmisleading information about the nature of the procedure, the attendant health risks and those of childbirth, and the "probable gestational age" of the fetus, those cases go too far, are inconsistent with *Roe*'s acknowledgment of an important interest in potential life, and are overruled. . . . It cannot be questioned that psychological well-being is a facet of health. Nor can it be doubted that most women considering an abortion would deem the impact on the fetus relevant, if not dispositive, to the decision. In attempting to ensure that a woman apprehend the full consequences of her decision, the State furthers the legitimate purpose of reducing the risk that a woman may elect an abortion, only to discover later, with devastating psychological consequences, that her decision was not fully informed. If the information the State requires to be made available to the woman is truthful and not misleading, the requirement may be permissible.

We also see no reason why the State may not require doctors to inform a woman seeking an abortion of the availability of materials relating to the consequences to the fetus, even when those consequences have no direct relation to her health. An example illustrates the point. We would think it constitutional for the State to require that in order for there to be informed consent to a kidney transplant operation the recipient must be supplied with information about risks to the donor as well as risks to himself or herself. . . .

[I]t is worth noting that the statute now before us does not require a physician to comply with the informed consent provisions "if he or she can demonstrate by a preponderance of the evidence, that he or she reasonably believed that furnishing the information would have resulted in a severely adverse effect on the physical or mental health of the patient." 18 Pa. Cons. Stat. §3205 (1990). In this respect, the statute does not prevent the physician from exercising his or her medical judgment. . . .

The idea that important decisions will be more informed and deliberate if they follow some period of reflection does not strike us as unreasonable, particularly where the statute directs that important information become part of the background of the decision. The statute, as construed by the Court of Appeals, permits avoidance of the waiting period in the event of a medical emergency and the record evidence shows that in the vast majority of cases, a 24-hour delay does not create any appreciable health risk. In theory, at least, the waiting period is a reasonable measure to implement the State's interest in protecting the life of the unborn, a measure that does not amount to an undue burden.

Whether the mandatory 24-hour waiting period is nonetheless invalid because in practice it is a substantial obstacle to a woman's choice to terminate her pregnancy is a closer question. The findings of fact by the District Court indicate that because of the distances many women must travel to reach an abortion provider, the practical effect will often be a delay of much more than a day because the waiting period requires that a woman seeking an abortion make at least two visits to the doctor. The District Court also found that in many instances this will increase the exposure of women seeking abortions to "the harassment and hostility of anti-abortion protestors demonstrating outside a clinic."... As a result, the District Court found that for those women who have the fewest financial resources, those who must travel long distances, and those who have difficulty explaining their whereabouts to husbands, employers, or others, the 24-hour waiting period will be "particularly burdensome." Id. at 1352.

These findings are troubling in some respects, but they do not demonstrate that the waiting period constitutes an undue burden. We do not doubt that, as the District Court held, the waiting period has the effect of "increasing the cost and risk of delay of abortions," id. at 1378, but the District Court did not conclude that the increased costs and potential delays amount to substantial obstacles....

C

Section 3209 of Pennsylvania's abortion law provides, except in cases of medical emergency, that no physician shall perform an abortion on a married woman without receiving a signed statement from the woman that she has notified her spouse that she is about to undergo an abortion. The woman has the option of providing an alternative signed statement certifying that her husband is not the man who impregnated her; that her husband could not be located; that the pregnancy is the result of spousal sexual assault which she has reported; or that the woman believes that notifying her husband will cause him or someone else to inflict bodily injury upon her. A physician who performs an abortion on a married woman without receiving the appropriate signed statement will have his or her license revoked, and is liable to the husband for damages.

[The District Court findings, with respect to the reasons some women do not consult their husbands about the decision to obtain an abortion, including domestic violence, sexual abuse, rape, and sexual mutilation, are omitted.]...

This information and the District Court's findings reinforce what common sense would suggest. In well-functioning marriages, spouses discuss important intimate decisions such as whether to bear a child. But there are millions of women in this country who are the victims of regular physical and psychological abuse at the hands of their husbands. Should these women become pregnant, they may have very good reasons for not wishing to inform their husbands of their decision to obtain an abortion. Many may have justifiable fears of physical abuse, but may be no less fearful of the consequences of reporting prior abuse to the Commonwealth of Pennsylvania. Many may have a reasonable fear that notifying their husbands will provoke further instances of child abuse; these women are not exempt from § 3209's notification requirement. Many may fear devastating forms of psychological abuse from their husbands, including verbal harassment, threats of future violence, the destruction of possessions, physical confinement to the home, the withdrawal of financial support, or the disclosure of the abortion to family and friends. These methods of psychological abuse may act as even more of a deterrent to notification than the possibility of physical violence, but women who are the victims of the abuse are not exempt from § 3209's notification requirement. And many women who are pregnant as a result of sexual assaults by their husbands will be unable to avail themselves of the exception for spousal sexual assault, § 3209(b)(3), because the exception requires that the woman have notified law enforcement authorities within 90 days of the assault, and her husband will be notified of her report once an investigation begins. § 3128(c). If anything in this field is certain, it is that victims of spousal sexual assault are extremely reluctant to report the abuse to the government; hence, a great many spousal rape victims will not be exempt from the notification requirement imposed by § 3209.

The spousal notification requirement is thus likely to prevent a significant number of women from obtaining an abortion. It does not merely make abortions a little more difficult or expensive to obtain; for many women, it will impose a substantial obstacle. We must not blind ourselves to the fact that the significant number of women who fear for their safety and the safety of their children are likely to be deterred from procuring an abortion as surely as if the Commonwealth had outlawed abortion in all cases....

This conclusion is in no way inconsistent with our decisions upholding parental notification or consent requirements. See, e.g., *Akron II* [Ohio v. Akron Center for Reproductive Health, 497 U.S. 502, 520 (1990)]; Bellotti v. Baird, 443 U.S. 622 (1979) (*Bellotti II*); Planned Parenthood of Central Mo. v. Danforth, [428 U.S. 52, 74 (1976)]. Those enactments, and our judgment that they are constitutional, are based on the quite reasonable assumption that minors will benefit from consultation with their parents and that children will often not realize that their parents have their best interests at heart. We cannot adopt a parallel assumption about adult women.

We recognize that a husband has a "deep and proper concern and interest...in his wife's pregnancy and in the growth and development of the fetus she is carrying." *Danforth*, [428 U.S.] at 69. With regard to the children he has fathered and raised, the Court has recognized his "cognizable and substantial" interest in their custody. Stanley v. Illinois, 405 U.S. 645, 651-652 (1972)....If this case concerned a State's ability to require the mother to notify the father before taking some action with respect to a living child raised by both, therefore, it would be reasonable to conclude as a general matter that the father's interest in the welfare of the child and the mother's interest are equal.

Before birth, however, the issue takes on a very different cast. It is an inescapable biological fact that state regulation with respect to the child a woman is carrying will have a far greater impact on the mother's liberty than on the father's. The effect of state regulation on a woman's protected liberty is doubly deserving of scrutiny in such a case, as the State has touched not only upon the private sphere of the family but upon the very bodily integrity of the pregnant woman. . . . The Court has held that "when the wife and the husband disagree on this decision, the view of only one of the two marriage partners can prevail. Inasmuch as it is the woman who physically bears the child and who is the more directly and immediately affected by the pregnancy, as between the two, the balance weighs in her favor." *Danforth*, [428 U.S.] at 71. . . .

Section 3209 embodies a view of marriage consonant with the common-law status of married women but repugnant to our present understanding of marriage and of the nature of the rights secured by the Constitution. Women do not lose their constitutionally protected liberty when they marry. The Constitution protects all individuals, male or female, married or unmarried, from the abuse of governmental power, even where that power is employed for the supposed benefit of a member of the individual's family. These considerations confirm our conclusion that § 3209 is invalid.

D

[The parental consent provision, requiring consent to an abortion, except in a medical emergency, for an unemancipated young woman under 18, unless the court determines that that the young woman is mature and capable of giving informed consent and has in fact given her informed consent, or that an abortion would be in her best interests, is constitutional.]

[The opinion of Justice Stevens, concurring in part and dissenting in part, is omitted.]

Justice BLACKMUN, concurring in part, concurring in the judgment in part, and dissenting in part.

I join parts I, II, III, V-A, V-C, and VI of the joint opinion of Justices O'Connor, Kennedy, and Souter. . . .

II

Today, no less than yesterday, the Constitution and decisions of this Court require that a State's abortion restrictions be subjected to the strictest of judicial scrutiny. Our precedents and the joint opinion's principles require us to subject all non-*de minimis* abortion regulations to strict scrutiny. Under this standard, the Pennsylvania statute's provisions requiring content-based counseling, a 24-hour delay, informed parental consent, and reporting of abortion-related information must be invalidated. . . .

A . . .

State restrictions on abortion violate a woman's right of privacy in two ways. First, compelled continuation of a pregnancy infringes upon a woman's right to bodily integrity by imposing substantial physical intrusions and significant risks of physical harm. . . .

Further, when the State restricts a woman's right to terminate her pregnancy, it deprives a woman of the right to make her own decision about reproduction and family planning — critical life choices that this Court long has deemed central to the right to privacy. The decision to terminate or continue a pregnancy has no less an impact on a woman's life than decisions about contraception or marriage. [*Roe* at 153.] Because motherhood has a dramatic impact on a woman's educational prospects, employment opportunities, and self-determination, restrictive abortion laws deprive her of basic control over her life. For these reasons, "the decision whether or not to beget or bear a child" lies at "the very heart of this cluster of constitutionally protected choices." Carey v. Population Services International, 431 U.S. 678, 685 (1977).

A State's restrictions on a woman's right to terminate her pregnancy also implicate constitutional guarantees of gender equality. State restrictions on abortion compel women to continue pregnancies they otherwise might terminate. By restricting the right to terminate pregnancies, the State conscripts women's bodies into its service, forcing women to continue their pregnancies, suffer the pains of childbirth, and in most instances, provide years of maternal care. The State does not compensate women for their services; instead, it assumes that they owe this duty as a matter of course. This assumption — that women can simply be forced to accept the "natural" status and incidents of motherhood — appears to rest upon a conception of women's role that has triggered the protection of the Equal Protection Clause. See, e.g., Mississippi Univ. for Women v. Hogan, 458 U.S. 718, 724-726 (1982); Craig v. Boren, 429 U.S. 190, 198-199 (1976). The joint opinion recognizes that these assumptions about women's place in society "are no longer consistent with our understanding of the family, the individual, or the Constitution."...

[The opinion of Chief Justice Rehnquist, with whom Justice White, Justice Scalia, and Justice Thomas join, concurring in the judgment in part and dissenting in part, and urging that Roe v. Wade be overruled, is omitted.]

Justice SCALIA, with whom THE CHIEF JUSTICE, Justice WHITE, and Justice THOMAS join, concurring in the judgment in part and dissenting in part....

The States may, if they wish, permit abortion-on-demand, but the Constitution does not require them to do so. The permissibility of abortion, and the limitations upon it, are to be resolved like most important questions in our democracy: by citizens trying to persuade one another and then voting....

That is, quite simply, the issue in this case: not whether the power of a woman to abort her unborn child is a "liberty" in the absolute sense; or even whether it is a liberty of great importance to many women. Of course it is both. The issue is whether it is a liberty protected by the Constitution of the United States. I am sure it is not. I reach that conclusion not because of anything so exalted as my views concerning the "concept of existence, of meaning, of the universe, and of the mystery of human life."...Rather, I reach it for the same reason I reach the conclusion that bigamy is not constitutionally protected — because of two simple facts: (1) the Constitution says absolutely nothing about it, and (2) the longstanding traditions of American society have permitted it to be legally proscribed. *Akron II,* [497 U.S.] at 520 (Scalia, J., concurring)....

The Court's reliance upon stare decisis can best be described as contrived....

I have always thought, and I think a lot of other people have always thought, that the arbitrary trimester framework, which the Court today discards, was quite as central to *Roe* as the arbitrary viability test, which the Court today retains. It seems particularly ungrateful to carve the trimester framework out of the core of *Roe*, since its very rigidity (in sharp contrast to the utter indeterminability of the "undue burden" test) is probably the only reason the Court is able to say, in urging stare decisis, that *Roe* "has in no sense proven 'unworkable.'"...[T]he following portions of *Roe* have not been saved:

> Under *Roe*, requiring that a woman seeking an abortion be provided truthful information about abortion before giving informed written consent is unconstitutional, if the information is designed to influence her choice, *Thornburgh*, 476 U.S. at 759-765; *Akron I*, 462 U.S. at 442-445. Under the joint opinion's "undue burden" regime (as applied today, at least) such a requirement is constitutional....
>
> Under *Roe*, requiring that information be provided by a doctor, rather than by nonphysician counselors, is unconstitutional, *Akron I*, [462 U.S.] at 446-449. Under the "undue burden" regime (as applied today, at least) it is not....
>
> Under *Roe*, requiring a 24-hour waiting period between the time the woman gives her informed consent and the time of the abortion is unconstitutional, *Akron I*, [462 U.S.] at 449-451. Under the "undue burden" regime (as applied today, at least) it is not....
>
> Under *Roe*, requiring detailed reports that include demographic data about each woman who seeks an abortion and various information about each abortion is unconstitutional, *Thornburgh*, [476 U.S.] at 765-768. Under the "undue burden" regime (as applied today, at least) it generally is not....

The Court's description of the place of *Roe* in the social history of the United States is unrecognizable. Not only did *Roe* not, as the Court suggests, resolve the deeply divisive issue of abortion; it did more than anything else to nourish it, by elevating it to the national level where it is infinitely more difficult to resolve. National politics were not plagued by abortion protests, national abortion lobbying, or abortion marches on Congress, before Roe v. Wade was decided. Profound disagreement existed among our citizens over the issue—as it does over other issues, such as the death penalty—but that disagreement was being worked out at the state level. As with many other issues, the division of sentiment within each State was not as closely balanced as it was among the population of the Nation as a whole, meaning not only that more people would be satisfied with the results of state-by-state resolution, but also that those results would be more stable. Pre-*Roe*, moreover, political compromise was possible.

Roe's mandate for abortion-on-demand destroyed the compromises of the past, rendered compromise impossible for the future, and required the entire issue to be resolved uniformly, at the national level. At the same time, *Roe* created a vast new class of abortion consumers and abortion proponents by eliminating the moral opprobrium that had attached to the act. ("If the Constitution *guarantees* abortion, how can it be bad?"—not an accurate line of thought, but a natural one.) Many favor all of those developments, and it is not for me to say that they are wrong. But to portray *Roe* as the statesmanlike "settlement" of a divisive issue, a jurisprudential Peace of Westphalia that is worth preserving, is nothing less than Orwellian. *Roe* fanned into life an issue that has inflamed our national politics in general, and has obscured with its smoke the selection of Justices to this Court in particular, ever since. And by keeping us in the abortion-umpiring business, it is the perpetuation of that disruption, rather than of any *pax Roeana*, that the Court's new majority decrees....

[W]hether it would "subvert the Court's legitimacy" or not, the notion that we would decide a case differently from the way we otherwise would have in order to show that we can stand firm against public disapproval is frightening. It is a bad enough idea, even in the head of someone like me, who believes that the text of the Constitution, and our traditions, say what they say and there is no fiddling with them. But when it is in the mind of a Court that believes the Constitution has an evolving meaning...; that the Ninth Amendment's reference to "othe[r]" rights is not a disclaimer, but a charter for action...; and that the function of this Court is to "speak before all others for [the people's] constitutional ideals" unrestrained by meaningful text or tradition—then the notion that the Court must adhere to a decision for as long as the decision faces "great opposition" and the Court is "under fire" acquires a character of almost czarist arrogance. We are offended by these marchers who descend upon us, every year on the anniversary of *Roe*, to protest our saying that the Constitution requires what our society has never thought the Constitution requires. These people who refuse to be "tested by following" must be taught a lesson. We have no Cossacks, but at least we can stubbornly refuse to abandon an erroneous opinion that we might otherwise change—to show how little they intimidate us....

In truth, I am as distressed as the Court is...about the "political pressure" directed to the Court: the marches, the mail, the protests aimed at inducing us to change our opinions. How upsetting it is, that so many of our citizens (good people, not lawless ones, on both sides of this abortion issue, and on various sides of other issues as well) think that we Justices should properly take into account their views, as though we were engaged not in ascertaining an objective law but in determining some kind of social consensus. The Court would profit, I think, from giving less attention to the fact of this distressing phenomenon, and more attention to the *cause* of it. That cause permeates today's opinion: a new mode of constitutional adjudication that relies not upon text and traditional practice to determine the law, but upon what the Court calls "reasoned judgment,"...which turns out to be nothing but philosophical predilection and moral intuition....

As long as this Court thought (and the people thought) that we Justices were doing essentially lawyers' work up here—reading text and discerning our society's traditional understanding of that text—the public pretty much left us alone. Texts and traditions are facts to study, not convictions to demonstrate about. But if in reality our process of constitutional adjudication consists primarily of making *value judgments*...then a free and intelligent people's attitude towards us can be expected to be (*ought* to be) quite different. The people know that their value judgments are quite as good as those taught in any law school—maybe better. If, indeed, the "liberties" protected by the Constitution are, as the Court says, undefined and unbounded, than the people *should* demonstrate, to protest that we do not implement their values instead of *ours*....

We should get out of this area, where we have no right to be, and where we do neither ourselves nor the country any good by remaining.

Notes

1. Stare Decisis, Reliance, and Autonomy. The joint O'Connor/ Kennedy/Souter opinion accepts the conventional wisdom that the strongest reliance interests, for stare decisis purposes, are in commercial cases. What values does this assumption reflect?

What is the nature of the reliance interests at stake in this context? In what sense can it be said that women have come to "rely upon" the right to choose abortion? One possibility is that they are accustomed to being reckless in using birth control in the knowledge that abortion exists as a "back-up." Can this be what the three Justices have in mind? A broader view of both reliance and the interests protected by *Roe* might be that women have come to see themselves as having some control and autonomy in personal decisionmaking, which *Roe* has come to symbolize, and it is this autonomy that enables them to see and plan their lives — their occupational lives as well as their reproductive lives — in long-range terms. Can *this* be what they have in mind? If so, this reasoning is specifically rejected by Justice Rehnquist, joined by four other Justices:

> The joint opinion . . . turns to what can only be described as an unconventional — and unconvincing — notion of reliance, a view based on the surmise that the availability of abortion since *Roe* has led to "two decades of economic and social developments that would be undercut if the error of *Roe* were recognized." . . . The joint opinion's assertion of this fact is undeveloped and totally conclusory. In fact, one can not be sure to what economic and social developments the opinion is referring. Surely it is dubious to suggest that women have reached their "places in society" in reliance upon *Roe*, rather than as a result of their determination to obtain higher education and compete with men in the job market, and of society's increasing recognition of their ability to fill positions that were previously thought to be reserved only for men.

Planned Parenthood v. Casey, 505 U.S. at 956, 957 (Rehnquist, C.J., dissenting). What different assumptions about individual autonomy and choice do Chief Justice Rehnquist and the authors of the joint opinion make?

What impact should public opinion have on abortion law? Public opinion polls consistently find that, depending on how the question is framed, between 50 and 60 percent of Americans favor keeping abortion legal and allowing women the right to choose whether to bear a child without government interference. See, e.g., Joan Biskupic, Abortion-Notification Case Could Test Changing Court, USA Today, Nov. 30, 2005, at A1 (USA Today/CNN/Gallup poll showed 56 percent of people think abortion should be legal under certain circumstances and 26 percent believe it should be legal in all circumstances). Do these figures reflect "reliance" on *Roe*?

For a state-by-state compendium of laws relating to abortion and contraception, see http://www.guttmacher.org/statecenter/spibs/spib_OAL.pdf (last visited March 13, 2006). See also NARAL Pro-Choice America & NARAL Pro-Choice America Foundation, Who Decides? The Status of Women's Reproductive Rights in the United States (14th ed. Jan. 2005).

2. Spousal Notice and Consent Provisions. In Planned Parenthood v. Danforth, 428 U.S. 52 (1976), the Supreme Court struck down Missouri's spousal consent provisions on the ground that the goal of fostering mutuality and trust in a marriage cannot reasonably be advanced by giving the husband a veto power over the abortion decision. Some lower court decisions had distinguished spousal consent from spousal notification and upheld the presumably less intrusive notification requirements. In *Casey*, the Court seems to have decided to treat consent and notification alike for spouses, in contrast to its decisions involving minors. See note 3, below.

What seems to be the concern of state legislators in attempting to mandate spousal notification? Is it simply one more barrier to abortion designed to curtail the number of abortions that occur in the state? Is it possible that the legislators have in mind some particular scenarios in which an abortion, without spousal notification, would be the wrong decision even from the woman's point of view? What if, for example, the woman decided in favor of an abortion, despite her wishes for a child, because she believed (erroneously) that her husband did not want another child but did not want to put him in the position of supporting an abortion? What if she believed (again, wrongly) that another child would create too much economic pressure on her husband but that his moral scruples opposing abortion would not permit him to take that economic pressure into account in advising her about whether to have an abortion? Chief Justice Rehnquist appears to have in mind these kinds of fact patterns. See *Casey*, 505 U.S. at 973 n.2 (Rehnquist, C.J., dissenting). Is it impermissible for a state legislature to attempt to protect a woman from these possible misperceptions? Or is the problem that in doing so it cannot infringe too greatly on the rights of women in the more common circumstances that did not fit such patterns?

Post-*Casey*, challenges persist by husbands or boyfriends seeking to protect their interests in a fetus continues. In one case, a Pennsylvania state judge responded to an ex-boyfriend's petition by entering a temporary order prohibiting a woman from carrying out her plans to have an abortion; the ban was lifted a week later. Stachokus v. Meyers, No. 67-E (Pa. Ct. of Common Pleas, August 5, 2002), available at http://news.findlaw.com/hdocs/docs/abortion/stachvmey080502ord.pdf. At a time when many feminists are urging measures to encourage fathers to be more engaged in child rearing, does it make sense to deny them the right to participate in the abortion decision?

3. Parental Notice and Consent Requirements. The parental consent with judicial bypass provision upheld in *Casey* essentially confirms the Court's prior decisions in *Danforth* and *Bellotti*, referred to above. Most (but not all) of the activity since then has concerned the issue of parental notification rather than parental consent.

In Hodgson v. Minnesota, 497 U.S. 417 (1990), the Court considered a challenge to a judicial bypass provision accompanying a parental notification requirement, as applied, which alleged that the bypass provision imposes additional trauma on minors, causes delays and hence increases the health risks of the procedure, and compels many minors to travel out of state to avoid the provision.

In Minnesota, as well as in Pennsylvania, waiting periods aggravate the burdens. See 497 U.S. at 464, 467-468 (Marshall, J., dissenting). To the dissenters in *Hodgson*, these burdens seemed particularly pointless in that the court hearing, for those with the stamina and resources to pursue the procedures, was in effect a "rubber stamp," with only an "extremely small" number of petitions denied. According to Justice Marshall, "[a]lthough they represent substantial intrusion on minors' privacy and take up significant amounts of court time, there is no evidence that they promote more reasoned decisionmaking or screen out adolescents who may be particularly immature or vulnerable." Id. at 477. This conclusion appears to conform with ten years of experience in Massachusetts, in which of 9,000 bypass petitions, all but 13 were granted, and of these 13, all but one was successfully appealed; in the one remaining case, the parents eventually gave consent, and the minor obtained the abortion. American Academy of Pediatrics v. Lungren, 940 P.2d 797, 836 n.12 (Cal. 1997) (dissenting opinion of Justice Kennard). For further discussion, see note 4, p. 883, infra.

In a case argued and decided along with *Hodgson*, Ohio v. Akron Center for Reproductive Health, 497 U.S. 502 (1990), the Court upheld an Ohio parental notification requirement with a judicial bypass procedure that required the minor to prove by clear and convincing evidence that (1) she is mature; (2) she has experienced a pattern of physical, emotional, or sexual abuse by one of her parents; or (3) notice is not in her best interests. Confronted with an attack to the statute on its face, the Court upheld the rule, concluding that allegations that the bypass procedure could delay an abortion 22 days did not render the statute unconstitutional. Parental notification and consent statutes continue to be upheld in the federal courts, and in most states, so long as they contain adequate judicial bypass provisions. See, e.g., WomanCare of Orlando Inc. v. Agwunobi, 15 BNA's Health L. Rep. 206 (N.D. Fla. Feb. 10, 2006) (upholding 48-hour parental notification period); Lambert v. Wicklund, 520 U.S. 292 (1997) (per curiam) (upholding parental notification statute with judicial bypass available when notification not in minor's best interest); see also Pro-Choice Mississippi v. Fordice, 716 So. 2d 645 (Miss. 1998) (upholding two-parent consent requirement with judicial bypass).

For examples of parental notice or consent provisions that have been invalidated because of inadequate bypass provisions, see Causeway Medical Suite v. Ieyoub, 109 F.3d 1096 (5th Cir. 1997), cert. denied, 522 U.S. 943 (1997) (invalidating amendment to Louisiana parental consent statute that granted judges discretion to deny abortion because it failed to specify time frame within which decision must be rendered, and permitted parental notification of bypass proceedings); Planned Parenthood, Sioux Falls Clinic v. Miller, 63 F.3d 1452 (8th Cir. 1995), cert. denied sub nom. Janklow v. Planned Parenthood, Sioux Falls Clinic, 517 U.S. 1174 (1996) (no judicial bypass procedure was available).

A few state courts have struck down parental consent or parental notification statutes, even when judicial bypass provisions were provided. See, e.g., N. Fla. Women's Health and Counseling Services, Inc. v. Florida, 866 So. 2d 612 (Fla. 2003) (invalidating one-parent notification requirement with bypass alternative, because state had no compelling interest in protecting minors from having abortions); Planned Parenthood of Central New Jersey v. Farmer,

762 A.2d 620 (N.J. 2000) (invalidating a parental notification provision that was shown to impose substantial costs in terms of delay, financial cost, and foregone abortions); Planned Parenthood League of Massachusetts v. Attorney General, 677 N.E.2d 101 (Mass. 1997) (on state constitutional grounds, invalidating two-parent consent requirement, even though it had a judicial bypass provision, because no state interest served). A California parental consent requirement with a judicial bypass provision was invalidated by the California Supreme Court, based on the reasoning that the state's contention of a strong state interest in the physical and emotional health of the minor was not consistent with its failure to require parental consent "for a minor to obtain medical care and make other important decisions in analogous contexts that pose at least equal or greater risks to the physical, emotional and psychological health of a minor and her child as those posed by the decision to terminate pregnancy." Academy of Pediatrics v. Lungren, supra. California voters subsequently rejected a ballot initiative that would have required parental notification before a minor could obtain an abortion. Bobby Caina Calvan, Costly Loss Softens Schwarzenegger, Boston Globe, Nov. 10, 2005, at A13.

New Hampshire's Parental Notification Prior to Abortion Act prohibits doctors from performing an abortion on a pregnant minor until 48 hours after notice of such procedure to her parent or guardian. Although the Act provides a judicial bypass provision, it does not provide for an abortion without notice in a medical emergency unless there is no time to give notice. The federal district court found the statute unconstitutional, which decision was affirmed by the U.S. Court of Appeals for the First Circuit. Planned Parenthood of Northern New England v. Heed, 390 F.3d 53 (1st Cir. 2004). In an opinion written by Justice O'Connor, the U.S. Supreme Court affirmed both that states have the constitutional right to require parental involvement when a minor considers terminating her pregnancy, and that the U.S. Constitution requires an exception for the preservation of life of health of the mother. Rather than invalidating the statute, however, the Court vacated and remanded the case, holding that the lower courts should have considered a narrower injunction on the Act's unconstitutional portion. Ayotte v. Planned Parenthood of Northern New England, 126 S. Ct. 961 (2006).

Ayotte contains citations to the parental notification statutes of all 44 states with such statutes, 38 of which have explicit exceptions for health or medical emergencies, two of which allow sufficient discretion to physicians to protect minors' health, and four of which, like New Hampshire, make no exception for minors' health in an emergency. See 126 S. Ct. at 966, n.1. For a continuously updated state-by-state survey of parental consent laws, see http://www.guttmacher.org/statecenter/spibs/spib_PIMA.pdf (last visited March 13, 2006).

4. Judicial Bypass Procedures. What do you think of the argument by the dissenting Justices in *Hodgson* (see note 3, supra) that judicial bypass procedures impose additional trauma on minors and cause unnecessary delay, without any improvement in decisionmaking, since most bypass petitions are granted? If judges were more scrupulous in determining either that a minor is mature or that an abortion is in her best interests, would the integrity, and thus the legitimacy, of the process be improved? Does the increase of parental notification measures across the country reflect a decreased confidence in minors' ability to make adult decisions? If so, how does this contrast with the public's willingness to broaden adult responsibility for juveniles who commit crimes? See Jon-Michael Foxworth, Note, An Unjust Act: The Schizophrenic State of Maturity and Culpability in Juvenile Justice and Minor Abortion Rights Law; Recent Trends in Virginia and Nationally, 9 Wm. & Mary J. Women & L. 295 (2003).

Notwithstanding the evidence in *Hodgson* that the judicial bypass procedure is a pointless procedure, bypass requests by minors are occasionally denied. In one case, reported in American Civil Liberties Union, Reproductive Freedom Project, 2 Reproductive Rights Update 3 (Thanksgiving 1990, No. 21), an Ohio judge denied a request, finding that "if [the minor in this case] was mature, she would have notified her parents." This case was later affirmed by the Ohio Supreme Court:

> On the one hand, appellant is a senior in high school who plans to attend college, and is a person who had a prior experience in the termination of a pregnancy. On the other hand, appellant testified that she had an abortion in June 1990 and is seeking to have another one performed less than a year later. Moreover, appellant testified that each pregnancy was the result of intercourse with a different man.... [A]ppellant was on a program of birth control, but discontinued it. In light of [this evidence], it was not unreasonable, arbitrary or unconscionable for the trial judge to dismiss the complaint by essentially finding that appellant did not prove her "maturity" allegation by clear and convincing evidence.

In re Jane Doe 1, 566 N.E.2d 1181 (Ohio 1991). See also In re Anonymous, 558 N.W.2d 784 (Neb. 1997) (upholding denial of minor to obtain abortion under judicial bypass procedure after court found minor not sufficiently mature to avoid notification requirement, and modifying provision to require notification of only one parent); In re Anonymous, 650 So. 2d 919 (Ala. Civ. App. 1994) (upholding trial court's denial of petition for judicial bypass when minor's primary reason for seeking bypass was to avoid disappointing her mother).

What information should judges seek in conducting a meaningful review of a minor's maturity or best interests? Under what circumstances would it be in the best interest of a minor too immature to make the abortion decision to be forced to have a child?

A significant barrier to adolescents seeking abortion without the consent of their parents is the accessibility of the court system. A 1997 study of Pennsylvania courts found that at least 40 of the state's 60 judicial districts were unprepared to handle judicial bypass inquiries, more than three years after the state's parental consent requirement had gone into effect. See Helena Silverstein, Road Closed: Evaluating the Judicial Bypass Provision of the Pennsylvania Control Act, 24 Law & Soc. Inquiry 73 (1999). See also Helena Silverstein & Leanne Speitel, "Honey, I Have No Idea": Court Readiness to Handle Petitions to Waive Parental Consent for Abortion, 88 Iowa L. Rev. 75 (2002).

5. Federal Policy Relating to Minors and Abortion. As part of the Adolescent Family Life Act, enacted to promote the involvement of parents and religious and charitable organizations in family planning services for adolescents, any grantee under the Act must obtain permission from a minor's parents before providing family planning services to her. 42 U.S.C. § 300z-5(a)(22)(A)(i) (2006). While the two-parent notification requirement has no judicial bypass provision, given the distinction the Supreme Court has made between a woman's constitutional right to choose an abortion and her right to obtain state funds in order to exercise that choice, discussed in note 7, p. 888, below, the provision is almost certainly constitutional. Other provisions of the Act have been upheld from challenge under the establishment clause in Bowen v. Kendrick, 487 U.S. 589 (1988), and counseling restrictions applicable to programs funded by Title X were upheld in the face of a broader First Amendment challenge in Rust v. Sullivan, 500 U.S. 173 (1991) (discussed below).

In recent years, federal funding for "abstinence-only" sex education programs has greatly increased; it is now over $170 million annually. Hazel Glenn Beh & Milton Diamond, The Failure of Abstinence-Only Education: Minors Have a Right to Honest Talk About Sex, 15 Colum. J. Gender & L. 12, 12 (2006) (citing Waxman Report). Qualifying programs must teach, among other things, that sexual activity outside of marriage is likely to have harmful physical and psychological effects. Maternal and Child Health Services Block Grant, 42 U.S.C. § 710(b)(2)(E) (2006). A recent congressional study concluded that 11 of the 13 most commonly used abstinence-only curricula contained errors and distortions — ranging from the exaggeration of condom failure rates to suggesting that abortion causes infertility. Staff of H. Comm. on Gov't Reform, The Content of Federally Funded Abstinence-Only Education Programs (Dec. 2004), http://www.democrats.reform.house.gov/Documents/20041201102153-50247.pdf (prepared by minority staff).

It has been argued that federal sponsorship of abstinence-only programs violates the constitutional rights of minors with respect to their sexual health and procreation decisions. See Beh & Diamond, supra. Another argument is that the programs violate the First Amendment, because of the explicitly religious message of some of the programs receiving federal support. Following this approach, a federal court in Louisiana held that the state's funding of abstinence-only programs that contained religious material violated the establishment clause. ACLU of Louisiana v. Foster, 2002 U.S. Dist. LEXIS 13778 (July 24, 2002) (issuing preliminary injunction against state disbursement of funds).

Adolescent pregnancy poses additional issues in terms of race and social class, which are explored in note 7, below, and in Section A, p. 766 of this chapter (statutory rape).

6. Litigating under the "Undue Burden" Test. State legislatures continue to pass abortion regulation, and pro-choice advocates continue to oppose it. A frequently updated website on abortion regulation state-by-state is http://www.guttmacher.org/sections/abortion.php. The main areas in contention include who can perform abortions, what information a state can require women seeking abortions to be furnished, how long a waiting period states can incorporate into their procedures, and at what point abortion can be prohibited except in extreme circumstances relating to saving a woman's life. As of March 1, 2006, 32 states require counseling and 29 of these require specific information be provided, such as the availability of assistance for pre-natal care, the names of referral agencies, the amount of pain the fetus can feel, or the link between abortion and breast cancer. See http://www.guttmacher.org/statecenter/ spibs/spib_MWPA.pdf. Twenty-four states require waiting periods between the counseling and the abortion procedure. Id. See also NARAL Pro-Choice America & NARAL Pro-Choice America Foundation, Who Decides? The Status of Women's Reproductive Rights in the United States 9 (14th ed. Jan. 2005).

After *Casey*, most successful challenges to mandatory delay and counseling requirements have been brought on the grounds that the statute lacked a health exception, or that the state constitution afforded greater privacy protections than the federal Constitution. See Planned Parenthood of Delaware v. Brady, No. Civ. 03-153-SLR, 2003 U.S. Dist. LEXIS 10099 at *3 (D. Del. 2003) (Delaware waiting period statute that did not contain a health exception was unenforceable); Planned Parenthood of Middle Tennessee v. Sundquist, 38 S.W.3d 1 (Tenn. 2000) (privacy protections in Tennessee constitution justified use of strict scrutiny to strike down mandatory waiting period requirement).

Two studies in Mississippi have examined the effects of that state's mandatory delay law, which requires that women seeking an abortion receive information in person from a health care provider 24 hours before the procedure. One study compared abortion rates in the year before and the year after the 1992 Mississippi law, which was the first mandatory delay law to go into effect in any state. It found that the total rate of abortions for Mississippi residents decreased by approximately 16 percent; that the proportion of Mississippi residents traveling to other states to obtain abortions increased 37 percent (from 18.6 percent to 25.4 percent); and that the proportion of second-trimester abortions among all Mississippi women obtaining abortions increased 40 percent (from 10.4 percent to 14.5 percent). See Theodore Joyce et al., The Impact of Mississippi's Mandatory Delay Law on Abortions and Births, 278 JAMA 653, 655 (1997). Another study showed that the rate of second-trimester abortions in Mississippi after enactment of the law increased by 53 percent (from 7.5 percent of abortions to 11.5 percent) among women whose closest health care provider is in-state, while it increased by only 8 percent (from 10.5 percent to 11.3 percent) among women whose closest provider was across the Mississippi border. All in all, this second study concluded that the mandatory delay law increased the mean gestational age of the fetus at the time of the procedure by approximately four days. Women living closest to abortion providers in other states were relatively unaffected by the law. See Ted Joyce & Robert Kaestner, The Impact of Mississippi's Mandatory Delay Law on the Timing of Abortion, 32 Family Planning Perspectives 4 (2000). By 2000, 60 percent of women in Mississippi traveled out of state to terminate their pregnancies. In Wyoming, the figure in 2000 was 95 percent. Eyal Press, Abortion, From a Distance, N.Y. Times, March 12, 2006, at WK13.

Other abortion regulations have focused on licensing and other requirements for abortion providers not imposed on other types of medical facilities. Some have been upheld and others have been invalidated. See, e.g., Greenville Women's Clinic v. Bryant, 222 F.3d 157 (4th Cir. 2000), cert. denied, 531 U.S.

1191 (2001) (upholding an extensive set of regulations in South Carolina affecting clinics performing any second-trimester abortions or more than five first-trimester abortions, on the grounds that the regulation did not strike at the abortion right itself and that any increased costs to women were modest and not shown to burden the ability of a woman to make the decision to have an abortion); Tucson Woman's Clinic v. Eden, 379 F.3d 531 (9th Cir. 2004) (affirming district court's ruling that regulation permitting state health department to conduct warrantless searches of abortion providers violated Fourth Amendment and remanding as to whether regulations as a whole constitute an "undue burden"); The Women's Center v. Tennessee, 2000 U.S. Dist. LEXIS 20198 (M.D. Tenn. Apr. 17, 2000) (issuing preliminary injunction against enforcement of Tennessee statute that imposed additional regulations upon ambulatory surgical treatment centers in which a "substantial number of medical or surgical pregnancy terminations are performed," on grounds that statute will likely be found to be unconstitutionally vague).

In Mazurek v. Armstrong, 520 U.S. 968 (1997), the United States Supreme Court vacated an injunction against enforcement of a Montana statute limiting performance of abortions to physicians. The court of appeals had thought such an injunction appropriate based on evidence that the motive for the Montana legislation was to make abortions more difficult, by preventing the sole physician's assistant performing abortions in the state from doing so. The Supreme Court held that even if the law targeted this single individual, there was insufficient evidence that the law created a substantial obstacle to abortion. Id. at 973-974. Similar limitations exist in at least 43 states.

Another site for litigation over abortion rights is state regulation prohibiting particular methods of abortion, often referred to as late-term or "partial-birth" abortions. In 2000, the United States Supreme Court invalidated a Nebraska statute banning partial-birth abortions, which lacked any exception for the preservation of the mother's health and proscribed the dilation and evacuation method used in most second-trimester abortions as well as the infrequently used dilation and extraction procedure. Stenberg v. Carhart, 530 U.S. 914 (2000). In 2003, Congress passed the federal Partial-Birth Abortion Ban Act, which more narrowly prohibited any procedure in which the physician "deliberately and intentionally vaginally delivers a living fetus," and then performs an "overt act, other than completion of delivery, that kills the partially delivered living fetus." The Act provides for an exception to preserve maternal life. 18 U.S.C. §1531. The federal courts that have addressed the statute to date have found it unconstitutional because it lacks a broader maternal health exception, and the U.S. Supreme Court has decided to review the issue. See, e.g., National Abortion Federation v. Gonzales, 2006 U.S. App. LEXIS 2386 (2d Cir. 2006); Planned Parenthood Federation of America v. Gonzales, 435 F.3d 1163 (9th Cir. 2006); Carhart v. Gonzales, 413 F.3d 791 (8th Cir. 2005), cert. granted, 126 S. Ct. 1314 (2006). See also Richmond Medical Center for Women v. Hicks, 407 F.3d 619 (4th Cir. 2005) (invalidating Virginia's partial-birth infanticide statute on the grounds that *Stenberg* established the maternal health exception as a constitutional requirement); Northland Family Planning Clinic, Inc. v. Cox, 2005 U.S. Dist. LEXIS 20358 (Sept. 12, 2005) (Michigan's Legal Birth Definition Act giving legal rights to a partially delivered fetus imposes an unreasonable burden on women seeking to terminate a pregnancy). As of March 1, 2006, 26 states had bans on late-term abortion, 18 of which had been specifically blocked by a court. For a complete listing which is regularly updated, see http://www.guttmacher .org/statecenter/spibs/spib_BPBA.pdf.

7. **The Class and Race Dimensions of the Abortion Right.** Other limitations on the abortion right include public funding restrictions. In the first decade after *Roe*, the Supreme Court upheld the withdrawal of funding for elective (i.e., not "medically necessary") abortions obtained by Medicaid-eligible, indigent clients, see Beal v. Doe, 432 U.S. 438 (1977), and Maher v. Roe, 432 U.S. 464 (1977). Annual federal funding legislation, known each year as the "Hyde Amendment," now limits federal reimbursement for abortions to very narrow exceptions, such as when necessary to save the life of the mother or to end pregnancies resulting from rape or incest; the restriction applies to funding provided through the Department of Health and Human Services and primarily affects Medicaid. See Harris v. McRae, 448 U.S. 297 (1980). Federal courts have held generally that state efforts to get around the federal Hyde Amendment restrictions are invalid, under the federal preemption clause. See, e.g., Elizabeth Blackwell Health Center for Women v. Knoll, 61 F.3d 170 (3d Cir.), reh'g en banc denied (1995), cert. denied, 516 U.S. 1093 (1996).

Federal funding restrictions do not affect any rights that might be established to state funds, under state law. See, e.g., Dalton v. Little Rock Family Planning Servs., 516 U.S. 474 (1996) (per curiam) (Hyde Amendment does not apply if compensation program entirely state-funded). But some states have interpreted their own state constitutions to require no more than the U.S. Constitution. See, e.g., Bell v. Low-Income Women of Texas, 95 S.W.3d 253 (Tex. 2002) (Texas constitution does not require state to fund all medically necessary abortions); Renee B. v. Florida Agency for Health Care Administration, 790 So. 2d 1036 (Fla. 2001) (failure to fund medically necessary abortions that are not required to save the life of the mother or to terminate a pregnancy caused by rape or incest does not violate Florida state constitution). For an inventory of state statutes relating to Medicaid funding for abortions, as well as an analysis of the Hyde Amendment's impact on the timing of poor women's abortions, see http://www.guttmacher.org/statecenter/spibs/spib_SFAM.pdf. It is clear that even restrictions that do not directly concern funding are especially disadvantageous to poor women.

> A forty-eight hour waiting period . . . may not be an "undue burden" for affluent professional women, and a hospitalization requirement may only serve to make her abortion more expensive. But for an 18-year-old girl in the rural South, unmarried, pregnant, hoping to finish school and build a decent life, who has little or no access to transportation, a hospitalization requirement can mean an abortion that will cost nearly one-thousand dollars and involve a trip of hundreds of miles; a waiting period can mean two long trips and an overnight stay in a strange and distant city.

Walter Dellinger & Gene B. Sperling, Abortion and the Supreme Court: The Retreat from Roe v. Wade, 138 U. Pa. L. Rev. 83, 102 (1989).

Access to abortion by poor women is also impeded by so-called "gag rules" which prohibit use of public funds to facilities which engage in counseling, referrals, or other services relating to abortion. In the face of statutory and constitutional challenges, a federal gag rule in the regulations applicable to Title X family planning programs was upheld by the U.S. Supreme Court in Rust v. Sullivan, 500 U.S. 173 (1991). In one of his first official acts as president, Bill Clinton suspended the rule by executive order, and the Title X regulations were eventually rewritten requiring federally funded programs to inform patients on all family planning options, and to counsel about abortion and make abortion referrals if asked. The regulations were published July 3, 2000, and are available at http://opa.osophs.dhhs.gov/titlex/gag_notice_07-02-2000.txt. Efforts to enact a congressional gag rule have not gained the necessary support, but the failure to increase Title X funding has meant that, in real terms, federal resources for family planning services are shrinking, while funding for abstinence-only programs is rapidly increasing. Some believe that the underfunding of Title X family planning programs may actually increase the number of abortions, since nearly half of the pregnancies occurring each year are unintended, and approximately half of those pregnancies are terminated by abortion. The Alan Guttmacher Institute, Facts in Brief, Induced Abortion (2003). Other restrictions on Title X funding, relating specifically to health care providers that refuse to provide medical care for religious reasons, is addressed in note 8, below.

A number of state statutes prohibit state employees, or organizations that receive state funds, from counseling or referring women for abortion services. See Ariz. Rev. Stat. Ann. § 36-2989(A)(9) (2005) (organizations funded under Children's Health Insurance Program may not include abortion counseling); Mich. Comp. Laws Ann. § 333.1091 (2005) (when allocating reproductive health services funds, Department of Community Health must give priority to organizations that do not perform or refer for elective abortions).

Funding restrictions that affect poor women in other countries reappeared in 2001. The Mexico City Policy, alternately known as the Global Gag Rule, restricts foreign non-governmental organizations that receive U.S. family planning funds from using their own, non-U.S. funds to provide abortions, provide counseling about abortions, or lobby their own governments for abortion reform. Julia L. Ernst et al., The Global Pattern of U.S. Initiatives Curtailing Women's Reproductive Rights: A Perspective on the Increasingly Anti-Choice Mosaic, 6 U. Pa. J. Const. L. 752, 774-775 (2004). The 2005 $15 billion HIV/AIDS assistance bill requires that at least one-third of the yearly disbursement of funds from prevention programs — roughly $200 million a year — be set aside for abstinence-only programs. For an examination of the effects the Rule has had on foreign NGOs and the countries in which they operate, see generally The Global Gag Rule Impact Project, Access Denied, available at http://www.globalgagrule.org/impacts.htm. See also Patty Skuster, Advocacy in Whispers: The Impact of the USAID Global Gag Rule upon Free Speech and Free Association in the Context of Abortion Law Reform in Three East African Countries, 11 Mich. J. Gender & L. 97 (2004).

Access to abortion in the U.S. is also affected by the number of physicians prepared to perform them. Only 46 percent of residency training programs in obstetrics and gynecology provide training in first-trimester abortion, and only 15 percent of chief residents in family medicine programs know how to perform the procedures. See R. Ameling et al., Abortion Training in U.S. Obstetrics & Gynecology Residency Programs 1998, 32 Family Planning Perspectives 268-271, 320 (2000). Since 1982, the number of abortion providers has fallen by 37 percent, and 57 percent of obstetricians who perform abortions are over 50 years of age. According to a survey conducted in 2000, 87 percent of U.S. counties have no abortion provider. See http://www.ms4c.org/issueshortage.htm. See also notes 8 and 9, below.

8. Catholic Hospitals and Abortion and Emergency Contraception Services. In 44 states, individuals and institutions are protected from performing controversial procedures under "conscience laws" enacted in the years following *Roe*. See Heather Rae Skeeles, Patient Autonomy Versus Religious Freedom: Should State Legislatures Require Catholic Hospitals to Provide Emergency Contraception to Rape Victims?, 60 Wash. & Lee L. Rev. 1007, 1022-1025 (2003). Accordingly, Catholic hospitals follow the National Conference of Bishops Ethical and Religious Directives for Catholic Health Care Services, available at http://www.ncc.buscc.org/bishops/directives.htm, which prohibit all forms of contraceptive services and counseling, medical and surgical abortions, sterilizations, and even emergency contraception to victims of rape. Leora Eisenstadt, Separation of Church and Hospital: Strategies to Protect Pro-Choice Physicans in Religiously Affiliated Hospitals, 15 Yale J.L. & Feminism 135, 137 (2003). The impact of these restrictions grows with the trend of religiously affiliated health care facilities to merge with non-sectarian institutions. Id. at 138.

Efforts to enact federal legislation that would require Catholic hospitals to provide access to a full range of reproductive services have not succeeded. A number of states, however, require all hospitals to provide either information about emergency contraception, a referral for the morning-after pill, or on-site emergency contraception treatment. These statutes are cited, and other proposed legislation discussed, in Skeeles, supra, at 1017-1019; see also Leonard J. Nelson, III, God and Woman in the Catholic Hospital, J. Legis. 69, 92-101 (2004) (discussing state emergency contraception requirements, as well as sexual assault protocols that challenge Catholic doctrine, from a perspective sympathetic to the Catholic Church). Skeeles concludes that in most jurisdictions, the "conscience clauses" apply only to procedures such as abortion sterilization, and artificial insemination, and not to emergency contraception. Id. at 1023.

In recent years, Catholic hospitals have not only refused to perform abortion and sterilization procedures, but some doctors with positions in these hospitals have been barred from performing medical procedures elsewhere, such as at private clinics not affiliated with the hospitals. For an account of three such cases, two of them involving the dismissal of the doctors from their positions at Catholic hospitals, and proposed legal theories for challenging these dismissals, see Eisenstadt, supra.

On the federal level, new legislation known as the Weldon Amendment, enacted as part of the 2005 Consolidated Appropriations Act, prohibits federal funding under Title X of the Public Health Service Act to any federal, state, or local agency that discriminates against any "health care entity," including health care providers and insurance plans, that does not provide for, pay for, provide coverage for, or refer for abortions. The Amendment was upheld at the federal district court level against a challenge that it was constitutionally vague. National Family Planning and Reproductive Health Association v. Gonzales, 391 F. Supp. 2d 200 (D.D.C. 2005).

California's Women's Contraception Equity Act requires Catholic institutions, including hospitals, to provide their employees with contraceptive coverage if they provide prescription drug coverage. Cal. Health & Safety Code § 1367.25 (West 2005); Cal. Ins. Code § 10123.196 (West 2005). This Act was upheld from First Amendment challenges in Catholic Charities of Sacramento, Inc. v. Superior Court, 85 P.3d 67 (Cal. 2004), cert. denied, 125 S. Ct. 53 (2004). The case is discussed, from a Roman Catholic perspective, in Maureen K. Bailey, Contraceptive Insurance Mandates and Catholic Charities v. Superior Court of Sacramento: Towards a New Understanding of Women's Health, 9 Tex. Rev. L. & Politics 367 (2005).

9. Anti-Abortion Activism. The right to abortion is increasingly contested through activities designed to discourage women from seeking abortions, and doctors from providing them. In an effort to stop demonstrations at abortion clinics in the Washington, D.C., area, various clinics sued to enjoin Operation Rescue from trespassing on, and obstructing general access to, the premises of abortion clinics under 42 U.S.C. § 1985(3), which provides a federal cause of action for private conspiracies to interfere with the civil rights of others. The Supreme Court in a 5-4 decision in Bray v. Alexandria Women's Health Clinic, 506 U.S. 263 (1993), concluded that plaintiffs had not established an animus against women based on their sex and that abortion is not "such an irrational object of disfavor" as to justify a presumption that opposition to that activity also constituted opposition to those who engage in that activity (i.e., women). Id. at 270. The majority also concluded that the deprivation of the right to abortion was not sufficient to constitute the object of a purely private conspiracy under § 1985. The right to travel might have provided a basis for a § 1985 action, but the Court found that traveling out of state to reach the a clinic did not implicate this right. Id. at 274-278.

What differentiates the activities of Operation Rescue from the mass "sit-ins" that were conducted for the purpose of promoting desegregation in the South in the 1960s? According to Justice Scalia in *Bray*, only a strictly construed race- or class-based animus requirement would prevent § 1985(3) from being used against such protests. Id. at 263. Justice Stevens disagreed, stating that at dispute is not the existence of a class-based animus requirement, but how to interpret it.

> [T]he demonstrations in the 1960's were motivated by a desire to extend the equal protection of the laws to all classes — not to impose burdens on any disadvantaged class. Those who engaged in the nonviolent "sit-ins" to which the Court refers were challenging "a political and economic system that had denied them the basic rights of dignity and equality that this country had fought a Civil War to secure." NAACP v. Claiborne Hardware Co., 458 U.S. 886, 918 (1982).

Id. at 344 (Stevens, J., dissenting). Assume that the 1960s sit-ins, like Operation Rescue's activities, violated state trespass laws. Is Justice Stevens's response anything other than a subjective judgment that some mass violations of law are beyond the reach of anti-conspiracy laws, while others are not, because of their respective substantive goals?

Bray revisits the arguments over whether discrimination affecting a characteristic or activity unique to women constitutes discrimination based on sex. Recall Geduldig v. Aiello, 417 U.S. 484 (1974), discussed in Chapter 2, pp. 219-221). Does it follow from *Geduldig* that activities aimed against persons seeking abortions are not discrimination based on sex? What do you make of Justice Scalia's observations that the activities are aimed also at those seeking to assist "persons" obtaining abortions (some of whom are men), and that there are other reasons for opposing abortion besides animus toward women?

Does the respondents' position that § 1985(3) should be available to help secure the autonomy of women in obtaining abortions require a state endorsement of abortion? As Justice Scalia points out, the Supreme Court's decisions upholding government abortion-funding restrictions (see note 5 in Section A, above) affirm that state policies disfavoring abortion are not necessarily unconstitutional. But to Justice Stevens, this observation misses the point, which is not whether the federal government is obligated to protect one right or another, but whether in enacting § 1985(3), it has attempted to do so. The question, in other words, is one of statutory construction.

Bray's impact on the federal remedies available to combat clinic violence was substantially altered by the 1994 passage of the Freedom of Access to Clinic Entrances Act (FACE). FACE allows for civil remedies and/or criminal penalties against anyone who

> by force or threat of force or by physical obstruction, intentionally injures, intimidates or interferes with or attempts to injure, intimidate or interfere with any person because that person is or has been, or in order to intimidate such person . . . from, obtaining or providing reproductive health services.

18 U.S.C. § 248(a)(1) (1994). Violators are subject to one year in prison or up to $10,000 in fines, or both, for the first violation, and up to three years in prison and up to $25,000 in fines for the second. If bodily injury or death results, other penalties are possible. The Act also authorizes a private right of action in favor of physicians, clinic staff, and patients who are injured by conduct proscribed by the Act.

Critics of FACE have argued that it violates the First Amendment, the Eighth Amendment, the Tenth Amendment, and the Religious Freedom Restoration Act. See, e.g., Lynn Wardle, The Quandary of Pro-Life Free Speech: A Lesson from Abolitionists, 62 Alb. L. Rev. 853 (1999) (law in this area threatens First Amendment, much as restrictions on abolitionist speech did before Civil War); Benjamin W. Roberson, Abortion as Commerce: The Impact of United States v. Lopez on Freedom of Access to Clinic Entrances Act of 1994, 50 Vand. L. Rev.

239 (1997) (arguing that FACE exceeds limits of the commerce clause and that state laws are better suited to deal with violent anti-abortion protests); Jill W. Rose & Chris Osborn, Note, FACE-ial Neutrality: A Free Speech Challenge to the Freedom of Access to Clinic Entrances Act, 80 Va. L. Rev. 1505 (1995) (arguing that FACE is a viewpoint-based regulation of speech and thus a violation of the First Amendment).

Nevertheless, FACE has survived numerous constitutional attacks at the federal appellate level. See, e.g., United States v. Bird, 401 F.3d 633 (5th Cir. 2005); United States v. Gregg, 226 F.3d 253 (3d Cir. 2000), cert. denied, 121 S. Ct. 855 (2001); United States v. Weslin, 156 F.3d 292 (2d Cir. 1998), cert. denied, 525 U.S. 1071 (1999).

In addition to FACE, the Supreme Court held in National Organization for Women v. Scheidler, 510 U.S. 249, reh'g denied, 510 U.S. 1215 (1994), that the Racketeer Influenced and Corrupt Organizations Act (RICO), 18 U.S.C. §§ 1961 et seq. (1994), does not require an economic motive. RICO may thus, under some circumstances, provide federal remedies, including treble damages, for some organized obstructions of health clinics involving extortion or actual or threatened violence. Twelve years later after several rounds in the same case, however, the Court held that the violence required to support a violation of the Hobbs Act, 18 U.S.C. § 1962, upon which the RICO findings supporting the injuction were predicated in *Scheidler*, must affect commerce by extortion or robbery, which was not shown in the case. Scheidler v. National Organization for Women, 126 S. Ct. 1264 (2006).

State laws provide some protection for health care providers and for women seeking abortions. These include general trespass laws and tort actions for tortious interference with business, false imprisonment, and intentional infliction of emotional distress. A few states have enacted statutes specifically targeted at physical acts intended to interfere with an individual entering or exiting a health care facility. See, e.g., Cal. Penal Code § 602.11 (West 2005). Some large verdicts have been obtained under state law claims, including an award of $204,585 in actual damages and $1,010,000 in punitive damages against Operation Rescue-National, Rescue America, and other anti-abortion groups, for interference with access to ten women's clinics in Houston during the time of the 1992 Republican National Convention. See Operation Rescue v. Planned Parenthood, 937 S.W.2d 60 (Tex. Ct. App. 1996) (affirming award). The effectiveness of these remedies has often been limited, however, by the difficulties (and expense) of attempting to collect the judgment from individual anti-abortion activists.

When injunctions are sought under either federal or state law, the Supreme Court has held that they must "burden no more speech than necessary to serve a significant government interest." Madsen v. Women's Health Center, Inc., 512 U.S. 753, 765 (1994). In *Madsen* itself, a 300-foot no-approach zone in which all uninvited approaches were prohibited was struck down, but the Court upheld a 36-foot buffer zone, prohibiting congregating or picketing around the property line of the clinic and prohibiting "singing, chanting, whistling, shouting, yelling, use of bullhorns, auto horns, sound amplification equipment, or other sounds or images observable to or within earshot of the patients inside the Clinic" during the hours of surgical procedures and recovery periods. A subsequent case upheld a

15-foot zone around a clinic from which protesters had to remain free and a "cease and desist" provision allowing patients to require sidewalk counselors to retreat, but invalidated an injunction creating floating 15-foot buffer zones around people and vehicles seeking access to the clinic. Schenck v. Pro-Choice Network of Western New York, 519 U.S. 357 (1997). The Court also upheld a Colorado statute making it unlawful for any person within 100 feet of a health care facility's entrance to "knowingly approach" within 8 feet of another person without that person's consent with leaflets, handbills, or signs or to engage in oral protest, education, or counseling with that person. Hill v. Colorado, 530 U.S. 703 (2000).

Anti-abortion activism has taken to the web. In one instance, the American Coalition of Life Activists portrayed a medical provider and its affiliated doctors on a website, in posters with the physicians' names and addresses labeled "GUILTY," "Deadly Dozen GUILTY," and "Nuremberg Files." This campaign followed in the wake of the murder of other doctors who had been identified in a series of posters labeled "WANTED" and "UNWANTED." In an action against the website developers under both FACE and RICO, plaintiffs originally won a verdict for over $108 million, all but $536,336 of which was punitive damages, along with an injunction shutting down the website. After multiple hearings, appeals, and remands, the verdict was affirmed but the punitive damages were reduced to nine times compensatory damages. See Planned Parenthood of the Columbia/Willamette, Inc. v. American Coalition of Life Activists, 422 F.3d 949 (9th Cir. 2005).

Putting Theory into Practice

5-7. Like all states, Kentucky requires that biological fathers pay child support for children born out of wedlock. One father claims that he should not have to pay child support because the law denies him the right women have to decide whether to terminate a pregnancy. He argues that Kentucky's statute has essentially forced him to become a father, thereby violating his constitutional rights.

Is there merit to his argument? See N.E. v. Hedges, 391 F.3d 832 (6th Cir. 2004). See also Melanie G. McCulley, The Male Abortion: The Putative Father's Right to Terminate His Interests in and Obligations to the Unborn Child, 7 J.L. & Pol'y 1 (1998) (arguing for state legislation that would grant the putative father the same ability to avoid the responsibility of an unwanted pregnancy as the mother).

5-8. An increasing number of states have enacted measures that would allow pharmacists to refuse to fill prescriptions based on personal convictions. In 1998, for example, South Dakota enacted a law making pharmacists immune from disciplinary action and civil liability if they refuse to dispense medication they believe will cause an abortion (i.e., the "morning-after pill"). See S.D. Codified Laws § 36-11-70 (2005). One of the nation's largest pharmacy chains, retail giant Wal-Mart, at first refused to stock emergency contraception, although it later changed its mind under public pressure. See Jyoti Thottam & Sean Scully, A Big Win for Plan B, Time, March 13, 2006, at 31.

Is the South Dakota law constitutional? Do pharmacists stand on the same footing as physicians who refuse to perform abortions even in contexts where no other providers are easily accessible? For a discussion of the issues, see Donald W. Herbe, Note, The Right to Refuse: A Call for Adequate Protection of a Pharmacist's Right to Refuse Facilitation of Abortion and Emergency Contraception, 17 J.L. & Health 77 (2002/2003).

5-9. Illinois law provides that "[u]pon receipt of a valid, lawful prescription for a contraceptive, a pharmacy must dispense the contraceptive, or a suitable alternative permitted by the prescriber, to the patient . . . without delay, consistent with the normal timeframe for filling any other prescription." 68 Ill. Admin. Code § 1330.91(j) (2005). Pursuant to this law, Walgreens requires its pharmacists to sign statements promising to fill contraceptive prescriptions. It suspended four pharmacists who refused to do so based on their religious beliefs. See Pharmacists Suspended Over Prescription Oath, NPR, Dec. 3, 2005 (Maria Hickey reporting), text available at http://www.npr.org/templates/story/story. php?storyId= 5038222&ft=1&f=2.

Should pharmacists who morally oppose contraception (especially the morning-after pill, which they consider a form of abortion) be protected from adverse employment action for acting on their consciences? What are the arguments on each side of this question?

5-10. Some abortion protestors photograph and videotape women entering abortion clinics; the photographs are later posted on the Internet, in some cases along with age, height and location. Protestors hope that the increased publicity will deter women from seeking abortions, and claim that they are protected under the First Amendment. Should they be? What remedies, if any, should be available to women whose photographs are published? See Lorna Collier, Patient Photos on Internet Test the Courts, Chi. Trib., May 15, 2002, at C1; P.J. Huffstutter, Kansas Prosecutor Wants Abortion Patients' Files, L.A. Times, Feb. 25, 2005, at A1.

b. Probing the Theoretical Foundations for an Abortion Right

Reva Siegel, Reasoning from the Body: A Historical Perspective on Abortion Regulation and Questions of Equal Protection
44 Stan. L. Rev. 261, 267-268, 273-277, 332, 350-351, 354, 357-363, 370 (1992)

Social forces play a powerful part in shaping the process of reproduction. Social forces define the circumstances under which a woman conceives a child, including how voluntary her participation in intercourse may be. Social forces determine whether a woman has access to methods of preventing and terminating a pregnancy, and whether it is acceptable for her to use them. Social forces determine the quality of health care available to a woman during pregnancy, and they determine whether a pregnant woman will be able to support herself throughout the term of gestation, or instead will be forced to depend on others for support. Social relations determine who cares for a child once it is born, and what resources, rewards, and penalties attend the work of gestating and nurturing human life. . . .

These observations, tenets of anthropological and feminist critical thought, do not inform the reasoning of those charged with interpreting the Constitution. In crafting equal protection and due process doctrine concerning reproductive regulation, the Court has typically reasoned from the premise that women's reproductive role is dictated by nature, and that regulation of women's reproductive conduct can be evaluated by consulting facts of nature. The result is that social relations enforced by the body politic often find constitutional justification in the organization of the female body itself. . . .

[*Roe*] presents decisions about motherhood as a private dilemma to be resolved by a woman and her doctor: a "woman's problem," in which the social organization of motherhood plays little part. In *Roe*, the Court repeatedly suggests that states should defer to private decisions respecting abortion because they reflect the expertise of a medical professional, not because the community owes any particular deference to women's decisions about whether to assume the obligations of motherhood. Because *Roe* and its progeny treat pregnancy as a physiological problem, they obscure the extent to which the community that would regulate a woman's reproductive choices is in fact implicated in them, responsible for defining motherhood in ways that impose material deprivations and dignitary injuries on those who perform its work. Analyzed within a medical framework, exclusion from employment, denial of unemployment and health insurance benefits, the stigma of unwed motherhood, and other of pregnancy's "natural sanctions" appear as consequences of a woman's body — not practices of the community that would regulate her conduct. *Roe*'s account of the abortion decision invites criticism of the abortion right as an instrument of feminine expedience (i.e. abortion "for convenience" or "on demand") because it presents the burdens of motherhood as woman's destiny and dilemma — a condition for which no other social actor bears responsibility. . . .

When the Court considers the pregnant woman from what it conceives to be a strictly physiological standpoint, in *Roe*, just as in equal protection cases like *Geduldig* [v. Aiello, 417 U.S. 484 (1974)], it sees her "situation [as] inherently different" from that of other citizens. The Court asserts that the pregnant woman's privacy rights are defeasible, without devoting a single sentence to explaining why this is so. The Court simply assumes that the existence of the embryo/fetus is sufficient to explain and justify the state's interest in regulating abortion; the opinion nowhere addresses the possibility that public interest in restricting abortion might be shaped by social judgments about the pregnant woman herself. As in its equal protection jurisprudence, the Court reasons from the premise that the physical reality of pregnancy can objectively substantiate public regulatory judgments concerning the pregnant woman . . . .

Roe thus holds that the state has an interest in potential life which becomes compelling at the point of viability. It defines this regulatory interest in potential life physiologically, without reference to the sorts of constitutional considerations that normally attend the use of state power against a citizen. In the Court's reasoning, facts concerning the physiological development of the unborn provide "logical and biological justifications" both limiting and legitimating state action directed against the pregnant woman. Because *Roe* analyzes an exercise of state power from a medical, rather than a social, point of view, it authorizes state action against the pregnant woman on the basis of physiological criteria, requiring no inquiry into the state's reasons for acting against the pregnant woman, or the impact of its actions on her. Indeed, *Roe* analyzes the state's interest in potential life as a benign exercise of state power for the protection of the unborn, and not as a coercive exercise of state power against pregnant women, often reasoning as if the state's interest in protecting potential life scarcely pertained to the pregnant woman herself. Thus, in the course of justifying its decision to protect the abortion decision as a right of privacy, the Court recognized an antagonistic state interest in restricting women's access to abortion on which it imposed temporal, but few principled, restraints.

In recognizing the state's interest in potential life, the Court ignored a simple social fact that should be of critical constitutional significance: When a state invokes an interest in potential life to justify fetal-protective regulation, the proposed use of public power concerns not merely the unborn, but women as well. Abortion-restrictive regulation is sex-based regulation, the use of public power to force women to bear children. Yet, the Court has never described the state's interest in protecting potential life as an interest in forcing women to bear children. *Roe*'s physiological reasoning obscures that simple social fact. "[I]f one accepts the medical definitions of the developing young in the human uterus" as a sufficient, objective, and authoritative framework for evaluating the state's regulatory interest in abortion — as *Roe* did — state action compelling women to perform the work of motherhood can be justified without ever acknowledging that the state is enforcing a gender status role. In part, this is because analyzing abortion-restricting regulation within physiological paradigms obscures its social logic, but also, and as importantly, it is because physiological reasons for regulating women's conduct are already laden with socio-political import: Facts about women's bodies have long served to justify regulation enforcing judgments about women's roles. . . .

Abortion-restrictive regulation is state action compelling pregnancy and motherhood, and this simple fact cannot be evaded by invoking nature or a woman's choices to explain the situation in which the pregnant woman subject to abortion restrictions finds herself. A pregnant woman seeking an abortion has the practical capacity to terminate a pregnancy, which she would exercise but for the community's decision to prevent or deter her. If the community successfully effectuates its will, it is the state, and not nature, which is responsible for causing her to continue the pregnancy. Similarly, a woman's choice to engage in sexual relations is no longer significant as a cause of pregnancy, if she would terminate that pregnancy, but for the interposition of communal force. A woman's "choice" to engage in (protected or unprotected) sex may be relevant to the state's justifications for enacting abortion-restrictive regulation, but it does not absolve the state from responsibility for compelling the pregnancy of a woman it prevents from obtaining an abortion. Indeed, if nature or a woman's "choices" play a prominent role in the state's justifications for imposing motherhood upon her, such explanations will obscure the fact that the state's decision to enact abortion restrictions rests on social judgments about the pregnant woman, just as they obscure the fact that such restrictions are an act of communal force against her.

In analyzing abortion-restrictive regulation from an antidiscrimination standpoint, I premise my discussion on the assumption that laws forbidding or impairing women's practical access to abortion are sex-based. I assume, as most commentators have, that when the Court revisits Geduldig v. Aiello, it should modify it to accord with the common social understanding and the amended terms of the Civil Rights Act of 1964, that regulation concerning women's capacity to gestate categorically differentiates on the basis of sex, and so is facially sex-based. . . .

Is the purpose of abortion-restrictive regulation a legitimate one? *Roe* describes a legislature's purpose in restricting women's access to abortion as protecting unborn life. Yet, from a social standpoint, that purpose can be differently described. A legislature's purpose in enacting restrictions on abortion is to pressure or compel women to carry a pregnancy to term which they would otherwise terminate — as the Court has acknowledged in the funding cases.

It is by no means clear that this legislative purpose is legitimate under equal protection doctrine. A legislature's effort to force women to bear children could easily be characterized as a "statutory objective [that] reflects archaic and stereotypic notions" about women. Motherhood is the role upon which this society has traditionally predicated "gross, stereotyped distinctions between the sexes." Thus, the objective of abortion-restrictive regulation is to force women to assume the role and perform the work that has traditionally defined their secondary social status. More particularly, the purpose of abortion-restrictive regulation appears constitutionally suspect if one considers (1) the role that stereotypes of women as "childrearers" played in the history of coerced childbearing (including laws criminalizing both abortion and contraception), (2) the role these same stereotypes played in justifying restrictions on women's participation in the workforce and the political arena during the era that federal and state law denied women access to abortion and contraception, and (3) the exclusions and indignities this society still inflicts upon women who gestate and nurture human life. . . .

Examining the relationship between a legislature's ends and means will identify stereotypical reasoning where the legislature misattributes characteristics of some group members to the group as a whole, and thus employs "gender as an inaccurate proxy for other, more germane bases of classification." But because a state's decision to save fetal life by compelling pregnancy entails a purely functional use of the pregnant woman, any traditional sex-role assumptions that may inform or prompt this regulatory decision cannot be detected by examining how closely the state's means are related to its ends. Rather, one has to ask, in what ways might assumptions about the proper roles of men and women have moved the state to engage in fetal life-saving by compelling pregnancy? What view of women prompted the state's decision to use them as a means to an end? Given the constitutionally suspect means that laws restricting abortion employ to promote the state's interest in potential life, and especially given their history of overt gender-based justifications, it is patently unreasonable to assume *a priori* that they are adopted by a process of legislative deliberation free from constitutionally illicit judgments about women.

[T]here is strong evidence that the attitudes which first prompted enactment of abortion-restrictive regulation still persist. Although the separate spheres tradition no longer receives official public sanction, the sex-role concepts it fostered continue to play a crucial part in the abortion controversy, supplying norms of sexual and maternal comportment for women that inform public judgments about the propriety of abortion. For example, in Louisiana, where the legislature recently attempted to enforce the state's nineteenth century criminal abortion statute and then enacted severe restrictions on abortion, a poll of the state's residents indicated they favored providing women access to abortion when pregnancy occurred because of incest or rape (89 percent); when the child is likely to have serious birth defects (67 percent); when childbirth might endanger a woman's health (64 percent), or when childbirth might endanger a woman's mental health (64 percent); but 79 percent of respondents were opposed to abortion "when childbirth might interrupt the woman's career."...National polls and sociological research confirm that such attitudes are widespread....

Thus, today, as in the nineteenth century, legislators enacting restrictions on abortion may act from judgments about the sexual and maternal conduct of the women they are regulating, and not merely from a concern about the welfare of the unborn. Legislators may condemn abortion because they assume that any pregnant woman who does not wish to be pregnant has committed some sexual indiscretion properly punishable by compelling pregnancy itself. Popular support for excusing women who are victims of rape or incest from the proscriptions of criminal abortion laws demonstrates that attitudes about abortion do indeed rest on normative judgments about women's sexual conduct. Opinion polls like Louisiana's suggest that the public assumes a woman can be coerced into continuing a pregnancy because the pregnancy is her sexual "fault."

Along distinct, but related lines, legislators may view abortion as repellant because it betrays a lack of maternal solicitude in women, or otherwise violates expectations of appropriately nurturing female conduct. If legislators assume that women are "child-rearers," they will take for granted the work women give to motherhood and ignore what it takes from them, and so will view women's efforts to avoid some two decades of life-consuming work as an act of casual expedience or unseemly egoism. Thus, they will condemn women for seeking abortion "on demand," or as a mere "convenience," judging women to be unnaturally egocentric because they do not give their lives over to the work of bearing and nurturing children—that is, because they fail to act like mothers, like normal women should....

Even if state actors have adopted restrictions on abortion out of a genuine and single-minded concern for the welfare of the unborn, archaic or stereotypical assumptions about women may nonetheless deeply bias their deliberations, making fetal life-saving by compelled pregnancy seem reasonable where otherwise it would not. A legislature's attitudes about women may cause it to underestimate or disregard the burdens it would impose on them by compelling pregnancy. A latent assumption that motherhood is women's "normal" condition can easily render state actors oblivious to the life-consuming consequences of forcing women to perform its work—just as a latent assumption that motherhood is women's "deserved" condition will cause indifference to the burdens the legislation will inflict. In short, a legislature may not decide that it is reasonable to save unborn life by compelling pregnancy, "but for" the archaic or stereotypic assumptions about women it holds. If restrictions on abortion are adopted in these circumstances, they offend constitutional guarantees of equal protection. . . .

[S]tate action restricting abortion injures women. . . . First, restrictions on abortion do not merely force women to bear children; powerful gender norms in this society ensure that almost all women who are forced to bear children will raise them as well, a result that legislatures adopting restrictions on abortion both desire and expect. Second, the work legislatures would force women to perform defines women's social status along predictable, gender-delineated lines. Women who perform the socially essential labor of bearing and rearing children face diverse forms of stigmatization and injury, none of which is ordained by the physiology of gestation, and all of which is the doing of the society that would force women to bear children. Third, when states adopt restrictions on abortion, they compel women to become mothers, while in no respect altering the conditions that make the institution of motherhood a principal cause of women's subordinate social status. When the gender-based impositions of abortion-restrictive regulation are considered in light of the forms of gender bias that may animate it, it is clear abortion-restrictive regulation is and remains caste legislation which subordinates women in ways that offend constitutional guarantees of equal protection. . . .

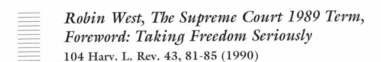

Robin West, *The Supreme Court 1989 Term, Foreword: Taking Freedom Seriously*
104 Harv. L. Rev. 43, 81-85 (1990)

[T]he standard liberal legalist argument for reproductive rights . . . may threaten our reproductive responsibilities. It is central to the liberal understanding of rights, including the right to an abortion, that the possession of a right insulates both the right-holder and the act that the right protects from the community's scrutiny, judgment, and understanding. Although the scope of the right may be limited by a compelling state interest, once the right is recognized, its exercise is no longer scrutinized for the moral quality of its exercise in any particular situation. In the reproductive context, then, the woman's "right" to exercise her choice to continue or terminate her pregnancy, assuming she has such a right, insulates her motives, reasons, or needs for doing so. Thus, the now standard liberal legalist argument for reproductive freedom rests on the claim that some pre-existing fundamental right—the right to privacy, the right to bodily integrity, or the right to nonsubordination—protects from majoritarian infringement a woman's decision either to carry a fetus to term or to abort and that state limits on that right are consequently invalid unless "compelling." The significance of the right is precisely that the reason for exercising it is not relevant to its existence.

The insularity of the decision to abort accorded by the liberal notion of "right" obviously broadens and deepens the scope of reproductive freedoms, *so long as the right is protected*. The clarity of the "rule" recognized in *Roe* consequently strengthens reproductive freedom. The insularity of the abortion decision accorded by the right also, however, has a cost: it obfuscates the moral quality of most abortion decisions. For that very reason, the standard liberal legalist understanding of the right to abort may become a liability in a world in which the public and state legislatures, rather than Herculean Supreme Court Justices, are the guardians of individual freedom. By insisting that the "right" to an abortion, like all rights, is not contingent on the morality of the right-holder or the moral quality of the conduct the right protects, the liberal legalist understanding may inadvertently bolster rather than challenge the pernicious and false claims that the decision to abort is more often than not based on nothing more than a woman's "convenience," is generally necessitated by her sexual promiscuity, and, at the extreme, is the moral equivalent of the decision to commit a premeditated murder. The overriding "insulating" logic of rights, generally embraced by the prochoice movement, that rights insulate conduct and the actor from scrutiny so that they can better protect the "worst of us" as well as the "worst in us" — may reinforce the damaging misperception that the demand for abortion reflects the irresponsible worst of us and worst within us. In a world, fast approaching since *Webster* and *Hodgson*, in which legislators, not courts, must bear the burden of decision in the reproductive field, that misperception may arguably do as much harm as the current conservative Court's continuing, interstitial retreat from the broad liberal promises of *Roe*.

From a postdemocratic liberal perspective, support for reproductive freedom — like all freedom — should rest on the demonstrated capacity of pregnant women to decide whether to carry a fetus to term or to abort responsibly. Correlatively, support for expanded reproductive freedom should rest on the claim that only by accepting the responsibility to make these judgments do women manifest their freedom to pursue their authentically chosen and desired life goals.... [W]hat a rights-focused liberalism obscures is that the meaningful distinction between murder and abortion is not in the nominal and question-begging difference between a "fetus" and a "baby," but rather in the moral quality of the underlying decision that liberal legalism insulates from scrutiny. Unlike the homicidal decision to take another's life, the decision to abort is more often than not a morally responsible decision. The abortion decision typically rests not on a desire to destroy fetal life but on a responsible and moral desire to ensure that a new life will be borne only if it will be nurtured and loved.

Such a shift in the focus of the abortion debate, however, does carry with it very real dangers. First, by resting the case for reproductive freedom on responsibility and rights, prochoice advocates would introduce a level of complexity to the debate that lacks the security of a clear constitutional rule. Like all freedoms, its security would rest on citizens' understanding that it is deserved, rather than on the legalistic ground that it is a right simply possessed regardless of the contrary whims or convictions of the community. Second and more important, explicitly basing reproductive freedom on the responsibility as well as the rights of women seems to invite a world in which each woman's decision to terminate her pregnancy would be monitored for compliance with some sort of responsibility-based moral code. . . . [F]rom a feminist perspective, no less than a Western liberal one, this solution looks like a *reductio ad absurdum*. In the very real world in which we live, . . . the good faith of any such relationship is likely to be—not just might be—badly tainted by the bias and simple meanness of a society still crippled by misogynist and racist perceptions of women. "Rights," by definition, insulate the individual and her freedom against this very danger. Responsibility-based arguments for reproductive freedom, on the other hand, seem to invite it.

A failure to rest reproductive freedom on a theory of responsibilities may ensure the complete erosion of the right, however. The Court's manifest ambivalence over the constitutional status of the right to privacy that undergirds reproductive freedom has compromised the persuasiveness of the appeal to rights and constitutional authority that has to date characterized the prochoice movement. Prochoice groups consequently must turn their attention away from courts and to the legislatures and the public who will increasingly be responsible for either protecting or obliterating this individual liberty. As the audience of the "prochoice/prolife" debate shifts away from courts and to legislatures, it may be prudent—whether or not philosophically wise—to focus attention on reproductive responsibility as well as on reproductive rights. If the premise of the rights-based argument—a Court willing to guard the individual liberty protected by the right against even well-intended state infringement—ceases to exist, the argument must change. Liberals and feminists must develop alternative, public-regarding arguments supporting those rights and the liberty they protect that transcend the circular and increasingly false insistence that they simply exist.

Minimally, a responsibility-based argument for reproductive freedom that would justify rather than supplant the rights-based claim of Roe v. Wade would more accurately correspond to the experience of women. Women need the freedom to make reproductive decisions not merely to vindicate a right to be left alone but often to strengthen their ties to others: to plan responsibly and have a family for which they can provide, to pursue professional or work commitments made to the outside world, or to continue supporting their families or communities. At other times the decision to abort is necessitated not by a murderous urge to end life, but by the harsh reality of a financially irresponsible partner, a society indifferent to the care of children, and a workplace incapable of accommodating or supporting the needs of working parents. At many other times the need to abort follows directly from a violent sexual assault. When made for any of these reasons, the decision to abort is not one made in an egoistic private vacuum. Whatever the reason, the decision to abort is almost invariably made within a web of interlocking, competing, and often irreconcilable responsibilities and commitments.

By focusing on the moral quality of reproductive decisions rather than insulating them from understanding, liberals could redirect societal attention toward this web of shared responsibilities and societal failures. We might then begin to recognize that we have a collective responsibility to address the variable causes that result in unwanted pregnancies, from the pervasive acceptance of sexual violence in our culture to our collective refusal to provide meaningful material assistance for the nurturing of children and families. Whatever the fate of *Roe*, widespread understanding of the moral nature of the abortion decision, the profound sense of responsibility that often accompanies it, and the societal failure to assume responsibility for the causes and effects of unwanted pregnancy, childbirth, and motherhood would strengthen, not weaken, the case for abortion rights and the freedoms those rights ought to protect. Without a Court willing to protect those rights in the face of societal opposition, however, that understanding may be necessary to the liberty's very existence.

Notes

1. The Right to Abortion as an Equality Right. *Casey* grounds the abortion right as a liberty interest, protected by the due process clause of the Fourteenth Amendment. This grounding represents a step beyond the right to privacy relied upon in Roe v. Wade itself, a right not stated expressly in the United States Constitution but rather articulated in "a line of decisions" based on the First, Fourth, Fifth, Ninth, and Fourteenth Amendments (and their "penumbras") defining those personal rights that are "implicit in the concept of ordered liberty." Roe v. Wade, 410 U.S. 113, 152 (1973) (citation omitted).

As the discussion in *Casey* suggests, the privacy theory of *Roe* has probably received more criticism than any other single example of constitutional jurisprudence. Critics have pointed to the absence of support for a privacy-based abortion right in the text of the Constitution and the failure of *Roe*'s trimester system to acknowledge the state's interest in protecting unborn life. See, e.g., John Hart Ely, The Wages of Crying Wolf: A Comment on Roe v. Wade, 82 Yale L.J. 920 (1973); Robert H. Bork, The Tempting of America: The Political Seduction of the Law 111-116 (1990). On the other side, some supporters of the constitutional right to choose an abortion criticize *Roe*'s failure to acknowledge the social dimensions of women's reproduction and note the meaninglessness of a privacy right for women who have insufficient power and resources to exercise it. See, e.g., Siegel, supra; Rosalind Petchesky, Abortion and Women's Choice: The State, Sexuality and Reproductive Freedom (rev. ed. 1990).

The equality principle, explored in the Siegel reading, above, has become the theoretical foundation for the abortion right that is favored by many feminist commentators. The Supreme Court has nodded a few times in the direction of equality analysis, without fully adopting it. See, e.g., Thornburgh v. American College of Obstetricians and Gynecologists, 476 U.S. 747, 772 (1986) ("promise that a certain private sphere of individual liberty will be kept largely beyond the reach of government . . . extends to women as well as men"); Webster v. Reproductive Health Servs., 492 U.S. 490, 538 (1989) (Blackmun, J., concurring in part and dissenting in part) (discussing both liberty and equality concerns); Bray v. Women's Health Clinic, 506 U.S. 263, 322-326 (1993) (Stevens, J., dissenting) (abortion protestors are motivated by discriminatory animus toward women). Do you find any traces of equal protection analysis in *Casey*?

Any equality-based theory, of course, would have to get around Geduldig v. Aiello, 417 U.S. 484 (1974), discussed in Chapter 2, pp. 219-221. As a matter of constitutional law, *Geduldig*, which held that singling out pregnancy as the only "disability" not covered by a state disability insurance plan discriminated between pregnant persons and nonpregnant persons, i.e., not on the basis of sex, has never been overruled. Siegel assumes that *Geduldig*, if looked at today, would — or at least should — be modified. That remains, of course, to be seen. See Bray v. Alexandria Women's Health Clinic, 506 U.S. 263 (1993), described on pp. 891-892, supra.

Setting *Geduldig* aside, is Siegel's analysis a sound application of equality analysis? Formal or substantive equality? Is nonsubordination theory more apt? Does her critique of *Roe* apply equally well to *Casey*?

Can the woman's right to choose an abortion rest entirely on the equality principle? Stephen J. Schnably argues that both privacy and equality analyses are necessary; equality analysis is necessary to understand that the right to make reproductive decisions is fundamentally a problem of unequal power, but the end goal remains private decisionmaking. See Schnably, Beyond *Griswold*: Foucauldian and Republican Approaches to Privacy, 23 Conn. L. Rev. 861, 932-934 (1991).

2. The Right to Abortion and Relational Feminism. Another theoretical foundation for the abortion right, which the West reading exemplifies, is drawn from relational/different voice feminism. Is a responsibility-based theory sound in this context?

For some, the emphasis on relational values is strategic, i.e., without underlining the moral difficulties for women faced with the abortion choice and the reverence for human life that typically accompanies that choice because tying the right to the liberal notion of choice, the case for abortion feeds too unattractive an image of mothers pursuing their own self-interest, an image that only serves to undercut the abortion right. Marjorie M. Shultz, for example, worries that the "uncritical embrace of extreme autonomy rhetoric and *exclusively* woman-regarding positions...undermine[s] our persuasiveness, [renders] us vulnerable on grounds of principle, and [damages] our aspirations for a humane and responsible world." Shultz, Abortion and the Maternal-Fetal Conflict: Broadening Our Concerns, 1 S. Cal. Rev. L. & Women's Stud. 79, 81 (1992). Shultz also raises concerns, on principle, that an unrestricted autonomy-based right would affect other legal principles in an undesirable way, such as undercutting the responsibility of doctors and employers to take reasonable measures to protect the safety of a fetus. Id.

Linda C. McClain cautions against responsibility-based theories for the abortion right, whether strategic or principled, on the ground that such theories will trigger too much second-guessing of women's decisions, without adequate societal or governmental commitment to reproductive health and to families. At the same time, it will also leave women vulnerable to charges of irresponsibility. Even the most compelling cases of constraint will still be found by some abortion opponents to be instances of mere "convenience." McClain, The Poverty of Privacy?, 3 Colum. J. Gender & L. 119, 173 (1992). See also Pamela S. Karlan & Daniel R. Ortiz, In a Diffident Voice: Relational Feminism, Abortion Rights, and the Feminist Legal Agenda, 87 Nw. U. L. Rev. 858 (1993) (criticizing relational approach to abortion as strategically defective).

Groups such as Feminists for Life of America (FFL), who base their opposition to the woman's right to an abortion on the principles of relational feminism, illustrate McClain's argument. FFL rejects the argument that abortion rights are necessary for women's equality and opposes abortion as a "quick fix," as oppressive of women, and as discriminatory against unborn children whom it is in women's interests to protect. The group's 2003 "Women Deserve Better" campaign argued that most women are coerced into abortions because of a lack of financial and emotional support. Marina Pisano, Roe v. Wade: 30 Years of Debate, San Antonio Express-News, Jan. 20, 2003, at A1. How might West or Siegel respond to this argument?

For still another view, consider the following:

> In the hundred-year-old nature versus nurture debate, contemporary feminists have taken the Rousseauist position that we are born good and society makes us bad. . . .
>
> The campaign for abortion rights, which has polarized America, was systematically mismanaged by feminist leaders, partly because of their refusal to acknowledge the violence inherent in any termination of life. . . .
>
> Unlike the feminist establishment, I recognize that abortion is killing. . . . We must philosophically strengthen feminist theory so that it can admit that abortion is an aggressive act, that it is a form of extermination. Modern woman has become an agent of Darwinian triage. . . .
>
> As a libertarian, I support unrestricted access to abortion because I have reasoned that my absolute right to my body takes precedence over the brute claims of mother nature, who wants to reduce women to their animal function as breeders. Women who want to achieve are at war with nature, as is shown by the hormonally disordering effects of career stress or extreme athletic training . . . In other words, in nature's eyes we are nothing but milk sacs and fat deposits. Women inspired by the Uranian Aphrodite to produce spiritual progeny should view abortion as a sword of self-defense put into their hands by Ares, the war god. Government, guaranteeing freedom of religion, has no right to interfere in our quarrel with our Creator, in this case pagan nature. Under the carnal constitution that precedes social citizenship, women have the right to bear arms. The battlefield is internal, and it belongs to us.

Camille Paglia, Vamps and Tramps: New Essays 38-41 (1994). Is this a more honest approach to the case for the abortion right? More autonomy-respecting? Does it have any appeal to you?

3. The Right to Abortion and Freedom from Bodily Invasion. Judith Jarvis Thomson presents this now-classic hypothetical:

> You wake up in the morning and find yourself back to back in bed with an unconscious violinist. A famous unconscious violinist. He has been found to have a fatal kidney ailment, and the Society of Music Lovers has canvassed all the available medical records and found that you alone have the right blood type to help. They have therefore kidnapped you, and last night the violinist's circulatory system

was plugged into yours, so that your kidneys can be used to extract poisons from his blood as well as your own. The director of the hospital now tells you, "Look, we're sorry the Society of Music Lovers did this to you — we would never have permitted it if we had known. But still, they did it, and the violinist now is plugged into you. To unplug you would be to kill him. But never mind, it's only for nine months. By then he will have recovered from his ailment, and can safely by unplugged from you."

Thomson, A Defense of Abortion, 1 Phil. & Pub. Affairs 47, 48-49 (1971).

What arguments in support of the woman's right to an abortion does this hypothetical suggest? Does it suggest limits to that right?

Is it relevant that a woman consented to the sexual intercourse that led to pregnancy? Shouldn't she be responsible for her actions? Recall Siegel's response, which looks beyond the pregnancy itself, to the question of who is responsible if she is prevented from choosing an abortion: "A pregnant women seeking an abortion has the practical capacity to terminate a pregnancy, which she would exercise but for the community's decision to prevent or deter her." Consider also the following:

> A person who consents to an action that has the foreseeable risk of a subsequent condition may be held morally responsible for that condition, should it occur, but that person is not presumed by law to have consented to the condition itself. A person who voluntarily smokes (action X), for example, may be considered responsible for the subsequent condition of lung cancer (condition Y), should it occur, but the person is not required to consent to the presence of the cancer in her body. So, too, with pregnancy. A woman who voluntarily engages in sexual intercourse (action X), may be partially morally responsible for the condition of pregnancy (condition Y), should it occur, but it does not follow that she is legally required to consent to that condition.

Eileen L. McDonagh, My Body, My Consent: Securing the Constitutional Right to Abortion Funding, 62 Alb. L. Rev. 1057, 1090-1091 (1999).

Robin West argues that this kind of reasoning "could conceivably find its way into the Supreme Court's reasoning over the next few years" because "[i]t is liberal and individualistic, respectful of the institutions as well as the moral precommitment of liberal legal jurisprudence." West, Liberalism and Abortion, 87 Geo. L.J. 2117, 2119 (1999). Is this medical treatment analogy compelling?

Building on the right-to-consent model, some have argued that restrictions on a woman's right to choose an abortion amount to involuntary servitude, in violation of the Thirteenth Amendment. See, e.g., Andrew Koppelman, Forced Labor: A Thirteenth Amendment Defense of Abortion, 84 Nw. U. L. Rev. 480 (1990); Donald H. Regan, Rewriting Roe v. Wade, 77 Mich. L. Rev. 1569, 1619 (1979). Does this principle add to the other theories already presented? For the argument that the slavery analogy is racist and polarizing, see Debora Threedy, Slavery Rhetoric and the Abortion Debate, 2 Mich. J. Gender & L. 3 (1994).

Putting Theory into Practice

5-11. Research shows consistently that boys are preferred to girls, especially as first or only children. See April L. Cherry, A Feminist Understanding of Sex-Selective Abortion: Solely a Matter of Choice?, 10 Wis. Women's L.J. 161, 171-172 (1995). In China, the combination of a restrictive "One Child" population control policy and a cultural preference for sons has resulted in an increasingly skewed sex ratio; the 2000 census put the birth rate at 119.8 boys for every 100 girls. Similar ratios occur in India, and both countries have banned the use of ultrasounds for sex determination. Peter Kammerer, Too Many Boys Means Trouble, South China Morning Post, Aug. 8, 2004, at 11. Some scholars have predicted the sex imbalance will result in increased violence and social upheaval. See Valerie M. Hudson and Andrea M. Den Boer, Bare Branches: The Security Implications of Asia's Surplus Male Population (2004).

Through amniocentesis, the sex of a fetus may be determined during the second trimester in time to obtain a legal abortion. One test promises a gender determination as early as five weeks in the gestational cycle through identification of fetal DNA. Carey Goldberg, Test Reveals Gender Early in Pregnancy, Boston Globe, June 27, 2005, at A1.

Illinois law prohibits abortions that are performed "with knowledge that the pregnant woman is seeking the abortion solely on account of the sex of the fetus." 720 Ill. Ann. Stat. 510/6(8) (2006). See also 18 Pa. Cons. Stat. Ann. § 3204(a) & (c) (2006) (providing that "[no] abortion which is sought solely because of the sex of the unborn child shall be deemed a necessary abortion"). Are these laws constitutional? Enforceable? Are they wise? What about laws to prevent sex selection in in vitro fertilization? See generally Farhat Moazam, Feminist Discourse on Sex Screening and Selective Abortion of Female Foetuses, 18 Bioethics 205 (2004); Alison Harvison Young, Let's Try Again . . . This Time With Feeling: Bill C-6 and New Reproductive Technologies, 38 U.B.C. L. Rev. 122, 131 (2005) (sex selection is illegal in Great Britain except to prevent, diagnose, or treat a sex-linked disorder or disease).

3. Pregnancy and Contractual Autonomy

In re Baby M.
525 A.2d 1128 (N.J. Super. Ct. Ch. Div. 1987),
rev'd, 537 A.2d 1227 (N.J. 1988)

SORKOW, J.S.C., Presiding Judge.

. . . This litigation began on May 5, 1986, when Mr. and Mrs. William Stern filed an ex-parte application for an order to show cause why this court should not issue an order for a summary judgment to enforce a surrogate-parenting contract. . . .

[A] verified complaint was filed seeking to enforce a surrogate-parenting agreement, compel the surrender to plaintiffs of the infant child born to Mrs. Mary Beth Whitehead, restrain any interference with plaintiffs' custody of the infant, terminate Mrs. Whitehead's parental rights and allow adoption of the child by Mrs. Stern. . . .

On February 6, 1986, Mr. Stern and Mr. and Mrs. Whitehead signed the surrogate parenting agreement. It was in all material respects the same contract [as one] that Mrs. Whitehead signed in the Spring of 1984. Mrs. Whitehead testified that her obligation was to attempt conception by artificial insemination, upon conception to carry the child to term, deliver and surrender the child to Mr. Stern renouncing at that time all of her parental rights and acknowledging that doing so would be in the child's best interest. It was also agreed that Mr. Stern's name would appear on the child's birth certificate.

In addition, the contract provided the following: Mrs. Whitehead would assume the risks of the pregnancy and child birth. She would submit to a psychiatric evaluation for which Mr. Stern would pay. Mr. Stern had the right to name the child. That in the event of the death of Mr. Stern, the child would be placed in the custody of Mr. Stern's wife. Mrs. Whitehead would not abort the child. In addition, she would undergo amniocentesis; and if the child was found to have a genetic or congenital abnormality, it would be aborted if Mr. Stern requested it.

That in the event the child possessed genetic or congenital abnormalities William Stern would assume legal responsibility for the child once it was born. . . .

Mrs. Whitehead was to be paid $10,000 and all medical expenses including dental expenses for performing her contractual obligations. . . .

The court was further told by the parties that they all understood their obligations under the contract. . . . Mrs. Stern, it must be noted, is not a party to the contract. This was to avoid any possible inference that there is a violation of N.J.S.A. 9:3-54 (which prohibits giving a consideration to obtain an adoptable child). Mr. Whitehead signed a certification pursuant to N.J.S.A. 9:17-44 establishing his non-paternity. Mr. Stern agreed to pay Mrs. Whitehead $10,000 for conceiving and bearing his child.

Fundamentally, when there were no time constraints, when Mrs. Whitehead was not pregnant, when each party had the opportunity to obtain advice (legal, medical and/or psychological), the parties expressed their respective offers and acceptances to each other and reduced their understanding to a writing. If the mutual promises were not sufficient to establish a valid consideration, then certainly there was consideration when there was conception. The male gave his sperm; the female gave her egg in their pre-planned effort to create a child — thus, a contract.

For the past year, there has been a child in being. She is alive and well. She is tangible proof of that which the Whiteheads and Mr. Stern in concert agreed to do. The child was conceived with a mutual understanding by the parties of her future life. Except that now, Mrs. Whitehead has failed to perform one of her last promises, which was to surrender the child and renounce parental rights. . . .

[T]here is no law governing surrogacy contracts in New Jersey and . . . the laws of adoption do not apply to surrogacy contracts. The sole legal concepts that control are parens patriae and best interests of the child. To wait for birth, to plan, pray and dream of the joy it will bring and then be told that the child will not come home, that a new set of rules applies and to ask a court to approve such a result deeply offends the conscience of this court. A person who has promised is entitled to rely on the concomitant promise of the other promisor. This court holds therefore that . . . once conception has occurred the parties' rights are fixed, the terms of the contract are firm and performance will be anticipated with the joy that only a newborn can bring. . . .

Defendants argue unconscionability. They claim the terms are manifestly unfair or oppressive. These terms were known to Mrs. Whitehead from her earlier surrogate contracting experience. She read the second contract, albeit briefly, prior to signing it. She was aware of her compensation. She had been pregnant before and had to be aware of the risks of pregnancy. Her obligation included physical examination for her own welfare as well as the welfare of the fetus. Mrs. Whitehead says that Mr. Stern undertook no risks. To compare the risk of pregnancy in a woman to the donation of sperm by the man would be unconscionable. This, however, is the bargain Mrs. Whitehead sought and obtained. Mr. Stern did take a risk, however, whether the child would be normal or abnormal, whether accepted or rejected he would have a lifetime obligation and responsibility to the child as its natural and biological father.

To the issue of unconscionability, defendants fail to show proof of overreaching or disproportionate bargaining that result in an unfair contract. Mrs. Whitehead was anxious to contract. At the New Brunswick meeting, she pressed for a definitive statement by the Sterns. She knew just what she was bargaining for. This court finds that she has changed her mind, reneged on her promise and now seeks to avoid her obligations. Unconscionability claims arise, more often than not, in consumer contracts for products or services. The seller is in the dominant position and the buyer must comply or there is no deal. Not so here — either party could have walked away from the other. Either party would then have continued on [the Infertility Clinic of New York's] roster of available surrogates and childless families seeking a surrogate. They chose not to do so. The bargain here was one for totally personal service. It was a very scarce service Mrs. Whitehead was providing. Indeed, it might even be said she had the dominant bargaining position for without her Mr. Stern had no other immediate source available. Each party sought each other to fulfill their needs.

It is argued by *amicus* that the $10,000 to be paid Mrs. Whitehead is so low as to be unconscionable. In counterpoint, it is stated that not all services can be compensated by money. Millions of men and women work for each other in their marital relationship. There may even be mutual inequality in the value of the work performed but the benefits obtained from the relationship serve to reject the concept of equating societal acts to a monetary balancing. Perhaps the risk was great for the money to be paid but the risk was what Mrs. Whitehead chose to assume and at the agreed upon fee. And it is assumed she received other intangible benefits and satisfaction from doing what she did. Her original application set forth her highly altruistic purpose. Notwithstanding *amicus'* position, all in this world cannot be equated to money. . . .

It is further argued that the contract is illusory; that is to say, that only one of the parties has an obligation, the other only benefits, that there is no mutuality of obligation. . . . Such is not the case. Mr. Stern gave his sperm; Mrs. Whitehead gave her egg. Together the miracle of a new life was obtained. Mrs. Whitehead argues Mr. Stern does not have to take the child under certain circumstances which have not happened and are not before this court. She is arguing hypothetically, "if." It is suggested again that the court is dealing with the facts before it. Even assuming arguendo, that the court were to address the issue of the illusory contract as stated by the defendants, the conclusion would be the same. The Whiteheads argue that Mr. Stern does not have to take the baby if it is imperfect; but the fact is the contract does provide that there is obligation and responsibility, that there is a life long responsibility by Mr. Stern for the child's support and welfare. The contract is not illusory....

An agreement between parents is inevitably subservient to the considerations of best interests of the child. The welfare of a child cannot be subscribed by an agreement of the parents.... It must follow that "best interests" are paramount to the contract and this court must answer a best interests inquiry if it is to specifically perform the surrogate parenting agreement.

What does "best interests of the child" mean? . . . It has many meanings for it is a concept general in meaning but specific in application....

[P]erhaps Dr. Salk gives the most quantified definition. He establishes nine criteria in defining "best interests of a child."

1) Was the child wanted and planned for? We now know the Sterns desperately wanted a child. They intended by the contract to have a child. They previously planned for the child by considering Mrs. Stern's own capability, inquiring about adoption and exploring surrogacy. They resolved in favor of surrogacy as the only viable vehicle for them to have a family. Mr. and Mrs. Stern contracted for Mrs. Whitehead's services. They created a nursery and made new wills to provide for the expected child. Mrs. Whitehead wanted to carry a child for a childless couple. It is clear that the Sterns planned for and wanted the child. Mrs. Whitehead did not. Her testimony is quite to that effect.

2) What is the emotional stability of the people in the child's home environment? The Sterns are found to have a strong and mutually supportive relationship. Any familial difficulties are handled through rational decision making. This is good evidence of mutual respect and empathy. Each recognizes and respects the other's needs, desires and goals. There is evidence of successful cooperative parenting of the infant child.

The Whiteheads appear to have a stable marriage now. It was earlier plagued with separations, domestic violence and severe financial difficulties requiring numerous house moves. There was a bankruptcy. Mrs. Whitehead dominates the family. Mr. Whitehead is clearly in a subordinate role. He has little to do with the subject child. Mrs. Whitehead is found to be thoroughly enmeshed with Baby M, unable to separate out her own needs from the baby's. This overbearing could inhibit the child's development of independence. The mental health professionals called by the guardian *ad litem* agree that Mrs. Whitehead may have trouble subordinating her own needs to the child's needs. Mrs. Whitehead has been shown, by clear and convincing proof to this court's satisfaction, to be impulsive, as shown by her unplanned future when dropping out of high school, the removal of her son from a second grade classroom without first making inquiry of the teacher and principal. Another example of impulsiveness is her flight to Florida in violation of a court order. She has been shown, by clear and convincing proof to this court's satisfaction, to be manipulative...[and] exploitive also. She uses her children for her own ends: witness the bringing of her older daughter to court where the child was terrorized by the crush of media, by her fawning use of the media to her own narcissistic ends. It appears she totally failed to consider the impact of the false sex abuse charge on her daughter. The placement of an infant's crib in Tuesday's room is without sensitivity or regard to Tuesday's feelings.

3) What is the stability and peacefulness of the families? Again, the Sterns are found to be living private unremarkable lives. The Whiteheads have known marital discord, domestic violence and many residential moves, although things are tranquil now.

4) What is the ability of the subject adults to recognize and respond to the child's physical and emotional needs? This court finds from clear and convincing proofs presented to it that Mrs. Whitehead has been shown to impose herself on her children. Her emphasis with the infant may impair the parenting of her other two children for whom she has been, with limited exception until now, a good mother. She exhibits an emotional overinvestment. It was argued by defendant's counsel that Mrs. Whitehead loves her children too much. This is not necessarily a strength. Too much love can smother a child's independence. Even an infant needs her own space.

The Sterns show sensitivity to the child's needs but at the same time allow her to develop independently. Both families recognize and satisfy the infant's physical needs.

5) What are the family attitudes towards education and their motivation to encourage curiosity and learning? The Sterns have demonstrated the strong role that education has played in their lives. They both hold doctoral degrees in the sciences. Mrs. Stern is a medical doctor. Mrs. Whitehead dropped out of the 10th grade in high school. Mr. Whitehead graduated high school doing enough, as he said, "to get by." Mrs. Whitehead has interposed herself in her son's education, denying the finding of a professional child study team and rejecting their recommendations.

6) What is the ability of the adults to make rational judgments? Mr. Whitehead permits his wife to make most of the important decisions in their family. His active participation in the May 5, 1986 elopement is hardly evidence of cogent thought. Mrs. Whitehead is found to be impulsive especially in crisis circumstances or moments of heightened concern. She doesn't think of the consequences: at age 15 she drops out of school, she withdraws her son from second grade for what she perceives to be an affront to him without first inquiring of the teacher or principal, she elopes to Florida in direct violation of a court order, without considering the economic and emotional consequences. She impulsively, not to say maliciously, makes an untruthful allegation about Mr. Stern. Mr. and Mrs. Stern have shown a capability to make logical reasoned decisions in all circumstances.

7) What is the capacity of the adults in the child's life to instill positive attitudes about matters concerning health? It is already noted that Mrs. Stern is a pediatrician. The court assumes her skill can but benefit the child. Other than failing to have the child vaccinated when Mrs. Whitehead was in Florida for the

first few months of the child's life, which is not to be minimized, there is no evidence that she would convey poor health habits to the child. Mr. Whitehead has been shown to be an episodic alcoholic "binging" for two week periods approximately every six months. He is doing nothing to eliminate this concern. To infuse a child into such a milieu is problematic.

8) What is the capacity of the adults in the baby's life to explain the circumstance of origin with least confusion and greatest emotional support? Mrs. Whitehead being the parent most invested with the infant's care, in all likelihood would be charged with the task of telling the child of her origins. This court doubts her capability to truthfully report Baby M's origin. She has shown little empathy for the Sterns and their role and even less ability to acknowledge the facts surrounding the original contract. Insofar as emotional support is concerned, the court doubts Mrs. Whitehead could or would subordinate herself for the child's benefit where there is a conflictual circumstance such as relating the child's origins to her. To this day she still appears to reject any role Mr. Stern played in the conception. She chooses to forget that but for him there would be no child. The quality of her reporting capabilities have been tested in these proceedings and found generally wanting. The Sterns have indicated a willingness to obtain professional advice on how and when to tell his daughter. Important in this equation is the child's trust that will have been constructed between custodial parent and child.

9) Which adults would better help the child cope with her own life? It has been shown that Mrs. Whitehead has trouble coping in crisis. She can manage the routine. The Sterns have shown no aberration in either circumstance.

The court also evaluates the climate to which the child may be exposed with the Whiteheads. In addition to a history of economic and domestic instability with another house move imminent, in addition to the reduced level of importance given to education in the Whitehead home and in addition to the character trait problems defined by almost all the mental health professionals including Mrs. Whitehead's own chosen experts, Mrs. Whitehead has a genuine problem in recognizing and reporting the truth.

While we here address best interest it is relevant to her entire posture before the court. Doctor Klein, her own expert, said she lies under stress. Dr. Schecter said she is a faulty reporter because of her "I don't know, I can't recall" answers; especially the number of such answers. The court found this to be so to such an extent it became apparent that Mrs. Whitehead testified to what she chose to, exercising a selective memory, intentionally not recalling or outright lying on the witness stand. This court is thoroughly satisfied that Mrs. Whitehead fully knew of the contents of this court's May 5, 1986 order [to show cause why the surrogate-parenting contract should not be enforced]. She testified on oath to the contrary but the content of her father's letter and [the letter of a witness, Hergenhan, who lied to the court] prove the contrary and it is Hergenhan's letter that also mitigates against Mrs. Whitehead for Mrs. Whitehead knew a lie was being perpetrated on the court; she knew it, participated in it and never acknowledged it. This fundamental inability to speak the truth establishes a tarnished Whitehead environment.

The foregoing recital shows that Mr. Whitehead is a benign force in the Whitehead household. The drive and direction are solely Mrs. Whitehead's prerogatives. This court is satisfied by clear and convincing proofs that Mrs. Whitehead is unreliable insofar as her promise is concerned. She breached her contract without regard to her legal obligations. There has been domestic violence in her household that she could not recall until the court documents refreshed her recollection. She should have known of these facts as she is the one who called the police. There were many house moves in the earlier years of marriage and another move appears imminent. The Whiteheads have had severe economic difficulties including a bankruptcy. In those court papers there appears to be a flawed statement of assets in that the Whiteheads omitted two assets thus misleading the court and their creditors. Mrs. Whitehead has been found too enmeshed with this infant child and unable to separate her own needs from those of the child. She tends to smother the child with her presence even to the exclusion of access by her other two children. She does not have the ability to subordinate herself to the needs of this child. The court is satisfied that based on the details above, Mrs. Whitehead is manipulative, impulsive and exploitive. She is also for the most part, untruthful choosing only to remember what may enhance her position, or altering the facts about which she is testifying or intentionally not remembering. Education plays a subordinate role in the Whiteheads' milieu. The judgment-making ability of Mrs. Whitehead is sorely tested. One outstanding example was her decision to run away in the face of a court order. While she claims fear of the system made her do it this court sees it, minimally, as a disregard of her legal and civic obligation to respond to a court's order, and, maximally, as a contempt of the court order. She does not concern herself with consequences of her acts. Her lack of candor makes her a poor candidate to report to the child in an age appropriate manner and time, the facts of the child's origins. She is a woman without empathy. She expresses none for her husband's problems with alcohol and her infusion of her other children into this process, exposing them rather than protecting them from the searing scrutiny of the media, mitigates against her claim for custody. She is a good mother for and to her older children. She would not be a good custodian for Baby M. . . .

Now having found that the best interest of the child will be enhanced and served in paternal custody, that there is no evidence of fraud, overreaching or violation of any other principle of equity by Mr. Stern, this court having evaluated the equities finds them weighted in favor of Mr. Stern. Enforcing the contract will leave Mr. and Mrs. Whitehead in the same position that they were in when the contract was made. To not enforce the contract will give them the child and deprive Mr. Stern of his promised benefits. This court therefore will specifically enforce the surrogate-parenting agreement to compel delivery of the child to the father and to terminate the mother's parental rights.

Notes

1. *Baby M.* Reversed.   The trial court opinion set forth above was reversed by the New Jersey Supreme Court in In re Baby M., 537 A.2d 1227 (N.J. 1988).

The court concluded that the surrogacy contract was invalid because it conflicted with state statutes the trial court had found inapplicable — statutes prohibiting the payment of money for adoption, statutes requiring consent of a birth mother to adoption *after* the birth of the child and regulating adoption in other ways, and statutes requiring proof of parental unfitness or abandonment before termination of parental rights. The court also held that the surrogate contract violated the public policy that "to the extent possible, children should remain with and be brought up by both of their natural parents." Id. at 1246-1247. The court proceeded to resolve the dispute as a custody dispute between two "natural" parents, awarding custody to Mr. Stern and visitation to Mrs. Whitehead. When faced with a similar legal issue, a California appellate court also found a surrogate parenting agreement unenforceable. Applying custody doctrine governing disputes between two legal parents, the court awarded joint physical and legal custody to the biological father and the surrogate mother. See In re Marriage of Moschetta, 30 Cal. Rptr. 2d 893 (Ct. App. 1994).

Although the trial court in *Baby M.* found the contract enforceable and the New Jersey Supreme Court did not, both courts arrived eventually at a best-interests-of-the-child analysis, and the courts agreed that the Sterns would offer the child a more stable upbringing. What do you think of the best-interests analysis applied by the trial court in the case? What assumptions underlie the analysis? The supreme court was more sympathetic to Mrs. Whitehead, stating that "given her predicament, Mrs. Whitehead was rather harshly judged." 537 A.2d at 1259. At the same time, in awarding custody to Mr. Stern, it relied on the same kinds of factors noted by the trial court. Using the facts provided in the opinion, is it possible to write a persuasive opinion, focused on the best interests of the child, to reach the opposite result?

2. Surrogacy and Intention. Approximately ten percent of U.S. women of reproductive age are affected by infertility, with about fifteen percent of them seeking some form of infertility service. Worldwide it is estimated that approximately two million children have been born through some means of assisted reproductive technology. Vanessa S. Browne-Barbour, Bartering For Babies: Are Preconception Agreements in the Best Interests of Children? 26 Whittier L. Rev. 429, 429-430 n.2 (2004) (citing sources).

Most reproductive technologies are not closely regulated at either the state or federal level. They are used in private in vitro fertilization (IVF) clinics, and how they are used is a result of decisionmaking by patients and their doctors. Margaret Foster Riley, with Richard A. Merrill, Regulating Reproductive Genetics: A Review of American Bioethics Commissions and Comparison to the British Human Fertilization and Embryology Authority, 6 Colum. Sci. & Tech. L. Rev. 1, 4 (2005).

Surrogacy arrangements have posed one of the most significant challenges to the laissez-faire approach to assisted reproduction. In the absence of clear statutory authority in most states, courts developed four approaches: (1) the intent-based approach, which seeks to fulfill the intentions of the parties (see below); (2) the genetic contribution test, which looks to the genetic tie between parent and child (see Johnson v. Calvert, discussed in note 4, below); (3) the gestational primacy test, giving preference to the mother who gestated and bore the child (adopted in cases in which surrogacy contracts are unenforceable, such as Arizona and North Dakota); and (4) the best-interests-of-the-child test (illustrated in *Baby M.*). Amy M. Larkey, Note, Redefining Motherhood: Determining Legal Maternity in Gestational Surrogacy Arrangements, 51 Drake L. Rev. 605, 622-627 (2003) (citing other cases and state legislation illustrating each approach).

Feminist scholars have divided over the issue of surrogacy generally and in particular over how the issue of autonomy should be analyzed. The principal feminist defense of surrogate contracts, which reflects the intent-based approach, credits the surrogate's expression of intent that her role will be limited to gestation. One of the chief objects of this approach is to avoid stereotypes about women as instinctive mothers that contribute to limiting gender roles. The approach also is said to assume, and thus reinforce, interest in and responsibility for parenting by both mothers and fathers:

> [L]egal rules . . . should recognize the importance and the legitimacy of individual efforts to project intentions and decisions into the future. Where such intentions are deliberate, explicit and bargained for, where they are the catalyst for reliance and expectations, as is the case in technologically-assisted reproductive arrangements, they should be honored. . . .
>
> By embracing the emerging opportunities provided by advancing technology, the law would enhance individual freedom, fulfillment and responsibility. Important additional gains would also accrue. Rules that would determine legal parenthood on the basis of individual intentions about procreation and parenting — at least in the context of reproductive technology — would recognize, encourage and reinforce men's choices to nurture children. By adopting a sex-neutral criterion such as intention, the law would partially offset the biological disadvantages men experience in accessing child-nurturing opportunities. The result would parallel recent legal efforts to offset the burdens that childbearing imposes on women who seek equal access to market employment.

Marjorie Maguire Shultz, Reproductive Technology and Intent-Based Parenthood: An Opportunity for Gender Neutrality, 1990 Wis. L. Rev. 297, 302-303. Note the objectives Shultz favors: individual freedom, sex neutrality, and offsetting the "biological disadvantages men experience in accessing child-nurturing opportunities." What is the vision of equality underlying this proposal?

Katharine K. Baker offers an even broader proposal for agreement-based parenthood, not only for "technologically produced" children, but for "regularly produced" children as well. Baker begins with Martha Fineman's notion that a gestational mother holds all initial rights and obligations to a child (Martha Albertson Fineman, The Neutered Mother, The Sexual Family and Other Twentieth Century Tragedies 1-9, 228-233 (1995)) and then proposes that fathers and partners acquire rights only by virtue of an agreement with the mothers, not genetics. See Baker, Bargaining or Biology? The History and Future of Paternity Law and Parental Status, 14 Cornell J.L. & Public Pol'y 1, 5-6 (2004). What conception of equality does this proposal reflect?

Is an intent-based approach to surrogacy arrangements realistic? Consider the New Jersey Supreme Court's concern:

> Under the contract, the natural mother is irrevocably committed before she knows the strength of her bond with her child. She never makes a totally voluntary, informed decision, for quite clearly any decision prior to the baby's birth is, in the most important sense, uninformed, and any decision after that, compelled by a pre-existing contractual commitment, the threat of a lawsuit, and the inducement of a $10,000 payment, is less than totally voluntary.

537 A.2d at 1248. Among courts that have followed this line of analysis, see R.R. v. M.H., 689 N.E.2d 790 (Mass. 1998) (surrogacy agreement unenforceable unless surrogate mother has a "reasonable" waiting period during which she could change her mind). See also Molly J. Walker Wilson, Precommitment in Free-Market Procreation: Surrogacy, Commissioned Adoption, and Limits on Human Decision Making Capacity, 31 J. Legis. 329, 330 (2005) (using behavioral research to argue that women who enter surrogacy contracts can never truly give informed consent "because there is no way that they can know before conceiving the child how they will feel about giving up the child once the time comes"); Marsha Garrison, Law Making for Baby Making: An Interpretive Approach to the Determination of Legal Parentage, 113 Harv. L. Rev. 835 (2000) (arguing that issues arising from new reproductive technologies should be resolved by interpreting existing family law rather than developing new track).

Of what significance to the debate over surrogacy arrangements are the economic pressures that might lead a surrogate to enter into an arrangement? One commentator, tongue in cheek, observes that these pressures, along with the "equation of (valued) femaleness with selflessness and motherhood, would seem to provide just the motivation necessary to cause a woman to enter into a contract that pays the equivalent of $1.57 per hour for nine months of life- and health-endangering, emotionally difficult work." Nancy Ehrenreich, Surrogacy as Resistance? The Misplaced Forces on Choice in the Surrogacy and Abortion Funding Contexts, 41 DePaul L. Rev. 1369, 1380-1381 (1992) (review essay).

From a law and economics or efficiency analysis, Judge Richard Posner argues that the financial constraints that push a woman toward becoming a surrogate are the same considerations as motivate all kinds of decisionmaking throughout the economy. See Posner, The Ethics and Economics of Enforcing Contracts of Surrogate Motherhood, 5 J. Contemp. Health L. & Pol'y 21, 26 (1989) (just as only wealthy people can afford butlers and expensive cars, so only wealthy people will be able to afford surrogate mothers). This is essentially the approach taken by one court:

> Although common sense suggests that women of lesser means serve as surrogate mothers more often than do wealthy women, there has been no proof that surrogacy contracts exploit poor women to any greater degree than economic necessity in general exploits them by inducing them to accept lower-paid or otherwise undesirable employment.

Johnson v. Calvert, 19 Cal. Rptr. 494, 503 (Cal. 1993) (discussed more fully in note 4, p. 920, below).

Who is right? Can women give meaningful consent to act as surrogates without any future parental rights, or are these arrangements exploitative?

Critics of surrogate contracts have also emphasized how surrogacy arrangements support ideological messages about having a child "of one's own" that have reinforced male dominance and women's sense of obligation to bear children:

> Given the discourse surrounding this issue, which treats infertility as a human tragedy of immense proportions and child rearing as an inviolable right, enforcing such contracts would seem to suggest that it is absolutely essential for women to become mothers by whatever means possible.

Ehrenreich, supra, at 1376.

> In Western, patriarchal societies, the classic where-do-babies-come-from tale we tell children is a variation on "Daddy planted a seed in Mommy."...
>
> In a mother-based system, a person is what mothers grow. People are made of the care and nurturance that bring a baby forth into the world and turn that baby into a member of society. In a patriarchal system, a person is what grows out of a seed; originally a man's seed, but now expanded in the sex-neutral language of "gametes." The essence of what a person is, in patriarchal thinking, is there when the seed is planted. Motherhood becomes, in such thinking, a place. Providing the place becomes a service. Under patriarchy, the place in which the seed grows does not really matter. It can be a wife, a "surrogate," or an artificial womb.

Barbara Katz Rothman, Daddy Plants a Seed, 47 Hastings L.J. 1241, 1244-1245 (1996). For the argument that "a woman's role as gestator is fundamentally different from the male role in reproduction," and thus should have primacy in a custody dispute, see Pamela Laufer-Ukeles, Approaching Surrogate Motherhood: Reconsidering Difference, 26 Vt. L. Rev. 407, 436 (2002).

Is there a race component to surrogacy arrangements? Consider the following:

> Minority women increasingly will be sought to serve as "mother machines" for embryos of middle and upper-class clients. It's a new, virulent form of racial and class discrimination. Within a decade, thousands of poor and minority women will be used as a "breeder class" for those who can afford $30,000 to $40,000 to avoid the inconvenience and danger of pregnancy.

Anita L. Allen, The Black Surrogate Mother, 8 Harv. Blackletter J. 17, 30 (1991). See also April L. Cherry, Nurturing the Service of White Culture: Racial Subordination, Gestational Surrogacy, and the Ideology of Motherhood, 10 Tex. J. Women & L. 83 (2001) (arguing that gestational surrogacy arrangements serve to reinforce notions of black women as nurturers of white children, while continuing to deny them legal rights as parents); Dorothy E. Roberts, Race and the New Reproduction, 47 Hastings L.J. 935 (1996) (new reproductive technologies reflect and reinforce racial hierarchy in America). Does this mean that surrogacy arrangements are not in the interests of African-American women?

In her intent-based defense of enforcing surrogate contracts, Marjorie Shultz does not ignore the constraints within which women make reproductive decisions or the negative ideological messages associated with surrogacy. She argues, however, that the risks of assuming universal consent must be weighed against the risks of assuming universal nonconsent:

> At best, sexist scripting is complex and contradictory. Who is to say what is merely "adaptive" and what is "free" choice? In the surrogacy example, which is the sexist conditioned script? A surrogate's wanting another child? Her feeling that she can give the ultimate altruistic gift of life? Her panic that it is unnatural to "give up" "her" child? Her belief that her gestational and genetic services are of major value and therefore might sell in the world? Is the intending mother controlled by sexist scripting in wanting to bring her husband's genetic child into their family? Or are her critics following a sexist script in feeling she deserves to be punished by losing the child she wanted to mother because she did not give up or postpone her career? Or because she was reluctant to risk her health to have her "own" baby? Similarly, is the intending father acting out a male chauvinist vanity in wanting a child that is "his," or is he expressing a male commitment to nurturing a child?
>
> The insight that choices may be adaptive is a useful theoretical construct; it challenges received ideas and aids reflection. But we still have functional and policy decisions to make. When a given choice is said to be adaptive, what should be done? Can we envision some pristine and separate self not shaped by outside persons, events and circumstances? The self is inevitably interactive and permeable. Identifying some pure component called individual will, unswayed and untainted by social, psychological or cultural conditioning is an illusion.
>
> If uncritically accepted to resolve conflicts over policy, the adaptive choice argument obscures as well as illumines. Identifying which pressures create "unfree choices" in order that individuals not be held accountable for them is a recurrent necessity in contract law. Doctrines like duress, coercion, lack of capacity and unconscionability establish criteria under which particular choices can be treated as voluntary exercises of meaningful choice or not. However, where an adaptive choice argument is used to justify a categorical bar on enforcement of all procreational or parenthood agreements—for example all surrogacy agreements—something different is happening. Given that pressures on such choices, as on all human choices, are uneven and multidirectional, if no possibility of a freely chosen surrogacy arrangement is envisioned, then the argument is not really about pressured choice. Rather, it is either about surrogacy per se, or about women as a group lacking the capacity for free decision-making.

Shultz, supra, at 353-354.

Lori B. Andrews, who has vigorously defended surrogacy contracts, is also concerned about the implications of assuming that women cannot make responsible reproductive decisions:

> Some feminists are comfortable with advocating disparate treatment on the grounds that gestation is such a unique experience that it has no male counterpart at law and so deserves a unique legal status. The special nature of gestation, according to this argument, gives rise to special rights—such as the right for the surrogate to change her mind and assert her legal parenthood after the child is born.

The other side of the gestational coin, which has not been sufficiently addressed by these feminists, is that with special rights come special responsibilities. If gestation can be viewed as unique in surrogacy, then it can be viewed as unique in other areas. Pregnant women could be held to have responsibilities that other members of society do not have—such as the responsibility to have a Cesarean section against their wishes in order to protect the health of a child (since only pregnant women are in the unique position of being able to influence the health of the child).

Some feminists have criticized surrogacy as turning participating women, albeit with their consent, into reproductive vessels. I see the danger of the anti-surrogacy arguments as potentially turning *all* women into reproductive vessels, without their consent, by providing government oversight for women's decisions and creating a disparate legal category for gestation.

Andrews, Surrogate Motherhood: The Challenge for Feminists, 16 Law, Med. & Health Care 72, 78 (1988).

3. The Commodification Critique. Alongside specific concerns about lack of consent and the potential exploitation of particular women surrogates, some commentators have focused on the more general dangers to society of conceiving of personal attributes as fungible objects. This, Margaret Radin argues, "detaches from the person that which is integral to the person." Margaret Jane Radin, Market-Inalienability, 100 Harv. L. Rev. 1849, 1881 (1987).

> In our understanding of personhood we are committed to an ideal of individual uniqueness that does not cohere with the idea that each person's attributes are fungible, that they have a monetary equivalent, and that they can be traded off against those of other people....
>
> Market rhetoric invites us to see the person as a self-interested maximizer in all respects. Freedom or autonomy, therefore, is seen as individual control over how to maximize one's overall gains.... [I]t is not satisfactory to think that marketing whatever one wishes defines freedom.

Id. at 1885. Applying the pragmatic analysis described earlier on pp. 821-822 of this chapter, Radin vacillates between an "incomplete commodification" approach and a "market-inalienable" approach to surrogacy, balancing the destructive effects of paid surrogacy against the benefits, under the non-ideal circumstances of this world, for women's empowerment. See id. at 1928-1936. See also Elizabeth S. Anderson, Is Women's Labor a Commodity?, 19 Phil. & Pub. Aff. 71 (1990) (supporting a more decisive conclusion that surrogacy constitutes an unconscionable commodification of children and women's reproductive capacities).

Is commodification a "given" in the surrogacy context? Stephen Schnably argues that it is a "tendency, not an overwhelming force," that Radin's analysis "effectively treats people as passive and unresisting objects of power," and that "her assumption that permitting surrogacy arrangements would result in commodification ignores women's capacity to fight the sexist and objectifying tendencies of paid surrogacy." Stephen J. Schnably, Property and Pragmatism: A Critique of Radin's Theory of Property and Personhood, 45 Stan. L. Rev.

347, 392, 396 (1993). Recall the discussion of prostitution on pp. 821-844 of this chapter. To what extent can the meaning of an activity like surrogacy or prostitution be controlled by those practice it?

4. Gestation-Only Surrogacy. In *Baby M.*, Mary Beth Whitehead was the child's biological mother, both because of her genetic contribution to the child and because she carried the child in her womb. Because she was the mother, after the New Jersey Supreme Court determined that her rights could not be terminated on the basis of a contract signed before the birth of the child, the custody of the child was adjudicated between her and the child's biological father under the customary test applied in custody disputes between biological parents: the best-interests-of-the-child test.

When the genetic and gestational functions are bifurcated, the issues become more complicated. In Johnson v. Calvert, 19 Cal. Rptr. 2d 494 (Cal. 1993), the gestational mother asserted parental rights against the contractual parents, who were also the genetic parents of the child. The California Supreme Court, interpreting the state's version of the Uniform Parentage Act to permit a finding of parenthood on either genetic or gestational grounds, concluded that "when the two means do not coincide in one woman, she who intended to procreate the child — that is, she who intended to bring about the birth of a child that she intended to raise as her own — is the natural mother under California law." Id., at 500. In so doing, the court adopted the approach advocated by Professor Shultz, outlined in note 2, above. As for the concern expressed by the New Jersey Supreme Court in *Baby M.* about when a prebirth contract could be truly voluntary, the court responded:

> The argument that a woman cannot knowingly and intelligently agree to gestate and deliver a baby for intending parents carries overtones of the reasoning that for centuries prevented woman from attaining equal economic rights and professional status under the law. To resurrect this view is both to foreclose a personal and economic choice on the part of the surrogate mother, and to deny intending parents what may be their only means of procreating a child of their own genes.

Id. at 503.

In a subsequent California case involving another surrogate who was not the genetic mother, it was the intended father who changed his mind; he no longer wished to be either married or a father. In re Marriage of Buzzanca, 61 Cal. Rptr. 2d 280 (Ct. App. 1998). In this case, as well, the intentional parenthood approach prevailed, and the father was held responsible for child support. Id.

Matters can become even more complicated when neither claimant is the genetic mother. In one egg donor case, a Pennsylvania court voided a surrogacy contract and declared that the legal mother of triplets was the gestational surrogate, not the contracting couple. J.F. v. D.B., 66 Pa. D. & C.4th 1 (Pa. Ct. Comm. Pl. 2004). The court determined that the egg donor was comparable to a sperm donor. Id.

Several cases involving lesbian parents and non-traditional reproductive procedures have recognized the parental status of both women. See, e.g., K.M. v.

E.G., 117 P.3d 673 (Cal. 2005) (recognizing rights of former lesbian partner, who supplied ova; court declined to treat partner like semen donor); Carvin v. Britain, 122 P.3d 161 (Wash. 2005) (lesbian partner standing to seeking custody rights after mother conceived child through artificial insemination). Issues involving lesbian parents are explored more fully in Chapter 3, at pp. 601-602.

5. Surrogacy and Legal Reform. The Uniform Status of Children of Assisted Conception Act, 9B U.L.A. 102-117, adopted by the National Conference of Commissioners on Uniform State Law in 1988, gives jurisdictions a choice about whether to allow surrogacy arrangements. Alternative A spells out the terms under which surrogacy arrangements are permissible. It requires that all relevant parties, including the husband of the surrogate mother, be parties to the agreement and that they obtain court approval of the agreement prior to conception. The court must find that the intended mother is unable to bear a child, that the surrogate has had at least one pregnancy prior to this arrangement and can have another child without unreasonable risk, that the parties have received counseling, and that home studies of the intended parents and the surrogate have been performed. Without court approval, the contract is void, and the woman who gives birth is the child's mother. A surrogate may change her mind and terminate the agreement without liability to the intended parents within six months of the last insemination. If she does not, the agreement is enforceable, and the intended parents are the legal parents. Under Alternative B of the Uniform Act, surrogacy agreements are void and unenforceable.

The Family Law Section of the American Bar Association approved a Model Surrogacy Act, which makes surrogacy agreements lawful and enforceable by specific performance. Under this Model Act, the allowable compensation to the surrogate ranges from $7,500 to $12,500. The surrogate may not renege on the agreement, but she may abort the pregnancy. The intended parents must be infertile. The Act substitutes a simplified procedure for the customary adoption requirements. Id. at 144-145.

Nearly half of the states address surrogacy arrangements either in case law or by statute. Seven jurisdictions treat surrogacy agreements as void and unenforceable, including Arizona, Indiana, Kansas, Michigan, New York, North Dakota, Utah, and the District of Columbia. See Vanessa S. Browne-Barbour, Bartering for Babies: Are Preconception Agreements in the Best Interests of Children? 26 Whittier L. Rev. 429, 447-449, 457 (2004). Another group of states allow surrogacy under some but not all circumstances. The most common restrictions are prohibitions or limits on what can be paid. Those states prohibiting compensation include Arkansas, Kentucky, Maryland (by Attorney General opinion), Nebraska, New Jersey, and Washington. States that regulate the fees and/or expenses that may be paid include California, Florida, Illinois, Kentucky, Nevada, and Virginia. Some states, such as Virginia, require that the surrogate mother be married, or has already had a child. Some states require prior court approval of surrogacy contracts. Jurisdictions imposing criminal sanctions for violation of the rules relating to surrogacy arrangements include the District of Columbia, Maryland, Michigan, New York, Virginia, and Washington. Id. at 449-458. Among the most detailed regulatory schemes are those in Florida, Illinois, New Hampshire,

Virginia, and Washington. See Fla. Stat. § 742.15(2) (2005); 750 Ill. Comp. Stat. § 45/6 (2005); N.H. Rev. Stat. Ann. § 168-B:16 (2005); Va. Code Ann. §§ 20-159 et seq. (2005); Wash. Rev. Code §§ 26.26.210 et seq. (2005).

The world community reflects similar divisions, with all pre-conception arrangements prohibited in most Middle Eastern countries, China, Denmark, Norway, Switzerland, Costa Rica and Germany, and unpaid surrogacy allowed in Korea, Australia, and India. In Great Britain, pregnancy-related expenses may be paid in connection with a surrogacy arrangement. Id. at 460-466.

One commentator, arguing as a general matter that "legal efforts to mark the specialness of intimate relationships by limiting or prohibiting economic exchange within them appear to have systematically adverse distributional consequences for women and poorer people" argues that surrogacy restrictions and prohibitions on the payment that a surrogate mother may receive exemplify the distributive inequality of the law's approach to intimate contracts. See Jill Elaine Hasday, Intimacy and Economic Exchange, 119 Harv. L. Rev. 491, 517, 526 (2005). Is she right? Are the regulatory efforts to control the exploitative potential of surrogacy arrangements misguided? See id. at 526 (proposing a fiduciary model, whereby the "law governing surrogacy could help safeguard the specialness of the parent-child relation by imposing a duty on both surrogate mothers and recipient parents to act as fiduciaries for each other and for the potential child").

6. Frozen "Pre-embryos": Balancing Wanted and Unwanted Parenthood. There are currently over 400,000 embryos in frozen storage. Jessica Berg, Owning Persons: The Application of Property Theory to Embryos and Fetuses, 40 Wake Forest L. Rev. 159, 161 (2005), with little clear law on how to resolve disputes that may arise over them.

In one case, a couple had planned on using frozen embryos to start a family, but divorced before a pregnancy had been achieved. At divorce, the wife sought custody of the embryos for possible future implantation and the husband sought authority to prevent implantation. The trial court declared that the embryos were "human beings" and awarded custody to the wife on the grounds that such action was the most likely to protect their best interests. Davis v. Davis, 1989 Tenn. App. LEXIS 641 (Blount County Cir. Ct., Sept. 26, 1989). The Tennessee Court of Appeals reversed, concluding that the parties shared an equal interest in the embryos, that the husband had a constitutionally protected right not to beget a child where no pregnancy had yet taken place, and that there was no compelling state interest to justify implantation against the will of either party. Davis v. Davis, 1990 Tenn. App. LEXIS 642 (Sept. 13, 1990).

On appeal to the state supreme court, the wife changed her position, deciding that rather than using the embryos to become pregnant herself, she wanted to donate them to a childless couple. The court rejected the approaches of both the trial court and the court of appeals, holding that "preembryos are not, strictly speaking, either 'persons' or 'property,' but occupy an interim category that entitles them to special respect because of their potential for human life." Davis v. Davis, 842 S.W.2d 588, 597 (Tenn. 1992), cert. denied sub nom. Stowe v. Davis, 507 U.S. 911 (1993). The court stated that, if possible, a contest over pre-embryos should be resolved according to prior agreement. Id. Where no such agreement exists, each party's constitutional privacy interests require that their particular positions, burdens, and interests in a particular case be weighed against the other's and the disposition ordered that avoids the most harm. Id. at 603-604. The court balanced the interests as follows:

> Beginning with the burden imposed on Junior Davis, we note that the consequences are obvious. Any disposition which results in the gestation of the preembryos would impose unwanted parenthood on him, with all of its possible financial and psychological consequences. The impact that this unwanted parenthood would have on Junior Davis can only be understood by considering his particular circumstances, as revealed in the record.
>
> Junior Davis testified that he was the fifth youngest of six children. When he was five years old, his parents divorced, his mother had a nervous break-down, and he and three of his brothers went to live at a home for boys run by the Lutheran Church. Another brother was taken in by an aunt, and his sister stayed with her mother. From that day forward, he had monthly visits with his mother but saw his father only three more times before he died in 1976. Junior Davis testified that, as a boy, he had severe problems caused by separation from his parents. He said that it was especially hard to leave his mother after each monthly visit. He clearly feels that he has suffered because of his lack of opportunity to establish a relationship with his parents and particularly because of the absence of his father.
>
> In light of his boyhood experiences, Junior Davis is vehemently opposed to fathering a child that would not live with both parents. Regardless of whether he or Mary Sue had custody, he feels that the child's bond with the non-custodial parent would not be satisfactory. He testified very clearly that his concern was for the psychological obstacles a child in such a situation would face, as well as the burdens it would impose on him. Likewise, he is opposed to donation because the recipient couple might divorce, leaving the child (which he definitely would consider his own) in a single-parent setting.
>
> Balanced against Junior Davis's interest in avoiding parenthood is Mary Sue Davis's interest in donating the preembryos to another couple for implantation. Refusal to permit donation of the preembryos would impose on her the burden of knowing that the lengthy IVF procedures she underwent were futile, and that the preembryos to which she contributed genetic material would never become children. While this is not an insubstantial emotional burden, we can only conclude that Mary Sue Davis's interest in donation is not as significant as the interest Junior Davis has in avoiding parenthood. If she were allowed to donate these preembryos, he would face a lifetime of either wondering about his parental status or knowing about his parental status but having no control over it. He testified quite clearly that if the preembryos were brought to term he would fight for custody of his child or children. Donation, if a child came of it, would rob him twice — his procreational autonomy would be defeated and his relationship with his offspring would be prohibited.
>
> The case would be closer if Mary Sue Davis were seeking to use the preembryos herself, but only if she could not achieve parenthood by any other reasonable means. We recognize the trauma that Mary Sue has already experienced and the additional discomfort to which she would be subjected if she opts to attempt IVF again. Still, she would have a reasonable opportunity, through IVF, to try once again to achieve parenthood in all its aspects — genetic, gestation, bearing, and rearing.
>
> Further, we note that if Mary Sue Davis were unable to undergo another round of IVF, or opted not to try, she could still achieve the child-rearing aspects of

> parenthood through adoption. The fact that she and Junior Davis pursued adoption indicates that, at least at one time, she was willing to forego genetic parenthood and would have been satisfied by the child-rearing aspects of parenthood alone.

Id.

Is this an example of the kind of contextualized legal reasoning discussed in Chapter 4? Is it an application of the "ethic of care"? Pragmatism? Stereotyped thinking? Resistance to stereotypes?

Mary Sue Davis was unable to conceive children through the usual means because after six painful tubal pregnancies, both of her fallopian tubes were inoperative. Each of the six IVF attempts involved a month of subcutaneous injections to shut down her pituitary gland and eight days of intermuscular injections to stimulate her ovaries to produce ova. She was anesthetized five times for the aspiration procedure and then returned for the transfer back to her uterus 48 to 72 hours later. Should this painful series of treatments be considered in the balancing of interests?

Is it clear to you why Junior Davis's strong feelings about not fathering children he could not raise himself in a nuclear family weighed more heavily than Mary Sue Davis's wish to succeed in her efforts to produce one or more children for herself or for others? The court stated that "[o]rdinarily, the party wishing to avoid procreation should prevail, assuming that the other party has a reasonable possibility of achieving parenthood by means other than use of the preembryos in question." 842 S.W.2d at 604. The court seemed to suggest that further IVF procedures or adoption would offer reasonable possibilities for Mary Sue Davis to achieve parenthood. What's going on here? How do you think the equities would be balanced if Junior Davis had wanted the embryos for implantation in his new wife and Mary Sue Davis had wanted the embryos discarded?

While the law is still emerging in this area, the trend in this context favors the right not to procreate over the right to procreate, as the court did in *Davis*. This approach usually means that the agreement the couple signed before the assisted reproductive procedures is unenforceable. See J.B. v. M.B., 783 A.2d 707 (N.J. 2001) (at divorce, wife entitled to have frozen embryos destroyed, notwithstanding agreement in contract to relinquish them to in vitro fertilization program if their marriage dissolved, because such contracts are contrary to public policy); A.Z. v. B.Z., 725 N.E.2d 1051 (Mass. 2000) (agreement that embryos would be wife's if the parties separated was unenforceable as a type of forced procreation; parenthood should not be forced on husband, notwithstanding his prior consent, once he objects to such an undertaking); see also Litowitz v. Litowitz, 48 P.3d 261 (Wash. 2002) (once donor eggs had been fertilized with husband's sperm, cryopreservation contract, not egg donor contract, controlled); Kass v. Kass, 696 N.E.2d 174 (N.Y. 1998) (enforcing preconception agreement expressing intention of parties to donate any disputed embryos to the IVF program for research purposes, notwithstanding woman's dispute of the agreement and desire to implant the embryos).

For analysis of these cases, and the questions raised in embryos disputes, see Berg, supra (urging use of property theory in addressing embryo disputes);

Olivia Lin, Note, Rehabilitating Bioethics: Recontextualizing In Vitro Fertilization Outside Contractual Autonomy, 54 Duke L.J. 485 (2004) (developing teleological, ethics-based approach to contracts relating to IVF, rather than individual autonomy contracts model); Paula J. Manning, Baby Needs a New Set of Rules: Using Adoption Doctrine to Regulate Embryo Donation, 5 Geo. J. Gender & L. 677 (2004) (advocating reliance on adoption law); Ellen Waldman, The Parent Trap: Uncovering the Myth of "Coerced Parenthood" in Frozen Embryo Disputes, 53 Am. U. J. Rev. 1021 (2004) (urging "greater empathy for, and judicial deference to, the interests of would-be mothers and fathers" in frozen embryo disputes); Karissa Hostrup Windsor, Note, Disposition of Cryopreserved Preembryos After Divorce, 88 Iowa L. Rev. 1001 (2003) (advocating federal legislation requiring enforceable agreements; in their absence, advocating that the party seeking to avoid procreation should prevail unless the other party seeks to use embryos personally and these embryos represent the only reasonable means to achieve biological parenthood).

A few states have enacted statutes addressing the status or use of cryopreserved pre-embryos. See Fla. Stat. Ann. § 742.17 (West 2005) (requiring couples and IVF programs to agree in advance about the disposition of pre-embryos in the event of a divorce or the death of a spouse); La. Rev. Stat. §§ 9:121 et seq. (West 2005) (requiring the treatment of pre-embryos as "juridical persons" and prohibiting destruction of pre-embryos or their use for research purposes); N.H. Rev. Stat. Ann. § 168-B:13 to 168-B:15 (West 2005) (regulating in vitro fertilization and pre-embryo transfer).

7. Technological Reproduction: A Constitutional Right? In 2004, in the midst of public debate about the regulation of cloning and stem cell research, President George W. Bush's Council on Bioethics released a report advocating increased restraints on in vitro fertilization (IVF). See President's Council on Bioethics, Reproduction and Responsibility: The Regulation of New Biotechnologies 205-224 (2004), available at http:www.bioethics.gov/reports/reproductionandresponsibility/_pcbe_final_reproduction_and_responsibility.pdf. In light of cases such as *Griswold*, *Roe*, and *Casey*, is there a constitutional right to IVF and other reproductive technologies? See Note, Assessing the Viability of a Substantive Due Process Right to In Vitro Fertilization, 118 Harv. L. Rev. 2792, 2813 (2005) (arguing that there should be such a right, but that it is not clear that courts will identify one).

Putting Theory into Practice

5-12. In 2002 Congress authorized the spending of nearly one million dollars to promote the donation of frozen embryos to a recipient who intend to use the embryos to bear and raise a child. Laura Meckler, "Embryo Adoption" Getting Push from $1 Million Awareness Drive, Chi. Trib., Aug. 21, 2004, at 9. Is this a good policy?

4. The Pregnant Woman and Fetus as Adversaries

Ferguson v. City of Charleston
532 U.S. 67 (2001)

Justice STEVENS delivered the opinion of the Court.

In this case, we must decide whether a state hospital's performance of a diagnostic test to obtain evidence of a patient's criminal conduct for law enforcement purposes is an unreasonable search if the patient has not consented to the procedure. More narrowly, the question is whether the interest in using the threat of criminal sanctions to deter pregnant women from using cocaine can justify a departure from the general rule that an official nonconsensual search is unconstitutional if not authorized by a valid warrant.

I

In the fall of 1988, staff members at the public hospital operated in the city of Charleston by the Medical University of South Carolina (MUSC) became concerned about an apparent increase in the use of cocaine by patients who were receiving prenatal treatment. In response to this perceived increase, as of April 1989, MUSC began to order drug screens to be performed on urine samples from maternity patients who were suspected of using cocaine. If a patient tested positive, she was then referred by MUSC staff to the county substance abuse commission for counseling and treatment. However, despite the referrals, the incidence of cocaine use among the patients at MUSC did not appear to change.

Some four months later, Nurse Shirley Brown, the case manager for the MUSC obstetrics department, heard a news broadcast reporting that the police in Greenville, South Carolina, were arresting pregnant users of cocaine on the theory that such use harmed the fetus and was therefore child abuse. Nurse Brown discussed the story with MUSC's general counsel, Joseph C. Good, Jr., who then contacted Charleston Solicitor Charles Condon in order to offer MUSC's cooperation in prosecuting mothers whose children tested positive for drugs at birth.

After receiving Good's letter, Solicitor Condon took the first steps in developing the policy at issue in this case. He organized the initial meetings, decided who would participate, and issued the invitations, in which he described his plan to prosecute women who tested positive for cocaine while pregnant. The task force that Condon formed included representatives of MUSC, the police, the County Substance Abuse Commission and the Department of Social Services. Their deliberations led to MUSC's adoption of a 12-page document entitled "POLICY M-7," dealing with the subject of "Management of Drug Abuse During Pregnancy."

The first three pages of Policy M-7 set forth the procedure to be followed by the hospital staff to "identify/assist pregnant patients suspected of drug abuse." The first section, entitled the "Identification of Drug Abusers," provided that a patient should be tested for cocaine through a urine drug screen if she met one or more of nine criteria.[4] It also stated that a chain of custody should be followed when obtaining and testing urine samples, presumably to make sure that the results could be used in subsequent criminal proceedings. The policy also provided for education and referral to a substance abuse clinic for patients who tested positive. Most important, it added the threat of law enforcement intervention that "provided the necessary 'leverage' to make the policy effective." That threat was, as respondents candidly acknowledge, essential to the program's success in getting women into treatment and keeping them there.

The threat of law enforcement involvement was set forth in two protocols, the first dealing with the identification of drug use during pregnancy, and the second with identification of drug use after labor. Under the latter protocol, the police were to be notified without delay and the patient promptly arrested. Under the former, after the initial positive drug test, the police were to be notified (and the patient arrested) only if the patient tested positive for cocaine a second time or if she missed an appointment with a substance abuse counselor.[5] In 1990, however, the policy was modified at the behest of the solicitor's office to give the patient who tested positive during labor, like the patient who tested positive during a prenatal care visit, an opportunity to avoid arrest by consenting to substance abuse treatment.

The last six pages of the policy contained forms for the patients to sign, as well as procedures for the police to follow when a patient was arrested. The policy also prescribed in detail the precise offenses with which a woman could be charged, depending on the stage of her pregnancy. If the pregnancy was 27 weeks or less, the patient was to be charged with simple possession. If it was 28 weeks or more, she was to be charged with possession and distribution to a person under the age of 18 — in this case, the fetus. If she delivered "while testing positive for illegal drugs," she was also to be charged with unlawful neglect of a child. Under the policy, the police were instructed to interrogate the arrestee in order "to ascertain the identity of the subject who provided illegal drugs to the suspect." Other than the provisions describing the substance abuse treatment to be offered to women who tested positive, the policy made no mention of any change in the prenatal care of such patients, nor did it prescribe any special treatment for the newborns.

---

4. Those criteria were as follows:

    1. No prenatal care
    2. Late prenatal care after 24 weeks gestation
    3. Incomplete prenatal care
    4. Abruptio placentae
    5. Intrauterine fetal death
    6. Preterm labor "of no obvious cause"
    7. IUGR [intrauterine growth retardation] "of no obvious cause"
    8. Previously known drug or alcohol abuse
    9. Unexplained congenital anomalies.

5. Despite the conditional description of the first category, when the policy was in its initial stages, a positive test was immediately reported to the police, who then promptly arrested the patient.

II

Petitioners are 10 women who received obstetrical care at MUSC and who were arrested after testing positive for cocaine. Four of them were arrested during the initial implementation of the policy; they were not offered the opportunity to receive drug treatment as an alternative to arrest. The others were arrested after the policy was modified in 1990; they either failed to comply with the terms of the drug treatment program or tested positive for a second time. Respondents include the city of Charleston, law enforcement officials who helped develop and enforce the policy, and representatives of MUSC.

Petitioners' complaint challenged the validity of the policy under various theories, including the claim that warrantless and nonconsensual drug tests conducted for criminal investigatory purposes were unconstitutional searches. Respondents advanced two principal defenses to the constitutional claim: (1) that, as a matter of fact, petitioners had consented to the searches; and (2) that, as a matter of law, the searches were reasonable, even absent consent, because they were justified by special non-law-enforcement purposes. The District Court rejected the second defense because the searches in question "were not done by the medical university for independent purposes. [Instead,] the police came in and there was an agreement reached that the positive screens would be shared with the police." Accordingly, the District Court submitted the factual defense to the jury with instructions that required a verdict in favor of petitioners unless the jury found consent. The jury found for respondents.

Petitioners appealed. . . . The Court of Appeals for the Fourth Circuit affirmed, but without reaching the question of consent. 186 F.3d 469 (1999). Disagreeing with the District Court, the majority of the appellate panel held that the searches were reasonable as a matter of law under our line of cases recognizing that "special needs" may, in certain exceptional circumstances, justify a search policy designed to serve non-law-enforcement ends. On the understanding "that MUSC personnel conducted the urine drug screens for medical purposes wholly independent of an intent to aid law enforcement efforts," the majority applied the balancing test used in Treasury Employees v. Von Raab, 489 U.S. 656 (1989), and Vernonia School Dist. 47J v. Acton, 515 U.S. 646 (1995), and concluded that the interest in curtailing the pregnancy complications and medical costs associated with maternal cocaine use outweighed what the majority termed a minimal intrusion on the privacy of the patients. . . .

We granted certiorari . . . to review the appellate court's holding on the "special needs" issue. Because we do not reach the question of the sufficiency of the evidence with respect to consent, we necessarily assume for purposes of our decision — as did the Court of Appeals — that the searches were conducted without the informed consent of the patients. We conclude that the judgment should be reversed and the case remanded for a decision on the consent issue.

III

Because MUSC is a state hospital, the members of its staff are government actors, subject to the strictures of the Fourth Amendment. . . . Moreover, the urine tests conducted by those staff members were indisputably searches within the meaning of the Fourth Amendment.... Neither the District Court nor the Court of Appeals concluded that any of the nine criteria used to identify the women to be searched provided either probable cause to believe that they were using cocaine, or even the basis for a reasonable suspicion of such use. Rather, the District Court and the Court of Appeals viewed the case as one involving MUSC's right to conduct searches without warrants or probable cause.

Because the hospital seeks to justify its authority to conduct drug tests and to turn the results over to law enforcement agents without the knowledge or consent of the patients, this case differs from the four previous cases in which we have considered whether comparable drug tests "fit within the closely guarded category of constitutionally permissible suspicionless searches." ... In three of those cases, we sustained drug tests for railway employees involved in train accidents, Skinner v. Railway Labor Executives' Assn., 489 U.S. 602 (1989), for United States Customs Service employees seeking promotion to certain sensitive positions, [*Von Raab*, supra], and for high school students participating in interscholastic sports, [*Vernonia School Dist.*, supra]. In the fourth case, we struck down such testing for candidates for designated state offices as unreasonable. Chandler v. Miller, 520 U.S. 305 (1997).

In each of those cases, we employed a balancing test that weighed the intrusion on the individual's interest in privacy against the "special needs" that supported the program. As an initial matter, we note that the invasion of privacy in this case is far more substantial than in those cases. In the previous four cases, there was no misunderstanding about the purpose of the test or the potential use of the test results, and there were protections against the dissemination of the results to third parties. The use of an adverse test result to disqualify one from eligibility for a particular benefit, such as a promotion or an opportunity to participate in an extracurricular activity, involves a less serious intrusion on privacy than the unauthorized dissemination of such results to third parties. The reasonable expectation of privacy enjoyed by the typical patient undergoing diagnostic tests in a hospital is that the results of those tests will not be shared with non-medical personnel without her consent.... In none of our prior cases was there any intrusion upon that kind of expectation.[14]

The critical difference between those four drug-testing cases and this one, however, lies in the nature of the "special need" asserted as justification for the warrantless searches. In each of those earlier cases, the "special need" that was advanced as a justification for the absence of a warrant or individualized suspicion was one divorced from the State's general interest in law enforcement.... In this case, however, the central and indispensable feature of the policy from its inception was the use of law enforcement to coerce the patients into substance abuse treatment. This fact distinguishes this case from circumstances in which physicians or psychologists, in the course of ordinary medical procedures aimed at helping the patient herself, come across information that under rules of law or ethics is

---

14. In fact, we have previously recognized that an intrusion on that expectation may have adverse consequences because it may deter patients from receiving needed medical care. Whalen v. Roe, 429 U.S. 589, 599-600 (1977)....

subject to reporting requirements, which no one has challenged here. See, e.g., Council on Ethical and Judicial Affairs, American Medical Association, Policy Finder, Current Opinions E-5.05 (2000) (requiring reporting where "a patient threatens to inflict serious bodily harm to another person or to him or herself and there is a reasonable probability that the patient may carry out the threat"); Ark. Code Ann. § 12-12-602 (1999) (requiring reporting of intentionally inflicted knife or gunshot wounds); Ariz. Rev. Stat. Ann. § 13-3620 (Supp. 2000) (requiring "any . . . person having responsibility for the care or treatment of children" to report suspected abuse or neglect to a peace officer or child protection agency).

Respondents argue in essence that their ultimate purpose — namely, protecting the health of both mother and child — is a beneficent one. In *Chandler,* however, we did not simply accept the State's invocation of a "special need." Instead, we carried out a "close review" of the scheme at issue before concluding that the need in question was not "special," as that term has been defined in our cases. 520 U.S. at 322. . . .

While the ultimate goal of the program may well have been to get the women in question into substance abuse treatment and off of drugs, the immediate objective of the searches was to generate evidence for law enforcement purposes in order to reach that goal. The threat of law enforcement may ultimately have been intended as a means to an end, but the direct and primary purpose of MUSC's policy was to ensure the use of those means. In our opinion, this distinction is critical. Because law enforcement involvement always serves some broader social purpose or objective, under respondents' view, virtually any non-consensual suspicionless search could be immunized under the special needs doctrine by defining the search solely in terms of its ultimate, rather than immediate, purpose. Such an approach is inconsistent with the Fourth Amendment. Given the primary purpose of the Charleston program, which was to use the threat of arrest and prosecution in order to force women into treatment, and given the extensive involvement of law enforcement officials at every stage of the policy, this case simply does not fit within the closely guarded category of "special needs."

Accordingly, the judgment of the Court of Appeals is reversed, and the case is remanded for further proceedings consistent with this opinion.

[The concurring opinion by Justice Kennedy is omitted.]

Dissenting opinion by Justice SCALIA, with whom THE CHIEF JUSTICE and Justice THOMAS join as to Part II.

There is always an unappealing aspect to the use of doctors and nurses, ministers of mercy, to obtain incriminating evidence against the supposed objects of their ministration — although here, it is correctly pointed out, the doctors and nurses were ministering not just to the mothers but also to the children whom their cooperation with the police was meant to protect. But whatever may be the correct social judgment concerning the desirability of what occurred here, that is not the issue in the present case. The Constitution does not resolve all difficult social questions, but leaves the vast majority of them to resolution by debate and the democratic process — which would produce a decision by the citizens of Charleston, through their elected representatives, to forbid or permit the police action at issue here. The question before us is a narrower one: whether, whatever the desirability of this police conduct, it violates the Fourth Amendment's prohibition of unreasonable searches and seizures. In my view, it plainly does not.

I

The first step in Fourth Amendment analysis is to identify the search or seizure at issue. What petitioners, the Court, and to a lesser extent the concurrence really object to is not the urine testing, but the hospital's reporting of positive drug-test results to police. But the latter is obviously not a search. At most it may be a "derivative use of the product of a past unlawful search," which, of course, "works no new Fourth Amendment wrong" and "presents a question, not of rights, but of remedies." United States v. Calandra, 414 U.S. 338, 354 (1974). There is only one act that could conceivably be regarded as a search of petitioners in the present case: the taking of the urine sample. I suppose the testing of that urine for traces of unlawful drugs could be considered a search of sorts, but the Fourth Amendment protects only against searches of citizens' "persons, houses, papers, and effects"; and it is entirely unrealistic to regard urine as one of the "effects" (i.e., part of the property) of the person who has passed and abandoned it. . . . Some would argue, I suppose, that testing of the urine is prohibited by some generalized privacy right "emanating" from the "penumbras" of the Constitution (a question that is not before us); but it is not even arguable that the testing of urine that has been lawfully obtained is a Fourth Amendment search. (I may add that, even if it were, the factors legitimizing the taking of the sample, which I discuss below, would likewise legitimize the testing of it.)

It is rudimentary Fourth Amendment law that a search which has been consented to is not unreasonable. There is no contention in the present case that the urine samples were extracted forcibly. The only conceivable bases for saying that they were obtained without consent are the contentions (1) that the consent was coerced by the patients' need for medical treatment, (2) that the consent was uninformed because the patients were not told that the tests would include testing for drugs, and (3) that the consent was uninformed because the patients were not told that the results of the tests would be provided to the police. . . .

Under our established Fourth Amendment law, the last two contentions would not suffice, even without reference to the special-needs doctrine. The Court's analogizing of this case to Miranda v. Arizona, 384 U.S. 436 (1966), and its claim that "standards of knowing waiver" apply are flatly contradicted by our jurisprudence, which shows that using lawfully (but deceivingly) obtained material for purposes other than those represented, and giving that material or information derived from it to the police, is not unconstitutional. . . .

Until today, we have never held — or even suggested — that material which a person voluntarily entrusts to someone else cannot be given by that person to the police, and used for whatever evidence it may contain. Without so much as discussing the point, the Court today opens a hole in our Fourth Amendment jurisprudence, the size and shape of which is entirely indeterminate. Today's holding would be remarkable enough if the confidential relationship violated by the police conduct were at least one protected by state law. It would be surprising to learn, for example, that in a State which recognizes a spousal evidentiary privilege the police cannot use evidence obtained from a cooperating husband or wife. But today's holding goes even beyond that, since there does not exist any physician-patient privilege in South Carolina....Since the Court declines even to discuss the issue, it leaves law enforcement officials entirely in the dark as to when they can use incriminating evidence obtained from "trusted" sources. Presumably the lines will be drawn in the case-by-case development of a whole new branch of Fourth Amendment jurisprudence, taking yet another social judgment (which confidential relationships ought not be invaded by the police) out of democratic control, and confiding it to the uncontrolled judgment of this Court—uncontrolled because there is no common-law precedent to guide it. I would adhere to our established law, which says that information obtained through violation of a relationship of trust is obtained consensually, and is hence not a search.

II

I think it clear, therefore, that there is no basis for saying that obtaining of the urine sample was unconstitutional. The special-needs doctrine is thus quite irrelevant, since it operates only to validate searches and seizures that are otherwise unlawful. In the ensuing discussion, however, I shall assume (contrary to legal precedent) that the taking of the urine sample was (either because of the patients' necessitous circumstances, or because of failure to disclose that the urine would be tested for drugs, or because of failure to disclose that the results of the test would be given to the police) coerced. Indeed, I shall even assume (contrary to common sense) that the testing of the urine constituted an unconsented search of the patients' effects. On those assumptions, the special-needs doctrine would become relevant; and, properly applied, would validate what was done here.

The conclusion of the Court that the special-needs doctrine is inapplicable rests upon its contention that respondents "undertook to obtain [drug] evidence from their patients" not for any medical purpose, but "for the specific purpose of incriminating those patients." In other words, the purported medical rationale was merely a pretext; there was no special need....This contention contradicts the District Court's finding of fact that the goal of the testing policy "was not to arrest patients but to facilitate their treatment and protect both the mother and unborn child."...This finding is binding upon us unless clearly erroneous, see Fed. Rule Civ. Proc. 52(a). Not only do I find it supportable; I think any other finding would have to be overturned.

The cocaine tests started in April 1989, neither at police suggestion nor with police involvement. Expectant mothers who tested positive were referred by hospital staff for substance-abuse treatment—an obvious health benefit to both mother and child....And, since "infants whose mothers abuse cocaine during pregnancy are born with a wide variety of physical and neurological abnormalities,"...which require medical attention,...the tests were of additional medical benefit in predicting needed postnatal treatment for the child.

Thus, in their origin—before the police were in any way involved—the tests had an immediate, not merely an "ultimate,"...purpose of improving maternal and infant health. Several months after the testing had been initiated, a nurse discovered that local police were arresting pregnant users of cocaine for child abuse, the hospital's general counsel wrote the county solicitor to ask "what, if anything, our Medical Center needs to do to assist you in this matter,"...(South Carolina law requires child abuse to be reported, see S.C. Code Ann. §20-7-510), the police suggested ways to avoid tainting evidence, and the hospital and police in conjunction used the testing program as a means of securing what the Court calls the "ultimate" health benefit of coercing drug-abusing mothers into drug treatment....Why would there be any reason to believe that, once this policy of using the drug tests for their "ultimate" health benefits had been adopted, use of them for their original, immediate, benefits somehow disappeared, and testing somehow became in its entirety nothing more than a "pretext" for obtaining grounds for arrest? On the face of it, this is incredible....

In sum, there can be no basis for the Court's purported ability to "distinguish this case from circumstances in which physicians or psychologists, in the course of ordinary medical procedures aimed at helping the patient herself, come across information that...is subject to reporting requirements,"...unless it is this: That the addition of a law-enforcement-related purpose to a legitimate medical purpose destroys applicability of the "special-needs" doctrine. But that is quite impossible, since the special-needs doctrine was developed, and is ordinarily employed, precisely to enable searches by law enforcement officials who, of course, ordinarily have a law enforcement objective....

[I]t is not the function of this Court—at least not in Fourth Amendment cases—to weigh petitioners' privacy interest against the State's interest in meeting the crisis of "crack babies" that developed in the late 1980's. I cannot refrain from observing, however, that the outcome of a wise weighing of those interests is by no means clear. The initial goal of the doctors and nurses who conducted cocaine-testing in this case was to refer pregnant drug addicts to treatment centers, and to prepare for necessary treatment of their possibly affected children. When the doctors and nurses agreed to the program providing test results to the police, they did so because (in addition to the fact that child abuse was required by law to be reported) they wanted to use the sanction of arrest as a strong incentive for their addicted patients to undertake drug-addiction treatment. And the police themselves used it for that benign purpose, as is shown by the fact that only 30 of 253 women testing positive for cocaine were ever arrested, and only 2 of those prosecuted....It would not be unreasonable to conclude that today's judgment, authorizing the assessment of damages against the county solicitor and individual doctors and nurses who participated in the program, proves once again that no good deed goes unpunished.

But as far as the Fourth Amendment is concerned: There was no unconsented search in this case. And if there was, it would have been validated by the special-needs doctrine. For these reasons, I respectfully dissent.

Notes

1. Criminal Prosecutions of Drug-Abusing Pregnant Women. According to the American Public Health Association, approximately ten percent of children who are born are exposed to some form of controlled substance — most often, crack cocaine. Heather Flynn Bell, Comment, In Utero Endangerment and Public Health: Prosecution vs. Treatment, 36 Tulsa L.J. 649, 649 (2001). While the degree of harm is still under study, there is no doubt that drug abuse by a pregnant woman enhances certain serious risks to the unborn child. Justice Kennedy in his concurring opinion in *Ferguson* summarizes some of the recent research:

> Infants whose mothers abuse cocaine during pregnancy are born with a wide variety of physical and neurological abnormalities. See Chiriboga, Brust, Bateman, & Hauser, Dose-Response Effect of Fetal Cocaine Exposure on Newborn Neurologic Function, 103 Pediatrics 79 (1999) (finding that, compared with unexposed infants, cocaine-exposed infants experienced higher rates of intrauterine growth retardation, smaller head circumference, global hypertonia, coarse tremor, and extensor leg posture). Prenatal exposure to cocaine can also result in developmental problems which persist long after birth. See Arendt, Angelopoulos, Salvator, & Singer, Motor Development of Cocaine-exposed Children at Age Two Years, 103 Pediatrics 86 (1999) (concluding that, at two years of age, children who were exposed to cocaine in utero exhibited significantly less fine and gross motor development than those not so exposed); Chasnoff et al., Prenatal Exposure to Cocaine and Other Drugs: Outcome at Four to Six Years, 846 Annals of the New York Academy of Sciences 314, 319-320 (J. Harvey and B. Kosofsky eds. 1998) (finding that four to six year olds who were exposed to cocaine in utero exhibit higher instances of depression, anxiety, social, thought, and attention problems, and delinquent and aggressive behaviors than their unexposed counterparts). There can be no doubt that a mother's ingesting this drug can cause tragic injury to a fetus and a child. There should be no doubt that South Carolina can impose punishment upon an expectant mother who has so little regard for her own unborn that she risks causing him or her lifelong damage and suffering. The State, by taking special measures to give rehabilitation and training to expectant mothers with this tragic addiction or weakness, acts well within its powers and its civic obligations.

121 S. Ct. 1281, 1294-1295 (Kennedy, J., concurring)

In light of these risks, pregnant women have been criminally charged under two different theories: delivery of a controlled substance to a minor and child abuse or endangerment. Courts have rejected the drug delivery theory on the grounds that the statutes under which charges were brought were not intended to apply to delivery of a controlled substance to a minor by way of the umbilical cord. See, e.g., Johnson v. State, 602 So. 2d 1288 (Fla. 1992). Most courts have also rejected the child abuse theory, on the grounds that a fetus is not a living child or "person" protected by child abuse statutes. See, e.g., Sheriff v. Encoe, 885 P.2d 596 (Nev. 1994); Commonwealth v. Welch, 864 S.W.2d 280 (Ky. 1993); State v. Gray, 584 N.E.2d 710 (Ohio 1993).

One state supreme court has upheld several such prosecutions. In State v. McKnight, Regina McKnight was convicted of homicide by child abuse after an autopsy performed on her stillborn child revealed traces of cocaine. 576 S.E.2d 168 (S.C. 2003), cert. denied, 540 U.S. 819 (2003). In holding that the legislature intended for the homicide by child abuse statute to apply to stillbirths, the court relied on Whitner v. State, 492 S.E.2d 777 (S.C. 1997), cert. denied, 523 U.S. 1145 (1998). In *Whitner*, the defendant pled guilty to charges of child neglect after smoking crack while pregnant, on advice of counsel who promised to get her into a drug treatment plan so that she could be reunited with her children. The judge, however, sentenced her to an eight-year prison term. After serving 19 months of her sentence, the local ACLU managed to get her conviction set aside, on grounds the statute under which she was convicted punished the unlawful neglect of a child, not a fetus. See Dorothy E. Roberts, Unshackling Black Motherhood, 95 Mich. L. Rev. 938, 944-945 (1997). In reinstating the conviction, the *Whitner* court reasoned that if wrongful death claims involving viable fetuses and criminal prosecutions for feticide against parties other than the mother can be sustained, it is not "absurd," as the defendant had contended, to prosecute drug-abusing mothers as well. 492 S.E.2d at 781-782. The court did not feel itself bound by the fact that the legislature had failed on 11 occasions to pass proposed bills specifically addressing drug abuse during pregnancy. Id. at 787 (Moore, J., dissenting). For a discussion of South Carolina's prosecutorial campaign against pregnant crack addicts, see Roberts, supra, at 941-946.

Many commentators have advocated criminal liability for prenatal drug abuse. The theory is that

> society sends out a clear message that it will condemn and punish those responsible for the harms caused by the substance abuse.... [P]rospective jail terms will motivate drug-addicted women either to seek treatment prior to becoming pregnant, or if already pregnant, to obtain what treatment is still available to them before giving birth and to continue treatment for future pregnancies after delivery.

Michael T. Flannery, Court-Ordered Prenatal Intervention: A Final Means to the End of Gestational Substance Abuse, 30 J. Fam. L. 519, 574-575 (1991-1992). For contrary views, see Lynn M. Paltrow, The War on Drugs and the War on Abortion: Some Initial Thoughts on the Connections, Intersections and the Effects. 36 Tulsa L. Rev. 649, 202 (2001) (efforts to control pregnant drug addicts "are rooted in forms of bigotry and prejudice" that ground other forms of control over women's right to an abortion, and are used "to draw attention away from real underlying issues like poverty, race discrimination, and lack of a coherent national health-care policy"); Michelle Mills, Fetal Abuse Prosecutions: The Triumph of Reaction over Reason, 47 DePaul L. Rev. 989 (1998) (urging caution because prosecutions for fetal abuse may worsen the problem of drug addiction).

Does the reasoning reflected in the pro-prosecution approach extend to criminalizing abuse of alcohol or tobacco during pregnancy? According to the American Public Health Association, of the four million women who give birth each year, 820,000 smoke cigarettes and 760,000 drink alcohol during pregnancy. Bell, supra, at 649.

An upstate New York woman was charged with child endangerment after she delivered a baby whose blood alcohol was 0.18 percent; the charges were later dismissed on the grounds that the state's child endangerment statute was not intended to apply to the unborn. Jordan Carleo, Evangelist, Charge Dropped in Drunken Baby Case, Albany Times Union, April 9, 2004, at B1; Lynn M. Paltrow, When Becoming Pregnant Is a Crime, 9 Crim. Just. Ethics 41, 43 (1990) (describing prosecutions of pregnant women for activities such as drinking alcohol and having sex against a doctor's advice). If the state amended the statute to include such conduct, what penalties would be appropriate? See James Drago, One for My Baby, One More for the Road: Legislation and Counseling to Prevent Prenatal Exposure to Alcohol, 7 Cardozo Women's L.J. 163 (2001) (reviewing legislation and case law, and recommending a combination of "a low level of criminal sanctions" and education). What about pregnant women who drive too fast, fail to use seat belts, or work extended hours against the advice of their doctors?

The effects of substance abuse can interact with other risk factors. For example, research shows that among women who drink at the same rate, children born to low-income women have a 70.9 percent rate of fetal alcohol syndrome, compared to a 4.5 percent rate for those of upper-income women. Roberts, supra, at 953 n.93 (citing study). Better nutrition is the difference. Id. at 953-954. A Northwestern University study also suggests that outcomes in pregnancies complicated by cocaine abuse may be improved by comprehensive prenatal care. Id. at 953 (citing study). See also id. at 947-948 (despite similar rates of substance abuse, some research has found that black women are ten times more likely than white women to be reported to government authorities).

McKnight expanded the homicide-by-child-abuse statute to encompass the pregnant woman who "allow[s] to be inflicted on the child physical injury," or who "fail[s] to supply the child with adequate health care." 576 S.E.2d at 174. Could the statute be used to convict a pregnant woman, in an abusive relationship, who does not leave her batterer? Federal legislation enacted in 2004 created a separate criminal offense for harm caused to a "child in utero" during the course of several predicate offenses. Opponents of the legislation argued that it exacerbated the maternal-fetal conflict by providing separate legal protection for a pregnancy; the law does not require a prosecution for the underlying offense against the mother. See Marc Santora, Albany Court Reverses Rule on Stillbirths, N.Y. Times, April 2, 2004, at B1.

Can the state's coercive powers be effective in changing the behavior of pregnant women and causing them to act more responsibly? The *Ferguson* court points out that criminal prosecution may deter pregnant women from seeking much-needed medical treatment. See also Dorothy E. Roberts, Punishing Drug Addicts Who Have Babies: Women of Color, Equality, and the Right of Privacy, 104 Harv. L. Rev. 1419 (1991) (punitive approach is both ineffective and racist). Do some women *choose* drug addiction? Even if they do not, is it clear that use of the criminal law in this context will not have *any* effect on deterring drug abuse by pregnant women?

A 2001 state-by-state compilation of case and statutory law addressing the regulation of drug and alcohol use by pregnant is available at Editorial Staff,

Synopsis of State Case and Statutory Law, 1 Yale J. Health Pol'y L. & Ethics 237 (2001).

2. Probationary Conditions and Civil Commitment. An alternative that some courts have pursued for controlling the reproductive decisions of women who are deemed irresponsible is to order a woman not to become pregnant as a condition of probation. In some cases, such conditions have been imposed for crimes unrelated to the woman's childbearing or childrearing conduct. These orders have not fared well on appeal if the condition is not reasonably related to the crime committed or to the goal of rehabilitation. See, e.g., People v. Zaring, 10 Cal. Rptr. 2d 263 (Ct. App. 1992) (invalidating probationary condition that defendant not become pregnant after conviction for possession of heroin).

When the underlying conviction is for child abuse or neglect, however, some trial courts have ordered women, as a condition of probation, either not to conceive or to use birth control. Appellate courts have overturned many of these cases as well, either on privacy grounds or on the grounds that such conditions are not reasonably related to the legitimate purposes of probation. See Trammell v. State, 751 N.E.2d 283 (Ind. Ct. App. 2001) (no-pregnancy condition excessively infringes on defendant's privacy rights and serves no rehabilitative purpose); Kansas v. Mosburg, 768 P.2d 313 (Kan. Ct. App. 1989) (probationary condition that defendant refrain from getting pregnant violates defendant's privacy interests); People v. Pointer, 199 Cal. Rptr. 357 (Ct. App. 1984) (invalidating no-conception term of probation for defendant convicted of felony child endangerment after her children were severely and irreparably harmed by her fanatical adherence to macrobiotic diet, on grounds less restrictive alternatives were available, including periodic pregnancy tests followed by prenatal monitoring if she became pregnant, and removal of the child from the defendant after birth if circumstances warranted).

In some cases, defendants have declined to appeal for fear of receiving a harsher penalty. See Stacey L. Arthur, The Norplant Prescription: Birth Control, Woman Control, or Crime Control?, 40 UCLA L. Rev. 1, 11-21 (1992). What outcome would you expect on appeal in a Tennessee case in which a woman and her husband were both convicted of molesting the woman's two sons and ordered to serve 20 years in prison, with the alternative of probation for both if the woman agreed to sterilization by tubal ligation? The woman accepted the terms. See AP, Woman Who Molested Sons Agrees to Sterilization, N.Y. Times, Jan. 31, 1993, at A29. Did the woman have a sex discrimination claim to raise on appeal? Did her husband?

Before Norplant was withdrawn from the market for safety reasons, some convicted child abusers may have preferred this contraceptive implant to prison terms. See Sarah Gill, Discrimination, Historical Abuse, and the New Norplant Problem, 16 Women's Rts. L. Rep. 43, 46 (Fall 1994) (citing sources); see also Arthur, supra, at 95 (probationary conditions requiring use of birth control should be allowed in some circumstances, as long as special care is taken to ensure that defendants understand and genuinely consent). Most feminist commentators, however, oppose the imposition of contraceptive probation conditions. See, e.g., Darci Elaine Burrell, The Norplant Solution: Norplant and the Control of African-American Motherhood, 5 UCLA Women's L.J. 401 (1995) (Norplant proposals directed at curtailing reproduction by poor women based on same view of African-American women as the views upon which slavery, the eugenics movement, and the sterilization abuses of the 1970s were based); Tracy Ballard, The Norplant Conditions: One Step Forward or Two Steps Back?, 16 Harv. Women's L.J. 139 (1993) (Norplant conditions violate equal protection by discriminating on the basis of gender, race, and status, and also the Eighth Amendment's prohibition against cruel and unusual punishment). Which approach best furthers women's autonomy?

What about a form of "civil commitment" for women who are in grave danger of drug abuse during a pregnancy? In 1998, South Dakota became the first state to require pregnant women who abuse alcohol or drugs to be taken into custody and undergo mandatory rehabilitation. Wisconsin soon followed, and several other states introduced legislation adopting a similar approach to the problem. See Christa J. Richer, Note, Fetal Abuse Law: Punitive Approach and the Honorable Status of Motherhood, 50 Syracuse L. Rev. 1127 (2000). Does such an approach present any different issues from those presented by imposing treatment, or isolation, as a condition of probation? For the case in favor of the approach, see Deborah Mathieu, Mandating Treatment for Pregnant Substance Abusers: A Compromise, 14 Pol. & Life Sci. 199, 204 (Aug. 1995) (recommending use of traditional civil commitment process, after refusal to receive treatment voluntarily in an outpatient program). Courts have not been as enthusiastic. See, e.g., State ex rel. Angela M.W. v. Kruzicki, 561 N.W.2d 729 (Wis. 1997) (state was not authorized, under statute governing child in need of protection, to keep pregnant woman who had repeatedly used cocaine in protective custody). See also Erin N. Linder, Note, Punishing Prenatal Alcohol Abuse: The Problems Inherent in Utilizing Civil Commitment to Address Addiction, 2005 U. Ill. L. Rev. 873.

3. Civil Child Abuse and Neglect. Use of a state's civil child abuse and neglect statutes is an alternative to criminal measures in controlling drug abuse by pregnant women. However these statutes, too, will be available only if the courts conclude they were intended to apply to prenatal conduct. See, e.g., In re Valerie D., 613 A.2d 748, 755, 758-762 (Conn. 1992) (maternal substance abuse constitutes parental neglect, but legislature did not intend for the termination statute to apply to prenatal parental conduct). Legislatures are free to amend their statutes and some have done so. See, e.g., Fla. Stat. Ann. § 415.503(9)(g)(1) (West 2004) (neglect of child includes "[u]se by the mother of a controlled substance or alcohol during pregnancy when the child, at birth, is demonstrably adversely affected by such usage"); 705 Ill. Comp. Stat. Ann. § 405/2-18(2)(c) & (d) (2006) (proof of fetal alcohol syndrome or "a medical diagnosis at birth of withdrawal symptoms from narcotics or barbiturates" is prima facie evidence of child neglect); Nev. Rev. Stat. Ann. § 432B.330(1)(b) (2004) (child is "in need of protection" if "he is suffering from congenital drug addiction or the fetal alcohol syndrome, because of the faults or habits of a person responsible for his welfare").

If drug abuse during pregnancy constitutes child neglect, what governmental responses are most appropriate? Removal of the child from the parent and even termination of parental rights may seem the most likely options. What will happen then, however, to the child? Babies who test positive for drugs are poor health risks, and disproportionately nonwhite, which means they are not strong adoption candidates and may face repeated recycling through the overloaded foster care system. See Michelle Oberman, Sex, Drugs, Pregnancy, and the Law: Rethinking the Problems of Pregnant Women Who Use Drugs, 43 Hastings L.J. 505, 525 (1992).

4. The Treatment Alternative. Several commentators urge that treatment is a better governmental response to pregnant drug addicts and substance abusers than punitive measures. See, e.g., Susan Fortney, A Jurisprudential Analysis of Government Intervention and Prenatal Drug Abuse, 17 J.L. & Health 11 (2002-2003) (prenatal drug abuse should be treated as a health care problem). According to one source, 33 states have adopted laws that pursue a public health approach, either by requiring research on the problem (13 states), initiating preventative public education campaigns (16 states), or providing drug treatment for pregnant addicts (11 states, including some pilot projects). See Jean Reith Schroedel & Pamela Fiber, Punitive Versus Public Health Oriented Responses to Drug Use by Pregnant Women, 1 Yale J. Health Pol'y L. & Ethics 217, 224-226, 233-235 (2001) (citing statutes).

Several of the women facing well-publicized prosecutions for criminal child abuse for using drugs during pregnancy had sought treatment during pregnancy but found either that waiting lists were long or that the drug treatment programs would not accept pregnant women. See Eileen McNamara, Fetal Endangerment Cases on the Rise, Boston Globe, Oct. 3, 1989, at 1. A 2000 study of services provided to female probationers revealed that 27 percent of probation programs offered no special services to pregnant probationers, 28 percent did not assist a pregnant probationer with obtaining prenatal care, and 82 percent had no state- or office-wide policy for dealing with pregnant probationers. David C. Brody & Heidee McMillin, Combating Fetal Substance Abuse and Governmental Foolhardiness Through Collaborative Linkages, Therapeutic Jurisprudence, and Common Sense: Helping Women Help Themselves, 12 Hastings Women's L.J. 243, 268 (2001).

One case challenged successfully the practices of substance abuse treatment programs that exclude pregnant women as sex-based discrimination under a state public accommodations statute. See Elaine W. v. Joint Diseases North General Hosp., Inc., 613 N.E.2d 523 (N.Y. 1993). In *Elaine W.*, the hospital had claimed that there were medical reasons for not providing drug detoxification treatment to pregnant women, but the court found the evidence supporting that claim inadequate.

In partial response to this problem, Congress passed the Alcohol, Drug Abuse, and Mental Health Administration Reorganization Act, Pub. L. No. 102-321, 106 Stat. 323 (codified as amended in scattered sections of 42 U.S.C.A. §§ 201-300 (West Supp. 1993)). This legislation expands block grants provided to states for drug treatment programs, including money targeted at addressing the particular needs of pregnant, drug-addicted women. The Act is discussed in Alys I. Cohen, Challenging Pregnancy Discrimination in Drug Treatment: Does the ADAMHA Reorganization Act Provide an Answer?, 6 Yale J.L. & Feminism 91 (1994). Six states have enacted legislation to prohibit drug treatment facilities from discriminating against pregnant women. See Schroedel & Fiber, supra, at 226.

It remains to be seen how realistic alternative drug treatment plans are. The cost for drug treatment programs for a pregnant cocaine addict is staggering, and few programs accept Medicaid. Michelle Oberman, Sex, Drugs, Pregnancy, and the Law: Rethinking the Problems of Pregnant Women Who Use Drugs, 43 Hastings L.J. 505, 517 (1992). Even advocates of the treatment alternatives point out that "there are few established methods for treating the addictions themselves, let alone for addressing the effect on the fetus of withdrawal from these drugs." Id. at 516. In addition to the medical complications associated with drug addiction, including a higher risk of contracting HIV, pregnant addicts are said to be poor patients, for example, missing almost 38 percent of their scheduled medical appointments. Id. at 518-519.

On the other hand, there seems little doubt that prenatal treatment for a drug-addicted woman is highly beneficial. From an economic perspective, the National Association for Perinatal Addiction Research and Education (NAPARE) estimates the prenatal costs of a cocaine-addicted woman at $7,000 (including maternal hospital stay and two days of neonatal care), while the costs incurred by an addict who fails to obtain prenatal care average $31,000, due to the increased need for neonatal intensive care. Id.

Putting Theory into Practice

5-13. A non-profit organization founded as Children Requiring A Caring Kommunity (C.R.A.C.K.), later renamed Project Prevention, was established to provide "effective prevention measures to reduce the tragedy of numerous drug affected pregnancies." The Project offers $200 dollars to females who promise to be sterilized or receive long-term birth control. The cash payment is made upon the showing of a certificate that the procedure has been performed. As of March 19, 2004, 1,181 individuals had consented to sterilization under the program. Of these, 1,156 were women and 25 were men. About 40 percent used Depo-Provera, another 40 percent had a tubal ligation, 166 women obtained IUDs, 37 received Norplant treatments, and the 25 men had vasectomies. Tiesha Rashon Peal, The Continuing Sterilization of *Undesirables* in America, 6 Rutgers Race & L. Rev. 225, 240 (2004) (citing http://www.projectprevention.org/reasons/statistics.html).

Is there any legal theory that would preclude this transaction? Is this a sensible policy? See Jane Gilbert Mauldon, Providing Subsidies for Norplant, Sterilization and Other Contraception: Allowing Economic Theory to Inform Ethical Analysis, 31 J.L. Med. & Ethics 351 (2003) (arguing that in certain circumstances, financial incentives belong among the policy methods used to reduce births to drug addicted mothers); Juli Horka-Ruiz, Note, Preventing the Birth of Drug-Addicted Babies Through Contract: An Examination of the C.R.A.C.K. Organization, 7 Wm. & Mary J. Women & L. 473 (2001) (arguing that the C.R.A.C.K. program creates a legally enforceable contract); Jennifer Mott Johnson, Reproductive Ability for Sale, Do I Hear $200?: Private Cash-for-Contraception Agreements as an Alternative to Maternal Substance Abuse, 43 Ariz. L. Rev. 205 (2001) (weighing competing constitutional and policy considerations and concluding that the scheme has merit).

Do you have any concerns about the program? See Peal, supra, at 238 (charging that this program "revives the eugenics movement of the past . . . bargain[ing] . . . with people's reproductive freedom"); Lynn Paltrow, Why Caring Communities Must Oppose C.R.A.C.K./Project Prevention: How C.R.A.C.K. Promotes Dangerous Propaganda and Undermines the Health and Well Being of Children and Families, 5 J.L. Soc'y 11, 13-15 (2003) (detailing "extensive outreach and ideologically-based public education campaign" that reinforces negative race and gender stereotypes and, "[u]nder the guise of openness, 'voluntary' choice, and personal empowerment," "promotes a vicious image of the 'eternal drug addict'"). Is the C.R.A.C.K. approach any more, or less, objectionable than the court-mandated probation conditions discussed previously?

For a range of views on C.R.A.C.K./Project Prevention, see the symposium issue in 5 J.L. Soc'y 1 (2003).

5-14. Research has established that a regimen of antepartum, intrapartum, and neonatal AZT treatment is successful in reducing the rate of HIV transmission from mother to child by approximately two-thirds. See David Lowe, HIV Study Raises Ethical Concerns for the Treatment of Pregnant Women, 10 Berkeley Women's L.J. 176, 176, 178 (1995) (citing study). Based on the above information, should AZT treatment be required for pregnant women who are HIV-positive? One federal panel recently issued a "strong recommendation" that clinicians screen all pregnant women for HIV, not just those at high risk. Press Release, Agency for Healthcare Research and Quality, Task Force Recommends HIV Screening for All Pregnant Women (July 4, 2005), http://www.ahrq.gov/news/press/pr2005/tfhivpr.htm. Should such a proposal be limited by the constitutional right to refuse medical treatment?

5-15. Since the age of 13, Jewel has suffered from cancer, for which she underwent major surgery several times, together with multiple radiation treatments and chemotherapy. At age 17, while her cancer was temporarily in remission, she became pregnant. During the 25th week of her pregnancy, she was diagnosed with an inoperable tumor in her right lung, from which her health quickly declined. Informed of her options, Jewel agreed to "palliative treatment" to extend her life until her 28th week of pregnancy to give her fetus a better chance of survival. Jewel expressed her wish "to live long enough to hold that baby." Jewel declined even more rapidly than was predicted, however, and in her 26th week, the attending doctors sought to deliver the fetus surgically. The doctors believed that while a "normal" 26-week fetus had a 50-50 percent chance of survival, the chance of survival of Jewel's fetus would be less than 20 percent because of the mother's condition and that the chances dropped virtually to zero if the surgery was not done immediately. Doctors also believed that the mother would probably die in the next couple of days without surgical intervention to deliver the child and that the surgery would accelerate her death. Jewel is semi-comatose and not competent to give consent to immediate surgery.

What legal standard should determine whether surgery should be permitted by a court in this case? What additional facts would be needed to apply this standard?

What if Jewel had previously made it clear that she would not consent to surgery before the 28th week? Do the circumstances presented—with surgery, the fetus's chance of survival moves from zero to slight; Jewel's death is accelerated from two days to one—justify surgery over her objections? See In re A.C., 573 A.2d 1235 (D.C. 1990). What if the woman's religious beliefs prevent her from receiving certain types of medical care? Should the courts balance the rights of the unborn fetus against the woman's right to refuse treatment? See In re Doe, 632 N.E.2d 326 (N.D. Ill 1994) (holding that no such balancing test was required because woman's right to refuse Cesarean section was controlling). See also Norwood Hosp. v. Munoz, 564 N.E.2d 1017 (Mass. 1991) (reversing probate court's order allowing forced blood transfusions because mother had minor child who would be abandoned if she died).

5-16. A 28-year-old woman from Salt Lake City failed to follow medical advice to have a Cesarean section. As a result, one of her twins was stillborn, although he could have been saved if the mother had had the procedure. She is arrested for first-degree criminal homicide and child endangerment. What defenses could be raised on her behalf? Should her conduct be criminalized?

The woman later pled guilty to two counts of child endangerment and the homicide charge was dropped. See Monica K. Miller, Refusal to Undergo a Cesarean Section: A Woman's Right of a Criminal Act?, 15 Health Matrix 383 (2005).

C. ECONOMIC AUTONOMY AND WOMEN'S POVERTY

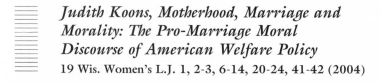

Judith Koons, Motherhood, Marriage and Morality: The Pro-Marriage Moral Discourse of American Welfare Policy
19 Wis. Women's L.J. 1, 2-3, 6-14, 20-24, 41-42 (2004)

During a campaign speech in 1991, Bill Clinton vowed to "put an end to welfare as we know it." Five years later, with the adoption of the Personal Responsibility and Work Opportunity Reconciliation Act (PRWORA), that promise was given effect. . . . Yet, the means adopted in TANF to "put an end to welfare"— work requirements, time requirements, state and local autonomy, and family values—have been components for many centuries of Euro-American policies on social provisioning. The "new tools" of welfare reform are part of an old, old story that is deeply etched with considerations of gender, race, and class. In that story, the single mother is "a hideous monster" to whom social policy gives two options: get a man or a low-wage job....

Welfare reform in the mid-1990s arose out of the appearance of a consensus on policy across party lines. Among the key provisions of the PRWORA were the Food Stamp Program, the Child Care and Development Block Grant, and the Temporary Aid to Needy Families Block Grant. In the Food Stamp Program, eligibility criteria were tightened and welfare families were no longer automatically enrolled in the program. Many programs for children were reworked in the PRWORA. Various food and childcare programs were consolidated into the Child Care and Development Block Grant. Funding was reduced or eliminated for child nutrition and meals programs. Child support enforcement efforts were bolstered. The Supplemental Security Income (SSI) definition of disability for children was narrowed.

Aid to Families with Dependent Children (AFDC), which had been construed to provide welfare assistance as a matter of statutory entitlement, was replaced by TANF, a fixed block grant program. With the adoption of the PRWORA, the framework for welfare was changed from a "statutory entitlement model" to a "devolved contractual model." Given flexibility to design work-oriented, transitional assistance programs, states were permitted to use TANF funds for cash assistance, childcare, education, training, and transportation....

For the central work requirement, the federal government required a welfare-reliant mother to engage in an approved work activity within two years of receiving her first welfare check or face sanctioning. The work activity requirement was slated to increase from twenty hours per week in 1996 to twenty-five hours per week in 1999 and to thirty hours per week in 2000. Optional individual responsibility plans were designed to move welfare recipients into the work force as quickly as possible....

Traditional "family values" were asserted in the PRWORA in five interrelated ways. First, the PRWORA explicitly expressed a purpose of promoting two-parent families. Construing the purpose as one of promoting marriage, a number of states adopted pro-marriage programs for welfare recipients. For example, Oklahoma announced a $10 million marriage initiative, financed by "unspent" TANF funds, to reduce the state's divorce rate by one-third by 2010. Arizona established a Marriage and Communication Skills Commission and appropriated TANF funds for marriage skills training vouchers. West Virginia adopted the "first unambiguous cash incentive for marriage," a $100 monthly marriage bonus for TANF recipients who are married. A growing Marriage Movement endorsed these and other pro-marriage and "responsible fatherhood" initiatives.

Second, the purpose of the PRWORA explicitly discouraged out-of-wedlock pregnancies. States were required to track out-of-wedlock pregnancy rates and to take steps to reduce illegitimate births. Bonuses for "Illegitimacy Reduction" were established for states that achieved the highest decreases of out-of-wedlock births without increases in abortions. In an effort to encourage abstinence and prevent teen pregnancy, federal funds were allocated to three different abstinence education programs.

Third, the PRWORA regulated non-marital sexuality by allowing states to impose "family caps" on recipient households. Under "family cap" legislation, a family could not receive additional benefits due to the birth of a child who was conceived during a period in which the family was eligible for TANF. Four states adopted family caps under federal waivers in the early 1990s. As of December 2003, twenty-four states had some form of family cap policy in place.

Fourth, the PRWORA opened the door for states to promote family planning and to encourage welfare-reliant mothers to relinquish their children for adoption. In fifteen states, family planning information and counseling initiatives were integrated into the TANF program. Three states devised programs to encourage mothers who receive welfare to give up children for adoption. In addition to offering services such as "positive information" about adoption, two states provided cash incentives for relinquishing newborns.

Fifth, the PRWORA demonstrated that welfare is a site of sexual regulation by mandating paternity identification as well as child support enforcement cooperation. Under the PRWORA, states were required to ensure that recipients cooperate with paternity identification and child support enforcement provisions. Furthermore, and with far-reaching consequences, the domestic violence exception to these procedures became optional. In addition, the PRWORA directed states to sanction uncooperative clients and, at the same time, expanded administrative powers and decreased judicial review.

With these measures, the PRWORA sought to codify — at the national and state levels — a conservative family values agenda. However, in the ensuing years, the rhetorical pitch has been elevated to advocate for more aggressive pro-marriage welfare policies. The PRWORA helped states over the threshold "toward what could become a robust and multi-front attack on the problem of family composition." . . . .

The rhetoric of welfare retrenchment of the late twentieth and early twenty-first centuries is, without question, a discourse of heterosexual marriage and conservative morality. That welfare retrenchment in the 1990s was, at heart, a marriage-based discourse is clearly reflected in the PRWORA's statement of purpose. Of the four purposes, three of them pointed toward marriage. Moreover, the structure of the section underscored the marital impetus of the PRWORA and the double-bind that it erected for poor women.

In subsection one, the purpose was to allow children to be "cared for in their own homes." However, subsection two created a critical inconsistency because "dependence of needy parents on government benefits" was to be ended. The contradiction was thus set: children should be cared for in their homes, but poor women must leave their homes and enter the low-wage labor market. Subsection four provided the answer to the conundrum — poor women should marry and become part of two-parent families so they may have the resources to care for their children. . . .

Moral reform continues to be offered as the solution to poverty. The prominent conservative view is that single motherhood and teenage pregnancy, by themselves, are causes of poverty and dependency. Into the twenty-first century, marriage is being proposed as the ideal anti-poverty program. In fact, the welfare system is seen as a result of "the collapse of marriage." Marriage is characterized as a "social good under attack." The reasons recited for the weakness of marriage are instructive. According to marriage advocates, over the past forty years there has been an "extraordinary shift in cultural norms concerning sex, marriage, and childbearing," including the advent of birth control, the entry of more women into the labor force, and the increasing acceptability of cohabitation outside of wedlock. Widened opportunities for women, including alternatives to marriage that were the fruits of the women's and civil rights movements are constitutive of this normative shift. . . .

Within the aligned "culture of poverty" rhetoric, structural economic factors — such as employment opportunities, the sex-segregated occupational structure, the shift from an industrial to a service- and technology-based economy, gendered pay inequity, access to education and training, and availability of child care — play an insignificant role in poverty. . . . Forcing women back into the marital fold is advanced as the means to end the economic misery of low-income women and to re-establish the social order. . . .

The pro-marriage rhetoric of welfare retrenchment is a package of loaded social symbols. Unbound, the discourse reveals the relic of the "good mother" from sixteenth-century Reformation Europe, the image of the "deserving" pauper of seventeenth-century colonial America, the deliberately split persona of the "independent" wage laborer and the "dependent" mother of the New Deal, and the icon of the "illegitimate" African-American mother and infant of the welfare rights era.

In pieces, the discourse shows that welfare retrenchment is a vehicle for the oppression of poor women in the labor market. The "bridefare or workfare" framework of welfare retrenchment exploits the labor of women, by mandating either unpaid work in the home or low-wage employment in the secondary labor market. In addition, welfare retrenchment is clearly redistributive, directing resources away from poor mothers and children and toward a newly valorized class of workers that is serving the middle and upper classes.

Shannon DeRouselle, Welfare Reform and the Administration for Children's Services: Subjecting Children and Families to Poverty and Then Punishing Them for It
25 N.Y.U. Rev. L. & Soc. Change 403, 405-413, 416, 424-426 (1999)

I. Federal and New York Welfare Reform

Tammy is a single, twenty-three-year-old mother of two children, Carl Jr. and Keisha, and has intermittently received AFDC benefits for the past seven years. Tammy became pregnant with Carl Jr. during her junior year of high school, and she subsequently dropped out of school during the summer before her senior year to take care of him. Tammy received AFDC benefits for Carl Jr. while living at home with her mother and three younger sisters. Carl Jr.'s father provided no financial or emotional support. A year later, Tammy became pregnant again. Tammy's mother refused to allow her to continue to live at home since she already had several children to support herself. Keisha's father also was not present in his child's life. Tammy and her children moved to a one bedroom apartment in the projects of East New York, Brooklyn.

Tammy's welfare caseworker told her that she would have to find a job or would have her benefits terminated pursuant to the new welfare reform work requirements that went into effect earlier that month. Tammy searched for, and eventually found a job as a part-time salesclerk at a local supermarket. She has worked in the past, but since she has no high school diploma and few skills, her previous jobs paid only slightly above minimum wage. Her current job pays the same. Tammy works from 3 p.m. to 9 p.m., five days a week. Tammy's mother and sisters help her by looking after her children when she is at work. This is a blessing, because she could not otherwise afford child care. But after Tammy had worked a few weeks at the supermarket, her caseworker informed her that she no longer qualified for cash assistance since her earnings were now just above the income eligibility maximum for a family of three. Tammy, confused, did not understand why her benefits were canceled, especially after she had complied with the new welfare rules and began her life as an independent, self-sufficient mother. Assuming that her loss of benefits also meant that she no longer qualified for Food Stamps and Medicaid, Tammy did not reapply for either program and has struggled to make ends meet ever since.

A. The Personal Responsibility and Work Opportunity Act of 1996...

The PRA required every state to design a plan outlining how it proposed to accomplish the goal of ending dependence on government benefits by promoting job preparation, work, and marriage. TANF provides each state increased flexibility to implement programs designed to achieve these objectives and address the individual needs of the particular state. The amount of each state's federal block grant is tied to its performance with respect to annual target rates of state employment percentages, teenage and out-of-wedlock pregnancy statistics, and welfare roll reduction figures set by Congress. However, the state block grant is capped.... Unfortunately, the incentive for states to maintain their levels of federal funding has resulted in stringent provisions which have already disqualified millions of needy families from welfare....

Through December 1996, three states—Iowa, Massachusetts, and Wisconsin—accounted for 13,000, or 72%, of the 18,000 terminations nationwide under the section 1315 waiver provision. A General Accounting Office (GAO) study found that failure to comply with work requirements was the most common reason for benefit termination in these three states. Hurried terminations resulted in high rates of error—in some states, more than half of the case terminations were reversed on appeal. In addition, the GAO found that a significant portion of the terminated families did not continue to receive Food Stamps and Medicaid, even though they might have remained eligible for these programs.... Explanations for this drop include the failure by many families to take the steps necessary to maintain eligibility and the doubt of many families that eligibility continued or was worth the effort....

B. New York's Welfare Reform Act of 1997

New York's welfare reform strategy, enacted to comply with the federal law, is known as the Welfare Reform Act of 1997 (NYRA). NYRA went into effect November 1, 1997.

The rules of NYRA generally coincide with corresponding federal requirements. NYRA's sixty month eligibility limit, adult work requirement, and teenage parent residency and school requirements incorporate the terms of PRA. But NYRA adds another restriction: a two year limit for state funded benefits, called Safety Net Assistance — receipt of which also counts toward the sixty month federal limit. Welfare recipients who have exceeded the time limit are permanently terminated from TANF-funded benefits. A benefit recipient who quits or reduces work hours without good cause becomes ineligible for benefits until she is willing to comply with work requirements. For a "second offense," she automatically becomes ineligible for benefits for at least three months — longer if she does not comply with the requirements. For a "third offense," she loses her benefits for a minimum of six months. NYRA exempts the following classifications of individuals from work requirements: the ill, incapacitated, elderly, disabled, caretakers of ill or incapacitated members of the household, parents and caretakers of children under the age of one, and pregnant women after the eighth month of pregnancy. Significantly, NYRA eliminates past exemptions for people without access to transportation and for teens who have been out of the house for more than a year.

C. Welfare Reform: Evaluations

Sponsors of welfare reform point to reports of shrinking welfare rolls and caseloads across the country as evidence of success. Welfare reform proponents boast that the current percentage of people in the United States on welfare is the lowest in thirty years. Fourteen months after the enactment of PRA, welfare rolls had fallen nationally by more than 1.7 million people.

Most reports claim that welfare rolls have diminished considerably because former recipients have moved from welfare into the workplace and no longer rely on public assistance. However, not all persons leaving welfare have made the transition to work — the reduction is largely the result of recipients who no longer qualify for aid for other reasons. . . .

Many families will be much worse off after benefit termination, yet these cases are frequently overlooked by reports that praise welfare reform.

Even when families do move from welfare to work, evidence indicates that reform gains are still tenuous. . . . Studies of the short-term effects of welfare-to-work programs found only moderate differences in earnings between program participants and control groups. In a study of the five-year impacts of four welfare-to-work programs, the Manpower Demonstration Research Corporation found somewhat more substantial gains in earnings for welfare-to-work program participants, but the greatest improvement was only $2076 annually. Moreover, once reductions in cash assistance are accounted for, the overall income of participants improved in only two of the four programs. Policy-makers can easily reduce welfare rolls, but the challenges for PRA and NYRA are to permanently keep the rolls low and reduce poverty at the same time. The failure to accomplish these objectives is a failure of welfare reform. . . .

II. New York City's Child Welfare System . . .

Tammy, in need of additional income since losing her public assistance, convinced the manager of the supermarket where she worked to increase her hours. The only problem was that the extra hours were during the day, which required her to find someone else to watch her children. The only person that she could afford had to leave one and a half hours before she returned home on Tuesdays. Tammy tried to work something out, but the babysitter had other obligations and could not stay until Tammy got home. Her options were to find another babysitter, or to ask the babysitter to have the kids take a nap before leaving, and to hope that nothing happened to them before she got home. Since Tammy barely had enough money for rent, bills, clothes and food, she reluctantly chose to leave the kids unattended. . . .

III. Tensions between [the Administration for Children's Services (ACS)] and Welfare Reform Policies

Three weeks later, on a Tuesday, Keisha woke up before Tammy came home. Scared, Keisha began to cry loudly for about a half-hour before a neighbor heard her screams. The neighbor, acting out of concern, immediately called the police, who then contacted ACS. Two officers and an ACS caseworker entered the apartment and found Carl Jr. and Keisha alone and frightened. In all of the commotion, during which onlookers had gathered to see what was going on, Tammy returned from work. Terrified that something had happened to her children, she rushed into the apartment. After the caseworker determined that Tammy had left the young children at home alone, the officers arrested her for endangering the children. Although unharmed, both children were immediately removed from Tammy's custody and placed in a foster care facility where they currently remain pending a family court hearing. Tammy also faces criminal charges.

A. Increased Child Maltreatment Allegations

It is my contention that ACS [New York's agency in charge of child protection] will see an increase in the number of abuse and neglect cases as a result of the changed welfare law. In 1991, the Los Angeles County Department of Children and Family Services found that "child abuse and neglect referrals jumped 12 percent following a 2.7 percent decrease in the state's AFDC grant and another 20 percent following AFDC cuts totaling 5.8 percent in 1992." Moreover, the National Incidence Study of Child Abuse and Neglect reports that children in families with incomes under $15,000 a year are twenty-two times more likely to experience maltreatment than children in families with incomes over $30,000. Finally, since PRA denies legal immigrants Food Stamp benefits and gives states the option to deny them TANF cash assistance, Medicaid, and child care services as well, many legal immigrant families are at risk of becoming involved with the child welfare system. States across the country with large immigrant populations will face particular challenges to meet these families needs, and to assess the impact of welfare reform on the child welfare system. Fortunately, New York has not exercised its option to eliminate TANF cash assistance to legal immigrants.

Families whose benefits are cut off may have no other resources on which to survive. The lack of alternative sources of income will result in a dangerously lower standard of living for thousands of families. Without monetary assistance or Food Stamps, parents will not be able to meet the nutritional needs of their children. Parents will barely, if at all, be able to afford living expenses such as rent and utilities. The incidence of parents leaving children unattended or in the hands of unqualified caretakers will become more frequent given that affordable quality child care is already virtually nonexistent. Combined, these financial strictures will have the effect of subjecting poor families to the threat of state intervention for neglect. Furthermore, the current trend towards the criminalization of neglect cases will result in poor women being inordinately penalized by the law....

B. Impairment of PRA Objectives . . .

Even assuming the validity of the premises which form the basis of the need for welfare reform, the inconsistencies between the two social welfare policies become obvious. Family structure and self-sufficiency are not promoted when parents are compelled to work in low-skill, low-wage, transitory jobs. Instead, the strict work requirements and aggressive child protection discourage family cohesiveness by leaving families in poverty and subsequently removing children for neglect when their parents are unable to provide for their care.

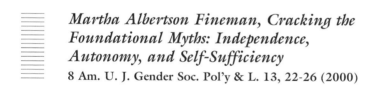 *Martha Albertson Fineman, Cracking the Foundational Myths: Independence, Autonomy, and Self-Sufficiency*
8 Am. U. J. Gender Soc. Pol'y & L. 13, 22-26 (2000)

In popular and political discourse, the idea of "subsidy" is viewed as an equally negative companion to dependence, the opposite of the ideal of self-sufficiency. But a subsidy is nothing more than the process of allocating collective resources to some persons or endeavors rather than other persons or endeavors because a social judgment is made that they are in some way "entitled" or the subsidy is justified....

Typically, subsidy is thought of as the provision of monetary or economic assistance. But subsidy can also be delivered through the organization of social structures and norms that create and enforce expectations. Taking this observation into account, along with the earlier discussion of inevitable and derivative dependency, it seems obvious that we must conclude that subsidy is also universal. We all exist in context, in social and cultural institutions, such as families, which facilitate, support and subsidize us and our endeavors.

...We all live subsidized lives. Sometimes the benefits we receive are public and financial, such as in governmental direct transfer programs to certain individuals like farmers or sugar growers. Public subsidies can also be indirect, such as the benefits given in tax policy. Private economic subsidy systems work in the forms of foundations, religions and charities. But a subsidy can also be non-monetary, such as the subsidy provided by the uncompensated labor of others in caring for us and our dependency needs.

It seems clear that all of us receive one or the other or both types of subsidy throughout our lives. The interesting question in our subsidy shaped society, therefore, has to be why only some subsidies are differentiated and stigmatized while others are hidden. In substantial part, subsidies are hidden when they are not called subsidy (or welfare, or the dole), but termed "investments," "incentives," or "earned" when they are supplied by government, and called "gifts," "charity," or the product of familial "love" when they are contributions of caretaking labor. . . .

As a result of such discussion, the very terms of independence and self-sufficiency might well be redefined or re-imagined in the public mind. Independence is not the same as being unattached. Independence from subsidy and support is not attainable, nor is it desirable — we want and need the contexts that sustain us. A different understanding of independence is needed and attainable. Independence is gained when an individual has the basic resources that enable her or him to act consistent with the tasks and expectations imposed by the society. This form of independence should be every citizen's birthright, but independence in this sense can only be achieved when individual choices are relatively unconstrained by inequalities, particularly those inequalities that arise from poverty. Independence, as well as justice, requires that those who are assigned a vital societal function are also provided with the wherewithal to do those tasks. This is a state or collective responsibility and may not be relegated to potentially exploitative private institutions.

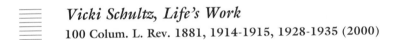

Vicki Schultz, Life's Work
100 Colum. L. Rev. 1881, 1914-1915, 1928-1935 (2000)

[T]raditional welfare strategies can be detrimental to women. . . . Joint property approaches [whereby individual men pay their partners for taking care of the house and children] rely on individual breadwinners to fund household labor, while welfare strategies rely on the state. State funding is advantageous for women, because it frees them from serving individual men and sheds class bias by funding household work at a uniform level regardless of the earnings of the family members who support it. Nonetheless, by paying women to stay home with their children rather than providing real support for parents (especially single parents) to work at paid jobs, welfare strategies still encourage women to invest in homemaking and caregiving to the exclusion of their job skills — which may harm women and their families in the long run. . . .

I realize that work alone is no panacea. It is the platform on which equal citizenship should be built, not the entire edifice. Still, the importance of work to the future cannot be overemphasized; abandoning work as a political and cultural ideal would be a serious mistake. People need more than money or property: We need life projects. We need goals and activities to which we can commit our hearts, minds, and bodies. We need to struggle with our capacities and our limits, in sustained ways in stable settings. We need to work alongside others in pursuit of common goals. We need to feel that we are contributing to something larger than ourselves and our own families. Most of us even need something that requires regular rhythms and structure, and provides a mechanism for deferring gratification. We need to feel that we are earning our keep — that we have a source of wherewithal that is our own. We also need public recognition for our labors. It is difficult to imagine any single activity that can fulfill all these purposes for the vast majority of people other than working. We have seen what happens to people when they don't have work to give life structure and meaning, and it is not exemplary. There is a reason why democratic societies have organized themselves as employment societies. Paid work is the only institution that can be sufficiently widely distributed to provide a stable foundation for a democratic order. It is also one of the few arenas — perhaps the only one — in which diverse groups of people can come together and develop respect for each other through shared experience. Can we think of a society anywhere in the world we would want to emulate in which most people do not work for a living? ...

The emphasis on work has been crucial to Second Wave feminism, which was born in part out of the recognition that even relatively well-off, white middle-class women were united with their minority, poor, and working-class sisters in the experience of being marginalized in the world of work — which in turn disempowered them in politics and in private life.... Older Americans have also demanded recognition as valid workers, and they won it in the Age Discrimination in Employment Act (ADEA).... The disability rights movement has also emphasized access to work, and they won an important victory with the Americans with Disabilities Act (ADA)....

We can also view the transition from welfare to work as part of this trend. I realize that the impetus for welfare-to-work programs has come from the political right, who may not have the best interests of poor people at heart. But it would be a mistake to attribute all of the new emphasis on work to conservatives alone. Some of the demand has come from members of the working poor who do not receive welfare, and who do not have the luxury of keeping a parent at home to take care of their own children....

Poor single parents have long expressed a desire for work that will allow them to support their children; they know that a decent job is the only path that provides real hope for their empowerment in the long run. Most people who receive welfare payments have been working for pay all along, as they must in order to ensure the survival of their families. But, partly because so many of them are women and racial minorities, single parents have not been perceived as "authentic" workers who have the capacity to contribute to productive endeavors beyond raising their own children. Women who draw on welfare are overrepresented among classic contingent workers, who fare worse on a variety of dimensions than people in more permanent employment. This is the legacy of the fact that our welfare system has been based on a family-wage model that sees women as inauthentic workers and cannot imagine mothers in economically-powerful provider roles.

Even if many welfare-to-work programs have been adopted for the wrong reasons, their existence does provide a political opening to turn things around. Not only is paid work important to people's ability to get ahead and their sense of community and self-esteem; it is also a more easily politicized setting than the privatized home. By creating social systems that allow poor (and other) parents to combine caregiving with stable employment, we enable them to move into the workforce — a space in which they can more easily engage in collective action to improve their situation. . . .

Viewed from this perspective, the best welfare-to-work programs push in the direction of a more expansive set of social programs that guarantee and support a right to work for everyone. If work is to provide the foundation for citizenship (as welfare-to-work programs imply), then everyone must have access to a suitable job, as well as the training and education needed to do the job. There is no reason to find or create jobs exclusively for people who have drawn on welfare, when so many others are struggling to find jobs, often under fiercely competitive conditions. The goal should be to ensure that everyone — mothers on welfare, fathers struggling to pay child support, poor women and men without children, people with disabilities, middle-class homemakers or divorcees, people in temporary jobs who want steady employment, older people, youth who are trying to finance continuing education, and, yes, even well educated displaced workers — has work.

Notes

1. From Worthy Mothers to Deviant Ones. Welfare began in the United States as state programs establishing "mother's pensions" for destitute mothers and their children. Use of the term "pension" connoted that the payment was a substitute for money that might otherwise be received in paid employment and contributed to the notion inherent in these early programs that motherhood was work and that a mother's devotion to the care of her children was important. See Jill Duerr Berrick, From Mother's Duty to Personal Responsibility: The Evolution of AFDC, 7 Hastings Women's L.J. 257, 258-259 (1996).

The initial purpose was to relieve impoverishment caused by mothers having been abandoned, or left widowed, by their husband — i.e., worthy mothers. From the very beginning, blacks, immigrants, and unwed mothers were systematically excluded, either by the failure to establish programs in locations where these populations were concentrated or through discriminatory eligibility requirements. In 1931, the first national survey of mother's pensions, broken down by race, found that only 3 percent of recipients were black. See Linda Gordon, Pitied but Not Entitled: Single Mothers and the History of Welfare 48 (1994).

With the Civil Rights movement of the 1960s and successful legal challenges to welfare criteria that excluded racial and ethnic minorities, including moral criteria and residency requirements, an increasingly larger proportion of welfare recipients were never married, non-Caucasian, and adolescent. By 1992, over 60 percent of welfare recipients were women of color. As this demographic transformation occurred, women on welfare were no longer viewed as worthy mothers, but as women engaged in irresponsible behavior. Accordingly, attention was focused less on the children in their care than on their sexual and procreative practices. Berrick, supra, at 264. For further historical background on the U.S. welfare system before the 1996 reforms, see Gwendolyn Mink, The Wages of Motherhood: Inequality in the Welfare State, 1917-1942 (1995); Theda Skocpol, Protecting Soldiers and Mothers: The Political Origins of Social Policy in the United States (1992); Michael B. Katz, The Undeserving Poor: From the War on Poverty to the War of Welfare (1989); Mimi Abramovitz, Regulating the Lives of Women: Social Welfare Policy from Colonial Times to the Present (1988). Specifically on the relationship between welfare and race, see Jill Quadagno, The Color of Welfare: How Racism Undermined the War on Poverty (1994); Dorothy E. Roberts, Welfare and the Problem of Black Citizenship, 105 Yale L.J. 1563 (1996) (book review).

2. Welfare Reform and Its Critics. In 1984, Charles Murray stated the basic case for conservative welfare reform, arguing that the system entrenched, rather than cured, poverty. Like all people, Murray argued, the poor make rational choices based on the existing incentive structures. Welfare rewarded having out-of-wedlock children. Murray not only defended shutting down the then-existing welfare system. He also supported public blame of the lazy and praise of the self-sufficient. Without the threat of degradation — i.e., without a distinction between the deserving and the undeserving poor — the poor, Murray argued, would have no reason to take responsibility for providing for themselves and their families. See Murray, Losing Ground: American Social Policy 1950-1980, at 154-162, 178-181 (1984).

Note the importance of individual agency in Murray's line of analysis. The poor are capable of acting rationally; as individual agents, they are also blame-worthy when they choose an option that is "immoral." The degree of choice exercised by the poor is, of course, a contested empirical fact. Murray assumes that the poor could work if only they chose to, while others describe an economic structure in which the opportunities for self-sufficiency, notwithstanding increasingly positive economic indicators for the "haves," are steadily worsening for the "have-nots."

Murray also assumes that the availability of welfare on a per-child basis increases the incentive for welfare mothers to have large families. The research is mixed. Some analysts have pointed to research showing that women do not make reproductive decisions based on the availability of welfare benefits. See Linda McClain, "Irresponsible" Reproduction, 47 Hastings L.J. 339, 383 n.179 (1996) (citing studies); Lucy A. Williams, The Ideology of Division: Behavior Modification Welfare Reform Proposals, 102 Yale L.J. 719, 739-741 (1992) (citing research). But see Marcia Carlson et al., The Effects of Welfare and Child Support Policies on Union Formation, 23 (5-6) Pop. Research & Pol'y Rev. 513 (2004) (reporting on recent longitudinal study which refutes the findings of earlier research and suggests that higher welfare benefits discourage couples from breaking up).

Research specifically on the experience of New Jersey with its family cap provisions exemplifies the conflict in the empirical data. Some studies indicate no statistically significant difference between birth rates of women who are subject to the cap and those who are not. McClain, supra, at 383 n.181 (citing research). One 1997 study suggests, however, that the family cap provision in New Jersey lessened the number of births to unmarried women; it also increased the number of abortions. Christie N. Love, Not in Our Country? A Critique of The United States Welfare System Through the Lens of China's One-Child Law, 14 Colum. J. Gender & Law 142, 169-170 (2005) (citing study estimating that the cap resulted in approximately 240 more abortions per year among women on welfare than would be expected without it). See also Susan Frelich Appleton, When Welfare Reforms Promote Abortion: "Personal Responsibility," "Family Values," and the Right to Choose, 85 Geo. L.J. 155 (1996).

The Koons reading describes the major overhaul of the U.S. welfare system that occurred with the passage of the Personal Responsibility and Work Opportunity Reconciliation Act of 1996, Pub. L. No. 104-193, 110 Stat. 2105 (codified as amended in various sections of 42 U.S.C.) (PRWORA). This Act replaced the Aid to Families with Dependent Children program (AFDC), the Job Opportunity and Basic Skills program (JOBS), and emergency assistance programs, with the Temporary Assistance for Needy Families Block Grant program (TANF), effective July 1, 1997. Many have questioned the workability of the new federal restrictions, including the time limits and the work requirements. See Joel F. Handler, "Ending Welfare as We Know It": The Win/Win Spin or the Stench of Victory, 5 J. Gender Race & Just. 131 (2001); Karen Czapansky, Parents, Children and Work-First Welfare Reform: Where Is the C in TANF?, 61 Md. L. Rev.308 (2002); Lucie E. White, Closing the Care Gap That Welfare Reform Left Behind, 577 Annals 131 (2001).

A comprehensive study using Census Bureau data from the Survey of Income and Program Participation compared the well-being of families before and after welfare reform. In the three years between December 1995 and February 2000, the study showed (1) a nine percentage point increase in paid employment among low-income single-mother household heads (from 59 to 68 percent); (2) increased monthly earnings of roughly $114 per month; (3) a decline in access the employment-based health insurance from 21 to 14 percent, despite work participation; (4) a decline in the share of low-income single-parent families with incomes below the official poverty line from 59 to 51 percent, although roughly 3.1 million families live in poverty after welfare reform, and 1.5 million live on incomes less than 50 percent of the poverty line; (5) a decrease in the percentage of low-income single parents who have acquired some college education from 24 to 17 percent; and (6) a decline in the percentage of non-Hispanic white welfare recipients from 34 to 24 percent, an increase of Hispanic welfare recipients from 20 to 30 percent, and stability in the percentage of black welfare recipients, although blacks are the only racial group to experience an increase in the percentage of non-welfare recipients who remain low income in this period (from 29 to 34 percent). Avis Jones-DeWeever et al., Before and After Welfare Reform: The Work and Well-Being of Low-Income Single Parent Families, Institute for Women's Policy Research (2003), at x-xi; full report available at http://www.iwpr.org/Poverty/Research_poverty.htm.

Other studies show that between 50 to 75 percent of those who have left the welfare rolls remained poor two years after leaving welfare. Shawn Fremstad, Recent Welfare Reform Research Findings, Center on Budget and Policy Priorities, at 5 (Jan. 20, 2004), available at http://www.cbpp.org/1-30-04wel.pdf (citing Rebecca M. Blank, Evaluating Welfare Reform in the United States, 40 J. Econ. Literature 1105 (2002)). One study of women in Michigan showed that, four years after receiving TANF benefits, only one-quarter were working in "good jobs," defined as jobs with health benefits that paid at least $7 an hour, or jobs without health benefits that paid at least $8.50 an hour. Id (citing study). Another study of 40,000 households found that about one-third of women who were no longer on welfare said they had to cut the size of meals, or skip meals, because they did not have enough money for food, and about half reported that they either often or sometimes run out of food and do not have money to buy more. Id. (citing study). A 2005 project of the Urban Institute to collect all available data on the experiences of low-income families and children during the major shift in U.S. welfare policy found that the median hourly wage of welfare recipients in 2002 was about $8.00, and that 13.8 percent of former welfare recipients in 2002 had no employment income, working spouse, TANF benefits or public disability benefits — up from 9.8 percent in 1999. Assessing the New Federalism: Eight Years Later, April 22, 2005, available at http://newfederalism.urban.org/publications/311198.html.

One problem for families who no longer qualify for cash benefits is that they do not realize that they may still qualify for child care assistance, health insurance, and food stamps. See Lolly Bowean, Children Are Uninsured Because Parents Don't Know They Qualify, Reports Says, Wall St. J., Aug. 10, 2000, at 12 (citing study by Robert Wood Johnson Foundation showing that six out of ten children are uninsured because their parents think that because they work and aren't on welfare, their children don't qualify for insurance); Roslyn Powell & Mia Cahill, Nowhere to Turn: New York City's Failure to Inform Parents on Public Assistance About Their Child Care Rights, 7 Geo. J. Poverty L. & Pol'y 363 (2000).

3. Welfare Reform and the Promotion of Marriage. An important objective of PRWORA is the reduction of out-of-wedlock pregnancies and childbirths. Is this a legitimate government goal? Proponents of marriage-based programs point to studies that have shown that children who grow up with both of their biological parents are more successful across a broad range of outcomes than children who grow up with only one parent, including higher educational attainment, better behavioral outcomes, and mental health, although some analysts believe that the positive outcomes typically associated with marriage are due to pre-existing characteristics of the people who choose to marry, and not divorce, rather than to marriage itself. See Sara McLanahan, Fragile Families and the Marriage Agenda, Center for Research on Child Wellbeing Working Paper # 03-16-FF, Dec. 2003, available at http://www.olin.wustl.edu/macarthur/bio/mclanahan.htm. For recent reviews of the various studies, which reach different conclusions, see Julia M. Fisher, Marriage Promotion Policies and the Working Poor: A Match Made in Heaven?, 25 B.C. Third World L.J. 475, 478-483 (2005) (favoring "Marriage Plus" solutions, discussed below);

Robin Fretwell Wilson, Evaluating Marriage: Does Marriage Matter to the Nurturing of Children?, 42 San Diego L. Rev. 847 (2005) (concluding that evidence provides "a compelling justification for state support of marriage"); Kim Yuracko, Does Marriage Make People Good or Do Good People Marry? 42 San Diego L. Rev. 889 (2005) (challenging causal link between marriage and child outcomes). See also Amy L. Wax, The Two-Parent Family in the Liberal State: The Case for Selective Subsidies, 1 Mich. J. Race & L. 491, 494 (1996) (arguing, with support of many studies, that it is appropriate for state to use subsidies to promote two-parent families).

Since 2002, the federal Administration for Children and Families (ACF), an agency of the Department of Health and Human Services, has dispersed grants to fund marriage promotion programs under President Bush's Healthy Marriages Initiative. Most states have responded in some way to the incentives. The vast majority of states, for example, have changed their rules to eliminate pre-1996 welfare eligibility barriers to two-parent families. Arizona, Louisiana, Michigan, New Mexico, Oklahoma, Utah, and Virginia have all created significant marriage promotion programs, which include such measures as marriage education programs, public service announcements, and courses in relationships skills both at the high-school level and for adults. See Fisher, supra, at 485 n.71.

The rewards to states can be significant. In 2005, New York received a "bonus" of $25 million from ACF, in recognition of the state's reduction in out-of-wedlock births and abortions. Marnie Eisenstadt, Birth Figures Deliver Bonus: State Receives $25 Million in Federal Money as Out-of-Wedlock Births Decline, The Post-Standard (Syracuse, New York), Oct. 14, 2004, at A8.

For a state-by-state listing of marriage promotion efforts, see Theodora Ooms et al., Center for Law and Social Policy, Beyond Marriage Licenses: Efforts in States to Strengthen Marriage and Two-Parent Families, April 2004, available at http://www.clasp.org/publications/beyond_marr.pdf. Over $90 million was spent on these programs in 2002-2003. Fisher, supra, at 486. Expansion of marriage promotion programs is an important part of the Bush Administration's second term agenda, the funds for which would come of out existing welfare spending. Robert Rector, How Not to Be Poor: When Will This Country Face the Facts About Marriage and Families?, National Review, Oct. 24, 2005, at 26.

Critics of the "healthy marriage" approach to welfare reform charge that, even if marriage is a legitimate government goal, "marriage alone is not sufficient to lift couples out of poverty." Fisher, supra, at 494. The Center for Law and Social Policy proposes "Marriage Plus" as an alternative, which would include not only marriage counseling and relationship training, but pregnancy prevention, mental health support, greater childcare services, reform of the child support system, employment training and placement. Id. at 494-496; Ooms, supra.

Census data show that five years after the overhaul of the welfare system, the proportion of black children living with two married parents increased from 34.8 percent to 38.9 percent. Blaine Harden, 2-Parent Families Rise After Change in Welfare Laws, N.Y. Times, Aug. 12, 2001, at A1. Should this viewed as a significant benefit of welfare reform? The proportion of white children living with two married parents remained stable at 78.2 percent, just slightly down from 78.5 percent. Id. What conclusions might we draw, if any, from these statistics?

4. Race, Gender, and Poverty. Poverty is strongly correlated to race and gender. The most current comprehensive Census Bureau data (2002) shows that 24 percent of blacks and 21.8 percent of Hispanics are below the federal poverty level, as compared with 10.2 percent of whites and 10.1 percent of Asians. U.S. Census Bureau, Statistical Abstract of the United States: 2004-2005, Table 686. While only 13.3 percent of women on average were below the poverty level in 2002, as compared to 10.9 percent of men, the poverty rate for single-mother families in 2002 was 33.7 percent, and by 2004 this rate had increased for the third year in a row, to 35.5 percent. National Women's Law Center, NWLC Analysis of New Census Data Finds Poverty of Women and Children Increases for Third Straight Year (August 26, 2004), available at http://www.nwlc.org/details.cfm?id=1986&section=newsroom. The gap is growing. In 2004, households in the bottom twenty percent of the income distribution — disproportionately female-headed households — received a smaller share of aggregate income than at any time in the 37 years that data had been collected. The bottom 20 percent of households received only 3.4 percent of income; the top 20 percent received nearly half. Id.

In 2003, the full-time weekly earnings median for all females in the U.S. was $552, as compared to $695 for men. By race, the median was $636 for whites, $514 for blacks, $693 for Asians, and $440 for Hispanics. The largest disparities were between female Hispanics ($410) and female blacks ($491), and white males ($715). Id. at Table 623. Median hourly earnings in 2003 ranged from $7.89 for blacks, $9.76 for Hispanics, $10.97 for whites, and $11.12 for Asians. U.S. Census Bureau, Statistical Abstract, supra, at Table 627. Annual income medians in 2002 ranged from $54,633 for whites and $60,984 for Asians, to $33,525 for blacks and $34,185 for Hispanics. Id. at Table 670.

5. Women and Social Security, Unemployment Insurance, and Minimum Wage. It is estimated that without Social Security benefits, more than half of women over the age of 65 would live in poverty. Currently, if a woman spends most of her career raising her family, her Social Security benefit is half of her husband's and, when her husband dies, she gets 100 percent of his benefits. Though the proportion of women who are entitled to benefits both as a worker and a spouse is rising, nearly one-third of women are eligible for benefits strictly as a wife or widow. Institute for Women's Policy Research, Who Are Social Security Beneficiaries?, IWPR Pub. No. D461 (March 2005).

Most policy analysts agree that stresses to the program will increase exponentially over the next twenty years, as the baby boom generation retires and begins to draw benefits. The most recent report by the Social Security Board of Trustees estimates that the program can pay full benefits until 2041, when the trust fund's reserves will be exhausted. H.R. Doc. No. 109-18, at 3 (2005). Current proposals to improve the program's solvency have focused either on a combination of reduced benefits and increased payroll taxes, or a change from the current defined-benefit system to a defined-contribution system, similar to 401(k) plans or individual retirement accounts (IRAs). Proponents of privatization argue that allowing workers to invest a portion of their retirement taxes would provide a better return on workers' investment. David C. John, The Heritage Foundation, How to Fix Social Security 3 (2004), www.heritage.org/Research/SocialSecurity/bg1811.cfm. However, the move away from a defined benefit program may have an adverse effect on women. Some commentators argue that the shift would mean that women and minorities will bear not only the financial burden of earning less over their lifetimes but also of receiving lesser benefits in retirement. Because women live longer, but tend to make more conservative investments, privatization may result in inadequate retirement savings. See Jane Elizabeth Zanglein, Investment Without Education: The Disparate Impact on Women and Minorities in Self-Directed Defined Contribution Plans, 5 Emp. Rts. & Emp. Pol'y J. 223 (2001); see also Dorothy A. Brown, Social Security Reform: Risks, Returns and Race, 9 Cornell J.L. & Pub. Pol'y 633, 649-650 (2000) (claiming that privatization would also perpetuate existing racial inequalities). Additionally, privatization particularly affects workers who have periods of unemployment in their early earning years, penalizing women who leave the workforce either full or part time to have children. William Spriggs, Social Security Privatization's Motherhood Penalty, Economic Policy Institute's Economic Snapshots (Feb. 2, 2005), available at http://www. epinet.org/content.cfm.webfeatures_snapshots_20050202.

Some experts have proposed the expansion of unemployment insurance for women who work part-time or who leave work for family-related reasons. See Testimony of Vicky Lovell, Institute for Women's Policy Research, Policy Alternatives for Improving Access to Unemployment Insurance for Women, Low-Wage and Part-Time Workers: The Case of Georgia, IWPR Pub. No. B236 (Dec. 15, 2000). For the argument that unemployment insurance is a poor vehicle for the kind of wealth distribution that low-wage and marginal working women may require, see Gillian Lester, Unemployment Insurance and Wealth Redistribution, 49 UCLA L. Rev. 335 (2001).

The most significant activity with respect to an improved wage structure is the Living Wage movement. This movement is an alliance between labor and religious leaders started in 1994 to campaign for local laws requiring city service contractors to pay a "living wage." Typically, living wage measures apply to employers who hold large city or county service contracts or receive substantial financial assistance from the city or county in the form of grants, loans, bond financing, tax abatements, or other economic development subsidies. As of May 2005, 130 ordinances had been passed, providing for minimum hourly wage levels ranging from $6.25 to $13.00. Minimums often depend on whether health benefits are provided, and indexing is typically provided. Among the cities with successful campaigns are Philadelphia, St. Louis, Tucson, Oakland, San Jose, San Francisco, New York, Milwaukee, New Orleans, Pittsburgh, Cleveland, Los Angeles, Denver, Miami, Detroit, Chicago, Boston, and Minneapolis. For a complete listing and details of the ordinances, see http://www.livingwagecampaign.org/index.php?id=2071.

6. Welfare and Autonomy. To what extent is autonomy a misguided goal for the welfare system? Can the views of Fineman and Schultz be reconciled? Who is right? Is it possible that the emphasis on women's autonomy actually has undermined their well-being? Consider this further analysis by Fineman:

[O]ur particular way of thinking about the desirability and attainability of autonomy for individuals and families has seriously limited the ways in which we think about equality. Ideas about individual autonomy and self-sufficiency create this limitation, as do corresponding institutional arrangements that support privatization and the market as an absolute good and governmental action and regulation as presumptively bad. One consequence of this has been the conceptual separation of the family from other societal institutions and the assignment to it of primary responsibility for the dependency of those deemed not autonomous and independent....

Rejection of the idea that there is some collective responsibility for dependency is not surprising in a society such as ours. American political ideology offers an iconic construct of the autonomous individual and trusts the abstraction of an efficiency-seeking market as an ordering mechanism. We have an historic and highly romanticized affair with the ideals of the private and the individual, as contrasted with the public and the collective, as the appropriate units of focus in determining social good.

After all, the very concept of the private defines the domain of the individual — an unregulated space where individual freedom reigns and in which each would-be king can construct *his* castle. If a child is part of that landscape, it is deemed a private matter, not the occasion for public subsidy or support. Children are considered to be like any other item of consumption, a matter of individual preference and individual responsibility.

The idea that the private is generally preferable as a means of responding to need and dependency has become more and more firmly enmeshed with our sense of social justice during the past few decades — informing the unwritten "social contract" that guides and gauges the relationship among individuals, societal institutions, and the state. As it evolves, what may be referred to as a distinctively American version of the social contract seems to be expanding along the private axis.

Privatization is increasingly seen as the solution to complicated social problems reflecting persistent inequality and poverty. The rhetoric surrounding many current policy debates urges previously public concerns to be transferred to the magic realm of the private solution. From welfare reform to the construction of ideal educational or prison systems, the assertion is that the private market can better address historic public issues than can the public government....

The theory of dependency I set forth develops a claim of "right" or entitlement to support and accommodation from the state and its institutions on the part of caretakers — those who care for dependents. Their labor should be treated as equally productive even if unwaged, and should be measured by its societal value, not by economic or market indicators. The fact that dependency work has been un- or undervalued in the market is an argument *for* governmental intervention and restructuring to mandate adjustment and market accommodation, as well as more direct reparations...

Martha Albertson Fineman, The Autonomy Myth: A Theory of Dependency xiii-xv (2004).

Putting Theory into Practice

5-17. How would you evaluate a proposal to give low-income individuals and couples who periodically attend parenting classes an annual tax deduction (or cash benefits if they do not pay taxes)? How about marriage relationship skills classes? How about an annual cash "bonus" for staying married?

D. RECONCEIVING AUTONOMY

Feminist scholars, prompted in part by some of the subjects studied in this chapter, have urged a reconceptualization of the liberal concept of autonomy. Kathryn Abrams, for example, proposes a theory of "partial agency."

> [L]aw tends most frequently to assume a simplified version of the liberal subject: a subject capable of uncompromised agentic self-determination, to whom legal authorities ascribe full responsibility for actions taken, and on whose behalf they are generally reluctant to intervene. The strength of these assumptions has often required lawyers seeking to depart from them to describe a sharply contrasting legal subject. In justifying legal intervention or a mitigation of legal sanction, lawyers have described, and judges have acknowledged, a female subject wholly incapable of self-direction, whom the law must rescue from her plight or relieve of responsibility for her actions. The pragmatic interest of feminist lawyers in securing positive outcomes for their clients has often made them complicit in this dichotomizing tendency. They have stressed the extent of their clients' subordination and constraint in ways that have muted any capacity for self-direction of agency.
>
> Most forms of partial agency . . . stand outside this Manichean view of legal subjectivity. [One example is Susan Keller's analysis of the variability that exists in the gaps between viewers' interpretation of a pornographic representation and their application of the representation in their own erotic lives, a variability which can serve as a salient route to self-exploration as well as a viable form of resistance and a way to problematize dominant sexual arrangements. Another example is Martha Mahoney's proposal that the unitary images of battered women offered by dominance theory be supplemented by accounts that incorporate the daily acts of self-preservation, familial protection, and outright resistance that she sees in the narrative of battered women. The works of both Keller and Mahoney] suggest a subject who is neither as unencumbered as the law's traditional subject nor as immobilized as the exceptional subject of the law's protection. If properly understood, these accounts not only have the potential to communicate new images of women living under conditions of oppression, but rather to revise the imagery, assumptions, and even the outcomes reflected in several areas of gender-related law.
>
> . . . Powerlessness is the description through which many legal proceedings simultaneously exonerate and stigmatize "good" victims of sexualized injury, those who conform to traditional gender roles. "Irresponsibility" — or full agency, culpably exercised — is the term with which legal authorities sanction non-conforming women: those who are sexually active, sexually aggressive, live outside the boundaries, or challenge the conventions of mainstream heterosexual family life.

A similar form of policing is frequently accomplished by means of the dichotomy between the wholly autonomous subject and the wholly compromised victim. Assimilation to the image of the wholly compromised or constructed victim is a price that women may be asked to pay for legal intervention in interactions or circumstances that were formerly not the province of law. Women may assert their divergence from unremitting victimization, but only at the risk of being assimilated to the autonomous subject who does not require, or requires considerably less, legal intervention. Highlighting this disciplinary use of the dichotomy may help some legal decisionmakers learn to see what exists of the human spectrum between those abstract poles: claimants who are functional and at least minimally self-directing, but also injured and in need of some degree of legal assistance.

. . . Dominance feminists' critics have sought to vindicate the submerged or repressed elements of the dominance vision: the partial agency women retain and the sexual pleasure we might hope to enjoy as we struggle toward greater equality. By framing these two positions not as mutual antagonists but as parts of a single program whose elements are sometimes in sync and sometimes in tension, women can secure our future power without sacrificing the quality or misrepresenting the character of our present lives.

Kathryn Abrams, Sex Wars Redux: Agency and Coercion in Feminist Legal Theory, 95 Colum. L. Rev. 304, 351-352, 374-376 (1995).

Abrams challenges both the liberal legal assumption of the dichotomized legal subject — one who is either autonomous or coerced, freely acting or incapable of self-direction, responsible or irresponsible — and dominance feminism's definition of woman as victim, which fails to move outside the liberal dichotomy. Abrams suggests a more complicated view of the subject, as an individual both free and constrained. What are the implications of the shift? This line of analysis is further developed in Chapter 6.

Another challenge to traditional liberal concepts of autonomy focuses on the premise of the individual, in competition with or in adversarial relationship to the collective community. Jennifer Nedelsky, for example, urges a shift from the conventional understanding of separate individuals whose interests are necessarily threatened by the collective power of the community, to a view in which the community is viewed as facilitative of individual flourishing and autonomy, and the obligations of government do not depend on the pre-identification of discrete individual rights.

> There is . . . a twofold objective in reconceiving autonomy: (1) to recognize that the irreducible tension between the individual and the collective makes choices or trade-offs necessary; and (2) at the same time, to move beyond a conception of human beings which sees them exclusively as separate individuals and focuses on the threat of the community. The collective is not simply a potential threat to individuals, but is constitutive of them, and thus is a source of their autonomy as well as a danger to it. . . . The task . . . is to think of autonomy in terms of the forms of human interactions in which it will develop and flourish. . . .
>
> It is hardly surprising that a tradition which has conceived of the relationship between the individual and the collective primarily in terms of the threat of the latter does not provide an adequate basis for defining individual rights in the context of affirmative responsibilities of the state. The dichotomy between individual rights and state power has meant that the courts have particular trouble in cases which require

them both to accept the state's intrusion into a previously private sphere and to develop a useful framework of individual rights.

Jennifer Nedelsky, Reconceiving Autonomy: Sources, Thoughts, and Possibilities, 1 Yale J.L. & Feminism 7, 21, 31-32 (1989). Linda C. McClain pursues a similar theme when she explores alternative, non-atomistic definitions of autonomy, including autonomy as self-government, which she explains may coexist with and include many forms of connection among citizens. See McClain, "Atomistic Man" Revisited: Liberalism, Connection, and Feminist Jurisprudence, 65 S. Cal. L. Rev. 1171, 1190 (1992).

Once separation from others is no longer viewed as the central premise of autonomy, the way is cleared for still a third reconceptualization of autonomy, one which views individual rights claims as claims not by an isolated, rights-bearing individual, but by an individual who is deeply interconnected with and dependent upon others.

> As I see it, individual autonomy is a capacity, not a static human characteristic to be posited as a presupposition of legal or political theory. This capacity must be developed; it can flourish or become moribund. What is essential to the development of autonomy is not protection against intrusion but constructive relationship. The central question for inquiries into autonomy (legal or otherwise) is then how to structure relationships so that they foster rather than undermine autonomy....
>
> If we understand autonomy as made possible by relationship rather than by exclusion, we can better understand the genuine problem of autonomy in the modern state. Our central problem today is not maintaining a sphere into which the state cannot penetrate but fostering autonomy where people are already within the sphere of state control or responsibility. The problem is best addressed by focusing on how the interactions between state and citizen are structured.

Jennifer Nedelsky, Law, Boundaries, and the Bounded Self, 30 Representations 162, 168-169 (1990). See also Martha Minow & Mary Lyndon Shanley, Relational Rights and Responsibilities: Revisioning the Family in Liberal Political Theory and Law, 11 Hypatia 4, 23 (Winter 1996) (defining relational rights in terms of "the claims that arise out of relationships of human interdependence"); Martha Minow, Interpreting Rights; An Essay for Robert Cover, 96 Yale L.J. 1860, 1888 (1987) (rights claims express relationships and interconnections at the very moment that the individual asserts his or her autonomy); Susan G. Kupfer, Autonomy and Community in Feminist Legal Thought, 22 Golden Gate U. L. Rev. 583 (1992) (reformulating autonomy in light of West's notion of the "authentic self" and feminist commitment to community); Anne C. Dailey, Feminism's Return to Liberalism, 102 Yale L.J. 1265, 1267 (1993) (book review) (describing shift in legal feminism to a "redeemed liberalism in which the philosophy of possessive individualism characteristic of classical liberalism has been tempered by a principle of empathy").

How does formulating the issue of autonomy in terms of the connections and relationships it enables make a difference to any of the issues raised in this chapter? Does the concept of relational autonomy avoid the problems of indeterminacy inherent in relational feminism more generally?

6

Non-Essentialism

Feminist legal scholars and activists in the United States have struggled to achieve equality between men and women. As this book illustrates, equality has had many meanings: identical treatment for men and women under the law; "special treatment" for women when women's experiences diverge biologically or culturally from those of men; the re-valuation of stereotypically "female" practices and qualities; the end of male domination; the achievement of autonomy. For each of these meanings, there is a tendency to attribute to women certain common characteristics — a process which has come to be referred to, critically, as "essentialism."

Essentialism in feminist legal critique refers to several related but distinct complaints. One is that use of the category "women" in feminist thought too often assumes characteristics that may be true for some women, but not all, thereby overemphasizing the situation of white, middle class, heterosexual, able-bodied — i.e., otherwise privileged — women. Some feminists have responded to this charge that while it is important to recognize differences among women, political action and reform requires us to speak in meaningful categories. This debate raises one of the main questions of this chapter: to what extent and in what contexts can we usefully generalize about women, or men for that matter?

Concerns about essentialism also sometimes arise in the context of values and goals that might conflict with American feminist efforts to obtain gender justice. This problem is not limited to, but is especially acute, when Western feminists attempt to take up the cause of women from other cultural traditions — sometimes in circumstances in which the women themselves do not wish to be "liberated." Are such efforts essentialist, in the sense of arrogant or imperialist? This chapter explores this question.

A third "essentialism" concern is that feminists inaccurately assume that the sex/gender system is inevitable and biologically determined. Feminists have long challenged the assumption that women's differences are natural, or biological givens — as they did when they challenged sex stereotypes and insisted that women were equals of men with respect to employment, political office, and virtually every other in which the law used to assume difference. See Chapter 1. Materials in Chapter 4 represent a revival in interest in the salience of biology. In this chapter, legal issues raised by transsexuals are used to question the fundamental distinction between sex and biology.

A fourth connotation of the term "essentialism" involves the vexed relationship between feminism and the cross-disciplinary academic movement known as "postmodernism." Postmodern theory seeks to undermine ordinary assumptions about truth and power by emphasizing the interrelationship between the two. Relations of power help determine what a society takes to be "true," and power thus has its most pervasive effects when it determines what we think we know. Postmodern feminists are skeptical of claims about universal "objective" truth, which have often been used to justify women's oppression. However, if all knowledge is socially constructed, how can feminists claim to be "right" about the fact and harms of gender inequality?

Anti-essentialist critiques have generated counter-critiques. One central concern is that anti-essentialism charges exhibit moral relativism, which ultimately disables political action. Several of the readings in this chapter attempt to resolve how feminism should proceed in the face of what may seem to be devastating theoretical critiques, and how feminism may be practiced in the context of the concerns about essentialism.

Although the term "essentialism" can refer to many different concepts, within feminist theory the term consistently is a derogatory label. As you work through the chapter, ask yourself whether it is always bad to be an essentialist. Are some forms of essentialism worse than others? Are some kinds of essentialism necessary or appropriate in certain contexts?

A. NON-ESSENTIALISM IN FEMINIST LEGAL THEORY

1. Differences and Intersectionality

a. Differences among Women

Sojourner Truth: Reminiscences by Frances D. Gage, Akron Convention (May 28-29, 1851)
History of Woman Suffrage, vol. I, 1848-1861, at 115-117
(Elizabeth Cady Stanton, Susan B. Anthony & Matilda Joslyn Gage eds., reprint ed. 1985)

The leaders of the movement trembled on seeing a tall, gaunt black woman in a gray dress and white turban, surmounted with an uncouth sun-bonnet, march deliberately into the church, walk with the air of a queen up the aisle, and take her seat upon the pulpit steps. A buzz of disapprobation was heard all over the house, and there fell on the listening ear, "An abolition affair!" "Woman's rights and niggers!" "I told you so!" "Go it, darkey!"

I chanced on that occasion to wear my first laurels in public life as president of the meeting. At my request order was restored, and the business of the Convention went on. Morning, afternoon, and evening exercises came and went. Through all these sessions old Sojourner, quiet and reticent as the "Lybian Statue," sat crouched against the wall on the corner of the pulpit stairs, her sunbonnet shading her eyes, her elbows on her knees, her chin resting upon her broad, hard palms. At intermission she was busy selling the "Life of Sojourner Truth," a narrative of her own strange and adventurous life. Again and again, timorous and trembling ones came to me and said, with earnestness, "Don't let her speak, Mrs. Gage, it will ruin us. Every newspaper in the land will have our cause mixed up with abolition and niggers, and we shall be utterly denounced." My only answer was, "We shall see when the time comes."

The second day the work waxed warm. Methodist, Baptist, Episcopal, Presbyterian, and Universalist ministers came in to hear and discuss the resolutions presented. One claimed superior rights and privileges for man, on the ground of "superior intellect"; another, because of the "manhood of Christ; if God had desired the equality of woman, He would have given some token of His will through the birth, life, and death of the Saviour." Another gave us a theological view of the "sin of our first mother."

There were very few women in those days who dared to "speak in meeting"; and the august teachers of the people were seemingly getting the better of us, while the boys in the galleries, and the sneerers among the pews, were hugely enjoying the discomfiture, as they supposed, of the "strong-minded." Some of the tender-skinned friends were on the point of losing dignity, and the atmosphere betokened a storm. When, slowly from her seat in the corner rose Sojourner Truth, who, till now, had scarcely lifted her head. "Don't let her speak!" gasped half a dozen in my ear. She moved slowly and solemnly to the front, laid her old bonnet at her feet, and turned her great speaking eyes to me. There was a hissing sound of disapprobation above and below. I rose and announced "Sojourner Truth," and begged the audience to keep silence for a few moments.

The tumult subsided at once, and every eye was fixed on this almost Amazon form, which stood nearly six feet high, head erect, and eyes piercing the upper air like one in a dream. At her first word there was a profound hush. She spoke in deep tones, which, though not loud, reached every ear in the house, and away through the throngs at the doors and windows.

"Wall, chilern, whar dar is so much racket dar must be somethin' out o' kilter. I think dat 'twixt de niggers of de Souf and de womin at de Norf, all talkin' 'bout rights, de white men will be in a fix pretty soon. But what's all this here talkin' 'bout?

"Dat man ober dar say dat womin needs to be helped into carriages, and lifted ober ditches, and to hab de best place everywhar. Nobody eber helps me into carriages, or ober mud-puddles, or gibs me any best place!" And raising herself to her full height, and her voice to a pitch to like rolling thunder, she asked, "And a'n't I a woman? Look at me! Look at my arm! (and she bared her right arm to the shoulder, showing her tremendous muscular power). I have ploughed, and planted, and gathered into barns, and no man could head me! And a'n't I a woman? I could work as much and eat as much as a man — when I could get it — and bear de lash as well! And a'n't I a woman? I have borne thirteen chilern, and seen 'em mos' all sold off to slavery, and when I cried out with my mother's grief, none but Jesus heard me! And a'n't I a woman?

"Den dey talks 'bout dis ting in de head; what dis dey call it?" ("Intellect," whispered some one near.) "Dat's it, honey. What's dat got to do wid womin's rights or nigger's rights? If my cup won't hold but a pint, and yourn holds a quart, wouldn't ye be mean not to let me have my little half-measure full?" And she pointed her significant finger, and sent a keen glance at the ministers who had made the argument. The cheering was long and loud.

"Den dat little man in black dar, he say women can't have as much rights as men, 'cause Christ wan't a woman! Whar did your Christ come from?" Rolling thunder couldn't have stilled that crowd, as did those deep, wonderful tones, as she stood there with outstretched arms and eyes of fire. Raising her voice still louder, she repeated, "Whar did your Christ come from? From God and a woman! Man had nothin' to do wid Him." Oh, what rebuke that was to that little man.

Turning again to another objector, she took up the defense of Mother Eve. I can not follow her through it all. It was pointed, and witty, and solemn; eliciting at almost every sentence deafening applause; and she ended by asserting: "If de fust woman God ever made was strong enough to turn de world upside down all alone, dese women togedder (and she glanced her eye over the platform) ought to be able to turn it back, and get it right side up again! And now dey is asking to do it, de men better let 'em." Long-continued cheering greeted this. "Bleeged to ye for hearin' on me, and now ole Sojourner han't got nothin' more to say."

Amid roars of applause, she returned to her corner, leaving more than one of us with streaming eyes, and hearts beating with gratitude. She had taken us up in her strong arms and carried us safely over the slough of difficulty turning the whole tide in our favor. I have never in my life seen anything like the magical influence that subdued the mobbish spirit of the day, and turned the sneers and jeers of an excited crowd into notes of respect and admiration. Hundreds rushed up to shake hands with her, and congratulate the glorious old mother, and bid her God-speed on her mission of "testifyin' agin concerning the wickedness of this 'ere people."

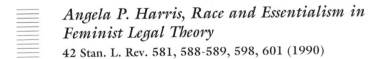

Angela P. Harris, Race and Essentialism in Feminist Legal Theory

42 Stan. L. Rev. 581, 588-589, 598, 601 (1990)

Since the beginning of the feminist movement in the United States, black women have been arguing that their experience calls into question the notion of a unitary "women's experience." In the first wave of the feminist movement, black women's realization that the white leaders of the suffrage movement intended to take neither issues of racial oppression nor black women themselves seriously was instrumental in destroying or preventing political alliances between black and white women within the movement. In the second wave, black women are again speaking loudly and persistently....Feminists have adopted the notion of multiple consciousness as appropriate to describe a world in which people are not oppressed only or primarily on the basis of gender, but on the bases of race, class, sexual orientation, and other categories in inextricable webs....

In feminist legal theory,...the voice of abstract categorization [is] still powerfully strong: "We the People" seems in danger of being replaced by "We the Women." And in feminist legal theory, as in the dominant culture, it is mostly white, straight, and socioeconomically privileged people who claim to speak for all of us....

The result of essentialism is to reduce the lives of people who experience multiple forms of oppression to addition problems: "racism + sexism = straight black women's experience," or "racism + sexism + homophobia = black lesbian experience." Thus, in an essentialist world, black women's experience will always be forcibly fragmented before being subjected to analysis, as those who are "only interested in race" and those who are "only interest in gender" take their separate slices of our lives....[F]eminist essentialism paves the way for unconscious racism....In a racist society like this one, the storytellers are usually white, and so "woman" turns out to be "white woman."...

For example, the paradigm experience of rape for black women has historically involved the white employer in the kitchen or bedroom as much as the strange black man in the bushes....[T]he experience of rape for black women includes not only a vulnerability to rape and a lack of legal protection radically different from that experienced by white women, but also a unique ambivalence. Black women have simultaneously acknowledged their own victimization and the victimization of black men by a system that has consistently ignored violence against women while perpetrating it against men.

Kimberlé Crenshaw, *Demarginalizing the Intersection of Race and Sex: A Black Feminist Critique of Antidiscrimination Doctrine, Feminist Theory, and Antiracist Politics*
1989 U. Chi. Legal F. 139, 140-143

With Black women as the starting point, it becomes more apparent how dominant conceptions of discrimination condition us to think about subordination as disadvantage occurring along a single categorical axis....[T]his single-axis framework erases Black women in the conceptualization, identification and remediation of race and sex discrimination by limiting inquiry to the experiences of otherwise-privileged members of the group. In other words, in race discrimination cases, discrimination tends to be viewed in terms of sex- or class-privileged Blacks; in sex discrimination cases, the focus is on race- and class-privileged women.

This focus on the most privileged group members marginalizes those who are multiply-burdened and obscures claims that cannot be understood as resulting from discrete sources of discrimination. [T]his focus on otherwise-privileged group members creates a distorted analysis of racism and sexism because the operative conceptions of race and sex become grounded in experiences that actually represent only a subset of a much more complex phenomenon.

Th[e] problems of exclusion cannot be solved simply by including Black women within an already established analytical structure. Because the intersectional experience is greater than the sum of racism and sexism, any analysis that does not take intersectionality into account cannot sufficiently address the particular manner in which Black women are subordinated.

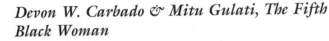

Devon W. Carbado & Mitu Gulati, *The Fifth Black Woman*

11 J. Contemp. Legal Issues 701, 710-720 (2001)

Consider the following hypothetical. Mary, a black woman, works in an elite corporate firm. There are eighty attorneys at the firm, twenty of whom are partners. Only two of the partners are black, and both are men. The firm has three female partners, and all three are white. There are no Asian American, Native American, or Latina/o partners. The firm is slightly more diverse at the associate rank. There are fifteen female associates: three, including Mary, are black, two are Asian American, and one is Latina. The remaining female associates are white. Of the forty-five male associates, two are black, two are Latino, three are Asian American, and the rest are white.

Mary is a seventh-year associate at the firm. She, along with five other associates, is up for partnership this year. Her annual reviews have been consistently strong. The partners for whom she has worked praise her intellectual creativity, her ability to perform well under pressure, her strong work ethic, her client-serving skills, and her commitment to the firm. She has not brought in many new clients, but, as one of the senior partners puts it, "that is not unusual for a person on the cusp of partnership."

For the past three years, the Chair of the Associate's Committee, the committee charged with making partnership recommendations to the entire partnership, has indicated to Mary that she is "on track." Being "on track" was important to Mary because, were she not on track, she would have seriously explored the option of moving either to another firm with better partnership prospects for her or in-house to an investment bank that provided greater job security. It was generally understood, however, and the Chair made sure to make it clear that "being on track is not a guarantee that you will ultimately make partner." . . .

The Associate Committee recommends that the firm promote all six. However, the partners vote only four into the partnership: one black man, one Asian American male, one white man, and one white woman. They deny partnership to Mary and a white male associate. The partnership's decision to depart from the Associate Committee's recommendation is not unusual. . . . [I]t accepts the committee's positive recommendation only half of the time.

Subsequently, Mary brings a disparate treatment discrimination suit under Title VII. She advances three separate theories: race discrimination, sex discrimination, and race and sex discrimination. She does not, however, have any direct evidence of animus against her on the part of the employer. In other words, Mary can point to no explicit statements such as "We don't like you because you are a woman," or "We think that you are incompetent; all blacks are." The evidence is all circumstantial: Mary was highly qualified, but was rejected for a position that was arguably open.

The court, ruling in favor of the firm's summary judgment motion, rejects all three of Mary's claims. With respect to the race discrimination claim, the court reasons that it is not supported by evidence of intentional or animus-based discrimination. According to the court, there is no evidence that the firm dislikes (or has a taste for discrimination against) blacks. In fact, argues the court, the evidence points in the other direction. The very year the firm denied partnership to Mary, it extended partnership to another African-American. Further, within the past five years, the firm had promoted two other African-Americans to the partnership. The court notes that both of these partners participated in the deliberations as to whether Mary would be granted partnership, and neither has suggested that the firm's decision to deny Mary partnership was discriminatorily motivated. The court concludes that the simple act of denying one black person a promotion is, especially when other blacks have been promoted, insufficient to establish discrimination.

The court disposes of Mary's gender discrimination claim in a similar way. That is, it concludes that the fact that the firm has in the past promoted women to the partnership, that the partners who voted to deny partnership to Mary extended partnership to another woman, and that women participated in the firm's deliberations as to whether Mary would be promoted, and none of these women have claimed that Mary was treated unfairly because she is a woman, suggests that the firm did not engage in sex-based discrimination against Mary.

The court concludes its dismissal of Mary's compound discrimination claim (the allegation of discrimination based on her race and sex) with an argument about cognizability. . . . According to the court, there is no indication in the legislative history of Title VII that the statute intended "to create a new classification of 'black women' who would have greater standing than, for example, a black male." According to the court, "the prospect of the creation of new classes of protected minorities, governed only by mathematical principles of permutation and combination, clearly raises the prospect of opening the hackneyed Pandora's box."

The foregoing hypothetical articulates the classic intersectionality problem wherein black women fall through an anti-discrimination gap constituted by black male and white female experiences. The problem can be framed in terms of essentialism. Consider first the court's response to Mary's race discrimination claim. In determining whether Mary experienced race discrimination, the court assumes that there is an essential black experience that is unmodified by gender. The court's adjudication of Mary's race discrimination claim conveys the idea that racism is necessarily total. It is a particular kind of animus that reaches across gender, and affects men and women in the same way. It is about race — a hostility against all black people. . . .

Consider now the court's adjudication of Mary's sex discrimination. Here, too, the court's analysis reflects essentialism. The essentialism in this context conveys the idea that women's experiences are unmodified by race. The court assumes that if a firm engages in sex discrimination, such discrimination will negatively affect all women — and in the same way....

Finally, consider the court's rejection of Mary's compound discrimination claim. Here, the court doctrinally erases black women's status identity as black women. Its conclusion that this identity status is not cognizable means that, for purposes of Title VII, black women exist only to the extent that their experiences comport with the experiences of black men or white women. Under the court's view, and in the absence of explicit race/gender animus, black women's discriminatory experiences as black women are beyond the remedial reach of Title VII....

To appreciate the identity performance problem, assume again that Mary is an African American female in a predominantly white elite corporate law firm. As before, Mary is up for partnership and her evaluations have been consistently strong. Stipulate now that four other black women are up for partnership, as are two white women and two white men. The Associate's Committee recommends that the firm extends partnership to all nine associates. The members of the partnership, however, decide to depart from this recommendation. They grant partnership to four of the black women. The fifth black woman, Mary, does not make partner. Of the four white associates, the firm extends partnership to one of the men and one of the women.

The partnership's decision creates a buzz around the firm. The firm had never before granted partnership to so many non-white attorneys. Moreover, in the firm's fifty year history, it had only ever promoted two black people to partnership. Both of these partners are men, and the firm promoted both of them in the mid-1980s, a period during which the firm, along with many others, had enjoyed a high level of prosperity.

Prior to 1980, the firm had never hired a black female associate. Furthermore, most of those who were hired after that date left within two to three years of their arrival. Given the history of black women at the firm — low hiring rate, high attrition rate, low promotion rate — associates at the firm dubbed this year the "year of the black woman."

Mary, however, does not agree. Subsequent to the partnership decision, she files a Title VII discrimination suit, alleging (1) race and sex compound discrimination, i.e., discrimination against her on account of her being a black woman, and (2) discrimination based on identity performance. The firm moves for summary judgment on two theories. First, it argues that Mary may not ground her discrimination claim on her race and sex. According to the firm, Mary may separately assert a race discrimination claim and/or a sex discrimination claim; however, she may not, under Title VII, advance a discrimination claim combining race and sex. Second, the firm contends that whatever identity Mary invokes to ground her claim, there is simply no evidence of intentional discrimination.

With respect to the first issue, the court agrees with Mary that a discrimination claim combining race and sex is, under Title VII, legally cognizable. The court has read, and understood, and it agrees with the literature on intersectionality.

Under the court's view, black women should be permitted to ground their discrimination claims on their specific status identity as black women. According to the court, failing to do so would be to ignore the complex ways in which race and gender interact to create social disadvantage: a result that would be inconsistent with the goals of Title VII.

With respect to second issue, the court agrees with the firm. The court reasons that recognizing Mary's status identity does not prove that the firm discriminated against her because of that identity. It explains that the firm promoted four associates with Mary's precise status identity—that is, four black women. Why, the court rhetorically asks, would a racist/sexist firm extend partnership to these women? The court suggests that when there is clear evidence of non-discrimination against the identity group within which the plaintiff is situated, that produces an inference that the plaintiff was not the victim of discrimination.

The court rejects the plaintiff's arguments that Title VII itself and the Supreme Court's interpretation of Title VII focuses on protecting individuals, not groups, from discrimination. . . .

The problem with the court's approach is that it fails to consider whether Mary was the victim of an intra-racial (or intra-gender) distinction based not simply on her identity status as a black woman but on her performance of that identity. In effect, the court's approach essentializes the identity status "black female." More specifically, the court assumes that Mary and the other four black women are similarly situated with respect to their vulnerability to discrimination. However, this might not be the case. The social meaning of being a black woman is not monolithic and static but contextual and dynamic. An important way in which it is shaped is by performance. In other words, how black women present their identity can (and often does) affect whether and how they are discriminated against.

Consider, for example, the extent to which the following performance issues might help to explain why Mary was not promoted, but the other black women were.

Dress. While Mary wears her hair in dreadlocks, the other black women relax their hair. On Casual Fridays, Mary sometimes wears West African influenced attire. The other black women typically wear khaki trousers or blue jeans with white cotton blouses.

Institutional Identity. Mary was the driving force behind two controversial committees: the committee for the Recruitment and Retention of Women and Minorities and the committee on Staff/Attorney Relations. She has been critical of the firm's hiring and work allocation practices. Finally, she has repeatedly raised concerns about the number of hours the firm allocates to pro bono work. None of the other four black women have ever participated on identity-related or employee relations-related committees. Nor have any of them commented on either the racial/gender demographics of the firm or the number of hours the firm allocates for pro bono work.

Social Identity. Mary rarely attends the firm's happy hours. Typically, the other four black women do. Unlike Mary, the four black women each have hosted at least one firm event at their home. All four play tennis, and two of them play golf. Mary plays neither. Finally, while all four black women are members of the country club to which many of the partners belong, Mary is not.

Educational Affiliations. Two of the other four black women graduated from Harvard Law School, one graduated from Yale, and the other graduated from Stanford. Mary attended a large local state law school at the bottom of the second tier of schools.

Marital Status. All four of the other black women are married. Two are married to white men and each of them is married to a professional. Mary is a single mother.

Residence. Each of the other four black women lives in predominantly white neighborhoods. Mary lives in the inner city, which is predominantly black.

Professional Affiliation. Mary is an active member of the local black bar association, the Legal Society Against Taxation, and the Women's Legal Caucus. None of the four black women belongs to any of these organizations. One of them is on the advisory board of the Federalist Society. One of the four black women is a Catholic, two are Episcopalian, and the other does not attend church. Mary is a member of the Nation of Islam. . . .

Intersectionality does not capture this form of preferential treatment. While intersectionality recognizes that institutions make intra-group distinctions, that understanding is situated in an anti-discrimination context that is buttressed by a status conception of identity.

Assuming the foregoing performance issues obtain in Mary's case, do they reflect impermissible discrimination? The answer is not obviously yes. Perhaps the partners simply do not like Mary. Based on the description of how Mary performs her identity, could one not reasonably conclude the following: She does not attend happy hours, she creates trouble, she is not a team player, she does not dress or act professionally. Redescribing Mary's performance in this way makes the employer's decision to deny her partnership appear non-discriminatory (and even legitimate). After all, working and succeeding in an organization is not only about doing work. It is also about getting along with people and getting them to like you. An argument can be made that Mary simply did not do much work in the direction of getting the people who mattered to like her. The other four black women did; and they got promoted. On its face some — perhaps — will see this as fair. Those who do the extra work of making people like them should get promoted. Given our claim that this line of reasoning is flawed, the question is: What exactly is the relationship between identity performance and workplace discrimination? . . .

Broadly speaking, there are two ways to make the point that intra-group distinctions based on identity performance implicate workplace discrimination. The first is to focus on the preferred group members. In our hypothetical, they are the four black women. The second way is to focus on the disfavored group members. Mary, the fifth black woman, falls into this category. . . .

In a prior article, *Working Identity* [85 Cornell L. Rev. 1259 (2000)], we argued that an employee's awareness that identity-based assumptions about her are at odds with the institutional norms and criteria of a firm creates an incentive for that employee to work her identity. There are a number of ways an employee might do this. The employee might laugh in response to, or engage in racist humor (signaling collegiality). She might socialize with her colleagues after work (signaling that she can fit in; is one of the boys). She might avoid contact with other employees with negative workplace standing (signaling that she is not really "one of them"). The list goes on. The point is that whatever particular strategy the employee deploys, her aim will likely be to comfort her supervisors/colleagues about her negative workplace standing. Specifically, the employee will attempt to signal that she can fit in, that she is not going to make her supervisors/colleagues uncomfortable about her identity—or theirs—and, at bottom, that the negative stereotypes that exist about her status identity are inapplicable to her. *Working Identity* refers to these strategies collectively as "comfort strategies." These strategies are constituted by identity performances.

Stipulate that the four black women in the hypothetical performed comfort strategies. The claim that the performance of such strategies constitutes discrimination is based on the idea that people with negative workplace standing (e.g., people of color) have a greater incentive to perform comfort strategies than people with positive workplace standing. This means that identity performances burden some employees (e.g., blacks) more than others (e.g., whites). Without more, this racial distribution of identity performances is problematic. The problem is compounded by the fact that identity performances constitute work, a kind of "shadow work." This work is simultaneously expected and unacknowledged. Plus, it is work that is often risky. Finally, this work can be at odds with the employee's sense of her identity. That is, the employee may perceive that she has to disassociate from or disidentify with her identity in order to fit in. To the extent the employee's continued existence and success in the workplace is contingent upon her behaving in ways that operate as a denial of self, there is a continual harm to that employee's dignity.

Recall that the claim is that the firm's discrimination against Mary derives from an intra-group distinction based on Mary's dress, institutional identity, marital status, professional and educational affiliations, and residence. The question becomes, why is this discrimination impermissible? The short answer is that the distinction creates an intra-racial and an inter-racial problem. The problem is that the firm draws a line between black people who do (or whom the firm perceives as performing) identity work to fit in at the firm and black people who do not perform (or whom the firm perceives as not performing) such work. The interracial problem is that white people are not subject to this sub-categorization.

Notes

1. Racial Tensions in the First Wave of Feminism. Sojourner Truth's speech at the Akron Convention in 1851, as well as the reporting of it, represents the historical racial tension in the women's movement. As a former slave and abolitionist missionary, Sojourner Truth was a strong voice for the rights of all women. Yet in order to assert her claims, she had to overcome resistance from women who were willing to exploit racial fears and to align themselves with pro-slavery advocates in order to advance the cause of white women. See bell hooks, Ain't I a Woman: Black Women and Feminism 127-131 (1981); Ellen Carol DuBois, Feminism and Suffrage: The Emergence of an Independent Women's Movement in America 1848-1869, at 95-96 (1978).

Among the most visible and effective suffragettes who seemed prepared to exploit the racism of the times was Elizabeth Cady Stanton, who claimed both affinity with Negro slaves, and superiority over them. Thus, for example, she reminds those in power of the obvious injustice that Blacks could vote while women could not: "[Y]ou place the [N]egro, so unjustly degraded by you, in a superior position to your own wives and mothers." Elizabeth Cady Stanton, Address to the Legislature of the State of New York (Feb. 14, 1854), History of Woman Suffrage, vol. I, 1848-1861, 597 (Elizabeth Cady Stanton, Susan B. Anthony & Matilda Joslyn Gage eds., reprint ed. 1985) (1881-1922). Later suffragettes used even more explicitly racist arguments asserting the desirability of diluting the Negro vote as a rationale for supporting women's suffrage. Historian Sara Evans quotes one Southern suffragist at a 1903 NAWSA convention as saying that "[t]he enfranchisement of women would insure immediate and durable white supremacy, honestly attained." Sara M. Evans, Born for Liberty: A History of Women in America 155 (1989).

Is any of this familiar? To what extent are the rights and welfare of minorities viewed, even today, as a kind of floor, below which the rights and welfare of whites should never fall?

For critiques of the analogy between slavery and women's subordination, see generally Serena Mayeri, A Common Fate of Discrimination: Race-Gender Analogies in Legal and Historical Perspective, 110 Yale L.J. 1045 (2001); bell hooks, supra, at 139 ("white women have used comparisons between 'women' and 'blacks' to exclude black women and to deflect attention away from their own racial caste system"); Joyce E. McDonnell, Beyond Metaphor: Battered Women, Involuntary Servitude, and the Thirteenth Amendment, 4 Yale J.L. & Feminism 207, 207-208 (1992) ("No matter how rhetorically useful [the metaphor of women as slaves] may have seemed then or may seem now, it was and remains grossly inaccurate and inherently racist").

2. The Intersectionality Critique. In what sense does the account of Sojourner Truth preview Harris' critique? Professor Crenshaw's? How can contemporary feminists avoid these critiques? To what extent have they done so? What follows from the Carbado/Gulati analysis? To what extent do presentational issues present unique problems for women?

A now-classic case used by some scholars to focus the issue of intersectionality is Rogers v. American Airlines, 527 F. Supp. 229 (S.D.N.Y. 1981). *Rogers* involved a challenge by an African-American woman to an airline grooming policy prohibiting employees from wearing an all-braided hairstyle. The court held that because the policy applied to all employees—women and men, black and white—it was not discrimination on the basis of either race or gender. Id. at 231-232. It also pointed out that the plaintiff did not begin to wear the hairstyle until just after a white actress, Bo Derek, popularized corn rows in the movie "10," rather than several years earlier when Cicely Tyson wore the hairstyle at the

Academy Awards. Id. at 232. Critics attacked the case for ignoring the interrelationships between race and gender.

> Wherever they exist in the world, black women braid their hair. They have done so in the United States for more than four centuries. African in origin, the practice of braiding is as American — black American — as sweet potato pie. A braided hairstyle was first worn in a nationally-televised media event in the United States — and in that sense "popularized" — by a black actress, Cicely Tyson, nearly a decade before the movie "10." More importantly Cicely Tyson's choice to popularize (i.e., to "go public" with) braids, like her choice of acting roles, was a political act made on her own behalf and on behalf of all black women.
>
> The very use of the term "popularized" to describe Bo Derek's wearing of braids — in the sense of rendering suitable to the majority — specifically subordinates and makes invisible all of the black women who for centuries have worn braids in places where they and their hair were not overt threats to the American aesthetic.

Paulette M. Caldwell, A Hair Piece: Perspectives on the Intersection of Race and Gender, 1991 Duke L.J. 365, 379; see also Michelle L. Turner, The Braided Uproar: A Defense of My Sister's Hair and a Contemporary Indictment of *Rogers v. American Airlines*, 7 Cardozo Women's L.J. 115 (2001); Harris, Race and Essentialism in Feminist Legal Theory, supra, at 596 (prevailing beauty standards create pain for Black women that is "different qualitatively, not merely quantitatively" from the pain of white women).

How compelling is this critique? Consider the following:

> [S]hould anti-discrimination law protect politically controversial, if racially salient, behavior advanced through the vehicle of physical grooming? Suppose some black women employed by American Airlines wished to wear cornrows and advance the political message they ostensibly embody, while others thought cornrows damaged the interests of black women in particular and reflected badly on the race as a whole (given the cultural politics of black America in the mid-to-late 1970s, there almost certainly were such black women employed by American Airlines and even more certainly there were such black women among its customers). Suppose further that the management of American Airlines, either formally or informally, sought out and considered the opinions of its employees as well as of its customers and made its grooming policies based at least in part on such information. Now Rogers's claim is no longer plausibly described as a claim on behalf of black women. Instead it is a claim on behalf of some black women over the possible objections of other black women.
>
> Rogers and her supporters might object: "What business is it of other black women whether we wear braids — no one will be forced to wear them." But this individualistic account of the stakes of the case flatly contradicts the proffered rationale for conceiving of the hairstyle as a legal right: cornrows are the "cultural essence," not of one black *woman*. If this claim is to be taken seriously then cornrows cannot be the cultural essence of only those black women who choose to wear them — they must be the cultural essence of *all* black women. And in this case *all* black women have a stake in the rights claim and the message about them that it will necessarily send — not only those who support the political and cultural statement conveyed by cornrows but also those who oppose that statement.

We'd need a fairly detailed account of the cultural and political stakes of cornrows to have a real sense of the political dimensions of this legal conflict. Does the wearing of cornrows track social class (are most cornrow wearers working class "authentics" or bourgeois trendies?) or ideological splits (nationalist v. integrationist?) within the black community? Do cornrows reflects a sophisticated racial politics in which the essentialist message is subordinate, ambiguous or even ironic or is a crude essentialism a central or indispensable part of the politics of cornrows? Is the symbolism of cornrows widely shared and well understood at least within some subset of American society or is it ambiguous?

Richard T. Ford, Racial Culture: A Critique 24-25 (2005).

Consider also the concern of heightened racial stereotyping in the context of sexual harassment law:

> The combined racial and sexual stereotyping experienced by women of color makes insertion of race into the reasonable woman standard risky. Inserting sexual orientation or class creates similar risks. When a target is not white, middle-class, and heterosexual, decision makers are likely to harbor negative stereotypes about the kind of woman she is. Thus highlighting a woman's race, class, or sexual orientation as well as her gender increases the risk of stereotypes such as "hot" Chicana, "submissive" Asian, "loose" African American, "macho" Lesbian, "trashy" lower-class white.... When the harm suffered is sexual or sexist, it is pragmatic to focus solely on that aspect of a person that is the fulcrum of her injury: gender. Similarly, when the harm suffered is racial harassment, it makes practical sense to focus solely on her race.

Caroline A. Forell & Donna M. Matthews, A Law of Her Own: The Reasonable Woman as a Measure of Man 88 (2000). What are the implications of this concern? See id. at 89 (plaintiff should be able to bring either a racial harassment claim or a sexual harassment claim; a combined claim should require sufficient facts to prove both).

What issues today most significantly divide black and white women? Consider the following:

> Domesticity divides women against themselves. Until feminists acknowledge this dynamic and diffuse it, alliances among women will remain fragile and difficult. Gender wars are not limited to conflicts between employed women and homemakers, for American women are not divided into two dichotomous groups. Instead, they are on a continuum. Some are as work-primary as "high-powered" men; others do no market work. But most American women lie somewhere in the middle, or shift between various points on the continuum at different stages of their lives. These infinite gradations are divisive, as each woman judges women more work-centered than herself as insensitive to their children's needs, and those less work-centered as having "dropped out," or "given up."...
> Gender has always seemed the most important axis of social power for privileged white women because it is the only one that blocks their way, privileged as they are by class and race. This is not to say that the injustice meted out to them is not injustice. It is. But if privileged women want others to join their struggles, they must

re-imagine themselves in ways that take into account the perspective their proposed allies.

Joan Williams, Implementing Anti-essentialism: How Gender Wars Turn into Race and Class Conflict, 15 Harv. Blackletter L.J. 41, 43, 51 (1999). See also Dorothy E. Roberts, Spiritual and Menial Housework, 9 Yale J.L. & Feminism 51, 59 (1997) (describing "[t]he dichotomy between spiritual and menial house-work" which "is inextricably connected to a racial division between domestic laborers, a division that has survived dramatic changes in women's relationship to the market"). The Roberts piece is excerpted on p. 233.

The literature on intersectionality analysis is extensive. For a few representa-tive examples, see Judy Scales-Trent, Black Women and the Constitution: Finding Our Place, Asserting Our Rights, 24 Harv. C.R.-C.L. L. Rev. 9 (1989) (arguing that black women should be viewed as a subset of blacks and afforded strict scrutiny under the Equal Protection Clause); Sumi K. Cho, Converging Stereo-types in Racialized Sexual Harassment: Where the Model Minority Meets Suzie Wong, 1 J. Gender Race & Just. 177 (1997) (focusing on the experience of Asian-Pacific women and describing process of objectification whereby various racia-lized ascriptions affect the nature of sexual harassment against women of different racial groups).

As the basic intersectionality critique has become accepted within feminist legal theory, it has reached increasingly beyond race to include other dimensions of oppression as well, including sexual orientation; some scholars have substituted the term "multidimensionality" for "intersectionality." Examples of this extension include Darren Lenard Hutchinson, Identity Crisis: "Intersection-ality," "Multidimensionality," and the Development of an Adequate Theory of Subordination, 6 Mich. J. Race & L. 285, 309-316 (2001); Francisco Valdes, Beyond Sexual Orientation in Queer Legal Theory: Majoritarianism, Multidi-mensionality, and Responsibility in Social Justice Scholarship or Legal Scholars as Cultural Warriors, 75 Denv. U. L. Rev. 1409, 1415 (1998); Elvia R. Arriola, Gendered Inequality: Lesbians, Gays, and Feminist Legal Theory, 9 Berkeley Women's L.J. 103, 139-141 (1994); Peter Kwan, Complicity and Com-plexity: Cosynthesis and Praxis, 49 DePaul L. Rev. 673, 688 (2000).

3. Intersectionality and the Problem of Categorization. To what extent is the intersetionality critique a problem of all categories? Can categories be eliminated? Consider the following:

> Every person, and perhaps even every object that we encounter in the world, is unique, but to treat each as such would be disastrous. Were we to perceive each object sui generis, we would rapidly be inundated by an unmanageable complexity that would quickly overwhelm our cognitive processing and storage capabilities. Similarly, if our species were "programmed" to refrain from drawing inferences or taking action until we had complete, situation-specific data about each person or object we encountered, we would have died out long ago. To function at all, we must design strategies for simplifying the perceptual environment and acting on less-than-perfect information. A major way we accomplish both goals is by creating categories. As cognitive psychologist Eleanor Rosch wrote in 1977, "Since no

organism can cope with infinite diversity, one of the most basic functions of all organisms is the cutting up of the environment into classifications by which non-identical stimuli can be treated as equivalent." Categories and categorization permit us to identify objects, make predictions about the future, infer the existence of unobservable traits or properties, and attribute the causation of events.

What happens when we group objects into categories? First, we tend to perceive members of the same category as being more similar to each other, and members of different categories as more dissimilar to each other, than when all the objects are viewed in aggregate. The same results adhere when the "objects" we categorize are other human beings.

This should come as no surprise. Categories are guardians against complexity. Their purpose is to simplify the perceptual field by distorting it, so that we experience it as less complex and more predictable than it actually is. Categorical structures can simplify the perceptual environment only if "fuzzy" differences are transformed into clear-cut distinctions. Complexity continually threatens the balance of our categorical structures. Assimilation and enhancement of contrast "guard the guardians." Thus, with object and social categories, one can predict a tendency towards thinking that "all x's are alike."

Second, although some debate exists on this issue, it appears that we create a mental prototype, often visual, of the "typical" category member. To determine whether an item is a member of a particular category, we match the object perceived with the category prototype and determine the "distance" between the two. We experience an object first as a member of its "basic" category — the category most accessible at the moment. Only with additional mental processing do we identify it as a member of its superordinate or subordinate categories. According to this view, we carry in our heads images of the "typical letter a," the "typical chair," the "typical law school professor," and the "typical urban gang member."

Cognitive psychologists refer to these categorical structures as "schemas." . . .

Schemas, like other categorical structures, "enable the perceiver to identify stimuli quickly, . . . fill in information missing from the stimulus configuration, and select a strategy for obtaining further information, solving a problem, or reaching a goal." But the price of this cognitive economy is that categorical structures — whether prototypes, stereotypes, or schemas — bias what we see, how we interpret it, how we encode and store it in memory, and what we remember about it later. In intergroup relations, these biases, mediated through perception, inference, and judgment, can result in discrimination, whether we intend it or not, whether we know it or not.

Linda Hamilton Krieger, The Content of Our Categories, 47 Stan. L. Rev. 1161, 1188-90 (1995).

b. Differences among Men

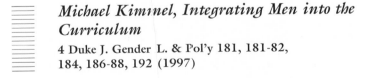

Michael Kimmel, Integrating Men into the Curriculum

4 Duke J. Gender L. & Pol'y 181, 181-82,
184, 186-88, 192 (1997)

There is a general failure to see men, or more accurately masculinity at every level of the educational endeavor — from what is taught, to who the teachers are, to the gender of the students, and to the gender of classroom dynamics. At every moment in the process, men are invisible.

"But wait," you will say, "men are not invisible. They are everywhere!" Quite true. Men are ubiquitous in universities, in professional schools, and in the public sphere in general. Most people would not dispute that men constitute over-whelming majority of corporate executives and CEOs, attorneys and law profes-sors, members of collegiate boards of trustees, and state, local, and national legislators. And of course it is true that in college curricula, every course that does not have the word women in the title is about men. For example, in the social sciences there may be courses called Women in Politics or Psychology of Women, but the courses with more generic titles like Social Change or Public Adminis-tration are courses in which the entire syllabus is organized around men. The course materials, however, focus almost exclusively on men in their public activ-ities: men are discussed as political leaders, military heroes, scientists, writers, artists, and the like. By contrast, when women are discussed at all, the class almost always includes a discussion of femininity, about how the women's experiences as women influenced their experiences in their public activities. Can one imagine a literature course in which the experience of Jane Austen or the Brontes, or a physics course in which the experience of Marie Curie was discussed without a discussion of their lives of women, about how their femininity contributed to, affected, or even determined their work? Can one imagine that same British literature course examining Charles Dickens' or William Thackeray's experience of masculinity, or that physics course examining Albert Einstein's or Sir Isaac Newton's efforts to prove their masculinity? It is in this sense that men themselves are invisible as men. . . . Everywhere one turns, it seems, there are courses on men, but little or no information on masculinity. . . .

Most feminist scholars have properly focused their attention on women, primarily on the "omissions, distorts, and trivializations" of women's experiences, and the spheres to which women have historically been consigned, like private life and the family . . . Now it is time to go a step further to include men as men. . . .

That scholars and students alike remain unaware of the centrality of gender in men's lives only helps to perpetuate inequalities based on gender in American society. This ignorance keeps in place the power of men over women, and the power of some men over other men, both of which are among the central mechanisms of power in our society. . . .

[W]hen gender is acknowledged, writers often endow manhood with a trans-cendental, almost mythic set of properties that still keep it invisible. For example, in the works of Robert Bly, Sam Keen, and other popular authors, manhood becomes an eternal, timeless essence that resides deep in the heart of every man. Manhood is thought of as a thing, a quality that one either has or does not have. Or manhood is considered innate, residing in the particular anatomical organization of the human male, or perhaps, as some transcendent tangible property that each man must manifest in the world, a reward presented with great ceremony to a young novice by his elders for having successfully completed an arduous initiation ritual. . . .

Definitions of masculinity, however, are not the manifestations of some inner essence, nor do they bubble up through biological composition. The search for a

transcendent, timeless definition of manhood is itself a sociological phenomenon — society tends to search for the timeless and eternal during moments of
crises, those points of transition when old definitions no longer work and new
definitions are yet to be firmly established. It is important to think of manhood in
a different way: as a constantly changing collection of meanings that are constructed through relationships with themselves, with other men, and with the
world. A social constructionist perspective understands gender definitions as
neither static nor timeless, but historically articulated within and through people's
interactions with their worlds.

There are four dimensions that comprise this social constructionist perspective on the development of gender ideologies. First, there is a cross-cultural
dimension. . . . Some cultures, like Western culture, encourage manly stoicism
and constant demonstration, while men in other cultures are even more preoc-
cupied with demonstrating sexual prowess than American men. Still other cultures prescribe a more relaxed definition of masculinity based on civic
participation, emotional responsiveness, and the collective provision for the community's needs. . . .

The second dimension of the social constructionist perspective suggests that
masculinity means different things at different times. What it meant to be a man in
the colonial era is quite different from what it means to be an American man
today. . . .

The third dimension of the social constructionist perspective explores the
multiple meanings of manhood in any one society at any one particular time. Not
all American men are the same. Experiences depend, for example, on class, race,
ethnicity, sexuality, age, even region of the country. Each of these axes modify the
others. . . .

The fourth and final dimension of the social constructionist perspective
involves individual development. Masculinity means different things to individual
men as they age and develop. The issues confronting a man about proving himself
and feeling successful, along with the social institutions in which he will attempt
to enact those experiences, all will change throughout his life. . . .

When educators survey their classes, they often work hard to degender
their students. Although many attempt to see their students as equals, they
also attempt to see them as different, to see both equality and difference simultaneously. They may see students with different experiences based on different
life circumstances, but equal in ability, talent, and motivation, and certainly
equal in educational opportunity. However, educators assign papers and
grade exams based on universal criteria that assume each student has had
equal experiences and has had equal access to the tools of the educational
trade. Is such putative equal treatment actually a subtle form of sex discrimination? Can educators continue to grade papers without acknowledging the different experiences students bring to the class? Can papers continue to be graded
as I was taught to grade, by turning the cover page over so as to conceal the
identity of the student? Does the failure to use such abstract and universalizing
criteria render invisible the very experiences of which this article is trying to take
account?

Notes

1. Feminism and Men. A few high-profile books for a popular audience have sympathetically explored issues of masculinity in contemporary social life. See Susan Faludi, Stiffed: The Betrayal of the American Man (2000); Christina Hoff Sommers, The War Against Boys: How Misguided Feminism Is Harming Our Young (2000). Similarly, a few legal theorists have suggested that understanding and combating violence against women necessitates attention to social norms of masculinity. See Katharine K. Baker, Sex, Rape, and Shame, 79 B.U. L. Rev. 663 (1999); Angela P. Harris, Gender, Violence, Race, and Criminal Justice, 52 Stan. L. Rev. 777 (2000).

Does Professor Kimmel ask the right questions? To what extent is the reason to study masculinity because without an understanding of it, women's progress will be limited? To what extent is the point that men, too, should be the beneficiaries of feminism?

Does feminist theory wrongly ignore the distinctive burdens faced by men in a gendered society? Is exploration of societal burdens on heterosexual men a fruitful avenue for feminist theorizing? If so, what are those burdens?

Has feminism encouraged male-bashing? The Roper Organization conducted surveys in 1970 and 1990 in which they asked 3,000 American women and 1,000 American men a set of questions about their perceptions of men. See Roper Organization, Opinions About Men, in The 1990 Virginia Slims Opinion Poll: A 20-Year Perspective of Women's Issues 54 (1990). In the 1970 survey, two-thirds of those questioned agreed that men were basically kind, gentle, and thoughtful. In 1990, only fifty-one percent agreed. In 1970, forty-one percent of those surveyed thought that all men wanted from a date was to go to bed; in 1990, fifty-four percent reached that conclusion. In 1970, thirty-two percent believed that men were basically selfish and self-centered; in 1990, forty-two percent agreed. In 1970, forty-nine percent believed that men's egos require that they put women down; in 1990, fifty-five percent agreed. In 1970, thirty-nine percent believed that men were interested only in their work, and not really interested in their families. By 1990, after two decades of a fatherhood revolution, fifty-three percent of those surveyed believed that men were only interested in their work, a fourteen percent increase. Michael S. Kimmel, Issues for Men in the 1990s, 46 U. Miami L. Rev. 671, 671-672 (1992). Are these shifts in views by women the healthy result of consciousness-raising? Or do they suggest a problematic willingness to blame "men" for complex structural problems? More than a decade later, the survey apparently has not been repeated: if it were, would you expect the same results?

The new "men's movement" may contribute to the sense of "gender war" described by Kimmel and such writers as Susan Faludi. See Faludi, Backlash: The Undeclared War Against American Women (1991). The most prominent spokesman for this movement, Robert Bly, urges that men "retreat from the world of women to temporary male sanctuaries in order to recapture some 'deep' or 'wild' masculinity that has become dormant in today's modern technological society in which women actively participate." Kimmel, supra, at 672, citing Robert Bly, Iron John: A Book About Men 6, 222-237, 244-249 (1990). Is there anything wrong with male "consciousness-raising"? What destructive, or constructive, impact might such a movement have on the role of gender in this society?

2. The Construction of Masculinity. An excellent, recent collection of essays on masculinity as a subject is Handbook of Studies on Men & Masculinities (Michael S. Kimmel et al. eds., 2005). This source contains an essay specifically on masculinity and feminist theory. See Judith Kegan Gardiner, Men, Masculinities, and Feminist Theory, in Handbook of Studies on Men & Masculinities, supra, at 35. Other leading treatments of the subject of masculinity are Michael S. Kimmel, The Gender of Desire: Essays on Male Sexuality (2005); R.W. Connell, The Men and the Boys (2000); R.W. Connell, Masculinities (1995); Lynne Segal, Slow Motion: Changing Masculinity, Changing Men (1990); Michael Kimmel, Manhood in America: A Cultural History (1996).

Is feminist legal theory the place for investigation of masculinity/masculinities? Or is there reason for feminist legal theory to focus only on "women" (with all the definitional problems this entails)? Richard Delgado's fictional character, "Rodrigo Crenshaw," argues:

> [O]ne should never adopt the perspective of the more powerful group, even strategically. Adopting another's perspective is always a mistake. One starts out thinking one can go along with the more numerous, better organized, and more influential group—say, white women in the case of sisters of color—and reap some benefits. You think that you can jump nimbly aside before the inevitable setbacks, disappointments and double crosses set in. But you can't. You will march strongly and determinedly in the wrong direction, alienating yourself in the process. You'll end up having the newly deployed rights cut back in your case, perhaps being criticized as irresponsible when you try to exercise them. Moreover, any small suggestion for deviation in the agenda, any polite request that the larger group consider your own concerns, will bring quick denunciation. You are being divisive. You are weakening the movement.

Richard Delgado, Rodrigo's Sixth Chronicle: Intersections, Essences, and the Dilemma of Social Reform, 68 N.Y.U. L. Rev. 639, 657 (1993). Is this an argument against coalition building? Does it suggest that trying to include men in feminism is not worth the price? If Delgado is correct, to what extent can white women and women of color work together? Is Rodrigo's argument "essentialist" in assuming there are clear distinctions between groups?

3. Men and the Intersection of Gender and Race. Should Black men, like Black women, be considered a separate category of analysis? Black men are disproportionately unemployed in most fields, and those who work are concentrated in low-status, low-paid occupations. Black men also have higher rates of incarceration and substance abuse, and lower rates of college attendance than Black women.

Is the subordinated status of men of color a feminist issue? Floyd Weatherspoon argues that African-American men suffer from a combination of race and gender discrimination both in employment and in the criminal justice system. See Floyd D. Weatherspoon, Remedying Employment Discrimination Against African American Males, 36 Washburn L.J. 23 (1996); Floyd D. Weatherspoon, The Devastating Impact of the Justice System on the Status of African-American Males: An Overview Perspective, 23 Cap. U. L. Rev. 23 (1994). In contrast, Devon Carbado asserts that "[h]eterosexual Black men occupy a privileged victim status in antiracist discourse."

> A central project of antiracist discourse is to reveal the extent to which Black men are victims of a racist criminal justice system. Given the statistics for Black male incarceration and the problems of discrimination in the criminal justice system, this project is undeniably important.
>
> Nevertheless, as a result of this focus on Black men without a similar focus on Black women, Black men are perceived to be significantly more vulnerable and significantly more "endangered" than Black women. Black men become the quintessential example of the effects of racial subordination. . . .
>
> As a consequence of this myth of racial authenticity and the currency of the endangered Black male trope, when an individual Black man is on trial for some criminal offense, the Black community sees first and foremost his status as a racial victim. Furthermore, when the alleged crime involves violence against women, the fact that a Black female or a woman of any race may be the victim of Black male aggression is subordinate to the concern that a Black man may be the victim of a racist criminal justice system.

Devon W. Carbado, Men in Black, 3 J. Gender, Race & Justice 427, 429 (2000); see also Kevin Brown, The Social Construction of a Rape Victim: Stories of African-American Males About the Rape of Desireé Washington, in Black Men on Race, Gender, and Sexuality: A Critical Reader (Devon W. Carbado ed., 1999). Could Weatherspoon and Carbado both be correct? How should feminists conceptualize the relationship between women of color and men of color in a society that is both racist and sexist?

2. The Primacy of Gender and Cultural Pluralism

Martinez v. Santa Clara Pueblo

402 F. Supp. 5 (D.N.M. 1975), rev'd and remanded, 540 F.2d 1039 (10th Cir. 1976), rev'd, 436 U.S. 49 (1978)

MECHEM, District Judge.

Julia Martinez and her daughter Audrey Martinez bring this suit, each individually and as the representative of a class, against the Santa Clara Pueblo and Governor Lucario Padilla, individually and in his capacity as governor of the Pueblo. Plaintiffs claim that a portion of a tribal ordinance which denies Pueblo membership to the children of female but not male members of the Pueblo who marry non-members of the Pueblo, violates 25 U.S.C. §1302(8), which prohibits a tribal government in the exercise of its powers of self-government from denying "to any persons within its jurisdiction the equal protection of its

laws or depriv(ing) any person of liberty or property without due process of law."
Plaintiffs seek an injunction against the further enforcement of the ordinance.

[25 U.S.C. § 1302, the Indian Civil Rights Act, was enacted by Congress
in 1968. The purpose of the Act was to "single out the more important civil
rights contained in the Constitution and to render those applicable to tribal
members who reside on the reservation," Martinez v. Santa Clara Pueblo, 540
F.2d 1039, 1042 (1976). Congress made some effort to square these new
rights with existing tribal law and custom; for example, the Fifteenth Amendment and the nonestablishment clause of the First Amendment were omitted
from the Act. Moreover, courts have held that the requirements of the ICRA
are not necessarily coextensive with the requirements of the U.S. Constitution.
Nevertheless, many Indian nations, including the Pueblo, were opposed to the
ICRA, seeing it as an effort to undermine tribal law. Martinez v. Santa Clara
Pueblo, 540 F.2d at 1045.]

The ordinance, passed in 1939, reads as follows: . . .

(1) All children born of marriage between members of the Santa Clara
Pueblo shall be members of the Santa Clara Pueblo.
(2) All children born of marriage between male members of the Santa Clara
Pueblo and non-members shall be members of the Santa Clara Pueblo.
(3) Children born of marriage between female members of the Santa Clara
Pueblo and non-members shall not be members of the Santa Clara
Pueblo.
(4) Persons shall not be naturalized as members of the Santa Clara Pueblo
under any circumstances.

Plaintiffs attack subparts two and three of the ordinance. . . .

The social and political organization of the Pueblo must be discussed first.
Santa Clara Pueblo was founded around 1300 A.D. The Pueblo now covers
roughly 48,000 acres, held by the United States in trust for the
Pueblo. Approximately 1,200 recognized members and between 150 and 200
non-members currently live on the Pueblo. Approximately 150 recognized members live elsewhere, one-third of them in other locations in New Mexico, and the
rest scattered across twenty-two different states.

In its early days, Santa Clara culture made no distinction between what
Anglo-Americans would term "political" and "religious" matters. However,
with the Spanish invasion in the early seventeenth century, the Pueblo instituted a "secular" government to distract Spanish attention from the caciques
(religious leaders) who were the real authorities in the Pueblo. The distinction
between religious and secular spheres is now well established in the Santa Clara
culture.

The membership of the Pueblo is and has been organized into what the
anthropologists refer to as "moieties," specifically the Winter people and the
Summer people. Each moiety is led by a cacique; and each is further divided
into factions. The precise function and significance of moiety membership is
not clear on the record; it is, however, clear that it is primarily a religious group-
ing. The caciques are still the dominant authorities in the Pueblo, nominating the

candidates for secular office and exercising an effective veto by influence over the actions of the secular government.

The division of the moieties into factions is a relatively recent development.... As reorganized [in 1935] the secular government retained many of its traditional institutions, such as the unity of the legislative and "appellate" judicial functions in the Council, while at the same time incorporating and instituting certain Anglo-American institutions, principally voting for secular officials. Thus, the present Pueblo government is neither wholly traditional nor wholly anglicized.

Under the Constitution and By-Laws there is a single governing body, the Council, which possesses both legislative and "appellate" judicial powers.... The Council consists of the secular officers of the Pueblo—the Governor, the Lieutenant Governor, the Secretary, the Treasurer, the Interpreter, and the Sheriff—and eight representatives.... As a matter of custom and practice, the representatives represent the factions, which still exist.

The Governor is the chief executive of the Pueblo charged with enforcing the law "civil and criminal, written and unwritten."... In addition he appears to have the initial responsibility for settling controversies among and concerning the members of the Pueblo. A person aggrieved by a ruling of the Governor may appeal to the Council, at which time the Governor may vote only to break a tie....

All other secular governmental power and responsibility is vested in the Council, including the power to enact ordinances governing Pueblo life.... Most important for the present case, the Constitution specifically grants the Council the power to determine which children of mixed marriages shall be recognized as members of the Pueblo,... and to determine who is a member for purposes of dealings in land and land use rights.... The 1939 Ordinance was enacted by the Council pursuant to these powers, and is agreed by all parties to be in force at this time.

The factual development of the equal protection claims of the parties is best begun by identifying the interests of plaintiffs and defendants affected or served by the Ordinance....

Audrey Martinez is the daughter of the marriage of plaintiff Julia Martinez, a recognized member of the Pueblo and Myles Martinez, a non-member of the Pueblo. It is undisputed that the 1939 Ordinance bars recognition of Audrey as a member of the Pueblo. If Myles were a member of the Pueblo and Julia Martinez were not—or if Julia were not married, and Audrey had been born out of wedlock, the Ordinance would not bar her recognition as a member and the Council would in fact so recognize her.

Julia Martinez has lived at the Pueblo all her life, with the exception of a relatively brief absence to further her education. Myles Martinez has lived at the Pueblo ever since his marriage to Julia, with the exception of a relatively brief absence while serving in the armed forces. Audrey Martinez grew up on the Pueblo, although she does leave to pursue her education. Aside from the fact that she is not recognized as a member of the Pueblo and is therefore denied certain rights, she has been raised in the culture of Santa Clara, speaks Tewa, the traditional language, and clearly considers herself to be a Santa Claran.

As a factual matter, recognition as a member of the Pueblo would give Audrey Martinez three distinct types of rights which she is presently denied. First, she would gain political rights, primarily the right to vote, to take matters before the Pueblo Council, and the qualification to hold office as a secular official.

Secondly, she would be entitled to share in the material benefits of Pueblo membership. The most important of the material benefits is that referred to as land use rights. . . . Other material benefits and privileges include the right to hunt and fish on the land, the use of irrigation water, and an equal share in any distribution of pecuniary benefits made by the Pueblo, or any other programs, present or future, undertaken by the Pueblo for the benefit of its members.

Third, as members, Audrey and other children similarly situated would as of right be able to continue living at the Pueblo. While it is true that the Martinez family and a number of other families in their position live at the Pueblo, this is not as a matter of right. If and when Mrs. Martinez dies, the rest of the family, as non-members would not have the right to continue living on the Pueblo, though it is not now known whether they would be forced to leave. Furthermore, under the Santa Clara Constitution, . . . non-members and only non-members may be expelled from the Pueblo for violating a Pueblo Ordinance.

Lack of membership does not now affect entitlement to federal benefits accorded Indians generally, or participation in the religious life of the Pueblo. In 1968, Mr. and Mrs. Martinez obtained BIA census numbers for their children, and since then the children have received all federal benefits generally available to Indians, including educational and medical benefits. As to religion, Audrey Martinez is already allowed to participate in Pueblo religious ceremonies to the same extent that she would be if she were a recognized member of the Pueblo. Thus, the question presented is one of membership in the Pueblo for purposes of purely internal, secular rights and privileges. . . .

In addition to these relatively precise and legally protectible interests, Julia and Audrey Martinez and many of those similarly situated share a strong emotional involvement with the Pueblo. Regardless of official definitions of membership, Julia Martinez feels that her children, having grown up in Santa Clara, should be recognized as Santa Clarans. Audrey Martinez, despite official definitions, clearly considers herself to be a Santa Clara Indian. While the law may not recognize or protect these interests, it would be foolish to pretend that they do not exist.

While the factual context of the legal claims made by Audrey and Julia Martinez differs, it is clear that both ultimately present the same legal question — whether the 1939 Ordinance violates their rights to equal protection of tribal laws, as secured to them by the Indian Civil Rights Act, 25 U.S.C. §1302(8).

The specific interests of the Pueblo in membership policies generally and in the particular policy of the 1939 Ordinance are of concern as well. Since 1680 the Pueblo has existed as a conquered people, identifiable as a group but surrounded by an alien culture, first Spanish and later American. From a practical political standpoint, the result has been a tension in the life of the Pueblo between traditional Pueblo customs and values and the "modern" customs and values of

Anglo-American society. As noted above, this tension was once so acute that the Pueblo became divided against itself. The differences were eventually resolved by the adoption of the Constitution, which drew upon both traditional Pueblo and modern Anglo-American institutions, synthesizing them into a unique structure neither wholly traditional nor wholly modern.

The function of membership policies must be examined within this context. . . . [Membership policies] are no more or less than a mechanism of social, and to an extent psychological and cultural, self-definition. The importance of this to Santa Clara or to any other Indian tribe cannot be overstressed. In deciding who is and who is not a member, the Pueblo decides what it is that makes its members unique, what distinguishes a Santa Clara Indian from everyone else in the United States. If its ability to do this is limited or restricted by an external authority, then a new definition of what it is to be a Santa Claran is imposed, and the culture of Santa Clara is inevitably changed.

The second major interest served by membership policies, and by the particular policy of the 1939 Ordinance, is that of economic survival of the tribal unit. As plaintiffs have demonstrated, the adoption of the 1939 Ordinance was in response to a sudden increase in mixed marriages, which had resulted in a proportionate strain on the economic resources of the Pueblo. Plaintiffs argue that economic integrity of the Pueblo is less important than cultural autonomy. The difficulty with this position is that the two are not easily separable. The ability of the Pueblo to control the use and distribution of its resources enhances its ability to maintain its cultural autonomy.

Plaintiffs do not challenge the power of the Pueblo, as delegated to and exercised by the Council, to make and enforce rules concerning membership. Their attack on the Ordinance is solely aimed at the criteria employed as to children of mixed marriages.

At trial the defendants sought to prove that the Ordinance was merely the written embodiment of ancient custom. . . . Before 1939 mixed marriages were relatively rare in the Pueblo, and consequently there was no need for a hard and fast rule concerning membership; rather, the Council considered each case separately. In that sense, the establishment of any one rule must be seen as a break with tradition.

On the other hand, the criteria employed in classifying children of mixed marriages as members or non-members are rooted in certain traditional values. It appears that Santa Clara was traditionally patrilineal and patrilocal — in other words, that kinship, name and location of residence generally were expected to follow the male rather than the female line. These cultural expectations have lost much of their force, but they are not entirely vitiated. . . . Furthermore, it is apparent that membership of the parents and marriage, either within or out of the Pueblo, has always been considered a highly significant factor in membership determinations as opposed to other possible criteria such as degree of Santa Clara ancestry. When a member of the Pueblo married a non-member, the status of children of the marriage was questionable. Consonant with this, children born to an unmarried Santa Clara woman traditionally have been and still are recognized as members, regardless of who the father is or might be. . . .

Plaintiffs do not suggest that the Indian Civil Rights Act should be interpreted in a manner which would impose an Anglo-American equal protection standard on tribes in derogation of their traditional values. To the contrary, they have consistently argued, as have the defendants, that the Act should be interpreted in such a manner as to preserve the cultural identity of Indian tribes in general and of Santa Clara in particular. Plaintiffs instead point out that the sex of the parent who is a member of the Pueblo bears little or no relationship to the strength of the parent's identification with traditional Santa Clara culture or the likelihood that the parent will attempt to pass the traditional cultural values on to the child. They point out, quite correctly, that Audrey Martinez and many other children similarly situated have been brought up on the Pueblo, speak the Tewa language, participate in its life, and are, culturally, for all practical purposes, Santa Clara Indians. On the other hand, there are certainly instances of children whose fathers are members of Santa Clara, but who have been raised far from the Pueblo, who cannot speak the language, who have not participated in the life of the Pueblo, and who know nothing of its values, customs and traditions, yet who are, under the 1939 Ordinance, recognized as members. Plaintiffs contend that this is not only irrational but actively destructive of the cultural identity of the Pueblo.

Even assuming plaintiffs are correct, the equal protection guarantee of the Indian Civil Rights Act should not be construed in a manner which would require or authorize this Court to determine which traditional values will promote cultural survival and therefore should be preserved and which of them are inimical to cultural survival and should therefore be abrogated. Such a determination should be made by the people of Santa Clara; not only because they can best decide what values are important, but also because they must live with the decision every day. . . .

Much has been written about tribal sovereignty. If those words have any meaning at all, they must mean that a tribe can make and enforce its decisions without regard to whether an external authority considers those decisions wise. To abrogate tribal decisions, particularly in the delicate area of membership, for whatever "good" reasons, is to destroy cultural identity under the guise of saving it. Congress has not indicated that it intended the Indian Civil Rights Act to be interpreted in such a manner.

In Re Fauziya Kasinga

U.S. Department of Justice Board of
Immigration Appeals File A73 476 695 (1996)

The applicant is a 19-year-old native and citizen of Togo. She attended 2 years of high school. She is a member of the Tchamba-Kunsuntu Tribe of northern Togo. She testified that young women of her tribe normally undergo ["female genital mutilation," abbreviated throughout as FGM] at age 15. However, she did not because she initially was protected from FGM by her influential, but now deceased, father.

The applicant stated that upon her father's death in 1993, under tribal custom her aunt, her father's sister, became the primary authority figure in the family.

The applicant's mother was driven from the family home, left Togo, and went to live with her family in Benin. The applicant testified that she does not currently know her mother's exact whereabouts.

The applicant further testified that her aunt forced her into a polygamous marriage in October 1994, when she was 17. The husband selected by her aunt was 45 years old and had three other wives at the time of marriage. The applicant testified that, under tribal custom, her aunt and her husband planned to force her to submit to FGM before the marriage was consummated.

The applicant testified that she feared imminent mutilation. With the help of her older sister, she fled Togo for Ghana. However, she was afraid that her aunt and her husband would locate her there. . . .

The applicant did not attempt a fraudulent entry into the United States. Rather, upon arrival at Newark International Airport on December 17, 1994, she immediately requested asylum. She remained in detention by the Immigration and Naturalization Service ("INS") until April 1996.

The applicant testified that the Togolese police and the Government of Togo were aware of FGM and would take no steps to protect her from the practice. She further testified that her aunt had reported her to the Togolese police. Upon return, she would be taken back to her husband by the police and forced to undergo FGM. She testified at several points that there would be nobody to protect her from FGM in Togo. . . .

According to the applicant's testimony, the FGM practiced by her tribe, the Tchamba-Kunsuntu, is of an extreme type involving cutting the genitalia with knives, extensive bleeding, and a 40-day recovery period. The background materials confirm that the FGM practiced in some African countries, such as Togo, is of an extreme nature causing permanent damage, and not just a minor form of genital ritual.

The record material establishes that FGM in its extreme forms is a practice in which portions of the female genitalia are cut away. In some cases, the vagina is sutured partially closed. This practice clearly inflicts harm or suffering upon the girl or woman who undergoes it.

FGM is extremely painful and at least temporarily incapacitating. It permanently disfigures the female genitalia. FGM exposes the girl or woman to the risk of serious, potentially life-threatening complications. These include, among others, bleeding, infection, urine retention, stress, shock, psychological trauma, and damage to the urethra and anus. It can result in permanent loss of genital sensation and can adversely affect sexual and erotic functions. . . .

The record also contains two reports compiled by the United States Department of State. The first of these, dated January 31, 1994, 1) confirms that FGM is practiced by some ethnic groups in Togo; 2) notes that while some reports indicate that the practice may be diminishing, an expert indicates that as many as 50% of Togolese females may have been mutilated; and 3) notes that various acts of violence against women occur in Togo with little police intervention.

[Section 101(a)(42)(A) of the Immigration and Nationality Act, 8 U.S.C. sec. 1101(a)(42)(A) (1994), defines a "refugee" eligible for asylum as any person "who is outside any country of such person's nationality . . . and who is unable or unwilling to return to, and is unable or unwilling to avail himself or herself of the protection of, that country because of . . . a well-founded fear of persecution on account of race, religion, nationality, membership in a particular social group, or political opinion."] . . . We agree with the parties that this level of harm can constitute "persecution" within the meaning of section 101(a)(42)(A) of the Act. . . .

In the context of this case, we find the particular social group to be the following: young women of the Tchamba-Kunsuntu Tribe who have not had FGM, as practiced by that tribe, and who oppose the practice. . . . In accordance with [precedent], the particular social group is defined by common characteristics that members of the group either cannot change, or should not be required to change because such characteristics are fundamental to their individual identities. The characteristics of being a "young woman" and a "member of the Tchamba-Kunsuntu Tribe" cannot be changed. The characteristic of having intact genitalia is one that is so fundamental to the individual identity of a young woman that she should not be required to change it. . . .

Both parties have advanced, and the background materials support, the proposition that there is no legitimate reason for FGM. Group Exhibit 4 contains materials showing that the practice has been condemned by such groups as the United Nations, the International Federation of Gynecology and Obstetrics, the Council on Scientific Affairs, the World Health Organization, the International Medical Association, and the American Medical Association.

Record materials state that FGM "has been used to control woman's sexuality." It also is characterized as a form of "sexual oppression" that is "based on the manipulation of women's sexuality in order to assure male dominance and exploitation. During oral argument before us, the INS General Counsel agreed with the latter characterization. He also stated that the practice is a "severely bodily invasion" that should be regarded as meeting the asylum standard even if done with "subjectively benign intent."

We agree with the parties that, as described and documented in this record, FGM is practiced, at least in some significant part, to overcome sexual characteristics of young women of the tribe who have not been, and do not wish to be, subjected to FGM. We therefore find that the persecution the applicant fears in Togo [is] "on account of" her status as a member of the defined group.

The INS suggests, in its brief and at oral argument, that a remand is necessary because the applicant has not established that she would be unable to avoid FGM by moving to some other part of Togo. As we found in Part I of our opinion, the applicant presented credible testimony that her husband is a well-known individual who is a friend of the police in Togo. She testified that her aunt and her husband were looking for her and that there could be no refuge for her because Togo is a small country and the police would not protect her.

The applicant's testimony is consistent with the background information in the record. That information confirms that 1) FGM is widely practiced in Togo; 2) acts of violence and abuse against women in Togo are tolerated by the police;

3) the Government of Togo has a poor human rights record; and 4) most African women can expect little governmental protection from FGM. We also take notice that Togo is a small country of approximately 22,000 square miles, slightly smaller than West Virginia. . . .

We have weighed the favorable and adverse factors and are satisfied that discretion should be exercised in favor of the applicant. Therefore, we will grant asylum to the applicant.

L. Amede Obiora, Bridges and Barricades: Rethinking Polemics and Intransigence in the Campaign Against Female Circumcision

47 Case W. Res. L. Rev. 275, 288-290, 295-299, 316-317, 329 (1997)

Genital scarification and reconstruction are time-honored and worldwide practices. As extant cultural traditions, the practices are particularly prevalent in Africa where they are reported to occur in about twenty-six countries; the exact number of women affected is unknown, but it is estimated between 80 and 110 million. Within the African context, the age at which it is performed varies between localities and it is possible to distinguish at least four major forms of incidence. The ritualized marking of female genitalia begins with the mildest forms of the procedures, where the clitoris is barely nicked or pricked to shed a few drops of blood. This procedure is innocuous and has a strictly symbolic connotation.

The next range of surgeries extend to the removal of the clitoral prepuce, hood, or outer skin. This is the form that ritual Muslims refer to as sunna, and medical data indicates that it poses minimal health risks if scientifically performed and monitored. Sunna is most comparable to male circumcision and there is some suggestion that it may serve the purpose of hygiene and cleanliness. A more radical form of female genital surgeries is known as excision or clitoridectomy. In this procedure, the clitoral glans and some of the nympha or labia minora, the narrow lip-like enclosures of the genital anatomy, are severed. The most extreme form of the surgeries is called infibulation, and it has been identified as the form that presents the most significant risks and hazards. This procedure entails scraping the labia majora, the two rounded folds of tissue that contour the external boundaries of the vulva, and stitching the remaining raw edges together in a manner that ensures that only a tiny opening will be left after the surgery heals.

The debate over the nomenclature of African genital surgeries reveals that Western-biased themes of bodily "integrity" and tightly bounded individuality tend to confuse and distort the issue. Several critics quarrel with the term "female circumcision," insisting that it is a misnomer for the more extensive practices of clitoridectomy and infibulation. Pontificating that any irreversible removal or a healthy organ or tissue is inherently mutilative, many of these critics maintain that "female genital mutilation" is the only appropriate characterization. Mary Daly, caught in a hyperbole of monocultural indignation, even goes so far as claiming that the varied surgeries all share the "common (slashing and mutilating) features of contemporary gang rape."

Describing a vital aspect of African cultural identity as "mutilation" has proven offensive, if not psychically mutilating, to critical African constituencies like the Premier Group des Femmes d'Afrique who prefer to employ the term "female circumcision."...

Female circumcision is embedded in an intricate web of habits, attitudes, and values, along with having both functional and symbolic connotations. In Africa, the practice is validated and undergirded by a wide spectrum of principles, in addition to temporal and spiritual beliefs. Recurring themes such as sexuality and fertility express preeminent indigenous values like solidarity among women, public recognition of lifecycle change, and procreation for social continuity. Some of these themes are not peculiar to cultures that practice circumcision. Adherence to rites of passage, for example, is an abiding phenomenon in the West.

[Obiora surveys a number of different symbolic meanings for female circumcision in different tribes, including circumcision as a test of courage; as a symbolic linking with tribal history; as a means of making the body symbolically fertile; as a sacrifice to a fertility deity; as a rite of purification; as a means of sex differentiation; as an aesthetic practice; as a symbol of individual identity; as a kind of cosmetic surgery akin to ear piercing; as a contraceptive device; as a means of inaugurating a girl into sexual womanhood; and finally as a way to discourage premarital sex. Obiora argues that it is this last function of female circumcision that Western critics have focused on to the exclusion of its other meanings and functions. She notes that female circumcision in the nineteenth-century West was primarily practiced for the control of female sexuality, and she suggests that Western observers therefore read their own cultural history onto the practice of female circumcision. Obiora also argues that Western academics tend to treat African people as lacking in agency, compelled by their "cultures" to behave in certain ways.]

Female circumcision, as it is conducted both in Africa and by African immigrants under foreign jurisdictions, has complicated several commonplace assumptions about social structure and agency. There is some indication that communitarian African social structures may not have the causal determinacy that gender relations and sexual stratification studies may suggest. Instead of being subject to a monolithic regime of patriarchs, it may well be that African women resort to female circumcision to recreate notions of womanhood adept for their peculiar conditions of existence. The world they know — with its intricate networks of kin relations, the accentuation of the dead and the unborn in their world views, the nature of production under dispersed and low technological infrastructure, the frailty of their ecological circumstances, the burdens of their structural incorporation into the global order — is not readily amenable to the conceptualization of polemic gender identity and politics.

The regrettable focus on determinism explains the inclination of some radical feminists to discount or marginalize the perspectives of African women who they perceive as merely condoning female circumcision. The failure to acknowledge and engage these women in dialogue does not extinguish their force or constituencies, constituencies that are equipped to foment subversive challenges to radical reform proposals. Interestingly enough, most studies on female circumcision seldom articulate personal discontent by its "victims." Instead, they tacitly or expressly convey a recalcitrance uncanny for victims of dismal abuse. Although attitudes regarding the practice appear to be gradually changing, some suggest that there has been no significant decline in the practice. It is certain that while academics and activists continue to wax eloquent at national and international forums about containment strategies, those directly affected by the issue remain faithful to their traditional obligation to circumcise. . . .

Through the years in Africa, outside interventionists, whether colonialist or missionary (and now feminist), continue to presume that it is their duty as the "advanced" to elevate and enlighten the "backward." It is characteristic of these interventionists to pay scant attention to crucial issues including the wishes and opinions of the supposed beneficiaries of their benevolence, the overall implications of intervention, and the possibility of more "benign" intervention. Not surprisingly, their campaigns, often couched in terms of virtual monopoly on good judgment, are perceived as unduly ethnocentric and presumptuous. Such campaigns conform to patterns and habits that have historically provoked righteous indignation and engendered cultural resistance to Western "missionary" exploits. Moreover, they tend to pre-judge and alienate the only forces — women, the "victims" and perpetrators — capable of facilitating or subverting meaningful change.

Leti Volpp, Feminism Versus Multiculturalism
101 Colum. L. Rev. 1181, 1204-1211, 1214-1216 (2001)

Society's excessive focus on minority and Third World sex-subordinating cultural practices has four detrimental effects. . . .

First, in concealing structural forces that shape cultural practices, what can be erased are forces that make culture. Specific cultural practices are connected to forces that deny women economic and political agency. These forces include global inequalities; new articulations of patriarchies in specific regions that are, for example, the result of emerging religious fundamentalisms; the legacies of colonialism and racism; and the flows of transnational capital. Our culture is not constructed within "hermetically sealed" boxes that travel with us from cradle to grave. While culture is often represented as the product of timeless ritual insular to particular communities, such forces profoundly shape culture.

As an example, the historical practice of sati — immolation of a widow on her husband's funeral pyre — is consistently singled-out as an expression of Indian culture or Hindu religion, and is often described as caused by religious and wifely devotion. But sati was not constituted as a practice through "Indian culture" or "Hindu religion" alone. Feminist theorist Lata Mani has examined how the "tradition" of sati was constructed through the collaboration of British colonial officials and Hindu pundits who attempted to find a religious basis for the practice as the colonial government sought to determine the appropriate legislative response. Officials and missionaries constructed such a basis by ignoring and marginalizing anything that did not accord with their presumptions. In individual descriptions of sati, even while European observers wrote of "wifely devotion" and a super-stitious and barbarous religion, nothing in the widows' explanations pointed to a religious basis for sati. Instead, their explanations consisted of concerns for future subsistence and financial support, concerns that were explicitly material and social. However, with the involvement of the British colonial government, reli-gion and culture were given the force of explanation, obscuring material reasons for the practice. Sati continues to be so understood, and in fact, is very often utilized in philosophical discourse to represent extreme cultural difference. . . .

As another example, amid the concern about gender apartheid under the Taliban, there has been little focus on the relationship between the intensification of religious fundamentalism and geopolitical economics. The United States gave aid to various mujahideen forces in Afghanistan to fight the Soviets. From these mujahideen groups, the Taliban emerged. The United States aided General Zia of Pakistan — whose government adopted the notorious hudood ordinances that among other provisions criminalized extramarital sex, so that women who accuse men of rape or become pregnant risk punishment for adultery — for the same reason. Feminists in the United States need to think critically about the relation-ship of this aid to states with policies inimical to women's concerns, instead of abstractly condemning Islam as the font of patriarchal oppression. At the same time, it is crucial for feminists to examine the importance of Christian funda-mentalism within the United States and its effect on the lives of millions of women around the world through funding and development that structure reproductive practices and politics. Such an examination would lead to a more nuanced analysis of differential birth rates in the global North and South than afforded by the often cited explanation that birth rates are the product of differ-ing cultural valuations about the worth of male children.

The second point is that the extreme focus on what is commonly concep-tualized as cultural violence or subordination makes it difficult to see forces beyond culture. There are other important social, political, and economic issues affecting women's lives other than the cultural practices that garner so much attention. . . . . The issues affecting immigrant or Third World women that receive the greatest attention are those that appear most easily identifiable as concerns to relatively privileged women in the West. These concerns include violations that threaten the freedom of movement, freedom of dress, freedom of bodily integrity, and freedom of control over one's sexuality, rather than violations of the right to shelter or basic sustenance. Thus, self-conception, in terms of what one fears for oneself, may play a role in generating concern about specific violations of women's rights. . . .

The insistent focus on immigrant and Third World women as victims also leads many to deny the existence of agency within patriarchy, ignoring that these women are capable of emancipatory change on their own behalf. The binary assumption that women in the West have choice, and that those in immigrant and Third World contexts have none, in part reflects the limits of our language in describing choice: Either one is an agent, or one is a victim. This binary also reflects historical representations of the West as the site of rugged individualism, and the East as the repository of passivity and culture. Furthermore, it reflects a legacy of feminist politics and theory that presents Third World women as bound by culture, as described above. This conceptualization has bled into discourses that can deny the subjectivity of immigrant and Third World women, both in terms of feminist empowerment and in terms of their enjoyment of pleasure.

A fourth effect of this intense focus on other women's sexist cultures is that it obscures violence at home, namely specific practices of violence against women within the United States, including those perpetrated by the state....

By accepting the contention that their lives are superior to the lives of women from "other" cultures, the attention of many women is diverted from the fact that they continue to be subordinate to men within their own culture....

It does not seem coincidental that the way some feminists have depicted gender oppression in immigrant and Third World communities reflects a failure to think about how women's concerns in those communities might implicate their own identities. There is a strong desire for innocence in many strands of feminist politics, supported by the definition of the essential female identity of woman as victim of male violence. But an individual can be subordinated in one social relation and dominant in another. There is an ease with which one slips into a position of subordination, for example, as a woman subject to the discrimination of the glass ceiling, without seeing how this very subordinate location may simultaneously reflect privilege, for example, as one that relies on domestic labor and child care by immigrant women of color. The missionary impulse to save immigrant and Third World women from their subordination is rarely turned to uplift domestic workers from exploitative work situations. The repressive cultures of these women, on the other hand, are a subject of feminist concerns. Thus, women in the First World can feel as though they have autonomy and agency in contrast to women in the Third World, at the same time that they feel victimized by men in the First, but will not conceptualize themselves to be agents of subordinating practices. This absolution of responsibility rests on the assumption that relations between women are presumed to be non-oppressive, whereas the bonds of race are presumed to oppress women of color. But this ignores the oppression of race and class among women. While to some extent this is understood in the context of the domestic politics of the United States, the innocence of the category "woman" seems to have been repackaged in the wrapping of the discourses of feminism versus multiculturalism and transnational women's rights.

A missionary feminist effort assuming West is Best incurs a defensive reaction from members of criticized communities, and thus plays into the hands of those who choose to defend sex subordinating behavior in the name of cultural nationalism. The cultural nationalist response to imperialist descriptions of other women functions as a problematic mirror image. Resistance becomes configured as the necessity of preserving culture, leading to the freezing of particular identifications of culture, which keeps women trapped within the binary logic. Blanket condemnation is less helpful in engendering dialogue than acknowledging that women in the West also have a problem with epidemic rates of male violence against women, sharing strategies that have been attempted to combat this violence, and asking how immigrant and Third World women are grappling with violence in their own communities. And beyond the mere equivalence of universal gender subordination, we also must understand and confront how gender subordination is related to other forces of subordination — including racism and transnational economic inequalities. This means paying attention to context, to the meaning of difference, and to global disparities of power....

═══
Madhavi Sunder, Piercing the Veil
112 Yale L.J. 1399, 1401-05 (2003)

The failure of the international community to intervene in Afghanistan prior to September 11th was more than a failure of politics. It was also a failure of law. To put it bluntly, human rights law has a problem with religion. In a postmodern world in which the nation-state has been deconstructed and eighteenth- and nineteenth-century notions of unmediated national sovereignty have been properly put to rest, religion—and its attendant category, culture—represent the New Sovereignty. Human rights abuses that since World War II are no longer acceptable when committed by states are paradoxically tolerated when justified in the name of religion or culture. September 11th crystallized this fact. The infamous Taliban regime in Afghanistan assumed power in 1996 and immediately began stripping women of fundamental human rights to education, healthcare, work, and movement. But war, not law, defeated what has been described as the world's most ruthless fundamentalist regime. For all its pomp and circumstance, international human rights had little to do with it.

Current scholarship posits an inherent conflict between women's rights and culture. But...religion qua religion is less the problem than is our traditional legal construction of this category. Premised on a centuries-old, Enlightenment compromise that justified reason in the public sphere by allowing deference to religious despotism in the private, human rights law continues to define religion in the twenty-first century as a sovereign, extralegal jurisdiction in which inequality is not only accepted, but expected. Law views religion as natural, irrational, incontestable, and imposed—in contrast to the public sphere, the only viable space for freedom and reason. Simply put, religion is the "other" of international law.

Today, fundamentalists are taking advantage of this legal tradition. Yet, contrary to law's centuries-old conception, religious communities are internally contested, heterogeneous, and constantly evolving over time through internal debate and interaction with outsiders. And this has never been so true as in the twenty-first century. Individuals in the modern world increasingly demand change within their religious communities in order to bring their faith in line with democratic norms and practices. Call this the New Enlightenment: Today, individuals seek reason, equality, and liberty not just in the public sphere, but also in the private spheres of religion, culture, and family. Current law, however, elides these claims for modernization. Failing to recognize cultural and religious communities as contested and subject to change, legal norms such as the "freedom of religion," the "right to culture," and the guarantee of "self-determination" defer to the claims of patriarchal, religious elites, buttressing their power over the claims of modernizers. Paradoxically, law's failure to question or revisit its old Enlightenment views is obstructing the emergence of the New Enlightenment. In short, human rights law, not religion, is the problem.

But on the ground, women's human rights activists are piercing the veil of religious sovereignty. [There is] a growing disconnect between human rights law and human rights practice. [A] close study of women's human rights activists working in Muslim communities and countries...demonstrates that, despite law's formal refusal to acknowledge claims of internal dissent, women are nonetheless claiming their rights to challenge religious and cultural authorities and to imagine religious community on more egalitarian and democratic terms. Just as we "pierce the veil" of corporate sovereignty in cases of injustice or fraud, women activists are asserting a right to confront oppressive laws and practices otherwise legally shielded in the name of religion.

Scholars have failed to recognize the full significance of these efforts. By insisting, in the words of President George W. Bush, "if you're not with us, you're against us," scholars celebrate campaigns for women's rights in Muslim communities for their similarities to Western women's rights movements, but elide what is different in these claims. In fact, these campaigns present powerful critiques of current law, which offers women a right to religious freedom (on leaders' terms) or to equality (within the public sphere), but no right to both. Envisioning a third way, women human rights activists in Muslim communities are pursuing equality and freedom within the context of religion, not just without it.

We ignore these activists at our peril. In an era of rising fundamentalism in which women's — and men's — lives are increasingly governed by private, not public, laws, securing human rights requires deconstructing religion and culture. As the anthropologist Lila Abu-Lughod writes, "We have become politicized about race and class, but not culture." [Abu-Lughod, Do Muslim Women Really Need Saving? Anthropological Reflections on Cultural Relativism and Its Others, 104 Am. Anthropologist 783, 789 (2002).] The same can be said — perhaps more forcefully — about religion, which law's Enlightenment origins have encouraged us to fear and to worship. Unmasking the politics and mutability of religion that traditional legal narratives have concealed, we must identify that part of religion that is a human or legal construction and thus requires justification and accountability....

This is nothing less than a question of life or death. In Pakistan last summer, a mentally disturbed young man was stoned to death for alleged blasphemy, and a tribal council ordered that a young woman be raped as revenge for a crime allegedly committed by her brother — all on the basis of traditional Islamic Shari'a law. In Nigeria, another woman, Amina Lawal, awaits her fate after an appeals court in that country upheld a Shari'a court's ruling that Lawal be stoned to death because she gave birth to a child outside of marriage. Nigeria's Supreme Court may ultimately decide the case. But as it currently stands, there is no legal theory — either under Nigerian national law or international human rights law — for overturning the pronouncements of a religious court.

In such cases, law's conception of religion and culture matters. So long as law continues to hold a fundamentalist view of religion and culture, it will transfer more power to fundamentalists and traditionalists at the expense of human rights.

Notes

1. *Martinez* Reversed. The Tenth Circuit Court of Appeals reversed the decision in *Martinez* on the merits; the court held that "there could have been a solution without discrimination." Santa Clara Pueblo v. Martinez, 540 F.2d 1039, 1047 (10th Cir. 1976). The Supreme Court reversed the decision of the Tenth Circuit, not on the merits, but on the grounds that Congress had failed to provide remedies for violation of the Indian Civil Rights Act other than habeas corpus. Santa Clara Pueblo v. Martinez, 436 U.S. 49 (1978).

Which court was correct on the merits? Consider Catharine MacKinnon's reflections on the case:

> I am told that the rule was made in 1939 after the General Allotment Act divided up communal lands into individually held parcels, in something like an attempt to make Indians into proper agrarians.... It appeared to the governing body of the Tribe that the offspring of mixed marriages threatened to swell the population of the Pueblo and diminished individual shares of the property. If this were the pressing problem it could have been solved without resorting to discrimination by simply excluding the offspring of both sexes where the parent, either male or female, married outside the Pueblo....
>
> Given this history, which the tribe did not choose or make, I imagine the tribe saying, we need this rule. I imagine Julia Martinez replying: I understand that history, it is also my history, but this is a male supremacist solution to a problem male supremacy created.... Why is it seen as a matter of cultural survival when men guarantee exclusive access to Indian women as a requirement of tribal membership, but when an Indian woman attempts to claim that her family is an Indian family, to choose who to make a family with, it's called a threat to cultural survival? Whose culture is this culture? Is male supremacy sacred because it has become a tribal tradition?

Catharine A. MacKinnon, Feminism Unmodified: Discourses on Life and Law 66-67 (1987).

Consider the case from each of the major perspectives developed in this book. Does support of Julia Martinez's challenge to the tribal rule necessarily mean giving gender justice priority over anti-colonial struggle?

2. Deconstructing "Culture" in the Navajo Nation. Leti Volpp suggests that one problem with a focus on "culture" is that is obscures the economic and political determinants of social behavior. Genevieve Chato and Christine Conte, in similar fashion, argue that the *Martinez* ordinance can better be understood when Indian nations are viewed as internal colonies of the United States, just as many "Third World" nations are former colonies of European powers. Genevieve Chato & Christine Conte, The Legal Rights of American Indian Women, in Readings in American Indian Law: Recalling the Rhythm of Survival 252 (Jo Carrillo ed., 1998).

Using the Navajo nation as an example, Chato and Conte argue that economic underdevelopment has hindered Navajo women's pursuit of equality in several interrelated ways. First, demographic pressure on a fixed land base has reduced the importance of livestock raising and farming, the traditional bases of Navajo women's authority in the household, and increased the incidence of welfare dependence. Id. at 259. Second, the economic marginalization of the Navajo has meant that most available jobs involve construction and other types of manual labor, job categories in which men are given preference. Id. As in the U.S. economy, women are clustered in low-paying, often part-time "pink collar" jobs. Third, Chato and Conte argue that in response to pressure from the United States government, the Navajo Nation adopted a political and judicial system on the model of the federal government. "This was a practical response providing parallel structures to negotiate sovereignty issues and resource royalties for the tribe. However, this model has also been extended into the realm of discrimination against women in the political and legal arenas. Navajo women are dismally underrepresented on the Navajo Tribal Council and in the judicial system." Id. at 260. Last and most importantly, according to Chato and Conte, "traditional Navajo beliefs against female leadership outside of the household have been reinforced by discriminatory Anglo norms." Id. Navajo women thus face a double struggle for equality.

How should Pueblo law respond to these circumstances? How should United States law respond?

3. The Indian Child Welfare Act. Application of the Indian Child Welfare Act of 1978 (ICWA), 25 U.S.C. §§ 1901-1963 (1982), presents another context in which rules designed to protect the cultural identity of American Indian nations may substantially curtail rights that women would otherwise possess. The ICWA is a jurisdictional act codifying previous state and federal law that requires, among other things, proceedings relating to the neglect, custody, or adoption of children of the tribe to be adjudicated in tribal courts. The Act was in response to the removal or placement of many Indian children away from Indian communities, which continues to threaten the survival of Indian culture. See Donna J. Goldsmith, Individual vs. Collective Rights: The Indian Child Welfare Act, 13 Harv. Women's L.J. 1, 4-5 (1990).

In Mississippi Choctaw Band of Indians v. Holyfield, 490 U.S. 30 (1989), the United States Supreme Court considered a case under the ICWA in which a Choctaw mother and father, who were unmarried, sought to place their newborn twins for adoption with a non-Indian family living off the reservation, in order that the children would have opportunities that the tribe would not be able to provide. The mother lived on the reservation at the time, but because there were no hospitals there, the children were born off the reservation. A Mississippi trial court, affirmed by the state supreme court, granted the adoption. The Supreme Court overruled on the grounds that because the mother was domiciled on the reservation, under the ICWA the state court had no jurisdiction to decide the adoption petition.

The effect of *Holyfield* was to preempt the desire of the mother (as well as the father) to put her children up for adoption outside the reservation. Should the tribe's interest in its own continued survival supersede that desire?

4. Feminist Analyses of the "Cultural Defense" in Criminal Law.
A related area of conflict among feminists has to do with the "cultural defense" in criminal law, namely, the use of evidence describing the culture of an immigrant defendant's native country in order to bolster a claim of justification or excuse. Two prominent examples are People v. Chen, No. 87-7774 (N.Y. Sup. Ct. Dec. 2, 1988) and People v. Wu, 286 Cal. Rptr. 868 (Ct. App. 1991) (both explored in Leti Volpp, (Mis)Identifying Culture: Asian Women and the "Cultural Defense," 17 Harv. Women's L.J. 57 (1994)). In *Chen*, the defendant was a 54-year-old Chinese immigrant who killed his wife by smashing her skull with a claw hammer. Chen argued that he lacked the intent to kill but rather had acted under "extreme emotional disturbance" in part because of his Chinese cultural values. Chen had become suspicious that his wife was having an affair, and attacked her after she admitted that she was seeing another man. Chen's attorney introduced an expert witness, a white anthropologist named Burton Pasternak, who testified that "In general terms, I think that one could expect a Chinese to react in a much more volatile, violent way to those circumstances than someone from our own society. I think there's no doubt about it." Pasternak elaborated by stating that social control is more strict and unchanging in China than in the West; that a Chinese man whose wife had committed adultery would be dishonored and that both parties would have difficulty remarrying; and that in the United States a Chinese "adulteress" would have no problem establishing a relationship with a white man, whereas a Chinese man whose wife had committed adultery would be considered a "pariah" among Chinese women and would have no chance finding a white woman. On cross-examination, Pasternak strongly contrasted Chinese people with "the average American," whom he described as a white professional male, and argued that Chinese immigrants assimilated into American society "very slowly, if ever." Impressed by this testimony, the trial judge found Chen guilty of manslaughter rather than murder and sentenced him to five years probation instead of time in prison.

In *Wu*, the defendant, Helen, who grew up in China, became romantically involved with a man, Gary Wu, who emigrated to the United States and married another woman. Many years later, however, he contacted Helen and told her he was unhappily married and that if Helen emigrated to the United States he would marry her and she could bear a child for him. Helen did emigrate to the United States, but Gary did not offer to marry her, even after the two of them had a child, a son named Sidney. Gary did divorce his wife, but did not tell Helen.

Helen, who was unable to speak English or drive a car, was unhappy in the United States, and eventually told Gary she would return to Macau. She did so without Sidney, but for the next eight years repeatedly asked Gary to visit her with Sidney. Gary continually asked for money, at one point proposing marriage after Helen showed him a certificate of deposit for a million Hong Kong dollars. Finally Helen and Gary were married in Las Vegas, but when pressed Gary would not say whether he had married her for her money. Shortly thereafter, Helen saw Gary beating their son, and Sidney told her the house they were staying in belonged to another woman, who was Gary's girlfriend. At that point, Helen told Sidney she wanted to die and asked if he would go too. He clung to her neck and cried.

Helen cut the cord off a window blind and strangled her son. She then attempted to kill herself by slashing her wrist with a kitchen knife, but she was revived at the local emergency room.

At the murder trial, the judge refused to instruct the jurors that they could choose to consider Helen's cultural background in determining the presence or absence of malice, and Wu was convicted of murder. On appeal, the California Court of Appeals reversed, holding that evidence of her cultural background was relevant to the issues of premeditation and deliberation and could potentially reduce the murder charge to one of voluntary manslaughter. The experts in this case were not anthropologists but "transcultural psychologists," who explained that Helen's behavior represented love and maternal altruism: "...in her own culture, in her own mind, there are no other options but to, for her at the time, but to kill herself and take the son along with her so that they could sort of step over to the next world where she could devote herself, all of herself to the caring of the son, caring of Sidney.... Her purpose...in many ways...is a benevolent one."

Leti Volpp, commenting on these cases, rejects the notion of a formalized "cultural defense" as likely to promote stereotyping, but also rejects the position that cultural evidence should never be admissible. She argues that the admission of cultural evidence was wrong in the *Chen* case, but correct in the *Wu* case, due to the value of "antisubordination." More specifically, Volpp offers guidelines for the admission of cultural evidence:

> There must be an acknowledgement of the fluid and interdynamic nature of cultures. Information that explains the actions of a defendant should be articulated by community members who are sensitive to the dynamics of power and subordination within the community of the defendant.... Information about the defendant's culture should never be reduced to stereotypes about a community but rather should concretely address the individual defendant's location in her community, her location in the diaspora and her history. The information should be provided so as to give insight into an individual's thoughts, and should not be used for purposes of explaining how an individual fits into stereotypes of group behavior.

Volpp, (Mis)Identifying Culture, supra, at 100. Are these guidelines workable in practice? Do they distinguish between the cultural evidence in *Chen* and in *Wu*?

A disproportionate number of the "cultural defense" cases involve Asian immigrants. Daina Chiu argues that the debate over the "cultural defense" itself is in large part a debate over the place of Asian Americans. In her view, the debate illustrates three different modes of "managing Asian difference" in American society. Those who argue for a cultural defense to protect immigrants see cultural difference as a reason for "special treatment," thereby preserving Americanness as white. Chiu calls this the "exclusion" approach to Asian Americans, and argues that it harms Asian women in particular, who have traditionally played a subordinate role in Asian culture. By contrast, the "assimilation" approach rejects the defense and demands conformity to dominant norms. An intermediate position, which would admit cultural evidence to show state of mind or mitigate punishment, reflects what Chiu calls "guilty liberalism." Chiu argues that the intermediate position necessarily fails because "the defendant benefits only to the extent that she shares the same values as dominant white culture. Therefore, white society is able to reinforce its prejudices through the other culture while purporting to act in tolerance of difference. In particular, this approach allows white society to reconstruct the subordination of women through the medium of another culture." Daina C. Chiu, The Cultural Defense: Beyond Exclusion, Assimilation, and Guilty Liberalism, 82 Cal. L. Rev. 1053, 1057 (1994). Chiu argues that the Chen case is an example of guilty liberalism. The judge in that case, she argues, reduced Chen's culpability not because he was acting under "different" cultural values, but because he held the "same" cultural values as Americans: "The subordination of women and the privileging of the male sex-right are common to both cultures." Id. at 1114.

A Maine case involved a father from Afghanistan who had lived in the United States for four years when he was arrested for kissing the penis of his nine-month-old son. Evidence in the case explained that kissing the penis of one's child is not considered either sexual or wrong in Afghanistan under Islamic law. The court rejected the cultural defense claim, and the defendant was given a suspended sentence. State v. Kargar, 679 A.2d 81 (Me. 1996), discussed in Nancy A. Wanderer & Catherine R. Connors, Culture and Crime: *Kargar* and the Existing Framework for a Cultural Defense, 47 Buff. L. Rev. 8129 (1999).

Should there be a cultural defense to female genital surgeries? The Federal Female Genital Mutilation Act, 18 U.S.C. §116(a) (2004), now makes it illegal to "knowingly circumcise[], excise[] or infibulate[] the whole or any part of the labia majora or labia minora or clitoris of another person who has not attained the age of 18 years." The maximum imprisonment term is five years. The cultural defense is explicitly excluded by the Act: "No account shall be taken of the effect on the person on whom the operation is to be performed of any belief on the part of that person, or any other person, that the operation is required as a matter of custom or ritual." 18 U.S.C. §116(c). At least two arrests have taken place under the statute. See Naomi Mendelsohn, Note, At the Crossroads: The Case For and Against a Cultural Defense to Female Genital Mutilation, 56 Rutgers L. Rev. 1011 (2004). Is this the right policy? See Doriane Lambelet Coleman, The Seattle Compromise: Multicultural Sensitivity and Americanization, 47 Duke L.J. 717 (1998) (approving a symbolic female circumcision that would have recognized the cultural interests of Somali immigrants in Seattle, in a way less injurious than male circumcision). What about male circumcision?

The "cultural defense" has been controversial among feminists. For further commentary, see Donna Kay Maeda, Subject to Justice: The "Cultural Defense" and Legal Constructions of Race, Culture, and Nation, in Postcolonial America 81 (C. Richard King ed., 2000); Doriane Lambelet Coleman, Individualizing Justice Through Multiculturalism: The Liberals' Dilemma, 96 Colum. L. Rev. 1093 (1996); Leti Volpp, Talking "Culture": Gender, Race, Nation, and the Politics of Multiculturalism, 96 Colum. L. Rev. 1573 (1996) (responding to Coleman); Holly Maguigan, Cultural Evidence and Male Violence: Are Feminist and Multiculturalist Reformers on a Collision Course in Criminal Courts?, 70

N.Y.U. L. Rev. 36 (1995) (rejecting all-or-nothing approach to cultural evidence and advocating its admissibility as to defendant's mental state, subject to refutation through conventional avenues).

There are now hundreds of cases in which individuals have attempted to invoke a cultural defense, involving a wide variety of cultural claims in a wide variety of contexts, including homicide and rape prosecutions, child abuse cases, drug use cases, treatment of animals, custody battles, employment discrimination suits, and the treatment of the dead. For a comprehensive account of these cases, see Alison Dundes Renteln, The Cultural Defense (2004).

5. Religious Freedom and Gender Equality in the United States. In EEOC v. Catholic University of America, 83 F.3d 455 (D.C. Cir. 1996), Sister Elizabeth McDonough, a Dominican nun and the first woman to be appointed to the canon law faculty at Catholic University, filed discrimination charges with the EEOC challenging her denial of tenure. She argued that Catholic University had engaged in sex discrimination and retaliatory conduct in violation of Title VII. The district judge dismissed the case without reaching the merits, on the ground that applying Title VII would violate both the free exercise and the establishment clauses of the First Amendment. In his view Sister McDonough's primary role in the Department of Canon Law was the functional equivalent of the role of a minister. EEOC v. Catholic University of America, 856 F. Supp. 1, 10 (D.D.C. 1994). The D.C. Circuit affirmed, taking note of a long line of cases holding that the free exercise clause exempts the selection of clergy from Title VII and similar statutes. In addition, the appellate court held that judicial review of Sister McDonough's case would entangle the court in religious matters in violation of the establishment clause. Indeed, the court rebuked the EEOC for investigating the claim and filing the first place. 83 F.3d at 467.

A more recent case involved the dismissal of a teacher at a Catholic girls' school in 2003, after she lent her name to an advertisement supporting abortion rights on the 30th anniversary of Roe v. Wade. The federal district court dismissed the case, on the ground that sorting out her Title VII claims would require the court to become entangled in church doctrine, in violation of the First Amendment. Curay-Cramer v. Ursuline Academy of Wilmington Del., Inc., 344 F. Supp. 2d 923 (D. Del. 2004). See also Fassl v. Our Lady of Perpetual Help Roman Catholic Church, 2005 U.S. Dist. LEXIS 22546 (Oct. 5, 2005) (refusing to hear employee Family and Medical Leave Act complaint against a Catholic Church, on First Amendment grounds); Combs v. Central Texas Annual Conference of the Methodist Church, 173 F.3d 343 (5th Cir. 1999) (upholding, on free exercise grounds, the dismissal of female minister after she was retroactively denied maternity benefits after she complained about pay equity).

Sexual harassment claims may escape religious defenses if the treatment complained of is not linked to religious beliefs, or a church's prerogatives with respect to choice of personnel. The lead case involves allegations of sexual harassment by a novice of the Society of Jesus against various superiors at two Jesuit institutions, who plaintiff claimed sent him pornographic material, made unwelcome sexual advances, and engaged him in inappropriate and unwelcome sexual discussions. The Ninth Circuit Court of Appeals held that the ministerial exception to Title VII did not apply because the church was "neither exercising its constitutionally protected prerogative to choose its ministers nor embracing the behavior at issue as a constitutionally protected religious practice." Bollard v. California Province of the Soc'y of Jesus, 196 F.3d 940, 944 (9th Cir. 1999), reh'g en banc denied, 211 F.3d 1331 (9th Cir. 2000). *Bollard* was applied and reaffirmed in Elvig v. Calvin Presbyterian Church, 375 F.3d 941 (9th Cir. 2004), reh'g en banc denied, 397 F.3d 790 (2005), a case in which a female minister alleged sexual harassment by her supervising pastor). Where the actions of the church or church personnel can be tied to religious beliefs, however, claims will not succeed even if they are cast in terms of sexual harassment. See, e.g., Bryce v. Episcopal Church in the Diocese of Colorado, 289 F.3d 648 (10th Cir. 2002) (upholding dismissal of sexual harassment charges stemming from church personnel action against youth minister after her civil commitment ceremony to another woman).

Does current sex discrimination law assume not only a white, middle-class, heterosexual woman, but also a woman without religious commitments? For the argument that employment discrimination law should apply to religious organizations, see Jane Rutherford, Equality as the Primary Constitutional Value: The Case for Applying Employment Discrimination Laws to Religion, 81 Cornell L. Rev. 1049 (1996); see also Linda L. Ammons, What's God Got To Do With It? Church and State Collaboration in the Subordination of Women and Domestic Violence, 51 Rutgers L. Rev. 1207 (1999); Keith E. Sealing, Polygamists Out of the Closet: Statutory and State Constitutional Prohibitions Against Polygamy Are Unconstitutional Under the Free Exercise Clause, 17 Ga. St. U. L. Rev. 691 (2001); see generally Cass Sunstein, Should Sex Equality Law Apply to Religious Institutions? in Is Multiculturalism Bad for Women? (Susan Moller Okin et al. eds., 1999).

Religious issues relating to the refusal of Roman Catholic hospitals to provide medical treatment relating to abortions and contraception, and the refusal of pharmacists to disburse morning-after pills based on claims of conscience, are discussed in Chapter 5, pp. 890-891, and problems 5-8 and 5-9, at pp. 894-895.

6. The International Dimension. In the international context, the conflict between women's nonsubordination and religious freedom becomes even more complicated. Is advocacy for women in these debates an appeal to basic "universal obligations to protect human functioning and its dignity" (see Martha Nussbaum, Sex & Social Justice 29-30 (1999)), or "Western-biased" "pontificating" (Obiora)? How does Sunder's approach fit into this debate?

There is a vast literature on issues relating to international human rights, women's equality, and the conflict between the goals of American feminism and religious fundamentalism in other countries, especially in Muslim cultures. A few of the leading, recent sources, which lead to many others, are International Law: Modern Feminist Approaches (Doris Buss & Ambreena Manji eds., 2005); Ayelet Shacher, Religion, State, and the Problem of Gender: New Modes of Citizenship and Governance in Diverse Societies, 50 McGill L.J. 49 (2005); Sally Engle Merry, Constructing a Global Law: Violence Against Women and the Human Rights System, 28 L. & Soc. Inquiry 941 (2003); Ann Laquer Estin, Embracing Tradition: Pluralism in American Family Law, 63 Md. L. Rev. 540 (2003); Women, Gender, Religion: A Reader (Elizabeth A. Castelli ed., 2001). For elaboration on the concept of the "New Sovereignty" to which Sunder refers, see Abram Chayes & Antonia Handler Chayes, The New Sovereignty: Compliance with International Regulatory Agreements (1995).

3. The Naturalist Error: Critiquing Biological Definitions of "Women"

Kantaras v. Kantaras
884 So. 2d 155 (Fla. Dist. Ct. App. 2004)

FULMER, Judge, joined by COVINGTON and WALLACE, JJ., concurring.

Linda Kantaras appeals from a final judgment dissolving her marriage to Michael Kantaras. This appeal presents an issue of first impression in Florida: whether a postoperative female-to-male transsexual person can validly marry a female under the current law of this state. We hold that the law of this state does not provide for or allow such a marriage; therefore, we reverse the final judgment and remand for the trial court to declare the marriage of the parties void ab initio.

In 1959 Margo Kantaras was born a female in Ohio. In 1986 Margo changed her name to Michael John Kantaras, and in 1987 Michael underwent sex reassignment, which included hormonal treatments, a total hysterectomy, and a double mastectomy. In 1988 Michael met Linda, and Linda learned of Michael's surgeries. Linda, who was pregnant by a former boyfriend, gave birth to a son in June 1989. Linda and Michael applied for a marriage license with Michael representing that he was male. The two married in July 1989 in Florida. In September 1989, Michael applied to adopt Linda's son, with Michael representing to the court that he was Linda's husband. Linda gave birth to a daughter in 1992 after Linda underwent artificial insemination with the sperm of Michael's brother.

In 1998 Michael filed a petition for dissolution of marriage seeking to dissolve his marriage to Linda and to obtain custody of both children. Linda answered and counterpetitioned for dissolution and/or annulment claiming that the marriage was void ab initio because it violated Florida law that bans same-sex marriage. Linda claimed that the adoption of her son was void because it violated Florida's ban on homosexual adoption, and she claimed that Michael was not the biological or legal father of her daughter. After a lengthy trial, the trial court entered an order finding that Michael was legally a male at the time of the marriage, and thus, the trial court concluded that the marriage was valid. The trial court also concluded that Michael was entitled to primary residential custody of the two children.

In outlining its reasons for determining that Michael was male at the time of the marriage, the trial court stated, in part:

24. Michael at the date of marriage was a male based on the persuasive weight of all the medical evidence and the testimony of lay witnesses in this case, including the following:

(a) As a child, while born female, Michael's parents and siblings observed his male characteristics and agreed he should have been born a "boy."

(b) Michael always has perceived himself as a male and assumed the male role doing house chores growing up, played male sports, refused to wear female clothing at home or in school and had his high school picture taken in male clothing.

(c) Prior to marriage he successfully completed the full process of transsexual reassignment, involving hormone treatment, irreversible medical surgery that removed all of his female organs inside of his body, including having a male reconstructed chest, a male voice, a male configured body and hair with beard and moustache, and a naturally developed penis.

(d) At the time of the marriage his bride, Linda was fully informed about his sex reassignment status, she accepted along with his friends, family and work colleagues that Michael in his appearance, characteristics and behavior was perceived as a man. At the time of the marriage he could not assume the role of a woman.

(e) Before and after the marriage he has been accepted as a man in a variety of social and legal ways, such as having a male driving license; male passport; male name change; male modification of his birth certificate by legal ruling; male participation in legal adoption proceedings in court; and as a male in an artificial insemination program, and participating for years in school activities with the children of this marriage as their father. All of this, was no different than what Michael presented himself as at the date of marriage.

25. Michael was born a heterosexual transsexual female. That condition [which] is now called "Gender Identity Dysphoria," was diagnosed for Michael in adulthood some twenty (20) years after birth. Today and at the date of marriage, Michael had no secondary female identifying characteristics and all reproductive female organs were absent, such as ovaries, fallopian tubes, cervix, womb, and breasts. The only feature left is a vagina which Dr. Cole testified was not typically female because it now had a penis or enlarged, elongated clitoris.

26. Michael after sex reassignment or triatic treatments would still have a chromosomal patter [sic] (XX) of a woman but that is a presumption. No chromosomal tests were performed on Michael during the course of his treatment at the Rosenberg Clinic.

27. Chromosomes are only one factor in the determination of sex and they do not overrule gender or self identity, which is the true test or identifying mark of sex. Michael has always, for a lifetime, had a self-identity of a male. Dr. Walter Bockting, Dr. Ted Huang and Dr. Collier Cole, all testified that Michael Kantaras is now and at the date of marriage was medically and legally "male."

28. Under the marriage statute of Florida, Michael is deemed to be male, and the marriage ceremony per formed in the Sandford [sic] County Court house on July 18, 1989, was legal.

The issue in this case involves the interplay between the Florida statutes governing marriage and the question of whether Michael Kantaras was legally male or female when he married Linda. We first address the relevant statutes and then discuss our reasons for concluding that the trial court erred in finding that Michael was male at the time of the marriage.

The Florida Legislature has expressly banned same-sex marriage. As amended in 1977 by chapter 77-139, Laws of Florida, the statute governing the issuance of a marriage license, at the time one was issued in this case, provided that no license shall be issued unless one party is a male and the other a female:

> No county court judge or clerk of the circuit court in this state shall issue a license for the marriage of any person unless there shall be first presented and filed with him an affidavit in writing, signed by both parties to the marriage, made and subscribed before some person authorized by law to administer an oath, . . . and unless one party is a male and the other party is a female.

§ 741.04(1), Fla. Stat. (1987). In 1997, the legislature enacted the Florida Defense of Marriage Act, prohibiting marriage between persons of the same sex . . .

Courts in Ohio, Kansas, Texas, and New York have addressed issues involving the marriage of a postoperative transsexual person, and in all cases the courts have invalidated or refused to allow the marriage on the grounds that it violated state statutes or public policy. In the case of In re Ladrach, 513 N.E.2d 828 (Ohio Probate 1987), the court found that a postoperative male-to-female transsexual was not permitted to marry a male. "There is no authority in Ohio for the issuance of a marriage license to consummate a marriage between a post-operative male to female transsexual person and a male person." Id. at 832. . . .

More recently an Ohio appellate court agreed with the decision in *Ladrach* and affirmed a trial court's denial of a marriage license to a postoperative female-to-male transsexual and a female. See In re A Marriage License for Nash, Nos. 2002-T-0149, 2002-T-0179, 2003 Ohio 7221, 2003 WL 23097095. Noting that "Ohio, like most states, has a clear public policy that authorizes and recognizes marriages only between members of the opposite sex," the court concluded that the term "male" as used in the marriage statute does not include a female-to-male postoperative transsexual. Id. at 32-33. Agreeing with the court in *Ladrach* that it was the responsibility of the legislature to change the public policy, the court stated that it was "loath to expand the statutory designation of individuals who may marry through judicial legislation." Id. at 34.

The Kansas Supreme Court declared a marriage void after it found that a postoperative male-to-female transsexual was not a woman. See In re Estate of Gardiner, 42 P.3d 120 (Kan. 2002), cert. denied, 537 U.S. 825 (2002). Gardiner, a probate case, involved the question of who was the rightful heir to the intestate estate of Marshall Gardiner: Gardiner's son, Joe, or J'Noel Gardiner, a male-to-female transsexual who married Marshall Gardiner the year before his death. Joe sought summary judgment on the ground that J'Noel's marriage to Marshall was void. . . .

The supreme court concluded that the issue on appeal was one of law, not fact, and it involved the interpretation of the Kansas statutes. . . . After discussing the common meaning of the terms sex, male, and female, the court stated:

The words "sex," "male," and "female" in everyday understanding do not encompass transsexuals. The plain, ordinary meaning of "persons of the opposite sex" contemplates a biological man and a biological woman and not persons who are experiencing gender dysphoria. . . .

Id. at 135. . . .

In Littleton v. Prange, 9 S.W.3d 223 (Tex. App. 1999), the Texas court found a marriage between a man and a postoperative male-to-female transsexual void. Christie Littleton, the transsexual, married Jonathon Mark Littleton in Kentucky in 1989. Id. at 225. After Jonathon's death in 1996, Christie sued Dr. Prange for medical malpractice in her capacity as Jonathon's surviving spouse. Id. The doctor moved for summary judgment asserting that Christie was a man and could not be the surviving spouse of another man. Id. The trial court agreed and granted summary judgment. Id. . . . The court concluded "as a matter of law, that Christie Littleton is a male. As a male, Christie cannot be married to another male. Her marriage to Jonathon was invalid, and she cannot bring a cause of action as his surviving spouse." . . .

There is one case in the United States that has permitted transsexual marriage. In M.T. v. J.T., 355 A.2d 204 (N.J. 1976), the husband sought an annulment on the ground that his wife was a male-to-female transsexual. The New Jersey court rejected the husband's argument, upheld the validity of the marriage, and affirmed a judgment of the lower court obligating the husband to support the transsexual as his wife. After considering the medical evidence, the court held that when a transsexual person has successfully undergone sex-reassignment and can fully function sexually in the reassigned sex, then the person could marry legally as a member of the sex finally indicated . . . .

In the case before us, the trial court relied heavily on the approach taken by an Australian family court in In re Kevin, (2001) 28 Fam. L.R. 158, aff'd, 30 Fam. L.R. 1 (Austl. Fam. Ct. 2003) which the trial court believed "correctly states the law in modern society's approach to transsexualism." In that case, the Australian court took the view that courts must recognize advances in medical knowledge and practice and found that a female-to-male transsexual should be considered a man for purposes of marriage. Australia prohibits same-sex marriage; nevertheless, the court ruled that a marriage between a woman and a postoperative female-to-male transsexual was valid. In affirming the trial court, the Family Court of Australia stated in its conclusion:

> Should the words "man" and "marriage" as used in the Marriage Act 1961 bear their contemporary ordinary everyday meaning? . . .
>
> Unless the context requires a different interpretation, the words "man" and "woman" when used in legislation have their ordinary contemporary meaning according to Australian usage. That meaning includes post-operative transsexuals as men or women in accordance with their sexual reassignment . . . .

30 Fam. L.R. 1 at 48.

On appeal, Michael argues that the trial court properly adopted the approach taken by the Australian court. He further argues that the approach taken by the majority of courts in the United States that have addressed the issue of transsexual marriage ignore modern medical science. We disagree.

The controlling issue in this case is whether, as a matter of law, the Florida statutes governing marriage authorize a postoperative transsexual to marry in the reassigned sex. We conclude they do not. We agree with the Kansas, Ohio, and Texas courts in their understanding of the common meaning of male and female, as those terms are used statutorily, to refer to immutable traits determined at birth. Therefore, we also conclude that the trial court erred by declaring that Michael is male for the purpose of the marriage statutes. Whether advances in medical science support a change in the meaning commonly attributed to the terms male and female as they are used in the Florida marriage statutes is a question that raises issues of public policy that should be addressed by the legislature. . . .

Our holding that the marriage is void ab initio does not take into consideration the best interests of the children involved in this case. While we recognize that the trial judge went to great lengths to determine the best interests of the children, the issue of deciding primary residential custody was dependent on the trial court's conclusion that the marriage was valid. We do not attempt to undertake a determination of the legal status of the children resulting from our conclusion that the marriage is void. The legal status of the children and the parties' property rights will be issues for the trial court to examine in the first instance on remand.

≡≡≡ *Smith v. Salem*
≡≡≡ 378 F.3d 566 (6th Cir. 2004)

COLE, Circuit Judge.

I. BACKGROUND . . .

Smith is — and has been, at all times relevant to this action — employed by the city of Salem, Ohio, as a lieutenant in the Salem Fire Department (the "Fire Department"). Prior to the events surrounding this action, Smith worked for the Fire Department for seven years without any negative incidents. Smith — biologically and by birth a male — is a transsexual and has been diagnosed with Gender Identity Disorder ("GID"), which the American Psychiatric Association characterizes as a disjunction between an individual's sexual organs and sexual identity. . . . After being diagnosed with GID, Smith began "expressing a more feminine appearance on a full-time basis" — including at work — in accordance with international medical protocols for treating GID. Soon thereafter, Smith's co-workers began questioning him about his appearance and commenting that his appearance and mannerisms were not "masculine enough." As a result, Smith notified his immediate supervisor, Defendant Thomas Eastek, about his GID diagnosis and treatment. He also informed Eastek of the likelihood that his treatment would eventually include complete physical transformation from male to female. Smith had approached Eastek in order to answer any questions Eastek might have concerning his appearance and manner and so that Eastek could address Smith's co-workers' comments and inquiries. Smith specifically asked Eastek, and Eastek promised, not to divulge the substance of their conversation to any of his superiors, particularly to

Defendant Walter Greenamyer, Chief of the Fire Department. In short order, however, Eastek told Greenamyer about Smith's behavior and his GID. [Smith was eventually suspended.]

The [EEOC] ultimately upheld Smith's suspension.... Smith then filed suit in the federal district court. In his complaint, he asserted Title VII claims of sex discrimination and retaliation, along with claims pursuant to 42 U.S.C. § 1983 and state law claims of invasion of privacy and civil conspiracy.... [T]he district court dismissed the federal claims and granted judgment on the pleadings to Defendants....

II. ANALYSIS

On appeal, Smith contends that the district court erred in holding that: (1) he failed to state a claim of sex stereotyping; (2) Title VII protection is unavailable to transsexuals; (3) even if he had stated a claim of sex stereotyping, he failed to demonstrate that he suffered an adverse employment action; and (4) he failed to state a claim based on the deprivation of a constitutional or federal statutory right, pursuant to 42 U.S.C. § 1983....

A. Title VII

1. Sex Stereotyping . . .

We first address whether Smith has stated a claim for relief, pursuant to *Price Waterhouse*'s prohibition of sex stereotyping, based on his gender non-conforming behavior and appearance. In *Price Waterhouse*, the plaintiff, a female senior manager in an accounting firm, was denied partnership in the firm, in part, because she was considered "macho." 490 U.S. at 235. She was advised that she could improve her chances for partnership if she were to take "a course at charm school," "walk more femininely, talk more femininely, dress more femininely, wear make-up, have her hair styled, and wear jewelry." Id. (internal quotation marks omitted). Six members of the Court agreed that such comments bespoke gender discrimination, holding that Title VII barred not just discrimination because Hopkins was a woman, but also sex stereotyping—that is, discrimination because she failed to act like a woman. Id. at 250-51 (plurality opinion of four Justices); id. at 258-61 (White, J., concurring); id. at 272-73 (O'Connor, J., concurring) (accepting plurality's sex stereotyping analysis and characterizing the "failure to conform to [gender] stereotypes" as a discriminatory criterion; concurring separately to clarify the separate issues of causation and allocation of the burden of proof). As Judge Posner has pointed out, the term "gender" is one "borrowed from grammar to designate the sexes as viewed as social rather than biological classes." Richard A. Posner, Sex and Reason, 24-25 (1992). The Supreme Court made clear that in the context of Title VII, discrimination because of "sex" includes gender discrimination: "In the context of sex stereotyping, an employer who acts on the basis of a belief that a woman cannot be aggressive, or that she must not be, has acted on the basis of gender." *Price Waterhouse*, 490 U.S. at 250. The Court emphasized that "we are beyond the day when an employer could evaluate employees by assuming or insisting that they matched the stereotype associated with their group." Id. at 251.

Smith contends that the same theory of sex stereotyping applies here. His complaint sets forth the conduct and mannerisms which, he alleges, did not conform with his employers' and co-workers' sex stereotypes of how a man should look and behave. Smith's complaint states that, after being diagnosed with GID, he began to express a more feminine appearance and manner on a regular basis, including at work. The complaint states that his co-workers began commenting on his appearance and mannerisms as not being masculine enough; and that his supervisors at the Fire Department and other municipal agents knew about this allegedly unmasculine conduct and appearance. The complaint then describes a high-level meeting among Smith's supervisors and other municipal officials regarding his employment. Defendants allegedly schemed to compel Smith's resignation by forcing him to undergo multiple psychological evaluations of his gender non-conforming behavior. The complaint makes clear that these meetings took place soon after Smith assumed a more feminine appearance and manner and after his conversation about this with Eastek. In addition, the complaint alleges that Smith was suspended for twenty-four hours for allegedly violating an unenacted municipal policy, and that the suspension was ordered in retaliation for his pursuing legal remedies after he had been informed about Defendants' plan to intimidate him into resigning. In short, Smith claims that the discrimination he experienced was based on his failure to conform to sex stereotypes by expressing less masculine, and more feminine mannerisms and appearance.

Having alleged that his failure to conform to sex stereotypes concerning how a man should look and behave was the driving force behind Defendants' actions, Smith has sufficiently pleaded claims of sex stereotyping and gender discrimination.

In so holding, we find that the district court erred in relying on a series of pre-*Price Waterhouse* cases from other federal appellate courts holding that transsexuals, as a class, are not entitled to Title VII protection because "Congress had a narrow view of sex in mind" and "never considered nor intended that [Title VII] apply to anything other than the traditional concept of sex." Ulane v. Eastern Airlines, Inc., 742 F.2d 1081, 1085, 1086 (7th Cir. 1984). . . . It is true that, in the past, federal appellate courts regarded Title VII as barring discrimination based only on "sex" (referring to an individual's anatomical and biological characteristics), but not on "gender" (referring to socially-constructed norms associated with a person's sex). . . .

However, the approach in [these cases] and by the district court in this case has been eviscerated by *Price Waterhouse*. See Schwenk v. Hartford, 204 F.3d 1187, 1201 (9th Cir. 2000) ("The initial judicial approach taken in cases such as *Holloway* [and *Ulane*] has been overruled by the logic and language of *Price Waterhouse*."). By holding that Title VII protected a woman who failed to conform to social expectations concerning how a woman should look and behave, the Supreme Court established that Title VII's reference to "sex" encompasses both the biological differences between men and women, and gender discrimination, that is, discrimination based on a failure to conform to stereotypical gender norms. See *Price Waterhouse*, 490 U.S. at 251....

After *Price Waterhouse*, an employer who discriminates against women because, for instance, they do not wear dresses or makeup, is engaging in sex discrimination because the discrimination would not occur but for the victim's sex. It follows that employers who discriminate against men because they *do* wear dresses and makeup, or otherwise act femininely, are also engaging in sex discrimination, because the discrimination would not occur but for the victim's sex. See, e.g., *Nichols*, 256 F.3d 864 (Title VII sex discrimination and hostile work environment claim upheld where plaintiff's male co-workers and supervisors repeatedly referred to him as "she" and "her" and where co-workers mocked him for walking and carrying his serving tray "like a woman"); Higgins v. New Balance Athletic Shoe, Inc., 194 F.3d 252, 261 n.4 (1st Cir. 1999) ("Just as a woman can ground an action on a claim that men discriminated against her because she did not meet stereotyped expectations of femininity, a man can ground a claim on evidence that other men discriminated against him because he did not meet stereotypical expectations of masculinity." (internal citation omitted))....

Yet some courts have held that this latter form of discrimination is of a different and somehow more permissible kind. For instance, the man who acts in ways typically associated with women is not described as engaging in the same activity as a woman who acts in ways typically associated with women, but is instead described as engaging in the different activity of being a transsexual (or in some instances, a homosexual or transvestite). Discrimination against the transsexual is then found not to be discrimination "because of...sex," but rather, discrimination against the plaintiff's unprotected status or mode of self-identification. In other words, these courts superimpose classifications such as "transsexual" on a plaintiff, and then legitimize discrimination based on the plaintiff's gender non-conformity by formalizing the non-conformity into an ostensibly unprotected classification. See, e.g., Dillon v. Frank, 952 F.2d 403 (6th Cir. 1992).

Such was the case here: despite the fact that Smith alleges that Defendants' discrimination was motivated by his appearance and mannerisms, which Defendants felt were inappropriate for his perceived sex, the district court expressly declined to discuss the applicability of *Price Waterhouse*. The district court therefore gave insufficient consideration to Smith's well-pleaded claims concerning his contra-gender behavior, but rather accounted for that behavior only insofar as it confirmed for the court Smith's status as a transsexual, which the district court held precluded Smith from Title VII protection.

Such analyses cannot be reconciled with *Price Waterhouse*, which does not make Title VII protection against sex stereotyping conditional or provide any reason to exclude Title VII coverage for non sex-stereotypical behavior simply because the person is a transsexual. As such, discrimination against a plaintiff who is a transsexual — and therefore fails to act and/or identify with his or her gender — is no different from the discrimination directed against Ann Hopkins in *Price Waterhouse*, who, in sex-stereotypical terms, did not act like a woman. Sex stereotyping based on a person's gender non-conforming behavior is impermissible discrimination, irrespective of the cause of that behavior; a label, such as "transsexual," is not fatal to a sex discrimination claim where the victim has suffered discrimination because of his or her gender non-conformity. Accordingly, we hold that Smith has stated a claim for relief pursuant to Title VII's prohibition of sex discrimination. . . .

B. 42 U.S.C. § 1983 Claims . . .

The facts Smith has alleged to support his claims of gender discrimination pursuant to Title VII easily constitute a claim of sex discrimination grounded in the Equal Protection Clause of the Constitution, pursuant to § 1983. See Back v. Hastings on Hudson Union Free Sch. Dist., 365 F.3d 107 (2d Cir. 2004) (holding that claims premised on *Price Waterhouse* sex stereotyping theory sufficiently constitute claim of sex discrimination pursuant to § 1983). . . .

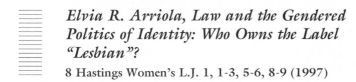

Elvia R. Arriola, Law and the Gendered Politics of Identity: Who Owns the Label "Lesbian"?
8 Hastings Women's L.J. 1, 1-3, 5-6, 8-9 (1997)

Several years ago, I was a member of a predominantly lesbian women's support group. The group offered a "womanspace" for individuals who wanted to share their experiences, strength, and hope as survivors of rape and sexual abuse. On a weekly basis, anywhere from fifteen to thirty women of all racial, ethnic and social backgrounds, who knew each other only by first name, rented a meeting room from a community church and shared stories of sexual victimization and abuse, with the singular goal of healing themselves through mutual support. . . . In the company of other survivors, the women felt safe enough, sometimes for the first time in their adult lives, to weep or get angry; for in this safe space they trusted that their companions would not mock, negate, or minimize their feelings. Of course, the critical sense of safety was ensured by the practice of someone standing guard at the door to make sure no man accidentally walked into the rented rooms. If that happened, all talk would suspend until the man was gone. This ground rule grew out of the plainly obvious fact that this was a meeting for women healing from sexual abuse by the men in their lives; only an all-women atmosphere could guarantee an emotionally safe environment.

Imagine, then, the turmoil created in this "womanspace" when one day a tall, quiet woman who had shown up regularly at meetings for several weeks suddenly came out to the group as a transsexual female. Not only that, she was a transsexual female who identified as a lesbian. Suddenly "Micki," who had simply appeared as an unusually tall, rather quiet and professionally dressed woman, looked very different to the group's members. Some of the women were too involved with their own issues to take in immediately what had just happened. In the following weeks, however, a few women, both lesbian and not, reacted strongly, sharing that they felt threatened by Micki's continued presence. Micki's feminine appearance bore witness to the wonders of modern medicine, but to some she was nothing but a fake. Her revelation explained at last the slightly masculine build around the shoulders and neck: this supposed woman was a man, or at least had been born male. Further, although she had given up her male identity, Micki's self confident demeanor betrayed residual hints of her socialization as a privileged white male.

Her chosen identity as a lesbian posed another gender and sexuality enigma. Having castrated "his" penis while leaving "his" sexual orientation unscathed, to what label was s/he entitled? The choice of a lesbian identity to express her (his) new identity as a "woman-loving-woman" communicated an unfamiliar sex and gender ambiguity. For some, the ambiguity only generated feelings of hostility and feelings of mockery for this once-man's appropriation of a label — lesbian — which they felt belonged only to "real women."

In the conflict and confusion that surfaced for several weeks after her coming out, Micki encountered both support and prejudice from fellow members of the incest survivors' group. A few sought out Micki's friendship, trying to assure her that she was welcome. Others kept their distance and in private conversations voiced their distrust and interest in removing Micki from the group. They felt abandoned by their group, angry and enraged that not everyone agreed that Micki should leave. Too many individuals supported Micki to force a formal demand that she leave and not come back. The resistors expressed a sense of betrayal by the group's unwillingness to oust Micki, whose perceived crime was in once having had a penis and now being viewed as neither truly female, nor woman, nor lesbian. She was at best a not-man. Eventually, the conflict led to a split, as Micki's resistors formed their own group, with membership limited to women who had been born into a female body. Micki herself eventually left the group. She ultimately formed her own support group, focusing on gender identity and abuse issues. . . .

By leaving to form another support group, Micki opened the door for healing from incest and sexual abuse to other transsexual females. Yet, the women who separated from the original group never had to examine the source of their fears. No one thought to ask whether some of their reactions to Micki, based upon preconceived ideas about the meaning of sex, gender or sexuality, might have stemmed from the same hetero-patriarchal value system which accounted for their own sexual victimization. Certainly no one felt the need to understand or address the unique form of gender oppression that leads an individual to such a drastic measure as sex reassignment surgery (SRS). The fact that Micki's recovery involved stories of how s/he had been shamed and traumatized from the time of his (her) childhood for engaging in gender-nonconforming behavior did not interest her opponents. Yet I wonder how the group never questioned the inclusion of "butchy" lesbians, some of whom dressed in very masculine attire, and who described similar childhood examples of abusive treatment for their own gender-nonconforming behavior. I have asked and answered my own question: it is all gender-based oppression. . . .

I have often wondered what would have happened in that group if Micki had not left. In the few weeks she was there, did it make any difference for someone like Micki, who had been raised as a boy and had become a man, to hear the depth of anger experienced by women who had survived male rape or incest and who now felt desperate at being unable to escape even a hint of residual male energy in a transgender female? Was it unreasonable for the women-from-birth to see Micki as a burden, rather than as someone who might help their healing by vouching as a once-man for the reality of abusive male power, and affirming to them, "yes, this is what men do and you were unjustly violated?" Could either side have seen the source of their fears and their unjust experiences as rooted in societal attitudes based on male power and privilege which continue to induce heightened levels of female sexual victimization, or which so oppress some boys/men that their only escape is to castrate the physical signs of the male gender identity they were assigned at birth?

Notes

1. What Is a Woman? Was "Micki" a woman? Was Michael Kantaras? What factors should determine the answer to that question? The *Kantaras* case catalogs much of the relevant case law on the subject, which by and large looks to a person's genitalia at birth as the most objective criterion, simple to apply. As one court cited in *Kantaras* states, "Every schoolchild, even of tender years, is confident he or she can tell the difference, especially if the person is wearing no clothes." Littleton v. Prange, 9 S.W.3d 223, 223 (Tex. App. 1999). But is it that simple?

Consider the situation of those who, by medical definitions, are neither completely "male" nor "female." According to Julie Greenberg, "Recent medical literature indicates that approximately one to four percent of the world's population may be intersexed and have either ambiguous or noncongruent sex features." Julie A. Greenberg, Defining Male and Female: Intersexuality and the Collision Between Law and Biology, 41 Ariz. L. Rev. 265, 267 (1999). The issue of surgery to "correct" intersexed individuals as infants so that they are more clearly male, or female, is controversial. Reassignment surgery on intersex infants has been a standard protocol since the late 1950s and early 1960s, but for the past decade the Intersex Society of North America has strongly opposed this surgery, preferring to have parents raise their intersex children as social males or females, and then let the children decide for themselves at puberty whether they would like to change their social sex, with or without surgical assistance. See E.J. Graff, The M/F Boxes, The Nation, Dec. 17, 2001, at 20, 21.

Feminists have found the issue a difficult one. Barbara Ehrenreich explores the arguments on both sides, concluding that intersex surgery is like female circumcision and other genital surgeries in that both are cultural practices with the potential to reinforce misogynist gender norms. Ehrenreich (with Mark Barr), Intersex Surgery, Female Genital Cutting, and the Selective Condemnation of "Cultural Practices," 40 Harv. C.R.-C.L. L. Rev. 71 (2005). For both medical and legal issues of gender assignment, see id.; Julie A. Greenberg, Legal Aspects of Gender Assignment, 13 Endocrinologist 277 (2003); Alyssa Connell Lareau, Note, Who Decides? Genital-Normalizing Surgery on Intersexed Infants, 92 Geo. L.J. 129 (2003).

Medical science seems to be less certain than "every schoolchild" that there are only two sexes, male and female. Consider Anne Fausto-Sterling's argument that there are really five sexes, not two:

> For some time medical investigators have recognized the concept of the intersexual body. But the standard medical literature uses the term intersex as a catch-all for three major subgroups with some mixture of male and female characteristics: the so-called true hermaphrodites, whom I call herms, who possess one testis and one ovary (the sperm- and egg-producing vessels, or gonads); the male pseudohermaphrodites (the "merms"), who have testes and some aspects of the female genitalia but no ovaries; and the female pseudohermaphrodites (the "ferms"), who have ovaries and some aspects of the male genitalia but lack testes. Each of those categories is in itself complex; the percentage of male and female characteristics, for instance, can vary enormously among members of the same subgroup. Moreover, the inner lives of the people in each subgroup — their special needs and their problems, attractions and repulsions — have gone unexplored by science. But on the basis of what is known about them I suggest that the three intersexes, herm, merm and ferm, deserve to be considered additional sexes each in its own right. Indeed, I would argue further that sex is a vast, infinitely malleable continuum that defies the constraints of even five categories.

Anne Fausto-Sterling, The Five Sexes: Why Male and Female Are Not Enough, The Sciences, March/April 1993, 20, 21. See also Dylan Vade, Expanding Gender and Expanding the Legal Conceptualization of Gender That Is More Inclusive of Transgender People, 11 Mich. J. Gender & L. 253, 261 (2005) (proposing a "non-linear alternative conceptualization" of transgender as a "gender galaxy" — "a three-dimensional, non-linear space in which every gender has a location that may or may not be fixed")." On what factors should feminists rely in deciding who is a woman?

Is *Kantaras* clearly a progressive opinion? See Elizabeth C. Barcena, Kantaras v. Kantaras: How a Victory for One Transsexual May Hinder the Sexual Minority Movement, 12 Buff. Women's L.J. 101 (2003/2004) (by focusing predominantly on gender identification rather than individual parenting qualities, opinion reinforces barriers to homosexuals in custody cases).

2. Transgender and the Law. The San Francisco Human Rights Commission Report defines transgender as:

> an umbrella term that includes male and female cross dressers, transvestites, female and male impersonators, pre-operative and post-operative transsexuals, and transsexuals who choose not to have genital reconstruction, and all persons whose perceived gender and anatomic sex may conflict with the gender expression, such as masculine-appearing women and feminine-appearing men. . . .
>
> All other terms — cross-dresser, transvestite, transsexual — are subsets of the umbrella term transgender.

Phyllis Randolph Frye, The International Bill of Gender Rights vs. the Cider House Rules: Transgenders Struggle With the Courts Over What Clothing They Are Allowed to Wear on the Job, Which Restroom They Are Allowed to

Use on the Job, Their Right to Marry, and the Very Definition of Their Sex, 7 Wm. & Mary J. Women & L. 133, 154 (2000).

As in *Kantaras*, many of the legal issues concerning transgender relate to marriage. In addition to the many cases cited in *Kantaras,* see In re Simmons, 825 N.E.2d 303 (Ill. App. Ct. 2005) (because marriage between involving transsexual was void, female-to-male transsexual not entitled to custody rights of child conceived through artificial insemination of his former "wife"); Mary Coombs, Sexual Dis-Orientation: Transgendered People and Same-Sex Marriage, 8 UCLA Women's L.J. 219 (1998); Mark Strasser, Marriage, Transsexuals, and the Meaning of Sex: On DOMA, Full Faith and Credit, and Statutory Interpretation, 3 Hous. J. Health L. & Pol'y 301 (2003).

The issue of transsexual marriage is explored in a transcultural context in Helen B. Berrigan, Transsexual Marriage: A Trans-Atlantic Judicial Dialogue, 12 L. & Sexuality 87 (2003); Leslie I. Lax, Is the United States Falling Behind? The Legal Recognition of Post-Operative Transsexuals' Acquired Sex in the United States and Abroad, 7 Quinnipiac Health L.J. 123 (2003). Immigration issues related to transsexual marriage are explored in John A. Fisher, Sex Determination for Federal Purposes: Is Transsexual Immigration Via Marriage Permissible Under the Defense of Marriage Act?, 10 Mich. J. Gender & L. 237 (2004).

3. Transgender Identity and Employment Discrimination Based on "Sex." In the employment context, until very recently, courts also have refused to recognize discrimination against transgender people as legally cognizable. Cases taking the traditional approach are summarized in Melinda Chow, *Smith v. Salem* Transgendered Jurisprudence and an Expanding Meaning of Sex Discrimination Under Title VII, 28 Harv. J.L. & Gender 207, 208-212 (2005); Laura Grenfell, Embracing Law's Categories: Anti-Discrimination Laws and Transgenderism, 15 Yale J.L. & Feminism 51, 56-60 (2003); Marvin Dunson III, Comment, Sex, Gender, and Transgender: The Present and Future of Employment Discrimination Law, 22 Berkeley J. Emp. & Lab. L. 465 (2001). See, e.g., Etsitty v. Utah Transit Authority, 2005 U.S. Dist. LEXIS 12634 (D. Utah June 24, 2005); Ulane v. Eastern Airlines, Inc., 742 F.2d 1081, 1085 (7th Cir. 1984) ("Title VII does not outlaw discrimination against a person who has a sexual identity disorder"); Dobre v. National R.R. Passenger Corp., 850 F. Supp. 284 (E.D. Pa. 1993) (requiring MTF (male-to-female) transition transsexual to use male washroom and dress in traditionally male attire is not discrimination "against a female because she is female"); James v. Ranch Mart Hardware Inc., 881 F. Supp. 478 (D. Kan. 1995) (permissible to discriminate against male transsexual, as long as also discriminate against female transsexuals).

Paisley Currah and Shannon Minter analyze the distinction made in these cases between sex and change of sex:

> [A]lthough it is difficult to see how an employer's decision to terminate an employee for undergoing sex-reassignment could plausibly be deemed anything other than a form of sex-based discrimination, courts have adopted the Orwellian notion that there is a meaningful legal distinction between discrimination because of sex and discrimination because of a change of sex. In Holloway v. Arthur Andersen

& Co., 566 F.2d 659 (9th Cir. 1977), for example, Ramona Holloway was fired for transitioning from male to female on the job. The Ninth Circuit held that Holloway was not discriminated against "because she is male or female, but rather because she is a transsexual who chose to change her sex. This type of claim is not actionable under Title VII." Similarly, in Underwood v. Archer Management Services, Inc., 857 F. Supp. 96 (D.D.C. 1994), the plaintiff alleged that she had been terminated from her job because, as a transsexual woman, she retained some masculine traits. The court held that insofar as "she was discriminated against because . . . she transformed herself into a woman" rather than "because she is a woman," she had failed to state a viable sex discrimination claim.

The incoherence of this purportedly meaningful distinction (between sex and change of sex) is apparent the moment one imagines a court applying a similar distinction in a case involving discrimination on any other ground. It is unlikely, for example, that an employer who terminated an employee for changing her religious affiliation or nationality would be absolved of liability on the ground that he did not object to the employee's new religion or national origin, but only to the change of religion or national origin. Yet, the only difference between these situations and that of a transsexual person is that while changing one's religion or nationality is generally considered to be a legitimate personal choice, "the very idea that one sex can change into another" is likely to engender "ridicule and horror."

Paisley Currah and Shannon Minter, Unprincipled Exclusions: The Struggle to Achieve Judicial and Legislative Equality for Transgender People, 7 Wm. & Mary J. Women & L. 37, 40-41 (2000). Similarly, courts have refused to recognize discrimination against transgender people as a form of anti-gay discrimination or as a form of discrimination against people with disabilities. Id.

Smith v. City of Salem is the first federal Court of Appeals decision to apply the *Price Waterhouse* rationale to a transgender Title VII plaintiff. Recall Rene v. MGM Grand Hotel, Inc., 305 F.3d 1061 (9th Cir. 2002) (en banc), cert. denied, 538 U.S. 922 (2003), holding that workplace harassment based upon a victim's sexual orientation can be a violation of Title VII, also under the sex-stereotyping theory of *Price Waterhouse*. (*Rene* is excerpted in Chapter 3, p. 443; *Price Waterhouse* is excerpted in Chapter 1, p. 59.) Is the reasoning persuasive? Is the result compelled by *Price Waterhouse*? See also Rosa v. Park West Bank & Trust Co., 214 F.3d (1st Cir. 2000) (failure to give a male cross-dresser a requested loan application could constitute a claim under the Equal Credit Opportunity Act); Schwenk v. Hartford, 204 F.3d 1187 (9th Cir. 2000) (in action by a pre-operative MTF transsexual inmate of a male prison under the Gender Motivated Violence Act, after attempted rape by a prison guard, court holds that term "gender" should be interpreted to encompass those who do not conform to gender expectations). For a highly publicized case involving a transgender former Army colonel whose job offer from the Library of Congress was withdrawn when his transgender status was discovered, see Schroer v. Library of Congress, reported at http://www.aclu.org//lgbt/transgender/12255res20050602.html.

The sex-stereotyping theory as applied to a variety of groups is explored in Chai Feldblum and Lisa Mottet, Gay People, Trans People, Women: Is It All About Gender?, 17 N.Y.L. Sch. J. Hum. Rts. 623, 642-647 (2000). As reported by Feldblum and Mottet, the Connecticut Commission on Human Rights and Opportunities issued a declaratory ruling that discrimination against an individual based on transgender status constitutes discrimination based on sex under Connecticut law. The Commission adopted a definition of transgender people, to include "transsexuals (both pre- and post-operative), intersexed people, anyone whose self-described gender identity is other than their sexual identity at birth (regardless of whether such individuals have had hormonal treatment or surgery), and also apparently effeminate men and masculine women. . . . As the [Connecticut] Commission noted, quite succinctly, "more and more courts have ruled that having specific expectations that a person will manifest certain behavior based upon his or her gender is not only conceptually outmoded sexual stereotyping, but also an unlawful form of sex discrimination." Id. at 647-648. For an explanation of the Canadian approach, which has endorsed the same view, see Grenfell, supra, at 77-84.

Can you explain the apparent difference between the judicial rejection of claims by transsexuals in *Kantaras* and the other marriage cases, and recent decisions in the employment context?

4. "Sex," "Gender," and Feminist Theory. Legal issues raised by transsexuals re-invokes a whole line of questions feminists have faced about the distinction between "sex" and "gender." Feminist theorist Linda Nicholson argues that feminists have used the word "gender" in two distinct ways.

> On the one hand, gender was developed and is still often used as a contrasting term to sex, to depict that which is socially constructed as opposed to that which is biologically given. On this usage, gender is typically thought to refer to personality traits and behavior in distinction from the body. Here, gender and sex are thought to be distinct. On the other hand, gender has increasingly become used to refer to any social construction having to do with the male/female distinction, including those constructions that separate "female" bodies from "male" bodies. This latter usage emerged when many came to realize that society not only shapes personality and behavior, it also shapes the ways in which the body appears. But if the body is itself always seen through social interpretation, then sex is not something that is separate from gender but is, rather, that which is subsumable under it.

Linda Nicholson, Interpreting Gender, 20 Signs 79 (1994).

Which conception of gender is more appropriate for feminism? Nicholson argues for the second. In her view, treating gender as something distinct from sex assumes that there is something called sexual difference that is always the same across cultures; this belief she calls "biological foundationalism." Id. at 82. Nicholson argues that biological foundationalism is inappropriate for feminists because it assumes without proof that all cultures experience sexual and bodily difference in the same way. Id. Similarly, Katherine Franke argues that it is gender that determines sex, and not the other way around. In Franke's view, "sexual equality jurisprudence has uncritically accepted the validity of biological sexual differences. By accepting these biological differences, equality jurisprudence reifies as foundational fact that which is really an effect of normative gender ideology." See Katherine M. Franke,

The Central Mistake of Sex Discrimination Law: The Disaggregation of Sex from Gender, 144 U. Pa. L. Rev. 1, 2 (1995). It follows for Franke, and other feminists, that discrimination against transgender people should be understood as a form of sex discrimination. See also Taylor Flynn, Transforming the Debate: Why We Need to Include Transgender Rights in the Struggles for Sex and Sexual Orientation Equality, 101 Colum. L. Rev. 392 (2001) (transgender rights advocacy helps to challenge break down traditional association of sex and biology).

Nicholson's and Franke's arguments seem to suggest that the distinction between "sex" and "gender" is not a useful one. Mary Anne Case argues, to the contrary, that unless sex and gender are "disaggregated," forms of discrimination that turn on gender role expectations rather than the physical attributes of sex will not be readily recognized. Case argues that *Price Waterhouse, VMI* (set forth in Chapter 2, pp. 260-274), and the numerous cases in which effeminate men have been penalized for breaching gender norms, are cases of gender, not sex, discrimination. Case, Disaggregating Gender from Sex and Sexual Orientation: The Effeminate Man in the Law and Feminist Jurisprudence, 105 Yale L.J. 1 (1995). See generally Francisco Valdes, Queers, Sissies, Dykes, and Tomboys: Deconstructing the Conflation of "Sex," "Gender," and "Sexual Orientation" in Euro-American Law and Society, 83 Cal. L. Rev. 1 (1995) (criticizing Anglo-American law and society for conflating "sex," "gender," and "sexual orientation").

Judges as well as academic feminists disagree about the proper relationship between the concepts of "sex" and "gender." Some members of the Supreme Court have begun using the terms "sex" and "gender" interchangeably. The issue became a matter of discussion between the justices in J.E.B. v. Alabama (set forth in Chapter 4, p. 772). The opinion for the court written by Justice Blackmun, along with separate concurring opinions by Justice O'Connor and Justice Kennedy and a dissenting opinion by Justice Rehnquist, all addressed whether the practice of making peremptory strikes of jurors based on whether they were men or women constitutes gender discrimination. Justice Scalia ridicules the change in terminology and uses the term "sex discrimination," explaining his usage as follows:

> [G]ender is to sex as feminine is to female and masculine to male. The present case does not involve peremptory strikes exercised on the basis of femininity or masculinity (as far as it appears, effeminate men did not survive the prosecution's peremptories). The case involves, therefore, sex discrimination plain and simple.

511 U.S. 127, 157 n.1 (1994) (Scalia, J., dissenting).

Justice Ginsburg had made the move from sex to gender by 1975, when she decided that the word "sex" was too disturbing in that it "may conjure up improper images" of what occurs in porno theaters. See Ruth Bader Ginsburg, Gender in the Supreme Court: The 1973 and 1974 Terms, 1975 Sup. Ct. Rev. 1, n.1.

For an account of the definitions of "gender" used in international human rights and refugee law, see Valerie Oosterveld, The Definition of "Gender" in the Rome Statute of the International Criminal Court: A Step Forward or Back for International Criminal Justice?, 28 Harv. Hum. Rts. J. 55, 66-71 (2005).

How should law distinguish the terms sex and gender?

4. Feminism and Knowledge

≡
≡ *Tracy E. Higgins, "By Reason of Their Sex":*
≡ *Feminist Theory, Postmodernism, and Justice*
   80 Cornell L. Rev. 1536, 1569-1572 (1995)

Postmodernism, broadly defined, rejects the role of philosophy as a foundation for social criticism. For example, Jean-Francois Lyotard defines the postmodern condition as one in which the "grand narratives" of legitimation, including narratives of historical progress, scientific rationality, reason, and justice, are no longer credible. These modern or Enlightenment accounts yield to a new "postmodern" view in which social criticism, including moral judgment, exists independent of any universalist theoretical ground. As Nancy Fraser and Linda Nicholson explain, "No longer anchored philosophically, the very shape or character of social criticism changes; it becomes more pragmatic, ad hoc, contextual, and local." This wide-ranging attack on metaphysics has led to skepticism of any overarching theory of justice and a call for what Lyotard describes as a "justice of multiplicities."

The postmodern skepticism of grand theory resonates with feminist legal theory's increasing distrust of universal claims about women. Postmodernism suggests that the problem lies not in ensuring that the representation of women's experience is accurate, but rather in the concept of representation itself. Sexual difference, however it may be measured, is irretrievably bound up with gender. In short, gender itself is a product of power and language and social institutions, including law, not a reality that preexists those structures. Thus, for postmodern feminist theorists, the problem of accounting for a range of feminist views and experiences is less an ontological than an epistemological difficulty.

Feminists, along with other groups on the margin of power, are reluctant to relinquish the hope that resort to some standard independent of politics and culture will strengthen their claims. Those who have been excluded from power continue to rely upon the possibility that those empowered who purport to respect that standard will respond to arguments for their inclusion. Although women have been largely excluded from the development of Western notions of justice (and indeed at times assumed incapable of reason), resort to claims of justice and equality has led to identifiable legal gains for women. Feminists therefore may fear that without an objectively defensible basis for distinguishing between truth and falsehood, women are left only with power to dictate the outcome of competing claims of truth. That prospect most frightens those who are oppressed. As Sabina Lovibond has asked, "How can any one ask me to say goodbye to 'emancipatory metanarratives' when my own emancipation is still such a patchy, hit-or-miss affair?"

Feminists may also be reluctant to embrace postmodernism because, despite the difficulty of giving content to the category "woman," that category seems necessary to feminist political advocacy. In other words, the lingering essentialism and tendency toward universalizing theoretical claims in feminist legal theory result, at least in part, from the political utility of making specific claims about women as a group. The perceived strategic cost of surrendering the claim to narrative authority is a product not only of the political structure but of the legal structure as well: the protection of civil rights laws is premised on the allegation of a group-based harm, thereby requiring an argument structured in terms of the characteristics, needs, and vulnerabilities of that group. These laws require feminist advocates not only to structure claims based on an allegation of harm to a particular woman but also to link that harm to the condition of women as a group.

Confronted with both the need to offer an authoritative account of women's experience and the consequences of exclusion implicit in offering such an account, feminist legal theorists have hoped for a middle path between postmodernism and foundationalism. They have revealed and criticized the partiality of law's description of womanhood while maintaining the possibility of a truer description, one freer from distortion and exclusion. In this sense, feminists' movement between critique and reaffirmation of gender categories parallels the Court's continuing quest for a principled basis for reviewing gender classifications. In sorting true from false accounts, however, feminists and the Court face a crisis of authority: Whose descriptions are valid? From what standpoint can mainstream accounts be criticized as incomplete?

Katharine T. Bartlett, Feminist Legal Methods
103 Harv. L. Rev. 829, 880-885 (1990)

Positionality is a stance from which a number of apparently inconsistent feminist "truths" make sense. The positional stance acknowledges the existence of empirical truths, values and knowledge, and also their contingency. It thereby provides a basis for feminist commitment and political action, but views these commitments as provisional and subject to further critical evaluation and revision. . . .

[P]ositionality retains a concept of knowledge based upon experience. Experience interacts with an individual's current perceptions to reveal new understandings and to help that individual, with others, make sense of those perceptions. Thus, from women's position of exclusion, women have come to "know" certain things about exclusion: its subtlety; its masking by "objective" rules and constructs; its pervasiveness; its pain; and the need to change it. These understandings make difficult issues decidable and answers non-arbitrary.

Like the postmodern [stance], however, positionality rejects the perfectibility, externality, or objectivity of truth. Instead, the positional knower conceives of truth as situated and partial. Truth is situated in that it emerges from particular involvements and relationships. These relationships, not some essential or innate characteristics of the individual, define the individual's perspective and provide the location for meaning, identity, and political commitment. Thus, for example, the meaning of pregnancy derives not just from its biological characteristics, but from the social place it occupies — how workplace structures, domestic arrangements, tort systems, high schools, prisons, and other societal institutions construct its meaning.

Truth is partial in that the individual perspectives that yield and judge truth are necessarily incomplete. No individual can understand except from some limited perspective. Thus, for example, a man experiences pornography as a man with a particular upbringing, set of relationships, race, social class, sexual preference, and so on, which affect what "truths" he perceives about pornography. A woman experiences pregnancy as a woman with a particular upbringing, race, social class, set of relationships, sexual preference, and so on, which affect what "truths" she perceives about pregnancy. As a result, there will always be "knowers" who have access to knowledge that other individuals do not have, and no one's truth can be deemed total or final.

Because knowledge arises within social contexts and in multiple forms, the key to increasing knowledge lies in the effort to extend one's limited perspective. Self-discipline is crucial. My perspective gives me a source of special knowledge, but a limited knowledge that I can improve by the effort to step beyond it, to understand other perspectives, and to expand my sources of identity. To be sure, I cannot transcend my perspective; by definition, whatever perspective I currently have limits my view. But I can improve my perspective by stretching my imagination to identify and understand the perspectives of others.

Positionality's requirement that other perspectives be sought out and examined checks the characteristic tendency of all individuals — including feminists — to want to stamp their own point of view upon the world. This requirement does not allow certain feminist positions to be set aside as immune from critical examination. When feminists oppose restrictive abortion laws, for example, positionality compels the effort to understand those whose views about the sanctity of potential human life are offended by assertion of women's unlimited right to choose abortion. When feminists debate the legal alternative of joint custody at divorce, positionality compels appreciation of the desire by some fathers to be responsible, co-equal parents. And (can it get worse?) when feminists urge drastic reform of rape laws, positionality compels consideration of the position of men whose social conditioning leads them to interpret the actions of some women as "inviting" rather than discouraging sexual encounter.

Although I must consider other points of view from the positional stance, I need not accept their truths as my own. Positionality is not a strategy of process and compromise that seeks to reconcile all competing interests. Rather, it imposes a twin obligation to make commitments based on the current truths and values that have emerged from methods of feminism, and to be open to previously unseen perspectives that might come to alter these commitments. As a practical matter, of course, I cannot do both simultaneously, evenly, and perpetually. Positionality, however, sets an ideal of self-critical commitment whereby I act, but consider the truths upon which I act subject to further refinement, amendment, and correction.

Some "truths" will emerge from the ongoing process of critical reexamination in a form that seems increasingly fixed or final. Propositions such as that I should love my children, that I should not murder others for sport, or that democracy is as a general matter better than authoritarianism seem so "essential" to my identity and my social world that I experience them as values that can never be overridden, even as standards by which I may judge others. These truths, indeed, seem to confirm the view that truth does exist (it must; these things are true) if only I could find it. For feminists, the commitment to ending gender-based oppression has become one of these "permanent truths." The problem is the human inclination to make this list of "truths" too long, to be too uncritical of its contents, and to defend it too harshly and dogmatically.

Positionality reconciles the existence of reliable, experience-based grounds for assertions of truth upon which politics should be based, with the need to question and improve these grounds. The understanding of truth as "real," in the sense of produced by the actual experiences of individuals in their concrete social relationships, permits the appreciation of plural truths. By the same token, if truth is understood as partial and contingent, each individual or group can approach its own truths with a more honest, self-critical attitude about the value and potential relevance of other truths.

The ideal presented by the positionality stance makes clear that current disagreements within society at large and among feminists—disagreements about abortion, child custody, pornography, the military, pregnancy, mother-hood, and the like—reflect value conflicts basic to the terms of social existence. If resolvable at all, these conflicts will not be settled by reference to external or pre-social standards of truth. From the positional stance, any resolutions that emerge are the products of human struggles about what social realities are better than others. Realities are deemed better not by comparison to some external, "discovered" moral truths or "essential" human characteristics, but by internal truths that make the most sense of experienced, social existence. Thus, social truths will emerge from social relationships and what, after critical examination, they tell social beings about what they want themselves, and their social world, to be. . . .

In this way, feminist positionality resists attempts at classification either as essentialism . . . or relativistic. . . . Positionality is both nonrelative and nonarbitrary. It assumes some means of distinguishing between better and worse understanding; truth claims are significant or "valid" for those who experience that validity. But positionality puts no stock in fixed, discoverable foundations. If there is any such thing as ultimate or objective truth, I can never, in my own lifetime, be absolutely sure that I have discovered it. I can know important and non-arbitrary truths, but these are necessarily mediated through human experiences and relationships. There can be no universal, final, or objective truth; there can be only "partial, locatable, critical knowledges"; no aperspectivity—only improved perspectives. . . .

Notes

1. Postmodernism in Feminist Legal Theory. As Maxine Eichner notes, postmodern theory (also referred to as poststructuralist theory) has "profoundly changed the ways that scholars in many disciplines approach the study of their fields." Maxine Eichner, On Postmodern Feminist Legal Theory, 36 Harv. C.R.-C.L. L. Rev. 1, 2 (2001). These fields include English, comparative literature, women's studies, "anthropology, art history, history, philosophy, political theory, sociology, and even the philosophy of science." Eichner, supra, at 2. Postmodernism has been slower, however, to make a mark on legal studies. Eichner speculates that this may be so because postmodern theory is better suited for critique than for building positive theory, and/or because the discipline of law—which relies on fixed categories and either/or logic—is "so closely associated with the vision of modernity against which postmodernists are reacting." Id. at 4.

Postmodernism, however, has deeply influenced feminist legal scholarship. For some theorists, postmodernist analytic techniques offer feminists the opportunity to "change how people think." Thus, Marie Ashe argues that "[t]he great relevance of poststructuralism for jurisprudence . . . is that it throws into question the categories and classifications upon which law has uncritically supported exercises of power that have silenced and opposed in the name of nature or in the name of practical necessity. . . . Law's recognition of its own limitation may open its ears to hearing the namings, the self-definitions, and the claims of oppressed persons, and more significantly, may permit Law's recognition that its customary namings and classifications have no greater claim to validity than do the self-narratives of those whom it has kept in silence." Marie Ashe, Mind's Opportunity: Birthing a Poststructuralist Feminist Jurisprudence, in Legal Studies as Cultural Studies: A Reader in (Post)Modern Critical Theory 116-117 (Jerry Leonard ed., 1995). Joan Williams argues that postmodernism can help theorists move beyond the sameness/difference debate in feminist legal theory. See Joan C. Williams, Dissolving the Sameness/Difference Debate: A Post-Modern Path Beyond Essentialism in Feminist and Critical Race Theory, 1991 Duke L.J. 296.

Some legal scholars have attempted to use postmodernist theory to construct positive programs for doctrinal reform. Drucilla Cornell has relied on frameworks of psychoanalyst Jacques Lacan to argue for doctrines affecting abortion, pornography, and sexual harassment that will protect women's freedom to exercise their sexual imaginations, thus sheltering women's right to imagine themselves as persons. See Drucilla Cornell, The Imaginary Domain: Abortion, Pornography, and Sexual Harassment (1995); see also Drucilla Cornell, At the Heart of Freedom: Feminism, Sex, and Equality (1998) (arguing that freedom, not equality with men, is what women need).

Maxine Eichner identifies four propositions that emerge from postmodernist theory:

> First, . . . postmodern feminists must use the link that they have so clearly demonstrated between power and identity to encourage women to resist dominant notions of gender roles.
>
> Second, . . . feminist legal theory should take to heart postmodern feminist insights regarding the importance of seeking more fluid notions of gender identity that are less closely linked to a particular sex. . . .
>
> Third, insofar as differences between women and men exist, feminist legal theorists should hesitate before celebrating them and touting their recognition as a mode of accepting "the Other." . . . [A] postmodernist legal theory must distinguish between traits and characteristics it seeks to revalue and those it seeks to make disappear through the elimination of oppression.

Fourth, and finally, a postmodern feminism based on differences and hetero-geneity must ultimately be grounded in a politics of material equality. Only within a system in which certain basic equalities exist can differences truly be valued rather than represent the visible scars of oppression.

Eichner, supra, at 65-66. Based on these principles, Eichner identifies an approach to guide the development of a feminist agenda:

[F]eminists must locate and support the legal conditions that would . . . [shield subordinate groups] from the pressure of dominant discourses emanating from the state, the market, and culture. These legal conditions would include allowing people the time and resources for social/civic participation through paid child-care benefits, shorter mandatory working hours, paid parental leave, and the deductibility of expenses for civic organizations, in addition to currently available tax deductions for donations to such organizations. . . .

Postmodern feminist theory should . . . place a high priority on broadening the definition of family beyond the stereotypical model (composed of a heterosexual adult male breadwinner and a heterosexual adult female caretaker along with their biological children), and on creating a network of protections that makes it costless for families to diverge from this model. . . .

[A] postmodern feminist agenda could seek laws to require television stations that receive public funding to produce programs featuring divergent depictions of gender roles. Similarly, postmodern feminists could seek to ensure that alternative gender discourses are communicated to children and young adults through federal or local mandates that require schools to expose students to examples of those who diverge from standard gender depictions of women and men. Such a requirement would go beyond simply presenting jobs and qualities in sex-neutral terms. Instead, students would be exposed to women and men in nontraditional occupations.

Id. at 68-69, 71. In addition, Eichner uses postmodern theory to argue for sex-neutral laws and rules whenever possible; for protection against domestic and street violence; for women's control over their bodies; for campaign finance laws that will make significant economic redistribution possible; for a progressive tax structure and a living wage; and for benefits for part-time workers. Id. at 72-76.

How does this agenda differ (if at all) from agendas that might emerge from the other varieties of feminist legal theory we have examined in this book?

2. Postmodern Theory and the Problem of Knowledge. Is worrying about epistemological questions of identity and truth a luxury for the privileged? bell hooks makes this suggestion, but then suggests that African Americans have much to gain from challenging the essentialist claims of those in authority. Patricia J. Williams has addressed this same issue with a bifurcated strategy. At times she has challenged the critical approaches that undermine the legal constructions that members of minority groups might use to improve their own status in existing society, such as individual rights. See, e.g., Williams, Alchemical Notes: Recon-structing Ideals from Deconstructed Rights, 22 Harv. C.R.-C.L. L. Rev. 401 (1987). At other times, she has struck piercing blows to the possibility of unified conceptions of identity that might be thought necessary to support any meaningful concept of individual rights. See, e.g., Williams, On Being the Object of Property, 14 Signs 5 (1988). Mari J. Matsuda's scholarship combines a similar set of political commitments with a contingent approach to questions of gender and race identity that challenges unitary foundations for such commitments. Compare, e.g., Matsuda, Looking to the Bottom: Critical Legal Studies and Reparations, 22 Harv. C.R.-C.L. L. Rev. 323 (1987), with Matsuda, When the First Quail Calls: Multiple Consciousness as Jurisprudential Method, 11 Women's Rts. L. Rep. 7 (1989). For an exploration of the need for a double, or integrated, strategy in the context of international women's rights issues, see Tracy E. Higgins, Anti-Essentialism, Relativism, and Human Rights, 19 Harv. Women's L.J. 89, 119 (1996) (urging a brand of "cross-cultural feminism" in which "[f]alse consciousness should be measured not against true consciousness (objective, absolute, pre-political) but against feminist consciousness (subjective, contested, political) and that "[f]eminist consciousness...must be understood as consisting of multiple and sometimes competing critical stances toward cultural oppression").

One method strongly associated with the concept of multiple, situational, and constructed truths is the use of experiential narratives. For a recent analysis of the role of experiential narrative in ascertaining, and conveying, the truth of women's lives, focusing on the constructed emotions they produce, see Kathryn Abrams, Legal Feminism and the Emotions: Three Moments in an Evolving Relationship, 28 Harv. J.L. & Gender 325 (2005) (foregrounding narratives by Marie Ashe, Patricia Williams, and Susan Estrich). Narratives can be used, of course, in different ways. For Catharine MacKinnon, narratives about women's experiences develop the consciousness through which women discover the truth of their common, systematic and total oppression by men. See Catharine A. MacKinnon, Toward a Feminist Theory of the State 83-105 (1989). To Abrams, however, it is not about a single, feminist truth, and not even all about women. Narratives of women's experiences have revealed, instead, truth that is variable, partial, and contested. Bringing into the analysis emotion as an anti-essentialist vehicle, Abrams writes that "truth revealed by emotion [is] not so simply truth, and the identity it communicate[s]...not unitary but plural and complex, [and] the woman (or even women) whose subjectivity it mapped [is] no longer the singular focus of feminist theory." Id. at 334. With what Abrams calls the "turn toward constructivism," "[i]nquiries into women's oppression were gradually supplemented or displaced by inquiries into processes of gendering. Feminist investigations were not only limited to exploring what women suffered and why, but began to focus on how gender — masculinity, femininity, or more ambivalent combinations of the two — were produced in women and men in different contexts." Id.

Does the focus on multiple, complex, variable truths obscure the central feminist insights about how gender oppression is reproduced, or does it make these insights more powerful?

3. Postmodernism and "Strategic Essentialism." Some scholars argue that presenting claims about women's experience as if they represented the unambiguous truth is more a strategic choice than an intellectual commitment. Frances Olsen, for example, writes that the uncompromising or "grand theory" character of MacKinnon's claims has galvanized feminism, helped to break habits of thought, and made feminism more understandable than would be possible through more complex explanations of women's subordination. See Olsen, Feminist Theory in Grand Style (book review), 89 Colum. L. Rev. 1147, 1170-1177 (1989). Outside legal discourse, Gayatri Spivak has famously endorsed "strategic essentialism" in pursuit of specific political goals. See Gayatri Spivak, Outside in the Teaching Machine 1-5 (1993); see also Diana Fuss, Essentially Speaking: Feminism, Nature and Difference 20 (1989) (essentialism may have strategic or interventionary value).

The problem, argues Kathryn Abrams, is that many essentialist claims that have been made by feminists — for example, the claim that women's "voluntary" desire for heterosexual sex is not real but, rather, an ideologically determined response to oppression, which then contributes to that oppression — are not good strategy. They are not good strategy because they offend women and distance them from feminist struggles, ignore the complicated responses of women that contain both compromise and resistance, and perpetuate the notion that women cannot be rational decisionmakers. See Abrams, Ideology and Women's Choices, 24 Ga. L. Rev. 761, 777-792 (1990).

Many feminists have criticized the effort to construct a "postmodern" feminism, on the grounds that the premises of postmodernism undermine feminist insights about the tangible, lived experience of women's subordination. Robin West has stated powerfully the basic critique. See, e.g., Robin West, Feminism in the Law: Theory, Practice and Criticism, 1989 U. Chi. Legal F. 59; Robin West, Caring for Justice (1997); see also Catharine A. MacKinnon, Points Against Postmodernism, 75 Chi.-Kent L. Rev. 687, 703 (2000) (arguing that postmodern theory, by erasing the distinction between truth and lies, makes it impossible for feminists to speak the truth about women's lives and be heard).

5. Responses to the Non-Essentialism Critiques

≡ *Janet Halley et al., Gender, Sexuality, and*
≡ *Power: Is Feminist Theory Enough?*
≡ 12 Colum. J. Gender & L. 601, 604-611 (2003)

Of course there are many, many forms of feminism. The variety is quite staggering. But I notice some elements that are virtually *essential* to feminism as it is practiced and performed in the United States today. I could be wrong about these essential elements; and feminism could change so that these elements fade out and/or new ones become definitional. So in the spirit of offering an impressionistic description of current conditions, here are the essential elements of feminism in the United States today.

First, to be feminism, a position must make a distinction between M and F. Different feminisms do this differently: some see men and women, some see male and female, some see masculine and feminine. While "men" and "women" will almost always be imagined as distinct human "groups," the other paired terms can describe many different things: traits, narratives, introjects. However a particular feminism manages these subsidiary questions, it is not "a feminism" unless it turns in some central or core way on the distinction between M and F.

And second, to be feminism in the United States today, a position must posit some kind of subordination as between M and F, in which F is the disadvantaged or subordinated element. At this point feminism is both descriptive and normative; it takes on the quality of a justice project while also becoming a subordination hypothesis. Feminism is feminism because, as between M and F, it carries a brief for F.

If the essentials are this minimal, there are many many features of contemporary and historically important feminism that are optional, however much they appear to their proponents as indispensable. For instance, the register on which subordination should be noticed is seriously contested. For Catharine A. MacKinnon, the relationship is one of power, whereas for cultural feminism, it is one of ethical ranking. In MacKinnon's power theory, the eroticization of domination *produces* men and women, male and female, masculine and feminine, *as* domination and subordination, and this is bad because, however much the subordinated feminine might desire domination, she also longs for liberation from it. For cultural feminism, male or men's or masculine values have trumped those of femaleness or women or femininity and this is bad because women's values are at least as good as—indeed are usually understood in cultural feminism to be *better than*—men's.

There are also profound disagreements within feminism about how to describe subordination. [These include] the debate that addresses childbearing, care work, and related matters. There are equally powerful debates on the place of sexuality in subordination. Countering MacKinnon's alliance with some cultural feminists to regulate heterosexual eroticism on the assumption that it is a key element in women's subordination and is always (or almost always or too often) bad for women, there have been powerful sex liberationist, sex radical, and more recently "sex positive" feminisms that understand sexuality to be a domain of "pleasure and danger" to which women need untrammelled access. And there have been breakaway movements like the anti-identitarian "politics of sexual acts" and "queer theory" which seek alternative theoretical, social, and political modes of assessing the relationships between sex and power—modes in which M and F are not necessarily presupposed to have the salience that they have in feminism.

Feminisms also differ a great deal in the degree to which they figure women's subordination as structural or episodic. A strictly structural theory would be one which posits the universal totality of male domination. MacKinnon's "feminism unmodified" is strongly structural in this sense. Many feminists resist this aspect of MacKinnon's theory, and seek to understand male dominance as having an "outside." Now that would be where they might also want to Take a Break from Feminism: if male dominance is not always already there, then we don't always need feminism.

I have noticed feminism resisting these moves in the direction of Taking a Break from Feminism in two chief ways. One is what my colleague, Duncan Kennedy, writing about something else, calls "paranoid structuralism." Feminist paranoid structuralism either hypothesizes or presupposes (please note a big difference there) that, although things in the world *seem* to be organized in a way that does not invoke M/F or require us to carry a brief for F, this perception is probably a deep error, and profoundly counterintuitive investigation will eventually reveal that, yep, it's M > F all over again. I am a huge fan of hypothetical paranoid structuralism. It is a crucial element of every radical theory that regards the very consciousness of those propounding it to be one of the "powers" against which it works. I love it also for how hard it works; it takes nothing for granted; it is a persistent incitement to critique. I love it for its love of the covert, its need for highly astute interpretive practices, and its constant yearning for a radical transformation of consciousness. But when paranoid structuralism is promoted from a hypothesis to a claim—when one *presupposes* the covert importance of one's favorite paranoid idea, or claims to see it precisely *because of* its seeming absence—it runs into the big downside of being, well, paranoid. It can lead you to not noticing other things that *are* going on, things that just can't and probably shouldn't be forced into the vocabulary of M > F.

The second mode in which feminism recuperates an ostensibly rejected structuralism is most noticeable in what I call the hybrid feminisms: socialist feminism, antiracist feminism, postcolonial feminism. These feminisms share the essential features of feminism as I have listed them; and they *also* posit that *some other system of social subordination,* operating according to *some other difference that defines the theory* and is essential to it in that sense, is also at work in the world. Class, race, empire: these are systematic social events that organize subordination in ways that are at least hypothetically distinct from M and F. There are two basic tendencies in these feminisms with respect to structuralism: a divergentist and a convergentist tendency. Divergentist hybrid feminism is ready to say that there are some things in, say, racism, that are simply not capable of being merged into the presupposition of M > F. There are tensions, splits, and sheer breakaway moments, in which an antiracist feminism would see things in terms of race *and not gender,* would be for a man *against a woman,* and so on. Work like this ends up performing a firm rejection of the structuralist wish. These feminisms have learned how to Take a Break from Feminism, and I would argue that the strength of so much of this work (or perhaps simply my own admiration for it) is directly the result of a willingness to do so. Rejecting this approach, convergentist hybrid feminism posits that the theory is not good enough, the explanation not worked out enough, until everything in the socialist dimension, the antiracist dimension, or the postcolonial dimension of the project can be fully referred to and merged into its feminism. . . . Oddly enough, it sometimes seems that feminism imagines that it will stand accused of racism and imperialism (or orientalism) if it does not posit its ambition to "top" both antiracism and anti-imperialism by emerging, when all is said and done, as their ultimate conceptual, normative, and political reference point. Structuralist ambitions figure in these gestures as an ultimate fealty to a transcendence, utopia, or harmonic convergence which, if we were only smart and good enough, we would be able to produce out of the terrible conflictual material we have to work with. . . .

There are costs to these recuperative strategies, to the structuralism they covertly reintroduce, as well as to the definitional demands of feminism itself: its precommitment to M/F and to carrying a brief for F.

Before offering a few thoughts on that, allow me to insist that there are costs to Taking a Break from Feminism as well. They include: relaxing the epistemic vigilance that is needed to resist male epistemic hegemony; risking further splits among feminists at a higher conceptual location than most other splits, and thus risking new fissures in the intellectual, social, political, and legal endeavor; demobilizing and demoralizing feminists; laying oneself and one's arguments open to cooptation by the enemies of women's well being; legitimating male dominance generally and specifically. If, for instance, feminism is our best weapon against the constant pressure of male sexual violence, weakening feminism in any of these ways could actually result in some guy's decision to rape a woman he would otherwise leave unmolested, or some prosecutor's willingness to see reasonable doubt in a rape case that would otherwise have seemed a clear prosecutorial priority. I see all that. Believe me, I do.

Still, I think it is also important for "us" to get clear about the costs of feminist structuralism, paranoid structuralism, and convergentism, and even of maintaining a constant focus on the conceptual priority of M/F, and the normative or political priority of perpetually carrying a brief for F.

Some of those costs are:

Brain drain. Everywhere I go women complain to me that academic feminism has lost its zing. Many key intellectual figures in feminism have decamped to other endeavors. Women's Studies Programs have undergone tumultuous transformations into Gender and/or Sexuality Studies Programs or disappeared altogether. Feminist journals accept articles only on the proviso that the authors produce the effect of M > F, so that important new work gets submitted and published elsewhere. Faced with these trends, feminists say they have been betrayed and abandoned, and urge one another—the saving remnant—to a renewed commitment to feminist tenets. (It has even been suggested at this conference that the situation is so bad that feminists should "go underground.") I think the feeling is misplaced and the remedy is probably counterproductive. One motive force driving the brain drain is, surely, the sheer preclusion imposed on inquisitive minds and avid justice seekers by the paranoid structuralist and convergentist presuppositions. Another is a widely-held and powerful hunch that, as Kendall Thomas put it at the conference, "women don't own gender": perhaps we need to examine M and F while suspending the stipulation that subordination is always their relation, and always takes the form of M > F. And then there is the hunch that many of the most devastating problems in the world might not be about M/F *even a little.*

Bad faith. If you look around the United States and Canada, at least, you see plenty of places where feminism, far from slinking about underground, is running things. Sex harassment, child sexual abuse, pornography, sexual violence: these feminist justice projects have moved off the street and into state and corporate bureaucracies. Schools and employers devote substantial resources now to extensive sexual harassment regulatory schemes. Child sexual abuse and rape enforcement have serious priority in many jurisdictions and frequently tap into "zero tolerance" enforcement modes much more readily than other kinds of child neglect and interpersonal violence. The Canadian Supreme Court has held that pornography that depicts the sexual subordination of women is an equality violation.

In some important senses, *feminism rules*. Governance feminism.

Not only that, it *wants* to rule. It has a will to power.

Here its commitment to M/F and to carrying a brief for F has real-world distributive consequences that feminism should not disavow. It wants to do, has done, and will do things on behalf of women *at the expense of men and other social interests*. This is not necessarily bad; justice in the real world sometimes means imposing costs. When it does this, feminism has effects. It gets blood on its hands. It needs — and I suggest it is utterly without — a theory and practice of its own role in governance, of itself as a responsible wielder of power.

Feminist convergentism and paranoid structuralism bring their own special contributions to the denial of feminist power, the maintenance of the myth that feminism remains an utterly underdog movement needing complete and unbroken solicitude. But the possibility of a more nearly responsible attitude to the problem of "feminism with blood on its hands" might also require Taking a Break from Feminism's definitional stakes of M/F and the subordination of F. I would suggest that these stakes not only make feminism what it is today, but also make it hard for it to see around corners of its own construction. Unless it Takes a Break from itself, it can't see injury to men. It can't see injury to men by women. It can't see other interests, other forms of power, other justice projects. It insists that all justice projects will track a subordination model. And this refusal to see, sustained while feminism imposes costs on interests and projects outside its purview, gives us a textbook case of *bad faith*.

Power masquerading as servitude. At this point in my argument, I frequently hear that I don't care about women, have belittled the harm suffered by women, have denied the harm suffered by women, and have silenced women. These are fascinating charges. More than that, they sting. . . . Whatever their merit, feminism imposes costs *on itself* when it makes these charges.

First, nothing in what I've said *requires* me to concede these charges. Saying that women might harm men, for instance, is not the same as saying that women are not harmed. Saying something feminist women disagree with does not silence them. To be sure, saying that we should Take a Break from Feminism might have as a *downstream consequence* harm to women, a silencing of women. I might get blood on my hands. But I can't help thinking that feminists who imagine that my critique not only risks those consequences but *contains* and intrinsically *performs* them are attributing to me the only kind of power they can imagine for themselves. Their implicit vision of themselves and their opponents as Gods capable of performative utterances on the level of "*Fiat Lux*" or "I sentence you . . ." is either very very flattering or very very scary.

Second, these accusations reassert precisely the presuppositions in feminism that I am calling into question. They redraw feminist disciplinary boundaries and implicitly require that feminists stay within them; a feminist will always describe everything in terms of M/F, and will always describe M/F as the domination of M and the subordination of F. That is, these charges are symptomatic of precisely the structuralism, with all the associated blind spots, which I am describing as costly *to* feminism.

Moral perfectionism and magic realism. Feminists hearing my line at this point have responded again and again with a formulation something like this:

if feminism had blood on its hands it would be because it had become a dominator; but feminism is definitionally *against* domination; and if it has dominated, if it has caused harm, it must chasten itself; but most likely feminism has not actually caused any harm; after all feminism is powerless and in fact *suffers* harm. This argument, for all its moral modesty, is actually quite strict: feminism (to be feminism) must be morally immaculate. It is either subordinated (and harmless) or not itself. A profound structural totalism—feminism is *the* subordination theory *par excellence*—subtends this formulation.

This willingness of feminism to undergo chastening in the name of its moral perfectionism is not necessarily meek all the way down. It stipulates for a binarized outcome: feminism can either assume guilt *or* deny harm. At moments when guilt has been the preferred stance, feminism has been notoriously not fun. Memories of these episodes have probably done a lot to fuel the brain drain. The fact that denial is framed as the chief alternative has produced certain magic realist tendency in feminism, and it has produced a lot of distrust in allied projects (antiracist projects, pro-gay projects, etc.) whose constituency arguably ends up bearing the costs of the decisions made by governance feminism. Finally, this denial has discouraged the investigation of internal ambivalence among self-identified feminists. Feminism in this mode does not particularly want to hear me say, "As a gay man, I...." And I might well decide to Take a Break from Feminism rather than give up on the hope of finding out what it might mean to say it.

Constituting women, heterosexuality, and women's suffering. One of the most crucial moments in the genealogy of United States feminism was the roughly simultaneous publication in 1990 of Judith Butler's Gender Trouble and Eve Kosofsky Sedgwick's Epistemology of the Closet. In different ways, and opening onto different consequences, both of them argued that what I have called here the definitional stake tying feminism to M/F also ties it, at the most fundamental level, to *the heterosexual*. To the extent that feminism defines itself as the -ism of this distinction, it *is* heterosexual; it *requires* heterosexuality and is basically not friendly to the homo-affirmative aim. Sedgwick responded by seeking a suspension of feminism; to articulate a "gay affirmative" agenda she felt the need to Take a Break from Feminism. She asked instead whether the homoerotic could be understood with richness and nuance in an account that did not turn substantially on M and F and proposed that study of same-sex eroticism might well return to feminism, but at an uncertain future date. Butler responded to the very same dilemma by turning feminism *against* the M/F distinction itself. A feminism that did not question its own role in producing the discursive strictures that require there to be women, the feminine, and femininity could not escape the charge of heteronormativity and thus could hardly merit the name of feminism.

A similar critical move can be performed on the definitional stake tying feminism to the subordination of F. What if, as well as *describing* and *opposing* this social and psychic event, feminism *helps to produce it*? What if the politics of injury and of traumatized sensibility which have almost completely occupied the space cleared by MacKinnon's politics of domination and subordination are helping to authorize and capacitate women as *sufferers*? If indeed feminism is a powerfully constitutive discourse, it might well have a shaping contribution to make *to women's suffering* when, for instance, it insists that a raped woman has suffered an injury from which she is unlikely ever to recover. What if real raped women, believing this feminist line, proceed never to recover? What if some men are "guided" by this bull's-eye to target women for rape rather than fomenting other aggressions, perhaps more manageable, perhaps directed elsewhere? When feminism insists that any effort to trace the causes of particular rapes in the woman's conduct blames the victim, revictimizes her, is a second rape, it might make rape seem more magical and random than it is, might make women more risk averse about it than they need to be, and might induce women to concede more social power to the threat of rape than they otherwise would. So much feminist rape discourse insists on women's object-like status in the rape situation: man fucks woman — subject verb object. Could feminism be contributing to, rather than resisting, the alienation of women from their own agency in narratives and events of sexual violence?

These questions pose a very profound problem about the nature of power and resistance. If a social subordination exists and an anti-subordination discourse ratifies it, fixes it, creates the discursive capacity for its experiential uptake by the subordinated, all the while hanging a bull's-eye on it, then where does one intervene to attack it? It has fascinated me, as I have begun to learn how to ask this question, to notice the strong feminist impulse to refuse it as unfeminist. The reaction has fueled my intuition that we might need to Take a Break from Feminism precisely to be *for women* and *against this increment of injury.*

Catharine A. MacKinnon, Women's Lives, Men's Laws
86-88, 89-90 (2005)

An analysis of women that is predicated on women's experience is based on observed social conditions, hence can assume no uniformity of gender, biological or otherwise, because women's concrete social experience is not uniform. Any regularities the analysis finds, it finds, its findings are then subject to examination by others. Discerning commonalities in experience is not the same as searching for an "essence." The socially constructed "woman" has no "essence." If women "as women" are social and concrete, they must encompass all of women's experiences of social hierarchy, because race, class, and sexual orientation (for instance) contribute to making women's concrete situation and status as women be what it is. A genuinely feminist method is thus open to real women in the social world and builds its category, "women," from them.

If, by contrast, an analysis of women proceeds from an abstract idea — a category that is not predicted on and built of women's social reality by is a priori or biological or otherwise pre-fixed in a social space (here Woman makes her appearance) — it is likely to be factually inaccurate as well as to impose a false sameness of woman and to obscure power divisions within the group.... "[S]ex can be an abstract category or it can be a concrete reality. It is concrete in feminist work. "Essentialism," by contrast, has become an abstraction.

Further, feminism does not take the view that gender is all there is. It takes the view that gender is almost never not there. Feminism claims not that all women are affected the same by male power or are similarly situated under it. It claims that no woman is unaffected by it. Feminism does not se all women as the same; it criticizes this view. It claims that all women are seen and treated as women in some way under male supremacy. This is not to say that feminism is always practiced, even by feminists. It certainly is not to say that feminism does not need to be more race-conscious; it does. Nor it is to say that some work, claiming to be feminist, has not been racist; it has. It is to say that some of the feminist analysis that has been dismissively tagged with what has become the academic epithet of "essentialism," as exemplary of the "straight, white, and economically privileged," is not....

The "essentialism" charge has become a sneer, a tool of woman-bashing, with consequences that far outrun its merits. The widespread acceptance of the claim seems due more to its choice of target than its accuracy in hitting it. Male power is ecstatic; its defenders love the accusation that feminism is "essentialist," even though they don't really know what is means. They do know that it has divided women, which sure takes a lot of heat off. The charge brings the moral authority of opposition to racism to the support of male dominance. "Essentialist" name-calling has become a weapon of choice against those who oppose pornography, prostitution, cliteridectomy, dowry burning, and other misogynist cultural practices, practices that target and harm women as women across cultures, although often in culturally specific forms. Avoiding "essentialism" has become a politically and intellectual respectable pretext for dismissing and ignoring gender and the realities of sexual politics....

The "essentialism" charge, which has become a vehicle for misogyny, has also undermined the contributions that dominance theory, as developed in feminism, could make to antiracist work. Feminist dominance theory is a theory of social and political inequality as such. It builds on antiracism and builds it in. It is time for it to come home. Instead, in strenuous attempt to avoid the hated label of "essentialism," the revulsion at the "sameness" of all women falsely said to be inherent in gender analysis has produced a reflexive affirmation of "difference" in much critical race theorizing during the past decade or so. During this time, there seems to be have been little or no awareness that sameness and different are the two roads to nowhere that mainstream equality theory confines the unequal to walking. In my opinion, failure to see this has crippled much antiracist legal work, including the fight for affirmative action, miring it in the same/difference equality trap that can only maintain white male power as is and fail to confront white male supremacy as such.

Anti-"essentialism," as practiced, thus corrodes group identification and solidarity and leaves us with one-at-a-time personhood; liberal individualism. What a coincidence. With the inability to assert a group reality — an ability that only the subordinated need — comes the shift away from realities of power in the world and toward the search for "identity," excuse me, "identities." It changes the subject, as it were, or tries to. But who wins? Can a postmodern humanism be far behind? "Identity" in its currently psychologically shrunk sense is not women's problem. Reality is: a reality of group oppression that exists whether we identify with our group or not.

6. Coalition-Building and Building a Non-Essentialist Practice

Mari J. Matsuda, Beside My Sister, Facing the Enemy: Legal Theory Out of Coalition
43 Stan. L. Rev. 1183, 1189-1191 (1993)

The way I try to understand the interconnection of all forms of subordination is through a method I call "ask the other question." When I see something that looks racist, I ask, "Where is the patriarchy in this?" When I see something that looks sexist, I ask, "Where is the heterosexism in this?" When I see something that looks homophobic, I ask, "Where are the class interests in this?" Working in coalition forces us to look for both the obvious and non-obvious relationships of domination, helping us to realize that no form of subordination ever stands alone.

If this is true, we've asked each other, then isn't it also true that dismantling any one form of subordination is impossible without dismantling every other? And more and more, particularly in the women of color movement, the answer is that "no person is free until the last and the least of us is free."

In trying to explain this to my own community, I sometimes try to shake people up by suggesting that patriarchy killed Vincent Chin [a Chinese man murdered in Detroit]. Most people think racism killed Vincent Chin. When white men with baseball bats, hurling racist hate speech, beat a man to death, it is obvious that racism is a cause. It is only slightly less obvious, however, when you walk down the aisles of Toys "R" Us, that little boys grow up in this culture with toys that teach dominance and aggression, while little girls grow up with toys that teach about being pretty, baking, and changing a diaper. And the little boy who is interested in learning how to nurture and play house is called a "sissy." When he is a little older he is called a "f-g." He learns that acceptance for men in this society is premised on rejecting the girl culture and taking on the boy culture, and I believe that this, as much as racism, killed Vincent Chin. I have come to see that homophobia is the disciplinary system that teaches men that they had better talk like 2 Live Crew or someone will think they "aren't real men," and I believe that this homophobia is a cause of rape and violence against women. I have come to see how that same homophobia makes women afraid to choose women, sending them instead into the arms of men who beat them. I have come to see how class oppression creates the same effect, cutting off the chance of economic independence that could free women from dependency upon abusive men.

I have come to see all of this from working in coalition: from my lesbian colleagues who have pointed out homophobia in places where I failed to see it; from my Native American colleagues who have said, "But remember that we were here first," when I have worked for the rights of immigrant women; from men of color who have risked my wrath to say, "But racism is what is killing us. Why can't I put that first on my agenda?"

The women of color movement has, of necessity, been a movement about intersecting structures of subordination. This movement suggests that anti-patriarchal struggle is linked to struggle against all forms of subordination. It has challenged communities of color to move beyond race alone in the quest for social justice. . . .

These are threatening suggestions for many of us who have worked primarily in organizations forged in the struggle for racial justice. Our political strength and our cultural self-worth is often grounded in racial pride. Our multi-racial coalitions have, in the past, succeeded because of a unifying commitment to end racist attacks on people of color. Moving beyond race to include discussion of other forms of subordination risks breaking coalition. Because I believe that the most progressive elements of any liberation movement are those who see the intersections (and the most regressive are those who insist on only one axis), I am willing to risk breaking coalition by pushing intersectional analysis.

An additional and more serious risk is that intersectional analysis done from on high, that is, from outside rather than inside a structure of subordination, risks misunderstanding the particularity of that structure. Feminists have spent years talking about, experiencing, and building theory around gender. Native Americans have spent years developing an understanding of colonialism and its effect on culture. That kind of situated, ground-up knowledge is irreplaceable. A casual effort to say, "Okay, I'll add gender to my analysis," without immersion in feminist practice, is likely to miss something. Adding on gender must involve active feminists, just as adding on considerations of indigenous peoples must include activists from native communities. Coalition is the way to achieve this inclusion.

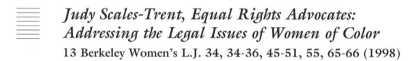

Judy Scales-Trent, Equal Rights Advocates: Addressing the Legal Issues of Women of Color
13 Berkeley Women's L.J. 34, 34-36, 45-51, 55, 65-66 (1998)

On February 21, 1991, reporters and television cameras crowded into a small conference room in San Francisco to hear an announcement by representatives of three local public interest law firms—Asian Law Caucus ("ALC"), Mexican American Legal Defense and Education Fund ("MALDEF"), and Equal Rights Advocates ("ERA"). The media had come to hear about the firms' victory in a case that would affect the rights of hundreds of thousands of workers in America. At the request of these attorneys, a federal district judge in Fresno had just ruled that undocumented workers in this country were protected by federal civil rights law. At the press briefing, the decision was announced and explained in English, Spanish, and Chinese. The story was covered not only by Bay area reporters, but also by Univision, a television station that broadcasts in Spanish throughout North and South America.

For Alicia Castrejon, an undocumented worker who was fired when she became pregnant, the victory meant that she might regain her job and receive back pay. But the decision had importance far beyond the particularities of her case. As one of the first federal rulings on the rights of undocumented workers in America, the case—EEOC v. Tortilleria "La Mejor"—sent a signal to those workers, and to their employers, that discrimination against undocumented workers would not be tolerated.

This was also an important moment in the life of ERA, a small public interest law firm in San Francisco. Since its creation in 1973, the firm had been addressing women's legal issues in a variety of ways, with an emphasis on employment discrimination law. ERA attorneys had taken many cases, including those involving sexual harassment, discriminatory wages, and the exclusion of women from nontraditional jobs. The case of Tortilleria "La Mejor," however, represented the more specialized focus on the legal issues of women of color — Latinas, Asian-American women, Native women, and African-American women — that the firm had come to adopt.

ERA's focus on women of color developed because of the continuing marginalization of these groups of women. In this country, it is common to speak about "women's issues" or "the race problem," and one often hears the phrase "minorities and women." Categorizing people this way obscures the fact that some minorities are women, and some women are members of minority groups. Because women who are minorities ("women of color") are not even visible in common parlance, their very real existence is obscured and their issues remain unaddressed.

Unfortunately, the invisibility of women of color persists even within the public interest law movement. Of the nearly 300 public interest legal organizations in this country, approximately seventeen, like the Women's Legal Defense Fund, were created to address women's legal issues, while approximately eleven others, like MALDEF, focus on those issues affecting a particular ethnic/racial group. These firms do, of course, perform work that has enormous value for women of color. When MALDEF wins a voting rights case, the importance of that victory for those Mexican Americans who are women cannot be understated. Similarly, the Women's Legal Defense Fund played a crucial role in getting Congress to pass the Pregnancy Discrimination Act, which prohibits discrimination in the workplace on the basis of pregnancy. Clearly, an important percentage of the women who benefit from this statute are African-American, Latina, Asian-American, and/or Native women. Yet the major focus of these groups is not the effect of the intersection of gender and race/ethnicity on the lives of these women. Thus, issues that arise at this juncture are sometimes not even seen, or are rejected as unimportant or irrelevant.

One notable example of this phenomenon is the case of Webster v. Reproductive Health Services. In 1988, as the Supreme Court was preparing to hear the case, many women's rights groups began to prepare briefs outlining their arguments for the continued protection of women's constitutional right to abortion. Because the National Association for the Advancement of Colored People ("NAACP") Legal Defense Fund had been a major public interest law firm for so long, and because of its national reputation as an important fighter for the oppressed, many activists thought that its support for the issue would send a powerful message to the Court. However, despite active lobbying by representatives of women's groups, the NAACP Legal Defense Fund refused to sign on to any of the briefs. In its view, abortion was a women's issue, not a race issue, and the NAACP Legal Defense Fund addressed only issues of race. Arguments that approximately half of all African Americans are women and that reproductive rights should, therefore, be important to an organization that cares about the lives of African Americans were to no avail.

Given this context, ERA's unique willingness and ability to see and explore the complications that arise at the intersection of gender and race/ethnicity in American society, and thus in American law, is of great importance....

[Scales-Trent describes the origins of ERA's "Women of Color Project" and the 1983 hiring of Terisa Chaw, ERA's first woman of color attorney.]

When Chaw joined ERA to begin the Women of Color Project, she did not know what this work would involve. However, she did know that she needed to start by contacting the many organizations in the area that addressed issues of race and ethnicity—organizations such as the ALC and La Raza Centro Legal. She also had the impression that many of these organizations did not know about ERA, primarily because they somehow did not see women's issues as connected with issues of race and ethnicity. She needed to increase ERA's visibility in minority communities....

Because of Chaw's contacts within the Asian community in the Bay area, the ALC asked ERA if it wanted to join them as co-counsel in a case involving the wages of some of the garment workers against Fritzi Manufacturing Company, a major San Francisco women's clothing manufacturer, and its contractor, T & W Fashions. ALC was representing thirteen former and present garment workers, all Chinese men and women. During this period, there were approximately 20,000 garment workers in the Bay area, most of whom worked in the 100 garment shops in Chinatown. The majority of these workers were immigrants who did not speak English and therefore had limited marketable skills, as well as little understanding of their employment rights. As a result, many of the workers received neither the minimum wage nor the overtime pay required by law.

When Chaw suggested that ERA join the ALC in this litigation, the other ERA attorneys and senior staff initially did not understand why the case might involve gender discrimination. Even if the majority of the class members were women, how could there be gender discrimination if both men and women were aggrieved by these practices? Why should a law firm created to address women's issues represent men? What would be the ramifications if it did?

Chaw conceptualized this case as a women's issue well-suited for ERA. She explained to the ERA staff and legal committee that the garment workers were primarily women—poor women of color who, because they spoke only Chinese, were even more vulnerable than other women. Because of their particular vulnerability, they were being exploited by the manufacturer. As a result of Chaw's persuasive arguments, ERA decided to join the ALC in representing these garment workers....

After only one year, Chaw left ERA in July of 1984....

As Chaw was leaving, Shauna Marshall, an African-American attorney, arrived at ERA. Because of her extensive litigation background at the Justice Department, Marshall immediately became involved in several ongoing cases. ...Six months later, in early 1985, ERA hired Marjorie Fujiki as director of the Women of Color Project. For the first time in the history of ERA, two of the three staff attorneys—the people who led the ERA program—were women of color.

Fujiki immediately began working with Marshall and the ALC on the garment workers' case. She had already worked with ALC as a law student and appreciated its approach to litigation, which was based in community education. The community education approach to litigation mirrored Fujiki's ideas, drawing her to ERA, where the attorneys spent approximately three-fourths of their time on litigation and the rest on community education. According to Fujiki, this community-based litigation was one of ERA's greatest strengths.

Consistent with this community-based approach, the attorneys not only held bi-weekly meetings with their clients during the litigation, but they also provided community education on the rights of garment workers as part of the Garment Workers' Educational Project created by ALC....

[A]t the close of this three-year struggle, both the contractor and the manufacturer settled the case for $172,000.00. It was the first time that a garment manufacturer had been forced to pay damages for labor violations to the workers of one of its contractors....

Several ERA projects grew out of the garment workers' case. After seeing how little money their clients received in the settlement, the ERA staff had a stronger understanding of how low the minimum wage was and of how legal work to increase the minimum wage could be a gender issue. As a result, ERA involved itself in the Coalition for a Fair Minimum Wage. According to former executive director Davis, ERA would never have seen this as a women's issue before its involvement in the garment workers' case....

Another offshoot of the garment workers' case was ERA's decision to take an active role in opposing Proposition 63, which would amend the state constitution to declare English the official language of California. Again, it was Fujiki who saw this as a gender issue that ERA should address. She pointed out that it is mainly the women in immigrant communities who bring their families to social services and that these women often speak no English. Therefore, any requirement limiting access to social services to those who speak English would adversely affect immigrant women, as well as their families. In California, most of these women are Latinas and Asian-American women....

With regard to defining issues, the impact of the garment workers' case on ERA was much larger than any monetary award it won for its clients. As Davis noted: "[this case] really broadened our thinking considerably." This was the case that opened up for the law firm both how they defined gender issues, and how ERA would provide services to its constituents. From now on ERA would conceptualize issues as "women's issues" when it could see an adverse impact on a group of women. They no longer would think that gender issues had to include only women, and exclude men. Also, ERA would no longer be limited to discrimination issues: it now understood that unfair labor practices, for example, could also be women's issues.

With respect to how ERA conducted its work, the impact of the garment workers' case was two-fold. First, ERA would no longer pursue litigation for its own sake, but would view litigation as a stepping stone to open up a range of other activity. Second, ERA would now be more involved in coalition work....

In her 1987 "Message from the Executive Director," Davis noted the transformation of ERA from a law firm specializing in sex discrimination to a law firm that "is dedicated to combating aggressively and affirmatively the disenfranchisement of women, especially low-income women and women of color." She continued:

> Easily the single most important factor in our metamorphosis was the establishment in 1983 of our Women of Color Project. The Project, more than any other aspect of ERA's program, compelled us to look at the phenomenon now known as the "feminization of poverty." The problems facing minority women are problems related to race, sex and class. For ERA, tackling these problems has meant working in coalitions with a broad range of organizations. Typically, these organizations were established to work on issues of race alone or race and class. Sex, if addressed at all, was a peripheral issue. In many instances, ERA has been the only feminist organization initiating contacts and participating in these coalitions and, as such, has served as a bridge linking the women's movement to the civil rights movement. . . .

The impact of the Women of Color Project extends beyond ERA's legal and policy work to influence the work of other groups in the larger community in at least two ways. First, other groups in the community have begun to see the intersection of sex and race/ethnicity in their own work and to act upon that new knowledge. Second, other groups have been empowered to act by their relationship with ERA.

For example, it became clear that Spanish radio and television had begun to see women's issues within the larger problem of ethnicity when they began to contact ERA for information. [The] Spanish-language media in the Bay area had never covered a story on abortion. But when ERA did work on abortion rights, Spanish radio and television contacted ERA for information and ran stories on this issue. [Legal] advocacy groups like MALDEF or ALC, which focus on issues of race/ethnicity, now see the related gender issues and refer these cases to ERA.

Another example of the effect that ERA's work has had on other community groups can be seen in Marshall's status as the only non-Chinese member of the twenty-five-member board of Chinese for Affirmative Action. When asking her to join the board, group members explained that they wanted her help in addressing black-Asian tensions within the community, and help in understanding both their own racism and the fact that the civil rights movement they are now a part of "was built on the backs of African Americans." Marshall noted that at one meeting, the board discussed what position they should take on the nomination of Clarence Thomas to the Supreme Court. She thought it significant that the board recognized this as an important question for an Asian advocacy group to consider. Marshall understood that the group wanted her on the board so she could push them to broaden their perspective on civil rights issues, as including women of color had helped ERA broaden its perspective on gender issues. Marshall continued, "[T]hey didn't ask one of our Asian staff or former staff members to be on the board. . . . They made a decision to really expand themselves and to push."

Putting Theory into Practice

6-1. You and your three best friends from law school decide to start a "feminist law firm." What kinds of work will you seek out? Whom will you seek to hire? What clients and communities do you hope to serve? Will your firm have the conventional status hierarchies between attorneys, paralegals, support staff, and maintenance workers? If not, what relationships will you create? Will your firm pursue litigation, community organizing, legislative work, direct action, some or all of the above? What principles will you adopt to keep true to your vision? Write a mission statement for your firm.

6-2. Consider the various approaches to feminist legal theory surveyed in this book. What would be a just world according to each perspective? Do these visions of justice differ from one another? Can the approaches be combined, or are some of them mutually exclusive?

6-3. What does it mean for feminism to "move on"? Would anything come in its place? In addition to the Janet Halley reading set forth above, consider Iris Marion Young, Lived Body versus Gender: Reflections on Social Structure and Subjectivity, in Recognition, Responsibility, and Rights: Feminist Ethics and Social Theory 3, 6 (Robin N. Fiore & Hilde Lindemann Nelson eds., 2003) (proposing replacement of gender by category of the "lived body," meaning the "unified idea of a physical body acting and experiencing in a specific sociocultural context"); see also Toril Moi, What Is a Woman? (1999).

6-4. What, if any, progress has been made in your lifetime for women? In what ways, if any, has life gotten worse for women? What issues will face a girl born today? Can you answer that question without specifying her race-ethnicity, language group, class, nation, sexuality, physical ability? Without being "essentialist" in any of the ways suggested in this chapter?

6-5. To what critiques explored in this chapter is this casebook vulnerable? Have the casebook authors engaged in any version of essentialism? Should they, or could they, have avoided it?

Table of Cases

Principal cases are in italics.

Index